**Foreign Relations of the
United States, 1950–1955**

The Intelligence Community 1950–1955

Editors   Douglas Keane
                    Michael Warner

General Editor   Edward C. Keefer

United States Government Printing Office
Washington
2007

DEPARTMENT OF STATE PUBLICATION 11441

OFFICE OF THE HISTORIAN

BUREAU OF PUBLIC AFFAIRS

For sale by the Superintendent of Documents, U.S. Government Printing Office
Internet: bookstore.gpo.gov   Phone: toll free (866) 512-1800;   DC area (202) 512-1800
Fax: (202) 512-2250 Mail: Stop IDCC, Washington, DC 20402-0001

ISBN 0-16-076468-8

Preface

The *Foreign Relations of the United States* series presents the official documentary historical record of major foreign policy decisions and significant diplomatic activity of the United States Government. The Historian of the Department of State is charged with the responsibility for the preparation of the *Foreign Relations* series. The staff of the Office of the Historian, Bureau of Public Affairs, under the direction of the General Editor of the *Foreign Relations* series, plans, researches, compiles, and edits the volumes in the series. Secretary of State Frank B. Kellogg first promulgated official regulations codifying specific standards for the selection and editing of documents for the series on March 26, 1925. These regulations, with minor modifications, guided the series through 1991.

Public Law 102–138, the Foreign Relations Authorization Act, which was signed by President George H.W. Bush on October 28, 1991, established a new statutory charter for the preparation of the series. Section 198 of P.L. 102–138 added a new Title IV to the Department of State's Basic Authorities Act of 1956 (22 U.S.C. 4351, et seq.).

The statute requires that the *Foreign Relations* series be a thorough, accurate, and reliable record of major United States foreign policy decisions and significant United States diplomatic activity. The volumes of the series should include all records needed to provide comprehensive documentation of major foreign policy decisions and actions of the United States Government. The statute also confirms the editing principles established by Secretary Kellogg: the *Foreign Relations* series is guided by the principles of historical objectivity and accuracy; records should not be altered or deletions made without indicating in the published text that a deletion has been made; the published record should omit no facts that were of major importance in reaching a decision; and nothing should be omitted for the purposes of concealing a defect in policy. The statute also requires that the *Foreign Relations* series be published not more than 30 years after the events recorded. The editors are convinced that this volume meets all regulatory, statutory, and scholarly standards of selection and editing.

Structure and Scope of the Foreign Relations *Series*

This volume is part of a retrospective subseries of volumes of the *Foreign Relations* series that fills in gaps in the volumes of the Truman and Eisenhower subseries. At the time the Truman and Eisenhower volumes were prepared, the Office of the Historian did not have access to documents related to intelligence. This is the second volume that documents the institutional foundations of the relationship between

foreign policy and intelligence. The first, *Foreign Relations, 1945–1950, Emergence of the Intelligence Establishment*, was published in 1996. This volume is a sequel, and it will be followed by a third volume with the same focus, covering the years 1956–1960. After 1960, the *Foreign Relations* volumes for the Kennedy, Johnson, and Nixon-Ford subseries include a chapter on intelligence and foreign policy in their volumes on the organization and management of foreign policy, thus negating the need for separate retrospective volumes.

Focus of Research and Principles of Selection for Foreign Relations, *1950–1955, Development of the Intelligence Community*

This volume is organized along chronological lines in one large chapter covering 1950–1955, and a second chapter that includes the key National Security Council Intelligence Directives of the period. The volume documents the institutional growth of the intelligence community during the first half of the 1950s. When Lt. General Walter Bedell Smith took over as Director of Central Intelligence in October 1950, he inherited an agency that was widely believed to have been unable to establish itself as the central institution of the U.S. intelligence community. Utilizing his great prestige, and a national security directive from President Truman, Smith established the multiple directorate structure within the Central Intelligence Agency (CIA) that has continued to this day, brought the clandestine service into the CIA, and worked to effect greater inter-agency coordination through a strengthened process to produce National Intelligence Estimates. The exponential growth of the national security establishment and of the intelligence community was due to the impact of two factors: NSC 68 (a clarion call for more active containment of the Soviet Union) and the Korean War. The Central Intelligence Agency was called upon to expand the clandestine service, and the intelligence community was required to provide better and more definitive intelligence on the Soviet bloc and China. When Allen Dulles took over as Director of Central Intelligence in February 1953, these pressures continued. By 1955, the general consensus of two commissions appointed by President Eisenhower to review the intelligence effort was that the clandestine service had grown too rapidly and was plagued by poor management. In general, the commission implied that the clandestine service's growth had come at the expense of the agency's intelligence analysts.

This volume presented the editors with documentary challenges. The documents used to compile this volume were unique by *Foreign Relations* standards. Rather than documenting the formulation of foreign policy decisions or important diplomatic negotiations, this volume is a record of high-level policy plans, discussions, administrative decisions, and managerial actions that transformed the intelligence community from its somewhat shaky establishment into a community

that collected intelligence worldwide; provided extensive analysis of that intelligence for policy makers; and carried out covert operations, as approved by the United States Government, on a global scale. The intelligence community under President Eisenhower in 1955 was a much more significant player and a more robust bureaucracy than it was under President Truman in the late 1940s. This volume documents that growth and development.

In preparing this volume, the editors sought to limit their selection of documents to those dealing with national intelligence coordination, planning, and policies. The editors did not seek to document the planning and implementation of specific intelligence operations, or to document the impact of intelligence appraisals upon specific foreign policy decisions or negotiations. Intelligence reports, estimates, and analyses dealing with particular regions, countries, or issues have not been included. The important intelligence operations of the Truman and Eisenhower years, missing in the coverage of *Foreign Relations* for 1945–1960, are covered in other retrospective volumes. The first, Guatemala, 1952–1954, was published in 2003. Others will follow.

The preparation of this volume raised special problems since many of the intelligence documents for 1950–1955 have been destroyed, or were widely scattered in multiple archival holdings. Documents were hard to locate because of the shifting and rapid growth of various intelligence organizations. It became obvious that some important decisions were probably reached without written records having been made. Still, this volume presents an extensive collection of documents that will go a long way to demonstrate the growth of the intelligence community during the key period 1950–1955. That growth and development was not without growing pains, as the documents reveal.

Editorial Methodology

The documents are presented chronologically according to Washington time. Memoranda of conversation are placed according to the date and time of the conversation, rather than the date a memorandum was drafted. Documents chosen for printing are authoritative or signed copies, unless otherwise noted.

Editorial treatment of the documents published in the *Foreign Relations* series follows Office style guidelines, supplemented by guidance from the General Editor. The documents are reproduced as exactly as possible, including marginalia or other notations, which are described in the footnotes. Texts are transcribed and printed according to accepted conventions for the publication of historical documents within the limitations of modern typography. A heading has been supplied by the editors for each document included in the volume. Spelling, capitalization, and punctuation are retained as found in the original text, except that obvious typographical errors are silently corrected. Other mistakes and omissions in the documents are corrected by bracketed insertions: a correction is set in italic type; an addition in roman type. Words or phrases underlined in the source text are printed in italics. Abbreviations and contractions are preserved as found in the original text, and a list of abbreviations is included in the front matter of each volume.

Bracketed insertions are also used to indicate omitted text that deals with an unrelated subject (in roman type) or that remains classified after declassification review (in italic type). The amount and, where possible, the nature of the material not declassified has been noted by indicating the number of lines or pages of text that were omitted. Entire documents withheld for declassification purposes have been accounted for and are listed with headings, source notes, and number of pages not declassified in their chronological place. All brackets that appear in the original text are so identified in footnotes. With the exception of Presidential recordings transcribed in the Office of the Historian by the editor(s) of the volume, all ellipses are in the original documents.

The first footnote to each document indicates the document's source, original classification, distribution, and drafting information. This note also provides the background of important documents and policies and indicates whether the President or his major policy advisers read the document.

Editorial notes and additional annotation summarize pertinent material not printed in the volume, indicate the location of additional documentary sources, provide references to important related documents printed in other volumes, describe key events, and provide summaries of and citations to public statements that supplement and elucidate the printed documents. Information derived from memoirs and other first-hand accounts has been used when appropriate to supplement or explicate the official record.

The numbers in the index refer to document numbers rather than to page numbers.

Advisory Committee on Historical Diplomatic Documentation

The Advisory Committee on Historical Diplomatic Documentation, established under the *Foreign Relations* statute, reviews records, advises, and makes recommendations concerning the *Foreign Relations* series. The Advisory Committee monitors the overall compilation and editorial process of the series and advises on all aspects of the preparation and declassification of the series. The Advisory Committee does not necessarily review the contents of individual volumes in the series, but it makes recommendations on issues that come to its attention and reviews volumes, as it deems necessary to fulfill its advisory and statutory obligations.

Declassification Review

The Office of Information Programs and Services, Bureau of Administration, conducted the declassification review for the Department of State of the documents published in this volume. The review was conducted in accordance with the standards set forth in Executive Order 12958, as amended, on Classified National Security Information and other applicable laws.

The principle guiding declassification review is to release all information, subject only to the current requirements of national security, as embodied in law and regulation. Declassification decisions entailed concurrence of the appropriate geographic and functional bureaus in the Department of State, other concerned agencies of the U.S. Government, and the appropriate foreign governments regarding specific documents of those governments. The declassification review of this volume, which began in 2002 and was completed in 2006, resulted in the decision to withhold 18 documents in full, excise a paragraph or more in 28 documents, and make minor excisions of less than a paragraph in 35 documents.

The Office of the Historian is confident, on the basis of the research conducted in preparing this volume and as a result of the declassification review process described above, that notwithstanding the number of denied and excised documents, the record presented in this volume presented here provides an accurate and comprehensive account the development of the intelligence community, 1950–1955.

Acknowledgments

The editors wish to acknowledge the assistance of officials at National Archives and Records Administration for their assistance in providing access to documents at the Truman and Eisenhower Presidential Libraries. David Haight at the Eisenhower Library was particularly helpful. The History Staff of the Center for the Study of Intelligence was extremely cooperative in assisting the editors in collecting relevant documents from Central Intelligence Agency files. Michael Warner, then Deputy Historian of the History Staff, was so instrumental in the production of this volume that he is listed as a co-editor. Special thanks to David Hatcher, Historian at the National Security Agency, and the historian at the Defense Intelligence Agency, who provided advice and key documents from their agencies.

The retrospective volumes on the organization and development of the intelligence community during the Truman and Eisenhower years was the brainchild of Neal Petersen, a long time editor of *Foreign Relations* and an expert on intelligence history. Petersen retired from the Office of the Historian before the first volume on the *Establishment of the Intelligence Community* was published in 1996, but the idea and basic concept was his. Douglas Keene and Michael Warner selected and annotated this volume under the supervision of David S. Patterson, then General Editor of the *Foreign Relations* series. The current General Editor, Edward C. Keefer, oversaw the final revisions and production of the volume. Susan Weetman and Dean Weatherhead coordinated the declassification of the volume and, with Edward Keefer and Renée Goings, prepared extensive declassification appeals which resulted in significantly more documentation being released. Florence Segura and Carl Ashley did the copy and technical editing. Caroline Sapp revised and updated the name list. Juniee Oneida prepared the index.

Bureau of Public Affairs   **Marc J. Susser**
December 2007   *The Historian*

Contents

Preface. III

Sources XI

Abbreviations and Terms XIX

Persons XXIII

The Intelligence Community, 1950–1955

    Organization of U.S. Intelligence. 1

    NSCIDs 790

Index. 811

Sources

In keeping with the statutory requirement of the *Foreign Relations* series, the editors have complete access to all the retired records and papers of the Department of State: the decimal central files; the special decentralized files ("lot files") at the bureau, office, and division levels; and the files of the Executive Secretariat. Virtually all the Department's files have been permanently transferred to the National Archives and Records Administration at College Park, Maryland (Archives II). All of these files, which the exception of the INR/IL historical files, and the administrative lot file that was later destroyed, are open for research at the National Archives.

The editors of the *Foreign Relations* series also have full access to the papers of Presidents Truman and Eisenhower, and other White House foreign policy records. Presidential papers maintained and preserved at the Truman and Eisenhower libraries include significant intelligence documentation from the Department of State and other federal agencies including the National Security Council, the Central Intelligence Agency, the Department of Defense, and the Joint Chiefs of Staff.

The editors also have full access to the files of the Central Intelligence Agency still in the possession of the Agency as well as to records transferred from the Agency to the National Archives. The Central Intelligence Agency files were crucial to the preparation of this volume and they will be discussed below.

Since this volume focuses on the development of intelligence, and not foreign policy and foreign relations, its sources are considerably different from most other *Foreign Relations* volumes. The decimal central files used for this volume are mainly intelligence-related, as reflected in the annotated source list below. The volume relies heavily on the retired files of the Bureau of Intelligence and Research (INR) at the Department of State. The most useful lot file was Lot 58 D 776, covering INR's work from 1945–1960. INR lot files subsequently have been consolidated at the National Archives, but Lot 58 D 776 provides core documentation for that consolidated file. The files of the Policy Planning Staff (S/P) of the Department of State also proved very valuable, especially S/P Files, Lot 64 D 563 and S/P–NSC Files, Lot 62 D 1, both of which had key material on psychological warfare and the Psychological Strategy Board. The lot files of the Executive Secretariat (S/S) of the Department of State were also very useful, particularly S/S–NSC, Lot 62 D 333, which contains the minutes and related papers of the Psychological Strategy Board, 1951–1953. Also of value are

S/S–NSC Files, Lot 63 D 351, the basic master files of the Department's NSC records for 1947–1961 and S/S–NSC Files, Lot 66 D and S/S–NSC Files, Lot 66 D 95, which both contain miscellaneous NSC records, with the latter containing NSC records of actions and some National Security Council Intelligence Directives (NSCIDs). Finally, the INR/IL Historical Files have documentation on the preparation and work-ing of NSC 10 series, the papers establishing and refining responsi-bilities for covert operations. All lots mentioned above, with the ex-ception of the INR/IL Historical Files, are available at the National Archives.

The best Central Intelligence Agency files listed are those of the Executive Registry, the Directorate of Operations, and the History Staff. They are of equal importance to the Department of State lot files. The History Staff files require special explanation. The History Staff collec-tion, maintained by the History Staff in the Center for the Study of In-telligence, contains documents selected over time by personnel of the various components of the Agency as having significant historical value and transferred to the physical custody of the History Staff to ensure their continued availability as part of the historical record. Documents in the historical collection tend to vary widely in nature and quality and usually provide only a partial record, but they are nonetheless a major resource and have been widely used in the preparation of this volume.

The Central Intelligence Agency files from the Executive Registry, the various directorates, and the Intelligence Community Management Staff, have a more direct provenance. The Executive Registry files are the official records of the Director of Central Intelligence and are there-fore crucial. The files of the Directorate of Operation were equally valu-able, while the files of the Directorate of Intelligence and Directorate of Science and Technology, and the Community Management Staff were important, but not to the standard of the Executive Registry, History Staff files, or the Operations files.

The editors did not do research in the massive files of the Na-tional Security Agency or the Defense Intelligence Agency, but instead relied upon the historians at those agencies to make available key doc-uments upon request or recommendation. At the National Archives, research in Record Group 218, the Records of the Joint Chiefs of Staff provided a few key documents. Record Group 263, the Central Intel-ligence Agency Files at the National Archives also fell into that same category. At the time the research for this volume was done, RG 263, contained basically sources made available to Thomas Troy for use in preparation of his book on the founding of the Agency, declassified National Intelligence Estimates and Special National Intelligence Es-timates, and declassified article from the Agency in-house journal,

Studies in Intelligence. Since the research for this volume was undertaken, the Central Intelligence Agency has transferred more records to the National Archives and made others available on its website. Finally, Record Group 273, the records of the National Security Council contains some key NSC policy papers, official minutes of NSC meetings, and NSCIDs.

Research at the Truman and Eisenhower presidential libraries provided important documents, but certainly not to the magnitude or importance as the records of the Department of State or Central Intelligence Agency. At the Truman Library in the Papers of the President, the President's Secretary's File was the most important, followed closely by the Subject File with documents on organizing covert operation and copies of NSCIDs. At the Eisenhower Library the best files were the Whitman File (records kept by Eisenhower's personal assistant Ann Whitman), the Staff Secretary Records, and the Records of the President's Special Assistant for National Security Affairs.

Two published works are worthy of consideration as starting points or research. The first is Michael Warner, editor, *The CIA Cold War Records: The CIA under Harry Truman,* which reproduces in facsimile format 81 documents covering 1945–1953, some of which are also produced in this volume. The other book is Ludwell Monatgue, *General Walter Bedell Smith as Director of Central Intelligence, October 1950– February 1953,* originally a classified five volume CIA study of the same name, but published in declassified form as a monograph by Pennsylvania State University Press. Montague was both a participant and an observer of the events of which he writes and supplemented his own recollections by research in CIA records and by extensive interviews of and correspondence with other key participants.

Unpublished Sources

Department of State

Central Files. See National Archives and Records Administration below.

Lot Files. For other lot files already transferred to the National Archives and Records Administration at College Park, Maryland, Record Group 59, see National Archives and Records Administration below.

A/MS Files: Lot 54 D 291

> Consolidated administrative files of the Department of State for 1949–1960, as maintained by the Management Staff of the Bureau of Administration (subsequently destroyed and not transferred to the National Archives).

INR/IL Historical Files

> Files of the Office of Intelligence Coordination, Bureau of Intelligence and Research.

National Archives and Records Administration, College Park, Maryland

Record Group 59, Records of the Department of State

Decimal Central Files, 1950-1955

100.4/PSB: Psychological Strategy Board
101.2: National Security Council
101.21: Central Intelligence Agency
103.11: U.S. federal agencies of non-Cabinet rank
103.1102: personnel of U.S. federal agencies of non-Cabinet rank
114.3: unauthorized or improper publication
120.201: workloads of diplomatic and consular representation
511.00: U.S. psychological warfare
611.00: U.S. international relations
611.61: U.S. relations with the Soviet Union
700.5411: U.S. overflights
711.5: U.S. national defense
711.52: U.S. intelligence activities
711.5200: U.S. intelligence activities
711.5261: U.S. intelligence activities in the Soviet Union
794.0221: Japanese occupied territory

Lot Files

Administration Files: Lot 62 D 220
    Top Secret records of the Bureau of Administration dealing with inter-agency relations from 1948–1961

INR Files: Lot 58 D 528
    Miscellaneous Top Secret files for the years 1949–1954 as retired by the Bureau of Intelligence and Research, including master files of Intelligence Estimates prepared by the Department of States Estimates Group

INR Files: Lot 58 D 776 (INR Lots 61 D 67 and 62 D 42 subsequently combined with this lot file)
    Subject files for 1945–1960, as maintained by the Office of the Special Assistant to the Secretary of State for Research and Intelligence, which includes information on the birth of the intelligence organization in the Department of State and a history of the national intelligence structure

INR Files: Lot 59 D 27
    Miscellaneous files for the years 1948–1954, including master file of minutes of the Intelligence Advisory Committee

INR Files, Lot 78 D 394
    Files relating to National Intelligence Estimates and Special Intelligence Estimates

Policy Planning Staff Files: Lot 67 D 548
    Subject files, country files, chronological files, documents, drafts and related correspondence for 1957–1961

S/P Files: Lot 64 D 563
    Master file of documents, drafts, records of meetings, memoranda, and related correspondence for 1947–1953 of the Policy Planning Staff

S/S–NSC OCB Files: Lot 61 D 385

Master set of the administrative and country files of the Operations Coordinating Board for the years 1953–1960, as maintained by the Executive Secretariat

S/P–NSC Files: Lot 62 D 1

Serial and subject master file of National Security Council documents and correspondence for the years 1948–1961 maintained by the Policy Planning Staff

S/S–NSC Files: Lot 62 D 333

Master file of minutes and papers of the Psychological Strategy Board for the years 1951–1953, as maintained by the Executive Secretariat

S/S–NSC Files: Lot 62 D 430

Master file of the Operations Coordinating Board for the years 1953–1960, as maintained by the Executive Secretariat

S/S–NSC Files: Lot 63 D 351

Serial master file of National Security Council documents and correspondence and related Department of State memoranda for 1947–1961, as maintained by the Executive Secretariat

S/S-NSC Files: Lot 66 D 148

Miscellaneous files concerning subjects considered by the National Security Council during 1949–1962, as maintained by the Executive Secretariat

S/S–NSC (Miscellaneous) Files: Lot 66 D 95

Administrative and miscellaneous National Security Council documentation, including NSC Records of Action for 1947–1963, as maintained by the Executive Secretariat

P Files: Lot 52 D 432

Files of Assistant Secretary of State for Public Affairs Edward W. Barrett for 1951

P Files: Lot 55 D 339

Files of the Assistant Secretary of State for Public Affairs, 1951–1952

S/S–RD Files

Files of restricted data materials maintained by the Executive Secretariat

Record Group 218, Records of the Joint Chiefs of Staff

Papers of the Joint Chiefs of Staff and the Chairman of the Joint Chiefs of Staff

Record Group 263, Records of the Central Intelligence Agency

Background documents from various sources made available to Thomas Troy in connection with the preparation of his book on the founding of the Central Intelligence Agency
Collection of NIE's, SNIE's and SE's
Declassified articles from *Studies in Intelligence,* a CIA publication

Record Group 273, Records of the National Security Council

Official NSC meeting minutes file
Records of the NSC Representative for Internal Security
Record set of NSC policy papers

Record Group 306

USIA Files, Lot 63 A 190, Files of the U.S. Information Agency

Record Group 457, Records of the National Security Agency

Special Research History Files

Library of Congress, Washington, D.C.

Radford Papers

National Security Council

Operations Coordination Board Records of Project Approvals

Central Intelligence Agency

Directorate for Intelligence files
   Job 80–R01440R

Directorate for Operations files
   Job 78–04513R
   Job 78–05091A
   Job 79–01228A
   Job 80–01795R
   Job 84–B00389R

Directorate for Science and Technology files
   Job 83–02415A

Community Management Staff files
   Job 82–00400R

Executive Registry files
   Files of the Directors of Central Intelligence
   Job 80–R01731R
   Job 83–01034R
   Job 85–500362R
   Job 86–T00268R
   Job 86–B00269R
   Job 95–G00278R

History Staff files
   Documents from various components of the Agency transferred to the custody of
   the History Staff, Center for the Study of Intelligence
   Job 83–00036R
   Job 83–00764R
   Job 83–01034R
   Job 84–00022R
   Job 84–00161R
   Job 84–T00286R
   Job 84–T00389R

Defense Intelligence Agency

Records made available by the Defense Intelligence Agency Historian

National Security Agency

Records held by or obtained through the Center for Cryptologic History, National Security Agency

Records of the President's Foreign Intelligence Advisory Board

Records of the meetings, reports and miscellaneous papers of the President's Board of Consultants for Foreign Intelligence Activities and, its successor, the President's Foreign Intelligence Advisory Board

Truman Library, Independence, Missouri

President's Secretary's Files
    Subject File
    Official File

Eisenhower Library, Abilene, Kansas

Dulles Papers
    Papers of John Foster Dulles, 1952–1959

Eisenhower Papers, Whitman File
    Papers of Dwight D. Eisenhower as President of the United States, 1953–1961, maintained by his personal secretary, Ann C. Whitman. The Whitman File includes: the Name Series, the Dulles-Herter Series, Eisenhower Diaries, Ann Whitman (ACW) Diaries, National Security Council Records, Miscellaneous Records, Cabinet Papers, Legislative Meetings, International Meetings, the Administration Series, and the International File

Eisenhower Records
    Records of Dwight D. Eisenhower as President of the United States, including the daily appointment book of the President

Hoover Commission Report on Intelligence Activities

Project "Clean Up"
    Records of Gordon Gray, Robert Cutler, Henry R. McPhee, and Andrew J. Goodpaster, 1953–1961

Staff Secretary Records
    Records of the office of the Staff Secretary, 1952–1961

Special Assistant to the President for National Security Affairs Records

Special Assistant to the President for Science and Technology Records

Published Sources

Benson, Robert L., and Michael Warner, eds., *Venona: Soviet Espionage and the American Response, 1939–1957*. Washington, D.C.: Central Intelligence Agency, 1996.

Montague, Ludwell Lee. *General Walter Bedell Smith as Director of Central Intelligence, October 1950–February 1953.* University Park: The Pennsylvania State University Press, 1992.

Pedlow, Gregory W., and Donald E. Welzenbach. *The CIA and the U–2 Program, 1954–1974.* Washington, D.C.: Central Intelligence Agency.

U.S. National Archives and Records Administration. *Public Papers of the Presidents of the United States: Harry S. Truman, 1950, 1951, 1952–1953.* Washington, D.C.: Government Printing Office, 1965–1966.

U.S. National Archives and Records Administration. *Public Papers of the Presidents of the United States: Dwight D. Eisenhower, 1953, 1954, 1955.* Washington, D.C.: Government Printing Office, 1959–1960.

Warner, Michael, ed., *The CIA Under Harry Truman,* Washington, D.C.: Central Intelligence Agency, 1994.

Abbreviations and Terms

AD/ORE, Assistant Director for Reports and Estimates
ADPC, Assistant Director for Policy Coordination, CIA
ADSO, Assistant Director for Special Operations (CIG and CIA)
AEC, Atomic Energy Commission
AFSA, Armed Forces Security Agency
AFSS, Air Force Security Service
ARC, Air Resupply and Communications
ARPA, Advanced Research Projects Agency
ASA, Army Security Agency
ATIC, Air Technical Intelligence Center

BOB, Bureau of the Budget
BW, biological warfare

CA, covert action; also circular airgram
CAS, Cleared American Source
CAT, Civil Air Transport
CE, Division of Central European Affairs, Department of State; also Counter-Espionage
CENTO, Central Treaty Organization
CERP, Combined Economic Reporting Program
CG, Commanding General
CI, Counter-intelligence
CIA, Central Intelligence Agency
CID, Criminal Investigative Division; also Counter-intelligence Division
CIG, Central Intelligence Group
CO, Commanding Officer
COAPS, Coordination, Operations and Policy/Planning Staff
COMINT, Communications Intelligence
CP, Communist party
CRITIC, Critical Intelligence Communications
CSP, Chief, Special Projects Division, Office of Policy Coordination
CW, chemical warfare

DCD, Domestic Contacts Division
DCI, Director of Central Intelligence (CIG and CIA)
DCID, Director of Central Intelligence Directive
DDCI, Deputy Director of Central Intelligence (CIG and CIA)
DDA, Deputy Director for Administration
DDC, Deputy Director for Coordination
DDI, Deputy Director for Intelligence
DDO, Deputy Director for Operations
DDP, Deputy Director for Plans
DD/S&T, Deputy Director for Science and Technology
DIRNSA, Director, National Security Agency
DNI, Director of Naval Intelligence
DOD, Department of Defense
DPD, Development Projects Division

E & E, escape and evasion
ECA, Economic Cooperation Administration

ECM, electronic counter-measures
ELINT, electronic intelligence
ES/NSC, Executive Secretary, National Security Council
EUCOM, European Command
EUR, Bureau of European Affairs, Department of State

FBI, Federal Bureau of Investigation
FBID, Foreign Broadcast Information Division
FBIS, Foreign Broadcast Information Service
FE, Office of Far Eastern Affairs, Department of State
FEA, Foreign Economic Administration
FEC, Free Europe Committee
FI, Foreign Intelligence
FOA, Foreign Operations Administration
FSO, Foreign Service Officer
FSR, Foreign Service Reserve
FTX, field training exercise
FY, fiscal year

G–2, intelligence section of divisional or higher staff
G–5, civil affairs section of divisional or higher staff
GAO, General Accounting Office
GCHQ, General Communications Headquarters (UK)
GMAIC, Guided Missile and Astronautics Intelligence Committee
GMIC, Guided Missile Intelligence Committee

HICOG, High Commissioner for Germany
HUMINT, human intelligence

IAB, Intelligence Advisory Board
IAC, Intelligence Advisory Committee
IAD, Acquisition and Distribution Division, Office of Research and Intelligence, Department of State
IBD, International Broadcasting Division
ICA, International Cooperation Administration
ICBM, intercontinental ballistic missile
ICIS, Interdepartmental Committee on Internal Security
ICS, Interdepartmental Coordinating Staff; also Intelligence Community Staff
IDP, Initial deployment plan
IFIO, International Foreign Information Organization
IFIS, International Foreign Information Staff
IG, Inspector General
IIC, Interdepartmental Intelligence Committee
IS, Intelligence Staff
ISA, International Security Affairs, Department of Defense
INR, Bureau of Intelligence and Research, Department of State

J–2, JCS intelligence organization
JAEIC, Joint Atomic Energy Intelligence Committee
JANIS, Joint Army-Navy Intelligence Studies
JCS, Joint Chiefs of Staff
JIC, Joint Intelligence Committee; also Joint Intelligence Center
JIS, Joint Intelligence Staff
JISPD, Joint Intelligence Studies Publication Board

JOT, junior officer trainee
JRC, Joint Reconnaissance Center
JRDB, Joint Research and Development Board
JSPD, Joint Subsidiary Plans Division
JTIS, Joint Technical Intelligence Subcommittee

L, Legal Adviser, Department of State

MAAG, Military Assistance Advisory Group
MI, military intelligence
MID, Military Intelligence Division, Department of the Army
MIS, Military Intelligence Staff, War Department General Staff; also military intelligence service

NATO, North Atlantic Treaty Organization
NCFE, National Committee for a Free Europe
NIA, National Intelligence Authority
NIC, National Indications Center of the IAC Watch Committee
NIE, National Intelligence Estimate
NIS, National Intelligence Survey; also National Intelligence Summary
NPIC, National Photographic Interpretation Center
NSA, National Security Agency
NSC, National Security Council
NSCID, National Security Council Intelligence Directive
NSG, Navy Security Group
NSRB, National Security Resources Board
NTPC, National Technical Processing Center

OB, order of battle
OCB, Operations Coordination Board
OCD, Office of Collection and Dissemination
OCI, Office of Current Intelligence
ODA, Office of Departmental Administration, Bureau of Administration, Department of State
ODM, Office of Defense Mobilization
OIR, Office of Intelligence Research
OLI, Office of Libraries and Intelligence Acquisition
ONE, Office of National Estimates
ONI, Office of Naval Intelligence, Department of Navy
ONR, Office of Naval Research
OO, Office of Operations
OPC, Office of Policy Coordination
OPD, Operations Division, War Department
ORE, Office of Research and Evaluation; also Office of Reports and Estimates
OSO, Office of Special Operations
OSS, Office of Strategic Services
OWI, Office of War Information

PACAF, Pacific Air Forces
PACOM, Pacific Command
PBCFIA, President's Board of Consultants for Foreign Intelligence Activities
PCG, Planning Coordination Group
PFIAB, President's Foreign Intelligence Advisory Board
PHOTINT, photographic intelligence

PIC, Photographic Interpretation Center
PM, Directorate of Politico-Military Affairs, Department of State; also paramilitary
PNG, persona non grata
PNIO, priority national intelligence objectives
POCC, Psychological Operations Coordinating Committee
PP, political and psychological
PSB, Psychological Strategy Board

R, Secretary of State's Special Assistant for Research and Intelligence
R&A, research and analysis
R&D, Research and development
RFA, Radio Free Asia
RFE, Radio Free Europe
RIAS, Radio in the American Sector
ROB, radar order of battle
ROKG, Republic of Korea Government
RTG, Reconnaissance Technical Group

S&T, Science and Technology
SAC, Strategic Air Command
SANACC, State-Army-Navy-Air Coordinating Committee
SE, Special Estimate
SEC, Scientific Estimates Committee
SESP, Special Electronic Airborne Search Operations
SHAPE, Supreme Headquarters Allied Powers Europe
SI, special intelligence
SIS, Special Intelligence Service
SNIE, Special National Intelligence Estimate
SO or SOPAG, Special Operations
SOVMAT, Soviet material
SWNCC, State-War-Navy Coordinating Committee

T/O, table of organization
TAC, Tactical Air Command

UNO, United Nations Organization
USAFE, U.S. Air Forces, Europe
USCIB, U.S. Communications Intelligence Board
USEB, U.S. Evaluation Board
USFA, U.S. Forces in Austria
USIA, U.S. Information Agency
USIB, U.S. Intelligence Board
USIE, U.S. Information and Education (Program)
USRO, U.S. Mission to NATO and European Regional Organizations
USSR, Union of Soviet Socialist Republics

VOA, Voice of America

ZI, zone of interior

Persons

Acheson, Dean, Secretary of State from January 21, 1949 to January 20, 1953

Adams, Sherman, White House Chief of Staff from January 20, 1953

Allen, George V., Assistant Secretary of State for Public Affairs from March 31, 1948 to November 28, 1949; Assistant Secretary of State for Near Eastern, South Asian and African Affairs from January 24, 1955 to November 1957; Director of the United States Information Agency from November 15, 1957 to 1960

Allen, Raymond B., Director of the Psychological Strategy Board from January to August 1952

Amory, Robert, Jr., Deputy Director for Intelligence of the Central Intelligence Agency from March 23, 1953 to 1962

Armstrong, W. Park, Jr., Special Assistant to the Secretary of State for Research and Intelligence from June 11, 1950; Chairman of the Communications Intelligence Board

Baker, William, Vice President, Bell Laboratories; Member of the President's Science Advisory Committee; Head of Baker Panel on Communications Intelligence

Balmer, Brigadier General Jesmond D., USA, member of the Joint Chiefs of Staff; the Assistant to the Director of Central Intelligence for Interagency Coordination

Barbour, Walworth, Director, Office of Eastern European Affairs from July 25, 1951 to May 1954; Deputy Assistant Secretary of State for European Affairs from May 26, 1954 to November 20, 1955

Barrett, Edward W., Assistant Secretary of State for Public Affairs from February 1, 1950 to February 20, 1952

Belmont, Alan H., Assistant Director, Federal Bureau of Investigation

Berding, Andrew H., Assistant Secretary of State for Public Affairs from March 22, 1957 to 1961

Bishop, Max, Consulate General at Dhahran from September 20, 1951 to January 6, 1954; Operations Coordinator, Office of the Under Secretary of State from November 2, 1954 to December 3, 1955

Bissell, Richard, Special Assistant to the Director of Central Intelligence from February 1, 1954 to 1958; Deputy Director for Plans from 1958 to February 1962

Boggs, Marion, Director of the National Security Council Secretariat until July 1959; Deputy Executive Secretary, from July 1959

Bohlen, Charles, Counselor, Department of State from March 13, 1951 to March 1953; Ambassador to the Soviet Union from March 27, 1953 to March 1957; Ambassador to the Philippines from March 13, 1957 to May 1959; Special Assistant to the Secretary of State from May 9, 1959

Booster, Davis E., Staff Assistant to Secretary of State Dulles

Bowie, Robert, Director of the Policy Planning Staff, Department of State from May 18, 1953 to August 1955; Department of State Representative on the National Security Planning Board from 1953 to 1957; Assistant Secretary of State for Policy Planning from August 10, 1955 to August 28, 1957

Braden, Thomas, Assistant to the Deputy Director of the Central Intelligence Agency, Office of Policy Coordination, International Organizations Division from 1951 to 1952; Chief, International Organizations Division, Central Intelligence Agency, from 1952 to 1954

Bradley, General Omar N., USA, Chairman, Joint Chiefs of Staff from August 16, 1949 to August 15, 1953

Breitweiser, Major General Robert, USAF, Director of Intelligence, Joint Staff from February 1957

Brownell, George, former military officer and lawyer; Head of Communications Intelligence Committee from December 28, 1951

Bruce, David K.E., Ambassador to France from 1949 to 1952; Under Secretary of State from February 7, 1952 to January 20, 1953; Observer to the Interim Committee of the European Defense Community from February 19, 1953; Representative to the European Coal and Steel Authority from 1954 to January 22, 1955; Ambassador to Germany from March 14, 1957 to 1959

Brundage, Percival E., Deputy Director, Bureau of the Budget from 1954 to 1956; Director, Bureau of the Budget from April 2, 1956 to March 17, 1958

Burke, Admiral Arleigh A., USN, Chief of Naval Operations from August 17, 1955 to 1961

Cabell, General Charles P., USAF, Director of Intelligence, Office of the Deputy Chief of Staff from 1951 to 1953; Intelligence Advisory Committee, Deputy Director of Central Intelligence from 1953 to 1962

Caccia, Sir Harold, British Ambassador to the United States from 1956 to 1961

Canine, Lieutenant General Ralph J., USA, Director, Armed Forces Security Agency from 1951; Director, National Security Agency from November 4, 1952 to 1956

Cassidy, Brigadier General John, USA, Staff Director, President's Board of Consultants on Foreign Intelligence Activities from January 1956

Clark, General (Ret.) Mark, USA, President of the Citadel from 1953 to 1955; Chairman of the Hoover Commission on the Organization of the Executive Branch for the Investigation of the Central Intelligence Agency from 1954 to 1955

Conant, James, B., Ambassador to Germany from May 17, 1955 to February 19, 1957

Connolly, Admiral Richard L., USN, President, Long Island University; member, President's Board of Consultants on Foreign Intelligence Activities from January 13, 1956

Coyne, J. Patrick, National Security Council Representative for Internal Security from 1947 to 1960; President's Board of Consultants on Foreign Intelligence Activities Staff Director from 1960

Cumming, Hugh, Foreign Service Officer, Moscow, Department of State from June 12, 1950 to August 14, 1951; Personal Rank of Minister to Moscow, Department of State, from August 14, 1951 to June 1952; Deputy Secretary General for Political Affairs, NATO, from June 30, 1952 to September 1953; Director of Intelligence and Research, Department of State from October 10, 1957

Cutler, Robert, Administrative Assistant to the President until 1953; Special Assistant to the President for National Security Affairs from March 23, 1953 to April 1955 and from January 1957 to July 1958

Dulles, Allen W., Chairman, National Security Council Survey Committee until 1948; Deputy Director for Operations, Central Intelligence Agency, 1951; Deputy Director Plans, Central Intelligence Agency in 1951; Deputy Director of Central Intelligence from 1951 to 1953; Director of Central Intelligence from 1953; member, Committee on Information Activities Abroad from February 17, 1960 to January 12, 1961

Dulles, John Foster, Secretary of State from January 21, 1953 to April 1959

Dodge, Joseph M., Director, Bureau of the Budget from 1953 to 1954; Chairman, Council on Foreign Economic Policy from December 1954 to 1956

Doolittle, General James, USAF; member, President's Board of Consultants on Foreign Intelligence Activities; Head of Doolittle Panel on Covert Activities from January 13, 1956

Eden, Anthony, Foreign Secretary of the United Kingdom from 1951 to 1955; Prime Minister of the United Kingdom from 1955 to 1957

Eisenhower, General Dwight D., USA, Supreme Allied Commander, Europe from December 1950 to May 31, 1952; President of the United States from January 20, 1953

Eisenhower, Major John S.D., USA, Assistant Staff Secretary to the President from 1953

Elbrick, C. Burke, General Deputy Assistant Secretary, Department of State, from May 26, 1954 to February 1957; Assistant Secretary of State for European Affairs from February 11, 1957 to April 22, 1958; Ambassador to Portugal from October 29, 1958

Erskine, General (Ret.) Graves, USMC, Special Assistant to the Secretary of Defense for Special Operations from June 1953 to October 31, 1961

Evans, Allan, Director, Office of Intelligence and Research, Department of State until September 15, 1957; Director, Office of Intelligence, Research, and Analysis from February 22, 1959

Fechteler, Admiral William M., USN, Chief of Naval Operations from August 1951 to August 1953

Foster, William C., Administrator, Economic Cooperation Administration from 1950 to 1951; member, Strategic Missile Evaluation Committee or "Teapot Committee", from June 16, 1953 to February 8, 1954; Deputy Secretary of Defense from September 24, 1951 to 1953

Frank, Joseph A., Office of Policy Coordination, Central Intelligence Agency from April 28, 1955

Furnas, Howard, Office of Research and Intelligence, Department of State from November 2, 1950 to September 1952 and from August 20, 1954 to September 1957; member Policy Planning Staff and Representative to the National Security Council Planning Board from January 13, 1958

Gaither, Rowan, Assistant Director of the Radiation Laboratory, MIT; member of the Board of Trustees, the RAND Corporation, from May 14, 1948; Chairman of the Ford Foundations from March 1951; Head of the Strategic Missile Evaluation Committee or "Teapot Committee," from June 16, 1953 to February 8, 1954; Head of Security Resources Board of Office of Defense Mobilization which issued "Deterrence-Survival in the Nuclear Age" from April 1957

Gardner, Trevor, USAF, Assistant Secretary of the Air Force for Research and Development from 1954 to February 1956

Gates, Thomas S., Under Secretary of the Navy from October 2, 1953 to 1957; Secretary of the Navy from 1957 to 1959; Deputy Secretary of Defense from June to December 1959; Secretary of Defense from December 2, 1959 to January 20, 1961

Gleason, S. Everett, Historian, Council on Foreign Relations from 1946 to 1950; Deputy Executive Secretary of the National Security Council from March 1953 to 1959; Cultural Attaché of the United States to the United Kingdom from 1959 to 1961

Goodpaster, Major General Andrew, USA, Staff Secretary to the President from October 10, 1954 to January 1961

Gray, Gordon, Secretary of the Army from June 20, 1949 to April 12, 1950; Director of the Psychological Strategy Board from 1951 to 1952; member, the President's Committee on International Information Activities from January 20, 1953 to June 30, 1953; Assistant Secretary of Defense for International Security Affairs from July 1955 to February 1957; Director of Defense Mobilization from March 1957 to July 1958; Special Assistant to the President for National Security Affairs from July 1958 to January 1961; member, Committee for Information Activities Abroad from February 17, 1960 to January 12, 1961

Guthe, Otto, Special Assistant to the Director, Office of Libraries and Intelligence Acquisition from January 23, 1948 to October 30, 1949; Assistant Director, Research and Reports, Directorate of Intelligence, Central Intelligence Committee from 1953 to 1965; Chairman, Economic Intelligence Committee from 1953 to 1965

Hagerty, James, Press Secretary to the President from January 1953 to 1961

Harlow, Bryce N., Administrative Assistant to the President from January 1953; Deputy Assistant to the President from 1953 to 1961

Harriman, W. Averell, Representative to Europe of the Economic Cooperation Administration from 1948 to 1950; Special Assistant to the President from 1950; Director of Mutual Security from 1951 to 1953

Helms, Richard, Office of Special Operations, Deputy Assistant Director for Special Operations, Central Intelligence Agency from 1951 to 1952; Acting Chief of Operations, Office of the Deputy Director for Plans from 1952 to 1953; Chief of Operations from 1953 to 1958; Deputy to the Deputy Director for Plans and Chief of Operations from 1958 to 1962

Henderson, Loy, Ambassador to Iran from September 19, 1951 to January 1956; member of the First and Second Suez Canal Conference, Suez Canal Committee in London and Cairo from August to September 1956; Deputy Under Secretary of State for Administration from January 26, 1955 to 1961

Herter, Christian, Under Secretary of State and Chairman, Operations Coordinating Board from February 1957 to April 1959; Secretary of State from April 1959 to January 1961

Hillenkoetter, Rear Admiral Roscoe, USN, Director of Central Intelligence, Central Intelligence Group and Central Intelligence Agency from May 1, 1947 to October 7, 1950

Hooker, Robert G., Jr., Policy Planning Staff, Department of State from January 23, 1950 to December 1951; Foreign Affairs Officer, Department of State, from November 13, 1953 to December 1954

Hoover, Herbert, former President; Chairman of the Commission on Organization of the Executive Branch of the Government from 1953

Hoover, Herbert, Jr. Under Secretary of State and Chairman, Operations Coordinating Board from October 1954 to February 1957

Hoover, J. Edgar, Director, Federal Bureau of Investigation

Houston, Lawrence, Assistant General Counsel of the Office of Strategic Services; General Counsel to the Central Intelligence Group and to the Central Intelligence Agency from 1946

Howe, Fisher, Deputy Special Assistant for Research and Intelligence, Department of State from March 1, 1950 to March 12, 1956; Director, Executive Secretariat, Department of State, from March 12, 1956 to October 1958

Hughes, John C., member, the President's Committee on International Information Activities from January 20, 1953 to June 30, 1953

Hughes, Rowland R., Director, Bureau of the Budget from 1954 to 1956

Hulick, Charles E., Jr., Deputy Operations Coordinator, Office of the Under Secretary of State from March 1, 1954 to August 12, 1956

Hull, General (Ret.) John E., USA, member, Strategic Missile Evaluation Committee or "Teapot Committee" from June 16, 1953 to February 8, 1954; Chairman of the President's Board of Consultants for Foreign Intelligence Activities from January 13, 1958

Humelsine, Carlisle H., Executive Secretary, Department of State from June 1947 to January 11, 1950; Deputy Assistant Secretary of State for Administration from January 1950; Assistant Secretary of State for Administration from July 29, 1950; Deputy Under Secretary of State for Administration from August 11, 1950 to 1953

Irwin, John N. II, member, the President's Committee on International Information Activities from January 20, 1953 to June 30, 1953; Deputy Assistant Secretary to the Assistant Secretary for Internal Security Affairs, Department of Defense from 1957 to 1961; Assistant Secretary of Defense for National Security Affairs from 1958 to 1961; member, Committee on Information Activities Abroad from February 17, 1960 to January 12, 1961

Jackson, C.D., Special Assistant to the President from January 26, 1953 to March 1954; President, Free Europe Committee in 1954; member, Committee on Information Activities Abroad from February 17, 1960 to January 12, 1961

Jackson, William H., member, National Security Council Survey Committee in 1948; Deputy Director of Central Intelligence from October 7, 1950 to 1951; Chairman, the President's Committee on International Information Activities from January 20, 1953 to June 30, 1953; Special Assistant to the Secretary of State from September 1955 to January 1956; Special Assistant to the President from January to September 1956; Acting Special Assistant to the President from September 1956 to January 1957

Jessup, Phillip, Ambassador at Large from March 2, 1949 to 1953

Johnson, Louis, Secretary of Defense from March 28, 1949 to September 19, 1950

Johnson, Roy W., Director, Advanced Research Projects Agency, Department of Defense from February 1958 to 1959

Joyce, Robert P., Office of Special Operations, Central Intelligence Group, Liaison to the Department of State from 1946 to June 1947; Political Adviser on Trieste from July 1, 1947 to October 27, 1948; Senior Consultant Representing the Secretary of State, Office of Policy Coordination from September 1948; Policy Planning Staff, Department of State from December 23, 1948 to December 22, 1952; Special Assistant, Bureau of Intelligence and Research from October 7, 1957 to April 19, 1959

Kennan, George F., Director, Policy Planning Staff, Department of State from March 7, 1948 to January 1, 1950; Counselor of the Department of State from August 4, 1949 to July 1951; Ambassador to the Soviet Union from March 14, 1952 to September 1952

Kent, Sherman, Head of the Office of the National Estimates from November 1953 to December 31, 1967; Chairman, Board of National Estimates, Central Intelligence Agency, November 1953 to December 31, 1967

Khrushchev, Nikita, Chairman of the Council of Ministers of the Soviet Union from September 7, 1953

Killian, James, member, Scientific Advisory Committee, Office of Defense Mobilization, from 1951 to 1957; Head Technical Capabilities Panel, Office of Defense Mobilization in June 1955; Chairman, President's Board of Consultants on Foreign Intelligence Activities from January 13, 1956 to 1958; Special Assistant to the President for Science and Technology from November 1957 to July 1959

Kirkpatrick, Lyman B., Deputy Assistant Director for Office of Operations, Central Intelligence Agency until 1950; Executive Assistant to the Director of Central Intelligence from 1950 to 1951; Assistant Director for Special Operations from 1951 to 1952, Chief of Operations, Deputy Directorate of Plans from 1952 to 1953; Special Assistant to the Deputy Director for Plans in 1953; Inspector General from April 1953 to 1962

Kistiakowsky, George, member, Strategic Missile Evaluation Committee or "Teapot Committee" from June 16, 1953 to February 8, 1954; staff member, White House Office of Science and Technology from 1957 to 1959; Director and Special Assistant to the President for Science and Technology from July 1959 to January 1961

Kohler, Foy, Chief, International Broadcasting Division, Department of State until November 1, 1949; Director, Voice of America Broadcasting from 1949 to 1952; Assistant Administrator, International Information Administration February 14 to November 1952; Policy Planning Staff from November 9, 1952 to February 2, 1953

Kyes, Roger, member, President's Committee on International Information Activities from January 20, 1953 to June 30, 1953; Deputy Secretary of Defense from February 2, 1953 to May 1, 1954

Land, Edwin, Founder of Polaroid; Chairman, Technical Capabilities Panel, Office of Defense Mobilization from 1954; member, President's Board of Consultants on Foreign Intelligence Activities from 1962

Larson, Arthur, Director, Under Secretary for Labor until 1956; United States Information Agency from 1956 to 1957; Special Assistant to the President for Speech Writing from 1957 to 1958

Lawrence, Harold, Deputy Staff Director, President's Board of Consultants for Foreign Intelligence Activities from January 1956

Lay, James S., Jr., member, Central Intelligence Group from January 1946; Secretary, Intelligence Advisory Board from January 1946 to September 1947; Office of Reports and Estimates, Central Intelligence Group in 1947; Assistant to the Executive Secretary, National Security Council from September 1947 to January 1950; Executive Secretary, National Security Council from January 1950 to 1961

LeMay, Curtis, USAF, Commander in Chief, Strategic Air Command from 1949 to 1957; Vice Chief of Staff of the Air Force from 1957 to 1961

Lemnitzer, General Lyman, USA, Vice Chief of Staff of the Army from April 8, 1957 to September 1960; Chairman, Joint Chiefs of Staff from September 1960 to 1962

Lloyd, Selwyn, Minister of Defense of the United Kingdom from 1954 to 1955; Secretary of State for Foreign Affairs of the United Kingdom from December 1955 to 1960

Lodge, Henry Cabot, Senator (R–MA); Permanent Representative to the United Nations from January 23, 1953 to 1960

Lovett, Robert A., Assistant Secretary of War for Air until December 1945; Under Secretary of State from July, 1, 1947 to January 20, 1949; Deputy Secretary of Defense from 1950 to 1951; Secretary of Defense from 1951 to 1953; member, Strategic Missile Evaluation Committee or "Teapot Committee" from June 16, 1953 to February 8, 1954; member, President's Board of Consultants on Foreign Intelligence Activities from January 13, 1956

MacArthur, Douglas II, Counselor of the Department of State from March 30, 1953 to July 20, 1956

MacMillan, Harold, British Prime Minister from January 1957 to October 1963

Macy, Robert M., Chief, International Division, Bureau of the Budget from 1950

Magruder, Brigadier General (Ret.) John, USA, United States Army, Senior Consultant representing the Secretary of Defense, Office of Policy Coordination from September 1948 to 1953

Makins, Sir Roger, British Ambassador to the United States from January 7, 1953 to November 9, 1956

Marshall, Charles Burton, member, Policy Planning Staff, Department of State, from June 1, 1950 to 1953

Marshall, General George C., USA, Chief of Staff, U.S. Army until November 1945; Secretary of State from January 21, 1947 to January 20, 1949; Secretary of Defense from September 21, 1950 to 1951

Matthews, H. Freeman, Deputy Under Secretary of State for Political Affairs from July 5, 1950 to 1953

McCone, John, Chairman, Atomic Energy Commission from 1958 to 1960; Director of Central Intelligence from November 29, 1961

McElroy, Neil H., Secretary of Defense from August 7, 1957 to December 1959

Merchant, Livingstone, Special Assistant to the Secretary of State from November 30, 1951 to March 24, 1952; Assistant Secretary of State for European Affairs from March 11, 1953 to May 7, 1956 and October 29, 1958 to August 12, 1959; Deputy Under Secretary of State for Political Affairs from August to December 1959; member, Committee on Information Activities Abroad from February 17, 1960 to January 12, 1961; Under Secretary of State for Political Affairs from June 24, 1960 to February 1, 1961

Meyer, Cord, International Organizations Division, Central Intelligence Agency from 1951 to 1954; Director, International Organizations Division from 1954

Morgan, George, Acting Director, Psychological Strategy Board from 1951 to 1952; Deputy Executive Officer, Operations Coordinating Board from March 23, 1953 to 1954

Murphy, Robert, Deputy Under Secretary of State for Political Affairs from November 1953 to 1959; Under Secretary of State for Political Affairs from August to December 1959

Nash, Frank C., Assistant to the Secretary of Defense for International Security Affairs from 1951 to 1953; Assistant Secretary of Defense for International Security Affairs from March 23, 1953 to 1954

Nitze, Paul H., Director of the Policy Planning Staff, Department of State, from January 1, 1950 to 1953; member, Strategic Missile Evaluation Committee or "Teapot Committee" from June 16, 1953 to February 8, 1954

Parrott, Thomas A., Office of Policy Coordination

Persons, Major General "Jerry" Wilton B., Deputy Assistant to the President from January 20, 1953 to October 7, 1958; Assistant to the President from October 7, 1958 to 1961

Peurifoy, John E., Assistant Secretary of State for Administration from March 17, 1947 to August 10, 1950

Quarles, Donald A., Assistant Secretary of Defense for Research and Development from October 1, 1953 to August 11, 1955; Secretary of the Air Force from August 15, 1955 to 1957; Deputy Secretary of Defense from April 30, 1957 to May 8, 1959

Radford, Admiral Arthur W., USN, Chairman of the Joint Chiefs of Staff from August 1953 to August 1957

Reber, James Q., Assistant Director for Intelligence Coordination, Central Intelligence Agency from 1950 to 1954

Robertson, Reuben, Deputy Secretary of Defense from August 1, 1955 to April 8, 1957

Rockefeller, Nelson A., Special Assistant to the President and Chairman of the Planning Coordination Group from 1954 to 1955

Rusk, Dean, Assistant Secretary of State for Far Eastern Affairs from March 28, 1950 to 1951

Samford, Lieutenant General John, USAF, Director of Intelligence for the United States Air Force from 1952 to 1956; Director, National Security Agency from November 1956 to November 1960

Sargeant, Howland H., Deputy to the Assistant Secretary of State for Public Affairs from October 1, 1947 to 1950

Savage, Carlton, member, Policy Planning Staff, Department of State from October 16, 1949

Smith, Gerard C., Consultant to the Secretary of State on Atomic Energy Affairs from April 12, 1954 to January 1, 1957; Assistant Secretary of State for Policy Planning from October 18, 1957 to 1961

Smith, Walter Bedell, Director of Central Intelligence from October 7, 1950 to February 20, 1953; Under Secretary of State from February 9, 1953 to 1954

Sprague, Mansfield, General Counsel, Department of Defense from 1955 to 1957; Assistant Secretary of Defense for International Security Affairs from 1957 to 1958; Head of the Committee on Information Activities Abroad from February 17, 1960 to January 12, 1961

Staats, Elmer B., Executive Officer of Operations Coordinating Board, National Security Council from 1953 to 1954

Stassen, Harold, Director for Mutual Security from January to May 1953; Director for Foreign Operations from August 1, 1953 to 1955; Special Assistant to the President for Disarmament from 1955 to 1958

Stevens, Vice Admiral (Ret.) Leslie C., Joint Plans Subsidiary Division, Joint Chiefs of Staff; Director, Psychological Strategy Board from September 1949

Stewart, Gordon, Chief, Foreign Intelligence, Central Intelligence Agency from July 1949

Strauss, Lewis L., Chairman, Atomic Energy Commission from July 1953 to 1958

Streibert, Theodore C., Director of the United States Information Agency from 1953 to 1956

Stubbs, Gail L., Office of Policy Coordination, Central Intelligence Agency

Symington, W. Stuart, Secretary of the Air Force from September 18, 1947 to April 24, 1950; Senator (D–MO)

Talbott, Harold E, Secretary of the Air Force from February 4, 1953 to August 1955

Trudeau, Major General Arthur G., USA, Assistant Chief of Staff, G–2 from November 16, 1953 to August 8, 1955

Truman, Harry S, President of the United States from April 12, 1945 to January 20, 1953

Truscott, Lieutenant General (Ret.) Lucian, the first Deputy Director for Coordination, Central Intelligence Agency from July 1, 1957 to July 1, 1960

Twining, General Nathan, USAF, Vice Chief of Staff from June 30, 1953 to August 1957; Chief of Staff from June 1953 to 1957; Chairman of the Joint Chiefs of Staff from August 15, 1957

Vandenberg, General Hoyt S., USAF, Director of Central Intelligence, Central Intelligence Group from June 10, 1946 to May 1, 1947; Chief of Staff, United States Air Force from April 30, 1948 to 1953

Webb, James E., Under Secretary of State from January 28, 1949 to 1952

Whearty, Raymond P., Chairman, Interdepartmental Committee on Internal Security

Wilson, Charles, E., Secretary of Defense from 1953 to 1957

Wisner, Frank G., Assistant Director for Policy Coordination, Central Intelligence Agency from September 1, 1948 to August 1, 1951; Deputy Director for Plans from August 23, 1951 to December 1, 1958

Yost, Charles W., Foreign Service Officer, Director, Office of Eastern European Affairs, Department of State from December 30, 1949 to September 29, 1950; member, Policy Planning Staff from April 20, 1958

The Intelligence Community, 1950–1955

Organization of U.S. Intelligence

1. Memorandum From Secretary of Defense Johnson[1]

Washington, January 19, 1950.

MEMORANDUM FOR

The Secretary of the Army
The Secretary of the Navy
The Secretary of the Air Force

SUBJECT

Support of Covert Operations of CIA

REFS

(a) Memorandum to the Director, CIA, on the above subject dtd 6 Oct '49[2]
(b) Reply of Director, CIA, to the Secretary of Defense, 18 Oct '49[3]

1. Pursuant to the last paragraph of the first reference you are authorized to support the covert operations of the Central Intelligence Agency in accordance with the terms of my memorandum of 6 October 1949.

2. The Joint Subsidiary Plans Division, Joint Staff, is the agency within the Department of Defense responsible, among other duties, for coordinating and facilitating operational support of approved covert operations of the CIA with the Services.

3. The responsibilities in this field of Brigadier General John Magruder, USA (Retired), Policy Consultant for this office with the State Department and the Central Intelligence Agency, remain as indicated in my letter of 7 October 1949, to the Secretary of State, a copy of which was provided you.[4]

Louis Johnson[5]

---

[1] Source: Central Intelligence Agency, Executive Registry, Job 95–G00278R, Box 1, Folder 5. Top Secret. Copies were sent to the Joint Chiefs of Staff; the Director, Subsidiary Plans Division; and the Director of Central Intelligence.

[2] See *Foreign Relations, 1945–1950, Emergence of the Intelligence Establishment,* Document 312.

[3] Ibid., Document 315.

[4] Ibid., Document 313.

[5] Printed from a copy that indicates Johnson signed the original.

2. National Security Council Report[1]

NSC 59/1   Washington, March 9, 1950.

THE FOREIGN INFORMATION PROGRAM AND PSYCHOLOGICAL WARFARE PLANNING

1. Foreign information programs in periods of peace and psychological warfare programs in periods of national emergency or war are established instruments of national policy and must be continuously directed toward the achievement of national aims. Foreign information activities and related facilities of all departments and agencies of the U. S. Government comprise the essential elements of a national foreign information program in time of peace and the essential nucleus for psychological warfare in periods of national emergency and the initial stages of war.

2. To achieve continuity between peacetime and wartime plans and programs and to provide for the strengthening and coordination of all foreign information activities in time of peace and psychological warfare activities in time of national emergency and the initial stages of war:

a. The Secretary of State shall be responsible for:

(1) The formulation of policies and plans for a national foreign information program in time of peace. This program shall include all foreign information activities conducted by departments and agencies of the U. S. Government.

(2) The formulation of national psychological warfare policy in time of national emergency and the initial stages of war.

(3) The coordination of policies and plans for the national foreign information program and for overt psychological warfare with the Department of Defense, with other appropriate departments and agencies of the U. S. Government, and with related planning under the NSC–10 series.[2]

---

[1] Source: National Archives, RG 59, S/S–NSC Files: Lot 66 D 148, Psychological Warfare. Secret. NSC Action No. 283 recorded that the Council approved NSC 59 as amended by memorandum action of March 9. The report in its approved form (printed here) was circulated as NSC 59/1 under cover of a March 9 note from Lay and submitted to the President for consideration. NSC Action No. 283 is ibid., S/S–NSC Files: Lot 66 D 95, Records of Action by the National Security Council. A memorandum from Lay to the National Security Council, March 10, indicates that the President approved NSC 59/1 on March 10. (Ibid., S/P–NSC Files: Lot 62 D 1, 1935–62, Box 115)

[2] For the NSC 10 series, see *Foreign Relations*, 1945–1950, Emergence of the Intelligence Establishment, Documents 283 ff.

b. All departments and agencies of the U.S. Government shall formulate detailed plans in support of the overall plans, and shall insure the most effective coordination and utilization of their appropriate activities and facilities for the implementation of approved plans, policies, and programs.

3. There shall be established within the Department of State an organization to:

a. Initiate and develop interdepartmental plans, make recommendations, and otherwise advise and assist the Secretary of State in discharging his responsibilities for the national foreign information program in time of peace.

b. Make plans for overt psychological warfare, including recommendations for preparations for national emergency and the initial stages of war. Such plans shall be continuously coordinated with joint war plans through the planning agencies of the Department of Defense and where such plans have a direct impact on war plans they shall be subject to the concurrence of the Joint Chiefs of Staff.

4. Plans prepared by this organization for overt psychological warfare in time of national emergency or the initial stages of war shall provide for:

a. Coordination of overt psychological warfare with:

(1) Covert psychological warfare.
(2) Censorship.
(3) Domestic information.

b. The employment and expansion, insofar as is feasible, of the activities and facilities which compose the national foreign information program in time of peace, in order to assure rapid transition to operations in time of national emergency or war.

c. Control of the execution of approved plans and policies by:

(1) the Department of Defense in theaters of military operations;
(2) the Department of State in areas other than theaters of military operations.

d. Transmittal of approved psychological warfare plans and policies to theater commanders through the Joint Chiefs of Staff.

5. The organization provided for in paragraph 3 above shall consist of:

a. A Director appointed by the Secretary of State after consultation with other departments and agencies represented on the National Security Council.

b. Policy consultants representing the Secretary of State, the Secretary of Defense, and the Chairman of the National Security Resources Board.

c. A consultant representing the Director of Central Intelligence for matters relating to coordination with planning under the NSC–10 series.

d. A consultant representing the Joint Chiefs of Staff on NSC 59 and NSC 10/2 matters.

e. A staff composed of full-time personnel representing the Department of State, the Department of Defense, and the Central Intelligence Agency.

f. A liaison representative to the staff from the National Security Resources Board and such liaison representation or staff membership from other departments and agencies of the government as may be determined by the Director after consultation with the consultants.

6. The Department of State shall provide necessary space, secretarial staff, and such other administrative services as may be required for this organization.[3]

7. The NSC–4 and the NSC–43 series are hereby rescinded.[4]

---

[3] See Document 17.

[4] The NSC 43 series, "Planning for Wartime Conduct of Overt Psychlogical Warfare," is in National Archives, RG 59, S/S–NSC Files: Lot 63 D 351, National Security Council Files. For text of NSC 4–A, December 9, 1947, see *Foreign Relations, 1945–1950*, Emergence of the Intelligence Establishment, Document 253. NSC 4, December 17, 1947, is ibid., Document 252.

---

3.   **Letter From the Department of State Member of the Standing Committee (Trueheart) to the Chief of the Coordination, Operations, and Policy Staff of the Central Intelligence Agency (Childs)[1]**

Washington, March 29, 1950.

Dear Mr. Childs:

Reference is made to your memorandum of March 6, 1950, forwarding a draft interagency operating procedure for the proposed Watch Committee.[2]

As you are aware, we are in full accord with the Watch Committee idea. We believe, however, that the specific procedures outlined in

---

[1] Source: Central Intelligence Agency, Executive Registry, Job 80–R01731R, Box 43, Folder 7. Top Secret. A handwritten notation indicates a copy was sent to AD/ORE on March 30.

[2] Not found.

the CIA proposal tend to obscure the method by which the Committee should operate and, indeed, the basic purpose for which the Committee needs to be established.

In considering procedures for the Watch Committee, it is important to bear in mind that a committee is not needed merely to effect an exchange of pertinent items of information. The unique feature of a committee—and the reason a committee is needed in this field—is that it provides a mechanism whereby all such items of information may be juxtaposed, compared with each other, discussed, and jointly evaluated by the members. Similarly, the committee structure permits joint consideration of the important question: What are the proper and significant categories of information (indicators) having a bearing on Soviet intentions to make war in the near future?

With this is mind we are submitting for your consideration a redraft of the agreement.[3] While there are a number of minor changes, the most important adjustments we propose are designed to emphasize this deliberative aspect of the Committee's work. I should be glad to discuss it with you in detail at your convenience.

I am sending copies of this letter to the other action addressees of your memorandum.[4]

Sincerely yours,

William C. Trueheart

---

[3] The enclosure, entitled "Draft of Proposed Interagency Operating Procedure," was not found.

[4] Not further identified.

---

4. **Memorandum From the Counselor of the Department of State (Kennan) to the Under Secretary of State (Webb)[1]**

Washington, March 30, 1950.

On June 18 [17], 1948, at its 13th meeting, the National Security Council approved a directive (NSC 10/2)[2] establishing in the Central

---

[1] Source: National Archives, RG 59, S/P Files: Lot 64 D 563, Chronological. Top Secret.

[2] For text of NSC 10/2, see *Foreign Relations*, 1945–1950, Emergence of the Intelligence Establishment, Document 292.

Intelligence Agency an Office of Special Projects[3] to plan and conduct covert operations, and in coordination with the Joint Chiefs of Staff to plan and prepare for the conduct of such operations in war time. The directive charged the Director of Central Intelligence with assuring *through designated representatives of the Secretary of State and of the Secretary of Defense* that covert operations be planned and conducted in a manner consistent with United States foreign and military policies and with overt activities.

Pursuant to this Directive, I was designated by General Marshall as his representative for the above purpose, and this designation was officially made known to the Executive Secretary of the National Security Council by a letter signed August 13, 1948 by Mr. Lovett.[4] Since that date, I have continued to bear this responsibility.

My present preoccupation with other duties and my pending departure from the Department oblige me to recommend that I now be relieved of this responsibility, and I do so recommend.

However, I do not think that any successor to me should be appointed in present circumstances; and I would urge that the National Security Council be informed that the Department will not be able to give further guidance on the exercise of this function by CIA until certain prerequisites are met which could alone assure the soundness of the operation of these arrangements. These are:

(a) There would have to be a marked improvement in the facilities for assuring the cooperation of security authorities of the Government in general, and the Department of Justice in particular, in the efforts of this Department and the Office of Special Projects to promote psychological warfare purposes.

It was never to be expected that covert operations could be so conducted as to produce appreciable political results unless those charged with their conduct could command the cooperation and the confidence of all agencies of the United States Government. In a memorandum of conversation and understanding initialed on August 12, 1948 by Mr. Souers, Admiral Hillenkoetter, Mr. Blum, Colonel Yeaton, Mr. Wisner and myself,[5] designed to serve as the basic premises underlying the conduct of this work, it was agreed that the activity was to be consid-

---

[3] The Office of Special Projects was the name originally proposed for the Office of Policy Coordination.

[4] Not printed. (National Archives, RG 59, S/P Files: Lot 64 D 563, Political and Psychological Warfare)

[5] The actual date of the meeting was August 6, 1948; the memorandum of conversation is printed in *Foreign Relations, 1945–1950*, Emergence of the Intelligence Establishment, Document 298.

ered "a major political operation" and that "the greatest flexibility and freedom from the regulations and administrative standards governing ordinary operations" would be required for its successful prosecution.

These requirements have not been adequately met. In particular, the Government has proven itself unable to take the necessary and appropriate action in matters concerning a number of the ex-communists and others who are the heart and soul of the potential ideological resistance to communism both here and abroad and whose movements in and out of this country are important to this purpose. Any political warfare efforts which purport to dispense with a free and flexible collaboration with these elements must be largely unrealistic. In addition to this, present restrictions on the exercise of executive discretion in the employment of persons by the United States Government place heavy handicaps on the fulfillment of the purposes of political and psychological warfare. I do not deny that positive results can still be obtained, in a fragmentary way and in limited areas of political warfare work where the cooperation of other agencies of the Government is not required. But in general the framework for the accomplishment of this work is so discouraging that prospects for success cannot be regarded as balancing out, in present circumstances, the other risks and disadvantages of the Department's participation in it.

(b) Some suitable arrangements would have to be devised to protect State Department personnel against personal damage to themselves arising out of their participation in this work.

Experience has indicated that the issuance of political guidance to the Director of Central Intelligence in these matters is, in present circumstances, liable to distortion and exploitation in ways dangerous to the reputations and positions of the persons concerned in this Department. We have already had one instance in which the issuance of such guidance in good faith, through the proper channels and with the full authority of superior officers in this Department, has—without notification to anyone in this Department—been reported by the CIA to the FBI as possible evidence of political unreliability on the part of the State Department official concerned. We have no protection against this happening again and no assurance that any one in this Department will even be aware of it when it does happen. In these circumstances, I would consider it unjust to permit any official of this Department to have anything to do with this work without warning him that his participation in it may very well be used, unbeknownst to him, for the purpose of throwing suspicion on his character and his loyalty. And since it is obviously not a tolerable state of affairs that men should be asked to work in this atmosphere and in this jeopardy, I think it necessary that this matter be clarified before the Department of State can participate further in this work.

On point (a), above, I think it may still be possible to bring about some improvement by direct discussion with the agencies concerned—particularly with the Attorney General. If this proves not to be the case, it seems to me that our only resort is the National Security Council.

On point (b), I think that this must in any event be taken up with the Executive Secretary of the National Security Council.

You will appreciate that it is not without great concern and disappointment that I make this recommendation. The idea of the establishment of an organization of this sort for covert operations in the political field was largely my own, as was the initiative which led to the Department's prominent part in launching this venture. It has been, and is, my conviction that the effective conduct of political warfare on the covert plane is indispensable to the prosecution of a successful policy toward the Soviet Union, designed to prevent a third world war and to reduce Soviet power and influence to tolerable dimensions. Anything which interferes, even temporarily, with the prosecution of this work seems to me to diminish materially the chances for defeating communist purposes on a world-wide scale.

I would also like to make it clear that the above recommendation is not meant to be in any sense critical of the conduct of the work of the Office of Special Projects by Mr. Wisner who, as far as I am able to observe, has struggled loyally and valiantly to make a success of this work under bitterly discouraging conditions and who has considerable accomplishments to his credit in those areas where conditions have permitted him to develop his official activity.

George F. Kennan[6]

---

[6] Printed from a copy that bears this typed signature.

---

5.   Editorial Note

NSC 68, "United States Objectives and Programs for National Security," April 14, 1950, is printed in *Foreign Relations, 1950*, volume I, pages 234–292. The National Security Council adopted NSC 68 on April 25, but President Truman did not approve it until September 30. The paper envisioned, among other things, a dramatic increase in defense spending, particularly in the form of covert action operations directed against the Soviet Union and its satellites. For subsequent papers in the NSC 68 series and related documentation, see the compilation on national security policy, ibid., 1951, volume I.

6. **Memorandum From the Joint Chiefs of Staff to Secretary of Defense Johnson**[1]

Washington, May 5, 1950.

SUBJECT

    Special Electronic Airborne Search Operations (SESP)

1. For several years since the end of the war, the Navy and the Air Force have been codirecting special electronic airborne search projects in the furtherance of a program of obtaining the maximum amount of intelligence concerning foreign electronic developments as a safeguard to the national defense. These operations have been carried on without a formal statement of policy but on the basis of an informal working agreement between the Navy and the Air Force. The information derived from these activities is of the utmost importance from both an operational and technical standpoint, and thus far has not been attainable from any other source.

2. As you undoubtedly know, the recent incident in the Baltic,[2] in which a Navy patrol plane engaged in a flight connected with this program was lost, resulted in a high-level decision, on 17 April 1950, to discontinue further projects of this program for a period of thirty days.

3. It is recognized that there is a risk of repetition of such incidents upon resumption of these flights, but it is felt that there would be more serious disadvantages accruing to the United States if the cessation of these operations were to be extended over an excessively long period.

4. Accordingly, the Joint Chiefs of Staff urge that the special electronic airborne search projects be resumed with the least practicable delay and that action be initiated at the highest governmental level to secure approval therefor. In this connection they have agreed upon the policies stated below as a definitive basis of operation when these flights are resumed:

a. The division of effort, geographically, will be that which most nearly follows normal peacetime deployment of air units, and at present is as follows:

---

[1] Source: National Security Agency, Center for Cryptologic History, Series V, L.1.2. Top Secret. A stamped notation on the memorandum indicates Johnson saw it.

[2] A U.S. Navy B–24 Privateer aircraft with 10 crewmen abroad was shot down by Soviet planes on April 8. The United States protested the Soviet action; see *Foreign Relations, 1950*, vol. IV, pp. 1140–1149.

(1) Europe:
  (a) To the Navy—Mediterranean and Black Sea Areas.
  (b) To the Air Force—Baltic, Gulf of Bothnia, Murmansk, and Caucasus Areas.
(2) Far East—To the Air Force.

The above division of responsibility does not preclude performance of Special Electronics Search Projects missions by either Service in any area, as may be locally agreed, when operational, cover, and other considerations so indicate. However, missions conducted by one Service which penetrate the area of the other Service will be coordinated thoroughly through the Commander concerned.

b. Aircraft engaged in these operations over routes normally flown by unarmed transport-type aircraft, i.e., the land masses of the Allied Occupation Zones and the Berlin and Vienna corridors, will continue to operate with or without armament. Aircraft engaged in these operations[3] over all other routes adjacent to the USSR or to USSR- or satellite-controlled territory will be armed and instructed to shoot in self-defense.[4]

c. Pending the availability of armed ECM aircraft, and in order to continue reconnaissance operations at the same tempo as was the case prior to the Baltic incident, flights will be conducted on the same schedules and routes as planned for ECM aircraft but with armed, and not necessarily ECM equipped, B–29 or B–50 aircraft.

d. Flights by single aircraft will, to the maximum extent possible, be scheduled so that the portion(s) of the flight near particularly sensitive or heavily defended areas will be under cover of darkness or weather.

e. Flights will not be made closer than twenty miles to the USSR or USSR- or satellite-controlled territory.

f. Emergency single-group code transmissions meaning "I am being attacked by VF," "I am being tracked by VF," etc., are prescribed for joint use.

g. Flights will not deviate from or alter planned flight courses for other than reasons of safety.

(Note: Although it is recognized that this paper is concerned primarily with SESP missions, it is considered that certain of the provi-

---

[3] "Which?" is handwritten in the margin, presumably by Johnson. In reply Secretary of the Navy Captain W.G. Lalor sent a memorandum to the Executive Secretary to the Secretary of Defense on May 22 explaining that the phrase "with or without armament" meant either armed or unarmed aircraft. (National Security Agency, Center for Cryptologic History, Series V, L.1.2.)

[4] President Truman wrote at the end of this sentence: "Good sense, it seems to me. HST."

sions contained herein are equally applicable to all aerial reconnaissance which may be conducted in sensitive areas adjacent to the USSR or to USSR- or satellite-controlled areas.)[5]

For the Joint Chiefs of Staff:
Omar N. Bradley
Chairman
Joint Chiefs of Staff

---

[5] President Truman wrote "Approved 5/19/50 Harry S Truman" below the signature block.

---

7.   Memorandum of Conversation[1]

Washington, May 5, 1950.

SUBJECT

OPC–Department of State Liaison

PARTICIPANTS

OPC–Mr. Wisner, P—Mr. Barrett, P—Mr. Sargeant, A—Mr. Humelsine, S/S—Mr. Sheppard, S/P—Mr. Joyce, and P—Mr. [*name not declassified*]

The following points of agreement were reached at the meeting in Mr. Humelsine's office on May 5.

1. The focal point of responsibility in the Department of State for providing coordinated propaganda policy guidance to OPC is the Assistant Secretary for Public Affairs.

2. There are two major segments to the problem of liaison so far as public affairs programs are concerned:

(a) Policy guidance and (b) coordination of operations.

3. To make certain that operations do in fact proceed in accordance with top-level decisions on propaganda policy, the following arrangements should be undertaken:

(a) Designation by the Assistant Secretary for Public Affairs of a deputy who would work with an OPC designee on (1) policy guidance

---

[1] Source: Central Intelligence Agency, Directorate of Operations, Job 80–01795R, Box 2, Folder 7. Top Secret. Drafted by [*name not declassified*]. A handwritten notation on the memorandum reads "Mr. Wisner (Your designee?)"

matters and, (2) coordination of operations. Once specific arrangements for coordination of operations are approved, agreed-on working-level relations can be started between OPC and P area units.

(b) Mr. Joyce will designate a person, to be associated with him, to work with OPC on propaganda projects. Mr. Barrett will arrange for this designee to work with his deputy for P–OPC liaison and with B/POL. The Joyce designee will have full access to P area policy guidance materials and meetings.

(c) Mr. Joyce will look to P for the coordination of propaganda policy guidance and coordination of operations under the above arrangements.

(d) Mr. Joyce, under these arrangements, will continue to have full access to the Assistant Secretary for Public Affairs and to the resources of the Public Affairs area. Proposals for modification of these arrangements or modification of major operational decisions will be the subject of prior discussion by P, Mr. Joyce and OPC.

---

8.   **Memorandum by the Assistant Director for Policy Coordination of the Central Intelligence Agency (Wisner)**[1]

Washington, May 8, 1950.

SUBJECT

Data for Consideration in Connection with NSC Studies

1. The attached data have been prepared in response to a request on 4 May from the Policy Planning Staff, Department of State, for budgetary estimates by OPC for the period from 1 July 1950 to 30 June 1957 in connection with certain studies being conducted with regard to NSC 68.[2] These estimates are based upon the assumptions understood to be applicable to NSC 68 and particularly the decision of the United States Government to make a major effort in the field of covert operations. The OPC charter is not elaborated here since it is assumed that those reviewing this paper will be familiar with NSC 10/2[3] and related documents.

2. The primary consideration is determination of the scale on which it may be possible to carry out covert operations in support of

---

[1] Source: National Archives, RG 59, S/P Files: Lot 64 D 563, NSC 68. Top Secret. The memorandum bears no indication of addressees.

[2] An annex of budgetary estimates for FY 1951–1957 is attached but not printed. The Policy Planning Staff request of May 4 has not been found.

[3] See footnote 2, Document 2.

United States foreign policy. In this connection it is apparent that two factors impose ceilings on covert operations:

a. The establishment of an organization such as OPC is unprecedented in the peacetime history of the United States. Because of this a significant body of knowledge, personnel reserves, techniques and philosophy of operations are not readily available. The difficulty of locating and inducing physically, intellectually and psychologically qualified American personnel to abandon their present activities and enlist in the cold war imposes a significant limitation on the capacity to plan and conduct covert operations. So long as the nation is technically at peace and manpower controls do not exist, recruitment of adequate numbers of personnel with ability to direct and execute these activities will be difficult and a fairly heavy attrition rate can be foreseen.

b. The second major limiting factor is the requirement that OPC activities be conducted in such a covert manner that they cannot be traced to the United States Government and in the event such activities are so traced, the Government shall be in a position plausibly to disavow responsibility. Covert operations are increasingly difficult to execute as they increase in size. Even such a relatively simple matter as the clandestine disbursement of funds grows difficult as the amounts involved increase to millions of dollars. These difficulties pyramid when complex activities are undertaken, such as the creation of large resistance organizations or the extensive employment of guerrilla units. The problems attendant on security are not insurmountable in themselves, but there are definite [limits?] above which it is not safe to go without willingness to face exposure which might entail hostile political and psychological exploitation.

3. A further difficulty inherent in the conduct of clandestine operations on behalf of this Government lies in the vast water area and various national borders interposed between the United States and its target areas. In contrast to the USSR operating from the center of the Eurasian land mass with interior lines of communication and dominating all areas between them and their primary targets in Eurasia, United States is confronted with major logistical and security problems that are not comparable. Even though logistical problems can be resolved the maintenance of adequate security in peacetime is a real limiting factor in the conduct of covert operations in Eurasia.

4. Responsive to the decision of the United States Government to make a major effort in the field of covert operations and to provide the basis on which the increased responsibilities of OPC may be accomplished, it is assumed that adequate administrative and logistical support will be available; specifically, that:

a. Prompt and final decision is made on NSC 50,[4] thus providing a firm basis for organization.

---

[4] For text of NSC 50, see *Foreign Relations, 1945–1950*, Emergence of the Intelligence Establishment, Document 384.

b. Adequate space is available to accommodate the Washington headquarters.

c. OPC (or the combined covert offices if OPC and OSO are consolidated under NSC 50) will have a high degree of administrative autonomy and control.

d. The FBI will conduct such personnel and other investigations as may be requested by OPC on a priority basis.

e. The Departments of Defense, State and other governmental agencies will provide adequate logistical and administrative support upon request of OPC.

f. In view of the dearth of personnel experienced in covert operations, military and foreign service personnel having appropriate qualifications will be made available to OPC on a high priority basis.

g. Recognition will be given to the fact that those conducting covert operations are in fact the front line troops in the cold war and should be given maximum support with administrative flexibility.

5. Since it is considered that 1954 is the crucial year, the estimates up to and including that time must necessarily include expenditures for establishing, stockpiling and operating overseas supply bases, the establishment and strengthening of effective organizations to direct and execute covert operations in and against each target area, the establishment of an adequate, world-wide communications system, and the conduct of extensive training with adequate facilities of all types, including paramilitary.

6. A series of independent projections coincide in establishing a figure of [number not declassified] as the maximum American field force that OPC can install and maintain overseas in 1954. This force will be disposed largely in Eurasia in considerable depth along the periphery of the Soviet Union. Prior to 1954 the primary limitation will be the size and inexperience of our overseas stations. However, by 1954 the bulk of the [number not declassified] personnel will have attained a degree of effectiveness which should have a significant effect on the cold war. The number of American personnel does not indicate the total size of the forces involved in covert operations, which must necessarily be conducted largely through apparati utilizing indigenous personnel.

7. The attached data which present estimates of OPC financial requirements by target areas as well as operational areas are considered as realistic as is possible within the framework of considerations and limitations outlined herein. Modifications of these estimates would be required in response to more specific policy guidance with respect to emphasis on certain programs or areas. For example, if covert economic warfare operations on any considerable scale were subsidized by OPC it would require sums greatly in excess of these estimates. Likewise, the share of financial responsibility to be borne by OPC in connection with certain types of joint operations undertaken with the Department of Defense may affect the estimates.

8. As is indicated above, the two major factors limiting the scale of covert operations are qualified and trained personnel willing and able to undertake these activities in the areas involved and the requirement that the activities be conducted in such a covert manner that they cannot be traced to the United States Government. Manpower controls designed to channel qualified personnel into the Government service on behalf of the cold war would ameliorate the first limitation. Likewise, if the international situation deteriorates further, the United States Government may be willing to authorize greater security risks in covert operations in order to step up such activities. For example, covert support of guerrilla or resistance forces on a large scale would be impossible to accomplish with the degree of security required by current United States policy. Should the Government's policy require such support on an enlarged scale with recognition of security factors involved, funds greatly in excess of those indicated on the attachment would be required.

Frank G. Wisner[5]

---

[5] Printed from a copy that bears this typed signature.

---

9.   Memorandum From the Secretary of State's Special Assistant for Intelligence (Armstrong) to the Under Secretary of State (Webb)

Washington, May 9, 1950.

[Source: Department of State, A/MS Files: Lot 54 D 291, CIA 1949–52. Top Secret. 2 pages not declassified.]

---

10.   Letter From the Under Secretary of State (Webb) to Director of Central Intelligence Hillenkoetter

Washington, June 6, 1950.

[Source: National Archives, RG 59, Central Files 1950–54, 103.1102/ 6–650. Top Secret. 2 pages not declassified.]

11.   Letter From Director of Central Intelligence Hillenkoetter to the Under Secretary of State (Webb)

Washington, June 12, 1950.

[Source: Central Intelligence Agency, Executive Registry Job 80–R01731R, Box 13, Folder 560. Secret. 2 pages not declassified.]

---

12.   Editorial Note

When North Korea invaded South Korea on June 25, 1950, the U.S. intelligence organizations had few resources or personnel dedicated to Korean matters. This situation changed quickly, with the Central Intelligence Agency and the armed forces' intelligence services devoting massive efforts to support the Korean war effort. The CIA Office of Policy Coordination began an immediate build-up. Its operational concepts were based on the Office of Strategic Services' (OSS) World War II experience and stressed stay-behind agents and guerrilla forces. For the CIA's intelligence analysis of the early phase of the Korean war, see Woodrow J. Kuhns, *Assessing the Soviet Threat: The Early Cold War Years* (Washington: Central Intelligence Agency, 1997).

After the second capture of Seoul by Communist forces in 1951, guerrilla forces, along with commando and reconnaissance raids, received the bulk of CIA attention. Eventually some 3,000 guerrillas were operating in the mountains of North Korea, and they briefly succeeded in tying up some North Korean and Chinese troops. The CIA also provided order of battle and targeting intelligence, intelligence to enforce the economic embargo against North Korea and China, and daily current intelligence publications on the situation in Korea.

For a time, following the entry of Chinese troops in late November 1950, there was widespread concern in the United States that the Korean invasion was the first phase of a Soviet-inspired World War III that would soon engulf Europe as well as Asia. Planning began to simultaneously provide massive support for anti-Communist guerrillas in China and paramilitary activity in Europe. Emergency war plans were drawn up. In this crisis atmosphere, the Department of Defense urged the CIA to begin to accelerate many other war-related programs: evasion and escape planning, the build-up of supplies, training of paramilitary forces, increased propaganda, encouragement of Soviet defections, economic defense programs, and the like. This led DCI Walter Bedell Smith to raise the issue of the appropriate scope and pace of CIA activities.

---

13.   **Memorandum From the Secretary of State's Deputy Special Assistant for Intelligence and Research (Howe) to the Deputy Assistant Secretary of State for Administration (Humelsine)**

Washington, June 28, 1950.

[Source: National Archives, RG 59, INR Files: Lot 58 D 776, State–CIA Relations. Top Secret. 1 page not declassified.]

---

14.   **Administrative Agreement Between the Department of State and the Central Intelligence Agency**

Washington, undated.

[Source: National Archives, RG 59, INR Files: Lot 54 D 291, CIA 1948–1952. Secret. 3 pages not declassified.]

---

15.   **Editorial Note**

The Central Intelligence Agency's Office of Policy Coordination sought to make use of ostensibly private organizations and businesses in carrying out its cold war covert action mandate. The National Committee for Free Europe (NCFE) was one of the first such organizations, incorporated in 1949. At the instigation of George Kennan of the Policy Planning Staff of the Department of State, NCFE was created to utilize anti-Communist refugees and émigrés to undermine Soviet control of Eastern Europe. In February 1950, the CIA gave NCFE a transmitter that was installed in Germany and went on the air as Radio Free Europe on July 4, 1950. A host of other organizations also worked with OPC, with more or less independence, in the early cold war years. These included the American Committee for Freedom for the Peoples of the USSR, the Committee for a Free Asia, the Congress for Cultural Freedom, and several youth and student organizations, including the National Student Association. One of the earliest Agency proprietary companies was Air America, which long provided CIA airlift capability in the Far East. CIA purchased Air America from Claire Chennault and his partner on August 23, 1950. Air America provided extensive support for CIA activities during the Korean war.

---

16.   Letter From the Director of the Federal Bureau of Investigation (Hoover) to the President's Special Consultant (Souers)[1]

Washington, July 7, 1950

My Dear Admiral:

For some months representatives of the FBI and of the Department of Justice have been formulating a plan of action for an emergency situation wherein it would be necessary to apprehend and detain persons who are potentially dangerous to the internal security of the country. I thought you would be interested in a brief outline of the plan.

Action to Be Taken By the Department of Justice

The plan envisions four types of emergency situations: (1) attack upon the United States; (2) threatened invasion; (3) attack upon United States troops in legally occupied territory; and (4) rebellion.

---

[1] Source: National Archives, RG 273, Files of the National Security Council Representative for Internal Security 1947–69, Box 36, Problem 11. Personal and Confidential; by Special Messenger. A handwritten notation reads: "Mr. Coyne has suggested that you probably will choose to discuss this with Mr. Lay and Mr. Coyne." This is followed by an initial that appears to be an "S". The initials JPC probably indicate that J. Patrick Coyne, NSC Representative for Internal Security, read the letter. Souers sent a noncommittal reply on July 14. (Ibid.)

The plan contains a prepared document which should be referred to the President immediately upon the existence of one of the emergency situations for the President's signature. Briefly, this proclamation recites the existence of the emergency situation and that in order to immediately protect the country against treason, espionage and sabotage the Attorney General is instructed to apprehend all individuals potentially dangerous to the internal security. In order to make effective these apprehensions, the proclamation suspends the Writ of Habeas Corpus for apprehensions made pursuant to it.

The plan also contains a prepared joint resolution to be passed by Congress and an Executive Order for the President which too will validate the previous Presidential proclamation.

The next step in the plan is a prepared order from the Attorney General to the Director of the FBI to apprehend dangerous individuals, conduct necessary searches and seize contraband as defined in the plan. Together with the order to the Director of the FBI the Attorney General will forward a master warrant attached to a list of names of individuals which names have previously been furnished from time to time to the Attorney General by the FBI as being individuals who are potentially dangerous to the internal security.

It should be pointed out that the plan does not distinguish between aliens and citizens and both are included in its purview. If for some reason the full plan is not put into operation it has so been drawn that the section applicable only to alien enemies may be put into effect.

Action to Be Taken By the FBI

For a long period of time the FBI has been accumulating the names, identities and activities of individuals found to be potentially dangerous to the internal security through investigation. These names have been compiled in an index which index has been kept up to date. The names in this index are the ones that have been furnished to the Department of Justice and will be attached to the master warrant referred to above. This master warrant will, therefore, serve as legal authority for the FBI to cause the apprehension and detention of the individuals maintained in this index. The index now contains approximately twelve thousand individuals, of which approximately ninety-seven per cent are citizens of the United States. Immediately upon receipt of instructions and the master warrant from the Attorney General the various FBI Field Divisions will be instructed by expeditious means to cause the apprehension of the individuals within their various territories. Each FBI Field Division maintains an index of the individuals within its territory, which index is so arranged that it may be used for ready apprehension purposes. Upon apprehension the individuals will be delivered to the nearest jail for temporary detention and action by the Attorney General.

Detention and Subsequent Procedures

The permanent detention of these individuals will take place in regularly established Federal detention facilities. These facilities have been confidentially surveyed and the facilities have been found to be adequate in all areas except in the territory covered by the FBI's New York, Los Angeles and San Francisco Offices. In these three areas arrangements have been perfected with the National Military Establishment for the temporary and permanent detention in Military facilities of the individuals apprehended.

The plan calls for a statement of charges to be served on each detainee and a hearing be afforded the individual within a specified period. The Hearing Board will consist of three members to be appointed by the Attorney General composed of one Judge of the United States or State Court and two citizens. The hearing procedure will give the detainee an opportunity to know why he is being detained and permit him to introduce material in the nature of evidence in his own behalf. The hearing procedure will not be bound by the rules of evidence. The Hearing Board may make one of three recommendations, that is; that the individual be detained, paroled or released. This action by the Board is subject to review by the Attorney General and the Attorney General's decision on the matter will be final except for appeal to the President.

The details of this plan as set forth in this communication have also been furnished on this date to Mr. James S. Lay, Jr., Executive Secretary, National Security Council.

With expressions of my highest esteem and best regards,

Sincerely yours,

J. Edgar Hoover

---

17.   Editorial Note

On July 10, 1950, NSC 74, a report to the National Security Council by Under Secretary of State James Webb on "A Plan for National Psychological Warfare," totalling 51 pages, was circulated to members of the Council and Secretary of the Treasury John W. Snyder. The report dealt largely with wartime contingency planning. It also recommended that a national psychological warfare organization be established. Pursuant to this recommendation and to NSC 59/1 (Document 2), the Department of State announced on August 17 the creation of a

National Psychological Strategy Board under the Secretary of State. For text of the announcement, see Department of State *Bulletin,* August 28, 1950, page 335. The board was in fact the Director and Consultants proposed in NSC 59/1, with representatives of the Joint Chiefs of Staff. NSC 74 never received the formal approval of the Council, but was used for reference in subsequent studies of this subject. A copy of NSC 74 is in the National Archives, RG 59, S/S–NSC Files: Lot 63 D 51, NSC 74.

---

18.   Director of Central Intelligence Directive 14/1[1]

Washington, July 17, 1950.

ESTABLISHMENT OF INTERAGENCY DEFECTOR COMMITTEE

1. Pursuant to the provisions of NSCIDs 13 and 14,[2] a permanent Interagency Defector Committee is hereby established, under the Chairmanship of the Central Intelligence Agency, composed of one representative each from the Central Intelligence Agency, the Department of State, the Departments of the Army, Navy, and the Air Force, the Atomic Energy Commission, and the Federal Bureau of Investigation.

2. The various Intelligence Advisory Committee representatives, acting for their chiefs, will exercise within the Committee all powers of decision defined by and allocated to the various Intelligence Agencies under the provisions of NSCIDs 13 and 14.

3. The Interagency Defector Committee will proceed immediately to implement the Defector Program in accordance with NSCIDs 13 and 14.

R.H. Hillenkoetter[3]
Director of Central Intelligence

---

[1] Source: Central Intelligence Agency, History Staff, Job 84–B00389R, HS/HC–600, Box 4. Secret; Security Information.

[2] Documents 252 and 253.

[3] Printed from a copy that bears this typed signature.

19.   Memorandum From the Chairman of the Communications Intelligence Board (Armstrong) to the Executive Secretary of the National Security Council (Lay)[1]

Washington, July 19, 1950.

SUBJECT

Communications Intelligence Requirements and Mobilization

1. At its Fifty-third meeting, 14 July 1950, the United States Communications Intelligence Board (USCIB) reviewed the status of the United States communications intelligence effort in the face of the world situation.

2. The members of the Board agreed unanimously that:

(a) the total communications intelligence requirements of the United States at this time transcend the specific requirements springing solely out of the Korean problem;
(b) the present scale of communications intelligence effort falls far short of meeting total requirements or even of enabling the United States to exploit available communications information to its full potential;
(c) the intensification of the effort to meet even current requirements can be accomplished only slowly because of the time factor involved in obtaining the indispensable security clearances of added personnel and in constructing the complex physical apparatus required;
(d) for the foregoing reasons, the expansion of the communications intelligence effort must be started now;
(e) partial mobilization in the communications intelligence field should be undertaken on a selective basis immediately.

3. In view of the above, the United States Communications Intelligence Board recommends to the National Security Council that as a matter of urgency:

(a) the National Security Council recognize that expansion of the United States communications intelligence effort is required and at the earliest possible moment;
(b) the National Security Council recommend to the President that the member departments and agencies of the United States Communications Intelligence Board be authorized to intensify without delay the communications intelligence effort by proceeding with the selec-

---

[1] Source: National Archives, RG 59, S/S–NSC Files: Lot 62 D 1, NSC Intelligence Directives. Top Secret. Lay circulated the memorandum to the NSC the next day. (Ibid.)

tive mobilization of reserves in this specialized field and with a general expansion of other personnel and equipment.[2]

For the United States
Communications Intelligence Board:

W. Park Armstrong, Jr.[3]

---

[2] The Intelligence Advisory Committee approved the recommendation, adding that "intensification" should apply to the entire intelligence structure, not just communications intelligence. Hillenkoetter informed NSC Executive Secretary Lay of this action in a memorandum of August 8, and Lay in turn informed the members of the NSC in a memorandum the same day. Both memoranda are ibid. The President approved the USCIB recommendation on July 27 in NSC Action No. 322. (Truman Library, President's Secretary File)

[3] Printed from a copy that indicates Armstrong signed the original.

---

20.   Letter From Director of Central Intelligence Hillenkoetter to the Under Secretary of State (Webb)[1]

Washington, July 26, 1950.

Dear Mr. Webb:

The State-Defense Staff Study of 1 May 1950, on "Production of National Intelligence", transmitted with your letter of 7 July[2] for my comments, points up the conflicting theories which have prevailed since the inception of CIA on the responsibility within our Government for intelligence relating to the national security, i.e., a responsible single Director versus a committee of co-equal directors of the several intelligence agencies.

The proposals set forth in the Staff Study would be so radical a departure from the concept of the Central Intelligence Agency as envisaged by the Congress that there exists at present no legal authority to adopt them.

---

[1] Source: National Archives, RG 59, INR Historical Files: Lot 58 D 776, National Intelligence Staff Study. Secret. All ellipses in the original letter.

[2] Not printed. (Ibid.) For the staff study, see *Foreign Relations, 1945–1950*, Emergence of the Intelligence Establishment, Document 420. Apparently, however, the staff study sent to Hillenkoetter mistakenly included pages from a "preliminary" or "early" version; see Document 22.

As an indication of this Congressional intent, I quote from the statement of the Chairman of the Special Subcommittee of the House Expenditures Committee Investigating Intelligence Activities of the Government (at the time of the Bogota crisis) dated 16 April 1948:

"It may be necessary for Congress to enact additional legislation to give the CIA the independent status it was generally presumed to enjoy .... Our Central Intelligence Agency must be protected against censorship or intimidation by any arm of the Executive Branch."

This position has been repeatedly made clear to me in virtually every committee session I have attended since assuming the Directorship. It is also a fact that in times of crisis the appropriate Congressional Committees have always called on the Director of Central Intelligence for an accounting and for briefing on the intelligence situation. The Congress has always made it amply clear in these situations that it holds the Director and this Agency completely responsible in the field of foreign intelligence, and it presumes that this Agency has the requisite powers and authorities to make that responsibility effective in the interests of our national security.

The effect of your Staff Study is to abrogate the statutory responsibility for the production of national intelligence of the Central Intelligence Agency and shift it as a collective responsibility to a committee. This is specified in your study as follows:

"Until the emergence of a national estimate or study from the IAC, collective responsibility is inescapable under the Act of 1947 ... The full statutory responsibility of the D/CI for the production of national intelligence becomes operative only when ... final drafts of national estimates or studies are recommended by the IAC to the D/CI."

Not only does the National Security Act contemplate no such doctrine of collective responsibility, but, in NSC 50,[3] the National Security Council specifically disavowed this doctrine in the following language:

"... we do not believe that the Director and the IAC should be bound by the concept of collective responsibility because this would inevitably reduce coordinated national intelligence to the lowest common denominator among the agencies concerned."

Careful thought and study has been given to the existing NSCID 1[4] in its relation to the statutory responsibilities of this Agency. The present directives and their implementation have not been satisfactory. There has been prepared for submission to the National Security Coun-

---

[3] For text of NSC 50, see *Foreign Relations*, 1945–1950, Emergence of the Intelligence Establishment, Document 384.

[4] Ibid., Document 432.

cil a basic NSCID which is attached herewith for your information.[5] This draft clearly establishes the minimum authorities necessary to enable this Agency to fulfill its statutory responsibilities and likewise establishes the responsibilities of the departmental agencies in support of national intelligence. Separate specific comments on your Staff Study are also attached.[6]

It is noted that you propose to submit your Staff Study with its proposed NSC Directive direct to the NSC. It is therefore requested that our comments and the inclosure accompany your submission.

As a matter of parallel interest the CIA has been instructed by the NSC to consider through normal NSCID procedure the following quoted comments of the Secretary of Defense, and to submit recommendations in connection therewith:

"I do not find the IAC comments on RECOMMENDATION 8 to be convincing. Existing directives fall far short of coming to grips with urgent and recognizable problems of coordination of intelligence in Washington and overseas. Furthermore, I do not concede that the 'rather elaborate committee structure' is either inevitable or desirable. On the contrary, it is my belief that the intricate committee structure is the consequence of compromises created by inter-bureau rivalries rather than the results of objective study of intelligence organization.

Dependable conclusions from . . . intelligence, as from every other subject matter of national intelligence, should result from evaluation and synthesis within the framework of the Central Agency of all available material from every Federal source. Final responsibility for coordinating the collection of this material as well as its processing should rest squarely in the same agency. With that responsibility should go corresponding authority, which now is ambiguous and obscured in the present interlocking committee structure."

In view of our instructions from the NSC in connection with this statement, it would in any case be incumbent on this Agency to submit our proposed revision of the NSCID through normal channels as it reflects our considered opinion of what is needed as a proper foundation for the national intelligence mission.

Sincerely,

R. H. Hillenkoetter[7]
Rear Admiral, USN

---

[5] Not found.

[6] A 7-page paper, July 25, signed by Hillenkoetter, is attached but not printed.

[7] Printed from a copy that indicates Hillenkoetter signed the original.

21.   Memorandum From the Chief of Staff of the Army (Collins) to Secretary of Defense Johnson[1]

Washington, July 28, 1950.

SUBJECT

Expanded Requirements of the Armed Forces Security Agency (AFSA) in View of Current World Situation

1. By a memorandum dated 22 June 1950[2] the Joint Chiefs of Staff recommended to you that funds be made available to permit commencing immediate recruiting of additional civilian personnel by the Armed Forces Security Agency (AFSA), in order to increase that Agency's output of communications intelligence. The Director, AFSA, was thereafter authorized by the Assistant Secretary of Defense (Comptroller) to commence recruiting, with ultimate ceiling to be determined later.

2. In the light of the current world situation, as it has developed since 22 June, the necessity for a large increase in output of communications intelligence has taken an added degree of urgency. In addition, the same developments have generated an additional need for greatly expedited production of cryptographic material required by the armed forces, and for stepped-up prosecution of already approved research and development projects in both the communications intelligence and communication security fields.

3. The Joint Chiefs of Staff, after careful study of the needs involved, recommend as a matter of urgency that the current direct resources of AFSA be increased as follows (these increases include the additional personnel recommended in the above mentioned memorandum of 22 June 1950):

a. *Personal Services (Civilian)*

	Additional positions	*Increased FY 1951 funds*
Communications intelligence	1253	$5,210,800
Communication security	389	$ 893,740
Totals	1642	$6,104,540

---

[1] Source: National Archives, RG 218, CCS 334 NSA (7–24–48) Sec. 4 (Formerly NSA). Top Secret. Copies were sent to the Assistant Chief of Staff, G–3, Assistant to the Chief of Naval Operations, Director, P&O Air, and Director of the Joint Staff.

[2] Not found.

Note—The increased funds include, in addition to salaries of new personnel, allowance for overtime to provide for a 6-day work-week for all civilian personnel.

    b. *Other Objects*

	Increased FY 1951 funds
Communications intelligence	$2,914,200
Communication security	$2,176,760
Total	$5,090,960

Note—The increased funds for objects other than personal services are chiefly to provide supplies and equipment entailed in increased and expedited effort represented by the recommended increase in personnel.

    4. The foregoing amounts include $2,998,000 for research and development, which amount has already been requested of the Chairman, Research and Development Board.

    5. In addition to the increases in funds and in civilian personnel recommended above, the Joint Chiefs of Staff have approved increases, amounting to 244 officers and 464 enlisted men, in the military personnel assigned to AFSA. A program for intercept facilities expansion to be provided for AFSA by the Services is now under consideration by the Armed Forces Security Agency Council. The expanded communications requirements related to this program will be determined as soon as practicable.

For the Joint Chiefs of Staff:
J. Lawton Collins[3]

---

[3] Printed from a copy that indicates Collins signed the original.

22.   Memorandum From the Secretary of State's Special Assistant for Intelligence and Research (Armstrong) to the Under Secretary of State (Webb)[1]

Washington, August 10, 1950.

SUBJECT

State–Defense Staff Study on "Production of National Intelligence"[2]

I regret to report the discovery that the staff study enclosed with your letter of July 7 to Admiral Hillenkoetter on this subject[3] was in fact a preliminary version containing three pages which were later amended. While the final version of the paper is not fundamentally different, the fact is that only the early version contained the reference to "collective responsibility"—to which Hillenkoetter took strong exception and on which he pinned much of his argument.[4]

This error, for which I am fully responsible, appears to have come about through the circumstance that the paper was amended in the interval between the time it was first presented to you (May 2) and the time when you considered it for the second time and forwarded it to Hillenkoetter (July 7). The amended pages were not substituted in the copies in your office, one of which apparently was transmitted to Hillenkoetter.

While we feel sure that the CIA reaction to either version of the paper would have been substantially the same, we must of course set the record straight by transmitting the final version of the paper on which there was State-Defense agreement. At the same time, there is the chance, however faint, that if Hillenkoetter has any inclination to modify his original and extreme position, forwarding of the later version will provide him with a convenient excuse for doing so.

In this connection, General Magruder and Admiral Souers yesterday discussed the CIA reaction to our proposals. According to Magruder, it is Souers's view that Hillenkoetter's position is wrong, that an effort should be made to make him see the constructive features of our proposals, and that the later version of the paper may provide him with a convenient "out." To this end, Souers has suggested that he

---

[1] Source: National Archives, RG 59, INR Historical Files: Lot 58 D 776, National Intelligence Staff Study. Secret. Drafted by Trueheart. Sent through the Executive Secretariat.

[2] Dated May 1, 1950; printed in *Foreign Relations, 1945–1950*, Emergence of the Intelligence Establishment, Document 420.

[3] Regarding Webb's July 7 letter, see footnote 2, Document 20. The enclosed "preliminary" or "early" version of the State–Defense staff study has not been found.

[4] See Document 20.

himself call Hillenkoetter and urge him to set up a meeting where Magruder could go over the paper with Hillenkoetter and his principal assistants.

Before that meeting, however, it will be important that we get to Hillenkoetter the correct final version of the paper. The simplest and best way of accomplishing this would be for you to telephone Admiral Hillenkoetter, inform him of the mistake and tell him that you are sending over the correct version of the paper. At the same time, you should mention that you understand that General Magruder will be discussing the subject of national intelligence with him.

Recommendation:

That you telephone Admiral Hillenkoetter along the above lines.

That you sign the attached letter after making the telephone call which will transmit the corrected paper.[5]

W. Park Armstrong, Jr.[6]

---

[5] The attached letter and "corrected paper" have not been found, but the list of attachments at the end of the letter identifies the corrected paper as the May 1, 1950, text (see footnote 2 above).

[6] Printed from a copy that bears this typed signature.

---

23.   Memorandum for the Record[1]

Washington, August 29, 1950.

Set forth below is a brief statement of some of the more pressing problems presently facing the Central Intelligence Agency. These are the subject of extensive studies within the Agency and are voluminously documented in Agency files.

---

[1] Source: National Archives, RG 263, History Staff/History Collection: History Research Project 82–2/00286, Box 4, HS/HC 500, National Intelligence Directives. Secret. Not signed but prepared by CIA General Counsel Lawrence Houston. According to Ludwell Montague, *General Walter Bedell Smith as Director of Central Intelligence, October 1950–February 1953*, p. 60, Smith had asked Houston for a review of the problems facing CIA and Houston responded on this date. A signed copy of Houston's August 29 covering memorandum to Smith and another copy of the memorandum for the record are printed in Michael Warner, ed., *The CIA Under Harry Truman*, pp. 341–347.

Appended hereto are certain documents which most clearly illustrate the issues involved and which indicate measures which would be basic steps in the solution thereof. These documents are identified in a list of tabs at the end of this paper.[2]

1. Coordination of Activities.

Difficulties in coordinating the intelligence activities of the Government, and of performing other functions imposed upon CIA by law, result from existing National Security Council directives which impose upon CIA the board of directors mechanism of the Intelligence Advisory Committee (IAC) in the following manner:

a. They require that recommendations and advice of the Director of Central Intelligence (DCI) to the National Security Council (NSC) must contain the concurrence or non-concurrence of the IAC;

b. They enable the IAC to assert the position that they are not merely advisory to the DCI, but are actually a board of directors, of which the DCI is but the executive secretary, i.e. one among equals;

c. Therefore the recommendations which go forward to the NSC are not CIA recommendations as contemplated by the law, but actually are watered-down compromises, replete with loop-holes, in an attempt to secure complete IAC support.

2. Intelligence Support for Production of Estimates.

Difficulties are encountered by CIA in producing adequate intelligence estimates, due to the refusal of the IAC agencies to honor CIA requests for necessary intelligence information, departmental intelligence, or collection action:

a. Information has been withheld from CIA by IAC agencies on the basis that it is "operational" rather than "intelligence information" and therefore not available to CIA; that it is "eyes only" information or on a highly limited dissemination basis; or that it is handled under special security provisions which by-pass CIA;

b. CIA is not empowered to enforce its collection requests on IAC agencies, or establish priorities;

c. There is a failure of spontaneous dissemination of certain material to CIA;

d. IAC agencies continue to cite the so-called "Third Agency Rule" as a basis for refusing to give intelligence to CIA.

3. Production and Dissemination of Estimates.

The furnishing of adequate national intelligence estimates to the President, the NSC, and other appropriate recipients is hampered by

---

[2] None of the tabs are attached.

the lack of complete material, (as set forth in paragraph 3, above), and by present procedures which require concurrence or substantial dissent to each estimate from the IAC agencies, but make no provision for setting time limits thereon:

a. Departmental agencies of the IAC cannot concur in intelligence estimates which conflict with agency substantive policy; nor can they free themselves from departmental bias or budgetary interests;

b. Coordination of CIA estimates often takes months, with the result a compromise position;

c. Departmental dissents to CIA estimates are frequently unsubstantial, quibbling or reflective of departmental policy.

4. *Special Problems.*

a. The IAC agencies resist the grant of authority to CIA to issue directives affecting the intelligence field in general and their activities or priorities in particular on the ground that it would violate the concept of command channels;

b. The status of CIA in relation to the President and the NSC must be redefined and clarified;

c. The relationships between CIA on the one hand, and the Department of Justice—particularly the FBI, on the other, especially in connection with the defector problem, must be improved and clarified.

d. Difficulties imposed by NSC directives in the field of unconventional warfare must be eliminated, particularly the policy control over CIA granted to the Departments of State and Defense. The separation of clandestine operations into two offices within CIA creates serious problems of efficiency, efficacy and, above all, security;

e. There is a failure of coordination of overt intelligence collection in the field, due in part to competition among the departments in the field, but also to lack of positive planning and action by CIA. This results in unnecessary duplication and overlaps, and the initial withholding of choice material. It is becoming necessary for CIA to take a strong position in the field of overt collection abroad.

5. *Nuclear Energy and Other Special Intelligence Subjects.*

Each has its own but related problems.

6. *Relationship Between JCS and CIA in the Event of War.*

This is an unresolved problem which has been the subject of considerable discussion, one aspect of which is covered by Tabs F and G attached. It may of course require urgent consideration at any time.

7. *Conclusion.*

Solution of the above problems lies in a grant of adequate authority to the DCI and CIA, and use of that authority to achieve the necessary coordination by direction rather than placing reliance in a spirit of cooperation and good will.

INDEX OF TABS

Tab A — CIA proposed revision of NSCID #1. This directive is believed by CIA to be necessary to give the Director the authority needed for exercise of his responsibilities. It has been forwarded to State for discussion, but no further action has been taken on it.

Tab B — Proposed "Memorandum to the National Security Council," which elaborates paragraphs 1–3 set forth in the memorandum above. This was prepared several months ago as an introduction to CIA's proposed revision to NSCID #1, included herewith under Tab A.

Tab C — National Security Council Intelligence Directive (NSCID) #1, under which CIA presently operates.[3]

Tab D — Memorandum entitled "Legal Responsibilities of the Central Intelligence Agency", which emphasizes particularly Congressional intent in regard to the national intelligence mission.

Tab E — Current State/Defense proposals for reorganization of intelligence production within CIA. A compromise version of this paper is still under discussion.

Tab E/1 — Compromise now urged by State/Defense thru Gen. Magruder.

Tab F — Joint Intelligence Committee report on war time status and responsibilities of CIA and its field agencies (JIC 455/1, 12 July 1950). This indicates an intention on the part of the JIC to have JCS take over control of all covert activities in the event of war.

Tab G — Memorandum for Brig. Gen. John Magruder, dated 16 August 1950, setting forth CIA's position on its war time relations to the Joint Chiefs. This memorandum was originally drafted for dispatch to the Secretary of Defense and was actually dispatched to General Magruder.

---

[3] *Foreign Relations,* 1945–1950, Emergence of the Intelligence Establishment, Document 432.

24. **Memorandum From the Secretary of State's Special Assistant for Intelligence and Research (Armstrong) to the Under Secretary of State (Webb)**[1]

Washington, September 14, 1950.

SUBJECT

Review of Relations with CIA

The purpose of this review is twofold:

1. To give you a general roundup of the state of our relations with the CIA at this juncture, as a new Director is coming in;

2. To ascertain which, if any, issues should be discussed with Admiral Hillenkoetter as a result of your letter,[2] written just prior to your departure for Europe, in which you suggested getting together with him to take up any problems which exist in relation to one particular phase of the Department's relations with CIA, namely, secret intelligence [1 line not declassified].

Any review such as this naturally focuses on areas of difficulty; these, however, must be kept in the perspective of our total relations which in a great number of areas are on the whole satisfactory. In this connection it should be pointed out that the Department's relations with CIA on the following important matters are of the best:

1. *Defectors*—each case invariably presents a knotty problem, but in the course of the last six months they have been smoothly and cooperatively dealt with by the Department, CIA, and the Military Services.

2. *Foreign Broadcast Monitoring*—an important "service of common concern" in which CIA produces for the Department and other agencies a vast quantity of voice monitoring reports.

3. *Scientific Intelligence*—A "service of common concern" and also a coordinating mechanism in which CIA's performance has been good. This office also works very closely with U/A, Mr. Arneson.

---

[1] Source: Department of State, A/MS Files: Lot 54 D 291, CIA 1948–1952. Top Secret. The memorandum was under cover of a September 19 memorandum from C.E. Johnson of the Management Staff of the Bureau of Administration to Humelsine, which indicates that a September 20 meeting was scheduled among Webb, Humelsine, Armstrong, and Howe to review relations with the CIA and Johnson's recommendations for changes in the proposed memorandum to Webb. Johnson recommended adding a statement on the inadequacy of CIA's intelligence collection and production. He further wanted to delete the reference to showing the memorandum to Smith, preferring this be conveyed to Webb orally. He also believed Smith should be invited to the Department for the meeting and briefed on the Department of State role in and capabilities for intelligence.

[2] Not found.

4. *Contacts Branch*—again a "service of common concern" in which CIA exploits the foreign intelligence available in the US through contacts with foreign nationality groups and individuals and US business firms with representatives abroad.

I should point out also that whereas the problems which I shall discuss below are focused primarily in OSO (secret intelligence) and ORE (research intelligence) it should not be construed that trouble exists with these offices on all points. Rather, there is a wide area of cooperative effort and useful collaboration and liaison with only a few, if significant, areas of disagreement on policy or method.

By way of general comment I would like to indicate that there are two factors in CIA attitude and method which we find difficult to deal with and which are often a source of misunderstanding:

a. CIA is reluctant to give us full information—especially voluntarily, but even after request. This applies to some intelligence information and also to activities in which they participate. In this it is our view that they carry security too far, or use security as an excuse for withholding information.

b. Similarly, we find CIA reluctant to come to us directly with their problems, to identify issues and seek solutions directly. We get complaints, but we find an unhealthy lack of direct approach to us by senior officers seeking constructive solutions to problems large and small which inevitably arise.

The following outline summarizes the points of difficulty, present and potential, in our relations with CIA.

I. Coordination of Intelligence Activities.

The Department has long felt that CIA has been deficient in fulfilling its responsibilities for leadership and direction in the coordination of intelligence throughout the Government. This responsibility within CIA is fulfilled essentially by two mechanisms:

a. The Intelligence Advisory Committee (IAC) composed of the Chiefs of each of the intelligence services, advisory to the Director.

b. A staff office (COAPS) composed of officers contributed by the various agencies and headed by a State Department officer, responsible to the Director and charged with formulating any procedures for the coordination of intelligence activities.

The Department is confident that change for the better can be anticipated not only by virtue of the new Director who will assume the chairmanship of the IAC and should fulfill the leadership expected of the Director of CIA in coordination matters, but also through the appointment of James Q. Reber as the State Department officer in charge of COAPS, who will also be Executive Secretary of the IAC.

I believe that no useful purpose would be served by discussion of this matter with the outgoing Director.

II. Intelligence Collection Programs.

This problem, which has very wide implications and is pointed up by the Korean incident, is discussed in a separate, accompanying memorandum.[3]

No useful purpose would be served by a discussion of the matter at this time with the Director.

III. Research Intelligence and "National Intelligence."

The difficulties which have arisen between the Department and CIA in this area stem from divergence of views as to the nature of "national intelligence" and the method of producing it on the one hand, and, on the other, a conflict of ideas on the location of responsibility in the Department and CIA for the production of research intelligence in the political and economic fields. The latter of these two problems is perennial and may in some measure be clarified with a solution to the problem of national intelligence. In any event, the steps necessary to bring this problem to a solution will only come in time and should be improved with the arrival of the new Director.

Some advance has been made in the problem of "national intelligence" which was sharpened by your exchange of letters with Admiral Hillenkoetter on the joint State-Defense proposal. General Magruder has made a preliminary exploration with Admiral Hillenkoetter and believes that an area of agreement may be possible.

Pending the outcome of these negotiations and the installation of the new Director on whose decision any final revision will depend, I believe no useful purpose would be served in raising this matter with Admiral Hillenkoetter.

IV. Organization for Secret Intelligence (OSO) and Secret Operations (OPC).

You will remember that some months ago general agreement was reached between the Department of Defense, CIA/OSO, CIA/OPC, and ourselves on a reorganization which would combine OSO and OPC and would take the form of an NSC directive (proposed NSC 10/3).[4] Further action on this document, however, was delayed pending a solution to the problem of personnel involved in the reorganization and now must await the new Director for action and implementation.

No useful purpose, therefore, would be served by discussions on this matter with Admiral Hillenkoetter. However, you should know

---

[3] Dated September 14; attached but not printed.

[4] Further information on the proposed merger is in *Foreign Relations, 1945–1950, Emergence of the Intelligence Establishment*, Document 419. The draft NSC 10/3 is printed as an attachment to that document.

that although there is no disagreement as between the Departments of State and Defense and CIA on this question, the Defense Department is currently considering a revision of authorities for wartime with respect both to OSO and OPC activities, and this may present some difficulties.

V. [Heading and 10 paragraphs (49 lines) not declassified]

VI. CIA Budget.

Each year the CIA submits an over-all budget figure to the NSC prior to submission to the Bureau of the Budget. It appears that over the course of the last few years no agency—neither the NSC nor the Budget Bureau nor the Office of the President, nor, for that matter, Congressional committees—examines the CIA budget with any thoroughness to warrant assumption of the responsibility for approval.

At best it is a very difficult matter to determine what degree of review should be made of the CIA budget to bring about a balance between the security factors which are obviously involved on the one hand, and the minimum requirements for assumption of responsibility by the Secretaries of State and Defense in the NSC, on the other.

Last year at your suggestion General Magruder and Halaby for Defense, and Sheppard and Howe for the State Department, were given an informal presentation of the budget programs for some of the offices of CIA. This was an initial step on the part of the NSC to form a basis for judgment for approval of the budget. Since that time an effort has been made by the Departments of State and Defense to arrive at a formula for an annual review of the budget. Consideration was given, for instance, to the possibility of appointing each year a special ad hoc high level group under the NSC for this specific purpose. More acceptable seems the possibility that the Director submit to the IAC on a secure basis for its comment the budget programs of the several CIA offices so that the NSC would at least have the benefit of the IAC advice.

This problem has advanced no further and almost surely should await the installation of the new Director and a new look at the problem with him. (As yet no discussions on this subject have been held with CIA itself.) In the meantime, no purpose would seem to be served in a discussion of the problem with Admiral Hillenkoetter.

General Conclusion.

1. The Department's relations with CIA are, with some exceptions, satisfactory.

2. The areas of difficultly are by no means impossible of solution and most, if not all, should be soluble with the new Director.

3. Although you asked to have a meeting with Admiral Hillenkoetter on your return, we know of no problems between the agencies which are of a kind that can be solved by such a discussion.

Recommendations:

1. That you take the opportunity to ask Admiral Hillenkoetter if he has any matters he wants to discuss, but you do not press for a meeting.

2. That you consider showing this memorandum to General Smith on a personal and informal basis soon after he takes office.[5]

W. Park Armstrong, Jr.[6]

---

[5] A handwritten comment in the margin just below this paragraph reads, "Is this adequate?"

[6] Printed from a copy that bears this typed signature.

---

25.   Director of Central Intelligence Directive No. 4/2[1]

Washington, September 28, 1950.

PRIORITY LIST OF CRITICAL NATIONAL INTELLIGENCE OBJECTIVES

In accordance with DCI 4/1,[2] paragraph 3, the following list of critical national intelligence objectives, with respect to the USSR, is established; so the highest priority shall be given to the collection of information and to the production of intelligence concerning Soviet capabilities and intentions for:

1. taking direct military action against the Continental United States;

2. taking direct military action, employing USSR Armed Forces, against vital U.S. possessions, areas peripheral to the Soviet Union, and Western Europe;

3. interfering with U.S. strategic air attack;

4. interfering with U.S. movement of men and material by water transport;

5. production and stockpiling, including location of installations and facilities, of atomic and related weapons, other critical weapons and equipment, and critical transportation equipment;

---

[1] Source: Central Intelligence Agency, Directorate of Operations, Job 78–04513R, Folder 35, Box 2. Secret.

[2] Not printed. (Ibid., History Staff, Job 84–B00389R, Box 4)

6. creating situations anywhere in the world dangerous to U.S. national security, short of commitment of Soviet Armed Forces, including foreign directed sabotage and espionage objectives;

7. interfering with U.S. political, psychological, and economic courses of action for the achievement of critical U.S. aims and objectives.

R. H. Hillenkoetter
Rear Admiral, USN
Director of Central Intelligence

---

26. **Memorandum From [*name not declassified*] of the Office of Policy Coordination of the Central Intelligence Agency to Thomas A. Parrott of the Office of Policy Coordination**[1]

Washington, October 10, 1950.

SUBJECT

Quarterly PW Guidance Report

1. Psychological warfare policy guidance for OPC activities was received from two principal sources during the past quarter. Much of this guidance came from the OPC Consultants, while some was received from the National Psychological Strategy Board (formerly the Interdepartmental Foreign Information Organization, on which OPC functioned in consultant status).

2. From the OPC Consultants, the following guidance was given OPC in matters of Psychological Warfare:

a. At the meeting of 9 August 1950, Mr. Joyce (State) agreed with the opinion that OPC should no longer engage in [*less than 1 line not declassified*] motion pictures. He stated that this should be treated as an overt matter and that such matters would be handled elsewhere.

b. On the same date, it was agreed that any possible use of propaganda balloons [*less than 1 line not declassified*] should not be publicized.

---

[1] Source: Central Intelligence Agency, Directorate of Operations, Job 80–01795R, Box 3. Top Secret.

c. On 23 August 1950, the consultants agreed that there was no objection on policy grounds to OPC proposals for the use of balloons from time to time [*less than 1 line not declassified*].

d. At the meeting of 13 September 1950, Admiral Stevens (JSPD) cautioned against any attempt to use Navy vessels as cover for [*less than 1 line not declassified*] psychological warfare operations. He stated that the Navy could furnish technical advice as to the feasibility of water-borne operations but that no warships would be made available for this purpose.

e. On 20 September 1950 the consultants stated that in planning and executing covert psychological warfare operations OPC should consider decisions of the National Psychological Strategy Board as constituting governing policy.

f. Again on 20 September, Mr. Hulick (OPC) referred to a recent decision of the National Psychological Strategy Board to the effect that balloons other than those of the toy variety would not be used for overt or covert propaganda against Iron Curtain countries without prior specific permission from the Board. Such a medium will be reserved for a particularly important message. It was stated that this policy is by no means irrevocable and that proposals for OPC action in this field would be considered on their merits.

3. Guidance received from the National Psychological Strategy Board:

a. On 14 July 1950, Mr. Barrett (State) announced the formation of an ad hoc coordinating group composed of State, Army, Navy, Air Force, and JSPD members, chaired by Mr. Jos. Phillips, State. This group was to coordinate information policy guidance in connection with the Korean situation. OPC made arrangements to have a member present at the ad hoc meetings, and overt guidance discussed therein was turned later into general materials for OPC Area Divisions. Guidance received at meetings for this inter-service group was indirect and irregular, and only used when appropriate to OPC methods and channels.

b. At the same meeting of 14 July, Mr. Wisner (OPC) referred to a decision, approved by the Department of State, to permit the National Committee for Free Europe to use certain material attributing responsibility of the Korean situation to the Soviets.

c. On Tuesday, 15 August 1950, the Board discussed attempts to defeat the admission of Communist China to the Security Council. The Board felt that [*less than 1 line not declassified*] propaganda identifying Communist China participation in the Korean situation might be extremely effective in certain limited areas. Mr. Phillips (State) referred to a suggestion that we might give circulation to reports or rumors that the Soviets did not actually want to seat the Chinese Communists in the UN. Mr. Barrett (State) saw no objection to this on policy grounds and undertook to review the policy question of limited covert use.

d. On 21 August 1950, Mr. Barrett (State) reported the recommendations of his department on identification of Chinese Communist participation in the Korean war. Such action was approved. (See entry above.)

e. At a special meeting of 13 September 1950, it was decided by the Board that the use of balloons as a propaganda carrying medium against the Iron Curtain countries would not at that time achieve any important advantage; the potential value of balloons was decided to have been sufficiently established to justify the further development and stockpiling of balloons for use in an emergency or in time of war. OPC was given the responsibility of doing so.

f. The [*less than 1 line not declassified*] was discussed on 18 September 1950, and Gen. Magruder (Defense) expressed the need for handout materials explaining [*less than 1 line not declassified*] to the public.

g. At the meeting of 25 September 1950, Mr. [*name not declassified*] (OPC) was asked to comment on the progress of the balloon project, and in doing so Mr. [*name not declassified*] requested authorization to coordinate with ONR on research, which was agreed to. A uniform reply to private inquiries re government use of balloons was agreed to: "The matter is under continuous study by agencies of the government, but disclosure of results at this time would not be in the public interest." The Board decided that utilization of large balloons would only be desirable on extraordinary basis to seek to reach large numbers behind the Curtain with important messages. The right of decision to use them was held by the NPSB. The Board further indicated at this time that any use of balloons for propaganda purposes, whether large or small (toy variety) would be a matter falling under its jurisdiction, and that such uses should be for Board decision. In view of the present situation, OPC was admonished to procure balloons for these purposes simultaneously with the fostering of training of personnel, additional research and experimentation. [*1½ lines not declassified*]

[*name not declassified*]

27. Memorandum From Theodore Babbitt, Ludwell Montague, and Forrest Van Slyck of the Office of Research and Evaluation of the Central Intelligence Agency to the Deputy Director of Central Intelligence (Jackson)[1]

Washington, October 10, 1950.

SUBJECT

Plan for a CIA Office of Estimates

1. Pursuant to your oral instructions given on 7 October we submit, in Enclosure A, an outline plan for a CIA Office of Estimates.

2. The end in view cannot be accomplished by reorganization within CIA alone. Successful implementation of this plan will require complementary action to ensure adequate research support by the departmental agencies and a cooperative attitude in the process of final coordination of estimates. The plan should not be put into effect until these requirements have been reasonably met.

3. Details of the structure and strength of the Office of Estimates will depend to a considerable extent on the composition and capabilities of the proposed Office of Research, as well as upon the degree of research support which can be reasonably expected from the departmental agencies, especially OIR. Consequently the elaboration of Enclosure A should be deferred until these matters are sufficiently clarified to afford a sound basis for further planning.

4. Some concrete problems which will arise in the course of reorganization with CIA and related negotiations with the IAC agencies are set forth in Enclosure B.[2]

---

[1] Source: Central Intelligence Agency, History Staff, Job 84–T00286R, Box 4, Folder 2. No classification marking. The memorandum is unsigned.

[2] Not found.

Enclosure A[3]

ROUGH PLAN FOR AN OFFICE OF ESTIMATES

This plan is based on the concepts held in 1945–46 and more recently set forth in the Dulles Report,[4] NSC 50,[5] and the "Webb Proposals".[6] One point must be made absolutely clear however, in order to avoid the patent defects of a joint committee system. It must be understood by all concerned that the Director at his level and the Assistant Director at his, having heard all the pertinent evidence and argument, have a power of decision with respect to the form and content of the estimate, other interested parties retaining the right to record divergent views when these relate to substantial issues and serve to increase the reader's comprehension of the problem, and then only.

The plan also presupposes:

a. The establishment of a Research Office in CIA to provide intelligence research reports in fields of common concern (e.g., scientific, economic, geographic).

b. Action to make sure of the availability of research support from the departmental agencies adequate to meet the requirements of the Estimates Office as to both timeliness and content. This condition cannot be met at present.

c. The recruitment of requisite senior personnel as rapidly as possible. The contemplated Office cannot be adequately manned with personnel now in CIA.

d. Thorough indoctrination of the IAC agencies in the new, cooperative concept, and a new start in relations with them. Initiation of the plan in the atmosphere which now exists would very probably be taken by them as an opportunity to impose on the partly imaginary CIA with which they have long contended. This plan will not work except on a basis of mutual confidence and cooperation in the national interest.

Organization and Functions

Office of the Assistant Director

Assistant Director and Deputy Assistant Director
Coordination and Liaison Staff
Administrative Staff

---

[3] Confidential.

[4] See *Foreign Relations*, 1945–1950, Emergence of the Intelligence Establishment, Document 358.

[5] Ibid., Document 384.

[6] Ibid., Documents 378, 380, and 404.

Coordination and Liaison Staff (For supporting argumentation see the Annex to this Enclosure.)[7]

   A. Composition.

   1. One full-time representative each designated by the IAC representatives of State, Army, Navy, and Air Force respectively.

   2. A similar representative of the CIA research office (or part-time representation of each of its major components?).

   3. CIA Staff Assistant, NSC Staff.

   4. A similar CIA representative with OSD and JIG.

   5. Executive Secretariat.

   B. Functions.

   1. In general, to represent the interest of their respective agencies in the Estimates Office, and the interest of the Estimates Office in their respective agencies.

   2. Specifically, to assist the Assistant Director in:

   a. Developing the estimates production program.
   b. Formulating the terms of reference for particular estimates.
   c. Formulating requests for research support and obtaining prompt and effective compliance therewith.
   d. Reviewing the estimates produced prior to their submission to the Director and the IAC.
   e. Securing IAC concurrence, or at least the formulation of dissent in the light of joint consideration.

Administrative Staff

   Personnel, fiscal, and administrative services.

   Receipt and dissemination services.

   Reproduction services.

Current Intelligence Division

   Production of the Daily Summary.

   Editing and publishing of other periodical reviews.

   Custody of sensitive material.

   Maintenance of situation room.

   Maintenance of off-hours watch.

---

[7] Not printed.

Five Regional Divisions: American, North Atlantic, East European, Southern, and Far Eastern.

A. Composition

1. Senior analysts well qualified by aptitude and experience for critical appraisal of current information and research data, for the perception of emergent trends, and for interpretation of the significance of current or anticipated developments. While every sort of expertise—political, economic, military, and area—should be represented, the emphasis should be on appreciation of the effect of all factors in combination.

2. Integral research support for these senior analysts, to assist them by keeping track of current developments, organizing research data from various sources, doing leg work, and drafting under their direction.

B. Functions

1. Surveillance of the developing situation, consultative guidance of the Current Intelligence Division, and the initiation of research projects and of estimates as required.

2. Production of estimates falling within Divisional competence.

3. Provision of appropriate expert participation in task groups formed to produce estimates of broader scope.

Functional Division

Provision of expertise (e.g., scientific, economic, geographic) as required on a functional rather than regional basis.

General Division

A very few analysts of broad competence rather than particular specialization, to concern themselves with the interrelationship of developments falling within the cognizance of two or more divisions and to provide leadership for task groups set up to deal with such problems.

28.   **Memorandum From the Under Secretary of State (Webb) to the Executive Secretary of the National Security Council (Lay)[1]**

Washington, October 17, 1950.

SUBJECT

Second Progress Report on NSC 59/1 "The Foreign Information Program and Psychological Warfare Planning"[2]

NSC 59/1 was approved as Government policy on March 10, 1950. It is requested that this Progress Report as of September 30, 1950, be circulated to the members of the Council for their information.

With the outbreak of hostilities in Korea, the Secretary of State took immediate steps to meet the urgent requirements of the situation. These steps included:

(1) the issuance of public policy guidance for all U. S. Government information media on Korea;

(2) the establishment within the Department of State of an ad hoc interdepartmental group to facilitate rapid coordination, especially between the Department of State and the Department of Defense, of psychological warfare policy matters in connection with the Korea situation;

(3) the establishment of communications with Toyko, with the Department of the Army as executive agent, and transmission to CINCFE of numerous suggestions for increasing the effectiveness of our psychological warfare effort in Korea;

(4) the assignment to the psychological warfare section established by General MacArthur in G–2 of Department of State information specialists normally attached to the information staff of Ambassador Muccio[3] in Korea.

In order to meet the requirements of further situations in which joint political and military action is required in the psychological warfare field, the Secretary of State took action to strengthen the existing organization under NSC 59/1.

With the concurrence of the Interdepartmental Foreign Information Organization, the Department of State on August 16, announced the establishment of a national psychological strategy board to carry

---

[1] Source: National Archives, RG 59, S/S–NSC Files: Lot 66 D 148, Psychological Warfare. Secret. This memorandum was circulated by Lay on October 17 as a National Security Council Progress Report. (Ibid.)

[2] For text of NSC 59/1, see Document 2; the text of the first progress report on NSC 59/1, June 21, is in the National Archives, RG 59, S/S–NSC Files: Lot 66 D 148, Psychological Warfare.

[3] Ambassador to Korea John J. Muccio.

out the functions assigned to the present Organization as established under NSC 59/1.[4] Instead of serving simply as policy consultants, the representatives of the Secretary of Defense, the Joint Chiefs of Staff and the Director of Central Intelligence are meeting regularly each week as members of the Board with the Assistant Secretary of State for Public Affairs as Chairman. Liaison representatives from the National Security Resources Board and the Economic Cooperation Administration are also meeting with the Board. A liaison representative from the Central Intelligence Agency will be available to attend Board meetings as required for intelligence matters. In addition to the responsibilities laid down in NSC 59/1, the Secretary of State is looking to the Board for concrete advice on both policy and operating problems in current situations where joint political and military action is required in the psychological warfare field.

The Board has taken action on a report forwarded by the Interdepartmental Foreign Information Staff (IFIS) on August 16, recommending adequate research and development on balloons for possible use as an alternative means of reaching the Soviet Union in the event of war or in the absence of diplomatic relations. The Central Intelligence Agency has been requested to arrange for the development and stocking of suitable types of balloons for possible use in emergency or war.

Other IFIS reports considered by the Organization include one on training of personnel for psychological warfare and foreign information.

The report prepared by the Organization on a Plan for Psychological Warfare was transmitted to the Executive Secretary, National Security Council on July 7, 1950.[5] This report has been distributed for consideration by the NSC and is now under study by the interested Departments and Agencies.

James E. Webb[6]

---

[4] Reference is to the National Psychological Strategy Board; see Document 17. With the establishment of the Psychological Strategy Board on April 4, 1951 (see Document 60), the National Psychological Strategy Board was redesignated the Psychological Operations Coordinating Committee.

[5] See Document 17.

[6] Printed from a copy that indicates Webb signed the original.

29.   Minutes of a Meeting of the Intelligence Advisory Committee[1]

IAC–M–1   Washington, October 20, 1950.

PARTICIPANTS

Director of Central Intelligence Lieutenant General Walter Bedell Smith, Presiding

MEMBERS PRESENT

Mr. W. Park Armstrong, Jr., Special Assistant, Intelligence, Department of State
Major General R. J. Canine, acting for Assistant Chief of Staff, G–2, Department
    of the Army
Rear Admiral Felix L. Johnson, Director of Naval Intelligence
Major General Charles P. Cabell, Director of Intelligence, Headquarters,
    United States Air Force
Dr. Walter F. Colby, Director of Intelligence, Atomic Energy Commission
Brigadier General Vernon E. Megee, Deputy Director for Intelligence,
    The Joint Staff
Mr. Meffert W. Kuhrtz, acting for Assistant to the Director, Federal Bureau
    of Investigation

ALSO PRESENT

Mr. William H. Jackson, Central Intelligence Agency
Mr. Fisher Howe, Department of State
Colonel Hamilton Howze, Department of the Army
Captain John M. Ocker, USN, Department of the Navy
Brigadier General E. Moore, Department of the Air Force
Dr. Malcolm C. Henderson, Atomic Energy Commission
Captain R. G. McCool, USN, The Joint Staff

1. The agenda of the meeting was "Policies and Procedures of the
Intelligence Advisory Committee."

CIA Developments

2. In opening the meeting, General Smith gave a brief résumé of
some of the problems affecting the Central Intelligence Agency which
were deemed of interest to the members of the Intelligence Advisory
Committee. He referred specifically to certain drafts of proposed NSC
directives, which were under discussion at the time General Smith took
over the duties of Director of Central Intelligence between representatives of the Central Intelligence Agency, the Department of State and
the Department of Defense. In general, the drafts under discussion were
designed to implement NSC 50.[2] By agreement of the Director of

---

[1] Source: National Archives, RG 59, INR Files: Lot 59 D 27, IAC Minutes 11/9/1950–
12/20/1951, Box 71. Secret. No drafting information appears on the minutes. The meeting was held in the Director's Conference Room at the Central Intelligence Agency.

[2] For text of NSC 50, see *Foreign Relations*, 1945–1950, Emergence of the Intelligence
Establishment, Document 384.

Central Intelligence, the Department of State and Department of Defense, further consideration of these drafts was terminated on the basis of General Smith's assurance that NSC 50 constituted a sufficient directive at the present time. General Smith stated that NSC 50, giving effect in substance to the recommendations of the so-called Dulles Committee Report, had not yet been carried out by the Central Intelligence Agency but that it was his intention promptly to carry out this directive except in one respect.

3. The exception related to the merger of the Office of Special Operations, the Office of Policy Coordination, and the Contact Branch of the Office of Operations. This merger was considered neither practical nor advisable at this time. General Smith said he believed the coordination of these offices, as recommended by the Dulles Report and incorporated in the directive from the National Security Council, could be achieved by more effective cooperation without actual merger. General Smith's position in regard to this aspect of NSC 50 had been made clear to the National Security Council at its meeting on 12 October 1950 and had been approved by the Council.[3]

4. General Smith also stated that he had encountered another problem in the Central Intelligence Agency which arose out of confusion as to the position of the Office of Policy Coordination in relation to the Central Intelligence Agency and to OPC's guidance from the Department of State and the Department of Defense. General Smith said that he construed NSC 10/2,[4] though somewhat ambiguous, as giving clear responsibility and authority to the Director of Central Intelligence for the activities of the Office of Policy Coordination. He said that guidance from the Department of State and the Department of Defense was essential for the success of these operations and that, as a matter of procedure, he was willing that such guidance be given by representatives of the Department of State and the Department of Defense directly to Mr. Wisner. However, Mr. Wisner would act under the authority and subject to the control of the Director of Central Intelligence, who, under NSC 10/2, was responsible for Mr. Wisner's operations.

Meetings of the IAC

5. In referring directly to the work of the Intelligence Advisory Committee in the future, General Smith expressed his opinion that this Committee should meet more often and for longer periods although,

---

[3] The NSC meeting of October 12 is mentioned in Montague, *Walter Bedell Smith as Director of Central Intelligence*, p. 66. Smith became DCI on October 7, 1950.

[4] See *Foreign Relations, 1945–1950*, Emergence of the Intelligence Establishment, Document 292.

as chairman, he would make every effort to keep the meetings as brief as possible. He stated that the Intelligence Advisory Committee must be geared for rapid cooperative work.

National Intelligence Estimates

6. In opening the subject of national intelligence estimates, General Smith read from a memorandum written by Mr. William H. Jackson, Deputy Director of Central Intelligence, as follows:[5]

The Responsibility of the Central Intelligence Agency for National Intelligence Estimates.

One of the principal duties assigned to the Central Intelligence Agency "for the purpose of coordinating the intelligence activities of the several Government departments and agencies in the interest of national security" is "to correlate and evaluate intelligence relating to the national security, and provide for its appropriate dissemination." The Central Intelligence Agency is thus given the responsibility of seeing to it that the United States has adequate central machinery for the examination and interpretation of intelligence so that the national security will not be jeopardized by failure to coordinate the best intelligence opinion in the country, based on all available information.

Although the Act[6] provides that "the departments and other agencies of the Government shall continue to collect, evaluate, correlate, and disseminate departmental intelligence," the statute does not limit the duties of the Central Intelligence Agency to correlate and evaluate intelligence, except by the standard of "national security."

The purport of the National Security Act can be understood and justified in the light of the history and general objectives of the Act. Behind the concept of a Central Intelligence Agency lay the necessity not only for the coordination of diversified intelligence activities, and for the performance by the central agency itself of certain services of common usefulness, but also for the coordination of intelligence opinion in the form of reports or estimates affecting generally the national security as a whole.

The Act apparently gives the Central Intelligence Agency the independent right of producing national intelligence. As a practical matter, such estimates can be written only with the collaboration of experts in many fields of intelligence and with the cooperation of several departments and agencies of the Government. A national intelligence report or estimate as assembled and produced by the Central Intelligence

---

[5] The full text of Jackson's memorandum has not been found.

[6] Reference is to the National Security Act of 1947 (P.L. 80–253), enacted July 26, 1947; 61 Stat. 495–510.

Agency should reflect the coordination of the best intelligence opinion, based on all available information. It should deal with topics of wide scope relevant to the determination of basic policy, such as the assessment of a country's war potential, its preparedness for war, its strategic capabilities and intentions, its vulnerability to various forms of direct attack or indirect pressures. An intelligence estimate of such scope would go beyond the competence of any single Department or Agency of the Government. A major objective, then, in establishing the Central Intelligence Agency was to provide the administrative machinery for the coordination of intelligence opinion, for its assembly and review, objectively and impartially, and for its expression in the form of estimates of national scope and importance.

The concept of national intelligence estimates underlying the statute is that of an authoritative interpretation and appraisal that will serve as a firm guide to policy-makers and planners. A national intelligence estimate should reflect the coordination of the best intelligence opinion, with notation of and reasons for dissent in the instances when there is not unanimity. It should be based on all available information and be prepared with full knowledge of our own plans and in the light of our own policy requirements. The estimate should be compiled and assembled centrally by an agency whose objectivity and disinterestedness are not open to question. Its ultimate approval should rest upon the collective judgment of the highest officials in the various intelligence agencies. Finally, it should command recognition and respect throughout the Government as the best available and presumably the most authoritative intelligence estimate.

Although the task is made more difficult by a lack of general acceptance of the concept of national intelligence estimates in the Government, it is, nevertheless, the clear duty and responsibility of the Central Intelligence Agency under the statute to assemble and produce such coordinated and authoritative estimates.

7. There followed a discussion of the above excerpt from the memorandum and there was general assent at the meeting to its statement of the responsibility of the Central Intelligence Agency for national intelligence estimates. General Smith stated that, in order to discharge this responsibility, he proposed at the earliest possible time to set up in the Central Intelligence Agency an Office of National Estimates. This division, in his opinion, would become the heart of the Central Intelligence Agency and of the national intelligence machinery. Services of common concern, now performed in the present Office of Reports and Estimates but not including the production of political intelligence, would be placed in a separate office or division which might properly be called the Office of Research and Reports. The latter would confine its activities to the production of reports as a service of common concern in fields assigned specifically by directives of the National Secu-

rity Council. It was pointed out by Mr. Jackson that the fact that the Office of Reports and Estimates has in the past produced both national estimates and miscellaneous reports in various fields, which could not possibly be construed as national estimates, had blurred and confused both the product and function of the Office of Reports and Estimates. There has been insufficient differentiation between the form and the coordination procedure in connection with the two products and in their methods of production.

8. General Smith said that, as to the matter of form, in the future intelligence estimates produced by the Central Intelligence Agency on the basis of intelligence contributions from the various intelligence agencies and concurred in or dissented from by the respective agencies would be published under a cover showing plainly that the estimate was a collective effort the result of which would be labeled as a national intelligence estimate.

Action

9. After discussion the following procedural steps were agreed upon in the production of national estimates:

a. The Intelligence Advisory Committee will adopt an intelligence plan, or more specifically, a list of required national estimates in an order of priority.

b. In the case of a particular estimate, a frame of reference and the assumptions on which the estimate is based will be discussed and approved by the Intelligence Advisory Committee.

c. Work on the estimate will be referred in the first instance to the Office of Reports and Estimates, or to the Office of National Estimates when it is established in the Central Intelligence Agency, and the several intelligence agencies will be consulted and a time-table fixed for contributions to the national estimate within the fields of their respective interests.

d. On the basis of these contributions, the Central Intelligence Agency will produce a first draft of the proposed national estimate.

e. This draft will be sent back to the agencies for comment and modification and for further discussion if required. On the basis of such comments and discussion, the Central Intelligence Agency will produce a second draft of the estimate.

f. This second, or later drafts if required, will be submitted to the Intelligence Advisory Committee for final discussion, resolution of differences and approval.

g. If differences cannot be resolved and approval obtained, the estimate will be published with notation of substantial dissent and reasons therefor.

It was made clear by General Smith that this procedure would not and could not be followed in the case of so-called "crisis estimates." In the event of need arising for a quick or crisis estimate, a procedure similar to that used in the recent instance when the President called for a series of estimates prior to his departure for the meeting with General

MacArthur would be followed.[7] That is, a special meeting of the Intelligence Advisory Committee will be called and representatives of the various intelligence agencies assigned at once to the production of a draft of the required estimate for immediate submission to the Intelligence Advisory Committee for discussion, revision and approval.

Agenda for the Next IAC Meeting

Action:

10. It was determined that at the next meeting of the Intelligence Advisory Committee there would be discussion of national estimates priorities and the frame of references and assumptions to form the basis of an intelligence estimate of the situation in Indo-China. It was also agreed that at a future date General Smith will produce a paper for submission to the Intelligence Advisory Committee indicating how the Central Intelligence Agency will function in the theater of operation in time of war. The next meeting of the Intelligence Advisory Committee was scheduled for Wednesday, 25 October, 3:00 P.M.

---

[7] The resultant Korean "estimates" are reprinted in Michael Warner, ed., *The CIA Under Harry Truman*, pp. 349–372.

---

30.   Memorandum From the Secretary of State's Special Assistant for Intelligence and Research (Armstrong) to Secretary of State Acheson[1]

Washington, October 23, 1950.

SUBJECT

NSC Consideration of CIA Budget

Annually the CIA has submitted for NSC approval a budget for which it proposes to seek appropriation. This "budget" usually has been stated simply as a total figure and, until last year, approved without extensive consideration by the NSC or its staff.

---

[1] Source: National Archives, RG 59, S/S–NSC Files: Lot 63 D 351, NSC 50 Series. Top Secret. This memorandum received the concurrence of Humelsine, Jessup, and Matthews. Document 24 provides background on this issue.

For the 1950–51 year representatives of State and Defense did review in a cursory fashion the budget programs of several of the CIA offices prior to NSC approval of the figure "for submission to the Bureau of the Budget." Subsequently, State and Defense gave some thought to the difficult problem of how, without compromising the security of the Agency, to fulfill its responsibility by a more satisfactory review of the CIA budget.

With the recent change in leadership in CIA, however, it no longer seems appropriate to suggest that a detailed NSC examination of the budget should take place; rather, there should be an indication that the NSC and the Departments of State and Defense have confidence in the new Director. It is quite likely that General Smith will volunteer to discuss some of his plans and programs with the Council.

Recommendations:

1. That the NSC approve the budget figure as submitted.

2. That, if appropriate and without indicating any lack of confidence, you might suggest in the course of the discussions that it would be helpful if General Smith, during the course of the year, would consider the problem of how the NSC can best fulfill its responsibilities with respect to the CIA budget and recommend procedures which would permit the fulfillment of those responsibilities without compromising the security of his Agency.

PA

---

31. **Memorandum for the Record by the Assistant Director for Policy Coordination of the Central Intelligence Agency (Wisner)**[1]

Washington, November 2, 1950.

SUBJECT

Relationship with ECA; conversations between top-ranking ECA and CIA officials on 2 November 1950

1. This memorandum will record the highlights of a conference which took place on Thursday 2 November between General Smith,

---

[1] Source: Central Intelligence Agency, Directorate of Operations, Job 80–01795R, Box 3. Top Secret. Drafted on November 7.

Mr. Jackson and the undersigned for CIA, and Messrs. Foster and Bissell for ECA. At the outset of the meeting, I was requested by General Smith to summarize the history of the relationship which I proceeded to do by giving a brief but general chronological account of the origin and development of our dealings with ECA, together with three or four illustrations of the activities in which we have been jointly engaged. At the conclusion of this résumé I emphasized our concern on the score of security breaches and operational and other improprieties as regards the use of counterpart funds. After giving a number of illustrations of these unhappy developments and after referring to several of the points made by Mr. Harriman in his most recent conversations with me, I stated that it seemed to me that there had been two chief types of insecurity and that there were two methods which should be employed in order to clear up as much of the difficulty as possible.

2. The two types of action which had given us concern and which promise to create much more serious problems for all who are involved unless they can be brought to an end are (a) loosetalk, i.e., the tendency on the part of certain ECA labor and public relations people to talk about matters which were none of their concern and with unauthorized people; and (b) clumsy and dangerously insecure attempts on the part of ECA labor and public relations officials [*less than 1 line not declassified*]. I acknowledged that we might not have been entirely without fault ourselves and I said that we had taken a number of steps to tighten up within our own organization, but I said that it seemed that action was in order on the part of Messrs. Foster and Bissell to clear up the difficulties within ECA. It was agreed by Messrs. Foster and Bissell that these actions should be taken and that as a first step fresh directives should be prepared to all ECA personnel concerned, [*1 line not declassified*]. It was further agreed that I should endeavor to work this out with Mr. Bissell at an early meeting (meeting set for two P.M., 10 Nov 50)[2] [*2 lines not declassified*].

3. [*1 paragraph (29 lines) not declassified*]

4. Mr. Foster then referred to a number of other projects which are pending before him at the present time. He said that he had not approved these projects because he had not received enough information about them to enable him to exercise his judgment. [*3 lines not declassified*] He requested that further information be supplied to him on these and the other projects before him and I agreed to furnish this information either to himself or in his absence to Mr. Bissell. (It seems to me that either Mr. Foster has forgotten what we have told him or that

---

[2] A handwritten note in the left margin reads, "Staff I to prepare draft." Staff I was part of OPC.

we have not done a proper job of providing details—with a third possibility that Mr. Tappin may not have passed on to Mr. Foster the information which we have provided to him about the projects under consideration.)[3]

5. I inquired as to whether Mr. Bissell would be authorized to act on matters of common concern, including the approval of projects in the absence of Mr. Foster, who will be out of the country for about 5 weeks on a round-the-world tour. Mr. Foster acknowledged that Mr. Bissell would have full authority in his absence. (Accordingly, we should endeavor to clear these matters with Mr. Bissell at a very early meeting and I should like to be reminded of this and provided with the papers and a reasonable oral briefing. I consider this to be the responsibility of Colonel Taylor as to the pending projects.)[4]

6. There were some very favorable comments made about the progress of our [less than 1 line not declassified] operations and all agreed that there was not only success here but immeasurable success in terms of evident results. The situation as regards [less than 1 line not declassified] operations was acknowledged to be by no means as clear. When called upon for an explanation of this, I said that the principal problem arose from the fact that the leadership of the [less than 1 line not declassified] has been weak and vacillating and that it has not been possible to press them as far as the [less than 1 line not declassified] have gone. I further said that our approach had been more along the lines of building up the younger and more vigorous elements [less than 1 line not declassified] and providing them with encouragement, guidance and funds for specific projects. General Smith commented that we should continue along this line especially that of building up vigorous younger elements—but that we should take our own independent soundings on the [less than 1 line not declassified] situation at a very early date with a view to reappraising the possibilities and reevaluating our efforts to date. It might be that we have been too soft about the old leadership and that we should undertake more stringent measures to move aside this leadership in order to make way for the other and better elements. Mr Bissell raised a question about the [less than 1 line not declassified] and General Smith replied that he did not think that they offered too promising a medium but that they should be looked at again.

F.G.W.[5]

---

[3] A handwritten notation in the left margin reads "SAA." This referred the issue to Wisner's Special Assistant for Action Colonel Robert Taylor.

[4] A handwritten notation in the left margin reads, "SAA." A handwritten notation in the right margin reads [text not declassified].

[5] Printed from a copy that bears these typed initials.

32.   Memorandum From Secretary of Defense Marshall to Director of Central Intelligence Smith[1]

Washington, November 27, 1950.

SUBJECT

Present Status of United States Intelligence

In the overall planning for our national security, an adequate and timely intelligence capability is felt to be a first priority consideration. In order to prevent strategic and tactical surprise we would wish to have:

(a) A 7- to 10-day warning of the imminence of hostilities, during which period our defense systems could be alerted and forces deployed or positioned as required.

(b) Provide additional warnings at least 12 to 48 hours prior to the initiation of hostilities which will indicate the location of bases on which atomic attacks are mounted and which will report the approximate time of launching of these attacks.

The foregoing provisions are obviously beyond our capabilities and possibly for a long time to come. However, they do provide a clear-cut target toward which your agency and the Department of Defense should point their intelligence efforts.

Satisfaction of these requirements necessitates detailed, comprehensive and continuing knowledge of the disposition, organization and state of readiness of the Soviet Armed Forces and the supporting economy. The current basis of estimates concerning the Soviet armed forces seems dangerously inadequate.

Because of the extraordinary security program of the Soviet Union virtually no intelligence contribution to these requirements is available through normal channels available to Service intelligence agencies.

In view of the basic requirement to prevent strategic and tactical surprise, our limited capability to meet this requirement and the potential for improvement of this capability through operations by the Central Intelligence Agency within the USSR and the satellites, particularly in the covert and defector fields, the Department of Defense is prepared to place support of CIA operations in these fields in Priority One.

---

[1] Source: Central Intelligence Agency, Directorate of Operations, Job 80–01795R, Box 3. Top Secret.

In view of the foregoing, a statement of your foreseeable quantitative and qualitative requirements in as much detail as possible is requested in order to enable the Department of Defense to arrange for this support.

With special reference to the matter of military equipment it is further requested that your requirements in this field be forwarded as soon as possible and separately from the more general requirements in support of the broader intelligence programs.

G. C. Marshall[2]

---

[2] Printed from a copy that indicates Marshall signed the original.

---

33.   Memorandum From the Assistant Director for Policy Coordination of the Central Intelligence Agency (Wisner) to Staff and Division Chiefs[1]

Washington, November 29, 1950.

SUBJECT

Policy Governing the Conduct of OPC Operations Within the United States

The following policy is announced to guide all concerned in judging the appropriateness of engaging in a given activity within the United States or its outlying possessions. This policy will not be construed as an alteration of existing procedures for obtaining approval to undertake a specific project or operation.

1. Basic Authority.

a. The following sources and limitations of authority are applicable to the subject of this paper:

(1) Sec. 102(d), National Security Act of 1947:

"... Provided, that the agency [CIA][2] shall have no police, subpoena, law-enforcement powers, or internal security functions...."

---

[1] Source: Central Intelligence Agency, Directorate of Operations Job 80–01795R, Box 3. Top Secret. Drafted in I/PR on November 21 and 24. All ellipses in the original.

[2] Brackets in the original.

(2) Excerpt from Memorandum of Agreement between ADPC and FBI:[3]

"... The Office of Policy Coordination recognizes the primary responsibility of the FBI in the field of United States domestic security. ..."

(3) NSC 10/2:

OPC was created by NSC 10/2 (under the authority of Sec. 102(d)(5) of the National Security Act of 1947) to supplement the overt foreign activities of the U.S. Government and to conduct covert operations in support of or to accomplish U.S. foreign policy objectives. The term covert operations is defined as embracing all activities (exclusive of operations to secure intelligence and of cover and deception for military operations) against hostile foreign states or groups or in support of friendly foreign states or groups, which are conducted so that any U.S. Government responsibility for them is not evident and that if uncovered the responsibility therefor can be denied. Foreign policy objectives are interpreted to be those objectives which are established by the President (usually acting through the Secretary of State) in pursuance of applicable laws, and enunciated and interpreted through various regulations and pronouncements. OPC's source for determination of what is U.S. foreign policy at a given time is the Department of State.

2. *Interpretation.*

a. General.

It is clear that by both law and charter OPC is precluded from engaging in operations concerned with the domestic affairs of the United States. OPC is authorized to conduct operations only against or in support of foreign states or elements thereof. Police, law-enforcement, and internal security functions are responsibilities of other U.S. Government agencies; OPC is bound by the presumption that these agencies are performing their functions faithfully and effectively.

What may not be clear is whether OPC is authorized to engage in operations within the United States against or in support of a foreign state or group and in so doing support U.S. foreign policy objectives. In many instances it might appear more practicable to carry out a given operation in the United States than elsewhere. OPC is not expressly authorized or forbidden by NSC 10/2 to conduct such operations. However, it appears to have been the intent of the NSC that covert op-

---

[3] Not found.

erations were only to be executed abroad (cf., purpose of establishing OPC: "to supplement the overt *foreign activities* of the U.S. Government" (underscoring supplied)). Moreover and more important, it would be very difficult if not impossible to undertake covert operations in the United States in such a manner that "any U.S. Government responsibility for them is not evident and that if uncovered the U.S. Government can plausibly disclaim any responsibility for them." The U.S. Government has certain responsibilities under international law for acts committed within its jurisdiction which might well make impossible disavowal of responsibility for a covert act committed by OPC in the United States. For these reasons it is considered that only in the most exceptional circumstances will it be desirable to propose operations which are to be executed within the United States.

   b. Auxiliary Activities.

   It is also evident, however, that OPC does have occasion to carry on certain activities within the United States. [*3½ lines not declassified*] The fact that these activities take place within the United States is, however, purely incidental to the main purpose of the OPC operation. The essential element is that they are part of operations to be executed abroad against hostile foreign states. Such activities have no other relation to the domestic affairs of the United States than that they physically take place, for reasons of necessity, convenience, security, etc., within the United States. The determinant as to the propriety, from the standpoint of OPC's charter, of an OPC undertaking within the United States is therefore the *objective* of the operation. The ultimate objective of any proposed undertaking must clearly be to produce an effect upon a foreign state or group. This effect may even be the ultimate reception abroad of an idea which has been produced and disseminated within the United States. It is not appropriate to undertake any activity which has the objective or primary effect of influencing the foreign or domestic policies of the United States, or of influencing the internal security of the United States; or which has as its target a domestic group in the United States.

   c. Preliminary Activities.

   There are certain other kinds of activity which OPC must carry on within the United States which are incidental but necessary to the execution of its substantive tasks. Some of these are self-evident and will not be dealt with here (e.g., personnel recruitment, domestic liaison, matériel procurement). Others are not so clearly defined and delineated and consequently provide opportunity for misunderstanding. Among these are:

   [*1 paragraph (20 lines) not declassified*]

(2) *External Research*—Preliminary to launching some operations it may be necessary to perform certain research or to acquire information which is necessary for realistic planning. Since OPC is not a research organization, it is often obliged to turn to external sources. The employment of private individuals and organizations outside the Government is sometimes required. In this activity OPC will finance only that research which (a) deals with matériel the need for which is essential to OPC operations, and (b) can not be obtained from established U.S. governmental research organizations. Here again, however, such contacts with U.S. groups, and their utilization, is solely for the support of OPC operations abroad.

(3) *Training*—Providing specialized training is an inherent prerequisite to the undertaking of many substantive activities. It is necessary to give indoctrination training to staff personnel. It is necessary to train staff agents and indigenous agents in doctrine and techniques of secret operations. It may be desirable to train individuals or groups of indigenous agents for execution of a particular clandestine operation. When it is more convenient and more practicable to do so, such training will be administered in the United States.

There are other types of training which involve personnel not under the permanent or complete control of OPC but which enable OPC indirectly to execute operations abroad. The training of a selected group of members of a foreign internal security service in anti-sabotage techniques might enable OPC effectively to discharge a requirement for protection of vital materials or installations in the country represented. [4 lines not declassified] It is appropriate for OPC to provide these types of training within the United States if (1) the *objective* of such training is within the charter of OPC, and (2) the training can, for reasons of convenience, security, control, or availability of facilities, most effectively be provided within the United States. OPC can of course provide this training through its own or through other available facilities where it is more desirable to do so.

(4) *Technological Research and Development*—In order that proficiency in execution of operations and capabilities for new operations may be constantly expanded, it is desirable to conduct research into and to sponsor the development of new devices, weapons, and equipment, including psychological warfare aids. It is necessary and appropriate to carry on this activity within the United States. In so doing, however, OPC will insofar as practicable conduct research and development through other Government agencies, OPC will not initiate research or development directly through private organizations in the United States, except where OPC has principal interest in the article to be developed, and where it is demonstrably impracticable to work through an established Government agency.

3. Chief, Staff III will promulgate this policy through appropriate regulations.[4]

Frank G. Wisner[5]

---

[4] A handwritten note in the margin next to paragraph 3 reads: "Done! see OPC Reg 50-15 dated 30 Nov 50. [*initials not declassified*] 30 Nov." [*text not declassified*]

[5] Printed from a copy that bears this typed signature.

---

34.   Memorandum of Agreement Between the Department of State and the Central Intelligence Agency[1]

Washington, December 4, 1950.

I. Purpose

This agreement is entered into between the Department of State (hereinafter referred to as the Department) and the Central Intelligence Agency (hereinafter referred to as CIA), to make administrative provisions for budget and finance procedures pertaining to the support of overt assignments of personnel of the Department (including Foreign Service personnel) to CIA Washington and field activities in the continental United States. This agreement also provides a basis for such other budget and finance arrangements as may be mutually agreed upon. This agreement does not cover those personnel details of a temporary nature [*less than 1 line not declassified*], or regular interservice assignments as provided for in the Foreign Service Act, or other nonreimbursable assignments mutually agreed upon. This agreement will cover all assignments of Departmental personnel now or hereafter made to all CIA Washington and domestic field office activities unless for security reasons appropriate officials determine that reimbursement should be made under the terms of the "covert" arrangements. Appendices may be added or amendments made to this agreement to cover other budget and finance arrangements of an overt nature as mutually agreed upon in writing by appropriate officials of the Department and CIA.

---

[1] Source: National Archives, RG 59, INR Historical Files: Lot 58 D 776, State–CIA Relationship 1949–56, Box 2. Secret.

II. Salaries

Advances will be made to the Department at the beginning of each quarter. Such payments will be based upon the salary compensation paid by the Department since other direct costs will be borne by CIA. Quarterly estimates will be based on known and anticipated needs for each quarter by grades, positions, and types of officials assigned. Adjustments will be made for over or under-payments for the preceding quarter. Fourth quarter adjustments should not normally be necessary.

III. Travel Arrangements

Any required temporary duty travel in the United States will be covered by appropriate CIA authorizations and all expenses will be paid to the officials concerned by CIA. Travel from overseas posts to the continental United States prior to detail to CIA and, in the event of assignment for overseas duty, the travel, salary, and other expenses incident thereto will be handled under the terms of costs arrangements consummated for such purposes.

IV. Liaison[2]

Liaison between the Department of State and the Central Intelligence Agency pertinent to this agreement shall be controlled at points designated by each agency for policy clearance, administrative coordination and implementation, and budgetary planning and reimbursement as follows:

a. The Policy Clearance Liaison Official shall be responsible for securing or ensuring operation and policy clearance, and establishing security standards for each activity requiring administrative support, and for advising the appropriate Administrative Liaison official thereon.

b. The Administrative Liaison Official of each Agency shall be responsible for intra-agency administrative coordination, implementation and maintenance of established security provisions.

c. The Budgetary and Finance Liaison Official shall be responsible for the establishment of cost factors, the transfer of funds between

---

[2] In a November 2 letter to DCI Smith, Humelsine reaffirmed the Department's liaison officers and agreed to establish an administrative control officer in the Office of the Special Assistant, Intelligence and Research, "to coordinate Departmental administrative support to CIA on all covert and overt matters except those pertaining to OPC." (National Archives, RG 59, Central Files 1950–54, 103.11/11–150) Deputy Director of Central Intelligence Jackson's letter to Humelsine, November 28, acceded to the Department liaison arrangements, named the CIA liaison officials, and enclosed copies of the covert and overt agreements for signature. (Ibid., 103.11/11–2850) The Department accepted the CIA's designated liaisons and signed each agreement. (Letter from Humelsine to Jackson, December 5; ibid., 103.11/12–550) The text of the December agreements has not been found.

Agencies, and the accomplishment of the necessary budgetary planning and allotment adjustments.

d. Additional liaison points at appropriate working levels may be established at the discretion and under the control of the Administrative Liaison Official.

e. Each Agency will determine if one or more officers will be designated to represent it in the discharge of the liaison responsibilities listed in a, b, and c above.

W. H. Jackson
Deputy Director of Central Intelligence

C. H. Humelsine[3]
Deputy Under Secretary for Administration
Department of State

---

[3] Printed from a copy that indicates the memorandum was signed by Jackson on November 28, and Humelsine on December 4.

---

35.   Minutes of a Meeting of the Intelligence Advisory Committee[1]

IAC–M–10   Washington, December 7, 1950.

Director of Central Intelligence
Lieutenant General Walter Bedell Smith
Presiding

MEMBERS PRESENT

Mr. W. Park Armstrong, Jr., Special Assistant, Intelligence, Department of State
Major General A. R. Bolling, Assistant Chief of Staff, G–2, Department
  of the Army
Rear Admiral Felix L. Johnson, Director of Naval Intelligence
Brigadier General Ernest B. Moore, acting for Director of Intelligence,
  Headquarters, United States Air Force
Dr. Walter F. Colby, Director of Intelligence, Atomic Energy Commission
Captain R. G. McCool, USN, acting for Deputy Director for Intelligence,
  The Joint Staff

---

[1] Source: National Archives, RG 59, INR Historical Files: Lot 58 D 776, Office of Libraries and Intelligence Acquisition, 1950–51, Box 18. Top Secret. No drafting information appears on the minutes. The meeting was held in the DCI's Conference Room.

Mr. Victor P. Keay, acting for Assistant to the Director, Federal Bureau of
Investigation

ALSO PRESENT

Mr. William H. Jackson, Central Intelligence Agency
Dr. William L. Langer, Central Intelligence Agency
Mr. [*name not declassified*], Central Intelligence Agency
Mr. Ludwell Montague, Central Intelligence Agency
Mr. Lyman B. Kirkpatrick, Central Intelligence Agency
Mr. Allan Evans, Department of State
Mr. William C. Trueheart, Department of State
Colonel Hamilton H. Howze, Department of the Army
Dr. Samuel McKee, Jr., Department of the Army
Mr. Roy S. Tod, Department of the Army
Captain John M. Ocker, USN, Department of the Navy
Colonel Edward H. Porter, Department of the Air Force
Lieut. Colonel J. C. Marchant, Department of the Air Force
Mr. C. D. DeLoach, Federal Bureau of Investigation

Acting Secretary Mr. James Q. Reber, Central Intelligence Agency

[Omitted here is discussion of minutes of previous meetings, a
comparative study of U.S.–USSR military and industrial strength,
China, NSRB request for an estimate, and intelligence requirements re
Spitzbergen.]

Watch Committee Terms of Reference (IAC–D–6)[2]

7. *Action:* Agreed that there should be a single Watch Committee
in the Government properly operated with the full participation of the
IAC members. This Committee should be the Watch Committee currently located in the Pentagon and headed by General Weckerling. General Smith stated that the Watch Committee headed by the CIA should
be abolished and that the terms of reference before the members would,
therefore, not need to be acted upon. He requested General Bolling to
have distributed to the member agencies the terms of reference under
which the present Watch Committee in the Pentagon is operating and
arrange for such modification as may be necessary to provide the U.S.
Government the service required. General Smith stated that it was his
responsibility to see that there is an arrangement in the Government
for carrying out the functions of a Watch Committee, that he did not
consider it necessary for the CIA to head it, that this Committee should
serve the entire Government and should accordingly be fully supported. He said that he was prepared to provide such financial or other
support as was necessary for this Committee to fulfill his needs under
the statute. It was understood that teletype facilities already exist which

---

[2] Not found.

would ensure communication necessary to meet the needs of the DCI and the IAC members.

[Omitted here is discussion of the German Defector Exploitation Center and crisis estimates on Germany, Iran, and Indochina.]

36.   Memorandum From Director of Central Intelligence Smith to Secretary of Defense Marshall[1]

Washington, December 26, 1950.

SUBJECT

Support Required by the Central Intelligence Agency from the Department of Defense

REFERENCE

Your Memorandum dated 27 November 1950, Subject: Present Status of United States Intelligence[2]

1. This Agency will make a maximum effort and will coordinate the collective efforts of all intelligence agencies toward attainment of the objectives set forth in reference memorandum. Defense plans cannot be based, however, on the assumption that timely warning of Soviet attack can be assured.

2. The following is a general statement of the support needed by the Central Intelligence Agency from the Department of Defense:

a. Assignment to CIA of one or two officers each from the Army, Navy, and Air Force, well qualified to assist in preparing national intelligence estimates.

b. [1 paragraph (7 lines) not declassified]

c. [1 paragraph (7 lines) not declassified]

d. [1 paragraph (2 lines) not declassified]

e. [1 paragraph (8 lines) not declassified]

f. Clarification of the relationship between representatives of CIA and the theater commanders in theaters of operations to insure that details of operations, covert personnel, and other highly sensitive material are known to a minimum number of individuals.

---

[1] Source: Central Intelligence Agency, Directorate of Operations, Job 80–01795R, Box 3. Top Secret.

[2] Document 32.

g. Arrangements by which CIA will be kept fully informed of those operational decisions and plans of the JCS which have a direct or indirect bearing on the functions of CIA. For the present, we believe that this would require providing this Agency, for carefully restricted use, copies of JCS, JIC and other papers bearing upon the duties and responsibilities of CIA.

h. Establishment of a permanent liaison between the JCS and appropriate elements of CIA, including a method for furnishing advice and guidance on essential elements of information which are considered of paramount importance for intelligence collection efforts.

3. The above are general statements of the requirements for the Central Intelligence Agency and indicate the major principles on which it is necessary to establish agreement between CIA and the JCS on the methods of support of this Agency.

Walter B. Smith[3]

---

[3] Printed from a copy that indicates Smith signed the original.

---

37.   Memorandum by J. L. Barnard of the Bureau of European Affairs[1]

Washington, January 4, 1951.

PRODUCTION OF NATIONAL INTELLIGENCE ESTIMATES

General Bedell Smith's direction of CIA has resulted in a significant change in that organization's production of finished intelligence. CIA is now in the business of producing what are called National Intelligence Estimates along the lines laid down in NSC 50. These papers are interdepartmental in character, designed to focus all available in-

---

[1] Source: National Archives, RG 59, INR Files: Lot 58 D 528, NIE Correspondence VI, 1950–54. Confidential. The memorandum was prepared to provide information to EUR on the production of National Intelligence Estimates. It was attached to a memorandum entitled "Background Paper for Mr. Armstrong's Statement at UM on National Intelligence Estimates." After that meeting, held on January 5, Special Assistant for Intelligence, W. Park Armstrong, Jr., circulated a list of completed and projected National Intelligence Estimates to 20 senior officials in 20 different offices and bureaus of the Department of State. (Ibid., Central Files 1950–54, 103.11/1–851)

telligence on a problem of importance to the national security. In the preparation of these Estimates, CIA is now relying on the State Department, rather than its own staff, for political and economic intelligence, the Department of the Army for military, etc., etc. A reorganization within CIA is in process with the emphasis on quality rather than quantity of personnel. CIA's Office of Reports and Evaluation (ORE) is being eliminated so far as political intelligence is concerned, and a small top level Office of National Estimates has been created to integrate the departmental drafts for the approval of the Intelligence Advisory Committee (IAC). (The IAC advises the Director of Central Intelligence and is made up of the chiefs of intelligence of State, Army, Navy, Air, AEC, FBI, and a representative from the Joint Staff in the Department of Defense.) Upon approval by the IAC, the paper becomes a National Intelligence Estimate and is sent by the Director of Central Intelligence to the President, appropriate officers of Cabinet level, and the NSC.

What all this means to EUR is simply this: heretofore reports written by CIA's former evaluation office (ORE) were sent to the R area of the Department for comment and concurrence or dissent. In this procedure, the Bureau's role was gauged to the relatively minor importance of these papers. The R area checked with the Bureau to insure that the Department was speaking with one voice, but the papers seldom dealt with major issues.

With the new CIA product, however, it is obvious that Bureau participation will be more important than it has been in the past. These National Intelligence Estimates, as can be seen by the auspices under which they are prepared and their eventual destination, carry considerable weight. What the new CIA Office of National Estimates wants and should have from State is the pooled intelligence of the Bureau and R. This approach does not mean that the Bureau will have to do any original drafting—such drafts will be prepared by the R area—but it does mean that the Bureau will share the responsibility for making State's contribution.

In practice, the preparation of a National Intelligence Estimate breaks down into the following steps: (1) the R area (OIR) prepares a first draft of the political and/or economic section of the paper under interdepartmental agreements as provided for in NSC 50; (2) these sections are then taken by the Office of National Estimates (CIA) and worked into a draft of the whole paper; (3) this CIA draft is sent to the contributing Departments for comment; (4) after consideration by the Departments, it is further discussed in CIA by an interdepartmental working group; (5) a final draft is then issued by CIA for approval by the IAC.

Although the Bureau may, on occasion, be consulted at stage (1), it will generally not enter the picture until stage (3) when the CIA draft of the whole paper is sent to the Departments for comment and suggestion. Stage (3) should be the beginning and the end of Bureau participation, unless the draft is radically changed in the course of its future development either in the working group discussion or the IAC (see below). The Bureau will receive its copy for comment through the Intelligence Adviser. Bureau comment may be made either in writing to the Intelligence Adviser, or directly to the OIR personnel involved (in which case the Intelligence Adviser should be informed). In the event that the Bureau or OIR feel that further discussion is needed in order to develop a unified Departmental position, they will notify the Intelligence Adviser who will then arrange a meeting for a reconciliation of views. If there is a fundamental divergence of interpretation between the Bureau and R, this fact and the opposing arguments will be presented to the Special Assistant for Intelligence who will follow the accepted principles of action and review by referring the matter to higher authority for a decision as to the Departmental position.

In this connection it should be noted that the Special Assistant speaks for the Department in the IAC. This role has its complications. The IAC, although formerly concerned almost exclusively with jurisdictional matters, has now been transformed under General Smith's chairmanship into a substantive group, which means that there is considerable give and take around the table before a final version of an Estimate is approved. Should the Special Assistant feel that in his judgment the final version is so changed by this give and take as to run counter to the Departmental position, he can either ask time for further consideration (in which case the Bureau will be apprised) or, if time does not permit, he can publish the Departmental position as a dissent in an appendix to the National Estimate.

Throughout this whole process, it must be recognized that once a National Estimate draft is underway, the timing on deadlines for contributions or comments is out of the hands of R. The Special Assistant will attempt to have these deadlines made realistic, but the ultimate decision as to their urgency rests with the IAC itself. Therefore, in order to incorporate the Bureau's views in this new and influential series of intelligence appraisals, it is essential that every effort be made within EUR to meet the due dates specified.

It is hoped that the procedure cited above will not place too great an additional burden on Bureau personnel, while, at the same time, it will ensure that the Bureau's role as a contributor of intelligence is being effectively played.

38. Memorandum From Director of Central Intelligence Smith to the Executive Secretary of the National Security Council (Lay)[1]

Washington, January 8, 1951.

SUBJECT

Draft of NSC Directive on Covert Operations and Clandestine Activities

1. On 14 December 1950, at my request, the National Security Council suspended paragraph 4 of NSC 10/2.[2]

2. I am submitting herewith the draft of a directive for issuance by the National Security Council which clearly defines the responsibilities for covert operations and clandestine activities in peace or in war.[3] This draft was prepared by representatives of this agency in consultation with Rear Admiral Leslie Stevens from the Joint Chiefs of Staff, Brigadier General John Magruder from the Office of the Secretary of Defense, and Mr. Robert Joyce from the Department of State.

3. It is my recommendation that this Directive be sent by the National Security Council to the Departments of State and Defense and the Joint Chiefs of Staff for comment.

4. A related subject which needs clarification is the distinction between covert operations such as may be planned and executed by this agency, and guerrilla warfare conducted by regular forces. I have directed that a paper on this subject be prepared for submission to the NSC.

Walter B. Smith[4]

---

[1] Source: Central Intelligence Agency, History Staff Job 83–00036R, Box 1. Secret. The date is taken from an attached document summary.

[2] NSC Action No. 400, approved December 14, 1950, suspended the provisions of paragraph 4 of NSC 10/2, at the request of the Director of Central Intelligence, until the issuance of a further directive. (National Archives, RG 59, S/S–NSC (Miscellaneous) Files: Lot 66 D 95, Records of Action by the National Security Council)

[3] The attachment printed below is a draft of NSC 10/3; see footnote 2, Document 42.

[4] Printed from a copy that indicates Smith signed the original.

Attachment[5]

NATIONAL SECURITY COUNCIL DIRECTIVE

COVERT OPERATIONS AND CLANDESTINE INTELLIGENCE ACTIVITIES

1. Under the authority of Section 102(d) (5) of the National Security Act of 1947 the National Security Council hereby directs that:

2. The Director of Central Intelligence shall be responsible for the planning, preparation and execution of covert operations and clandestine intelligence activities in peace or in war and for insuring that such operations are planned and conducted in a manner consistent with and in support of U.S. foreign and military policies and with overt activities.

3. The following relationships shall prevail in wartime or in peacetime in areas where U.S. military forces are engaged in combat:

a. The DCI shall coordinate covert operations and clandestine intelligence activities with the Secretary of Defense and the Joint Chiefs of Staff and the appropriate non-military U.S. government departments and agencies, and insure that plans for such activities are accepted by JCS as being consistent with and complementary to approved plans for wartime or emergency military operations.

b. Covert operations and clandestine intelligence activities in a theater of military command shall come within the responsibility of the theater commander and the DCI shall designate a senior representative to be on the General Staff of each theater commander concerned with such operations and activities, responsible to the theater commander through the Chief of Staff, to assist in the planning, direction and command of such operations and activities. Policy direction and control of the execution of such operations and activities in the theater shall be through the JCS via the theater commander.

c. Theater commanders shall be advised of such covert operations and clandestine intelligence activities as are based in their respective areas but with objectives that transcend or do not directly affect the responsibilities of the respective theater commanders.

d. The DCI shall coordinate with the Secretary of State in order to insure that plans and activities are consistent with the political strategy and political operations and objectives of the United States.

e. In areas other than theaters of military operations, the senior representative of the DCI shall keep the respective senior political rep-

---

[5] Secret.

resentatives, in the countries concerned, generally advised of covert operations and clandestine intelligence activities affecting the area of their responsibility or based thereon, and shall obtain political guidance from such representatives with respect thereto.

f. For reasons of security and adequate liaison, the DCI shall maintain independent communications with his representatives overseas, including lateral communications between theaters. Arrangements for such communications shall be coordinated with those of the military.

g. The Departments of State and Defense and the JCS shall provide continuous guidance and support of the DCI in planning covert operations and clandestine intelligence activities and insure that such operations and activities receive the necessary and appropriate support.

4. As used herein clandestine intelligence includes espionage and counterespionage; covert operations include guerrilla warfare (as defined in NSC_____), sabotage, covert demolitions, covert countersabotage, covert removal of personnel including escape and evasion evacuation and exfiltration, covert propaganda, covert political warfare and covert economic warfare. Such operations do not include armed conflict by organized military forces or cover and deception for military purposes.

5. The foregoing rescinds paragraph 4 of NSC 10/2 and all other provisions of NSC 10/2 and NSCID–5[6] which may be inconsistent with the provisions of this directive.

---

[6] For text of NSCID No. 5, December 12, 1947, see *Foreign Relations*, 1945–1950, Emergence of the Intelligence Establishment, Document 423.

---

39.   Memorandum From the Secretary of State's Deputy Special Assistant for Intelligence and Research (Howe) to the Special Assistant for Intelligence and Research (Armstrong)

Washington, January 9, 1951.

[Source: National Archives, RG 59, Central Files, 103.11/1–951. Secret; R Distribution Only. 1 page not declassified.]

40.   Report by the Chairman of the Armed Forces Security Agency Council (Stone) to the Joint Chiefs of Staff[1]

J.C.S. 2010/25   Washington, January 11, 1951.

SUCCESSION OF DIRECTORS, ARMED FORCES SECURITY AGENCY
Reference: J.C.S. 2010

The Problem

1. In light of the directive in the Appendix to J.C.S. 2010,[2] to recommend a procedure by which the successors to the office of Director, Armed Forces Security Agency (AFSA), will be appointed.

Facts Bearing on the Problem and Discussion

2. Paragraph 2b of the Appendix to J.C.S. 2010 provides that a Flag or General Officer of the Army, Navy, or Air Force be appointed by the Joint Chiefs of Staff as Director, Armed Forces Security Agency, subject to the approval of the Secretary of Defense. It further provides that the Director's normal tour of duty shall be two years, and that the directorship be rotated among the Services. No procedure has yet been established whereby successors to the Director, AFSA, will be appointed.

3. The first Director, AFSA, was nominated to the Joint Chiefs of Staff by an ad hoc committee (appointed by the Joint Chiefs of Staff) composed of two members from each of the three Services; his appointment was made by the Joint Chiefs of Staff, with the approval of the Secretary of Defense.

4. The first Director (Rear Admiral Earl E. Stone, U.S. Navy) took office on 15 July 1949; his tour of duty will be completed on 15 July 1951.

5. A proposed procedure to determine the succession of Directors, Armed Forces Security Agency, has been concurred in by the Armed Forces Security Agency Council (Enclosure).

---

[1] Source: National Archives, RG 218, CCS 334 NSA (7–24–48) Sec. 4 (formerly 334 AFSA). Top Secret; Limited Distribution. A covering note from W.G. Lalor and L.K. Ladue of the Joint Secretariat indicates that on January 19 the Joint Chiefs of Staff approved the recommendations and the conclusion in JCS 2010/25 and issued the directive in the enclosure.

[2] Not found.

Conclusion

6. It is concluded that a requirement exists for a definite procedure to be established whereby the succession of Directors, Armed Forces Security Agency, will be determined.

Recommedations

7. It is recommended that the Joint Chiefs of Staff:

a. Approve the above conclusion.
b. Issue the directive in the Enclosure to the Chairman, Armed Forces Security Agency Council.

Enclosure[3]

DIRECTIVE FOR THE CHAIRMAN, ARMED FORCES SECURITY AGENCY COUNCIL

SUBJECT

Procedures for Nominating and Appointing the Director, Armed Forces Security Agency

1. An ad hoc committee of the Armed Forces Security Agency Council (AFSAC), composed of two Flag or General Officer members of each Service, shall convene on or about 1 February 1951 for the purpose of nominating the second Director, Armed Forces Security Agency (AFSA). The Army and the Air Force will indicate not later than 1 February their General Officer candidate or candidates for the Office of Director, who are considered to be suitably qualified, and available if appointed. (The first and present Director is a Navy Flag Officer.)

2. This committee shall nominate one officer from among those indicated as candidates by the Army and Air Force, and will report this nomination to AFSAC for forwarding to the Joint Chiefs of Staff for appropriate action, not later than 1 March 1951.

3. The Joint Chiefs of Staff, upon approving the nomination, and subject to the approval of the Secretary of Defense, will appoint that General Officer to assume the duties of Director, AFSA, on or about 15 July 1951, for two years.

4. The third Director, AFSA, shall be a General Officer of the Service not previously represented in this position.

5. Biennially thereafter, the succeeding Director of AFSA will be from the appropriate Service, as determined by the rotation thus established.

---

[3] Top Secret.

41.   Airgram From the Department of State to Certain Diplomatic Missions and Consulates[1]

Washington, January 15, 1951, 2:15 p.m.

NATIONAL INTELLIGENCE SURVEYS (NIS)

Reference is made to the Department's unnumbered circular instruction dated November 5, 1948 entitled "National Intelligence Studies".[2] In the above instruction the general outline of the program for production of NIS was announced, and a brief description given, both of the purpose of NIS, and the responsibilities of the Department in its production. Since the issuance of this instruction, a number of chapters and sections of NIS relating to various countries have been completed. Copies of these portions have regularly been forwarded to the principal post in the area concerned under cover of Form DS–4.

The present international situation has emphasized and greatly increased our requirements of both current and basic intelligence. The present greater emphasis on current information is obviously in order, but it must not obscure and completely supplant the collection and reporting of needed basic information. Planning and the establishment of policy relative to national security require basic intelligence, too. Therefore, where at all possible, increased attention should be devoted to providing the basic information needed for the preparation of the NIS and to filling in and bringing up-to-date chapters and sections which have already been completed.

In preparing portions of NIS, every effort is made by the producing agency to utilize all pertinent information available in Washington. It has been and will continue to be necessary, however, to request additional data and information from Foreign Service posts. In some cases it will be expedient to forward to the post concerned preliminary drafts of sections for revision or correction and return to the Department.

It is, of course, very important that portions of NIS which have been produced be revised and kept up-to-date. In the preparation of occasional and voluntary reports, Foreign Service personnel are urged to consult available NIS material, and wherever possible, endeavor to

---

[1] Source: National Archives, RG 59, Central Files 1950–54, 103.11/1–1551. Secret; R Distribution Only. Drafted on January 5 by OLI/IAD: Theodore M. Nordbeck. Cleared by R/NIS: John B. Appleton, EUR: John L. Barnard, FE: Cyrus Peake, NEA: Edwin M. Wright, ARA: Hobart A. Spalding, GER: John R. Kennedy. The airgram was sent to 66 Embassies and Legations and 10 Consulates.

[2] Not printed. (Ibid., 101.61/11–548)

augment the information contained therein. Each NIS section and sub-section concludes with a paragraph entitled "Comments on Principal Sources", which contains a brief survey of the information gaps and weaknesses in the preceding section. These comments are a valuable guide to the basic information which is currently not available in Washington and which should, if possible, be acquired and reported.

The Department, and the other agencies cooperating in the NIS program, welcome and request comments and suggestions from the field concerning NIS. It is requested that completed sections and subsections forwarded to posts be brought to the attention of all appropriate personnel at the post.

Acheson

---

42.   **Note From the Executive Secretary of the National Security Council (Lay) to the National Security Council**[1]

NSC 10/4   Washington, January 16, 1951.

RESPONSIBILITIES OF CIA (OPC) WITH RESPECT TO
GUERRILLA WARFARE

References: NSC 10/2 and NSC 10/3[2]

Upon the recommendation of the Acting Director of Central Intelligence, his enclosed memorandum and its attached draft Directive on the subject are circulated herewith for consideration by the National Security Council.

As recommended in paragraph 3 of the enclosed memorandum, the Departments of State and Defense and the Joint Chiefs of Staff are being requested to transmit to this office their respective comments for Council consideration in connection with the enclosed draft Directive.

---

[1] Source: Truman Library, Papers of Harry S. Truman, President's Secretary's Files, Subject File. Top Secret.

[2] For text of NSC 10/2, see *Foreign Relations*, 1945–1950, Emergence of the Intelligence Establishment, Document 292. DCI Smith's interpretation of NSC 10/2 as conveyed by Wisner to the Departments of State and Defense and JCS is printed in *The CIA Under Harry Truman*, p. 347. A draft of NSC 10/3 is in *Foreign Relations*, 1945–1950, Emergence of the Intelligence Establishment, Document 419. Other versions are attachments to Documents 38 and 43.

It is requested that special security precautions be taken in the handling of this matter.

James S. Lay, Jr.[3]

Enclosure

Memorandum From Acting Director of Central Intelligence Jackson to the Executive Secretary of the National Security Council (Lay)[4]

Washington, January 15, 1951.

SUBJECT

> Draft of NSC Directive on Responsibilities of CIA (OPC) with Respect to Guerrilla Warfare

1. Under date of January 8, 1951, the Director of Central Intelligence transmitted to the Executive Secretary, National Security Council, a draft NSC directive on covert operations and clandestine activities.[5] In paragraph 4 of the memorandum of transmittal, which accompanied this draft, he stated that a paper dealing with a related subject requiring NSC clarification would shortly be submitted to the NSC.

2. Submitted herewith is the draft of a directive for issuance by the NSC which defines and delimits the responsibilities of CIA (OPC) with respect to guerrilla warfare. This draft was prepared in collaboration with representatives of the Office of the Secretary of Defense and of the Joint Chiefs of Staff.

3. It is recommended that this draft be sent by the NSC to the Departments of State and Defense and to the Joint Chiefs of Staff for consideration and comment.

William H. Jackson[6]

---

[3] Printed from a copy that bears this typed signature.
[4] Top Secret.
[5] Document 38.
[6] Printed from a copy that indicates Jackson signed the original.

Enclosure[7]

Washington, January 11, 1951.

DRAFT NATIONAL SECURITY COUNCIL DIRECTIVE
on
RESPONSIBILITIES OF CIA (OPC) WITH RESPECT TO
GUERRILLA WARFARE

The Problem

1. To determine the appropriate responsibilities of CIA (OPC) in the field of guerrilla warfare.

Definitions

2. For the purpose of this study the several types of military or paramilitary forces which may be involved in armed conflict are defined as follows:

a. *National Military Forces.* Organized and uniformed military elements which are organically components of a national military establishment.

b. *Guerrilla Forces.* Organized bodies of politically motivated and predominantly indigenous irregulars, in or out of uniform, not organically a part of national military forces, trained and equipped for armed conflict of specialized character and for limited objectives.

c. *Underground Resistance Forces.* Politically motivated and predominantly indigenous individuals and groups organized and trained clandestinely for covert subversive operations against the state and, when opportunity offers, for semi-covert physical operations, including armed conflict. In the latter stages, underground resistance movements tend to become identical with guerrilla organizations.

Discussion

3. This study deals with the respective roles of the U.S. Military Forces and CIA (OPC) in the exploitation of friendly guerrilla forces in order to determine the responsibilities of CIA (OPC) in this field.

General Responsibilities of CIA (OPC) in Guerrilla Warfare

a. This organization is the national agency responsible under specified conditions for the "planning, preparation and execution" of the various types of covert operations enumerated in NSC 10/2. Some of these operations do not involve armed conflict and will not be discussed in this study. Some of the physical types of covert operations might indirectly involve armed conflict but it is primarily in the field

---

[7] Top Secret.

of guerrilla warfare that responsibilities of CIA (OPC) and the national military forces overlap.

b. The responsibility of CIA (OPC) with respect to guerrilla operations differs in peace and war. In peacetime, OPC formulates doctrine and technique for utilization and employment of guerrilla warfare, plans guerrilla warfare operations to be implemented in case of war in response to and consistent with the requirements of the military authorities, and within the limits of feasibility, makes the physical preparations necessary for such implementation. It foments, supports and conducts only such peacetime guerrilla operations as may be authorized by the State Department with the approval of the Department of Defense. In wartime, OPC implements plans previously prepared, and continues the planning and execution of guerrilla warfare operations within the framework of organization and command specified in NSC_____.[8]

Characteristics and Capabilities of CIA (OPC) in Support of Guerrilla Warfare

4. a. The covert operations of CIA (OPC) "do not include armed conflict by organized military forces." Therefore CIA (OPC) has no responsibility for the organization, training or operations of such units as "Commandos," "Rangers," etc., which are in all respects organic components of national military forces. This does not, however, prevent mutual arrangements between the national military forces and CIA (OPC) for employing the same facilities, when appropriate, for the training of individuals or groups in subjects of common interest.

b. A distinguishing characteristic of guerrilla operations by CIA (OPC) is the employment of relatively limited numbers of American CIA (OPC) personnel. This consists of individual operatives and leaders rather than large bodies of men. Such personnel, however, must have specialized qualifications, including linguistic and political background, imagination, resourcefulness and initiative. They must have access to clandestine intelligence sources. They will be concerned with such intricate matters as establishing initial contacts with appropriate leaders of underground or guerrilla forces in enemy territory, gaining their confidence and developing their capabilities by furnishing communications, weapons, equipment and training, and by exercising such controls over their organization and operations as will insure that their activities support U.S. political and military objectives.

c. These operations will generally be strategic rather than tactical in nature. Initially and usually they will be deep in enemy territory and will require special intelligence, communications and covert trans-

---

[8] NSC 10/3, as approved. [Footnote in the original.]

portation facilities. In the initial phases, the fomentation, development and exploitation of indigenous underground and guerrilla forces should be exclusively a responsibility of CIA (OPC). Without wasteful duplication, the national military forces could not be expected to have the assembled talent and flexibility of organization for such operations.

d. Most resistance activities and movements in their earlier stages are covert in character, and have their origins in the successful establishment and operation of underground organizations. As they begin to develop strength, these movements have a tendency to come out into the open and under proper circumstances, including support by the local population, favorable terrain, and assistance from the outside, develop into organized resistance movements on a major scale. Assuming the successful development of large-scale and relatively well organized resistance movements behind enemy lines resulting from successful covert operations or originating spontaneously, the control and exploitation as well as the support and provisioning of such resistance movements should become the responsibility of the theater commanders whose interests are most directly affected or benefited.

e. However, such guerrilla movements never entirely lose their covert characteristics in that they maintain contacts with underground operatives located in cities and in or near centers of enemy control; and moreover, in that they depend for their survival upon extreme mobility and secrecy as to their location and movements as of any given time. Finally, they remain highly political in their nature and inspiration, and for this as well as other reasons already mentioned, cannot be used against all types of objectives and targets. It follows that even though control and direction of large organized resistance movements should pass to the senior military commanders, there remains the necessity for close cooperation by and assistance from those experienced in covert operations.

Responsibility of the National Military Forces in Unconventional Combat Methods

5. a. As previously stated, guerrilla forces are not to be confused with organizations such as "Commandos" and "Rangers". These latter are organized by and are organically a part of the national military forces. The combat operations of these types of units will often require methods similar to those employed by guerrillas. The training of such organizations will, in some respects, be analogous to that of guerrillas. Their operations can best be described as employment of "unconventional combat methods" by orthodox forces—unconventional only in the sense that they have been little exploited in the American Military Forces and are more flexible and adaptable to circumstances than those of conventional combat units.

b. Independent Commando-type units can accomplish close-in or distant raids for a variety of purposes. They may include airborne or landing operations. Ranger-type units, organic to the division, consist of specially equipped personnel trained in hand-to-hand combat, furtive movement and individual resourcefulness in all situations. They are adept at infiltration and disruptive tactics behind enemy lines. The activity of these units is limited to the zone of combat of the parent division and is employed to assist the division in carrying out its specific missions. These units may at times employ local indigenous inhabitants. While they employ tactics similar to guerrillas, neither Commando nor Ranger operations are deemed to be guerrilla operations, and CIA (OPC) has no responsibility respecting them.

Responsibility of the National Military Forces in Guerrilla Warfare

6. a. The national military forces rarely, if ever, will be in position to assume responsibility for the covert techniques required in fomenting guerrilla movements, establishing initial contacts with existing ones, and in the early development of the movements into appreciable military assets. This is the mission of CIA (OPC) and that agency should be afforded all feasible logistical support by the military forces.

b. In wartime, a guerrilla movement having successfully been built up to a certain magnitude, may require military direction and logistical support from an appropriate military commander similar to that furnished regularly constituted forces under his command. Such direction and support will exceed the resources of CIA (OPC). At this time, control, exploitation and supply of the movement should be assumed by or assigned to the appropriate military commander. Nevertheless, for reasons stated in paragraph 4–e, CIA (OPC) personnel should either serve as, or continue to be a part of, the operating link between that commander and the guerrilla forces.

In some cases a decision by the theater commander becomes necessary as to whether or not command of the guerrillas should pass. In a few cases, attended by profound political implications, consultation in the matter of command will be advisable between the theater commander and higher authority.

Conclusions

7. a. Guerrilla warfare is defined as the operations of organized bodies of politically motivated and predominantly indigenous irregulars, in or out of uniform, not organically a part of national military forces, trained and equipped for armed conflict of specialized character and for limited objectives.

b. CIA (OPC) is the agency of this Government which in peacetime has the sole responsibility under specified conditions for the planning, preparation and conduct of guerrilla operations. In wartime CIA (OPC) is responsible for continued planning and conduct of guerrilla warfare, subject to the provisions of NSC_____,[9] and in collaboration with the national military forces as follows:

CIA (OPC) is responsible for the development of existing guerrilla movements and the fomentation of new ones; and for the control and support of guerrilla operations until their magnitude requires that such control and support be passed to an appropriate military commander. Such elements of CIA (OPC) as may be required should either serve as, or continue to be a part of, the operating link between that commander and the guerrilla forces.

Recommendations

8. That the National Security Council accept the Discussion as guiding principles and approve the Conclusions.

---

[9] NSC 10/4, as approved. [Footnote in the original. NSC 10/4 was withdrawn at the request of the Deputy Director of Central Intelligence following approval of NSC 10/5 on October 23 (see Document 90).]

---

43.   Memorandum From Robert P. Joyce of the Policy Planning Staff to the Ambassador at Large (Jessup)[1]

Washington, January 16, 1951.

SUBJECT

NSC 10/3

I think you will find the attached file[2] to be self-explanatory and I believe that you will desire to review it before the Under Secretary considers signing the attached draft memorandum addressed to Mr. James S. Lay, Jr. The following considerations with respect to NSC 10/3 have been suggested to me within the Department:

1. The document as presently worded does not sufficiently assert Department of State responsibility, authority and control over the activities set forth in 10/3. Specifically paragraph 3a would seem to

---

[1] Source: Department of State, INR Historical Files: NSC 10 Series, 1951. Top Secret.

[2] Joyce apparently clipped this memorandum to a file folder holding several documents on this topic. The folder has not been found.

place complete control of covert operations and clandestine intelligence activities within the JCS. Similarly the last sentence in paragraph 3b reenforces JCS control. (In active military theatres)[3]

2. Paragraph 3d then produces [*reduces*?] the "coordinating" role of the Secretary of State vis-à-vis the Director of Central Intelligence in Washington. It has been suggested that this coordinating role is insufficiently explicit and does not extend down to the theatre commanders through the JCS.

It has been suggested to me that the Department should ask for a great deal more in that the roles between the Department and the Military Establishment have now reached a point where the Department of State is in a position to obtain a great deal more than this document provides for. It was therefore suggested that the two alterations marked on page 2 and page 3 of the draft 10/3 might now be included in the Department's comment requested by Mr. Lay.

I have the following comments to make:

1. General Smith and Allen W. Dulles feel that it is necessary at this time to obtain for CIA what is set forth in 10/3. They both feel that they have gone as far as possible in asserting CIA's role vis-à-vis the JCS in Washington and as related to theatre commanders. As long as the present JCS position remains in its present state, nothing further can be accomplished in increasing the responsibility and authority of the CIA particularly in military theatres. As you know, General Smith and Allen Dulles are presently in Tokyo in an endeavor to accomplish something with General MacArthur and General Willoughby which will make it possible for CIA to play some role in the intelligence field in General MacArthur's theatre. (Has his theatre ever been defined geographically?)

2. The Director of Central Intelligence feels that if he tries to get more than 10/3 calls for, he might end up by getting much less. In other words, General Smith is prepared to settle for 10/3 as presently drafted on the theory that this gives him enough to work out CIA's problems in the command structure given present thinking within the JCS and the personalities of theatre commanders in time of war. General Smith does not feel that it would be wise at this time, in his endeavor to obtain the necessary degree of authority and control over secret operations and clandestine activities, to engage in a jurisdictional battle with the JCS which would raise basic issues, generate heat and

---

[3] The parenthetical phrase was added by hand. References to paragraphs 3a and 3d under points 1 and 2 of this memorandum apparently refer to the earlier draft attached to Document 38.

conflict and probably result in jeopardizing what CIA now has and can get in the present circumstances.

3. My own feeling is that the Department of State can probably not go beyond the present language of draft NSC 10/3 in asserting civilian responsibility and authority. General Magruder and Admiral Stevens agree that this is a fact. General Magruder is an outstanding exponent of the theory that war is too serious a business for the generals, is an extension of politics, etc., etc. He advises against the Department's trying to assert itself further than is now outlined in the present draft and believes that if it did so the JCS would react violently, and immediate conflict would develop and there would be little or no hope of getting even what is set forth in the present language of 10/3.

I think it will be most useful if Messrs. Matthews and Webb could have your comments on the foregoing.[4]

Robert P. Joyce

Attachment[5]

DRAFT NATIONAL SECURITY COUNCIL DIRECTIVE

on

COVERT OPERATIONS AND CLANDESTINE INTELLIGENCE ACTIVITIES

1. Under the authority of Section 102(d)(5) of the National Security Act of 1947, the National Security Council hereby directs that:

2. The Director of Central Intelligence shall be responsible for the planning, preparation and execution of covert operations and clandestine intelligence activities in peace or in war and for insuring that such operations are planned and conducted in a manner consistent with and in support of U.S. foreign and military policies and with overt activities.

3. The DCI shall coordinate with the Secretary of State in order to insure that plans and activities are consistent with the political strategy and political operations and objectives of the United States.

4. In areas other than theaters of military operations, the senior representative of the DCI shall keep the respective senior political representatives, in the countries concerned, generally advised of covert

---

[4] A handwritten postscript by Joyce reads, "... Another consideration: If this Dept. causes difficulties with the JCS which hold up indefinitely W.B. Smith's new charter, he and C.I.A., I think, will not appreciate this Dept's role therein. RPJ." Ellipsis in the original.

[5] Top Secret.

operations and clandestine intelligence activities affecting the area of their responsibility or based thereon, and shall obtain political guidance from such representatives with respect thereto.

5. The following relationships shall prevail in wartime or in peacetime in areas where U.S. military forces are engaged in combat:

a. The DCI shall coordinate covert operations and clandestine intelligence activities with the Secretary of Defense and the Joint Chiefs of Staff and the appropriate non-military U.S. Government departments and agencies, and insure that plans for such activities are accepted by JCS as being consistent with and complementary to approved plans for wartime or emergency military operations.

b. Covert operations and clandestine intelligence activities in a theater of military command shall come within the responsibility of the theater commander and the DCI shall designate a senior representative to be on the General Staff of each theater commander concerned with such operations and activities, responsible to the theater commander through the Chief of Staff, to assist in the planning, direction and command of such operations and activities. Policy direction and control of the execution of such operations and activities in the theater shall be through the JCS via the theater commander.

c. Theater commanders shall be advised of such covert operations and clandestine intelligence activities as are based in their respective areas but with objectives that transcend or do not directly affect the responsibilities of the respective theater commanders.

d. For reasons of security and adequate liaison, the DCI shall maintain independent communications with his representatives overseas, including lateral communications between theaters. Arrangements for such communications shall be coordinated with those of the military.

6. The Secretaries of State and Defense, the Chairman of the National Security Resources Board, and the Joint Chiefs of Staff shall provide continuous guidance and support of the DCI in planning covert operations and clandestine intelligence activities and insure that such operations and activities receive the necessary and appropriate support.

7. As used herein clandestine intelligence includes espionage and counterespionage; covert operations include guerilla warfare (as defined in NSC_____), sabotage, covert demolitions, covert countersabotage, covert removal of personnel including escape and evasion evacuation and exfiltration, covert propaganda, covert political warfare and covert economic warfare. Such operations do not include armed conflict by organized military forces or cover and deception for military purposes.

8. The foregoing rescinds paragraph 4 of NSC 10/2 and all other provisions of NSC 10/2 and NSCID No. 5 which may be inconsistent with the provisions of this directive.

44.   Memorandum From Acting Director of Central Intelligence Jackson to the Executive Secretary of the National Security Council (Lay)[1]

NSC 66/1   Washington, January 18, 1951.

SUBJECT
>   Intelligence Support for the Voice of America with regard to Soviet Jamming

1. Reference is made to my memorandum of 7 September 1950 on the above subject,[2] forwarding the Report of the Ad Hoc Committee on Voice of America Jamming, and noting that Recommendation 3 of the Report regarding establishment of an additional monitoring facility would be referred to the United States Communications Intelligence Board.

2. The Chairman of USCIB has now forwarded to me the attached report[3] which recommends, in brief, that an additional monitoring facility be established under the operational direction of AFSA and delineates the requirements in terms of facilities, personnel and equipment for the establishment of such a facility. This USCIB report and its recommendations have the unanimous approval of the IAC.

3. In the light of the USCIB report and further consideration of the problem, the IAC now submits, for the consideration of the Council in connection with NSC 66, the following final recommendations which incorporate the recommendations of the USCIB report and the recommendations of the earlier IAC report, appropriately revised:

a. That a readjustment of priorities among existing intelligence tasks or a reallocation of the use of existing intelligence facilities should not be undertaken.

b. That there should be established an additional monitoring activity to obtain and provide information on current Soviet jamming activities which will assist the VOA in its program and assist other U. S. Government communications services in combatting present and future Soviet radio interference, and that this additional monitoring activity be established, coordinated and operated as follows:

---

[1] Source: National Archives, RG 59, S/P–NSC Files: Lot 62 D 21, 1935–62, no label, Box 115. Secret.

[2] Memo for NSC from Executive Secretary subject: "Support for the Voice of America in the Fields of Intelligence and of Research and Development," dated September 11, 1950. [Footnote in the original. This memorandum has not been found.]

[3] Not found.

(1) The initial program for this activity should be undertaken along the lines suggested in Enclosure 2 of the USCIB Report of 28 November 1950.[4]

(2) This activity should monitor and locate Russian jamming signals and other interfering transmitters and should convey promptly and continuously to the VOA and other interested U. S. communications services such resulting information as will assist them to improve their reception.

(3) This activity should not interfere with existing monitoring programs, particularly from the standpoint of equipment and personnel.

(4) This activity will be coordinated by CIA with existing non-AFSA monitoring activities.

(5) In view of the COMINT aspects of this program, USCIB should be assigned the function of general coordination of this activity. In the performance of this function USCIB should be governed by the provisions of NSCID No. 9.[5]

(6) This activity should be placed under the operational direction of AFSA, and appropriate provision should be made for Service procurement of the necessary equipment and personnel.

c. That the CIA assume over-all responsibility to:

(1) Coordinate the collection of information concerning Russian jamming from all sources.

(2) Serve as the collection point for this information and assure that such of this information as will assist the VOA and other government communications services to improve their reception on a daily basis is passed promptly and continuously to these services. The CIA, with the assistance of the Special Assistant, Intelligence, Department of State, should determine and establish such security arrangements and channels of dissemination as may be required to pass this information to the VOA; these arrangements and channels to be determined in the light of materials made available.

(3) Undertake, in conjunction with the other intelligence agencies, a coordinated program for the collation, evaluation and dissemination of such information as will be useful in the long-range analysis of Russian radio interference and in the development of counter-measures.[6]

W. H. Jackson[7]

---

[4] Attached hereto. [Footnote in the original. Enclosure 2, IAC–D–11, is not attached.]

[5] For text of NSCID No. 9, March 10, 1950, see Foreign Relations, 1945–1950, Emergence of the Intelligence Establishment, Document 435.

[6] The President approved the recommendations on February 28. (Memorandum from Lay to the National Security Council, February 28; National Archives, RG 59, S/P–NSC Files: Lot 62 D 21, 1935–62, no label, Box 115)

[7] Printed from a copy that indicates Jackson signed the original.

45.   **Memorandum From the Executive Secretary of the Department of State (McWilliams) to the Deputy Under Secretary of State for Administration (Humelsine)[1]**

Washington, January 19, 1951.

I am attaching herewith a copy of a draft directive on the national psychological effort which was left with Mr. Webb by Mr. Souers today.

Mr. Webb informs me that Mr. Souers made a very strong plea that we accept this arrangement, and it had been Souers' desire to go direct to the Secretary with this proposal.

Mr. Webb has asked me to put the paper into the proper hands for staff study and presentation of recommendations to the Secretary. He considers this a matter of urgency since Souers intends to go to the President about this in a short time.

Mr. Webb specifically asked that you and Mr. Barrett collaborate on the staff paper for the Secretary. I am forwarding this to you for action with the request that you prepare a paper in coordination with Mr. Barrett and such other offices as you might think necessary.

W.J. McWilliams[2]

Attachment[3]

Washington, January 18, 1951.

DRAFT DIRECTIVE ON THE NATIONAL
PSYCHOLOGICAL EFFORT

There is hereby established under the National Security Council a Psychological Strategy Board responsible at the national level for psychological policy formulation within the framework of approved national policies, and for coordination and evaluation of the national psychological effort, including authority to issue policy guidance to all departments and agencies of the Government executing major portions of the psychological effort abroad:

The Board shall be composed of:

a. a full-time chairman, who shall be designated by the President on the recommendation of the National Security Council, and who shall

---

[1] Source: National Archives, RG 59, P Files: Lot 52 D 432. Secret.

[2] Printed from a copy that bears this typed signature.

[3] Secret.

be the head thereof and shall, subject to review by the National Security Council at the request of any Council member, have the power of decision upon matters falling within the jurisdiction of the Board;

b. one representative each of the Secretary of State, the Secretary of Defense, the Joint Chiefs of Staff, and the Director of Central Intelligence;

c. one representative each of the heads of such other departments and agencies of the Government as may from time to time be determined by the Board.

In the event of an objection by any member of the National Security Council to a decision of the Board or its Chairman, an effort shall be made by the Council member and the Board, or its Chairman, to resolve the divergency prior to any consideration by the National Security Council.

The Chairman of the Board, subject to the direction of the National Security Council, shall be authorized to employ such consultants as may be necessary and to organize a staff composed of individuals employed for this purpose and of individuals detailed from the participating departments and agencies.

The Board and its staff shall perform no psychological operations.

---

46.   Letter From the Deputy Director of Central Intelligence (Jackson) to the Secretary of State's Special Assistant for Intelligence and Research (Armstrong)[1]

Washington, February 1, 1951.

Dear Mr. Armstrong:

As you know, General Smith has written to the Secretary of State[2] to indicate in broad terms how he envisions the allocation of certain intelligence responsibilities, in line with National Security Council Directives, as between the Department of State and the Central Intelligence Agency. This letter was based on the principles agreed to in our recent discussions on the responsibilities of the Department and

---

[1] Source: National Archives, RG 59, INR Historical Files: Lot 58 D 776, State–CIA Relationship 1949–56. Confidential.

[2] Dated February 1. (Ibid.)

Central Intelligence Agency with reference to certain functions formerly performed in Central Intelligence Agency by the Office of Reports and Estimates. To assist you in planning to meet the additional burden which will fall on the Department, I am outlining my understanding of the agreements upon which General Smith's letter is based.

The Department has responsibility for intelligence research in the political, cultural and sociological fields. The research work hitherto performed in these fields by our former Office of Reports and Estimates is discontinued and the Department will be responsible for meeting the requests from all departments and agencies previously handled by the Office of Reports and Estimates. This will include initiation of requirements for intelligence collection and evaluation of raw information reports in these fields. The Department will undoubtedly have further demands on its resources arising from its increasing participation in the preparation of National Intelligence Estimates.

As a guide towards estimating the increased burden on the Department, I might point out that Central Intelligence Agency is discontinuing, among other activities, the following:

1. Political research to meet the requests of the National Security Council, the Joint Chiefs of Staff and other departments and agencies;
2. Intelligence research for psychological warfare;
3. Intelligence research on international organizations, particularly United Nations;
4. Intelligence research on world Communism;
5. Intelligence research in the political, cultural and sociological fields for the internal needs of Central Intelligence Agency.

The Central Intelligence Agency wishes to assist the Department in meeting these new responsibilities, as is indicated in General Smith's letter. To fulfill this obligation, Central Intelligence Agency is prepared to:

1. Provide, for the remainder of fiscal 1951, funds for additional personnel up to the amount of $200,000. We have both estimated that the number of additional personnel which the Department may need is approximately 150.
2. Cooperate in the detail or transfer to the Department of any available personnel formerly engaged in the Office of Research and Estimates. The Department is free to discuss such detail or transfer directly with the personnel involved.[3]

I understand that working negotiations are under way on these points. Copies of this letter have been distributed to the appropriate

---

[3] This assistance was presumably to tide the Department over until the positions were properly authorized and budgeted.

officers in this organization for policy guidance. I hope you and I may meet for further discussions if the need arises in the course of these negotiations.

Sincerely,

William H. Jackson[4]

---

[4] Printed from a copy that bears this typed signature.

---

47. Memorandum From the Under Secretary of State (Webb) to the Executive Secretary of the Department of State (McWilliams)[1]

Washington, February 2, 1951.

Admiral Souers has spoken to the Secretary regarding the discussions Admiral Souers and I have been having about the proposed Cabinet Committee on psychological warfare, to be headed by a full-time chairman and report to the NSC.[2]

Admiral Souers made the point to the Secretary that there were a number of programs going in this field which we were not aware of and which he did not think could be coordinated without some procedure such as he has suggested. He said his main objective was to get all these things out on the table so they could be looked at and put together as a program.

The Secretary desires Mr. Humelsine or Mr. Barrett, or the proper person, to prepare for him a short paper on the programs that are being discussed with Admiral Souers. He wants to know particularly what programs are going which are not subject to our coordination now. What is the subject matter of these programs, both overt and covert?

After the Secretary has studied this matter, he is inclined to agree to a meeting that would include himself, Admiral Souers, Fred Lawton, Bedell Smith and Bob Lovett to thrash the matter out.

JW

---

[1] Source: National Archives, RG 59, P Files: Lot 52 D 432. Top Secret. Copies were sent to Barrett for action and to Humelsine.

[2] See Document 45.

48.   Memorandum of Conversation[1]

Washington, February 5, 1951.

PARTICIPANTS

    CIA—Messrs. Reber, Smith, Webb, [name not declassified]

    State—Messrs. Barnes S/S, Manfull S/S–R, Trueheart R

SUBJECT

    CIA Daily Summary

In opening the meeting, Mr. Reber stated in substance that: 1) After consultations with the President, CIA had decided to continue to publish its Daily Summary but to recast the publication in the form of a true "Intelligence Summary" rather than a mere summary of telegrams; and 2) CIA desired to obtain from the Department an additional copy of all S/S telegrams for a new Office of Current Intelligence, which will be established to publish the new Daily.

Mr. Barnes[2] stated that while the Department had always desired to keep the CIA Director and the analysts in the Office of National Estimates fully informed of current developments of a sensitive nature, we had always had certain reservations regarding the Daily Summary, particularly with respect to its distribution. He pointed out that the CIA Daily Summary had never been an "Intelligence Summary" as such and that we have been concerned at times in the past regarding the use of sensitive and operational S/S telegrams in that publication, particularly after the distribution of the Summary had been extended to include persons not normally receiving S/S–R telegrams.

Mr. Reber expressed the view that the distribution of the Summary was an incidental question; that it was necessary in the first instance to determine the intelligence need to be met by the new Summary; and that it was necessary in any event for the new Office of Current Intelligence to receive all pertinent information, including S/S telegrams, in order to do an adequate job.

At this point there was a long and inconclusive discussion of whether it was necessary for the editors of the new Daily to have access to all sensitive and operational materials in order for them to select intelligently the significant items for reporting and whether it was feasible to publish a true "Intelligence Summary" on a daily basis. In

---

[1] Source: National Archives, RG 59, Central Files 1950–54, 114.3/2–551. Secret. Drafted by Melvin L. Manfull.

[2] Robert G. Barnes, Chief of the Policy Reports Staff, Executive Secretariat.

this connection, there was a divergence of opinion among the CIA people themselves as to whether they could publish on a periodic basis the type of "Intelligence Summary" they apparently had in mind.

Mr. Barnes explained the various channels through which CIA received Department telegrams and expressed doubt that the Office of National Estimates and Office of Current Intelligence in CIA required equal treatment with respect to S/S telegrams. He stressed in this connection overall responsibilities of S/S concerning the distribution of sensitive material to other agencies and the relationship of the CIA Daily Summary to this problem.

It was finally agreed that: 1) CIA would develop and present to the Department more concrete proposals with respect to the type of publication they had in mind, the distribution it should receive, etc, in justification of their request; and 2) in the interim, Mr. Smith was authorized to make available to the editor of the new Summary copies of "information only" S/S telegrams on a trial basis in order for CIA to determine its possible future need for this type of material in connection with the new Summary.

---

49.   Memorandum From the Assistant Secretary of State for Public Affairs (Barrett) to Secretary of State Acheson[1]

Washington, February 13, 1951.

SUBJECT

Meeting with Admiral Souers

Regarding your meeting with Admiral Souers:

When the parties concerned were unable to resolve their differences over who should supervise psychological strategy now and in event of war, the question was referred to the NSC.[2] The President then directed Admiral Souers, with the assistance of the Bureau of the Budget, to study the subject and make recommendations.

The Admiral came up with what he considered a compromise plan. This was a plan for a board as proposed by the Defense Department,

---

[1] Source: National Archives, RG 59, Central Files 1950–54, 511.00/2–1351. Secret. Sent through the Executive Secretariat.

[2] See Documents 45 and 47.

consisting of one representative each from State, Defense, Joint Chiefs and CIA, plus an "independent" chairman. However, the Admiral proposed that the chairman should report to the National Security Council—not to the President as recommended by Defense.

We have objected strenuously to this plan, and accordingly, we understand it hasn't been presented to the President.

Subsequent discussion with Admiral Souers developed the fact that he had in mind a board whose field would be far broader than that discussed in any of the NSC 74 papers.[3] The original papers all specified that the board would give broad direction to overt information and psychological warfare matters and just "coordinate with" covert psychological operations. The Admiral, it developed, was thinking in terms of a board that would plan general strategy for virtually all unconventional warfare measures. These would include overt psychological strategy, covert psychological strategy (whispering campaigns, etc.), covert operations of the old OSS variety, and perhaps certain economic warfare measures (like pre-emptive buying).

Admiral Souers has implied in private conversations that he believes the planning for perfectly overt psychological operations should continue under the coordination of the Secretary of State, as is now the case with our Psychological Strategy Board, which presently operates under the authority given the Secretary in NSC 59[4] and which would be strengthened under State's version of NSC 74. He seems, however, inclined to advocate the creation under NSC of a superboard to coordinate overt psychological planning with planning in all the other unconventional warfare fields mentioned above.

The following is a listing of U.S. foreign propaganda programs in being or planned and the state of coordination with each:

In addition to the Department's USIE program, programs are now being carried on or are planned by CIA, ECA, Army, Air Forces, NATO and SHAPE.

The Department, ECA, Army, NATO and SHAPE are now engaged in overt information activity abroad.

Coordination of overt operations by the Department is undertaken through the National Psychological Strategy Board (members: State, as Chairman, Defense, JCS, CIA, ECA and NSRB) which has been set up under NSC 59, and through direct liaison in the U.S. and abroad between the Department and the agencies concerned. The independent charters held by ECA and the Army occasion a lack of coordination

---

[3] See Document 17.
[4] For the text of NSC 59/1, see Document 2.

and/or duplication in some operations such as the Armed Forces Radio Service and the activity of some ECA country units.

Covert propaganda operations are centered in CIA although the ECA and Army, in some instances, appear to be involved in activity of this nature (to the apparent annoyance of CIA).

CIA covert propaganda operations are coordinated with the Department through an agreement for direct liaison between P and CIA's Office of Policy Coordination (OPC), through the role of Mr. Joyce (S/P) as CIA consultant, and through CIA participation in the National Psychological Strategy Board. I consider that coordination in this field is satisfactory, but do not know and do not need to know the substance of all of CIA's programs. ECA and Army covert or semi-covert operations are not coordinated with State or CIA in all cases. NATO and SHAPE information operations are in the formative stage, and we are working out the problems of coordination. No major problems here have been uncovered so far.

Psychological warfare in areas of military operations is under the control of the theatre commander, as in Korea.

There is a substantial lack of coordination in relation to psychological operations in Korea. This is a problem not only for the Department but for the JCS, the Department of the Army and CIA.

Research in psychological warfare is being undertaken by State, Army, Air Forces, and CIA.

There is a definite lack of coordination in the field of psychological warfare research, particularly within the defense establishment.

---

50.   Memorandum for the Record by the Director of Central Intelligence's Executive Assistant (Kirkpatrick)[1]

Washington, February 14, 1951.

SUBJECT

Meeting on Integration of O/SO and O/PC

---

[1] Source: Central Intelligence Agency, Directorate of Operations, Job 78–05091A, Box 1. Secret.

PRESENT

Mr. Dulles, [*name not declassified*], W.C. Wyman, Mr. Wisner

Col. Johnston, [*name not declassified*], Mr. Angleton, Mr. Helms, and Mr. Kirkpatrick

1. It was proposed by Mr. Dulles that a basic step toward integration might be the adjustment of the geographical divisions in the two offices so that they correspond to each other. Mr. Wisner said that this might prove difficult in certain instances and cited Italy as an example. He said that O/PC in Italy falls naturally into the Western Hemisphere bloc, whereas in O/SO it is in the Mediterranean-Balkan area. It was pointed out that [*less than 1 line not declassified*]. It was concluded that this matter would be studied and that there probably would be adjustments necessary on both sides.

2. There was discussion of making the staffs in both offices correspond to each other. It was pointed out that Mr. O'Gara has plans for the administrative staffs of both offices which will make them identical. It was decided that a committee composed of Col. Johnston, Mr. Helms, and Mr. O'Gara should study this problem and come up with recommendations.

3. There was discussion of the level on which O/SO and O/PC operations should be coordinated. O/PC feels that there should be specialists at a certain level. It was suggested that this level might be the area region which would be the bottom of the merger. It was suggested that each area division be combined with the deputy for each activity. The pattern by area may vary. It was pointed out that the "confidential" activities of O/PC as distinguished from the "secret" operations might be separated. The general operations of the two offices break down into political-economic, paramilitary, and intelligence. It was also suggested that perhaps area divisions might have a deputy for each of these activities rather than a deputy for O/SO and one for O/PC.

4. O/PC raised the question of the responsibility for dealing directly with resistance groups. It was pointed out that it was the O/PC function to run resistance groups although it is recognized that it is the O/SO function to get intelligence from these groups. A task force composed of Mr. Angleton, Mr. [*name not declassified*], and Mr. Rositzke was named to reach an agreement on this subject and to present any points of controversy to the Assistant Directors for referral, if necessary, to the Deputy Director.

5. There was talk of the fact that three offices, OO [Office of Operations],[2] O/SO and O/PC were all in contact with the [*less than 1 line not declassified*]. It was agreed that this was a very sensitive subject and

---

[2] Brackets in the original.

that there should be a unified approach. A task force composed of Mr. Thompson, Mr. Houck, Mr. Hunter, and Mr. Ashcraft was named to determine a policy on dealing with labor.

6. A similar problem of three offices all dealing with the [*less than 1 line not declassified*] was raised. A task force composed of Mr. Horton, Mr. Ashcraft and Mr. Lloyd was named to determine an agency policy for dealing with the [*less than 1 line not declassified*].

7. The question of training was brought up and Mr. Kirkpatrick was asked to prepare for Mr. Dulles a statement on training.

Lyman B. Kirkpatrick[3]

---

[3] Printed from a copy that bears this typed signature.

---

51.   Memorandum of Agreement Between the Central Intelligence Agency and the Department of State[1]

Washington, February 19, 1951.

RE SS CABLES

Because of certain changes in CIA organization the Department of State and CIA have considered it useful to re-examine arrangements whereby the Department has been making available to CIA certain special cables through the Office of the Secretary of State. The following understandings have been reached as a result of the re-examination:

a. The Department of State will make every effort to supply directly to CIA, through direct distribution or through the IAD liaison channel, all intelligence reports of interest to CIA. In addition the Department will continue to supply to the Central Intelligence Agency, through the channel indicated in paragraph f. below, two copies of operational and policy telegrams of interest and concern to CIA which may be considered so sensitive as to not be placed within the normal liaison channel.

b. The external distribution of the Daily Intelligence Bulletin, which will replace the CIA Daily Summary,[2] is:

---

[1] Source: National Archives, RG 59, INR Historical Files: Lot 58 D 776, State–CIA Relationships, 1949–56. Confidential.

[2] See Document 48.

The President
Secretary of State
Secretary of Defense

c. Inclusion of materials from the special State Department distribution in the Daily Intelligence Bulletin will be based on importance in terms of intelligence rather than operations or policy developments. The agencies will rely upon close contact between the Office of Current Intelligence and SS to develop understandings regarding inclusion of sensitive materials.

d. Because of State Department's legitimate concern with regard to the extent of third agency use of State Department sensitive cables, any extension of the proposed distribution (see paragraph b. above) will be done only after consultation with the State Department.

e. The responsibility for receipt and internal CIA distribution of telegrams under consideration shall be the Office of Current Intelligence with the understanding that distribution will be limited to: the Office of the Director, the Office of National Estimates, and to Daily Intelligence Bulletin editors as necessary for their background information.

f. As of the beginning of business Tuesday, February 20th, the Office of Current Intelligence will assume the responsibility for receipt and dissemination, a function discharged at present by the Office of National Estimates. Specifically the officer in charge and his address is:

[3 lines not declassified]

g. In the Department of State this special liaison will be handled by the Policy Reports Staff of the Executive Secretariat.

For the Director of Central Intelligence:
James Q. Reber[3]
Acting Assistant Director,
Intelligence Coordination

---

[3] Printed from a copy that bears this typed signature. Below the signature is typed: "Endorsed: Agreed: Robert G. Barnes, February 19, 1951" with an indication that Barnes signed the original.

52.   Memorandum From the Deputy Assistant Secretary of State for Administration (Scott) to the Under Secretary of State (Webb)[1]

Washington, undated.

SUBJECT

NSC–74 Background

This is in response to your request for a full statement of the inter-departmental arrangements and planning leading up to NSC–74[2] and the assignment of the psychological problem to Admiral Souers.

1. NSC–10/2

NSC–10/2 (attached as Tab A),[3] approved in June 1948 fixed responsibility for covert operations and directed the responsible officer to assure coordination of such activities with U.S. foreign and military policies and overt activities. This decision has remained in effect and has not been at issue in the planning of organization for overt psychological operations until Admiral Souers' assignment.

2. NSC–4 and NSC–43

NSC–4[4] (attached as Tab B), which was approved by the NSC in December, 1947, made provision for the coordination of foreign information measures. NSC–43[5] (attached as Tab C), which was approved by the NSC in March, 1949, made certain provisions on planning for wartime conduct of *overt* psychological warfare. In December, 1949, the provisions of these two papers were consolidated with minor changes and approved as NSC–59.[6]

3. NSC–59

NSC–59 (attached as Tab D), approved in March, 1950, charges the Secretary of State with responsibilities for:

---

[1] Source: National Archives, RG 59, P Files: Lot 55 D 339. Top Secret. Although this memorandum is attached to one from Barrett to Webb, March 14, the content of Scott's memorandum indicates that it was probably drafted about February 20.

[2] See Document 17.

[3] An attached list of Tabs A–M is not printed. None of the tabs are attached to the memorandum. For NSC 10/2, see *Foreign Relations,* 1945–1950, Emergence of the Intelligence Establishment, Document 292.

[4] Ibid., Document 252.

[5] See ibid., Documents 392 and 401.

[6] See Document 2.

(1) Formulation of policies and plans for peacetime information program, including all foreign information activity conducted by departments and agencies of the U.S. Government.

(2) Formulation of National Psychological Warfare policy in time of national emergency and the initial stages of war.

(3) Coordination of policies and plans for the information program and for overt psychological warfare with the Department of Defense, with other appropriate departments and with related planning under the NSC–10 series.

There was directed to be established within the Department of State an organization to consist of: "(a) A Director appointed by Secretary of State after consultation with other departments and agencies represented on the National Security Council. (b) Policy consultants representing the Secretary of the State, the Secretary of Defense, and the Chairman of the National Security Resources Board. (c) A consultant representing the Director of Central Intelligence for matters relating to coordination with planning under the NSC–10 series. (d) A consultant representing the Joint Chiefs of Staff on NSC–59 and NSC–10/2 matters. (e) A staff composed of full-time personnel representing the Department of State, the Department of Defense, and the Central Intelligence Agency. (f) A liaison representative to the staff from the National Security Resources Board and such liaison representation or staff membership from other departments and agencies of the government as may be determined by the Director after consultation with the consultants."

This organization was directed to:

"(a) Initiate and develop interdepartmental plans, make recommendations, and otherwise advise and assist the Secretary of State in discharging his responsibilities for the national foreign information program in time of peace.

(b) Make plans for overt psychological warfare, including recommendations for the preparations for national emergency and the initial stages of war. Such plans shall be continuously coordinated with joint war plans through the planning agencies of the Department of Defense and where such plans have a direct impact on war plans they shall be subject to the concurrence of the Joint Chiefs of Staff."

4. Psychological Strategy Board

On August 17, 1950, the Department of State issued a press release (attached as Tab E) announcing the establishment of a national psychological strategy board under the Secretary of State.[7] This Strategy Board was in fact nothing more than the "Director" and the "Consultants" under NSC–59, including the JCS representative. This step was

---

[7] Printed in Department of State *Bulletin*, August 28, 1950, p. 335.

taken in recognition of the necessity for conducting psychological measures in connection with the hostilities in Korea and the increasingly critical world-wide situation. The activities of the "organization" were in fact intensified, as the Board has met more frequently since the announcement and has dealt with more problems of a psychological character requiring joint political and military action.

5. NSC–74

In July, 1950 the Under Secretary of State transmitted to the NSC a report prepared by the Organization established pursuant to NSC–59. This report was issued for clearance as NSC–74 (attached as Tab F).

This paper has been prepared principally during the period prior to Korea and was based on the tacit assumption that any war would be general and would break out without warning. It provided an "initial stage" of psychological warfare organization to be invoked on D–day, or earlier at the discretion of the President, and a plan for the "subsequent stages" to be established as rapidly thereafter as possible.

The plan for the initial stages of war recognized the responsibility of the Secretary of State to "formulate national psychological warfare policy and issue psychological warfare policy directives to appropriate departments and agencies of the U.S. Government" and to "coordinate policies and plans for overt psychological warfare with the Department of Defense" and other agencies. The plan also directed the Secretary of State to make "detailed plans and preparations to employ psychological warfare to the maximum in consonance with this plan." It was recognized that overt psychological warfare would be executed in theaters of military operations by theater commanders and in other areas by the Department of State.

For the "initial stages" the Interdepartmental Foreign Information Organization was to be "augmented" and established as an Interim Psychological Warfare Board to act as the "Executive Agent" of the Secretary of State in the execution of his planning and coordinating responsibility for psychological warfare. The Board was to be composed of a Chairman representing the Secretary of State, a Vice-Chairman representing the Joint Chiefs of Staff, and one representative each from State, Defense, and ECA.

The plan for the "subsequent stages" provided a National Psychological Warfare Board "composed of a Chairman, appointed by the President and directly responsible to him; a member designated by and representing the Department of State; a member chosen from the Joint Chiefs of Staff organization, designated by and representing the Department of Defense; and a member designated by and representing the Central Intelligence Agency."

On September 13, 1950, Secretary Johnson submitted to the Executive Secretary of NSC his comments on NSC–74[8] (attached as Tab G). He proposed the immediate implementation of the plan for the "initial stages", but he considered it inadequate even for the situation at that time and thought that "we should move to create immediately an independent psychological planning board in the Executive Office of the President." The chairman would have been directly responsible to the President and the board members would have been full-time appointees not representing the Departments.

Also on September 14, the Under Secretary of State advised the NSC that the Department of State approved NSC–74 except for the subsequent stages plan, which he believed required further study.[9] (See Tab H.) He also stated that he had "taken steps to strengthen the Inter-departmental Foreign Information Organization established under NSC–59/1, so that it may meet the requirements of situations where joint military and political action is necessary in the field of psychological warfare", referring to the establishment of the psychological strategy board.

After further study within the Department, a draft NSC–74/1 (attached as Tab I) was developed.[10] In an effort to meet the requirements of the present situation, this paper provided for the establishment of a National Psychological Strategy Board (or National Psychological Warfare Board in time of war) "as the coordinating agent for the Secretary of State" with respect to his responsibility to "recommend broad policies and plans for the national psychological effort designed to achieve a maximum support of U.S. national objectives" and to "review the plans and programs of agencies executing psychological measures for conformity with national policy." The chairman was to be designated by the Secretary of State, the vice-chairman by JCS and additional members by State, Defense, and CIA. This paper spoke of the "National Psychological Effort" in order to avoid the controversy about whether "psychological warfare" is conducted in time of peace, and to make adequate provision for the present situation. It was the position of the Department of State that organization in time of war should be subjected to further study.

Following discussion of the new State Department draft by the NSC senior staff, it was determined that agreement between the Departments could not be secured. A memorandum of disagreement was prepared

---

[8] Not found.
[9] Not found.
[10] Not found.

(attached as Tab J) and submitted for NSC consideration, together with an additional memorandum from the JCS[11] (attached as Tab K). The senior staff memorandum stated the essential issue as follows:

"Should responsibility at the national level for psychological policy formulation, within the framework of approved national policies, and for the coordination and evaluation of the national psychological effort, including authority to issue policy guidance to all Departments and agencies of the Government executing portions of the psychological effort (1) be assigned to the Secretary of State, or, (2) be assigned to an official independent of any Department and responsible to the President."

After NSC consideration on January 4, the President referred these memoranda "to Mr. Souers and the Bureau of the Budget for further study and recommendation to the President."[12]

On January 18, Mr. Souers presented to you the proposal for a Board "under the NSC" with a chairman to be appointed by the President[13] (attached as Tab L).

Last week there was a meeting at the Bureau of the Budget for discussion of this problem which was attended by Admiral Souers; Messrs. Lawton and Staats of the Bureau; Messrs. Barrett, Matthews, Joyce, and Scott. A revised draft of the Souers directive was circulated and discussed, but no copies were given out. An analysis of this revised draft is attached as Tab M.[14]

W. K. Scott[15]

---

[11] Neither found.

[12] Not further identified.

[13] See attachment to Document 45.

[14] Memorandum from Scott to Webb, February 16. (National Archives, RG 59, P Files: Lot 55 D 339)

[15] Printed from a copy that bears this typed signature.

53. Memorandum From Director of Central Intelligence Smith to President Truman[1]

Washington, February 28, 1951.

Your copy of the initial issue of the daily Current Intelligence Bulletin, which is based upon information from all sources, is enclosed.[2] The former summary, which was based solely upon cables from diplomatic representatives, has been discontinued.[3]

It is hoped that the broad representative current intelligence presented in the new Bulletin, with immediate comments of analysts, will be of more comprehensive value to you. It should be emphasized that the comments do not necessarily represent the mature appreciation of the Central Intelligence Agency and have not been coordinated with the other agencies represented on the Intelligence Advisory Committee. They are actually the first impressions of CIA on "spot" information, and are subject to later revision. The next and following copies will contain selected items received directly from CIA sources.

Walter B. Smith

---

[1] Source: Truman Library, Papers of Harry S. Truman, President's Secretary's Files. Top Secret.

[2] Not found. A description of the enclosure at the end of the memorandum identifies it as the Current Intelligence Bulletin of February 28, 1951. A copy is in Central Intelligence Agency, Directorate of Intelligence, Job 97–T00975A, Box 1.

[3] The former summary, called the Daily Summary, was based on collateral sources, primarily news media and Department of State telegrams from U.S. Embassies abroad. It was designed for the use of the President and the National Security Council. The Current Intelligence Bulletin drew on all-source material, including COMINT-derived information. Distribution outside of CIA was to the President, the Secretary of State, and the Secretary of Defense. See also Documents 48 and 51.

54.   Letter From Director of Central Intelligence Smith to the Chairman of the Joint Chiefs of Staff (Bradley)[1]

Washington, March 2, 1951.

Dear General Bradley:

Herewith as discussed during our conference last Monday (see Annex 1)[2] are estimates of the support which is or which may be needed by CIA from the Department of Defense in order to carry out projects which have already been approved or which it is possible may be approved within the near future in accordance with our estimate of present trends of policy. Our estimated requirements are listed under three categories as follow: those already requested under approved projects; those required for the support of approved projects, requests for which will be made within the next thirty days; those required for the support of projects which are still tentative or which are still in the discussion state.

These latter are largely guesswork but the guesswork is educated to the extent that it is based on past experience and on our estimate of future possibilities.

For cross reference, in Annex 2,[3] we have indicated the requirements for covert operations by project, listing those which fall within the above three categories.

As I mentioned during Monday's conference, the responsibilities which are being placed upon us under our Charter and under NSC directives, particularly in the field of planning and execution of guerrilla warfare activities, go beyond our current capabilities and indeed embrace operations of such magnitude that they threaten to absorb the resources of this Agency to a point which might be detrimental to its other responsibilities.

In order to bring these activities into proper focus a statement will be submitted to the Joint Chiefs of Staff within the next 60 days,[4] giving CIA estimate of support required from the Department of Defense

---

[1] Source: Central Intelligence Agency, Executive Registry, Job 80–B01731R, Box 10. Top Secret.

[2] Attached but not printed.

[3] Not found.

[4] Smith sent a follow-up letter to Bradley on May 4 stating that NSC consideration of his request for a determination of the appropriate scope and pace of CIA operations was pending. He was therefore withholding providing his overall requirements for Department of Defense support until the NSC had made its decision. (Central Intelligence Agency, Executive Registry, Job 95–G00278R, Box 1, Folder 9)

in order to meet our dual responsibilities in the field of operations and accordingly to enable it to:

(1) complete the organization of a professional clandestine intelligence service, adequate to meet all peacetime requirements plus an estimate of expansion to meet conditions of general war;
(2) conduct effective covert operations on a global basis under continued conditions of cold war and including guerrilla activities on the mainland of Asia and in Eastern Europe.

The above would require, in my opinion, detailed planning, guidance, and control, participated in by the three Armed services, the Department of State, and probably the Office of Defense Mobilization, as well as the Central Intelligence Agency. This Agency will be glad to participate in discussions directed toward the formation of a staff or syndicate competent to give such guidance and control.

Faithfully,

Walter B. Smith[5]

---

[5] Printed from a copy that bears this typed signature.

---

55. Letter From President Truman to Director of Central Intelligence Smith[1]

U.S. Naval Station, Key West, March 8, 1951.

Dear Bedell:

I have been reading the Intelligence Bulletin[2] and I am highly impressed with it.

I believe you have hit the jackpot with this one.

Sincerely,

Harry S. Truman[3]

---

[1] Source: Truman Library, Papers of Harry S. Truman, President's Secretary's Files. No classification marking. President Truman was on vacation at the Little White House in Key West, Florida. A handwritten notation on the letter reads, "air mailed from Key West."
[2] See Document 53.
[3] Printed from a copy that indicates Truman signed the original.

56.   Letter From the Chairman of the Joint Chiefs of Staff (Bradley) to Director of Central Intelligence Smith[1]

Washington, March 9, 1951.

Dear General Smith:

I have read your letter (TS #43690) of 2 March 1951[2] with interest, and note that you are preparing a statement for submittal to the Joint Chiefs of Staff giving your estimate of the support required from the Department of Defense in order to meet your responsibilities in the field of operations.

The assets which may be generated by requirements for operations in the cold war can be expected to be of proportionate value in case overt global war should intervene, and for some time all of us have been acquiring a considerable body of experience in learning the mechanics of dealing with the complex elements that are involved.

It seems to me that much of the support which is visualized in the enclosures to your letter can be provided by arrangements which have already been set in motion and are well advanced. This leads me to hope that we will not have too much difficulty in handling the situation within the current framework, but it is, of course, a proper subject for further exploration and discussion with the Joint Chiefs of Staff.

Financing appears to be a matter between you and the Congress, but you may be assured that I shall support your efforts to obtain funds for any conception of your plans and operations which has been accepted by Defense.

Sincerely,

Omar N. Bradley[3]

---

[1] Source: Central Intelligence Agency, Executive Registry, Job 95–G00278R, Box 1, Folder 9. Top Secret.

[2] Document 54.

[3] Printed from a copy that indicates Bradley signed the original.

57.   Memorandum to the Executive Secretary of the National
      Security Council (Lay)[1]

Washington, undated.

SUBJECT

   Third Progress Report on NSC 59/1, "The Foreign Information Program and
   Psychological Warfare Planning"[2]

1. NSC 59/1 was approved as Government policy on March 10,
1950. It is requested that this Progress Report as of March 6, 1951, be
circulated to the members of the Council for their information.

2. In addition to steps taken to strengthen the existing organization under NSC 59/1 as reported in the second progress report,[3] further measures have been taken in this direction. Twenty-one weekly or
semi-weekly meetings of the National Psychological Strategy Board
have been held since the last progress report. The new procedures for
expediting the conduct of Board meetings were approved in December 1950, and the appointment of a full-time Executive Secretary to the
Board is pending.

3. New arrangements were made for closer interdepartmental coordination of information policy guidances.

4. A survey team composed of Colonel W.J. Bohnaker, Joint Sub-
sidiary Plans Division of the Joint Chiefs of Staff, Lt. Col. Frederick R.
Young, Psychological Warfare Division, Department of the Army, and
Mr. W. Bradley Connors, Department of State, was sent to Tokyo and
Korea in October. Findings of the survey group were reviewed by the
Interdepartmental Foreign Information Organization at its meeting of
November 13, 1950, and on 18 January 1951 the Director, Mr. Barrett,
transmitted to executing agencies the following statement on psycho-
logical warfare activities in Korea:

"The Interdepartmental Foreign Information Organization, having
reviewed psychological warfare activities in Korea on the basis of information now available, which is admittedly incomplete, and noting that
psychological warfare activities in the Department of the Army have been
elevated to the status of a Special Staff Division, concludes that:

"1. The importance of psychological warfare as an instrument of
national policy should be emphasized to all executing agencies in the
field;

---

[1] Source: National Archives, RG 59, Central Files 1950–54, 711.5200/3–751. Secret.
Drafted by Oechsner.

[2] For text of NSC 59/1, see Document 2.

[3] Document 28.

"2. Executing agencies should give psychological warfare the priority commensurate with its importance.

"3. The fullest use should be made of all known techniques and facilities now available for psychological warfare.

"4. To assure the most effective coordination of psychological warfare measures at the national level, it is desirable that agencies executing psychological warfare programs in the field provide full reports on current plans and operations."

Periodic reviews of psychological warfare activities in Korea have been made subsequently by the Board with the purpose of implementing the above conclusions. It is the view of the Department of State, however, that proper status and importance have not yet been given psychological warfare in Korea.

5. A Plan for National Psychological Warfare for General War, prepared by the Interdepartmental Foreign Information Staff under the terms of NSC 59/1, has been forwarded to the Director and is under consideration by the Board.

6. The staff has also notified the Director of completion of a study on "Detailed Functions of a National Psychological Warfare Organization," pending a decision on the location of the organization under NSC 74/3.[4]

7. Plans for the following areas have been developed interdepartmentally or by the Department of State and have been accepted by the Board for implementation or are under present consideration:

Korea
China
Indo-China
Russia
Germany

8. "Project Troy".[5] A report developed by the Department of State after consultation with the National Psychological Strategy Board, has been submitted; its implementation is now under consideration. The report covers only the first stages of the study described below, and

---

[4] Regarding NSC 74, see Document 17. NSC 74 and NSC 74/1 are in National Archives, RG 59, S/P–NSC Files: Lot 63 D 351, NSC 74. NSC 74/3 was not found.

[5] Project Troy, initiated in October 1950, was a research study undertaken by a group of scientists and social scientists assembled by the Massachusetts Institute of Technology. The "Project Troy Report to the Secretary of State" was submitted on February 1, 1951. It proposed technical means to get around Soviet jamming of VOA and ideas for political and psychological warfare. A copy is in National Archives, RG 59, INR Historical Files: Lot 58 D 776, Project Troy, Perforating the Iron Curtain. Documentation on the report and consideration of it within the Department of State is ibid., Central Files 1950–54, 511.00, 611.00, 711.5, and ibid., S/P Files: Lot 64 D 563. See also Document 59.

will be available to other departments shortly. Under this project, the Massachusetts Institute of Technology assembled 30 of the nation's top scientists and other experts to explore all means—conventional and un-conventional—for penetrating the Iron Curtain. The report endorses the large scale expansion of radio facilities, already initiated, and calls for even further expansion along lines which should facilitate further piercing the curtain by means which will not interfere with other telecommunications channels (military).

9. "Project Vagabond". Under this project, a study has been made of the use of seaborne portable radio transmitters to be mounted for stationary operations at negotiated bases in our overt information ac-tivities, but also to be available for covert operations and for military psychological warfare in the event of war.

10. "Project Brain Wave". The Department of State is developing and has reported to the Board a project designed to stimulate display of indigenous anti-Communist sentiment in the countries of Western Europe.

11. "Project Nobel". The Board has approved a project for the issuance of a pro-Western statement by all surviving holders of the Nobel peace prize.

12. The Board has continued to study the use of balloons as prop-aganda carriers. CIA has been assigned the project of a continuing study in this field and has also been instructed to stockpile one thousand large-sized propaganda balloons of the best type presently available.

13. The Board has at various meetings studied the question of de-fectors and their possible use in the information and psychological war-fare programs.

14. The subject of the relationship between SHAPE, NATO, State and Defense, with respect to both the current information program and psychological warfare planning, is under active study by staff and Board.

---

58.   **Memorandum From Director of Central Intelligence Smith to President Truman**

Washington, March 20, 1951.

[Source: Truman Library, Papers of Harry S. Truman, President's Secretary's Files. Top Secret. 1 page not declassified.]

59.   Memorandum From Robert J. Hooker of the Policy Planning Staff to the Director of the Policy Planning Staff (Nitze)[1]

Washington, March 26, 1951.

SUBJECT

Troy Report[2]

The Troy Report almost uniformly reflects a very high order of technical competence, political sophistication, and common sense. It deserves the most serious consideration. It lays down principles and techniques for the conduct of political warfare which, with few exceptions, seem worthy of adoption. On the non-technical side its value is not so much its originality—few of the ideas will seem original to anyone who has sat around the S/P table—as its cogency. Development of Staff views as to what recommendations should be adopted, and how we can secure their adoption, would seem to be in order.[3]

Following are its highlights. I am intruding my own comments only with respect to recommendations which seem to be questionable.

Volume I—Foreword

Explains that although the initial study was directed primarily toward the technical problems confronting VOA because of Soviet jamming, it was agreed that other methods of piercing the Iron Curtain should be examined, "and that the nature of any technical facility was inevitably tied to the target and to the content of the material to be conveyed and finally to the effect which was ultimately desired." (p. viii) Thus the study has emerged with the concept of "political warfare". "The newness of our idea, if any, lies in the understanding of the strategic power of the several elements when combined as a well rounded and coordinated whole.... the idea that the United States must develop a coordinated political warfare effort is the most important idea in the report." (p. ix)

---

[1] Source: National Archives, RG 59, S/P Files: Lot 64 D 563, Political and Psychological Warfare 1951–1953, Box 11A. Top Secret. Drafted by Hooker. All ellipses in the original.

[2] See numbered paragraph 8 of Document 57 and footnote 5 thereto.

[3] Another evaluation of the Troy report is in a memorandum from Armstrong to Barrett, March 26, which complimented the report for "its appreciation of the nature of political warfare and in its proposals as to the techniques that could be employed in disseminating our propaganda and otherwise carrying on political warfare activities." In his memorandum Armstrong also offered a critique of the "over-all substantive approach" of the Troy report. (National Archives, RG 59, INR Files: Lot 58 D 776, Box 14)

Part I—Political Warfare

Chapter I—Political Warfare

Urges the "unification of political warfare", which "should be organized like any form of warfare, with specialized weapons, strategy, tactics, logistics, and training". (p. 3)

Part II—Communication Into Shielded Areas

Deals with means of communication for piercing the Iron Curtain, mentioning, besides radio and balloons, and other existing ways, the use of direct mail to send professional journals and industrial and commercial publications and questions "Impulsive emotional blockades of this kind of communication, such as the recent ban on shipments of *The Iron Age*". It also mentions sending of objects, typical of American life, drugs, flash lights, fountain pens, small radio receivers, etc.

Chapter II—Radio

"Really important advances can be made along two complementary lines: a) by developing a broadcasting system which combines standard elements in a special way to achieve the effect of enormous power and, b) by developing a tiny, cheap, self-contained, durable receiver that could eventually be distributed in large numbers over the world." (p. 11) It notes that a hundred, perhaps a thousand, Soviet jamming transmitters are in use, which "appear to be *centrally controlled*, although the individual transmitters are widely distributed". (p. 13) "The evidence suggests that the operation is growing in scale and is a direct and major threat to high-frequency radio communication *within* and *to* Europe generally". (p. 14)

Recommends use of "the coherent transmitter" technique whereby a ten unit cluster, radiating one megawatt each, costing about 1.5 million dollars apiece, would have the same power as a single one hundred megawatt unit, "and if well-located could reach most of Eastern Europe at night. . . . (a) it cannot easily be jammed over a large area; (b) it can be heard with a receiver as insensitive as a simple crystal set". (p. 21)

Recommends also "a concerted effort to develop crystal and transistor receivers for mass production". (p. 22)

Points out "The Russian jamming operation seems to us to have clear and serious implications extending beyond the immediate problems of the Voice of America. . . . Already there have been instances of deliberate, effective jamming of intercontinental point-to-point transmissions, both United States and British. . . . If our high-frequency transmissions were jammed (they could be jammed tomorrow) and the Atlantic cables cut by submarine action, air mail would be our only means of communication with Europe. . . . the problem must be faced, as a matter of national security, now. . . . A wideband transatlantic communication facility, reliable and secure against jamming, can and must be provided. The appropriate agency should at once sponsor a thorough engineering study of the several possible methods. The national telecommunications policy must be reexamined. . . . The challenge of the electro-magnetic war is serious and we are not organized to meet it." (pp. 24–27)

Chapter III—Balloons

"An area of a million square miles could be saturated with a billion propaganda sheets in a single balloon operation costing a few million dollars. . . . If the area of dispersal in such an operation were restricted to 30,000 square miles, which may be practicable, there would be a leaflet laid down, on the average, for each area of 30 by 30 feet. . . . The dispersion of balloons in flight and the dispersion of leaflets in falling from altitude both lend themselves to saturation operations. . . . Production specifications should be established now and productive capacity should be located. . . . The operational testing and production program should be undertaken now. It may cost about one million dollars. . . . In order to coordinate balloon use with other political warfare operations, organizational planning for the final operations should start now. . . . A stockpile sufficient for an actual operation should be created now, and the questions of size and type of stock should be reviewed periodically as the program develops". (pp. 29–35)

Part III—Notes on Target Areas

Introduction

Observes that VOA "programs should deal insofar as possible with subjects that are matters of real *emotional concern* to the members of the audience. . . . There is a real danger . . . that heavy emphasis on news will lead to a neglect of longer range types of programs dealing with the local concerns of people behind the curtain". (p. 40)

Chapter IV—Russia

Notes that appeals to reason or efforts to modify ideological views have small chance of success. Suggests efforts should be directed toward undermining Soviet rulers' confidence in themselves and each other: noting possibility of producing deterioration in administrative structure "by overloading the system with material introduced from outside"; disturbing confidence of the leaders by increasing defection; stimulating mutual distrust by artificial means, bogus letters, etc.; promoting distrust of dependability of military and political organizations among the satellites. Comments that although the "full and fair" formula is officially abandoned, it remains in the habits of psychological warfare operators. Recommends "We should avoid the position, express or implied, that communism is bad, or any implication of contempt for communism ... rather ... that Stalinism has betrayed certain ideals of Marxism which have actually had a peaceful evolution in the West. ... Discord in the United States is not only tolerable but actually necessary. Variation and divergence ... are ... an evidence of strength, not weakness. ... There should be no direct or indirect disparaging of Soviet culture." (pp. 44–45)

Our principal targets should be the intelligentsia, skilled workers, bureaucrats, personnel of the mechanized armed forces, rural areas. Major themes should be "The Soviet peoples have proven themselves capable, patriotic, hard-working ... having with their sweat and blood built up a large scale industry and modern agriculture, are now being denied the fruits of their labor by a harsh and grasping regime. ... the USSR and the United States ... have ... common interests and common attitudes. ... Americans grant that the teachings of Marx, Engels, and Lenin have great historical importance. Yet the Stalinist system has not evolved ... as Marx and Engels would have wished". (p. 46) The handling of the material "should be persistent, simple and consistent ... based on genuine sophistication in Stalinist thinking ... truly personal ... occasionally seek the opportunity for drama ... should get on the band-wagon at the earliest possible moment for programs which are certain to be widely popular among the Russian people, even if they also have official Russian support." (pp. 46–47)

Chapter V—Europe

Proposes "a program based on the concept of European unity. ... one must look to European tradition itself. ... Nor will mere verbal argument suffice if in our other acts we appear to encourage the continuance of inequities or special privilege long associated with the managerial elites of European society." (pp. 51–55)

Recommends exploiting the opportunities offered by Yugoslavia.

Recommends considering seriously the inclusion of satellite and possibly Russian units in the all-European Army and, with suitable acknowledgment of the difficulty of the problem, emphasizes the importance and the genuine possibility of organizing a European Army with national units as small as companies. (Comment: The inclusion of satellite and Russian units under their own flags or so organized as to appear to the world as national units would seem questionable prior to an outbreak of hostilities. But they should be so organized that they can readily be converted into national units. The Report's unwillingness to accept the assumption that national units in the European Army must be of division size seems warranted, provided the problem is approached with suitable realism and flexibility.) The economic program should be designed to reduce the inequalities between social classes, reduce the feeling of isolation from sources of raw materials and markets for manufactures, eliminate barriers between the nations of Europe and encourage increase in productivity.

Recommends emergency aid and all possible support to Yugoslavia.

Chapter VI—China and Southeast Asia

"We cannot appeal to them to align themselves with us against Russia, save in terms of the fact that we, rather than Russia, can aid them in their struggles for development. . . . There is needed now a special Presidential Commission on Aid to Asia". (p. 66) Political warfare operations "should operate at the local level and specially trained technical personnel should participate at the local level. . . . projects must fit local needs, local customs, and local requirements".

Chapter VII—The Defector

Makes the highly questionable recommendation that an experimental Russian government-in-exile should be set up, "a small but responsible state with its own territory and a more or less free hand to develop social and political institutions which could fit the needs of present day Russians. . . . the creation of Russian troop units to serve in the all European Army . . . almost immediately". (p. 71)

The remaining recommendations are closely similar to the policy decisions already taken and now pending with respect to defectors, except for a recommendation, the necessity for which seems questionable, "that the defector program be set up under a single individual with authority to draw on necessary resources and personnel wherever located within the government". (p. 72)

Part IV—Some General Conclusions

Chapter VIII—General Conclusions

"In the absence of plans the conduct of political warfare tends to become a series of defensive responses to enemy action. . . . The success of our political warfare depends finally, upon the public support of national policies. . . . What is needed, what is indeed indispensable, is a planned research effort to insure first, that scarce resources of personnel, wherever located, are assigned tasks of the highest priority and second, that pieces of the research mosaic not lying clearly within the responsibility of existing agencies are supplied to complete the whole picture. . . . there must be some *single authority* concerned with political warfare exclusively, with the capacity to design a comprehensive program and the power to obtain execution of this program through the effective action of all the agencies and departments that are now engaged in waging political warfare." (pp. 79–81)

Volume II

Annex 1—Political Warfare

Points out that "the rise of technology has so changed the play of economic and social forces that the questions that now divide nations . . . go too deep to yield easily to negotiation . . . international relations must therefore increasingly be conducted through channels that reach the mass of people directly". (pp. 1–2)

Observes that U.S. Civil War was the first since the religious wars of the 17th Century to be fought consciously over an idea, and was fought not by professional armies but by masses of men representative of the whole society, with spectacular losses on both sides, won less by superior tactical skill than by overwhelming weight, and ended in unconditional surrender. "Technological advance has now put in our hands logistical weapons of such power that we find ourselves literally unable to use them for limited objectives. War has become for us not only all-out but all-or-none. . . . Even though such a weapon might win a war, it probably would not do so in a way that will lead to a satisfactory peace. Atomic war thus falls outside the Clausewitz definition. Its possession gives us time to develop a united world, but its use will not continue that policy." (p. 3)

Thus, we must seek other ways of reaching our international objectives. "Fear of all-out war has so far kept us from aggressive steps to halt the Russian advance. This is just the wrong attitude. A carefully planned series of forward steps that erode the Russian power provides the best way of avoiding, not provoking, the last great battle of the West . . . we must remember clearly that all international actions—wars included—are directed at the minds and emotions of men. . . . This interconnected simultaneous use of all instruments of international action to obtain a single objective is what we call, in this Report, political warfare. . . . a political war consisting of well-planned attacks on a series of limited objectives will make an all-out shooting war impossible for Russia and unnecessary for us." (pp. 3–4)

Annex 2—Briefing Travelers

Points out desirability of briefing travelers and U.S. soldiers abroad to make a good impression and answer intelligently the types of questions they will be asked.

Annex 3—The Mails

Points out value of use of the mails for "some sort of access to the U.S.S.R. and easy access to some of the satellites. . . . this channel should be used for what it is worth. . . . suited to a long-range background program. . . . can provide an equal-status contact—a professional talking to an already-sympathetic professional. . . . of non-government origin. . . . Lists of appropriate printed material, commercial or non-commercial should . . . be selected from *that now distributed in the United States.* . . . (1) of a high standard (2) non-political." (pp. 1–2)

Annex 4—Distribution of Objects

Seems far-fetched, with the all-important exception of crystal radios capable of receiving new and future VOA programs.

Annex 5—Overload and Delay

An "attack . . . should be directed at those weaknesses which could not be corrected without seriously reducing the power held by those few at the top. We might, for instance, take actions which would result in a serious overloading of the top levels by a crippling increase in the number of problems referred upward for a decision. How far could the Soviet system go in increasing the decision-making powers at the lower ranks before it fell below the critical level of centralized control for maintaining a dictatorship? We should explore all the 'input' points available to us, and we should deliberately embark on a program for increasing them, particularly at the lower levels. . . . deliberately experiment in this area . . . investigate the nature of departures from routine which make any local action improbable. . . . We might create many difficulties for the system by making as many of the situations it must meet highly conditional." (pp. 3–4)

Annex 6—Albania

Discusses possible defection of Albania in terms which add nothing to our understanding of this problem and its potentialities.

Annex 7—Two Doctors

Skip it.

Annex 8—Political Warfare—United States vs. Russia

". . . propaganda against the U.S.S.R. will be a squandering of money and of personnel and may actually be harmful unless there is a certain minimum coordination of words and acts. . . . unless its policy makers know in advance of significant military, economic, and political moves which are to be undertaken by all Government agencies . . . our programs of attack must be derived from the properties of the target, not from the properties of the weapons we happen to have." (pp. 2–3)

As objectives for VOA discusses friendship, creating doubt, resistance, and social groupings by classes, sex and age, the peasantry, nationality groups, party affiliation, and military-civil.

It recommends strongly against "the non-Party people being set off against the Party members. This has long been a shaky proposition, because it neglected the structure of the Party and the diversity of its actual roles in Soviet society. . . . A very high proportion of displaced persons . . . maintain that a large number of the Party people are blame-less, were forced into their membership, and do their best not to harm people. . . . To stress the theme of Party as against non-Party people might serve to push them deeper into the Party rather than away from it." The crucial differentiation is between "we" and "they", "between the ordinary, poor driven people both within and without the Party, and those in power or associated and/or identified with it". (p. 12)

"The suggested approach does not slight, minimize, or debunk So-viet accomplishments. A series error is often made in assuming that because so many Soviet citizens seem to have so strong a rejection of the Soviet regime, they equally reject all of its works and institutions. Nothing could be further from the truth. Work with defectors indicates that even among the most disaffected there tends to be strong personal, even emotional, identification with many of the features of society de-veloped under Soviet rule. . . .

"By the same token, we should be exceedingly cautious in attack-ing the Soviet system not to permit the impression that this means for us the sweeping away of all the basic institutions of contemporary So-viet society and their replacement by institutions imported from the West. Our central appeal is the promise of an end to the oppressive, compulsive totalitarian aspects of the Soviet regime. . . .

". . . There are two closely related themes which meet the require-ments indicated. The first stresses that the Soviet regime is impersonal, harsh, capricious, with little or no respect for the human dignity or for the basic rights to justice and fair play of a hardworking, decent, long-suffering people. The second stresses that the Soviet people have made great sacrifices and endured extraordinary hardship and suffering to build up in the Soviet Union a great and powerful industry and a prom-ising agricultural establishment, but they are being denied the fruits of their labor and the just reward for their suffering—which itself need never have been so great or so long-lasting—by a regime which is ex-ploiting the ordinary people, peasant, worker, and intelligent [sic][4] alike, for purposes of its own having nothing to do with the welfare of the people." (pp. 15–16)

Volume III

Annex 9—Personnel for Southeast Asia and Other Backward Areas

Proposes "the recruiting of a group of American youth willing and able to spend two to four years of their lives in intimate personal con-tact with the village people of Asia. Their primary task would be the demonstration of suitably modified western techniques of public health

---

[4] Brackets in the original.

and agriculture. . . . The training program would have, of course, to be elaborated with care and modified on the basis of future experience . . . whether the scheme proposed here can actually meet the need in practice can only be found out by trying. The importance of the problem certainly justifies a pilot project to test the possibilities." (pp. 1–3)

Annex 10—Population Problems

Notes futility of economic aid when "no ingenuity of Marxist dialectic, and no Point IV can reason away or buy off the rules of biology." In the not-very-long run the various proposed measures of assistance "will increase in even greater proportion the number of mouths".

Suggests efforts to build up in such areas of the Far East "somewhat different attitudes toward individual life than now exists. Specifically, this change can be described in terms of encouraging mothers to recognize the value of having a limited number of healthy, energetic and well-nourished children rather than a succession of sick, feeble and starving ones. . . . Demonstration that medicine and public health provide a more certain means of survival may well reduce the exaggerated drive towards numbers". (pp. 1–2)

Annex 11—Research in Support of Political Warfare

". . . it is particularly crucial that research be instituted which will guide the central coordinating body charged with fashioning the overall national political welfare [*warfare?*] strategy. . . . [it][5] must be of such a kind that it provides partial predictions concerning the psychological repercussions at home and abroad of economic, military, diplomatic, and informational policies."

Recommends study of the political control systems utilized for influencing the decisions of groups holding or seeking power, analysis of the social structure of key target areas, and of basic attitudes of target populations, investigation of major channels of communication within a country and existing attitudes towards materials carried in these channels, continuing studies of domestic vulnerability to political warfare, and research on the changing of attitudes.

Also recommends research in support of the defector program, on the use of radio, the creation of the image of America, methods of disrupting Russian administrative systems, vulnerabilities of Russian satellite armed forces, revolutionary role of Russian intellectuals, the concept of "United Europe", the problem of inventing things for Southeast Asian requirements, the effectiveness of the exchange of persons, and political warfare administration.

---

[5] Brackets in the original.

Annex 12—Defectors

"The lesson of history is clear that exiles or defectors have played a key role in revolutionary or counterrevolutionary movements. To the extent that they have been supported and aided by foreign governments ... such support has usually paid good dividends in terms of national interests to the foreign government ... [*1½ lines not declassified*]. If so, however, the consequences of such techniques for our general defection program must be carefully evaluated before any such decision is made. ... [*6 lines not declassified*] ... The intelligentsia and the middle occupational elite are more strongly represented in the defector group than in the total Russian population. A third (at least) of the defectors had Party and/or Komsomol membership—this is *much* higher than a random sample. This fact militates strongly against the contention that defectors overwhelmingly represent the rejects of Soviet society or people who were *never* able to adjust to the Soviet regime." (pp. 5–19)

Annex 13—Forward Planning

Deals with the possible impact on our society of the developing situation and its "threat to some of the historic qualities that we have heretofore assumed to be an inherent part of our way of life", diversity, mobility, curiosity, and affection or sympathy. "We earnestly recommend a research program that will pool the energies and wisdom of historians, anthropologists, economists and psychologists to analyze the possible effects of a prolonged preparedness upon this society and provide us with a basis for dealing intelligently with the life that lies immediately before us." (pp. 2–4)

[Comment: This might well be a desirable project for the Ford Foundation to undertake.][6]

Annex 14—Public Opinion

"A special problem of public support might arise if Russia were to appear to relax or stabilize her aggressive pressure. ... Other problems of public support may well arise if the government adopts a policy of aggressive political warfare." (p. 1)

Discusses, among the type of problems which can be anticipated: How does public opinion influence foreign policy? How can policy be best presented to earn support? How can public understanding and support be increased? and America's image of itself.

Annex 15—Stalin

"Since Stalin's death offers the best opportunity for exploiting the fear and self-interest of the Soviet elite with the aim of weakening the

---

[6] Brackets in the original.

regime to the point where it can no longer threaten our world objectives, and since the death of the dictator can occur at any time, it is of the utmost importance to initiate planning for this eventuality without delay. . . . it is proposed that a special section be set up within the Political Warfare Executive to concentrate exclusively on this task. . . . to collect the views of the most competent students of Soviet Government and society and those of recent refugees from the U.S.S.R. as to what is likely to take place when Stalin dies. From these views, several hypotheses should be developed. . . . For each one of these hypotheses the general outline of a political warfare campaign would be developed. Failure to have a strategy worked out might permit consolidation of power under a new dictator, and we might have to wait another quarter of a century (if we survive that long) for another opportunity."

Annex 16—Biography of Team

Annex 17—Consultants

Annex 18—Project Troy Briefing

Volume IV

The annexes contained in Volume IV, 19 through 26 inclusive, all deal with the various technical problems of breaking through the Soviet jamming of VOA.

---

60.   Editorial Note

In a directive of April 4, 1951, to the Secretary of State, the Secretary of Defense, and the Director of Central Intelligence, President Truman established the Psychological Strategy Board. His goal was to promote "more effective planning, coordination and conduct, within the framework of approved national policies, of psychological operations." The Board, consisting of the Under Secretary of State, the Deputy Secretary of Defense, and the Director of Central Intelligence, was to report to the National Security Council. For text of the directive of April 4, see *Foreign Relations, 1951*, volume I, pages 58–60. See also ibid., pages 902–965. President Truman appointed Gordon Gray as the first Director of the Psychological Strategy Board.

The White House released an abbreviated version of the President's directive on June 20. See *Public Papers: Truman, 1951*, pages 341–342.

The Department of State initially opposed the creation of the Board and later maintained that a Department member should chair the

Board, arguing that it was "impossible . . . to entrust the formulation and execution of policies and programs of political warfare to an agency not subject or subordinate to the Department of State." (Memorandum from Under Secretary of State Webb to the Director, Bureau of the Budget, March 15; National Archives, RG 59, Central Files 1950–54, 100.4 PSB/4–451) Ellipsis in the original.

Master files of minutes and papers of the PSB for the years of its existence are ibid., S/S–NSC Files: Lot 62 D 333. Additional material on the establishment of the PSB and its operations is ibid., P Files: Lot 55 D 339, Barrett Files and ibid., Central Files 1950–54, 100.4/PSB, 511.00, and 711.5200.

---

61.   Paper Prepared in the Office of Policy Coordination of the Central Intelligence Agency[1]

Washington, April 4, 1951.

CIA/OPC STRATEGIC WAR PLAN
IN SUPPORT OF
THE JOINT OUTLINE EMERGENCY WAR PLAN

I. General

1. Purpose

This plan provides for conversion of peacetime covert operations to wartime needs in support of military war plans based on forces available. This plan is limited to such operations and excludes consideration of the manifold CIA/OPC responsibilities for covert operations in peace, in cold war and in overt war not in direct support of military war plans.

2. Definitions

a. For the purposes of this paper, "D (The) Day" refers to the day on which actual, active combat operations of conventional warfare start in a general war.

b. "Peace" as used herein refers to all situations short of overt general war.

---

[1] Source: Central Intelligence Agency, Office of the Deputy Director for Operations, Job 79–01228A, Box 6. Top Secret. Printed from a copy that indicates that the last three pages were revised on November 1.

3. Assumptions

At any time after 1 January 1951, war may be forced upon the United States and her Allies by acts of aggression on the part of the USSR and/or her satellites.

a. (1) *Basic Assumption* (JCS). This plan may be effective at any moment, but full implementation of the plan is predicated on actual hostilities not starting before 30 June 1952.

b. *Special Assumptions* (JCS).

(1) M–Day and D–Day may be the same.

(2) The USSR will have the following Allies:

Poland	Bulgaria
Eastern Germany	Communist China
Czechoslovakia	Outer Mongolia
Hungary	Albania (probably)
Rumania	

The political alignment of Korea will depend on the outcome of the UN actions there.

(3) The Western bloc will consist of the following:

(a) Allied with the United States at the outbreak of war:

United Kingdom	Italy
France	Portugal
Benelux	Australia
Denmark	New Zealand
Norway	South Africa
Iceland	Ceylon
Canada	

(b) Bound to Allies by treaty commitments (subject to provisions of the UN Charter):

    1 UK and Turkey, Egypt, Jordan, Iraq
    2 US and Philippines
    3 US and Latin American countries (in varying degrees of cooperation)

(c) The Arab States are favorably disposed toward the Allies but are unlikely to fight, especially outside of their own territory.

(d) The Allies will have base facilities at least in Japan.

(e) The status of the governments of Western Germany and Austria is dependent upon plans under NATO.

(f) Greece is entirely sympathetic and will help as far as possible.

(g) Sympathetic to the Western bloc but probably not belligerents at the outset:

    India
    Pakistan

(4) Neutral Countries

(a) Probable neutral countries unless attacked:

Switzerland	Afghanistan	Iran
Sweden	Burma	Yugoslavia
Spain	Thailand	
Finland	Indonesia	
Ireland	Israel	

(5) Western European countries under NATO will have improved economically and militarily but, except for the UK, will be unable to resist effectively, being overrun and occupied.

(6) Atomic weapons will be used by both sides.

(7) Biological warfare *may* be used by either side.

(8) War may start with little or no warning. At best, it will be preceded by a period of political negotiations and tension which will give the Allies a few months warning. The Allies may decide to start the main attack.

(9) Part of the oil of the Middle East will become vital to the Allied effort at some stage of the war.

(10) It is expected that the Soviets will employ subversive activities and unconventional warfare on a global scale and to an extent unparalleled in history.

c. *Added Assumptions* (CIA). For the Armed Forces to capitalize on CIA effort, they should on a top priority basis:

(1) *General*

(a) Provide material, logistical, and administrative (communication) support from the Army.

(b) Ear-mark, effective for use on "D–Day" (or earlier if the imminence of Soviet invasion is unmistakable), the necessary Air Support from the Air Force to include coordinated and simultaneous attack by both Air and Unconventional Forces and the execution of night operations for the purpose of infiltrating personnel and sabotage stores.

(c) Detail for duty with CIA the selected Department of Defense officer and enlisted personnel who are trained in Clandestine Warfare under CIA auspices.

(2) *For Covert Operations in Europe*

(a) Authorize a limited relaxation of security measures and activities in Europe under Army and/or Air Force cover and the allocation to CIA of a safe Military training area in Germany for processing, billeting, and administering limited number of CIA recruited Austrian and German indigenes now available for training.

(b) Authorize the utilization by CIA of selected personnel from U.S. controlled indigenous labor battalions in Germany as a source for recruiting personnel to be trained and employed in Clandestine Operations.

(c) Expedite procurement of and authorize CIA participation in the screening and selection of indigenous personnel to be recruited by the Army under the Lodge Bill, so that an adequate percentage of the personnel screened and accepted can be made available to CIA.

(d) In conjunction with CIA, set up without delay in the European Theater a planning team to effectuate the above. This team to consist of one each member from the Army, Air Forces, and CIA.

II. Mission

4. Strategic Concept Peace and War

a. *Peace.* To conduct covert operations in support of U. S. foreign policy objectives and to plan and prepare for support of military war plans.

b. *War.* In time of war to conduct covert operations in military theaters in support of military war plans as well as covert operations in support of U.S. foreign policy directives. In areas outside of military theaters, to conduct covert operations in support of over-all politico-military war plans to reduce the Soviet war potential.

5. Basic Missions

a. *Peace.* In general CIA/OPC's present basic activities are specifically prescribed in NSC 10/2 as follows:

(1) Propaganda

(2) Economic warfare

(3) Preventive direct action, including:

(a) Sabotage
(b) Anti-sabotage
(c) Demolition
(d) Evacuation.

(4) Subversion against hostile states, including:

(a) Assistance to underground resistance movements
(b) Assistance to guerrillas
(c) Assistance to refugee liberation groups
(d) Support of anti-Communist elements in threatened countries.

(5) Planning and preparation, in conjunction with the JCS, for the conduct of covert operations in wartime.

CIA/OPC has intensified and amplified certain of these cold war activities in response to NSC 68, NSC 58/2, NSC 59, NSC 103/1, NSC 104 and other significant NSC documents.[2]

---

[2] Regarding NSC 68 and NSC 59, see Documents 5 and 2, respectively. For NSC 58/2, see *Foreign Relations,* 1949, vol. V, pp. 42–54. For NSC 103/1, see ibid., 1950, vol. V, pp. 463–466. For NSC 104, see ibid., 1951, vol. I, pp. 1023–1034.

b. *War.* In time of war, or when the President directs, all plans for covert operations shall be coordinated with the Joint Chiefs of Staff with a view to the accomplishment of the following mission:

THE UTILIZATION OF COVERT OPERATIONS TO THE FULLEST PRACTICABLE EXTENT TO ASSIST IN ACCOMPLISHING THE MILITARY DEFEAT OF THE U.S.S.R. AND HER SATELLITES. HIGHEST PRIORITY AMONG COVERT OPERATIONS IN SUPPORT OF MILITARY WAR PLANS WILL BE GIVEN TO THE RETARDATION OF THE SOVIET ADVANCE IN WESTERN EUROPE.

6. Specific Undertakings

a. Support by covert means the following military undertakings:

(1) Essential defensive tasks

(a) Protection of the Western Hemisphere outside of the continental U.S.
(b) Defense of the U.K.
(c) Holding of Northwest Africa and the Cairo–Suez area.

(2) Strategic air offensive

(a) The strategic air offensive will be directed against:

　　1 Soviet atomic air offensive
　　2 Support elements of Soviet offensive
　　3 Soviet industrial potential with emphasis on POL and transportation facilities

(3) Operations in Western Eurasia

(a) Operations in Western Europe will include defensive operations; if the situation renders it imperative, withdrawal until assumption of offensive operations and reoccupation of lost territory. The defensive operations by unconventional warfare forces in support of military war plans will include, on highest priority, the retardation of the Soviet advance and attacks on Soviet forces and lines of communications at the *outset* of hostilities. Maximum pressure will be maintained during the time that the Allied forces are engaged in the Western European defense.

(4) Control of essential lines of communication as follows:

(a) Western Hemisphere to U.K.
(b) Western Hemisphere to Gibraltar
(c) East coast of U.S. to South America and South Africa
(d) West coast of U.S. to Japan, Okinawa, Philippines Anzam area, and Alaska
(e) U.K. to Gibraltar and Central and South Atlantic
(f) Gibraltar to Suez

b. Unconventional warfare against Soviet submarine and mining potential.

c. Increase of psychological warfare upon the outbreak of general overt war.

d. Increase of unconventional warfare upon the outbreak of general overt war.

7. *Phasing of Tasks—General*

a. *Present to "D Day"*

(1) Preparation of CIA war plan and coordination of this plan with that of the military theaters. Procurement and training of covert personnel, stockpiling of supplies, and matériel to be used in support of war plans. Conduct of approved covert operations.

(2) The activation and effectuation of such covert operations in support of war plans (e.g., evacuation, sabotage, or counter-sabotage) as may be ordered by competent authority.

(3) Preparation for the transition from peacetime execution of covert operations to the wartime execution under the command of the American Theater Commander. This will include activation of a special CIA staff at the American Theater Commander's headquarters.

b. *First Phase (D to D + 3 Months)*

The implementation of covert operations in support of theater war plans to cover withdrawals and in support of an air offensive. During this phase and beginning at the outset of hostilities, highest priority will be given to retardation of the Soviet advance, attacks on Soviet forces, and interruption of Soviet LOC's.

c. *Second Phase (D + 3 Months to D + 12 Months)*

Continuation of basic strategy of first phase to include the emphasis on the retardation of the Soviet advance.

d. *Third Phase (D + 12 Months to D + 24 Months)*

The implementation of covert operations in support of theater war plans aimed at stabilizing the Soviet offensive. Upon stabilization of the Soviet offensive, such covert operations will be directed toward enhancing the Allied position and toward initiating an Allied offensive either in this phase or phase IV.

e. *Fourth Phase (D + 24 Months to End of War)*

Continuation of basic strategy of second and third phase with increasing emphasis on covert operations in support of an Allied offensive and in support of the establishment of military government. Operations to nullify "scorched earth" tactics on the part of the retreating enemy will be mounted at this time.

III. TASKS FOR CIA/OPC DIVISIONS IN SUPPORT OF MILITARY WAR OPERATIONS

8. *General*

Each geographical division will plan, develop facilities for, and execute upon direction, covert operations in the countries within its area, in coordination with and in support of the programs of other United States Government agencies, as follows:

a. *Eastern Europe:*[3] Assist U.S. armed forces to

(1) Retard from the *outset* of hostilities, the Soviet advance, attack the Soviet forces, destroy their lines of communication, and exert the maximum pressure on them during the period that the Allied forces are engaged in the defense of Western Europe. This is of highest priority.

(2) Incite discontent amongst Soviet peoples with the Kremlin-controlled government and keep alive and strengthen their hope for eventual liberation therefrom.

(3) Develop the resistance potential of opposition elements within the USSR and countries under its domination.

(4) Induce, by every stratagem and means possible, the defection of satellite states and their separation from the USSR.

(5) After the Western Allies are prepared to capitalize thereon, instigate revolts in selected countries in the area with a view to deposing the communist regimes and replacing them with governments which are friendly to the cause and subscribe to the principles set forth in the U.N. Charter.

(6) Inhibit the growth of Soviet political and military capabilities for further offensive action against the non-communist world.

(7) In countries in the area not under control of the USSR, strengthen the will and ability of the peoples and the governments to resist efforts at communist subversion.

(8) Assist the military theater commanders, in the event of hostilities, in conducting such operations against the Soviet Union and its satellites as will destroy the effectiveness of their combined military forces, and the effectiveness of supporting communist parties, resulting in their replacement by governments sympathetic to the free world.

(9) Provide support to other competently authorized operations and activities directed from or toward the area.

(10) Priority in CIA preparations for wartime operations insofar as Western Europe is concerned will be in areas *east* of the Rhine–Alps line.

b. *Western Europe*[4]

(1) Assist U.S. Armed Forces to retard, where and when applicable, the Soviet advance, attack the Soviet forces, destroy their lines of communication, and exert the maximum pressure on them during the

---

[3] Balkans, Greece, Czechoslovakia, Baltic States, Poland, Hungary, Germany, Austria, Switzerland, USSR. [Footnote in the original.]

[4] Scandinavian Countries, Benelux, United Kingdom, France, Iberia, Italy, Trieste. [Footnote in the original.]

period that the Allied forces are engaged in the defense of Western Europe. This is of highest priority.

(2) Disaffect local Communist parties from the Cominform and the CPSU(B).

(3) Dissipate the support and strength of the Communist party in each country.

(4) Strengthen the will and ability of the peoples in the area to resist both the internal and external forces of Communism.

(5) Prepare the peoples of the area, in case of attack by external Communist forces, to engage in resistance activities and the Western powers to communicate with, assist, and direct this resistance.

(6) Provide support to other competently authorized operations and activities directed from or toward the area.

(7) Every possible precaution must be taken to insure that the pattern of recruiting, organizing, and coordinating activities in North Atlantic Treaty Organization areas does not indicate that the United States lacks confidence that the line of the Rhine–Alps can be held. Such precautions may require the use of cover plans to conceal the true purpose of preparations in the North Atlantic Treaty Organization areas.

c. *Near East and Africa*[5]

(1) Acquaint the peoples in critical parts of the area with the imperialist and subversive aims of the USSR and local communist movements.

(2) Strengthen the will and ability of the peoples in the area to resist the internal and external encroachments of communist forces.

(3) Enroll the peoples and governments in the area on the side of the West in the East-West conflict.

(4) Ensure the availability to the Western world, and the denial to the USSR and satellites, of the strategically important resources of the area.

(5) Alleviate the conflicts and differences between or among countries within the area with a view to establishing harmonious relations between the various states in the area.

(6) Prepare the peoples of those areas likely to be overrun by hostile forces in case of war to carry on resistance activities, and the Western allies to communicate with, assist, and direct this resistance.

(7) Provide support to other competently authorized operations and activities directed from or towards the area.

---

[5] All of Africa, Israel, Arab States, Iraq, Syria, Lebanon, Jordania, Saudi Arabia, Yemen, Turkey, Iran, India, Pakistan, Afghanistan, Nepal, Ceylon, Tibet. [Footnote in the original.]

d. *Far East*[6]

(1) Frustrate by all possible means the efforts of the USSR to establish a regime in China subservient to the interests of the USSR; and to consolidate its control over the territories and peoples of China.

(2) Foster the emergence of and develop a Chinese political leadership which can command popular support of the Chinese people and not be subject to domination by the USSR.

(3) Dissipate the support and strength of local Communist parties in those countries where such parties are actively functioning.

(4) In countries in the area not under the control of the USSR or the Communist Party of China, acquaint the peoples and governments with Communist aims and strengthen their will and ability to resist efforts at Communist subversion.

(5) In countries in the area likely to be overrun by Communist forces, prepare the peoples thereof to engage in resistance activities and the Western Allies to communicate with, assist, and direct this resistance.

(6) Develop the resistance potential of opposition elements in Eastern USSR.

(7) Provide support to other competently authorized operations or activities directed from or toward the area.

e. *Western Hemisphere*[7]

(1) Dissipate the support and strength of the local Communist party in those countries where one is actively functioning.

(2) Strengthen the will and ability of the peoples in the area to resist both the internal and external forces of communism.

(3) Ensure the availability to the United States and its Allies, and the denial to the USSR and satellites, of those strategically important resources designated by compotent authority.

(4) Provide support to other competently authorized operations and activities directed from or toward the area.

f. *Psychological Staff Division*

(1) To provide the over-all direction, technical guidance, and means (as required) to Area Divisions for exploitation of economic, political, propaganda, and scientific situations.

(2) To plan and develop facilities for covert economic, political, propaganda, and scientific operations, and execute those operations requiring centralized control and which transcend military theaters of operations and are not within the operational capabilities of the Area Divisions, to:

---

[6] Siam, Malaya, Indonesia, Philippines, Burma, China, Japan, Okinawa, Korea, New Zealand, Australia, Pacific Islands. [Footnote in the original.]

[7] South and Central Americas. [Footnote in the original.]

(a) Weaken the position of the Soviet Bloc and strengthen the position of the U.S. and Allies.

(b) Combat the activities of Communist-controlled international organizations.

(c) Strengthen the will and ability of non-Communist international organizations to resist Communist effort at subversion, and encourage these organizations in anti-Communist activities.

(d) Encourage the subjects of the USSR and its Satellites to desert Communist jurisdiction, renounce allegiance to their rulers, and seek haven in non-Communist jurisdiction; provide interim sanctuary and support to such disaffected peoples and other refugees from USSR and Satellite jurisdiction; and prepare for their employment in the task of liberating their respective homelands.

(e) Accomplish such other missions as may be assigned from time to time in the pursuit of opportunities or support of other projects.

9. Operational Forces

a. Tab "A"[8] outlines the CIA/OPC operational forces available on a phased basis.

b. Tab "B" outlines the Air Force support requirements.

c. Tab "C" outlines the Naval support requirements.

IV. Administrative and Logistical Matters

Requirements for logistical support, bases, and personnel and materiel in the ZI for period from 1 July 1952 to 1 July 1954 will follow.[9]

V. Command, Communications, and Liaison Matters

11. The command and communications channel of CIA will be from the Headquarters in Washington to its principal headquarters in the field. In active theaters of war where American forces are engaged, covert operations will be conducted under the direct command of the American Theater Commander and orders therefore will be transmitted through the Joint Chiefs of Staff unless otherwise directed by the President.

12. For reasons of security and adequate liaison, the DCI shall maintain independent communications with designated representatives overseas, including lateral communications between theaters. Arrangements for such communications shall be coordinated with those of the military.

13. Command and Liaison Procedures for War Planning of Covert Operations in Theaters (see Annex 1).[10]

---

[8] None of the tabs are printed.

[9] Not printed. (Central Intelligence Agency, Office of the Deputy Director for Operations, Job 79–01228A, Box 6)

[10] Not printed.

62.   **Memorandum From the Director of the Policy Planning Staff
(Nitze) to the Under Secretary of State (Webb)**[1]

Washington, April 9, 1951.

Mr. McWilliams asked me to set down briefly my ideas concerning the functions of the new Psychological Strategy Board.[2] In particular I want to state my exceptions to Mr. Barrett's memorandum to you of March 29, 1951, on the subject: Plans for Psychological Strategy Board.[3]

That memorandum speaks of the board's jurisdiction as including "the development of proposals in the field of military, political and economic action geared for psychological effect and to the development of campaigns directed toward important psychological objectives and embracing action in these fields as well as the fields of purely psychological activity". It envisages the board as operating as a central authority on political warfare—"as recommended by the Troy group".[4]

The Troy group, you will recall, was originally given warrant to study the problem of defeating Russian jamming of the Voice of America. The group widened its own jurisdiction to include the content of the programs to be protected against jamming. The group interpreted this widened jurisdiction to include the substance of "political warfare". The group interpreted "political warfare" to include the Marshall Plan, Point IV, ECA operations in the Far East, and the like. The group referred to political warfare as "inter-connected simultaneous use of all instruments of international action". The group envisaged political warfare as the range of activities which, if successful, "will make an all-out shooting war impossible for Russia and unnecessary for us".

The group then called for an "aggressive" political warfare program instead of the current efforts, which the group labeled "defensive".

The group discovered a need that "the many elements of our national power, political, economic, military," be "wielded as an integrated effort". In the group's phrasing, "We therefore urge the unification of political warfare".

The group thus called for "some single authority". This was to have "capacity to design a comprehensive program and power to

---

[1] Source: National Archives, RG 59, S/P Files: Lot 64 D 563, Chronological. Top Secret. Drafted by Marshall.

[2] See Document 60.

[3] The memorandum by Barrett has not been found. An unsigned March 26 draft prepared by Leon Crutcher of the Management Staff is in National Archives, RG 59, P Files: Lot 55 D 339.

[4] See footnote 5, Document 57 and Document 58.

obtain execution of this program". The authority was to be "concerned with political warfare exclusively", but the phrase, as we have seen, was interpreted to embrace all aspects of foreign policy.

The Troy group went vastly beyond its original terms of reference and explored a field for which it had no special competence and about which it had little information. In effect it proposed a new board to take over the jurisdiction of all the agencies operating in the foreign field, of the NSC, and in part of the President himself.

I think I have stated sufficiently my misgivings about the Troy report as a frame of reference for the new board. I have the same misgivings about the reference in Mr. Barrett's memorandum to "the development of proposals in the field of military, political and economic action geared for psychological effect and to the development of campaigns directed toward important psychological objectives and embracing action in these fields as well as fields of purely psychological activity".

In my view, if the board were to follow out the implications of the Troy report and the language cited from Mr. Barrett's memorandum, the result would be a harmful duplication and conflict of authority with established agencies and a missing of the potentially very valuable objective set up for the board in the establishing directive.

The board obviously is not intended as a new agency to determine or formulate the ends of our foreign policy. Its primary jurisdiction has to do with means of our policy—those means devoted directly to affecting the state of mind within the adversary's camp. I employ the word "directly" advisedly. I am aware that all of our policy—ends and means—relates in some way to the state of mind in the adversary's camp. Certain of the means for carrying out that policy act indirectly on his state of mind as a collateral effect. I do not believe these means fall within the board's primary jurisdiction. Other means are designed for direct effect on that state of mind. These clearly do fall within the board's primary jurisdiction.

I believe the board should bring about a sharpening of effort in regard to our behind-the-iron-curtain information program, our defector program, our covert activities within the adversary's fold, and the like. It should seek to ensure that no opportunity for such activities goes unexploited and that the activities are consistent among the various agencies carrying them out. When this part of our effort might be helped by a clarification of policy or broadening the effort to interpret that policy on some other front, the board should be alert to the opportunity to call the matter to the attention of the agency or agencies concerned. If the board should undertake to formulate programs "geared for psychological effect" in the field of military, political and economic action and "embracing action in these fields as well as fields of purely psychological activity", there would be no stopping place short of assuming jurisdiction over the whole range of our foreign policy—ends and means.

Paul H. Nitze[5]

---

[5] Printed from a copy that bears this typed signature.

---

63. Memorandum From the Executive Secretary of the National Security Council (Lay) to the National Security Council[1]

Washington, April 9, 1951.

SUBJECT

NSC 10/3 and NSC 10/4[2]

REFERENCES

A. NSC 10/2[3]
B. Memos for NSC from Executive Secretary, subject: "NSC 10/3" and subject: "NSC 10/3 and NSC 10/4", dated February 6 and March 30, 1951, respectively[4]

The enclosed memorandum by the Director of Central Intelligence on the subject reports is submitted herewith for consideration by the National Security Council of the proposal contained in paragraph 1 thereof.

Accordingly, it is requested that each Council member indicate his action with respect to the proposal contained in the first paragraph of

---

[1] Source: Truman Library, Harry S. Truman Papers, President's Secretary's Files, Subject File. Top Secret.

[2] For a draft of NSC 10/3, see the attachment to Document 43. For NSC 10/4, January 16, see Document 42. NSC 10/4 was withdrawn on December 13, after the approval of NSC 10/5; see Document 90.

[3] For text, see Foreign Relations, 1945–1950, Emergence of the Intelligence Establishment, Document 292. This text cites the 1951 revised language of paragraph 4 that includes the added final phase "unless otherwise directed by the President." See footnote 6 below.

[4] Lay's February 6 memorandum to the National Security Council transmitted the CIA's draft directive on NSC 10/3 along with a memorandum from Under Secretary Webb outlining the views of the Department of State. Lay's memorandum also indicated that the National Security Resources Board concurred in the proposed directive. (National Archives, RG 273, Policy Papers, NSC 10/3, Box 3) Lay's March 30 memorandum has not been found (see footnote 6 below).

the enclosure by completing and returning the attached memorandum form.[5]

Furthermore, if the proposal in paragraph 1 of the enclosure is approved,[6] it is requested that all copies of NSC 10/3 and of the reference memorandum of March 30 be returned to this office in accordance with the recommendation contained in paragraph 2 of the enclosure.

With respect to NSC 10/4, it is suggested that further Council consideration of that report be deferred until additional recommendations regarding it are submitted by the Director of Central Intelligence at a later date, as indicated in the last paragraph of the enclosure.

It is requested that special security precautions be taken in the handling of this material and that access be limited to individuals requiring the information contained herein in order to carry out their official duties.

James S. Lay, Jr.

Enclosure

Memorandum From Director of Central Intelligence Smith to the National Security Council[7]

Washington, April 9, 1951.

SUBJECT

NSC 10/3 and NSC 10/4

1. As a result of a conference held on 5 April 1951 by the Deputy Secretary of Defense Lovett, Under Secretary of State Webb, General Bradley, and the undersigned,[8] it was agreed that the differences among

---

[5] Not found.

[6] Truman approved the proposal for a new paragraph 4 of NSC 10/2 in an April 16 memorandum to Lay. In a handwritten note he added: "It is a proper suggestion. I approve it." (Truman Library, Papers of Harry S. Truman, President's Secretary's Files, Subject File) Lay informed the Council by memorandum of April 16 that the statutory members of the Council had approved the new paragraph 4. This settled the controversy between CIA and the JCS (see Document 42) and draft NSC 10/3 was withdrawn. The President's copy of Lay's April 16 memorandum bears a handwritten notation dated May 25, 1951, by Rose A. Conway, Administrative Assistant in the President's office, indicating that copies of NSC 10/3 and Lay's memorandum of March 30 had been returned to Lay for destruction.

[7] Top Secret.

[8] The conference is described in Montague, *General Walter Bedell Smith as Director of Central Intelligence*, p. 207.

the interested agencies with regard to the proposed changes in NSC 10/2 could best be composed by substituting for paragraph 4 thereof the following:

"4. In time of war, or when the President directs, all plans for covert operations shall be coordinated with the Joint Chiefs of Staff. In active theaters of war where American forces are engaged, covert operations will be conducted under the direct command of the American Theater Commander and orders therefor will be transmitted through the Joint Chiefs of Staff unless otherwise directed by the President."

2. Accordingly, it is recommended that NSC 10/3, and the commenting paper thereon by the Joint Chiefs of Staff, dated 27 March 1951,[9] be withdrawn.

3. If this recommendation is accepted by the National Security Council, the basic directive for covert operations by the Office of Policy Coordination of the Central Intelligence Agency (NSC 10/2) will remain in effect with paragraph 4 thereof changed as indicated in paragraph 1, above. This document leaves something to be desired but it is workable. Discussions relative to the details of authority and responsibility, which appear inevitably to follow any significant change, can thus be minimized. Those which cannot be avoided when two or more agencies of Government are cooperating in pursuit of a common objective can be continued indefinitely on the staff level without militating against the effectiveness of important operations now in progress.

4. Further recommendations regarding final action on NSC 10/4 (Responsibilities of CIA with Respect to Guerrilla Warfare) will be submitted at a later date when it is determined to what extent, if any, these responsibilities can be transferred or decentralized to other agencies of the Government.

Walter B. Smith[10]

---

[9] Not found.

[10] Printed from a copy that indicates Smith signed the original.

64.   Letter From Secretary of Defense Marshall to Director of
Central Intelligence Smith[1]

Washington, April 13, 1951.

Dear General Smith:

Reference is made to your memorandum of 26 December 1950,
transmitting a general statement of the support needed by the Central
Intelligence Agency (CIA) from the Department of Defense.[2]

The military agencies accept the commitment for furnishing one
or two officers each to CIA to aid in the preparation of national intelligence estimates.

Your request for special consideration in obtaining military personnel for use in clandestine intelligence and covert operations entails
budgetary, personnel and training implications which must be considered by the three Services in their manpower plans. If you will furnish
the Department of Defense with more detailed breakdown with respect
to the numbers of enlisted and officer personnel desired from each of
the Services, the qualifications desired in such personnel, and the rate
at which you desire they be supplied, I will be glad to consider the
matter further.

With respect to the use of certain facilities at Army, Navy and Air
Force installations, the Joint Chiefs of Staff will welcome discussion of
the details of such requirements and be receptive to any reasonable demands which will further the national security.

[1 paragraph (12 lines) not declassified]

The assignment of CIA representatives to the military staffs in theaters of operations will be dependent upon the relationship between
those representatives and the theater commanders. This is now under
consideration in NSC 10/3 proposed by CIA.[3]

With reference to your request that you be kept fully informed of
operational decisions and plans of the Joint Chiefs of Staff, I am informed that the policy of the Joint Chiefs of Staff on this matter has
been transmitted to you in JICM–1205 of 25 September 1950.[4]

Permanent liaison between elements of the Central Intelligence
Agency and the Joint Chiefs of Staff, including a method of furnishing

---

[1] Source: Central Intelligence Agency, Executive Registry, Job 95–G00278R, Box 1,
Folder 9. Top Secret.

[2] Document 36.

[3] For the draft text of NSC 10/3, see the attachment to Document 43.

[4] Not found.

advice and guidance on essential elements of information, appears to be established through frequent working-level contacts with the Service intelligence agencies and the representative of the Joint Chiefs of Staff on the Intelligence Advisory Committee. Should any deficiencies exist under this arrangement, I would appreciate having them brought to my attention.

As the remaining proposals made in your memorandum will be directly affected by the decisions reached with respect to revision of NSC 10/2 and NSCID 5,[5] it is believed advisable to defer a definite reply until final action on the proposed revisions has been taken.

Faithfully yours,

G. C. Marshall[6]

---

[5] See Document 255 for the revision of NSCID No. 5.

[6] Printed from a copy that indicates Marshall signed the original.

---

65.   Memorandum From Director of Central Intelligence Smith to the Chairman of the Interdepartmental Intelligence Conference (Hoover)[1]

Washington, April 17, 1951.

SUBJECT

Need for Specific Intelligence and Counter-Intelligence Information

Your memorandum of 28 February 1951,[2] outlining the need for specific intelligence and counter-intelligence information on the part of the Interdepartmental Intelligence Conference, was handed to us on 22 March 1951 by Major General Bolling. This Agency realizes that the type of information which you describe is becoming more and more necessary and vital to the internal security of the United States, appreciates your action in specifying the types of information desired by your Committee and welcomes the opportunity to comment on the problem you have presented.

---

[1] Source: Central Intelligence Agency, Executive Registry, Job 80–B01731R, Box 29. Secret.

[2] Not found.

In our overseas operations our ability to achieve satisfactory results in the fields of interest to the IIC depends in some areas upon obtaining the cooperation of local intelligence and security organizations. These local organizations have, in varying degrees, useful information on the specific targets listed in your memorandum. We could secure more information from these local agencies if we were able, within the limits prescribed by the primary requirements of our own security, to work out an exchange of information and to furnish them on a basis of reciprocity some information on these subjects developed within the United States.

Furthermore, we could more effectively address the work of this Agency to the targets set out in your memorandum if there were a closer coordination of the intelligence on Soviet controlled espionage activities abroad and the intelligence on such activities in this country.

To this end, the CIA would be glad to consider with the IIC agencies the desirability of designating a CIA liaison representative to attend meetings of the IIC or to serve as a member of a working group of the IIC in order to facilitate the exchange of information which will be mutually helpful.

Walter B. Smith[3]

---

[3] Printed from a copy that indicates Smith signed the original.

---

66.   Letter From the Chairman of the Interdepartmental Intelligence Conference (Hoover) to Director of Central Intelligence Smith[1]

Washington, May 2, 1951.

Dear General Smith:

Your memorandum of April 17, 1951,[2] concerning the IIC need for specific intelligence and counterintelligence information, has been received and considered by the Interdepartmental Intelligence Conference.

---

[1] Source: Central Intelligence Agency, Executive Registry, Job 80–B01731R, Box 29. Confidential; Via Liaison. The letter is on FBI stationery.

[2] Document 65.

It will not be possible for the IIC agencies to furnish to you on a regular basis information of a confidential nature, or that developed from confidential sources, for use in bartering with foreign intelligence and security organizations. Where there is a specific problem or special circumstances existing, we will, of course, be glad to consider any specific requests or suggestions and, where possible, information in such cases will be made available for your use in this manner.

When the IIC or its Subcommittee is considering a specific problem concerning the coordination of domestic intelligence with foreign intelligence matters, you will, of course, be invited to designate a representative to attend, as contemplated in the IIC Charter. Generally, however, it is felt that the appropriate media for the coordination of the intelligence on Soviet-controlled espionage activities abroad and the intelligence on such activities in this country exists in the Intelligence Advisory Committee and in the close liaison facilities which are maintained with CIA.

The IIC agencies desire to cooperate with you in any manner possible in connection with the obtaining of this vital information, which can for the most part only be obtained in the foreign field. As previously indicated, it is most urgent that this type of information be developed as its receipt could, when considered in the light of domestic problems, possibly be the means of averting serious Communist-controlled Fifth Column or sabotage operations within our borders. It will be appreciated if you will furnish at your earliest convenience any studies or information which you may presently have in connection with the type of information listed in the IIC memorandum of February 28, 1951.[3]

Sincerely yours,

J. Edgar Hoover

---

[3] Not found.

67.   **Memorandum From the Assistant Secretary of State for
Public Affairs (Barrett) to the Under Secretary of State
(Webb)[1]**

Washington, May 14, 1951.

SUBJECT

Plans for New PSB

On Tuesday, May 8, a meeting was called by General Smith in CIA to discuss plans for the new PSB. This meeting was attended by Mr. Dulles, Admiral Stevens, General Magruder, Mr. Wisner and myself. Minutes of the meeting are being prepared by CIA and a copy will be sent to your office in case you would like to look at them.[2]

No firm recommendations were made as to the substantive problems which the Board should attack. General Smith expressed the opinion, however, that the PSB should have as one of its functions taking high policy from NSC and other sources and translating this into psychological warfare objectives. Admiral Stevens felt that the Board should concern itself largely with use of psychological warfare in the cold war and General Smith believes it might constitute a "general staff" for the cold war.

At the end of the meeting General Smith requested that each agency concerned designate two men to draft recommendations for the consideration of the Board members. This working group is to address itself to the following questions:

1. What kind of a staff will the Board need?
2. How should this staff proceed?
3. What mechanisms are presently available which could be used for the conduct of the Board's business.
4. What should be the initial program of the Board?

Allen Dulles and I registered mild objections to the above. We felt that the Board should consume as little time as possible on formal consideration of mechanisms, organizational problems, etc.—and certainly should not get involved in a lot of formal papers on this subject. Both of us expressed the belief that we would like to see the Board get going immediately on certain substantive problems—like our over-all strategy with regard to Iran, or overloading the Soviet administrative

---

[1] Source: National Archives, RG 59, Central Files 1950–54, 100.4–PSB/5–1451. Secret. Sent through S/S, and initialed by Webb.

[2] The minutes have not been found.

system. The General seemed to agree in part, but, I gather, felt that some minimum organizational planning would be necessary.

I have asked Mr. Phillips Davison, Executive Secretary of the Psychological Operations Coordinating Board, to represent the Department on this working group. He would be accompanied by Mr. Crutcher from Mr. Humelsine's office when organizational problems are being considered, and by Mr. Phillips from this office when policy matters are under discussion.

The first meeting of this working group has been called for next Wednesday.

E.W.B.

68.   **Memorandum From the Executive Secretary of the National Security Council (Lay) to the Director of the Policy Planning Staff (Nitze), the Department of Defense Representative on the National Security Council Senior Staff (Nash), the Joint Chiefs of Staff Representative on the National Security Council Senior Staff (Wooldridge), and the Deputy Director of Central Intelligence (Jackson)[1]**

Washington, May 14, 1951.

SUBJECT

Scope and Pace of Covert Operations

At the direction of the President you have been designated as a special group of the Senior NSC Staff to consider the attached memorandum on the subject from the Director of Central Intelligence, and to prepare for the Council's consideration appropriate recommendations with respect thereto.

In performing this function it is anticipated that you will work in close collaboration with your respective principals in order to reflect their views during the staff work, and with the designated representatives of your respective departments and agencies under NSC 10/2[2]

---

[1] Source: Truman Library, Papers of Harry S. Truman, President's Secretary's Files, Subject File. Top Secret; Eyes Only.

[2] Regarding NSC 10/2, see footnote 2, Document 42.

in order to realize the advantages of their knowledge and experience in this field.

After allowing time for your study of the attached memorandum, a meeting will be scheduled within the next week or so.

It is requested that extraordinary security precautions be taken in the handling of this project and that knowledge of and access to the attached memorandum and subsequent documents be restricted to the minimum required for adequate staff work. Copies of or extracts from this and subsequent documents should not be made without permission of this office.

James S. Lay, Jr.[3]

Attachment

Memorandum From the Director of Central Intelligence (Smith) to the National Security Council[4]

Washington, May 8, 1951.

SUBJECT

Scope and Pace of Covert Operations

The Problem

1. To obtain more specific guidance from the National Security Council in order to define the projected scope and pace of covert operations in aid of current overt cold-war and of military preparations to meet overt global war, and to insure timely and effective support for such operations.

Pertinent Facts

2. The following facts highlight the need for this guidance and support:

a. To meet its responsibilities for covert operations, the Central Intelligence Agency has already had to increase its personnel and expenditures to an extent believed to exceed the scope contemplated by the National Security Council when it authorized covert operations in the summer of 1948.

b. Even more considerable increases will be required in the near future if this agency is to discharge the missions already specifically

---

[3] Printed from a copy that bears this typed signature.
[4] Top Secret; Eyes Only.

proposed to it by the Departments of State and Defense and the Joint Chiefs of Staff or undertaken on the initiative of CIA with the approval of such Departments. Still greater increases would be required to accomplish the missions which are apparently envisioned under the NSC 68 series (and of which segments are found in various other NSC papers; e.g., NSC 58/2, NSC 59, NSC 103/1, and NSC 104).[5] These increases are beyond CIA's present administrative support capabilities.

c. High level policy decisions are required not only on the issue of these increases in themselves, but on the direction and nature of covert operations. For example, to what extent will the United States support counter-revolution in the slave states? A Joint Chiefs of Staff memorandum to the Director of Central Intelligence, 28 March 1951,[6] raises a related issue: The view of the JCS that CIA give maximum emphasis to preparations for the retardation of Soviet advances in Europe beginning on D Day. In view of CIA's presently limited facilities this request raises the issue of the priorities as between covert-cold-war activities and covert activities to support the military in the event of a general war.

Discussion

3. Pursuant to the provisions of NSC 10/2, CIA has been actively engaged for over two years in the planning and conduct of covert operations in the general fields of activity specifically provided for therein, viz:

a. propaganda
b. economic warfare
c. preventive direct action, including—

(1) sabotage
(2) anti-sabotage
(3) demolition
(4) evacuation

d. subversion against hostile states, including—

(1) assistance to underground resistance movements
(2) assistance to guerrillas
(3) assistance to refugee liberation groups
(4) support of anti-Communist elements in threatened countries

e. Planning and preparation, in conjunction with the JCS, for the conduct of covert operations in wartime.

---

[5] Regarding the NSC 68 series, see Document 5. For NSC 58/2, "U.S. Policy Toward the Soviet Satellite States in Eastern Europe," December 8, 1949, see *Foreign Relations, 1949*, vol. V, pp. 42–54. Regarding NSC 59, NSC 103/1, and NSC 104, see footnote 2, Document 61.

[6] Not found.

4. Subsequent to NSC 10/2, the NSC 68 series called for an intensification of covert operations in the fields of economic, political and psychological warfare with the purpose of rolling back the perimeter of Soviet power and the ultimate frustration of the Kremlin design. As a result, the covert activities of CIA have been stepped up considerably, even though the policies established by NSC 68 have never been spelled out in terms of a specific covert program directive to CIA.

5. Specifically, the currently stepped-up covert projects of CIA (see more detailed listing at Tab "A") are being prosecuted in five areas of the world as follows [1 *line not declassified*]:

Western Europe [*dollar amount not declassified*]

Emphasis on: psychological and labor operations especially [*less than 1 line not declassified*], organization of stay-behind and resistance groups in all Western Europe [*less than 1 line not declassified*], political action [*less than 1 line not declassified*] and a pilot economic warfare operation [*less than 1 line not declassified*].

Eastern Europe [*dollar amount not declassified*]

Emphasis on: psychological warfare [*less than 1 line not declassified*]; extensive special political operations [*less than 1 line not declassified*]; organization of resistance groups in Eastern Europe and the Baltic; and expansion of the [*less than 1 line not declassified*] underground.

Near East [*dollar amount not declassified*]

Emphasis on: preliminary exploratory activities [*less than 1 line not declassified*]; denial of [*less than 1 line not declassified*] oil fields; psychological and labor operations throughout the Near East.

Far East [*dollar amount not declassified*]

Emphasis on: guerrilla warfare and escape and evasion in [*less than 1 line not declassified*]; stay-behind preparations [*less than 1 line not declassified*]; psychological and labor activities throughout the Far East; preclusive buying; [*2 lines not declassified*].

Latin America [*dollar amount not declassified*]

Emphasis on: preliminary exploratory activities, propaganda, and the establishment of a mechanism for these and other activities on an expanded scale.

Special Projects [*dollar amount not declassified*]

Emphasis on: National Committee for Free Europe and its agency, Radio Free Europe; training foreign agents in the United States; support of international anti-Communist labor and youth organizations; and the development of outlets for propaganda against foreign targets.

Research and Development [*dollar amount not declassified*]

Overhead [*dollar amount not declassified*]

6. [*1 paragraph (4 lines) not declassified*]

7. [*7 paragraphs (26 lines) not declassified*]

8. The above missions, current and proposed, representing a very considerable number of covert cold-war projects, constitute in themselves a rather extensive preparation to conduct covert operations in support of the military effort in the event of the outbreak of a general war. Nevertheless, they do not comprise the comprehensive cold-war program clearly contemplated by NSC 68. In the absence of a specific detailed plan for conducting a comprehensive cold-war program, it is not possible to make an accurate estimate of manpower, matériel, and money required. Nor, in the absence of detailed overt war plans is it possible to make an accurate estimate of the requirements of full-scale covert operational support of an all-out military effort. Nevertheless, it is possible, on the basis of the requirements of the programs already under way or in the planning stage, to make an informed guess of the general order of magnitude of a covert apparatus capable of supporting either an effort to prevent overt war or an all-out military effort in the event of such war. [*1½ line not declassified*] (These estimates exclude additional requirements for military personnel and for funds to stockpile and resupply certain standard military items for guerrillas and resistance groups. For further detail see Tab "B".)

9. Thus, the Central Intelligence Agency is faced with the fact that its covert operations are outstripping its present administrative capabilities. Even an apparatus of the magnitude required to discharge the relatively limited cold war and military support programs, outlined by paragraphs 5 and 7 above, calls for an administrative organization of considerably greater strength than now present in CIA to solve effectively the complex planning and logistical problems involved. Specifically, there would be required a staff comparable to that of a Major Command, procurement and production machinery for those items not properly assignable to the Department of Defense, and additional facilities for: training, security clearances, communications, headquarters office space, and other requisite administrative and logistical services. Without such augmentation the growing magnitude of covert operations will tend to divert an ever increasing share of the time and attention of CIA key personnel from the basic intelligence mission of the Agency, with the attendant risk that such mission will not be adequately accomplished.

10. Although the cumulation of missions already undertaken by CIA, to say nothing of those now proposed to CIA, may transcend the original intentions of NSC 10/2, the NSC 68 series leaves little doubt that it is our national policy to conduct covert operations on a very large scale. It is the view of CIA that all of these things can and should be done. But before launching CIA into such large activities, a number of high level policy decisions and certain vital assurances are required from the National Security Council. The following paragraphs deal with the qualitative nature of the required guidance.

11. It appears that the Office of Policy Coordination was originally created to be primarily an agency to execute covert support to cold war activities (with planning and preparation for covert support in the event of hot war as an additional responsibility). However, the increasing scope and pace of hot war preparation is tending to overshadow this original purpose. The cold war program (though essentially political in conception) is heavily weighted with military considerations; equally, the hot war preparations (though essentially military in conception) are heavily weighted with political considerations. Because CIA's present responsibilities cover both current cold war covert operations and certain covert aspects of preparations for hot war, it has perhaps been more immediately aware than other interested agencies of the need for delineation of policies and priorities as between these programs and of the need for more definitive machinery to give both programs politico-military guidance on a continuing basis. The machinery established under NSC 10/2, i.e., the designated representatives of the Departments of State and Defense, has consisted of individuals of the most exceptional qualifications, who have been of the greatest assistance in developing projects. The efforts of these representatives have been augmented by those of an equally well qualified and helpful representative of the Joint Chiefs of Staff. However, this machinery was not designed to develop strategic guidance of the order required by the far-reaching policy determination of NSC 68 and other post-NSC 10/2 policy papers.

12. An illustration of the need for such strategic guidance is the problem raised by the view of the Joint Chiefs of Staff, as expressed in its memorandum of 28 March 1951, that the Central Intelligence Agency should give top priority to preparations for the retardation of a Soviet military advance across Europe. The responsibilities of the Director of Central Intelligence under NSC 10/2 are such that he cannot accept this view as controlling without assurance that this military policy will also be consistent with the foreign policy of the United States. Only a National Security Council decision can give this assurance in a matter of such moment. Such a decision will require a determination of relative priorities and of the extent to which the United States is willing to support and follow up on counter-revolution in the slave states. Polit-

ical and matériel support on a national scale is required to back up and capitalize on any counter-revolution which may be engendered. Only the National Security Council can insure such support.

13. It is true that the covert apparatus needed for the cold war is similar to that needed to support the military effort in a hot war. However, there are numerous important differences in detail and in timing. For example, it is clearly desirable from the standpoint of either cold war or hot war to develop the potential of resistance groups in Eastern Europe. How much of this potential to develop, when to release it, and how much to hold in reserve are problems which can be and are argued differently by the military and by the political experts. Again CIA must seek politico-military guidance at the NSC level to determine where and how to build and utilize its covert assets.

14. Another area requiring such guidance pertains to the question of concealing U.S. participation in covert activities which cannot remain completely covert. The training of indigenous personnel for resistance and guerrilla activity, the mounting of guerrilla operations, all become more difficult to cover as the size of the effort increases and the time for field operations approaches. [3 *lines not declassified*] Somewhere in the process it becomes pointless to attempt to deceive the enemy on U.S. participation, just as it would have been naive for the U.S.S.R. to expect the U.S. to believe it had no part in supporting and directing the Greek Communist guerrilla operations. Only continuing guidance from the National Security Council level can insure sound decisions in this field.

15. Finally, it is urged that these matters call for immediate resolution by the National Security Council. It requires approximately eighteen months to build the base from which all-out covert operations can be launched. The building of the U.S. covert base and apparatus is not proceeding at the required pace and cannot until the specific determination and guidance discussed above have been issued by the National Security Council.

Conclusions and Recommendations

16. The above discussion leads to the following conclusions which are stated in the form of recommendations to the National Security Council:

a. That in view of the magnitude issue as well as the guidance needed to give proper direction to stepped up covert operations, the National Security Council initiate a comprehensive review of the covert operations situation.

b. That this review contain a restatement or redetermination as appropriate of the several responsibilities and authorities involved in U.S. covert operations.

c. That if the above review results in a reaffirmation of the decision to place covert operational responsibility within the Central Intelligence Agency—the Central Intelligence Agency should be provided necessary support from other agencies of the government to insure the successful discharge of this responsibility including the following specific assurances:

(1) Adequate provisions for joint planning with the Armed Forces for covert activities and operations in support of wartime military operations, spelling out a clear delineation of authorities, duties and responsibilities.

(2) Specific guidance for dealing with the military in fields where the same covert apparatus is being developed to engage in high priority cold war missions as well as to be available to the military in the event of overt war.

(3) More specific provision for insuring that the foreign policy and political considerations which are involved in covert operations are brought to bear on determinations of politico-military significance.

(4) Specific provisions to insure that the type and quantities of personnel, administrative and logistical support required of other governmental departments and agencies for the prosecution of the covert effort will be forthcoming as necessary.

d. That where guidance for covert operations is of concern to more than one Department, this guidance be coordinated and issued to the Central Intelligence Agency (and to other participating agencies) by the new Psychological Strategy Board.

Walter B. Smith[7]

Tab A[8]

[2 *pages not declassified*]

Tab B[9]

[1 *page not declassified*]

---

[7] Printed from a copy that indicates Smith signed the original.

[8] Top Secret; Eyes Only.

[9] Eyes Only.

69.   **Memorandum From the Deputy Assistant Secretary of State for Public Affairs (Sargeant) to the Under Secretary of State (Webb)**[1]

Washington, May 24, 1951.

Program Planning for Psychological Warfare

The National Security Council has directed that in any actual theater of war the Department of Defense will be responsible for psychological activities. However, as it is agreed that the State Department's program of International Information and Educational Exchange will be called on to assist the military the following steps have been taken:

1. An emergency plan has been prepared which covers the necessary general directives for providing propaganda activities in the country attacked and in adjacent countries, not only for the United States forces which might be involved but for the government under attack. While this plan is general, it was drawn with two special countries in view—Iran and Yugoslavia.

2. A stockpile of necessary basic supplies, including paper, ink, mimeograph, and necessary sound equipment is being prepared.

3. A basic stockpile of propaganda output in the form of research materials on various subjects that will probably need to be covered in an emergency as well as some semi-prepared press releases, pamphlets, leaflets and other similar forms of propaganda is being prepared.

Further, an informal meeting has been held with the British to provide for the beginning of active policy and operations liaison.

In a situation short of actual warfare the State Department is responsible for overt propaganda activities. Through the National Psychological Strategy Board we are in constant liaison with other agencies in the field. As an acknowledged agency of the United States Government we do not engage in activities which will seriously embarrass the government.

However, recognizing the seriousness of the international situation we began to prepare almost two years ago for a vigorous Psychological Offensive. The Offensive has the dual purpose of (1) strengthening the alliance of free nations, and (2) weakening the Soviet Union and its satellites. We distinguish between the short

---

[1] Source: National Archives, RG 59, P Files: Lot 52 D 432, Office of Assistant Secretary Edward Barrett, 1950–51, Box 5. Restricted. The unsigned original appears to be a draft. There is no indication whether it was sent to Webb. It bears the handwritten note, "Hand-carried to Wilber's office this PM."

term objective in psychological warfare of persuading the enemy to make a false move and the longer term objective in our psychological offensive of both encouraging our friends and discouraging our enemies.

In preparation for our special program we prepared a plan known as the Campaign of Truth, which contains the following devices to concentrate our efforts on our specialized objectives:

1. A system of country priorities in which we analyzed propaganda strategy on a global basis.

2. Country papers which aimed our efforts more precisely by stating:

a. Those propaganda themes or objectives which in each country would best contribute to our overall objectives.

b. Target group priorities in which we chose those social classes in each country which it was most expedient for us to reach; and

c. Media priorities by which we determined what devices are most effective in each country for reaching our target groups.

3. Special Propaganda Plans—Special plans spelling out in great detail the psychological vulnerability of the peoples and the appeals useful in reaching them, have been prepared for Russia, China, Indo-China and the Eastern European satellites and South Asia. Others are in process.

4. Guidances—There are four types of guidances used to assure that our operators use the most effective messages:

a. The country paper or basic guidance for each area.

b. The overnight guidance which covers day to day events.

c. The weekly guidance which takes care of events of continuing concern; and

d. Special guidances which cover either special propaganda problems or special events which lend themselves to propaganda exploitation.

Among the State Department activities which might be pointed to as vigorous implementation of the propaganda responsibility of the State Department, I include the following:

(1) Radio—We have two radio stations—RIAS in Berlin and Red-White-Red in Vienna beaming a strong signal and a hard-hitting message into the Eastern European areas constantly. The Radio Division is now constructing studios in Munich in addition to increasing the strength of its transmitters and from there will beam still a third program into Russia and Eastern Europe soon. The next step calls for a fourth program to be beamed out of Salonika to the Near East. The Ring Plan which calls for encircling Russia and her satellites with the most powerful radio transmitters ever built, and Project Vagabond, in which radio transmitters are mounted on ships, are examples of the

new planning of IBD.[2] A further effort to get our message into the crucial areas, has already resulted in contracting for radio receivers to be distributed in Korea, Indo-China, Greece, Iran and Turkey. The 1952 budget provides for further increase of this program. Further, IBD has begun to broadcast in many minority languages of China and Russia, as for example, Ukrainian, Georgian, Lithuanian, Amoy, Mandarin, Cantonese and Swatow dialect, as well as Urdu and Hindi to South Asia, and is actively working toward programs in Central Asian dialects in the very near future.

(2) Press—The major changes under the Campaign of Truth in the press program are that regional and local production in not only standard languages but important dialects is being stressed and that a great deal of material which is either tied to the local interests of the people or is anti-Soviet in character is being produced under the imprint of private groups. This is one way in which we have been able to aid organizations interested in furthering the same objectives we have.

(3) Motion Pictures—The new developments in the motion picture program are ever-increasing emphasis on production in the field, particularly in priority countries and the speeding up of the production of a newsreel so that it can become a fast medium for propaganda messages.

(4) Exchange of Persons—Priority emphasis worldwide has been given to labor leaders and journalists, as labor is a most important target group for us in almost every priority country and opinion leaders are also a first priority group. The trend has been away from academic exchanges toward political exchanges.

(5) Libraries and Institutes—In addition to more careful selection of types of books and languages in the translation program the whole concept of the library has been sharpened into that of an Information Center which specializes in books, magazines and exhibits which contribute directly to our basic purposes of strengthening ourselves and weakening the enemy.

In policy formulation USIE plays an active role in the Department. Mr. Barrett participates in Mr. Webb's meetings. Representatives of the Policy Staff are members of working groups on special problems, as for example, the CFM meetings in Paris, the Forced Labor issue, the NATO information program for which we have the responsibility in the United States Government. A special Policy Implementation Staff makes news for us to exploit. We help to determine the content of various intelligence reports sent out to the missions, and we receive propaganda guidance reports from our missions at regular intervals, some daily.

---

[2] International Broadcasting Division.

Although the planning for our program began quite some time ago it should be noted that little could be done to really effect significant improvement until last October when additional funds were granted by the Congress. The Campaign of Truth is dependent on having adequate resources.

---

70. Memorandum From the Secretary of State's Special Assistant for Intelligence and Research (Armstrong) to the Director of the Policy Planning Staff (Nitze)[1]

Washington, May 26, 1951.

SUBJECT

Scope and Pace of Covert Operations

General Smith's memorandum of May 8 to the NSC on the above subject[2] raises a number of not clearly separable problems and issues. In an admittedly arbitrary delineation, the following discussion and recommendations for a Departmental position in the Senior Staff are offered, with an indication, where possible, of the views expressed by General Magruder and Admiral Stevens.[3]

1. Increased Scope of OPC Operations

The great increase in number and size of projects which OPC has been called on to perform and can anticipate since the approval of NSC 10/2,[4] and particularly since the Korean war, requires, in General Smith's view, a reaffirmation by the NSC of its directive to CIA contained in 10/2. He as much as says that the character of the mission for OPC has changed by the change in size and he believes this should be recognized by NSC.

---

[1] Source: National Archives, RG 59, Central Files 1950–54, 611.61/5–2651. Top Secret. This memorandum is virtually identical to a draft by Robert P. Joyce of the Policy Planning Staff to Nitze, May 26; ibid., INR Files: Lot 58 D 776, OPC. The difference in attribution has not been explained. Memoranda from Joyce to Nitze of May 18 and May (misdated March) 25, and an unsigned memorandum to Armstrong of May 17 on the same subject, are ibid.

[2] See the attachment to Document 68.

[3] See Annex 1 and Annex 2 below.

[4] See footnote 2, Document 42.

There seems to be no disagreement in the Department or with General Magruder, Admiral Stevens, or CIA itself that there is no alternative but to pursue vigorously the covert operations and to re-affirm the 10/2 in the light of the changes noted by General Smith.

2. Cold War Operations vs. Preparation for Hot War

General Smith points out the gradual but pronounced shift of emphasis in OPC projects from those in support of cold war activities to those involved in the planning and preparation for covert support in the event of war. This presents to OPC a competing claim upon personnel and facilities and General Smith requires further guidance.

The Department would join with General Magruder and Admiral Stevens in believing that we have no course but to pursue both objectives simultaneously. However, the Department would feel that, in the light of the continuing and understandable pressure from the Military for activities in support of a hot war, it is necessary to re-affirm that a fundamental mission of OPC is to promote national policy which has been most recently set forth in the NSC–68 series,[5] and that therefore *primary* emphasis must be upon the cold war psychological objectives. This would include the underlying principle that every effort, including psychological, should be made to prevent the coming of a Third World War, while not overlooking the possibility that such a war will break out and we will need to be fully prepared for it.

3. Guidance Mechanism; Support

General Smith directly and indirectly inquires whether OPC should look to the Psychological Strategy Board for guidance and co-ordination. At the same time he points out that OPC will not be able to fulfill its mission unless it gets more support in terms of personnel and assistance in military and political plans and policies.

The Department would agree with General Magruder and particularly with Admiral Stevens that the PSB was established for just this purpose and it should be utilized to the fullest possible extent. The PSB can and should be called upon for giving or obtaining from the NSC decision where decision is needed, for giving continual guidance, for coordinating the various agencies and for marshalling from the agencies the support required by OPC.

4. Decision and Guidance on Specific Projects

General Smith asks for guidance on a number of specific projects some of which will be in conflict in terms of either the objectives or

---

[5] See Document 5.

claims upon personnel or facilities in short supply. Notably General Smith has pointed out that with respect to the problem of support of counter-revolution in the slave states—how much support should be given, when to release it, how much reserve to maintain—presents a conflict in terms of the objectives of the cold war on the one hand, and of preparation for hot war on the other.

Although General Magruder does not address this point, Admiral Stevens points out, and the Department of State would warmly endorse his position, that such problems cannot be answered without further plans and proposals by the CIA and impliedly what the issues are as between the conflicting objectives. This and every other project on which CIA needs specific guidance or decision must be presented in terms of the specific problem to the PSB for coordination, and where necessary presentation to the NSC and the President.

5. *Cover Problems*

General Smith's memorandum points out that under the rigid specifications of 10/2, all OPC operations must be carried out in such a way as to remain covert and not disclose the interest of the US Government; that this tends to limit the effectiveness of OPC, particularly in para-military type operations which, on the one hand cannot disguise US Government interest and on the other can be more effectively carried out under quasi-military aegis.

Admiral Stevens suggests and General Magruder would apparently concur that this problem too should be presented in terms of individual projects and specific recommendations thereto to the PSB for resolution. There is no apparent inclination to disagree with General Smith on this.

[1 *paragraph (12 lines) not declassified*]

6. *Organization*

General Smith's memorandum does not directly address this question but implicit in his approach as well as in the memoranda of General Magruder and Admiral Stevens is the problem of organization for covert activities. The Department would join with Magruder and Stevens in feeling that within OPC and CIA organizational changes, particularly in any distinction between wholly covert type operations and para-military operations, should be handled by CIA itself and should not be of concern to the other agencies except where they may impinge upon the responsibilities of the other agencies or upon the intelligence effort of the Government. On the other hand, with respect to the organizational location of covert operations in the Government as a whole, the Department would agree with Magruder and Stevens that there is no alternative to the present allocation of this responsibility, almost in toto, to CIA–OPC.

Proposed Action

Only Admiral Stevens has suggested what specific action should be taken on General Smith's memorandum. Even General Smith's recommendations call for "guidance", without any indication as to the nature or form of such guidance.

The Department would concur in Admiral Stevens's specific suggestion that the Senior Staff recommend that the NSC approve a statement of policy with respect to General Smith's memorandum. In brief, Admiral Stevens recommends that this statement of policy contain the following points:

a. CIA should increase the scope and pace of its cold-war activities without jeopardizing its planning and preparation for covert, hot-war activities.

b. There should be no change in the present Governmental organization for covert activities, but that the newly created Psychological Strategy Board should be fully utilized.

c. (1) Present mechanisms for coordination on planning for hot war are available with elements of the Military Establishment.

(2) The PSB should give the necessary guidance on any conflicts which arise in pursuing the objectives for the cold and the hot war.

(3) The PSB can and should ensure that political and military considerations are applied to covert activities.

(4) All agencies should give fullest possible support to the covert activities and this support should be insured and coordinated through PSB.

d. PSB should be specifically directed (by the NSC and the President) to provide or obtain the guidance required by CIA.

Annex 1

Memorandum From Brigadier General John Magruder to the Department of Defense Representative on the Senior Staff of the National Security Council (Nash)[6]

Washington, May 23, 1951.

SUBJECT

Scope and Pace of Covert Operations (memo to NSC from Director, Central Intelligence dated 8 May 1951)

1. The Director, Central Intelligence is faced by problems created by the cold war in which our enemy has the initiative and by the fact

---

[6] Top Secret; Eyes Only. General Magruder was the Department of Defense consultant to the Office of Policy Coordination.

that our Government as a whole has not adapted itself to the flexibility of action demanded in the circumstances. The Departments of State and Defense in the face of swift and uninhibited manuevers by the Kremlin are still bound by formal traditions of political action and conventional war planning as if peace and war were absolute conditions. CIA alone has been conceived and patterned to exercise relative freedom of action in a world situation which is more akin to war than peace.

2. Nationally we are not mobilized to face the kind of challenge forced upon us by the Kremlin. That challenge obviously cannot be met by the CIA alone, or by the totality of our so-called psychological resources. The Soviets have enlarged the cold war by the coordinated employment actively or potentially of all their resources, orthodox as well as unorthodox.

3. The issues raised by the DCI are not administrative or jurisdictional. They can be understood only in light of the inflexibility of our governmental organization and concepts in facing urgent and unusual requirements. While the orthodox departments think and plan too largely in terms of a D–Day that no man can predict, we deprive ourselves of full resources in fighting a cold war which might be decisive. While our psychological and covert agencies remain a "thin red line of heroes", there is no authoritative agency geared to ensure them mutual and continuous support from orthodox national forces.

4. The National Security Council cannot serve as this agency. Nor can it solve the problems of CIA by any broad statements of principle or detailed delineation of functions. The Council can, however, urge expedition in the activation of the required agency and ensure its unquestioned authority to solve the major issues raised by the DCI, as well as other varied problems yet to be created by the cold war

5. I refer to the Psychological Strategy Board. When activated this organization, within the terms of the Presidential Directive of 4 April 1951,[7] can resolve most of the difficulties facing the DCI through its authority to:

(a) Consider on the national level major covert projects coordinated with all other psychological operations.
(b) Give authoritative decision with respect to the necessity and propriety of CIA undertaking major projects requiring resources balanced as between cold war demands and future war plans.
(c) Provide coordination and guidance which will ensure that covert operations at all times are contributory to the attainment of national objectives.
(d) Promulgate programs which will include provisions for such supplementary support as may be required from other departments and agencies, including manpower, money and general logistics.

---

[7] See Document 60.

6. In view of the foregoing considerations, the following comments are pertinent to the *Conclusions and Recommendations* in paragraph 16 of the basic paper, by sub-paragraphs as numbered therein:

Sub-paragraph a and b. It is useless to belabor the question as to whether or not CIA should continue to be the agency primarily responsible for conducting "covert" operations. This matter has long been debated with the same conclusion. The answer should be affirmative for two reasons: one, there is no other agency of government which can as logically be assigned the responsibility; two, the cold war is on, and the ground lost by any major reorganization at this time would be hazardous. The reasonable concern of the DCI regarding guidance he requires in the stepped-up covert operations can be dispelled by the coordination and guidance forthcoming from the Psychological Strategy Board which should be expected to make logical distribution of responsibilities in the conduct of cold war operations.

If this statement of the scope and authority of the Psychological Strategy Board should be in question, the National Security Council should recommend in unequivocal terms to the President an interpretation of his Directive which would establish the validity of the concept.

Sub-paragraph c(1). Provisions for joint planning with the armed forces for covert operations in war time exist in the established procedures for the preparation of covert annexes to joint war plans through the mechanism of the Joint Subsidiary Plans Division of the Joint Chiefs of Staff in Washington and the Commander's Staff in theaters of operations. Unusual adjustments should be provided in PSB programs.

Sub-paragraph c(2). Guidance in the allocation of available resources of CIA for covert operations as between cold war missions and preparations for overt war should be made in the programs promulgated by the PSB.

Sub-paragraph c(3). The PSB should have the authority and responsibility for determining the relative weight to be ascribed to political and military considerations involved in covert operations, and be the arbiter as to whether the operations should or should not be undertaken by CIA.

Sub-paragraph c(4). The administrative and logistical provisions of projects or programs promulgated to operational agencies, including CIA, by the PSB should provide authoritatively for the necessary supplementary support, if required, in types and quantities of personnel, and other administrative and logistical assistance.

Sub-paragraph d. The guidance herein requested is a normal responsibility of the PSB as prescribed in the President's Directive.

7. It is probably true that the major departments have looked to CIA for accomplishments wholly beyond its capabilities, particularly in available manpower. Furthermore, the same departments, when requested by CIA for assistance in supporting its overload, have been loathe to depart from administrative rigidity and war mobilization objectives in order to aid CIA. The recruitment of types of Americans with talents required by the varied operations of CIA is rendered almost impossible by favorable employment conditions in civil life and the absorption of such types into the armed forces. It is literally impossible for CIA to expand operations unduly unless the armed forces make available manpower in keeping with the tasks imposed. Decision must be made as to whether the manpower demands for war mobilization or cold war operations are to have precedence in a rational division of scarce categories of personnel. If it be assumed that the cold war can be won, then it is rational to divert manpower for psychological operations at a relatively minor charge against orthodox mobilization plans and routine administrative conveniences.

8. Reconsideration should be given to the provision of NSC 10/2 which requires that covert operations be "so planned and executed that any U.S. Government responsibility for them is not evident to unauthorized persons and that if uncovered the U.S. Government can plausibly disclaim any responsibility for them." It is obvious that the international atmosphere and conditions requiring this highly restrictive security provision no longer exist. Publicly announced national policy asserts the determination of the Government to fight Soviet aggression wherever it appears and implicitly by any means necessary. If for no other reason, the magnitude and variety of cold war effort renders the security formula invalid except for *genuinely covert operations*. Certainly it is not a secret to the enemy that the U.S. Government supports unconventional warfare. We should not accept the handicaps of unduly rigid security measures respecting para-military types of operations beyond those required to obscure our strategy and tactics. The acceptance of this reasoning is important in that it facilitates all administrative and logistical steps in combining overt and covert national resources in pursuing the cold war.

A clear differentiation can be made between two categories of "covert" operations to the first of which the security formula in NSC 10/2 should remain applicable, and to the second of which the formula should be modified. These two categories are:

(a) Covert operations of a political, economic and psychological character, which by their nature remain truly covert and which are employed abroad to influence developments favorable to the United States, and

(b) Operations which, while initially covert, are by their nature designed to create psychical manifestations which cease to be covert, such as, sabotage, support of underground and guerilla movements and para-military activities.

John Magruder[8]

Annex 2

Memorandum From the Chief of the Joint Subsidiary Plans Division, Joint Chiefs of Staff (Stevens) to the Joint Chiefs of Staff Representative on the Senior Staff of the National Security Council (Wooldridge)[9]

SPDM–208–51   Washington, May 17, 1951.

SUBJECT

Scope and Pace of Covert Operations

1. The action to be taken by the National Security Council on the Central Intelligence Agency memorandum of 8 May 1951, "Scope and Pace of Covert Operations," hinges on the acceptance or rejection of two propositions which are implied but not discussed in that memorandum. They are:

a. Although global overt war may occur at any time, the possibility that the cold war will continue is sufficiently great to warrant a strong effort in the planning and conduct of the cold war as well as of a hot war.

b. There is a possibility that by the planned use of all our capabilities, including covert ones, we can win the cold war, thereby averting global hot war.

2. Acceptance of these two propositions means that we play it both ways, for either war or a continuation of the uneasy "peace," without putting all our eggs in either basket. Although there may be differences of opinion as regards the degree of probability of both of the two above propositions, there seems to be general agreement as to their validity as stated, and consequently as to the desirability of our playing it both ways. This is the only course which seems consistent with our intelligence and the national thinking behind the great bulk of National Security Council papers in recent years.

3. As a result of past experiences, we are better organized to deal with overt war than with the unprecedented situation of a protracted

---

[8] Printed from a copy that bears this typed signature.

[9] Top Secret; Eyes Only. Two copies were sent to Magruder. Admiral Stevens was the Joint Chiefs of Staff consultant to OPC.

all out cold war. The President's directive of April 4, 1951, establishing the new Psychological Strategy Board but requiring maximum use of existing agencies, seems to go far towards providing the necessary mechanism. PSB can be expected to function not only as a coordinating agency for guidance, but, when it is unable to reach decisions and provide guidance itself in the light of approved policy, to formulate and recommend in the premises to the National Security Council and the President.

4. A decision to play it for both hot war and a continuation of the cold war gives a definite answer to the basic question raised by the CIA memorandum. CIA should increase the scope and pace of its capabilities and action directed towards the winning of the cold war, but should not jeopardize its effectiveness for hot war, including planning and preparations therefor by so doing. When detailed and specific conflicts in priorities arise, they can and should be settled through the Psychological Strategy Board. CIA is also required to insure that its intelligence activities will not suffer by such an increase in scope and pace, and its internal arrangements should take this into consideration.

5. The extent to which the United States will support and follow up on counter-revolution in the slave states, how much of that potential to develop, when to release it, and how much to hold in reserve, cannot be answered without the development of more concrete plans and proposals to this end. Such plans and proposals are entirely suitable for presentation by CIA to the PSB, which, after study, criticism and coordination, should obtain final decision from the President via the National Security Council. The potential forces for counter-revolution may, with sufficient time and skill in their development, be capable of eventually providing a final solution for the cold war, or, in case hot war intervenes, of raising covert operations from a series of minor conspiracies to the stature of a weapon on a par with land, sea and air forces.

6. [1 paragraph (9 lines) not declassified]

7. Consistent with the foregoing, it is suggested that the following action be proposed to the National Security Council on the specific recommendations of the CIA memorandum:

a. As a result of a comprehensive review of the covert operations situation, the CIA should increase the scope and pace of its capabilities and action directed towards the winning of the cold war, but should not by so doing jeopardize its effectiveness for hot war.

b. Covert operational responsibility should remain as now directed. Although all organizational problems are not completely solved, there is no reason to believe that they cannot be solved within the existing framework. Moreover, the urgencies of the situation will not permit major structural alterations, which would in themselves create new problems. Such clarifications of present broad responsibilities as may be essential should be handled through the PSB.

c. (1) Directives are in existence which appear to make basic adequate provisions for joint planning with the Armed Forces for covert activities and operations in support of wartime military operations. The mechanism of the PSB should be employed for any clarifications which may be necessary.

(2) Specific guidance for dealing with the military in fields where the same covert apparatus is being developed for both cold and hot war purposes should be obtained from the PSB.

(3) The PSB should insure that the foreign policy and political considerations which are involved in covert operations are brought to bear on determinations of politico-military significance. To accomplish this, the PSB has recourse up to the NSC and the President, and down to operating agencies either directly or through the consultant mechanisms that are established by NSC 10/2 and NSC 59/1.

(4) Within the limits of security, all government agencies should be directed to provide appropriate personnel, administrative, and logistic support for the covert effort. The detailed nature of this support should be coordinated through the PSB.

d. The Psychological Strategy Board should be directed to provide or obtain guidance as necessary to the covert effort.

L. C. Stevens[10]
Rear Admiral, USN

---

[10] Printed from a copy that bears this typed signature.

---

71.   Memorandum of a Meeting of the Senior Staff of the National Security Council[1]

Washington, May 28, 1951.

SUBJECT

General Smith's memorandum to the NSC of May 8 on the *"Scope and Pace of Covert Operations"*[2]

---

[1] Source: National Archives, RG 59, INR Historical Files: Lot 58 D 776, OPC. Top Secret. Printed from an unsigned carbon copy. The first page bears the initials "PA", indicating that this copy was intended for W. Park Armstrong, Jr. The drafting officer and those present at the meeting have not been identified.

[2] Attachment to Document 68.

Action

It was agreed that CIA–OPC would prepare a written and oral presentation of two projects[3]—Guerrillas in China, and Resistance in Eastern Europe—by which the Senior Staff could become more familiar with the details and therefore the problems involved in such projects, including such issues as:

a. Personnel and logistic support in short supply and possibly in conflict with other projects;
b. Possible conflicts on objectives of the project, particularly as between the cold war and preparation for hot war;
c. Alternative methods such as covert, semi-covert, and paramilitary;
d. Potentialities, including an analysis of the political and military risks involved in the fulfillment of the project.

Discussion

The discussion touched on the following points:

1. *Personnel.* OPC is experiencing serious difficulty in obtaining the necessary personnel to carry out its operations, and notably headquarters personnel, most of whom would come from the Military Establishment—either regular officers or special call-up of reserves. One estimate of their needs called for 50 officers per year, of special qualifications in various areas and military specialties.

2. *Supplies and Stock Piling.* There was no disagreement in the responsibility of CIA to budget for its own supplies, but to procure them through the facilities of the Military.

3. *Funds.* CIA pointed out that to date funds were not a limitation upon their effectiveness in carrying out planned projects, but rather the limitations were in personnel and logistics.

4. *Priorities.* It was pointed out that there were three types of projects, the allocation of resources to which represented the basic priority difficulty, namely: (a) political and psychological targets, purely for the cold war; (b) guerrilla operations which could be activated now or in the event of hot war; and (c) development of resistance in preparation for hot war. In this connection it was pointed out that any cold-war activity would be helpful toward the preparation for hot war, but at the same time preoccupation with (b) and (c) above could not help but hurt the effective prosecution of (a).

---

[3] Frank G. Wisner forwarded these studies to the NSC senior staff under cover of a memorandum dated June 8. (Central Intelligence Agency, Office of the Deputy Director for Operations, Job 79–01228A, Box 6)

5. *Potentialities and Risks.* Considerable concern was felt that the fulfillment of many of the projects under way might materially increase the risk of general war. Obviously the more successful we are in reaching our cold-war objectives of containment through strengthening of free-world forces, the more we are risking a general war. On the other hand the OPC projects may inherently be more provocative than the general factors of success because they are designed positively to weaken the potential enemy, and in some cases to cause clashes.

6. *Psychological Strategy Board.* It was generally felt that the PSB, when it becomes operative, will be in a position to coordinate the direction given to OPC projects. Two important matters in this connection were pointed out:

a. The PSB charter may have to be expanded if it is to be effective in insuring *the support* as distinct from guidance for OPC from the various agencies.
b. Initiative in presenting the issues involved in projects must rest heavily upon CIA, which should identify the various issues and conflicting priorities—whether of matériel or objectives—for presentation to the PSB and, where appropriate, the NSC.

7. *Scope and Organization.* There was no disagreement that CIA must continue to increase the scope of its activities to fulfill the enlarged mission given to it. It was apparent that with possibly minor exceptions CIA should continue to have full responsibility for all of this type of work.

In this connection it was pointed out that General Smith's memorandum was indicative of the growth and success of the OPC operations because it raised such problems as conflicting priorities and the effects of successful operations which heretofore have not been necessary to raise since all of the effort was going into a build-up. At the same time the memorandum indicated the need for CIA to put forward full analysis of the issues involved in projects in which some decision is necessary and the need for the development of such a facility as PSB for the resolution of such problems. These problems could not any longer be decided on a blanket and over-all basis but would require the specific analysis of the issues in individual projects.

72.   Terms of Reference for the Economic Intelligence Committee[1]

IAC D–22/1 (Revised)   Washington, May 29, 1951.

1. The Director of Central Intelligence with the concurrence of the members of the IAC has established an Economic Intelligence Committee, on which shall sit designated representatives of those agencies charged with primary responsibility for foreign national security intelligence, i.e., the Departments of the Army, Navy, Air Force, State, the Joint Chiefs of Staff, and the Central Intelligence Agency. Any other agency whose interest or competence may be relevant to the particular problem under examination may be invited also to sit with the Economic Intelligence Committee.

2. The representative from the Central Intelligence Agency shall serve as Chairman of the Economic Intelligence Committee, and he shall supply the secretariat.

3. The Economic Intelligence Committee shall:

a. Arrange concerted economic intelligence support, on selected major issues, for studies of interagency interest requested by the Intelligence Advisory Committee, the Joint Chiefs of Staff, etc.

b. Arrange for the mobilization of the data and analysis available, relevant to appropriate operating problems of any member agency requesting assistance, or of any other agency dealing with economic security problems, which may request assistance.

c. Examine continuing programs of fundamental economic research relating to the national security throughout the United States Government and recommend to the IAC for appropriate action allocation of responsibility for specific fields of inquiry where such allocation appears appropriate.

d. Review and report to the IAC from time to time, on the pertinence, extent, and quality of the data and analyses available, bearing on the issues analyzed.

e. Recommend to the IAC for appropriate action priorities and allocation of responsibilities for the collection and analysis to fill specific gaps in the economic intelligence needed for national security.

f. Maintain a continuing review of the foreign economic intelligence activities of the United States Government as they relate to the national security.

g. Make such special reviews of economic intelligence distribution and processing procedures as may appear useful, and make rec-

---

[1] Source: Central Intelligence Agency, Executive Registry, Job 85–500362R, Box 3, Folder 10. Secret. The document was forwarded, presumably to members of the Intelligence Advisory Committee (there is no list of addressees), under cover of a memorandum from James Q. Reber, Secretary, Intelligence Advisory Committee. (Ibid.)

ommendations for improvement to the Intelligence Advisory Committee, which shall have responsibility for instituting such action as it may judge appropriate.

h. Prepare coordinated reports which present the best available foreign economic intelligence.

4. In carrying out its responsibilities, the Economic Intelligence Committee may set up such subcommittees and working parties as may be judged necessary.

5. When any member agency is unable to accept a recommendation of the Committee, the matter may be referred to the Intelligence Advisory Committee. All agencies directly concerned shall be asked to sit with the Intelligence Advisory Committee for the consideration of such questions.

73.   Memorandum From the Deputy Director of Central Intelligence (Jackson) to the Executive Secretary of the National Security Council (Lay)[1]

Washington, May 31, 1951.

SUBJECT

Appraisal of Foreign Economic Intelligence Requirements, Facilities and Arrangements Related to the National Security

1. In accordance with the instructions of the National Security Council in NSC Action 282,[2] the Central Intelligence Agency has conducted a study of foreign economic intelligence requirements relating to the national security and of the facilities and arrangements currently employed for meeting those requirements.

2. As the study has progressed, both the requirements and the facilities and arrangements have been changing in response to changes

---

[1] Source: Truman Library, Papers of Harry S. Truman, President's Secretary's Files. Secret. Jackson's report was circulated to NSC members under cover of a June 1 memorandum from Lay.

[2] NSC Action No. 282, February 7, 1950, requested a study of economic intelligence and existing facilities and arrangements, and a plan for satisfying national needs for such intelligence through coordinated inter-agency effort. (National Archives, RG 273, NSC Records of Action, Box 1)

in the international situation and in the organization of various agencies of the Government.

3. It is believed that the facilities and arrangements now in effect or contemplated by the various agencies will go far toward providing the basis for the adequate coverage of economic intelligence relating to the national security whose lack prompted NSC Action 282. The Central Intelligence Agency itself is engaged in strengthening its work in economic intelligence production as a service of common concern. The Office of Research and Reports has been established to coordinate the economic intelligence activities of other agencies and to produce such economic intelligence as it not otherwise allocated.

4. For reasons explained in Tab A,[3] it is believed that it is neither practicable nor desirable to recommend at this time a formal allocation by the National Security Council of responsibility for economic intelligence production among the various agencies.

5. What is immediately needed is machinery to insure regular procedures whereby (1) the full economic knowledge and technical talent available in the Government can be brought to bear on specific issues involving the national security, and (2) important gaps in the collective economic knowledge of the Government can be identified on a continuing basis and responsibility for filling them be allocated as they are disclosed.

6. To meet this need, the Director of Central Intelligence proposes to establish an Economic Intelligence Committee. This proposal and the terms of reference of the Committee[4] described in Tab A (tabbed in red) have the concurrence of the members of the Intelligence Advisory Committee. To clarify the role of the Central Intelligence Agency in the coordination and production of economic intelligence, it is recommended that the National Security Council issue the attached proposed NSCID (Tab B[5]—also tabbed in red). This proposed NSCID has also received the concurrence of the Intelligence Advisory Committee. It would be desirable to invite the Economic Cooperation Administration and the Department of Commerce to sit with the National Security Council when this document is being considered. Upon the approval of the proposed NSCID, the Director of Central Intelligence will establish the Economic Intelligence Committee.

---

[3] Memorandum to the Intelligence Advisory Committee from the Director of Central Intelligence entitled "Proposed Economic Intelligence Committee," undated, not printed.

[4] Document 72.

[5] Not printed. The draft NSCID is identical to NSCID No. 15, June 13, corrected on June 22, Document 254.

7. It is further recommended that the National Security Council call to the attention of the relevant agencies of the Government the urgency of a collaborative effort to exploit the intelligence resources of the Government for security purposes. A draft of a proposed communication from the National Security Council asking that high priority be given to requests for cooperation from the Economic Intelligence Committee is attached (Tab C).[6]

8. The Director of Central Intelligence will keep under continuing review the arrangements of the United States Government for the production of economic intelligence and will make further recommendations concerning specific allocations of responsibility should this appear desirable at any time in the future.

William H. Jackson[7]

---

[6] Not printed.

[7] Printed from a copy that indicates Jackson signed the original.

---

74.   Department of State Press Release[1]

No. 532   Washington, June 20, 1951.

In answer to questions as to the relationship between the Psychological Strategy Board, announced today by the President,[2] and the Interdepartmental Committee which has been working in this field under the chairmanship of Mr. Edward W. Barrett, Assistant Secretary of State for Public Affairs, the following statement was issued by Under Secretary of State James E. Webb:

"By agreement with my two colleagues on the Psychological Strategy Board, I can state it is now planned that the Interdepartmental Committee which has been serving under the chairmanship of the Assistant Secretary of State for Public Affairs will continue in existence with responsibility for coordinating the execution of United States foreign information programs under the name 'Psychological Operations

---

[1] Source: National Archives, RG 59, S/S–NSC Files: Lot 63 D 351, NSC 59/1, Box 55. No classification marking.

[2] The President approved the Psychological Strategy Board on April 4; see Document 60. This press release made the President's directive available to the public.

Coordinating Committee.' This Committee, which has been serving in this field for the past year, includes representatives from the Department of Defense, the Joint Chiefs of Staff, the Central Intelligence Agency, the Economic Cooperation Administration, and the Department of State.[3]

"Other activities in the Department of State will continue as presently organized under the broad guidance of the new Psychological Strategy Board announced by the President."

---

[3] Under Secretary of State Webb wrote Director of Central Intelligence Smith on May 2 informing him that this change was taking place, and asking that a CIA officer be made available to serve with the Psychological Operations Coordinating Committee. Smith replied in the affirmative in an undated letter. (Both in Central Intelligence Agency, History Staff, Job 83–00036R, Box 5)

---

75.   Memorandum From Robert P. Joyce of the Policy Planning Staff to the Director of the Policy Planning Staff (Nitze)[1]

Washington, June 21, 1951.

SUBJECT

The Director of Central Intelligence on the Scope and Pace of CIA Activities with Particular Reference to Para-Military Operations and Preparations for Operations

General Walter B. Smith met this morning with the ad hoc committee of the Senior Staff of the NSC to set forth verbally his ideas on the above-mentioned subject. The representatives of the Departments of State, Defense and the JCS who act as consultants to OPC of CIA were also present.[2]

General Smith started by querying whether it was desirable for CIA to operate as a sort of "covert War Department" for the conduct of large-scale guerrilla operations. He added that para-military, large-scale guerrilla operations might go on for a period of years in this pres-

---

[1] Source: Department of State, INR Historical Files, NSC 10 Series, 1951. Top Secret. Drafted by Joyce.

[2] The consultants to the Office of Policy Coordination were Joyce (for the Department of State), Brigadier General John Magruder (for the Department of Defense) and Rear Admiral Leslie C. Stevens (for the Joint Chiefs of Staff).

ent era of the tepid war. He commented that no commander should accept responsibility for important missions unless he is assured of receiving proper support. He went on to speak of CIA's present support of guerrilla warfare on the China Mainland. He stated that it was possible that these operations might develop into a very large military effort involving perhaps two or three hundred thousand men who would have to be equipped and supplied. If this situation did in fact develop it would naturally involve a large production program for specialized light weapons and would mean in addition, a large-scale training, shipping and air-supply and re-supply program which would amount to a military operation. In other words an "operation of war" on a grand scale.

General Smith doubted that the CIA was the proper agency to undertake such a program. He stated that our Military Establishment would undoubtedly feel uncomfortable with such an operation left to a civilian agency. He added that although the Secretary of Defense and the top echelon of the three services might agree with such an operation to be undertaken by the CIA, nevertheless the working levels in the armed services would not be prepared to go along and the end result would be that necessary logistic and other support would not be forthcoming in a degree which would permit the CIA successfully to fulfill its responsibilities. General Smith cited several instances whereby support for CIA in terms of personnel had been agreed to by the Secretary of Defense but that long delays and whittling down by the lower echelons of the three services had resulted in his obtaining only a minimum of support. For example, the Secretary of Defense had agreed that CIA should receive from 400 to 500 officers but that after a period of four months only 40 officers had been supplied to the CIA. He emphasized that the delays in the staff echelons and the reluctance to make available qualified personnel had made it virtually impossible for the Director of Central Intelligence to meet the requirements which had been laid upon him by the JCS itself. General Smith then spoke of the responsibility and authority vested in a theatre commander to accomplish certain missions and added that he did not see how the Director of Central Intelligence or his representatives could ever obtain in peacetime like authority to accomplish missions of great magnitude which had been laid upon the CIA. He then stated that it might be possible for high ranking and highly competent generals loaned to CIA to obtain such authority but there were very few of these and they were most difficult to obtain from the Military Establishment. In other words, available talent in this category was limited.

General Smith went on to say that he, acting on his own responsibility, could do and did do certain things in the field of special operations. As an illustration he mentioned activities designed to impede the supply of aviation gasoline to the Chinese communists which was presently entering the Portuguese port of Macao. He said that an operation of this kind would only require a few men and his organization could handle it. On the other hand, however, a large para-military support program for anti-communist guerrillas in China is entirely another thing and perhaps beyond the capabilities of the CIA given present dispositions and attitudes within the working levels of the Military Establishment.

General Smith went on to say that the major mission of the CIA is intelligence and that the operations tail are now starting to wag the intelligence dog and that CIA was already spread very thin. He added that the obtaining of necessary funds was not presently a problem as the honeymoon with Congress was still going on. He added, however, that these honeymoons never lasted forever and that sooner or later he would probably have to justify to the Congress programs and large projects involving the expenditure of several hundred million dollars.

General Smith stated that as the Director of Central Intelligence it would afford him great relief if he could wrap up in one package this whole problem of guerrilla warfare and present it to the military as a military and not a CIA responsibility. He felt that he must do this for the reasons which he had already set forth and unless there should be enthusiastic, timely and real support from the Military Establishment which was not presently forthcoming and which he did not anticipate. He went on to point out that the military were apparently placing great hopes in the so-called retardation project. He feared that these D–Day hopes of what could be done were unrealistic and therefore dangerous. He spoke of the large preparations which would be required and stated that it had been his experience that by the time an adequate force could be equipped and trained it would undoubtedly be penetrated. He mentioned the difficulties faced by the French resistance due to enemy penetration and stated that in the present case the dangers of communist-penetration were much greater and that whole groups which had been painfully prepared might be gobbled up almost instantly when and if D–Day came. He emphasized that there was a high degree of wishful thinking and unreality within the Military Establishment as to what could be accomplished by special operations in wartime and that this was a dangerous situation to be allowed to develop further. He stated that the conventional army officer did not understand the enormous difficulties involved due to an understandable lack of knowledge of just what guerrilla warfare behind the enemy lines involved. He added that there should be a careful auditing of the requirements the military were placing upon the CIA in this field with a view to there being a complete understanding as to the probable capabilities of the CIA. This would avoid misunderstandings as well as erroneous military planning based on false assumptions.

General Smith stated that, as a minimum, there should be joint CIA-military participation in planning and operations in order that the military should bear its responsibility for large-scale guerrilla operations. This would assure that the necessary support from the military for the CIA would be forthcoming. He stated that there might be set up within the JCS a joint staff where CIA and military officers could plan para-military operations. General Smith suggested that CIA specialized personnel might assume responsibility for first contacts with underground leaders and guerrilla commanders. The CIA might even assume the responsibility for providing modest supplies to guerrilla movements in order to see how their capabilities develop. If such guerrilla capabilities develop in a large way and turn into important military operations, then the CIA responsibility should cease and the military should take over and be charged with the responsibilities for supply, re-supply and other logistic support.

Admiral Stevens stated that there was already in progress joint planning as between the CIA and the representatives of the JCS and that he considered that this situation was working out well. He added that naturally there was a time lag in getting projects approved due to the fact that the JCS had a continually clogged agenda. He added that, in his opinion, the military generally speaking were trained and held responsible for formal military operations and that they were incapable of waging cold war. General Magruder agreed that there was insufficient flexibility in the formal Military Establishment or in the formal military mind successfully to carry on delicate covert operations where a great deal of flexibility and sophistication in political matters was called for.

It was generally agreed that a great deal of educational work was necessary before the military could realize the nature and potentialities of covert operations. It was suggested that perhaps the best way for the CIA to obtain the requisite support from the Military Establishment would be for General Marshall to issue orders to the effect that the CIA operation was a national effort of the greatest importance and that the heads of the military services should see to it down the line that it received what it needed to have in an expeditious manner as a matter closely related to the national security. There was discussion as to whether it might or might not be desirable for the President to issue the necessary instructions in order that CIA should receive unstinted and generous support.

Robert P. Joyce

**76.   Memorandum From the Acting Executive Secretary of the
National Security Council (Gleason) to the National Security
Council**[1]

Washington, June 27, 1951.

SUBJECT

Scope and Pace of Covert Operations

REFERENCES

A. Memo for Special Committee of Senior NSC Staff from Executive Secretary,
same subject, dated May 14, 1951[2]
B. NSC 10 Series[3]

At the direction of the President, a Special Committee of the Senior
NSC Staff has been studying the scope and pace of covert operations as
outlined in the enclosed memorandum from the Director of Central Intelligence.[4] In this connection, the Special Committee has had the benefit of further elucidation of the problem by officials of the Central Intelligence Agency responsible for covert operations. The Director of Central
Intelligence has expressed to the Special Committee his serious concern
that covert operations of the scope and magnitude described in the enclosure are beyond the capabilities of CIA without greatly increased and
accelerated support from the Departments of State and Defense.[5]

On the basis of its study and consideration of the subject, the Special Committee of the Senior NSC Staff recommends that the National
Security Council take the following actions:

1. Approve in principle as a national responsibility the immediate expansion of the covert organization established in NSC 10/2, and
the intensification of covert operations designed in general order of
emphasis to:

a. Place the maximum strain on the Soviet structure of power, including the relationships between the USSR, its satellites, and Communist China; and when and where appropriate in the light of U.S.
and Soviet capabilities and the risk of war, contribute to the retraction
and reduction of Soviet power and influence to limits which no longer
constitute a threat to U.S. security.

---

[1] Source: Truman Library, Papers of Harry S. Truman, President's Secretary's Files,
Subject File. Top Secret; Eyes Only. A copy was sent to the Director of Central Intelligence.
A handwritten notation on the memorandum indicates that it was the President's copy.

[2] Document 68.

[3] See Document 42 and footnote 2 thereto.

[4] Not attached; presumably it was a copy of Smith's May 8 memorandum attached
to Document 68.

[5] See Document 75.

b. Strengthen the orientation toward the United States of the peoples and nations of the free world, and increase their capacity and will to resist Soviet domination.

c. Develop underground resistance and facilitate covert and guerrilla operations in strategic areas to the maximum practicable extent consistent with 1-a above, and ensure availability of these forces in the event of war.

2. Reaffirm the responsibility and authority of the Director of Central Intelligence for the conduct of covert operations in accordance with NSC 10/2 and subject to the general policy guidance prescribed therein, and further subject to the approval of the Psychological Strategy Board which shall be responsible for:

a. Determining the desirability and feasibility of programs and of individual major projects for covert operations formulated by or proposed to the Director of Central Intelligence.

b. Establishing the scope, pace, and timing of covert operations and the allocation of priorities among these operations.

c. Ensuring the provision of adequate personnel, funds, and logistical and other support to the Director of Central Intelligence by the Departments of State and Defense for carrying out any approved program of covert operations.

3. Request the Secretary of Defense to provide adequate means whereby the Director of Central Intelligence may be assured of the continuing advice and collaboration of the Joint Chiefs of Staff in the formulation of plans for paramilitary operations during the period of the cold war.

4. In view of the necessity for immediate decision prior to the coming into operation of the Psychological Strategy Board, authorize the conduct of expanded guerrilla activities in China, as outlined in the attached memorandum and pursuant to the appropriate provisions of NSC 48/56.[6]

It is requested that you indicate your action with respect to the above recommendations by completing and returning, *as a matter of priority*, the attached memorandum form.[7]

It is requested that special security precautions be taken in the handling of this material and that access be limited to individuals requiring the information contained herein in order to carry out their official duties.

S. Everett Gleason

---

[6] For NSC 48/5, "U.S. Objectives, Policies and Courses of Action in Asia," May 17, see *Foreign Relations*, 1951, vol. VI, pp. 33–63.

[7] The attached memorandum form, not printed, bears no indication of approval or disapproval by President Truman or the National Security Council.

77.   Letter From Director of Central Intelligence Smith to Secretary of Defense Marshall[1]

Washington, July 2, 1951.

Dear General Marshall:

I have carefully studied the proposed revision of NSCID–5 as prepared by the Joint Chiefs of Staff[2] and have compared it with the original directive which it is designed to replace.[3] The proposal of the Joint Chiefs of Staff appears to disregard the intent of Congress as expressed in the National Security Act of 1947 and as revealed in the record of Congressional hearings prior to the passage of the Act. During these hearings it was made clear that the purpose of Congress in enacting the law was to centralize control of clandestine activities abroad. The term, "services of common concern," as finally written into the law was used, among other subjects, to cover clandestine espionage operations.

The proposed revision seems also (see paragraph 1, sub-paragraph a of the draft) to disregard the fact that the responsibility of the Director of Central Intelligence is to the National Security Council and the President—a status which was reaffirmed recently in the President's handwritten comments on the Joint Chiefs of Staff document proposing revision of NSC 10/2, which also pertains to this Agency.[4] The special operations of this Agency are designed to support in every possible way the requirements of the Departments and Services which operate under the statutory members of the National Security Council but the channel of responsibility to the National Security Council remains clear.

From the practical point of view, it is unwise to have a number of different authorities conducting clandestine operations. When I assumed my present duties, I found that a number of Government Departments were operating their own "spy nets" abroad. One or two of these were voluntarily transferred to CIA control in accordance with the intent of law. Others remain in existence, and we cross trails from time to time; sometimes with ludicrous and occasionally with rather tragic results. On the whole, however, this multiplicity of control of a very sensitive type of operation is a thoroughly bad business. I believe it can be corrected in time by establishing a broader base of confidence and cooperation in CIA

---

[1] Source: Central Intelligence Agency, History Staff Job 83–01034R, Box 4, Folder 6. Top Secret.

[2] The JCS revision was not found.

[3] For NSCID No. 5, December 12, 1947, see *Foreign Relations*, 1945–1950, The Emergence of the Intelligence Establishment, Document 423.

[4] Not found.

operations and by improving those operations to the point where they meet the needs of the agencies CIA is designed to serve.

NSCID–5 as presently in effect, after stating in paragraph 1 that the Director of Central Intelligence shall conduct all organized Federal espionage operations outside the United States and its possessions for the collection of foreign intelligence information required to meet the needs of all Departments and Agencies concerned in connection with the national security, makes exception "for certain agreed activities by other Departments and Agencies." I am prepared at any time to discuss any such activities proposed by other Departments and Agencies and to endeavor to reach an agreement with respect to them. Furthermore, I am obligated under paragraph 4 of NSCID–5 to coordinate such agreed activities of "casual agents" with the organized covert activities.

I wish to make it clear that this Agency is entirely willing to place its personnel under the American theater commander in any theater of active military operations where American troops are engaged and is equally willing, and indeed anxious, to coordinate its activities with the Joint Chiefs of Staff. If it is necessary to formalize this attitude, a brief statement like that embodied in the recently approved revision of paragraph 4, NSC 10/2,[5] should be sufficient. Accordingly, I do not believe that the proposed revision merits consideration by the National Security Council. The present directive seems quite adequate.

Faithfully,

Bedell Smith[6]

---

[5] See footnote 2, Document 38.

[6] Printed from a copy that indicates Smith signed the original.

---

78. Minutes of a Meeting of the Psychological Strategy Board[1]

PSB M–1   Washington, July 2, 1951.

PRESENT

Lieut. General W. Bedell Smith, Director of Central Intelligence
Mr. Robert Lovett, Deputy Secretary of Defense

---

[1] Source: National Archives, RG 59, S/S–NSC Files: Lot 62 D 333, PSB Minutes. Secret. This was the first meeting of the PSB. It was held in the DCI's conference room.

Mr. Edward Barrett, for the Under Secretary of State
Mr. Gordon Gray, Director, Psychological Strategy Board
Mr. Allen Dulles, Central Intelligence Agency
Mr. James Q. Reber, Central Intelligence Agency
Mr. [*name not declassified*], Central Intelligence Agency

Functions of the Board and Staff

1. Initial discussion was based on the agenda proposed in the memorandum of 1 June 1951 from Mr. Dulles to the Director of Central Intelligence.[2] In view of Mr. Gray's appointment, discussion of the proposed interim procedure (Tab A of that memorandum) was not necessary. The proposed functions and organization of the Staff (Tab B) was passed over as it was considered a non-controversial paper. The basic difference of view brought out in General Magruder's and Mr. Sargeant's papers was discussed briefly but no decision or recommendation was made. It was agreed that Mr. Gray should have an opportunity to discuss the matter with various interested people before forming an opinion.

2. General Smith stated his view that the principal factor missing in our psychological set-up at the present time is a "master plan" similar to the plan of the Combined Chiefs of Staff in the last war when it was decided to concentrate first on Germany and then turn on Japan. He pointed out that everything else would logically flow from such a plan and that economic programs, covert missions, and VOA policies should be related to it.

3. General Smith felt that the PSB and its Staff should work on the preparation of this master plan and act as a high-level project review board to allocate missions to the various agencies and to survey the effectiveness of operations in progress.

Funds, Space, and Personnel

4. The Board agreed that Mr. Gray and his Staff should be physically located on "neutral ground" apart from any one of the participating agencies.

5. It was understood that Mr. Peel of CIA would assist Mr. Gray in working out with Mr. Finan of the Bureau of the Budget[3] and representatives of State and Defense the necessary arrangements regarding funds and office space for the Board and Staff. General Smith agreed to try to make certain slots available for the immediate hiring of some high-level consultants to be assigned to the PSB.

---

[2] A copy is in the Central Intelligence Agency, Executive Registry, Job 80–R01731R, Box 33, Folder 1089.

[3] William F. Finan, Assistant Director for Administrative Management, Bureau of the Budget.

Relations With Other Groups

6. The relation of the Board to the NSC was discussed briefly, and it was understood that the Board would occupy a position somewhat similar to that of the Senior Staff, reporting directly to the NSC. Coordination with the Joint Chiefs of Staff would be effected through their representative with the Board, Admiral Stevens.

7. The supporting role of the O/PC Consultants and Mr. Barrett's Psychological Operations Coordinating Board was mentioned and the possibility was raised of combining these two groups while preserving separate overt and covert staffs. It was agreed, however, that no change should be made at the present time inasmuch as both groups were operating satisfactorily.

Scope of "Psychological Operations"

8. The point was made that the scope of the Board's responsibility is very broad and covers every kind of activity in support of U.S. policies except overt shooting and overt economic warfare.

---

79.   **Memorandum From the Chairman of the Interdepartmental Committee on Internal Security (Whearty) to the National Security Council Representative on Internal Security (Coyne)[1]**

NSC 68/17   Washington, July 23, 1951.

SUBJECT

> ICIS Section of Internal Security Annex for Report on Status and Timing of Current U.S. Programs for National Security

In accordance with the memorandum for the Senior NSC Staff by the NSC Executive Secretary, dated July 16, 1951,[2] attached hereto is the ICIS Section of the Internal Security Annex for the report on this subject. It is noted that the Executive Secretary indicated that the initial drafts of the annexes should be available to the drafting team

---

[1] Source: National Archives, RG 273, Records of the National Security Council Representative on Internal Security, 1947–69, NSC 68 (Internal Security), Box 46. Top Secret.

[2] Not found.

not later than July 23, 1951. As you know, this report is to be prepared pursuant to the President's directive to the NSC with respect to the review of the NSC 68 programs.

Raymond P. Whearty

Attachment[3]

1. Utilizing the personnel and facilities of all Federal agencies concerned, the ICIS is developing a program designed to bring about the highest practicable state of internal security. The program includes the following major elements:

a. Protection of critical governmental, industrial, port and other installations and facilities.

b. Measures designed to afford preventive security against unconventional attack, including atomic, chemical, biological and radiological.

c. To establish more effective controls to prevent the entry into the United States of persons who are actually or potentially dangerous to the national security and the exit of those whose departure would constitute a security threat.

d. To strengthen the controls over the importation and exportation of materials, the entry or exit of which would endanger the national security.

e. Procedures designed to protect classified government information.

f. Procedures for federal advice to state and local authorities and private business in voluntarily restricting the dissemination within the United States of unclassified technological information, the release of which might endanger the national security.

g. Assurance that responsible federal agencies have made adequate plans and preparations for the administration of various internal security programs, the implementation of which is contingent upon a state of war or war-related emergency.

h. Coordinating the provisions of emergency legislation and regulations pertaining to internal security matters.

2. A summary of the progress made to date under items a. to h. above follows:

a. (1) A study, in two parts, covering industrial security, was submitted to the NSC which approved its recommendations. As a consequence thereof, an Industry Evaluation Board and a Facilities Protec-

---

[3] Secret.

tion Board have been established; the former under the Secretary of Commerce and the latter, while administered by the Department of Commerce, responsible to the ICIS. The functions of these boards are to evaluate industrial plant and related resources; to assign to the appropriate departments and agencies of government the responsibility for preparation and supervision of security programs; to establish overall protection policies; to insure the preparation of detailed plans by each agency in its area of responsibility; and to review and monitor the implementation of such plans.

(2) A plan for the protection of government buildings, prepared by the General Services Administration, is currently awaiting final ICIS approval.

(3) A study on port security submitted to the Treasury Department has resulted in the preparation of a detailed plan for augmenting Coast Guard activities in this respect. The plan has been approved and is currently being implemented.

b. Several studies have been prepared and approved covering possible preventive measures against unconventional attack. Some thirty-five (35) studies by various departments and agencies have been submitted to ICIS covering the vulnerability of their respective areas of responsibility. A study proposing that an overall intelligence evaluation be prepared by CIA, utilizing the IAC agencies, has been submitted to, and is under consideration by, the NSC. Such an evaluation is essential upon which to predicate the degree of implementation not only of protective measures against unconventional attack but also should prove invaluable in the consideration of defense measures against all forms of covert and overt attack.

c. (1) Comprehensive reports covering entry and exit safeguards have been prepared and approved by ICIS. Their provisions and recommendations for strengthening controls have been referred to and are being implemented by the responsible agencies such as the Immigration and Naturalization Service (Justice), Visa and Passport Divisions (State), Customs (Treasury).

(2) The "Wartime Regulations Covering Entry and Exit" have been completely revised and redrafted, and are currently being circulated by State Department to all interested departments and agencies for concurrence.

d. (1) A detailed study covering the means of clandestine introduction of unconventional attack media and other materials. Predicated upon its conclusions, recommendations have been made to the Bureau of Customs and other agencies for the augmentation of already existing machinery for detection and prevention of entry.

(2) The authority to control the export of strategic materials is vested in the Secretary of Commerce. The determination of what

materials are strategic or which for reasons of economics, etc., should not, in the interest of national security, be exported is not within the purview of ICIS.

(3) The control of export of unclassified, published technological information to the Soviet bloc has, at the request of the Secretary of Commerce, been actively studied and interim recommendations made. No final solution to this extremely complex problem has been devised. Special emphasis is currently being placed on finding a solution.

e. (1) Regulations establishing "Minimum Standards for the Handling and Transmission of Classified Government Information" have been submitted to, and approved by, the NSC and the President, contingent upon the resolution of the provisions of a single paragraph thereof by the Department of Justice and the Department of Defense.

(2) Regulations establishing "Minimum Standards for Security Clearance for Access to Classified Government Information" have been submitted to and approved by the NSC and the President who has directed their publication concurrently with, or immediately following, the publication of the regulations referred to in (1) above.

(3) Regulations prescribing security procedures to determine the eligibility of foreign visitors to have access to classified U.S. Government information have been submitted to the NSC and are currently under consideration by it.

f. A study was prepared by the ICIS which has led to the establishment of an agency in the Department of Commerce to provide advice and guidance in this field to state and local authorities and to private business. Appropriate liaison has been established in all departments and agencies concerned whereby recommendations are made as to the guidance to be given regarding the specific matters coming under their respective jurisdictions. Appropriate publicity has been given this project, and it is now functioning.

g. This is a general problem which is receiving continuing consideration. In applying the principle it is usually determined that specific measures fall under one of the categories listed in a. through f. above and progress thereunder has been discussed previously.

h. This also is a general problem of a continuing and varied nature. In addition to generating such regulations, for example, as shown in e. above, the ICIS reviews proposed regulations and legislation originating in various departments and agencies with a view to evaluating and recommending the resolution of differences pertaining to the interests and requirements of other agencies. Since the various departments and agencies of the executive branch have become more and more cognizant of the coordinative function of ICIS, the effectiveness of its efforts in this area of interest has improved.

3. There has been almost unqualified cooperation by the various departments and agencies in support of ICIS activities. However, many of the programs and projects advocated by the ICIS for implementation by these agencies have met with the obstacle of lack of funds. For example, the Department of Commerce has found it difficult to provide for the essential staff and administrative cost of the Industry Evaluation Board and the Facilities Protection Board. Agencies such as the Federal Communications Commission are finding it difficult to undertake even the planning for physical security of the communications industry. Once such plans are completed the cost of supervision and enforcement of protective measures will be an additional obstacle. As a further example, plans for removing subversives from critical plants and facilities must provide, not only for security checks of employees which is of itself an expensive procedure, but also for the equally important protection of the rights of individuals through hearings and appeals procedures. The latter will doubtless entail the establishment of regional appeals boards across the country, probably under the jurisdiction of the Department of Labor. That Department consequently must be provided the funds for their establishment and functioning. Plans are not yet crystalized to the degree that specific costs can be estimated but it is anticipated that impediments and difficulties of this nature will be encountered.

4. The program, as outlined, is considered adequate. Additional specific problems under the broad outline are constantly arising and are being incorporated thereunder for active consideration. The entire program is an immediate one, and the corrective actions determined to be necessary are being implemented on an urgent basis as soon as the requirement is established. Those measures which are earmarked for implementation only in the event of general hostilities nevertheless are envisaged as being equally urgent for determination as those which are required to be implemented currently.

5. Inasmuch as all of its functions are considered to be current and immediate, the target date for readiness is *now* and not in the future. The ICIS will continue to impart a sense of urgency to all of its deliberations and will endeavor to instill the same in the agencies charged with the responsibility of carrying out agreed upon internal security measures.

80.   Memorandum From the Joint Chiefs of Staff to Secretary of Defense Marshall[1]

Washington, July 27, 1951.

SUBJECT

A Project to Provide a More Adequate Basis for Planning for the Security of the United States

1. In response to your memorandum dated 8 June 1951,[2] the Joint Chiefs of Staff have considered the report of the Interdepartmental Committee on Internal Security (ICIS) on the above subject.[3] They have considered also a memorandum, dated 13 July 1951, by the Director of Central Intelligence[4] which was forwarded to the Joint Chiefs of Staff by your memorandum of 19 July 1951.[5]

2. The ICIS report considers Soviet capabilities, Soviet intentions, and U.S. plans for the internal security of the United States. It suggests the need for further coordination and integration of such matters. The draft directive proposed in the report, addressed to the Director of Central Intelligence as Chairman, Intelligence Advisory Committee (IAC), is intended to remedy these inadequacies by establishing a project to develop a comprehensive appraisal of Soviet capabilities to injure the continental United States. The draft directive contemplates further that key Defense Department personnel be assigned to the project full time for an estimated period of six months and examination by the IAC of certain aspects of United States military war plans.

3. In the opinion of the Joint Chiefs of Staff the project proposed in the ICIS report involves four distinct steps as follows:

a. An estimate of the capability of the USSR to launch a military attack on the continental United States.
Comment: This estimate should be prepared under the direction of the Director of Central Intelligence as Chairman of the IAC.
b. An estimate of the capability of the USSR to conduct sabotage and otherwise disrupt internal U.S. activities.

---

[1] Source: Central Intelligence Agency, Directorate of Intelligence, Job 80–R01440R, Box 3, Folder 10. Top Secret. The memorandum was sent to the members of the National Security Council at the request of the Secretary of Defense on July 30.

[2] Not found.

[3] Apparent reference to Document 79. A memorandum from DAH (not identified) to DCI Smith, July 23, which summarizes a June 1 draft of the ICIS report is attached but not printed.

[4] See the attachment below.

[5] Not found.

Comment: This estimate also should be prepared under the direction of the Director of Central Intelligence as Chairman of the IAC.[6]

c. An evaluation of our military capability to counter potential enemy capabilities as estimated in subparagraph 3 a above, and an estimate and report of the probable damage to the United States resulting from such attack.

Comment: This is a responsibility of the Joint Chiefs of Staff.

d. An evaluation of ways and means available to counter potential enemy capabilities as estimated in subparagraph 3 b above, and an estimate and report of the probable damage to the United States resulting from such enemy actions.

Comment: This should be accomplished under the direction of the ICIS.

4. Procedures now in effect, whereby members of the IAC provide information and advice to the Director of Central Intelligence, assure assistance in the preparation of estimates 3 a and 3 b above by those qualified in such matters. Accordingly, such intelligence as is required for the project is available through normal channels without the assignment of additional Department of Defense personnel on a full-time basis to CIA. In addition, the ICIS is so organized that portions of the project allocated to that agency will not entail assignment of additional full-time personnel.

5. In view of the above, it is believed that the enclosed draft directives provide a more satisfactory means of accomplishing the purposes of the project than the one proposed in the ICIS report. It is recommended, therefore, that the enclosed directives be issued by the National Security Council in lieu of the directive proposed by the ICIS.

For the Joint Chiefs of Staff:

Omar N. Bradley[7]
Chairman
Joint Chiefs of Staff

---

[6] A handwritten notation at the end of this paragraph reads: "Interdepartmental Int. Conf." Regarding the subsequent assignment of this estimate to the Interdepartmental Intelligence Conference, see footnote 4, Document 86.

[7] Printed from a copy that indicates Bradley signed the original.

Enclosure "A"[8]

PROPOSED NATIONAL SECURITY COUNCIL DIRECTIVE

APPRAISAL OF SOVIET CAPABILITIES AND PROBABLE COURSES OF ACTION FOR A SURPRISE ATTACK UPON THE CONTINENTAL UNITED STATES DURING 1951–52

1. Pursuant to authorization by the President, the Director of Central Intelligence, as Chairman of the Intelligence Advisory Committee (IAC), is hereby directed to develop, with the assistance and guidance of IAC agencies and the advice of other appropriate Government departments and agencies, comprehensive intelligence estimates concerning:

a. The capabilities of the USSR to launch military attacks against the continental United States, and

b. The capabilities of the USSR to injure or damage persons, property or morale within the United States by subversion and sabotage.

2. For the purpose of implementing this directive, the departments and agencies of the executive branch of the Government shall make available to the Director of Central Intelligence such intelligence information and advice as appropriate to the solution of the problem.

3. It is desired that these estimates be completed as soon as practicable and, upon completion, a report be forwarded to the National Security Council.

Enclosure "B"[9]

PROPOSED NATIONAL SECURITY COUNCIL DIRECTIVE

MEASURES FOR THE INTERNAL SECURITY OF THE UNITED STATES

1. Pursuant to authorization by the President, the Interdepartmental Committee on Internal Security (ICIS) is hereby directed to evaluate, with military advice and guidance from the Joint Chiefs of Staff, ways and means available other than those within the purview of the Joint Chiefs of Staff, to counter potential enemy capabilities to conduct sabotage and otherwise disrupt internal U.S. activities.

2. The Director of Central Intelligence, as Chairman of the Intelligence Advisory Committee (IAC), has been directed to furnish ICIS a comprehensive intelligence estimate of Soviet capabilities to injure or

---

[8] Top Secret.
[9] Top Secret.

damage persons, property, or morale, within the United States by subversion and sabotage. ICIS, within its normal functions, will devise measures to counter such Soviet capabilities.

3. It is desired that this evaluation be completed as soon as practicable after receipt of the intelligence estimate (paragraph 2 above) and that a report be forwarded to the National Security Council.

Attachment

Memorandum From Director of Central Intelligence Smith to the Executive Secretary of the National Security Council (Lay)[10]

Washington, July 13, 1951.

SUBJECT

A Project to Provide a More Adequate Basis for Planning for the Security of the United States

REFERENCE

Memorandum for the Director of Central Intelligence from the Executive Secretary, National Security Council, same subject, 5 June 1951[11]

1. There is no doubt of the great need for, and value of, the proposed project. The conclusions and recommendations of the Interdepartmental Committee on Internal Security are concurred in.

2. It should be noted, however, that the appraisal envisaged is of much broader scope than the usual National Intelligence Estimate. It involves the integration of intelligence on the USSR with various types of information on the United States. It is therefore essential that, as provided in Paragraph 2 of the proposed NSC Directive, all Government departments and agencies "shall make available to the Director of Central Intelligence such information in their possession as is necessary to the solution of the problem . . ." as well as "the full-time services, on a temporary loan basis, . . . of those individuals who are best qualified by experience and knowledge to assist in the project."

Walter B. Smith[12]

---

[10] Secret. All ellipses in the original.

[11] Not printed. Other memoranda are attached that relate to NSC discussion of the issue in June, including a memorandum from Lay to the National Security Council, June 5, which encloses a June 1 memorandum from Whearty to Coyne that transmits the June 1 draft ICIS report and a proposed National Security Council directive. The latter two are not attached, however, and none of these attachments is printed.

[12] Printed from a copy that indicates Smith signed the original.

81.   Memorandum From the Director of the Policy Planning Staff (Nitze) to the Under Secretary of State (Webb)[1]

Washington, August 3, 1951.

Before leaving on my vacation I want to set down my views in relation to developments concerning the Psychological Strategy Board.

1. The Presidential Directive of April 4, 1951,[2] is somewhat unclear in setting forth the scope of the Board's jurisdiction in that it

a. Refers to psychological objectives, strategy and operations without precisely delimiting the meaning of "psychological."

b. Covers by reference NSC 59/1[3] and 10/2[4] in the jurisdiction of the Board without saying specifically whether the inclusion is definitive or illustrative.

c. Vests the Board with power to "formulate policy" in respect to psychological activities without defining the relationship between such policy and the national foreign policy.

2. In the efforts to get the Psychological Board operating two general approaches to the question of the Board's purpose and jurisdiction have developed—

a. The first is generally advocated for by members of CIA active in the initial phases of the Board's work. It is that the Board has primary authority with regard to all matters of the conduct of foreign policy short of formal hostilities.

b. The second represents the viewpoint of the Department of State and has support from the military. It is that the Psychological Strategy Board should exercise—

(1) Primary authority in ensuring among all agencies concerned maximum effectiveness and unity of objective and effort in regard to activities set forth in NSC 59/1 and 10/2.

(2) Secondary authority to see that full account of psychological factors—that is, aspects having impact on the mind, will, and morale of foreign peoples—is taken in the planning and execution of other activities bearing on the field of foreign relations, including the planning of the national objectives themselves.

3. These two points of view have been made apparent in all critical stages of the efforts to establish the understandings and the organizational arrangements to get the Board's work under way. To clear

---

[1] Source: National Archives, RG 59, S/P Files: Lot 64 D 563, Psychological Warfare. Secret. Drafted by Charles Burton Marshall, member of the Policy Planning Staff.

[2] See Document 60.

[3] For NSC 59/1, see Document 2.

[4] Regarding NSC 10/2, see footnote 2, Document 42.

the matter up, the Director of the Board[5] sought to bring about an agreed definition of psychological operations as concerned in the Board's jurisdiction. This effort produced two drafts which typify the conflicting approaches:

a. The first representing the radically broad concept of the Board's scope is:

"Psychological operations," as used in the President's directive, is a cover name to describe those activities of the United States in peace and in war through which all elements of national power are systematically brought to bear on other nations for the attainment of U.S. foreign policy objectives.

b. The second, representing the more restricted view, is:

Psychological operations are interpreted within the terms of the Presidential Directive of 4 April 1951 to consist of activities designed to influence the attitudes, actions and capabilities of foreign peoples, so as to further U.S. national objectives.

The role of PSB is:

a. To formulate basic plans for the systematic employment of those psychological operations encompassed by NSC 59/1 and NSC 10/2, to coordinate their execution, and to evaluate their effect.

b. To ensure in the formulation and application of national political, economic and military policies, that the symbolic and psychological aspects thereof are adequately exploited.

In face of the prospect that the two definitions were irreconcilable, the Director decided to lay aside the effort to remedy the issue by definition and to concentrate instead on particular problems and the creation of a staff.

4. It is necessary and desirable, however, to clear up in the beginning the difference as to the Board's purpose and jurisdiction and to resolve the issue by adopting the narrower concept. This is based on the following considerations:

a. It would be counter to the interests of the Board and to the Government in general to have friction develop between the Board and other agencies concerned over conflicting assumptions about authority. The principle that good fences make good neighbors is just as important in Government as it is anywhere else.

b. Clarity of view as to purpose and function is desirable not only to avoid jurisdictional conflicts at the top level but also to develop harmonious collaboration in day-to-day relationships at all levels.

c. Clarification is necessary in order to clear the way for going ahead with planning the Board's work. In laying out the work it is necessary to know not only what the Board's and its Staff's problems will be but also to what relationship to the problems the Board and its Staff will have. Under the radically broad definition, any problem might be expounded by inference to cover the sum total of national policy. To

---

[5] Gordon Gray.

make particular problems manageable, it is necessary to relate them to some restriction in basic concept. It would prove vexatious to everyone concerned if the Board and its Staff were to commence their labors without some clear view as to goal and limits.

d. It is well to confine the Board to a commitment which it can fulfill and which will make it most useful to the Government rather than attempting to fulfill a vast responsibility all too likely to result in duplication, conflict, and frustration running counter to the Board's usefulness.

5. In the discussions of the organizational problem the Director and some of his immediate assistants have repeatedly stressed that a premium will be placed on staffing the organization with individuals from outside the Government service. This may be desirable in avoiding the draining away of talents needed in other agencies and in widening the sum of capabilities available to the Government. At the same time, the idea can be pushed too far. A unit composed preponderantly of individuals unfamiliar with the labyrinthine ways of the Government would all too likely find itself unable to make headway. It would find itself frustrated in trying to get its own work done. Others would find it getting in the way. It is better therefore that a balance be struck between new resources of imagination and old wisdom in the ways of the Government.

6. The following are recommended:

a. That the Under Secretary seek, at the next meeting of the Board, to bring about an agreement as to the underlying concept of the Board's direction and limits in harmony with the principles stated in the more restrictive view of the Board's role.[6]

b. As a matter of less urgency, that the Under Secretary give a caveat against the attitude which discounts the usefulness of individuals already in the Government and seeks a preponderance of individuals from outside the Government in staffing the Board.

Paul H. Nitze[7]

---

[6] The Psychological Strategy Board adopted a statement on September 25 that favored the more restrictive view of its role. It is printed in *Foreign Relations*, 1951, vol. I, pp. 178–180.

[7] Printed from a copy that bears this typed signature.

82.   Minutes of a Meeting of the Psychological Strategy Board[1]

PSB M–2   Washington, August 13, 1951, 2:30–4:30 p.m.

PRESENT

Members

> Lt. General W. Bedell Smith, Director of Central Intelligence, Acting Chairman
> Mr. James E. Webb, Under Secretary of State
> Mr. Robert Lovett, Deputy Secretary of Defense

Others

> Mr. Gordon Gray, Director, Psychological Strategy Board
> Col. Armand Hopkins, JCS Representative
> Major General John Magruder, Department of Defense
> Mr. Frank Wisner, Central Intelligence Agency
> Mr. Charles E. Johnson, Acting Executive Secretary, Psychological Strategy Board
> Mr. Robert G. Efteland, Secretary

Progress Report by the Director (PSB D–1)

1. In addition to his statement in *Progress Report by the Director* (PSB D–1),[2] Mr. Gray commented that efforts are being made to recruit individuals for permanent appointment to the staff of the Psychological Strategy Board (PSB). He noted that Task Panel "A" (PSB D–1/1)[3] was the outgrowth of a meeting at the White House in which Assistant Secretaries of State Rusk and Barrett had participated.

Procedure for Conduct of Board Business

2. The Board agreed that it would meet only when there are important problems to discuss. The Acting Chairman and the Director will schedule meetings on a rotation basis at any one of the three Agencies at the convenience of the Board. The members are free to bring their alternates as they deem desirable.

3. In the matter of briefing, Mr. Gray suggested that his staff brief the members' alternates a few days before meetings of the Board. The alternates would then brief the members in advance of Board meetings. General Smith and Mr. Lovett favored this procedure. Mr. Lovett urged that papers be held to a minimum for security reasons. Mr. Webb stated that he had not decided how to handle the briefing problem.

---

[1] Source: National Archives, RG 59, S/S–NSC Files: Lot 62 D 333, PSB Minutes. Top Secret. Drafted on August 14. The meeting was held in the Director's Office, Psychological Strategy Board Building.

[2] A copy is in the Central Intelligence Agency, Executive Registry Job 80–R01731R, Box 32, Folder 1060.

[3] A copy is ibid.

4. To prevent problems being placed before the Board for decision until the members have had a chance to study them, it was the consensus that the Director should determine whether a problem is within the competence of the Board and whether it is necessary for the PSB staff to present its views to the PSB.

List of Problems of Interest to the Board (PSB D–2)[4]

5. Mr. Gray, in presenting his views on *List of Problems for the Director and Staff in Order to Work Priority* (PSB D–2), called the Board's attention to paragraph 4 in which he states his concern that the Board should not assume too many problems without careful consideration. He said this document is an effort to translate NSC papers into action. It is necessary to convert NSC policies into specific objectives and formulate plans which will achieve these objectives. As the problems listed in Sections II–A, II–B and II–C on page 2 are solved, the remaining problems will become clearer. The staff intends to give top priority to the substantive problems I through II–C which fall generally into a category of psychological strategy planning not previously initiated. Section II–D will then be considered. Section II–E will be considered concurrently inasmuch as these problems are largely concerned with relationships. Mr. Gray explained that it is not necessary to reconcile differing definitions as to what psychological operations mean because the same work is necessary under either concept. Consequently, it was decided to list the problems facing the PSB to provide the Board with specific terms of reference which would enable it to get on with its work. Therefore, the list of problems (PSB D–2) illustrates the area of interest of the PSB and the Staff. At the same time it provides for Mr. Gray the basis for planning a functioning staff organization.

6. General Smith said that the list of problems appears to be monumental. He asked Mr. Gray how he expected to accomplish these projects and still attack current problems. Mr. Gray replied that the Staff intends to use ad hoc groups whenever necessary on new problems. General Smith said that in his opinion the PSB staff would require many reinforcements to accomplish the work outlined in PSB D–2. He believed that completion of the problems listed would require two years of effort by the PSB staff and that there was not that much time available. He said that the problems listed in Sections I–A (4), I–A (5), and I–A (7) are enough to keep the PSB staff busy for quite some time. In addition, as he looked over the list of problems, it appeared that many others were going to require work by the staff in the very near future. He noted, as an example, that the problem in Section II–K had not yet

---

[4] Not found.

been assigned a work priority. However, it is a problem which must be met right now.

7. Mr. Webb said that the Kremlin has a special group which devotes all of its efforts to maximizing the strength of the USSR and to fractionating and weakening that of the United States. He hoped that the members would conceive the function of the PSB as drawing together U.S. efforts in the same way as the Kremlin group does for Russia. Moreover, he believed the Board should discuss further many of the problems listed in PSB D–2 before the Staff completes its work and reaches a final position on the problems. He said surveys take time and that we should not overlook each Board member's ignorance of the work of other agencies. He looked upon the PSB as a central place for the members to meet, discuss problems and make policy. The PSB should be a central place where guidance would be available. It would give Mr. Webb the feeling that here is a group of knowledgable Government Officials who can meet our major problems in the psychological area.

8. Mr. Lovett said that this list is an encyclopedic approach and gives the Board something to shoot at. He suggested that the Board approve the document (PSB D–2) as an identification of problems which call for discrimination as to which should be undertaken first. He suggested that the Board undertake as a matter of urgency the problems listed in Section I–A (4), I–A (5) and I–A (7). This will enable the Board to find out what is being done by Government agencies, what general directives they are following and what they plan to do. Mr. Webb agreed with Mr. Lovett and said that if these three problems were worked out, the PSB would then know what the agencies in the U.S. Government are working on. It could bring together whatever additional resources are necessary to achieve our goals and could make the necessary plans for any gaps which might be found to exist. General Smith agreed with: a) the above, b) that the staff of the Board should undertake the necessary work in connection with these three points; and c) that the Board should consider at a later date the other problems listed in the document. Mr. Gray said that the list will naturally be subject to constant revision. He suggested that the staff, in addition to the study of Sections I–A (4), I–A (5) and I–A (7), be allowed to take up any urgent matter which the Board might direct.

Section II–D of PSB D–2

9. The Board discussed at length the problem stated in this section of the paper. It was the consensus of the Board that the Russians are planning some disruptive action to embarrass us. Possibly they will reaffirm their disarmament suggestions and intensify their peace drive. It will have the same old sugar coating and will attempt to show that the United States is preventing disarmament in the world. The Shvernik

letter possibly gives a guide to the Russian attitude. No doubt the Russians will say to small countries "if you don't go along with us and accept our position, you must bear the consequences." The Board agreed that the United States must take action to meet these Russian maneuvers both abroad and in the United States.

Section II–E of PSB D–2

10. Mr. Gray said that he planned to have a Special Assistant handle the relationships of PSB with congressmen and representatives of private agencies who are interested generally in psychological developments. He does not anticipate any problems in this connection. The main thing will be to keep others from doing things we don't want them to do rather than the need to encourage cooperation by outsiders. Mr. Webb asked Mr. Gray if he intended to use other executive agencies of the Government to talk to representatives of private groups. Mr. Gray said that he would use Government agencies but that it would be necessary to have someone available in PSB to talk with them so that they feel they are being given consideration. General Smith believed it would be desirable for Mr. Gray to have such an officer to deal with interested private agencies. Mr. Lovett said that the Department of Defense would handle most inquiries itself but that it would push off general inquiries to the PSB. It was the consensus of the Board that the procedure outlined by Mr. Lovett should be followed.

Organization, Functions, and Budget (PSB D–3)[5]

11. The Board's consideration was limited to page 5 of PSB document D–3. In explaining this estimate, Mr. Gray said that he expects that the staff will be increased somewhat to meet the problems the PSB must handle. However, he believed that any increase would be reasonable and in no case would the staff be increased to anywhere near double the size called for in the document. The Board agreed that the necessary funds would be provided from appropriate Agency budgets.

Other Business

12. Mr. Gray discussed two papers as examples of problems which contain psychological implications. He asked that the members caution their Agencies to make available to the PSB copies of paper of importance to the work of the Board and its Staff. The members agreed that they would instruct their agencies to cooperate in this matter.

13. General Smith discussed the question of preventing uncontrolled activity in the psychological field now that the PSB has been organized. He said that there is a need to develop an over-all psycholog-

---

[5] Not found.

ical strategy plan. Other Agencies and the Army, which is concerned only with the tactical military phase of operations, would then be able to carry out assigned missions. General Magruder stated that he would discuss the Army's role with Mr. Lovett (who had left the meeting) and that the Department of Defense would handle the matter internally. He said that the Services would deal with the Board through the JSPD which was established for this purpose. General Magruder said that two papers are being prepared concerning the Army's interpretation of its function and that copies will be submitted to the PSB. It was the consensus that an over-all psychological strategy plan should be developed so that all activity in the Government is in consonance with it.

---

83.   **Memorandum From the Joint Chiefs of Staff to Secretary of Defense Marshall[1]**

Washington, August 15, 1951.

SUBJECT

Scope and Pace of Covert Operations

1. In accordance with the request contained in your memorandum dated 29 June 1951,[2] the Joint Chiefs of Staff have studied the recommendations of the Special Committee of the Senior National Security Council Staff regarding the "Scope and Pace of Covert Operations", forwarded by a memorandum from the Executive Secretary of the National Security Council (NSC), dated 27 June 1951.[3]

2. The Joint Chiefs of Staff have prepared a Study, a copy of which is attached hereto.[4] The Conclusions to this Study are quoted below for ready reference:

"a. In the light of the world situation, the United States should, within its capabilities, bring to bear upon the USSR appropriate cold-war resources and weapons during peacetime with the objective of

---

[1] Source: Truman Library, President's Secretary's Files, Subject File. Top Secret; Eyes Only. Lay circulated the memorandum to the National Security Council on August 22. (Ibid.)

[2] Not found.

[3] Document 76.

[4] Not printed.

weakening the power and will of the Kremlin to wage either cold or hot war;

"b. It is possible that the present cold war may continue over a period of many years. However, the implementation of a well-planned United States program of covert operations (as defined in NSC 10/2)[5] against the Kremlin conceivably might shorten the period of the struggle, might also be decisive in winning the cold war, and thus might prevent the eventuation of overt war. These possibilities appear sufficient to justify the United States in undertaking a covert effort of great magnitude;

"c. In order to assure a well-planned United States program of covert operations against the Kremlin during peacetime:

"(1) The Psychological Strategy Board (PSB) should develop the strategic concept and national program, based upon national objectives, consistent with current military planning and within available economic means;

"(2) After approval by the National Security Council (NSC) of the concept and program, necessary operational plans, including costing and other appropriate estimates, should be prepared by the appropriate agencies under the direction of the PSB and subject to its review and approval;

"(3) In the event of any conflict of interests among the agencies directly concerned, the NSC should be the final arbiter in each case; and

"(4) All elements of the national program of covert operations should be reviewed by the NSC at least quarterly;

"d. Responsibility for the conduct of covert operations in wartime must be as directed in NSC 10/2. In this connection, it is axiomatic that all wartime operations in any military theater or area (specifically including covert) shall be under the direction of the military commander of the theater or area. On the other hand, responsibility for the conduct of covert operations in peacetime should rest in the Director of Central Intelligence (DCI);

"e. On the long-range basis, the Central Intelligence Agency (CIA) should procure and maintain its own personnel;

"f. On both long-range and short-range bases, the Department of Defense should support CIA peacetime covert operations by:

"(1) Providing for approved projects, appropriate equipment and services as practicable which either cannot or should not be obtained elsewhere; and

---

[5] NSC 10/2 is in *Foreign Relations*, 1945–1950, Emergence of the Intelligence Establishment, Document 292.

"(2) Assisting in training, as practicable, and in providing necessary training facilities (such as not to interfere with research and development installations and installations required to be maintained in a combat-ready status) particularly when cover is an inherent requirement for the training;

"g. Department of Defense support of CIA peacetime covert operations at an increased scope and pace will call for some expansion of the mobilization base and mobilization requirements. This expansion should, in general, be related to the increase in CIA covert operations;

"h. In view of the present restricted capability of CIA, such peacetime projects as can be justified by reason of their immediate urgency and of the national importance of the results reasonably to be expected therefrom, should be supported by the Department of Defense. On the short-term basis, this support in terms of military personnel will include a limited number of specially qualified active duty officers and men and certain retired and/or reserve officers not on active duty. Some of these reserve officers may, on the short-term basis, be called to active duty for assignment to CIA for a specific project. This must be subject, however, to an overriding priority for the Services whenever a Service specialty qualification is involved. In addition, assistance by the Department of Defense to CIA probably will be necessary with respect to the duty status and process of procurement of certain potential inductees and personnel with reserve commissions:

"i. The following procedures and restrictions must apply to the assignment of military personnel to CIA:

"(1) Arrangements for assignment of active duty officers and men will be made with the Services through the Joint Chiefs of Staff organization;

"(2) The need for personnel must be justified in each instance. Numbers will be limited to the minimum for performance of specific tasks in approved projects and programs;

"(3) As far as practicable, all details or assignments will be on a voluntary basis and under no circumstances will an individual be assigned to CIA against his will. All details will be temporary in nature and subject to Services practices of rotation;

"(4) No individuals in the Reserve Officers Training Corps (ROTC) or in other officer candidate groups will be made available to CIA; and

"(5) CIA must make every effort to assure to the military personnel assigned to it an equality of opportunity for advancement (in pay and allowances or rank, etc.) commensurate with that of their contemporaries serving on active duty with their parent Service; and, where applicable and feasible, to obtain for individuals concerned a remuneration consistent with that paid to personnel obtained from other sources and performing comparable duties;

"j. In order for the Department of Defense to support a CIA accelerated program the requirements for personnel, supply, and services should, except in extreme emergency, be forecast sufficiently in advance to enable the Services to include such requirements in their mobilization base and requirements. Personnel provided to CIA by the Services should be on a reimbursable basis so that they will not be charged against the authorized strength of the Services; and

"k. All matters concerning the support to be rendered CIA by the Department of Defense will be subject to the overriding reservation that such support either for a single project or for the total of all projects will not jeopardize seriously the capabilities of the Department of Defense to carry out its responsibilities. If the conflicting needs of the Department of Defense and the projects for covert operations impinge upon the question of the security of the United States, the question should be decided on a level no lower than the President."

3. The Joint Chiefs of Staff recommend that the recommendations in the memorandum, subject as above, dated 27 June 1951, from the Executive Secretary of the NSC, be approved, subject to:

a. Acceptance by the NSC of the military considerations, together with the reservations of the Joint Chiefs of Staff as set forth in paragraph 2 above, and

b. The revision of paragraphs 1 and 2 of the recommendations to read as indicated below (with appropriate renumbering of the succeeding paragraphs):

"1. Direct the Psychological Strategy Board (PSB) to submit at the earliest practicable date a strategic concept for a national program of covert operations directed against the Kremlin under cold war conditions designed in general order of emphasis to:

"a. Place the maximum strain on the Soviet structure of power, including the relationships between the USSR, its satellites, and Communist China; and when and where appropriate in the light of U.S. and Soviet capabilities and the risk of war, contribute to the retraction and reduction of Soviet power and influence to limits which no longer constitute a threat to U.S. security.

"b. Strengthen the orientation toward the United States of the peoples and nations of the free world, and increase their capacity and will to resist Soviet domination.

"c. Develop underground resistance and provide assistance to underground resistance movements and guerrillas in strategic areas to the maximum practicable extent consistent with 1–a above, and to provide the base upon which the military may expand these forces on a military basis in time of war within activated theatres of operations.

"2. As an interim measure, and subject to future NSC action on the report to be submitted by the PSB as directed in paragraph 1 above, approve in principle as a national responsibility the immediate expansion of the covert organization established in NSC 10/2, and the intensification of covert operations designed to accomplish the objectives set forth in the three preceding subparagraphs, in accordance with approved plans and projects."

For the Joint Chiefs of Staff:

Omar N. Bradley[6]
Chairman, Joint Chiefs of Staff

---

[6] Printed from a copy that indicates Bradley signed the original.

---

84.   Memorandum for President Truman of Discussion at the 100th Meeting of the National Security Council[1]

Washington, August 22, 1951.

[Omitted here is discussion of agenda items 1: The Situation in the Far East, 2: The Kaesong Negotiations, 3: Probable Soviet Actions at the San Francisco Conference on the Japanese Peace Treaty, 4: The Situation in Iran, and 5: Relations between India and Pakistan.]

6. *NSC 26/2* (Progress Report, dated July 26, 1951, by the Department of State on NSC 26/2)[2]

In response to The President's request for comments on this Progress Report, General Smith outlined briefly the activities of representatives of CIA in the areas in question. [2 *lines not declassified*]. In conclusion, General Smith stated to the Council the need which he felt for clearer authorization from the Secretary of State or from the Council in order to permit CIA to carry out its responsibilities under this policy.

Mr. Lay pointed out that all that was necessary was a formalization by the Secretary of State of CIA's responsibility to carry out policies set forth in NSC 26/2.

---

[1] Source: Truman Library, Memo for the President, Meeting Discussions, 1951. Top Secret. Drafted on August 23, but no drafter is indicated.

[2] NSC 26/2 is in National Archives, RG 59, S/S–NSC Files: Lot 63 D 351, Box 51. The July 26 progress report has not been found, but for the fourth progress report, April 7, 1952, see Document 105.

The National Security Council:

Discussed the reference Progress Report and noted that the Secretary of State would issue a directive to the Director of Central Intelligence formalizing the responsibilities of the Central Intelligence Agency in implementing the policies set forth in NSC 26/2.

[Omitted here is discussion of agenda items 7: Security of Strategically Important Industrial Operations in Foreign Countries, 8: The Position of the United States With Respect to the Philippines, and 9: NSC Status of Projects.]

---

85.   Memorandum for the Record by the Deputy Director for Plans of the Central Intelligence Agency (Wisner)[1]

Washington, August 27, 1951.

SUBJECT

> Consideration of the JCS memorandum concerning the "Magnitude Paper" by ad hoc committee of NSC Senior Staff

This memorandum will record the highlights of a meeting of the ad hoc committee of the NSC Senior Staff which was held in Mr. Lay's office on 27 August to consider the JCS memorandum to the Secretary of Defense[2] commenting upon and proposing certain revisions of the NSC Staff paper on this subject.[3] The following individuals were present at the meeting: Mr. Lay and Mr. Gleason (NSC); Messrs. Bohlen and Joyce (State); Mr. Nash and General Magruder (Defense); Admiral Wooldridge (JCS); Mr. Gray (PSB); and Messrs. Jackson and Wisner (CIA).

In the outset of the meeting it became evident that the majority if not all of those present considered the JCS memorandum to be confusing and obscure. Numerous questions were addressed to Admiral Wooldridge in the effort to obtain clarifications of various points in the JCS paper. For example, Mr. Lay stated and others agreed that they could not understand the intent of the changes made by the JCS paper

---

[1] Source: Central Intelligence Agency, Deputy Director for Operations, Job 79–01228A, Box 6. Top Secret. Drafted on August 29. The original was sent to Jackson; copies were sent to Dulles (DD/CI) and Johnston (AD/PC). All ellipses in the original.

[2] Document 83.

[3] Document 76.

in paragraph 1c of the NSC Staff paper. These changes propose the deletion of the words "facilitate covert and guerrilla operations" and the substitution of "provide assistance to underground resistance movements and guerrillas"; and the deletion of the words "insure availability of these forces in the event of war" and the substitution of "to provide *the base* upon which the military may expand these forces on a military basis in time of war within activated theaters of operation". It was concluded that the original language should remain unchanged in the absence of any clear reason for changing it. However it was agreed to add the following language to the end of the original paragraph 1c:

". . . insure availability of these forces in the event of war *for utilization in accordance with principles established by the National Security Council, including wherever practicable provision of a base upon which the military may expand these forces on a military basis in time of war within active theaters of operation.*" (underscored language added)[4]

Mr. Nash proceeded to analyze the JCS memorandum and made the point that the paper in its entire latter portions dealt with matters which were not suitable for inclusion in an NSC paper but which should be the subject matter of internal Defense Department determination and disposition. Mr. Nash recommended that the attention of the meeting be focused on the forepart of the paper to the exclusion of the very detailed administrative provisions of the latter paragraphs. It was agreed that Mr. Nash's recommendation was sound and that the latter paragraphs of the paper should be the subject of consideration and decision within the Department of Defense and the military services. Presumably there would be an opportunity for CIA to participate in the deliberations leading to the development of the Defense Department position and papers covering the administrative provisions.

Admiral Wooldridge urged on behalf of the JCS that two changes be made in the paper in order to take into account and adequately reflect the points of chief concern to the JCS. He proposed the addition of a new paragraph 2 in the paper to read as follows:

"Direct the Psychological Strategy Board to assure that its strategic concept for a national psychological program includes provision for covert operations designed to achieve the objectives stated in paragraph 1 above."

It was agreed to adopt this paragraph in order to make manifest within the paper the responsibility of the Psychological Strategy Board for insuring that the specified objectives should be provided for in the strategic plan which it is required to develop under the directive which

---

[4] Printed here as italics.

sets up the PSB. It was understood that nothing in the new paragraph would require the submission to and approval by the PSB of existing programs and activities of the CIA in order for these to proceed or obtain the necessary support of the Defense establishment.

Admiral Wooldridge's other point was that paragraph 2c should be changed to provide that the PSB would coordinate the provision of personnel, funds and other support to the CIA by the Departments of State and Defense, rather than *insure* the provision of such support. Admiral Wooldridge contended that the PSB as such had no authority to "insure" the provision of support by the other departments. Mr. Jackson while acknowledging the technical accuracy of Admiral Wooldridge's point nevertheless maintained that the assurance of support for the CIA was essential from the point of view of the Director of CIA, and that whatever words might be added it should be very clear that the CIA should not be called upon to execute programs without the assurance that the necessary support would be forthcoming. Mr. Jackson's position was fully supported by all present at the meeting and it was agreed to adopt the following language to give expression to the technical point raised by Admiral Wooldridge:

"Coordinating action to insure the provision of adequate personnel . . ."—continues as original.

There being no other points offered or suggested by Admiral Wooldridge or any others at the meeting, it was agreed that the above indicated changes would be all that were necessary. Mr. Nash indicated that he would recommend to the Secretary of Defense that the latter send forward to Mr. Lay a statement to the effect that the NSC Senior Staff paper is approved by the Department of Defense subject only to the three indicated changes in language.

Frank G. Wisner[5]

---

[5] Printed from a copy that indicates Wisner signed the original.

86.   Record of Action No. 543 of the National Security Council[1]

Washington, August 30, 1951.

A Project To Provide a More Adequate Basis for Planning for the Security of the United States (Memos for NSC from Executive Secretary, same subject, dated June 5[2] and August 7, 1951;[3] NSC Action No. 519[4])

Approved the draft directive on the subject prepared by the Director of Central Intelligence pursuant to NSC Action No. 519 and attached to the reference memorandum of August 7 on the subject, in lieu of the draft directive proposed by the Interdepartmental Committee on Internal Security in the enclosure to the reference memorandum of June 5. The Acting Attorney General approved with the following comment:

"Since the Interdepartmental Intelligence Conference deals only with the internal security aspects of the Nation's security, it is presumably understood that the IIC should prepare the estimate provided for in paragraph 1 (b) of the draft directive only in so far as it pertains to the internal aspects of the capability of the USSR to conduct sabotage and otherwise disrupt internal U. S. activities. The foreign aspects of Russia's ability to commit sabotage, of course, are not within the purview of the IIC, and would appear properly a matter of study by the CIA and the subject of a separate report."

Note: The Acting Attorney General participated in the above action with the Council, the Secretary of the Treasury and the Director of Defense Mobilization. The approved directive and comment by the Acting Attorney General subsequently circulated for Council information and transmitted to the appropriate agencies for implementation.

---

[1] Source: Central Intelligence Agency, Office of the Deputy Director for Intelligence, Job 80–R01440R, Box 3, Folder 10. Top Secret.

[2] See footnote 9, Document 80.

[3] Not found.

[4] NSC Action No. 519, approved August 1, noted NSC discussion of the report by the Interdepartmental Committee on Internal Security (Document 79) and the views of Joint Chiefs of Staff and the Director of Central Intelligence, and agreed to the four points in the third paragraph of the Joint Chiefs of Staff memorandum (see Document 80), subject to the assignment of paragraph 3–b to the Interdepartmental Intelligence Conference and the integration and coordination of the resulting reports by representatives of the appropriate departments and agencies by the Director of Central Intelligence into a single report for the National Security Council; and noted that the Director of Central Intelligence would prepare a directive derived from the NSC guidelines. (National Archives, RG 59, S/S–NSC (Miscellaneous) Files: Lot 66 D 95, Records of Actions by the National Security Council)

87.   Report on the Office of Special Operations of the Central Intelligence Agency by the Deputy Assistant Director of Special Operations (Kirkpatrick)[1]

Washington, August 31, 1951.

I. Introduction

History of the Organization. The Office of Special Operations is a direct carry-over from the Office of Strategic Services. When that organization was disbanded at the end of the war, the Secret Intelligence Branch and the X–2 Branch (Counterespionage) were retained as the Strategic Services Unit under the Office of the Assistant Secretary of War. When the President created the Central Intelligence Group in January 1946, the Strategic Services Unit was transferred to that organization and became the Office of Special Operations.

Principal assets brought forward from OSS days included some experienced personnel; the nucleus of organizations operating principally in Germany and China; the counterespionage files of OSS; and established liaisons with certain foreign intelligence services. While the organization in China has been largely destroyed by the Communists, the organization in Germany has been developed and expanded. Inherited after the conclusion of World War II was the responsibility for coverage of Latin America, previously held by the Federal Bureau of Investigation.

Today the Office of Special Operations is organized into seven foreign divisions operating 131 fixed field stations, three principal staffs and six subordinate staffs. [*3 lines not declassified*]

II. Findings—General

1. There is a high degree of professional competence among the Division and Staff Chiefs in OSO, although it is apparent that this pro-

---

[1] Source: Central Intelligence Agency, Directorate of Operations, Job 80–B01795R, Box 6. Top Secret. In an August 31 covering memorandum to Deputy Director of Central Intelligence Jackson, Kirkpatrick wrote in part: "The attached report on the Office of Special Operations is based upon my participation in certain parts of your survey of OSO during July and August 1951, plus independent conversations which I have held with Staff, Division and Branch Chiefs, reports which I had prepared, and research into various OSO files." He also noted certain discrepancies in personnel figures which were attributable, he said, to personnel in transit from headquarters to the field and vice versa. The body of the report includes sections on the Staffs, the Foreign Divisions, Miscellaneous, and Recommendations, followed by charts showing OSO Organization, Staffing, Field Stations, Distribution of CIA/OSO Intelligence Material, Reports Disseminated by OSO, and Estimated Personnel Strength of the British Secret Services.

fessional competence has not always been utilized to its fullest extent in the development of an espionage service directed at the principal targets of intelligence.

2. No particular emphasis is being placed by OSO on espionage against the USSR.[2]

3. There is an extreme shortage of personnel in all classes, ranging from the Branch Chief level to the clerical level. Further, it is obvious that a considerable amount of valuable OSO effort is lost as a result of a shortage of clerical personnel to handle the paper work.

4. Considerable OSO effort is being dissipated from the major mission of establishing a long-term clandestine espionage organization. Particular examples of the dissipation of effort is the emphasis on supporting the 8th Army in Korea with an intelligence detachment. Actually OSO does not have the trained personnel to do this job at the present time, and the net gains for CIA will be minor in contrast with the gains by use of the same personnel on long-term espionage operations.

5. There is not sufficient emphasis in OSO on counterespionage operations.

6. OSO rules and regulations should be reviewed, to allow greater initiative and judgment by responsible branch, division, staff, and station chiefs.

7. The tremendous support-load that OSO performs for other offices of CIA and other agencies of the Government, should be lessened.

8. There is too great concentration on collection of short-range, tactical information, and not sufficient attention to collection of high-level political and strategic information.

9. The policy of shifting personnel between areas, and of a two-year tour of duty overseas, should be reviewed.

10. [3 lines not declassified]

11. There has been insufficient liaison between OSO headquarters and the field.

12. There is no standard system for checking on the activity of field stations. In one instance, the only report received from a field representative was a request for supplies—no intelligence has yet been received from this station.

---

[2] In June 1951, CIA formalized the Redcap program to monitor Soviet officials abroad and encourage them to defect. See Robert L. Benson and Michael Warner, eds., *Venona: Soviet Espionage and the American Response, 1939–1957*, p. xxxii. This required considerable liaison with foreign intelligence services. Attempts were also made to infiltrate agents into the Soviet Union, but, given stringent Soviet controls, these attempts, codenamed Redsox, enjoyed very limited success. This was recognized by 1954 and a program using legal travelers for short term observation of the Soviet Union was set up under the codename Redskin.

13. There is no standard divisional organization.

14. The delay between collection of information and its dissemination to consumer intelligence agencies is in the nature of two to three months except for cabled reports. Two major bottlenecks are responsible for this: official pouches are extremely slow; and reports control has been allowed to take three to six weeks as an average to produce reports (this is after the reports are prepared for publication by the foreign divisions).

15. [2 lines not declassified]

[Omitted here is the body of the report.]

---

88.   Memorandum From the Acting Assistant Director of Special Operations of the Central Intelligence Agency (Kirkpatrick) to the Deputy Director of Central Intelligence (Jackson)

Washington, September 25, 1951.

[Source: Central Intelligence Agency, Executive Registry, Job 95–G600278R, Box 1, Folder 7. Secret. 3 pages not declassified.]

---

89.   Memorandum From the Executive Secretary of the National Security Council (Lay) to the National Security Council[1]

Washington, October 9, 1951.

SUBJECT

Scope and Pace of Covert Operations

REFERENCE

Memo for NSC from Acting Executive Secretary, same subject, dated 27 June 1951,[2] and references therein

---

[1] Source: Truman Library, Papers of Harry S. Truman, President's Secretary's File, Subject File. Top Secret; Eyes Only. A copy was sent to the Director of Central Intelligence. Ellipsis in the original.

[2] Document 76.

The Under Secretary of State and the Acting Chairman of the National Security Resources Board have approved the recommendations contained in the reference memorandum. The Director of Central Intelligence has concurred therein.

The Acting Secretary of Defense, however, on October 8, 1951 approved the recommendations contained in the reference memorandum, subject to the following changes:[3]

1. Change paragraph 1–e to read as follows:

"Develop underground resistance and facilitate covert and guerrilla operations in strategic areas to the maximum practicable extent consistent with 1–a above, and ensure availability of these forces in the event of war for utilization in accordance with principles established by the National Security Council, including wherever practicable provision of a base upon which the military may expand these forces on a military basis in time of war within active theaters of operations."

2. Insert a new paragraph 2 to read as follows, renumbering the ensuing paragraphs accordingly:

"Direct the Psychological Strategy Board to assure that its strategic concept for a national psychological program includes provision for covert operations designed to achieve the objectives stated in paragraph 1 above."

3. Change the original paragraph 2–c (now paragraph 3–c) to read as follows:

"Coordinating action to ensure the provision of adequate personnel. . . ."—continues as in original.

Accordingly, it is requested that you indicate your action with respect to the above changes by completing and returning, *as a matter of priority*, the attached memorandum form.[4]

It is requested that special security precautions be taken in the handling of this material and that access be limited to individuals requiring the information contained herein in order to carry out their official duties.

James S. Lay, Jr.

---

[3] See Document 85.

[4] The attached memorandum form, not printed, indicates that President Truman gave his approval on October 23; see Document 90.

90.   Note From the Executive Secretary of the National Security Council (Lay) to the National Security Council[1]

NSC 10/5   Washington, October 23, 1951.

SCOPE AND PACE OF COVERT OPERATIONS

REFERENCES

   A. Memo for NSC from Acting Executive Secretary, same subject, dated June 27, 1951[2]

   B. Memo for NSC from Executive Secretary, same subject, dated August 22, 1951[3]

   C. Memo for NSC from Executive Secretary, same subject, dated October 9, 1951[4]

As of October 23, 1951, the statutory members of the National Security Council approved the recommendations contained in Reference A as amended by the changes contained in Reference C. The Director of Central Intelligence had concurred therein.

Accordingly, the report as amended and approved is enclosed herewith for information and appropriate implementation by all departments and agencies concerned, as indicated therein.

It is requested that special security precautions be taken in the handling of this report and that access be limited strictly to individuals requiring the information contained therein to carry out their official duties.

It is further requested that all copies of the reference memoranda be withdrawn and returned to this office upon receipt of this report.

James S. Lay, Jr.[5]

---

[1] Source: Truman Library, Papers of Harry S. Truman, President's Secretary's Files, Subject File. Top Secret. NSC 10/4 (Document 42) was withdrawn on December 13, after the approval of NSC 10/5. (Memorandum from Lay to the National Security Council, December 13; Truman Library, Papers of Harry S. Truman, President's Secretary File, Subject File)

[2] Document 76.

[3] The August 22 memorandum transmitted the JCS views (Document 83) to the National Security Council.

[4] Document 89.

[5] Printed from a copy that bears this typed signature.

Enclosure[6]

ACTIONS TAKEN BY THE NATIONAL SECURITY COUNCIL ON SCOPE AND PACE OF COVERT OPERATIONS

1. The National Security Council approves in principle as a national responsibility the immediate expansion of the covert organization established in NSC 10/2, and the intensification of covert operations designed in general order of emphasis to:

a. Place the maximum strain on the Soviet structure of power, including the relationships between the USSR, its satellites, and Communist China; and when and where appropriate in the light of U.S. and Soviet capabilities and the risk of war, contribute to the retraction and reduction of Soviet power and influence to limits which no longer constitute a threat to U.S. security.

b. Strengthen the orientation toward the United States of the peoples and nations of the free world, and increase their capacity and will to resist Soviet domination.

c. Develop underground resistance and facilitate covert and guerrilla operations in strategic areas to the maximum practicable extent consistent with 1–a above, and ensure availability of these forces in the event of war for utilization in accordance with principles established by the National Security Council, including wherever practicable provision of a base upon which the military may expand these forces on a military basis in time of war within active theaters of operations.

2. The National Security Council directs the Psychological Strategy Board to assure that its strategic concept for a national psychological program includes provision for covert operations designed to achieve the objectives stated in paragraph 1 above.

3. The National Security Council reaffirms the responsibility and authority of the Director of Central Intelligence for the conduct of covert operations in accordance with NSC 10/2 and subject to the general policy guidance prescribed therein, and further subject to the approval of the Psychological Strategy Board which shall be responsible for:

a. Determining the desirability and feasibility of programs and of individual major projects for covert operations formulated by or proposed to the Director of Central Intelligence.

b. Establishing the scope, pace, and timing of covert operations and the allocation of priorities among these operations.

---

[6] Top Secret. Also printed in Michael Warner, ed., *The CIA Under Harry Truman*, pp. 437–439.

c. Coordinating action to ensure the provision of adequate personnel, funds, and logistical and other support to the Director of Central Intelligence by the Departments of State and Defense for carrying out any approved program of covert operations.

4. The National Security Council requests the Secretary of Defense to provide adequate means whereby the Director of Central Intelligence may be assured of the continuing advice and collaboration of the Joint Chiefs of Staff in the formulation of plans for paramilitary operations during the period of the cold war.

5. In view of the necessity for immediate decision prior to the coming into operation of the Psychological Strategy Board, the National Security Council authorizes the conduct of expanded guerrilla activities in China, as outlined in the memorandum from the Director of Central Intelligence enclosed with the reference memorandum of June 27, 1951 (Reference A), and pursuant to the appropriate provisions of NSC 48/5.[7]

---

[7] NSC 48/5, "U.S. Objectives, Policies and Courses of Action in Asia," is printed in *Foreign Relations*, 1951, vol. VI, pp. 33–63.

91.　Fact Sheet[1]

Washington, November 8, 1951.

1. *Name*: IAC Watch Committee

2. *Established*: Established in its present form by IAC decision of 7 December 1950.[2] It was preceded by the Joint Intelligence Indications Committee (JIIC), which consisted of full members from the military services and members of other IAC agencies participating informally.

3. *Chairman*: Brig. General John Weckerling, Chief, Intelligence Div., G–2.

---

[1] Source: National Archives, RG 59, Administration Files: Lot 62 D 220, Top Secret Records on Inter-Agency Relations, 1948–61, Committee Status Book, Box 1. Top Secret. The date is handwritten at the bottom of the page.

[2] See Document 35.

4. *Membership*: CIA JCS
State (Mose Harvey, DRS; Air Force
Alternates: Boris Klosson & Army
Howard Wiedemann, DRS) Navy
AEC
FBI

5. *Terms of Reference*: Terms of reference, as authorized by the IAC, are given in G–2 memorandum (G2–IWW–319.26) dated 20 December 1950.[3] The Committee's mission is to collect, evaluate, analyze and report indications of Soviet-Communist intentions of hostile action and it is responsible for issuing a weekly report on Indications of Soviet-Communist Intention of Hostile Action.

6. *Secretariat*: G–2 provides the secretariat which a) regularly collects from all IAC agencies material bearing on the determination of Soviet-Communist intentions, and b) drafts, reproduces and distributes the weekly report.

7. *Activity*: The Committee meets regularly once a week (Wednesdays from 10 a.m. to about 1 p.m.) and has crash sessions when required.

8. *Background*: See memorandum referred to in point 5 above.

9. *Effectiveness*: The IAC Watch Committee is performing an extremely important function and, in effect, may be regarded as the intelligence body charged with the responsibility of alerting the US Government of Soviet-Communist intentions to initiate war. The Department's participation has priority over most other intelligence functions performed by DRS and to a large extent the work of DRS is geared to the intentions problems with which the Committee is concerned.

---

[3] Not found.

92.   **Memorandum From the Under Secretary of State (Webb) to the Executive Secretary of the National Security Council (Lay)[1]**

Washington, November 8, 1951.

SUBJECT

Third Progress Report on NSC 59/1, "The Foreign Information Program and Psychological Warfare Planning"

1. NSC 59/1 was approved as governmental policy on March 10, 1950. It is requested that this Progress Report, as of October 17, 1951, be circulated to the members of the Council for their information.

2. The activities described in this report were undertaken in implementation of NSC 59/1.

3. The Interdepartmental Foreign Information Organization was redesignated the Psychological Operations Coordinating Committee[2] following the issuance of the Presidential Directive of April 4, 1951, establishing a Psychological Strategy Board.[3] It will therefore be referred to hereafter in this report as the "Committee." Formal announcement of the redesignation is being withheld pending decision on certain organizational details.

4. In addition to the Chairman, representatives of the following agencies regularly attend the weekly meetings: Department of Defense, Joint Chiefs of Staff, Executive Office of the President, Department of State, Economic Cooperation Administration, and Central Intelligence Agency. The Army, Navy and Air Force chiefs of psychological warfare attend when matters of interest to their respective services are before the Committee.

5. On the Committee's recommendation, a survey team was sent to Tokyo and Korea in October 1950 to study psychological warfare activities there. The findings of this group were reviewed by the Committee at its meeting November 13, 1950. The Committee has subsequently made periodic reviews of psychological warfare activities in Korea in order to help implement the recommendations of the survey team.

---

[1] Source: National Archives, RG 59, S/P–NSC Files: Lot 62 D 1, 1935–62, Box 115, no label. Secret; Security Information.

[2] See Document 74.

[3] See Document 60.

6. A National Psychological Warfare Plan for General War[4] was prepared by the Interdepartmental Foreign Information Staff (now the Secretariat of the Committee) under the provisions of NSC 59/1. This Plan was approved by the Committee and forwarded to the National Security Council. The National Security Council has since received comments on the Plan from the Joint Chiefs of Staff, which were referred to the Psychological Strategy Board. The Department of State has also submitted a version of the Plan to the Psychological Strategy Board.

7. Psychological warfare plans for Russia, Korea and Indochina have been developed and approved. Plans for Germany, the Middle East and the Satellite areas are being prepared in the Department of State. A China plan is also being prepared on the basis of comments from the field on the Interim Plan for China, approved by the Committee in March, 1951.

8. *Project Troy*[5]

Under this project, thirty of the nation's top scientists and other experts were assembled by the Massachusetts Institute of Technology under contract to the Department of State to explore all conventional and unconventional means of penetrating the Iron Curtain. Particular attention was given to the possibilities of utilizing in psychological warfare the new developments in the electro-magnetic field. The report submitted by the group calls for a substantial expansion of our radio facilities, which has already been undertaken. A vest-pocket radio is being developed along the lines recommended by the group, making use of the "transistor," a remarkable device which increases battery-life several hundred times and makes it possible to build a radio set of this size.

Funds to complete the project, although requested, have not been appropriated by Congress.

9. *Propaganda Balloons*

There has been continued study of the possibility of using balloons to carry our propaganda to the people of Russia and her satellites. Following Committee approval, the appropriate government agency, in cooperation with private organizations including the Crusade for Freedom in New York, launched an experimental propaganda balloon project from Western Germany with Czechoslovakia as a target. This project was begun the week of August 12, 1951. Balloons were subsequently

---

[4] The plan, which was discussed at an October 25 meeting of the PSB, is in the National Archives, RG 59, S/S–NSC Files: Lot 62 D 333, PSB D–8, Box 1.

[5] See Document 59.

launched to Poland. Details of the project have since appeared in the press. The effectiveness of the project is currently being evaluated.

10. *Defectors*

At the Committee's request, the Department of State prepared a detailed history of United States handling of Russian and Satellite defectors during and since World War II. This study was turned over to the Policy Advisory Staff of the Department of State for its use in treating information aspects of the defector question.

11. *Exploitation of Economic Themes*

The Committee has recommended that a full-time consultant be employed to study the problem of coordinating government output on economic matters and exploiting economic themes more fully.

Working with the Economic Cooperation Administration the Psychological Operations Coordinating Committee actively promoted several economic themes in psychological operations. One of the most important of these is the ECA Production-Productivity drive in Western Europe. This is a concerted effort to increase Western Europe's gross production by $100 billion yearly. The project has become front-page news in most of Europe's newspapers. By agreement between the Department of State and ECA the Production-Productivity drive is now a major U.S. project.

12. *Prisoners-of-war*

A study on propaganda exploitation of Chinese and North Korean Prisoners-of-war was approved by the Committee on August 13 and recommended as guidance to the Far East Command.

13. *Contingency of Soviet Leaders' Death*

A contingency plan against the possible death of certain Soviet leaders has been prepared by an inter-agency working group at the request of the Committee and is in process of final coordination.

14. *Current projects*

Some of the more important current activities of the Committee or the Secretariat are as follows:

a) With the approval of the Psychological Strategy Board an interdepartmental working group has been established to study the broad range of psychological problems growing out of the presence of U.S. military units overseas.

b) A military working group charged with developing key themes for use in propaganda directed to Soviet and Satellite troops has made an interim report to the Committee.

c) On recommendation of the Committee an expanded program of on-the-job training has been undertaken in the State Department for military officers in psychological warfare. The military services have expressed their desire to continue participation in this program.

d) The Committee is considering a Navy Department study encompassing plans to exploit the psychological potential in Soviet submarine operations.

e) The Committee is engaged in making plans for the implementation of two Korean contingency plans which were prepared by the Psychological Strategy Board.

f) The Secretariat is developing stand-by psychological operations plans for implementation immediately following the outbreak of a possible general war. When completed and approved by the Committee, these plans will be forwarded to the Psychological Strategy Board for consideration.

James E. Webb[6]

---

[6] Printed from a copy that indicates Webb signed the original.

---

93.   Memorandum From the Assistant Director for Special Operations (Wyman) and the Assistant Director for Policy Coordination of the Central Intelligence Agency (Johnston) to Director of Central Intelligence Smith[1]

Washington, November 14, 1951.

SUBJECT

Draft Report on Special Operations

1. From early October until the present date, OPC/OSO and members of the Joint Subsidiary Plans Division have engaged in the consideration of three successive drafts of a JCS paper, subject as above.

2. This paper is of utmost significance to CIA's responsibilities for war planning in both Europe and for any extension of NATO to the Middle East. It established three principles:

a. That overall guidance for clandestine activities at SHAPE or any NATO countries to be established, will be channeled through the Standing Group, Washington, D.C.

---

[1] Source: Central Intelligence Agency, Executive Registry, Job 80–B01731R, Box 8, Folder 333. Top Secret; Security Information.

b. That, while in time of war Commanders within NATO will exercise operational control of U.S. clandestine resources in direct support of military operations to the extent necessary to ensure coordination, the command of such resources will be retained in both peace and war by the U.S.

c. It reaffirms the NSC directive that clandestine operations conducted in active Theaters of War where American Forces are engaged will come under the American Theater Commander or such other U.S. Commanders as may be designated by the JCS. (The problems of U.S. command responsibilities in Europe are currently under discussion. The outcome of these discussions will determine whether CIA will be responsive to a single U.S. Commander or some other U.S. military mechanism.)

3. The subject paper recommends in paragraph 3.h, page 5, Enclosure "A,"[2] the establishment of an "ad hoc" committee under the Standing Group to advise it on clandestine matters. It will be noted that the proposed DCI memorandum reserves the right later to ask for establishment of a permanent committee if such is considered necessary.

4. Similarly, the subject paper, in paragraph 21., suggests direct coordination between OSO and JCS, through the JSPD. In the proposed DCI memorandum to the Chief, JSPD, concurrence is made with the principle advanced, but resolution of what office is to handle the direct coordination is left to the JCS as an internal matter.

5. In the main, the Report of the JSPD to the JCS guards our respective OPC and OSO interests and those of CIA as a whole;[3] and agreeable to the request contained in paragraph 2. of TS 62654 (Tab "A"),[4] it is recommended that the accompanying memorandum from DCI to the Chief of the Joint Subsidiary Plans Division, the Joint Chiefs of Staff, be signed and dispatched.

W. G. Wyman
Kilbourne Johnston

---

[2] According to the list of enclosures at the end of the memorandum, Enclosure "A" was a memorandum from the DCI to the Chief, JSPD. It has not been found.

[3] The enclosed draft report, identified as Enclosure "B," has not been found.

[4] Tab "A" was a memorandum from JSPD to the DCI, dated October 26, not found.

94.   Memorandum for the Files[1]

Washington, November 23, 1951.

SUBJECT

Meeting at Mr. Barrett's Home on Tuesday Evening, November 20, 1951 to discuss USIE and OPC Relationships

Those Present were as follows:[2]

For CIA	For State
Mr. Dulles	Mr. Barrett
Mr. Wisner	Mr. Kohler
Mr. Lloyd	Mr. Joyce
Mr. Braden	Mr. Barbour
	Mr. Devine

Conclusions:

It was agreed that:

(1) The proposed RFE Baltic broadcasts would not go on the air as scheduled and that a joint RFE–VOA effort would be made to take care of the displaced personnel. Kohler to confer with NCFE officials re details.

(2) That the next Crusade for Freedom would not be of the high-pressure and spectacular nature of this year's but would be something in the nature of a magazine and directmail approach with all copy carefully cleared.

(3) That Radio Free Asia would undergo no further expansion until the future course of the Committee for Free Asia had been settled in a manner satisfactory to both CIA and State.

Discussion:

At the opening of the meeting an agenda was distributed in which was included brief statements proposing what the proper spheres of operation of RFE and VOA should be. These proposals were as follows:

---

[1] Source: Central Intelligence Agency, History Staff, Job 83–00036R, Box 7. Top Secret.

[2] Officers not otherwise identified are: For CIA, Lloyd was Deputy Chief, Psychological Staff Division and Braden was Chief, International Organizations Branch, Psychological Division, Office of Policy Coordination. For State, John E. Devine was in the Press Office.

1. *Sphere of Activity for RFE and, by extension, RFA*

To provide radio facilities so that the potentially most effective émigré groups can speak from nearby points to their captive fellow-countrymen. By implication this would preclude acknowledged sponsorship by American, British or any group other than the speaking émigrés. It also implies that the broadcasts would be in the standard broadcast band.

2. *Sphere of Activity for VOA*

To deliver a radio message, by both medium and short wave, in the name of the United States Government and the American people.

These proposals were not agreed to in the meeting.

Following the first reading of these proposals, Mr. Dulles pointed out that the RFE Czech program does not now credit émigré groups but rather puts forward effective individuals many of whom are anonymous.

Mr. Wisner advanced the suggestion that perhaps RFE activities should only be continued if they are supplementary and noncompetitive with VOA.

Mr. Kohler generalized this thought in a proposal that RFE should carry on covert or supplementary activities which will aid the official United States Government radio. Mr. Wisner did not think the term "Covert" could be logically applied in the case of RFE.

Mr. Joyce commented that at the present time the émigré committees connected with NCFE are so divided that RFE cannot ordinarily get authority to attribute items to any one of the émigré groups. He did add that the committees are serving one of their original purposes in that they are keeping émigré group pressure from officials in the State Department.

Mr. Lloyd, in response to a question, said that there is now very little recording of program material by émigré groups in New York. That was previously the basic arrangement but now the bulk of the material is originating overseas.

Mr. Barrett referred to the four questions which were posed by Mr. Barnard at the previous meeting and said that we ought to examine all RFE activities in the light of the following questions:

1. Is the activity one that is serving a useful enough purpose to justify the funds involved?
2. Can it be done better by this organization than by Government directly or by other existing organizations?
3. Is it jeopardizing the existence and success of other important activities?
4. How can it best be financed?

Mr. Barrett went on to say that according to best available estimates the USSR is now spending about two billion dollars a year on propaganda and directly related activities. Hence, there is considerable justification for multiple activities—provided they don't adversely affect one another. He also said that some of the need for non-Governmental groups to participate in a "no holds barred" campaign has disappeared with the toughening attitude of the United States Government vis-à-vis USSR, but that we should study carefully the extent to which such more-extreme-than-government activities are still justified.

Mr. Barbour stated that the limit on what the United States Government may say is probably getting less and less but there will always be some such area which can better be handled by a non-Governmental organization.

Mr. Kohler stated that he does not see in practical terms what this non-Governmental area is. He mentioned that VOA is now using very strong anti-Stalin material and the principal yardstick is whether an item is effective propaganda or not. He pointed out that this same criterion would apply to the operations of a non-Governmental organization. Mr. Kohler added that he thinks that the RFE programming is probably a little more conservative than VOA because RFE is not so near policy and has to tread carefully on a number of issues. Mr. Braden asked whether in the Far East, Radio Free Asia can say things that the United States Government cannot say. Mr. Kohler said that he was not aware that it could. He added that if a third force group appeared which had something to say that we wanted said and could not say ourselves it would then be time to give them radio facilities.

Mr. Barbour stated that he feels that RFE could as a general rule take a more strident line than VOA.

Mr. Barrett raised the question as to whether the Czech operation was actually ideal and suggested that we ought to get more information on it.

Mr. Wisner reported that the French are now taking active steps to form a national committee. He also said that the British were making some moves in that direction but had not gotten far. Mr. Barrett said that instead of a national committee for France, Britain, U.S., and so on, there ought to be a committee for Free Europe which would really be international in character. Mr. Dulles said that an international committee would be very difficult to organize and even more difficult to operate. What would be better in his opinion would be three national committees with a permanently sitting coordinating group, probably in Paris.

Mr. Barrett said that he felt we might somehow profit by the devices worked out by American political parties—organizations such as "New Dealers for Willkie", "Young Democrats for Dewey" and so on.

Mr. Kohler raised the question of what we are really after in Eastern Europe. He said that he didn't think we needed propaganda in Eastern Europe because the Russians are doing our work for us.

Mr. Joyce did not agree with this and referred to the NSC basic documents in which we are directed to increase tension in Eastern Europe and try to release the USSR's hold over its satellites and roll back the Soviet borders to the 1939 line.

Mr. Barrett said that he felt it was most important for us to get news and ideas to the people in Eastern Europe. Mr. Kohler added that two radio voices—VOA and RFE—are worse than one when they are not clearly distinguishable by the audience. Mr. Wisner said if we needed more volume to Eastern Europe we should step up the Voice of America.

Mr. Barrett recalled the fact that Mr. Kohler feels that there is nothing that needs to be said to the Baltic that cannot be said quite adequately by the Voice of America. Mr. Dulles raised the question of how the Baltic plans of RFE could be called off if it is decided not to put the programs on the air. Mr. Kohler said that in his talks with John Hughes[3] and Adolph Berle[4] he had the definite impression that the personnel which had so far been lined up for the Baltic program could be taken care of in other ways. He said it would be better to have a headache for a couple of weeks than to live the problem for a couple of years. Mr. Dulles pointed out that a responsible group of American citizens had participated in the planning for this and other RFE activities and that they and their proposals could not just be casually dismissed. Mr. Wisner said he felt that a perfectly logical explanation could be advanced, that political conditions have changed and that the State Department is now able to carry on the Baltic job; therefore, RFE's resources could be applied to other directions. Mr. Barrett recalled that the request from the State Department for the Baltic broadcast by RFE had come at a time when State did not have the financial resources to undertake such programs. Mr. Kohler said that the Baltic program need had first come to his attention in the winter of 1949–50. Mr. Dulles reminded the group that in May, 1951 the Department of State had approved RFE broadcasts in the Baltic languages. Mr. Joyce said that this same approval had come as recently as August 8 of this year from the Department. It was generally agreed that in spite of these commitments conditions had changed and it was important now that RFE broadcasts did not go on in the Baltic languages. Mr. Kohler then said that he would get together in New York with RFE representatives to help them take the head off RFE in connection with any cancellation

---

[3] Hughes was a prominent businessman, Ambassador to the Atlantic Council, and member of the NCFE.

[4] Berle was a prominent lawyer, former Assistant Secretary of State, and a member of the NCFE.

of the Baltic language broadcast plans. He said that he would do this within a week.

Mr. Wisner asked if the present policy of the Department would allow subversive broadcasts to this area. Mr. Kohler said there was no necessity for subversive broadcasts since we had not recognized the Soviet rule in these areas and were working with what we felt were the legal governments.

Mr. Dulles said that close liaison between IBD and RFE in New York was needed and he was told that arrangements had already been made for regular meetings between Mr. Kretzmann[5] and Mr. [*name not declassified*] of RFE.

Mr. Lloyd said that RFE has just about completed work on three stations in Lisbon which are powered with 50 kilowatts each. These have been intended for relaying purposes only, with the programs originating in Munich being sent to Portugal and then played back by short wave to Hungary, Romania, and so on. Mr. Barrett made the suggestion that perhaps more radio operations could be justified simply on the basis of tying up Russian facilities and making some progress in the electronic war.

Mr. Dulles raised the question of what should be done about the Crusade for Freedom next year. Mr. Barrett said that he felt that the present type of campaign was harming the total United States effort and making people ask the question whether the Voice of America is really needed. He did not say that to his surprise no serious questions came up in the last Congress concerning the apparent duplication between Radio Free Europe and VOA. Mr. Barrett suggested that instead of the present type of Crusade for Freedom, a low-pressure program should be conducted. He said that something along the line of the tuberculosis seal campaign in magazines, with coupons, and so on, ought to be tried out. Mr. Lloyd then said that Abbott Washburn[6] was only getting into high speed on the Crusade and that in the next few years he hoped to be able to work the Crusade for Freedom up to a point where 15 or 20 million dollars could be raised. Mr. Dulles suggested that Mr. Washburn be brought down to Washington at an early date and given the idea of the low-pressure campaign. Mr. Barrett raised the question of explaining the rest of the RFE budget if the mail order approach raises only about $750,000. He felt than an anonymous donor could take care of that problem but Mr. Dulles did not agree on this point. Mr. Dulles raised the question of whether the Crusade for Freedom has value in making the public more aware of the international

---

[5] Roger Kretzmann of IBD.
[6] Executive vice chairman of the Crusade for Freedom.

political situation. It was said that this question could not really be answered. Mr. Barrett felt that it probably made the public more aware in certain respects but on the whole created more problems than it solved.

Mr. Barrett raised the question about Radio Free Asia and Mr. Braden replied that RFA is staying right where it is until they are given further orders. Mr. Barrett said that in regard to the radio audience in China it was his understanding that there is a small and decreasing audience as the result of Communist repressive measures. He felt that it was better for OPC to put its RFA money into local, non-U.S.-labeled operations in the Far East. He said that we did not need another American voice in the area. Mr. Dulles then suggested that RFA be kept going on its present basis along with CFA for the next few weeks until the new head of the organization is selected. He should then be brought in for a discussion of this whole problem. In closing, Mr. Barrett suggested that the four questions posed by Mr. Barnard be applied to all NCFE and CFA projects. He suggested that CIA appoint one person and that State appoint another to work as a team to do this job. Mr. Dulles said that he would prefer to see a record of this meeting and have a chance to discuss it with his colleagues before appointing such a person.

---

95.   Memorandum From the Deputy Assistant Director for Special Operations of the Central Intelligence Agency (Kirkpatrick) to Director of Central Intelligence Smith[1]

Washington, November 30, 1951.

SUBJECT:

Request from G–2 for Discussion of Agreed Activities under NSCID #5[2]

1. Reference is made to our memorandum to you dated 17 November 1951[3] concerning the above subject. On 23 November 1951, prior to the receipt of the attached memo and proposed agreement from General Bolling to you, Mr. Roy Tod of G–2 informally coordinated

---

[1] Source: Central Intelligence Agency, History Staff, Job 83–01034R, Box 4. Top Secret.

[2] Document 255.

[3] Not found.

with OSO the draft of the proposed agreement entitled "Establishment of 'Agreed Activities' by the Department of the Army Under the Provisions of NSCID #5."

2. The draft has been successfully revised by OSO, and in the opinion of this Office represents a sound statement of the problem. Complete coordination with the CIA of the espionage and counterespionage activities being conducted by the Services has never taken place and would be of great benefit and assistance in reducing duplication, eliminating the undue dissipation of intelligence assets, and providing an orderly controlled maximum utilization of the entire U.S. intelligence potential.

3. It is recommended that the proposals in the attached agreement be concurred in and implemented and that the same proposals be extended to include the Navy and the Air Force.

Lyman B. Kirkpatrick[4]

Attachment

Draft Department of the Army Paper[5]

Washington, November 23, 1951.

SUBJECT

Establishment of "Agreed Activities" by the Department of the Army Under the Provisions of NSCID #5

1. NSCID #5 authorizes and directs that the DCI shall conduct all *organized* Federal espionage operations outside the United States and its possessions for the collection of foreign intelligence information required to meet the needs of all Departments and Agencies concerned, in connection with the national security, *except for certain agreed activities by other Departments and Agencies.* (The same policy applies to counter-espionage activities.) This directive further provides that the use of casual agents in a covert capacity by any IAC agency shall be coordinated by the DCI with the organized covert activities.

---

[4] Printed from a copy that bears this typed signature.
[5] Top Secret.

2. For varying reasons, largely beyond the control of the intelligence agencies, the entire provisions of NSCID #5 have never been effectively implemented nor has the U.S. attained the position where it can now accomplish espionage operations on the scale required to meet completely the continually expanding needs of all the Departments and Agencies concerned. Since the original issuance of NSCID #5 in January 1947 there has been a steady expansion in the scope and volume of the intelligence information required by the military services and other agencies. Because this has been paralleled by an expansion in the security measures of the USSR and its satellites, the U.S. Government has been faced with an ever increasing dependence upon espionage and related clandestine activities as the primary means for obtaining the information required.

3. Through necessity and with the tacit approval of CIA, the Army intelligence elements within the overseas command areas have been conducting espionage operations, to varying degrees, since the end of World War II. Under a strictly legal interpretation of NSCID #5 in the absence of any official arrangements for "agreed activities" by the Department of the Army, the Army is not empowered to conduct organized espionage operations and CIA remains responsible for the conduct of espionage operations to meet both the tactical requirements of the overseas commanders and to meet the long range strategic requirements originating at the Washington level. However, the Army possesses, by virtue of its trained complements in overseas areas and its present and past "unagreed activities", espionage assets which should be utilized to the fullest extent in order to meet the ever increasing need for that intelligence information which, under present conditions, is procureable only through clandestine operations. In order to regularize these necessary and desirable espionage activities being conducted by the Army, they should be "legalized" by agreement between the DCI and the Department of the Army as provided in NSCID #5. Such agreement would permit the Army, in large measure, to conduct espionage operations to meet those tactical information requirements which are in direct support of an overseas commander's mission and would place CIA in a better position to concentrate on long range strategic requirements which usually necessitate deeper and more permanent operations.

4. Various ad hoc arrangements have been made between the Army and CIA in an attempt to solve the problem of conducting espionage operations on a closely coordinated basis as envisaged by NSCID #5. During the period 1949–50, G–2, in collaboration with CIA, prepared and issued to the intelligence chiefs of FECOM, USFA, and EUCOM, policy letters calling for joint planning and coordination of operations between CIA and these overseas commands. However, these policies have not been implemented to a productive and satisfactory extent.

5. There are established responsibilities for the implementation of National Security Council Intelligence Directives. First, NSCID #1[6] provides that "the respective intelligence chiefs shall be responsible for insuring that NSC orders or directives, when applicable, are implemented within their intelligence organizations". In this connection, the revised NSCID #5 (dated 28 Aug 51)[7] was sent by the NSC to the Director of Central Intelligence *and the IAC agencies* for appropriate action; Second, JCS 202/70 charges the JIC with responsibility for preparation of joint guidance to unified commands (under further provision of JCS 1259/27)[8] on national policy pertaining to intelligence activities. The unified commands have not been notified officially of the recent revision of NSCID #5 nor have the service intelligence chiefs on the IAC taken formal action to implement the "agreed activities" portion of this directive, and officially establish the current and continuing espionage operations of the military services as "agreed activities" under the provisions of NSCID #5.

6. It is deemed essential that action be taken to remedy these deficiencies with the least possible delay so that espionage operations being conducted by the Army shall be officially recognized by the DCI as "agreed activities" under the provisions of NSCID #5 and fully coordinated by him within the framework of an overall program to insure the most effective use of all espionage capabilities currently or potentially available to the U.S. Government.

7. The current situation may be sumarized as follows:

a. The United States government is not now in a position to meet the full extent of its present needs for clandestine collection of intelligence information. Fulfillment of these needs can only be met through centrally coordinated utilization of *all* espionage capabilities currently or potentially available to the U.S. Government.

b. Army intelligence elements within the overseas command areas are conducting espionage operations without their "accreditation" as "agreed activities" under the provisions of NSCID #5.

c. The overseas commands have information requirements, based upon their assigned missions, which can only be met through espionage operations.

d. [*1 paragraph (4 lines) not declassified*]

---

[6] For NSCID No. 1, see *Foreign Relations*, 1945–1950, Emergence of the Intelligence Establishment, Document 432.

[7] Not found, but see Document 77.

[8] Neither JCS paper has been found.

e. As additional areas of the world become critical or sensitive, in terms of their involvement with the struggle between the USSR and the Western Powers, there will be a further increase in the scope and variety of information targets requiring espionage activity on the part of the U.S. Government.

f. It has now become mandatory that *all* U.S. espionage capabilities be put to use and that they be conducted in such a manner that each capability will be so applied as to best meet the overall interests of the U.S. Government.

8. It is believed that action should be taken to accomplish the following:

a. Development of a basic agreement between the DCI and the Department of the Army that will establish the conditions, including type of espionage operations, and the extent to which Army intelligence elements within the overseas command areas may conduct, as "agreed activities" under the provisions of NSCID #5, espionage operations in direct support of the overseas commander's mission or for such purposes as the DCI and the A.C. of S, G–2 may mutually agree to be in the overall interests of the U.S. Government.

b. Development of specific agreements to meet the particular requirements and conditions existing within each overseas command area, with particular reference to the areas in or from which the Army intelligence elements may conduct espionage operations as "agreed activities."

c. Development of a mechanism for centralized coordination and control of U.S. espionage operations both at the Washington level and in the field, that will:

(1) Promote the most effective use of all espionage capabilities currently or potentially available to the U.S. Government;
(2) Avoid duplication of effort, unwitting multiple use of the same sources, false confirmation, and the dissipation of those intelligence asset which are available.

e. Preparation of the necessary directives to implement the action, outlined in sub-paragraphs a. through d. above, within the Army elements of the overseas commands and appropriate CIA stations overseas.

9. It is recommended that G–2 discuss this proposal informally with the DCI and suggest to him that appropriate representatives of G–2 and CIA/SO be appointed to develop the action outlined in paragraph 8 above. This proposal has been informally coordinated with the OSO/CIA and it is understood that the DCI has been informed.

96.   Notes of a Meeting[1]

Washington, December 5, 1951.

SUBJECT

Psychological Strategy Board

PRESENT

S/P—	PSB—Admiral Stevens
Mr. Nitze	PSB—Mr. Philbin
Mr. Ferguson (part)	C—Mr. Bohlen (part)
Mr. Savage	P—Mr. Phillips
Mr. Koch	P—Mr. Schwinn
Mr. Marshall	R—Mr. Trezise
Miss Fosdick	S—Mr. Compton
Mr. Tufts	
Mr. Stelle	
Mr. Villard	
Mr. Watts	

Admiral Stevens opened the meeting by saying he was chairman of a small group in PSB charged with "formulating a national strategic concept for psychological action" as called for in the directive establishing the PSB and as envisioned in NSC 59/1 and NSC 10/2 which include both covert and overt propaganda activities.

Mr. Nitze said he thought the covert and overt activities should be kept separate.

Admiral Stevens said that people were worried today because they felt that our foreign policy was "gone at piecemeal—on a hand to mouth basis" with no over-all strategic concept. A strategic concept, he said was a "point of view—a tentative plan of action, always under review but not rigid" and he thought that such a concept or plan should be put down on paper, difficult as it might be to do.

A discussion ensued about the difficulties of getting "everything down" in NSC papers and the danger of parts being lifted out of context to fit particular situations.

Admiral Stevens said that, at present, NSC papers are the only approved guides to national policy and cited the NSC paper on the U.S.S.R. in which the policy of reducing the threat of Soviet power and

---

[1] Source: National Archives, RG 59, S/P Files: Lot 64 D 563, Political and Psychological Warfare. Top Secret. Drafted by Phillip H. Watts, Executive Secretary of the Policy Planning Staff.

influence is set forth. How far, he asked, do you have to reduce the power and influence to have meaning. The fomenting of revolution within the U.S.S.R. is to be treated separately because the U.S. is not prepared for such an undertaking and would have no assurance of success, but in order to form an over-all concept it has to be considered.

Admiral Stevens referred to the PSB paper dated 15 November, entitled *National Psychological Strategy*,[2] which had been sent to the Department informally the previous week. He said it was only a working draft intended to evince reactions from State and CIA. What he'd like, would be to have Bohlen, Nitze, Joyce and Wisner get together and see if they couldn't come up with a "central strategic concept."

Mr. Nitze suggested that perhaps it would be better to start at the narrowest part of the problem, i.e. how to reduce the threat of Soviet power and influence.

Admiral Stevens said that the PSB draft was an attempt to outline the steps necessary to create a central strategic concept and that NSC 10/5[3] was a "holding operation" which he defined as "placing the maximum strain on the Soviet structure of power."

Mr. Nitze pointed out that "maximum strain" were meaningless words—that we should get down to the concrete.

Admiral Stevens returned to the PSB draft and said that what State had been asked for was (a) its point of view about creating revolutions in the satellites, (b) what political actions would be undertaken for the holding operation set forth in NSC 10/5, and (c) what could be accomplished by other actions including propaganda controlled by State.

Mr. Nitze again urged that we take a concrete problem such as the retraction and reduction of Soviet power and influence. This is *one* policy objective of the U.S. Government but *not* the sum total of U.S. policy—there are a whole hierarchy of objectives. It would be fine if Soviet power would retract but as you get down to accomplishing this you get into many complex problems. Stimulating a revolution in the U.S.S.R. is not now a current practical objective.

Admiral Stevens said a statement to this effect should be put out and approved by the NSC. OPC needs this kind of a statement as part of a central concept.

Mr. Bohlen said there is no single policy but a multiplicity of policies like the multiplicity of dots which make the whole image on a radarscope. He said he wasn't clear how a central concept would be helpful—we should look at specific areas—Albania, for example. There

---

[2] A copy is in National Archives, RG 59, Central Files 1950–54, 100.4–PSB/5–1551.

[3] Document 90.

are many serious complications which flow from creating a revolution in any satellite country.

Mr. Nitze said he felt that we should develop our capabilities in the covert field as far as possible. We should move up in successive first approximations on an area by area, technique by technique basis.

Admiral Stevens agreed with the area by area approach and said that OPC must then come in with what it is capable of doing. He said he realized that a central concept wouldn't solve all our problems but that we ought to try to put one down on paper.

Mr. Bohlen suggested that it might be possible to take specific areas such as East Germany, Poland, Czechoslovakia, etc., and assuming that we had certain covert action capabilities, take a look at what the political implications of such actions would be. At the same time we might select certain areas and assuming the existence of favorable political factors have OPC determine what their covert capabilities were. Then the two determinations might be married.

Mr. Nitze said he worried about theoretical situations. Where there existed a clear problem with concrete possibilities of accomplishing something, this approach might be OK, but taking a series of hypothetical situations and trying to see through all the branching implications and reactions would be a negative exercise.

Admiral Stevens said that some of the fringe areas around the U.S.S.R. are vulnerable and we should look carefully to see what can be done. He said OPC was capable of carrying out several simultaneous operations if it seemed desirable to do so.

Mr. Bohlen said that Wisner needs to know the general direction in which we want to proceed so that he can lay out his plans and have his agents prepared. Therefore, we should take a look at individual areas.

Admiral Stevens said it still gets back to a central strategic concept. Put down on paper that we don't want to create a revolution in the U.S.S.R. as well as some of the "lesser things" we do want to do. It will just be an approximation to be used as guidelines for PSB and OPC.

Mr. Nitze again emphasized the difficulty of setting forth general principles until you get down to specific problems. There is always the danger that people will think that by having broad principles lots of specific problems will be solved.

Admiral Stevens said he still thought that we'd make the biggest advance if State would undertake to respond to the request in the PSB paper.

Mr. Nitze said he thought that joint work with OPC and PSB was called for so that everyone would be clear on the dimensions of the problem and just what was to be accomplished. He suggested that we address ourselves to the specific question of the retraction and reduction of Soviet power and influence. He said he could envisage a paper broken down somewhat as follows:

a. Reduction and retraction of Soviet power to acceptable proportions over a 10-year period.
b. Any thought of revolution in the U.S.S.R. must come at the end of the 10-year period.
c. Reduction of Soviet power in the Satellites in the near term.
d. The development of techniques to accomplish a, b, and c.

This is a first approximation and should be kept under continuing review.

Admiral Stevens said he would like to have a "good" State Department man sit with his committee to coordinate the responses to the PSB paper.

Mr. Nitze replied that taking responses and putting them together wouldn't work—what was needed was joint work by State, OPC, and PSB.

There followed an inconclusive discussion of the term "psychological strategy", during which Mr. Nitze pointed out the dangers involved in trying to marry propaganda and covert operations. They should be kept separate and made concrete and definable.

Admiral Stevens returned to the PSB paper and asked if State could put anything on paper which would be helpful—could it, for instance, redraft the three requests made of it?

Mr. Nitze said he considered the framework of the paper wrong. It appeared that the retraction and reduction of Soviet power and influence was the "be all" and "end all" of our policy. If this phase of our policy could be taken as a specific problem and so addressed, he thought we could come up with something useful. He ended the meeting by saying that we would get together with someone from OPC and PSB and try to map out a course of action.

97.   **Memorandum From Director of Central Intelligence Smith to the Executive Secretary of the National Security Council (Lay)**[1]

Washington, December 10, 1951.

SUBJECT

Proposed Survey of Communications Intelligence Activities

1. In view of the duties and responsibilities imposed upon the Director of Central Intelligence and the Central Intelligence Agency by Section 102(d) of the National Security Act of 1947, as amended, the DCI herewith advises the National Security Council that he is gravely concerned as to the security and effectiveness with which the Communications Intelligence activities of the Government are being conducted.

2. It is believed that existing means of control over, and coordination of, the collection and processing of Communications Intelligence have proved ineffective to assess and reconcile the Communications Intelligence requirements of the various interested Departments and Agencies and, as well, the national intelligence requirements in this field.

3. It is further believed that the system of divided authorities and multiple responsibilities which prevails with respect to Communications Intelligence will, if uncorrected, preclude the development of the consistent, firmly administered security program which is required in order to preserve this invaluable intelligence source. In recent years a number of losses have occurred which it is difficult to attribute to coincidence.

4. Because of the unique value of Communications Intelligence, this matter directly affects the national security. Any corrective measures to be taken should be based upon a thorough investigation of the facts and should give due regard to the needs of the National Security Establishment and those of the various Departments and Agencies concerned.

5. Accordingly, it is recommended that the Secretary of State and the Secretary of Defense, assisted by the Director of Central Intelligence, be asked to have the Communications Intelligence activities of the Government surveyed, with the view of recommending any corrective measures that may be required to insure the most secure and effective conduct of such activities.

Walter B. Smith

---

[1] Source: National Security Agency, Center for Cryptologic History, Series XVI, C–3 (CIA Reports). Top Secret. "Approved Dec 13 '51 /s/ Harry S Truman" is handwritten in the bottom left corner of the memorandum.

98.   Letter From Director of Central Intelligence Smith to Secretary of Defense Lovett[1]

Washington, December 11, 1951.

Dear Mr. Secretary:

In anticipation of the probability of a military cease-fire in Korea, as well as the possibility of a breakdown in negotiations, it becomes important to review our assets in China proper and the effect thereon of either development. A year ago the Chinese Nationalist Government claimed the existence of 1,500,000 guerrillas on the Mainland of China, and although we believe that this figure was exaggerated, we know that during the past year the effective action of the Chinese Communist forces has greatly reduced the number of guerrillas. The current CIA estimate is approximately 165,000. A military cease-fire on the Korean peninsula will probably restore freedom of movement to a major portion of Chinese forces now confronting us, and it is to be assumed that the Chinese Communist Government will then take action to intensify the anti-guerrilla campaign.

Another asset is the Chinese Nationalist Forces on Taiwan. Their army now consists of about 450,000 ground troops in fair state of small unit training but with inadequate equipment and in a poor state of combat effectiveness. Their small Navy and Air Force have both deteriorated militarily as a result of lack of equipment and training facilities. These forces will within four years begin to undergo a rapid deterioration through age alone. They, like the guerrillas on the Mainland, represent a waning asset which will have to be strengthened, built up, and used within the immediate foreseeable future if we are to get any benefit from them.

The military and economic programs for the support of Taiwan, such as they are, have attained only limited success. This is due in part at least to Nationalist refusal to effect political reform and particularly to the failure of the Nationalist Government to eliminate corruption among its officials. Our support to guerrillas has so far failed to produce the results which had been initially anticipated, due primarily to Nationalist reluctance to commit their guerrilla assets to action and secondarily to the difficulty of Chinese Nationalist regular officers of senior grade to adapt themselves to the conditions and requirements of guerrilla warfare.

---

[1] Source: Central Intelligence Agency, Office of the Deputy Director for Operations, Job 79–01228A, Box 11. Top Secret.

Recent studies based on personal observation on the spot by several qualified officers serving with this Agency indicate the following:

(a) The Chinese Nationalist forces are not as ineffective potentially as the pessimistic reports made a year ago, by our Service Attachés then on Taiwan, would indicate. Neither are they as effective as the optimistic reports of Americans now employed directly or indirectly by the Chinese Nationalist Government would indicate. My belief is that they can be made effective and that if U.N. policy permitted, and if the Nationalist Government would cooperate effectively, Chinese Nationalist divisions could be rotated to Korea and might serve very creditably. It is the opinion of General Wyman[2] and other qualified observers that the presence of a Nationalist division in Korea in contact with former Nationalist troops now serving the Communist Government would have a marked psychological effect.

(b) The existing scattered and relatively ineffective guerrilla forces on the Mainland, if well led, armed, and given a political rallying point, could be made a potent weapon and might contain much stronger Chinese Communist forces.

(c) The presence on Taiwan of a Chinese Nationalist force gaining in strength as the result of training, improved morale, and improved equipment, would, particularly if its combat training should include repeated and aggressive raids and temporary thrusts onto the Mainland, immobilize for coastal defense a considerable portion of the better troops of the Chinese Communist Army and a large quantity of its military transport. The Nationalist troops on certain offshore islands are doing this at the present time on a small scale and the threat could be intensified.

In my opinion if we are to obtain the full effect of the possibilities enumerated above, two things are required. The first is a change in our own policy with respect to employment of Chinese Nationalist forces and a more aggressive approach to the use of guerrillas. Second: political reform of the Chinese Nationalist Government is essential. So far U.S. efforts to encourage such reform have been almost without success as the controlling clique of the KMT has been unwilling to loosen its stranglehold on the Government. It is probable that this intransigeance stems from the belief that maintenance of the status quo gives this clique an exclusive claim to reinheritance of the Mainland as a byproduct of U.S. victory in World War III.

Attached are two studies[3] bearing on the basic subject which I suggest be given military staff consideration. One of these represents the

---

[2] Major General Willard G. Wyman, a so-called China hand, serving as Commander of US Forces, Southeastern Europe at this time.

[3] Not printed.

views of the Estimates Division of this Agency[4] which, although not an IAC coordinated paper, reflects the most recent estimates of the military intelligence agencies. As will be noted, this paper does not concern itself with the beneficial effects which would result from an improvement of the political situation on Taiwan. The other study which represents the views of the operating divisions of CIA points up the difficulties resulting from the present unsatisfactory political situation and concentrates upon the importance of a housecleaning in Taiwan and a clarification of U.S. policy if significant results are to be achieved.

These are my personal views, based on conversations with all those in this Agency who are giving consideration to the exploitation of our assets in the Far East. I recommend, however, that the Joint Chiefs of Staff consider this general subject and the attached papers as a matter of urgency for the purpose of amplifying and firming up our present program and, if indicated by mature consideration, producing recommendations which will crystallize our governmental policy toward the strengthening of Taiwan as an anti-Communist base militarily, economically, politically, and psychologically. It seems to me that the self-interest of the United States demands this.

Personnel of CIA are prepared to participate and assist in this study and in the planning which should follow. For this purpose I have arranged to secure the services of General Frank Merrill[5] who, as you know, is experienced in commando-type operations in the Far East and he would head the CIA contribution to any planning syndicate which you may desire to establish.

Sincerely,

Walter B. Smith[6]

---

[4] Estimates Division is the Office of National Estimates.

[5] Major General Merrill (Ret.) was a veteran of both the China and Burma Theaters.

[6] Printed from a copy that indicates Smith signed the original.

99.   Editorial Note

On December 13, 1951, President Truman directed the Secretary of State and the Secretary of Defense, assisted by the Director of Central Intelligence, to appoint a committee to examine United States Government Communications Intelligence (COMINT) efforts and to recommend measures to improve their conduct and security. (Truman Library, President's Secretary's File) The committee was headed by prominent New York attorney George A. Brownell and included Charles E. Bohlen, representing the Department of State, General John Magruder, representing the Department of Defense, and William H. Jackson, representing the Central Intelligence Agency. The committee submitted a five-part report on June 13, 1952. Part I was a history of U.S. COMINT efforts, Part II dealt with the role of COMINT, Part III laid out the then-current organization of the COMINT community, Part IV detailed the actual conduct of COMINT activities, and Part V consisted of the report's conclusions and recommendations.

The major findings of the report were that the four existing COMINT organizations (Army, Navy, Air Force, and Armed Forces Security Agency (AFSA), which was controlled by the JCS) were conducting duplicative operations in many areas and that the U.S. Communications Intelligence Board (USCIB) lacked adequate authority to correct the situation. The report recommended that AFSA be given greatly expanded authority over the service organizations, that the AFSA director report directly to the Secretary of Defense, and that USCIB be replaced by a new, strengthened COMINT Board chaired by the DCI.

In October 1952, the President and the NSC adopted most of the Brownell Committee's recommendations and issued a revised version of NSCID No. 9 on October 24, 1952 (Document 257). In place of AFSA, the National Security Agency was created. NSA had the same resources as AFSA, but a different charter. The JCS was removed from the chain of command. The Secretary of Defense was made executive agent for the government as a whole for COMINT, subordinate to a special committee of the NSC consisting of himself and the Secretary of State, advised by the Director of Central Intelligence.

The Brownell Committee report is in National Archives, RG 457, SRH–123, Brownell Committee Report; a declassified version is available in George A. Brownell, *The Origins and Development of the National Security Agency* (Laguna Hills, CA: Aegean Park Press, 1981).

100.   Memorandum of Conversation[1]

Washington, January 17, 1952.

SUBJECT

> Meeting to Discuss the Crusade for Freedom held in Mr. Barrett's Office on
> January 17, 1952

PARTICIPANTS

> CIA—Mr. Allen Dulles, Mr. Frank Wisner, Mr. Tom Braden and Mr. Gates Lloyd
>
> NCFE—Mr. C. D. Jackson and Mr. Abbott Washburn
>
> State—Mr. Edward W. Barrett, Mr. Howland H. Sargeant, Mr. Foy Kohler, Mr.
> Robert P. Joyce and Mr. John Devine

Agreement:

As the result of the discussion it was agreed that the Crusade for
Freedom would be continued in 1952 but in a considerably lower key
in comparison with the 1951 Crusade. The precise nature of the Crusade is to be worked out cooperatively by NCFE, CIA and the Department of State.

Discussion:

Mr. Jackson said that he and his colleagues realize that they cannot repeat the 1951 type Crusade. He raised the question of whether
there should be a Crusade at all and answered it by saying that he felt
that some sort of Crusade had to continue. He said that the major question was what sort of Crusade could be organized and still not present serious problems for the Department of State. Mr. Jackson said
that the most troublesome aspect of the 1951 Crusade was its length of
three months. He said that a shorter Crusade pitched at a lower level
would solve many of the problems that had occurred in the past year.
He said that one good idea that had been developed by local committees was to have a one-day civic organization doorbell ringing campaign. Some buildup of publicity would be necessary for a national
doorbell ringing campaign but it would be nothing to compare with
the extended Crusade of this year. Mr. Jackson said that the direct mail
approach had been tried this year with some success and could be expanded. He added that he felt the short campaign would have the additional advantage of removing the possibility of the public's making
invidious comparisons between RFE and VOA. He said that with the

---

[1] Source: National Archives, RG 59, S/S–NSC Files: Lot 63 D 351, no folder title,
Box 48. Top Secret; Security Information. Drafted by John Devine of the Bureau of Public Affairs on January 21.

short campaign there would not be time for the public to reflect on such issues.

Mr. Barrett reminded the group that NCFE had started as an organization to look after and make use of the various Eastern European refugee groups. He recalled that giving these groups a radio voice was something of a later development. He also recalled that the Crusade was established primarily as a cover for the governmental support of the enterprise. Mr. Barrett raised the question of whether or not the Crusade had grown to such proportions that it was now a case of the tail wagging the dog. He also raised the question of whether the two or three million dollars that might be raised in the Crusade might be endangering the $85,000,000 involved in the appropriations for the USIE operations. He thought it was important to get back to the idea of just enough of a Crusade to give the minimum necessary cover to NCFE. Mr. Barrett suggested direct mail solicitation of funds, magazine advertisements and coupons, and corporation solicitations. He also said that he thought the device of large anonymous gifts might be looked into further.

Mr. Jackson said that after the 1951 campaign it became clear to him that the Crusade had actually done an important selling job on the American public in the matter of psychological warfare and the importance of such an effort to our nation. He felt that this was a most important aspect of the Crusade and one that had been usually overlooked. Mr. Jackson said also that an efficient field organization had been built up for the Crusade and it was one which could respond to almost any kind of stimuli we wanted to apply.

Mr. Kohler suggested that the Crusade's national organization might be used to communicate to the public other messages which would be useful in connection with the United States' psychological warfare effort.

Mr. Sargeant said that if the Crusade's national organization were really going to continue to be a force in the situation, it would be necessary to keep it busy the year around with useful projects such as film shows, publicizing the visits of foreign labor leaders, and participating in other activities relating to the international propaganda situation.

Mr. Barrett said that it was important to secure international sponsorship for the RFE broadcasts as had been done for the balloon operations.

Mr. Jackson said that the international nature of the balloon message did not add anything to its effectiveness. He said that current attempts to set up committees in France and England along the lines of NCFE were not succeeding and he doubted seriously whether that was a fruitful line of further endeavor. Mr. Jackson said that he felt the development should be toward the Munich-type of operation to Czechoslovakia where the program has acquired such a predominantly local coloration that the American connection is almost completely submerged. Mr. Dulles agreed that an international committee was not a workable arrangement.

Mr. Washburn said that two million dollars gross had been raised in the Crusade this year when there was a stated goal. He thought that the next Crusade need not have a specific goal and that such a change would help keep things in a low key.

Mr. Kohler commented that in the 1951 Crusade, the impression was given that the combined efforts of RFE and RFA were covering the world as far as radio propaganda needs were concerned.

Mr. Sargeant said that he felt a Crusade national organization could serve a useful purpose in developing popular interest in psychological warfare and could at the same time assign tasks to local groups which would actually assist in the psychological warfare effort. He mentioned writing of letters and essay contests.

Mr. Dulles said that he hoped that the group could agree on the Crusade's going ahead this year on a program that will be worked out in close coordination with VOA.

Mr. Jackson said that he hoped a four point decision could be reached:

1. That the Crusade should go ahead this year.
2. That it should take place in September at the earliest and not last more than two weeks.
3. That the Crusade national organization should proceed in the meantime with the jobs of general education on psychological warfare matters, and an explanation of VOA–RFE relationships.
4. That NCFE should collaborate with the Department of State on what should be said to local groups.

Mr. Jackson's suggestions were discussed but there was no general agreement.

Mr. Barrett felt that agreement at this time should be limited to saying that the Crusade organization should not be disbanded, that there should be a Crusade in 1952 of a considerably lower pitched nature, and that the precise character of the 1952 Crusade should be worked out in close consultation between NCFE, CIA and State. This was agreed to by all present.

101. Memorandum From the Deputy Director for Plans of the Central Intelligence Agency (Wisner) to the Chief of Staff of the Air Force (Vandenberg)[1]

Washington, January 22, 1952.

SUBJECT

Civil Air Transport's Application for Commercial Rights in Okinawa

REFERENCE

a. GHQ Far East Command Letter AG 095 (22 November 1951) GD/D, dated November 22, 1951, Subject: Civil Air Transport's Application for Commercial Rights in Okinawa[2]

1. It is understood that reference a. has been forwarded by the Department of the Army to the Department of the Air Force for action. The Psychological Warfare Division of the latter Department has informally requested this Agency to make a statement of its interest in the matter.

2. Civil Air Transport (CAT, Incorporated) is a Chinese flag airline wholly owned by the United States Government and controlled by this Agency. As a commercial airline, Civil Air Transport performs a wide variety of covert services for the Agency throughout the Far East [2 lines not declassified]. It is the single most valuable asset of the CIA in the Far East, without which the Agency would find it impossible either to discharge its operational tasks or to plan the greatly increased activities envisaged under NSC 68[3] and 10/5.[4]

3. [1 paragraph (15 lines) not declassified]

4. Apart from the U.S. Government's interest outlined above, there appears to be ample justification for approving Civil Air Transport's application on strictly commercial grounds. Firstly, whereas under the terms of the Sino-U.S. bilateral agreement a United States carrier is permitted to serve Formosa, the Chinese Government's designated instrument, Civil Air Transport, by virtue of its aircraft limitations, has been unable to avail itself of rights to serve points in the U.S. territories specified in the route annex of the agreement. Notwithstanding the precise terms of the agreement, it would seem in order, as a matter of

---

[1] Source: Central Intelligence Agency, Executive Registry, Job 95–G00278R, Box 1, Folder 15. Top Secret. Security Information. Drafted in the Far East Division of OPC on January 11. Sent to Vandenberg through the Joint Subsidiary Plans Division of the Joint Chiefs of Staff.

[2] Not found.

[3] See Foreign Relations, 1950, vol. I, pp. 234–292.

[4] Document 90.

comity, to grant the designated airline of China traffic rights to serve an alternate point under United States control which is within the airline's capabilities to serve. Secondly, the routes flown by Civil Air Transport naturally include Okinawa and it is hardly justifiable that Okinawa, a point in the immediate trading area of Formosa, should be denied the service of the international airline of China. Thirdly, Civil Air Transport is the only airline in the area which has the capacity and the willingness to render low cost cargo and passenger service commensurate with the economy of the area; this factor is expected to attract substantial traffic of U.S. contractors and others on Okinawa employing indigenous personnel. It is not calculated, however, that any appreciable inroad will be made on the business of other competitive airlines inasmuch as the type of traffic which could be carried by Civil Air Transport would not, in any event, be moved by other commercial air carriers. Lastly, it would constitute an economic hardship to the airline in serving its routes from Korea to Thailand to have no traffic rights at Okinawa inasmuch as it would still be necessary to make technical stops at Okinawa for the purpose of fueling.

5. With reference to the final paragraph of reference a. it should be noted that the Civil Aeronautics Board does not have jurisdiction over civil air operations at Okinawa except where carriers of the United States are involved. This Agency does not desire that the United States Government's interests in Civil Air Transport be disclosed to the Board at this time; conversely, it is believed that coordination with the Board, without disclosure of United States Government interest might lead to unnecessary delays and possible obstructions by representations of interested United States carriers. It is requested, therefore, that the matter not be coordinated with Civil Aeronautics Board as suggested. The subject has, however, been discussed with Mr. Alexis Johnson, Deputy Assistant Secretary for Far Eastern Affairs, Department of State, who has stated that the Department will interpose no objection to approval of Civil Air Transport's application.

6. The Agency considers it a matter of great importance and urgency that the subject application be approved. Failure to obtain such approval will result in the most serious setbacks to the Agency's operations.

Frank G. Wisner[5]

---

[5] Printed from a copy that bears this typed signature.

102.   Memorandum for the Record[1]

Washington, February 15, 1952.

SUBJECT

Meeting with USAF Representatives Regarding USAF Photo Reconnaissance Requirements

1. [name not declassified] and 1st Lt. C. W. Matt[2] attended a meeting with representatives of USAF to discuss and explore the requirement for a pre-D-Day reconnaissance of the USSR. Air Force representatives included officers from Requirements, Plans, Operations, Intelligence, Development and the AF State Department representative. Brig. Gen. Garland was the senior officer present.

2. In opening the discussions, the Chairman stated that it was necessary to develop a firm requirement in order to sell State Department in the need for relaxing the diplomatic side enough to permit violations of sovereignty. It will be necessary to impress on State the degree to which our offensive will rely on pre-D-Day reconnaissance in order to carry out our post-D-Day strikes. Secondly, Air Force must point out the large vacuum existing in intelligence regarding the USSR. The Chairman stated that SAC had been asked to participate in developing a requirement. SAC, however, declined, stating that in their view the requirement should be based on the need for intelligence. SAC did not want to raise the implication that their offensive would be delayed by waiting for reconnaissance!!!

3. The representative from Development outlined what was on hand or would be available in the future. He stated that it was necessary to obtain guidance on which item or items to push. In other words, where will they put their money? He discussed balloons, drones, a recon version of the Snark[3] and piloted aircraft. The recon Snark should be available in 1954 and will have speed of Mach .95 and altitude of 52,000. Drones can now be controlled up to 50 miles and this can probably be raised to 200 miles. Gopher balloons will be available in the fall of 1952.

4. Requirements representative stated that recon was needed on (1) new industrial complexes and air facilities for which there is no

---

[1] Source: Central Intelligence Agency, History Staff, Job 83–00036R, Box 11. Secret; Security Information. Drafted by [name not declassified], Air Maritime Division, Office of Policy Coordination, Central Intelligence Agency.

[2] Both of CIA's Air Maritime Division.

[3] Snark was a proposed Air Force strategic cruise missile.

intelligence or for which we need new intelligence, (2) area from Urals to FE on which there is no photo coverage and (3) general recon to uncover new targets developed since WW II. It was also pointed out that warning requirement was also of prime importance.

5. Air Force State representative reported that State had formerly taken a dim view of violations such as photo recon would involve. However, he believed that now that international affairs had gotten to present condition, State might not take as serious objections as before. They might agree that the planes, etc., might get shot down the indicent would not start a war. [sic] He stated balloons might cause misgivings in State because of their lack of directional control and possible aimless wanderings. Representative seemed to think State might go along with Snark, drones, etc., if requirement strongly presented.

6. CIA representative was asked how CIA might contribute. It was pointed out that only a very limited capability existed at present. A CIA capability might be developed but will require a large amount of support from Air Force. At best, and for some time in the future, CIA capability will be largely peripheral.

7. It was decided that Intelligence Section of USAF would develop the draft requirement from the intelligence viewpoint. Other sections would assist as required. Presumably, CIA will be specifically asked for any future information if Air Force so desires.

[name not declassified][4]

---

[4] Printed from a copy that bears this typed signature.

---

103. Memorandum From the Acting Assistant Director for Special Operations of the Central Intelligence Agency (Helms) to the Deputy Director for Plans of the Central Intelligence Agency (Wisner)

Washington, February 16, 1952.

[Source: Central Intelligence Agency, Directorate of Operations, Job 75–05091R, Box 1, Folder 37. Secret; Security Information. 3 pages not declassified.]

104. Memorandum From the Director of the Psychological Strategy Board (Allen) to Board Members[1]

Washington, February 20, 1952.

SUBJECT

Procedure for Handling 10/5 Matters in PSB

I recommend that the following arrangements and procedures be formally approved by the Psychological Strategy Board in order that it may most effectively discharge its responsibilities under paragraph 3 of NSC 10/5:[2]

1. A special panel will be created by PSB, the membership of which will consist of the same representatives of the Secretary of State and of the Secretary of Defense who now advise the Central Intelligence Agency's Office of Policy Coordination pursuant to NSC 10/2, and the representative of the Joint Chiefs of Staff who acts in a similar capacity.[3] The membership will also include a representative of the Central Intelligence Agency and two representatives of the Psychological Strategy Board, designated by the Director, Psychological Strategy Board, one of whom shall act as Chairman of the panel.

2. This panel shall consider all programs and individual major projects within the scope of NSC 10/5 which are submitted to the panel for review by the Director of Central Intelligence.

3. In the light of national policy and preliminary and tentative estimates of available resources, the panel will review the desirability of the programs and major projects which have been referred to it and reach agreement or disagreement as to recommendations for approval, modification, or disapproval.

---

[1] Source: National Archives, RG 59, S/S–NSC Files: Lot 62 D 333. Top Secret; Security Information. Forwarded to Under Secretary of State Webb under cover of a letter from Allen of the same date. The letter was returned to Allen with a note dated February 25. A handwritten notation on the letter indicates that it was approved by Webb. (Ibid.)

[2] Document 90. In a letter of March 14 Allen informed H. Freeman Matthews, Deputy Under Secretary of State, that he had received written approval from each member of the Board. Allen further stated that C. Tracy Barnes, his deputy, was being designated chairman of the special panel to be established under the approved procedure. (National Archives, RG 59, S/S Files: Lot 56 D 459, Secretary's Letters, Defense 1952)

[3] For text of NSC 10/2, see Foreign Relations, 1945–1950, Emergence of the Intelligence Establishment, Document 292. The representatives were Robert P. Joyce (State), Brigadier General John Magruder (Defense), and Rear Admiral Leslie C. Stevens (JCS).

4. All of the following projects or programs will be referred by the panel to the Director of PSB for submission to the PSB:

(a) Any program or "major" project on which the panel as a whole cannot reach unanimous agreement;

(b) Any program or "major" project which in the opinion of any member of the panel raises a question of policy, desirability or feasibility of sufficient importance to warrant formal consideration by the PSB.

5. Any program or "major" project on which the panel as a whole has reached unanimous agreement and which has not been referred to the Director of PSB for submission to the PSB under the provisions of paragraph 4 (b) above shall be handled as follows:

(a) The representative of the Director of Central Intelligence on the panel shall present the program or project to the Director of Central Intelligence for his approval if not already formally recommended by him. If he approves, the Director of Central Intelligence shall sign and file with the Director of PSB a written statement approving such project or program and agreeing that the Central Intelligence Agency will provide such support as such project or program requires from the Central Intelligence Agency as evidenced by the requirements approved by the panel.

(b) The representative of the Secretary of State on the panel shall present the program or project to the Under Secretary of State for his approval. If he approves, the Under Secretary of State shall sign and file with the Director of PSB a written statement approving such project or program from the standpoint of national policy and agreeing that the Department of State will provide such support as such project or program requires from the Department of State as evidenced by the requirements approved by the panel.

(c) The representative of the Secretary of Defense on the panel shall present the program or project to the Deputy Secretary of Defense for his approval. If he approves, the Deputy Secretary of Defense shall sign and file with the Director of PSB a written statement approving such project or program from the standpoint of national policy and agreeing that the Department of Defense will provide such support as such project or program requires from the Department of Defense as evidenced by the requirements approved by the panel.

6. Any program or project which has received the approval of the Director of Central Intelligence, the Under Secretary of State and the Deputy Secretary of Defense, under the provisions of paragraph 5, above, shall be deemed to have received the approval of the Psychological Strategy Board in accordance with the requirements of NSC 10/5.

7. In the event that the Director of Central Intelligence, the Under Secretary of State or the Deputy Secretary of Defense shall report that his Department or Agency, respectively, is unwilling or unable to provide the approval and agreement set forth in paragraphs 5 (a), 5 (b), or 5 (c) above, the project or program in question shall be referred by the panel to the Director of the Psychological Strategy Board for submission to the Psychological Strategy Board for its further action.

8. In the event that the Director of Central Intelligence, the Under Secretary of State, or the Deputy Secretary of Defense recommend any amendment, modification, or other changes to the program or project, the program or project, together with such recommendations, will be referred back to the panel for further action, under procedures identical to those applicable to the original submission of programs and projects to the panel.

RBA

---

105. Memorandum From the Under Secretary of State (Bruce) to the Executive Secretary of the National Security Council (Lay)[1]

Washington, April 7, 1952.

SUBJECT

Fourth Progress Report on NSC 26 Series, "Removal and Demolition of Oil Facilities, Equipment and Supplies in the Middle East"

NSC 26/2,[2] NSC 26/4 and NSC 26/5[3] were approved as governmental policy on January 10, 1949, August 18, 1950 and May 3, 1951, respectively. It is requested that this fourth progress report as of March 10, 1952 be circulated to the members of the Council for their information.

Important Developments:

1. July 9, 1951, the Secretary of Defense stated that due to worsening world conditions and increased global requirements, "the earmarking of a military contingent for the specific use in connection

---

[1] Source: Truman Library, Papers of Harry S. Truman, President's Secretary's File, Subject File. Top Secret; Special Handling.

[2] Not printed. (National Archives, RG 59, S/S–NSC Files: Lot 63 D 351, Box 51)

[3] Neither printed. (Ibid., RG 273, Policy Papers of the NSC: NSC 26, Box 9)

with NSC 26/2 should not be done in advance".[4] He added that the JCS were of the opinion that although "under certain circumstances a force such as the Battalion of Marines now in the Mediterranean might be available for this mission", "the sending of a force to Saudi Arabia must be decided at the time (of the emergency) in view of the overall situation confronting us".

2. [4 paragraphs (39 lines) not declassified]

3. On August 14, 1951 it was recommended by State [less than 1 line not declassified] field representatives in Dhahran, Saudi Arabia in consultation with local US military officials that the company notify the Saudi Arabian Government in a most general way of denial and evacuation plans.[5] On August 21, 1951 it was decided by the Departments of State and Defense in consultation [less than 1 line not declassified] that not only denial plans, but also broader national policies in the area, would be jeopardized by such disclosure to SAG officials at that time and that no indication should be given that the Western powers might abandon the area.[6]

4. On August 22, 1951 the National Security Council discussed the third progress report and noted that the Secretary of State would issue a directive [3 lines not declassified].[7]

5. On September 10, 1951 the Bahrein Petroleum Company informed the Department of State of its acceptance of the denial policy provided: (a) concurrence of the local government were obtained before the program could be put into effect, and (b) company claims for reimbursement would be "treated upon the same footing as claims of other companies elsewhere who cooperate in like measures".[8]

6. [3 paragraphs (11 lines) not declassified]

7. [16 lines not declassified] Similar problems in Saudi Arabia have been presented to the US military for resolution. No problems have arisen that require action on the NSC level."[9]

8. January 16–February 3, 1952, a mission of State–Defense–CIA–US oil company representatives visited Middle East oil areas of United States denial responsibility, i.e. Saudi Arabia, Kuwait, Bahrein, Qatar, to review NSC 26 progress, plans, policies and problems. Conclusions and recommendations, which are now under State–Defense–CIA study, will be presented in the next progress report.

---

[4] Not printed. (Ibid.)

[5] Not found.

[6] Not found.

[7] See Document 84.

[8] Not found.

[9] Not found.

Action Now Contemplated

Further action required to implement NSC 26 includes further development of Aramco-type denial plans to Kuwait, Kuwait Neutral Zone, Bahrein and Qatar; [*less than 1 line not declassified*]; continual examination of the situation re protective forces; and inter-Departmental consideration of problems observed during the January field mission, i.e. implementation of the denial plans in the event of local opposition, status of company personnel engaged in denial operations, degree of denial throughout Middle East oil areas, clearer definition of the national interest in preserving oil reservoirs, notification of local authorities regarding denial plans, delegation of field responsibility for NSC 26, security of denial plans, coordination of denial plans with production plans, rehabilitation plans, personnel protection, evacuation, and counter-sabotage plans.

Policy Evaluation

Policy evaluation will be withheld pending a resolution of the problems mentioned in the above paragraph, following which recommendations will be made as to whether new Council action, including the revision of NSC 26, is desirable.

David Bruce[10]

---

[10] Printed from a copy that indicates Bruce signed the original.

---

106. Memorandum From the Deputy Director for Plans of the Central Intelligence Agency (Wisner) to Director of Central Intelligence Smith and the Deputy Director of Central Intelligence (Dulles)[1]

Washington, April 10, 1952.

SUBJECT

United States Policies on Support for Anti-Communist Chinese Forces

---

[1] Source: Central Intelligence Agency, Office of the Deputy Director for Operations, Job 79–01228A, Box 11. Top Secret; Security Information; Eyes Only.

1. This memorandum is prepared for the information and use of the Director and the Deputy Director only. It summarizes the discussion which took place at the JCS Conference Room at 11:00 a.m. Wednesday, 9 April 1952. The State Department was represented by Messrs. Bohlen, Nitze, Allison and Ferguson. The JCS was represented by General Bradley, Admiral Fechteler, General Twining, General Hull and General Cabell. The Department of Defense was represented by Mr. Nash, and Mr. Lay was present for the NSC staff. Messrs. Dulles and Wisner represented CIA.

2. The stated subject matter of the meeting was the JCS paper to the NSC on Formosa,[2] although General Bradley pointed out that the subject matter was much broader and stemmed from the Director's December letter to the Secretary of Defense.[3] The composition of the meeting had been determined at the NSC meeting of the preceding week, at the conclusion of which it had been decided that there would be a direct discussion of the policy questions raised by the JCS paper as between State, Defense, JCS and CIA, as a preliminary to a possible NSC staff study of the matter. CIA had been included because of the matter having been originally raised by the Director's letter and also because of the importance of the policy review to large and significant CIA operations in the area concerned.

3. Mr. Bohlen began for State by giving a brief résumé of our present policy with respect to Formosa and the Chinese Nationalists, which is largely spelled out in NSC 48/5.[4] Following this, Mr. Bohlen said that he would like to take up the points in the JCS paper of 22 March 1952, one by one, in order to clarify certain doubts which the State Department had as to the significance and underlying meaning of these points. It was not clear to the Department whether the paper refers to what the policy should be on the assumption of a truce in Korea, or whether it proposed modifications of the existing policy either at the present time or on the basis of some other assumption. He asked whether subparagraph (c) meant that the JCS were proposing the lifting of restrictions now in order to allow the Chinese Nationalists to attack the mainland.

4. Admiral Fechteler replied that the meaning of this paragraph is that we should not close the door to movements westward from Formosa. It did not mean that the ban against westward movements should be lifted immediately, but only if conditions should warrant this in the light of developing circumstances.

5. Mr. Nitze replied that this was a very helpful clarification and one quite satisfactory to State. The Department had been concerned

---

[2] Dated March 22; see *Foreign Relations,* 1952–1954, vol. XIV, Part 1, pp. 20–21.

[3] Document 98.

[4] For NSC 48/5, see *Foreign Relations,* 1951, vol. VI, pp. 33–63.

lest this mean a recommendation for an overt policy change at the present time—since such a policy change would be interpreted world-wide as a full engagement of U.S. power and prestige in the destruction of the Chinese Communist regime on the mainland.

6. Admiral Fechteler asked what the situation would be if the Chinese Nationalists should attempt to launch raids against the mainland from Formosa now. What would we do; would we try to stop this; and if so, by what means would we seek to stop it—by diplomatic or by military means? Messrs. Allison and Nitze replied that they regarded this as an academic question at the present time, since the Nationalists are not in a position to launch significant landings against the mainland without our help.

7. General Bradley asked Mr. Dulles whether CIA operations have suffered or are suffering from the existing policy, which prohibits movements east or west, and if so, what changes we consider necessary in order to remove the interferences.

8. [11 lines not declassified] (At a later point in the discussion, Mr. Dulles raised the question as to whether the present policy means that the Nationalists are prevented from reinforcing the offshore islands from Formosa. It was the unanimous response that the present policy does not prohibit the reinforcement or re-supply of the offshore islands from Formosa, since the policy is restrictive only against attacks upon the China mainland. It was further stated that what happens as between the offshore islands and the mainland is not affected by the present policy and that it need not be a concern of this Government.)

9. Mr. Nitze stated with respect to subparagraph (c) that State could accept the explanation and interpretation given by Admiral Fechteler provided its meaning were clearly spelled out as requiring a re-examination of all of the circumstances which might be applicable at the appropriate moment in connection with a determination of whether the circumstances might warrant a lifting of the ban on movement westward.

10. General Hull stated that he considered the question somewhat more fundamental and not so easy to dismiss. The existence of the westward ban implies that we have a substantially negative policy on the use of present and potential resources on Formosa. The question is, "Do we build up or don't we?" If there is to be a build-up, there must be at the very least a philosophy understood and accepted at the top levels of this Government that we are building toward a positive or affirmative exploitation of the Formosa potential. Lacking this philosophy, Formosa will simply fail to receive the priorities and hence won't get the stuff. The other competitive demands for our military aid will eat up all of the matériel, and Formosa will get nothing.

11. Mr. Nitze thought the present language of NSC 48/5 is both broad enough and sufficiently flexible to permit a build-up not only

for defensive purposes but also for possible offensive purposes. He quoted portions of the language of this paper in support of his point.

12. Mr. Bohlen said he was inclined to agree with General Hull's position that the language could be amended slightly to give it a more positive ring, provided that it was clearly understood that we would not tell the Chinese Nationalists that we were changing the policy and undertaking the support of a build-up for offensive purposes. He explained that the Chinese Nationalists would surely exploit any such statement or information on a world-wide basis with grave embarrassment to our over-all position and at a time when it is still difficult to foresee what future developments will bring.

13. Mr. Dulles said that he was troubled about the fact that this is the only spot in the world where we are using our own forces to protect the Communists. Mr. Bohlen replied that this was perhaps theoretically so, but he said that we would no doubt move to restrain any others over whom we have influence if we thought they were likely to launch overt aggressive attacks against the USSR or the satellites. He said, moreover, the "protection of the Communists" is at this time illusory since there is nothing at the moment to protect the Chinese Communists *from*.

14. General Hull in reply to a question from Mr. Allison stated that the JCS did not deem it within the realm of possibility to build up the Chinese Nationalists to the point where they could successfully undertake an invasion of the Chinese mainland without extensive military assistance from us. He said, "If they go back, we have got to put them back."

15. Reverting to an earlier point in the conversation, Mr. Allison said that it might clarify the situation somewhat if we would state now that if there should be an overt Communist attack against Southeast Asia, we would employ the Chinese Nationalist potential against Hainan or such other places as might be most effectively attacked by these forces.

16. General Hull said this would be helpful. General Bradley said that this last point tended to confuse him somewhat. He was trying to sort out in his mind the difference between the paper now under consideration and discussions of another paper relating to what actions we would take in the event of an attack by the Chinese Communists against Southeast Asia. He reminded the meeting that the present discussion grew out of and had been touched off by General Smith's letter, which had taken the line that if we are going to do anything about Formosa, time is of the essence.

17. Mr. Dulles stated that this was as he understood it to be. General Smith's letter had clearly pointed up the aspect of wasting assets and the disintegration of the situation on Formosa from both a military and political standpoint. There are disquieting reports about the political and military situation on Formosa—reports of sagging morale and other things which open up alarming possibilities as to what may

happen if we do not firm up our policy for that area and take appropriate action under the new policy.

18. General Bradley said that this obviously raises the entire question of the validity of our support to Formosa. Why should we be spending several hundreds of millions of dollars and pouring in military supplies and equipment if we are not willing to take the additional steps necessary to insure against a collapse. We are faced with several distasteful conclusions:

a. As matters now stand, we are allowing a useful potential to waste away and are merely throwing good money after bad.

b. It would appear that our present methods cannot be expected to unseat the Communist regime, and that the adoption of the additional military measures to accomplish this result at this time would risk our involvement in a general war, at least against China, and possibly Russia as well.

c. If we withhold or withdraw our aid now, Formosa will collapse in short order.

With respect to this latter point, General Bradley said that the JCS has repeatedly taken the position that the loss of Formosa would be highly damaging to our over-all strategic position, but that this was not sufficiently critical to warrant our putting in U.S. forces to hold Formosa.

19. Mr. Nash stated that the decision of the NSC had, as he understood it, been to review the entire situation and not just one or two isolated features of it. He proposed that a working group comprised of State, Defense, JCS, CIA and NSC representatives should immediately address itself to the broader task.

20. Mr. Bohlen agreed that this was the problem. He said there should be an immediate study of everything that can be done to solidify and stabilize the situation on Formosa.

21. General Bradley also agreed and added that he would like to adopt Mr. Bohlen's proposal of a slight modification of the pertinent language of NSC 48/5. He also said that he thought subparagraphs (d) and (e) of the JCS paper of 22 March represent existing policy and therefore raise no new questions.

22. Mr. Bohlen remarked that General Chase[5] had said when he was here that the average age of the Chinese Nationalist forces on Formosa was some four years younger than the average age of the Division which he had led in the invasion of the Philippines. (Mr. Dulles requested the undersigned to check this point.)

23. Messrs. Nash and Lay reaffirmed Mr. Nash's earlier recommendation that a five-ply working group needs to study the problem in the broad context of General Smith's letter to the Secretary of Defense.

---

[5] Chief of the Military Assistance Advisory Group, Formosa.

24. Just at the conclusion of the discussion, Mr. Dulles stated that CIA would be very glad to continue its participation in this examination of the problem, not only because of what we might be able to contribute from the intelligence standpoint but also because of the large operational stake which we have in the outcome of the deliberation. He reminded General Bradley that CIA had no wish to continue the conduct of such large-scale operations and that General Smith had pointed this out repeatedly and had offered to divest himself of this responsibility if only the JCS or someone else would pick it up. These remarks prompted a ripple of polite laughter around the table, and General Bradley stated (with a smile and a bow towards Mr. Dulles) that he saw no reason to revise the present situation or alter the responsibilities as they now stand.

Frank G. Wisner[6]

---

[6] Printed from a copy that bears this typed signature.

---

107.   Memorandum From Director of Central Intelligence Smith to the National Security Council[1]

Washington, April 23, 1952.

SUBJECT

Report by the Director of Central Intelligence

In July 1949, the National Security Council directed that certain changes be made in the organization of the Central Intelligence Agency. The instructions contained in this Directive—NSC 50[2]—have been carried out in all substantial respects.

There is attached, marked Tab A, a chart of the organization of the Central Intelligence Agency as of October 1950 and an organization chart as of 31 December 1951. A comparison of these charts will indicate the general scope of this reorganization.

---

[1] Source: National Archives, RG 59, S/S–NSC Files: Lot 63 D 351, NSC 50 Series. Top Secret. The memorandum was circulated by NSC Executive Secretary Lay on April 28 as a National Security Council Progress Report on the implementation of NSC 50, "The Central Intelligence Agency and National Organization for Intelligence," July 1, 1949. (Ibid.)

[2] See *Foreign Relations*, 1945–1950, Emergence of the Intelligence Establishment, Document 384.

Specifically, there has been established an Office of National Estimates to produce intelligence estimates of national concern, both in acute situations and on a long-term basis. In its operations this Office utilizes the resources of the total United States intelligence community. The members of the Council are acquainted with the production of the Office of National Estimates, but, for ready reference, there is attached, marked Tab B, a list of the National Intelligence Estimates which were prepared in 1951.[3]

To provide the National Security Council and appropriate offices of the Government with all-source intelligence on a current basis, there was also established during 1951 an Office of Current Intelligence. Council members are acquainted with the publications of this Office.

An Office of Research and Reports has been set up to provide coordinated intelligence, primarily on economic matters, as a service of common concern to interested Government agencies. Although accurate appraisal of an enemy's economic potential is a most important factor in estimating his military capabilities, this crucially-important task had previously been scattered among twenty-four separate agencies of the Government.

An Interdepartmental Economic Intelligence Committee has also been established, and the Agency's Assistant Director for Research and Reports is its Chairman. His Office is the clearing house for study and analysis of the economy of the Soviet Orbit and for exploring and filling the gaps that had developed in the previously unrelated system of collection and evaluation.[4]

In cooperation with the Department of Defense, there has been established the Interdepartmental Watch Committee. Its function is to provide constant and periodic review of indications of possible enemy action. The Central Intelligence Agency also maintains a twenty-four hour watch on behalf of the Agency.[5]

Continuity of high caliber personnel, possessing specialized training and experience, is essential for the conduct of the Agency's activities. Accordingly, plans for a career service within the Central Intelligence Agency are being worked out and the first groups of prospective junior career officers are in training.

After sufficient career personnel have been recruited and trained in this service, it will be possible eventually to select senior officials of the Central Intelligence Agency from among their number. This development will take time. Meanwhile, one of the Agency's continuing

---

[3] Not printed.
[4] See Documents 72 and 73.
[5] See Document 91.

problems will be the difficulty of securing adequately qualified personnel, particularly for senior positions.

Four NSC papers approved during the period under review required the special services of the Central Intelligence Agency:

1. [1 *paragraph (9 lines) not declassified*]

2. NSC 86/1[6] confirmed the operational responsibility abroad of the Central Intelligence Agency with respect to handling defectors. To meet this responsibility, improved machinery has been provided by the Agency for interrogating and caring for the high level defectors, [2 *lines not declassified*]. Nevertheless, both the number and quality of defectors have been disappointing. Studies are being made of inducement programs to improve this situation, and appropriate recommendations will be made in due course to the Interagency Defector Committee. It should be noted in this connection that the care and rehabilitation of escapees and refugees, as distinguished from high level defectors, are not, and should not be, a Central Intelligence Agency responsibility. [2 *lines not declassified*]

3. The third NSC paper—NSC 66/1[7]—directed the Central Intelligence Agency to provide intelligence support for the Voice of America with respect to Soviet jamming. This is being done, but the establishment of an additional monitoring facility to locate Soviet jamming stations, requested by NSC 66/1 of the Armed Forces Security Agency has not been performed, due to technical difficulties. The National Security Council subsequently authorized the Central Intelligence Agency and the Department of State to implement this aspect of NSC 66/1 as a pilot operation, pending further consideration of the plan on technical grounds within the Department of Defense structure. This is being done.

4. The remaining paper—NSC 10/5[8]—redefines the Central Intelligence Agency's responsibilities in a field which was probably not envisaged at the time the National Security Act of 1947, under which the Agency was established, was framed. This is the field of cold war covert activities, including guerrilla warfare. We have accepted these responsibilities as agents for the major Departments concerned and for projects which are approved by the Psychological Strategy Board. The Departments of State and Defense are charged with providing the Central Intelligence Agency with the necessary support to accomplish these missions. The presently projected scope of these activities has, during the

---

[6] NSC 86/1, "U.S. Policy on Soviet and Satellite Defectors," approved by Truman on April 19, 1951, is in National Archives, RG 59, S/S–NSC Files: Lot 63 D 351, NSC 86 Series.

[7] For NSC 66/1, "Intelligence Support for the Voice of America With Regard to Soviet Jamming," see Document 46.

[8] Document 90.

past three years, produced a three-fold increase in the clandestine operations of this Agency and will require next year a budget three times larger than that required for our intelligence activities. These cold war projects are worldwide in scope (with the effort intensified in the Far East) and they include psychological warfare as well as paramilitary operations; denial programs with respect to strategic materials; stockpiling on a limited scale in strategic areas to assist the military in the event of war; the organization and planning of sabotage teams to support resistance operations; and the planning and organization of escape and evasion networks and stay-behind movements for use in the event of war.

Given the necessary support, it will be possible for the Central Intelligence Agency to fulfill these requirements; but since they have resulted in such a large expansion in the Agency's budget and personnel strength, it should be noted that:

1. They are not functions essential to the performance by Central Intelligence Agency of its intelligence responsibilities.

2. They were placed in this Agency because there was no other Department or Agency of the Government which could undertake them at that time.

3. They will inevitably militate against the performance by Central Intelligence Agency of its primary intelligence functions and are a continuing and increasing risk to its security. Regrettably, (from my personal viewpoint) it seems impracticable, for reasons of coordination and security, to divorce these from other covert operations.

There remain a number of unsolved problems—major and minor. The following examples will indicate their nature and range:

1. *Interrelationship Between Intelligence and Operational Planning.* It is not necessary for an intelligence officer to know very much about plans, either civilian or military, but if his product is to be timely he must have adequate advance information at least of the general nature and objectives of any plans toward which he can make an intelligence contribution, as well as of such national or international policies and agreements as precede them. The liaison arrangements of CIA and the Department of State on such matters are reasonably satisfactory, although there remains room for betterment. Such arrangements with the Armed Services are still somewhat less than satisfactory, although some improvement is being made.

2. *Security.* The utmost diligence has been exercised to insure the security of the Central Intelligence Agency, and I am now convinced that it is at least as secure as any activity of the Government. My remaining concern in this regard is largely based on the fact that the Agency is scattered among twenty-eight buildings in the Washington area. Every effort will be made to obtain funds for the construction of a reasonably secure building.

3. *Communications Intelligence.* Responsibility for this activity is presently divided. It is of particular concern since it affects a highly important source of raw intelligence. The President has directed that a survey be made by the Secretaries of State and Defense, assisted by the Director of Central Intelligence, to determine what, if any, organizational changes might improve the security and productivity of this service. This survey is now in progress under the supervision of an independent committee, appointed for the purpose.[9]

4. *Scientific and Technical Intelligence.* The least progress in coordinating intelligence activities has been made in certain fields of scientific and technical intelligence. An interagency committee is presently studying this problem, with the view of recommending the proper steps for the improvement of this situation.

The Council is generally acquainted with the Central Intelligence Agency's secret operations designed to produce raw intelligence. Although we are making every effort to develop these latter sources, our experience so far has been in general disappointing. They are costly by comparison with other intelligence operations and they present in most cases a gambler's chance of obtaining really significant critical strategic information, although they consistently produce a significant quantity of useable information. We must and shall devote our best effort to their improvement and to the exploitation of every reasonable chance for penetration. On a few rare occasions there have been really brilliant accomplishments.

In conclusion, it should be pointed out that, in view of the efficiency of the Soviet security organization, it is not believed that the present United States intelligence system, or any instrumentality which the United States is presently capable of providing, including the available intelligence assets of other friendly states, can produce strategic intelligence on the Soviet with the degree of accuracy and timeliness which the National Security Council would like to have and which I would like to provide. Moreover, despite the utmost vigilance, despite watch committees, and all of the other mechanics for the prompt evaluation and transmission of intelligence, there is no real assurance that, in the event of sudden undeclared hostilities, certain advance warning can be provided.

As far as our intelligence production is concerned, the Central Intelligence Agency is basically an assembly plant for information produced by collaborating organizations of the Government, and its final product is necessarily dependent upon the quality of the contributions of these collaborating organizations.

Walter B. Smith[10]

---

[9] See Documents 97 and 99.

[10] Printed from a copy that indicates Smith signed the original.

Tab A

CENTRAL INTELLIGENCE AGENCY
(Organization as of 1 October 1950)

DIRECTOR OF CENTRAL INTELLIGENCE

DEPUTY DIRECTOR

INTELLIGENCE ADVISORY COMMITTEE

EXECUTIVE

DEPUTY EXECUTIVE

BUDGET STAFF

MANAGEMENT STAFF

PERSONNEL STAFF

PROCUREMENT REQUIREMENTS STAFF

SPECIAL SUPPORT STAFF

ADMINISTRATIVE STAFF

INSPECTION & SECURITY STAFF

MEDICAL STAFF

OFFICE OF SPECIAL OPERATIONS

OFFICE OF OPERATIONS

OFFICE OF POLICY COORDINATION

ADVISORY STAFF

LEGAL STAFF

COORDINATON, OPERATIONS & POLICY STAFF

OFFICE OF COLLECTION & DISSEMINATION

OFFICE OF SCIENTIFIC INTELLIGENCE

OFFICE OF REPORTS & ESTIMATES

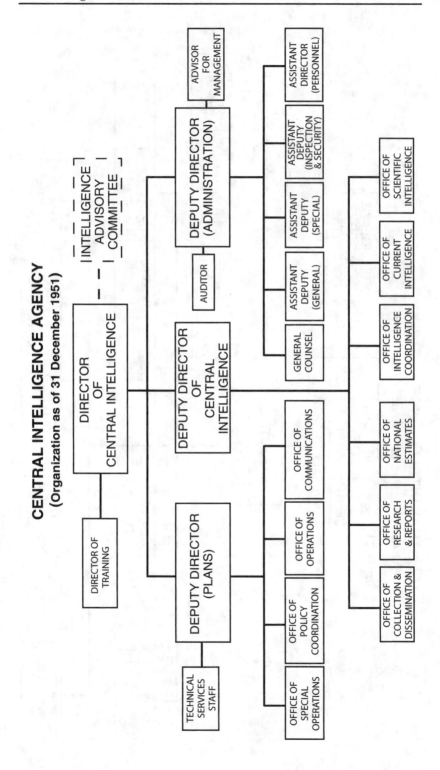

CENTRAL INTELLIGENCE AGENCY
(Organization as of 31 December 1951)

108. Briefing Paper Prepared by the Chairman of the 10/5 Panel (Barnes)[1]

Washington, May 7, 1952.

BRIEFING TO THE PSYCHOLOGICAL STRATEGY BOARD
ON SOME 10/5 PROBLEMS

A. The Purpose of the Briefing

The word "briefing" on the agenda is somewhat misleading. I should be extremely reluctant to "brief" the Board on 10/5,[2] as each of you already has considerable familiarity with the subject, quite aside from the fact that General Smith is the undisputed expert. What I am really doing is asking for a "briefing in reverse"; or, in other words, seeking the Board's help and guidance on behalf of the 10/5 Panel so that it can function as the Board's screening agent, as completely and intelligently as possible. Study of the famous "Packet" has shown us as members of the Panel that there are some issues which should be submitted for Board consideration.

B. Summary of the Steps Leading Up to the Briefing

To provide the proper framework for the issues which we wish to raise, I believe it will be of advantage to review briefly the background of NSC 10/5.

NSC 10/2, approved by the President in June 1948,[3] directed the undertaking of covert operations by OPC (then called the Office of Special Projects) on behalf of the U.S. Government. The DCI was given the ultimate responsibility and was instructed to ensure, through representatives of State and Defense, that such covert operations were consistent with U.S. policy. The 10/2 Representatives, consisting of General Magruder, General Balmer, and Mr. Joyce, have been meeting with the Chief of OPC each week to give such policy guidance. In addition, there is day-to-day liaison by CIA, not only with State and Defense, but also with other appropriate departments and agencies.

---

[1] Source: National Archives, RG 59, S/P Files: Lot 64 D 563, Political and Psychological Warfare. Top Secret; Eyes Only. The distribution of the paper is indicated in the Annex. Not printed here is a brief table of contents. The May 8 minutes of the 12th meeting of the Psychological Strategy Board indicate that this paper was discussed at that time. (Ibid., S/S–NSC Files: Lot 62 D 333, PSB Minutes) All ellipses in the original.

[2] Document 90.

[3] Printed in *Foreign Relations*, 1945–1950, Emergence of the Intelligence Establishment, Document 292.

The normal growth of CIA operations under 10/2, the approval and implementation of the NSC 68 Series,[4] and additional requirements placed on CIA by State, Defense, and the JCS (such as support for programs in Korea and China; the retardation program; resistance programs; stockpiling; and oil-denial programs), indicated to DCI that the covert program was fast expanding beyond the horizons seen at the time of its creation. Accordingly, CIA sought additional guidance from NSC in the "Scope and Pace" or "Magnitude" Paper of May 8, 1951,[5] in which were set forth two fundamental issues, clarification of which was considered essential to orderly growth. These were—

1. High policy approval of increases in personnel and expenditures required by requested programs, but going beyond limits thought to have been intended by NSC in June 1948, plus approval of substantial additional increases, if all the programs being thrust upon OPC were even to be attempted;
2. High policy decisions as to the direction and nature of covert operations.

[2 paragraphs (12 lines) not declassified]

With respect to the direction and nature of the covert program OPC was faced with major decisions. CIA interpreted the NSC 68 Series as establishing the desirability of large scale covert operations but felt that these policies had not been translated into a directive sufficiently specific for the operational guidance of OPC.

Here is a sampling of the kind of decisions then troubling CIA:

1. Should OPC emphasize covert activities in support of cold war or in support of preparation for hot war? For example, should OPC properly give top priority to a European retardation plan as requested by the JCS?
2. How should OPC resolve the differing military and political concepts relating to the build-up, maintenance and use of resistance groups?
3. Should activities, such as paramilitary, be changed from covert to overt? If so, when and how?

These basic problems prompted CIA to ask for guidance in four areas: (1) the scope and pace of covert operations for cold war and preparation for hot war; (2) redetermination of responsibilities for covert operations; (3) assurance of logistical support; and (4) coordinated guidance from PSB.

The NSC responded to the "Magnitude" Paper in NSC 10/5, approved by the President on October 23, 1951. This stated that the NSC "approves in principle as a national responsibility the immediate expansion of the covert organization established in NSC 10/2", thereby

---

[4] See Document 5.
[5] Attachment to Document 68.

answering at least in part the primary CIA worry as to OPC's increase in size. This answer, however, merely emphasizes the rest of 10/5, which is devoted to the question of objectives and how to develop a covert program.

Obviously, the best size for OPC can never be determined with engineering accuracy. But equally obviously, the size of OPC should be responsive, in a general way, to various considerations, among which, in our opinion, are three important ones that will be discussed in greater detail in a moment. These considerations are:

1. What are the correct interpretations of national objectives?
2. What is the national program for achieving them?
3. How large can the OPC program become without disclosing the hand of the U.S.?

As to objectives the NSC called for an intensification of covert operations designed to: (1) place maximum strain on the Soviet structure of power; (2) contribute towards retraction of Soviet power and influence; (3) orient the free world towards the U.S., and (4) develop resistance and guerrilla operations.

With regard to program, 10/5 in effect says to CIA, "We recognize your need for guidance; we will not spell it out for you ourselves; we will, however, provide you with a mechanism which should resolve your dilemmas."

The mechanism was PSB, then a young and only just fluttering fledgling. PSB was directed to include in its strategic concept provision for covert operations to achieve the objectives just mentioned. Moreover, PSB was given the responsibility for: (1) determining desirability and feasibility of covert programs and major projects, and (2) establishing the scope, pace, and timing of covert operations.

In furtherance of these responsibilities, the Board on February 27, 1952 approved the creation of a panel that includes the 10/2 Representatives already described, plus two PSB members, Barnes and Putnam. At the same time, an administrative procedure was adopted for reviewing programs and projects.[6]

On March 20, 1952, CIA submitted to PSB the "Packet", which consists of the CIA/OPC Strategic Plan, a Budget Analysis for FY 1953, Programs and Major Projects over $50,000, and their Support Requirements—a total documentation of about 300 pages, including descriptions of some 100-odd projects.[7]

---

[6] See Document 104.

[7] The "Packet" has not been found, but several documents dealing with Department of State consideration of it are in National Archives, RG 59, S/P Files: Lot 64 D 563, Political and Psychological Warfare. The CIA/OPC Strategic War Plan is Document 61.

The 10/5 Panel has now studied the "Packet", in the light of 10/2, the "Magnitude" Paper, 10/5 and other NSC papers. This study has convinced us that many of the "Magnitude"-type issues still demand clarification and that serious Board consideration is essential. Whatever time may be required for this consideration, however, the Board in our opinion need not delay its approval of much, perhaps all, of the "Packet".

C. Approval of the "Packet"

Without prejudice to any strategy which PSB may later evolve, via the Stevens Group or by other means; without prejudice to further analysis of the "Packet" (such as the information which has been requested by the JCS representative in order to provide more readily comparable figures on supporting personnel and materiel being supplied by Defense); and without prejudice to questions which any of the Board may wish to ask; it is our belief that in general the "Packet" should be endorsed.

Despite the rapid growth of OPC, the total FY 1953 program still only calls for about one per cent of the federal budget and, at most, only [number not declassified] men.

Unquestionably, the establishment of facilities and the training of personnel are the top priority needs of OPC today.

OPC can reasonably continue this build-up without losing operating flexibility. In the meantime, the individual training plus the consolidation of organization will be assets to OPC whatever jobs are assigned to it in the future. Consequently, although no decision is today requested of the Board, the 10/5 Panel does plan soon to submit the "Packet", or as much of it as is appropriate, to the Board for its approval.

Obviously, any Board approval of an OPC Packet must be subject to continuous review, as national policy evolves.

But, in particular, the approval which the 10/5 Panel will soon recommend to the Board must be subsequently reviewed by both the Panel and the Board in the light of future clarifications of national policy and objectives.

D. Certain Unresolved Issues

Our study of the "Packet" has made us realize that soon the Board is to be presented with some difficult but unavoidable issues.

To eliminate any possible ambiguity—the Board will not be expected to *make* policy, but if the 10/5 Panel is to operate, it needs some *interpretations* of policy.

For example, before the Board, or the Panel acting for it, can pass on the "desirability" of a project as required by 10/5, it seems to us that the Board must provide answers to quite a number of basic questions, of which I will give two rather closely related examples:

1. Does U.S. policy, as properly interpreted, contemplate supplying overt physical support to revolutionary factions that might emerge in the wake of Stalin's death, if the situation offered a reasonable chance of changing a regime to suit U.S. interests without precipitating general war?

It seems to us that if U.S. policy excludes this possibility, then OPC would prepare for quite a different program than it would if U.S. policy either included the possibility of such overt physical support or merely reserved to the nation the freedom to make the decision at a later date.

2. Does U.S. policy, as properly interpreted, include or exclude efforts under any circumstances to overthrow or subvert the governments of the satellites or the U.S.S.R.?

If U.S. policy excludes such efforts, then any OPC projects directed primarily or largely to those ends should be eliminated or should be retained only on the ground that preparations for such efforts may give the U.S. some freedom of decision.

If, on the other hand, the answer is "yes", or merely "maybe", then, in order to have freedom of decision at the proper moment, it would seem important for the Board to know now, and for the 10/5 Panel to find out for the Board, how much military support and what type of military support will be available. For example, do we plan to go in on foot? If not, are airborne divisions available or on order? If on order, is the lead time synchronized with the estimated date of need?

In stating these examples, no inference is intended that the Board is responsible for resolving the questions. However, in order that the Board may discharge its obligation with respect to the OPC program, it must, in our judgment, be fully acquainted with the answers from whatever source derived. The 10/5 Panel, in turn, must seek such answers when attempting to perform its delegated functions.

The following passages from a lead article in the April 26, 1952, issue of the London *Economist* express a similar dilemma in the public mind:

"The discreet silence of western diplomacy about its hopes and purposes in Eastern Europe becomes more and more conspicuous. . . .
"From the viewpoint of the Kremlin this silence of embarrassment must look like the silence of conspiracy. From London and Paris, from the land and sea stations of the Voice of America, from Radio Free Europe in Munich, and from such guerilla bases as Madrid and Belgrade and so-called 'black' stations, there comes hour after hour a stream of criticism and exhortation directed at the Soviet Union and its satellites. The effort is comparable only to that of the Cominform itself. To Moscow monitoring services and to the Russians who read analyses of western output, it must all look systematic and sinister. To experienced Communists, who themselves plan ahead and think in terms of political

warfare, it must seem incredible that all this activity is not harnessed to a plan for war and civil war among the western marches of the Soviet Union. *To encourage resistance by words and to have no intention of supporting it later by arms does not, the Russian would argue, make sense."* (emphasis supplied)

". . . the general atmosphere of conspiracy is heightened by the actual and alleged activities of the Central Intelligence Agency behind the Iron curtain."

"There can, indeed, be little doubt that there is in Eastern Europe a widespread belief that time will bring what the rulers call a war of aggression and what the ruled call liberation."

". . . This is obviously an unsatisfactory state of affairs, which might become dangerous. It may mean that American and British policies are out of step and that there are two policies in Washington. It may mean that planning has moved from containment pure and simple to containment plus all such interference with the Russian sphere of influence as can be safely got away with. . . . In a decision to pass in Europe from containment to political, economic and social counterattack there is nothing whatever to be ashamed of. . . . What is wrong is that policy in such a matter should be formed piecemeal under the pressure of special requirements without any formulation of how far it is to go and what its ultimate objectives are to be. . . ."

". . . The policy of 'containment plus' is just beginning to hurt the East; but unless it is formulated and explained, public opinion will not support it and accept its consequences."

E. Responsibilities of the 10/5 Panel

To assist in reaching a sensible working relationship between the Board and the 10/5 Panel, I am including in this final section some specific requests for guidance.

1. We should like the Board to confirm in principle the conclusion that OPC cannot create a useful apparatus unless it be authorized to develop an over-all program, in dollars and personnel, covering a period of, let us say, two or three years.

The 10/5 Panel feels that OPC, like the Army, must be allowed to tailor its apparatus to an order of magnitude. It cannot today determine precisely what operation will be needed tomorrow any more than the Army can prophesy what particular campaign it will be directed to fight. The 10/5 procedure is presently focused on approval of particular programs and projects. If the 10/5 Panel should formalize and perpetuate this type of approval, to the exclusion of more general approval, it would tend to stultify OPC's healthy development, especially if this procedure were in any way construed as requiring OPC to delay the creation and training of a useful apparatus until the Board had approved particular programs and projects.

Such approval, of course, will not affect in any way the Board's existing responsibility to review all particular programs and projects submitted under the 10/5 procedure.

It will, however, ensure OPC the flexibility essential for the development of quality as well as of quantity, and it will permit the 10/5 Panel to prepare an over-all program for Board consideration.

Moreover, such approval in our opinion would be in keeping with the NSC decision in 10/5 already mentioned; namely, to approve "in principle as a national responsibility the immediate expansion of the covert organization established in NSC 10/2. . ." This was an approval of an increase in order of magnitude.

2. With respect to the Panel's job of screening particular programs and projects for the Board, the following are some suggested conclusions which are submitted for ratification by the Board. As you will see, they are efforts to hang flesh on the 10/5 skeleton.

a. The 10/5 Panel should *not* be called upon to act like a general manager of the program. This is properly the function of CIA/OPC.

For example, one project calls for [*less than 1 line not declassified*]. We believe that the PSB should *not* be responsible for approving such matters as (1) the exact type or amount of stores cached, (2) the location of the caches, or (3) safeguards to prevent physical deterioration or loss of secrecy. Anything recommended by the Case Officer and approved by CIA and the 10/2 [*10/5?*] mechanism will be considered reasonable, in the absence of actual evidence to the contrary.

The PSB *should* be responsible for determining that:

(1) The procurement and caching of stores for retardation is reasonable;
(2) [*less than 1 line not declassified*] is a reasonable country in which to prepare for retardation; and that
(3) The scale of the effort is reasonable.

b. Other recommendations are:

(1) That the 10/2 Representatives continue to provide the detailed, day-to-day guidance to CIA, while the 10/5 Panel provides the more general guidance, including the strategic concepts to be developed by the PSB. Details should be worked out between the 10/2 Representatives and the 10/5 Panel.
(2) That when a program appears to contribute towards the achievement of a national objective, but also appears either to be inconsistent with current national policy, or to be in an area where national policy is not clearly defined, the 10/5 Panel should bring the program to the attention of the Board.

For example, CIA has two major programs for China: (a) support of Nationalist Government-controlled guerillas and resistance groups on the mainland [*less than 1 line not declassified*], and (b) support of "any and all" anti-Nationalist anti-communist resistance groups on the mainland [*less than 1 line not declassified*]. Each program contributes towards the national objective of reducing communist power in China.

The programs, however, raise a basic question: Is U.S. Policy: (a) to strengthen the Nationalist Government as a rallying point for all anti-communist activities in China, (b) to encourage the development of a "Third Force" to assume control of all anti-communist activities in China at the expense of the Nationalists, or (c) to support at least for the time being both the Nationalist Government and to develop a "Third Force".

(3) That the 10/5 Panel may become concerned with the possible desirability of conducting a 10/5 program overtly rather than covertly.

For example, the "Magnitude" paper points out that after guerilla forces have reached a certain size, attempts to maintain cover are ridiculous. Therefore, an increase in guerilla or resistance forces would require a further judgment as to the desirability of making the operation overt.

c. The 10/5 Panel should be authorized to ask questions designed to uncover hidden assumptions and implications in connection with any matter germane to the responsibilities delegated to it by the Board.

Annex

Distribution is as follows:	Copy No.
General Walter Bedell Smith	
Director of Central Intelligence Agency	1
William C. Foster	
Deputy Secretary of Defense	2
David K. Bruce	
Under Secretary of State	8
Raymond B. Allen, Director	
Psychological Strategy Board	4
Frank G. Wisner, Deputy Director/Plans	
Central Intelligence Agency	5
[name not declassified]	
Central Intelligence Agency	6
Colonel Kilbourne Johnston	
Assistant Director, Central Intelligence Agency	7
Robert P. Joyce, Policy Planning Staff	
Department of State	9
Brigadier General Jesmond D. Balmer	
Chief, Joint Subsidiary Plans Division	
Joint Chiefs of Staff	10
Brigadier General John Magruder	
Deputy Assistant to the Secretary of Defense	
for International Security Affairs–Psychological Policy	11

C. Tracy Barnes, Deputy Director
  Psychological Strategy Board   3
Palmer Putnam, Special Assistant to the Director
  Psychological Strategy Board   12
Philip H. Watts, Policy Planning Staff
  Department of State   13

---

109. Memorandum From the Under Secretary of State (Bruce) to the Executive Secretary of the National Security Council (Lay)[1]

Washington, May 7, 1952.

SUBJECT

Fourth Progress Report on NSC 59/1, "The Foreign Information Program and Psychological Warfare Planning"

1. NSC 59/1[2] was approved as governmental policy on March 10, 1950. It is requested that this progress report, as of April 15, 1952, of activities undertaken in implementation of NSC 59/1, be circulated to the members of the Council for their information.

2. The organization referred to in NSC 59/1 has been designated The Psychological Operations Coordinating Committee (POC). It will be referred to in this report as "the Committee."

3. This report describes only those foreign information operations and plans which, being interdepartmental in nature, were coordinated through the Committee.

4. Consequent to a reorganization of foreign information activities within the Department of State, the Chairmanship of the Committee has been assumed by the Administrator, International Information Administration. The following are regularly represented at the weekly meetings of the Committee: Secretary of Defense, Joint Chiefs of Staff, the Mutual Security Agency, Central Intelligence Agency, Assistant Secretary for Public Affairs, Department of State, and the Army, Navy

---

[1] Source: National Archives, RG 59, Miscellaneous Lot Files: Lot 62 D 385, NSC 59, Box 56. Top Secret; Security Information. Forwarded to NSC members under cover of a memorandum from Lay, May 7. (Ibid.)

[2] Document 2.

and Air Force chiefs of psychological warfare and the Psychological Strategy Board staff.

5. *Troop Acceptability Program*

An operational plan for handling psychological problems growing out of the presence of United States military personnel in Europe, has been approved by the Committee. The interdepartmental working group which prepared this plan is now preparing another for dealing with psychological problems connected with the presence of United States military personnel in other areas of the world.

6. *Soviet-Dominated Military Personnel*

A plan for conducting overt psychological operations vis-à-vis the armed forces of the Soviet-dominated world was prepared by an interdepartmental working group by direction of the Committee. The Committee also approved and referred to appropriate operating divisions a number of interdepartmentally-developed propaganda themes to be used in output directed towards military personnel of the USSR and its captive countries.

7. *General Assembly*

On the Committee's recommendation qualified information specialists were obtained from the Department of Defense and another agency to support the public information staff of the United States Delegation to the United Nations General Assembly in Paris in November, 1951. These officers provided valuable assistance to the Delegation in the conduct of its information operations.

8. *NATO Anniversary*

The Committee provided advice and support in the preparation of interdepartmental plans for a broad program of information activity of the U.S. and other NATO member countries to commemorate the third anniversary of the signing of the North Atlantic Treaty in April, 1952. The Committee and its staff participated in arrangements for the issuance of a special postage stamp commemorating the anniversary.

9. *Television in Propaganda*

An interdepartmental working group established by the Committee has laid the groundwork for interdepartmental cooperation in the further development of television as a propaganda medium.

10. *Operations Newsletter*

A "Psychological Operations Newsletter" is issued monthly by the Staff. The purpose of the newsletter is to keep appropriate officers of POC member agencies, both in Washington and in field establishments, informed of current activities in this field.

11. *Training Program*

In accordance with the Committee's recommendation, an expanded program of on-the-job training is being conducted in the State Department for military officers assigned to psychological warfare organizations. Fourteen officers have completed the six-months course, or are now following the course.

12. *Project Nobel*

The Committee has approved and referred to the International Information Administration in the Department of State, for implementation, a project designed to associate the living recipients of the Nobel peace prize with the ideals of the Free World.

13. *Current Activities*

Some of the more significant current activities of the Committee or its staff, in conjunction with the appropriate operating agencies, are as follows:

a. Considering overt psychological warfare operations plans for handling Communist charges that UN Forces are using bacteriological warfare in Korea.

b. Coordination, at the request of the Psychological Strategy Board, of overt psychological warfare operations plans to exploit the success or failure of the Korean truce negotiations.

c. Coordinating interdepartmental propaganda activity with respect to the Soviet note of March 10 dealing with a German peace treaty.

d. Review of a proposed statement on Communist sabotage of peace negotiations in Korea, which could be issued by General Ridgway in event of failure of the negotiations.

e. Interdepartmental planning for overt psychological warfare operations following possible outbreak of general war. Known as the "X-Day Project," the plans will be forwarded to the Psychological Strategy Board when completed and approved by the Committee.

f. Establishment of liaison arrangements between the Committee and the Information Liaison Group, a U.S. interdepartmental committee established in Paris to consider information and propaganda problems in the European area.

g. Development of overt psychological operations plans to help maintain continued Yugoslav independence from Soviet domination.

David Bruce[3]

---

[3] Printed from a copy that indicates Bruce signed the original.

110. Memorandum From the Secretary of State's Special Assistant for Intelligence and Research (Armstrong) to Secretary of State Acheson[1]

Washington, May 9, 1952.

SUBJECT

Progress Report on NSC 50:[2] The Central Intelligence Agency and National Organization for Intelligence

The subject report represents General Smith's account of his stewardship of the Central Intelligence Agency since he assumed office in October 1950; I believe that you will want to read it in full.[3] It sets forth the considerable accomplishments of CIA during this period, the major problems which remain to be solved and a caveat as to what may be reasonably expected of the U.S. intelligence system, given the efficiency of the Soviet security organization. I would recommend that you compliment General Smith on the report and on the progress it records, which in a very large measure is attributable to his personal leadership.

There are three points to which your attention should be drawn and which may be discussed in connection with the review of this Progress Report:

1. *Covert Operations.* You will observe that General Smith lays considerable stress on the greatly increased scope of this phase of CIA's responsibilities (page 3, paragraph 4), pointing out that in the coming year the [2 *lines not declassified*]. While it would be undesirable to take exception to the preview given by General Smith of increased activities in this field, it would be well to indicate, in connection with this paragraph of the Progress Report, that the Department, for its part, is constantly seeking to evaluate the effects of covert CIA operations in terms of overall U.S. objectives and in the light of changing international conditions.

2. *Departmental Information.* General Smith states on page 4 that arrangements whereby CIA obtains information on the Department's planning and policy "are reasonably satisfactory, although there remains room for betterment." (Similar arrangements with the military services are described as "somewhat less than satisfactory.") You

---

[1] Source: National Archives, RG 59, S/S–NSC Files: Lot 63 D 351, NSC 50 Series. Top Secret. Concurred in by G, S/P, and C. Transmitted through the Under Secretary and the Executive Secretariat.

[2] For NSC 50, see *Foreign Relations, 1945–1950,* Emergence of the Intelligence Establishment, Document 384.

[3] Document 107.

should know that since the issuance of NSC 50 on July 1, 1949, the Department has made intensive efforts to make available to CIA all information believed to be of concern to it. The Secretariat furnishes to CIA by rapid means a most comprehensive selection of the Department's telegrams, including telegrams of a policy nature. Similar non-telegraphic materials are furnished through one of my divisions. In addition, a representative of CIA/OPC has access in Mr. Joyce's office to the complete file of messages comparable to your daily "log", save only those items deleted by Mr. Joyce. Finally, arrangements have been made whereby certain highly sensitive materials identified as of interest to intelligence, such as the record of your recent conversations with the British Ambassador regarding Indochina, are made available by my office to the Director of Central Intelligence for highly-limited CIA internal distribution. In view of the nature of the planning and policy-making process, and the high degree of security required, it is very doubtful that intelligence will ever be fully satisfied with the state of its information in this regard.

On the other hand, you should be aware that the flow of information described above is by no means reciprocated by CIA. Planning and operational data are made available only as CIA determines that the Department's interests are affected. Some information of direct concern to the Department is not made available and access to CIA telegrams, which would provide a check on the adequacy of CIA's practices in this regard, is not permitted.

3. *Current Intelligence.* The Department has some reservations on the discussion in the report of "current intelligence", to which General Smith makes brief reference on page 1. The Dulles–Jackson Correa report of January 1949,[4] on which NSC 50 is based, took exception to the various current intelligence summaries (daily, weekly, and monthly) which were then being published by CIA. The Committee questioned the need for such publications, pointing out that they consisted almost entirely of summaries of departmental telegrams (90 percent State), including both operational and intelligence material. The result, according to the Committee, was "a fragmentary publication which deals with operations as well as intelligence, without necessarily being based on the most significant materials in either category." The Committee concluded that (a) "in a summary of this type, circulated to the President and the highest officials of the Government, there is an inherent danger that it will be misleading to its consumers"; and (b) it duplicates at considerable expense of manpower and money, summaries circulated by the Department and other agencies.

---

[4] For a summary of the Dulles Report, see *Foreign Relations, 1945–1950*, Emergence of the Intelligence Establishment, Document 358.

The production of these summaries has been improved and it is our understanding that the President finds them of great value which, in itself, is reason for a continued effort in their production. The Department, however, still finds many of the same objections that existed in 1949 and itself finds the summaries of little value. In particular, we are concerned that the summaries frequently are the vehicle whereby foreign policy problems, with CIA comment, are brought to the attention of high officials of other agencies and the President, during the period when policy recommendations are being formulated and before the Department is prepared to suggest courses of action. We believe that with due regard for timeliness the provision of certain current intelligence to the President and to the operating agencies of the Government could and should be based on the same principles of contribution and coordination among the agencies as is now effected with respect to National Intelligence Estimates.

Recommendations:

1. That you warmly commend General Smith on this report and on the leadership he has brought to the Intelligence community.

2. That you state, with reference to CIA covert operations, that the Department, for its part, is constantly seeking to evaluate the effects of covert CIA operations in terms of over-all U.S. objectives and in the light of changing international conditions.

3. That, if the question is raised regarding the furnishing to CIA of information from the Department, you invite General Smith to suggest ways in which the existing liaison could be improved, bearing in mind that (a) his principal problem appears to be with the Pentagon and (b) the flow of information from CIA likewise leaves something to be desired.

4. That, if the question is raised regarding current intelligence, you indicate that, while you recognize such publications are necessary and appropriate for the President, you believe they would serve a more useful purpose if the principles of contribution and coordination which apply to National Intelligence were applied insofar as possible to current intelligence.

W. Park Armstrong, Jr.

111.   Memorandum From Robert P. Joyce of the Policy Planning Staff to the Under Secretary of State (Bruce)[1]

Washington, May 22, 1952.

SUBJECT

Magnitude of CIA Operations

It occurred to me that you might be interested in some sort of recapitulation of the points brought out in the meeting in your office yesterday afternoon in connection with today's meeting of the PSB. There are one or two new elements in the situation that came out of the regular Wednesday meeting of the 10/2 Consultants yesterday afternoon. (I did not attend this meeting myself but my representative, William A. McFadden, reported to me this morning.) The two new elements are:

1. Assistant Director of CIA for OPC, Colonel Johnston, stated that if the PSB tomorrow (today) generally bought the CIA "Packet",[2] OPC would consider that it had finally obtained a charter which would permit it to expand in a large way and start creating on a world-wide basis an impressive covert apparatus necessary to accomplish the requirements laid upon OPC of CIA. Colonel Johnston indicated that favorable action today by the PSB would have CIA budgetary significance as well. The implication of this is that the CIA could move forward to obtain the vast amount specified in the "Packet".

2. General Balmer of the Joint Strategic Plans Division advised at the meeting yesterday that the JCS had finally approved the OPC "war plan"[3] and would communicate such approval with its comments within about one week.

In connection with paragraph one above, there is quoted an excerpt from a memorandum presented to the Senior Staff of the NSC on June 8, 1951 by Frank G. Wisner:[4]

"Unless the decision is made now to provide the resources and apparatus capable of undertaking covert operations of this magnitude, the United States will not be in a position to conduct such covert activities as national policy may require. Therefore, failure to reach a decision at this time is in effect a decision *not* to proceed with the

---

[1] Source: Department of State, INR Historical Files: NSC 10 Series, 1952. Top Secret; Security Information. Drafted by Joyce. Copy 1 of 6. A handwritten note on memorandum reads "Copies 3, 4 and 5, sent to, seen by & returned by, Nitze, Sargeant and Armstrong—destroyed on 9.11.53." All elipses in the original.

[2] See footnote 7, Document 107.

[3] Document 61.

[4] Not found.

build-up required to implement current national policy as expressed in NSC 68 and other applicable NSC directives".

I think you might desire to keep in mind the following considerations at the PSB meeting this afternoon:

a. Paragraph 5 of NSC 10/2 of June 18, 1948[5] states: "As used in this directive 'covert operations' are understood to be all activities (except as noted herein) which are conducted or sponsored by this Government against hostile foreign states or groups or in support of friendly states or groups but which are so planned and executed that the United States Government responsibility for them is not evident to unauthorized persons and if uncovered the United States Government can plausibly disclaim any responsibility for them. . . ." The question might reasonably be asked General Smith if present plans to create a very large "covert apparatus" can possibly meet the requirements of the foregoing provisions of NSC 10/2. Will not large CIA bases on a world-wide scale soon be recognized for what they are? Will it not be impossible under these circumstances for this Government plausibly to disclaim any responsibility?

b. Although NSC 10/2 authorizes OPC "in coordination with the JCS to plan and prepare for the conduct of such operations in wartime", will not in fact the establishment of large bases for training guerrilla warriors and for staging air drops behind the lines in case of war, etc., have important political repercussions in peacetime?

c. If the CIA proceeds to establish such large and necessarily at least semi-overt bases throughout the world, all in the line of preparations for a hot war, will not the impression be created in the Kremlin that this Government is busily preparing to attack the Soviet Union? Will not the Russians point to these large and populous bases as evidence to support their thesis that the United States intends to unleash a global war against the motherland of the workers? Will not our allies in the West react unfavorably and themselves be fearful that the United States is in fact preparing perhaps not to bring about a war but at least engaging in provocative action which might inspire reaction from the East leading to increasing danger of war?

d. Does General Smith himself think that he can create a huge "covert apparatus" on a world-wide basis which has any chance whatever of maintaining its covert nature?

e. How effective does General Smith consider the retardation plan would be in case of a hot war? Does problematical assistance to the military effort in case of a hot war over-balance the moral and psychological factors referred to in the previous paragraphs?

---

[5] For NSC 10/2, see *Foreign Relations, 1945–1950, Emergence of the Intelligence Establishment*, Document 292.

f. By generally approving of the "Packet" does the Department of State endorse in a blanket fashion JCS and CIA plans for preparing for a hot war?

g. Is it a fact, as we understood General Smith to believe a year ago, that CIA planning for a hot war de-emphasizes and limits the effectiveness of CIA as an intelligence agency and an agency designed to operate covertly in the field of political warfare for the ultimate objective of achieving cold war objectives thus lessening the chances of and perhaps preventing the outbreak of all-out warfare?

I believe that these questions trouble us here in the State Department. You may care to recommend that some of these considerations should be studied by the 10/5 Panel before it recommends to the PSB that the CIA "Packet" should at this time be generally approved.

Robert P. Joyce

---

112. Letter From the Secretary of State's Special Assistant for Intelligence and Research (Armstrong) to Director of Central Intelligence Smith[1]

Washington, June 3, 1952.

Dear General Smith:

As you know, National Security Council Intelligence Directive No. 10[2] places upon the Department of State primary responsibility for the collection abroad, by overt means, of information in the basic sciences. The Department, under this directive, has additional secondary responsibilities for collection in other scientific and technical fields.

On a limited scale, the Department has, during the past two years, endeavored to meet these responsibilities. The experience gained during this period of time has confirmed the importance of several factors in the collection of scientific information:

a. Except in the case of the USSR and its satellites (including China), the traditional and normal channels of intercommunication between US and foreign scientists are capable of furnishing a large portion of the

---

[1] Source: National Archives, RG 59, INR Files: Lot 58 D 776, Atomic Energy. Secret; Security Information. Drafted by Theodore M. Nordbeck on May 29.

[2] For NSCID No. 10, see *Foreign Relations, 1945–1950, Emergence of the Intelligence Establishment*, Document 429.

information required for intelligence purposes. The normal channels comprise interchange of published works and scientific periodicals, reciprocal visits and attendance at international meetings and conferences.

b. In the case of the USSR and satellites, the limited information available through normal channels can be effectively supplemented only by carefully planned covert activities.

c. In the case of non-Soviet areas, the information which is needed to supplement that received through the normal and traditional channels mentioned above principally relates either to a specific field of scientific effort and to research which has not yet reached the publication stage, or to an overall evaluation of scientific potential in one or more broad fields.

d. The types of information mentioned in (c) above can be acquired most efficiently and economically through overt means, provided the following factors are kept in mind:

1. The use of relatively young or scientifically unknown individuals will, in most cases, not only be ineffective, but may tend to dry up even the normal channels of intercommunication. Profitable contact with foreign scientists can usually be expected only where there is a reasonable quid pro quo, that is, when the US scientist is a qualified leader in a given field, and when the basis of the contact is a legitimate exchange of scientific ideas and experiences. Relatively unknown individuals who only ask questions quickly arouse resentment and reluctance, since it is obvious that their principal purpose is to extract information, giving nothing in return.

2. Every effort must be made to keep the collection of basic scientific information removed from the taint of intelligence. Infraction of this principle may not only hinder the overt operation, but may jeopardize contacts and sources essential to the success of covert operations.

3. The degree to which a US scientist can be successful in collecting information on a specific or general scientific field depends upon his own ability and competence in that field rather than upon any detailed briefing by intelligence.

The Department is keenly aware of the importance of carrying out its responsibilities under NSCID–10, and desires to expand its current activities in this respect. The following steps should be taken in this direction, some of which can be accomplished within the Department's present resources; others will require additional support.

a. The Department can collect the bulk of basic scientific material available in published form which CIA requires.

b. The existing scientific attachés can undertake to collect specific additional information which CIA may require within their individual fields of competence.

c. With appropriate financial assistance, known and competent specialists can be selected and sent overseas for limited periods of two to three months to cover specific fields of science on a strictly overt basis. These consultants would function in the same manner as normal science attachés, and would make their reports to the office of the Science Advisor, Department of State. They would have no direct connection with CIA in any way.

d. The office of the Science Advisor, with additional staffing assistance, could undertake a more extensive program of debriefing scientists and engineers who have visited foreign areas under private sponsorship. The use of this office, which while it has no apparent connection with intelligence, is directly and openly concerned with science, will in many cases be more fruitful than debriefing by the intelligence agencies themselves.

e. With adequate financial assistance the Department can increase the competence and scope of coverage of US representation to international scientific conferences and congresses abroad. It is believed that such meetings are extremely profitable occasions for the interchange of scientific information and ideas, particularly in acquiring prepublication knowledge of work in progress.

In accordance with paragraphs 1,d and 1,f of NSCID–10, the above views and suggestions are submitted to the Central Intelligence Agency for consideration, both as to their validity, and as a basis for further discussion as to the degree of support to the overt scientific collection activities of the Department which might be appropriate and justifiable.

Sincerely yours,

W. Park Armstrong, Jr.[3]

---

[3] Printed from a copy that indicates Armstrong signed the original.

---

113.   Memorandum by the Director of Naval Intelligence (Johnson)[1]

ONI Instruction 003820.36A   Washington, June 3, 1952.

SUBJECT

Exploitation of maritime sources for intelligence purposes

---

[1] Source: Central Intelligence Agency, Executive Registry, Job 95–G00278R, Box 1, Folder 17. Secret; Security Information. The memorandum was sent to "Distribution List F28 (less DIC–17ND)," which has not been identified.

1. *Purpose.* This instruction outlines an agreement between the Office of Naval Intelligence and the Central Intelligence Agency concerning the exploitation of maritime sources for intelligence purposes.[2]

2. *Cancellation.* ONI Instruction 003820.36[3] is cancelled and superseded by this instruction.

3. *Background.* The National Security Council places the responsibility for the collection of foreign intelligence from domestic sources with the Central Intelligence Agency. Because of the extensive naval interest in maritime matters, and the capabilities of the DIOs in exploiting this field, a mutually satisfactory agreement has been reached by ONI and CIA.

4. *Procedure.*

a. *Counter-Intelligence and Security.* The exploitation of maritime Sources, including but not limited to, masters, officers, crews, operators, owners and agents for counter-intelligence and security purposes, is the responsibility of the District Intelligence Officers without prior clearance or coordination with CIA.

b. *Foreign Intelligence, Owners, Operators and Agents.* Exploitation of owners, operators and agents for the purposes of foreign intelligence is the primary responsibility of CIA. If deemed advisable however, and subject to prior coordination with the CIA field office, these sources may be exploited for foreign intelligence purposes by the DIOs. Such interviews will be arranged, and at his option participated in, by the cognizant field representative of CIA. Primary responsibility of the CIA in this field does not restrict or affect in any way the responsibility of the DIOs under paragraph 4a of this instruction.

c. *Foreign Intelligence, Masters, Officers and Crews.* The exploitation of masters, officers and crews of merchant vessels for foreign intelligence purposes is the responsibility of the DIOs. Direct access by CIA to such sources, in exceptional cases, is not precluded by this agreement; however such special interviews will be arranged by the DIOs.

d. *Dissemination.*

(1) *Foreign Positive Intelligence.* Foreign positive intelligence obtained by DIOs from maritime sources, either afloat or ashore, shall be made available to the CIA field office for ultimate appropriate dissemination by CIA in Washington. The DIOs shall simultaneously submit reports of such intelligence to ONI for dissemination within the Naval establishment. Every effort will be made to secure duplicate copies of enclosures, in order that the CIA field office and the DIO may

---

[2] Known as the "Salt Water Agreement."
[3] Not found.

each forward a copy to Washington. In the event that only a single copy of enclosures is available, and reproduction is impracticable, they shall be forwarded to CIA.

(2) *Counter-Intelligence.* All counter intelligence and information secured under the SOMM plan[4] will be forwarded to ONI for analysis and dissemination. No lateral distribution of such reports will be made to CIA field offices by the DIOs.

e. *Sources.*

(1) *Counter-Intelligence.* The names of counter-intelligence informants shall not be disclosed to CIA.

(2) *Foreign Intelligence Sources.* The names of sources furnishing foreign intelligence exclusively, whether connected with the maritime field or not, will be furnished to CIA field offices.

(3) *Overlapping Sources.* It is considered probable that some maritime sources, as listed in paragraph 4c of this instruction, will also be classified by the DIOs as counter-intelligence informants or SOMM plan participants. The release of names of such sources to the CIA field office is subject to the discretion of the DIO. Sufficient source description will be furnished the CIA field office to obviate false confirmation, but extreme care is urged in such disclosure that sensitive sources supplying both types of information are not jeopardized.

f. *Requirements.* IAC requirements for foreign intelligence from sources in paragraph 4c of this instruction will be coordinated by CIA, as necessary. General Navy requirements covering the exploitation of these sources are presently in the hands of the DIOs, and further specific requirements will be furnished from time to time by ONI. DIOs will make every effort to alert the pertinent CIA field office to the arrival of ships from high priority areas, or of unusual foreign intelligence potential. In such cases a CIA representative may furnish interagency requirements or participate in the interview if necessary.

g. *DIO–CIA Field Office Relationship.* It is manifestly impossible to exactly delimit all rights, responsibilities or privileges under an interagency agreement, such as this one, developed within the framework of NSCID No. 7.[5] It is possible, however, to fashion such an agreement into an effective instrument for the complete intelligence exploitation of the maritime field. The catalyst required is an amicable working relationship between the DIOs and the CIA field offices, which can only be based upon a sympathetic understanding of each other's problems and a desire to cooperate in a common effort. District Intelligence Officers are directed to make every effort consistent with existing

---

[4] Not further identified.

[5] See *Foreign Relations,* 1945–1950, Emergence of the Intelligence Establishment, Document 427.

directives to formulate such a working relationship at the earliest moment, and resolve such local problems as arise in connection with this agreement.

R. F. Stout[6]

---

[6] Printed from a copy that bears the typed signature of Deputy Director of Naval Intelligence Stout who signed for Johnson.

---

114.   Editorial Note

NSC 114/3, "United States Programs for National Security," June 5, 1952, included Summary Statement No. 7—Foreign Intelligence and Related Activities, prepared by the Central Intelligence Agency. For text of Summary Statement No. 7, see *Foreign Relations, 1952–1954*, volume II, Part 1, pages 50–53.

---

115.   Minutes of a Meeting of the Intelligence Advisory Committee[1]

IAC–M–73   Washington, June 5, 1952.

Director of Central Intelligence
General Walter Bedell Smith
Presiding*[2]

Deputy Director (Intelligence)
Central Intelligence Agency
Mr. Loftus E. Becker
Presiding*

---

[1] Source: Central Intelligence Agency, Community Management Staff, Job 82–00400R, Box 1. Secret; Security Information. The meeting was held in the DCI's conference room.

[2] Asterisks refer to footnote in the original minutes reading, "For part of the meeting."

MEMBERS PRESENT

Mr. W. Park Armstrong, Jr., Special Assistant, Intelligence, Department of State
Brigadier General John Weckerling, acting for Assistant Chief of Staff, G–2,
    Department of the Army
Rear Admiral Felix L. Johnson, Director of Naval Intelligence, Department
    of the Navy
Colonel Edward H. Porter, acting for Director of Intelligence, Headquarters,
    United States Air Force
*Dr. Malcolm C. Henderson, acting for Director of Intelligence, Atomic Energy
    Commission
Brigadier General Richard C. Partridge, Deputy Director for Intelligence,
    The Joint Staff
Mr. Victor P. Keay, acting for Assistant to the Director, Federal Bureau of
    Investigation

ALSO PRESENT

Dr. Sherman Kent, Central Intelligence Agency
*Mr. Robert Amory, Jr., Central Intelligence Agency
Mr. Ralph Clark, Central Intelligence Agency
*Mr. R. J. Sontag, Central Intelligence Agency
Mr. Paul Borel, Central Intelligence Agency
Mr. Ludwell L. Montague, Central Intelligence Agency
Mr. Edgar Hoover, Central Intelligence Agency
*Mr. William P. Bundy, Central Intelligence Agency
*Mr. Chester Cooper, Central Intelligence Agency
*Mr. Harold Ford, Central Intelligence Agency
Mr. Richard Drain, Central Intelligence Agency
*Mr. [name not declassified], Central Intelligence Agency
Mr. William C. Trueheart, Department of State
Mr. R. M. Scammon, Department of State
Mr. Mose L. Harvey, Department of State
Mr. Joseph A. Yeager, Department of State
Colonel O. B. Sykes, Department of the Army
Lieut. Colonel H. N. Maples, Department of the Army
Captain Ray Malpass, USN, Department of the Navy
Colonel Charles F. Gillis, Department of the Air Force
Colonel S. M. Lansing, The Joint Staff
Colonel John D. Tolman, The Joint Staff

James Q. Reber[3]
Secretary

Approval of Minutes

1. *Action:* The minutes of the last meeting, 29 May 1952,
(IAC–M–72) were approved.[4]

---

[3] Printed from a copy that bears this typed signature.

[4] IAC minutes are in Central Intelligence Agency, Community Management Staff
Job 82–00400R, Box 1.

RDB Request for Intelligence Estimate of Soviet Scientific and Technological Capabilities (IAC–D–51)[5]

2. *Action:* Agreed that the RDB request would be met by the JIC if this proved to be within the latter's capability. In this event it was understood that the JIC would arrange for the RDB promptly to withdraw their request on the DCI.

3. *Discussion:* It was pointed out that the JIC had a study now in progress (JIC 603/1)[6] which was along the lines of the RDB request. It was thought probable that with some adaptation this study would satisfy the RDB request and also serve as a scientific and technological contribution for NIE–65.[7] General Smith stated that a component of the Defense Department, such as RDB, should, where possible, get its intelligence support from the military intelligence agencies. The DCI satisfies the intelligence requirements of the NSC and, although willing to satisfy a need of such organizations as RDB, if practicable, will be glad to have such needs satisfied elsewhere. In response to a question General Smith agreed that CIA components would be willing to give informal assistance to the military analysts, to the extent that was practicable in the light of their other duties, but made it clear that CIA does not participate in JIC estimates and assumes no responsibility therefor. If it should develop that the JIC could not without outside contributions meet the RDB need and the RDB request is not withdrawn, then the DCI stated he would expect to try to satisfy the request on a community basis.

[Omitted here is discussion of other subjects.]

---

[5] Not found.

[6] Not found.

[7] NIE 65, "Soviet Bloc Capabilities Through 1957," approved June 16, 1953. (National Archives, RG 263, Central Intelligence Agency Files)

116. Memorandum From the Executive Secretary of the National Security Council (Lay) to the National Security Council[1]

Washington, June 12, 1952.

SUBJECT

Organized and Coordinated Program of Covert Preclusive Buying

REFERENCES

A. Memo for NSC from Acting Executive Secretary, same subject, dated February 11, 1952[2]
B. NSC 104/2, pars. 11 and 12[3]
C. Memos for NSC from Executive Secretary, subject, "Assignment of Responsibilities for Economic Defense," dated November 7, 1951 and January 25, 1952[4]

Pursuant to Reference A, the Senior NSC Staff requested the Economic Defense Advisory Committee (formerly the Mutual Trade Security Advisory Committee) to prepare a study of the desirability and feasibility of the initiation of a preclusive buying program. The enclosed report[5] was prepared by the Economic Defense Advisory Committee in response to this request; was submitted through the Department of State; and was discussed by the Senior NSC Staff which concurred in it with amendments incorporated therein. The Senior NSC Staff considered that the recommendations in paragraph 10 of the enclosure are in accordance with existing policy contained in NSC 104/2, and that action by the National Security Council on these recommendations is, therefore, not required.

In the light of the above, the Secretary of State, pursuant to Reference C, is directing the implementation of the recommendations contained in the enclosure through the Economic Defense Advisory Committee. The enclosed report is accordingly circulated herewith for the information of the National Security Council to indicate the action which is being taken on the basis of the memorandum of the Chairman, National Security Resources Board, in Reference A.

James S. Lay, Jr.

---

[1] Source: Truman Library, Papers of Harry S. Truman, President's Secretary's Files. Secret; Security Information. Copies were sent to the Secretary of the Treasury, Secretary of Commerce, Acting Director of Defense Mobilization, and the Director of the Bureau of the Budget.

[2] Not printed. (Ibid.)

[3] For NSC 104/2, see Foreign Relations, 1951, vol. I, pp. 1059–1064.

[4] The November 7, 1951, memorandum circulated to the National Security Council a November 6 memorandum on the subject from President Truman, which is printed ibid., p. 1214. The January 25 memorandum is in National Archives, RG 59, Central Files 1950–54, 460.509/1–2552.

[5] Not printed.

117.   Director of Central Intelligence Directive No. 4/2 (Revised)[1]

Washington, June 12, 1952.

PRIORITY LIST OF CRITICAL NATIONAL INTELLIGENCE OBJECTIVES

In accordance with DCI 4/1,[2] paragraph 3, the following list in order of priority of critical national intelligence objectives, with respect to the USSR and its Satellites (including Communist China) is established; so the highest priority shall be given to the collection of information and to the production of intelligence concerning Soviet and Satellite capabilities and intentions for:

1. taking direct military action against the Continental United States;

2. taking direct military action, employing USSR and Satellite Armed Forces, against vital U.S. possessions, areas peripheral to the Soviet Orbit, and Western Europe;

3. interfering with U.S. strategic air attack;

4. interfering with U.S. movement of men and material by water transport;

5. production and stockpiling, including location of installations and facilities, of atomic and related weapons, other critical weapons and equipment, and critical transportation equipment;

6. creating situations anywhere in the world dangerous to U.S. national security, short of commitment of Soviet and Satellite Armed Forces, including foreign directed sabotage and espionage objectives;

7. interfering with U.S. political, psychological, and economic courses of action for the achievement of critical U.S. aims and objectives.

Walter B. Smith[3]
Director of Central Intelligence

---

[1] Source: Central Intelligence Agency, Directorate of Operations, Job 78–04513R, Box 1. Secret; Security Information.

[2] Not printed. (Ibid., History Staff Job 84–T00389R, HS/HC–600, Box 4)

[3] Printed from a copy that bears this typed signature.

118. Letter From the Ambassador to the Soviet Union (Kennan) to the Deputy Under Secretary of State (Matthews)[1]

Moscow, June 18, 1952.

Dear Doc:

I propose in this letter to speak about matters of such delicacy that I want you to know before you get into it that it is a letter of which I am keeping no copy, and one which you will probably wish to destroy as soon as you have read it.

Since my arrival in Moscow I have become increasingly aware of a situation which not only gives me great concern but which seems to involve a very important question of principle concerning the attitude of our Government as a whole toward this mission and the functions which it is supposed to perform. I am prepared to go ahead and decide these questions on my own formal responsibility here, but in doing so I wish to make sure that the situation is clearly understood in Washington and that my decision here is in accord with the view of authoritative circles in our Government. It is for this reason that I am mentioning the matter to you.

I find upon arrival here and upon closer acquaintance with the activities of the staff that during the past two or three years this mission—and by that I mean its personnel, premises and extraterritorial status—has been intensively and somewhat recklessly exploited by the military intelligence-gathering agencies of the Government for their particular purposes. Their representatives here have, I am afraid, been encouraged by their home offices to utilize intensively such facilities as they enjoy here by virtue of their diplomatic status, for the purpose of assembling every possible shred of information on military subjects. I do not find that their instructions have called upon them to take adequate account of the effects their actions might have on the straight political and diplomatic potential of the mission, or on those very privileges and facilities from which they were profiting. So far as I can analyze the point of view which lies behind these activities, it is one which has not considered the diplomatic potential of this mission as a factor to be seriously taken into account, and which assumes the very existence of the mission as a short term provisorium, to be ruthlessly and intensively exploited while it lasts.

---

[1] Source: National Archives, RG 59, Central Files 1950–54, 120.32161/6–1852. Top Secret.

I would like to be able to list for you a number of the factual incidents which lead me to make these observations. Actually, I cannot bring myself to put them on paper for obvious reasons. I can only say the following about them:

1. Many of them are quite shocking and surprising, almost incredible to anyone who has had any extensive familiarity with the diplomatic profession.

2. In several instances little or no effort has been made to avoid detection by the Soviet authorities. In certain instances actions have been performed here under the very lenses of Soviet photographers appointed for the purpose of photographing them, and those actions were ones which the Soviet Government had specifically warned us were contrary to local law.

3. Many of these actions seem to me to have been of a childish and "Boy Scout" nature, which, in addition to serving as proof to the Soviet Government of systematic misuse of our diplomatic status, must have brought smiles to the faces of higher Soviet authorities and cannot have contributed to Soviet respect for the mission.

4. Many of the targets are ones which I think could easily have been reached by other and less dangerous methods.

5. In general, these activities have been the result not of spontaneous initiative on the part of the men out here, but of pressures put upon them by their own superiors in Washington.

These activities have had and are having three effects which I think it is important for our Government to note:

1. They are self-defeating in that they lead to a steady and gradual curtailment of the very facilities which they exploit.

I have no doubt whatsoever that the curtailment of travel for this mission represents a reaction of the Soviet authorities to the extensive exploitation of travel facilities by this and other missions for purposes which cannot be viewed by them as legitimate. The same is true of the drastic and total isolation of the diplomatic corps here, including even neutral missions, from contact with the Soviet people. These things have probably had a good deal to do with the extraordinary pressures put on the servant and custodial staffs of diplomatic missions. If they are continued, we must expect a steady increase in the severity of these restrictions to a point where life will become practically impossible for foreigners in this city unless they wish to sit like prisoners within their buildings and be served by imported servants. The upshot of this is that activities of this nature must be predicated upon a lack of concern for maintenance of those very facilities whose existence they assume and exploit.

2. These activities have a deleterious effect on the actual diplomatic potential of the mission, i.e., of its value as a political reporting

unit and a channel of communication with the Soviet Government, and have already probably reduced its possibilities significantly in these fields.

What has been said above about the exhaustion of these channels for intelligence purposes has its application in even greater degree to the normal purposes that these facilities were supposed to serve. With the increasing isolation of the diplomatic corps, the curtailment of travel facilities, and the constant increase in Soviet vigilance vis-à-vis foreigners, you have the ruin of those last vestigial positions which made possible, even in a minor way, something resembling normal life and travel in this country. Not only that, but one cannot help feeling that the attitude of members of the Soviet Government and officials of the Foreign Office toward individual diplomatic officers of our mission must be affected by what they know of the uses to which the mission is daily being put. This applies particularly to the ambassador here, for the Soviet authorities can only conclude either that he is aware of and responsible for this employment of his mission, or that he is not aware of it or is powerless to stop it. In the first case, they must regard him as the major offender. In either of the latter cases they must regard him as a secondary figure-head who is only being put up for formal and protocol purposes like their own ambassadors abroad. I hardly need emphasize to you how serious a factor this is. In the end, the great political judgments about the nature of Soviet power, its psychology and its intentions, are of vastly greater importance to our Government than detailed tidbits of tactical information about the Soviet armed forces, much of which can be obtained in other places of (if really well-trained people are used) by other and more desirable methods. Yet we are seriously handicapped, in our ability to arrive at these major judgments, by the retaliatory actions brought upon us by these peripheral activities of the mission. Furthermore, the maintenance of the mission as a channel of communication with the Soviet Government is something which may be rarely of practical importance but when the moment does come that it is of any value at all, then its importance can be enormous. In the burdening and reduction of the ambassadorial position by the tolerance of these activities our Government is really taking a heavy responsibility in the face of the uncertainties of the future.

3. The continuance of this type of activity actually places in jeopardy, in my opinion, the physical security of the members of the mission and their families.

Thus far the Soviet authorities have been very correct in this respect, and no American official or employee has, in recent years, suffered (to my knowledge) any physical damage or open unpleasantness. However, we know very well that the Soviet authorities are assembling a careful, and, I fear, impressive record of all of our activities. The Grow diary is only a small part, I am sure, of what they have in their pocket. We also know that in the more remote past there have been instances when unwise Americans met with physical violence, judicial summonses and other forms of unpleasantness. We must remember that our American employees here—and by this I mean all those persons not on the diplomatic list—are by Soviet usage completely devoid of diplomatic immunity for any violations of Soviet law. We have not seen fit to challenge seriously this position of the Soviet authorities. That means that these people are all extremely vulnerable and can in most instances very easily be framed and made subject to court action at any time.

Finally, you have the several possibilities that out of the present delicate international situation there might arise either a rupture of relations between our countries or an actual state of war. In either of these events, I think it entirely possible, if not likely, that individual members of our staff, and perhaps the whole staff might suffer seriously by virtue of these activities that have been conducted in the past. Our Government must therefore realize that if it wishes such activities to be continued at this post, it cannot hold the ambassador and other officers of the mission responsible for the maximum safety of members of the staff in the face of possible consequences that may ensue.

I am aware that this is hardly a matter on which direct written instructions can be issued to this mission, and not even one about which there can be official correspondence. I do not wish to place the Government in the position of having to give me any written instructions of an undesirable nature. I am therefore writing this letter to tell you, first of all, that I propose to issue orders to all members of this mission that they are expected to comply strictly with Soviet laws and regulations so far as they are known, and also they are to avoid every form of public behavior which might be expected to give the impression to local citizens and officials that they are engaged in improper activities. This applies particularly to the use of cameras, radio receiving sets, and other electrical and auditory devices, and to the visiting or inspection of installations or areas of a known military significance. I have already discussed these matters with the service attachés, who have taken my observations in good part. But one of them points out that this will mean important modifications in his policies and activities, and that these modifications are not apt to be agreeable to his home office.

Secondly, I would like to ask that you call to the attention of the heads of the various intelligence-gathering agencies the fact that this is my intention, and that you ascertain whether any of them is in disagreement with this position and considers that it is, on balance, detrimental to United States interests.

Thirdly, in case there is this feeling on the part of any of the responsible heads of the agencies involved, I would earnestly request that you have this matter taken to a high interdepartmental agency for thorough discussion and settlement.

Fourth, if my proposed position here meets with the full understanding and approval of the Government—so that I need not feel that any subsequent reproach will rest upon me or this mission for its conduct in this matter—then I will expect no reply of any sort to this communication, and I will understand that silence means consent.

Fifth, if, on the other hand, it is the considered view of the appropriate higher authorities of our Government that the practices I have in mind are of an importance such as to override the disadvantages to which I have pointed, and if, therefore, it is the desire of the Government that I not alter any of the existing practices, then I would appreciate it if you could find means simply to inform me that my letter of this date has been duly considered but that the Government sees no grounds for alteration of existing practices. In such case, however, I want it clearly understood, both by the Secretary and the President, that I cannot properly be held responsible for such deterioration as may ensue in the value of this mission both as an observation post and as a channel of communication with the Soviet Government, or for any other unhappy consequences.

I am sorry to have to write this letter, but if you will put yourself in my place you will see that I have no choice but to do so. I cannot allow to proceed a progressive deterioration in the actual diplomatic potential of a mission entrusted to my care, on a vague assumption that this is what the Government wants. On the other hand, I cannot, without at least apprising the Government of what I am doing and giving it an opportunity to overrule me, take administrative measures here which might later conceivably lead to my being charged with having deprived the United States Government of valuable information, and prejudiced the military interests of the country.[2]

Very sincerely yours,

George F. Kennan[3]

---

[2] On July 7, Fisher Howe, Deputy Special Assistant to the Secretary of State for Intelligence and Research, sent a note to Matthews and followed up with a letter on July 15 informing him that the Services were asking for copies of Kennan's letter. Howe suggested that the Department obtain Kennan's agreement to show it to them. (Ibid.) In a July 22 memorandum, Howe stated that Matthews agreed, Kennan was queried and agreed, and that he and Walworth Barbour discussed it with senior representatives of the Services. All said they had no serious objection to Kennan's proposals. (Ibid.) According to a handwritten note by Howe on the July 22 memorandum, Matthews sent a letter to Kennan to this effect, but Matthews' letter has not been found.

[3] Printed from a copy that indicates Kennan signed the original.

P.S. Two afterthoughts:

I neglected to mention above that I am afraid the situation I have described in this letter has led to a certain amount of bitterness against this mission on the part of other missions in the city, who feel that their status has also been worsened and their opportunities reduced as a result of our activities. I think there is something in this, if we take into consideration, in addition to the activities discussed in this letter, indiscretions that have been committed by individual Americans in the form of publication or leakage of information about their relations with other missions and with Soviet citizens here.

Secondly, I should make it plain that the reason I am addressing this letter to you now is that the first severe test of the policy I propose to enforce here will come in connection with the Soviet Air Force Day on June 28. I shall not be here myself, but I have given instructions through Hugh Cumming that there is to be no photographing or listening activity on the roofs of Embassy premises here which can be detected and photographed from other roofs (as has been done in the past). If the consensus of authoritative opinion in Washington wish to indicate that to Hugh by telegraphic message as suggested above we will permit the activities; but my own feeling is that it is highly unwise and is bound to appear some day in a propaganda white book or some other disagreeable form, as proof of the systematic abuse by the American Embassy of its diplomatic status and of its violation of local Soviet laws and regulations.

G.F.K.[4]

---

[4] The initials are typed.

119. Memorandum From President Truman to the Chairman of the Psychological Strategy Board (Smith)[1]

Washington, June 21, 1952.

SUBJECT

Organization of Psychological Strategy Board

I have been giving consideration to the organization of the Psychological Strategy Board and particularly to the question of whether the directive of April 4, 1951,[2] establishing it should be amended. In addition to the recommendations of the Board's first Director and the recommendations of the Board included in your useful and constructive memorandum of May 16,[3] I have had the report of a study undertaken at my direction by the Director of the Bureau of the Budget.

It is my view that, as you recommend, no change in the directive of April 4, 1951, or in the organization of the Board should be made at this time. The Board's decision to rotate the chairmanship, with the Director taking his turn as presiding officer is consistent with the intent of the directive of April 4, 1951.

Adjustments in the relationships of the Director with the National Security Council and of the Board with the Joint Chiefs of Staff recommended in your memorandum similarly can be made within the framework of the existing directive and are consistent with it. I shall speak with the Executive Secretary of the National Security Council relative to the former. Appropriate representation of the Joint Chiefs of Staff with the Board can be arranged by the Secretary of Defense.

I believe that it would be helpful to me if the Board could suggest occasions when I might become more directly informed of its work, particularly of its evaluation of the national psychological effort, through a meeting with the Board, the Director and the Executive Secretary of the National Security Council.

I am transmitting the report of the Director of the Bureau of the Budget on the organization of the Psychological Strategy Board for study and appropriate action by the Board.[4] The report emphasizes the

---

[1] Source: Truman Library, Papers of Harry S. Truman, Confidential File. Top Secret, Security Information. A June 13 memorandum from Bureau of the Budget Director F. J. Lawton to President Truman indicates that the proposed memorandum to Smith had been discussed with Souers, Lay, and Smith, and that all were in agreement with it. (Ibid.)

[2] See Document 60.

[3] Not printed. (Truman Library, Papers of Harry S. Truman, Confidential File)

[4] Attached but not printed is the April 21 report entitled "The Psychological Strategy Board: Selected Aspects of Its Concept, Organization and Operations."

primary usefulness of the Board as an instrument for more effective planning through the organized utilization of the resources of the participating agencies. The report further stresses the need for increased emphasis upon the Board's responsibilities for forward planning and in the evaluation of the total national psychological effort. I particularly commend these sections of the report to the attention of the Board.

Harry S. Truman[5]

---

[5] Printed from a copy that indicates Truman signed the original.

---

120. Memorandum From the Assistant Director of National Estimates of the Central Intelligence Agency (Kent) to the Deputy Director of Intelligence of the Central Intelligence Agency (Becker)[1]

Washington, July 1, 1952.

SUBJECT

The Problem of Scientific and Technical Intelligence

1. Herewith some thoughts on the problem of scientific and technical intelligence which are pretty close to convictions with me.

2. Without in any way trying to derogate the importance and the extraordinary difficulty of your administrative problems, let me repeat that had O/NE not had the assistance of O/SI in drafting the text of SIE–5,[2] that estimate would have been a quite different and far, far less useful document. In fact, it is my belief that without O/SI's interpretation of the evidence and with no corrective for service interpretation of the evidence, C/NE could have done nothing but accept the service interpretation which in the light of what I learned from O/SI would have been an over-reassuring one.

---

[1] Source: Central Intelligence Agency, History Staff Job 84–00022R, Box 3, Folder 12. Secret.

[2] Reference is presumably to NIE–5, "The Scale and Nature of the Soviet Air Defense Effort, 1952–54," December 3, 1951. (Ibid., National Intelligence Council, Job 79–S01011A, Box 2, Folder 1)

3. Obviously this is for your private eye and just as obviously if I give it any further circulation it will be to Washington Platt on an "Eyes Only" basis.

Sherman Kent[3]

Attachment[4]

Some Thoughts on the Problem of Scientific and Technical Intelligence

1. In any country's security system there are elements upon which the country in question places great store. These are truly its secrets of security.

2. Generally speaking these secrets of security if they are not in themselves scientific and technical at least rest on scientific and technological developments. Ask yourself: Knowledge of what twenty US secrets of security would I be most concerned to keep from the USSR? How many of the twenty really lie outside the scientific/technical area?

3. The importance which a country attaches to any of these elements in its security system is an index of that country's desire to keep them secret from all outsiders. Thus the more important they are the more difficult they become as intelligence targets.

4. The security measures in operation in the USSR have been peculiarly successful in the scientific/technical areas. It would be my guess that in no part of our knowledge of Soviet secrets of security is the ratio of fixed points to voids so large. In the matter of the gadgets around which Soviet air defense capabilities are built, the paucity of fixed points is dramatic in the extreme.

5. In the last analysis the mission of intelligence is to draw the meaningful and objective generalization from the data.

a. If the data, or fixed points, are numerous and the voids between them small, then meaningful, objective, and probably correct generalizations can be drawn.

b. If the data, or fixed points, are few and the voids between them large, meaningful generalizations can still be drawn. But who is to say that they are objective and/or probably correct? Who is to say they are anything but pure fiction?

---

[3] Printed from a copy that bears this typed signature.
[4] Secret.

6. In case 5b above, the generalizer, minimally confined and directed by fixed points, may be engulfed by forces wholly extraneous to the problem at hand. It is here that he may be consciously or unconsciously taken over by his hopes, his wishes, and his fears, or by those of his friends or the institution he works for. (I refer you to the men who have designed maps of the heavens and who have generalized the muscular Orion and his club, belt, and lion skin from a dozen or so stars.) What he comes up with is something far different from and usually far more or less than the meager suggestions of the fixed points. The added something is not from the data; it is from him.

7. As long as the national intelligence community can fix only relatively few points in key scientific and technical developments of the USSR and as long as the voids between these points are very large, generalizations by any single individual or single intelligence institution may be dangerously skewed by individual wish or institution policy.

8. Ask yourself: "What would I wish if my future were interwoven with that of one of the armed services?" You would wish to be a part of the best damn outfit of its sort in existence—an outfit that could deliver enough lethal power to destroy any enemy in a single attack and do it without losing a man.

9. Ask yourself the next question: What do I do to get my wish?" If you are in intelligence you may do two things.

a. To assure yourself that your service will get the funds to make it the best damn outfit of its sort in existence you will not play down the enemy. You will build him up, especially in gross terms of his offensive capability.

b. To assure yourself that once you've got the best damn outfit in the world, it will carry out its mission you begin to take away from the enemy. You will take away notably in the area of his defensive capabilities. You are not quite so certain to do this as to build up his offensive capabilities, because of the perils involved. You know that if you significantly undervalue his defensive capabilities and plans are drawn upon your evaluation your service may be cruelly hurt in the clash. You finally fix the point of his defensive capabilities at the place where the curve of your wish intersects the curve of your fear. The fixed points are so few that you can easily draw your curves to accommodate them.

10. When you have done these two things you have done little more than describe the ideal enemy; the enemy big enough to warrant the perfection of your outfit, but an enemy who is nevertheless a pushover in a showdown.

11. You can do this in the field of scientific and technical intelligence on the USSR, and no one can say you may [nay?] so long as the ratio of fixed points to voids remains what it is.

12. The above is a long way of spelling out my doubts as to the virtues of assigning to given departmental intelligence organizations a

"primary" responsibility in any of the specific areas of scientific and technical intelligence. All along I have feared the generalizations, say, that ONI may make of the fixed points and voids re Soviet underwater warfare techniques, that G–2 may make re Soviet tank design, that A–2 may make re Soviet GCI and A–2 radar and AAA. I have however been somewhat comforted by realizing that if any single service comes up with a wishful generalization, this generalization may be opposed to the wish of another service; that the other service will possess all the data of the first and that it will be capable of drawing its own variant or opposing generalization.

13. If a service is duly invested with "primary" responsibility and if at the same time it possesses sources of information which it may or may not share with other services and if it chooses not to share, the chances of another service developing a variant or opposing generalization have shrunk considerably and may have shrunk to approximate zero.

14. We are in a position today where we cannot anticipate either (a) a dramatic decrease in the ratio of voids to fixed points in the area of scientific and technical developments in the USSR or (b) a dramatic change in human nature. As long as we do not take out insurance against the acceptance of a generalization that must perforce partake heavily of the wish, we are asking for trouble. If I were carrying the statutory responsibilities of the DCI the minimum insurance I would take out would be as follows:

a. Keep O/SI in business pretty much as it is today—even endeavor to strengthen some of its divisions. The ones I would strengthen would be those dealing with the most important subject matter irrespective of whether another agency had been awarded "primary" responsibility in this subject matter.

b. Set up a machinery to insure that no one scientific/technical intelligence outfit withheld information which it may have developed and which it found useful in drawing its own generalizations.

121. Memorandum From the Director of the Armed Forces Security Agency (Canine) to Secretary of Defense Lovett[1]

Washington, July 8, 1952.

SUBJECT

Brownell Committee Report[2]

REFERENCE

Your Memorandum of 23 June 1952[3]

1. After a careful study of the report of the Brownell Committee, I have concluded that it presents a fair and essentially accurate picture of the history and development of COMINT and of its present functioning. I have followed closely the work of the Committee throughout their investigation and have been greatly impressed with their objective approach to and deep penetration of the extremely complicated problem which confronted them. It is my opinion that they have reached eminently sound conclusions.

2. In those portions of the report containing historical and other background information, there are a few errors in fact, and also certain statements which may convey erroneous impressions. While these appear to have had no significant effect on the Committee's obviously thorough understanding of the essentials involved, and their whole background, it is desirable that certain of these errors be set straight for the record; this is done in inclosure 1.[4]

3. In my opinion the organization of COMINT activities proposed by the Brownell Committee is both workable and practical at all three levels, subject to the comment given below. It would constitute an extension on a joint basis of the vertical principle of organization which, as the Committee points out, now exists in each of the three Armed Services separately. I regard as particularly important the degree of authority which the Committee proposes to vest in the Director of AFSA, an authority which, for the first time since the creation of the Agency, will be commensurate with his responsibilities.

4. It is noted that the Committee apparently intends that the responsibilities of the Director of AFSA be extended in the Communication Security field to embrace the production and protection of the

---

[1] Source: National Security Agency, Center for Cryptologic History, Series V, F.7.12. Top Secret; Security Information.

[2] See Document 99.

[3] Not found.

[4] Not printed.

codes and ciphers of the entire U.S. Government, rather than merely the Department of Defense as is now the case. I consider such an extension of jurisdiction in the Communication Security field to be desirable. However, the Committee has not seen fit to elaborate upon this proposal and, in fact, has included in its report very little comment on the problems involved. Moreover, the proposed directive contains no specific provisions as to organization above, within, or below AFSA for the purpose of conducting communication security activities on a national basis. In this connection it is desirable to invite to your attention two facts:

a. There is in existence an Executive Order dated 3 July 1945,[5] which created a National Cryptographic Security Board charged with responsibility for the efficient coordination and supervision of all cryptographic systems and related procedures of the Federal departments and agencies. This Board was established as a body apart from the then existing Communication Intelligence Board for the reason that different interests were involved.

b. The United States Communication Intelligence Board (USCIB) has considered at some length the advisability of extending its responsibilities to include communication security matters but has thus far failed to reach agreement.

In view of the foregoing facts, I believe that further study is required to determine the best national structure for communication security activities. Accordingly, the comments and proposed changes set forth herein have to do with COMINT activities only. I will have a separate study made of the communication security problem with a view toward preparing a separate directive. It is believed advisable to treat the two categories separately, and this can be done without detriment to either. An attempt to combine the two in a single directive would probably introduce complications which could result in delaying implementation of the Committee's clear-cut recommendations on COMINT.

5. With respect to the latter recommendations, the following comment is submitted in response to paragraphs 3 and 4 of your memorandum:

a. *Recommendations as to Changes in Organization Above AFSA*

(1) Retention in USCIB of the principle of decision and action on certain matters by unanimous agreement would serve to perpetuate one of the chief difficulties which according to the Committee now hamper USCIB, since the matters where this would apply are essentially those to which the Board has confined its attention in the past. This would particularly affect the protection of COMINT sources. The net result would be to preserve for each Department and Agency

---

[5] Not found.

virtual autonomy in the application of COMINT security measures, despite the fact that the maintenance of such security is vital to all. It is true that the right of appeal to higher authority is provided for in the proposed Board procedures. Nevertheless, this would place the burden of such appeal on the majority, where it would be reluctantly exercised, whereas in matters involving the common interest the burden of obtaining exception should rest on the minority. Extension of the majority-rule principle to all of the Board's decisions and actions would not only accomplish the latter but would also simplify the Board's procedures. Certainly it would appear desirable to extend this rule at least to security matters.

(2) Paragraph d. (5) of the proposed Presidential Memorandum provides for certain special consideration in matters of appeal which involve the responsibilities of the Secretary of Defense as Executive Agent. These responsibilities pertain to those matters which fall within the jurisdiction of the Director of AFSA. The propriety of according this consideration to appeals made by the representative of the Secretary of Defense is appreciated; nevertheless, since the Director of AFSA is also directly under the Secretary and is the individual immediately responsible, it would appear a less complicated arrangement to have the Director rather than the representative of the Secretary of Defense, given this special consideration in appeals. Accordingly, it is suggested that consideration be given to the advisability of this change.

(3) Experience has demonstrated that the special nature of COMINT activities requires that they be treated in all respects as being outside the framework of other or general intelligence activities. If this is not done the protection of COMINT sources is seriously jeopardized. In recognition of this fact, the current charter of USCIB (see paragraphs 6 and 8 of National Security Council Intelligence Directive #9)[6] contains certain provisions which I strongly urge be carried over into the new directive.

b. *Recommendations as to Organization within AFSA*

(1) The introductory statement to this section of the Committee's conclusions and recommendations appears to imply that there are serious weaknesses in the present organizational structure of AFSA. I agree in general with what are apparently intended to be supporting comments of the Committee, but it strikes me that these comments are not, in fact, criticisms of structure but are remarks pertaining to personnel policies applicable to AFSA. They actually deal with incumbency of the Directorship and other key positions, the alleged high rate of turnover of personnel, and various other personnel problems. I assume therefore, that the Committee found no basic faults in the AFSA structure as such.

(2) With regard to the recommendation that the Director should have a civilian chief technical assistant who would have under him all research and development in the cryptanalytic field, it is to be noted that the Chief of the Office of Research and Development, one of the

---

[6] See *Foreign Relations*, 1945–1950, Emergence of the Intelligence Establishment, Document 435.

three principal subdivisions of AFSA, has been a civilian since January 1952. As a result of recommendations of the Special Cryptologic Advisory Group (SCAG) a plan for improving the organization of these activities is now in the process of development with the assistance of SCAG members.

(3) It is noted that paragraph 2. a. of the Committee's proposed Presidential Memorandum *excludes* from the meaning of COMINT and the mission of AFSA the evaluation and dissemination of information obtained from intercepted communications, and its synthesis with information from other sources. It is noted further that paragraph 2. c. (2) of the same memorandum states that the responsibility assigned to the Director of AFSA *does not contravene* the responsibilities of the departments and agencies in respect to these same functions. Whereas the former statement is positively preclusive, the latter appears to afford the Director some freedom of action provided he does not interfere with the legitimate work of other agencies. Some latitude in this is essential for technical purposes, especially in the field of traffic analysis. It is, therefore, recommended that the former statement be omitted and the latter be retained, with a slight modification, as a separate and final provision of the proposed memorandum.

c. *Recommendations as to Changes in Organization Below the AFSA Level (In the Service COMINT Organizations)*

(1) While the meaning of "COMINT activities" as used in Public Law 513 is probably clear from the context of that Law it may be well to define more specifically the scope of the term for the purposes of the proposed directive. When read out of context, the definition of Communication Intelligence contained in the Law could be interpreted to include postal censorship and the monitoring and processing of foreign press and propaganda broadcasts. It is believed advisable to make it clear that such activities are not to be included under the provisions of the new directive.

6. Attached hereto as inclosure 2[7] is a suggested redraft of the proposed Presidential Memorandum for the Secretary of State and the Secretary of Defense. In addition to certain substantive changes which are recommended on the basis of the foregoing comment, there is some rearrangement of the section which deals with the directive to USCIB. This rearrangement is considered advisable because of the recommended change in Board procedure. I consider that the proposed executive memorandum contains no information of classification higher than Secret, and have reclassified the proposed revision of Exhibit K accordingly.

Ralph J. Canine[8]
Major General, US Army

---

[7] Not printed.
[8] Printed from a copy that bears this typed signature.

122. Memorandum of Conversation[1]

Pasadena, California, July 17, 1952.

PARTICIPANTS

Cal Tech
President L. A. DuBridge
Dean E. C. Watson
Professor C. C. Lauritsen
Professor R. F. Bacher
Professor J. L. Greenstein (Part time)

PSB
Palmer Putnam

CIA
Willis A. Gibbons
[*name not declassified*]

SUBJECT

Discussion of the Feasibility and Utility of a Satellite Vehicle for Reconnaissance Purposes

1. *Background.* At the request of Mr. Palmer Putnam (PSB), and of Admiral Luis deFlorez (OTS/CIA), I called Dean E. C. Watson, California Institute of Technology (Cal Tech) on 10 July 1952 and asked if he could arrange for himself, President DuBridge and Professors Lauritsen, Bacher and Millikan to meet with us in Pasadena on Thursday, July 17th for the purpose of discussing this subject. Dean Watson said that he would be delighted to arrange the discussion. Upon arrival we found that Professor Millikan had been called out of town and could not meet with us. Dean Watson said that Professor J. L. Greenstein, an astrophysicist, had conducted some discussion with the Rand Corporation people regarding the vehicle and suggested that Greenstein's knowledge would be helpful if we were agreeable to inviting him into the discussion. We thereupon asked Professor Greenstein to consult with us.

2. Putnam had brought with him several copies of a paper which he had prepared outlining current capabilities of the Soviets and indicating that by 1957 the Soviets will possess the capability of a saturation attack with atomic weapons against the United States and against which the United States can have no effective defense. Putnam held

---

[1] Source: Central Intelligence Agency, History Staff, Job 83–00036R, Box 11. Secret; Security Information. Drafted on July 25 by [*name not declassified*], Special Assistant for Research, Office of Policy Coordination, Central Intelligence Agency.

that some drastic policies are required and that we need to increase our intelligence take regarding the Soviet Union. He suggested that the utilization of a satellite vehicle for reconnaissance purposes might be one means of increasing our intelligence concerning the Soviet Union and of physical structures and the characteristics relating thereto.

3. We made reference to the Rand Corporation report "Utility of a Satellite Vehicle for Reconnaissance," R–217. The scientists present from Cal Tech had read the report.

4. The report contemplated and discussed the feasibility of building and launching a so-called satellite vehicle which would orbit around the earth at an altitude of some 350 miles above the earth travelling at a speed of five miles per second, thus completing from 14 to 18 complete orbits every 24 hours earth time. The satellite would be powered by an isotope of cerium (Ce–144), a beta emitter, which would heat mercury into a vapor which in turn would drive an engine which would drive generators for production of power. The power would be utilized, once the satellite was on orbit, for operating the navigational controls and a television camera and transmitter which would be incorporated in the satellite. The orbit of the vehicle would be predetermined with respect to the earth's latitude and longitude thereby permitting intensive coverage from the standpoint of photography of certain portions of the earth. The Rand study contemplated that five television receiving stations would be erected on the earth to receive the television signals and transmissions from the vehicle. The vehicle would not be man-carrying.

5. It was the general consensus of the Cal Tech scientists:

a. That it was probably feasible to build such a vehicle;

b. That there would be unforeseen difficulties, which probably could be surmounted, in "marrying" the different technical systems to be contained within the satellite;

c. That the problem of insuring sufficient reliability of electronic equipment installed in the satellite when such equipment could not be got at or serviced would be great;

d. Serious question was raised as to the value of pictures taken from an altitude of 350 miles.

(1) Resolution of presently available television camera equipment was recognized to be of not much significance for objects of less than 200' × 200' in size. Question was therefore raised as to the net addition to be made by such photographs to our intelligence knowledge concerning Soviet territory.

(2) Question was raised as to whether the gross information thus obtainable would be worth the cost and the time interval which necessarily must take place before such a vehicle could be developed and successfully operated.

e. Factors relating to the pitch, roll and yaw characteristics of the vehicle were discussed. It was considered that very slight pitches and rolls might seriously interfere with picture collection and might make difficult the identification of areas of which pictures were taken;

f. Inasmuch as almost no facts are available concerning temperatures at altitudes above 100 miles from the earth's surface, it was considered that heating and cooling aspects of the satellite vehicle would be subject to considerable speculation and experimentation;

g. Normal atmospheric turbulence was considered to be a factor which might interfere with picture taking;

h. It was considered that four or five such satellites might have to be built and launched before one could be launched that would stay on orbit and operate as we required.

6. Professor Lauritsen appeared to be the least impressed by the possibility of use of a satellite vehicle for such reconnaissance purposes. He asserted that in his opinion it would require from eight to ten years to develop and construct such a vehicle for launching. He considered also that the same or better reconnaissance information could be secured by the employment of from six to twelve jet aircraft flying at an altitude of 50,000 feet over the Soviet Union. He further asserted that such aircraft in one day could secure the photographic information of better resolution and quality than could the satellite vehicle camera. Lauritsen asserted that this could be done immediately with presently available equipment and that such aircraft could not be picked up by radar.

7. At the conclusion of our discussion I posed substantially the following question to the scientists present: "If you were at present the Director of Central Intelligence what would be your attitude and action regarding the satellite vehicle for reconnaissance purposes?" President DuBridge and Dean Watson responded substantially as follows:

a. They would continue to consider the possibility of utilization of such a satellite vehicle and in so doing they would

(1) consult with the scientists at the Rand Corporation who have studied the matter intensively and have prepared the reports;

b. They would insure that additional and continuing feasibility studies regarding the development and construction of such a vehicle were pursued;

c. They would seriously investigate the nature and quality of pictures (information) that could be secured from operation of such a vehicle;

d. They would consider whether the additional intelligence information that theoretically could be secured from such a vehicle would be worth the possible cost and the time lag necessary to create and produce it;

e. They would consider whether alternative means for securing the information might not be more effective. Among such alternative means they mentioned clandestine operations and aerial photography from aircraft or balloons;

f. They suggested that aerial photographic analysis people of the Air Force be consulted as to their ability to interpret photographs of the approximate resolution to be expected from the satellite vehicle.

8. At the conclusion of our discussion at Cal Tech, President DuBridge arranged for Messrs. Gibbons and Putnam to go to Santa Monica to discuss the matter further with the Rand Corporation people. I did not accompany them for this discussion.

[*name not declassified*]

---

123.   Editorial Note

On July 25, 1952, President Truman approved NSC 127/1, "Plan for Conducting Psychological Operations During General Hostilities," of the same date. NSC 127/1 was an amended version of NSC 127, same title, March 3, 1952. NSC 127 and NSC 127/1 are in National Archives, RG 59, S/S–NSC Files: Lot 63 D 351, NSC 127 Series, Box 67.

124. Memorandum From the Under Secretary of State (Bruce) to the Executive Secretary of the National Security Council (Lay)[1]

Washington, July 31, 1952.

SUBJECT

> Fifth Progress Report on NSC 59/1, "The Foreign Information Program and Psychological Warfare Planning"[2]

1. NSC 59/1 was approved as governmental policy on March 10, 1950. It is requested that this progress report covering the period April 15–July 31, 1952, of activities untaken in implementation of NSC 59/1 be circulated to the members of the Council for their information. In accordance with the provisions of the third paragraph of the President's directive of April 4, 1951,[3] a copy of this report is being referred to the Psychological Strategy Board for use in its evaluation of the national psychological effort.

2. The organization referred to in NSC 59/1 has been designated The Psychological Operations Coordinating Committee (POC).[4] It will be referred to in this report as "the Committee."

3. This report describes only those foreign information operations and plans which, being interdepartmental in nature, were coordinated through the Committee.

4. Under the Chairmanship of the Administrator, the International Information Administration, the following are regularly represented at the weekly meetings of the Committee: Secretary of Defense, the Defense Department Office of Information, Joint Chiefs of Staff, the Mutual Security Agency, Central Intelligence Agency, Assistant Secretary for Public Affairs, Department of State, the Army, Navy and Air Force chiefs of psychological warfare and the Psychological Strategy Board staff. In accordance with the terms of the President's directive of April 4, 1951, which among other things authorized the Secretary of State to effect readjustments in the organization established under NSC 59/1, the POC secretariat was transformed into a full time interdepartmental planning staff.

5. During the period covered by this report the Committee concentrated its attention on psychological problems connected with the

---

[1] Source: National Archives, RG 59, S/P–NSC Files: Lot 62 D 1, no label, Box 115. Top Secret; Security Information. Lay circulated the report to NSC members under cover of a July 31 memorandum. (Ibid.)

[2] For NSC 59/1, see Document 2.

[3] See Document 60.

[4] See Document 74.

Korean situation, particularly with respect to the prisoner of war issue, both as regards the physical control of prisoners of the United Nations Command and also as regards the prisoner issue in the truce negotiations. The recommendations of the Committee were designed to contribute to the ability of the UN Command to gain and maintain the psychological initiative in Korea. However, our psychological efforts in Korea were directed toward the achievement of the principal UN aim in Korea—the conclusion of an armistice.

6. Ascertaining that the United Nations Command was in a position of serious disadvantage in handling the problems described above, the Committee took prompt action resulting in the following:

a. An on-the-scene survey of psychological warfare support arrangements in Japan and Korea by a team comprised of the Administrator, the International Information Administration, Dept. of State; the Chief of Psychological Warfare, Department of the Army; and the Policy Advisor, International Broadcasting Service, Department of State.

b. The establishment in Washington on June 12 of a watch committee, with representation from the Departments of Defense and State and the Central Intelligence Agency, whose purpose is to supply a daily summary of news, editorials and public comments originating in the U.S. and foreign countries, both Communist and non-Communist, concerning the Korean situation, and to provide suggestions, information and advice on psychological matters for fast transmission to Tokyo, Pusan and Panmunjom.

c. The establishment of a corresponding unit within FECOM comprised of military, psychological warfare and public information experts whose function is to inform FECOM of current world wide public reaction to developments in Korea, and to provide, in quantity, material and suggestions which may be useful in advancing the UNC propaganda position relative to Korea.

d. The preparation of an action plan to provide for such activities as the following:

1. Exploitation of signed-in-blood petitions of UNC-held prisoners resisting repatriation;
2. Stockpiling, for possible later use, recorded and press interviews with prisoners of war, and motion pictures of the prisoner-screening process;
3. Exploitation of UNC information and education work among prisoners of war;
4. Exploitation of rehabilitation work in South Korea.

7. *Bacteriological Warfare Charges*

The Committee gave considerable attention to Communist charges concerning bacteriological warfare in Korea. The Committee audited the activities of a working group comprised of representatives of the

Departments of Defense and State and the Central Intelligence Agency, under State leadership for the purpose of developing psychological plans for: (1) countering the Communist charges, and (2) developing when possible new measures which would be designed to seize and maintain the propaganda initiative. The group is effectively coordinating the efforts of the agencies concerned with handling the problem.

8. *Troop Acceptance in Japan*

The Committee provided interdepartmental coordination of a plan for developing an attitude of acceptance and an active sense of responsibility on the part of the Japanese Government and people with regard to the mission of the United States armed forces stationed in and about Japan as a consequence of the United States–Japan Security Treaty.

9. *X-Day Planning*

The Committee has continued to monitor the planning of its X-Day Working Group, which is preparing complete contingency plans for overt psychological operations during the initial stages of general hostilities. When completed and approved by the Committee the plans will be forwarded to the Psychological Strategy Board.

10. *Yugoslav Plan*

The Committee noted and referred to the staff of the Psychological Strategy Board for further development a working paper on maintenance of Yugoslav independence from Soviet domination.

11. *Review of POC Business*

The committee has undertaken an extensive review of unfinished POC business and is currently completing action on such business. The committee also is reviewing past POC recommendations and is monitoring the implementation of approved projects.

12. *POC Recommendation Regarding Communist Military Buildup in Korea*

The POC recommended that there be a full public exposition of the facts on the nature and extent of the Communist military buildup in Korea during the course of the truce negotiations. As a result of POC's recommendation appropriate statements were issued by the UN Command, by the British and by other governments having forces in Korea.

David Bruce[5]

---

[5] Printed from a copy that indicates Bruce signed the original.

125. Report by the Psychological Strategy Board[1]

PSB D–30   Washington, August 1, 1952.

STATUS REPORT ON THE NATIONAL PSYCHOLOGICAL EFFORT
AND FIRST PROGRESS REPORT OF THE PSYCHOLOGICAL
STRATEGY BOARD

[Omitted here are a list of references and a brief summary of the report.]

I. Status of the National Psychological Effort

The Board presents below a statement on the status of national psychological programs as of 30 June 1952. In submitting this statement the Board desires to emphasize the following general conclusions:

1. To be fully effective, psychological planning at the strategic level should ideally be based on an agreed overall strategic concept for our national psychological programs. While efforts to date underline the difficulties of formulating such a concept, some progress has been made in achieving agreement on certain broad criteria to be utilized in establishing relative priorities within existing capabilities. Further progress toward the development and implementation of an agreed strategic concept for our psychological effort can take place only in conjunction with a corresponding development of capabilities and resources and an accompanying adjustment of basic national policy.

2. The United States is not making significant progress in the psychological field toward its objective of reduction and retraction of Soviet power as laid down in NSC 20/4.[2] In considering the total cold war position of the United States as contrasted with that position a year ago, it is evident that in certain areas, such as Western Europe, our position has been strengthened by the good progress recorded under NATO. However, there has been some deterioration of strength in certain other areas, notably in the Near East. But this should not necessarily be attributed to superior effectiveness of Soviet propaganda.

3. A major handicap in psychological operations outside of the Iron Curtain derives from growing resentment in parts of Asia and throughout much of Europe to a "made in America" label on part of our psychological output. Of even graver significance is the increasing

---

[1] Source: National Archives, RG 59, S/S–NSC Files: Lot 62 D 333, PSB Files, PSB D–30. Top Secret; Security Information. The report contains Annexes A–E. None is printed except for Annexes D and E, which are enclosures 1 and 2 to Document 127.

[2] See *Foreign Relations*, 1948, vol. I, Part 2, pp. 662–669.

reaction against the military character of some of our political and economic activity. Programs designed to have a deterrent effect on the Soviet Union are distorted and exploited by communist or anti-American propaganda and thus are occasioning resistance, neutralism, and charges of agressiveness to the detriment of our psychological effort.

The statement which follows is based on an analysis of current reports of the Department of State and the Department of Defense, of a report by field staff representatives of the Mutual Security Agency, and of a report by the Central Intelligence Agency, concerning their activities related to the national psychological effort during the fiscal year ending 30 June 1952.[3]

This statement is not presented as a full evaluation of the national psychological program during the period in question, the Board having decided that such an evaluation is not possible at this time. However, the reports on which it is based throw significant light on some aspects of the existing "cold war" situation. There emerges from them a picture of some substantial progress, mixed with many problems and obstacles which hinder a more complete achievement of our psychological objectives.

A. Outside the Iron Curtain

The general psychological situation in the non-Soviet world is not bright, but progress has been made in some areas.

In *Western Europe* the picture is spotty. On the one hand, progress is reported in containing Soviet communism and in the development of unity and readiness to build indigenous military strength in the area. On the other hand there are disturbing reports of the growth of neutralism and anti-Americanism in France and Britain, if not in Western Europe as a whole.

In *the Middle East,* irresponsible nationalism is the current major threat to free world interests. United States capabilities for effective psychological action have declined though some slow progress is reported in certain sections of the Moslem world.

In *Africa,* intensive communist efforts to gain control over the colored races are having some success. A modest start has been made at laying the groundwork for future activities aimed at checking them.

In *Latin America,* there has been a recent increase in our capabilities for effective psychological action, and some indication of substantial progress in combatting anti-American feeling in certain countries.

---

[3] For the text of the report of the Department of State to the NSC, and summaries of the other three reports mentioned, see Annexes A, B, and C, and specially classified Annex D. [Footnote in the original. Regarding these annexes, see footnote 1 above.]

In South and Southeast Asia, anti-colonialism and associated racial resentments have been far more important elements in the psychological developments in the military struggle against rebel forces in the area. On the other hand, communist electoral gains in India have forced the Nehru Government to modify perceptibly its former position of neutrality in the East-West conflict.

In Formosa and Japan, some gains are reported as a result of United States psychological activities.

In addition to the above comments on specific areas, the following general observations on the non-Soviet world, drawn from the departmental reports, may be warranted.

1. A steady operational trend toward the use of indigenous groups for propaganda purposes reflects a recognition that in many areas overt propaganda bearing the United States label is meeting with increasing indifference or resistance. Further development of non-attributed psychological methods, together with a de-emphasis of overt channels, appears to be logical in this situation.

2. In underdeveloped countries some progress has been made in developing psychological approaches which appeal to local aspirations and emphasize local participation and initiative. Such approaches are particularly relevant in these areas, where the memory or actuality of domination by the white man is a far greater psychological reality than the Soviet menace.

3. The overriding abhorrence of another possible war in some areas, particularly Western Europe, constitutes an important psychological liability for the United States. This attitude tends to inhibit actions which may seem to involve any increased risk of war, and manifests itself in neutralism, anti-Americanism, and extreme sensitivity to occasional warlike statements by leading Americans. The spread of this attitude makes possible the continued effective use of "peace" as a leading theme in Soviet psychological aggression.

4. Certain national policies of the United States are psychologically damaging in various areas of the non-Soviet world. In the Moslem world this is true of United States policy toward Israel; in areas under European domination it is true of United States identification with its NATO allies which makes it difficult for the United States to avoid the psychological effects of the colonial policies of those allies; in Britain and elsewhere it is true of United States policy toward China.

The same may be said of certain primarily domestic matters. For instance, efforts to counteract communist exploitation of the race relations problem in the United States have not been fully successful. Likewise, the restrictive immigration policy of the United States, most recently embodied in the McCarran Act, has damaging psychological repercussions abroad. Finally, United States tariff laws severely hurt the ability of foreign countries to export to this country and thus are seen abroad as running directly counter to United States policy of building up economic stability in the free world by expanding international trade.

B. Behind the Iron Curtain

The Soviet grip in the Communist-dominated areas of Europe and of the Far East appeared to be even firmer at the end of the fiscal year 1952 than at the beginning. There was no evidence of progress toward achievement of the basic objectives set forth in NSC 20/4, namely, the reduction and retraction of Soviet communist power. Moreover, short-term possibilities of any improvement in this respect appeared so slight as to be negligible. In this area of the world our national psychological effort, both overt and covert, must continue for some time to emphasize long-term objectives and the discovery of means to build up resources and capabilities.

Among the many problems incident to this buildup, one in particular may be mentioned. Our capabilities for effective action against the communist regime in China are limited in part by the absence of a stable and more universal rallying point outside China to which overseas Chinese could look for political and psychological leadership, and by the related need for a thorough-going reform of Nationalist Chinese military and political institutions.

In the overt information field behind the Iron Curtain, the Voice of America and Radio Free Europe clearly emerge from the reports as the only significant remaining programs which effectively reach the people of either or both the USSR and the Satellites. The reports are equally clear, however, as to the need for making the Voice still more powerful. Meanwhile there are ominous indications that we may be falling behind in the electromagnetic war.

Some good use has been made of defectors and escapees from behind the Iron Curtain during the year, both on the programs of the Voice and America and in non-attributable activities of other agencies. Results point to the desirability of a still more highly organized effort in this direction.

C. Related Activities

Certain related activities of a highly restricted nature are not covered in the body of this report. For an evaluative summary of these activities, reference is made to the specially classified Annex D.

D. Organizational Progress

An improvement is noted in the effectiveness of policy guidance during the period covered by this report. In part, the improvement has resulted from closer cooperation of the departments and agencies involved. Quicker and more effective action both in Washington and in the field, and a consequent improvement in the coordination of our psychological effort, has resulted from a number of forward steps in organization. The reports make it clear, however, that much still remains to be done.

II. Progress in Formulating and Promulgating Over-All National Psychological Objectives, Policies and Programs

During its first year of operation the Psychological Strategy Board has taken a number of steps to carry out its responsibility "for the formulation and promulgation, as guidance to the departments and agencies responsible for psychological operations, of over-all national psychological objectives, policies and programs, and for the coordination and evaluation of the national psychological effort." The major effort has been in the planning field. The chief steps taken are as follows:[4]

A. Plans completed and in effect:

(1) Psychological Operations Plan for the Reduction of Communist Power in France—designed to encourage and support French Government efforts to reduce communist power in their country to a point where it will no longer threaten United States national objectives in the area. Under this Plan and the parallel Plan for Italy (see below), the initiative for the most important actions lies with the indigenous governments. Supporting actions by the United States are under the control of the Ambassador. Progress in France has been considerable during the past two months and prospects for the future appear good.

(2) Psychological Operations Plan for the Reduction of Communist Power in Italy—parallel to the above plan for France. Although progress in Italy is less substantial than in France, the Italian Government is actively considering further effective action in this field.

(3) Psychological Operations Plan for Soviet Orbit Escapees (Phase "A")—designed to provide care and resettlement for current escapees and facilitate their use by CIA and the Armed Forces. Reception, supplemental care, and resettlement operations have already begun on a small scale and will be considerably expanded within the limits of the 4.3 million dollars made available to the Department of State for this activity by the Director for Mutual Security.

---

[4] For a more detailed report on planning activities, see specially classified Annex E. [Footnote in the original.]

B. *Plans and guidances completed but not yet being executed:*

(1) Plans for immediate execution: None

(2) Stand-by plans:

a. *General war:*

i. A plan for the conduct of psychological operations in the event of general war has been submitted by the Board to the National Security Council and was under study by them as of 30 June 1952.[5]

ii. A national overt propaganda policy guidance for general war has been approved by the Board and serves as guidance for current operational planning on this subject in the Government.

b. *Korean Armistice Negotiations:* Two psychological operations plans have been promulgated. One is partly operational at present and provides for further actions in the event that an armistice is achieved. The other plan provides for the contingency that armistice negotiations are conclusively broken off and full hostilities are resumed.

C. *Plans and projects authorized and in process of development* involve most of the critical areas in the world struggle.

A plan for national psychological strategy with respect to *Germany,* nearly completed, is to deal with the integration of the Federal Republic into Western Europe, the reduction of Soviet capabilities in Western Germany, the problem of German unification, and the role of a unified Germany in the unification of Europe.

Psychological strategy plans to advance national objectives in the *Middle East, Southeast Asia,* and *Japan* are in earlier stages of preparation. With respect to the *Soviet Union* a psychological operations plan for exploiting Stalin's passing from power has been drafted and is receiving further staff study.

Other plans and papers in preparation, not confined to any geographic area, include:

(1) an over-all strategic concept for the national psychological effort;

(2) a plan for stimulating and utilizing defection from the Soviet Orbit beyond the existing flow of escapees (this plan will supplement the "Phase A" plan mentioned in A. (3) above);

(3) an inventory of "cold war" instrumentalities, some of them novel, with a view to harassment and retaliation against the USSR and the Soviet Orbit;

(4) an analysis of communist "germ warfare" and other "hate America" propaganda and the psychological problems arising therefrom; and

---

[5] This plan was approved by the President on 25 July 1952. [Footnote in the original. See Document 123.]

(5) a plan designed both to gain greater acceptance in the free world for United States economic security objectives vis-à-vis the Soviet Orbit, and to capitalize on and obstruct Soviet economic exploitation of captive Europe and Communist China.

---

126. Director of Central Intelligence Directive No. 3/4[1]

Washington, August 14, 1952.

PRODUCTION OF SCIENTIFIC AND TECHNICAL INTELLIGENCE

Pursuant to the provisions of NSCID No. 3,[2] and for the purpose of strengthening the over-all governmental intelligence structure for the production of scientific and technical intelligence, the following policies and operating procedures are hereby established:

1. Policies

In discharging allocated responsibilities and effecting integration of intelligence, the interested departments and agencies will apply the following basic principles:

a. No complete separation of areas of interest is possible or necessarily desirable in scientific and technical intelligence activities.

b. Full and free interchange of all intelligence information and finished intelligence between all agencies concerned is essential.

c. No one agency is considered to be the final authority in any field; conclusions may be questioned by other IAC agencies and dissents recorded.

d. Any agency may make such studies as it believes necessary to supplement intelligence obtained from other agencies in order to fulfill its agency functions, but such studies should not normally be disseminated outside the producing agency without advance consultation with the agency having primary responsibility for the subject-matter involved.

---

[1] Source: Central Intelligence Agency, History Staff, Job 84–00022R, Box 3. Secret; Security Information. The Ad Hoc Committee to Survey Existing Arrangements Relating to the Production of Scientific and Technical Intelligence produced a lengthy interagency report that formed the basis for DCID 3/4. The report is ibid. Annexes A and B are attached but not printed.

[2] For NSCID No. 3, see *Foreign Relations, 1945–1950, Emergence of the Intelligence Establishment*, Document 426.

e. An agency charged with primary responsibility in a particular field will develop special competence in that field and will normally carry out all or most of the research in that field.

f. Each intelligence agency will endeavor to coordinate the intelligence activities of its Technical Services and its other facilities having intelligence production capabilities with the work of the IAC intelligence agencies and to make available to those agencies the intelligence produced by such Services and facilities.

2. *Procedures:*

a. *Delineation of Dominant Interests.* The general field of scientific and technical intelligence production is subdivided into three basic major areas, and allocation of primary production responsibilities therein is made as follows:

(1) Intelligence on all weapons, weapons systems, military equipment and techniques, plus intelligence on pertinent research and development leading to new military material and techniques—primary production responsibility of the departments of the Department of Defense, as exemplified in Annex A.

(2) Intelligence on fundamental research in the basic sciences, on scientific resources, and on medicine (other than military medicine) plus intelligence on pertinent applied research and development—primary production responsibility of Central Intelligence Agency, as exemplified in Annex B.

(3) Intelligence on Atomic Energy—production responsibility of all interested agencies.

b. It is recognized that despite the above-mentioned specific allocations of primary production responsibilities to the Military Services and CIA, the Military Services will also require intelligence indicating trends from fundamental research in basic sciencies, which they normally will obtain from CIA. Conversely, CIA will also require intelligence on applied research relating to weapons, weapons systems, military equipment and techniques, and the technical characteristics of existing equipment, which it normally will obtain from the Military Services. Accordingly, there continue to exist areas of common or overlapping interest which require continuing inter-agency liaison and such working-level conferences as may be appropriate.

c. *Coordinating Mechanisms*

(1) The Joint Atomic Energy Intelligence Committee is hereby reconstituted as a permanent interdepartmental committee with the same structure and functions as before.

(2) Subject to the foregoing, there is hereby established the Scientific Estimates Committee, a permanent interdepartmental committee, to integrate scientific and technical intelligence, as and when required

for the production of national intelligence, to stimulate and guide inter-agency liaison and such working-level conferences as may be appropriate, and to coordinate the production of Chapter VII of the NIS.

(3) The Scientific Estimates Committee shall be composed of designated representatives as members from CIA, the Joint Staff, the Departments of State, Army, Navy, and Air Force, the Atomic Energy Commission, and such other ad hoc representatives as may be determined necessary by the regular committee members. In order to maintain continuity and stability, each department and agency mentioned above will designate a regular member and, if desired, an alternate by transmitting names and titles to the Director of Central Intelligence. This action will not preclude the designation of such additional persons as may be technically and otherwise qualified to discuss or report on a particular subject under consideration by the Committee. The Chairman will be elected annually. The Committee will establish its methods of procedure. The Central Intelligence Agency shall provide an executive secretary and secretariat as required.

(4) It is recommended that the SEC concentrate on the integration of intelligence opinion (other than that for which the JAEIC is responsible) as and when required for the purposes of national intelligence, and only incidentally assist in the coordination of production of other intelligence in scientific and technical fields. The principal occasion for activity on the part of the committee will arise when contributions are required for national intelligence purposes. The Committee's activities will be directed to synthesizing departmental intelligence, and while so doing to bring to light any inconsistencies resulting from the production activities of the respective departments and agencies, each operating within its assigned sphere of responsibility, and to resolve conflicting conclusions, or have appropriate dissenting views registered for the benefit of the national intelligence production organization.

(5) The SEC can best assist in the coordination of production of intelligence in scientific and technical fields by stimulating and guiding inter-agency liaison and working-level conferences.

3. Director of Central Intelligence Directive 3/3[3] is herewith rescinded.

Walter B. Smith[4]
Director of Central Intelligence

---

[3] Not printed. (Central Intelligence Agency, History Staff, Job 84–T00389R, Box 4)
[4] Printed from a copy that bears this typed signature.

127.   Memorandum From the Executive Secretary of the National Security Council (Lay) to the National Security Council[1]

Washington, August 19, 1952.

SUBJECT

    Status of United States Programs for National Security as of June 30, 1952

REFERENCES

    A. NSC 135[2]
    B. Memo for NSC from Executive Secretary same subject, dated August 19, 1952[3]

The following sensitive portions of two of the status reports attached to the reference memorandum of August 19 on the subject,[4] are transmitted herewith for the information of the statutory members of the National Security Council as part of NSC 135:

Annex D to No. 6, The National Psychological Program, entitled "Summary of a Report from the Central Intelligence Agency".

Annex E to No. 6, The National Psychological Program, entitled "Planning Activities of the Psychological Strategy Board Through June 30, 1952".

Paragraph IX, 5 of No. 7, The Foreign Intelligence Program.

It is requested that special security precautions be observed in handling the enclosures and that access thereto be limited to a need-to-know basis.

James S. Lay, Jr.

---

[1] Source: National Archives, RG 59, S/P–NSC Files: Lot 64 D 563, NSC 135. Top Secret; Security Information; Eyes Only.

[2] Regarding NSC 135, "Status of U.S. Programs for National Security as of June 30, 1952," see Foreign Relations, 1952–1954, vol. II, Part 1, pp. 56–57.

[3] Not printed. (National Archives, RG 59, S/S–NSC Files: Lot 63 D 351, NSC 135 Series)

[4] The PSB status report, PSB D–30, is printed as Document 125.

Enclosure 1

Annex D to No. 6, "The National Psychological Program" of NSC 135[5]

Washington, August 1, 1952.

SUMMARY OF A REPORT FROM THE CENTRAL INTELLIGENCE AGENCY

There has been some progress in achieving the national objectives set forth in NSC 10/2 and 10/5.[6] This progress, however, has been slow and in most areas severely restricted, partly by the limited nature of available resources and capabilities, but even more by time limitations. It takes a long time to develop the apparatus and the trained personnel for covert activities and the development of concepts and doctrine of the kind discussed in this report. The United States has been engaged in covert activities for too brief a period, and therefore present developments fall far short of ultimate potential.

Europe

In France and Italy, CIA reports that Soviet power and influence apparently are being contained. Increased and more effective covert psychological operations in Western Europe may account for the increasingly violent and indiscriminate nature of the Soviet and indigenous Communist propaganda barrage against the anti-Communist organizations in that area.

[*2 paragraphs (22 lines) not declassified*]

In Eastern Europe, Soviet power and influence have not been reduced to any measurable extent. However, U.S. capabilities for future covert operations have increased, [*less than 1 line not declassified*]. Recent covert operations have revealed that the Communist authorities do not have complete control of the situation in these countries, and that the area can be successfully penetrated. Thanks to much valuable experience gained in the techniques of covert psychological warfare and political action in Eastern Europe, CIA now possesses capabilities for influencing large segments of labor, youth, refugees, persecutees, women, religious groups, and political parties.

---

[5] Top Secret; Eyes Only. This is Annex D to PSB D–30 (Document 125).

[6] For NSC 10/2, see *Foreign Relations*, 1945–1950, Emergence of the Intelligence Establishment, Document 292. For NSC 10/5, see Document 90.

In the satellite countries of Southeastern Europe, CIA capabilities for psychological operations have increased considerably, though Soviet power and influence have not been reduced in the area.

The power and influence of the Kremlin within the USSR has not been affected by U.S. covert activities, and short-term possibilities in this direction are so slight as to be insignificant. CIA's effort in this area is now being focused on progressively developing capabilities for long-term exploitation.

Pointing out that present policy provides for U.S. support of anti-regime resistance of the Great Russians, CIA sees a definite need for resolving the policy question of the extent to which it will be permitted to support clandestinely and exploit operationally *any* group or individual actively interested in the destruction of the Bolshevik regime.

Middle East

A decline in U.S. capabilities throughout most of the Middle East is noted, though this is felt to be only temporary. To some extent, the decrease in U.S. covert capabilities in the Middle East is attributed to the policy conflict arising out of U.S. support for the maintenance of France's position in North Africa, which has psychological repercussions throughout the African, Arab, and Asian worlds. Similarly, an impediment to U.S. capabilities in the area is found in the disparity of our attitudes toward Israel and the Arab States despite a stated policy of impartiality.

In the particularly important field of the Moslem world, some progress has been achieved along the following lines:

1. In utilizing nationalist forces for our own purposes, by endeavoring to direct them away from their more destructive tendencies and into channels which will be relatively compatible with U.S. interests; namely, to endeavor to turn the force of nationalism against the Communists, to direct it against political corruption, to focus it upon demands for social reform and economic progress;

2. In stimulating an increased awareness among the religious hierarchy of the threat of international Communism;

3. In increasing the degree of understanding of the status of Moslems living inside the Soviet orbit; and

4. In laying the groundwork for further expanded activities along similar lines. Progress will continue to be slow in this field because of the most delicate and dangerous aspect of Near Eastern affairs from the point of view of foreign intervention.

Far East

Support of the Chinese Nationalist Government on Formosa is described as the most significant program now being undertaken by CIA in the Far East, where the Agency is also actively supporting the military authorities in Korea and laying the groundwork for penetration of Manchuria and North China.

While, on balance, the U.S. has achieved some psychological gains in the overt field (Treaty of Peace with Japan, Pacific Military Alliances, etc.), Soviet power has not been measurably reduced in the Far Eastern areas under its dominance, and progress toward our objectives in the field of covert activities has been negligible, [*less than 1 line not declassified*]. There, CIA's activities directed toward discrediting Soviet Russia, Communist China, the [*less than 1 line not declassified*], and Communism in general, are having some success.

Korea

CIA regards coordinating machinery between civilian and military authorities in the field of psychological warfare as inadequate in certain respects. A coordinating mechanism (CCRAK) was set up, for example, but failed to include the operations of USIE services in Korea. Close cooperation with the military exists in the field on intelligence and tactical psychological warfare measures. However, a completely effective coordination of two major strategic plans with respect to Korea has not been realized with respect to coordination of command and logistical support, but steps are being taken to remedy this situation. These are expected to result in some modifications of CIA's responsibilities to ensure that CIA does not commit itself to actions which are beyond its present or anticipated capabilities.

Latin America

Despite evidence that the Soviet Union is now placing greater emphasis on its covert mechanisms in Latin America, U.S. covert capabilities there have substantially increased during the past year through the expansion of personnel and facilities. Such expansion, it is planned, may increasingly turn toward the formation or support of indigenous, nationalistic, free-enterprise groups or political parties. Some substantial results in combating pro-Communist and anti-American influences have been achieved through covert means [*less than 1 line not declassified*]. It is to be noted that Latin America is an area unique for the United States, because of the overt Good Neighbor and non-intervention policies of long standing, and the powerful reasons necessitating those overt policies. The security of covert operations and the further development of policy and management systems which protect such security both in Washington and in the field are of peculiar importance for this area. Therefore, CIA capabilities have been developed to be operative only under special conditions.

Africa

In Africa a beginning has been made in laying the groundwork for future activities to check Communist efforts to get control over the colored races; but this work has so far been purely preparatory and no progress toward actual achievement in that field is recorded.

General

In general, CIA emphasizes the importance of setting up increased capabilities, particularly in the form of thoroughly-trained American and indigenous personnel and long-term cover mechanisms. An apparent need exists for establishing at all possible points radio broadcast facilities capable of reaching the USSR.

CIA's capabilities need to be reinforced for building up an apparatus capable of long-term exploitation against the Chinese Communist regime. For the shorter terms CIA has had only very limited success in the penetration either of Communist China or the USSR itself.

CIA points up the vital importance of VOA as constituting at present the only effective means the U.S. possesses for conducting psychological operations within the confines of the USSR. Covert penetration has been carried out primarily for the purpose of procuring intelligence, and because of the rigid controls impeding the movement of agents inside that country, no psychological warfare under present conditions can be undertaken in the USSR by any other medium except radio.

Through its covert channels CIA has discovered that VOA broadcasts have been audible in the USSR throughout 1950 and 1951. Although Soviet jamming has considerably reduced the audibility of these broadcasts, nevertheless information [*1½ lines not declassified*] indicates that considerable segments of the Soviet peoples continue to listen to VOA broadcasts despite technical difficulties and personal risk. Some of these refugees have criticised the VOA broadcasts for not being sufficiently forceful and for devoting a considerable portion of the programs to irrelevant matters not bearing directly on the current East-West struggle. Furthermore, ethnic groups such as the Ukrainians have complained that the broadcasts are not sufficiently representative of the desires and aspirations of the minority groups within the USSR. But when all this is said, the fact remains that information obtained by CIA indicates that the VOA broadcasts do play an important role in reminding the peoples of the Soviet Union that there is an alternative way of life, and in providing them with hope of ultimate liberation.

[*1 paragraph (5 lines) not declassified*]

In Western Europe especially, there was marked progress in CIA's efforts to work through various anti-Communist groups—both urban and rural. At the same time, there have as yet been no very tangible results from attempts to penetrate indigenous Communist parties. On the other hand, efforts to combat Communist influence in the labor unions, [*1 line not declassified*] have met with considerable success, [*less than 1 line not declassified*], and the view is expressed that capabilities in this direction should be increased.

Enclosure 2

Annex E to No. 6, "The National Psychological Program" of NSC 135[7]

Washington, August 1, 1952.

PLANNING ACTIVITIES OF THE PSYCHOLOGICAL
STRATEGY BOARD THROUGH JUNE 30, 1952

1. Plans Completed and Being Executed

A. Psychological Operations Plan for the Reduction of Communist Power in France. (PSB D–14/c).

This plan and the corresponding one for Italy (Paragraph 1B) were developed by the same PSB planning panel and actions under both plans are being coordinated by the same group. Both plans resulted from extensive inquiry during the summer and fall of 1951, as a result of which the Board concluded that the French and Italian Communist apparati, the two most powerful in Western Europe, constituted a serious threat to American foreign policy and to NATO plans for defense of Western Europe. In consequence, the Board prescribed specific courses of action for reduction of Communist power in both France and Italy.

Upon approval of both plans on February 21, 1952, a Washington interdepartmental coordinating committee was established under the chairmanship of a member of the PSB staff, and comparable panels were established in Paris and Rome. These groups are in communication with each other with respect to implementation of the plans.

Analysis of the Communist position in both France and Italy resulted in the conclusion that in both countries the primary sources of Communist power was in their organized control over trade unions. Therefore, the main emphasis in both plans is devoted to reduction of Communist power over trade unions and the encouragement of the free trade union movement. The most important actions that can be taken in both countries are for the government to give positive support to the democratic unions in their struggle against Communist

---

[7] Top Secret; Security Information; Eyes Only. This is Annex E to PSB D–30 (Document 125).

domination of organized labor, to stop subsidizing and to stop dealing with the Communist unions, and to work towards a more equitable share of the national income for labor.

With regard to the French plan, progress toward achieving the major objectives appears hopeful under the present Pinay Government. Unlike its predecessors, the Pinay Government has demonstrated far more courage and affirmative leadership, and on its own initiative, has been moving vigorously against the Communists within the last two months. However, this is no guarantee of stability. The government has given us assurances that it will continue this campaign and that it intends to take specific action to reduce Communist power in the trade union field. While making known to the government our continuing interest in this problem, we have withheld more affirmative participation and are watching the French initiative with hope in its promise for the future.

B. *Psychological Operations Plan for the Reduction of Communist Power in Italy. (PSB D–15/b).*

As stated in connection with the similar plan for reduction of Communist power in France reported in the previous paragraph, this plan was approved by the Board on February 21, 1952. Development of the plan, which was in conjunction with the development of the French plan, is reported on in the previous paragraph.

With regard to progress concerning the achievement of the objectives of the Italian plan, since September 1951 we have made high level representations expressing our concern over the continued strength of Communist power in Italy. The DeGasperi Government has repeatedly assured us that it intends to take vigorous measures to reduce the strength and influence of the Communist movement. Up to the May 1952 elections, the government had done very little along these lines and, particularly, had not moved against the main sources of Communist power in the trade union field.

The local elections throughout Italy in 1951 and 1952 indicated no diminution and perhaps a slight increase of electoral support for the Communist-left socialist bloc. Since the 1948 national elections, when this bloc polled 31.4%, it has for the first time made substantial inroads into the agricultural South. In contrast to this, the electoral support for the four democratic center parties was substantially reduced compared to 1948 due to a sharp fall off in support for the Christian-Democrat Party, while the extreme right received a sharp increase in support.

Since the May elections we have received renewed and more positive assurances that the government means to move against the Communists and there have been indications of formal action. The government will put its main reliance on new legislation. The situation now appears more promising and hopeful than it has been for a long time, but we are awaiting positive results. Since the Communists appear to be avoiding the provocation of the Italian Government, we are hopeful that the latter will take positive action on its own initiative.

C. *Psychological Operations Plan for Soviet Orbit Escapees—Phase "A" (PSB D–18a).*

This plan, approved by PSB December 20, 1951, includes programs to care for and resettle current escapees, and envisages maximum possible utilization of escapees [*less than 1 line not declassified*] under Public Law 51 (Lodge Amendment), which permits recruitment of escapees into the U.S. Armed Forces. (For discussion of Phase "B" see paragraph 3A below.)

On April 7, pursuant to approval by the President, $4.3 million dollars were made available by the Director of Mutual Security to the Department of State, which had been given responsibility for the program.

The time since funds were made available has been used to build the organization and staff for the continuing administration of the program; and to identify and care for the most urgent immediate needs of escapees.

Organization. Small staffs are being established and activities have begun in each of the countries which border the iron curtain. A regional office in HICOG and a policy and coordination unit in the Department of State have been established.

Resettlement and Supplemental Care. A general contract was signed on June 16, 1952, with the Provisional Committee for the Movement of Migrants from Europe (PICMME, an international body organized in November, 1951) for the overseas transport of up to 14,000 escapees during one year at an estimated rate of $100 per capita. The number thus far moved under the program is negligible, but it is anticipated that a scheduled flow may be attained in August.

Projects have been authorized to care for urgent immediate needs of escapees resident in Greece, Germany, Austria, Turkey and Italy, needs such as food, clothing, shoes, repair and decontamination of barracks, and medical treatment. In every country of operation the immediate needs of the escapees are being met.

Propaganda Utilization. No general propaganda utilization of the plans and activities of the escapee program is now contemplated by State Department. Newsworthy projects and assistance to key individuals will be used in media reaching iron curtain areas when appropriate. When the program has greater accomplishments to point to, the State Department plans more general treatment. Similar policies govern domestic information activity.

Funds. Of the initial authorization of $4,300,000, an estimated $1,500,000 was obligated during the fiscal year 1952. An additional $1,460,500 is being requested to cover an increase in the estimated number of escapees already requiring assistance.

Accomplishment of Other Purposes. As requested under this phase of the plan, the Department of Defense has somewhat liberalized the conditions under which escapees may be recruited under the authorization of the Lodge Amendment. Of 5194 applications, 3916 have been rejected, 295 have been accepted (262 on active duty), and 982 are being processed.

[*1 paragraph (2 lines) not declassified*]

D. *Public Statements with Respect to Certain Weapons. (PSB D–17d)*

In February 1952, following a series of conflicting statements by public officials as to atomic and related developments, the PSB approved and forwarded to the Executive Secretary, NSC, recommendations for a guidance to appropriate agencies on public statements with respect to certain weapons. On May 9, 1952, a memorandum on this subject was issued by the President, setting forth the criteria recommended by the PSB and directing compliance therewith.[8] At present the PSB staff is reviewing the action which has been taken by the agencies and the effect of the application of the criteria.

2. Plans Completed But Not Yet Being Executed—
Stand-By Plans

A. *Psychological Operations Plan Incident to Korean Cease-Fire Negotiations (PSB D–7c).*

This plan was approved by the Psychological Strategy Board on October 25, 1951. It is designed to establish special psychological objectives to be implemented toward our allies as well as our adversaries, with respect to the Korean conflict. Some of the desired courses of action are at present in effect, but the majority of the recommended actions are directly related to the progress made in connection with the cease-fire. The operational planning is substantially complete. An alert network has been established among the affected agencies so that the appropriate action can be put into effect without delay as developments make this necessary.

---

[8] NSC Action No. 622; NSC 126; and memo for NSC from Executive Secretary, subject, "Public Statements with Respect to Certain American Weapons", dated March 28, 1952. [Footnote in the original. For NSC 126, see *Foreign Relations,* 1952–1954, vol. II, Part 2, pp. 869–872.]

B. *Emergency Plan for Breakoff of Korean Armistice Negotiations (PSB J–19d).*

This plan was approved by the Psychological Strategy Board on September 18, 1951. It endeavors to establish for governmental departments and agencies engaged in psychological operations courses of action for application in preparation for, and in the event of, a breakdown in the Korean armistice negotiations. The operational planning is substantially complete. The receipt of certain assurances from the Far Eastern Command with respect to logistical support is necessary in order that the affected agencies can establish the appropriate contingent plan without delay, should developments make this necessary.

C. *Plan for Conducting Psychological Operations During General Hostilities (PSB D–8b).*

This plan was approved by the Board on February 21, 1952 and submitted to the National Security Council as NSC 127. (As amended and approved by the NSC and approved by the President, this was circulated as NSC 127/1.)[9] This plan was designed in order that the proper agencies would be able to conduct psychological operations in pursuance of prescribed national objectives during general hostilities. This plan shall be executed upon Presidential proclamation in the event of war or at such time as the President may direct.

D. *National Overt Propaganda Policy Guidance for General War (PSB D–11/b).*

This plan was approved by the Board on November 15, 1951. It sets forth the objectives which will govern the national overt propaganda effort in a general war forced upon the United States by the USSR or any of its satellites. The objectives and tasks which should be followed by the United States with respect to the world as a whole, the USSR and its satellites, our allies and friends, and neutral nations are set forth. This guidance has been distributed to the various departments and agencies for their use. The Psychological Operations Coordinating Committee (POC) has established an X-Day Committee which is concerned with the inter-departmental coordination of policies and operations in the event of war. This guidance is being used in the implementation of their planning.

---

[9] See Document 123.

3. Plans Authorized and in Process of Development

A. *Psychological Operations Plan for Soviet Orbit Escapees—Phase "B" (PSB D–18a/1).*

This project is concerned with the stimulation of defection and examination of the psychological and subsidiary military advantages which would result from the proper utilization of these escapees. Phase "A", concerned with the care, resettlement, and possible utilization of current escapees, is reported on in Paragraph 1C of this paper.

B. *Inventory of Instrumentalities for Countering Soviet Orbit Blackmail Tactics (PSB D–19/1).*

The Board has had prepared an "Inventory of Cold War Weapons", consisting of a list of certain agencies and instrumentalities (some of which are of a novel character). The Board has further directed study toward the feasibility of harassment and retaliation against the Soviets by use of appropriate instrumentalities.

C. *Psychological Operations Plan Prescribing Specific Courses of Action with Respect to Germany (PSB D–21a).*

This plan is designed to prescribe certain courses of action with respect to: (a) the integration of Western Germany into Western Europe, (b) the reduction of Soviet capabilities in Eastern Germany, (c) the achievement of German unity, and (d) the role of a unified Germany in the unification of Europe.

D. *Psychological Strategy Planning for the Middle East (PSB D–22).*

This plan is to devise by means of coordinated psychological operations a national psychological plan, taking into account both long-range and short-range considerations, in order to overcome or prevent instability within this area which would threaten Western interests. It seeks to prevent the extension of Soviet influence and at the same time to strengthen Western influence and to establish within the community of nations a new relationship with the states of the area that recognizes their desire to achieve status and respects their sovereign equality.

E. *Psychological Strategy Planning for Southeast Asia (PSB D–23).*

This plan is designed to assist by means of coordinated psychological operations in preventing the free countries of Southeast Asia from passing into the Communist orbit and in developing in these countries the will and ability to resist Communism from within and without, and to contribute to the strengthening of the free world.

F. *Psychological Operations Plan for the Exploitation of Stalin's Passing from Power (PSB D–24).*

This plan is designed to study the actions the United States should take to develop the maximum psychological results at the time of Stalin's death.

G. *Preliminary Analysis of the Communist B.W. Propaganda Campaign (PSB D–25).*

This study concerns itself with the psychological problems which the current "Hate America" Communist propaganda campaign have presented.

H. *Statement of U.S. Aims in the Cold War ("Princeton Statement"—PSB D–26).*

This paper was designed to devise the maximum psychological effect which could be achieved by a statement of high U.S. or foreign officials relative to the liberation of peoples now under Soviet Communist control.

I. *Psychological Strategy Plan for the Pro-U.S. Orientation of Japan (PSB D–27).*

This plan is designed to develop a psychological strategy for co-ordinated psychological operations to strengthen Japan and other non-communist powers in Asia. It would promote Japan's economic and military capacity to contribute to collective security, assure Japan's continuing commitment to close association and joint action with the U.S. and would assist in restoring Japan to a position of strength in a co-operative endeavor to secure the non-communist nations of Asia from Communist subversion or attack.

J. *Psychological Strategy for Economic Security Vis-à-vis the Soviet Orbit (PSB D–28).*

This plan is designed to prepare national psychological strategy and specific courses of action with respect to the psychological aspects of U.S. economic security programs concerned with the Soviet orbit by increasing the degree of acceptance in the Free World of U.S. economic security objectives vis-à-vis the Soviet orbit. It also seeks to weaken Soviet control over the orbit countries by capitalizing on and obstructing Soviet economic exploitation of captive Europe and China through psychological operations.

Enclosure 3

Paragraph IX, 5 (page 8) of No. 7, "The Foreign Intelligence Program" of NSC 135[10]

Washington, August 15, 1952.

5. ESPIONAGE AND COUNTERESPIONAGE

U.S. espionage and counterespionage activities outside the Continental limits of the U.S., with certain exceptions, are conducted by CIA. Through these activities, including the operation of secret agents, [1½ lines not declassified] CIA has collected significant amounts of valuable intelligence from areas outside the USSR and the Soviet Orbit. A number of high quality, secret sources have been developed in selected areas, capable of producing important clandestine intelligence, often with strategic implications.

Although substantial progress has been made, CIA has not yet achieved a satisfactory collection of intelligence on and from the USSR and the satellites. The tremendously effective State Security apparatus of the USSR and the Soviet Orbit make this primary target extremely difficult to attack. Intensive efforts have been expended in an attempt to develop within the USSR and the satellite countries a secure clandestine intelligence apparatus capable of supporting and providing communications for agent operations. The collection of intelligence from these areas is increasing.

The reduction of available overt intelligence sources by Soviet and satellite security precautions imposes upon CIA a responsibility for the collection of intelligence through espionage and counterespionage to a degree unparalleled in the past. In view of this and since available espionage and counterespionage facilities are not sufficient to fulfill present intelligence requirements, a mechanism for assigning over-all priorities to intelligence requirements levied on CIA by the various U.S. intelligence agencies has been established through the Interagency Priorities Committee, a subcommittee of the Intelligence Advisory Committee. In general terms, the topmost priority within this framework is being afforded to Soviet and satellite intentions and capabilities.

Substantial progress has been made in organizing stay-behind agents in areas likely to be overrun in the event of further hostilities. In the face of known Soviet occupation and control techniques, the

---

[10] Top Secret; Security Information; Eyes Only. For a summary of Report No. 7 of NSC 135, see Document 128.

durability of such stay-behind nets and their ability to function for an appreciable period of time after the outbreak of hostilities have not been firmly established. The effective establishment of stay-behind and other war planning operations is conditioned upon over-all war planning by Defense agencies which is on a continuing basis.

Counterespionage operations abroad gradually have been built up and concentrated against the Soviet and satellite intelligence services. They are becoming increasingly effective.

128.   Report From the National Security Council to President Truman[1]

Washington, September 2, 1952.

SUBJECT

Brief on No. 7, "The Foreign Intelligence Program," NSC 135

The basic handicap of the program is, of course, the paucity of intelligence of all types, covert and overt, on the Soviet Orbit. Nevertheless, atomic estimates, though still uncertain, are more reliable than a year ago. A number of "finds" in Soviet electronics and telecommunications have been made. Intelligence on air defense and on basic scientific research is improved. New economic sources and techniques promise better intelligence on Soviet military production. Use of foreign radio broadcasts was good. Target research progressed. The NIS program (world-wide encyclopedic data) is 45% complete on the 24 highest-priority areas, and 22% complete as a whole. NATO intelligence requirements are being met.

Despite the fact that espionage within the Orbit has failed to produce significant results, outside the Orbit it is generally good. A number of stay-behind nets have been established.

Improvement is needed in coordination between intelligence and policy and between intelligence and operational planning, although the

---

[1] Source: Truman Library, Papers of Harry S. Truman, President's Secretary's Files. Top Secret; Security Information. This is a summary prepared by the NSC Reporting Unit of a 12-page report (Report No. 7 of NSC 135, "Status of United States Programs for National Security") prepared by CIA with the concurrence of the Intelligence Advisory Committee. The full report is ibid. It omits paragraph 5, which is printed as Enclosure 3 to Document 127.

national estimates are now effectively drawing upon governmental resources. Political, social, and cultural intelligence research-in-depth is
needed for areas outside the Orbit. Enemy long-range plans and intentions, especially in Korea, are not known. Knowledge of the Soviet
guided missile program is poor. Collection by the Service attachés is
inadequate. Further exploitation of aerial reconnaissance is indicated.
Knowledge of Soviet work in the field of radio jamming and in biological and chemical warfare is inadequate. Psychological and economic warfare have created unparalleled demands for intelligence.

There is no guarantee that intelligence will be able to furnish adequate warning of attack prior to actual detection of hostile formations.
Certain last-minute defensive and offensive preparations may, however, be detected; opportunities for such detection vary from fair (in
Germany and Korea) to extremely poor (in Transcaucasia and Southeast Asia).

---

129.   Memorandum From Robert P. Joyce of the Policy Planning Staff to the Under Secretary of State (Bruce)[1]

Washington, October 15, 1952.

SUBJECT

PSB and General Smith's Proposal

I refer to the memorandum[2] handed you by the Director of Central Intelligence at the PSB meeting last Thursday, October 9, which
outlines General Smith's recommendation that (in his own words):
"The responsibility for guiding policy, for approving projects, and for
assessing the results of all covert cold war operations be placed upon
the Psychological Strategy Board; and b) the present representatives of
the Departments of State, Defense and Joint Chiefs of Staff now charged
with giving policy guidance to the operating divisions of this Agency
(or personnel of equal stature and experience) be grouped as a cold
war general staff with the Director of the PSB staff as Chief thereof,
and be given additional responsibility of considering proposed proj-

---

[1] Source: National Archives, RG 59, P Files: Lot 55 D 339, New Proposals for PSB.
Top Secret.

[2] Printed below as Attachment 1.

ects, of recommending these projects for approval or disapproval by the Board, of periodic evaluation of the conduct of these projects, and of recommending periodically whether they are to be continued or discontinued." General Smith goes on to say that "The PSB, as presently constituted, has not so far accomplished all of the results which I myself had hoped for." He believes that the concepts and suggestions he makes in these informal memoranda would make the PSB "a really meaningful body as it would in fact become the device through which all of our major cold war activities are considered and approved."

A meeting was held in Mr. Frank G. Wisner's office on October 10 at which were present in addition to Mr. Wisner, Admiral Kirk, General Magruder, Mr. Tracy Barnes, and myself, at your direction. As you know, Mr. Barnes took over a week ago as Assistant Director of the CIA for OPC. The purpose of the meeting was to discuss General Smith's memorandum and it was thoroughly understood that the meeting was exploratory and that no commitments were expected or would be made until the important suggestions and recommendations in General Smith's memorandum were thoroughly understood. Admiral Kirk stated that he had had long conversations with General Smith about the latter's thinking relating to the PSB role in clandestine political warfare. He remarked that he was in general agreement with General Smith. Both General Magruder and Mr. Wisner had also discussed the matter with General Smith and they had clear ideas as to what the latter was driving at. It was generally agreed that the kernel of General Smith's thought was contained in the sentence starting at the bottom of page 1 of his memorandum which states: "Moreover, under the existing mechanism for providing policy guidance and program approval, the Agency has continued in the position of having to assume too much responsibility and authority for its own good." He goes on to say that "the rapidly increasing cost of covert operations, coupled with the missing elements of objective review and substantive audit, leave it open to departmental and Congressional criticism."

During the meeting I took occasion to clarify certain points in General Smith's memorandum which did not appear to me entirely clear:

1) In speaking of "all of our major cold war activities," did General Smith confine his recommendations only to political warfare by clandestine means or was he thinking in terms of overt propaganda as well? The answer was that he was thinking only of covert activity.

2) In outlining his concept of the duties of the "advisers and staff officers of the three principals," it was not clear as to whether these persons would be PSB officials or officials of their respective departments and agencies, i.e., State, Defense, CIA and perhaps the JCS. The answer was that these persons who would backstop the Board members would be representatives of their respective departments and agencies where they would have their offices and perform their functions.

3) When General Smith spoke of his objection to the formal reference of cold war projects to the routine machinery of the major departments and the inevitable delays and breaches of security that this process involves, did he mean to shut off the sometimes necessary and fruitful direct working relationships between senior CIA officials and senior State Department officials on the working level? The answer to this question was no, but it was believed that General Smith desired a rigidly controlled, lateral working relationship held to more senior and responsible officials who were in a better position to give the necessary advice and clearances.

General Magruder stated that he was very much in favor of General Smith's basic concept. He commented that the atmosphere within the Defense establishment relating to clandestine and unconventional activities had changed very greatly over the past two years. These activities at their outset were not clearly understood or appreciated by the Military who took an understandably negative view of mysteries and "unconventionality" which cut across established orthodox channels and straightforward military concepts. These attitudes within the Defense establishment had been greatly ameliorated and now the attitudes of top people within the Services and within the JCS vis-à-vis covert operations reflected much more awareness of the necessity for political warfare and all types of covert activities. He went on to say that, although it was still difficult for any group including a representative of the Secretary of Defense to commit the three Services to logistical support, nevertheless these difficulties could now be met much more easily within the Defense establishment. General Magruder commented that, in his opinion, expeditious clearances for covert activities and Department of Defense "no objection" or "yes, please do the most you can" were now possible as long as the activities did not impinge upon the basic constitutional and legislative powers and authority of the Military establishment.

I think that we should examine very closely General Smith's concept of the assistant, staff officer, or deputy to support each PSB member. He envisages "highly qualified officers ... upon whom the principals could rely completely as their technical advisers and *whom their respective Departments would accept in that status.* It would be essential that these selected officers would have the competence to speak authoritatively and definitively on the various matters to be considered ...." General Smith qualifies this rather startling allocation of authority by stating that: "The selected staff officers would have to be held responsible by the principals for the necessary amount of coordinating and checking in their departments."

I do not believe that this is a workable concept. No State Department official would have the necessary qualifications to fulfill such responsible functions as I believe are envisaged under General Smith's concept of a "Board of Directors for all covert cold war activities." I do not think that the Secretary or Under Secretary would consider giving off-the-cuff clearances for highly sensitive political operations without first consulting the most competent persons in the Department of State. Certainly, no staff officer or assistant could or should be clothed with any such power or responsibility as this would cut across basic concepts of departmental handling of policy decisions. If, in any such group as envisaged by General Smith, I or my successor should presume to provide policy clearance in highly sensitive fields of intimate interest to, let us say, EUR, and in which, let us say, NEA has a profound interest, I should certainly be assassinated instanter by the Assistant Secretaries of these two Bureaus, and quite rightly so. It is my opinion that the present mechanism for providing policy guidance to OPC of CIA works pretty well. It is perhaps administratively somewhat unorthodox, but the activity itself is "unconventional" and is not easily fitted into conventional and institutionally correct procedures.

I inquired of Frank Wisner if he thought that General Smith considered that the Department of State was not providing adequate policy guidance under the present mechanism or whether there were long delays in obtaining clearances due to some of the factors set forth in General Smith's memorandum. Mr. Wisner replied that he did not think that this was in the General's mind, but rather General Smith's basic thought was that "no objection" on the part of the Department of State was not sufficient. He rather desired a mechanism which would more closely commit the Department to responsibility for sensitive and exceedingly costly activities directly in the field of foreign policy by other means, i.e., political warfare. I may add that whenever the CIA required a policy decision on an important matter where time was of the essence, such decision has been forthcoming sometimes within a matter of hours. The Deputy Under Secretary is constantly available for these high level decisions which have always been made in the past without their being referred to the lower levels and fought over by relatively junior officials. In other words, it is my view that General Smith's memorandum in this respect refers primarily to the delays, lack of sufficient logistic support, and security breaches which have been experienced for understandable reasons within the Department of Defense and the JCS.

With regard to the General's insistence upon this Department assuming more responsibility for these activities, we must, of course, look closely into the degree of authority and control which must be concomitant with such responsibility. As you know, it was the concept of General Marshall, Mr. Forrestal, Mr. Lovett and Mr. Kennan, when OPC was set up in the spring of 1948, that political warfare activities of covert means (excluding para-military operations and planning therefor in case of overt hostilities) was of primary interest to the Department of State. The idea was explored of placing such activity directly within this Department, but I believe it was finally decided that the operation should be one step removed from this Department, and it was for this reason that it was placed, faute de mieux, within the framework of the CIA. We are still the Department primarily interested in political warfare by covert means. If this is so, we should accept General Smith's basic thesis and accept more responsibility but at the same time exercise closer control over operations. I inquired whether General Smith had in mind a "theater commander" concept which would mean that the Department would say "go ahead" and then his organization would take over and all implementation would be considered operational and within his exclusive responsibility. Mr. Wisner replied that this was not in General Smith's mind as evidenced by the part of the latter's memorandum where he refers to "periodic evaluation of the conduct of these projects and of recommending periodically whether they are to be continued or discontinued." This concept would mean a much greater degree of State Department control than is presently exercised. When he took over the CIA, General Smith told the Chief of Foreign Service Personnel Durbrow that he could use perhaps fifty qualified Foreign Service Officers in a delicate operation where political know-how and area expertise is essential. We have never been able to meet this request, and presently there are only three or four qualified Foreign Service Officers serving in OPC of CIA.

As you are well aware, a green light for an operation or a "no objection" is entirely inadequate. My office has endeavored, through the weekly 10/2 representatives forum and by personal contacts with senior operational personnel of the OPC to keep abreast of political warfare operations. This has been difficult and sometimes these operations inevitably get off the beam. It is axiomatic that delicate political operations are about as good as the operators. Perhaps this adds up to the conclusion that if this Department accepts more responsibility, it will mean that senior officers of this Department must themselves devote increasing personal attention to monitoring CIA political warfare activities.

I think that recent events in the Soviet Union fully justify General Smith's observation that "it is inevitable that cold war operations will continue over a long period of time." If our conflict with Stalinism, Russian Imperialism, International Communism, or whatever name we give it may more and more assume the pattern of what we call "cold war" over an indefinite period, it seems to me that political warfare by clandestine means will increasingly assume major significance. The NSC in 10/5[3] affirmed this conclusion and called for increased scope

---

[3] Document 90.

and magnitude in covert operations. General Smith speaks of the happy combination of personality and experience, the continuity of which is not insured. I would place more stress than he apparently does on his phrase "the continuity of which is not insured." An institutional arrangement made at this particular juncture and based to some degree on personalities might be dangerous. It might work very well up until January 20, 1953. With regard to the State Department end of General Smith's concept, I should like to see, if possible, the focal point within the Department providing policy guidance and control for political warfare activities placed upon as high a "professional level" as possible.

I attach hereto a memorandum addressed to me on October 10 by Mr. Krentz as well as a memorandum I have just received from Mr. Tracy Barnes. I think that both of these memoranda will assist in our study of the problem presented by General Smith's memoranda.

Robert P. Joyce[4]

Attachment 1

Draft Memorandum by Director of Central Intelligence Smith[5]

Washington, October 8, 1952.

In the field of unconventional and psychological operations the Central Intelligence Agency is an executive and operating agency charged with carrying out projects in support of national policies. These projects include political and paramilitary operations, the general desirability of which have been determined by the senior departments of the Executive Branch of the Government. As an operating agent for these departments, CIA requires more than policy guidance. The actual projects which it proposes to undertake in furthering national policy should be carefully scrutinized before final approval, and the net value of the operations themselves should be periodically assessed by some authority outside the Agency but representative both of it and of

---

[4] Printed from a copy that bears this typed signature.

[5] Secret; Security Information. For text of the October 30 version of this paper endorsed by the Psychological Strategy Board, see Document 135.

the interested executive departments. The mounting cost of these operations makes such prior assessment and continuous audit a matter of great urgency.

Ever since I assumed my present responsibilities I have been trying to arrive at the best method of establishing within the Agency an objective method of project review and analysis, but without really satisfactory results. Moreover, under the existing mechanism for providing policy guidance and program approval, the Agency has continued in the position of having to assume too much responsibility and authority for its own good. Thus, the rapidly increasing cost of covert operations, coupled with the missing elements of objective review and substantive audit, leave it open to departmental and Congressional criticism. The simple fact is that in the field of cold war, vision and imagination are essential, but these two essential qualities must be held under wraps. Otherwise, the number of ways they will conjure up to spend money is really surprising, and the selective judgment of a detached, objective authority must be applied.

It is inevitable that cold war operations will continue over a long period of time. The involve activities which do not lend themselves to precise evaluation and it is impossible to judge in absolute terms the successes or failures of particular programs. Unlike military operations which require the continuous and increasing application of force toward an abrupt and conclusive ending, those in which we engage usually require a fluctuating effort with no clear termination in prospect. For this reason, it is all the more important that they should not be undertaken unless all concerned are satisfied as to their desirability.

The ideal situation would be for all cold war projects to be considered in detail and passed upon by a committee consisting of the Under Secretary of State, the Deputy Secretary of Defense, and the Director of Central Intelligence (the present PSB). However, it is not possible for these fully occupied individuals to devote the amount of time necessary for such direct analysis, and they would need competent and fully trusted advisors from their respective staffs in order to be adequately informed. I believe, however, that the three officials mentioned, sitting as the Psychological Strategy Board, can *if adequately supported* perform these functions without too much additional burden, and they are already doing a good deal of it in an informal way at their weekly luncheon meetings. This, however, is the result of a happy combination of personalities and experience, the continuity of which is not insured. It can be insured only if there is a genuine acceptance of certain essential principles. The first of these is full recognition by the three Board members of the true significance of their role which would be actually to approve, guide, and assess the value of covert cold war operations, as well as to give the policy guidance under which these operations are planned and executed. In this capacity, they would be in effect a board of directors for all covert cold war activities. Second and somewhat more difficult of attainment would be the provision of a few highly qualified officers within the P.S.B. staff upon whom the principals could rely completely as their technical advisors, and whom their respective departments would accept in that status. It would be essential that these selected officers have competence to speak authoritatively and definitively on the various matters to be considered, both in their capacity as advisors and staff officers of the three principals and as representatives of the departments from which they are seconded. Time would be lost and insecurity would result from formal reference of cold war projects to the routine machinery of the major departments, since this would have the inevitable result of allowing these matters to get down into the depths of departmental staffs and to be fought over and widely discussed by a large number of relatively junior officials. Hence, the selected staff officers would have to be held responsible by the principals for the necessary amount of coordinating and checking within their departments.

The three presently designated representatives of the Departments of State and Defense and the Joint Chiefs of Staff are all top quality individuals. We could not hope to get and would not want to have better people. It seems to me that the only difficulty is that they are not set up in the proper framework at the present time. They or others of equivalent caliber could serve as the principal advisors and assistants of the two Under Secretaries. I recommend, therefore, that: (a) the responsibility for guiding policy, for approving projects, and for assessing the results of all covert cold war operations be placed upon the Psychological Strategy Board; and (b) the present representatives of the Departments of State, Defense, and the Joint Chiefs of Staff now charged with giving policy guidance to the operating divisions of this Agency (or personnel of equal stature and experience) be grouped as a cold war general staff with the Director of the PSB staff as chief thereof, and be given the additional responsibility of considering proposed projects, of recommending these projects for approval or disapproval by the Board, of periodic evaluation of the conduct of these projects, and of recommending periodically whether they are to be continued or discontinued.

The PSB, as presently constituted, has not so far accomplished all of the results which I myself had hoped for. The concept outlined above would, to a certain extent, change its present character and would make it a really meaningful body as it would in fact become the device through which all of our major cold war activities are considered and approved. The present staff of the PSB would undergo a corresponding change with respect to its composition, functions and responsibilities.

These are general recommendations. If they are favorably considered, they will require detailed analysis and staff action.

Attachment 2

**Memorandum From Kenneth C. Krentz of the Policy
Planning Staff to Robert P. Joyce[6]**

Washington, October 10, 1952.

General Smith's draft memorandum of October 8[7] presents a logical and convincing case for the appointment of deputies to the PSB members who would be responsible, each under the aegis of his own department, for formulating policy guidance and evaluation for all covert political and psychological operations. There is little doubt that such a set-up would enable CIA to function more effectively and responsibly in this field and I can see certain advantages from the Department of State's point of view in that decisions be by a departmental group rather than solely by State with tacit or other concurrence by Defense. However, I can foresee several serious dangers from our point of view unless this project were to be extremely carefully worked out in terms of our own organization.

First, it seems to me that our present small office, functioning for and under the direct control of Mr. Matthews is, while not perfect, a very effective means of pulling together day-to-day operations on the covert side with all the responsible political officers of the Department. We know what is going on and can work very closely with the Assistant Secretaries and their Deputies and are in a position constantly to guide the thinking of working-level people in CIA/opc.

Covert political warfare is so alien to the normal concepts of American government in the past, is so labyrinthine and delicate, that it seems to me maturity of judgment and experience plus the career officer's intuitive sense of political factors are essential factors in dealing with the problem on the day-to-day working levels of the bureaus. Experience, I believe, will demonstrate that the deputies proposed would in a very short time tend to become involved exclusively in high-level decisions and relationships which would isolate them from the intimate contact with the diverse parts of the Department and CIA, which we now maintain.

To set up a new mechanism within the Department to perform our function seems to me dangerous to our ends. I think particularly the

---

[6] Secret; Security Information.

[7] See Attachment 1 above.

"Secretariat" approach would tend to place these functions in a routine and perhaps an unimaginative context in which I do not believe they can be fitted. I am quite aware that our present set-up is viewed with horror by organizational and managerial eyes. Nevertheless, I believe the nature of the problem requires an unorthodox approach. In other words, if we appoint the deputies to sit in the PSB, I believe they should be supported by practically the same set-up which we now have under Mr. Matthews.

We must also consider that the Deputy Under Secretary for Substantive Affairs is likely always to be a high-calibre substantive officer. Under the vicissitudes of our system this would not necessarily be true for future Under Secretaries.

General Smith says, "It would be essential that these selected officers (the deputies) have competence to speak authoritatively and definitively on the various matters to be considered, both in their capacity as advisors and staff officers of the three principals and as representatives of the departments from which they are seconded (sic). Time would be lost and insecurity would result from formal reference of cold war projects to the routine machinery of the major departments, since this would have the inevitable result of allowing these matters to get down into the depths of departmental staffs and to be fought over and widely discussed by a large number of relatively junior officials. Hence, the selected staff officers would have to be held responsible by the principals for the necessary amount of coordinating and checking within their departments."

In the last analysis this becomes a question of individuals. If we were to set this proposal up tomorrow the individuals would be yourself and General Magruder. This would work beautifully because both of you have several years of intimate experience, knowledge of pitfalls, extensive cooperating contacts—built up over several years also through selected individuals—and the requisite qualities of mind for the job. Here also we would run into the violent objection of managers that you cannot rely upon individuals. Any comparably competent officers must be able to take over at any time. I think this is the exception that proves the rule. With the departure of yourself shortly and the possible departure of General Magruder at any time, I have a strong feeling that we might be getting into a very undesirable position. Furthermore, I do not think General Smith's generalization as to Departmental staffs can be applied to the Department of State as it could to CIA or to the Pentagon. Our substantive staffs are relatively small and highly coordinated in the traditional pattern of Foreign Office operation.

This matter of our own internal set-up should have the most careful consideration before we agree to modifications. This is something which is going to take a large amount of thought and foresight, but my first reaction is that to be successful we should have to maintain something within our own building very similar to what we have now.

I am thoroughly in accord with General Smith's stresses on the need for constant evaluation of covert programs and auditing even as to detail. Carefully worked out, the mechanism he proposes might be the best means of achieving this.

Kenneth C. Krentz[8]

---

[8] Printed from a copy that bears this typed signature.

---

130. Memorandum From Robert P. Joyce of the Policy Planning Staff to the Director of the Bureau of German Affairs (Riddleberger)[1]

Washington, October 10, 1952.

SUBJECT

Liaison Relationships between OPC of CIA and the Department of State[2]

As you are aware, under NSC Directives the Department of State has certain responsibilities for providing political guidance to the organization within the CIA which engages in certain activities which might be generally referred to as within the field of political warfare. Primary responsibility for providing this counsel, advice, guidance and control is vested in Mr. H. Freeman Matthews, and I have responsibility as his subordinate for the day to day operation of this function. In the performance of these duties, members of this office and I on occasion consult with you when important policy matters are under consideration. The ordinary relationship is, however, with the various Deputy Assistant Secretaries and the office Directors and their

---

[1] Source: National Archives, RG 59, Central Files 1950–54, 103.11/10–1052. Top Secret; Security Information. Copies were sent to EUR–Perkins, FE–Allison, NEA–Byroade, and ARA–Miller. Riddleberger's handwritten note on the first page reads: "Discussed with Joyce. No answer required. JWR, 10/16/52."

[2] On August 1, OPC merged with the CIA's Office of Special Operations to form the Directorate of Plans, under Deputy Director for Plans Frank G. Wisner. The acronym OPC was not used in CIA after that date.

Deputies. On occasion, when a particular situation in a particular country demands and is receiving close attention by the CIA, officers in charge are brought in.

My colleagues (Kenneth C. Krentz, Lampton Berry, William McFadden) and I arrange personal meetings where the appropriate official of the CIA is able to consult directly with the appropriate official of the Department of State. I have found it desirable to attend these meetings or to see to it that one of my colleagues is present. On occasion, when the CIA is engaging in important operations in a particular country in a rapidly developing situation, my office has authorized a continuing and sometimes daily direct relationship between the CIA official concerned and the appropriate officer of the Department. In all these contacts, however, my office is kept advised as to the nature of the business and the decisions, if any, which were taken. This liaison control has proved to be necessary in order that I may be in a position to be continuously aware of the political advice being supplied to OPC of CIA and in order that matters of importance may be brought to the attention of Mr. Matthews for final decision.

OPC of CIA has expanded very rapidly indeed during the past four years. From a small group of about [number not declassified] persons in 1948, I believe the organization now has on its rolls some [number not declassified] persons. The activities of this section of CIA have expanded enormously in scope and magnitude on a world wide basis. This situation has meant (up until recently, for reasons which need not be gone into here) that requests for political guidance and consequently the need for increasing direct contact between CIA officials and officers of the Department of State has greatly increased. The job of channelizing and controlling these contacts has been difficult but, in my opinion, necessary both in the interests of security and efficiency in seeing to it that OPC obtains the most carefully considered advice from the most competent and responsible officers in the Department.

A great number of officers of OPC of CIA are on terms of personal friendship with many political officers of this Department, and there has been a continuing tendency for informal contacts between such persons on both sides of the house. It is very difficult, and sometimes undesirable, to endeavor to control too stringently these relationships which are occasionally fruitful. On the other hand, these personal relationships sometimes work against important security considerations, and on occasion the CIA man talks operations with his Department of State friend who may talk policy. There have been occasions when contacts of this nature result in the CIA man considering that he has obtained a policy view or even on occasion a green light from his Departmental contact. In addition to these informal contacts, there is a constant disposition on the part of some CIA officials to deal directly with his "opposite number" in the Department of State at times without clearance within the CIA or with my office. I believe it will be understood that although certain "opposite number" contacts are on occasion desirable, they should nevertheless be controlled. There have been instances in the past when CIA officials have considered and reported that they have received policy decisions or "no objection" responses from certain Departmental officers following direct and uncoordinated contacts.

This situation has been discussed on many occasions with Mr. Frank Wisner, who has had his own difficulties within the CIA in controlling and channeling relationships between OPC and the Department of State. Recently Ambassador Lewis Clark, who is presently with the CIA, has been placed in control of liaison between OPC of CIA and this Department. He is preparing an inventory of all contacts between OPC officials and political officers of this Department. He is discovering that there have developed relationships such as described in the preceding paragraph and that these contacts sometimes caused confusion and duplication. Mr. Clark is tightening up this liaison relationship within OPC, and his office will be the clearing house for all meetings between OPC officers and the political officers of the Department of State. He has requested, and I have agreed, that a renewed endeavor be made within this Department to insure that all meetings involving policy guidance shall be arranged for or passed upon by my office.

The purpose of this memorandum is to request that you bring this matter to the attention of your Deputy and your office Directors. It might be suggested to them that they should have no further direct dealings with CIA officials on policy matters without clearance with my office. Only in exceptional cases, should contact be below the Deputy office director level. Exceptions should be cleared by my office and the office director concerned. I am sure that you will understand that there is no desire on my part to interpose myself or to choke off useful and desirable contacts between officials of the CIA and appropriate political officers of the Department. I believe that you will agree that this degree of control is necessary in order to 1) prevent misunderstandings of the Department's position from developing within the CIA; 2) insure that political advice and guidance proffered by one Departmental official is coordinated with other areas of the Department; 3) maintain a necessary degree of security with regard to the operations of the CIA and the relationship between OPC and the Department of State under NSC Directives, and 4) insure that all substantive and important policy guidance decisions are placed before Deputy Under Secretary Matthews.

RPJ

131. Memorandum From Director of Central Intelligence Smith to the Executive Secretary of the National Security Council (Lay)[1]

Washington, October 14, 1952.

SUBJECT

A Project to Provide a More Adequate Basis for Planning for the Security of the United States (NSC Action No. 543)[2]

1. On August 30, 1951, by NSC Action No. 543, the National Security Council directed that the Director of Central Intelligence prepare, in collaboration with the Interdepartmental Committee on Internal Security (ICIS), the Interdepartmental Intelligence Conference (IIC), and the Joint Chiefs of Staff (JCS), a summary evaluation of the net capability of the USSR to injure the Continental United States. The NSC directive required that this summary evaluation be prepared upon completion of basic studies by the Intelligence Advisory Committee (IAC) under the direction of its Chairman, the Director of Central Intelligence; by the IIC; by the JCS with collaboration, as required, of the Federal Civil Defense Administration, (FCDA); and by the ICIS with collaboration, as required, of the FCDA, as indicated Tab A.

2. The IAC study was published on October 23, 1951 as Special Estimate 14, "Soviet Capabilities for a Military Attack on the United States before July 1952."[3] The IIC study dated October 10, 1951, and the ICIS study of May 15, 1952 are enclosed herewith as Tab B.[4] Because of the sensitive nature of the JCS study, it was not distributed outside the JCS organization. Members of the working group which drafted the summary evaluation were briefed orally on its contents.

3. The attached summary evaluation represents a step forward in planning for the security of the United States and is transmitted as an example of the caliber of work currently to be expected. In the

---

[1] Source: Central Intelligence Agency, Office of the Deputy Director for Intelligence Job 80–R1440R, Box 3, Folder 10. Top Secret; Security Information. Smith's memorandum is attached to an October 21 covering memorandum from Acting Executive Secretary Gleason to the NSC, which indicates that the NSC would "at an early meeting" consider the recommendations contained in paragraph 5 of Smith's memorandum. See Document 137.

[2] Document 86.

[3] Not printed. A copy is in National Archives, RG 263, Central Intelligence Agency Files.

[4] Not enclosed but available upon request to the Executive Secretary. [Footnote in the original.]

following important respects, however, it falls far short of supplying the estimates essential to security planning:

a. An evaluation of the USSR's capability to injure the United States should contain a plain statement of the estimated percentage of reduction in US capabilities likely to result from Soviet attack; specifically, percentage reduction in the fields of: US military strength in being, atomic counterattack capability, industrial production, and ability to produce new weapons of critical importance.

b. To provide guidance in current planning for US security, evaluations on this subject should be projected into the future and contain an estimate of prospective developments in USSR's offensive capabilities.

c. A more adequate and realistic evaluation would cover the probable Soviet capabilities to injure US facilities and strengths in all parts of the world, and not merely the capability of USSR to injure the Continental United States. Such an evaluation should include some estimate of Soviet intentions in the light of net capabilities.

4. Three primary reasons why the attached paper does not meet these requirements are:

a. We lack knowledge of Soviet plans and intentions and our knowledge of Soviet capabilities cannot be considered complete.

b. The basic underlying studies required to produce the statement mentioned in paragraph 3-a do not exist.

c. There is at present no machinery to plan, guide, coordinate and produce an appraisal or estimate based on the integration of national intelligence with military, political and economic operational data dealing with our own capabilities.

5. It is believed that an appraisal of the type referred to in paragraph 4-c would serve to provide a more adequate basis for planning for the security of the United States. To this end it is recommended that the National Security Council:

a. Note the attached summary evaluation as an initial effort in response to the NSC directive issued by NSC Action No. 543, and as an example of the kind of work currently to be expected on this type of problem.

b. As an interim measure instruct the Director of Central Intelligence to prepare, in collaboration with officials of other governmental bodies as required,[5] terms of reference for a more adequate evaluation of the USSR's capability to injure the United States.

c. Concurrently, instruct the Director of Central Intelligence to examine, in collaboration with officials of other governmental bodies as

---

[5] From this point, a line is drawn to the bottom of the page where the words "including IIC & ICIS" were added by hand.

needed,[6] the adequacy of present machinery, and the character of any new machinery that may be required in order to plan, guide, coordinate, and produce for the National Security Council, upon request, evaluations in the nature of "Commander's Estimates," of the USSR's capabilities and intentions vis-à-vis the United States, based upon the integration of military, political, and economic operational data dealing with United States' capabilities and intentions, and national intelligence.

Walter B. Smith[7]

Enclosure[8]

Washington, October 6, 1952.

NET CAPABILITY OF THE USSR TO INJURE THE
CONTINENTAL US

Problem

1. To prepare a summary evaluation of the net capability of the USSR, as of mid-1952, to injure the continental United States.

Scope

2. This evaluation considers the injury which could be inflicted on the continental United States by USSR military action and Soviet-inspired sabotage in connection with the initial attack and in connection with attacks immediately following. The US has substantial strengths in being outside the continental United States, and no estimate is expressed herein as to the effect of a Soviet attack on such strengths or the likelihood that the Soviet will allocate parts of its striking power to such an attack.

Conclusions

3. The Soviet Union, as of mid-1952, has the net capability to inflict serious but not permanently crippling damage to the continental strengths of the United States.

4. This Soviet capability is primarily that of surprise air attack using atomic bombs. The Soviet capability for inflicting direct damage on the US by sabotage is small by comparison with damage that could be inflicted by an atomic air attack. However, sabotage in conjunction with

---

[6] From this point, a line is drawn connecting to the line noted in footnote 5 above.

[7] Printed from a copy that indicates Smith signed the original.

[8] Top Secret; Security Information.

an atomic air attack could significantly increase the total physical and psychological impact. Such sabotage could include the use of atomic weapons smuggled into the US if the Kremlin were disposed to accept the considerably increased risk of premature disclosure which this operation would entail.

5. The Soviet stockpile of atomic bombs, as of mid-1952, is probably appreciably less than 100. The nature and extent of the damage that could be inflicted by a surprise air attack, involving the launching against US targets of the entire Soviet stockpile of atomic bombs, would vary according to the objectives governing the selection of targets.

a. An attack on US targets selected with the objective of inflicting maximum overall damage to US armament production capacity and military power would probably prevent the US from regaining its current armament production capacity and military power for a period of the order of 2 years.

b. An attack on US targets selected with the primary objective of neutralizing US atomic capabilities (see sub-paragraph 6-a) would probably not prevent an atomic counter attack from the continental US of a size unacceptable to the Soviet Union in the light of its present defenses and vulnerabilities.

c. An attack on US targets selected with the primary objective of neutralizing US ability to sustain large scale military operations and to produce new weapons of critical importance (see sub-paragraphs 6-b and 6-c), could, under circumstances considered probable for the enemy, achieve such neutralization for a period of the order of 6 to 12 months.

d. Regardless of the primary objective of the attack or the basis of target selection, the USSR is incapable of inflicting by such attack sufficient mass casualties or disorganization to force US government changes or decisions acceptable to the USSR (see sub-paragraph 6-d).

Objectives of the Attacks

6. We believe that any military action or sabotage undertaken by the USSR against the continental US would be for the purposes listed below. Achievement of the first three of these objectives is, for the present at least, essential to the ultimate success of any Soviet war plan against the western powers.

a. To prevent the launching of atomic attacks against the Soviet Union in the light of its defenses and vulnerabilities. Probable primary targets would include Strategic Air Command bases, aircraft and control centers, atomic production facilities and storage sites.

b. To neutralize US ability to sustain large scale military operations. Probable primary targets would include concentrated industries critical and basic to war production; basic services, including power and transport; ports and Naval bases; and atomic production facilities.

c. To neutralize US ability to develop or produce any new weapons of critical importance. Probable primary targets would include Atomic Energy key facilities for new development, guided missile production and test installations, and applied research facilities.

d. To so neutralize the general industrial, economic, and psychological strength of the US that government decisions or changes acceptable to the Soviet Union would occur, or could be forced by additional pressures elsewhere in the world. Pursuit of this objective would probably involve an effort to inflict mass casualities and cause disorganization in urban areas. Probable primary targets would include all those listed for other more specific purposes in sub-paragraphs 6-a, 6-b, and 6-c above, with the additional targets of government control centers, population centers, and miscellaneous industry and supplies wherever concentrated.

Method and Effectiveness of Attacks

7. *Air Attacks.* By far the most effective means available to the USSR for injuring the continental United States in the initial stage of hostilities is air attack with atomic bombs. It is estimated that the USSR is capable of carrying out air attacks against any target in the continental United States and Canada. Some targets listed as essential to its objectives would be difficult to reach with Soviet capability of mid-1952. USSR capabilities for air attack are estimated in detail as follows:

a. *Penetration of US Defenses.*

(1) The capability exists for the USSR to penetrate US, Alaskan and Canadian defense with air attack at any time and place which it might select. The factors favoring this capability are:

(a) The USSR has the initiative.
(b) The US aircraft control and warning net is not completed.
(c) The USSR can jam and reduce the efficiency of the aircraft control and warning system. The extent to which the USSR can do this is not known.
(d) The radar net will not detect low flying aircraft at distances which would make interception feasible.
(e) The US Ground Observer Corps is not yet fully effective.
(f) The regulation of air traffic into the United States is not sufficiently rigid to make identification positive. Also electronic identification equipment is not available to supply all friendly aircraft.
(g) Sufficient all-weather fighters for US air defense forces are not yet available. Crew deficiencies also exist.
(h) Russian bombers can overfly the range of US anti-aircraft artillery.

(2) The net success in penetrating the US defenses in terms of bombs on target would vary with the avenues chosen, the methods of attack and depth of targets inside peripheral defenses, character of individual targets and their local defenses, and the degree of surprise attained. It is estimated that 65 to 85 per cent of bombs launched could

be delivered on target in an attack aimed at US armament production facilities and military strength in general.

b. *Effectiveness of Air Attack with Atomic Bombs.* As of mid-1952, the USSR probably had a stockpile of 50 bombs of approximately 20 KT yield, or the equivalent in bombs of different yields. It is possible that the number of bombs was as low as 25 or as high as 100.

(1) Assuming that (1) the USSR had a stockpile of 100 bombs, (2) all were allotted to the optimum targets in the US, (3) all were dropped with near optimum placement, and (4) the entire attack was delivered in a short period, the Soviet Union could inflict sufficient damage to prevent the US from regaining its present armament production capacity and military power for at least two years. However, the actual USSR stockpile is probably appreciably less than 100 atomic weapons; optimum target selection is improbable; and it is probable that the number of bombs delivered on target would be only 65 to 85 per cent of those launched. Consequently the probable delay in recovery of US armament production capacity and military power might well be less than two years.

(2) If the probable Soviet stockpile of atomic bombs were used against US targets selected with a view to preventing the launching of US atomic weapons (see sub-paragraph 6-a), we believe that the percentage of bombs on target would be substantially less than 65 to 85 percent. This estimate is based on the nature and location of the targets and on the fact that the aircraft element in these targets is mobile. Such an attack, under circumstances considered probable for the enemy, would probably not prevent an atomic counter attack from the continental US of a size unacceptable to the Soviet Union in the light of its present defenses and vulnerabilities.[9]

(3) If the probable Soviet stockpile were directed at the ability of the US to sustain large scale military operations and to produce new weapons of critical importance (see sub-paragraphs 6-b and 6-c), delivery capability should be high. Under circumstances considered probable for the enemy, substantial neutralization of these US capabilities could probably be achieved for a period of the order of 6 to 12 months.[10]

(4) If the probable Soviet stockpile were used to achieve any of the purposes stated in paragraph 6, some progress might be made toward achieving the purpose described in sub-paragraph 6-d. However, the degree of destruction required to achieve that purpose is believed to be well beyond current Soviet capabilities.

c. *Effectiveness of Air Attack with Conventional Bombs.* Using conventional bombs, the USSR could not at the present time inflict injury on the continental United States that would be significant in achieving any of the purposes listed in paragraph 6.

---

[9] As noted in paragraph 2 above, no estimate is expressed herein as to the effect of a Soviet attack on US strengths overseas, or as to the likelihood that the Kremlin would allocate parts of its striking power to such an attack. [Footnote in the original.]

[10] US ability to sustain large scale military operations is considered here as a general ability. If effects were analyzed in terms of sustaining particular military operations, i.e. land operations, sea operations, air operations, amphibious and joint operations, different predictions would likely result for each. [Footnote in the original.]

d. *Effectiveness of Air Attack with Chemical, BW and Other Unconventional Weapons.* At the present time the USSR does not have the capability to use chemical, BW, or other unconventional weapons in air attacks to achieve any of the purposes listed in paragraph 6.

8. *Effectiveness of Airborne Troop Attacks.* The USSR could not materially contribute to the achievement of any of the purposes listed in paragraph 6 by the use of airborne troop or commando air drops.

9. *Effectiveness of Sea Attack.*

a. *Surface Forces.* The USSR could not inflict significant injury on continental United States by use of Naval surface forces, as these surface forces lack the strength and composition necessary for operations against the continental United States.

b. *Sub-surface Forces.* Soviet submarines are capable of reaching, with little chance of detection, positions off the US coasts from which personnel could be landed and missiles fired at land targets. There is no evidence that the USSR as yet possesses an atomic missile that can be fired from a submarine. Although the possibility exists that the USSR does have such a weapon, we consider the damage resulting from such attacks would be minor by comparison to that of atomic air attack, and would not materially change the results to be expected from an air attack which delivered the entire available stockpile.

10. *Sabotage.* The Soviet capability for inflicting direct damage on the US by sabotage is small by comparison with damage that could be inflicted by an atomic air attack. However, sabotage in conjunction with an atomic air attack could significantly increase the total physical and psychological impact. Such sabotage could include the use of atomic weapons smuggled into the US if the Kremlin were disposed to accept the considerably increased risk of premature disclosure which this operation would entail. USSR sabotage capabilities are estimated as follows:

a. *Use of Saboteurs.* Measures to control the movement of potential saboteurs across the borders of or within the United States do not completely prevent access to most sabotage targets in the United States. If war occurs, however, the entry and departure of potential saboteurs probably would be quickly and substantially curtailed. The freedom of action of potential saboteurs also in this event would probably be quickly and substantially curtailed by U.S. Government detention of those Communists and others who are regarded as potential saboteurs and of resident enemy aliens (including Soviet Bloc diplomatic and official personnel). Plans for the accomplishment of such detention have been prepared.[11]

---

[11] See Document 16.

b. *Physical Sabotage Capabilities against Specific Types of Targets* are estimated as follows:

(1) *Industrial Installations and Facilities.* Sabotage capabilities are high against facilities upon which a war mobilization, war production and wartime civilian economy depend. Security supervision is maintained in critical plants engaged in industrial contracts with defense agencies and also in certain essential supporting facilities. No like supervision is maintained in plants serving the essential civilian wartime economy. Inadequate visitor control in, and absence of authority to remove potential saboteurs from, vital non-classified-contract plants and inability to prevent Soviet inspired disruptive strikes, even in classified-contract plants, further add to the vulnerability of these industrial installations.

(2) *Key Military Installations* (including command facilities and other facilities essential for logistical support of the military within an area). Sabotage capabilities are slight in view of present deployment and readiness of area military forces and other protective countermeasures.

(3) *Port Facilities.* Substantial sabotage capabilities exist, since the program for safeguarding port facilities, adopted after evaluation of the risks involved, has necessarily been limited primarily to major ports. Even this limited program is proving difficult to implement in full.

(4) *Forests.* Sabotage capabilities consist chiefly of arson. Present forest protection facilities are inadequate to prevent a substantial increase in forest fire loss through sabotage. However, it is believed that such losses would be limited to an extent that U.S. war strength would not be critically affected.

(5) *Crops and Livestock.* While existing measure for safeguarding the nation's food supply are not adequate to prevent unconventional attacks, they might serve to minimize damage thereto from such attacks. It is believed that losses in this category would be limited to an extent that U.S. war strength would not be critically affected.

(6) *Public Water Supplies* are generally vulnerable to temporary and local BW contamination. The introduction of contaminants into water already in a circulating system is a greater danger than such introduction on watersheds or in reservoirs.

(7) *Essential Government Administrative Operations.* Saboteurs have some capability for assassination of key government officials, notwithstanding protective measures to which they have been alerted. Saboteurs also have the capability for disrupting the continuity of essential and other government operations by the clandestine introduction of chemical or biological agents into public buildings. Against this capability, existing countermeasures are only slightly effective.

c. *Sabotage Devices.* Potential saboteurs can readily obtain a wide variety of sabotage devices, including chemical and biological agents. They can also obtain or produce non-fissionable component parts of atomic bombs. Each of the foregoing is available in the United States or procurable through smuggling, for which substantial opportunities exist over United States land and sea frontiers and through abuse of diplomatic immunity and courtesy. There also exists the possibility of introducing assembled atomic bombs from abroad by such smuggling. The effective limit on sabotage capability will continue to be determined by

US controls on movements of persons and materials and on access to critical targets rather than by the availability of sabotage devices.

With regard to BW agents, programs pertaining to disease reporting, immunization, research, training, stockpiling, alertness, protection of veterinary biologicals and physical security of essential buildings are under way in the appropriate agencies. Satisfactory execution of these programs is essential to adequate defense against overt as well as clandestine biological warfare attack.

d. *Non-physical Sabotage.* While the continued propaganda and other subversive efforts of the Communists probably are not without some result, the prosecutions of national and local Communist leaders, plus the increasing awareness of the American public of the seriousness of this threat, are reducing the Communist potential in this field.

Tab A[12]

NATIONAL SECURITY COUNCIL DIRECTIVE

on

A PROJECT TO PROVIDE A MORE ADEQUATE BASIS FOR PLANNING FOR THE SECURITY OF THE UNITED STATES

1. Pursuant to authorization by the President there is hereby directed the development of the following comprehensive studies in order to provide a more adequate basis for planning for the security of the United States.

a. An estimate of the capability of the USSR to launch a military attack on the Continental United States, to be prepared under the direction of the Director of Central Intelligence as Chairman of the Intelligence Advisory Committee.

b. An estimate of the capability of the USSR to conduct sabotage and otherwise disrupt internal U.S. activities, to be prepared by the Interdepartmental Intelligence Conference.

c. An evaluation of U.S. military capability to counter potential enemy capabilities as estimated in subparagraph a above, and an estimate of the probable damage to the United States resulting from such attack, to be prepared by the Joint Chiefs of Staff with the collaboration, as required, of the Federal Civil Defense Administration.

d. An evaluation of ways and means available to counter potential enemy capabilities as estimated in subparagraph b above, and an estimate of the probable damage to the United States resulting from such enemy actions, to be prepared by the Interdepartmental Committee on Internal Security with the collaboration, as required of the Federal Civil Defense Administration.

---

[12] Top Secret; Security Information.

2. Upon the completion of the foregoing studies there will be prepared by the Director of Central Intelligence in collaboration with the Interdepartmental Committee on Internal Security, the Interdepartmental Intelligence Conference and the Joint Chiefs of Staff, a summary evaluation of the net capability of the USSR to injure the Continental United States.

3. The summary evaluation referred to in paragraph 2 above shall be completed as soon as possible and shall be forwarded to the National Security Council. Access thereto will be restricted to as few individuals as possible and only on an absolute need-to-know basis.

---

132. Memorandum From President Truman to Secretary of State Acheson and Secretary of Defense Lovett[1]

Washington, October 24, 1952.

SUBJECT

Communications Intelligence Activities

The communications intelligence (COMINT) activities of the United States are a national responsibility. They must be so organized and managed as to exploit to the maximum the available resources in all participating departments and agencies and to satisfy the legitimate intelligence requirements of all such departments and agencies.

I therefore designate the Secretaries of State and Defense as a Special Committee of the National Security Council for COMINT, which Committee shall, with the assistance of the Director of Central Intelligence, establish policies governing COMINT activities, and keep me advised of such policies through the Executive Secretary of the National Security Council.

I further designate the Department of Defense as executive agent of the Government, for the production of COMINT information.

I direct this Special Committee to prepare and issue directives which shall include the provisions set forth below and such other provisions as the Special Committee may determine to be necessary.

1. *A directive to the United States Communications Intelligence Board (USCIB).* This directive will replace the National Security Council In-

---

[1] Source: National Security Agency, Center For Cryptologic History. Top Secret.

telligence Directive No. 9,[2] and shall prescribe USCIB's new composition, responsibilities and procedures in the COMINT fields. This directive shall include the following provisions:

a. USCIB shall be reconstituted as a body acting for and under the Special Committee, and shall operate in accordance with the provisions of the new directive. Only those departments or agencies represented in USCIB are authorized to engage in COMINT activities.

b. The Board shall be composed of the following members:

(1) The Director of Central Intelligence, who shall be the Chairman of the Board.
(2) A representative of the Secretary of State.
(3) A representative of the Secretary of Defense.
(4) A representative of the Director of the Federal Bureau of Investigation.
(5) The Director of the National Security Agency.
(6) A representative of the Department of the Army.
(7) A representative of the Department of the Navy.
(8) A representative of the Department of the Air Force.
(9) A representative of the Central Intelligence Agency.

c. The Board shall have a staff headed by an executive secretary who shall be appointed by the Chairman with the approval of the majority of the Board.

d. It shall be the duty of the Board to advise and make recommendations to the Secretary of Defense, in accordance with the following procedure, with respect to any matter relating to communications intelligence which falls within the jurisdiction of the Director of NSA.

(1) The Board shall reach its decision by a majority vote. Each member of the Board shall have one vote except the representatives of the Secretary of State and of the Central Intelligence Agency who shall each have two votes. The Director of Central Intelligence, as Chairman, will have no vote. In the event that the Board votes and reaches a decision, any dissenting member of the Board may appeal from such decision within 7 days to the Special Committee. In the event that the Board votes but fails to reach a decision, any member of the Board may appeal within 7 days to the Special Committee. In either event the Special Committee shall review the matter, and its determination thereon shall be final. Appeals by the Director of NSA and/or the representatives of the Military Departments shall only be filed with the approval of the Secretary of Defense.

(2) If any matter is voted on by the Board but—

---

[2] Dated March 10, 1950; see *Foreign Relations*, 1945–1950, Emergence of the Intelligence Establishment, Document 435. NSCID No. 9 Revised is printed as Document 257.

(a) no decision is reached and any member files an appeal;

(b) a decision is reached in which the representative of the Secretary of Defense does not concur and files an appeal; no action shall be taken with respect to the subject matter until the appeal is decided, provided that, if the Secretary of Defense determines, after consultation with the Secretary of State, that the subject matter presents a problem of an emergency nature and requires immediate action, his decision shall govern, pending the result of the appeal. In such an emergency situation the appeal may be taken directly to the President.

(3) Recommendations of the Board adopted in accordance with the foregoing procedures shall be binding on the Secretary of Defense. Except on matters which have been voted on by the Board, the Director of NSA shall discharge his responsibilities in accordance with his own judgment, subject to the direction of the Secretary of Defense.

(4) The Director of NSA shall make such reports and furnish such information from time to time to the Board, either orally or in writing, as the Board may request, and shall bring to the attention of the Board either in such reports or otherwise any new major policies or programs in advance of their adoption by him.

e. It shall also be the duty of the Board as to matters not falling within the jurisdiction of NSA;

(1) To coordinate the communications intelligence activities among all departments and agencies authorized by the President to participate therein;

(2) To initiate, to formulate policies concerning, and subject to the provisions of NSCID No. 5,[3] to supervise all arrangements with foreign governments in the field of communications intelligence; and

(3) to consider and make recommendations concerning policies relating to communications intelligence of common interest to the departments and agencies, including security standards and practices, and, for this purpose, to investigate and study the standards and practices of such departments and agencies in utilizing and protecting COMINT information.

f. Any recommendation of the Board with respect to the matters described in paragraph e above shall be binding on all departments or agencies of the Government if it is adopted by the unanimous vote of the members of the Board. Recommendations approved by a majority, but not all, of the members of the Board shall be transmitted by it to the Special Committee for such action as the Special Committee may see fit to take.

g. The Board will meet monthly, or oftener at the call of the Chairman or any member, and shall determine its own procedures.

---

[3] Document 255.

2. *A directive to the Secretary of Defense.* This directive shall include the following provisions:

a. Subject to the specific provisions of this directive, the Secretary of Defense may delegate in whole or in part authority over the Director of NSA within his department as he sees fit.

b. The COMINT mission of the National Security Agency (NSA) shall be to provide an effective, unified organization and control of the communications intelligence activities of the United States conducted against foreign governments, to provide for integrated operational policies and procedures pertaining thereto. As used in this directive, the terms "communications intelligence" or "COMINT" shall be construed to mean all procedures and methods used in the interception of communications other than foreign press and propaganda broadcasts and the obtaining of information from such communications by other than the intended recipients,[4] but shall exclude censorship and the production and dissemination of finished intelligence.

c. NSA shall be administered by a Director, designated by the Secretary of Defense after consultation with the Joint Chiefs of Staff, who shall serve for a minimum term of 4 years and who shall be eligible for reappointment. The Director shall be a career commissioned officer of the armed services on active or reactivated status, and shall enjoy at least 3-star rank during the period of his incumbency.

d. Under the Secretary of Defense, and in accordance with approved policies of USCIB, the Director of NSA shall be responsible for accomplishing the mission of NSA. For this purpose all COMINT collection and production resources of the United States are placed under his operational and technical control. When action by the Chiefs of the operating agencies of the Services or civilian departments or agencies is required, the Director shall normally issue instructions pertaining to COMINT operations through them. However, due to the unique technical character of COMINT operations, the Director is authorized to issue direct to any operating elements under his operational control task assignments and pertinent instructions which are within the capacity of such elements to accomplish. He shall also have direct access to, and direct communication with, any elements of the Service or civilian COMINT agencies on any other matters of operational and technical control as may be necessary, and he is authorized to obtain such information and intelligence material from them as he may require. All instructions issued by the Director under the authority provided in this paragraph shall be mandatory, subject only to appeal to the Secretary of Defense by the Chief of Service or head of civilian department or agency concerned.

---

[4] See Public Law 513–81st Congress 1950. [Footnote in the original.]

e. Specific responsibilities of the Director of NSA include the following:

(1) Formulating necessary operational plans and policies for the conduct of the U.S. COMINT activities.

(2) Conducting COMINT activities, including research and development, as required to meet the needs of the departments and agencies which are authorized to receive the products of COMINT.

(3) Determining, and submitting to appropriate authorities, requirements for logistic support for the conduct of COMINT activities, together with specific recommendations as to what each of the responsible departments and agencies of the Government should supply.

(4) Within NSA's field of authorized operations prescribing requisite security regulations covering operating practices, including the transmission, handling and distribution of COMINT material within and among the COMINT elements under his operational or technical control; and exercising the necessary monitoring and supervisory control, including inspections if necessary, to ensure compliance with the regulations.

(5) Subject to the authorities granted the Director of Central Intelligence under NSCID No. 5, conducting all liaison on COMINT matters with foreign governmental communications intelligence agencies.

f. To the extent he deems feasible and in consonance with the aims of maximum over-all efficiency, economy, and effectiveness, the Director shall centralize or consolidate the performance of COMINT functions for which he is responsible. It is recognized that in certain circumstances elements of the Armed Forces and other agencies being served will require close COMINT support. Where necessary for this close support, direct operational control of specified COMINT facilities and resources will be delegated by the Director, during such periods and for such tasks as are determined by him, to military commanders or to the Chiefs of other agencies supported.

g. The Director shall exercise such administrative control over COMINT activities as he deems necessary to the effective performance of his mission. Otherwise, administrative control of personnel and facilities will remain with the departments and agencies providing them.

h. The Director shall make provision for participation by representatives of each of the departments and agencies eligible to receive COMINT products in those offices of NSA where priorities of intercept and processing are finally planned.

i. The Director shall have a civilian deputy whose primary responsibility shall be to ensure the mobilization and effective employment of the best available human and scientific resources in the field of cryptologic research and development.

j. Nothing in this directive shall contravene the responsibilities of the individual departments and agencies for the final evaluation of COMINT information, its synthesis with information from other sources, and the dissemination of finished intelligence to users.

3. The special nature of COMINT activities requires that they be treated in all respects as being outside the framework of other or general intelligence activities. Orders, directives, policies, or recommendations of any authority of the Executive Branch relating to the collection, production, security, handling, dissemination, or utilization of intelligence, and/or classified material, shall not be applicable to COMINT activities, unless specifically so stated and issued by competent departmental or agency authority represented on the Board. Other National Security Council Intelligence Directives to the Director of Central Intelligence shall be construed as non-applicable to COMINT activities, unless the National Security Council has made its directive specifically applicable to COMINT.[5]

---

[5] Pursuant to this revision of NSCID No. 9, the National Security Agency was established on November 4.

---

133. Report by the Psychological Strategy Board[1]

PSB D–34   Washington, October 30, 1952.

NATIONAL PSYCHOLOGICAL EFFORT FOR THE
PERIOD JULY 1, 1952 THROUGH SEPTEMBER 30, 1952

[Omitted here are a title page, a copy of the November 3 transmittal memorandum from Director Alan G. Kirk to NSC Executive Secretary Lay, and a Table of Contents.]

I. Significant Psychological Activities During the
Period Under Review

1. The Board presents below a brief evaluative summary of psychological activities during the reporting period on the part of the departments and agencies responsible for psychological operations.

Capabilities by Area

2. Some progress toward our psychological goals has been achieved in certain areas. Wide geographical gaps remain, however, in

---

[1] Source: National Archives, RG 59, S/S–NSC Files: Lot 62 D 333, PSB D–34. Top Secret; Security Information; Eyes Only.

our capabilities for making an immediately effective psychological contribution to the reduction and retraction of Soviet power and influence. These gaps include the USSR itself, Communist China and most of the European satellites. In other areas there has been progress, especially in building capabilities for future development.

3. Radio broadcasting currently is the major active element being employed in the psychological field against the USSR. The Russian "jamming" continues to be a serious obstacle, and poses a problem in the whole field of communications. Insofar as Communist China is concerned, the situation is about the same but probably with less receptivity due to shortages of receiving facilities among the masses.

Anti-American Attitudes

4. In the free world and especially in Western Europe, specific grievances and generalized discontents continue to find expression in anti-American sentiments and resentments of overt United States propaganda and pressure. During the reporting period a substantial increase was made in the volume of guidance and support material for indirect and non-attributable propaganda. However, the above trend makes clear the importance of still further increasing our efforts to develop indirect and non-attributable information activities.

Western Europe

5. The benefactor-beneficiary relationship in this area continues to cause difficulty for our psychological efforts to develop attitudes favorable to the position-of-strength strategy. European enthusiasm continues to lag for institutions looked on as specifically military, i.e., NATO and EDC. However, U.S. psychological action has contributed to an increasing awareness of the communist danger in some countries, notably France and Sweden; to the development of pro-integration attitudes in Western Germany; and to progress toward European functional and political unity. All these gains, taken together with the growth of military strength in Europe, contributed to counteracting the spread of neutralist sentiments.

Middle East

6. The political crisis in Iran has materially reduced U.S. capabilities to influence the present trend of events in that country, though some limited results of non-attributable activities are reported. The danger of further deterioration in Iran emphasizes the importance of rapid preparation of psychological activities in neighboring countries, where repercussions of such deterioration would be felt. In Egypt, the political crisis similarly reduced current capabilities, but the present situation contains both favorable and unfavorable elements that make the future uncertain. In the area as a whole, little progress in the psy-

chological field can be reported for the quarter toward the achievement of national policy objectives. A notable contribution to the national psychological effort in the area, however, was the airlift by the United States Air Force of some 3,800 Moslem pilgrims from Beirut to Jidda.

Far East

7. In Southeast Asia, awareness of United States aid was increased appreciably during the reporting period by the psychological impact of TCA and MSA agricultural, public health, and other aid programs. Psychological capabilities in Southeast Asia have been expanded, especially in the non-attributable field, but little increase in current effectiveness is reported. The tendency in the area to identify the United States with European colonial powers, and with indigenous leadership groups which are opposed by revolutionary nationalist movements, continues to present a psychological obstacle. In Japan, certain non-attributable activities in the labor field continue to make progress.

Korea

8. Aside from direct psychological warfare in support of hostilities, the psychological effort in Korea has exerted pressure on the communists for an armistice and has stressed the principle of voluntary repatriation of prisoners of war. This principle has gained widespread acceptance in the non-communist world.

"Hate America" Propaganda

9. All the reporting departments and agencies have been concerned with combatting the Soviet-Communist "Hate America" propaganda campaign. A large volume of guidance and support material on this subject was provided for both overt and non-attributable propaganda channels. Emphasis was placed on the absurdity and evil purpose of the hate campaign. Special steps were taken to coordinate the release by the Department of Defense and its components of information on biological and chemical warfare. The effectiveness of these activities cannot be gauged in isolation from other United States operations.

Military Assets for the "Cold War"

10. A number of actions and programs of the Department of Defense and the military services during the reporting period, particularly in Western Europe and the Middle East, illustrate the type of contribution these services can make to the national psychological effort. However, it is noted that there remains an unexploited potential for the use of military psychological warfare assets in support of approved national peacetime programs; but that considerable difficulty is encountered in exploiting this potential in the absence of specific authority and missions upon which military psychological activities in peacetime may be based. The feasibility of making such a delineation is under study.

[Omitted here are Part II, "The Work of the PSB;" Part III, "Summaries of Reports": A. Department of State, B. Department of Defense, C. Central Intelligence Agency, and D. Field Representatives of Mutual Security Agency; and Annexes A and B.]

134. Editorial Note

On November 5, 1952, James S. Lay, Jr., Executive Secretary of the National Security Council, transmitted a "Key Data Book" prepared by the NSC Reporting Unit to President Truman. This briefing book contained sections on the national psychological program and the foreign intelligence program. For text, see *Foreign Relations, 1952–1954*, volume II, Part 1, pages 165–181.

135. Memorandum From the Executive Secretary of the National Security Council (Lay) to the National Security Council[1]

Washington, November 13, 1952.

SUBJECT

Procedure for NSC 10/5 Matters

At the request of the Director of Central Intelligence, his memorandum outlining the procedures which the Psychological Strategy Board has agreed to follow in carrying out its responsibilities under NSC 10/5,[2] is transmitted herewith for the information of the statutory members of the Council.

It is requested that special security precautions be taken in the handling of this memorandum.

James S. Lay, Jr.

---

[1] Source: Truman Library, Papers of Harry S. Truman, President's Secretary's Files, Subject File. Top Secret. Copies were sent to the Chairman of the Joint Chiefs of Staff, the Director of Central Intelligence (without enclosure), and the Director of the Psychological Strategy Board (without enclosure).

[2] For NSC 10/5, see Document 90.

Annex

Memorandum From Director of Central Intelligence Smith to the Members of the Psychological Strategy Board[3]

Washington, October 30, 1952.

SUBJECT

Procedure for NSC 10/5 Matters

In the field of unconventional and psychological operations the Central Intelligence Agency is an executive and operating agency charged with carrying out projects in support of national policies. These projects include political and paramilitary operations, the general desirability of which have been determined by the senior departments of the Executive Branch of the Government. As an operating agent for these departments, CIA requires more than policy guidance. The programs and major projects which it proposes to undertake in furthering national policy should be carefully scrutinized before final approval, and the net value of the operations themselves should be periodically assessed by some authority outside the Agency, but representative both of it and of the interested executive departments. The mounting cost of these operations makes such prior assessment and continuous audit a matter of great urgency.

Under the existing mechanism for providing policy guidance and program approval, the Agency has continued in the position of having to assume too much responsibility and authority. While in the field of cold war both vision and imagination are essential, yet these qualities must be controlled by selective judgment of a detached, objective authority.

It is inevitable that cold war operations will continue over a long period of time. They involve activities which do not lend themselves to precise evaluation and it is impossible to judge in absolute terms the successes or failures of particular programs. Unlike military operations which require the continuous and increasing application of force toward an abrupt and conclusive ending, activities of this type require a

---

[3] Top Secret; Security Information. For an earlier draft of this memorandum and Joyce's comments on it, see Document 129. There had been considerable discussion of the inadequacies of the PSB preceding this memorandum. Documentation is in National Archives, RG 59, Central Files 1950–54, 100.4–PSB/9–352, and ibid., S/S-NSC Files: Lot 62 D 333.

fluctuating effort with no clear termination in prospect. For this reason, it is all the more important that they should not be undertaken unless all concerned are satisfied as to their desirability.

The responsibilities in their respective departments of the individuals who make up the PSB, and the demands made upon their time, are such as to preclude their giving detailed study, analysis and review to the covert operations of CIA. There is needed a method by which these persons can depend, in the exercise of their responsibilities as members of PSB, on the recommendations of qualified subordinates, reserving their personal detailed consideration for those cases and matters which, by their nature, require their direct attention.

Here I have in mind the provision of a few highly qualified officers upon whom the principals could rely completely as their technical advisers, and whom their respective departments would accept in that status. It would be essential that these selected officers have competence to speak with the greatest degree of authority compatible with the individual responsibilities of the members of the PSB on the various matters to be considered, both in their capacity as advisers and staff officers of the three principals and as representatives of the departments from which they are seconded. Time would be lost and insecurity would result from formal reference of cold war projects to the routine machinery of the major departments, since this would have the inevitable result of allowing these matters to get down into the depths of departmental staffs and to be fought over and widely discussed by a large number of relatively junior officials. Hence, the selected staff officers would have to be held responsible by the principals for the necessary amount of coordinating and checking within their departments.

The Board set up a Panel in its paper dated February 20, 1952, subject: "Procedure for Handling 10/5 Matters in PSB".[4] It is not equipped nor staffed for prompt and decisive action. Panels of this size and nature tend to be slowed down by procedural matters, and their energy dissipated.

I believe a smaller group consisting of one representative from each of the Departments of State and Defense and CIA, and with the Director of PSB as permanent chairman, can produce the results we desire, provided these representatives have the work of this group to which they are assigned as their primary responsibility, to take priority over any other work even, if necessary, to the exclusion of other duties. I believe the Joint Chiefs of Staff should provide an advisor to this Group and the Departments and Agency should furnish aides and clerical assistance as may be necessary.

---

[4] Document 104.

I would stress to each Member of the Board the importance of selecting a high-quality representative for this Group. Representatives on the present Panel are excellent, but unhappily will not be available to us much longer. Replacements must be found of similar stature, and who will have the complete confidence of their respective departments and agency. Needless to say, they require full support from the very top. The success of this project will depend upon the persons selected by us.

Specifically, I recommend the Board amend its previous decisions in this field and follow the procedure set forth below except in such cases as may be otherwise provided by the President.

(1) Each Board member should designate as a member of a reviewing group a senior representative from his department or agency who will be competent to represent such member in the review of NSC 10/5 programs and projects and to make recommendations thereon. When designated, such individual should be fully empowered to obtain quick, responsive and effective action on any such program and project from any level of his department. The work incident to his assignment to this group should have priority over any other work so that he will be sufficiently free of other duties to give all the time necessary for such review. In the case of the Department of Defense, a general or flag officer representative of the Joint Chiefs of Staff should also be designated as military adviser to the reviewing group.

(2) The Director of PSB should chair the reviewing group.

(3) The reviewing group should not only review NSC 10/5 programs and major projects in the first instance and recommend their approval or disapproval either in whole or in part, but should also periodically review such programs and projects and recommend whether they are to be continued or discontinued, speeded or slowed, increased or decreased.

(4) The reviewing group should propose to the PSB such amendments to the present 10/5 Procedure as will implement the above recommendations, and thereafter propose to the PSB any further procedures which will enable the group efficiently to expedite its review responsibility.

(5) Final action in each case will be taken by the PSB.

If this procedure is concurred in, I recommend that it be brought formally to the notice of the National Security Council as the method which will be followed by the Board in carrying out its responsibilities under NSC 10/5.

Walter B. Smith[5]

---

[5] Printed from a copy that indicates Smith signed the original.

136. Memorandum From the Director of the National Security Agency (Canine) and Representatives of the Military Services and Joint Chiefs of Staff to Secretary of Defense Lovett[1]

Washington, November 20, 1952.

SUBJECT

Formal Implementation of the Provisions of NSCID No. 9 Revised[2]

REFERENCE

Secretary of Defense Memorandum of 4 November 1952,[3] subject: Interim Implementation of NSCID No. 9 Revised

1. Pursuant to the requirements expressed in paragraph 3 of the reference, a working group was formed and developed the inclosed directives.

2. The proposed directives, concurred in by the undersigned, are submitted for your approval.

3. In accordance with paragraph 1d of the reference, a list of directives, orders, or instructions relating to Communications Intelligence matters issued by any authorities within the Department of Defense inconsistent or at variance with the provisions of NSCID No. 9 Revised or with the proposed implementing directives inclosed herewith will be forwarded as soon as compiled.

Ralph J. Canine
Major General, US Army
Director, National Security Agency
Chairman

Robinson E. Duff
Major General, USA
Representing the Secretary of the Army

L.S. Howeth
Captain, USN
Representing the Secretary of the Navy

John B. Ackerman
Brigadier General, USAF
Representing the Secretary of the Air Force

---

[1] Source: National Security Agency, Center for Cryptologic History, Series V, A.28. Top Secret; Security Information.

[2] See Document 132. NSCID No. 9 Revised is printed as Document 257.

[3] Not found.

Edward H. Porter
Brigadier General, USAF
Representing the Joint Chiefs of Staff

Enclosure

Memorandum From Secretary of Defense Lovett[5]

Washington, December 5, 1952.

MEMORANDUM FOR THE

Secretary of the Army
Secretary of the Navy
Secretary of the Air Force
Joint Chiefs of Staff
Director, Communications-Electronics
Director, National Security Agency

SUBJECT

Implementation of NSCID No. 9 Revised

REFERENCES

(a) NSCID No. 9 Revised, dated 24 October 1952
(b) Memorandum of 4 November 1952 from Secretary of Defense subject:
Interim Implementation of NSCID No. 9 Revised

1. This Directive is issued for the purpose of implementing the provisions of reference (a) and supersedes reference (b).

2. The National Security Agency (NSA) is hereby established as an agency within the framework of the Department of Defense with the mission assigned to it in reference (a). For the purposes of this Directive, NSA will be understood to consist of the Headquarters, subordinate units, and facilities, including the personnel thereof, that are specifically assigned or attached to, or provided for, NSA by the Secretary of Defense or other competent authority, and over which the Director, NSA, exercises administrative, operational and technical control.

3. Pursuant to the provisions of reference (a), all Communications Intelligence (COMINT) collection and production resources of the Department of Defense are hereby placed under the operational and technical control of the Director, NSA.

4. The Director, NSA, will arrange with the appropriate authorities of other departments and agencies of the government for his assumption

---

[5] Top Secret; Security Information. Copies were sent to the Secretary of State, Director of Central Intelligence, and the Director of the Federal Bureau of Investigation. The date is handwritten on the enclosure.

of operational and technical control of the COMINT collection and COMINT production resources of those departments and agencies.

5. All military and civilian personnel, funds, records, equipment, facilities, and other support available to or authorized for the Armed Forces Security Agency (AFSA) are hereby made available to and authorized for the National Security Agency. Arrangements heretofore in effect for the provision of personnel, fiscal and other support for AFSA shall continue in effect for NSA unless otherwise modified.

6. All directives, orders or instructions relating to COMINT matters issued by any authorities within the Department of Defense inconsistent or at variance with the provisions of reference (a) will be immediately brought to the attention of the Secretary of Defense by the initiating authorities and/or the Director, NSA.

7. In fulfilling his assigned responsibilities, the Director, NSA, will be guided by the provisions of reference (a) and he will:

a. Transmit the budget estimates and civilian manpower requirements of NSA, as approved by the Secretary of Defense, to appropriate authorities for inclusion in designated appropriations of the Military Departments or the Office of the Secretary of Defense. These approved estimates and manpower requirements will not be subject to review by the Military Departments.

b. Conform to the personnel, fiscal, and property accounting policies of the Secretary of Defense. A departmental property account is authorized for NSA.

c. Review COMINT requirements, programs and budget estimates of the Military Departments, insure the provision of an adequate balanced program, and support these items in cooperation with the Departments concerned.

d. Establish procedures for production and procurement of specialized COMINT equipments under the cognizance of NSA.

e. Assure to the maximum practicable extent, in consonance with Department of Defense policies, standardization of specialized COMINT equipments and facilities.

f. Determine and make known to the Director, Communications-Electronics, the requirements for rapid communications to meet the needs of NSA. These will include a statement of anticipated traffic loads and such additional data as will assist in fulfilling the requirements.

g. Determine and make known to appropriate authorities courier service requirements as needed for the expeditious handling of COMINT traffic and material.

h. In consonance with the policies of the Department of Defense, provide means for review, coordination, and approval of all COMINT research and development requirements.

i. Establish a research and development program adequate to accomplish the COMINT mission, and control the assignment and implementation of all COMINT research and development projects.

j. In consonance with the policies of the Department of Defense, provide technical guidance and support for COMINT training conducted by the Military Departments and, to insure necessary levels of technical competence, prescribe minimum standards for their COMINT training curricula.

k. Conduct necessary specialized and advance COMINT training.

8. With reference to paragraph 7f above, the Director, Communications-Electronics, with the assistance of the Joint Communications-Electronics Committee, shall have the authority and responsibility for insuring that the Military Departments, within their capabilities, fulfill the military communications requirements of NSA.

9. The COMINT responsibilities of the Military Departments will include, among others, the following:

a. Providing the necessary COMINT facilities and resources for the support of military operations and of the National COMINT effort in accordance with assigned responsibilities.

b. Procuring, organizing, training, equipping, administering, budgeting, and providing logistic support to their respective COMINT units. This will include provision of adequate reserve programs to meet emergency or wartime requirements.

c. Within the limits prescribed by public law and Department of Defense policies, assigning military personnel to NSA for a minimum period of thirty-six months. Longer assignment of specially qualified personnel is authorized as may be arranged with the Department concerned. The Military Departments may add, withdraw, or substitute personnel within the authorized personnel strength of NSA, subject to approval by the Director, NSA.

d. Advising the Director, NSA, regarding close support matters and recommending the number and composition of COMINT units needed to fulfill the close support requirements of the Departments.

e. Performing COMINT collection and production tasks as specified by the Director, NSA.

f. Submitting COMINT research and development requirements directly to the Director, NSA, for his action, and accomplishing such COMINT research and development and service testing as approved or assigned by him. This does not preclude the Military Departments from initiating and pursuing, subject to prompt notification to and approval by the Director, NSA, such research and development as may be necessary to support their COMINT activities.

10. Where delegation of control is required in close support of a military commander, the Director, NSA, will normally delegate operational control of specified COMINT facilities and resources to the COMINT agency of the appropriate Military Department for assignment to a subordinate unit.

11. The Director, NSA, is authorized to make requests of the Joint Chiefs of Staff, the Military Departments, and all other government agencies and activities for information and assistance which his functions and responsibilities may require and to furnish such agencies and activities with information and assistance as appropriate.

Lovett[6]

---

[6] Printed from a copy that indicates Lovett signed the original.

Enclosure

Memorandum From Secretary of Defense Lovett[7]

Washington, undated.

MEMORANDUM FOR THE
> Secretary of the Army
> Secretary of the Navy
> Secretary of the Air Force
> Joint Chiefs of Staff
> Director, Communications-Electronics
> Director, National Security Agency

SUBJECT
> Interim Responsibility for Communication Security

Pending the issuance of additional instructions, the responsibilities for Communication Security (COMSEC) activities and related matters assigned to the Director, Armed Forces Security Agency, shall continue to be assigned to the Director, National Security Agency.

Lovett[8]

---

[7] Top Secret; Security Information.
[8] Printed from a copy that indicates Lovett signed the original.

---

137.   Memorandum From the Acting Deputy Director for Intelligence of the Central Intelligence Agency (Amory) to Director of Central Intelligence Smith[1]

Washington, November 25, 1952.

SUBJECT
> Senior Staff Action on the Summary Evaluation

---

[1] Source: Central Intelligence Agency, Office of the Deputy Director for Intelligence, Job 80–R01440R, Box 3, Folder 10. Top Secret. A handwritten notation on the memorandum indicates it was prepared in the Office of National Estimates. A stamped notation indicates that Smith saw the memorandum on November 26.

1. The Senior Staff approved paragraphs a. and b. of Enclosure A as its recommendation for action at tomorrow's meeting of the NSC.

2. In paragraph a., the reference to specific limitations of the summary evaluation as noted in your transmittal memorandum[2] was deleted. Various individual members of the Senior Staff felt that there are still other defects in the summary evaluation.

3. In paragraph b., your proposal for the preparation of terms of reference was adopted, and it was further recommended that the NSC instruct you to report on the needs for improved machinery for preparing a more adequate evaluation of the USSR's net capability to inflict direct injury on the United States.

4. The main point of controversy was your recommendation c., as clarified in paragraph c. of the attached Enclosure. On this point the Senior Staff decided to take no action at this time, on the understanding that you might feel free to put the proposal before the NSC yourself.

5. The opposition to a Senior Staff recommendation at this time came primarily from the military. JCS has just submitted to the Secretary of Defense a lengthy memorandum on the subject,[3] which it was felt could not be adequately considered prior to the NSC meeting. It was evident from Admiral Wooldridge's oral paraphrase that the JCS view is that no additional machinery is needed to produce "Commander's Estimates," the JCS being the agency responsible for and capable of producing such estimates.

Robert Amory, Jr.

Enclosure A[4]

SENIOR STAFF RECOMMENDATIONS FOR NSC ACTION

The National Security Council:

5. a.[5] Receives the summary evaluation, *Net Capability of the USSR to Injure the Continental U.S.*, as an initial effort in response to the NSC Directive issued by NSC Action No. 543,[6] and notes that it is characterized by a number of limitations and inadequacies, including the fact

---

[2] Not found, but presumably it transmitted to the NSC a revised version of Smith's paper attached to Document 131.

[3] Not found.

[4] Top Secret.

[5] The number "5" is handwritten in front of paragraphs a, b, and c.

[6] Document 86.

that developments since the evaluation was prepared have rendered it, in part, out of date.

5. b. Instructs the Director of Central Intelligence, in collaboration with the Joint Chiefs of Staff, the Interdepartmental Intelligence Conference, the Interdepartmental Committee on Internal Security and Officials of other governmental bodies as required, to prepare for early submission to the NSC, terms of reference for a more adequate evaluation of the USSR's net capability to inflict direct injury on the United States, and recommendations concerning the machinery necessary to produce for the NSC such a coordinated evaluation.

DCI RECOMMENDATION (No Senior Staff Action)

5. c. Instructs the Director of Central Intelligence, in collaboration with Officials of other governmental bodies as required, to examine the adequacies of the present machinery, and to make recommendations to the NSC concerning the character of any new machinery that may be required in order to produce for the NSC coordinated evaluations, in the nature of "Commander's Estimates," of the Soviet Bloc's net capabilities and probable courses of action vis à vis the United States' security interests. Such evaluations require the integration of national intelligence with adequate military, political, and economic operational information on the United States' capabilities and contemplated courses of action.[7]

---

[7] For the discussion and the decision taken at the November 26 NSC meeting, see Document 138. Additional documentation on this initiative, which led to the creation of the Special Evaluation Subcommittee of the National Security Council (NSC 140), approved by President Truman on January 19, 1953, is in Foreign Relations, 1952–1954, vol II., Part 1, pp. 205–208.

138.   Memorandum for President Truman of Discussion at the 126th Meeting of the National Security Council[1]

Washington, November 26, 1952.

[Omitted here are a short paragraph that indicates the President presided at the meeting and discussion of agenda item 1: The Situation in the Far East.]

2. *A Project To Provide a More Adequate Basis for Planning for the Security of the United States* (Memo for NSC from Acting Executive Secretary, same subject, dated October 21, 1952; Memos for NSC from Executive Secretary, same subject, dated November 25 and 26, 1952, and August 30, 1951;[2] Memo for NSC from Executive Secretary, subject: "Summary Evaluation of the Net Capability of the USSR to Injure the Continental United States", dated November 25, 1952;[3] NSC Action No. 543;[4] SE–14)[5]

When the President turned to the second item on the Agenda Mr. Lay called the Council's attention to the views of the Joint Chiefs of Staff on the report and to the latest changes recommended by the Director of Central Intelligence at the instance of the Internal Security Committees and finally, to the two alternative recommendations made by the Senior Staff to replace the first two recommendations by the Director of Central Intelligence. Mr. Lay pointed out that the Senior Staff had taken no action on the third recommendation in General Smith's memorandum.

The President then asked General Smith to comment on the proposals in his memorandum. After explaining briefly the background of the present evaluation, General Smith summarized what he had heard of the discussions in the Senior Staff on the first two of his three recommendations and called the Council's attention to his most recent revision of his third recommendation, which was at this point distributed to the members of the Council. General Smith then turned to the views of the Joint Chiefs of Staff and stated that he agreed with a number of the points made therein and disagreed with others. Firstly, there could be no question of the need for the production of so-called "Commander's Estimates" for the use of the President and the National

---

[1] Source: Truman Library, President's Secretary's Files, National Security Council. Top Secret; Security Information. Drafted on November 28, presumably by Lay.

[2] None of these memoranda has been found, but presumably they transmitted to the NSC versions of and comments on the paper attached to Document 131.

[3] Not found.

[4] Document 86.

[5] See footnote 3, Document 131.

Security Council. The Joint Chiefs, said General Smith, do not believe that the production of such estimates requires the creation of any new machinery. With this view General Smith said he could not agree, but added that if the present evaluation actually met all the requirements of the President and the Council there was, of course, nothing more to be done.

General Smith then noted that the Joint Chiefs of Staff did not believe that the Director of Central Intelligence was the appropriate official to prepare Commander's Estimates. With this view General Smith found himself in agreement, but he went on to say that he did not think that the Joint Chiefs of Staff were, themselves, the appropriate body to prepare the kind of estimate which the President and the Council required. The data which must be amassed to provide the kind of report that was required would by no means be purely military data. Those agencies of the Government which were concerned with passive defense, civilian defense, sabotage and the like, were also directly or indirectly involved in the preparation of such estimates. Plainly, he continued, the problem was too large and too complicated for any one Government agency to solve by itself. It seemed obvious to General Smith that the National Security Council alone was the proper agency to guide and coordinate such studies. Obviously it could not do this directly, but it could do so by calling on the instrumentalities available to it. With all deference to the Joint Chiefs of Staff, concluded General Smith, the problem which concerned the Council transcends the purely military sphere, although General Smith conceded that it might well be possible, as suggested by the Joint Chiefs of Staff, to have that body monitor such a study provided the National Security Council was assured that the Joint Chiefs of Staff would make use, in its preparation, of the resources of all the Government agencies which were required.

The President then turned to Secretary Foster for his comment, stating that the problem was obviously very controversial.

Secretary Foster said he would prefer to listen first to the views of Mr. Gorrie, Mr. Wadsworth and others before stating his own.

Mr. Gorrie[6] expressed general agreement with the views stated by General Smith and said that he agreed with the recommendations offered to the Council by the Senior NSC Staff.

Mr. Wadsworth[7] also expressed agreement with the view of General Smith that the civilian agencies would have very significant contributions to make in the preparation of such evaluations in the future. Mr. Wadsworth further pointed out that he was not in a position to be

---

[6] Jack Gorrie, Chairman of the National Security Resources Board.

[7] James J. Wadsworth, Acting Administrator of the Federal Civil Defense Administration.

as clear on this problem as he would have liked, since he had not been permitted to examine the basic studies prepared by the Joint Chiefs and others, to back up the conclusions which appeared in the current report. Mr. Wadsworth concluded by stating his anxiety to be of maximum use in any future attempts along these lines.

Again called upon for his views, Secretary Foster stated that it seemed to him that there were two fundamental points at issue. The first of these was the adequacy of the present report on the net capability of the Soviet Union to inflict damage on the United States. Secretary Foster said he was frank to admit that there were serious gaps in this report as far as it constituted the basis for planning United States courses of action. Some of these shortcomings, he added, derived from the very nature of the beast. Such evaluations as the one in question naturally involved the war plans of the United States. These plans are, of course, very sensitive and the Chiefs of Staff quite properly leaned over backward to protect the security of these plans. The inevitable result was to create difficulties for the civilian agencies, though it seemed to him that these agencies could not appropriately expect the Joint Chiefs to reveal the details of such plans. However, continued Secretary Foster, he felt certain that he was speaking for the Joint Chiefs of Staff when he stated that they would make available everything that is really necessary to the production of this type of study to the appropriate civilian officials if the latter were in a position to establish their need to know. Furthermore, continued Secretary Foster, the Joint Chiefs had expressed their readiness to provide oral presentations on the problem to whatever group of the National Security Council it was determined should receive such information. All-in-all, said Secretary Foster, the present methods for producing such estimates were the best that had been found so far and he believed, as a first attempt, the present paper represented real progress even if it were obvious that further progress was necessary. As a suggestion to that end, Secretary Foster thought an ad hoc committee should be set up to take a careful look at the problem raised by General Smith's memorandum and to try to determine whether further evaluations of the type under consideration should be coordinated by the Joint Chiefs of Staff or the Director of Central Intelligence, or by an augmented NSC staff.

Summing up, Secretary Foster said that he recommended that the Council accept the first recommendation proposed by the Senior Staff. As to the second Senior Staff recommendation, with respect to the preparation of new terms of reference, there was some question as to whether the Council ought to accept it. Whether, as Secretary Foster put it, they patient can actually diagnose his own disease. Nevertheless, Secretary Foster stated that he had no specific recommendation to substitute for the one proposed by the Senior Staff.

The President then asked General Bradley if he desired to make any comment.

General Bradley stated that he did not differ fundamentally with the views expressed by General Smith. On the whole he was inclined to believe that the NSC Staff was the group best fitted to undertake studies such as these in the future. No single agency could do such studies and no single agency should try. As to the furnishing of information on United States capabilities and possible courses of action in the military field, General Bradley emphasized that the Joint Chiefs were wholly in favor of the "need to know" rule on sensitive material. Within this reservation, however, the Chiefs were prepared to reveal whatever was necessary for the preparation of such studies. In point of fact, there were too many people who were curious about our war plans and had no legitimate interest in them. General Bradley promised that the Joint Chiefs would do anything in their power in order to achieve the kind of estimate needed, but would only monitor the effort as a last resort.

Asked for his views by the President, Secretary Bruce stated briefly that he was in agreement with the recommendations proposed by the Senior Staff.

General Smith then entered the discussion with the statement that he was sure the Council could clean this matter up and that the differences could be ironed out. This was, he said, a phase of the old argument between G–2 and G–3. He illustrated the dilemma with which he had been confronted in carrying out the task of preparing the present report by noting that he had recently required certain assumptions with respect to the civil defense capabilities of the USSR in the contingency of an attack by the United States. We obtained these assumptions, he stated, from the Joint Strategic planners orally, but when we came to cast up the score and to write these vital assumptions into the report, this was not permitted because the Joint Chiefs of Staff had not acted on these assumptions. It was impossible to prepare a study of the net capability of the USSR to damage the United States under such procedures. Nevertheless, continued General Smith, by the use of assumptions supplied by the military it was certainly possible to prepare an adequate evaluation without jeopardizing the security of war plans.

The President stated that the current discussion had been extremely interesting and productive, but that it seemed to him that the problem posed in General Smith's third recommendation ought to have more study before the Council reached any conclusions on it. He expressed the hope that all the requisite agencies would get together to provide a reasonable basis for Council action at a future meeting.

General Smith said that he thought it would be most helpful if Mr. Amory, as a representative of the Director of Central Intelligence, could sit down with representatives of the Joint Chiefs of Staff in order to explain what was needed to achieve the right result.

With this proposal Secretary Foster expressed agreement and added that he, himself, would be glad to talk with Mr. Amory.

Mr. Lay then inquired whether it was the desire of the Council to accept the two recommendations proposed by the Senior Staff, but to defer action on the third recommendation proposed by General Smith and amended by the paper which he had circulated earlier in the meeting. The Council concurred in Mr. Lay's understanding of the desired action.

Mr. Murray,[8] speaking for the Attorney General, stated that he had one small point which involved the transposition of the words "as required" in the second recommendation by the Senior Staff. Mr. Murray stated that he was merely anxious to be assured that it was requisite for the Director of Central Intelligence to collaborate with all the agencies mentioned in this paragraph in the production of the next estimate.

Mr. Lay pointed out that this was the intention of the present language and the Council agreed to the wording suggested by Mr. Murray.

In conclusion, Mr. Lay stated that he desired to emphasize the fact that the NSC Staff had long recognized the need for more adequate staff studies, not only of the type which the Council was today considering, but to provide the basis for better policy statements generally. Where such studies could best be made, whether under the NSC Staff or elsewhere, was of course, he added, for the Council to decide, but there could be no doubt that the NSC Staff was generally agreed on the desirability of improvement. He felt that the NSC Staff could undertake this work, but some reorganization would be required.

The President then repeated his view that the Council could come to no firm conclusion on General Smith's final recommendation at this meeting, but that the matter should be the subject of further study.

The National Security Council:[9]

a. Received the summary evaluation, "Net Capability of the USSR to Injure the Continental United States", transmitted by the reference memorandum of October 21 and amended by the reference memorandum of November 25 on the same subject, as an initial effort in response to the NSC directive issued by NSC Action No. 543, and noted that it is characterized by a number of limitations and inadequacies,

---

[8] Not further identified.

[9] Paragraphs a–c constituted NSC Action No. 687. (National Archives, RG 59, S/S–NSC (Miscellaneous) File: Lot 66 D 95, Records of Action by the National Security Council)

including the fact that developments since the evaluation was prepared have rendered it, in part, out of date.

b. Instructed the Director of Central Intelligence, in collaboration with the Joint Chiefs of Staff, the Interdepartmental Intelligence Conference, the Interdepartmental Committee on Internal Security, and, as required, officials of other governmental bodies, to prepare for early submission to the National Security Council, terms of reference for a more adequate evaluation of the USSR's net capability to inflict direct injury on the United States, and recommendations for the machinery necessary to produce for the National Security Council such a coordinated evaluation.

c. Deferred action, pending further study, on the recommendation in paragraph 5-c of the memorandum by the Director of Central Intelligence enclosed with the reference memorandum of October 21, amended as follows by the Director of Central Intelligence and circulated at the meeting.

"c. Instruct the Director of Central Intelligence, in collaboration with Officials of other governmental bodies as required, to examine the inadequacies of the present machinery, and to make recommendations to the NSC concerning the character of any new machinery that may be required to produce for the NSC coordinated evaluations, in the nature of 'Commander's Estimates,' of the Soviet Bloc's net capabilities and probable courses of action vis-à-vis the United States' security interests. Such evaluations require the integration of national intelligence with adequate military, political, and economic operational information on the United States' capabilities and contemplated courses of action."

Note: The action in b above subsequently transmitted to the Director of Central Intelligence for implementation.

[Omitted here is discussion of agenda items 3: Reappraisal of United States Objectives and Strategy for National Security, 4: The National Psychological Effort, and 5: NSC Status of Projects.]

139. Paper Prepared by the Psychological Strategy Board[1]

PSB D–31   Washington, November 26, 1952.

A STRATEGIC CONCEPT FOR A NATIONAL PSYCHOLOGICAL PROGRAM WITH PARTICULAR REFERENCE TO COLD WAR OPERATIONS UNDER NSC 10/5[2]

1. Almost all governmental policies and actions have psychological content in that they bear on the minds and wills of other peoples. An attempt to formulate a national psychological strategy covering every intention and action having psychological impact in this sense would encompass every aspect of governmental activity. This would be an effort of unmanageable proportions. In order to formulate a national psychological strategy that will usefully subserve the national policy it is necessary to divide the task into separate aspects of manageable proportions. When we ask, "What can usefully be said about ways and means of bringing about a retraction of Soviet power and influence?" we have selected one such aspect and have stated it in such a way that we can perhaps deal with it. The following does not attempt to deal with the problems involved in the distribution of resources between cold war operations and preparations in support of overt war.

2. NSC 10/5, paragraph 1, approved "the intensification of covert operations designed in general order of emphasis to:

a. Place the maximum strain on the Soviet structure of power, including the relationships between the USSR, its satellites and Communist China; and when and where appropriate in the light of U.S. and Soviet capabilities and the risk of war, contribute to the retraction and reduction of Soviet power and influence to limits which no longer constitute a threat to U.S. security.

---

[1] Source: National Archives, RG 59, S/S–NSC Files: Lot 62 D 333, PSB D–31. Top Secret; Security Information. A draft of this paper was sent to Under Secretary of State Bruce, Deputy Secretary of Defense Foster, and Director of Central Intelligence Smith on August 20 by the Director of the PSB, who described the paper as the product of half a year's work by a high level group under Admiral Stevens. (Ibid.) In analyzing the paper for Bruce in an August 26 memorandum, Nitze stated that the chief virtue of the paper was a negative: "it admits inability . . . to propose a strategic concept which outlines a program designed to bring about a final solution of the cold war." (Ibid.) Nitze had made this same point to Stevens in a December 5, 1951, meeting (see Document 96). All ellipses in the original.

[2] In accordance with Presidential Directive of 4 April 1951, which establishes the PSB as responsible for the formulation and promulgation, as guidance to the departments and agencies represented for psychological operations of over-all national psychological objectives, policies and programs, and which defines psychological operations as including all activities under NSC 59/1 and 10/2. [Footnote in the original. For the Presidential Directive, see Document 60. For the text of NSC 59/1, see Document 2. For NSC 10/2, see *Foreign Relations, 1945–1950, Emergence of the Intelligence Establishment,* Document 292. For NSC 10/5, see Document 90.]

b. Strengthen the orientation toward the United States of the peoples and nations of the free world, and increase their capacity and will to resist Soviet domination.

c. Develop underground resistance and facilitate covert and guerrilla operations in strategic areas to the maximum practicable extent consistent with 1-a above. . . ."

3. NSC 10/5, paragraph 2, directed "the Psychological Strategy Board to assure that its strategic concept for a national psychological program includes provision for covert operations designed to achieve the objectives in paragraph 1 above."

4. It is the object of this paper to outline a strategic concept for a national psychological program with particular reference to cold war operations under NSC 10/5. These operations are primarily covert in character, but we believe a paper addressed to such operations will provide a concept valuable to overt psychological operations under NSC 59/1 as well, especially those which are concerned with bringing about the retraction of Soviet power and influence.

5. The general objective of psychological operations in the cold war can be subsumed under the general heading of contributing to the "retraction and reduction of Soviet power and influence" whether by operations designed to weaken Soviet power in the Communist orbit or by operations designed to weaken Soviet influence by strengthening the free world.

6. Our national strategy, as defined in NSC 20/4,[3] paragraph 20, is to "endeavor to achieve our general objectives by methods short of war." This national strategy calls for efforts to "encourage and promote the gradual retraction of undue Russian power and influence from the present perimeter areas around traditional Russian boundaries . . . ; to eradicate the myth by which people remote from Soviet military influence are held in a position of subservience to Moscow . . . ; (and) to create situations which will compel the Soviet government to recognize the practical undesirability of acting on the basis of its present concepts . . ."

7. In the absence of open hostilities, the cold war can be expected to continue in one form or another as long as the Soviet Union, which is to say, the Bolshevik Party, adheres to the aims and methods which it has pursued ever since its accession to power, within as well as outside the Party. Recognition of this—particularly public recognition—is necessary for understanding and support of continuity of effort. The overthrow of the Party by war or successful revolution appears to be the only certain means of forcing such changes. One is excluded, and the other so far beyond our current capabilities as to be presently unfeasible.

---

[3] For NSC 20/4, see *Foreign Relations, 1948*, vol. I, Part 2, pp. 662–669.

8. We are unable at present to propose a strategic concept which outlines a program designed to bring about a final solution of the cold war because (a) we do not have and cannot clearly foresee the time when we will have the capabilities, and (b), because without adequate capabilities the risks involved are clearly disproportionate to the probabilities of success. The time required to develop the necessary capabilities is so great that the nature of an acceptable solution cannot be determined with sufficient accuracy to serve as a guide. As our capabilities increase, flexibility and opportunism in the light of events appear presently more desirable than commitment to too specific a goal.

9. We should continue to develop our capabilities for assisting revolution and continue to re-appraise the situation. This will require both the development of further capabilities for the exploitation of existing techniques and a major program for the development of new techniques and approaches. It is possible that the cumulative effect of retraction of Soviet power and influence, together with future events and the inherent problems with which the Soviet government and the Bolshevik Party are faced may eventually bring about sufficient change in their aims and methods to provide an acceptable solution. Efforts to develop our capabilities and to bring about such a retraction as opposed to a program for a definitive solution may be regarded as the interim strategic concept for a national psychological program.

10. Within the limits imposed by the terms of our national strategy and the present level of our covert capabilities it is possible to advance certain general criteria for operations under 10/5, to test broad fields of possible covert action against these criteria, and from a combination of the two to give more precise form to the psychological operations which should be prosecuted in accordance with the interim strategic concept, and to provide an indication of priorities. Overt propaganda should give appropriate support in accordance with priorities as may be determined.

11. The general criteria which present covert operations under the interim strategic concept should meet are those of effectiveness, feasibility, acceptable risk, and flexibility.

a. *Effectiveness:* The importance of the effects which successful operations may be calculated to have in reducing Soviet influence and power or in strengthening the free world against the exertion of Soviet influence and power must be appreciable and must warrant the effort, cost and risk of the operation. In general, priorities should be proportional to anticipated effectiveness.

b. *Feasibility:* Our capabilities in terms of trained manpower or material, and local or international support, must be adequate to give reasonable promise of success to the operation in the face of such capabilities as the Communists may have to frustrate it.

c. *Acceptable risk:* The degree to which the undertaking or successful conclusion of the operations may be calculated to provoke military reaction from the Communists must be sufficiently limited as to be an acceptable risk in terms of our national strategy.

d. *Flexibility:* Operations should be of a type which lend themselves within reasonable limits to adaptation or modification to exploit such opportunities or undertake such objectives as may become possible or advisable subsequent to actual initiation of the operation.

12. There is a wide range of activity currently in process to bring about the retraction of Soviet power and influence which should continue. Many of these activities, although in themselves incapable of producing clear and incontrovertible gains, are of great value in supporting overt policies which can be expected to be effective. Omission from the following discussion of many existing projects, does not imply that they are not considered of value, but rather that the approved projects should continue as presently conceived and planned, insofar as they meet the above criteria.

13. Within the field of cold war covert operations, it is considered that greatest emphasis should be placed upon the following broad fields of activity, not necessarily in order of priority:

a. Weakening of Kremlin control over the internal assets of the Soviet-controlled bloc, and increasingly occupying the Kremlin with problems within this area.

b. Direct action to reduce subversive Soviet influence in those areas of the free world that are most immediately threatened thereby.

c. Covert manipulation of key elements in unstable countries of the free world to increase the stability and utility to the objectives of U.S. foreign policy of those countries.

14. Within these three broad fields of activity, the following categories meet the criteria outlined above and should be given greater emphasis than they are currently receiving. Detailed studies may reveal that effective action within some of these categories is beyond our capabilities. Also, events will undoubtedly indicate the desirability of concentration on other lines of effort. This will require continuous review of interim strategic policy.

a. *Disintegration of Communist Parties Outside the Iron Curtain.* Communist parties in the free world are principal vehicles for Soviet subversion. They are also much more accessible to us than are those within the Iron Curtain. By a combination of covert and overt action their effectiveness can be appreciably reduced and in some areas totally nullified. Some of the means that can be employed are (a) reduction of financial support, (b) penetration and exposure, (c) instigation of internal conflicts and dissensions among individuals and groups, (d) outlawing of local parties, (e) legal action of all types against individuals and groups, (f) promotion of ideological deviations, (g) creating and intensifying difficulties with local governments and public opinion.

Individual priority studies should be made by CIA of the detailed methods which can be most effectively employed against the CPs in France, Italy, India, Japan, Iran, and Guatemala, and an appraisal of the probable over-all effectiveness of such an effort should be made for each of those countries.

A special study should be made by CIA, similar in scope, directed towards disintegrating the influence of the CP and individual communists on the present Argentine government.

b. *Detachment of Albania.* Because of Albania's unique geographical position, its detachment from the Soviet orbit may be feasible. The principal advantage gained would be its psychological effects both in subjugated countries and in areas under intense Soviet pressure, although there would also be useful additional by-products of a military nature, especially as regards the position of Yugoslavia and Greece. It would be a demonstration that a continuing Soviet advance is not inevitable and that a retraction of Soviet power is practically possible. A preliminary estimate indicates that detachment could be accomplished by Albanian personnel and without the overt participation of Western military forces.

A detailed plan should be made [*less than 1 line not declassified*] covering each step in such action up to its successful completion, including time phasing and all logistic aspects. Estimates should be made of personnel and material requirements, together with plans for meeting them. Detailed appraisal should be made of the probable degree of secrecy that could be maintained throughout [*1½ lines not declassified*]. The extent to which preliminary disorganizing of the Albanian economy would contribute to the success of the operation should be appraised.

If such studies continue to indicate feasibility, the State Department should investigate the feasibility and effectiveness of obtaining the acquiescence or the active support of Great Britain as well as Yugoslavia, Greece and Italy, together with the practicability of reaching agreements on political objectives which would preclude such future difficulties as efforts at domination by these neighboring countries. The necessity of recognition of such a revolutionary government should be appraised, and the necessity, feasibility and timing of overt economic and logistic assistance, together with its amount and cost.

c. *Breeding Suspicion and Dissension Within the Communist System.*

The inherent suspicion and lack of mutual trust and confidence within the communist system and our own experience in exploiting them gives grounds for belief that we would be able to increase this suspicion far beyond what we have hitherto accomplished, to the point of systematic removal or elimination of personnel in important and effective positions. The communist reservoir of able and experienced personnel is not unlimited, and individuals of demonstrated power and effectiveness would be excellent targets. Many techniques are available to apply to these ends, but our access to and knowledge of conditions within the satellites indicate that the best chances of success would be obtained by breeding distrust among satellite personnel and between those individuals and Moscow, although such efforts within the Soviet Union should be included to the maximum of our capabilities. It should be noted that this category involves a narrower objective than broad attempts to disrupt the system by a variety of means other than marking individuals for suspicion and distrust. It has a definite relationship to and should be correlated with the defective program.

[1 paragraph (1½ lines) not declassified]

d. *Efforts Directed Towards Disruption of Soviet and European Satellite Economies [less than 1 line not declassified].*

The special vulnerabilities of the Soviet economic system are subject to exploitation on a strategic basis. Such exploitation can be used to produce a reduction in economic and military potential and indirectly to bring about the defection of key Communist officials. [2 *lines not declassified*]

(1) [1 *paragraph (7 lines) not declassified*]
(2) Covert activities against illegal trade channels still offer possibilities of effecting further appreciable reduction in the volume of imports of strategic commodities into the Soviet orbit, [1 *line not declassified*].
(3) A wide range of passive economic sabotage activities may be undertaken by Eastern Europeans under present conditions with relative safety. If the incentive of self-interest is added, effectiveness of such a program would be increased [2 *lines not declassified*].
(4) [1 *paragraph (6 lines) not declassified*]

e. *Covert Political Action to Strengthen Critical Free World Areas Against Developments Which Might be Favorable to Communist Objectives.*

Covert action in this category, directed largely toward covert manipulation of key individuals, should be designed to shore up and orient favorably to U.S. interests the governments of areas which are critical to U.S. interests and which are in danger of developing regimes or conditions inimical to U.S. interests. Egypt, Iran, Japan, India and certain Latin American countries should receive priority in this category.[4]

---

[4] The priority for these countries shall not be at the expense of continuing efforts in Germany, Italy and France. [Footnote in the original.]

Operations on Formosa and among the Overseas Chinese, directed towards broadening the base of support of the Chinese Nationalist Government would also fall into this category.

[1½ lines not declassified] should make concrete correlated proposals within the foregoing framework.

Recommendations

1. It is recommended that the progressive retraction and reduction of Soviet power and influence in accordance with our capabilities and subject to the limitation of acceptable risk be accepted as the interim strategic concept for a national psychological program with particular reference to cold war operations under NSC 10/5.

2. It is recommended that the responsible agencies place greatest emphasis in these operations on the three broad fields of activity identified in paragraph 13 above. This recommendation is without prejudice to those arrangements now in effect whereby a responsible agency is to make preparations for activities after D-Day in support of approved war plans.

3. It is recommended that the responsible agencies give priority within those broad fields to determining the detailed practicability and desirability of proceeding along the lines indicted under each category described in paragraph 14 above. It is further recommended that where such studies indicate that the foregoing criteria will be met, the indicated actions be given priority in both national and agency programs proportionate to their probable effectiveness.

4. It is also recommended that our covert capabilities continue to be developed with increasing vigor along all lines whose eventual employment may be expected to bring about more drastic reductions in Soviet power and influence.

5. It is also recommended that this interim strategic concept be kept under continuous review, and revised in the light of future developments at least annually and also as additional categories of action appear to meet the specified criteria.

Feasibility of Logistic Support

Acceptance of this concept is without prejudice to later logistic feasibility testing by the Department of Defense of specific courses of action which would require logistic support of that Department.

140. Memorandum From Director of Central Intelligence Smith to the Chairman of the Joint Chiefs of Staff (Bradley)[1]

Washington, December 12, 1952.

SUBJECT

Overseas CIA Logistical Support Bases

REFERENCES[2]

a) Secretary of Defense TS Memo #23579, dated 6 October 1949, Support of Covert Operations of CIA

b) TS Memo #81056 from CIA to Joint Subsidiary Plans Division/Joint Chiefs of Staff, dated 13 June 1952, subject as above

c) TS Memo #81111 from Joint Subsidiary Plans Division/Joint Chiefs of Staff to CIA, dated 26 June 1952, subject as above (SPDM–257–52)

d) TS Memo #81949 from CIA to Joint Subsidiary Plans Division/Joint Chiefs of Staff, dated 19 August 1952, subject as above

1. In accordance with NSC 10/2[3] CIA is not only charged with the mission of conducting cold war but also that of planning for covert operations in time of war in collaboration with the Joint Chiefs of Staff. It is essential to establish logistical support for hot war plans prior to D-Day. Rather than create separate parallel lines of supply for similar materiels with the military services, it is desired to continue in collaboration with the Department of Defense in the establishment of support installations, to be used not only for hot war requirements but also for CIA's cold war support. Further, it is believed appropriate that the agency should use Department of Defense hot war stocks for cold war needs on a reimbursable basis.

2. Based on our operational plans, a world-wide support base concept was formed locating the bases at military installations. The CIA

---

[1] Source: Central Intelligence Agency, Executive Registry, Job 80–B01731R, Box 8. Top Secret; Security Information. Sent through the Chief of the Joint Subsidiary Plans Division. An attached note from RWF (not identified) to DCI Smith, December 10, indicates that DD/P prepared the memorandum, which was approved in CPM, DD/P (with Wisner recommending signature), and DD/A. The note indicated that JSPD had coordinated the logistical planning and added that the military did not wish to go further with detailed planning until the JCS approved the planning concept, and signing the memorandum meant only approving the support and base concept, not the actual authorization of funds. A notation on the note indicates that Smith saw it on December 12. The enclosures, a table entitled Recapitulation for CIA Logistical Support and an earlier December 8 draft of the memorandum, are not printed. Ellipsis in the original.

[2] None of the references (a–d) was found.

[3] For NSC 10/2, see *Foreign Relations, 1945–1950, Emergence of the Intelligence Establishment,* Document 292.

base will be considered a tenant unit on the military base. It is contemplated that the major bases will be located [4½ *lines not declassified*].

3. A major logistical support base will consist of a CIA base headquarters, training, communications, medical accommodation for evacuees and storage for six months' hot war requirements as well as provide logistical support for CIA operational groups or headquarters. The latest revised estimate of requirements on a broad basis is listed in the attached enclosure. Informal planning along the lines indicated has been carried out by elements of CIA with the Joint Subsidiary Plans Division of the Joint Chiefs of Staff and the general planning is consistent with and complementary to approved plans for wartime military operations.

4. At such time as detailed plans are firm and approved by the Department of Defense and this Agency, CIA accepts the obligation to reimburse the Department of Defense for its proportionate share of these construction requirements in accordance with Reference (a) as follows:

"Personnel, Supplies, and Equipment will be transported to overseas storage points under military control and supplies and equipment will be stored and protected at such points without reimbursement where additional, extraordinary expenses to the Department of Defense are not involved. . . Where the service incurs additional, extraordinary expenses in providing transportation or establishing and maintaining at overseas points, dumps for covert operations, the CIA must make reimbursement therefor."

5. It is requested that the strategic planning of this base concept be approved, and that the military services be so advised and directed to assist in the preparation of detailed plans.

Walter B. Smith[4]

---

[4] Printed from a copy that indicates Smith signed the original.

141. Letter From the Executive Secretary of the National Security Council (Lay) to the Director of the Federal Bureau of Investigation (Hoover)[1]

Washington, December 17, 1952.

My Dear Mr. Hoover:

On October 31 you formally advised this office of certain observations in connection with National Security Council Intelligence Directive No. 9 (NSCID 9) as revised on October 24,[2] and you requested that they be brought to the attention of the appropriate members of the NSC. Those observations were, in effect, as follows:

1. The Attorney General, as Chief Legal Officer of the Government, should be a member of the Special Committee of the NSC whenever matters of interest to the Federal Bureau of Investigation (FBI) are before that Committee; and it should be made explicit that the FBI is to assist the Attorney General and the Special Committee when such matters are before the Committee.

2. The right granted to the United States Communications Intelligence Board (USCIB) "to investigate and study the standards and practices of its member agencies and departments in utilizing and protecting COMINT (communications intelligence) information" is too broad and may lead to abuse.

3. The authority granted to the Director, NSA "to have direct access to . . . any elements of the . . . civilian COMINT agencies on any matters of operational and technical control as may be necessary" also is too broad, as is the Director's authority "to obtain such information and intelligence material from (those agencies) as he may require."

With reference to the first point above, I am informed that it was the understanding when the Directive was drafted, that the Attorney General, under the established procedures of the NSC, would be a member of the Special Committee whenever matters of interest to the FBI were before that Committee; and that in such instances, the Attorney General could, as a matter of course, have the assistance of the Bureau. That understanding has been confirmed by the President when, in approving this Directive, he directed that this procedure is to be followed. NSCID 9 will be revised accordingly regarding the membership of the Special Committee.

In connection with your second and third points, the Secretaries of State and Defense acting as the Special Committee of the NSC for

---

[1] Source: National Security Agency, Center for Cryptologic History, Series XVI, C.6 (Other Staff Papers). Top Secret; Security Information. Ellipsis in the original.

[2] See Document 132. Hoover's comments have not been found.

COMINT with the assistance of the Director of Central Intelligence, have directed me to advise you as follows.

It is understood that your concern regarding these latter two points is that they might result in encroachment upon or interference with the unique responsibilities of the FBI in the internal security field and that, consequently, you desire that the FBI be granted explicit exemption from those portions of the Directive.

With specific reference to your second point, paragraph 1f of the Directive states that the Board's authority in the matter under discussion shall be binding only if it is adopted by the unanimous vote of the members of the Board. Furthermore, this paragraph prescribes that any recommendation of this sort approved by a majority, but not all, of the members of the Board shall automatically be transmitted by the Board to the Special Committee. No such action of the Board therefore can be binding on you unless you agree to it and, in the event of disagreement, the matter would be considered by the Special Committee, augmented by the Attorney General, as a matter of course and not as a matter of formal appeal on your part.

With specific reference to your third point, above, paragraph 2f of the Directive recognizes that elements of the Armed Forces and other agencies will require close COMINT support and that necessary direct operational control of specified COMINT facilities and resources will be delegated by the Director to the chiefs of other agencies. The types of operations contemplated by the FBI undoubtedly would fall within the meaning of a close support requirement for the accomplishment of your mission, in which case it would be possible for you to arrange with the Director, NSA, for the assignment to your Bureau of such facilities as are needed for this requirement.

In connection with the authority granted to the Director, NSA, to have direct access to any elements of civilian COMINT agencies and to obtain information and intelligence material from those agencies, such access is always established through mutually prescribed channels. However, the vital element of security would be eliminated if normal channels of interdepartmental exchange were prescribed for the conduct of COMINT business. On the other hand, all members of the Board would be handicapped severely if they could not participate laterally in all phases of the COMINT operation through mutually acceptable channels.

With reference to your reservation regarding the allocation of votes in USCIB, which was raised orally by your representatives in addition to the points made in your letter, this device was only designed as an administrative mechanism to provide a reasonable dividing line between civilian and non-civilian issues if such were to arise. In view of your reservation, however, the Special Committee has decided that the

FBI representative should cast two votes at Board meetings—as is provided for the representative of the Secretary of State and the Director of Central Intelligence—and that the representative of the Secretary of Defense should also cast two votes. This would equalize your voting strength with that of the other civilian members and still provide the possible advantage of the reasonable dividing line. NSCID 9 will be amended accordingly.

It may be pertinent in conclusion to review the reasons for the existence of NSCID 9. That Directive was issued for the following reasons:

1. To set forth with exactitude the fundamental principle that the COMINT activities of the U.S. are a national responsibility rather than a matter of primary interest to any one of the departments or agencies concerned.
2. To delineate clearly the broad lines of policy which will govern this mutual assumption of responsibility.
3. To reconstitute USCIB in a manner which will assure an orderly, precise, secure and effective complex of COMINT activities.
4. To set up the most rapid and equitable system which not only would give full protection to the individual agencies and departments on the Board but also would provide final adjudication, as needed, by the Chief Executive.

The Directive, amended as indicated above, would appear to accomplish the foregoing as regards all agencies participating in COMINT activities. On the other hand, excepting the FBI from adherence to portions of the Directive would weaken the Directive to a point where it would have little meaning or value because the fundamental principle of its creation would have been destroyed. Since COMINT must be set apart from the normal operations of Government and a special mechanism created to handle COMINT activities, those activities must be coordinated by the bodies which have been created to handle them—namely, the Special Committee and USCIB—on a basis of mutual responsibility with equitable representation of all interested departments and agencies.

In summary, however, nothing in the directive should be construed to encroach upon or interfere with the unique responsibilities of the Federal Bureau of Investigation in the field of internal security. This will be made explicit by adding a paragraph to this effect in NSCID 9.

Sincerely yours,

James S. Lay, Jr.[3]

---

[3] Printed from a copy that bears this typed signature.

142. **Memorandum From Robert P. Joyce of the Policy Planning Staff to the Deputy Under Secretary of State (Matthews)**[1]

Washington, December 31, 1952.

SUBJECT

[less than 1 line not declassified] Activities directed against Poland

I attach hereto a copy of Warsaw's cable No. 338 of December 27, midnight.[2] Yesterday I called [less than 1 line not declassified] to meet with me and Mr. Vedeler of EE for a discussion of the implications of this cable and the broadcast on December 29 by the Warsaw station in English Morse which sets forth the Polish line on American espionage activities in Poland, etc. I attach hereto FBIS Report No. 252,[3] which I think you will desire to read in full.

[1 paragraph (14 lines) not declassified]

At the meeting of the Consultants to OPC yesterday afternoon (General Magruder for Defense, Colonel Wright representing General Young of the JCS, and myself representing this Department), the whole Polish operation was gone into at length [less than 1 line not declassified]. The following facts and assumptions emerged:

[6 paragraphs (18½ lines) not declassified]

I need not point out that this affair represents an appalling setback [less than 1 line not declassified] the U.S. Government. There may be political repercussions which might make it exceedingly difficult or impossible for our diplomatic mission to maintain itself in Warsaw. Another telegram in from our Embassy on December 27 pointed out that the Polish Foreign Office had advised the Embassy that only American Embassy officers on the diplomatic list would be immune from Polish jurisdiction, including the provisions of the Polish legislation on espionage activity.[4] We know too little today to arrive at any conclusion as to whether [less than 1 line not declassified] activities in Poland over the past two years are directly related to recent moves indicating that the Polish authorities are moving in on the American Embassy in the same pattern that has been established in other Eastern Satellite capitals. EE is watching this entire situation closely, and I have arranged

---

[1] Source: Department of State, INR/IL Historical Files, NSC 10 Series, 1952. Top Secret. A notation on the memorandum reads: "Please return to S/P—Joyce."

[2] This telegram transmitted a Polish newspaper account that reported that Polish authorities had apprehended two U.S. spies who had parachuted from a plane into Poland. (National Archives, RG 59, Central Files 1950–54, 711.5248/12–2752)

[3] Not found.

[4] Not found.

for [*less than 1 line not declassified*] to bring in as soon as it is received all information received from abroad [*less than 1 line not declassified*].

[*3½ lines not declassified*] You will recall that the Korean war was already three or four months old, and that there was a very strong feeling within the Military Establishment that the Korean war, as an act of overt Communist military aggression, probably represented the opening stage of Soviet aggression involving real danger of an all-out conflict. Late in 1950 and early in 1951 the Military Establishment became intensely interested in the concept of "retardation". This concept meant that everything possible should be done [*less than 1 line not declassified*] to develop resistance mechanisms within the Eastern European Satellite area which might be activated and heavily re-supplied in the event of war. The objective was to develop large-scale guerrilla warfare and sabotage forces behind the Soviet lines. [*less than 1 line not declassified*] heavy pressure by our Military Establishment to accelerate these activities.

You will recall that early in 1951 General Smith produced his so-called Scope, Pace and Magnitude Paper, and there was consideration by the NSC of the CIA's mission.[5] More than anything else, this U.S. Military requirement for retardation on a vast scale impelled General Smith to have the NSC re-affirm his charter, particularly as related to the vastly expensive activities in connection with the development of retardation.

During this period almost two years ago, both the State Department, the CIA and notably General Magruder were convinced that the Psychological Warfare Division (General McClure) in the Department of the Army as well as other senior officers in the Army and Air Force were engaging in a very great deal of wishful thinking as to what could be done by clandestine means in Eastern Europe to develop resistance mechanisms capable of producing a massive retardation contribution. This thinking within the Military resulted from, in my opinion, almost complete ignorance of Eastern Europe and what a highly developed totalitarian police state could accomplish in the way of snuffing out anything remotely related to so-called resistance organizations. Nevertheless, the CIA, General Magruder and I did not feel that we could block what the Army desired to see accomplished in this field. We could only, and we did what we could, endeavor to educate the Army to the realities of life in an Eastern European Soviet Satellite and to warn that perhaps very little indeed could be accomplished in peace time in the way of setting up an organized mechanism capable of springing into

---

[5] Reference is to Smith's paper (see Document 68) which was the basis of NSC 10/5 (Document 90).

being on D-Europe Day. The State Department representatives naturally could not oppose covert activities, the objectives of which related to the national security and were designed to contribute to the military effort of the Western Allies in resisting Soviet attack on Western Europe. As stated above, General Magruder and I, as well as General Balmer, the Joint Chiefs of Staff representative as a consultant to OPC of CIA, could only point out the extreme difficulties of accomplishing anything and endeavor to persuade the Military that their Planners should not, repeat not, in the development of strategic plans, count on a resistance potential behind the enemy lines in the first stages of an all-out war.

In the meeting [*less than 1 line not declassified*] yesterday both General Magruder and General Balmer stated that there still exists in the Department of the Army a highly optimistic appreciation of what can be done in the way of guerrilla activity in time of war based on resistance mechanisms developed in times of peace. General Magruder recalled that recently in a briefing General Collins himself had referred to the destruction by resistance elements of bridges behind the enemy lines in Eastern Europe in case of war, his idea apparently being that such actions present no great difficulties of accomplishment. The fact is that large bridges to be destroyed by demolition require charges involving tons and tons of explosives which must be carefully and sometimes painfully placed. Needless to say, all strategic bridges will be heavily guarded by military detachments in time of war.[6]

The Air Force has also exerted pressure on the CIA to develop escape and evasion capabilities in Eastern Europe in time of war. The Air Force interest is, of course, easily explained and quite understandable. The fact remains that the setting up of escape and evasion routes, safe houses and recruiting of native personnel in peace time is an infinitely complicated, dangerous and time-consuming process.

Prior to the meeting in Paris early in March, 1952 of the Eastern European Chiefs of Mission, I addressed a memorandum on February 1, 1952 to Messrs. Bonbright, Barbour and Campbell,[7] which contains the following paragraphs:

"A general explanation might be given to the chiefs of mission alone, as to the aspects of so-called positive political action within the Soviet orbit, i.e., plans and preparations which are designed to lay the groundwork for massive internal resistance in case of war. In the light of these considerations, do the chiefs of mission consider that the risks involved should and must be taken?

---

[6] A handwritten notation in the margin reads, "and peace!"

[7] Not found.

"What suggestions have the chiefs of mission for the timing, phasing, scope and pace of positive political action by covert means behind the Iron Curtain? This question might be dealt with country by country and individually with the several chiefs of mission.

"It seems to me that these questions lie close to the heart of our strategy for the cold war for the next few years. I believe that our representatives on the spot not only could contribute a great deal which would be helpful in Washington but also that they should be aware of current plans and activities in the countries to which they are assigned."

The Record of Discussions of the meeting in Paris contains the following paragraph under "Conclusions and Recommendations":[8]

"II. 3. *Covert Operations.* Such operations are a necessary part of the total effort aimed at weakening the Soviet grip on the satellites. They should be aimed not only at securing a maximum of intelligence but also at breaking down the Soviet system of control and *building organizations for future action.* It must be recognized, however, that operations of this character may endanger the continued functioning of our diplomatic missions in the countries concerned."

The point of the foregoing is to illustrate that all of the Chiefs of Mission present at the Paris meeting agreed that in the national interest it was necessary for the CIA to do what it could to develop covert mechanisms within the Eastern European satellite countries. With respect to Poland, I talked in Paris individually with Ambassador Flack. He referred to the fact that the United States had more friends to the square inch in Poland than perhaps in any other satellite country and mentioned the five million Poles in the United States. He did point out, however, that the Sovietization of Poland had moved forward rapidly and that Poland had now become an efficient Police State with informers everywhere and with Soviet officials in all key points of the government, particularly in the US. In other words, in spite of the extreme difficulties and risk, Flack's own judgment was that it might be possible to do something in Poland, and in any event the attempt should be made.

[1 paragraph (11½ lines) not declassified]

General Balmer of the Joint Chiefs of Staff attended the meetings with the British and was provided with a copy of the agreed minutes. He has advised me that the somewhat pessimistic evaluation of capabilities for clandestine activities in Eastern Europe which came out of these meetings with the British was very useful indeed in counteracting some of the far too optimistic ideas existing within the Departments of the Army and the Air Force.

---

[8] Not found.

The Military Establishment for obvious strategic reasons was primarily interested in Poland insofar as retardation and escape and evasion were concerned. In addition, opportunities within Poland were regarded as much greater than in the other satellites, with the possible exception of Albania. The Poles historically hate and fear the Russians. The Poles have perhaps the strongest feeling of nationalism in Eastern Europe and a long tradition of conspiratorial and underground activity. [3 lines not declassified] To sum up, the situation was about as follows:

1. Pressure on the CIA by our Military Establishment to develop something in Poland was very great indeed.
2. The Department of State could not and did not oppose [less than 1 line not declassified] efforts to develop resistance organizations in Poland, and the Department was constantly advised of what was being done [less than 1 line not declassified].

The end result was as set forth in the first part of this memorandum. In other words, the efforts in Poland resulted in an extremely important set back which might have serious repercussions on the operations of our Embassy in Warsaw. In addition, the Polish UB has obtained information on the techniques and objectives of American clandestine activities. The Warsaw Government has made extremely clever and probably most effective propaganda use out of this fiasco. (See FBIS Report No. 252–1952)

[4 lines not declassified] I suggest that the following conclusions might possibly be derived from this experience in Poland:

1. It has become impossible, with only the existing techniques and contacts, [less than 1 line not declassified] to operate in the satellite area of Eastern Europe. The perfection of totalitarian police state techniques is approaching "1984" efficiency to a degree where "resistance" can probably exist only in the minds of the enslaved peoples of the Soviet orbit in Europe.
2. No resistance organization can survive in the Soviet orbit, with the possible exception of Albania.
3. [8 lines not declassified]
4. Unless new techniques are developed, perhaps nothing can be accomplished in the Soviet orbit in Eastern Europe except by a mass approach through the air waves, balloon operations and leaflet drops.

Recommendations:

1. The Department of State should devote careful study to [less than 1 line not declassified] operations within Poland. The Department should then provide political guidance [less than 1 line not declassified] in terms of long-range political objectives in Eastern Europe, such guidance to provide the framework within which covert operations should or should not be attempted.
2. The entire subject of cold war activities by clandestine means directed against the Soviet orbit in Eastern Europe should be studied

by the Psychological Strategy Board or whatever top level agency might succeed it under the new Administration. (Perhaps the committee presided over by Mr. William H. Jackson[9] might review the documentation mentioned in this memorandum. I understand this committee will review "cold war" activities, particularly in the Soviet orbit in Europe.)

Robert P. Joyce[10]

---

[9] See Document 151.
[10] Printed from a copy that bears this typed signature.

---

143.   Report by the Psychological Strategy Board[1]

PSB D–35   Washington, January 5, 1953.

NATIONAL PSYCHOLOGICAL EFFORT AS OF
DECEMBER 31, 1952

[Omitted here is Section I, "Purpose and Framework."]

II. Summary of Significant Psychological Activities

1. The Board presents below a brief evaluative summary of the status of our national psychological programs as of December 31, 1952, based on the appended Progress Reports of recent significant activities by the departments and agencies responsible for psychological operations.

General Comments

2. U.S. capabilities for psychological action, within the limits of the world power position, are slowly but steadily improving, but they remain inadequate for taking immediately effective psychological action contributing to a retraction of the Kremlin's power and influence.

---

[1] Source: National Archives, RG 59, S/S–NSC Files: Lot 62 D 333, PSB D–35. Top Secret; Security Information. Annex A, Report of the Department of State; Annex B, Report of the Department of Defense; Annex C, Report of the Central Intelligence Agency; and Annex D, Report of the Mutual Security Agency, are not printed. Annex C was specially classified and was not found. A covering note, which reads, "This report was approved by the Board at its Seventeenth Meeting, January 15, 1953," was signed by Secretary to the Board Charles E. Johnson.

3. Progress has been made in planning and coordinating interdepartmental and inter-agency action, in making use of indigenous resources for "gray" or unattributed operations, in building up potentialities for increased "black" or covert activity, and in expanding under existing programs technical facilities for radio broadcasting.

4. Our national psychological effort is at greatest disadvantage in the USSR and Communist China. In these areas, radio broadcasting remains almost the only weapon we are now employing on any significant scale. Even here, Russian jamming presents a very serious problem, although evidence continues to appear that broadcasts are heard by a limited audience on whom they have some effect. In Communist China listening facilities for the masses are severely limited.

5. In the Soviet satellite states of Eastern Europe also, radio broadcasting constitutes the major active element at our disposal. In these countries, too, jamming constitutes an obstacle, although at present a less serious one, perhaps, than in the USSR. In the case of some of the satellites, however, some progress has been made in building up other capabilities for psychological activities.

6. More positive psychological action directed against the Soviet orbit necessarily awaits a greater development of our over-all capabilities, and an accompanying adjustment of our basic national policy. In the present interim position, until a more aggressive strategic concept becomes feasible, psychological planning and programming against the orbit has gone ahead on the basis of doing everything possible to aggravate its internal conflicts in the hope that this will subsequently help to bring about a retraction of Kremlin control and influence.

7. U.S. psychological programs outside the Iron Curtain, where the major portion of the national psychological effort has been applied, have moved with moderate success toward the achievement of our objectives in certain areas. The psychological impact of American aid programs has, despite some difficulties, in most respects been favorable. With regard to the psychological problems arising from the large numbers of American personnel abroad, considerable progress has been made in respect to U.S. troops. Some progress is recorded toward meeting the "neutralist" menace. The US–UN stand against forcible repatriation of Korean prisoners of war has gained general acceptance with good psychological effect. There is closer and more effective cooperation between the various agencies carrying out American psychological programs abroad, and steadily increasing recognition of the role of psychological operations in world affairs.

Related Activities

8. Certain related activities are covered in a specially classified section of this report, Annex C.

Area Summary

9. In *Western Europe* there have been set-backs, such as the delay in ratification of the European Defense Community accords and the decision of the European member governments to cut their defense contributions under NATO. But the over-all picture contains bright elements as well. The reports of all PSB reporting agencies indicate that, as 1952 ends, communism is on a slow but definitely perceptible decline (with the possible exception of Italy). Furthermore, there is agreement that U.S. psychological programs have made an effective if modest contribution to this decline. Communism remains the major long-term threat, of course; but other forces tending to disrupt free world solidarity, and other forms of anti-Americanism, such as "neutralism," constitute more immediate problems.

10. In the *Middle East* the picture is not so bright. Iran is an obvious danger spot and a classic example of the difficulties and potential dangers confronting the continued existence of freedom in countries where extreme nationalism exists as a major problem in itself, and one that is aggravated and complicated by the fact that it can be easily inflamed and exploited by communism. Tension arising from some of the same elements that are found in Iran is growing in Iraq. In both these cases, as in the other Arab countries of the area, it can not be confidently asserted that there has been progress in the psychological field. In *North Africa*, nationalist ferment presents increasingly complex problems of a psychological character, rendered more acute by the presence of important American air bases within the area.

11. This does not mean, however, that the picture in the Middle East is entirely dark. Favorable effects continue from such psychological initiatives as the Mecca airlift, and the visit of the Fleet to the area. Our economic and military aid programs, and their active psychological exploitation, have produced good results, particularly in *Turkey*, which represents an encouragingly stable and friendly factor.

12. In *South and Southeast Asia*, all the problems and potential dangers in the situation are still present; but from the reports emerges the impression that gradually U.S. capabilities for holding our own in the psychological struggle there are being improved. Both on the overt information side and in non-attributable activities significant gains have been registered, particularly in the Philippines, Indo-China, and Thailand. In the *Indian sub-Continent* too, slow progress continues. Wise exploitation of the psychological possibilities of our aid programs, the agreement to extend military aid to Pakistan, and U.S. acceptance in the UN of the Indian Resolution on Korea—subsequently rejected out of hand by the Soviet bloc—have all had a favorable effect.

13. In the *Far East*, psychological activities are steadily if slowly expanding. A psychological plan to deal with the problems raised by the

presence of U.S. troops in *Japan* is now being prepared. Better use is being made of Japanese indigenous organizations and other resources in combatting communism. New psychological activities under the Far East Command include moves to build up escape operations in *Korea* and strengthen and improve the organization responsible for unconventional warfare. A number of psychological programs designed to take advantage of the proximity of U.S. and communist forces in Korea have been undertaken. Efforts to penetrate *Red China* were being slowly developed, with a significant increase in leaflet dropping, radio broadcasting, and some other activities of a non-attributable nature.

14. In *Latin America*, likewise, the spread of communism and the growing threat of Peronism have led us to increase our capabilities for combatting these and other anti-American forces. Overt information efforts are combining with TCA aid programs and non-attributable activities on an increasing scale. It is evident from current reports, however, that more will be required before we can take care of the dual Communist-Peronista threat to hemisphere unity.

Special Problems

15. Coordinated efforts of all the departments and agencies concerned had, by the year's end, been undertaken to minimize the impact of the communist germ warfare charges. Similarly, the Soviet "Hate America" campaign, as well as the so-called Campaign of Peace, seem to be declining in effectiveness outside the Iron Curtain, thanks, in part at least, to persistent and better-coordinated U.S. efforts to counteract them. The long-term implications of these campaigns remain serious, however. There are manifest indications of the effectiveness of the "Hate America" campaign inside the Iron Curtain countries, and the need for more effective counter measures continues great.

16. Major psychological problems continue to be raised by our commercial and immigration policies. The repercussions of our trade and tariff restrictions tend in some countries to diminish the psychological effects of our economic aid programs. The restrictions on immigration and the complications of our visa policy continue to offset some of the best efforts of our psychological operations.

17. Quietly effective use appears to have been made of the psychological possibilities inherent in our development of novel atomic and other weapons.

[Omitted here are Section III, "The Work of PSB," and the annexes.]

144.   Memorandum From Secretary of State Acheson and the Director for Mutual Security (Harriman) to the Executive Secretary of the National Security Council (Lay)[1]

Washington, January 19, 1953.

SUBJECT

Sixth Progress Report on NSC 104/2, "U.S. Policies and Programs in the Economic Field which may Affect the War Potential of the Soviet Bloc"[2]

REFERENCES

A. NSC 104/2
B. Memorandum for NSC from Executive Secretary, "Assignment of Responsibilities for Economic Defense", dated November 7, 1951,[3] transmitting Memorandum by the President on this subject
C. Memorandum for NSC from Executive Secretary, "Assignment of Responsibilities for Economic Defense", dated January 25, 1952[4] transmitting Memorandum of Agreement between the Secretary of State and the Administrator of the Mutual Defense Assistance Control Act

In accordance with the President's directive on the assignment of responsibilities for economic defense under NSC 104/2 and the memorandum of agreement between the Secretary of State and the Administrator of the Mutual Defense Assistance Control Act, there is submitted herewith the sixth progress report on NSC 104/2.[5] It is requested that this be circulated to the members of the Council for their information.

Dean Acheson[6]

Appendix II[7]

RESEARCH AND INTELLIGENCE FOR ECONOMIC DEFENSE

There are two principal tasks of the intelligence and research underlying the operations and policy formulation of economic defense.

---

[1] Source: National Archives, RG 59, S/S–NSC Files: Lot 63 D 351, OCB Files, NSC 104, Memoranda 1952–53, Box 61. Secret; Security Information. A handwritten notation on the memorandum indicates that it was delivered to Lay at the NSC on January 19 by security messenger.

[2] NSC 104/2 is printed in Foreign Relations, 1951, vol. I, pp. 1059–1064.

[3] See footnote 4, Document 116.

[4] Ibid.

[5] The 24-page progress report and Appendix 1, Replies from COCOM Countries on Prior Commitments Issue, are attached but not printed.

[6] Printed from a copy that bears this typed signature. The signature block for the Director of Mutual Security is blank.

[7] Secret; Security Information.

One is the task of appraising the overall relative economic capabilities and vulnerabilities of the Soviet bloc and the West in terms of economic defense measures and programs; this is a long range problem of large dimensions. The other task is that of keeping close and continuous touch with current East-West trade patterns and practices and economic developments within the Soviet bloc and the West; this is essential to provide the basic facts on specific relative vulnerabilities for purposes of current economic defense operations and negotiations.

The drafts prepared in connection with the proposed National Intelligence Estimate (NIE) 59 represent a systematic attempt to appraise the relative overall vulnerabilities of the Free World and the Soviet bloc. It is clear, however, that the materials available for any accurate appraisal of specific Soviet bloc vulnerabilities are still meager. Furthermore, the analysis of such materials is still in a very early stage of development, and much more work is needed in this important area. Meanwhile, the demands for basic trade analysis and other data needed for day-to-day operations continue to be insistent and continue on the increase. The problem is to plan the work for both the short-run or current operating and policy needs and the broader, longer run needs so as to achieve the maximum benefit for the East-West trade program.

The progress made in recent months in the fields of shipping and foreign trade intelligence for economic defense backstopping is summarized below.

There has been a notable increase in attention given to shipping intelligence, and a number of papers on this subject have been prepared; considerable work remains to be done, however. Included in this effort has been the joint development with the British of an agreed intelligence estimate of the facts concerning trade with Communist China, including the volume of trade and the number and capacity of vessels engaged in the trade.

A second area in which progress has been made in the past several months is the preparation of commodity studies of strategic items entering into East-West trade. In connection with the work of the OIT technical task groups, (see *Title II Activities* in body of report) CIA and the Department of State prepared, and Intelligence Advisory Committee (IAC) agencies have to some extent reviewed, commodity analyses of a number of International List II and III items. A few of these studies, on lead, pyrites, electrical machinery, marine boilers and tires and tubes, represented comprehensive analyses. An intensive study of rubber has also been in progress. A great many others, although not comprehensive, represented very considerable efforts in the utilization of available data. The work was extensive and, though not exhaustive because of the time element and competing priorities, represents an important step forward. It is hoped that by the end of 1953 comprehensive analyses will be available on the requirements, production, and trade of the Soviet bloc in each of the major items considered to be of important strategic value to the bloc, particularly those items subject to less-than-embargo control.

The companion project to the commodity studies was initiated early in 1952, and is a series of country-by-country studies analyzing the trade relations between the principal Western European countries and the important Soviet bloc countries with which they trade. Work on these analyses has only begun. The analyses are needed in policy planning on "decreasing reliance" and in implementing the Battle Act, and are aimed at affording policy officers a better factual background in gauging the bargaining positions of the individual countries trading with the Soviet bloc. The analyses would also serve to uncover prospective difficulties before they have come to a head. Given more time, it is sometimes possible to avoid the shipment of strategic goods by a Western country without prejudicing its economic and political position. This intelligence need in the trade field was stressed in the fourth progress report on NSC 104/2.[8]

To date, two comprehensive bilateral trade studies have been prepared, and three others are in process. These studies involve considerable expenditure of man-hours, but the results justify more work in this field.

In addition to the above analyses, The Department of Commerce has been pursuing two projects in the compilation of trade statistics, in accordance with interdepartmental arrangements made early in 1952. One is the compilation, from published and supplementary trade material, of the trade of each of the significant Free World countries with the Soviet bloc, by country and commodity. Useful reference tables have been issued quarterly on many of these countries and, on others, less frequently. The second part of the project is the collation of classified data which the individual COCOM countries submit monthly on their exports (or licenses granted for export) to the Soviet bloc of items included in the International Lists. The Department of Commerce summaries provide data from which the trends and pattern of this trade can be more readily discerned in certain cases and from which answers to specific commodity or country problems can be developed with much less effort than was formerly required in dealing with the individual monthly reports. This work, which marks an important initial step in the development of the needed statistical base, is being reviewed in an interagency committee.

The Intelligence Working Group (IWG) established under EDAC–IAC sponsorship was quite active in the second half of 1952.

---

[8] Not printed. (National Archives, RG 59, S/S–NSC Files: Lot 63 D 351, OCB Files, NSC 104, Memoranda 1952–53, Box 61)

The IWG has provided closer working relationships between the intelligence agencies, on one hand, and the policy and operating sections, on the other, with the latter able to indicate directly their needs and to assist in providing necessary background for the work they initiate. Although there is inevitably room for considerable improvement in the treatment of specific problems, the IWG is improving intelligence support of economic defense policy and operations. One of its most significant current projects is the establishment of a unit which will collate the extensive data now being received on Soviet bloc procurement efforts, particularly those efforts which involve evasions of Western economic security controls. The details of the project are not yet fully worked out, but it has been approved in principle.

In conclusion, there should be mentioned the general problem of disseminating National Intelligence to foreign Governments and international bodies. One difficulty which has impeded United States negotiations on economic defense matters could be eliminated by establishing a better procedure so that our negotiators might use the material contained in intelligence documents to maximum advantage. Such use of intelligence is inhibited by the pervasive difficulty of ensuring that security is maintained in the course of using such material. This problem should be explored to determine whether amendments to pertinent NSC directives and other regulations would be desirable.

---

145. Memorandum From Robert P. Joyce of the Policy Planning Staff to the Deputy Under Secretary of State (Matthews)[1]

Washington, January 27, 1953.

There is forwarded to you herewith two memoranda, both dated yesterday, on the general subject of the secret intelligence activities and the covert operations abroad of the CIA. The first memorandum, signed by me, is designed to provide background material and to set in the proper framework the second memorandum, which is signed by Outerbridge Horsey and prepared by all of us in this Office (Horsey, Berry, Strong, McFadden and myself).[2]

---

[1] Source: National Archives, RG 59, INR Files: Lot 58 D 776, State–CIA Relations. Top Secret. A handwritten notation on the memorandum reads, "R—Mr. Howe" (Fisher Howe, Deputy Special Assistant for Research and Intelligence).

[2] J. Lampton Berry, Robert C. Strong, and William McFadden.

The basic purpose of these memoranda is to raise fundamental problems with regard to the CIA operation abroad and the guidance and control of these activities to insure that they shall be closely geared in with our overall strategy and political objectives. The memorandum signed by Horsey has been shown to Messrs. Armstrong and Howe, who have indicated to us that they are in general agreement with the analysis plus the conclusions and recommendations which flow therefrom. Armstrong's office, of course, has a large interest in the subject of the relations between this Department and the CIA, and I am sure you will want to bring Armstrong and Howe into any discussions based on this material.

The memorandum signed by me I have drafted in a manner and with the idea in mind that it might be read and discussed in due course by General Smith and Mr. Allen W. Dulles.[3] I am sure you will have your own ideas as to the timing and manner in which this might be accomplished if you agree with me that it should be. It would also be my suggestion that these two memoranda, together with the material referred to in them, might very well be placed before the William H. Jackson Committee,[4] which will study the psychological warfare effect of the government.

Robert P. Joyce[5]

Annex 1

Memorandum From Robert P. Joyce of the Policy Planning Staff to the Deputy Under Secretary of State (Matthews)[6]

Washington, January 26, 1953.

SUBJECT

The Department of State and the CIA

---

[3] Allen W. Dulles succeeded Walter Bedell Smith, who resigned as Director of Central Intelligence on February 9 and became Under Secretary of State on the same day. Allen W. Dulles was appointed Director of Central Intelligence the same day, was confirmed by the Senate on February 23, and was sworn in on February 26.

[4] See Document 151 regarding the June 30 Jackson Committee report.

[5] Printed from a copy that bears this typed signature.

[6] Top Secret; Security Information.

There is forwarded to you herewith a memorandum dated January 26, 1953[7] which has been prepared in this office by Messrs. Horsey, Berry, Strong, McFadden and myself. In this connection, I refer to my memorandum addressed to you on December 17, 1952 with particular reference to the so-called Kaji case in Tokyo as well as to my memorandum addressed to you on December 31, 1952 entitled "CIA Activities Directed Against Poland".[8] In the former memorandum I suggested that before my departure I should write a memorandum for you embodying certain conclusions I have reached as a result of four years close working relationship with OPC of CIA. The memorandum forwarded to you today endeavors to pose important problems which have recently arisen as a result of CIA covert activities in the field which have caused, are still causing, and will probably continue to cause serious embarrassment to the conduct of U.S. foreign relations. In the memorandum referred to in the previous sentence, my colleagues and I have endeavored to pose the basic questions with regard to Department of State and CIA relationships which we believe the new administration will desire to deal with in the immediate future as they relate to the presumed new policy of more "dynamism" with regard to the conduct of the cold war.

The kernel of the problem, as I see it, is that the operations abroad, in the field of secret intelligence as well as secret operations, have increasingly tended to be less and less geared into what I understand to be the present overall strategy of the United States in the management of its foreign relations. Perhaps a better way of stating it would be to say that CIA covert activities lack sufficient policy guidance and control, the inevitable result being that such activities, on occasion, are not in the national interest nor do they support our overall policy objectives. The memorandum of January 26, 1953 endeavors to meet this problem head on in the hope that CIA activities abroad may be restudied on the National Security Council level and perhaps a new look be taken by President Eisenhower himself.

I set forth below certain thoughts and conclusions I have arrived at which might be helpful in providing information of a background and historical nature relating to the organization, growth and present operations of the Central Intelligence Agency. These observations relate primarily to OPC of CIA.

---

[7] Printed below.

[8] The memorandum on the Kaji case was not found, although documentation on the repercussions of the arrest and detection in Japan of Waturu Kaji, a Japanese national, by U.S. authorities is in National Archives, RG 59, Central Files, 794.0221. For the memorandum on Poland, see Document 142.

I. Political Background—1949 and 1950

In the autumn of 1949, OPC of CIA was a relatively small and compact unit within the framework of but somewhat independently situated in the CIA organization. It was busily preparing to set up mechanisms through which it could engage in so-called psychological and political warfare by covert means as defined in NSC 10/2.[9] In September, 1949, the Russians produced their first atomic explosion several years ahead of what I understand to be the best calculated estimates. Soviet political warfare on a world-wide scale was constantly being stepped up to subvert, divide, weaken and eventually control large and important areas of the free world in which the U.S. had a vital stake. On June 25, 1950 the North Korean Communists, under Russian control, crossed one of the frontiers of the free world by military force. The Communist guerrilla attacks against the French and the Vietnamese were assuming the proportions of a major war; Soviet pressure against Iran was increasing; Communist guerrilla warfare in Malaya was being stepped up; the Chinese Communists were taking over Tibet; the Communists were succeeding in Guatemala, etc., etc. Tito's Yugoslavia was under constant menace of a military attack by the Soviet satellites of Eastern Europe.

All of these facts produced within the United States Government and among the American people a sense of urgency to prepare for the possibility of additional Communist attacks against the free world which might lead to an all out military conflict, including an attack against the United States. We started our military build-up on a vast scale during the last part of 1950. During this period, both within the government as well as outside, there suddenly developed an intense interest in so-called psychological or political warfare. This caused considerable pressure to be exerted against OPC of CIA immediately to engage in psychological and political warfare activities by covert means. At the same time, exceedingly strong pressure was exerted upon OPC of CIA by the Defense Establishment to accomplish in the shortest possible time those responsibilities set forth in NSC 10/2 relating to preparing for resistance activities and guerrilla warfare behind the enemy lines in case of war. You will recall that during the last part of 1950 powerful elements within the Military Establishment considered that perhaps the Russians in 1954 or 1955 would attain a degree of military preparation and atomic capability which might lead the leaders in the Kremlin either to endeavor to obtain their objectives by the use of overt military force on a grand scale, or the Kremlin would exert the threat of force and subversion to obtain control of strategic portions of

---

[9] For NSC 10/2, see *Foreign Relations, 1945–1950, Emergence of the Intelligence Establishment*, Document 292.

the non-Communist world. This would necessarily lead to such reactions upon our part that the danger of an all out conflict would indeed be very great. Underlying these considerations, was the over-riding fact that China was added to the Communist world and Chinese Communist military forces threatened Southeast Asia.

II. Expansion of OPC

The objective world situation late in 1950 and early in 1951 (or at least the subjective reaction thereto on the part of the Government and the people of the United States) and the pressures referred to above led to a vast expansion of OPC of CIA. The emphasis understandably given by the Military to prepare for war and the pressures to organize behind-the-lines resistance, led to constantly increasing emphasis within the OPC on preparations for a hot war. (In this connection, I refer to my memorandum of December 31, 1952 with regard to [less than 1 line not declassified] activities in Poland.) OPC tended to become more and more of a military and para-military planning agency. At the same time, OPC was endeavoring to meet the demands and pressures for increased activity in the field of covert political action. I believe that the end result of this situation was that OPC tried to do too much in too little time with inadequate personnel. I believe that Mr. Frank G. Wisner would agree with this estimate. I may say that qualified personnel in this country for OPC planning and operations is extraordinarily difficult to come by and difficult to train.

Some unhappy results of this haste inevitably followed:

[7 paragraphs (74 lines) not declassified]

III. Learning the Hard Way

For the reasons stated above, it is my conclusion that these failures of the CIA are not exclusively CIA failures, but are rather *American failures* attributable, to sum up, to the following factors:

1. The American characteristic of impatience and "wanting to get the job done". The American belief that if enough money, personnel and effort are applied, everything is possible and can be accomplished either instanter or certainly within a year or two.

2. The CIA approach during the past three years has been far too heavily influenced by the thinking within and without the Government that we had very little time. It is my personal view that NSC 68[10] gave expression to and reflected much of this thinking.

3. The role of covert operations in the conduct of foreign policy has been exaggerated. Quietly, securely, and expertly handled political

---

[10] Regarding NSC 68, "United States Objectives and Programs for National Security," April 14, 1950, see Document 5.

and intelligence operations can undoubtedly make a valuable and, on rare occasions, a crucial contribution to the national security, but only if such activities are of a highly professional character. They can never "win the cold war", but only make a modest but significant contribution.

4. The CIA, as General Smith himself has stated repeatedly, has tried to take on too much in too little time. CIA has obtained the services of a great number of highly talented, loyal and high caliber Americans. Many of them, however, have the characteristics mentioned in paragraph No. 1 above. In the medium levels of CIA there are many persons who consider the Department of State to be negative and timid. These persons over-estimate the role of special operations by clandestine methods and under-rate the difficulties and pitfalls in our dealings with both our allies and our opponents. The *Congressional Record,* issue of January 14, 1953, No. 6, page A–157, contains the following statement from a study of "psychological strategy" prepared by former Congressman O.K. Armstrong:

"High success in the performances of its [the CIA's][11] important tasks, has been due in largest measure to the leadership and direction of Bedell Smith and Allen Dulles. Major handicap, according to a summary of *interviews by key personnel* is due to lack of coordination, or more accurately cooperation, by some echelons of the State Department *in following recommendations* made by CIA for the security of the nation." (Italics supplied)

IV. Observations and Suggestions

[*11 paragraphs (59 lines) not declassified*]

V. Conclusions

The foregoing, I fear, may sound perhaps captiously critical and negative insofar as the CIA is concerned. I hope that it is not taken in this sense. There is a great deal of light in the picture.

My own feeling is that the CIA has made remarkable progress during the past five years in perhaps the most tricky, sensitive and delicate of all governmental operations demanding the highest degree of sophistication and experience. It takes many, many years to build up what we may term a covert apparatus. The Russians have had thirty-five years experience. We have had five. The only way to learn the intelligence business is to engage in it. The CIA has been actively engaging in this business under the enormous pressures referred to in previous sections of this memorandum. Glaring mistakes have been made, but solid accomplishments have already been achieved. It is my belief that the senior officials of the CIA are entirely aware of the de-

---

[11] Brackets in the original.

ficiencies of the organization in its field activities, and remedial action is being taken to tighten up and increase security. The training and indoctrination process has been vastly improved and men who have shown no talent for the intelligence business have been released.

The CIA organization has made progress in recruiting, training and seasoning a group of highly talented men who are coming to consider American Intelligence their life career. Amateurism is giving place to an increasing degree of professionalism. It is being realized that an intelligence bull is misplaced in the world china shop of 1953 and that a cat and later a soft-treading leopard is a more suitable and effective animal. I believe that a greater degree of discipline has been established and that there is a real understanding growing up within the secret intelligence activities and special operations fields that intelligence is not a policy-creating function within the Government and can never be. Although there are still some officers within the CIA who have a feeling that intelligence operations abroad are an end in themselves and should be conducted independently of and without interference from policy-making and implementing American officials. I believe this must and will be corrected with time and a greater degree of discipline in government. The U.S. responsibility is such that amateurism, free-wheeling and heavy-handedness cannot be permitted in 1953. Our friends and allies must have confidence not only in the goodness of our intentions and objectives but also in our judgment, discretion and methods. Our dangerous adversaries turn our mistakes against us with telling effect, and this does not make for the confidence in our leadership which we must have to exercise it effectively in the crucial years to come.

One more observation: If we comport ourselves in the international arena as though we are urgently preparing for a perhaps inevitable conflict with the Soviet world, we add fuel to fears and inspire counteraction which increase the danger of just such a conflict. This is a most difficult problem—to prepare for war to prevent it—but we must somehow solve it in the next few years to come.

Robert P. Joyce[12]

---

[12] Printed from a copy that bears this typed signature.

Annex 2

Memorandum From Outerbridge Horsey of the Policy Planning Staff to the Deputy Under Secretary of State (Matthews)[13]

Washington, January 26, 1953.

SUBJECT

The Department of State and CIA Operations Abroad

Problem:

To review CIA–State relationships, in secret intelligence and in covert operations, with the double objective (a) of insuring that *all* CIA field activities are of optimum value in the prosecution of United States foreign policy objectives and (b) of diminishing the risk of results harmful to those objectives.

Discussion:

Recent integration within CIA, at headquarters and in the field, of the two main fields, "secret intelligence" and "covert operations," emphasizes their interdependence. Even in the previous state of more or less water-tight separation of the two activities, *either* might have affected, and indeed did affect, the conduct of foreign policy.

"Secret intelligence" is used herein to describe what NSCID–5[14] defines as "all organized federal espionage operations outside the United States . . . for the collection of foreign intelligence information . . . in connection with the national security . . ." (Counter-espionage is excluded from this discussion) Secret intelligence activities are conducted by the Director of Central Intelligence. Moreover, he has responsibility for coordinating covert and overt intelligence activities. The senior U.S. representative in each country has the responsibility for coordinating *overt* intelligence collection activities, but there is no recognition in theory or in practice of the fact that *secret* intelligence activities can affect the conduct of foreign policy. By law the Director of Central Intelligence is responsible for the protection of intelligence sources and methods from unauthorized disclosure. In general this has in practice resulted in the withholding of detailed information on se-

---

[13] Top Secret; Security Information. Drafted by Horsey, Joyce, Berry, Strong and McFadden. Ellipsis in the original.

[14] Document 255.

cret intelligence activities in both the planning and execution stages. The Department and Chiefs of Mission in the field are briefed from time to time on the broad lines of secret intelligence activities in a particular country. The positive intelligence information developed by CIA is furnished, in some measure and with varying degrees of promptness to Chiefs of Mission in the field, and in greater measure and considerably more delay to the Department in Washington. Occasionally, CIA will seek policy guidance before or while a particular operation is being conducted, but it does not necessarily follow the advice given; nor is it obliged to do so. In general, information on intelligence collection operations themselves is not sufficiently specific or timely to permit effective policy guidance, even if the Department were required to provide such guidance, which it is not.

NSC 50[15] calls for "closer liaison" between CIA and State and for strengthening the "guidance" received by CIA from intelligence consumers, but the context of these references makes it clear that they relate to the nature of the intelligence to be collected and not to the policy implications of the conduct of intelligence collection activities. Any operations in a foreign country, however, are bound to have implications for the overt conduct of relations with the country concerned. Indeed they can have very serious results, leading to the undermining of the stability of a friendly government, the loss of public confidence in the U.S. or giving substance to Soviet anti-U.S. charges. The judgment as to whether and in what manner a covert proceeding of any kind is likely to affect overall objectives in the country concerned is one which in the final analysis can be made only by the agency responsible for the conduct of overall policy.

The British meet the problem of political guidance on secret intelligence activities, as well as the larger problem of coordinating all other foreign intelligence activities, by giving an inter-agency committee, of which the Foreign Office representative is automatically Chairman, close policy control over the entire foreign intelligence effort of the U.K. The MI–6 man in the field, although he belongs to an independent organization whose chief reports directly to the Prime Minister, is given the specific responsibility of clearing with the Ambassador when his activities are likely to affect the conduct of overt relations. The MI–6 man is able to discern the likelihood of political consequences because he is part of a small highly-trained professional corps, and because awareness of political factors is an essential qualification. A serious failure to do so costs him his job.

---

[15] See *Foreign Relations, 1945–1950, Emergence of the Intelligence Establishment,* Document 384.

The immense range of CIA's secret intelligence activities, the paucity of trained personnel with good political judgment, the extent of our involvement in many foreign countries and the serious results of mistakes, would seem to require that the authority of the Secretary of State and of the principal U.S. representatives in each foreign country be extended in some measure into the "secret intelligence" field. This is all the more necessary because of the recent merging of the "secret intelligence" and "covert operations" functions within CIA. Since the necessity of continuous political guidance in the second category is unquestioned, such extension of the Department's authority would seem to be the logical corollary of that merging.

The exclusion of the Department and its representatives in the field from any right to full knowledge of what is going on in the intelligence field, and of giving policy guidance thereon, has been applied in practice not only to the subject matter of NSCID–5 but also to the preliminary or fact-finding stages of "covert operations." (The latter are defined for the present purpose as activities authorized by NSC 10/2 and NSC 10/5.)[16] These fact-finding operations can, however, have just as serious political consequences, for good or for ill, as the actual operations themselves. Moreover, it is hard to draw the dividing line in a given case between the "intelligence" phase and the "operations" phase when a "project" is submitted through the joint machinery for clearance under paragraph 3(d)(1) of NSC 10/2. And CIA is the agency which under the present system draws the dividing line.

As to "covert operations" themselves, NSC 10/2 of course recognized their intimate relationship to the overt conduct of policy. This relationship was emphasized by providing that the Secretary of State should nominate the man initially in charge of these operations. NSC 10/2 said further that covert operations should be "planned and conducted in a manner consistent with U.S. foreign and military policies and with covert activities" but it left with the Director of Central Intelligence the responsibility for insuring that they were so conducted. Committee machinery for inter-departmental clearance was established, with the right of appeal to the NSC itself in case of serious differences.

The very nature of covert operations, the necessary use of a separate communications system and considerations of security in practice leave the initiative largely in the hands of CIA Headquarters and CIA representatives in the field. Because of lack of knowledge, the policy makers are often precluded from giving the necessary guidance. Because many of the questions involved do not concern two of the members (JCS and Defense) of the Committee of "OPC Consultants," be-

---

[16] For NSC 10/2, see ibid., Document 292. For NSC 10/5, see Document 90.

cause a number of personal relationships between CIA and State opposite numbers have grown up, and because it is not always used by CIA, this Committee machinery has not been fully effective. In spite of full cooperation at the top levels of CIA on policy coordination in accordance with the letter and spirit of NSC 10/2 there has been a tendency toward free-wheeling[17] at the operating level. There have been a number of failures recently to obtain State Department clearance, sometimes the explanation being given that the matter was not thought to involve a policy question, sometimes that the responsible officers in the State Department could not be reached in time, and at least once with no valid explanation. A number of recent experiences underline the necessity of CIA also recognizing in practice the mandate of NSC 10/2 to clear with State as well as with JCS and Defense the political implications of projects of a para-military nature. On the other hand, there are a number of examples of close and fruitful relations between CIA and the State Department. This type of cooperation, as well as close relationships which have developed at some posts in the field is, however, largely the accidental result of the personalities involved rather than of the system itself. The momentum of a large and organizationally independent government organization inevitably pulls away from cooperation.

If covert operations are to be a really effective arm of foreign policy, the policy officers of the State Department must, through tightly organized machinery, be brought into more intimate relationship with *all* stages of covert operations and particularly the planning or "intelligence" stages.

In summary, political guidance by the State Department on "covert operations" is increasingly difficult to get across in view of (1) the merging within CIA of responsibility for these operations with that for secret intelligence collection; (2) the difficulty in practice of distinguishing between the two types of operation and CIA freedom from policy guidance on the second; (3) the immense range of both types of activity, particularly in view of the military pressure to develop resistance and stay-behind organizations; (4) the lack of full knowledge on the part of the Department of State of what is going on in both fields until and unless CIA chooses to give such information or something "blows."

Recommendation:

The Secretary of State and the principal U.S. representative in each country, as part of their overall responsibility for the conduct of U.S.

---

[17] An attached handwritten note reads, "It is interesting and pertinent to note that it is current in CIA to say that the State Dept calls anything 'free wheeling' which represents a new idea."

foreign relations, should have authority, acting through designated representatives agreeable to CIA in a manner which will not prejudice security or limit effectiveness, to insure that *all* covert activities abroad, including those defined earlier as "secret intelligence", are *planned and conducted* consistently with U.S. foreign policy and with the overt execution of that policy.[18]

Outerbridge Horsey[19]

---

[18] There is no indication as to what action, if any, was taken in the Department to implement this recommendation.

[19] Printed from a copy that bears this typed signature.

---

146.   National Security Council Report[1]

NSC 142   Washington, February 10, 1953.

[Omitted here are a table of contents and Section I, "Objective," consisting of a quote from the National Security Act of 1947 outlining the duties of the CIA.]

II. STATUS OF UNITED STATES PROGRAMS FOR NATIONAL SECURITY AS OF DECEMBER 31, 1952

[Omitted here are Parts 1–6. Part 1, The Military Program, was prepared by the Department of Defense. Part 2, The Mobilization Program, was prepared by the Office of Defense Mobilization. Part 3, The Mutual Security Program, was prepared by the Office of the Director for Mutual Security. Part 4, The Civil Defense Program, was prepared by the Federal Civil Defense Administration. Part 5, The Stockpiling Program, was prepared by the Department of Defense. Part 6, The Psychological Program was prepared by the Psychological Strategy Board.]

---

[1] Source: National Archives, RG 59, S/S–NSC Files: Lot 63 D 351, NSC 142, Box 69. Top Secret, Security Information. NSC 142 consisted of eight parts, each prepared by the agency having primary responsibility for that particular national security program. The composite report was circulated to the NSC by NSC Executive Secretary Lay on February 10. Only Parts 7 and 8 are printed. Part 7 was prepared by the CIA, dated February 6, and concurred in by the IAC. Part 8 was not found attached but a text from another Record Group is included here.

No. 7—The Foreign Intelligence Program

II. Coordination[2]

Coordination among the intelligence agencies, so essential to producing adequate intelligence for national security purposes, is generally good. Although no recommendations on this subject have been made to the NSC during the year by the Director of Central Intelligence, several improvements in intelligence coordination have been accomplished by mutual agreement among the intelligence agencies and others. Such activities are under constant review and improvements can also be expected during 1953.

III. National Estimates

1. The organization and procedures established since October 1950 for the production of national intelligence estimates have now been proved in practice. The totality of resources of the entire intelligence community is drawn upon to produce national intelligence estimates, and they can be improved only as we strengthen these resources. These estimates derive authority from the manner of their preparation and from the active participation of all the responsible intelligence agency heads in their final review and adoption. Agency dissents are recorded where estimates would be watered down by further efforts to secure agreement.

2. A production program for national intelligence estimates has been initiated. It provides for a re-examination of existing estimates on critical areas or problems as well as the production of new estimates designed to improve the coverage of important topics. Special effort is being made to schedule the completion of basic estimates on the USSR in advance of the review of budget estimates and NATO plans.

3. Close coordination between planners and policy-makers on the one hand and the intelligence community on the other is continually being pressed in an effort to make the intelligence produced both useful and timely. The IAC mechanism is most useful when the NSC is furnished with a coordinated intelligence view in advance of the time when the policy is fixed.

4. "Post-mortems," designed to reveal deficiencies in the preparation of selected estimates and to stimulate corrective action, have been continued. The experience of past months in this procedure, particularly as applied in the case of estimates on the Far East, indicates that the results are beneficial.

IV. Political, Social, and Cultural Intelligence

1. The status of political, social and cultural intelligence is very good, due allowance being made for the paucity of information on the

---

[2] There is no section I.

Soviet Orbit and the difficulties of collecting it. Facilities for the production of such intelligence, however, are adequate only for the most urgent needs of the IAC agencies. Less pressing demands can be met only partially and inadequately.

2. The principal deficiency in this field is in the effort devoted to the exhaustive research on which sound estimates and analysis on current development depend. Only the USSR can be regarded as adequately covered in this respect, the European Satellites and Western Europe nearly so. The agencies have applied special effort to developing intelligence on China. Surveys of present programs both within the Government and in private research are making possible an integrated and maximal use of resources. On medium priority areas, such as Iran, Indochina and India, there is considerable lag between production of immediate interpretation and analysis of longer term factors. On low priority areas, such as Africa and Latin America, such factors receive even less study. World Communism, outside the Soviet Orbit, is satisfactorily covered with respect to party strength, political maneuverings and relationships to the Moscow propaganda lines. Research into matters of organization, financial support and infiltration into political and social organizations is inadequate.

V. Armed Forces Intelligence

1. Operational Intelligence

Intelligence needed in support of current military operations in Korea is generally excellent. Information on installations and on developments in Manchuria, such as the movement and activities of the Chinese Communist Forces and North Korean units north of the Yalu River, is inadequate. Reliable information of the enemy's long-range plans and intentions is practically non-existent. Little improvement in these deficiencies can be expected in the near future despite our efforts.

2. Order of Battle and Equipment

Order of battle and equipment information on the USSR, Communist China, and—to a lesser degree—the European Satellites is partial and inadequate, primarily because of the extreme difficulty of collection. Intelligence on Communist Bloc units and equipment in most areas with which the United States or nations friendly to the United States are in contact is more nearly complete and reliable.

Information on the navies of the Soviet Bloc is, however, in general, satisfactory and adequate because of the greater accessibility of naval forces to observation. Coverage on order of battle intelligence and equipment is generally adequate in respect of nations outside of the Iron Curtain, except in the case of some neutral nations whose national policy restricts our access to such information.

The Intelligence Community   413

3. Targeting

The assembly and analysis of encyclopedic target data on economic and industrial vulnerabilities is well along for the Soviet Orbit and is in intermediate research stages for Western Europe and the Far East; increased research emphasis is being placed upon military targets. Current target systems studies are reasonably adequate to support joint operational planning but more vigorous data collection efforts will be required to maintain these studies on a current basis. In particular, target intelligence required to counter the Soviet atomic threat is handicapped by gaps in current information on Soviet weapons, stockpiling arrangements and delivery capabilities. Production of dossiers for priority combat targets is almost complete for the USSR but coverage varies considerably for the Satellite and approach areas. Finally, extensive tactical target coverage has been completed on areas adjoining the Korean theater but on other areas is in various stages of completion.

4. Support for the North Atlantic Treaty Organization (NATO)

NATO requests have been filled with the best available intelligence consistent with the National Disclosure Policy. Intelligence studies and intelligence to assist in the establishment of basic intelligence files for the NATO echelons are provided to the NATO Standing Group. Releasable current studies and reports pertinent to the area and the mission of the NATO major commands are continuously provided.

VI. Economic Intelligence

1. Foreign economic intelligence on the free world presents few serious problems, mainly those that arise from the wealth of material and multiplicity of sources. For the Soviet Bloc, however, such intelligence is far from adequate. Apart from aggregate statistics of uncertain reliability published by the Soviet government, the intelligence community is confined to exploiting a diminishing flow of low-grade data, much of which is becoming increasingly out-of-date. Only by taking advantage of every possible item of information in the course of a comprehensive, thoroughly planned, and coordinated study can national security needs for knowledge of the Bloc's economic capabilities and vulnerabilities be met. This may mean the subordination of short-term requirements to the long-range program and a resolute and imaginative attack on problems of centralized indexing and exploitation of all pertinent materials, whether overt or classified. Within the limits of available materials, the next twelve months are expected to see the production of individual industry studies of greater substance than any now available. These will form the foundation for inter-industry studies and other over-all analysis.

2. In the field of economic warfare and support for collective controls, machinery has been established to speed up the processing and evaluation of spot data into intelligence on which action can be taken by the Economic Defense Advisory Committee and the covert services. There has been established a coordinating committee which is assisting in bringing available intelligence more quickly and fully to bear on questions arising under this program.

3. The target analysis and production activities outlined in Section V, *Armed Forces Intelligence*, involve the large-scale processing of foreign economic and technological data.

4. The heavy research requirements in the economic field make it imperative that duplicate efforts be kept at an absolute minimum. An even more determined effort to accomplish this objective will be made during the coming year.

VII. Scientific and Technical Intelligence

1. Scientific and technical intelligence regarding the USSR and Satellites made important progress during 1952; however, current knowledge is still inadequate in terms of national security needs. In order to obtain sounder scientific estimates in many fields, it is now more apparent than ever that there is a need for serious interagency study and development of new and unconventional technical means of collecting scientific intelligence information. Efforts with this type of collection show considerable promise, and the development and expansion of these and other techniques is being explored.

2. With the concurrence of the IAC, the DCI on 14 August 1952 issued a directive delineating areas of dominant interests in the general field of scientific and technical intelligence,[3] allocating primary production responsibility between CIA and the intelligence agencies of the Department of Defense. At the same time he established a Scientific Estimates Committee (SEC), primarily concerned with integrating scientific and technical intelligence opinion for the production of national intelligence. Coordination of technical intelligence for purposes other than the production of national intelligence is the responsibility of the military intelligence agencies, with CIA and the SEC maintaining appropriate liaison.

3. There has been continued improvement in our knowledge of Soviet accomplishments in the production of fissionable materials and their conversion to atomic weapons. Intelligence estimates on the status of USSR plutonium production are now reasonably sound, and good bases have been established for estimating Soviet capabilities for

---

[3] Document 126.

future expansion of the production of this material. However, the absence of sufficient evidence on which to base conclusions on installed or planned isotope separation capacity for the production of U–235 is one of the most important gaps in intelligence on the Soviet Atomic Energy Program. Also, the evidence on activities in the thermonuclear field is poor. Extensive collection and research programs have been undertaken which may result in improvement during the coming year.

4. Scientific and technical intelligence on conventional military weapons and equipment of all types is good so far as standardized items in current use are concerned. Necessarily, knowledge of weapons improvements in many cases must await Service use. In regard to development of air weapons, information is partial and inadequate. Knowledge of current Soviet guided missiles programs is poor, although certain projects based on German developments are fairly well known.

5. While our knowledge of Soviet biological and chemical warfare programs continues to be poor, the agencies have undertaken collection and research programs which may result in improvement during 1953.

6. On basic scientific research, which is CIA's responsibility, major gaps exist in the intelligence in the countries behind the Iron Curtain, and present estimates of long-range development are very weak. However, knowledge of the current status of over-all Soviet scientific research and development is believed to be more nearly adequate. During 1953, further improvements, particularly in long-range predictions, are expected to result from present plans for improving overt collection of pertinent information, a more complete and systematic exploitation of open scientific literature, and a concerted intelligence research effort on basic foreign scientific activities.

VIII. Psychological Intelligence

Overt and covert propaganda and psychological warfare programs have developed to an unprecedented degree in the past two years. The intelligence needs of these programs fall largely within the framework of political and sociological intelligence. The orientation and organization of the material for the psychological warfare user calls for unaccustomed depth and detail both in the field reporting and in analysis. State is initiating a reorganization designed to increase coordination of governmental and private research in this field. Inasmuch as research contracts of military operational agencies involve social science projects of use to intelligence, the coordination of these with intelligence agencies is important. The Research and Development Board has established a psychological warfare committee to integrate such contact within Defense. Liaison between State, Defense, and CIA should insure coordination for mutual benefit.

IX. Geographic Intelligence

1. Geographic research of IAC agencies on foreign areas, including evaluations of foreign mapping activities, is providing regional reports and staff studies for policy and operational planning. Coordinated geographic and map intelligence studies are also undertaken in support of the National Intelligence Survey program.

2. Current geographic and mapping information on the Soviet Bloc and adjacent areas is grossly inadequate. Geographic intelligence research gives particular attention to the regional analysis of those geographic facts that are required in support of planning and operational intelligence for these areas. Within CIA, emphasis is also placed on the study of current developments in Soviet mapping activities and programs.

X. Basic Intelligence

1. The program of National Intelligence Surveys (NIS), which was begun in 1949 as an interdepartmental cooperative venture, was intended to meet with U.S. Government's demands for encyclopedic factual intelligence on a world-wide basis. Since the NIS program was begun 1,490 individual sections have been produced on 59 of the 108 NIS areas, which is the equivalent of approximately 23 complete NIS. Based upon the rate of production established during the last quarter of FY 1952, a production goal of the equivalent of approximately 10 complete NIS has been set for FY 1953, and production to December 31, 1952 indicates that this goal will probably be attained.

2. NIS production is scheduled in accordance with JCS priorities and intelligence agency capabilities. Limitations of the latter have precluded production of NIS on *all* JCS high priority areas and made it necessary to undertake partial surveys on some other areas. However, NIS production on the group of 24 areas of highest priority is approximately 48% complete, whereas the entire program is about 22% complete. NIS on ten individual areas are over 75% complete, and five of these are in the JCS high priority list. Geographic research support for NIS has been excellent.

3. In general the quality of the NIS is good, and can be expected to improve as the gaps in information are filled and revisions are published under the Maintenance Program which was started in FY 1952. Coordination within and between all IAC and non-IAC agencies engaged in the NIS program is excellent and suitable liaison is maintained with the JCS.

XI. Warning of Attack—Current Intelligence

1. As noted above, current information on the Soviet Orbit is partial and inadequate. Accordingly, conclusions concerning Soviet and Communist intentions to initiate hostilities at any given time must be tentative generalizations drawn from inadequate evidence. They are

often based on estimates of the over-all situation rather than on detailed factual information.

2. The IAC Watch Committee provides a sound foundation for extracting intelligence from partial and inadequate information. In supporting the work of the committee, the intelligence agencies make careful cross-checks of information from all sources against an elaborate analysis of possible indicators of Soviet intentions. This method is not relied on exclusively; other approaches are constantly being tried.

3. In general there has been improvement during the past two years in the ability of current intelligence to provide prompt notice and preliminary evaluations of events and developments in the Soviet as well as in the neutral and friendly areas. This improvement is attributable to increased skill and knowledge of intelligence analysts and to a deepening sense of common purpose among the IAC agencies.

4. *There is no guarantee that intelligence will be able to give adequate warning of attack prior to actual detection of hostile formations.* Under certain circumstances, some last-minute defensive and offensive preparations on the Soviet periphery may, however, be detected. Opportunity for detection of indications of Soviet or Satellite attack varies from fair in the border areas of Germany and Korea to extremely poor in the Transcaucasus and Southeast Asia. Each agency maintains its own 24-hour Watch arrangements to handle any information that is received.

XII. Collection

1. The Foreign Service

In general, the collection activities of the Foreign Service are satisfactory. Intelligence needs are met most adequately in the political field, less so in certain aspects of the economic field, and least satisfactorily in the scientific, technical and psychological fields. These deficiencies are generally attributable to a lack of specialized competence in those fields which are not closely related to the basic diplomatic functions of the Foreign Service. Remedial action has been taken by establishing a comprehensive economic reporting program and a continuing program of providing Foreign Service posts with more complete and effective guidance on intelligence needs. Additional remedial measures in progress concern:

a. the greater use of overseas personnel of certain operational programs in collecting basic intelligence information, particularly in the psychological and sociological fields; and

b. the recognition of the role of the Foreign Service in the national intelligence effort through the revision of the Foreign Service Manual to include for the first time specific and detailed intelligence instructions.

As a result of a recent study measures to meet the needs for basic scientific information are being carried out.

2. Service Attaché System

The Service Attaché System furnishes extensive useful military information on countries outside the Iron Curtain. Attachés in the Soviet-bloc countries obtain and transmit a considerable volume of valuable information although, under the restrictions imposed on them by Communist governments, the coverage which they provide cannot be considered adequate. The Service Attaché System has been strengthened since the beginning of the Korean conflict through the opening of new offices and the assignment of additional officers to important posts. Constant efforts are being made to improve the collection capabilities of Service Attachés by the development of new collection guides and techniques.

3. Overseas Commands

Armed Forces Commands in Europe are acquiring extensive information. While intelligence collection on the Soviet Union itself is partial and inadequate, it is good in the Eastern Zones of Germany and Austria. Considerable information is gathered by European Commands from returned PW's, escapees, and refugees.

Collection of intelligence in the Far East is adequate on friendly and neutral areas but is partial and inadequate on Communist China and Eastern Siberia. Tripartite Agreements among the respective service agencies for exchange of intelligence on Southeast Asia have considerably enhanced collection capabilities in the area and are expected to improve this situation.

4. Aerial Reconnaissance

Because of overriding considerations of other than an intelligence nature, the Armed Services have not as yet exploited fully their overflight capabilities in aerial reconnaissance. Photo reconnaissance capabilities have increased, with a resulting improvement in contributions in this field. The contributions of radar reconnaissance are only fair, as compared to photo reconnaissance, but are being improved. Photo interpretation capability is generally deficient in the Armed Services; corrective measures are underway. The use of photo intelligence in the analysis of economic and scientific developments in respect of the Soviet Orbit is being strengthened. Research and development effort is being expended on free balloons, piloted and pilotless vehicles ("guided missiles" and satellites) to overcome a lack of special reconnaissance vehicles. Research continues in the improvement of various detecting devices.

5. (This paragraph is being given separate limited distribution for security reasons.)[4]

---

[4] Not found.

6. Domestic Collection

Through offices located in key cities throughout the U.S., CIA performs a service of common concern in actively collecting foreign intelligence information from business, financial, educational, and other nongovernmental organizations and private individuals. The cooperation of these organizations and individuals has consistently been, and continues to be, excellent. Particular effort has been recently directed to the collection of data on foreign scientific and technical developments, and to the exploitation of the dwindling sources of economic and political information on Communist China. Because the interests of the intelligence-producing agencies have become more sharply directed toward the Soviet Orbit, the domestic collection effort is increasingly pointed in that direction, with particular emphasis on foreign nationality groups within the United States, defectors, and other recently arrived aliens.

7. Foreign Radio Broadcasts

a. Monitoring

Immediate and extensive coverage of foreign news, information, and propaganda broadcasts is provided by a world-wide monitoring network, maintained by CIA as a service of common concern. A Moscow broadcast can be received in Washington in translation or summary within one hour. Coverage of the Soviet Orbit is excellent, except for parts of Asia and the Baltic States. Progress made during 1952 towards closing these gaps included: the activation of a station at Hokkaido, Japan, to monitor northeast Asian broadcasts; negotiations with the British Broadcasting Company for monitoring of Baltic and northwestern USSR transmitters by the BBC under existing reciprocal arrangements; and a monitoring survey in Pakistan to explore the possibilities of covering hitherto unmonitorable Central Asian broadcasts.

b. Propaganda Analysis

Propaganda Analysis in support of psychological warfare activities and overt programs such as the VOA, has been further improved. Quantitative and content analysis of radio propaganda has been supplemented by some analysis of published propaganda and press material. More rapid and specialized support on radio propaganda is now provided to "watch" groups and estimating offices.

8. Foreign Materials and Equipment

The collection and technical analysis of Soviet Orbit products has continued to aid in the assessment of USSR scientific, economic, and technological capabilities, although the procurement during 1952 of significant items has not come up to expectations. Foreign materials and equipment are vital to the factory markings analysis program. Owing to the relative stability of the fighting front in Korea, the amount of captured materiel of intelligence importance has declined. At present the most productive channels for selective procurement of Soviet manufactured items and raw materials are official U.S. missions and covert CIA components overseas. Items procured reasonably successfully through such channels during the year included power tools, pharmaceuticals, rubber products, and metallurgical samples. Improvement in the coordination, through the Joint Materiel Intelligence Agency, of technical analysis requirements and exploitation activities has resulted in a greater yield of information from Soviet objects acquired.

9. Monitoring of Radio Jamming

Under NSC 66/1[5] the agencies undertook the construction and organization of a monitoring system to obtain information on Soviet jamming and related activities in the radio frequency spectrum. A pilot operation involving a very limited number of stations is being established. Adequate information as to the extent of Soviet jamming, concentration of the jamming stations, and related information must await the initiation and implementation of a much-expanded program.

XIII. Support and Collation Facilities

1. Availability of Materials

With a few exceptions, all pertinent foreign positive intelligence, both raw and finished, is distributed among all interested IAC agencies. In addition to the distribution of current material, there is a continuing effort to locate and extract pertinent information from the large volume of intelligence material that was collected during and after the war, and from other collections in overseas files. The sheer volume of these materials presents formidable and as yet unsolved problems. No IAC agency, utilizing existing techniques, is in a position to record and store all this material and to make the information contained therein readily available to analysts requiring it. Remedy for this problem is being sought through the refinement of agency responsibilities and the development of machine indexing techniques.

2. Library Facilities

While the libraries of the IAC agencies are not yet self-sufficient, they are equipped to satisfy most of the major needs of their users. Their utility can be increased and their effectiveness can be improved in connection with current plans for improving central reference facilities.

---

[5] For NSC 66/1, "Intelligence Support for the Voice of America With Regard to Soviet Jamming," see Document 44.

3. Biographic Information

Each IAC agency maintains files of biographic data on foreign personalities for its own particular purposes and makes such data available to the other agencies upon request. Excellent data can be made available on political, military, and scientific personalities outside the Iron Curtain; coverage within the Soviet Orbit is necessarily partial and inadequate. Personalities in the economic and industrial fields are poorly covered at present although there is considerable information available. Means of improvement are currently being studied. As a result of recent arrangements between the State Department and CIA, the latter is discontinuing biographic intelligence in the political, social, and cultural fields and will in the future depend on the Department of State for such intelligence.

4. Photographic Files

The several Defense agencies and CIA each maintain photographic and related documentary libraries consistent with their requirements and responsibilities. Material in each library is available to the IAC community. Continuing effort must be exerted to increase the quality and quantity of this source of intelligence.

5. Map Procurement and Reference Services

[2½ lines not declassified] Results during the past three years have proved the effectiveness of overt collection of maps and related information through the Foreign Service Geographic Attaché program. Increased emphasis is being placed on the collection of maps and engineering drawings from domestic sources. Service Attaché channels are also being used. The currently published foreign maps required for intelligence activities are received on a continuing basis through exchange arrangements between the Department of State and many foreign official mapping agencies. These exchanges are in addition to those of an operational character maintained by the Military Services. Excellent map reference services in support of intelligence requirements are maintained by close working arrangements between the map libraries.

6. Foreign Language Publications

The exploitation of foreign language publications for intelligence purposes is presently undertaken in varying degrees by each agency. [2½ lines not declassified] Currently, the IAC agencies are considering plans with reference to the exploitation of foreign language publications which might result in improved coordination in procurement, exploitation, and indexing for intelligence purposes.

Translation is also done by each agency, though coordination is effected to prevent duplication. Overseas abstracting from foreign language publications is presently performed at a number of diplomatic posts. This work is coordinated with similar CIA and departmental activities in the U.S. to avoid duplication and to make the maximum use of available linguists.

Most publications needed for the intelligence effort are now being obtained, though major gaps exist in regard to Soviet Bloc materials. Through overt and covert channels there is an increasing effort to improve procurement in this latter category.

7. External Research

External research in the social sciences of particular interest to intelligence has presented difficult problems of coordination. In order to improve coordination CIA and the Department of State are jointly strengthening the latter's External Research Staff, and the Department of Defense has taken steps to ensure necessary coordination of external research contacts on psychological warfare among military agencies. It is expected that liaison arrangements between the Department of Defense, Department of State, and CIA in this field will produce substantial progress during the current year in minimizing duplication, ensuring community benefit of finished research and facilitate more rational letting of external research contracts. Evaluation of this program as it affects the Department of Defense cannot as yet be given.

No. 8. The Internal Security Program[6]

Recent information regarding the feasibility of hand-portable atomic weapons makes possible their clandestine use and thus requires a complete reappraisal, which is underway, of virtually the whole internal security program. Action on initial countermeasures, approved by the President on December 29, 1952, is being taken by the IIC, the ICIS, and the AEC.

Domestic counter-intelligence has been improved by a great expansion of informant coverage, with emphasis on subversive movements and key industrial facilities. By vigorous prosecution of functionaries of the Communist Party, USA under the Smith Act, and by action to compel registration of the Party as a Communist action organization under the Internal Security Act of 1950, the Party's National Board has been neutralized, its leaders convicted or forced into hiding, Party and bail funds depleted, membership reduced appreciably and recruitment drastically hampered. However, such vigorous action

---

[6] Source: National Archives, RG 273, NSC Representative on Internal Security, NSC 142, Box 46. Top Secret; Security Information. Prepared jointly by the Interdepartmental Intelligence Conference and the Interdepartmental Committee on Internal Security. An attached statement on the objective of the internal security program, consisting of a quotation from NSC 142, is not printed.

has also driven the Party further underground and made counter-intelligence and continued prosecution more difficult. Investigative agencies assert the need for more intelligence regarding Soviet and satellite espionage and sabotage organizations, additional manpower, and additional funds for military internal security programs.

In the event of war, plans are ready for immediate apprehension of 20,000 dangerous civilians. Related programs are being prepared to neutralize dangerous U.S. military personnel, enemy aliens and diplomatic personnel. Accordingly, most potentially dangerous individuals should be neutralized within the initial period of a Soviet attack.

Although Executive Order 10290[7] on the safeguarding of classified security information is in force, an acceptable degree of security for such information will not be achieved until satisfactory standards of clearance are established for access to such information by government employees and consultants, by non-government personnel in classified contract work, and by representatives of foreign governments. ICIS recommendations on personnel security and access have been made but not adopted. (The ICIS has not participated in the Loyalty program.)

There is a high degree of installation security for some sensitive government buildings and areas, but uniform standards have not yet been generally achieved. Some progress has been made in industrial installation security, but protective programs do not include control of sub-contracting plants of classified contractors nor essential civilian wartime industrial facilities. Legal sanction is lacking to remove security risks in industry and there is difficulty in preventing strikes by Communist-infiltrated unions. Plant visitors are inadequately identified and checked. Accordingly, it should come as no surprise if acts of sabotage occur.

The port security program, limited to major ports, has not achieved reasonable security as regards fire protection and harbor entrance guarding. No effective security program is in force for telecommunications.

Control over the entry of dangerous aliens has not been achieved, largely because of personnel limitations in the Coast Guard and the Customs and Immigration Service, lack of control over alien crewmen, inadequate surveillance of foreign vessels, and poor control over foreign diplomatic and official personnel. The Omnibus Immigration Act, effective December 24, 1952,[8] provides authority for remedying some inadequacies in entry control. There is little control over illegal entry by coastal or plane landings. On departures from the U.S., there are few effective exit controls operative, although there is limited screening of

---

[7] For E.O. 10290, see 3 CFR 1949–53 compilation, pp. 790–797 or 16 FR 9795.
[8] 66 Stat. 163–281.

crewmen under the Magnuson Act. Export and monetary controls present no significant problems.

Arrangements to report unconventional attacks have been made, but countermeasures provide little security against clandestine AW, BW and CW unconventional attacks.

---

147.   Memorandum From Director of Central Intelligence Dulles to the Chief of Staff of the Air Force (Vandenberg)[1]

Washington, May 20, 1953.

SUBJECT

Air Resupply and Communications (ARC) Wing Program

1. In the fall of 1950, you informed this Agency[2] that, in anticipation of CIA requirements for support of covert operations, the U.S. Air Force was organizing several Special Operational Wings. At that time, it was contemplated that a total of seven such wings, which are now designated Air Resupply and Communications (ARC) Wings, would be organized. About a year later, the magnitude of this program was reconsidered in the light of over-all manpower limitations and the number of wings was reduced from seven to four. We now understand that consideration is being given to a still further curtailment which will reduce the number of wings to two, and that as a part of this plan the 500th ARC Wing will move from Wheelus Field, Libya, to Molesworth Air Force Base, England, and the 581st ARC Wing from Clark Field, R. F., to Okinawa.

2. We are, of course, cognizant of the many problems which confront the USAF at this time. However, the reduction of the number of ARC Wings to only two has serious implications upon our plans both for current operations and in the event of a "hot" war.

3. During the "cold war," CIA has a very substantial and growing requirement for support in the serial transport, handling and storage of its matériel and supplies. This Agency depends upon the ARC Wings to furnish a major part of such support. Manifestly, full utiliza-

---

[1] Source: Central Intelligence Agency, Office of the Deputy Director for Operations, Job 79–01228A, Box 8. Top Secret; Security Information. Cleared by Wisner and Cabell.

[2] This communication has not been further identified.

tion of the capabilities of the ARC Wings cannot be achieved rapidly, but it is believed that a good beginning toward such full utilization has been made and we are looking forward to a continuing expansion of our joint operations.

4. The wartime mission of the ARC Wings is stated to be: (1) air support of Unconventional Warfare Operations; and (2) the preparation and dissemination of Psychological Warfare materials. While no formal agreement exists that the Wings will be available to support CIA covert operations, this Agency has always assumed that they would be, and war plans have been made on that basis. These war plans require the availability of effective air support facilities on D-Day for the immediate support of guerrilla and resistance operations. Following D-Day, there will be an increasing requirement for this type support to meet war plans jointly developed by the CIA and the JCS. As I am sure you are aware, air support of covert operations requires that the personnel be highly trained in the peculiar techniques involved and have the specialized equipment to implement these techniques.

5. If our understanding of the planned reduction to two wings is correct, it appears to us that improved utilization of the capabilities of the ARC Wings under both "cold war" and "hot war" conditions, could be effected if storage and packaging facilities could be retained in the Tripoli area, thus giving greater flexibility to the support which the 580th ARC Wing could render to us in the European-Near Eastern-African area. In effect, therefore, the Tripoli facilities would be a satellite of the permanent base at Molesworth. Similarly, in the Far East we would very much like to see comparable satellite facilities maintained at Clark Field because of the vital necessity of maintaining an adequate base in the sensitive Southeast Asia area. Our objective, which we believe is apparent, is to insure the maximum utility of ARC by the maintenance of additional packing and storage facilities at Tripoli and at Clark. These facilities would give ARC, and in turn CIA, greatly increased flexibility and would enhance the operational utility of these organizations. By maintaining these additional packing and storage facilities, the reduction in the ARC program from four to two wings, in our opinion, would be minimized.

6. For obvious reasons, it is impossible for this Agency to predict accurately the time and place where ARC Wing facilities will be most needed. However, in an endeavor to exploit to the utmost the capabilities of the two wings to give maximum support to the conduct of covert operations, the possibility of creating satellite facilities as outlined above is offered. While the movement of aircraft presents no major problem, the transfer of substantial amounts of supplies and matériel is very difficult to achieve, especially so under wartime conditions.

7. Request that USAF units capable of rendering the above support be included in the over-all Air Force program.

8. In the event that you feel that this memorandum should have been addressed to the Secretary of Defense, request you so advise.

Allen W. Dulles[3]

---

[3] Printed from a copy that indicates Dulles signed the original.

---

148. Editorial Note

The United States Government supported the creation of a Volunteer Freedom Corps, to comprise nationals of Eastern European countries (other than East Germany). Major U.S. allies opposed the proposal, and consequently, it died a slow death. Consideration of the Volunteer Freedom Corps is covered extensively in *Foreign Relations, 1952–1954*, volume VIII. The Department of State had major reservations about the proposals, some of which were raised by Under Secretary Smith in the 145th meeting of the National Security Council, May 20, 1953. (Ibid., pages 213–218)

---

149. Memorandum From William P. Bundy of the Office of National Estimates of the Central Intelligence Agency to Director of Central Intelligence Dulles[1]

Washington, May 26, 1953.

SUBJECT

NSC 140/1, the Edwards Report[2]

---

[1] Source: Central Intelligence Agency, Office of the Deputy Director for Intelligence, Job 80–R01440R, Box 3. Top Secret; Security Information; Special Security Handling. A stamped notation on the memorandum indicates that Dulles saw it on June 3.

[2] Documentation on NSC 140/1, May 18, 1953, also known as the Edwards Report, is in *Foreign Relations, 1952–1954*, vol. II, Part 1, pp. 328–349, 355–360, and 367–370.

1. Attached is the Edwards Report,[3] just in case it should arise in the discussion of the Armaments question.[4]

2. For your present purposes, the following are worth noting:

a. The Report assumes a Soviet stockpile of 120 in mid-1953 and 300 in mid-1955, and proceeds from these figures with an allocation of these levels between: (1) SAC bases in US; (2) SAC bases overseas; (3) other US targets. The assumed stockpile levels are the median JAEIC figures, and the presumed allocations are regarded as logical attempts to inflict maximum damage on the US—they do not claim to be *the* allocation the Soviets would necessarily make. As General Edwards is pointing out in his separate letter, a need exists for a systematic study of Soviet strategy in the event of war.

b. General Webster of the JCS "neither concurs nor non-concurs." This unfortunate position is the result of the fact that the original terms of reference called for considering overseas installations, with reference to their importance to defence of the continental US and to a US counteroffensive. This limitation was insisted on by General Bradley personally, in the original oral discussions with General Smith, specifically in order to avoid covering "every PT boat in the Adriatic." It was the understanding of all who participated in the original laying out of the project that we would stick to the fewest possible bases abroad, and those would be related to the *air* effort. Unfortunately the word "air" was omitted from the written form, although the Edwards Committee orally agreed to interpret it in this way. Thus, the JCS working group got off and allocated a very small number of bombs (10, I believe) to *non-air* targets such as ports and major ground supply dumps. The Committee threw out this allocation and stuck to the air bases—and at the last minute General Webster took the stand that he could not sign the report! The actual difference is minimal, and should not really affect the substance. But there it is.

3. In its basic conclusions, the report fully supports statements that the Soviets could probably damage the US critically in the next few years. While the damage predicated for mid-1955 is less than some thought it would be, the curve of bombs-on-target is obviously rising between mid-1953 and mid-1955. The Committee did not consider the possible effect of the early warning McGill and Lincoln lines, since it was thought they could not be effective by mid-1955. Whether the curve can be levelled off by defensive measures is now in controversy.

WPB

---

[3] Attached but not printed.

[4] Reference may be to Allen Dulles' participation in the May 27 NSC meeting which discussed armaments and American policy. A memorandum of that discussion is ibid., Part 2, pp. 1169–1174.

150.   Letter From Director of Central Intelligence Dulles to the Chairman of the Continental Defense Committee (Bull)[1]

Washington, June 30, 1953.

Dear General Bull:

In response to your request of June 15,[2] for the views of this Agency on organizational arrangements to provide the best possible continuing production of Net Capability Estimates, the following thoughts are submitted:

There is no need to argue the necessity for reliable estimates of net capabilities as the basis for national policy formulation. These can only be prepared by careful integration of gross-capability intelligence of the enemy with our capabilities and plans, so that the net result of the interplay may be forecast as accurately as possible. This need is not confined to the problem of defense of North America but is equally inescapable for planning US requirements and commitments in any part of the globe.

The President and the NSC in practice and pursuant to statutory authority depend on the Director of Central Intelligence, representing the coordinated views of the Intelligence Agencies, for foreign intelligence estimates, and on the Chairman of the Joint Chiefs of Staff, speaking as their representative, for military advice. Thus what is required to furnish the President and Council with guidance in the most useful and complete form is the effective amalgamation of the functions of the two.

Responsibility for such combined analysis cannot rightly be assigned to one of these advisers to the exclusion of the other, for both are coordinate staff officers serving the same commander. Each must consider the factors developed by the other in order to eliminate reliance on arbitrary assumptions and produce valid and realistic forecasts.

It is my view, therefore, that the President and Council should establish a permanent subcommittee on Net Capability Estimates to be composed of:

The Chairman of the Joint Chiefs of Staff
The Director of Central Intelligence

---

[1] Source: Central Intelligence Agency, Office of the Deputy Director for Intelligence, Job 80–R01440R, Box 3. Top Secret. Security Information. In connection with the NSC's evaluation of the net capabilities of the Soviet Union (NSC 140/1), General Bull chaired a committee on continental defense, which was supposed to complete its report in mid-July. See *Foreign Relations, 1952–1954*, vol. II, Part 1, p. 368.

[2] Not further identified.

and that this subcommittee be charged with providing, on its initiative or as requested by the Council, estimates of net capabilities as needed to support the formulation of national policy.

The manner in which this subcommittee would discharge its function should be left flexible and might very well differ substantially according to the nature of the estimate undertaken. It should have authority to secure support and information from all executive branches of the government and should be required to consult with such agencies and interdepartmental committees as may be able to contribute significantly to any estimate. The subcommittee should take such action as may be necessary to preserve the security of highly sensitive information such as U.S. war plans and intelligence sources.

I believe you will find that the views expressed herein are substantially the same as those stated by General Smith in his memorandum of 14 October 1952 to the Executive Secretary of the National Security Council,[3] and orally to the National Security Council on 26 November 1952,[4] and to the Joint Chiefs of Staff on 17 December 1952.[5] Thus, though the need has long been recognized, no general or continuing machinery has yet been established. It is my earnest hope that as a result of the recommendations of your Committee, the Council will take necessary action along the lines I have indicated.

Sincerely yours,

Allen W. Dulles[6]

---

[3] Document 131.
[4] See Document 138.
[5] No record of these oral comments has been found.
[6] Printed from a copy that indicates Dulles signed the original.

---

151. Editorial Note

The Report of the President's Committee on International Information Activities (the Jackson Committee report), June 30, 1953, dealt in part with intelligence and intelligence-related activities. For the text of the report, see *Foreign Relations*, 1952–1954, volume II, Part 2, pages 1795–1874. For a progress report on implementation of the report, prepared by the Operations Coordinating Board and circulated on October 1, 1953, see ibid., pages 1877–1899.

152. Memorandum From the Deputy Secretary of Defense (Kyes)[1]

Washington, July 15, 1953.

MEMORANDUM FOR THE

Secretaries of the Military Departments
Joint Chiefs of Staff
Assistant Secretaries of Defense
Chairmen of Boards, Committees and Councils, OSD
Assistants to the Secretary of Defense
Directors of Offices, OSD

SUBJECT

Reorganization—Office of Special Operations, Office of the Secretary of Defense

REFERENCES

Department of Defense Directive C-5132.1
Department of Defense Directive S-3140.1[2]

General Graves B. Erskine, USMC (Retired), has been appointed Assistant to the Secretary of Defense and Director, Office of Special Operations, Office of the Secretary of Defense. His office and responsibilities are within the immediate purview of the Deputy Secretary of Defense, to whom he will report.

All functions formerly assigned to the Deputy for Psychological Policy and to the Office of Psychological Policy, Office of the Secretary of Defense, are hereby assigned to the Office of Special Operations; the Office of Psychological Policy is therefore abolished; and personnel thereof assigned to the Office of Special Operations.

The functions of the Office of Special Operations encompass all psychological operations activities in which the Department of Defense participates, including monitorship of psychological warfare planning, operations, and research and development; as well as unconventional warfare, international information activities, and other operations of a similar nature which are within the cognizance of the Psychological Strategy Board, its successor agencies, or within the provisions of NSC 10/2,[3]

---

[1] Source: Central Intelligence Agency, Office of the Deputy Director for Operations, Job 79–01228A, Box 8. Secret; Security Information.

[2] The two references were not found.

[3] See *Foreign Relations*, 1945–1950, Emergence of the Intelligence Establishment, Document 292.

NSC 10/5,[4] NSC 59/1,[5] and the report by the President's Committee on International Information Activities.[6]

It is also the function of the Office of Special Operations to advise and assist the Secretary of Defense and his staff on all matters pertaining to the national intelligence effort, including those provided under NSCID No. 9 Revised,[7] in which the Office of the Secretary of Defense has a direct interest or designated responsibility.

It is the duty of the Director, Office of Special Operations, to provide staff support for the Secretary of Defense and the Deputy Secretary of Defense in these fields and to perform such other duties as may be assigned. The Director, Office of Special Operations, will provide principal staff representation for the Office of the Secretary of Defense in all such matters with other departments and agencies of the U.S. Government.

For these purposes the Director, Office of Special Operations, is herewith delegated the authority to obtain such reports and information from the military departments as are necessary to carry out his responsibilities, and is authorized to request the military departments to issue the necessary directives to obtain such reports and information.

In the performance of these functions, the Director, Office of Special Operations, will to the extent practical, utilize the advice, assistance, and appropriate facilities of the military departments. Such utilization shall not, however, be construed or so utilized as to circumvent the existing command channels through the Secretaries of the military departments for the formal communication of approved policies, plans, or other directives.

The reference directives remain in effect except as modified by this memorandum with respect to subordination and title of office pending their reissuance or recision after completion of anticipated National Security Council–Executive Branch reorganization now under consideration.

Roger M. Kyes[8]

---

[4] Document 90.

[5] Document 2.

[6] See Document 151.

[7] Document 257.

[8] Printed from a copy that indicates Kyes signed the original.

153. Report by the Psychological Strategy Board[1]

PSB D–47   Washington, July 29, 1953.

STATUS REPORT ON THE NATIONAL PSYCHOLOGICAL EFFORT AS OF JUNE 30, 1953

[Omitted here are a cover page, title page, and table of contents.]

I. Status of the Program on June 30, 1953

1. The Board presents below a brief evaluative summary of the status of our national psychological programs as of June 30, 1953, based largely on the appended Progress Reports by the departments and agencies responsible for operations.

General

2. While the President's Committee on International Information Activities studied the whole problem of the world struggle with a view to basic improvements in the U.S. position, the struggle, on the psychological as on other fronts, was conducted with increased vigor. The most far-reaching opportunity came with Stalin's death. The President's speech of April 16[2] was signally successful in capitalizing on the situation by appealing to the new leaders for an era of worldwide peace and friendship. The world at large received the speech with great enthusiasm, and the follow up support through psychological exploitation added to the initial success.

3. Further exploitation of events behind the Iron Curtain has been guided by the requirement that psychological operations must be keyed in with political action. After Stalin's death, the next major occasion for such action followed the outbreaks in Czechoslovakia and East Germany. Plans and operations were stepped up accordingly, with prospect of conducting a major campaign in the long-range contest to take full advantage of the consequences of Stalin's death.

4. Outside of the Soviet orbit the developments on the psychological front have been characterized by a disappointing deterioration

---

[1] Source: National Archives, RG 59, S/S–NSC Files: Lot 62 D 333, PSB D–47. Top Secret. PSB D–47, a Progress Report by the Psychological Strategy Board, was submitted to the President and the National Security Council on July 29. The title page of the report indicates that it was prepared pursuant to a May 27 memorandum from NSC Executive Secretary Lay to the Acting Director of the Psychological Strategy Board which has not been found. Also on the title page is a note by Charles E. Johnson, Secretary to the Board, indicating that the Board approved the report at its July 29 meeting.

[2] Reference is to President Eisenhower's "The Chance for Peace" speech; text in *Public Papers: Eisenhower, 1953*, pp. 179–188.

in the attitudes towards the U.S. Non-Communist press and public opinion in Western Europe has reflected mounting criticism of U.S. foreign policy (the possible trend back to isolationism), and alleged anti-Communist "hysteria". These unfavorable attitudes in combination with a generally more receptive reaction among Western European peoples to the Soviet "peace offensive" now constitute an intensification of anti-American feeling among significant elements of European opinion.

5. World opinion has also been markedly unfavorable towards the development of U.S. foreign trade policies. At the same time that we are sharply reducing our programs for economic assistance, it has felt that we are providing little indication that our markets are to be opened up to foreign goods. Congressional criticism of our allies for their practices in the field of East-West trade, in combination with the new Soviet line on expansion of trade with the free world, has begun to have an adverse psychological impact around the world.

6. Urgent planning for stronger psychological measures based on Thailand was set in motion as the result of the invasion of Laos and the accompanying threat of Communist aggression in Southeast Asia.

7. While our overt psychological capabilities have been reduced by personnel difficulties, pressures in the Congress and appropriations cuts, covert capabilities continued to make sound progress, and faster and more energetic teamwork was secured through closer relations with the NSC and the operating agencies.

Areas

8. Within the *USSR* itself, radio still constitutes the only important means used currently to reach the Russian people. Jamming by the Russian radio of our broadcasts continues to present a major problem. There was however, a perceptible increase in effectiveness of our radio resources in the last six months due to the inauguration of Radio Liberation and the stepped-up activity of Radio Free Russia. In addition to the radio, leaflet distribution was utilized to reach Soviet military forces stationed outside the USSR.

9. Similarly, in *Communist China*, the major psychological activities presently available are radio and leaflet drops. Both of these are being substantially increased. Through *Hongkong*, increased use is being made of overt, grey and black propaganda channels with the Chinese Mainland.

10. In the *European Satellites* likewise, radio is our major propaganda communications medium. RIAS, RFE, and VOA have contributed to the building up of pressures that may be instrumental in weakening the Kremlin's control of the satellites. In most of these *Satellite States*, progress in other forms of psychological activity, mainly unattributable, has been slow, and has centered on the build-up of operating potential. There

has, however, been increased action, including leaflet drops, in certain satellites—notably Albania, Bulgaria, and Rumania.

11. A high degree of access to *East Germany* was maintained despite increasing Soviet security restriction. Virtually the entire area has been continuously subjected to U.S. psychological programs through mainly indigenous channels.

12. In *Western Europe,* the presence of U.S. Armed Forces and the Military Aid program provided a significant psychological impact. Increased emphasis on troop acceptance programs enlisting the positive cooperation of the governments and the local authorities has brought about a definite improvement in most areas in the problem of avoiding friction between U.S. military personnel and foreign populations.

13. Among the principal problems that have confronted U.S. psychological efforts in Western Europe during the past six months are increased criticism of the U.S. and, especially since Stalin's death, the Soviet "Peace Offensive". It is evident that many, if not all, Western European governments have been influenced to some extent by the Kremlin's tension-reducing tactics. The effect has been to retard progress toward a number of our objectives, including the build-up of Western defenses, the ratification of EDC, and attainment of European integration.

14. The U.S. counter-offensive has included fullest exploitation by the Department of State's Information Program of the President's Inaugural address[3] and of his April 16 speech challenging the new leaders of the USSR to prove their peaceful professions by deeds, not words. Copies of the latter were presented to Foreign Offices all over the world in advance of delivery and kinescopes of the entire speech were sent to seventy-three posts within a day of its delivery. One of these was shown over BBC television on April 20 to an estimated audience of 6,000,000. Five million pamphlets, handbills, and leaflets on the speech were prepared and distributed, and a documentary film of it in thirty-five languages had been produced and shipped by May 2.

15. In *Italy,* U.S. efforts to aid the reelection of the Democratic Center Parties fell considerably short of their objective. The DeGasperi Coalition was returned to office by a slender margin and the Communists and extreme Rightists registered significant gains.

16. In *France,* the municipal elections in May showed that the Communists had suffered a slight set-back in rural areas, but had maintained their position in the industrial areas in larger cities. Governmental instability was a troublesome factor during the period and a relaxation of earlier French official measures to reduce the power of the Communist Party in France resulted. The repercussions of some Con-

---

[3] Ibid., pp. 1–8.

gressional investigations, as well as of the Rosenberg executions, in conjunction with the Kremlin's peace campaign, appear to have contributed to an increase in neutralism.

17. In the *United Kingdom* also, there appears to have been a marked increase in neutralism in its special British form of Bevanism. Although the belief is still widely held that Western unity must be preserved, three major elements contribute to the growth of anti-American feeling:

(1) The belief that the U.S. is deeply divided on basic international policies,
(2) The development of the Soviet "peace offensive", and
(3) The desire to exercise a more positive and independent initiative in international affairs.

18. In *West Germany and Berlin*, the recent riots touched off greatly increased pressures for unification, complicating the problems of German ratification of the EDC. With this exception, however, U.S. psychological programs in Berlin and West Germany, as well as their projection into East Germany, appear to have been fairly effective in promoting progress toward our major goal of a Democratic Germany integrated into Western defense efforts. Since late March German press opinion has reflected a decline in confidence in U.S. leadership. This was temporarily halted by the President's April 16 speech, but has since been resumed. The two major factors contributing to this are: (1) the Soviet "peace offensive" and (2) lack of agreement within the U.S. on policy towards Germany.

19. In the *Near and Middle East and South Asia*, neutralism, and the tendency to associate the U.S. with "colonialism", continued to present a major obstacle to the attainment of U.S. psychological objectives. In the Arab States, the alleged pro-Israel bias on the part of the U.S. remained a major handicap, although the visits to Middle Eastern capitals by Secretary Dulles and Mr. Stassen may have alleviated this problem, at least temporarily. IIA has continuously exploited the beneficial aspects of these visits in its output to the area. Turkey, Pakistan, and Greece appear to be the brightest spots in this area, psychologically speaking.

20. In the *Far East*, the resumption of Korean truce talks raised major psychological problems. The exchange of sick and wounded prisoners necessitated special measures to deal with "brain washing". Steps were taken to achieve more effectively coordinated guidance on information matters concerning Korea through the channels of the Psychological Operations Coordinating Committee. The offer of a reward to MIG pilot defectors was followed by an immediate and significant shift in Communist air tactics over the Korean battle area.

21. In *Japan*, severe economic problems and growing neutralist resistance to the U.S. objective of Japanese rearmament have been

trouble spots in a picture otherwise fairly satisfactory. "Grey" and unattributable activities have progressed favorably.

22. In *Latin America,* our capabilities for effective psychological action increased in a number of countries, for the most part in the field of unattributable activity. There has been growing dissatisfaction in many Latin American countries directed mainly against American economic policies. To help offset this, a major psychological move was Dr. Milton Eisenhower's goodwill tour of South America initiated late in June.

Special Items

23. Emergency assistance provided by U.S. Armed Forces in cases of national catastrophe has made material contributions to U.S. psychological efforts in *The Netherlands, England, Turkey, Greece, Iran, Ecuador,* and *Japan.*

24. A grant of 1,000,000 tons of wheat to *Pakistan* has had a similarly favorable effect.

25. Carefully planned exploitation of U.S. leadership in the atomic field, with a coordinated public information program on the Nevada weapons tests and other special weapons, as well as certain news leaks that gave rise to widespread speculation as to the explosion of a thermo-nuclear device at Eniwetok atoll, contributed to the U.S. psychological effort.

[Omitted here are Section II. The Work of PSB; Annex A, Report of the Department of State; Annex B, Report of the Department of Defense; Annex C, Report of the Mutual Security Agency; and Annex D, General Appraisal.]

---

154.   Editorial Note

In March 1951, Jacobo Arbenz Guzman was sworn in as President of Guatemala. A climate of labor unrest and fears of a possible Sovietization of Guatemala soon prompted opposition groups to begin plotting against the Arbenz regime. Prominent among the plotters was an exiled army colonel, Carlos Castillo Armas. Castillo Armas, based in Honduras, had the active support of Nicaragua's Anastasio Somoza and the United Fruit Company. By early 1952, the CIA, concerned about Arbenz's growing reliance on left-wing activists, including members of the Communist Party, had made contact with Castillo Armas. Plans for assistance were dropped in October 1952, however, after rumors of U.S. involvement became widespread and Arbenz's forces began taking preemptive action.

Guatemala re-emerged as a priority during the Eisenhower administration. On August 12, 1953, the Guatemalans announced their second expropriation of United Fruit Company land. On that same day, the Operations Coordinating Board authorized the CIA to proceed "on a basis of high priority" on the project which was to become PBSUCCESS. Utilizing a $3 million budget, the CIA trained Castillo Armas' men and expanded contacts with Guatemalan army officers in hopes of persuading them to overthrow the government from inside. Fears that Arbenz would form an open alliance with the Communists were reinforced when a Swedish ship carrying Communist-bloc weaponry arrived in Guatemala in May 1954. American officials used this event to reinforce Guatemalan army fears that Arbenz wanted to arm a people's militia, under party discipline, to nullify the army's power.

Castillo Armas and his men invaded Guatemala from Honduran territory on June 18, 1954, and were soon engaged in a series of inconclusive battles with larger Guatemalan army formations. Intense American diplomatic and propaganda pressure, as well as airstrikes by World War II era fighters flown by CIA contract pilots, created a sense of confusion and crisis among Arbenz and his regime. Meanwhile, clandestine CIA contacts with the regular army finally persuaded several powerful officers to confront Arbenz, who resigned on June 27, 1954. Over the next few days, American diplomats and intelligence officers helped broker the ticklish negotiations between Castillo Armas and the officers who led the coup. Castillo Armas was eventually installed as President of Guatemala. See *Foreign Relations, 1952–1954, Guatemala.*

155. National Security Council Report[1]

NSC 161   Washington, August 14, 1953.

STATUS OF UNITED STATES PROGRAMS FOR
NATIONAL SECURITY AS OF JUNE 30, 1953

[Omitted here are Parts 1–8 of the report.]

No. 9—The Foreign Intelligence Program

(In concurring in this report, the IAC agencies wish to point out that the effects of recent budget cuts on intelligence activities cannot be assessed at this time, and are therefore not reflected in this report.)

I. Coordination

1. Coordination among the intelligence agencies, so essential to producing adequate intelligence for national security purposes and to reducing cost by avoiding duplication, is improving. There is still some duplication of effort which adds to the cost of intelligence, but steps are being taken continually to reduce this to a minimum.

2. On March 7, at the recommendation of the Director of Central Intelligence, with the concurrence of the members of the Intelligence Advisory Committee, the NSC issued NSCID No. 16,[2] directing the DCI to ensure coordination of procurement and processing of foreign language publications. No other recommendations for coordination have been made to the NSC during the past six months; however, several improvements in intelligence coordination have been accomplished by mutual agreement among the intelligence agencies and others. There are at present, in addition to the Intelligence Advisory Committee established by NSCID No. 1,[3] nine interdepartmental committees to coordinate important intelligence programs in atomic energy, domestic exploitation, defection, watch procedures, economic intelligence, economic warfare intelligence, scientific intelligence, clandestine intelligence priorities and foreign language publications.

---

[1] Source: National Archives, RG 59, S/S–NSC Files: Lot 63 D 351, NSC 161 Memoranda, Box 74. Top Secret; Security Information. NSC 161 replaced NSC 142. For NSC 142, see Document 146. Although NSC 161 was dated and circulated on August 14, Part No. 9 was completed, concurred in, and dated August 4.

[2] Document 258.

[3] See *Foreign Relations, 1945–1950*, Emergence of the Intelligence Establishment, Document 432.

II. National Estimates

1. The organization and procedures established since October 1950 for the production of national intelligence estimates continue to operate satisfactorily. The totality of resources of the entire intelligence community is drawn upon to produce national intelligence estimates, and they can be improved only as we strengthen these resources. These estimates derive authority from the manner of their preparation and from the active participation of all the responsible intelligence agency heads in their final review and adoption. Agency dissents are recorded where estimates would be watered down by further efforts to secure agreement.

2. A production program for national intelligence estimates is prepared annually and reviewed quarterly at which time obligatory changes are made. This program provides for a re-examination of existing estimates on critical areas or problems as well as the production of new estimates designed to improve the coverage of important topics. Continued emphasis is placed on the completion of basic estimates on the USSR in advance of the review of U.S. budget estimates and NATO plans.

3. Close coordination between planners and policy-makers on the one hand and the intelligence community on the other is continually being pressed in an effort to make the intelligence produced both useful and timely. The IAC mechanism is most useful when the NSC is furnished with a coordinated intelligence view in advance of the time when the policy is fixed. This is being done with increasing frequency and directness of application to the policy issues.

4. Special efforts are being made to get greater precision and clarity in estimates generally. As a particular case, considerable progress was made in NIE–65, "Soviet Bloc Capabilities through 1957", (16 June 1953), over NIE–64, "Soviet Bloc Capabilities through Mid-1954", (12 November 1952):[4]

a. Greater analytical precision in the section on political warfare capabilities, which concentrates upon the critical areas of the world, and which distinguishes between the capability to overthrow governments and the capability to influence governments and peoples.

b. Greater emphasis on scientific and technical factors, which occupy about a quarter of the discussion in NIE–65.

c. Greater clarity in the military strengths and capabilities sections, with fewer figures, more emphasis on military programs, and a more specific analysis of Bloc air defenses and of Soviet capabilities to deliver atomic weapons in the U.S.

---

[4] Extracts of NIE 65 are printed ibid., 1952–1954, vol. VIII, Document 599. A declassified text of NIE 64 is in National Archives, RG 263, National Intelligence Estimates.

III. Political, Social and Cultural Intelligence

1. The status of political, social and cultural intelligence has been very good, due allowance being made for the paucity of information on the Soviet Orbit and the difficulties of collecting it. Facilities for the production of such intelligence, however, have been adequate only for the needs of the NSC and the most urgent needs of the IAC agencies. Less pressing demands have been met only partially and inadequately.

2. The principal deficiency in this field, which varies from slight to serious, has been in the resources devoted to the exhaustive coverage and research on which sound estimates and analyses depend. Coverage of the USSR, the Eastern European Satellite complex, and China, has been most nearly adequate. Relatively lower priority has been given to research on other areas, with Western Europe, Japan and Southeast Asia at the upper end of the scale, graduating downward to Latin America and Africa. The inadequacy of resources has been reflected chiefly in an inability to prosecute sustained research programs at all desired points. Nonetheless, there has remained sufficient flexibility to produce individual studies of considerable depth on selected major problems. World Communism, outside the Soviet Orbit, has been satisfactorily covered with respect to party strength, political maneuverings and relationships to the Moscow propaganda lines. Research into matters of organization, financial support and infiltration into political and social organizations has been less satisfactory.

IV. Armed Forces Intelligence

1. Operational Intelligence

Intelligence covering the combat zone area for the support of current military operations in Korea is generally adequate. There still remains a serious deficiency in our ability to obtain timely identification of or information on the movements or locations of Chinese forces in all areas behind the immediate front line armies in Korea back through Manchuria into China. Information on installations and on developments in Manchuria, such as types and extent of training, reorganization and resupply of the Chinese Communist Forces and North Korean units north of the Yalu River is inadequate. This deficiency remains substantially unchanged. Reliable information on the enemy's long-range plans and intentions is practically non-existent.

The extent of our information on Chinese Communist activities in South China is inadequate. The United States is dependent on French and Associated States sources for operational intelligence concerning the Viet Minh and to a lesser extent for information on the Chinese Communists in the border areas contiguous to Indochina. The present level of information would be inadequate for support of operations by U.S. forces; however, inherent in any commitment of U.S. forces would be the rapid development of combat and operational intelligence efforts. The Five-power Intelligence Conference exchanges have increased U.S. knowledge of the Viet Minh.

A possible early augmentation of U.S. intelligence personnel in Indochina should improve present U.S. coverage in that area. However, the picture for the major target area in Asia, i.e., Communist China, is very dark.

The achievement of any major improvement must depend on the increase in scope and efficiency of clandestine operations against military targets.

2. Order of Battle and Equipment

Order of battle and equipment information on the USSR, Communist China and—to a lesser degree—the European Satellites is partial and inadequate, primarily because of the extreme difficulty of collection. Intelligence on Communist Bloc units and equipment in most areas with which the United States or nations friendly to the United States are in contact is more nearly complete and reliable.

Coverage on order of battle intelligence and equipment is generally adequate in respect of nations outside of the Iron Curtain, except in the case of some neutral nations whose national policy restricts our access to such information.

3. Targeting

The assembly and analysis of encyclopedic target data on economic and industrial vulnerabilities is well along for the Soviet Orbit and is in intermediate research stages for Western Europe and the Far East; increasing research emphasis continues on military targets. Current target systems studies are reasonably adequate to support joint operational planning but more vigorous data collection efforts will be required to maintain these studies on a current basis and to support extended systems analysis to meet detailed service requirements.

Target intelligence required to counter the Soviet atomic threat continues to be handicapped by gaps in current information on Soviet weapons, stockpiling arrangements, delivery capabilities and specific air base potentials.

Initial production of dossiers for priority combat targets is almost complete for the USSR but coverage varies considerably for the satellite and approach areas. Extensive tactical target coverage has been completed on areas adjoining Korean theater but on other areas is in various stages of completion.

4. Support for the North Atlantic Treaty Organization (NATO)

NATO requests have been filled with the best available intelligence consistent with the National Disclosure Policy. Intelligence studies and intelligence to assist in the establishment of basic intelligence files are provided to the NATO Standing Group and NATO major commands. Releasable current studies and reports pertinent to the area and the mission of the NATO major commands are continuously provided.

V. Economic Intelligence

1. Foreign economic intelligence on the free world presents few serious problems, mainly those that arise from the wealth of material of variable quality and from the multiplicity of sources. For the Soviet Bloc, however, such intelligence is far from adequate. The Soviet government does publish some aggregate statistics of uncertain reliability which, however, can be profitably utilized by careful analysis. Apart from this source, the intelligence community is confined to exploiting a diminishing flow of low-grade data, much of which is becoming increasingly out of date. Only by taking advantage of every possible item of information in the course of a comprehensive, thoroughly planned and coordinated study can national security needs for knowledge of the Bloc's economic capabilities and vulnerabilities by met. This may mean the subordination of short-term requirements to the long-range program and a resolute and imaginative attack on problems of centralized indexing and exploitation of all pertinent materials, whether overt or classified. Individual industry studies now being produced will form the foundation for interindustry and other over-all analyses. Maximum utilization of available data will result from the application of improved statistical and other techniques.

2. In the field of economic warfare and support for allied collective controls, intelligence coverage of movements of carriers engaged in trade with the Soviet Bloc is excellent; however, information on the cargoes of these carriers is inadequate. Machinery has been established to speed up the processing and evaluation of spot data into intelligence on which action can be taken by the Economic Defense Advisory Committee and the covert services. In this regard, increased attention is being given to current trade transactions. There has been established a coordinating committee which is assisting in bringing available intelligence more quickly and fully to bear on questions arising under this program.

3. The target analysis and production activities outlined in Section IV, *Armed Forces Intelligence,* continue to involve the large-scale processing of foreign economic and technological data.

4. The heavy research requirements in the economic field make it imperative that duplicate efforts be kept at an absolute minimum. Closer integration of research programming among the various agencies concerned with economic research for intelligence is being developed through the Economic Intelligence Committee.

VI. Scientific and Technical Intelligence

1. Scientific and technical intelligence regarding the USSR and Satellites continued to make some progress during the first half of 1953. However, in the last analysis, production of realistic estimates is still dependent upon securing information on Soviet objectives and progress. There continues to be improvement in the analysis and evaluation of available information; however, the flow of information of a scientific and technical nature from conventional sources is becoming increasingly inadequate. As a consequence, there is an urgent need for the further development and utilization of new and improved methods and techniques for the collection of scientific and technical intelligence information. Efforts along these lines have progressed slowly in the past six months, notwithstanding present potential in the fields of non-communication electromagnetic interception ("noise-listening") and photographic reconnaissance.

2. A review of the effects of DCID 3/4[5] (which allocated primary production responsibilities between CIA and the departments of the Department of Defense and established the Scientific Estimates Committee (SEC)) was scheduled for the first half of 1953. In order to provide more time for an appraisal of the effects of this directive, the review has been postponed until August 1953.

3. Through detailed studies of Soviet scientific personnel, scientific literature, and through improvements in long-range detection techniques, continued improvement has been achieved in knowledge of Soviet accomplishments in the production of fissionable materials which form the basis of the Soviet atomic weapons stockpile. A reasonably good basis has been established for estimates of plutonium production to date and for predicting Soviet capabilities for future expansion in the production of this material. However, the absence of sufficient evidence on which to base conclusions on installed or planned isotope separation capacity for the production of uranium–235 results at the present time in one of the most important gaps in intelligence on the Soviet atomic energy program. Of equal significance is the lack of evidence in the thermonuclear field. In the face of increasing difficulties in the collection of relevant information, studies in depth of personnel and research activities looking toward the selection of additional useful targets offers some hope of further improvement in our knowledge during the forthcoming year. To protect sources of intelligence in this field, and assure the availability of a maximum amount of significant technical intelligence data, the DCI, with the concurrence of the IAC,

---

[5] Document 126.

on 11 April 1953 issued a directive establishing controls for the dissemination of information on the detection of atomic weapons tests within the USSR.[6]

4. Existing scientific and technical intelligence on conventional Soviet armaments other than naval continues to be good so far as standardized items in current use are concerned. However, intelligence on weapons and equipments pertaining to the Soviet air offensive and defensive capabilities remains generally inadequate. Information regarding Soviet guided missiles programs is also poor, although certain projects based on German developments are becoming better known. In general, knowledge of key scientists, test facilities, and trends in military research and development remains too inadequate to be a sound basis for predicting future Soviet weapons and equipment.

5. While the existence of a Soviet biological warfare program has not been positively confirmed, there continue to be indications supporting the belief that such a program does exist. Existence of a Soviet chemical warfare program has been confirmed; however, very little additional information related to this program has been received in the past six months. The limited progress obtained in chemical warfare intelligence has come from increased utilization of Soviet open literature in related fields. The extreme scarcity of intelligence in both fields offers an opportunity for the Soviets to obtain technological surprise.

6. Some progress has been made in the exploitation of open scientific literature and in research in depth on institutions, but knowledge of basic scientific research and development behind the Iron Curtain remains inadequate. Information on Soviet long-range scientific development programs is similarly poor. Information on the quantity of Soviet scientific and engineering manpower is reasonably adequate, but estimates of its quality remain less satisfactory. In view of the increasing importance of such basic scientific information to the prediction of future Soviet potential, a concentrated effort to improve intelligence in this field is planned for the coming months.

VII. *Psychological Intelligence*

1. Overt and covert propaganda and psychological warfare programs have developed to an unprecedented degree in the past two years. The intelligence needs of these programs fall largely within the framework of political and sociological intelligence. The orientation and organization of the material for the psychological warfare user calls for unaccustomed depth and detail both in the field reporting and in analysis.

---

[6] Not further identified.

2. The Department of State has created a Psychological Intelligence Research Staff designed to increase coordination of governmental and private research in this field.

3. The final report of the Advisory Group on Psychological and Unconventional Warfare to the Research and Development Board recommended methods by which research in these fields might be better balanced and integrated within the Department of Defense. Because of the pending reorganization of the research and development structure in the Department of Defense, the report has not been acted upon.

4. A major deficiency in this field is the lack of information and of coordinated effort among intelligence agencies in determining resistance potential, psychological vulnerabilities, and of our propaganda effectiveness with respect to target audiences behind the Iron Curtain. Encouraging progress has been made individually by intelligence agencies in the development of an intelligence basis for the support of psychological warfare activities. The results produced thus far do not meet operational requirements, in part because of the difficulty of defining those needs.

VIII. Geographic Intelligence

1. Geographic research of IAC agencies on foreign areas, including evaluations of foreign mapping activities, is providing (a) regional studies, (b) objective and area analyses in support of covert operations, and (c) staff studies for policy and operational planning. Coordinated geographic and map intelligence studies are also undertaken in support of the National Intelligence Survey program.

2. Current geographic and mapping information on the Soviet Bloc and adjacent areas is inadequate. Geographic intelligence research gives particular attention to the regional analysis of those geographic facts that are required in support of planning and operational intelligence for these areas. Emphasis has been placed on the exploitation and utilization of available Russian technical literature in filling critical gaps. Within CIA, particular attention has also been given to the study of current developments in Soviet mapping activities and programs.

IX. Basic Intelligence

1. The program of National Intelligence Surveys (NIS), which was begun in 1948 as an interdepartmental cooperative venture, was intended to meet the U.S. Government's demands for encyclopedic factual intelligence on a world-wide basis. Since the NIS program was begun 1,729 individual sections have been produced on 66 of the 108 NIS areas, which is the equivalent of approximately 26 complete NIS. Of this number, 1,224 have been published. For the first time during the history of the program, the rate of production by contributing

agencies equivalent to 8 NIS, as established by the JCS, was attained in fiscal year 1953. Based on this performance, a similar production program has been established for fiscal year 1954.

2. NIS production is scheduled in accordance with JCS priorities and intelligence agency capabilities. Limitations of the latter have precluded production of NIS on *all* JCS high priority areas and made it necessary to undertake partial surveys on some other areas. However, NIS production on the group of 19 areas and 4 ocean areas of highest priority is approximately 54% complete, whereas the entire program is about 28% complete. NIS on twelve individual areas are over 75% complete, and five of these are in the JCS high priority list. Geographic research support for NIS has been excellent.

3. In general the quality of the NIS is good, and can be expected to improve as the gaps in information are filled and revisions are published under the Maintenance Program which was started in fiscal year 1952. However, the time lag between production and publication still remains a problem. Coordination within and between all IAC and non-IAC agencies engaged in the NIS program is excellent and suitable liaison is maintained with the JCS.

X. *Warning of Attack*

1. Conclusions concerning Soviet and Communist intentions to initiate hostilities at any given time must be tentative generalizations drawn from inadequate evidence. They must usually be based on estimates of the overall situation, adjusted to available current factual information.

2. The IAC Watch Committee provides an interagency mechanism for assuring that new, detailed information is quickly pooled and evaluated. Maximum use is thus made of partial and inadequate information. In supporting the work of the committee, the intelligence agencies make careful cross-checks of information from all sources against an elaborate analysis of possible indicators of Soviet intentions. This method is not relied on exclusively; other approaches are constantly being tried.

3. In general there has been improvement during the past two and one half years in the ability of intelligence to provide prompt notice and preliminary evaluations of events and developments in the Soviet as well as in the neutral and friendly areas.

4. Intelligence cannot assure adequate warning of attack prior to actual detection of hostile formations. Under certain circumstances, some indications of defensive and offensive preparations on the Soviet periphery may, however, be detected. Capability for detection of indications of Soviet or Satellite attack varies from fair in the border areas of Germany and Austria to extremely poor in the Transcaucasus and

Far East. Each agency maintains its own 24-hour Watch arrangements to handle any information that is received.

XI. Collection

1. The Foreign Service

In general, the collection activities of the Foreign Service have been satisfactory. Intelligence needs have been met most adequately in the political field, less so in certain aspects of the economic field, and least satisfactorily in the scientific, technical and psychological fields. These deficiencies have been generally attributable to a lack of specialized personnel in those fields which are not closely related to the basic diplomatic functions of the Foreign Service. Remedial action has been taken by establishing a comprehensive economic reporting program and a continuing program of providing Foreign Service posts with more complete and effective guidance on intelligence needs. Additional remedial measures in progress concern:

a. the greater use of overseas personnel of certain operational programs in collecting basic intelligence information, particularly in the psychological and sociological fields, and,

b. the recognition of the role of the Foreign Service in the national intelligence effort through the revision of the Foreign Service Manual to include for the first time specific and detailed intelligence instructions.

As a result of a recent study, measures to meet the needs for basic scientific information are being carried out.

2. Service Attaché System

The Service Attaché System furnishes extensive useful military information on countries outside the Iron Curtain. Attachés in the Soviet Bloc countries obtain and transmit a considerable volume of valuable information, although under the restrictions imposed on them by Communist governments, the coverage which they provide cannot be considered adequate. The Service Attaché System has been strengthened since the beginning of the Korean conflict through the opening of new offices and the assignment of additional officers to important posts. Constant efforts are being made to improve the collection capabilities of Service Attachés by the development of new collection guides and techniques.

3. Overseas Commands

Armed Forces Commands in Europe are acquiring extensive information. While intelligence collection on the Soviet Union itself is partial and inadequate, it is good in the Eastern Zone of Germany and Austria. Considerable information is gathered by European Commands from returned PW's, escapees and refugees.

Collection of intelligence in the Far East is adequate on friendly and neutral areas but is partial and inadequate on Communist China and Eastern Siberia.

4. Aerial Reconnaissance

Because of the overriding considerations of other than intelligence nature, the Armed Services have not as yet exploited fully their overflight capabilities in aerial reconnaissance. Photo reconnaissance capabilities have increased, with a resulting improvement in contributions in this field. The contributions of radar reconnaissance are only fair as compared to photo reconnaissance, but are being improved. Photo interpretation capability is generally deficient in the Armed Services; corrective measures are underway. The use of photo intelligence in the analysis of economic and scientific developments in respect of the Soviet Orbit is being strengthened. Research and development effort is being expended on free balloons, piloted and pilotless vehicles ("guided missiles" and satellites) to overcome a lack of special reconnaissance vehicles. Research continues in the improvement of various detecting devices.

5. (This paragraph is being given separate limited distribution for security reasons.)[7]

6. Domestic Collection

As a service of common concern for the entire intelligence community, CIA collects foreign intelligence information from nongovernmental organizations and individuals in the U.S., through field offices and resident agencies in 28 cities. During the past six months, the rate of production of intelligence information reports has dropped slightly, due to: (a) increased emphasis on quality and selectivity in reporting, (b) distribution of information of limited interest to one or two consumers only, rather than wide dissemination in report form, and (c) servicing of special requirements for information in support of intelligence operations. To improve the collection of foreign technical information, arrangements have been made with the Air Technical Intelligence Center for the assignment of three air technical officers to three CIA field offices, in accordance with the provisions of NSCID No. 7.[8] Methods of exploiting foreign nationality groups and aliens within the U.S. are being intensively studied in an effort to increase the flow of information on the Soviet Bloc.

---

[7] A handwritten note at the end of this sentence reads, "(see next page)." The inserted page was filed at the end of the report and is printed below as an attachment.

[8] For text, see *Foreign Relations, 1945–1950*, Emergence of the Intelligence Establishment, Document 427.

7. *Foreign Radio Broadcasts*

a. *Monitoring*

CIA's world-wide monitoring network provides rapid and voluminous coverage of foreign news, information and propaganda broadcasts as a service of common concern. Speed in field operations and in reporting of important information to Washington is such that the intelligence agencies may receive, by wire service, the translated text of the first part of a long Moscow broadcast while the Russian station is still transmitting the final portions of the broadcast. The Soviet Orbit is well covered, except for Central Asia and the Baltic States. During the past six months, the possibility of establishing a station in Pakistan to monitor Central Asian broadcasts has been explored but the plan is now tabled, with IAC concurrence, in favor of further developing Asian coverage from existing stations in Cyprus and Japan. Tentative discussions have been held with Japanese Government officials concerning eventual joint monitoring operations, and a survey made of the monitoring potential on the west coast of Honshu. Coverage of Baltic and northwestern USSR transmitters by the British Broadcasting Company still awaits BBC budgetary approval.

b. *Propaganda Analysis*

Requirements of estimating offices and psychological warfare activities have resulted in a slight shift in emphasis in the propaganda analysis effort, leading away from the preparation of weekly reviews of the whole propaganda field and towards the production of more numerous specialized propaganda studies on substantive intelligence problems.

8. *Foreign Materials and Equipment*

Collection of Soviet bloc items from overt sources has increased appreciably during the past six months and has provided useful data to economic and scientific intelligence and to the factory markings program. While military operations in Korea have not led to the capture of many important military end-items since January, plans are under consideration for more intensive exploitation and analysis of captured explosives, propellants and other material available in the Far Eastern theater. Significant information on aircraft components was obtained from inspection of the MIG 15's which landed in Denmark. Nonmilitary items recently acquired through covert channels include several Soviet electronics measuring machines and a teletype printer of the type currently used in the Soviet communications system. The Joint Technical Intelligence Subcommittee of the JIC has absorbed the functions of the former Joint Materiel Intelligence Agency in the collection and exploitation of foreign materials.

9. Monitoring of Radio Jamming

Under NSC 66/1[9] the agencies undertook the construction and organization of a monitoring system to obtain information on Soviet jamming and related activities in the radio frequency spectrum. A pilot operation involving a very limited number of stations is being established. Adequate information as to the extent of Soviet jamming, concentration of the jamming stations, and related information must await the initiation and implementation of a much-expanded program.

10. Travel Folder Program

The IAC has instituted a program for guiding and facilitating the collection of intelligence information through U.S. and U.K. official travel within the Soviet Orbit. Travel briefs to orient travelers and training of potential travelers to observe industrial, military and scientific facilities should improve collection.

XII. Support and Collation Facilities

1. Availability of Materials

With few exceptions, all pertinent foreign positive intelligence is distributed among all interested IAC agencies. In addition to the distribution of current material, there is a continuing effort to locate and extract pertinent information from the large volume of intelligence material that was collected during and after the war, both in the United States and overseas. The sheer volume of these materials presents difficult problems of storage, analysis, and collation before they can be made readily available for research analysts and current intelligence purposes. The use of microfilm and machine techniques is providing assistance in dealing with these problems.

2. Reference Facilities

CIA provides a central reference facility for the IAC agencies through its collection of basic intelligence documents received from all sources. In addition, separate files of specialized intelligence data and materials are maintained to supplement the basic collection of the IAC agencies. These include biographic data, industrial data, photographs and motion picture films.

3. Library Facilities

Library services in the IAC agencies should become increasingly effective as a result of new measures for interlibrary cooperation in publications procurement, indexing and reference service.

---

[9] Document 44.

Another measure, stemming from the scarcity of Soviet Orbit publications, is CIA sponsorship of publication by the Library of Congress of the *Monthly List of Russian Accessions* and the *Cyrillic Subject Union Catalog*. Both services are based on cooperative reporting of holdings by all major U.S. libraries specializing in Slavic publications.

4. Biographic Information

Each IAC agency maintains a file of biographic data on foreign personalities in the categories for which they have been assigned basic responsibility, and makes such data available to the other agencies upon request. Excellent data can be made available on political, military, economic, and scientific personalities. The depth of coverage varies with the intelligence interest, and with availability of source material. In those Iron Curtain areas where information is not easily obtained, the IAC agencies provide for more comprehensive coverage of the press, radio, and scientific and technical literature. There are extensive programs for the exploitation of displaced persons, returning PW's, and defectors, as well as other personnel having a knowledge of personalities in various areas. Every effort is made to include in dossiers that biographic information which is needed by intelligence researchers, such as political orientation, ability, susceptibility to psychological warfare, probable course of action, past career, religion, marital status, associates, membership in cliques, location, etc.

5. Industrial Information

Specialized data to meet departmental needs are maintained by the Defense Agencies. CIA collates all other types of foreign industrial information, including research establishments doing industrial research and development work. The material is maintained by individual establishment and is controlled by a tabulating card indexing system. References to industrial end-products are being indexed by tabulating machine methods to speed the analysis of data being supplied to all IAC agencies.

6. Photographs and Motion Picture Films

The several Defense agencies and CIA each maintain photographic and related documentary libraries, including motion picture films, consistent with their requirements and responsibilities. Except for postwar coverage of Soviet and Satellite Areas, the photographic support is nearly adequate for present needs.

7. Map Procurement and Reference Service

Procurement of foreign-published maps and information on mapping abroad is coordinated by a staff within CIA serving an interagency map committee. Results during the past three years have proved the effectiveness of overt collection of maps and related information through the Foreign Service Geographic Attaché program. Increased emphasis is being placed on the collection of maps and engineering drawings from domestic sources. Service Attaché channels are also being used. The currently published foreign maps required for intelligence activities are received on a continuing basis through exchange arrangements between the Department of State and many foreign official mapping agencies. These exchanges are in addition to those of an operational character maintained by the Military Service. Excellent map reference services in support of intelligence requirements are maintained by close working arrangements between the map libraries.

8. Foreign Language Publications

Approval of NSCID 16[10] has given new impetus to cooperative IAC activity in this field, and definite progress is being made toward implementation of the directive. An interagency advisory committee and its subcommittees are working on methods of improving the coordination of procurement and exploitation of foreign language publications for intelligence purposes. CIA is taking action to centralize its library, reference, and indexing services for foreign language books and periodicals, and to facilitate the use of such services by other agencies. Efforts are being made to coordinate operations, apportion the workload, and reduce duplication between the following activities: overseas abstracting by US missions to satisfy the local and departmental needs; exploitation by various agencies of technical and other publications to fulfill specific requirements; and exploitation by CIA of foreign language publications for information of interest to more than one intelligence agency. A central index of translations, maintained by CIA, prevents duplication between the translating activities carried on by each agency, and makes the translated product accessible to other intelligence consumers.

Good coverage of foreign publications needed for the intelligence effort is now being obtained, although further intensive collection action should be undertaken with regard to Soviet Bloc and Communist Chinese publications.

9. External Research

Plans for developing further coordination of external and contractual research in the social sciences (i.e., non-governmental) of interest to intelligence suffered modification when the Department of State felt obliged to cut back severely its expenditure in the External

---

[10] Document 258.

Research Staff. Contributions from CIA and the Department of Defense will permit continuation of the existing program, but by no means full realization of the scale of operation which seemed to be in sight before the current budgetary allocations were determined. For the foreseeable future, therefore, there will continue to be imperfections in the efforts to minimize duplication in external research, to insure community benefit from such research and to facilitate the rational letting of external research contracts.

Positive recommendations for a better balanced and integrated program of research in the fields of psychological and unconventional warfare within the Department of Defense have been made by an advisory group to the RDB. Action on the report has been deferred pending reorganizations of the research and development program of the Defense Department.

The Economic Intelligence Committee plans to compile a report of all government sponsored economic external research on the Soviet Bloc classified through Secret. The report would include completed research, research in progress, and contemplated research.

Note: In lieu of a financial statement, not included in the above report, the Director of Central Intelligence will make an oral report to the National Security Council on CIA's expenditures. The oral report will pertain only to CIA data and will not include expenditures on intelligence made by the other members of the intelligence community.

Attachment[11]

Paragraph 5, "Espionage", of Part XI, "Collection",
in No. 9, The Foreign Intelligence Program

Since the submission of the last report, the difficulties incident to the collection of covert intelligence within the Soviet and Satellite orbit remain unchanged. Basic control procedures exercised by the various opposition security services make it more and more apparent that "black" penetration of denied areas is increasingly hazardous, and because of its illegal nature does not insure accessibility to strategic targets. In addition, the pressure of these control procedures is a continuing and serious threat to the limited assets painfully created by successful operations in the past. Although the situation is relatively less critical in Satellite areas, particularly East Germany, recent events may even endanger this coverage.

---

[11] Top Secret; Eyes Only; Security Information. See footnote 7 above.

In an effort to meet this situation, the covert mechanism has maintained a high degree of flexibility in order that all possible avenues of
approach are carefully examined in relation to changing conditions. In
this regard steps have been taken to exploit the recent tempering of controls on foreign travel to the Soviet orbit. The validity of this approach
will depend largely on the extent to which the Soviet Union wishes to
push its "peace offensive" by a relaxation of travel controls, and the
availability of properly motivated individuals who will naturally blend
into this framework. These contingencies do not permit an optimistic
outlook but represent a possible alternative, and perhaps in time may
serve to avoid an almost complete dependence on illegal entry.

Suffice it to say that progress in the delicate and highly specialized field of covert intelligence collection is hardly perceptible on a
short-range reporting base and significant successes in the immediate
future do not seem likely. At the same time meaningful and usable intelligence is being produced, support facilities developed and strengthened, and valuable experience, both in operations and career development of personnel, is being acquired.

156. Editorial Note

[*text not declassified*]

157. White House Press Release[1]

Denver, September 2, 1953.

EXECUTIVE ORDER 10483 ESTABLISHING THE OPERATIONS COORDINATING BOARD

By virtue of the authority vested in me by the Constitution and
statutes, and as President of the United States, it is hereby ordered as
follows:

---

[1] Source: National Archives, RG 59, S/S–NSC Files: Lot 66 D 148, PCG. No classification marking. The press release was issued from Lowry Air Force Base. Eisenhower
was vacationing at the "Summer White House" in Colorado.

Section 1. (a) In order to provide for the integrated implementation of national security policies by the several agencies, there is hereby established an Operations Coordinating Board, hereinafter referred to as the Board, which shall report to the National Security Council.

(b) The Board shall have as members the following: (1) the Under Secretary of State, who shall represent the Secretary of State and shall be the chairman of the Board, (2) the Deputy Secretary of Defense, who shall represent the Secretary of Defense, (3) the Director of the Foreign Operations Administration, (4) the Director of Central Intelligence, and (5) a representative of the President to be designated by the President. Each head of agency referred to in items (1) to (4), inclusive, in this section 1(b) may provide for an alternate member who shall serve as a member of the Board in lieu of the regular member representing the agency concerned when such regular member is for reasons beyond his control unable to attend any meeting of the Board; and any alternate member shall while serving as such have in all respects the same status as a member of the Board as does the regular member in lieu of whom he serves.

(c) The head of any agency (other than any agency represented under section 1(b) hereof) to which the President from time to time assigns responsibilities for the implementation of national security policies, shall assign a representative to serve on the Board when the Board is dealing with subjects bearing directly upon the responsibilities of such head. Each such representative shall be an Under Secretary or corresponding official and when so serving such representative shall have the same status on the Board as the members provided for in the said section 1(b).

(d) The Special Assistant to the President for National Security Affairs may attend any meeting of the Board. The Director of the United States Information Agency shall advise the Board at its request.

Section 2. The National Security Council having recommended a national security policy and the President having approved it, the Board shall (1) whenever the President shall hereafter so direct, advise with the agencies concerned as to (a) their detailed operational planning responsibilities respecting such policy, (b) the coordination of the interdepartmental aspects of the detailed operational plans developed by the agencies to carry out such policy, (c) the timely and coordinated execution of such policy and plans, and (d) the execution of each security action or project so that it shall make its full contribution to the attainment of national security objectives and to the particular climate of opinion the United States is seeking to achieve in the world, and (2) initiate new proposals for action within the framework of national security policies in response to opportunity and changes in the situation. The Board shall perform such other advisory functions as the President may assign to it and shall from time to time make reports to the National Security Council with respect to the carrying out of this order.

Section 3. Consonant with law, each agency represented on the Board shall, as may be necessary for the purpose of effectuating this order, furnish assistance to the Board in accordance with section 214 of the Act of May 3, 1945, 59 Stat. 134 (31 U.S.C. 691).[2] Such assistance may include detailing employees to the Board, one of whom may serve as its Executive Officer, to perform such functions, consistent with the purposes of this order, as the Board may assign to them.

Section 4. The Psychological Strategy Board shall be abolished not later than sixty days after the date of this order and its outstanding affairs shall be wound up by the Operations Coordinating Board.

Section 5. As used herein, the word "agency" may be construed to mean any instrumentality of the executive branch of the Government, including any executive department.

Section 6. Nothing in this order shall be construed either to confer upon the Board any function with respect to internal security or to in any manner abrogate or restrict any function vested by law in, or assigned pursuant to law to, any agency or head of agency (including the Office of Defense Mobilization and the Director of the Office of Defense Mobilization).

Dwight D. Eisenhower[3]

---

[2] This section of the act authorizes Executive branch departments to use appropriations to support interagency boards.

[3] Printed from a copy that indicates Eisenhower signed the original.

---

158.   Memorandum From President Eisenhower to the Executive Secretary of the National Security Council (Lay)[1]

Denver, September 2, 1953.

I have signed today Executive Order 10483[2] establishing the Operations Coordinating Board and abolishing the Psychological Strategy Board.

---

[1] Source: National Archives, RG 59, S/S–NSC Files: Lot 62 D 430, Establishing Executive Order. Top Secret; Special Security; Eyes Only. By memorandum of September 3, Lay transmitted the memorandum to the Under Secretary of State, Deputy Secretary of Defense, Director of the Foreign Operations Administration, Director of Central Intelligence, and to C.D. Jackson, Special Assistant to the President, for appropriate implementation. (Ibid., OCG Files: Lot 62 D 430, Establishing Executive Order)

[2] Document 157.

Supplementary to that Executive Order, I hereby direct that the necessary classified actions be taken to accomplish the following:

Additional Functions of the Operations Coordinating Board

The following are assigned as additional functions of the Operations Coordinating Board:

a. The functions of the Psychological Strategy Board assigned in paragraphs 2 and 3 of NSC 10/5[3] approved October 23, 1951, insofar as those functions relate to major programs.

b. The policy coordinating functions provided for in paragraph 3d(1) of NSC 10/2[4] approved June 18, 1948, under such procedures as the Board shall determine in order to insure the proper degree of security.

c. The functions of the Psychological Operations Coordinating Committee established pursuant to NSC 59/1[5] approved March 9, 1950, as modified by the President's directive of April 4, 1951[6] directing the establishment of the Psychological Strategy Board.

Coastal Raiding and Maritime Interdiction Operations (China)

a. Responsibility for the support of, and training for, the above operations shall be transferred from the Central Intelligence Agency to the Department of Defense at such time or times as appropriate arrangements may be made and approved by the OCB.

b. Those clandestine operations presently conducted by CIA in conjunction with such operations shall remain the responsibility of the Director of Central Intelligence, or be discontinued as appropriate.

c. The Director of the Bureau of the Budget shall determine, on the basis of the plans and recommendations of the agencies concerned, how much of the personnel, property, record, and unexpended balances of appropriations and other funds available, or to be made available in connection with these operations, shall be transferred to the Department of Defense.

Other

a. The President's directive of April 4, 1951, directing the establishment of the Psychological Strategy Board, is rescinded.

b. The Consultants Group established pursuant to NSC 10/2, approved June 18, 1948, is to be abolished.

---

[3] Document 90.

[4] See *Foreign Relations*, 1945–1950, Emergence of the Intelligence Establishment, Document 292.

[5] Document 2.

[6] See Document 60.

c. The Psychological Operations Coordinating Committee referred to above is to be abolished.

d. The Operations Coordinating Board shall not perform any of the functions assigned in the NSC 17 series[7] to the Interdepartmental Committee for Internal Security and to the Interdepartmental Intelligence Conference.

Dwight D. Eisenhower[8]

---

[7] The NSC 17 series of 1948–1949 dealt with internal security. No reports in this series are printed. Documentation is in the National Archives, RG 59, S/P–NSC Files: Lot 63 D 351, NSC 17, Box 49.

[8] Printed from a copy that indicates Eisenhower signed the original.

---

159.   Letter From the Secretary of State's Special Assistant for Intelligence and Research (Armstrong) to the Deputy Director of Central Intelligence (Cabell)[1]

Washington, September 9, 1953.

Dear General Cabell:

The 1954 budget of the Foreign Service has been substantially reduced. This reduction comes at a time when there are demands, requirements, many of particular concern to CIA, for an increase in intelligence collection activities. Moreover, this reduction will no doubt continue in effect in subsequent years, and will thus have a long-term effect on the functions of the Foreign Service, including the collection of intelligence information from overt sources. Such collection has included: (a) collection of foreign publications; (b) collection of maps and cartographic data; (c) peripheral reporting; (d) collection of scientific information; (e) foreign press monitoring services.

The Department recognizes that these overt collection activities are responsibilities of the Foreign Service and are important to the national security. They are hence of concern to the Director of Central Intelligence in view of his duty to advise the National Security Council in such matters.

In an effort to satisfy these demands of intelligence and to continue to carry out the Department's responsibilities for the direction

---

[1] Source: Central Intelligence Agency, History Staff, Job 84–00161R, HS/HC–195, Box 3. Confidential. This copy is "Tab A to IAC–D–73."

and management of the Foreign Service of the United States, the Department proposes in the attached document[2] a framework within which, on the basis of national security needs, it would be possible for the Director to meet his responsibilities. Under this proposal, CIA could provide financial support for collection activities beyond a stated minimum which the Department can provide under its budget.

The Department believes that, if this framework is acceptable, it would probably be desirable to consult or at least inform IAC on this proposal and, if appropriate, advise the NSC. Furthermore, the Department believes that, when and as appropriate, there should be consultation with the Bureau of the Budget and with the proper committees of Congress.

Sincerely yours,

W. Park Armstrong, Jr.[3]

---

[2] Not found.

[3] Printed from a copy that indicates Armstrong signed the original.

---

160. Minutes of the First Meeting of the Operations Coordinating Board[1]

Washington, September 17, 1953, 12:30 p.m.

PRESENT

> General Walter B. Smith, Under Secretary of State—Chairman
> Mr. Allen Dulles, Director of Central Intelligence
> Mr. C. D. Jackson, Special Assistant to the President for Cold War Operations
> Mr. William H. Godel, alternate for the Deputy Secretary of Defense
> Mr. William M. Rand, alternate for the Director, Foreign Operations Administration
> Mr. Robert Cutler, Special Assistant to the President for National Security Affairs
> Mr. George A. Morgan

1. The Board designated Mr. C. D. Jackson to serve for the time being as its Acting Executive Officer and George A. Morgan to serve as his Acting Deputy.

---

[1] Source: National Archives, RG 59, S/S–NSC Files: Lot 62 D 430, Minutes. Secret; Security Information. The meeting was held in C.D. Jackson's office.

2. The Board authorized the Acting Executive Officer to use the PSB staff and resources for OCB work until other arrangements are made.

3. The Board decided that the general pattern of present PSB administrative support arrangement should be continued for the balance of this fiscal year.

4. Noting that the table of organization for OCB staff should be authorized and an administrative support agreement concluded by September 30, the Board instructed Mr. Morgan to prepare drafts for consideration at the next Board meeting. The Board indicated that the OCB staff should be kept to a minimum and developed only as the workload demands. The basic function should be that of a working secretariat, including that of acting as chairmen and executive secretaries of meetings and generally serving as catalysts in the coordination process, but there should also be a small nucleus of planners.

5. The Board noted that all PSB approved papers and projects remain in force until specifically dealt with by OCB.

6. It was agreed that Mr. Jackson should review existing PSB projects and approved papers and make recommendations to the Board for their disposition.

7. The need for good backstopping of the Board in the member agencies was discussed. It was agreed that each Board member would have a principal assistant for this purpose who would attend formal Board meetings. It was also suggested that these assistants and Mr. Morgan serve as a senior staff to screen work for the Board, but decision on this proposal was reserved pending further study.

8. The need for close liaison and a sound division of labor with the NSC Planning Board was stressed. Mr. Morgan was instructed to circulate OCB papers to Mr. Cutler for information, notify him of meetings, and in consultation with him recommend any further arrangements needed for OCB–NSC liaison. Mr. Cutler designated Mr. T. B. Koons of the NSC Staff to maintain standing liaison with Mr. Morgan on OCB matters, and also noted that Mr. Morgan attends Planning Board meetings as an adviser. With regard to assignments to OCB from NSC, Mr. Cutler mentioned a number of implementation assignments to other agencies now in force. It was agreed that these assignments would stay as they are rather than being transferred to OCB at this time, thus giving OCB a chance to start without assuming such a backload of accumulated responsibilities. Mr. Cutler agreed to put a memorandum of this agreement in the NSC records and to send Mr. Morgan a copy.

9. The Board noted its obligation to make progress reports to the NSC and decided that these should ordinarily be made at intervals of six months, and otherwise only when specially needed.

10. The Board decided to continue existing arrangements for handling 10/2 matters through a panel composed of representatives of State, Defense and CIA, with the addition that the panel is to be chaired by Mr. Jackson and that FOA is to designate one officer who will be invited to attend meetings when matters of concern to FOA are discussed. Mr. Dulles reserved the right to bring certain matters in this field directly to the Board.

11. It was agreed that Mr. Morgan should hold a meeting of appropriate representatives next week to discuss recommendations for OCB assuming the functions of POCC.

12. The Board decided to continue meeting usually on Wednesdays at 12:30 and to follow the informal meeting with a formal meeting at 1:30, which would also be attended by the principal assistant of each Board member and necessary secretariat.

13. The Board directed that staff work on the two Christmas projects[2] begun by PSB should be completed in time for the Board to make the necessary decisions at its next meeting, including a decision on relative investment in the two projects in proportion to their relative value.

Walter B. Smith
Chairman

---

[2] The projects are documented in *Foreign Relations*, 1952–1954, vol. VIII, pp. 103–108.

---

161. Memorandum From Director of Central Intelligence Dulles to the President's Special Assistant (Jackson)[1]

Washington, September 25, 1953.

SUBJECT

Russian Satellite Minorities

REFERENCE

Memorandum from Mr. Jackson to the members of the PSB, dated 1 September 1953[2]

---

[1] Source: Central Intelligence Agency, History Staff, Job 83–00764R, HS/CSG–2291, Box 1. Secret; Security Information. Drafted by [*name not declassified*] on September 15 and rewritten by Wisner on September 16. Copies were sent to the Under Secretary of Defense, the Under Secretary of State, the Director of the Foreign Operations Administration, Robert Cutler, and George Morgan.

[2] Not found.

1. We agree with your suggestion that a thorough review of our present policy toward the Soviet nationalities should be made. It appears that most of the decisions reached affecting the development of psychological warfare against the USSR may not have given the most appropriate emphasis to the exploitation of the non-Russian ethnic groups within the Soviet Union. As I understand the matter, the old State Department policy has rested in large part upon the contention that a showing of interest, on our part, in the non-Russian peoples will arouse the antagonism of the Great Russians, who would interpret our actions as designed to dismember the Soviet Union, and could, for that reason, be turned against us propagandistically as well as exploited within Russia as a strong appeal for internal unity and support of the Kremlin regime. Within the framework of this approach a policy of non-predetermination or ultimate self-determination has been adopted and adhered to by all covert asset facilities under our control. Since Beria's liquidation,[3] and in view of the latest developments in the Soviet Union, however, we feel that re-evaluation of our present position is desirable. The purpose of such a review should be not to abandon the policy of non-predetermination, but rather to extend its application to permit fuller exploitation of the vulnerabilities inherent in the Soviet system.

2. In this connection, it is my understanding that as a result of the proposed merger of the two PSB documents, i.e. D–40 and D–45,[4] the Soviet nationalities issue will be once more reviewed by the new OCB working group. Their findings and recommendations will then be submitted either through the Department of State or Mr. George Morgan,[5] to the NSC Planning Board. We can, therefore, expect that the final document will be presented to the NSC, and after its approval it will serve as policy authorization for implementation of activities in connection with this important issue.

3. I have one further observation to make in this connection, even though I appreciate that it is at the risk of going into certain details with which I believe you are quite familiar. The old policy upon which we have been basing our actions and certain of our more important operations, has never, to the best of my knowledge, achieved formal

---

[3] Lavrenty Beria, head of Soviet internal security, was arrested in the Soviet Union in July 1953. His execution was publicly announced December 23, 1953.

[4] PSB D–40, April 23, is in National Archives, RG 59, S/S–NSC Files: Lot 62 D 333, PSB Documents. PSB D–45 is in Eisenhower Library, PSB Documents, Master Book of, Vol. IV, folder 1, Interim US Psychological Strategy Plan for the Exploitation of Unrest in Satellite Europe, NSC Registry Series, NSC Staff Papers, Box 16.

[5] Acting Director, Psychological Strategy Board.

"governmental status". By this I mean that the policy has never been threshed out at the higher policy levels of Government or gone into with sufficient thoroughness, and certainly I do not think it has been gone into by the present Administration to the depth that I consider warranted by a matter of such importance. I know that you are well acquainted with the various sharply-conflicting points of view which make this such a controversial issue both within the ranks of the Soviet emigration and also in American public opinion (including congressional opinion). One of the unfortunate results of this controversy is that in the present atmosphere and in the absence of a sufficiently authoritative policy determination, the governmental officials charged with responsibility for the execution of the policy are subject to criticism and attack to a degree which is unnecessary, and which would, in my judgment, be minimized if we had a sufficiently clear and high-level determination of policy.

Allen W. Dulles[6]

---

[6] Printed from a copy that indicates Dulles signed the original.

---

162. Memorandum From the Deputy Director for Plans of the Central Intelligence Agency (Wisner) to Director of Central Intelligence Dulles[1]

Washington, October 7, 1953.

SUBJECT

> Comments of DD/P on Certain of the Proposed Additions and Deletions in the Revision of NSC 10/2 and NSC 10/5

1. I question the desirability of deleting in its entirety the language of old paragraph 2. of NSC 10/2[2] for the reason that by such complete deletion it seems to me that we deprive ourselves unnecessarily of the evidence that there has been a deliberate and conscious determination

---

[1] Source: Central Intelligence Agency Office of the Deputy Director for Operations, Job 79–01228A. Top Secret; Security Information. Copies to COP/DD/P, C/PP, C/PPC, and C/PM.

[2] Printed in Foreign Relations, 1945–1950, Emergence of the Intelligence Establishment, Document 292. The comments referred to have not been further identified.

on the part of the NSC that covert operations and espionage and counter-espionage operations should be placed within the structure of the Central Intelligence Agency, and that the two should be correlated under the control of the Director of Central Intelligence. I agree that portions of the old language should be deleted for various reasons, since they are no longer applicable and may be undesirable. However, because of the lengthy and often heated philosophical and bureaucratic discussions about the desirability of having CIA made responsible for covert operations other than intelligence—and in view of the criticisms and attacks which are still being leveled against the Agency along this very line—it seems to me useful for us to be able to point to this language which is a clear and unequivocal indication of a determination of the long disputed issue by the NSC. My purposes in this regard could be accomplished by the following minor changes in the language of the paragraph. I would retain the first sentence as written, since this is a useful reconfirmation of the fact that the CIA is charged by the NSC with conducting espionage and counter-espionage operations abroad. (We are having enough trouble with other members of the intelligence community at the present time to render it undesirable for us to voluntarily sacrifice any language from an important Governmental document which either provides or confirms our authority in this particular field.) The last sentence could be changed to read as follows:

"It is therefore determined to be desirable that the responsibility for covert operations should be retained within the structure of the Central Intelligence Agency where they can best be correlated with espionage and counter-espionage operations under the control of the Director of Central Intelligence."

2. Concerning the proposed deletion of paragraph 2. of NSC 10/5,[3] I assume that this is deleted for the reason that the responsibility and authority of the OCB is sufficiently spelled out in the Executive Order 10483[4] plus the present supplemental memorandum of 3 September 1953.[5]

3. I question the abandonment of the language of paragraph 3.c. of NSC 10/5. This language we fought hard to get into NSC 10/5 and felt at the time that we required it in order to receive the most satisfactory assurance available that we would have some help in lining up support for our activities and operations from the Departments of State

---

[3] Document 90.

[4] Document 157.

[5] An apparent reference to Document 158, or Wisner may have been referring to the September 3 date when NSC Executive Secretary Lay transmitted the Executive order to the involved government officials for implementation.

and Defense. If this language is deleted in its entirety, we are thrown back on our own resources entirely and will have no tangible "legal" basis for levying demands upon the other departments and no approved mechanism for laying on such demands. If anything, further consideration should be given to the inclusion of the newly created IIA organization and FOA (formerly ECA–MSA) as departments or agencies upon which we should be in a position to call for such assistance and support as they may be capable of providing.

4. In paragraph 3.b. at the bottom of page 3 of Attachment A, I would recommend the insertion of the word "official" between the words "with" and "overt." The present language dangles a bit since the overt activities referred to are not in any way specified.

5. In paragraph 4. I notice that the old language of NSC 10/2 is retained intact, and although the language is pretty good from our standpoint in its present form, it does not provide for situations such as Korea. The present language speaks of "active theaters of *war* where American forces are engaged." It is my recollection that General Smith worked out language with the Pentagon and the Far East Command to cover the in-between situation and undeclared hostilities, and the language of the telegrams by which this agreement was arrived at and established might be profitably consulted in this connection.

6. For better clarification of the proposed new sentence at the end of paragraph 5. I would recommend the insertion of the words "conceived as" between the words "initially" and "covert"; and also the inclusion of a comma between the words "definitions" and "and responsibility".

Frank G. Wisner[6]

---

[6] Printed from a copy that indicates Wisner signed the original.

---

163. Editorial Note

NSC 162/2 of October 30, 1953, "Basic National Security Policy," set forth President Eisenhower's Cold War strategy, which included several policy formulations of importance to the intelligence community. NSC 162/2 declared that United States security required the development and maintenance of an intelligence system capable of: "1) collecting and analyzing indications of hostile intentions that would give maximum prior warning of possible aggression or subversion in any area of the world; 2) accurately evaluating the capabilities of foreign countries, friendly and neutral as well as enemy, to undertake military, political, economic and subversive courses of action affecting U.S. security; and 3) forecasting potential foreign developments having a bearing on U.S. national security."

As a means to reduce Soviet capabilities to control or influence the free world, NSC 162/2 also called on the government to: "a) take overt and covert measures to discredit Soviet prestige and ideology as effective instruments of Soviet power, and to reduce the strength of communist parties and other pro-Soviet elements; b) take all feasible diplomatic, political, economic and covert measures to counter any threat of a party or individuals directly or indirectly responsive to Soviet control to achieve dominant power in a free world country; and c) undertake selective, positive actions to eliminate Soviet-Communist control over any areas of the free world." NSC 162/2 is printed in full in *Foreign Relations, 1952–1954*, volume II, Part 1, pages 577–597.

---

164. Memorandum From Colonel Brad J. Smith in the Office of Special Operations of the Department of Defense to the Secretary of Defense's Assistant for Special Operations (Erskine)[1]

Washington, November 18, 1953.

SUBJECT

Overflights

1. In a conversation with Fred Ayer (Special Assistant to the Secretary of the Air Force for Intelligence) today, I learned that at the IAC meeting on 17 November, General Samford brought up the subject of overflights to Mr. Allen Dulles.[2] General Samford is reported to have said that he was "tired of pushing on one end of a strand of limp spaghetti," and Mr. Dulles agreed to bring the matter of overflights up before the NSC.

2. We have a copy of a paper on overflights which was written some time ago by Fred Ayer.[3] It is possible that this may be of interest

---

[1] Source: National Archives, RG 330, OSD Files, Office of Special Operations, OSO Chronological File Jan. 1–Nov. 30, 1953. Top Secret; Security Information.

[2] The minutes of the November 17 meeting have not been found.

[3] Not found.

to you and might be worth bringing to Mr. Kyes' attention for introduction at an OCB discussion some time, especially since it appears
that the subject will be introduced at an NSC meeting.

3. Mr. Ayer also mentioned having sent to you a paper on balloon
overflights.[4] Balloon overflights seem to me to present a very interesting possibility in that the balloons will travel at approximately 80,000
feet, some thousands of feet out of interception range.

4. The Air Force is presently planning a test of the balloon overflight capability which involves releasing the balloons in Hawaii and
hoping to pick them up some place on the West Coast. If the test proves
successful, the Air Force will then be able to present the Secretary of
Defense with a film strip of pictures taken at five-minute intervals from
80,000 feet of the path followed by the balloon for 2400 miles, along
with a recommendation that we investigate the possibility of balloon
overflights in the Soviet Union.

5. I understand the balloon project (in USSR)[5] will cost about
$40,000,000.

B.J. Smith[6]

---

[4] Not found.

[5] The words "(in USSR)" were inserted by hand.

[6] Printed from a copy that bears this typed signature.

---

165. Letter From the Deputy Secretary of Defense (Kyes) to Director of Central Intelligence Dulles[1]

Washington, December 4, 1953.

Dear Allen:

In the course of my trip through Europe in September, my attention was drawn to a number of areas in which there appear to be serious weaknesses in the furtherance of our over-all intelligence effort.
While I do not have personal knowledge of some of the items which I
shall mention, General Erskine, at my request, examined the intelligence picture from the field commanders' point of view and provided

---

[1] Source: Central Intelligence Agency, Executive Registry, Job 95–G00278R, Box 1.
Top Secret; Security Information.

me with the benefit of his observations. I realize, of course, that most, if not all these matters are no strangers to you, but perhaps my views will not be amiss as a slightly different slant.

I am fully convinced that the successful prosecution of any military program has its very foundation in the quantity, quality, and proper dissemination of intelligence. I am very aware that deficiencies exist in the Department of Defense intelligence agencies and am taking steps to correct those faults. Correction of the following deficiencies, which lie in the covert field and, therefore, fall within your purview, appears to be of vital importance to the country:

a. Lateral dissemination of information by CIA field agencies to local commanders appears necessary and logical. For example, it seems that USCINCEUR should receive CIA field reports directly and not be required to wait for distribution of screened material from Washington.

b. The penetration of the "iron curtain" by covert means falls far short of our requirements. [5½ lines not declassified]

c. [1 paragraph (7 lines) not declassified]

d. [1 paragraph (9½ lines) not declassified]

There are other points which should be discussed in detail. I'm sure you will agree that improved coordination between our agencies will improve the efficiency of our respective intelligence operations. I therefore suggest that our appropriate staff officers meet as soon as possible to go over these matters of common interest. General Erskine will represent the Department of Defense if you concur.

With best personal regards,

Yours sincerely,

Roger M. Kyes[2]

---

[2] Printed from a copy that indicates Kyes signed the original.

---

166.   Memorandum From Director of Central Intelligence Dulles to Deputy Secretary of Defense Kyes

Washington, December 29, 1953.

[Source: Central Intelligence Agency, Office of the Deputy Director for Operations, Job 79–01228A, Box 13. Top Secret. 1 page not declassified.]

167. Draft Memorandum From the Deputy Director for Plans of the Central Intelligence Agency (Wisner) to Director of Central Intelligence Dulles[1]

Washington, January 8, 1954.

SUBJECT

> Policy Guidance for CIA planning to "capitalize on and exploit new uprisings in the satellites"

1. Referring to our conversations of Wednesday afternoon, 6 January, at which time you informed me of certain statements made to you by Mr. C. D. Jackson at or following the OCB meeting of the same day, I have looked into the questions of policy guidance and the status of our own planning in this field. I do not find that we have ever received definitive or authoritative policy guidance of the kind which would authorize us to proceed with the development of plans of a general character to either whip up or exploit uprisings which may occur in the satellites. The only policy guidance which tends to bear on this subject which I have been able to locate is as follows:

a. The guidance which we have received to "keep the pot simmering—but to avoid boiling it over".

FILL IN APPROPRIATE REFERENCES HERE, INCLUDING EXCHANGES WITH HICOG, ETC., AS WELL AS REFERENCES TO MR. DULLES' OWN EXCHANGES WITH TRUSCOTT ON THIS SUBJECT[2] (about the end of the summer).[3]

b. The "Winter of Unrest" paper,[4] the salient features of which are

_____

_____

_____

c. The OCB instruction—already executed—to stockpile certain quantities of explosives and demolition materials at forward points in Europe. These materials have been so stockpiled in order to be available

---

[1] Source: Central Intelligence Agency, Office of the Deputy Director for Operations, Job 79–01228A, Box 18. Secret. Drafted by Wisner and Helms. A note in the upper right corner reads, "Orig. To C/ w/note asking him to get together w/C/PPC and concert on rounding this out and filling in the gaps. CC sent to Ballmer w/similar message."

[2] Not found.

[3] A handwritten note in the margin next to this paragraph reads, "NSC 174? [two illegible words] a balanced program." NSC 174 is printed in *Foreign Relations, 1952–1954,* vol. VIII, pp. 110–127.

[4] Not found.

in case of need, but we have NO policy guidance governing the infiltration thereof either at the present time or under any specific set of circumstances in the future.

2. The fact that there appears to be a lack of understanding at higher governmental levels on this general subject is, I believe, a very serious matter. I think it is essential that we take steps promptly with a view to either

a. Disabusing the minds of those who believe we are all set to go, or are in the process of developing plans to touch off or support uprisings in the satellites; or

b. Getting some governmental policy direction in this field which will clarify our responsibilities and position.

3. Actually, it is my own understanding, which is shared by Dick Helms and by Tracy Barnes—with both of whom I have discussed the matter—that present governmental policy does not provide for or support the stirring up or the provision of significant quantities of support to satellite uprisings. I have never understood how it is possible to support from outside a satellite country a revolt or unrest of any kind which is not sufficiently strong, in and of itself, to unseat the government in power. This support can only be provided by armed military forces prepared to march to the active assistance of the revolutionists for the purpose of helping them complete their attempted coup and providing the strength necessary to consolidate and hold their gains. To the best of my knowledge there is no historical precedent for a successful revolt in a country where the weight of a large army of a foreign power, supporting the existing regime, is either in the country or standing on its borders ready to move. Nor is it my understanding that there is any US policy decision in being, nor any adequate US forces to back up any such decision, to move in and give support to an attempted revolt.

4. None of the foregoing is to say that we should not continue to encourage resistance to the Soviet satellite regimes in order to keep the pressure on and to retard the consolidation of Soviet controls in those areas. This is what I understand our policy directives to amount to at the present time, but it is one of the most difficult, unanswered questions of the day as to what US or Western policy would be in case of an attempted revolt occurring in any of the satellites within the foreseeable future and prior to the withdrawal of Soviet military power from the immediate or adjacent area. This is the question which has been posed to us repeatedly by European statesmen, of whom Ernst Reuter was one of the most succinct propounders. You may recall his repeated predictions that there would be further outbreaks of unrest, perhaps as early as the Spring of this year, in Eastern Germany, and he asked just what the West would propose to do in such event. He tended

to answer his own question by speculating that we would probably be forced to stand idly by wringing our hands and seeing all possibility of future resistance go down in bloody liquidation unless we were able meanwhile, through diplomatic action of the most courageous and forceful character, to bring about a retraction of Soviet power.

168.   Letter From Director of Central Intelligence Dulles to the Assistant Chief of Staff (G–2) of the Army (Trudeau)[1]

Washington, January 25, 1954.

Dear General Trudeau:

In your letter of 24 December 1953[2] you suggested that problems relating to clandestine intelligence required a clarification of NSCID #5[3] rather than an "Agreed Activities" paper.

NSCID #5 is a fundamental statement of policy. Prior to its issuance the underlying philosophies and problems were debated at length at all levels in the interested offices of the Executive Branch of the Government and by appropriate congressional groups. Each formal study of the problem of clandestine intelligence operations, after debate of the various views presented, came without exception to an acceptance of the principles reflected in NSCID #5.

A revision was issued on 28 August 1951[4] to meet new conditions arising from the Korean War and the establishment of NATO, but the paper as revised is still a statement of basic responsibilities rather than an attempt to spell out the conditions that will govern all conceivable relationships and circumstances. There is, however, ample flexibility in the concept stated in NSCID #5 to meet all such circumstances, and changing needs can best be met by corollary agreements, based on NSCID #5, which can be readily achieved without calling into play the full machinery of the National Security Council, which inevitably would require a rather prolonged procedure.

---

[1] Source: Central Intelligence Agency, Executive Registry, Job 95–G00278R, Box 1, Folder 27. Secret. Drafted on January 4, and rewritten by C.P. Cabell on January 22. A legal opinion by CIA General Counsel Lawrence Houston is ibid.

[2] Not printed. (Ibid., Folder 24)

[3] See *Foreign Relations*, 1945–1950, Emergence of the Intelligence Establishment, Document 423.

[4] Document 255.

Therefore, rather than seek a change in NSCID #5, I would prefer to pursue the problem of a coordinated program on the basis of the "Agreed Activities" paper which representatives of the Armed Services prepared in collaboration with representatives of this Agency, in June of last year. We are now awaiting with interest the return of this draft agreement which I understand the JIC ad hoc committee dealing with this problem planned to rework on the basis of comments from commanders in the field.

I would therefore urge that you use your influence to bring about early resumption of negotiation leading to a final "Agreed Activities" paper.

Sincerely,

Allen W. Dulles[5]

---

[5] Printed from a copy that indicates Dulles signed the original.

---

169.   Director of Central Intelligence Directive 15/1[1]

Washington, February 4, 1954.

RESPONSIBILITY FOR PRODUCTION OF ECONOMIC INTELLIGENCE: SOVIET BLOC[2]

Pursuant to the provisions of NSCID–1, NSCID–3, and NSCID–15,[3] and for the purpose of strengthening the over-all governmental intelligence structure for the production of economic intelligence on the Soviet Bloc, the following policies and allocations are hereby established:

---

[1] Source: National Archives, RG 59, INR Historical Files: Lot 58 D 776, DCI Directives. Confidential. A typed note reads: "Agreed text CIA/State 2/5/54." For a revised version of this directive, see Document 191.

[2] The term "Soviet Bloc" as used in this Directive covers the USSR; Poland, Czechoslovakia, Hungary, Rumania, Bulgaria, Albania, East Germany; Communist China and North Korea. Supplements to this directive may reduce this coverage or extend it to other areas under Soviet domination, if such modification is warranted. [Footnote in the original.]

[3] For NSCID No. 1, see Document 256; for NSCID No. 3, see *Foreign Relations*, 1945–1950, Emergence of the Intelligence Establishment, Document 426; for NSCID No. 15, see Document 254.

1. Policies

1.1 In discharging allocated responsibilities and effecting integration of economic intelligence, the interested departments and agencies will apply the following basic principles:

a. No complete separation of areas of interest is possible or necessarily desirable in economic intelligence activities.

b. Full and free interchange of all intelligence information and finished intelligence and schedules of research programs, including external research, between all agencies concerned is essential.

c. No one agency is considered to be the final authority in any field; conclusions may be questioned by other IAC agencies and dissents recorded.

1.2 An agency charged with primary responsibility in a particular field will develop special competence in that field and will normally carry out most of the research in that field.

1.3 Any agency may make such studies as it believes necessary to supplement intelligence obtained from other agencies in order to fulfill its departmental functions; however, basic research studies should not normally be undertaken without prior discussion with the agencies having primary responsibility for the subject matter involved.

1.4 Each intelligence agency will endeavor to coordinate the intelligence activities of its technical services and its other facilities having economic intelligence production capabilities with the work of the IAC intelligence agencies and to make available to those agencies the intelligence produced by such services and facilities.

2. Responsibility for Economic Intelligence Production

2.1 Responsibility for research and for the production of economic intelligence on the Soviet Bloc is allocated as follows:

a. The Department of State shall have primary responsibility for those aspects of intelligence production in which economic and political analysis are interdependent. It will produce intelligence on economic policy and politico-economic trends and will undertake such other analyses and studies as may be required in fulfilling its assigned primary production responsibilities.

b. The Department of Defense shall have primary responsibility for the production of intelligence on the military aspects of the economy. They will produce intelligence on military requirements, logistics, ships and ship movements, and on production of military end items, and will undertake such other analyses and studies as may be required in fulfilling their assigned primary production responsibilities.

c. The CIA shall have primary responsibility, as a service of common concern, for intelligence production on all aspects and all sectors of the economy, except for those specified in 2.1 (a) and (b). With full recognition given to the intelligence produced by other agencies, it shall supplement this intelligence by such independent analyses and studies as may be necessary to produce integrated economic intelligence on the total economy of the Soviet Bloc.

2.2 It is recognized that, despite the above-mentioned allocations of primary production responsibilities, there will be areas of common or overlapping interest which require continuing interagency liaison and such working-level conferences as may be appropriate.

3. *Responsibility for Economic Intelligence Coordination*

3.1 To assist the Central Intelligence Agency is carrying out its coordinating responsibility, the Economic Intelligence Committee shall continue to perform the functions outlined in IAC D–22/1 (revised).[4]

3.2 In accordance therewith, the Economic Intelligence Committee shall, upon request of the Office of National Estimates, prepare coordinated contributions to comprehensive estimates of Soviet Bloc Capabilities scheduled in the approved program of National Intelligence Estimates.[5]

---

[4] Document 72.
[5] Printed from an unsigned copy.

---

170.   Editorial Note

Sections of NSC 5407 (which replaced NSC 161), "Status of United States Programs for National Security as of December 31, 1953," were circulated on February 17, 1954, and in subsequent circulars as they were prepared. The report was discussed at the 187th, 188th, and 190th meetings of the NSC on March 4, 11, and 25, 1954. (National Archives, RG 59, S/S–NSC Files: Lot 63 D 351, NSC 5407) Part 8, "The Foreign Intelligence Program" was prepared by the Central Intelligence Agency. (Eisenhower Library, White House Office, Office of the Special Assistant for National Security Affairs, NSC Series, Status of Projects, NSC 5407, Boxes 4–5) NSC 5407 is discussed in an editorial note in *Foreign Relations, 1952–1954*, volume II, Part 1, page 633.

171. **Note From the Executive Secretary of the National Security Council (Lay) to the National Security Council**[1]

NSC 5412   Washington, March 15, 1954.

COVERT OPERATIONS

REFERENCES

    A. Memo for the Statutory Members of the NSC from Executive Secretary, subject: "The NSC 10 Series", dated March 3, 1954[2]
    B. NSC 10/2[3]
    C. NSC 10/5[4]

The President has this date approved the enclosed National Security Council directive on the subject, as submitted by the reference memorandum and adopted by the other statutory members of the National Security Council, and directs its implementation by all executive departments and agencies of the U.S. Government concerned, as indicated therein.

Accordingly, as set forth in paragraph 7 of the enclosure, NSC 10/2, NSC 10/5 and certain provisions relating thereto of the President's memorandum to the Executive Secretary, NSC, supplementing Executive Order 10483,[5] are hereby superseded.

It is requested that special security precautions be observed in the handling of the enclosed directive and that access to it be very strictly limited on an absolute need-to-know basis.

It is further requested that all copies of the reference memorandum be returned to this office for destruction upon receipt of this report.

James S. Lay, Jr.[6]

---

    [1] Source: Eisenhower Library, Special Assistant to the President for National Security Affairs Records. Top Secret. Copies were sent to the Chairman of the Joint Chiefs of Staff, the Director of Central Intelligence, and the Executive Officer, Operations Coordinating Board.
    [2] Not found.
    [3] See *Foreign Relations, 1945–1950, Emergence of the Intelligence Establishment,* Document 292.
    [4] Document 90.
    [5] See Documents 157 and 158.
    [6] Printed from a copy that bears this typed signature.

Enclosure[7]

NATIONAL SECURITY COUNCIL DIRECTIVE
ON COVERT OPERATIONS

1. The National Security Council, taking cognizance of the vicious covert activities of the USSR and Communist China and the governments, parties and groups dominated by them (hereinafter collectively referred to as "International Communism") to discredit and defeat the aims and activities of the United States and other powers of the free world, determined, as set forth in NSC directives 10/2 and 10/5, that, in the interests of world peace and U.S. national security, the overt foreign activities of the U.S. Government should be supplemented by covert operations.

2. The Central Intelligence Agency had already been charged by the National Security Council with conducting espionage and counterespionage operations abroad. It therefore seemed desirable, for operational reasons, not to create a new agency for covert operations, but, subject to directives from the NSC, to place the responsibility for them on the Central Intelligence Agency and correlate them with espionage and counterespionage operations under the over-all control of the Director of Central Intelligence.

3. The NSC has determined that such covert operations shall to the greatest extent practicable, in the light of U.S. and Soviet capabilities and taking into account the risk of war, be designed to:

a. Create and exploit troublesome problems for International Communism, impair relations between the USSR and Communist China and between them and their satellites, complicate control within the USSR, Communist China and between them and their satellites, and retard the growth of the military and economic potential of the Soviet bloc.

b. Discredit the prestige and ideology of International Communism, and reduce the strength of its parties and other elements.

c. Counter any threat of a party or individuals directly or indirectly responsive to Communist control to achieve dominant power in a free world country.

d. Reduce International Communist control over any areas of the world.

e. Strengthen the orientation toward the United States of the peoples and nations of the free world, accentuate, wherever possible, the identity of interest between such peoples and nations and the United States as well as favoring, where appropriate, those groups genuinely advocating or believing in the advancement of such mutual interests,

---

[7] Top Secret.

and increase the capacity and will of such peoples and nations to resist International Communism.

f. In accordance with established policies and to the extent practicable in areas dominated or threatened by International Communism, develop underground resistance and facilitate covert and guerrilla operations and ensure availability of those forces in the event of war, including wherever practicable provisions of a base upon which the military may expand these forces in time of war within acting theaters of operations as well as provision for stay-behind assets and escape and evasion facilities.

4. Under the authority of Section 102(d)(5) of the National Security Act of 1947, the National Security Council hereby directs that the Director of Central Intelligence shall be responsible for:

a. Ensuring, through designated representatives of the Secretary of State and of the Secretary of Defense, that covert operations are planned and conducted in a manner consistent with United States foreign and military policies and with overt activities, and consulting with and obtaining advice from the Operations Coordinating Board and other departments or agencies as appropriate.

b. Informing, through appropriate channels and on a need-to-know basis, agencies of the U.S. Government, both at home and abroad (including diplomatic and military representatives), of such operations as will affect them.

5. In addition to the provisions of paragraph 4, the following provisions shall apply to wartime covert operations:

a. Plans for covert operations to be conducted in active theaters of war and any other areas in which U.S. forces are engaged in combat operations will be drawn up with the assistance of the Department of Defense and will be in consonance with and complementary to approved war plans of the Joint Chiefs of Staff.

b. Covert operations in active theaters of war and any other areas in which U.S. forces are engaged in combat operations will be conducted under such command and control relationships as have been or may in the future be approved by the Department of Defense.

6. As used in this directive, "covert operations" shall be understood to be all activities conducted pursuant to this directive which are so planned and executed that any U.S. Government responsibility for them is not evident to unauthorized persons and that if uncovered the U.S. Government can plausibly disclaim any responsibility for them. Specifically, such operations shall include any covert activities related to: propaganda; political action; economic warfare; preventive direct action, including sabotage, anti-sabotage, demolition; escape and evasion and evacuation measures; subversion against hostile states or groups including assistance to underground resistance movements, guerrillas and refugee liberation groups; support of indigenous and anti-communist elements in threatened countries of the free world; deception plans and operations; and all activities compatible with this

directive necessary to accomplish the foregoing. Such operations shall not include: armed conflict by recognized military forces, espionage and counterespionage, nor cover and deception for military operations.

7. This directive supersedes and rescinds NSC 10/2 and NSC 10/5. Subparagraphs "a" and "b" under the heading "Additional Functions of the Operations Coordinating Board" on page 1 of the President's memorandum for the Executive Secretary, National Security Council, supplementing Executive Order 10483, are superseded by the following provisions:

a. Except as the President otherwise directs, the members of the Operations Coordinating Board shall, under appropriate security arrangements, be advised in advance of major programs involving covert operations related to National Security Council policies.

b. The designated representatives of the Secretaries of State and Defense referred to in paragraph 4-a above shall keep the Board Members of their respective departments advised as to matters on which they are consulted by the Director of Central Intelligence, and which have been or are to be referred to the Operations Coordinating Board.

c. The Operations Coordinating Board will be the normal channel for securing coordination of support among the Departments of State and Defense and the Central Intelligence Agency.

---

172.   Minutes of a Meeting of the Intelligence Advisory Committee[1]

IAC–M–145   Washington, March 16, 1954.

Director of Central Intelligence
Allen W. Dulles
Presiding

MEMBERS PRESENT

Mr. W. Park Armstrong, Special Assistant for Intelligence, Department of State

Major General Arthur G. Trudeau, Assistant Chief of Staff, G-2, Department of the Army

Rear Admiral H. C. Daniel, acting for Director of Naval Intelligence, Department of the Navy

Major General John A. Samford, Director of Intelligence, Headquarters, United States Air Force

---

[1] Source: Central Intelligence Agency, Executive Registry, Job 85–500362R, Box 2. Secret. The meeting was held in the DCI's conference room.

Colonel Samuel M. Lansing, acting for Deputy Director for Intelligence, The Joint Staff

Dr. Charles H. Reichardt, Atomic Energy Commission Representative to the IAC

Mr. Victor P. Keay, acting for Assistant to the Director, Federal Bureau of Investigation

ALSO PRESENT

Lt. Gen. Charles P. Cabell, Central Intelligence Agency
Dr. Sherman Kent, Central Intelligence Agency
**Dr. H. Marshall Chadwell, Central Intelligence Agency[2]
Mr. James Q. Reber, Central Intelligence Agency
[name not declassified], Central Intelligence Agency
Lt. Gen. Harold R. Bull (Ret.), Central Intelligence Agency
*Mr. Ludwell L. Montague, Central Intelligence Agency[3]
[name not declassified], Central Intelligence Agency
*Mr. William P. Bundy, Central Intelligence Agency
[name not declassified], Central Intelligence Agency
[name not declassified], Central Intelligence Agency[2]
[name not declassified], Central Intelligence Agency
[name not declassified], Central Intelligence Agency[3]
[name not declassified], Central Intelligence Agency
[name not declassified], USMCR, Central Intelligence Agency[3]
Mr. William C. Trueheart, Department of State
*Mr. E. W. Doherty, Department of State[3]
*Mr. Miron Burgin, Department of State[3]
*Mr. J. W. Lydman, Department of State[3]
Lt. Col. Roland L. Kolb, Department of the Army
Lt. Col. James G. Martin, Department of the Army
Lt. Col. Vasco J. Fenili, Department of the Army
Captain Allan L. Reed, USN, Department of the Navy
Cmdr. James G. Thorburn, Jr., Department of the Navy
Colonel Donald H. Ainsworth, United States Air Force
Colonel John J. Morrow, United States Air Force
Colonel Charles F. Gillis, United States Air Force
Mr. John A. Power, United States Air Force
Captain Ray E. Malpass, USN, The Joint Staff
Colonel Orin H. Moore, The Joint Staff
Lt. Col. Perry H. Penn, The Joint Staff
*Mr. John Easton, The Joint Staff[3]

Richard D. Drain[4]
Secretary

[Omitted here is discussion of unrelated agenda items.]

---

[2] Attended Executive Session. [Footnote in the original.]
[3] [Attended] Part of Meeting. [Footnote in the original.]
[4] Printed from a copy that bears this typed signature.

Soviet Capabilities in Guided Missiles (IAC–D–81, 10 March)[5]

6. *Action:* Agreed to defer action until a later meeeting.

7. *Discussion:* Admiral Daniel and Colonel Lansing felt that the subject was one allocated to the departments of the Department of Defense by DCID 3/4[6] and that to handle a matter primarily in the weapons field through the national intelligence machinery might lead to overcrowding an already overworked mechanism. General Trudeau suggested that the entire community is concerned with at least the collection effort in this field, an effort which needs stepping up before existing estimates can be much improved. Mention was made of a current JIC study (603/16, November 1953)[7] pertinent extracts from which the service members felt might be made available to the Federal Civil Defense Administration.

8. General Samford thought it desirable to respond as fully as possible to present and future requestors involved with this subject. He doubted that less than a National Estimate would meet the need.

9. Mr. Dulles recognized that this subject had grown in importance since DCID 3/4 was issued almost two years ago and may require treatment different from that suggested in the Directive. He invited members to consider the matter further, pending a full discussion at a later meeting.

[Omitted here is discussion of unrelated agenda items.]

---

[5] Not found.
[6] Document 126.
[7] Not further identified.

173. Paper Prepared in the Central Intelligence Agency[1]

Washington, March 25, 1954.

PREPARATION OF COORDINATED EVALUATIONS
OF THE NET CAPABILITIES OF THE USSR TO INFLICT
DIRECT INJURY ON THE UNITED STATES

Problem

1. To create appropriate organizational machinery for the preparation of continuing coordinated evaluations of the net capabilities of the USSR to inflict direct injury on the United States, and to direct the preparation of such an evaluation.

Discussion

Introduction

2. By memorandum dated 10 March 1954, pursuant to NSC Action 873-d., the Director of Defense Mobilization has submitted certain recommendations relative to the organizational aspects of the continental defense program.[2] These recommendations do not cover parts of Chapter VI of NSC 159,[3] specifically paragraphs 129–131 relating to questions of "net evaluation" organization. Since these questions are substantially different from the issues of operational organization, it is appropriate to deal with the two in separate papers, whether final action is taken by the National Security Council itself or by the Planning Board.

---

[1] Source: Central Intelligence Agency, Office of the Deputy Director for Intelligence, Job 80–R01440R, Box 3. Secret. A note on the paper indicates that the DCI and DD/I saw it on May 4, 1954. All ellipses in the original.

[2] Memorandum from ODM Director Arthur S. Flemming to Cutler, March 10. (Eisenhower Library, White House Office, NSC Staff Papers, Disaster File Series, Box 22, Continental Defense) NSC Action No. 873, taken at the 158th meeting of the NSC on August 6, 1953, directed the Joint Chiefs of Staff and the NSC Planning Board to submit further recommendations on continental defense to the Council. In addition, Flemming was directed by the President to establish a special task force to study and make recommendations on improving government organization with respect to internal security functions. A copy of NSC Action No. 873 is in National Archives, RG 59, S/S–NSC (Miscellaneous) Files: Lot 66 D 95, NSC Records of Action.

[3] NSC 159, "Continental Defense," circulated to the NSC on July 22, was the report of the Continental Defense Committee chaired by General Bull (see footnote 1, Document 150). A copy of NSC 159 is in National Archives, RG 59, S/S–NSC Files: Lot 63 D 351, NSC 159 Series.

History

3. Two previous evaluations in this field have been prepared for the Council, the history being as follows:

a. On August 30, 1951, the Council directed that the Director of Central Intelligence, in collaboration with the Joint Chiefs of Staff (JCS), the Interdepartmental Committee on Internal Security (ICIS), and the Interdepartmental Intelligence Conference (IIC), prepare a summary evaluation, covering Soviet net capability against the continental United States as of mid-1952.[4] After considerable delay and difficulty, such an evaluation was submitted to the Council on October 14, 1952, with an accompanying memorandum by the then Director pointing out shortcomings of the report and recommending that he, DCI, be directed to examine into the creation of new and better machinery to integrate operational data with intelligence in this field.[5] On November 25, 1952, the Secretary of Defense forwarded to the Council the views of the JCS on the question,[6] and there ensued negotiations in which JCS, CIA, ICIS, and IIC participated and which eventuated in the directive set forth as NSC 140, approved by the President on January 19, 1953.[7]

b. Under this directive, a Subcommittee headed by Lt. General Idwal H. Edwards (USAF ret.) completed and submitted to the Council on May 18, 1953 its report, NSC 140/1.[8] This differed from the previous study in that (1) it was projected for two years into the future, through mid-1955; (2) in addition to the continental United States, defined key installations overseas were considered; (3) instead of using maximum estimates of Soviet strength, as had been substantially done before, the evaluation used a probable estimate level in this regard, and assumed a Soviet strategy regarded as being consistent with these estimated capabilities. The Report was given to the Planning Board's Continental Defense Committee, the so-called Bull Committee, and was used by that Committee along with other relevant materials in the preparation of NSC 159.

4. The Report of the Bull Committee, NSC 159, July 22, 1953, referred to the substance of the Edwards Report (para. 9), and also considered in some detail the problem of permanent organization (paras. 129–131) recommending that a new evaluation be undertaken in two phases, the first covering Soviet attack capabilities—to be done jointly by the JCS and CIA—and the second covering damage, or vulnerability to the estimated attack capabilities—to be done by a separate Committee under NSC direction. NSC 159, para. 30, further noted that the Council "might well wish to establish a permanent subcommittee on

---

[4] See Document 86.

[5] The evaluation and the accompanying memorandum have not been found. See Document 138.

[6] Not found.

[7] See *Foreign Relations*, 1952–1954, vol. II, Part 1, pp. 205–208.

[8] NSC 140/1 is ibid., pp. 328–349.

'Net Capabilities Estimates' composed of the Chairman of the JCS and the Director of Central Intelligence . . ."

5. Concurrently, the question of net evaluations in general was considered by The President's Committee on International Information Activities, the Jackson Committee. In its Report submitted to the Council on June 30, 1953, the Jackson Committee specifically recommended that machinery for the preparation of such evaluations should be created.[9] (Jackson Committee Report, pp. 3, 118, Recommendation No. 1) Action by the Council or any agency on this recommendation was deferred pending the submission of the ODM report directed by NSC Action 873 d. to be submitted pursuant to NSC 159 and NSC 159/4.

Importance of the Net Evaluation

6. In view of the usefulness of the Edwards Report and the subsequent recommendations of the Bull and Jackson Committees, the importance and desirability of continuing net evaluations of Soviet capability to injure the United States may be regarded as established. For purposes of Council consideration of problems relating to continental defense or the defense of US installations overseas, it is meaningless to have gross estimates of Soviet nuclear capabilities, air strength, etc., unless these are merged with existing US and Allied defensive capabilities so as to produce an evaluation of the net Soviet capability, present and prospective.

Organizational Problems

7. *Method of Operation.* Experience with the 1951–52 project demonstrated emphatically that it was not satisfactory to conduct a net evaluation on the basis of one-shot contributions by several agencies, melded by one agency or by a group. The Edwards Subcommittee operated on the basis of continuing exchange of material by a tightly-knit operating group producing in effect "successive approximations" leading to a final refined product. Wherever the responsibility may be placed, and on whatever basis agencies participate, this method of operation is essential. Moreover, this method of operation can also be employed—as it was by the Edwards group—to minimize the security problem involved in the handling of sensitive information that must be supplied particularly by JCS, CIA, and FBI.

8. *Allocation of Responsibility.* Three allocations have so far been tried or proposed. *The Edwards Subcommittee* consisted of a Chairman appointed by the Council (General Edwards was actually nominated by the JCS), and representatives of JCS, CIA, the ICIS, and IIC. Other

---

[9] Extracts from the Jackson Committee Report are ibid., Part 2, pp. 1795–1874. See also Document 151.

agencies, notably ODM and FCDA, were in the position of contributors and advisors, but did not participate in the final work of the Subcommittee. *The NSC 159 recommendation* would divide the work into two stages, with JCS and CIA acting jointly in the first, and with the second, or damage, stage handled by an ad hoc committee chaired by an NSC representative and including Defense, ICIS, IIC, ODM and FCDA. *The JCS views on NSC 159*, submitted to the Council on September 1, 1953, take the position that the Department of Defense has adequate resources in conjunction with "other agencies," to prepare the needed evaluation without resort to additional machinery. This appears to mean that primary responsibility should be placed solely in Defense, with power to call on other agencies as needed. The great difference between these three methods illustrates the complexity of the problem of allocating responsibility so as to bring in all interested agencies to an appropriate degree and at the same time to have a workable set-up. The following points appear relevant:

a. A fully refined net evaluation involves consideration of several elements, for which different agencies have primary responsibility. At a minimum, these include Soviet gross overt attack and defense capabilities. CIA and Intelligence Advisory Committee (IAC) agencies concerned with foreign intelligence),[10] Soviet gross clandestine attack capabilities (IIC, CIA, AEC principally), Soviet strategy (all intelligence agencies), US military defensive and gross retaliatory capabilities (JCS), US non-military defensive capabilities (ODM, FCDA), US internal security capabilities (ICIS), and US vulnerability in terms of damage to be expected from various scales and types of attack (Defense, ODM, FCDA principally). None of these can be considered in isolation. To illustrate, the Soviet attack strategy would be based in part on the Soviet estimate of US weaknesses and gaps in defense, and in part also on the Soviet estimate of the degree of damage that might be inflicted.[11] Hence, it becomes necessary to take theoretical possibilities of attack and "war-game" them through from a Soviet standpoint. In theory at least, this could not be done properly without constant and full participation of all interested agencies.

b. On the other hand, such a multi-agency exercise is on its face impractical and endlessly time-consuming. Some compromise must be struck, as was done in setting up the Edwards Subcommittee.

c. It is readily possible to separate out the elements relating to US vulnerability in terms of damage. Moreover, although, as indicated in a above these are theoretically interlinked with Soviet strategy, in practice damage estimates based on assumed hypothetical levels of attack would be adequate, since in any event such estimates would be "broadbrush" in character. Thus it is reasonable to separate out the damage aspect, and charge this phase to a separate group.

---

[10] The principal IAC agencies are State, the three services, and the Joint Intelligence Group of the Joint Staff. [Footnote in the original.]

[11] [5 lines not declassified.] [Footnote in the original.]

d. However, it appears neither logical nor practicable to combine that damage aspect with the internal security aspect for which ICIS and IIC are primarily responsible. The principal internal security problem belongs in the "capabilities" rather than the "damage" category, since it concerns Soviet clandestine introduction of nuclear or other weapons. Thus, the Edwards Subcommittee setup was logical on this point. As a practical matter, the internal security agencies are believed to have felt that the Edwards and Bull Reports placed at too low a level the likelihood of Soviet employment of clandestine capabilities. However, assuming the internal security agencies have produced an estimate of the likelihood of detection if the Soviets used clandestine means, the ultimate question of whether the Soviets would be prepared to take this risk is certainly one of basic Soviet strategy involving broader considerations than those for which the internal security agencies are responsible. The split shown by Mr. McDonnell's dissent to NSC 159 cannot be remedied by any organizational changes, although of course the internal security agencies should participate fully in the final judgment.

e. As to the position stated in the JCS views on NSC 159, it is not known whether the views are firmly held by the JCS or by the Department of Defense. The particular subject of Continental Defense is one aspect of the larger problem of a permanent organization for producing net evaluations on Soviet capabilities, and CIA's views on this matter have been stated in the Director's letter to General Bull, dated 30 June 1953,[12] a copy of which has been circulated to the Planning Board. In brief, it appears to CIA that to place pre-eminent responsibility in the JCS would be to overlook the legal responsibilities of the Director of Central Intelligence in the field of national intelligence, under the National Security Act of 1947. The President and the NSC in practice and pursuant to statutory authority depend on the Director of Central Intelligence, representing the coordinated views of the Intelligence Agencies, for foreign intelligence estimates, and on the Chairman of the Joint Chiefs of Staff, speaking as the representative of the services, for military advice. Thus, the President and Council can best receive guidance in the most useful and complete form through an effective amalgamation of the functions of the two.

9. *Personnel and Facilities.* If it is accepted that a tightly-knit operating group is the appropriate method of operation, questions of personnel and facilities become important. In the case of the Edwards Subcommittee, these were handled by the furnishing of facilities in the JCS area of the Department of Defense and by the furnishing of secretarial and other personnel by the JCS and CIA. It is believed that these arrangements were satisfactory, and that they could be repeated without strain on the contributing agencies.

Target Date, Scope and Projection Period

10. *Target Date.* Since national policy in the field of continental defense is now laid down comprehensively in NSC 5408,[13] with programs

---

[12] Document 150.

[13] See *Foreign Relations*, 1952–1954, vol. II, Part 1, pp. 609–633.

extended for some years into the future, it appears unlikely that there will be a major overhauling of this policy during 1954, barring drastic changes in the intelligence picture of Soviet capabilities or intentions.

11. The Edwards Subcommittee completed its work in four months, but found that this was too short a period in which to go into all of the important aspects. The Edwards Subcommittee had particular difficulty with the question of Soviet strategy in the event of war, whether the Soviets would allocate the bulk of their stockpile to the US or a large part of it against non-US targets. A successor group may find it desirable to submit this question to thorough intelligence consideration, based on the material on capabilities and damage developed by the group. This question was referred to by General Edwards in a personal memorandum to the Executive Secretary, NSC, dated 19 May 1953.[14] General Edwards also referred to the desirability of covering the extent of strategic warning that might be expected, of a vulnerability study, and of a psychological study of the effects on the people of the US of assumed levels of atomic attacks. In view of the complexity of these problems, it appears highly desirable that the new study be allowed at least six months, and if possible longer, for completion.

12. To allow six months or more for a new evaluation would throw the completion after 1 October 1954, and would eliminate its usefulness as a supporting element for work on the FY 1956 budget. However, this disadvantage appears outweighed by the considerations stated in paragraph 11.

13. *Scope.* The Edwards Report considered not only the continental United States but also key US installations outside the US, considered in terms of the usefulness of such installations to US counteroffensive action. There was some difficulty about the definition of such overseas installations, leading to a misunderstanding affecting the JCS submission. Apart from avoiding a repetition of this, the scope of the Edwards Report appeared workable.

14. *Projection.* The Edwards Report projected its conclusions forward for two years, and General Edwards recommended that future studies adopt a projection period not greater than this. For planning purposes it would be desirable to have a longer projection period, since many policy decisions cannot bear fruit for three or more years. However, from a working standpoint, it would be extremely difficult to get a firm enough picture of either Soviet or US capabilities, in order to do

---

[14] General Edwards' memorandum to the NSC Executive Secretary, May 19, provided comments by the Special Evaluation Subcommittee concerning future evaluations of the Soviet Union's net capabilities to damage the United States. (National Archives, RG 273, Policy Papers, NSC 140, Box 56)

the "war-gaming" exercise. The Planning Board should consider whether the policy considerations should outweigh working difficulties and limitations.

Recommendations

In the light of the foregoing, it is recommended that the National Security Council issue an appropriate directive or directives:

a.[15] Establishing a Net Evaluation Subcommittee composed of the Chairman of the Joint Chiefs of Staff and the Director of Central Intelligence.

b.[15] Charging this Subcommittee with the responsibility for providing estimates of net capabilities as needed to support the formulation of national policy.

c. Directing that this Subcommittee prepare by 1 March 1955 an evaluation, covering the period through (mid-1957), of the net capabilities of the USSR to inflict direct injury on the continental United States and on key US installations overseas, the latter being defined in terms of their importance to US counter-offensive action.

d. Attaching to the Subcommittee, for the purpose of this evaluation, the Chairman of the ICIS and IIC respectively, with full right of participation on all matters concerning Soviet capabilities that involve internal security of the US, and of the likelihood of Soviet employment of such capabilities in the event of attack.

e. Establishing a Vulnerability Subcommittee composed of the Secretary of Defense, the Director of Defense Mobilization, and the Federal Civil Defense Administrator, with power to call upon other agencies for contributions.

f. Directing this Vulnerability Subcommittee to prepare appropriate studies of the damage, both material and psychological, that might be inflicted on the US under assumed levels of Soviet delivery of nuclear weapons or other attack, such studies to be furnished to the Net Evaluation Subcommittee and to be incorporated in the evaluation directed under paragraph c above. For this purpose, the Chairman of the Vulnerability Subcommittee, or his representative, should be attached to the Net Evaluation Subcommittee in the preparation of the final evaluation.

---

[15] Items a. and b. could be separated from the rest. Arguably the others would require only Planning Board action. [Footnote in the original. NSC 5423, "Directive for a Net Capabilities Evaluation Subcommittee," June 23, 1954, subsequently established the subcommittee. Additional documentation on the creation and work of the subcommittee is in *Foreign Relations*, 1952–1954, vol. II, Part 1, pp. 800–802, and ibid., 1955–1957, vol. XIX, pp. 1, 2, passim.]

174. Draft Memorandum From Director of Central Intelligence Dulles to the Director of the Bureau of the Budget (Dodge)[1]

Washington, March 30, 1954.

I am writing this memorandum with reference to the policy, recommended by the National Security Council and approved by the President, for increasing observation of Soviet Bloc diplomatic representatives, including personnel with international organizations, while within the continental United States, with special reference to those whose activities are suspected to extend beyond the scope of normal diplomatic assignments. This policy was most recently stated in par. 20b(9) of NSC 5408.[2] As you know, the President has approved this program being undertaken by the Federal Bureau of Investigation.

It is our opinion that it may be very helpful to our activities outside of the United States to have such a selective surveillance intensified within the United States, and that such a program may have a potential in the field of foreign intelligence information which could be exploited on a continuing basis. The individuals who would be under surveillance are in this country temporarily and eventually will depart for their own or other countries. Information and leads derived from this program would be of assistance to the Central Intelligence Agency in carrying out its responsibilities with regard to this class of persons outside the United States.

We understand that the Federal Bureau of Investigation's budget for Fiscal Year 1955, which has been approved by the Bureau of the Budget and is before the committees of the Congress, made no provision for this increased activity and contains no funds which can be allocated to its support. Because a program for observation of foreign diplomats is one of considerable sensitivity, it is not considered desirable to reopen the Bureau's budget for Fiscal Year 1955, which is now before the Congress, in view of the obviously attendant publicity. We

---

[1] Source: Eisenhower Library, Special Assistant for National Security Affairs Records, NSC Series, Briefing Notes, CIA-Funds, Box 4. Top Secret. A copy was sent to the Attorney General for the Director, Federal Bureau of Investigation. Two handwritten notations in the upper right corner read: "Copy given to Cabell March 31" and, in a different handwriting, "RC draft after talking with P." RC was Robert Cutler, the Special Assistant to the President for National Security Affairs. A brief memorandum of conversation by Cutler describing his talk with the President, at 11:30 a.m. on March 30, is in ibid. The President's views are reflected in this draft memorandum, which Cutler presumably prepared for Dulles' signature.

[2] NSC 5408 is printed in *Foreign Relations, 1952–1954*, vol. II, Part 1, pp. 609–633. Paragraph 20b(9) is redacted, however. The fully declassified text of NSC 5408 is in National Archives, RG 59, S/S–NSC Files: Lot 63 D 351, NSC 5408.

are, therefore, proposing, because of our interest in developing this program on an experimental basis, that the Central Intelligence Agency make available during Fiscal Year 1955 to the Federal Bureau of Investigation, funds from its Contingency Reserve up to an amount to bring the program to the full stage of development considered desirable by the FBI by the end of Fiscal Year 1955; [1 *line not declassified*].

If the program is deemed successful during the course of its development in Fiscal Year 1955, it is understood that the Federal Bureau of Investigation would provide for the entire activity for Fiscal Year 1956 and thereafter in its regular budget requests to the Congress, and would continue to make available to the Central Intelligence Agency the information and leads derived from thereafter carrying out the program which would be of assistance to the Central Intelligence Agency.

The Special Assistant to the President for National Security Affairs has explained to the President how this matter is to be arranged. Your approval of this proposal is, accordingly, requested.[3] Upon receipt of such approval, I will discuss the matter with the Chairmen of the House and Senate Appropriation Committees.

Director
Central Intelligence Agency[4]

---

[3] A March 15 letter from Dodge to Dulles indicates Bureau of the Budget approval of the monetary transfer. (Eisenhower Library, Special Assistant for National Security Affairs Records, NSC Series, Briefing Notes, CIA-Funds, Box 4)

[4] The draft memorandum is unsigned.

175. Minutes of a Meeting of the Intelligence Advisory Committee[1]

IAC–M–150   Washington, May 4, 1954.

Director of Central Intelligence
Allen W. Dulles
Presiding[2]

Lt. Gen. Harold R. Bull (Ret.)
Presiding[2]

MEMBERS PRESENT

Mr. W. Park Armstrong, Special Assistant for Intelligence, Department of State
Brigadier General John M. Willems, acting for Assistant Chief of Staff, G–2, Department of the Army
Rear Admiral H. C. Daniel, acting for Director of Naval Intelligence, Department of the Navy
Major General John A. Samford, Director of Intelligence, Headquarters, United States Air Force
Brigadier General Edward H. Porter, Deputy Director for Intelligence, The Joint Staff
Dr. Charles H. Reichardt, Atomic Energy Commission Representative to the IAC
Mr. Meffert W. Kuhrtz, acting for Assistant to the Director, Federal Bureau of Investigation

ALSO PRESENT

Mr. Robert Amory, Jr., Central Intelligence Agency
Mr. Huntington D. Sheldon, Central Intelligence Agency
*Dr. H. Marshall Chadwell, Central Intelligence Agency
[name not declassified] Central Intelligence Agency
*[name not declassified] Central Intelligence Agency
*Mr. Ludwell L. Montague, Central Intelligence Agency
*[name not declassified] Central Intelligence Agency
*Mr. R. Jack Smith, Central Intelligence Agency
Mr. Harold P. Ford, Central Intelligence Agency
*[name not declassified] Central Intelligence Agency
[name not declassified] Central Intelligence Agency
Dr. Allan Evans, Department of State
Lt. Colonel Vasco J. Fenili, Department of the Army
Lt. Colonel James P. Barry, Department of the Army
Lt. Colonel H. N. Maples, Department of the Army
Captain N. E. Smith, USN, Department of the Navy
Mr. Lawrence Healey, Department of the Navy
Brigadier General Millard Lewis, United States Air Force

---

[1] Source: Central Intelligence Agency, Executive Registry, Job 85–S00362R, Box 2. Secret. The meeting was held in the DCI's conference room.

[2] Part of meeting. [Footnote in the original.]

Colonel Donald H. Ainsworth, United States Air Force
Colonel John J. Morrow, United States Air Force
Colonel Robert Totten, United States Air Force
Mr. Donald F. Benjamin, United States Air Force
Mr. Samuel S. Rockwell, United States Air Force
Rear Admiral Edwin T. Layton, The Joint Staff
Colonel Samuel M. Lansing, The Joint Staff
Captain Ray E. Malpass, USN, The Joint Staff

Richard D. Drain[3]
Secretary

Approval of Minutes (IAC–M–149, 28 April)[4]

1. *Action:* Approved.

Progress Report, Ad Hoc Committee (Watch) (IAC–D–6/1 (Revised) 26 April 1954)[5]

2. *Action:* Approved the ad hoc committee's recommendations as follows:

a. The Terms of Reference (attachment 1)[6] were approved as amended, subject to final concurrence by the FBI member before issuance as DCID 1/2.[7]

b. Implementation of the Terms of Reference and activation of the Indications Center (see attachment 2) should be effected on 1 July 1954 or earlier if practicable.

c. The Ad Hoc IAC Committee (Watch) should continue in existence at least until activation of the Indications Center, should continue supervision of the preparation of the Indications Intelligence Plan (see attachment 3), should prepare for the convening of the proposed conference to systematize and coordinate collection of indications information and intelligence, and should continue its examination of relevant systems, procedures, and channels. The ad hoc committee, in its continuing examination of channels for transmission of warning, was asked to develop procedures to insure timely alerting of IAC members, IAC agencies, and other appropriate Government bodies.

3. *Discussion:* Mr. Dulles stressed the great importance of adequately performing the watch function, as exemplified by its recognition in

---

[3] Printed from a copy that bears this typed signature.
[4] Not printed.
[5] Not found.
[6] Attachments 1–3 were not found.
[7] Document 179.

NSC 162/2[8] as a major intelligence objective. He proposed to take up with the Council, on the basis of this paper as issued, how materials available to the NSC and Government agencies may be provided to the Watch Committee in connection with performing its mission and functions.

4. It was brought out by discussion of proposed changes to the draft terms of reference that it is desirable sharply to focus the watch function as one of providing maximum prior warning of the imminence of hostile action. At the same time, the watch machinery must have unrestricted access to a great variety of materials in order to perform that function. Experience has shown that without such access, and without recognition of the high priority to be accorded the watch process, that process tends to become static.

5. Various members commented on the subordinate relation of the Watch Committee to the IAC. It was recognized that the Watch Committee could present to the IAC any problem, substantive or procedural, affecting its operation and that the IAC's review of the Watch Committee's operation would tend to prevent the development of misunderstanding as to the Watch function or product.

6. It was understood that the proposed approach to field intelligence activities would include non-military as well as military activities.

[Omitted here is discussion of agenda item 7: Annex to NSC Action No. 1074.]

---

[8] See Document 163.

176.   Memorandum for the Record[1]

Washington, May 4, 1954.

SUBJECT

Meeting in Office of Chairman of the Joint Chiefs of Staff on Tuesday, 4 May 1954, with Admiral Radford; Mr. Amory, and General Bull were present with the DCI and Rear Admiral Layton, General Porter, and two other officers were also present

1. In the meeting which started at 3 P. M., Mr. Dulles explained his purpose by stating that he was hopeful that the Director of Central Intelligence and the Chairman of the Joint Chiefs of Staff could by exchanging views come to an agreement on the proposal for proper "Organizational Arrangements for Continental Defense."

2. Mr. Dulles noted the divergence of judgments between the Joint Chiefs of Staff and others on one side, and CIA and others on the other side as indicated in the two solutions (alternatives A and B of para. 9 to NSC Action 873–d)[2] recommended in papers relating to the "Net capabilities of the USSR to inflict damage on the US," which is now up for resolution by the NSC. He felt that this discussion today could clear up some misapprehension and lead to an agreed view.

3. Mr. Dulles explained that there was a dual responsibility shared equally by the Director of CIA and the JCS for advising the NSC on the intelligence and operational features respectively of an appraisal of the net capabilities of the USSR to inflict direct injury on the US. He noted that other agencies would have responsibility also but only in limited areas requiring only part time participation to the extent necessary to insure that their responsibilities are fully met but not to the extent requiring a disclosure of war plans, or the extensive use of other highly secret documents. He emphasized also that CIA participation would be on a very limited high level basis, and that the few CIA representatives involved would be professional men who could be trusted to protect all information made available to them. He did not expect that revelation of war plans as such would be found necessary but that operational information would be required. He pointed out that he could not carry out his full responsibility as DCI without such knowledge of our own capabilities.

---

[1] Source: Central Intelligence Agency, Office of the Deputy Director for Intelligence, Job 80–R01440R, Box 3. Secret. Drafted by General Bull on May 27. Amory wrote "Concur" followed by his signature below General Bull's initials at the end of the memorandum.

[2] See footnote 2, Document 173.

4. Admiral Radford replied that he frankly didn't understand why there was any necessity for this high level organization to make a commanders estimate. He felt that if CIA made its coordinated intelligence estimate, the JCS and the Defense Department were, with this estimate available, competent to do the rest of the evaluation for the NSC and the President, based on their own knowledge of and responsibility for operational matters and war plans. He saw no need for setting up another coordinating agency. He didn't see this need as recently carried out in the Continental Defense field.

5. General Bull pointed out that a single intelligence estimate of gross capabilities was not the final word on intelligence—that it was necessary to work by phases in a process of comparing gross intelligence estimates with our operational capabilities. This procedure would result in new intelligence estimates based on a knowledge of our own strengths and dispositions such as the Kremlin is believed to have to guide its decisions. This knowledge is not now available to our own national intelligence agency. Such a procedure for comparing capabilities on both sides, we believe, is essential and is a shared responsibility of DCI and Defense.

6. Mr. Dulles again emphasized that he did not want to pry into those areas of classified information not essential to carrying out his responsibility and stated that although the NSC planning for developing the net evaluation was stated as urgent he would not press for action at the next NSC meeting pending further consideration by Admiral Radford.

7. Mr. Amory called Admiral Radford's attention to the fact that since no defense can be perfect, there will always be a portion of any major attacking force that will get through. This hostile force, representing the remaining net capability of the enemy at that time, retains a capability for attack. It continues to be the Director's responsibility to evaluate this capability as it was his responsibility before and during the operation.

8. In response to Admiral Radford's expressed desire to give it more thought, the Director, in leaving, stated he would be pleased to discuss the problem further and felt sure they could work it out.

H. R. B.[3]

---

[3] Printed from a copy that bears these typed initials.

177. Memorandum From the Chairman of the Continental Defense Committee (Bull) to Director of Central Intelligence Dulles[1]

Washington, May 5, 1954.

SUBJECT

   Net Evaluation Procedures

1. In addition to the point that we have been making that the DCI has a *legal responsibility* to advise the Commander (and his NSC) on his intelligence estimates of both gross and net capabilities, probable intentions and probable courses of action, there are much more potent arguments in favor of joint intelligence operational consideration as follows:

a. Admiral Radford and others infer that all they need is the normal estimate of *gross capabilities* which they in the Defense Department can then use in working out the net capabilities. This view is not only an oversimplification of the problem but it puts the Director in the position of abdicating his responsibilities for estimating for "The Commander" the Bloc's probable *intentions and probable courses of action*. This the Director *cannot do* in a satisfactory and useful manner in a vacuum, *excluded from knowledge* of our *own deployments* and our *own capabilities*. If the Director's estimates are done in this manner he is asked to estimate the thinking of the Kremlin leaders which is based on their intelligence of our capabilities which they most certainly know in great detail, whereas the Director in his estimate is permitted to have no such comparable knowledge. The Director's knowledge of US and allied capabilities and dispositions must be at least comparable to the intelligence possessed by the Kremlin leadership. To think, as I believe Admiral Radford and the military in general do, that the Commander's estimate is made by G–3 after receiving a G–2 contribution overlooks the sound procedures which govern all good staff operations in the G–2/G–3 field.

b. No G–2 makes his estimates of enemy capabilities, probable courses of action, or probable intentions or advises his Commander in an operational vacuum. By the closest hour by hour contact and joint daily or more frequent briefings, he is always able to make his estimate of probable hostile courses of action based on not only the enemy new

---

[1] Source: Central Intelligence Agency, Office of the Deputy Director for Intelligence, Job 80–R0440R, Box 3. Secret. The typed words "Condensed by Robert Amory, Jr." (with Amory's handwritten initials) appear below Bull's signature at the end of the memorandum.

capabilities in manpower, weapons, organization, training, leadership, dispositions, etc. but also from his estimate of what the enemy probably knows concerning our own strengths, dispositions and intentions.

c. The Director as our National G–2 should have the same rights and duties as any G–2 in the lower echelons has. Otherwise he cannot fulfill his legal responsibilities.

2. Although I recognize that a case can be made that the "national level" presents different problems with a justified restriction on revelation of war plans, certain planned courses of action, certain dispositions, weapons development, etc. should be made available to DCI and IAC on a very strict "need-to-know" basis, I believe a clear definition of intelligence requirements in the operational field could be worked out jointly and I doubt that a knowledge of detailed war plans would be necessary. In general, DCI should get only operational information which it is reasonable to expect the enemy to have in whole or in part.

We have no present mechanism to meet our minimum needs. We are blocked by self imposed departmental restrictions or ground rules which severely limit our intelligence investigation of our own force—a handicap not imposed on our enemies.

3. I want to point out also from my experience a real stumbling block in getting Defense to accept our proposal. That is, the broadening of the responsible group to include other agencies such as IIC and ICIS who have a similar justification for full responsibility in their more limited field—hostile attack on the Continental US by Soviet agents. Their exclusion from overall responsibility can be justified on practical grounds only but I think it must be done to make the joint effort work. I think it might be acceptable to insure them the right and duty to be heard at appropriate times and to comment on the final report or at least segments thereof that bear in any way on their responsible interests. I believe you should support the probable Defense Department desire to exclude them but to do so on a practical basis related to their total lack of *responsibility* in the fields of foreign intelligence and foreign deployments and war plans which quite rightly should be kept on a strict "need-to-know". They will resist as we have but I believe the exclusion can be justified on grounds acceptable to the NSC.

H.R. Bull

178. Memorandum for the Record[1]

Washington, May 10, 1954.

SUBJECT

Supplement to Minutes of OCB Meeting of May 5, 1954

At the luncheon meeting of the OCB on May 5, the Board concurred in a proposal to allocate additional funds to support a series of projects designed to encourage ratification of the European Defense Community. This proposal, originating with the Department of State, is based on the view that activities in this request to date have been useful but need to be accelerated to the extent practicable. The acceleration and the additional allocation of funds would be designed to support EDC ratification through such media as the press, radio, speeches, labor groups, etc.

The Board concurred in a request [less than 1 line not declassified] to the Director of the Budget for an allocation of such additional funds as may be necessary to expand and accelerate this program. [5 lines not declassified]

Elmer B. Staats
Executive Officer

---

[1] Source: National Security Council, OCB Record of Project Approvals, 1953–1955. Top Secret. Copies were sent to Dulles, Smith, Anderson, and Cutler.

179.   Director of Central Intelligence Directive No. 1/2[1]

Washington, May 11, 1954.

TERMS OF REFERENCE, WATCH COMMITTEE OF THE IAC

Pursuant to the provisions of paragraph 6, NSCID No. 1,[2] and paragraph 10,a,(1) of NSC 162/2,[3] approved by the President on 30 October 1953, the following terms of reference for the Watch Committee of the IAC are hereby established:

Preamble

The Soviet/Communist bloc, as a potential aggressor, has the capability to initiate suddenly at any time and in a place and by methods of its own choosing, hostile action[4] in such strength as to gravely threaten the security of the United States. The mission of providing earliest possible warning of hostile action will be undertaken by the IAC agencies, within the scope of their responsibilities, as of the highest priority. The proper discharge of this mission depends upon the carrying out of complementary watch and estimating functions.

A. Name

Watch Committee of the IAC

B. Mission

To provide earliest possible warning to the United States Government of hostile action by the USSR, or its allies, which endangers the security of the United States.

C. Functions

1. To develop and operate on a current and continuing basis an intelligence plan for the levying upon IAC members, and the requesting from other U.S. agencies through appropriate channels, of the intelligence requirements necessary to provide the maximum degree of advance warning and for recommending the collection priorities of these requirements.

2. To analyze and evaluate information and intelligence, both current and cumulative, on an all-source basis, furnished by the IAC agen-

---

[1] Source: National Archives, RG 59, S/S–NSC Files: Lot 66 D 148, Misc. NSC Memos. Secret. NSC Executive Secretary Lay circulated this directive under cover of a memorandum to the National Security Council dated June 1.

[2] Document 255.

[3] Text in *Foreign Relations, 1952–1954*, vol. II, Part 1, p. 577–597.

[4] Aggressive action by armed forces, or by organizations or individuals in support of military strategy. [Footnote in the original.]

cies relating to the imminence of hostilities, and to develop therefrom the conclusions as to indications of:

a. Soviet/Communist intentions to initiate hostilities against

1 the continental United States, U.S. possessions, or U.S. forces abroad,
2 U.S. allies or their forces,
3 areas peripheral to the Soviet Orbit.

b. any other development, actual or potential, susceptible of direct exploitation by Soviet/Communist hostile action which would jeopardize the security of the United States.

3. To report promptly their conclusions, together with significant indications, to the principals of the IAC and other appropriate recipients. In the event of an impending critical situation, IAC principals will be immediately advised after which the provisions of paragraph 6, NSCID No. 1, will apply.

4. To make recommendations to the IAC, or member agencies thereof, including such divergent views as may be recorded.

5. The Watch Committee shall avoid duplicating IAC estimative functions.

D. *Composition and Organization*

1. The Watch Committee will be composed of a Senior Officer representing each IAC member organization, one of whom will be designated by the DCI, after consultation with the IAC, as Chairman for a specified period. The Committee will be supported by an Indications Center, headed by a Director to be provided by CIA and consisting of an administrative Secretariat and an Indications Group.

[Omitted here is an organizational chart of the Watch Committee.]

2. The Watch Committee will meet on a regular schedule as determined by the Committee and on special occasions when requested by one or more of its members or their principals.

E. *Duties and Responsibilities*

The Watch Committee shall discharge, or direct the Indications Center in the discharge of, the below-listed duties and responsibilities.

1. Develop and operate on a current and continuing basis the Watch Committee Intelligence Plan for systematizing, energizing, and coordinating through appropriate channels the world-wide collection by U.S. agencies of information and intelligence pertinent to the Watch Committee mission.

2. Arrange through the IAC or the appropriate member thereof for exploitation of every domestic and foreign source of information and intelligence pertinent to the Watch Committee mission; and, among other actions, arrange, at appropriate times, that representatives of IAC

field intelligence activities confer with the IAC and the Watch Committee in order effectively to coordinate, but not direct, field intelligence activities with the activities of the Watch Committee.

3. Arrange with the IAC agencies for a systematic screening of all information and intelligence received by them by any means for the purpose of immediately extracting and forwarding to the Indications Center all items which may contain indications of Soviet/Communist intentions as set forth in C, 2 above (this procedure is in addition to the action called for in paragraph 6 of NSCID No. 1); an agency evaluation, where appropriate, will be forwarded as soon as possible.

4. Members will maintain close and intimate liaison with their respective parent agencies to assist them in ensuring that all pertinent information and intelligence is being made available to the Indications Center.

5. Continuously screen all pertinent information and intelligence received from all IAC agencies for indications relating to the Watch Committee mission.

6. Develop promptly an early evaluation and analysis of each indication in coordination with the intelligence agency or agencies best qualified to deal with the field of intelligence to which the indication belongs.

7. Coordinate with the individual members of the Watch Committee the selection of indications for consideration by the Committee in regular and special meetings.

8. Prepare material for use by the Watch Committee to assist in its deliberations and the formulation of its conclusions.

9. Coordinate the reproduction and dissemination of approved Watch Committee reports.

10. Maintain in readily usable form a complete and integrated file of all available information and intelligence pertinent to the Watch Committee mission.

11. Maintain wall maps, charts and other display material which will most effectively assist in illustrating and interpreting graphically the current and cumulative indications.

12. Concurrently, but not as a substitute for current methods of analysis and evaluation, develop and test (with outside assistance if desirable) the application of mechanical aids and techniques to the problem on an experimental basis with a view to their eventual use in assisting effectively the Watch Committee in the accomplishment of its mission.

13. Perform such additional tasks as shall be required by the IAC in the discharge of the Watch Committee mission.[5]

---

[5] Printed from an unsigned copy.

180. **Memorandum From the Chief of the International Organizations Division, Central Intelligence Agency (Brader) to the Deputy Director for Plans of the Central Intelligence Agency (Wisner)**

Washington, May 14, 1954.

[Source: Central Intelligence Agency, Office of the Deputy Director for Operations, Job 79–01228A, Box 24. Secret. 2 pages not declassified.]

---

181. **Paper Prepared by the Operations Coordinating Board**[1]

Washington, May 14, 1954.

PRINCIPLES TO ASSURE COORDINATION
OF GRAY ACTIVITIES

1. Purpose

1.1 To assure coordination of information (which term as used in this paper includes propaganda and other related activities) unattributed to the U.S. Government, the National Security Council, in NSC 165/1,[2] dated 24 October 1953:

a. Authorized the U.S. Information Agency, when considered advisable, and except in the case of operations of the Voice of America, to communicate with other peoples without attribution to the U.S. Government on matters for which attribution could be assumed by the Government if necessary, and

b. Directed that the Operations Coordinating Board agree upon principles which will govern such unattributed activities (hereinafter such activities are included in the definition of gray).

These principles, having been agreed upon by the OCB, are published herewith for the guidance of officials concerned.

1.2 The intent of this paper is to underline the need for field coordination, to insure that all information activities are conducted

---

[1] Source: Central Intelligence Agency, History Staff, Job 83–00036R, Box 5. Secret. OCB Executive Officer Staats circulated this paper to the Operations Coordinating Board by memorandum on May 18. (Ibid.)

[2] Entitled "Mission of USIA"; text in *Foreign Relations*, 1952–1954, vol. II, Part 2, pp. 1752–1754.

securely and effectively, to prevent duplication and to avoid embarrassment to the U.S. Government. Responsibilities in the white and black fields are clearly established, but in the gray field responsibility has been assigned to more than one agency. Therefore, this paper concerns itself primarily with the criteria to use in determining whether USIA or the Department of State or the OCB designee will undertake a particular gray activity. Thus to carry out fully the intent of this paper, there must be close liaison in the field among representatives of the agencies concerned so that each item of gray activity will be considered in light of:

a. The assignments of responsibility and the criteria set forth in Paragraph 3.

b. The merits of the case, assets available, and other considerations which may apply locally.

1.3 Chiefs of Diplomatic Missions or Principal Officers (the ranking State Department official at a subordinate post) have the overall responsibility for insuring that field coordination at all posts for which they have supervisory responsibility is satisfactory (Paragraph 4.2). Moreover, State and USIA both at headquarters and in the field will be responsible for initiating liaison with the OCB designee concerning their respective gray activities, so that the latter knows of existing or contemplated activities and can preserve the security of its own activities.

2. Definitions

For the purpose of this paper, the following definitions of terms are used in describing both the content of information and the type of activity.

White	Acknowledged as an official statement or act of the U.S. Government, or emanates from a source associated closely enough with the U.S. Government to reflect an official viewpoint. The information is true and factual. It also includes all output identified as coming from U.S. official sources.
Gray	The true source (U.S. Government) is not revealed to the target audience. The activity engaged in plausibly appears to emanate from a non-official American source, or an indigenous, non-hostile source, or there may be no attribution.[3] Gray is that information whose content is such that the effect will be increased if the hand of the U.S. Government and in some cases any American partic-

---

[3] In areas where activity is conducted without any attribution and it may result in embarrassment to an agency of the U.S. Government, liaison officers will carefully weigh all aspects of the proposed activity before deciding whether such an operation should be undertaken. [Footnote in the original.]

ipation are not revealed. It is simply a means for the U.S. to present viewpoints which are in the interest of U.S. foreign policy, but which will be acceptable or more acceptable to the intended target audience than will an official government statement.

Black   The activity engaged in appears to emanate from a source (government, party, group, organization, person) usually hostile in nature. The interest of the U.S. Government is concealed and the U.S. Government would deny responsibility. The content may be partially or completely fabricated, but that which is fabricated is made to appear credible to the target audience. Black activity is also usually designed to cause embarrassment to the ostensible source or to force the ostensible source to take action against its will.

3. Responsibility for Operations

3.1 Since the responsibility is assigned for gray activity to more than one agency, liaison officers in the field, and in Washington whenever necessary, must determine which agency will undertake an activity. The inherent risk must be assessed by means of criteria set forth in Paragraph 3.4, bearing in mind that activities in which USIA or State engage must be those which the U.S. Government could acknowledge if necessary.

3.2 Authorized to engage in white activity directed at foreign audiences are: The State Department, USIA, the Foreign Operations Administration (as assigned in Reorganization Plans 7 and 8) the Defense Department and other U.S. Government departments and agencies as necessary.

3.3 Responsibility for engaging in black propaganda and other related activities is assigned solely to the designee of the OCB. Likewise it should be kept in mind that activities, either gray or black, conducted into denied areas from their peripheries, other than radio, are the sole responsibility of the OCB designee.

3.4 Responsibility for gray is assigned to the OCB designee, USIA and State. The following criteria will assist in determining the responsibility for the execution of a proposed gray activity. If the answer to any of the three questions below is affirmative, the activity is the sole responsibility of the OCB designee. If government interest is not to be revealed but the answer to all three questions listed below is negative, the activity may fall within the charter of State, USIA or the OCB designee:

a. Would the disclosure of the source occasion serious embarrassment to the U.S. Government or to the agencies responsible for the information activity?

b. Would the activity or the materials disseminated be seriously discredited if it were to become known that the U.S. Government were responsible?

c. Would the outlet be seriously damaged if it were to become known that the activity is subsidized or otherwise assisted by the U.S. Government?

3.5 The Department of State and USIA may engage in gray activity which can be acknowledged by the U.S. Government if necessary, provided that before a decision or commitment is made, the OCB designee's representative, wherever one is stationed, is consulted and his concurrence obtained. Concurrence shall be given unless the OCB designee is of the opinion that a proposed operation will jeopardize its activities or established mechanisms, or does not comply with the criteria in 3.4. In giving its concurrence the OCB designee is not assuming responsibility for the successful completion of an activity conducted by another agency. Necessary coordination between State and USIA and the OCB designee will be undertaken through liaison channels described in paragraph 4. Wherever the OCB designee has no such representative approval of the Chief of Diplomatic Mission or Principal Officer will be obtained.

4. Machinery for Application of the Criteria

4.1 The coordination required for application of the criteria stated in Paragraph 3.4 is to be achieved by creation and use of appropriate liaison arrangements in the field and in Washington.

4.2 The Assistant Secretary of State for Public Affairs, the Director of USIA and the designee of the OCB will each designate mutually acceptable points of contact in selected missions for field coordination. In any case in which an agency authorized to engage in gray activities proposes to use the personnel or facilities of the Department of Defense abroad, the Assistant to the Secretary of Defense (Special Operations) will designate a mutually acceptable point of contact at the appropriate location. Responsibility is vested in the Chiefs of Diplomatic Missions or Principal Officers for insuring that field coordination at all posts for which they have supervisory responsibility is adequate, that criteria are correctly applied, and that decisions are within the framework of national policy.

4.3 Coordination in Washington, to supplement that in the field, is the responsibility of the Assistant Secretary of State for Public Affairs and the Director of USIA. They will be responsible for initiating appropriate liaison arrangements and clearances within and between their respective departments and with the designee of the OCB.

4.4 Whenever deemed necessary by the Assistant Secretary of State for Public Affairs, the Director of USIA and the OCB designee, representatives of other United States Agencies engaged in information activities abroad will be included in such coordination machinery.

In any case in which an agency authorized to engage in gray activities proposes to use the personnel or facilities of the Department of Defense abroad, the representative of that Department designated pursuant to paragraph 4.2 shall be informed of the nature of the activity.

4.5 Whenever the field representatives of the agencies herein concerned are unable to reach an agreement as to which agency will undertake a gray project, the matter will be referred to Washington for advice and decision by the appropriate representatives of the agencies involved. Communications from the field on such matters will be via the channels of the OCB designee whenever the OCB designee is mentioned.

4.6 The designated liaison officers at each station in the field will meet at the earliest practicable date to review all gray operations of State and USIA which are currently functioning, and apply the criteria herein described to determine if they should be continued, transferred to the OCB designee, or terminated.

---

182. Draft National Security Council Directive[1]

NSC 5423   Washington, June 23, 1954.

NATIONAL SECURITY COUNCIL DIRECTIVE FOR A NET CAPABILITIES EVALUATION SUBCOMMITTEE

1. Pursuant to authorization of the President there is hereby directed the preparation of a report assessing the net capabilities of the USSR, in the event of general war, to inflict direct injury upon the continental United States and key U.S. installations overseas. This net capabilities report will cover the period through July 1, 1957 and should be submitted to the Council on or before November 1, 1954. It will cover all types of attack, direct or clandestine, and will deal primarily with the initial phases of war, i.e., the period during which all or most of the Soviet stockpile of nuclear weapons might be expended. It will

---

[1] Source: National Archives, RG 273, NSC Policy Papers, NSC 5432, Box 32. Top Secret. The draft was circulated to the National Security Council under cover of a June 23 note from NSC Executive Secretary Lay. The draft was approved by the President on June 24. (National Archives, RG 59, S/S–NSC Files: Lot 63 D 351, Annotated List of Individual NSC Papers) NSC 5423 superseded NSC 140. For documentation on the NSC 140 series, see *Foreign Relations, 1952–1954*, vol. II, Part 1, pp. 205–208, 328–349, 355–360, 368–370, and ibid., Part 2, 1177–1178. For a CIA view of the evolution of Net Capabilities Estimates, see Document 189.

include consideration of the several courses of action which the USSR is capable of executing and in support of which the Soviet nuclear weapons stockpile might be expended. In determining the net effect of an attack, the report will take into account the mid-1957 status of presently approved defense programs.

2. In order to carry out this directive, there is hereby established a Net Capabilities Evaluation Subcommittee of the NSC composed of the Chairman of the Joint Chiefs of Staff, the Director of Central Intelligence, and the following members for the specific purposes noted below:

a. The Chairman of the Interdepartmental Intelligence Conference and the Chairman of the Interdepartmental Committee on Internal Security for matters relating to internal security;

b. The Director, Office of Defense Mobilization, for matters relating to continuity of government, sufficiency and continuity of industry, and urban vulnerability;

c. The Federal Civil Defense Administrator for matters relating to civil defense;

d. The Chairman, Atomic Energy Commission, for matters relating to Atomic Energy Commission activities.

3. The Chairman of the Joint Chiefs of Staff will serve as Chairman of the Net Capabilities Evaluation Subcommittee. The Subcommittee will have a temporary staff, composed of individuals assigned by the participating agencies and headed by a Director chosen by the Chairman of the Joint Chiefs of Staff and the Director of Central Intelligence. It is expected that members of this staff will be assigned to this project as their primary duty during the period of preparation of the net capabilities report.

4. The functions of the Net Capabilities Evaluation Subcommittee will include:

a. Responsibility for the security of the project during the period of preparation of the report.

b. General supervision of the project at all stages including:

(1) Preparation of subsidiary terms of reference as a guide for preliminary reports on selected factors essential to the assessment, these preliminary reports to be contributed to the project by the various agencies concerned.

(2) Preparation of planning or intelligence assumptions to be used as a basis for preliminary reports by the various agencies.

(3) Review of preliminary reports contributed and issuance of requests for reconsideration or amplification.

(4) Examination of data used in preparation of preliminary reports as necessary and provided that war plans and intelligence sources and methods are not unnecessarily disclosed.

(5) Decisions concerning handling and distribution of preliminary reports and data contributed by the various agencies.

c. Preparation of intermediate working papers as required.

d. Preparation and submission of the final report for consideration by the NSC.

5. The National Security Council staff will furnish an Executive Secretary for the Subcommittee. The agencies participating in the work of the Subcommittee are hereby requested to furnish appropriate administrative services. All personnel participating in the work of the Subcommittee will have appropriate security clearances and will be instructed in whatever special security measures the Subcommittee adopts.

6. The Net Capabilities Evaluation Subcommittee hereby established is empowered under the terms of this directive to call on any agency of the government for relevant information, evaluations, and estimates, subject only to establishment of appropriate security arrangements and careful limitation of access to highly sensitive material so that there will not be any unnecessary disclosure of war plans or intelligence sources and methods.

7. Distribution of the final report of the Subcommittee will be determined by the President.

---

183. Report by the Operations Coordinating Board[1]

Washington, July 21, 1954.

REPORT ON NSC 59/1[2] AND NSC 127/1[3]

1. NSC 59/1, "The Foreign Information Program and Psychological Warfare Planning," approved by the President March 19, 1950, has been largely superseded by subsequent directives, notably: Reorganization Plan No. 8,[4] which established the United States Information Agency; the President's letter of June 1, 1953, to heads of Executive

---

[1] Source: National Archives, RG 273, National Security Council Files, NSC 127/1. Secret. Attached to the report is OCB Acting Executive Officer George Morgan's July 22 covering memorandum to NSC Executive Secretary Lay, which indicated that the Operations Coordinating Board approved the report on July 21. The report was forwarded to the National Security Council under cover of a July 23 memorandum from NSC Executive Secretary Lay. (Ibid.)

[2] Document 2.

[3] See Document 123.

[4] See *Foreign Relations*, 1952–1954, vol. II, Part 2, pp. 1709–1711.

Departments;[5] and Executive Order No. 10483,[6] which established the Operations Coordinating Board. The functions of the Psychological Operations Coordinating Committee, established pursuant to NSC 59/1, were transferred by the President by a special memorandum to the NSC dated September 3, 1953,[7] to the Operations Coordinating Board. The POCC has been discontinued as a separate coordinating arrangement. OCB arrangements for former POCC functions are described in Annex "A".[8]

2. The OCB has noted with approval certain interagency relationships and arrangements as indicated in Annex "A". It is considered that these arrangements will serve the requirements of interdepartmental coordination of international information activities until such time and under such conditions of hostilities as the President may otherwise direct. In the event that the NSC in its consideration of over-all policy and organizational arrangements with respect to prescribed theaters of war determines that an information and psychological warfare arrangement may be required different from that set forth in Annex "A", the OCB when directed by the NSC, will develop specific recommendations for its consideration.

3. NSC 127/1, approved by the National Security Council on July 24, 1952, NSC Action No. 657, concurred in a plan for conducting psychological operations during general hostilities submitted by the Psychological Strategy Board, subject to two modifications:

a. Overt information facilities and personnel in military theaters of operations were to be made available to the U.S. military commander designated by the JCS during a period of hostilities. Determination of the facilities and personnel so transferred and their later return were to be coordinated by the Psychological Strategy Board.

b. Subsequently, the responsibility for the determination was placed upon the organization established pursuant to NSC 59/1.

4. The President approved NSC 127/1 as a basis for emergency planning related to sudden general hostilities and directed that subsidiary plans and measures should provide maximum flexibility for the President in determining the ultimate organization required for full scale general hostilities.

5. NSC 127/1 was designed for a period of full mobilization or general hostilities and therefore did not apply to the hostilities in Korea. Subsequent to the approval of NSC 127/1, the President on March 12, 1953 assigned responsibility to the ODM and the Bureau of the

---

[5] Text in *Public Papers: Eisenhower, 1953*, pp. 351–354.

[6] Document 157.

[7] The memorandum is dated September 2; see Document 158.

[8] Entitled "Interagency Liaison with U.S. Information Agency," dated June 28. Not printed.

Budget, under the coordination of the President's Advisory Committee on Reorganization, for the development of a plan of organization for full mobilization required for general hostilities. No specific plan related to information and psychological warfare activities has yet been developed. The OCB apparently has no responsibility under NSC 127/1 for any aspects of this planning.

6. A PSB contingency plan, D–11b, "National Overt Propaganda Policy Guidance for General War,"[9] is still in effect and will continue to be utilized as appropriate. The OCB will refer it for revision or other disposal by the appropriate authority as indicated by the plan of organization for full mobilization (par. 5 above) when provisions for information and psychological warfare activities have been developed and approved.

Recommendation

It is recommended:

7. That the NSC, recognizing that the organizational aspects of NSC 59/1 and NSC 127/1 are obsolete, rescind these papers without prejudice to the principles of operation and the responsibilities of departments and agencies to engage in psychological warfare and psychological warfare planning enunciated therein or elsewhere.

8. That the NSC note that the OCB serves as the body for dealing with requirements for interdepartmental coordination concerning overseas information and psychological warfare activities in carrying out NSC assignments or upon specific request by participating departments and agencies.

9. That the NSC note that the OCB developed, on an urgent basis, a detailed contingency plan for information and psychological warfare activities in Indochina and that the OCB will not develop any further detailed subsidiary plans of this type for designated areas unless so directed by the NSC.

---

[9] Not found.

---

184.   Editorial Note

In July 1953 Congress created the Commission on the Organization of the Executive Branch of the Government to look into the organization of the Executive Branch and report back to the Congress. (P.L. 108, approved July 10, 1953; 67 Stat. 142) On July 24, 1953, President Eisenhower named former President Herbert Hoover as chairman of the commission. (*Public Papers: Eisenhower, 1953*, page 516) The Hoover Commission, as it was called, delegated a small sub-group, or task force, under General Mark W. Clark to review the relationship of the intelligence organizations to the executive.

President Eisenhower, wanting a separate report on the CIA's Directorate of Plans to be presented to him personally and not to Congress, asked General James H. Doolittle to conduct a special study. See Document 185. For the Doolittle report, see Document 192.

The Doolittle report was made available to General Clark's task force, which completed classified and unclassified reports in May 1955. A May 4, 1955, memorandum from the Secretary of State's Acting Special Assistant for Intelligence and Research Fisher Howe to Under Secretary of State Hoover described the work of the Clark task force, its members' contacts with Department of State officials, and the Department's views on areas needing improvement. (National Archives, RG 59, Central Files 1955–60, 711.5200/5–455) The classified version of the Clark report is Document 220; the unclassified version is Document 221.

---

185.   Letter From President Eisenhower to General James H. Doolittle[1]

Washington, July 26, 1954.

RE

Panel of Consultants on Covert Activities of the Central Intelligence Agency

Dear General Doolittle:

I have requested you, and you have agreed, to act as Chairman of a panel of consultants to conduct a study of the covert activities of the Central Intelligence Agency. With your concurrence I have invited Messrs. William B. Franke, Morris Hadley, and William Pawley to act with you as members of the panel. Mr. S. Paul Johnston has kindly agreed to serve as Executive Director of the panel.

It is my desire that the Panel of Consultants should undertake a comprehensive study of the covert activities of the Central Intelligence Agency, in particular those carried out under the terms of NSCID #5

---

[1] Source: Eisenhower Library, Administration Series. Secret.

of August 28, 1951,[2] and NSC 5412 of March 15, 1954.[3] You will consider the personnel factors, the security, the adequacy, the efficacy and the relative costs of these operations and, as far as possible, equate the cost of the over-all efforts to the results achieved. You will make any recommendations calculated to improve the conduct of these operations. To the extent that agencies of the Government, other than the Central Intelligence Agency, are engaged in covert operations which may parallel, duplicate, or supplement the operations of CIA, you may investigate such other operations conducted by any other department or agency of the Government in order to insure, insofar as practicable, that the field of foreign clandestine operations is adequately covered and that there is no unnecessary duplication of effort or expense.

In view of the particularly sensitive nature of these covert operations, their relation to the conduct of our foreign policy, and the fact that these sensitive operations are carried on pursuant to National Security Council action approved by me, I desire that your report be made to me personally and classified Top Secret. I will determine whether or not the report or any part thereof should have any further dissemination. I should appreciate it if your report could be available to me prior to October 1, 1954.

As you know, the Commission on Organization of the Executive Branch of the Government, generally known as the Hoover Commission, is constituting a Task Force to study and make recommendations with respect to the organization and methods of operations of the CIA.[4] General Mark W. Clark has been designated by Mr. Hoover to head this Task Force which, I understand, will probably be organized and start its work sometime in September next. Under the law constituting the Hoover Commission, the Task Force shall study and investigate the present organization and methods of operation of the Agency to determine what changes therein are necessary to accomplish the policy of Congress to promote economy, efficiency, and improved service by:

a. recommending methods and procedures for reducing expenditures to the lowest amount consistent with the efficient performance of essential services, activities and functions;

b. eliminating duplication and overlapping of services, activities, and functions;

c. consolidating services, activities, and functions of a similar nature;

d. abolishing services, activities, and functions not necessary to the efficient conduct of Government;

e. eliminating nonessential services, functions, and activities which are competitive with private enterprise;

f. defining responsibilities of officials; and

---

[2] Document 255.

[3] Document 171.

[4] See Documents 184, 220, and 221.

g. relocating agencies now responsible directly to the President in departments or other agencies.

As the work of the Hoover Task Force will get under way shortly, I suggest that you and General Clark confer in order to avoid any unnecessary duplication of work as between you. The distinction between the work of your Study Group and of the Hoover Task Force is this:

You will deal with the covert activities of the CIA as indicated in paragraph (2) above, and your report will be submitted to me. General Clark's Task Force will deal largely with the organization and methods of operation of the CIA and other related agencies within the limits prescribed in the law as outlined in paragraph (4) above. Reports of the Hoover Commission are made to the Congress.

The purpose of these studies, both that of the Hoover Task Force and that of your Group, is to insure that the United States Government develops an appropriate mechanism for carrying out its over-all intelligence responsibilities and the related covert operations. I consider these operations are essential to our national security in these days when international Communism is aggressively pressing its worldwide subversive program.

Sincerely,[5]

---

[5] Printed from an unsigned copy.

---

186. Memorandum From the Joint Chiefs of Staff to Secretary of Defense Wilson[1]

Washington, August 3, 1954.

SUBJECT

Information and Recommendation Concerning Warning Facilities of the Intelligence Community

1. The Joint Chiefs of Staff have been informed that the Director of Central Intelligence has submitted a memorandum to the National

---

[1] Source: National Archives, RG 59, S/P Files: Lot 62 D 1. Secret. A covering memorandum from NSC Executive Secretary Lay, August 4, forwarded the JCS memorandum to the National Security Council, in connection with discussion of the warning facilities of the intelligence community at its August 5 meeting. For the discussion at that meeting, see Document 187.

Security Council (NSC)[2] recommending that the President direct all appropriate departments and agencies of the government to keep the Intelligence Advisory Committee (IAC) Watch Committee informed concerning diplomatic, political, military, or other courses of action by the United States, contemplated or in process of execution, which might bring about military reaction or early hostile action by the USSR, or its allies, endangering the security of the United States. The Director of Central Intelligence further recommends that all information and intelligence pertinent to its mission, without restriction because of source, policy or operational sensitivity, be made available to the Watch Committee.

2. The directive recommended by the Director of Central Intelligence is not interpreted to mean that either the Watch Committee or the National Indications Center (NIC) will be furnished U.S. War Plans because under the present policy the United States will not initiate hostilities with the USSR or its allies.

3. The Joint Chiefs of Staff recognize that this directive will make available to the Watch Committee information on operations of a very sensitive nature that should be strictly maintained in a "need-to-know" status to reduce danger of disclosure to a minimum. However, the Joint Chiefs of Staff consider that knowledge of such sensitive operations must be provided the Watch Committee if it is to carry out its mission of providing early warning to the United States of hostile action by the USSR, or its allies, which endangers the security of the United States. Therefore, the Joint Chiefs of Staff recommend that the Secretary of Defense support the recommendation of the Director of Central Intelligence in principle.

4. The method recommended by the Director of Central Intelligence by which the information is transmitted to the Watch Committee and its subordinate organization, the National Indications Center, and the handling of such information by that Committee and Center thereafter requires clarification to make it more precise. Also, to ensure that the Services will not be expected to furnish the Watch Committee with a myriad of small details of operations, the transmission and handling of which would overload the Service organizations as well as the NIC, it is considered that the governmental departments and agencies should be required to furnish the NIC only with the information which they believe to be of sufficient importance to cause military reaction or early hostile action by the USSR, or its allies.

5. The Joint Chiefs of Staff therefore recommend that you support the recommendations of the Director of Central Intelligence as modified by the changes below (changes to the Director of Central Intelligence recommendations indicated in the usual manner):

---

[2] Dated July 22. A copy of DCID 1/2 is attached. (National Archives, RG 273, Official Minutes, 1947–1961, 209th Meeting, Box 42)

"Ask the Council to recommend that the President direct all appropriate departments and agencies of the Government:

"a. To keep the IAC Watch Committee (as established by DCID 1/2) informed, ~~through arrangements with the Director, National Indications Center, on behalf of the Chairman of the Watch Committee,~~ concerning diplomatic, political, military, or other courses of action by the U.S., ~~contemplated~~ *approved for immediate implementation* or in process of execution, which *they believe to be of sufficient import that it* might bring about military reaction or early hostile action by the USSR, or its allies, *thus engandering the security of the U.S. This information is for the explicit and express use of the Watch Committee and those members of the NIC who need to know of it in order to perform their functions.*

"b. To make fully available to the IAC Watch Committee ~~through appropriate arrangements with the Director, National Indications Center, on behalf of the Chairman~~, all information and intelligence pertinent to its mission, without restriction because of source, policy or operational sensitivity."

6. The Joint Chiefs of Staff urge that full consideration be given by the NSC to the need for careful development of the method of transmitting and using this information. They consider that this method should be developed by the IAC, which is the agency responsible for the Watch function. Furthermore, the Joint Chiefs of Staff consider it extremely important that information of action to be taken by the United States not be transmitted until the action is approved for immediate implementation. If a directive on this subject should provide otherwise, the strategic planning of the United States would be given an undesirable dissemination. To further insure against undesirable dissemination, the recommendation of the Joint Chiefs of Staff includes a provision that information of an operational nature is for exclusive use within the Watch Committee.

For the Joint Chiefs of Staff:

N. F. Twining[3]
Chief of Staff, United States Air Force

---

[3] Printed from a copy that indicates Twining signed the original.

187. Memorandum of Discussion at the 209th Meeting of the National Security Council[1]

Washington, August 5, 1954.

SUBJECT

Discussion at the 209th Meeting of the National Security Council, Thursday, August 5, 1954

Present at the 209th meeting of the Council were the President of the United States, presiding; the Vice President of the United States; the Secretary of State; the Secretary of Defense; the Director, Foreign Operations Administration; and the Director, Office of Defense Mobilization. Also present were the Secretary of the Treasury; the Attorney General (for Items 1, 2 and 3); the Director, Bureau of the Budget; the Chairman, Atomic Energy Commission (for Items 1 and 2); the Federal Civil Defense Administrator (for Items 1 and 2); the Chairman, Council of Economic Advisers (for Items 1 and 2); the Acting Director, U. S. Information Agency (for Item 5); the Acting Secretary of the Army, the Acting Secretary of the Navy, and the Secretary of the Air Force (for Items 1 and 2); General Twining for the Chairman, Joint Chiefs of Staff (for Items 1 and 2); the Chief of Staff, U.S. Army, the Chief of Naval Operations, and the Commandant, U.S. Marine Corps (for Items 1 and 2); Elbert P. Tuttle, Department of the Treasury; Robert R. Bowie, Department of State; the Director of Central Intelligence; the Assistant to the President; Robert Cutler, Special Assistant to the President; the Deputy Assistant to the President; the Executive Secretary, NSC; and the Coordinator, NSC Planning Board Assistants.

There follows a summary of the discussion at the meeting and the main points taken.

[Omitted here are agenda Item 1: Review of Past Activities and the Future Program of the National Security Council, and Item 2: Guidelines Under NSC 162/2 for FY 1956 (NSC 5422/1). Agenda Item 2 is printed in *Foreign Relations, 1952–1954*, vol. II, Part 1, pp. 700–715.]

---

[1] Source: Eisenhower Library, Whitman File, NSC Records. Top Secret; Eyes Only. Drafted by Marion W. Boggs, Coordinator, NSC Planning Board Assistants, on August 6.

3. *Transmittal of Information and Recommendation for Future Action Concerning Warning Facilities of the Intelligence Community*
(Memos for NSC from Executive Secretary, same subject, dated July 26 and August 4, 1954)[2]

Mr. Cutler briefed the Council on the background of this problem. Revised CIA recommendations, entitled "Suggested NSC Action, Item 3", were distributed, and paragraph 2 of this document was read aloud (copy filed in the minutes of the meeting).[3]

Mr. Allen Dulles said that an effort was being made to improve the intelligence mechanism for providing early warning of a possible attack. An indication center was being set up under the Watch Committee to study all possible items which might alert us to danger. This center would need to have not only foreign intelligence, but also information on U.S. policies which might produce hostile reactions in enemy countries. Mr. Dulles felt that it would be unwise to adopt the formula suggested by the Defense agencies, to the effect that the Watch Committee would be kept informed only of those U.S. policies which in the judgment of the agency passing on the information might bring about hostile enemy reaction.

The President said the only purpose of these arrangements was to get the right information to the people who had to study it. He would not want a lot of inconsequential information to be passed on to the Watch Committee. He suggested that significant information on U.S. policies might be transmitted to the Watch Committee.

The Attorney General felt that the CIA recommendations tended to set up a kind of supervision over the FBI. He requested assurance that adoption of these recommendations would require no change in FBI methods or operations. He asked whether CIA was not now receiving all the information it needed. Mr. Dulles said he did not know, because he did not know what information was being held back.

The President called attention to paragraph 2-c of the CIA recommendations. He said that decision as to withholding information from the Watch Committee should be referred to him only if the Director of Central Intelligence and the other agency involved disagreed. He reiterated his desire that the Watch Committee get all the information that could be of real use to it, and suggested that the CIA recommendations, as amended at the meeting, be adopted subject to the Director of Central Intelligence and the Director of the FBI agreeing on editorial changes not affecting the substance.

---

[2] See Document 186 and footnotes 1 and 2 thereto.

[3] Not found, but for substance, see NSC Action No. 1195, below.

The National Security Council:[4]

a. Noted that Director of Central Intelligence Directive 1/2[5] states the following mission of the Watch Committee of the Intelligence Advisory Committee:

To provide earliest possible warning to the United States Government of hostile action by the USSR, or its allies, which endangers the security of the United States.

b. Recommended that the President, subject to the Director of Central Intelligence and the Director, Federal Bureau of Investigation, agreeing upon editorial changes not affecting the substance, issue the following directive to all appropriate departments and agencies of the Government:

(1) To make fully available to the IAC Watch Committee all significant information and intelligence pertinent to its mission and functions (as defined in DCID 1/2), without restriction because of source, policy or operational sensitivity.

(2) To keep the IAC Watch Committee informed concerning significant diplomatic, political, military, or other courses of action by the U.S., approved for immediate implementation or in process of execution, which might bring about military reaction or early hostile action by the USSR, or its allies, thus endangering the security of the U.S. This information is for the explicit and express use of the Watch Committee and those members of the NIC who need to know of it in order to perform their functions.

(3) When, in the opinion of an agency or department, overriding considerations affecting the national security exist which justify an exception to (1) or (2) above, the decision as to withholding or delaying the transmission of the information to the Watch Committee shall be taken up with the Director of Central Intelligence and, if there is disagreement, referred to the President.

Note: The action in b above subsequently transmitted to the Director of Central Intelligence for appropriate action.

[Omitted here is Agenda Item 4: Significant Developments Affecting U.S. Security.]

---

[4] The following constituted NSC Action No. 1195, August 5. (National Archives, RG 59, S/S–NSC (Miscellaneous) Files: Lot 66 D 95, Records of Action by the National Security Council) The directive adopted in NSC Action 1195–b was subsequently approved by the Director of Central Intelligence and the Director of the FBI with some editorial changes that did not affect substance, and by President Eisenhower on November 30. The approved directive was circulated as NSC 5438 of the same date. (National Archives, RG 59, S/S–NSC Files: Lot 63 D 351, NSC 5438)

[5] Document 179.

5. *Coordination of Economic, Psychological and Political Warfare, and Foreign Information Activities* (NSC Action No. 1183)[6]

Discussion of this question arose in connection with Item 6 below, "The Foreign Information Program and Psychological Warfare Planning".

The President recalled that he had previously emphasized the need for coordination of economic warfare activities (NSC Action No. 1183). It now seemed to him that his previous idea—that we needed a Director of Economic Warfare—had been too narrow. Perhaps we needed a director of unconventional or non-military warfare. Policy decisions in this field should, of course, be taken by the Council, but we also need a mechanism for objective study, for digesting information, and for coordinating implementation. He did not want half a dozen different agencies reporting to the Council on this subject. Perhaps the Planning Board might be supplemented by a special group to study this neglected field.

The President then noted that the Bureau of the Budget is now studying the coordination of economic warfare. He requested the Director, Bureau of the Budget, to broaden this study to include the placing of responsibility within the Executive Branch for coordinating economic warfare, psychological warfare, political warfare, and foreign information.

Mr. Cutler said that a large part of the issue in this field revolved around the question of who would run psychological warfare in the event of war—the military or State. The President said neither one; in time of war these operations would have to be conducted under the general direction of the President.

The National Security Council:[7]

Noted the President's request that the Bureau of the Budget expand its study regarding the coordination of economic warfare activities pursuant to NSC Action No. 1183, to include the placing of responsibility within the Executive Branch for coordinating economic warfare, psychological warfare, political warfare, and foreign information activities.

Note: The above action subsequently transmitted to the Director, Bureau of the Budget.

---

[6] In NSC Action No. 1183, taken at its 207th meeting, July 22, the Council noted the President's request that the Bureau of the Budget prepare recommendations regarding responsibility for coordination of economic warfare activities. (National Archives, RG 59, S/S–NSC (Miscellaneous) Files: Lot 66 D 95, Records of Action by the National Security Council)

[7] The following constituted NSC Action No. 1197, August 5. (Ibid.)

6. *The Foreign Information Program and Psychological Warfare Planning*
(Memos for NSC from Executive Secretary, same subject, dated
July 23 and August 4, 1954; NSC 59/1; NSC 127/1)[8]

Mr. Lay briefed the Council on the background of this problem,
calling attention to the OCB recommendations transmitted by the reference memorandum of July 23, and the views of the Joint Chiefs of
Staff transmitted by the reference memorandum of August 4. Mr. Cutler felt that the President's request for the study described in the preceding item did not entirely obviate the need for rescinding NSC 59/1
and NSC 127/1, as recommended by OCB. These papers were antique
wreckage; they were completely out of date and referred to agencies
which no longer existed.

The President said he hesitated to rescind these policies since the
Joint Chiefs of Staff, by the reference memorandum of August 4, objected to such a course. He thought we could let this antique wreckage stay on the books, even though it was recognized as obsolete, until the Council received a further report on the coordination of
economic, psychological and political warfare.

The National Security Council:[9]

Noted that NSC 59/1 and NSC 127/1 are deemed obsolete, but
deferred further action with respect thereto pending receipt of the study
described in the preceding item.

Marion W. Boggs

---

[8] Lay's July 23 memorandum transmitted the OCB report, dated July 21 (Document
183). For NSC 59/1, March 9, 1950, see Document 2. For NSC 127/1, see Document 123.

[9] The following constituted NSC Action No. 1198, August 5, 1954. (National
Archives, RG 59, S/S–NSC (Miscellaneous) File: Lot 66 D 95, Records of Action by the
National Security Council)

188.   Memorandum From the Deputy Operations Coordinator in the Office of the Under Secretary of State (Hulick) to the Under Secretary of State (Hoover)[1]

Washington, August 23, 1954.

SUBJECT

The Doolittle Survey

I have reduced to writing some ideas contained in the attached memorandum which I thought I might use in briefing the Doolittle team on covert operations of CIA. I am far from certain, however, in my own mind, as to whether the two examples I have singled out as illustrative of where improvement is needed and is actively being sought are the kind of things you consider as appropriate for the Department to raise before the Doolittle group. I should appreciate receiving your guidance on this matter.

As to the list of questions, I discussed these with Frank Wisner. He thought they were appropriate. He was concerned, however, about the possibility of the Assistant Secretaries striking a critical note, due to the fact that in some instances operations have been carried out without their knowledge but with a higher clearance from you. He hoped that in the morning briefing it would be made clear to the survey group that there have been occasions when an operation was cleared only at the top; and that these instances could give cause for an Assistant Secretary to believe the operation had had no policy clearance whatsoever.

Attachment[2]

BRIEFING NOTES

I. The office of the Deputy Operations Coordinator, directly responsible to the Under Secretary, performs the functions called for under paragraph 4 of NSC 5412.[3] All covert operations are cleared in advance with the Department through this office, which provides the Agency with written policy guidances. The office consists of three officers, one responsible for Western and Eastern Europe, one for the Far

---

[1] Source: Department of State, INR/IL Historical Files, NSC 5412, 1954–57, NSC 10 Series. Top Secret. Drafted by Hulick.

[2] Top Secret.

[3] Document 171.

East and South East Asia and one for the Near and Middle East and Latin America. Working closely with this office but not physically located in it are a Special Assistant in the Public Affairs office of the Department and a Special Assistant for Emigré matters in the Office of Eastern European Affairs. It provides a two-way channel of communication between the substantive offices of the Department and operational offices of the Agency.

In order to provide maximum security and control over the coordination of covert operations all personal contact between officers in the Department and the Agency on specific projects is supposed to be channeled through this office. To a very large degree that is now the case. The exceptions are occasions when the Director of CIA approaches the Secretary or Under Secretary directly on highly sensitive matters. All records of written communications are filed in this office. No copies are permitted to be filed elsewhere in the Department. While policy guidance is obtained from the responsible substantive areas, the final guidances in written form are prepared in this office only.

CIA covert annexes to OCB progress reports on NSC policy papers are presented to the Under Secretary through this office, which can also make them available to the State Department members of OCB Working Groups.

II. There are two outstanding problems in the field of covert operations which have not yet been satisfactorily resolved.

1. The Free Europe Committee (FEC) and Radio Free Europe (RFE) are powerful propaganda and psychological political instruments which are controlled by the Agency and are supposed to operate under policy guidance from the Department. The FEC was created in 1949 as a private organization, financed partly by private donations and partly by funds from the Agency, the latter accounting for about two thirds to three fourths of the money.

The purpose of FEC was to provide a means of supporting and utilizing prominent political exiles from communist-dominated countries without recognizing these groups as Governments in Exile and to avoid complications for the Department which maintained diplomatic relations with the Communist Governments of the countries from which they fled.

The two major functions performed by FEC are (1) support and utilization of émigré groups as symbols of resistance and (2) broadcasts to the peoples of Eastern Europe through RFE. Both FEC and RFE, which has its base in Munich, Germany, have grown into very large establishments, staffed by highly competent people. They produce their own analysis of developments behind the Iron Curtain and develop their own programs to influence the people and cause difficulties for the Communist regimes.

While FEC and RFE are supposed to function within the framework of official US policy and under policy guidance from the Department, they have been gradually assuming a degree of independence of operation, which has created a control problem. Decisions involving matters of policy consequence are frequently taken by FEC and RFE without reference to the Department through the Agency. This is a matter of real concern which the Department and the Agency are currently attempting to resolve.

2. The second outstanding problem is that of evolving ways and means of coping more satisfactorily with the political repercussions when a covert operation is uncovered. We are deeply involved in many countries in the use of covert assets to influence developments in a manner favorable to US objectives. While each such case must be handled to a large degree on its own merits, there is a need for establishing a few basic principles of operation. Due to a still prevalent lack of knowledge and understanding of the support role of CIA under NSC 5412 on the part of some officials, both in Washington and in the field, there is often a division of opinion as to how such emergencies should be handled. This division can freeze initiative and timely action and produce compromise positions which are not adequate to meet the problem. The division of opinion, it is believed, stems in part at least from an underlying opposition on the part of some officials to covert operations of CIA.

The solution to this problem must be sought through an educational process with more briefings in depth by CIA of State Department and Foreign Service officers on the task of CIA and the manner in which it attempts to discharge its responsibility. Improvements should also result gradually through the efforts of this office to bring about an ever closer coordination between the Department and CIA, so that carefully considered policy guidance is provided in advance by the substantive offices of the Department for each covert operation in support of overt policies as defined in the various NSC documents.

On the part of CIA officials it is necessary that they deal with complete frankness with this office and leave to its judgment which officers in the Department are to be consulted in order to obtain proper policy guidance for specific covert operations. There is still a tendency on the part of some CIA officials to be so secretive that even this office sometimes has the feeling that it does not know all that it should in order to discharge its responsibility. In order to establish the requisite degree of mutual confidence between the Agency and the Department both sides must contribute so that the inhibitions and respective reserves developed on both sides during the early formative years of CIA gradually fade away.

It is of the utmost importance that all responsible officials in State and CIA recognize the fact that NSC 5412 provides for joint CIA-State

implementation on NSC policies; that use of covert operations in support of our overt efforts in the field of foreign policy is an established
fact; that final decision on the timing and nature of such covert operations rests with the Department; that when a covert operation goes
sour it is a matter of concern to the US Government and not just CIA;
and that problems arising out of exposed covert operations must be
met and minimized by the joint efforts of CIA and State as a team.

III. The following are types of questions which might be asked of
the Assistant Secretaries:

1. Have the Agency's covert operations been generally effective in
furthering implementation of overt US policy objectives? If so, can you
cite specific examples?

2. If there have been instances in which covert operations have
been harmful, do you believe they could have been avoided? Did they
result from failure of the Agency to coordinate or did they represent
coordinated operations involving a calculated risk?

3. Are you satisfied that there is proper coordination and prior
policy guidance for all covert operations conducted by the Agency in
your area?

---

189.   Paper Prepared in the Central Intelligence Agency[1]

Washington, August 25, 1954.

THE "NET ESTIMATES" PROBLEM

Introduction. One of the most basic problems faced by intelligence
agencies is that of obtaining adequate information of operational matters and of using such information to produce meaningful "net estimates" of the capabilities and intentions of other nations, taking account of our own acts and facts as they must appear to others. In
general, U.S. doctrine in the military services has prescribed a sharper
separation between intelligence and operations than exists in the UK
and some, if not most, other nations, although in the practical operation of field staffs this separation is usually mitigated or overcome

---

[1] Source: National Archives, RG 263, HS/HC: HRP 82–2/00022, Box 1, HS/HC 111,
Misc. Documents. Secret. The original went to General Clark; copies were sent to Assistant Director for National Estimates (Kent), Deputy Director for Intelligence (Amory),
and William Bundy.

through working understandings. At the highest levels in the services, however, and even in the State Department, there is a strong tendency either to keep operational matters wholly in "operational" channels, or, if they are conveyed to intelligence offices, to impose restrictions against discussion with outside agencies. This memorandum deals with efforts made by CIA since the fall of 1950 to meet this problem, in three contexts: (1) National Intelligence Estimates handled through regular machinery; (2) specific "net estimates" or "net evaluations" handled by special machinery; (3) the Watch Committee, handling intelligence from the warning standpoint.

1. Operational Information and National Intelligence Estimates.

In the NIE field, a distinction must be made between the furnishing of operational *assumptions* and the furnishing of specific operational *facts*, especially concerning our own capabilities. The former has never presented great difficulties, and is now in satisfactory shape. The latter, however, has been troublesome on several occasions, and no satisfactory overall solution has been reached.

In one type of estimate, dealing with the consequences of possible U. S. courses of action, operational assumptions as to U.S. policy are the foundation of the estimate. The only problem is that of ensuring that the assumptions have appropriate backing, and this is now usually done through the CIA Adviser to the NSC Planning Board, who may consult the Planning Board as a whole or may deal directly with the departments most concerned. Assumptions are cleared at whatever level is necessary to assure their solidity.

In the more general type of estimate, dealing with probable developments in a given situation, it is occasionally necessary to have—in addition to the always implicit assumption of no drastic change in overall US policy—specific assumptions on such matters as US aid levels, where the US may affect the situation drastically and immediately. Since the estimate may be designed to provide the basis for policy in these very respects, it is sometimes necessary to make an arbitrary assumption for the future. For example, the currently pending estimate on developments in Taiwan, to be completed for submission to the Planning Board when the question of aid levels is discussed, will be based on the assumption that the scope and nature of US programs remains as at present. Thus, the estimate will not purport to be definitive (even within the usual limits of predictability) but will be a benchmark obviously subject to adjustment if a decision is made to alter the scope and nature of the programs . . . .[2] In any event, there is no substantial present problem in obtaining such assumptions, which

---

[2] Ellipsis in the original.

are usually framed in consultation with the CIA Advisor to the NSC Planning Board, or occasionally directly by departments principally concerned.

In contrast with the relative simplicity of the policy-assumptions problem, the problem of obtaining specific own-capability facts—or even assumptions—has been complex and difficult. Early in the history of the present NIE machinery, in April 1951, an ad hoc solution was reached for one case, an estimate (NIE 27)[2] on the likelihood of invasion of Taiwan. For this estimate, it was obvious that the intelligence community needed to know, generally at least, the dispositions of US forces in the area, since these forces were the principal obstacle to Chinese Communist action. After some negotiation via the service intelligence heads, appropriate "assumptions" approximating the real facts were provided and used.

This specific case was not then made the basis for a general solution, although the need was discussed at the working level. No specific proposal was submitted by O/NE to the Director, or by him to other agencies.

In two major fields, experience has subsequently highlighted the vacuity of estimates prepared without clear knowledge of our own capabilities. With respect to Soviet Bloc capabilities to attack Western Europe, all estimates through 1950 had been able to proceed on the assumption of virtually no Western opposition. From 1951 onward, this assumption became increasingly less valid, and in the preparation of the estimates there were prolonged discussions leading finally to the use of a fairly meaningless formula that the Soviet Bloc could "launch" a lot of campaigns, including a full-scale offensive in Western Europe. Whether any meaningful answer could have been provided in Washington without duplicating the activities of SHAPE is doubtful, but the fact is that no machinery existed even for getting and incorporating (with proper credit) the current conclusions of SHAPE. As they finally stood the estimates were certainly not helpful to anyone on this point.

It was the second field, however, that of air defense of the Soviet Union, which seemed to General Smith even more forceful, and the experience in this field, in the spring and summer of 1952, contributed heavily to the campaign launched by him in October 1952, as discussed in the next section. What happened was simple. A pioneer national estimate on Soviet air defense capabilities ran into prolonged agency disagreements, in which it became more and more clear that any description of the effectiveness of Soviet defenses depended entirely on assumptions as to our capabilities and strategy of attack. Eventually, it

---

[2] For NIE 27, see *Foreign Relations*, 1951, vol. VII, Part 2, pp. 1623–1624.

was recognized that without clear guidance on these matters the estimate was, in the words of General Smith, merely an inventory of Soviet assets, and it was finally approved by the Intelligence Advisory Committee after most qualitative statements had been cut out, and after the title had been altered to, "The Scale and Nature of the Soviet Air Defense Effort 1952–54."[3]

So far as National Intelligence Estimates are concerned, the situation since then has been as before—that operational information is not made available to the intelligence community on any systematic basis adequate for its employment in such estimates. With the development of increasingly close and cordial working relationships both in the IAC itself and at the National Estimates Board and Staff levels, it is safe to say that a great deal of such information is in fact fed informally into the estimates. But much operational information is still withheld wholly, and the overall situation is far from satisfactory.

2. Special Machinery for "Net Estimates"

In the summer of 1951, concern over continental defense, within the National Security Council, led to discussion of the need for an authoritative "evaluation" of the net capability of the USSR to injure the United States. Although General Smith made no affirmative effort to have sole primary responsibility for the effort—and in fact is believed to have expressed his opposition to the assignment—the Joint Chiefs of Staff were diffident, and the upshot was an NSC directive, of August 30, 1951,[4] that DCI prepare a "summary evaluation" in collaboration with the Joint Chiefs of Staff and with the internal security committees.

The resulting exercise, handled through regular channels and without any central mechanism, was a nightmare. The Intelligence Advisory Committee speedily produced the necessary basic estimate of Soviet gross capabilities (SE–14, 18 October 1951),[5] and the internal security committees furnished adequate contributions. However, the Joint Chiefs of Staff contribution was delayed for several months and when finally produced, in May 1952, proved to be based on the most extreme possible estimates of Soviet capabilities and on several other questionable assumptions, of a largely intelligence nature, concerning Soviet attack strategy. General Smith regarded this contribution as unsatisfactory and assigned two members of the Board of National Estimates, Mr. E. M. Hoover and Vice Admiral B. M. Bieri (former Deputy

---

[3] See footnote 2, Document 120.

[4] NSC Action No. 543, Document 86.

[5] Not printed. (National Archives, RG 263, Soviet NIEs, 1950–1955, # 20, Box 1) The actual date of SE–14 is October 23, 1951.

Chief of Naval Operations), to the task of producing an integrated evaluation merging all contributions, and modifying the JCS contribution. The ensuing procedure was trying to all concerned. It finally produced a report which General Smith accepted as the best obtainable in the circumstances, and which he forwarded to the NSC on 14 October 1952.[6]

In his accompanying memorandum General Smith noted the defects of the report, and gave three "primary reasons" for them. The third of these was:

"c. There is at present no machinery to plan, guide, coordinate and produce an appraisal or estimate based on the integration of national intelligence with military, political, and economic operational data dealing with our own capabilities."

General Smith recommended that as an interim measure he be instructed to prepare terms of reference for a more adequate study of the problem, and that the Council:

"c. Concurrently, instruct the Director of Central Intelligence to examine, in collaboration with officials of other governmental bodies as needed, the adequacy of present machinery, and the character of any new machinery that may be required in order to plan, guide, coordinate, and produce for the National Security Council, upon request, evaluations in the nature of 'Commander's Estimates,' of the USSR's capabilities and intentions vis-à-vis the United States, based upon the integration of military, political, and economic operational data dealing with United States' capabilities and intentions, and national intelligence."

When General Smith's recommendations were forwarded by the Secretary of Defense to the Joint Chiefs of Staff for comment, the JCS responded by a sharply critical memorandum, dated November 21, 1952.[7] There ensued negotiations, which were limited to the terms of reference and procedure for a new study, but which also gave an opportunity for General Smith to clarify his ideas to the Joint Chiefs of Staff on the overall problem. In the light of the change of administrations then in process it was finally decided to let the overall recommendation (subparagraph c. quoted above) lie over, while proceeding with a new "net evaluation" on the basis of an entirely novel procedure. This procedure, embodied in NSC 140,[8] was approved by President Truman on January 19, 1953, and accepted by the Eisenhower Administration without change. It created a Special Evaluation Subcommittee, chaired by a direct Presidential appointee, Lt. General Idwal H. Edwards, USAF (Ret.)—who was in fact nominated by the Joint Chiefs of Staff under a gentlemen's agreement with General

---

[6] Document 131.

[7] Not found, but see Document 137 and footnote 3 thereto.

[8] For NSC 140, see *Foreign Relations*, 1952–1954, vol. II, Part 1, pp. 205–208.

Smith—with representatives of the JCS, CIA, and the internal security committees as full members.

The so-called Edwards Committee was given a very short dead-line, May 15, 1953, for the preparation of a new net evaluation to serve as the basis for a policy appraisal of the whole field of continental defense. Through the able leadership of General Edwards and with a large share of credit also to Lt. General H. R. Bull, representing CIA, the deadline was met. The resulting report (NSC 140/1, May 18, 1953)[9] although slightly marred by one misunderstanding with the JCS working level on terms of reference, was a highly valuable effort substantively. Organizationally it seemed to CIA, and, it is believed, to the NSC Secretariat and to others familiar with the earlier failure and with the general problem, to prove that net evaluations or estimates could be done, even on the most complex problems, through a process of constant interchange of intelligence and operational information (under appropriate security safeguards), and that the resulting net papers were a vast improvement on anything that could be done by intelligence and operations working at arms' length from each other.

With this pioneer demonstration, attention turned for a time back to the more general problem. Largely as a result of CIA urging, the report of the President's Committee on International Information Activities (Jackson Committee), published June 30, 1953,[10] included as its very first recommendation the following:

"1. The necessary measures should be taken to provide net estimates of political, economic and military capabilities." (Page 3)

While this recommendation might have provided a lever for reopening the over-all question and resurrecting General Smith's recommendation c. of the preceding October (which was still technically unfinished business in the NSC), two factors combined to make this appear undesirable to the DCI. One was the replacement of most of the Joint Chiefs of Staff in August 1953; the other was the fact that in its policy consideration of continental defense (NSC 159 series)[11] the NSC referred all organization questions to the Office of Defense Mobilization for study (NSC action No. 873 d., August 1953).[12] Since it was at first thought that Office of Defense Mobilization's study would be quickly completed, it seemed clearly wiser to await it, and to work out agreement with the Joint Chiefs of Staff on a proper procedure in

---

[9] Text is ibid, pp. 328–349. See also Document 149.
[10] See Document 151.
[11] See Foreign Relations, 1952–1954, vol. II, Part 1, pp. 465–489.
[12] See footnote 2, Document 173.

the limited field of continental defense before taking up the over-all question again.

As it worked out, ODM encountered substantial delay both in preparing its recommendations and in getting them cleared by the NSC Planning Board. Only in April 1954 did ODM's paper become available to NSC.[13] At this point the JCS comment on the ODM proposals revealed that the "new Chiefs" were not happy about a net estimates procedure under which ultimate final responsibility was not vested solely in them, and there ensued a round of negotiations between Mr. Dulles and Admiral Radford, which clarified the issue but failed to produce agreement.[14] A split paper was finally submitted to the President and the NSC on June 9, 1954,[15] and the issue was resolved by the President in favor of joint responsibility in the Chairman of the Joint Chiefs of Staff and the Director of Central Intelligence, with other government agencies represented on an appropriate basis.[16] The President designated Admiral Radford as Chairman for the exercise, which is now proceeding with a deadline of 1 November 1954. Rear Admiral Robbins is directing the project on Admiral Radford's behalf, while General Bull is again representing CIA. Substantively the scope of the study has been broadened to cover specifically all key US installations overseas, thus making possible a far more refined and comprehensive view of Soviet attack strategy than was possible in the Edwards group. Procedurally, it appears at this writing that the project is being handled at the working level with a greater degree of close cooperation even than in the Edwards group.

During the course of the negotiations on the particular continental defense problem, the over-all issue was discussed, and the Director, of Central Intelligence proposed that the device of joint responsibility in DCI and the Chairman of the JCS, the one as intelligence adviser, the other as military adviser, to the President and the NSC, be extended generally to cover problems for which a specific net evaluation, or net estimate, procedure is appropriate. (Such problems, generally speaking, would be those of substantial scope, involving a complicated study of the interplay of US action and Soviet counteraction. In situations where action on both sides would be simple and predictable, the use of joint machinery might not be warranted.) For the present, this suggestion is not being pressed, since the success of the new continental defense project appears to be important in any decision.

---

[13] Not found.
[14] See Documents 176 and 177.
[15] Not found.
[16] See Document 182.

3. The Watch Committee and Operational Information

For that part of the intelligence community that concentrates on providing warning of hostile action, knowledge of US or allied operations may be even more vital than for more long-range intelligence efforts. Without such knowledge false warnings may be given, available intelligence may be seriously misconstrued (in either direction), and intelligence effort may not be focused properly at points and areas of tension.

The 1948–54 history of this problem is covered in detail in reports prepared by the Office of Current Intelligence, the CIA component particularly charged with the watch function and with support of the Watch Committee. The essence of the story is that there has been no remotely adequate procedure for keeping the Watch Committee informed of operational matters that could have a bearing on its activities. However, as a result of the work of an ad hoc Committee designated by the IAC in 1953 to review the whole Watch Committee process, the Director of Central Intelligence, in July 1954, submitted to the NSC, and the President approved in principle, a directive that operational information necessary to the Watch Committee's mission be furnished to it, under appropriate security safeguards.[17] At the date of writing, the exact wording of this directive remains to be ironed out with the FBI Director. In CIA's judgment the substance of this directive will provide a broad and adequate basis for the proper functioning of the Watch Committee in this respect, though no doubt particular problems of detail and interpretation will arise. The directive provides that in cases where an agency believes that overriding security considerations preclude release of information (conceded to be significant to the Watch Committee), the matter shall be referred initially to DCI, thereafter to the President if DCI and the referring agency are unable to resolve it. Thus, the Director should be in a position to iron out difficulties as they arise.

It is significant that this directive has had the full support of the JCS, in principle and in its general breadth.[18] This JCS attitude may be a significant indication of the possibilities for further improvement in the fields of national estimates and of special net evaluation machinery, discussed in the earlier sections of this memorandum.

---

[17] President Eisenhower approved at the 209th meeting of the NSC; see Document 187.

[18] See Document 186.

190.   **Papers Prepared by a Working Group of the Operations Coordinating Board Assistants for the Operations Coordinating Board[1]**

Washington, August 25, 1954.

LIST OF AGREED COURSES OF ACTION
JULY 1, 1954 TO DECEMBER 31, 1954
TO IMPLEMENT NSC 174[2]

During the six-month period beginning July 1, 1954 the departments and agencies plan to take the following specific actions having a relationship to courses of action set forth in NSC 174 and other pertinent NSC documents. Underlining indicates quotations from paragraphs of NSC 174. Where actions are not cited, this indicates that while the department or agency follows in its day-to-day operations the policies set forth, no explicit project in regard to those paragraphs can presently be specified.

The responsibility of the working group is to suggest general courses of action to implement the specific objectives set forth in NSC 174. The development of detailed plans to carry out such courses of action is the function of the several responsible agencies.

1. *Take overt and covert measures to discredit Soviet prestige and ideology as effective instruments of Soviet power, and to reduce the strength of Communist parties and other pro-Soviet elements.*[3] (NSC 162/2, Para. 43a.) (NSC 174, Para. 9)

---

[1] Source: National Archives, RG 59, S/P–NSC Files: Lot 62 D 1, NSC 174. Top Secret. Circulated to the OCB on August 20 by Staats for discussion at the OCB's August 25 meeting. A September 7 memorandum by Staats indicates that the OCB approved the two papers at its meeting. (Ibid.)

[2] NSC 174, "U.S. Policy Toward the Soviet Satellites," is dated December 11. (National Archives, RG 59, S/S–NSC Files: Lot 63 D 351, NSC 174 Series) Extracts from NSC 174 and NSC discussion of the issue are in *Foreign Relations, 1952–1954,* vol. VIII, pp. 110–128. NSC 174 was referred to the Operations Coordinating Board as the coordinating agency designated by the President.

[3] Although NSC 162/2 does not appear to provide specific policy guidelines for the starred courses of action when applied to the USSR, it is understood that NSC 162/2 does not direct the abandonment of current operating policies and programs whether overt or covert along these lines. Furthermore, NSC 174, Para. 9, provides as follows ... "feasible political, economic, propaganda and covert measures are required to create and exploit troublesome problems for the USSR. . ." Accordingly, in the absence of detailed NSC guidance on policy toward the Soviet Union it is assumed that these courses of action are applicable to the USSR. New projects should be carefully considered, however, in terms of the Policy Conclusions set forth in NSC 162/2. *Note:* Above footnote applies to all asterisks. [Footnote in the original. Underlined text is printed in italics. NSC 162/2, "Basic National Security Policy," is dated October 30, 1953. (National Archives, RG 59. S/S–NSC Files: Lot 63 D 351, NSC 162 Series)]

Actions to be taken:

a. At the General Assembly of the United Nations beginning September 21, 1954, support the following actions which are expected to have the result of discrediting the position of the USSR:

(1) Review of the report of the Disarmament Commission.
(2) Review of the report of the UN Commission for the unification and rehabilitation of Korea.
(3) Review of the report of the Collective Measures Committee on methods which might be used to maintain and strengthen international peace and security.
(4) Review of the question of admission of new members to the UN.
(5) Review of report of ECOSOC on evidence of existence of forced labor.
(6) Review of the Special Committee on the question of defining aggression.

b. Initiate or resume discussion in the UN General Assembly of:

(1) The Austrian Treaty question.
(2) Various items regarding human rights.
(3) Measures for the peaceful solution of the problem of prisoners of war.

c. Anticipate and counteract Soviet moves in the UN General Assembly concerning:

(1) Admission of Communist China.
(2) East-West trade.
(3) Guatemala.

d. Assure effective propaganda support of the U.S. position on the issues set forth in a., b., and c., above. (State, primary—USIA and CIA supporting)

e. The case of the F–84 shot down by Czech fighters in 1953 will be expedited for presentation before the International Court of Justice. If good case is developed for B–29 and RB–50 shot down in Far East by Soviet fighters, these cases should be presented to I.C.J. (State, primary—Defense, supporting)

f. Press representations for return of U.S. citizens held in USSR— if no favorable response appropriate publicity will be considered. Also continue efforts to secure release of U.S. citizens held in jail in Czechoslovakia. (State, primary—USIA and CIA, supporting)

g. Develop and use for overseas distribution three special films designed to demonstrate the Communist technique of takeover and control of sovereign nations. (USIA, primary)

h. Spotlight policies and problems of agriculture in Soviet bloc— exposing failures and playing up ingenious peasant passive resistance. (USIA, primary)

i. *Problems of Communism* is being published as an attributed bi-monthly publication and plans are now well advanced for an unattributed monthly publication which will be devoted to problems of the Soviet orbit. (USIA, primary)

j. Place emphasis upon the fact the satellites are captive countries controlled through various techniques by the Soviet military machine, as supporting materials are developed and opportunities are presented. (USIA, primary—CIA and Defense, supporting)

k. Employ selected persons who have lived under or suffered at the hands of Communist tyranny for speaking tours sponsored by civic organizations in U.S. and selected areas abroad. (State and USIA, primary—FOA and Defense, supporting)

2. *Strengthen covert activities in support of the Basic Objectives set forth in paragraphs 10 and 11 of NSC 174.*

Actions to be taken:

CIA to report on separately. (CIA, primary)

3. *Use appropriate means short of military force to oppose, and to contribute to the eventual elimination of, Soviet domination over the satellites; including, when appropriate, concert with NATO or other friendly powers, resort to UN procedures, and, if possible, negotiation with the USSR.* (NSC 174, Para. 12)

Actions to be taken:

a. Take such actions as may be appropriate to exploit the Greek-Turk-Yugoslav Friendship Pact as a factor influencing the satellites. (State, primary—USIA, Defense and CIA, supporting)

4. *Encourage and assist the satellite peoples in resistance to their Soviet-dominated regimes, maintaining their hopes of eventual freedom from Soviet domination, while avoiding:*

a. *Incitement to premature revolt.*

b. *Commitments on the nature and timing of any U.S. action to bring about liberation.*

c. *Incitement to action when the probable reprisals or other results would yield a net loss in terms of U.S. objectives.*[4] (NSC 174, Para. 13)

Actions to be taken:

a. Emphasize in appropriate ways our continued interest in Eastern Europe and our refusal to recognize Soviet domination of the area as permanent. (State, primary—USIA and CIA, supporting)

---

[4] *For example, account should be taken of the undesirability of provoking the liquidation of important resistance movements or creating false hopes of U.S. intervention.* [Footnote in the original. Subsequent asterisks apparently refer to this note.]

b. Support and offer guidance where appropriate to the Kersten Committee. (State, primary—USIA, supporting)

c. Exploit the elections in Czechoslovakia. (State, primary—CIA and USIA, supporting)

d. In the event EDC ratification occurs during the period, issue a statement or emphasize the concept of a free European Community open to countries of Eastern Europe upon their liberation from Soviet Communist tyranny. (State, primary—USIA and CIA, supporting)

5. *Develop and encourage, as appropriate, increased use of passive resistance by the peoples of the [USSR and] satellites.** (NSC 174, Para. 14)[5]

6. *Be prepared to exploit any future disturbances similar to the East German riots of 1953 by planning courses of action which would best serve U.S. interests in such events.* (NSC 174, Para. 15)

Actions to be taken:

a. Keep harvest results for the current year under review and be prepared to exploit significant shortages with offers of food or other appropriate action. (State, primary—CIA and FOA, supporting)

b. On the basis of an analysis of the June 17, 1953 East German uprising develop specific courses of action to be taken in the event of a similar occurrence in the future and report thereon by December 1, 1954. (USIA and CIA, primary)

7. *Foster satellite nationalism as a force against Soviet imperialism, while avoiding commitments to national ambitions which would interfere with U.S. post-liberation objectives.* (NSC 174, Para. 16)

Actions to be taken:

a. Appropriate statements will be issued and exploited commemorating the following national holidays of the satellite states and other suitable occasions, such as: August 15, Commemoration of Poles stopping Russians on Vistula; August 20, Commemoration of Warsaw Uprising; August 20, St. Stephens Day (Hungarian National Holiday); September 28, Anniversary of Petkov's Execution (Bulgaria); October 28, Czechoslovakian Independence Day; November 18, Latvian Independence Day; December 25, Christmas (Gregorian calendar). (State, primary—USIA and CIA, support)

8. *Cooperate with other forces—such as religious, cultural, social— which are natural allies in the struggle against Soviet imperialism.** (NSC 174, Para. 17)

Actions to be taken:

a. Determine whether a practical program of cultural and technical exchange of persons with the Soviet bloc can be developed. (State, primary—CIA and USIA, supporting)

---

[5] All brackets in the original.

b. Ensure maximum exploitation in the interest of the U.S. of visits to the U.S. by delegations from countries behind the iron curtain. (State and USIA, primary—Defense and CIA, supporting)

9. *Stimulate and exploit conflicts within the communist ruling groups in [the USSR and in] each satellite, among such groups, and between them and the Kremlin.** (NSC 174, Para. 18)

Actions to be taken:

a. Continue to exploit indications of internal conflict within the satellite ruling groups and between them and the Kremlin, such as conflicts growing out of the:

(1) "New economic courses." (USIA, primary—CIA, supporting)
(2) The satellite government reorganizations undertaken in conformity with the Kremlin's desire to emphasize a collective leadership. (USIA, primary—CIA, supporting)
(3) Instances of difficulty between a satellite and the USSR as, for example, deliberate snubs of cultural delegations in the USSR or trouble with Soviet occupation (and line of communication) troops in the satellites. (USIA, primary)

10. *Foster disaffection in [the USSR and] satellite armed forces and police, to diminish their reliability in suppressing domestic disturbances and their will to fight in the event of war.** (NSC 174, Para. 19)

Actions to be taken:

a. Display military strength of U.S. whenever appropriate, such as the visits of U.S. Fleet units to Baltic, or visits of U.S. Air Force aircraft to significant points where news of the event will reach target nations. (Defense and State jointly)

b. As opportunity offers and material is available, emphasize any conflicts within Soviet and satellite security forces and between them and other elements of the population. (USIA, primary—CIA, supporting)

c. Wherever found, exploit dissatisfaction with Soviet "advisors" and key personnel among officers and men of the satellite armies. (USIA, primary—CIA and State, supporting)

d. Exploit as a propaganda theme the idea that the USSR will use the satellite armed forces as cannon fodder in the event of war. (CIA, primary—USIA, supporting)

11. *Encourage defection of [USSR and] key satellite personnel and possible VFC recruits, but not mass defection [in the case of the satellites]; and assist in the resettlement and rehabilitation of refugees who do escape.** (NSC 174, Para. 22)

Actions to be taken:

a. Support implementation of the extensive operational plan for Phase A of Escapee Program approved by OCB, including the expeditious implementation of the Refugee Relief Act of 1953. (FOA and State, primary—CIA, Defense and USIA, supporting)

12. *Support or make use of refugees or exile organizations which can contribute to the attainment of U.S. objectives, but do not recognize governments-in-exile.** (NSC 174, Para. 23)

Actions to be taken:

a. Take appropriate action such as messages on national days, speeches by government officials, etc., to bolster the prestige of exile organizations meeting the above criteria. (State, primary—USIA and CIA, supporting)

b. Support relief and rehabilitation projects which are advanced by accredited groups or organizations affecting refugee or exile organizations which can contribute to the attainment of U.S. objectives. (FOA, primary)

13. *Maintain flexibility in U.S. economic policies toward the Soviet bloc, and toward individual satellites, in order to gain maximum advantage with the limited economic weapons at hand (both restrictions and incentives).* (NSC 174, Para. 25)

Actions to be taken:

a. The Economic Defense Advisory Committee (EDAC) and its member agencies, in line with the decisions of the April and July, 1954 meetings of the Consultative Group in Paris, are carrying out U.S. responsibilities for the following:

(1) Implementing, in coordination with COCOM countries, provisions for the more effective enforcement of strategic trade controls on a more limited list of commodities exported to the Soviet bloc. (FOA, primary)

(2) Implementing plans approved by the Consultative Group for expanded exchange of information among members of COCOM and views on Soviet bloc trade trends and tactics. (FOA, primary)

b. Develop plans for making available surplus agricultural commodities in the U.S. to the peoples of the Soviet bloc, as "targets of opportunity" present themselves in accordance with basic guidelines and criteria approved by the OCB for the disposal of such commodities. (State and FOA, primary—CIA, supporting)

14. *Continue U.S. diplomatic missions in Poland, Czechoslovakia, Hungary, and Rumania as long as may be in the U.S. interest, and keep under review the possibility of resuming diplomatic relations with Bulgaria and Albania.* (NSC 174, Para. 26)

Actions to be taken:

a. Consider the desirability of consulting further with Congress concerning resumption of diplomatic relations with Bulgaria. (State, primary)

15. *Exploit the existence, and encourage the development, of the Yugoslav-Greek-Turkish entente as a means of weakening Soviet power in*

the Balkan satellites and as an example of free association of independent Balkan nations serving as a potential alternative to Soviet rule. (NSC 174, Para. 27)

Actions to be taken:

a. Continue negotiations for a solution to the Trieste problem in order to clear way for further integration of Yugoslavia into the Western Defense pattern and the strengthening of the Western position. (State, primary)

b. Take such actions as may be appropriate to exploit the Greek-Turk-Yugoslav Friendship Pact as a factor influencing the satellites. (State, primary—USIA, Defense and CIA, supporting)

c. Explore the advisability of encouraging the Greek and Turkish governments to seek the cooperation of the Bulgarian Government in a survey of the upper Meric-Evros River looking to joint development of the river. (State and FOA, primary—CIA, supporting)

16. *Keep the situation with respect to Albania under continuing surveillance with a view to the possibility of detachment of that country from the Soviet bloc at such time as its detachment might be judged to serve the overall U.S. interest.* (NSC 174, Para. 28)

Actions to be taken:

a. Upon completion of present negotiations for a favorable settlement of the Trieste problem, examine the situation with respect to Albania and the possibility of detachment of that country from the Soviet bloc. (CIA, primary—State and Defense, supporting)

17. *Exploit to the fullest extent compatible with the policies regarding Germany as a whole and Berlin, the special opportunities offered by West Berlin and the facilities of the Federal Republic to undermine Soviet power in East Germany. Place the Soviets in East Germany on the defensive by such measures as may be taken to keep alive the hope of German reunification.* (NSC 174, Para. 29)

Actions to be taken:

Detailed plans for action against East Germany are set forth in the Progress Report of the Working Group for NSC 5404/1, dated June 8, 1954.[6] That Group has primary responsibility for coordinating activities concerning Berlin.

18. *Emphasize (a) the right of the peoples of Eastern Europe to independent governments of their own choosing, and (b) the violation of international agreements by the Soviet and satellite governments, whereby they have been deprived of that right, particularly the Yalta Declaration on Liberated*

---

[6] For text of the financial appendix to NSC 5404/1, January 25, see *Foreign Relations, 1952–1954*, vol. VII, Part 2, pp. 1390–1394. The full text of and the progress reports on NSC 5404/1 are in the National Archives, RG 59, S/S–NSC Files: Lot 63 D 351, NSC 5404 Series, Box 77.

Europe and the Treaties of Peace with Bulgaria, Hungary and Rumania. (NSC 174, Para. 30)

Actions to be taken:

a. Develop opportunities for high U.S. officials through speeches and other means to emphasize the right of the peoples of Eastern Europe to independent governments of their own choosing and the violation of international agreements by the Soviet and satellite states. (State, primary)

b. Develop opportunities to exploit the voluminous documentary materials being compiled in the Department of State to demonstrate satellite treaty violations. (State, primary—USIA and CIA, supporting)

ADDITIONAL ACTIONS TO IMPLEMENT NSC 174 WHICH HAVE NOT BEEN ACCEPTED BY WORKING GROUP[7]

There follows a list of additional actions to implement NSC 174 which have not been accepted by the Working Group for the reasons stated therein:

1. Distribute inexpensive commodities by balloon or other similar means to people in the Soviet orbit in such a way that it will be non-attributable to the U.S. Government.

Reason for non-acceptance:

On September 23 and October 21, 1953 the OCB approved purchase and stockpiling of balloons but determined that final decision for use of balloons for this purpose would be made by the Board. Subsequent to that date no agency has recommended a specific project and no target of opportunity has arisen.

2. Implement the plan to detach Albania from the Soviet orbit.

Reason for non-acceptance:

a. State believes no action should be taken to implement this plan while negotiations over Trieste are underway.

b. If Trieste problem is satisfactorily resolved, agreement covering future status of Albania should be obtained from neighboring states (Yugoslavia, Greece, Italy) before any action for liberation is undertaken. (See paragraph 16 of "Operational Plans for Period July 1, 1954 to December 31, 1954" for current Working Group recommendations.)

3. Train leaders and prepare plans for supplying weapons and equipment for use in future riots and disturbances in the satellite areas.

Reason for non-acceptance:

CIA will make separate submission.

---

[7] This is the second paper circulated to the OCB.

4. Develop extensive covert operations to organize resistance groups among the peoples of the satellites which, in the event of war, can offer significant armed resistance to communist forces or, in the event of an upsurge of popular feeling similar to the East German riots of 1953, can stage a coup d'etat.

Reasons for non-acceptance:

CIA will make separate submission.

---

191.   Director of Central Intelligence Directive 15/1[1]

Washington, September 14, 1954.

PRODUCTION AND COORDINATION OF FOREIGN ECONOMIC INTELLIGENCE

Pursuant to the provisions of NSCID Nos. 1, 3, and 15,[2] and for the purpose of strengthening the over-all governmental intelligence structure for the production and coordination of foreign economic intelligence relating to the national security, the following policies and operating procedures are hereby established:

1. Policies

In carrying out their foreign economic intelligence activities and responsibilities, and in order to effect a better coordination in the production and exchange of foreign economic intelligence, the interested departments and agencies will apply the following basic principles:

a. No complete separation of interests is possible or necessarily desirable in economic intelligence activities.

b. Full and free interchange of all pertinent information, finished intelligence, and schedules of research programs, including external research, between all agencies concerned is essential.

c. No one agency is considered to be the undisputed authority in any field; conclusions may be questioned by other IAC agencies and dissents recorded.

---

[1] Source: Central Intelligence Agency, History Staff, Job 84–B00389R, Box 4, Folder 43. Confidential. This directive is an updated text of Document 169.

[2] For NSCID No. 1 Revised, see Document 256; for NSCID No. 3, see *Foreign Relations, 1945–1950, Emergence of the Intelligence Establishment,* Document 426; for NSCID No. 15, see Document 254.

d. Each agency will be responsible for fulfilling its departmental requirements for economic intelligence; it will give full recognition to the finished intelligence produced by other agencies, but any agency may make such studies as it believes necessary to supplement the intelligence produced by other agencies. However, basic research studies should not normally be undertaken or disseminated outside the producing agency without consultation with the agency having primary responsibility for the subject matter involved.

e. An agency charged with primary responsibility in a particular field will develop special competence in that field and will normally carry out most of the research in that field.

f. Each intelligence agency will endeavor to coordinate the intelligence activities of its Technical Services and its other facilities having economic intelligence production capabilities with the work of the IAC intelligence agencies and to make available to those agencies the intelligence produced by such Services and facilities.

2. Allocation of Primary Production Responsibilities

a. Production of military-economic intelligence on all foreign countries, including by way of illustration intelligence on military requirements, military materiel production, shipbuilding and ship movements, logistic capabilities, economic vulnerabilities to all forms of military attack, and target system analysis (including specific location, physical vulnerability, and supplementary studies as required), is the responsibility of the departments of the Department of Defense.

b. Production of intelligence on all foreign countries on economic doctrines, political and social aspects of economic organizations and institutions such as trade unions, and on the relationships between political and economic policies, is the responsibility of the Department of State.

c. Production of all economic intelligence on the Soviet Bloc[3] is the responsibility of the Central Intelligence Agency except as indicated herein. In addition, it will supplement the intelligence produced by other agencies by conducting such independent analyses and studies as may be necessary to produce integrated economic intelligence on the Bloc.

d. Production of all economic intelligence on foreign countries outside the Soviet Bloc is the responsibility of the Department of State except as indicated in paragraph 2.a.

---

[3] As used herein, "Soviet Bloc" includes USSR, Communist China, Poland, Czechoslovakia, Hungary, Rumania, Bulgaria, Albania, Soviet occupied portions of Germany and Austria, and Communist dominated portions of Korea and Indo-China. [Footnote in the original.]

e. Despite the above mentioned allocations of primary production responsibilities, there will be areas of common or overlapping interest (including, for example, Soviet Bloc economic policies, East-West trade, and inland transportation) which will require continuing interagency liaison and cooperation.

f. The existing allocations of production responsibility for National Intelligence Surveys (NIS) are not changed by this directive even though such allocations may, in some instances, be at variance with agency responsibilities specified in paragraphs 2.a., b., c., and d. However, the EIC will from time to time examine such allocations and after consulting with the NIS Committee will make appropriate recommendations.

3. Responsibility for Economic Intelligence Coordination

a. To assist the Central Intelligence Agency in carrying out its responsibilities with respect to coordination, the Economic Intelligence Committee (EIC) will continue to perform the functions outlined in IAC–D–22/1 (Revised), 29 May 1951.[4] Further, the EIC will be responsible for (1) reviewing from time to time the allocations of responsibility assigned herein; (2) determining how the provisions of this directive apply, particularly in areas of common or overlapping interest; and (3) recommending to the IAC appropriate changes in the allocations of responsibility assigned herein.

b. In order to minimize the duplication of effort and expense: (1) the EIC will prepare and circulate consolidated periodic lists of the economic research being conducted within the intelligence agencies; and (2) agencies sponsoring external research projects, involving more than $5,000, in support of economic intelligence production will submit descriptions of the scope of such projects to the EIC for review. The EIC will endeavor to present its recommendations in advance of final approval by the contracting agency. In its periodic reports to the IAC the EIC will include a summary of actions on these projects.

Allen W. Dulles[5]
Director of Central Intelligence

---

[4] Document 72.
[5] Printed from a copy that bears this typed signature.

192. Report by the Special Study Group[1]

Washington, undated.

REPORT ON THE COVERT ACTIVITIES OF THE CENTRAL
INTELLIGENCE AGENCY

I. Introduction

The acquisition and proper evaluation of adequate and reliable intelligence on the capabilities and intentions of Soviet Russia is today's most important military and political requirement. Several agencies of Government and many thousands of capable and dedicated people are engaged in the accomplishment of this task. Because the United States is relatively new at the game, and because we are opposed by a police state enemy whose social discipline and whose security measures have been built up and maintained at a high level for many years, the usable information we are obtaining is still far short of our needs.

As long as it remains national policy, another important requirement is an aggressive covert psychological, political and paramilitary organization more effective, more unique and, if necessary, more ruthless than that employed by the enemy. No one should be permitted to stand in the way of the prompt, efficient and secure accomplishment of this mission.

In the carrying out of this policy and in order to reach minimal standards for national safety under present world conditions, two things must be done. First, the agencies charged by law with the collection, evaluation and distribution of intelligence must be strengthened and coordinated to the greatest practicable degree. This is a primary concern of the National Security Council and must be accomplished at the national policy level. Those elements of the problem that fall within the scope of our directive are dealt with in the report which follows. The second consideration is less tangible but equally important. It is now clear that we are facing an implacable enemy whose avowed objective is world domination by whatever means and at whatever cost. There are no rules in such a game. Hitherto acceptable norms of human conduct do not apply. If the United States is to

---

[1] Source: Central Intelligence Agency, Community Management Staff, Job 82–M0311R, Box 1, Folder 23. Top Secret. Regarding the origins of this report, also known as the Doolittle Report, see Documents 184 and 185. It was forwarded to the President under cover of a September 30 letter signed by J.H. Doolittle, Chairman, and members of the Special Study Group William B. Franke, Morris Hadley, and William D. Pawley. The covering letter, the table of contents, and the appendices (B–D) are not printed. Appendix A is a copy of Document 185.

survive, long-standing American concepts of "fair play" must be reconsidered. We must develop effective espionage and counterespionage services and must learn to subvert, sabotage and destroy our enemies by more clever, more sophisticated and more effective methods than those used against us. It may become necessary that the American people be made acquainted with, understand and support this fundamentally repugnant philosophy.

Because of the tight security controls that have been established by the U.S.S.R. and its satellites, the problem of infiltration by human agents is extremely difficult. Most borders are made physically secure by elaborate systems of fencing, lights, mines, etc., backed up by constant surveillance. Once across borders—by parachute, or by any other means—escape from detection is extremely difficult because of constant checks on personnel activities and personal documentation. The information we have obtained by this method of acquisition has been negligible and the cost in effort, dollars and human lives prohibitive.

The defection of Soviet and satellite personnel offers a more profitable field for exploitation. The Agency is properly focusing a great deal of its effort in this direction, [1 line not declassified]. The information obtained from this source has been of value but is sporadic and incomplete.

A still greater potential lies in communications intelligence. This leads to the conviction that much more effort should be expended in exploring every possible scientific and technical avenue of approach to the intelligence problem. The study group has been extensively briefed by C.I.A. personnel and by the Armed Services in the methods and equipment that are presently in use and under development in this area. We have also had the benefit of advice from certain civilian consultants who are working on such special projects. We are impressed by what has been done, but feel that there is an immense potential yet to be explored. We believe that every known technique should be intensively applied and new ones should be developed to increase our intelligence acquisition by communications and electronic surveillance, high altitude visual, photographic and radar reconnaissance with manned or unmanned vehicles, upper atmosphere and oceanographic studies, physical and chemical research, etc. From such sources may come early warning of impending attack. No price is too high to pay for this knowledge.

In the short time that has been available to us we have been intensively briefed by the Director and staff of the Central Intelligence Agency, by the rest of the intelligence community, and by the principal users of the intelligence product. We have conferred with representatives of other interested Government agencies and with certain knowledgable individuals whose past experience and present thinking have made their views of value. The procedures which have been followed, and the list of witnesses who have been heard are detailed in Appendix B, attached. Our findings and recommendations follow.

II. Conclusions and Recommendations

With respect to the Central Intelligence Agency in general we conclude: (a) that its placement in the overall organization of the Government is proper; (b) that the laws under which it operates are adequate; (c) that the established provisions for its financial support are sufficiently flexible to meet its current operational needs; (d) that in spite of the limitations imposed by its relatively short life and rapid expansion it is doing a creditable job; (e) that it is gradually improving its capabilities, and (f) that it is exercising care to insure the loyalty of its personnel.

There are, however, important areas in which the C.I.A. covert organization, administration and operations can and should be improved. The Agency is aware of these deficiencies and in many cases steps are being taken toward their solution.

While we believe our study to have been as comprehensive as possible in the time available to us, we realize that it is not complete. We are well aware of the tremendous problems facing the Director and staff of an organization such as C.I.A. and appreciate the sincere efforts being made to solve them. In an attempt to be constructive and in the hope that we may be helpful, we make the following recommendations:

A. With Respect to Personnel

That the Agency personnel competence level be raised. The Agency should continually strive to achieve this and if necessary reduce its present work load to expedite its realization. Necessary steps are:

1. Elimination of personnel who can never achieve a sufficiently high degree of competence to meet the C.I.A. standard. This will entail a substantial reduction in present personnel. There is no place in C.I.A. for mediocrity.

2. Review and improvement of recruitment plans and procedures in order to obtain higher quality applicants for Agency jobs. The time required to process them should be reduced.

3. Continual improvement of the present excellent training facilities and capabilities in all covert activities to keep step with future requirements.

4. An intensified training program to include those key personnel in the covert services who require additional training, by rotation through C.I.A. training facilities. At present at least 10 percent of total covert personnel should be in training.

5. Assignment to field stations and to country areas of only those people who are fully qualified to handle the highly specialized problems involved.

6. Maintaining the position of Director above political considerations in order to assure tenure and continuity as in the F.B.I.

B. With Respect to Security

That greater security be developed at all levels of the Agency to the end that the good name of the United States and the fulfilment of C.I.A.'s important mission may not be jeopardized. The following steps should be taken to accomplish these objectives:

1. Elimination, to the maximum extent practicable, of provisional and preliminary clearances in the security processing of prospective Agency personnel.

2. Improved and more standardized security processing of alien operational personnel prior to their use by the covert services overseas.

3. Immediate completion of full field investigations and polygraph examinations of the several hundred Agency personnel who have not yet been fully processed.

4. Establishing of uniform and tighter security procedures at headquarters and suitable safeguards in the field the better to insure the security of the Agency's facilities, operations, sources and methods.

5. Insurance of the closest possible coordination of the counterespionage activities of the covert services with the over-all counterintelligence activities of the Office of Security to prevent, or detect and eliminate, any penetrations of C.I.A.

6. Augmentation of the present sound policy of polygraphing all new employees and all personnel returning from overseas assignments to include periodic rechecks of all personnel, on a more comprehensive basis, whenever effective counterintelligence practices indicate.

7. Creation of greater security consciousness on the part of all personnel by improving initial indoctrination courses and by conducting regular "security awareness" programs.

8. Imposition of severe penalties upon employees at any and all levels who advertently or inadvertently violate security.

9. Establishment of a uniform system for the submission by all overseas missions of regular reports on the status of personnel, physical, documentary and related elements of security. Such reports should be submitted to the Office of Security with copies to the Inspector General and to the appropriate division of the Deputy Director of Plans.

10. Periodic security inspections by the Security Office of overseas missions and of DD/P's divisions, staffs and facilities in the United States.

11. Rigid adherence to the "need-to-know" requirement as the basis for dissemination of classified intelligence developed by the covert services and for intra-Agency dissemination of classified data.

12. Continuous indoctrination and guidance to correct the natural tendency to overclassify documents originating in the Agency.

13. Promulgation of definitive standards and procedures governing cover for the guidance of all personnel. There should be a continuing program of monitoring cover in foreign installations. Personnel departing for overseas assignments should be more adequately briefed concerning the importance of cover generally, and in particular their mission and personal cover.

14. Insurance that officials of proprietary organizations adhere to C.I.A.'s security regulations in order to avoid disclosure, breach, or compromise of the Agency's covert association with such organizations.

15. Assignment of qualified security officers to the larger proprietary organizations to aid in avoiding security compromises.

16. Formulation for immediate implementation of emergency plans and preparations, geared to the specific needs of each overseas mission and station, to insure, as far as possible, adequate safeguarding of personnel and safeguarding or destruction of material, in the event of emergency.

17. Concentration of C.I.A.'s headquarters operations in fewer buildings with increased emphasis in the interim on improvement of the physical security of C.I.A.'s many buildings and the classified data and materials contained therein.

C. With Respect to Coordination and Operations

That one agency be charged with the coordination of all covert operations in peacetime, subject to the provision that necessary flexibility be achievable in time of war. The covert operating capabilities of C.I.A. must be continually improved. Steps toward these ends are:

1. Implementation of NSC 5412[2] which now makes C.I.A. the coordinating agency pending a national emergency.

2. Preparation and test of a readily implementable plan for the immediate and effective availability of local covert assets to theater commanders at the outbreak of war in their areas.

3. Immediate resolution, by the National Security Council, of the misunderstandings that still exist between C.I.A. and some of the Armed Services with respect to "agreed activities."

4. Development of better understanding between other agencies and C.I.A. relative to exploitation of Soviet and satellite defectors.

---

[2] Document 171.

5. A greater interchange of information, at all working levels, between C.I.A. and the military services regarding their intelligence programs and policies.

6. Improvement at all levels of coordination of C.I.A. covert activities with the State Department.

7. Establishment of definite world-wide objectives for the future, and formulation of a comprehensive long-range plan for their achievement.

8. Use, in all areas, of governmental cover by C.I.A. personnel only when other cover is not suitable or cannot be made available.

9. Active development of non-governmental cover.

10. The planting of agents under very deep cover in all areas including those that may not be of immediate interest, and the careful preservation of such assets.

11. More effective use of "proprietary project" cover through better planning and by using personnel having adequate business and area experience.

D. *With Respect to Organization and Administration*

That an intensive organizational study be made to the end of streamlining functions, clarifying lines of responsibility and authority, reducing overhead and increasing efficiency and effectiveness. From our relatively brief examination of organization it is obvious that:

1. The present elaborate staff structure of the Deputy Director for Plans should be simplified.

2. The covert organization should be so located, organized and administered as to maintain maximum security with reference to personnel and activities.

3. The Inspector General should operate on an Agency-wide basis with authority and responsibility to investigate and report on all activities of the Agency.

4. The activities of the Operations Coordination Board under the N.S.C. should be broadened to provide the D.C.I. with adequate support on the more important covert projects.

5. Despite the recommended reduction in present personnel and budgetary economies that the C.I.A. must continue to grow in capacity until it is able to meet, entirely, its national commitments.

6. Centralized accommodations, hand-tailored to its needs, should be provided to house the Agency.

E. *With Respect to Cost Factors*

That although the activities of C.I.A. should be expanded, costs of present operations should be reduced. This can be in part, accomplished through:

1. The exercise of better control over expenditures for all covert projects, and specifically that (except for those of an extremely sensitive nature) they be made subject to review and approval by the Agency's Project Review Committee.

2. Furnishing the Comptroller (under proper security provisions) with sufficient information on all covert projects to enable him to exercise proper accounting control on a fiscal year basis.

III. Discussion

Introduction—History and Growth of C.I.A.

The Central Intelligence Agency is an organization of mixed origins and recent growth.

The overt side of C.I.A., well described by the Agency's title, took over in 1947 from the former Central Intelligence Group. It receives the intelligence collected by all government agencies, processes it, disseminates and files it. This phase of the work is well administered under the Deputy Director of Intelligence and serves the whole intelligence community. Since 1947 it has grown to its present size of approximately [*number not declassified*].

The covert side of C.I.A. started with O.S.O. (Office of Special Operations) which was a remnant of the former O.S.S. Next came O.P.C. (Office of Policy Coordination) which was the "Cold War Shop," an offshoot of the State Department. The two operated under C.I.A. in virtual independence of each other until they underwent a shot-gun marriage in 1952, and were put under a Deputy Director for Plans. This covert side now numbers approximately [*number not declassified*] on the regular table of organization, and approximately as many more engaged in special projects, or about [*number not declassified*] in all.

Supporting and serving Intelligence and Plans are about [*number not declassified*] more persons, of whom about two-thirds are grouped under a Deputy Director for Administration, and about one-third are under Directors or Assistant Directors reporting directly to the Director of Central Intelligence himself, as in the case of Personnel, Training, and Communications. The work of these [*number not declassified*] is largely in support of covert operations, as the requirements of the overt intelligence side are relatively simpler, whether for training or for support.

Additional personnel on special projects bring the current total to approximately [*number not declassified*]. In 1947 the total was less than [*number not declassified*]. This represents a [*number not declassified*] increase in seven years.

(*Note:* Throughout this report we have considered as "covert" all activities that are not "overt." Specifically, we have included under "covert" the operations assigned to the Agency by NSC 5412 as well as its clandestine espionage and counterespionage operations.)

A. The Personnel Factors

The most important elements in the successful conduct of covert intelligence operations are the people who run them, —from top management down to the agent under deepest cover. First consideration, therefore, must be given to the recruitment, selection, training and evaluation of the most highly competent people available. They must then be assigned to jobs where they can be used most effectively and be given whatever support they require to enable them to carry out their missions.

In the past this Agency has not been entirely successful in achieving this result. In its short history it has suffered from lack of continuity in policy direction and management. At its inception it suffered from an inheritance of mixed and sometimes mutually antagonistic elements from O.S.S. and other predecessor agencies. Then, at a stage when still groping toward a stabilized peacetime program, it was suddenly called upon to meet the requirements of the Korean War.

Under this pressure it "ballooned" out into a vast and sprawling organization manned by a large number of people some of whom were of doubtful competence. Of necessity, sensitive positions were sometimes filled with people having little or no training for their jobs.

Fortunately, the Agency did possess an invaluable asset in the form of a hard core of capable and devoted men as a part of its World War II inheritance, and did succeed in attracting to this cadre an appreciable number of capable people. In some areas they have done, and are doing, an excellent job, but it appears from a personnel standpoint, that C.I.A. tends to accept more commitments than are warranted by its human assets. This leads us to the belief that an immediate re-evaluation of all programs should be undertaken by the Project Review Committee to eliminate those of lesser importance and to cut back the activity rates of all but the most essential to bring the over-all program into a more realistic coincidence with current Agency capabilities. When improved recruitment, adequate training and over-all experience level justify, Agency activity may again be accelerated.

We have made a study of the educational and experience background of the 34 key people in the Agency's chain of command. From this the following composite figures emerge: all are natural born U.S. citizens; they range in age from 38 to 66 yrs., averaging 47.9 yrs; 32 are married; 17 have 1 or more dependent children; 21 are wholly dependent on government salary; all but 2 are college graduates; 13 have advanced degrees. Twelve have had 1 or more years business experience; all but 6 have served in the U.S. Armed Forces; 15 have had intelligence experience (O.S.S., Armed Forces, etc.) prior to 1947; and 10 have had specialized C.I.A. training. Of this group 32 have had 3 years or more service with C.I.A., 20 have had 5 years or more, and 15 have been with the Agency for the full 7 years since it was established in its present form in 1947.

The Office of Personnel supplied an excellent statistical study covering [*number not declassified*] staff employees and agents on the roster as of 30 June 1954 from which the following data were taken: males make up 58 percent of total, females, 42 percent; average age is 34.2 years and two-thirds are in the 25–39 year age bracket. As for education, approximately 68 percent of the total are high school graduates, some 47 percent have B.A. (or equivalent) degrees, and about 24 percent have done post-graduate work or possess advanced degrees. Forty-five percent have served 3 years or more with the C.I.A. Looking at prior intelligence experience, which includes service with the Armed Forces or with the Agency's predecessor organizations, and realizing that all Agency personnel do not require such training, 71 percent had none, but 29 percent have had 1 year or more and 11 percent 2 or more years. Of the Agency total, 73 percent have had some foreign language training or experience, and nearly half have had some prior foreign area knowledge. Slightly over 50 percent are Armed Service veterans.

From the above we feel that the present personnel potential of the Agency is reasonably good. There is convincing evidence, however, that "dead wood" exists at virtually all levels. We have heard critics remark to the effect that there are too many ex-military people. We have been advised that some people coming back to headquarters from overseas assignments are sometimes not assigned to new jobs for long periods. Uncertainties in policy, frequent internal reorganizations, together with competition from industry frequently cause good people to seek employment outside. As in other governmental agencies, there is a tendency through inertia or because of a desire for financial security, for the mediocre to stay. As a result, despite the continual and necessary acquisition of additional good people, the competence level of the Agency is not rising as rapidly as is desirable. Prompt and drastic action to increase the rate of improvement is indicated. We are of the opinion that a planned reduction of at least 10 percent in present personnel can and should be achieved without reducing the amount and quality of Agency output.

We have been briefed on the Career Service Plan by means of which the Agency hopes to increase personnel stability. Whether the plan will achieve this result is as yet unknown, but it will not in itself solve the Agency's personnel problems. Nevertheless we believe that a sound Career Service Plan is desirable and should be implemented as promptly as possible.

The C.I.A. has a recruitment program operating in colleges and universities throughout the United States. This program has not been entirely successful in producing either the quantity or the quality of applicants needed for Agency requirements.

In part, this is due to the general shortage of technically trained people vis-à-vis heavy current demands by industry in practically all fields. On the other hand we have heard criticism from scholastic sources that the C.I.A. approach, both to the school and to the individual, is not what it should be, and furthermore, that many potentially good people are lost because of the very great length of time that now elapses between initial contact and entry into the job.

Clearance of new personnel at present averages 90 days. The F.B.I. takes only 30 days maximum for clearing its own personnel. Although we appreciate fully the special problems involved in C.I.A., we believe it is both practical and essential to reduce the present 90 day period as much as possible.

Many applicants find the necessary clearance procedures unpalatable and annoying. Some are repelled by misunderstanding of the purpose of polygraphic examination and the techniques employed. Some (particularly in scientific fields where future professional reputation may depend upon publication of papers, etc.) are unwilling to accept the implications of a lifetime of anonymity, or of life under a pseudonym. We do not suggest that these requirements be abandoned or relaxed in any degree. We are certain that they are necessary for maximum security and success of covert operations. But some better means of approach should be developed to assure the prospective employee that he is necessary, and to persuade him that in this Agency he can find a desirable career and at the same time perform a vital service to his country.

We have been impressed by the excellence of the Agency's training facilities and the competence of its instructor personnel. Our comment is that insufficient use is made of these facilities. It is obvious that the language, communication and clandestine agent training centers which we inspected are being operated far under capacity levels. This, of course, is a reflection of the slacking off in recruiting programs, but it suggests also that adequate use of the facilities is not now being made to improve the over-all quality of Agency covert activities by new training or refresher training of personnel already in the Agency.

We are aware that the present tendency of the Agency to take on more work than it can handle satisfactorily has limited optimum use of the training facilities, but it cannot be repeated too frequently that in C.I.A. covert operations quality is more important than quantity. A small number of competent people in a sensitive agency can be more useful than a large number of incompetents. In the long run it will pay to stop some of the less essential operations now to permit 10–15 percent of Agency covert personnel to go into training. As the backlog of inadequately trained personnel is reduced and the competence level of Agency personnel increased, this percentage may be lowered.

B. The Security Factors

Nothing is more important in the planning and execution of C.I.A.'s covert activities than continuing recognition at all levels throughout the Agency of the importance of security in all of its aspects. Although many sound and important security steps have already been put into effect by the Agency, in view of the outstanding importance of C.I.A.'s mission to the national security, constant effort must be made to improve security wherever possible.

We have been thoroughly briefed by the Security Office of the Deputy Director of Administration (DD/A), and by appropriate offices of the Deputy Director of Plans (DD/P) on personnel, physical, documentary, operational and cover security. We have examined the Agency's methods of screening out undesirable applicants or present employees by interrogation, field investigation and polygraph techniques. We have also examined DD/P's methods of processing alien operational personnel prior to their use by the covert services overseas.

We believe that C.I.A.'s security clearance criteria for prospective Agency personnel are sound. Without exception, they should be fully adhered to in practice. The granting of provisional or other interim clearances should be minimized. Full background investigations and polygraph examinations should continue to be prerequisite to hiring for all positions. Individuals now on the rolls who have not had the benefit of these full security clearance procedures should be so processed at the earliest possible date. (At the time of our study there were 132 headquarters and 531 field personnel who had not been polygraphed because they had entered on duty prior to the institution of the polygraph program in 1948.)

We are impressed with the competent manner in which the polygraph program is handled in the Agency and with the results obtained therefrom. Polygraph examination has proved extremely useful in identifying sexual perverts and other security risks. To September 1, 1954, [*number not declassified*] polygraph examinations had been conducted, resulting in the elimination of [*number not declassified*] individuals as security risks. We endorse the Agency's continuation of the polygraph program as an aid to investigation and interrogation as long as the present high standards govern the use of this device.

There is considerable room for improvement in existing security processing procedures for alien operational personnel. Because some personnel must be used for immediate short term operations, it may sometimes be difficult to apply full security clearance procedures to them. [*11½ lines not declassified.*]

[*1 paragraph (10 lines) not declassified*]

A uniform requirement should be established for the submission by all overseas missions of regular reports on the status of personnel, physical, documentary and related elements of security. Such reports should be submitted to the Office of Security with copies to the Inspector General and the appropriate division of DD/P. We recommend that periodic security inspections should be made by the Office of Security of all overseas missions and of DD/P's headquarters and other facilities in the United States. Tighter security procedures at headquarters and particularly in the field will better insure the security of the Agency's facilities, operations, sources and methods. Implementation of these recommendations should aid in raising the level of security throughout the entire Agency, particularly throughout the covert services.

If such a system of reporting and inspecting is adopted, the Director can, for the first time, look to one office for the security of the entire Agency. He will then have a more precise and timely picture of security-related developments throughout the Agency.

We cannot emphasize too strongly the importance of the continuation and intensification of C.I.A.'s counterintelligence efforts to prevent, or detect and eliminate penetrations of C.I.A. We endorse fully the present counterintelligence practices of the Agency which include polygraphing all personnel returning from overseas assignments, automatic security checks and file reviews of personnel being considered for transfer in the field or reassignment at headquarters, security checks of personnel nominated for special types of clearance, etc. We do not think that periodic re-investigation of all personnel is now necessary, but we believe that comprehensive rechecks of personnel should be made on a selective basis whenever sound counterintelligence practices dictate. Questionable cases should be intensively investigated and expeditiously resolved.

The counterespionage activities of the clandestine services can be one of the most fertile sources of information concerning attempted penetrations of C.I.A. Appropriate steps should be taken to insure the closest possible coordination of DD/P's counterespionage activities in this field with the over-all counterintelligence activities of the Office of Security. Any penetration attempt made against C.I.A., whether it involves Agency personnel and/or clandestine intelligence operations, can never be fully controlled and exploited until all information concerning such attempts—whether made in the United States or overseas—is channeled through one focal point, preferably the Security Office.

"Security consciousness" is an obvious "must" for all C.I.A. personnel. Constant efforts should be made to improve the Agency's security indoctrination courses. Regular "security awareness" programs should be inaugurated in order that all personnel may be reminded of the continuing need for "security consciousness" in the conduct of their day-to-day affairs.

Most breaches of security committed by C.I.A. personnel appear to be inadvertent rather than intentional. The net effect of such breaches on the national security is the same regardless of intent. Without exception, an inflexible attitude must be adopted with respect to security breaches and severe penalties meted out to employees at all levels who advertently or inadvertently violate security.

Too easy access to much of C.I.A.'s classified data is a potential source of trouble. Except for the tight restrictions drawn around supersensitive material, large segments of C.I.A.'s files are open to inspection and use by Agency personnel without qualification as to "need-to-know." Improvement is needed in carrying out the "need-to-know" rule as a basis for intra-Agency, as well as interdepartmental, distribution of C.I.A.'s classified data. This situation is aggravated considerably by the fact that there are too many duplicate records. The security of C.I.A.'s data is further jeopardized by a tendency to over-classify documentary data originating in the Agency, a condition which operates in derogation of the security classification system as a whole.

Considering C.I.A.'s unduly dispersed headquarters (43 buildings in the Washington area), its physical security program is reasonably good. The potential security risks inherent in such wide-spread dispersal make it essential that the Agency continue its efforts to consolidate the headquarters facilities into fewer, more adequate buildings.

The physical security measures in effect at C.I.A. installations which were visited in the general vicinity of Washington are excellent. The physical security of overseas installations visited by representatives of our study group appeared to vary with local circumstances and conditions. The limited number of inspections made was not sufficient to allow of definitive conclusions as to the general security of all overseas missions. There appear to be, however, no basic, minimum physical security requirements governing these missions or stations, except for the safeguarding of classified documents. We believe that acceptable minimum standards should be promulgated immediately and that regular inspections by qualified Security Office personnel should be made to enforce them.

Detailed plans and preparations should be made for immediate implementation of war-emergency measures by all overseas missions and stations, tailored to the local conditions. They should provide for maximum safeguarding of Agency personnel and operations, and for adequate safeguarding or destruction of classified data and material in the custody of the installations in question.

Secure cover is an inherent part of all clandestine operations. The security of some of the Agency's cover devices is excellent, security of others is inadequate. Cover security is a problem that requires continuous and exhaustive study. Detailed standards and procedures, policies and regulations, should be issued for the guidance of the personnel concerned. There is need for more adequate briefing of personnel departing for overseas assignments concerning the cover of their missions and their personal cover problems. The Office of Security should continually monitor the cover devices used in all foreign stations.

Maintaining proper cover in proprietary organizations requires that all personnel concerned actually live within the cover framework at all times. Vulnerable points are the channels of communications between C.I.A. and the proprietary organizations as well as contacts between personnel of such organizations and other personnel of the Agency. Another vulnerable feature is in the assignment of personnel from the Agency to the proprietary organizations and the hiring of outside personnel. Any person who has previously served in a known capacity with the Agency is a potential security hazard if associated with any proprietary organization. A like hazard exists if a person is hired on the outside by the organization without first obtaining a complete clearance from the Agency.

Professionally qualified security officers should be placed on the staff of the larger proprietary organizations. Experience shows that organizations so staffed usually have fewer security compromises. Close coordination should be maintained with the Agency on the matter of requesting surveys of proposed "business" sites before they are acquired, so that any potential security hazard on or near the premises may be disclosed. All officials of proprietary organizations must be indoctrinated in the necessity of conforming with the security requirements of the Agency. Neglect of certain basic security requirements by such officials can lead to disclosure, breach, or compromise of the covert association.

C. Coordination and Operations

The success of the covert operations of C.I.A. depends upon how efficiently they are conducted and how well they are coordinated with other agencies of the Government. These criteria prevail both in peace and in war, but both coordination and operations are necessarily somewhat different during each of these periods. Peace in any ordinarily accepted sense of the word, appears to be impossible of achievement in the foreseeable future. The covert operations of the Agency must therefore be planned and coordinated in order to meet the requirements of a continuing cold war situation as well as the requirements of possible hot war. C.I.A. has this obligation under NSCD 5412 (March 15, 1954).

Looking toward the possible outbreak of actual hostilities in any theater of operations, a detailed plan should be developed now delineating the wartime headquarters responsibilities of C.I.A. to insure that appropriate policy guidance, integrated with N.S.C. and J.C.S. plans, be furnished to C.I.A. representatives in the field. In an emergency situation time obviously will not permit referral of all critical covert operational questions to Washington. Furthermore, the needs of commanders in the field may require the immediate transfer of many local C.I.A. covert operational assets to their commands. It is absolutely essential, therefore, that well-considered, well-implemented and pretested plans be prepared in advance to insure smooth transfer of such assets and to deal with any other local covert operational problems.

In the case of espionage and counterespionage operations there is disagreement between C.I.A. and some of the military services which has yet to be resolved. This relates to the area of "agreed activities" (NSCID 5, August 28, 1951)[3] as to which a dispute has dragged on for years. Some of the services feel that certain foreign espionage and counterespionage operations must be run directly by them. The Director of Central Intelligence has been desirous of securing the voluntary agreement of the Armed Services, and has submitted various proposals to them as to the delimitation of these areas of "agreed activities." To date the attempts to resolve the differences have been unavailing. We believe that the prime responsibility for the failure does not lie with C.I.A., but with these services. In fact, we believe that the Director of Central Intelligence, in his desire to reach an amicable solution, has gone further than was intended by the N.S.C. directives. Since agreement has not been reached on a voluntary basis, the dispute should be resolved by the N.S.C. In the settlement of this dispute, in addition to recognizing the right of the Armed Services to perform counterintelligence activities for the security of their own installations and personnel, the Armed Services should be allowed to engage in espionage and counterespionage operations (provided they are coordinated by the Director of Central Intelligence) until such time as C.I.A. has the capability to perform all espionage and counterespionage operations outside the United States.

In order to avoid undue delay in the resolution of such problems in the future, the Director of Central Intelligence (as coordinator of all foreign intelligence) should report regularly to the N.S.C. on the status of efforts to implement N.S.C. directives, with particular emphasis on major unresolved questions.

Inasmuch as the exploitation of Soviet and satellite defectors outside the United States has been a source of annoyance (and even hostility) on the part of some of the military services and other agencies toward C.I.A. and vice versa, we believe that steps should be taken immediately to insure full implementation of the defector program in accordance with the spirit and letter of NSCID 13 (Jan. 19, 1950).[4]

---

[3] Document 255.

[4] Referenced in *Foreign Relations*, 1945–1950, Emergence of the Intelligence Establishment, Document 433.

The misunderstandings which exist between C.I.A. and the Armed Services stem largely from insufficient exchange of information and coordination with respect to espionage, counterespionage, and covert operations. We have been advised, for example, that in certain instances C.I.A. operators appear to have been too secretive with respect to information which is of direct interest to the military services and vice versa. We have been told of incidents where important covert operations have been "blown" because C.I.A. and military intelligence units were operating *against* each other, without knowledge of each other's interest or activity. The relationship that exists in various countries between covert C.I.A. personnel and the military attachés is not always satisfactory. Attachés and MAAG's are playing important roles in the collection of foreign intelligence and in the defector program, and it is, therefore, essential that closer coordination and greater exchange of information be established between C.I.A.'s representatives and the military at every foreign station.

Misunderstandings between some of the services and the Agency are not confined to overseas operations. A lack of knowledge of plans, facilities, and operations seems to exist in some areas between the Pentagon and C.I.A. Compartmentation can be carried too far. Improvement in collaboration at the working levels is particularly essential.

Relations with C.I.A.'s other principal customer, the Department of State, also are not entirely satisfactory. In Washington, coordination seems to be reasonably good with well-established liaison channels, but misunderstandings seem to exist at many overseas stations. There is a feeling that C.I.A. is making too much use of [*less than 1 line not declassified*] cover in many places. Such official cover is thin, at best, and any compromise creates embarrassing situations. In some areas C.I.A. personnel have not coordinated their activities sufficiently with those who should know of them in our embassies. As a result, people have worked at cross purposes, with unfortunate results. It is realized that there are situations in which disclosure of plan and purpose should be held to a minimum number of people, but in all cases the Senior U.S. Representative should be sufficiently advised to insure proper coordination in accordance with approved N.S.C. intelligence directives.

D. Organization and Administration

In the course of investigating the covert operations of the Agency, we were briefed on the organization of the individual components of the DD/P complex. We also had the benefit of the thinking of a number of key Agency people with respect to the DD/P organization as a whole. As a result certain general observations with respect to DD/P organization have emerged which are germane to the problem of the efficiency and economy of its operations.

From the remarks that have been made on the subject of Agency history and personnel problems, it is clear that the organization is still in an evolutionary stage. It has suffered from a mixed inheritance, a lack of policy continuity, tremendous pressures to accept commitments beyond its capacity to perform, and a mushroom expansion. As a result there has been an absence of long-range planning with consequent organizational difficulties. We are strongly of the opinion that further streamlining of organization, clarification of functions, and straightening of lines of authority will result in more and better work with fewer people at lower costs.

The covert activities of C.I.A. fall under the direction of the Deputy Director for Plans (DD/P). They are presently conducted by a complicated organization of a mixed straight-line and functional type in which staff has been superimposed on staff to such an extent that duplication of effort, conflicting command authority, and division of responsibility have inevitably resulted in dilution of the total effort.

There are six principal staffs in the DD/P complex ranging in size from [number not declassified] people, totaling [number not declassified]. These are superimposed over seven area divisions ranging in size from [number not declassified]. Five of the staffs have subordinate divisions, and two of the staffs have subordinate staffs. In addition, each of the divisions has its own set of staffs. Altogether, the DD/P complex totals over 40 major units.

We are strongly of the opinion, based upon our limited review of the DD/P element, that consideration of a complete reorganization of the element is needed. As an indication of the type organization that might be more effective and less costly, we have included in this report for consideration purposes only, a revised organization chart as Appendix D. A chart of the present DD/P organization is also included, for purposes of comparison, as Appendix C. The personnel contemplated under the revised DD/P organization would number approximately 1,000 less than are presently employed by this element.

In considering any reorganization, we cannot emphasize too strongly our feelings with respect to the need for greater security in all DD/P operations. As the covert side of C.I.A., it should operate with a maximum of anonymity. Knowledge of its physical location, operation and the identity of its personnel should be kept on an absolutely need-to-know basis.

We feel that continuous inspection and closer control (both fiscal and operational) over covert activities are necessary. We realize that certain security risks are involved but we believe they can be handled properly.

The subject of fiscal control, and the relationship of the Comptroller to the organization are discussed under Section E following.

The concept of an Inspector General for the Agency is sound. He should report only to the Director. He should be given the greatest possible latitude and authority to inspect all aspects of the Agency at any time, including the Director's own office and the DD/P complex. We believe that any limitations that have been placed on this function in the past should be completely removed.

Because of the rapid expansion of the Agency, its operations are conducted in some 43 buildings in the Washington area. Some of these buildings are of temporary wartime construction and constitute a fire hazard. This forced decentralization of operations results in great loss of time of personnel whose duties require them frequently to visit various buildings of the Agency; it increases security problems; and it results in a great reduction in over-all efficiency. We recommend that sympathetic consideration be given to the Agency's effort to obtain funds with which to provide centralized accommodations for its activities, and we suggest that these accommodations would best serve the peculiar requirements of the Agency if they were hand-tailored to its needs. We are of the opinion that in a relatively short time the expenditure required would be self-liquidating.

Although in the present organizational plan of the Government C.I.A. seems to be well integrated into the Intelligence Community at the National Security Council level, events have occurred recently (for example—Guatemala) which indicate that gaps exist in high level planning and coordination of important covert operations which may expose the U.S. Government to unnecessary risks of compromise. Overall policy guidance comes from N.S.C., and is satisfactory, but better coordination is needed for the more important covert activities of C.I.A. at the national level. This is the function of the Operations Coordination Board, but at the present time it does not appear to be giving the Agency adequate guidance and advice on the more important covert projects. The activities of the Board should be broadened in order to provide the D.C.I. with the support he needs on such projects.

E. The Cost Factors

The budgetary procedures of the Agency were reviewed with the Agency Comptroller and representatives of the Bureau of the Budget and appear to be satisfactory. Between the fiscal years ended June 30, 1947 and 1955 the total budget has increased from approximately [*dollar figures not declassified*], the latter figure including a reserve fund of [*dollar figure not declassified*]. The 1955 fiscal year budget exclusive of the reserve fund is divided approximately as follows:

Direct costs:
  Covert operations   [*dollar figure not declassified*]
  Overt operations   [*dollar figure not declassified*]
Indirect or support costs: [*dollar figure not declassified*]
                              [*dollar figure not declassified*]

Since indirect or support costs are relatively proportionate to direct costs, the total budget may be considered to be approximately [*number not declassified*] for covert and [*number not declassified*] for overt operations.

The number of civilian employees of the Agency under personnel ceilings has increased from [*number not declassified*] at June 30, 1947, to an estimated [*number not declassified*] for the fiscal year ending June 30, 1955, and military personnel has increased during the same period from [*number not declassified*] to [*number not declassified*]. The aggregate of [*number not declassified*] for the fiscal year ending June 30, 1955 will be allocated as follows:

Covert operations:

Foreign Intelligence	[*dollar amount not declassified*]
Political & Psychological	[*dollar amount not declassified*]
Paramilitary	[*dollar amount not declassified*]
Overt operations	[*dollar amount not declassified*]
Indirect or support elements	[*dollar amount not declassified*]
	[*dollar amount not declassified*]

This total does not include individuals under contract, who are not regular employees of the Agency, individuals under deep cover and those engaged in proprietary enterprises, and indigenous personnel. The aggregate of persons in these categories is estimated at [*number not declassified*], most of whom are engaged in covert operations.

The actual number of individuals to be engaged on Agency activities for the fiscal year 1955 will, therefore, be approximately [*number not declassified*].

The covert operations of the Agency are budgeted and accounted for on a project basis except for headquarters and overseas support costs. Political and psychological and paramilitary projects exceeding a specified minimum dollar total are in general reviewed and approved by a Project Review Committee. Foreign Intelligence projects are not subject to review by this committee but are authorized by the Director of the Agency, the Deputy Director of the Agency, the Deputy Director of Plans, or certain other individuals depending upon the estimated dollar costs of individual projects. We believe that for purposes of control and as an aid in auditing, Foreign Intelligence projects (except those of an extremely sensitive nature) should be made subject to review and approval by the Project Review Committee.

Due to DD/P's present secrecy policies with respect to Foreign Intelligence projects, the Comptroller of the Agency is unable to maintain meaningful records showing the expenditures made for individual projects in this category. The Foreign Intelligence Staff keeps certain records of such expenditures but on the basis of a calendar rather than a fiscal year. We believe that the Comptroller should be furnished with information which will enable him to record, control and account for the costs of the individual projects of this element of the Agency. Adequate protection for security purposes can and should be provided within the Office of the Comptroller.

Certain other projects in the political and psychological and paramilitary areas, of a sensitive nature are occasionally developed and processed without full information with respect thereto being given to the Deputy Director for Administration and the Comptroller. Since, of necessity, the funds must be made available by the Comptroller, it is inevitable that he will have knowledge that operations of this nature are being conducted and it is unlikely that more specific information relating to the projects can long be kept secret from him. In one particular instance where substantial sums were expended, the Comptroller was called upon to make the expenditures with no supporting data being furnished to him at the time or at any future date. When we requested breakdowns of costs of the operation we found that they were available only in the area division involved and that they were incomplete and unsatisfactory. We are of the opinion that this deviation from the normal procedure of placing upon the Comptroller the responsibility of accounting for expenditures is unsound, and is not justified by the claim that the security of the operation is improved by this deviation.

We are of the opinion that the administrative plans for individual covert projects are not in all instances as complete in detail as is desirable and that if they were amplified the Comptroller and the Auditor-in-Chief would be in a much better position to carry out their respective duties and responsibilities.

---

193. Memorandum of Conversation[1]

Washington, October 19, 1954.

The President saw General Doolittle and other members of the Committee appointed to investigate the activities of the CIA.

---

[1] Source: Eisenhower Library, Whitman File, Administrative Series, Dulles, Allen, Box 13. No classification marking. No drafting information appears on the memorandum.

The report was presented by General Doolittle,[2] who said they had gone over it with Allen Dulles for three reasons: (1) to be absolutely fair; (2) to study Mr. Dulles better to watch for his reactions to a report not wholly favorable; (3) and their hope that the maximum good would come out of the report. Mr. Dulles made several recommendations that were incorporated in the report.

The President prefaced his remarks by saying that of course Mr. Dulles knew, as does everyone, that no two men would have the same judgments about certain things. That what we wanted to know was did we have a good man for the CIA head, and was he being selective and skillful in getting his assistants, and was his team working together in the best interests of the United States.

General Doolittle emphasized that the report was constructive criticism and in no sense a white wash. Some of the recommendations were very technical.

About Dulles: his principal strength is his unique knowledge of his subject; he has his whole heart in it, his life, he is a man of great honesty, integrity, loyally supported by his staff. His weakness, or the weakness of the CIA is in the organization—it grew like topsy, sloppy organization. Mr. Dulles surrounds himself with people in whom he has loyalty but not competence. There is a lack of discipline in the organization. There is a complete lack of security consciousness throughout organization. Too much information is leaked at cocktail party.

There is the family relationship with the Secretary of State. Such relationship can be important as it leads to protection of one by the other or influence of one by the other. Doolittle feels that it is a relationship that it would be better not to have exist. The President thought, however, there was something more favorable to be said about the relationship; he appointed Allen Dulles in full knowledge of the relationship and thinks it might be beneficial.

About Dulles' two chief assistants. Frank Wisner is a chap of great promise but not a good organizer.

About Dulles' readiness to accept criticism, Doolittle said he is highly emotional; wherever criticism was against him he took it well; he fought for his staff people, however, to the point of becoming emotional.

Doolittle had said that Bedell Smith had at one time said that Dulles was too emotional to be in this critical spot. He said further he thought his emotionalism was far worse than it appeared on the surface. The President said he had never seen him show the slightest disturbance. He said further that we must remember that here is one of

---

[2] For the written report, see Document 192.

the most peculiar types of operation any government can have, and that it probably takes a strange kind of genius to run it. The President said that what did disturb him was what the Committee reported about his assistants—Wisner and Cabell. Doolittle said in his opinion Allen Dulles did not have an administrative individual in either. Eisenhower said he was convinced no military man could do the job. President pointed out importance of Allen Dulles' contacts throughout world. President further said, with reference to lack of security, that it was completely frustrating to find always evidence that people are talking. Security Council has gotten pretty good.

President said his next move would be to get Dulles in and talk to him about it. The relationship with Secretary of State did not disturb him because part of CIA's work is extension of work of State Department. He further feels the confidential relationship between the two brothers is a good thing.

Someone in room said Bissell was not a good man. Also that Amory was an exceptionally fine man.

President said we were interested in two things: (1) improvement within CIA itself; (2) improvement in relationship and better understanding between CIA and rest of intelligence committees in government.

President said he was astonished at the difficulty of getting good administrators in government; that he had found a good many fine administrators throughout his long career.

---

194. **Letter From Edwin H. Land, Chairman of the Technological Capabilities Panel of the Science Advisory Committee, Office of Defense Mobilization, to Director of Central Intelligence Dulles[1]**

Washington, November 5, 1954.

Dear Mr. Dulles:

Here is the brief report from our panel telling why we think overflight is urgent and presently feasible. I am not sure that we have made

---

[1] Source: Central Intelligence Agency, Office of the Deputy Director for Science and Technology, Job 33–02415A, Box 1, Folder 7. Top Secret; Eyes Only. The role of the Technological Capabilities Panel in the development of the U–2 is discussed at length in Chapter 1 of *The CIA and the U–2 Program, 1954–1974*, by Gregory W. Pedlow and Donald E. Welzenbach.

it clear that we feel there are many reasons why this activity is appropriate for CIA, always with Air Force assistance. We told you that this seems to us the kind of action and technique that is right for the contemporary version of CIA; a modern and scientific way for an Agency that is always supposed to be looking, to do its looking. Quite strongly, we feel that you must always assert your first right to pioneer in scientific techniques for collecting intelligence—and choosing such partners to assist you as may be needed. This present opportunity for aerial photography seems to us a fine place to start.

With best wishes,

Edwin H. Land

For: Project 3, Technological Capabilities Panel
Office of Defense Mobilization
Executive Office of the President

Project Members:
E. H. Land
James G. Baker
Joseph W. Kennedy
Edward M. Purcell
John W. Tukey[2]

Attachment

Memorandum for Director of Central Intelligence Dulles[3]

Washington, November 5, 1954.

SUBJECT

A Unique Opportunity for Comprehensive Intelligence

For many years it has been clear that aerial photographs of Russia would provide direct knowledge of her growth, of new centers of activity in obscure regions, and of military targets that would be important if ever we were forced into war. During a period in which Russia has free access to the geography of all our bases and major nuclear facilities, as well as to our entire military and civilian economy, we have

---

[2] Baker and Purcell were at Harvard University, Kennedy at Washington University in St. Louis, and Tukey at Princeton University.

[3] Top Secret; Eyes Only.

been blocked from the corresponding knowledge about Russia. We have been forced to imagine what her program is, and it could well be argued that peace is always in danger when one great power is essentially ignorant of the major economic, military, and political activities within the interior zone of another great power. This ignorance leads to somewhat frantic preparations for both offensive and defensive action, and may lead to a state of unbearable national tension. Unfortunately, it is the U.S., the more mature, more civilized, and more responsible country that must bear the burden of not knowing what is happening in Russia. We cannot fulfill our responsibility for maintaining the peace if we are left in ignorance of Russian activity.

While aerial photography could be the most powerful single tool for acquiring information, it has until now been dangerous to fly over Russia. Up till now, the planes might rather readily be detected, less readily attacked, and possibly even destroyed. Thus no statesman could have run the risk of provocation toward war that an intensive program of overflights might produce. The Air Force has, for a long time, studied a program of overflight as a natural aspect of its Reconnaissance mission and has, in recent months, considered several proposals for airplanes designed for this purpose. While it is important that such research and development continue in the Air Force, for the present it seems rather dangerous for one of our military arms to engage directly in extensive overflight.

On the other hand, because it is vital that certain knowledge about industrial growth, strategic targets, and guided missile sites be obtained at once, we recommend that CIA, as a civilian organization, undertake (with the Air Force assistance) a covert program of selected flights. Fortunately, a jet powered glider has been carefully studied by Lockheed Aircraft Corporation for overflight purposes. This manufacturer proposes to take full responsibility for the design, mock-up, building, secret testing and field maintenance of this extraordinary and unorthodox vehicle, making it feasible for a CIA task force to undertake this vital activity. Such a task force requires highly specialized and able guidance in procurement and operation (by Air Force officers for aircraft, by scientists for photographic and electronic equipment). The Lockheed super glider will fly at 70,000 feet, well out of reach of present Russian interception and high enough to have a good chance of avoiding detection. The plane itself is so light (15,000 lbs.), so obviously unarmed and devoid of military usefulness, that it would minimize affront to the Russians even if through some remote mischance it were detected and identified.

Since the proposed mission of this plane is first of all photographic, and only secondarily electronic, a word should be said about the information expected from the photographs, as well as about the effects of the cloud cover over Russia. Photographs are appended[4] that demonstrate the large information content of pictures taken from these great altitudes. A single mission in clear weather can photograph in revealing detail a strip of Russia 200 miles wide by 2,500 miles long. Cloud cover will reduce completeness, of course, but clouds are not a serious obstacle because one can afford to wait for good weather; alternate routes over clear areas can be selected in flight; and finally, the number of intelligence targets accessible during a single mission is so large that even a partial sampling would yield an extraordinary amount of intelligence.

The opportunity for safe overflight may last only a few years, because the Russians will develop radars and interceptors or guided missile defenses for the 70,000 foot region. We therefore recommend immediate action through special channels in CIA in procuring the Lockheed glider and in establishing the CIA task force. No proposal or program that we have seen in intelligence planning can so quickly bring so much vital information at so little risk and at so little cost. We believe that these planes can go where we need to have them go efficiently and safely, and that no amount of fragmentary and indirect intelligence can be pieced together to be equivalent to such positive information as can thus be provided.

It is recommended that

(a) The Central Intelligence Agency establish an initial task force to complete any necessary feasibility studies in a few weeks, and that, assuming successful completion of the studies, the following further actions be taken.

(b) A permanent task force, including Air Force supporting elements, be set up under suitable cover to provide guidance on procurement, to consolidate requirements and plan missions in view of priority and feasibility, to maintain the operation on a continuing basis, and to carry out the dissemination of the resulting information in a manner consistent with its special security requirements.

(c) The procurement of a coordinated system from Lockheed, consisting of CL–282 aircraft with photographic and electronic equipment, be authorized.

(d) Such high altitude overflights be authorized in principle.

---

[4] Not found.

Attachment[5]

A UNIQUE OPPORTUNITY FOR COMPREHENSIVE
INTELLIGENCE—A SUMMARY

Opportunity

Collection of large amounts of information at a minimum of risk through prompt development of a special, high altitude airplane. Assurance of thousands of photographs that will yield critical analysis of vast Soviet complexes. Protection of mission by decisive altitude advantage over Soviet interception. This protection good for only a few years, thus assured only through very prompt action.

Objectives

Providing adequate locations and analyses of Russian targets (including those newly discovered).

More accurate assessment of Soviet Order of Battle and of early warning indicators, thus improving our defenses against surprise attack.

Appraising Soviet guided missile development (through photos of test range, etc.).

Improving estimates of Soviet ability to deliver nuclear weapons and of their capacity to produce them.

Disclosing new developments which might otherwise lead to technological surprise.

Appraising Soviet industrial and economic progress.

Organization

Secret task force under Central Intelligence Agency with strong Air Force staff assistance to equip and carry out entire mission up to point where flow of useful new intelligence is established. Task force to include top experts selected from Government agencies, armed services, universities and industry to provide for most effective application of science and technology toward fulfillment of this objective.

Vehicle

Special "powered glider" CL–282 aircraft proposed by Lockheed. ALTITUDE–70,000 feet. SPEED–500 kt. RANGE–3,000 n. mi. GROSS WEIGHT–15,000 lbs. TAKE-OFF DISTANCE–1,200 feet. CREW–lone

---

[5] Top Secret; Eyes Only.

pilot in heated, pressurized suit. AVAILABILITY–four aircraft for field use in 17 months assured by Lockheed.

Cameras

Standard Trimetrogon for charting entire overflown strip. Focal lengths from 12–48 inches to be used in multiple mounts for main work load. Special long focal length spotting camera for detailing concentrated areas down to objects as small as a man. Clear identification of Roads, Railroads, Power Lines, Industrial Plants, Air Fields, Parked Aircraft, Missile Sites and the like within a strip 200 miles wide by 2,500 miles long per flight.

Electronics

Electronics intercept [*less than 1 line not declassified*] data to be recorded on special automatic recorders preset for selected frequencies. More extensive electronic data available by optional use of additional electronic gear in place of photographic gear.

Schedule

New intelligence to start flowing within twenty months.

Cost

$22,000,000 to initial flow of significant intelligence. (Includes procurement of design, development and test of six CL–282 aircraft, training and operation of special task force and initial logistic support.)

---

195. Editorial Note

Director of Central Intelligence Allen Dulles prepared a paper for a review of national security policy then underway on November 18, 1954. Dulles reviewed the evolving dynamics of the superpower competition, predicting that, over the next few years, the Soviet Union would become a more formidable competitor with the West in all regions of the world. To respond to this growing competition (which Dulles believed would remain primarily diplomatic, economic, and cultural, and was not likely to result in a ground war), Dulles noted that the United States needed "to employ in a closely coordinated fashion all the cold war weapons at its disposal." To do so, the government required "the decisive coordination of political, military, economic and covert actions." The text is in *Foreign Relations, 1952–1954*, volume II, Part 1, pages 776–781.

196. Memorandum for Record[1]

Washington, November 19, 1954.

Following attended luncheon given by Secretary of Air Force, Talbott:

Mr. Trevor Gardner, Asst. to Sec. A.F.
Lt. Gen. Donald Putt A.F.
Dr. Land
Mr. Clarence Kelly Johnson, Lockheed A/C Co.
Mr. Fred Ayers, Asst. to Sec. A.F.
Mr. Allen Dulles, DCI
Lt. Gen. C.P. Cabell, DDCI

It was agreed that the special item of matériel described by Lockheed was practical and desirable and would be sought in addition to the matériel item suggested by Gen. Twining at the earlier meeting with him.[2]

It was agreed that the Project should be a joint Air Force–CIA one but that regardless of the source of the funds, whether A.F or CIA, CIA unvouchered channels would be needed to pass the funds.

CPC

---

[1] Source: Central Intelligence Agency, Office of the Director for Science and Technology, Job 33–02415A, Box 1, Folder 7. Top Secret. The memorandum was handwritten by Cabell.

[2] The meeting has not been further identified.

197.   Memorandum by the Intelligence Advisory Committee[1]

Washington, November 23, 1954.

SUBJECT

Intelligence

In our opinion there are serious gaps in our Intelligence covering the Soviet Bloc areas, particularly in relation to our ability to determine the capabilities of the Soviet Union to launch nuclear attacks against the U.S. and to detect indications of their intentions to do so. We believe that we could have a substantially improved capability of filling these gaps through the use of aerial reconnaissance and photography, and that today these methods are the most practicable additional means to this end.

Allen W. Dulles
Director of Central Intelligence

W. Park Armstrong, Jr.
Spec. Asst. for Intelligence
Department of State

Arthur G. Trudeau
Major General, USA
Asst. Chief of Staff, G–2
Department of the Army

John A. Samford
Major General, USAF
Director of Intelligence
Department of the Air Force

Carl F. Espe
Rear Admiral, USN
Director of Naval Intelligence

Edwin T. Layton
Rear Admiral, USN
Dep. Director for Intelligence
The Joint Staff, JCS

Harry S. Traynor
Atomic Energy Commission
Representative to the IAD

Ralph R. Roach[2]
Acting Asst. to the Director
Federal Bureau of Investigation

---

[1] Source: Central Intelligence Agency, Office of the Deputy Director for Science and Technology, Job 33–02415A, Box 1. Top Secret. Although no addressee is given on the memorandum, it went to the President who alone made the decision on overflights.

[2] Printed from a copy that shows that Carl Reichardt signed for Traynor above Traynor's typed signature and that shows only Roach's typed signature.

198. Memorandum by Director of Central Intelligence Dulles[1]

Washington, November 24, 1954.

SUBJECT

Reconnaissance

You are familiar with the large gaps in our Intelligence coverage of the Soviet Union which prevent us from obtaining adequate knowledge of Soviet intentions and, in important respects, of Soviet capabilities; and in particular, with respect to their capabilities and intentions to launch nuclear attacks on the United States. You are familiar, too, with the current and growing difficulties in the way of filling those gaps by the more classic means.

In my considered judgment, as well as that of the other members of the Intelligence Community, there is not the prospect of gaining this vital Intelligence without the conduct of systematic and repeated air reconnaissance over the Soviet Union itself. (Even this does not assure adequacy, but will certainly provide a much closer approach to adequacy.) The members of the Doolittle Committee in their report,[2] expressed their belief that every known technique should be used and new ones developed to increase our Intelligence by high altitude photographic reconnaissance and other means, and that no price would be too high to pay for the knowledge to be derived therefrom. Thus, there is a definite and urgent National requirement for photographic and electronic reconnaissance overflights of the Soviet Bloc.

While we have been considering the problem for a long time (you may recall a discussion I had with you some months ago concerning overflights), Dr. James R. Killian, Jr., and members of Project 3, Technological Capabilities Panel, Office of Defense Mobilization, (E.H. Land, James G. Baker, Joseph W. Kennedy, Edward M. Purcell and John W. Tukey) have independently arrived at essentially the same conclusion.[3] I have also discussed it with Secretary Talbott and with General Twining.[4] We are all agreed that the requirement is an urgent one and

---

[1] Source: Central Intelligence Agency, Office of the Deputy Director for Science and Technology, Job 33–02415A, Box 1. Top Secret. The date is handwritten. Although no addressee is shown, internal references indicate the memorandum was addressed to President Eisenhower, who made the decision on overflights.

[2] Document 192.

[3] Document 194.

[4] Document 196.

that with suitable direction and support, it is feasible of accomplishment with minimum risk.

An existing Air Force aircraft type (the Canberra)[5] is considered capable of modification to give it a ceiling of around 65,000 feet. At such an altitude now, the expectation that it would be detected is very low indeed, and the possibility that it would be intercepted and shot down is practically nil. The possibility of forced landing in enemy territory exists, but the chances of that are low. The repercussions of its falling into enemy hands can be mitigated if the aircraft should be manned by non-official U.S. personnel. To the extent practicable, we would try to man the aircraft with Poles or other non-U.S. nationals. The aircraft itself, if not completely destroyed, would bear no markings that would clearly identify its origin. (The Canberra itself is nearly identical with its British prototype.)

As a follow-on to the Canberra, we would simultaneously proceed with the procurement of specially designed reconnaissance aircraft with more advanced performance characteristics, that would take it to around 70,000 feet.[6]

In addition to this high altitude day reconnaissance, we would resort to very low altitude reconnaissance at night with appropriate aircraft. Whereas the night reconnaissance would not provide a substitute for the high altitude day photography, nevertheless it would give an opportunity for supplementary reconnaissance, exploiting such technical developments as infrared photography and certain electronics techniques.

Of course, not even the 70,000 foot opportunity will be of indefinite duration. Our problem will be one of keeping ahead and creating new opportunities as the old disappear.

We are all agreed also that, in order to attain a status of readiness to launch these flights as early as desired, and then to conduct them, extraordinary procedures would have to be adopted for aircraft, crew and equipment procurement, testing, training, and for operations. This would require the greatest possible collaboration between the Air Force and the Central Intelligence Agency.

I recommend that you:

a. Approve the existence of a National requirement for the above reconnaissance overflights.
b. By approval of this document, direct the Secretary of the Air Force and the Director of Central Intelligence to establish as a matter

---

[5] The aircraft became known as the RB–69.
[6] This aircraft would become the U–2.

of urgency, a collaborative project for the procurement and testing of the necessary aircraft and equipment, and for the procurement and training of the necessary crews (such crews to be [*less than 1 line not declassified*] to the extent practicable). The Director of Central Intelligence is also hereby authorized to obligate in Fiscal Year 1955 an amount not to exceed [*dollar amount not declassified*] from the [*less than 1 line not declassified*] for aircraft procurement, and it is expected as the project develops additional authority will be sought by him for funds for maintenance, training, operations, etc.

c. By approval of this document, direct the Secretary of the Air Force and the Director of Central Intelligence, subject to appropriate policy guidance as directed, to conduct at the earliest possible date, the reconnaissance overflights, and to do so in such a way as to reduce the risk of involvement of the U.S. to the minimum practicable.

Allen W. Dulles[7]

---

[7] Printed from a copy that bears this typed signature.

---

199. Memorandum of Conference With President Eisenhower[1]

Washington, November 24, 1954, 8:10 a.m.

OTHERS PRESENT

Secretary of State (for part of meeting)
Secretary of Defense
Mr. Allen Dulles
Secretary of Air Force
General Twining
Lt. General Cabell
Lt. General Putt
Colonel Goodpaster

Authorization was sought from the President to go ahead on a program to produce thirty special high performance aircraft at a cost of about $35 million. The President approved this action. Mr. Allen Dulles indicated that his organization could not finance this whole sum without drawing attention to it, and it was agreed that Defense would seek to carry a substantial part of the financing.

---

[1] Source: Eisenhower Library, Whitman File, Ann Whitman Diary. Top Secret. Drafted by Goodpaster on November 24.

The Secretary of Defense sought the President's agreement to taking one last look at the type of operations planned when the aircraft are available. The President indicated agreement.

To a question by the President, the Secretary of State indicated that difficulties might arise out of these operations, but that "we could live through them."

In summary, the President directed those present to go ahead and get the equipment, but before initiating operations to come in for one last look at the plans.

G.

200. Director of Central Intelligence Directive No. 4/3[1]

Washington, December 14, 1954.

COMPREHENSIVE NATIONAL INTELLIGENCE OBJECTIVES

1. Pursuant to National Security Council Intelligence Directive No. 4,[2] paragraph 1, the following comprehensive national intelligence objectives, generally applicable to all foreign countries and areas, are hereby established:

a. Basic descriptive data as outlined in NIS Standard Instructions.

b. Social, economic, and political stability and trends of development; susceptibility to foreign influence or coercion; vulnerability to subversion.

c. Military capabilities and vulnerabilities, offensive and defensive, including economic, scientific and technical, and psychological factors.

---

[1] Source: National Archives, RG 59, S/P–NSC Files: Lot 62 D 1, NSC Intelligence Directives. Secret. DCID 4/3 and DCID 4/4 (Document 201) were attached to a single cover page, which indicated that both had been prepared by the Director of Central Intelligence in collaboration with members of the Intelligence Advisory Committee pursuant to National Security Council Intelligence Directive No. 4, and that they were approved on December 14.

[2] Text in *Foreign Relations,* 1945–1950, Emergence of the Intelligence Establishment, Document 422.

d. Capabilities to influence, coerce, or subvert other governments and peoples; capabilities for espionage, sabotage, and other clandestine operations in other countries.

e. Foreign policy, including strategic concepts and intentions; international alignment, with particular reference to alignment with or against the US or the USSR; disposition and intention to interfere in the internal affairs of other states; preparation for and intention to resort to armed action against other states.

2. Priority national intelligence objectives, with reference to specific countries and subjects, will be set forth in a separate DCID.

3. DCID 4/1 "National Intelligence Objectives," 5 February 1948,[3] is hereby rescinded.

Allen W. Dulles[4]
Director of Central Intelligence

---

[3] Not printed. (Central Intelligence Agency, History Staff, Job 84–B00389R, HS/HC–600, Box 4)

[4] Printed from a copy that bears this typed signature.

---

201. Director of Central Intelligence Directive No. 4/4[1]

Washington, December 14, 1954.

PRIORITY NATIONAL INTELLIGENCE OBJECTIVES

1. Pursuant to National Security Council Intelligence Directive No. 4,[2] paragraph 2, the following list of priority national intelligence objectives is established as a guide for the coordination of intelligence collection and production in response to requirements relating to the formulation and execution of national security policy.

2. By definition, all items in this listing are deemed to be critical national intelligence factors requiring priority attention and effort.

---

[1] Source: National Archives, RG 59, S/P–NSC Files: Lot 62 D 1, Box 2517, NSC Intelligence Directives. Secret. DCID 4/3 and DCID 4/4 were attached to a single cover page; see footnote 1, Document 200.

[2] Text in *Foreign Relations*, 1945–1950, Emergence of the Intelligence Establishment, Document 422.

Distinction is made, however, between three levels of priority within the general priority category. Order of listing within these three groups is a matter of convenience in presentation and has no significance with respect to the relative priority of specific items within the group.

[Omitted here is a graphic depicting priority levels.]

3. In order to afford a stable basis for intelligence planning, this directive is designed to remain valid over an extended period. It will be reviewed semiannually, or on the request of any member of the IAC. It is recognized that urgent interim requirements may arise requiring ad hoc treatment, and that the criteria on which the following priorities are established shall remain under continuing review.

4. DCID 4/2 is hereby rescinded.[3]

I. Highest Priority Objectives:[4] Those of such critical importance as to require a maximum intelligence effort.

a. Soviet over-all politico-military strategy, intentions, and plans, particularly Soviet intentions and plans to initiate hostilities using Soviet or Satellite armed forces.

b. Chinese Communist over-all politico-military strategy, intentions, and plans, particularly Chinese Communist intentions and plans to initiate hostilities using Chinese Communist armed forces.

c. Soviet development, production, disposition, and employment of weapons and other components of weapons systems requisite for nuclear attack on the United States and/or key US overseas installations or for defense of the Soviet Bloc against air attack. Particular reference is made to the development, production, and employment of: (1) nuclear weapons; (2) delivery systems, including aircraft, guided missiles, and related base facilities; and (3) the components of the Soviet air defense systems.

d. Soviet capabilities, plans, and intentions for the clandestine delivery of nuclear, biological, or chemical weapons.

---

[3] DCID 4/2, "Priority List of Critical National Intelligence Objectives," was issued 28 September 1950 and revised 12 June 1952 and 4 August 1953. [Footnote in the original DCID 4/2 is Document 25]

[4] Note: Order of listing within Category I is a matter of convenience in presentation and has no significance with respect to the relative priority of specific items within that category. [Footnote in the original.]

II. High Priority Objectives:[5] Those of such high importance as to warrant an intensive intelligence effort.

The USSR and European Satellites

a. The Soviet estimate of US and allied capabilities and intentions, of US and allied economic and political stability, and of the strength, cohesion, and probable development of the NATO Bloc.

b. Major Soviet international political objectives and courses of action, including economic policies and actions, with particular reference to courses designed to weaken and disrupt the NATO alliance or to foment antagonism between Western and Asian powers.

c. Soviet political strengths and weaknesses: the actual locus of political power in the USSR; actual or potential personal or policy conflicts within the ruling group; Soviet-Satellite relations, with particular reference to the character and degree of Soviet control; the strengths and weaknesses of the Soviet and Satellite apparatus of police control; the extent of actual disaffection and of potential resistance in the Soviet and Satellite populations.

d. The character of the Soviet (including Satellite) economy, with particular reference to its ability to support a major war; the motivation, character, and magnitude of current economic development programs, their implementation, and their effect upon the economic, political, and military strength of the Soviet Bloc.

e. Soviet and Satellite scientific and technical strengths and weaknesses affecting Soviet economic and military capabilities.

f. The strength, composition, disposition, capabilities, and weaknesses of the Soviet and Satellite armed forces, including their strategic and tactical doctrine, their political reliability, their logistical support, and military production and stockpiling.

[29 paragraphs (86½ lines) not declassified]

Allen W. Dulles[6]
Director of Central Intelligence

---

[5] *[2½ lines not declassified.]* [Footnote in the original.]
[6] Printed from a copy that bears this typed signature.

202. Paper by James Q. Reber of the Planning and Coordination Staff of the Central Intelligence Agency[1]

Washington, December 23, 1954.

INTELLIGENCE INFORMATION COLLECTION PROGRAM AND
THE COORDINATION OF REQUIREMENTS

1. Coordination of collection requirements which are responsive to the intelligence production programs of the IAC and its member agencies is fundamental to obtain the maximum benefit from the collection activities of the Government. A number of these production programs have been fairly defined. They include: the NIS (now in its eighth year), National Intelligence Estimates with its annual program and postmortem procedures, research in economic, scientific and technical intelligence, and the Watch Committee and the National Indications Center. The recently approved Priority National Intelligence Objectives (DCID–4/4)[2] are intended to provide more discriminating guidance than heretofore to these production programs, from which, in the main, requirements for collection stem directly rather than from the DCID–4/4.

2. Because of the size and number of the research elements in the intelligence community and their remoteness from collection activities, the function of collection requirements is the vital link which warrants constant and careful attention in order to assure that collection activities are supporting, without duplication or other needless collection, the priority production programs.

3. It is believed that a first step in providing such attention is to bring together in one place the essential, factual material on what collection mechanisms exist and how requirements are today levied and coordinated. The attached paper purports to be an initial, though admittedly incomplete, statement of such.

4. This paper has been prepared through the cooperation of officers within CIA who are close to and have some responsibility for matters described herein. As it may be amended and improved, it might serve several purposes:

(a) The Director and the IAC might use it in budget presentations to inform the Bureau of the Budget of this segment of intelligence activities

---

[1] Source: National Archives, RG 59, INR Files: Lot 58 D 776, Collection and Dissemination. Secret.

[2] Document 201.

(b) It might serve as a bench mark established at this time and place which would later serve as a point of reference and measurement of our program in the future

(c) It might acquaint any reader with some of the problems and activities involved in the coordination of collection requirements and in ways not previously possible, thus serving as an educational paper

(d) Insofar as it is complete and authorative, it should serve as a base for those who have the responsibility for seeking to effect improvements in directing the collection of intelligence information toward the most useful purposes.

5. Facts about big bureaucracy with its many people and many procedures are difficult to come by. Accordingly suggestions from the readers of this document as to how it can be made more accurate and useful would be appreciated.

6. It has been recommended to the Director by the Board of National Estimates in connection with its proposed review of DCID–4/2 (National Intelligence Objectives)[3] that the Director initiate a review of the coordination of collection requirements. Such a review would necessarily require among other things an understanding of the way in which the collection mechanisms themselves are administered, their capabilities and their relations with producers as well as requirements officers. While a general review, such as proposed, is appealing it should also be kept in mind that there are continual efforts directed toward improvement in specific areas. For example, as a means of effecting improvement in the handling of defector exploitation for intelligence purposes the IAC at its meeting of 20 December 1954 instituted certain new arrangements. Of course, a general review and special attention to specific collection problems could go forward hand in hand.

James Q. Reber[4]

---

[3] Document 25.
[4] Printed from a copy that bears this typed signature.

Attachment

Paper Prepared in the Central Intelligence Agency[5]

Washington, December 23, 1954.

INTELLIGENCE INFORMATION COLLECTION PROGRAM AND
THE COORDINATION OF REQUIREMENTS

1. *The Foreign Service of the United States:* Instructions to the Foreign Service for collection are in the last analysis the responsibility of the Assistant Secretaries of the respective bureaus in the Department of State. Except for agricultural reporting which is now administered by law directly[6] by the Department of Agriculture, the Department of State must provide reporting of interest to the U.S. Government with its many non-intelligence interests as well as to the IAC Community. It must also be recalled that this same Foreign Service has other major responsibilities, namely, representation to foreign governments and protection of U.S. interests abroad. The desk officers in each political bureau depend to a considerable extent upon the intelligence organization of the Department of State for the preparation and coordination of requirements for intelligence reporting.

Increased attention to the collection of information abroad for the use of intelligence is reflected in the new chapter (900) of the Foreign Service Manual which deals with this subject. In the economic field the "R" Area in the Department of State cooperates with the Division of Foreign Service Reporting to insure that insofar as possible available resources of the Foreign Service are not requested to collect information available in Washington and that requirements relevant to national security are given precedence over those for less vital functions of the Government (such as development of information about possible markets for U.S. products abroad). State "R" has invited the assistance of ORR and the Economic Intelligence Committee (EIC) to assist in the preparation of guides for economic reporting. The intelligence organ-

---

[5] Secret. There is no drafting information on the paper.

[6] There are current negotiations between the Departments of State and Agriculture which have resulted in a temporary agreement for the continuance of agricultural reporting on the Soviet Bloc by State. These talks are continuing with regard to State's assistance to Agriculture for agricultural reporting on the Free World (many areas not covered by AAs [Agricultural Attachés] can be covered in part by State). [Footnote in the original.]

ization in State has also invited CIA/OCI to participate in the preparation of instructions for political reporting.

It should also be borne in mind that the "R" Area itself is an important originator of requirements for reporting in the political, cultural and social field and that while it has access to other collection mechanisms, the Foreign Service is a prime collector of information in the area of intelligence assigned to State. The establishment of a national intelligence estimating program and the demand on the "R" Area of State for contributions thereto represent an important influence in guiding the "R" Area to requisition information on gaps of fundamental importance. There are comparable effects upon reporting by virtue of the "R" Area's participation in the Watch process, as well as in the NIS production.

2. *Peripheral Reporting Program:* This program was established as a separate collection device within the Foreign Service under the Chiefs of Mission. Its purpose is to obtain information on the Soviet Bloc countries by the assignment of competent officers to certain posts contiguous to the Soviet Bloc where the potential data on that area is substantial. This was necessary as a means of supplementing the reporting from missions behind the Iron Curtain area where many local restrictions are imposed on our staffs. At present, peripheral reporting units are located in Frankfurt, Vienna, Paris, Tel Aviv and Istanbul. In Frankfurt the peripheral reporting unit prepares comprehensive studies in the political, cultural, sociological and economical fields based on information collected on the USSR; these reports are called SPONGE reports.

The peripheral reporting officers make use of a variety of sources including defectors, escapees, refugees, travelers and officials of other governments located in the same areas as the peripheral units. The original emphasis was upon collection from arrivals from behind the Iron Curtain. Peripheral officers are now encouraged to develop other sources among the indigenous travelers to and from the Soviet Bloc and staffs of other government located in the same countries as the peripheral reporting unit. While the peripheral units are encouraged to develop sources as indicated above, the main sources at present are as follows:

> Frankfurt (defectors)
> Vienna (refugees)
> Paris (émigrés and groups of émigrés)
> Tel Aviv (refugees and recent émigrés from Iron Curtain countries)
> Istanbul (émigrés and a few arrivals from Bulgaria)

3. *Foreign Map Procurement:* The requirements of all the mapping agencies of the U.S. Government for foreign maps are coordinated by CIA and the Interagency Map Procurement Coordinating Committee

on which sit the representatives of the mapping agencies. The MPC is chaired by the Chief of the Map Library Division, CIA/ORR, who also serves as the Special Assistant to the Director, Office of Libraries and Intelligence Acquisition, Department of State (also designated informally, "Special Assistant for Maps"). Under the direction of the Special Assistant for Maps, foreign maps are procured through the Department of State and Foreign Service. Although the function of overt collection of maps abroad rests with the Department of State, the geographic research function has been transferred from State to CIA; hence, the CIA direction of a State collection program. Four map procurement officers are stationed in the field and part-time map procurement activity is assigned to other foreign service officers stationed in other areas. Salaries and administrative support of these field officers are the responsibility of State and during recent budget reductions two map procurement officers were dropped despite the efforts of CIA to persuade the Department of State to retain them.

The above program for the collection of foreign maps has been in existence seven years. Procurement has been routinized by the establishment of informal exchange agreements (140) with certain countries under which new map production is received in Washington through the Foreign Service posts.

Requirements of CIA and Department of Defense components for maps, air photography and other map information which is available from U.S. firms engaged overseas in mapping and intelligence photography are prepared in the Map Library Division, ORR/CIA for procurement by CIA/OO/C.

Frequently, an approaching assignment for production of an NIS Chapter IX (Map and Chart Approval) on a given area has provided a stimulus for procurement of foreign maps on that area in time for use in Washington in producing the Chapter. In other cases foreign map requirements are in direct response to individual agency research projects or to recognized gaps in foreign map coverage.

The coordinated interagency map procurement program does not conflict with the map exchange agreements between the mapping components of Defense and the opposite agencies in foreign countries. Some of these agreements pertain to joint mapping programs with other NATO countries. Agreements between the Army Map Service and the NATO countries' mapping agencies provide the bulk of topographical maps on NATO countries (and their colonies).

4. *Foreign Publications Procurement* is coordinated by the DCI in pursuance of the responsibility placed upon him in NSCID–16.[7] An in-

---

[7] Document 258.

teragency committee has been established which seeks to identify those areas in which needed publications may be obtained through the cooperative action of agencies who have collecting capabilities as well as to be alert to new means of procurement. Overt publications procurement in the field is divided among military attachés, collection arms of military commands overseas, and personnel of the Foreign Service. The attachés and overseas commands concentrate on publications required by their parent organizations, while Foreign Service personnel fill the requirements of the Department of State, CIA and about 20 other Government agencies such as the Library of Congress and the Department of Agriculture. For this purpose the Foreign Service maintains at the present time six full-time Publications Procurement Officers (in Moscow, Paris, Berlin, New Delhi, Tokyo, and Hong Kong) and assigns the function on a part-time basis to an officer in other important posts. The degree of coordination and cooperation among service attachés and Foreign Service officers varies greatly from post to post. The Foreign Branch of the CIA Library, serving for this purpose as an operating arm of the Division of Acquisition and Distribution of the Department of State, in the last two years since its establishment, has attempted to improve procurement by formulating more detailed guidance for publications procurement officers, by providing them with evaluation on their efforts, and by working closely with those personnel in the defense departments engaged in preparing collection requirements for the service attachés in order that the most effective field procurement channel may be utilized in any given procurement situation. When publications are not available through overt channels, arrangements are made whenever possible to obtain the materials through clandestine collection by CIA. As a result of the USIA Survey, the NSCID–16 subcommittee on Procurement will explore with USIA the extent to which their library centers abroad can assist in procurement.

   5. *Military Attachés:* The attachés of the military services are guided by the "Essential Elements of Information" published in one form or another under the direction of the Chiefs of Intelligence in G–2, ONI and AFOIN. The EEI have been developed painstakingly and represent the comprehensive needs of the individual services. Within this general framework specific or ad hoc requirements are levied upon the attachés as current needs arise or, more systematically, as required to meet the needs of each service and the JIC in its service to the JCS, in response to the national intelligence estimating program for military contributions and in response to both the original and maintenance production of NIS sections assigned to the military.

   6. *General Comment With Regard to 1 to 5 above:* The foregoing is in accordance with the allocation of responsibility for overt collection

abroad as outlined in NSCID–2.[8] Each agency is free to collect economic and scientific and technical intelligence information in accordance with its needs. Under NSCID–2 injunction, information, by whomever collected, shall immediately be transmitted to the agency most concerned as well as made available to all other interested agencies. These facilities are to be utilized so as to avoid unproductive duplication and uncoordinated overlap; "within budgetary limitations" they are to insure that "full flow of intelligence information which is the major need of all departments and agencies for the accomplishment of their respective missions". In the field, the senior U.S. representative in each foreign area is responsible for the coordination of "all normal collection activities in his area". The manner in which this is done will vary from post to post, both in respect to the personalities involved and the size and importance of the mission. In March 1954 the Department of State sent a special instruction to all Chiefs of Mission reiterating the coordinating role of mission chiefs under NSCID–2 and urging maximum use of all available personnel including military attachés. At the same time, the Army, Navy and Air Force dispatched similar messages to all attachés, urging maximum cooperation with mission chiefs in developing coordinated collection programs.

7. *Regular Collection Offices:* Each intelligence agency maintains a collection office to coordinate requirements from its research offices, assist their research offices in determining the availability of the information in Washington (either in its own agency or another agency), levy requirements on collectors (either its own collection arm or those of other agencies) and disseminate the information collected against requirements.

CIA/OCD/LD's liaison officers, initially working through cleared liaison authorities in other (non-IAC) government agencies, ferret through those "non intelligence" government agencies known or believed to have (or capable of obtaining) foreign intelligence. CIA/OCD/LD collects such intelligence either against specific requests or spontaneously.

CIA/OCD/LD administers a debriefing program, making available to CIA the knowledge of government officials who have been abroad. The debriefing program is not limited as to area or subject but is, of course, limited only by the knowledge of the returned officials.

8. *Collection of Foreign Intelligence Within The United States from Nongovernmental sources:* On a selective basis is the responsibility of CIA

---

[8] For text, see *Foreign Relations*, 1945–1950, Emergence of the Intelligence Establishment, Document 425.

(OO/C) as a service of common concern (NSCID–7).[9] Guidance in this selection is provided by the continuing requirements statements of the research elements of CIA and the other IAC agencies, in addition to consumer evaluations of reports and supplemented by continuous liaison to discuss specific needs and individual sources.

To assure that this service is of maximum value to consumers, conferences are being scheduled at the working level in all of the member agencies. In addition, four specific interagency arrangements are either completed or well on the way to completion:

(a) Three specialized ATIC officers have been placed in domestic field offices to guide and actually engage in the collection of technical information. The assignment of a fourth officer, trained in air electronics, is expected shortly.

(b) A similar arrangement has been worked out through G–2 for the assignment of two Signal Corps Intelligence officers to domestic field offices in an effort to increase the quantity and quality of telecommunications-intelligence collection. One of these officers is already being processed.

(c) Arrangements have been completed with the Director of Intelligence of the Air Force and with the Air Research and Development Command to facilitate the exploitation of civilian employees at the various ARDC centers for intelligence information not otherwise available to the member agencies.

(d) Tentative arrangements have been concluded with G–2 for a similar program to be established in the near future with the seven Army Technical Services.

A fifth specific effort to produce more effective and coordinated intelligence collection consisted of a program to analyze critically all requirements which have been received by Contact Division from the producing elements of CIA and the other IAC agencies, and to codify in readily usable form all basic requirements currently outstanding.

9. *Radio Monitoring:* Under NSCID–6[10] a central radio monitoring service (CIA/FBID) is established and the monitoring of foreign propaganda and press broadcasts for the collection of intelligence information by other federal agencies is specifically precluded.

Since radio monitoring does not lend itself to exploitation for specific information on specific subjects, guides or "targets" are provided by IAC offices each week. These are requests for translation of what is said by area transmitters in comment on, reaction to, or mention of specific subjects, events or people. Additionally, a list of long-range or

---

[9] Ibid., Document 427.
[10] Ibid., Document 424.

standing requirements stated in broad terms is provided quarterly. Both target lists are distributed to field installations in order that the desired information may be selected from the great volume of monitored radio broadcasting.

Specific collection requests, especially on the technical aspects of radio monitoring, but sometimes on the content of radio broadcasts, are levied on CIA/FBID either formally by the requester through CIA/OCD, or informally to the Liaison Officer, FBID.

Additional guidance is obtained from study of intelligence deficiencies and the NIS and NIE programs. Some requirements are self-evident, e.g., radio monitoring coverage of Central Asia provides unique information on an area of the world not otherwise covered to any appreciable extent by intelligence collection activities. Before investing funds and personnel in meeting a requirement such as this, FBID solicits the IAC agencies to determine their interest.

10. *The Collection and Exploitation of Soviet Materials for Intelligence Purposes* is carried out under two programs which are coordinated. On the one hand the military has established a committee known as the Joint Technical Intelligence Subcommittee (JTIS) with the responsibility for coordinating military requirements for Soviet materials, relaying them to field components with a capability for collection and coordination of the exploitation of Soviet material. Civilian requirements (those of CIA, State and AEC) are coordinated by a "Sovmat Staff" in CIA/OO which levies requirements against not only foreign service and military collection units but also, when appropriate, against CIA's clandestine collection service. Through the participation of the Chief of the Sovmat Staff as an Advisor to the Chairman of JTIS coordination between these two programs is provided.

11. *The Travel Folder Program* is designed to obtain the maximum information from within the Soviet Orbit by direct personal observations on the part of American officials stationed in U.S. Missions behind the Iron Curtain. Approved by the IAC, the program is supervised by CIA in consultation with the Economic Intelligence Committee. The program consists of the coordination of IAC requirements (mainly economic, scientific, technical, and military), briefing and debriefing of travelers, the preparation of comprehensive reports of their observations, [3½ lines not declassified].

12. *Research Units Abroad* sponsored by CIA (strategic divisions) attempt to bring to the field more intimately the kind of guidance which would make field collection more meaningful in terms of headquarters programs. [5 lines not declassified]

13. *Collection of U.S. Files Abroad* was undertaken by CIA in 1951. A team microfilmed documents containing intelligence information in the files of the U.S. agencies all over Europe, in anticipation of the pos-

sible overruning of Europe by Russia and the consequent loss of the information in such documents. In general, such microfilming was not conducted in response to specific requirements and was mainly composed of industrial data regarding West European countries.

The entire collection of some 2,000 reels of film is available in the CIA Industrial Register. Few of the files microfilmed have been indexed, but the team identified them in terms of subject matter whenever possible and in terms of source or area when subject matter information was not available. Selected portions of the collection have been incorporated into IR files, and a more complete index is being prepared on a low priority basis.

No direct requirements are levied against the file. The IR analysts use this information, among other sources in their files, when incoming requirements indicate its utility, as do other research analysts when using IR files.

14. *Captured Enemy Documents:* Plans have been established for coordination in the exploitation of captured enemy documents in wartime under a joint military agency known as the Armed Services Documents Intelligence Center. Civilian agencies requirements will be satisfied in this program by virtue of a CIA representative serving as an Assistant Director in the Center who coordinates the requirements of CIA, State and AEC.

15. *The National Security Agency* is guided in its collection activities through a USCIB subcommittee (Intelligence Committee) whose function includes requirements coordination. This subcommittee, composed of the intelligence agencies representatives, operates under a rather highly sophisticated system of identifying priorities.

16. *In the Field of Indications* responsibility to improve the coordination of collection is set forth in DCID–1/2.[11] The Watch Committee is supposed to "develop and operate on a current and continuing basis the Watch Committee Intelligence Plan for systematizing, energizing and coordinating through the appropriate channels the world-wide collection by U.S. agencies of information and intelligence pertinent to the Watch Committee mission."

17. [*1 paragraph (24 lines) not declassified*]

18. *External Research:* Members of the intelligence community, as well as several other Government agencies, sponsor external research projects on foreign areas, thus providing an additional source of foreign intelligence. This research is performed by Government agencies and private institutions, each of them using whatever sources are available to them. Government agencies, contracting for private research on

---

[11] Document 179.

foreign areas, frequently supply such contractors with intelligence information which is, of course, supplemented by the contractors' own resources. Government agencies conducting research on behalf of other Government agencies are exploited by informal interagency contact and by such regular collection offices as CIA/OCD.

External research on foreign areas, although performed in response to departmental needs, is subject to certain coordination efforts by the intelligence community. These efforts are:

a. A clearing house for information provided by the External Research Staff, Department of State (ERS), a joint operation of State, CIA and Defense;

b. Informal monthly discussions among external research administrators of various agencies to exchange information on what they are doing and what needs to be done;

c. An Advisory Panel on Research in Special Operations appointed by the Assistant Secretary of Defense for Research and Development consisting of outside specialists to provide guidance to the Department of Defense. USIA, CIA, State, FOA and OCB are represented on the Panel by associate members; and

d. On 11 December 1954 the DCI proposed to USIA, State, Defense, OCB and FOA that agencies with intelligence needs in the propaganda and psychological warfare and foreign information fields cooperate in the development of a government-wide program of external research in support of such activities. Each agency would retain complete responsibility for its departmental external research program but would benefit by coordination of its program with other agencies having related missions.

19. *ELINT:* Collection of information by the detection, reception and recording of non-communication electronic radiations is carried on by the three services and by CIA/DDP. Analysis of material which has been collected is conducted separately by the Air Force and jointly by Army and Navy through the Army-Navy Electronic Evaluation Group, (NAEEG). There is limited and spasmodic coordination in the field with respect to detection, reception and recording of ELINT collection. There is little or no coordination between the groups working on the analysis of collected material. Present ELINT collection activities carried on by the services are primarily directed toward OB type information such as the identification and location of radio stations, long-range navigation systems and so forth. Insofar as it has developed, the CIA/DDP collection effort is directed toward the detection of new and unusual electronic emanations.

20. *Interrogations* of returning POWs, refugees and defectors have been the subject of various activities by the IAC agencies—[*19 lines not declassified*].

[*1 paragraph (3 lines) not declassified*]

Coordination of the U.S. Defector Program at the Washington level is accomplished by the Interagency Defector Committee (IDC). [*6½ lines not declassified*]

The Armed Services have established a center (Armed Services Prisoner Interrogation Center) to coordinate the exploitation of POWs. CIA, State and AEC's interests are represented by an Assistant Director at the Center. Although its mission is interrogation of captured prisoners, it participated in the interrogation of American POWs who had been held and then released by the Chinese.

21. *Clandestine Collection Activities of the U.S. Government* include CIA/FI, which also has access to any intelligence products of clandestine operations, the clandestine services of the three military agencies and AFOAT. The coordination of requirements for clandestine collection by CIA has been effected through the establishment of the Interagency Priorities Committee for Clandestine Collection. Further development in the efficient utilization of all sources of the Government for clandestine collection is being developed through the proposal for agreed activities under NSCID–5[12] now under negotiation between the Director and the intelligence chiefs of the military agencies. The coordination of information collected by AFOAT and all other sources is assured, insofar as possible, under DCID 11/1.[13] In the main, as far as the direction of collection is concerned, the effect of this would be to alert AFOAT in the event that information regarding an atomic explosion by the Russians were detected by one of the services other than AFOAT in order that it could promptly institute collection activity.

22. *Press Monitoring* is done by some of the posts of the Foreign Service in order to provide themselves with current press opinion. This press monitoring activity varies from post to post; in Latin America only one post (Rio de Janeiro), in Europe 19 posts, in Far East 11 posts and in Near East and Africa 22 posts conduct press monitoring.

Current monitoring of the press of our two major enemies, USSR and Red China, is performed in Moscow and Hong Kong respectively. In Moscow there is the Joint Press Reading Service (JPRS), [*less than 1 line not declassified*]. The JPRS reviews and abstracts from the major newspapers and periodicals of the USSR and issues two translated

---

[12] For NSCID No. 5, December 12, 1947, see *Foreign Relations, 1945–1950, Emergence of the Intelligence Establishment*, Document 423. For the revision of August 28, 1951, see Document 255.

[13] DCID 11/1, December 7, 1954, "Control of Information Regarding Foreign Nuclear Explosions," is in Central Intelligence Agency, History Staff, Job 84–B00389R, Box 4, Folder: HS/HC–600.

series, Section A covers foreign affairs and Section B domestic news. In addition, abstracts of leading periodicals are prepared separately. Dissemination is made by State within the Government and to a few private institutions. The Hong Kong Press Monitoring Service has access to (a) [2 lines not declassified] as well as (b) to U.S. procured Chinese mainland publications. The HKPMS issues three press summaries titles: Review of the Hong Kong Press (issued almost daily covering the main articles of the Hong Kong press), Summary of the Chinese Mainland Press (produced on the average of three or four issues per week covering the main topics of the Chinese language press and dividing the topics in catagories of subject interest), and Current Background (a study of various topics of political, economic and sociological significance based on press articles extending over an indefinite period of time). Wide dissemination of these press summaries is given within the U.S. Government and to 25 private academic institutions or individuals.

In addition to the press summaries prepared by embassy employees (whether Foreign Service or USIA, etc.) the missions frequently obtain press summaries from other governments. In approximately 15 posts, press summaries of the British are obtained while to a much lesser extent, press summaries prepared by the French are received. In nine posts, press summaries prepared by the host government are received and in one post (Tehran) a press summary prepared by the USSR is received. Dissemination of press summaries back to Washington and within the Government varies from post to post. A review of the press monitoring activities was prepared by State/IAD and distributed within the Government for the information of the users.

No headquarters requirements are levied for overseas press monitoring and consequently no coordination is required.

23. *Photographic Intelligence Collection and Requirements:* Intelligence photography is collected from the air, on the ground, or as records from radarscope presentations. The U.S. Air Force and U.S. Navy operating squadrons and attachés collect approximately 75% and 15% respectively with the rest attributable to U.S. Army, CIA, and other miscellaneous sources. Most of the aerial photography collected by the Army for the Army Map Service is purchased from commercial organizations. CIA concentrates its effort toward the collection of aerial photos from certain firms and foreign governments.

Aerial and ground photographs are required by the intelligence analysts and mapping agencies throughout the IAC to corroborate other intelligence data and fill existing gaps in intelligence. They are essential to the production and maintenance of accurate large-scale topographic maps and the preparation of strategic and tactical target programs (Air Force) now in progress. CIA intelligence analysts require photographic intelligence in support of intelligence objectives, which may be geographic, economic, scientific, or military in nature and to support clandestine operations.

While procedures exist in each agency for the coordination of its photographic requirements, there has been established, on the invitation of AFOIN in 1948, an Interagency Graphics Research Coordinating Group. Orginally, the group was composed of the three services; it was joined by CIA in 1951. This Group, meeting monthly, exchanges information regarding photo requirements, location of desired photography, overseas commercial mapping activities and related matters. Highly classified and highest priority aerial photographic requirements are reviewed and coordinated by JCS Plans and Policy with final concurrence of State, Military and CIA.

---

203. Paper Prepared by a Working Group of the Operations Coordinating Board[1]

Washington, January 5, 1955.

ANALYSIS OF THE SITUATION WITH RESPECT TO POSSIBLE DETACHMENT OF A MAJOR EUROPEAN SOVIET SATELLITE

Summary

1. Acting on the suggestion of the Board Assistants, the OCB, at its meeting of August 25, 1954,[2] requested the Working Group to review additional possible actions to implement NSC 174,[3] particularly a major coordinated effort by appropriate agencies designed to detach one of the important European satellites from the Soviet bloc. The Working Group was requested to submit a preliminary staff analysis to the Board which would point up the policy and strategic implications and feasibility factors that would be involved in such an effort.

---

[1] Source: National Archives, RG 59, S/S–OCB Files: Lot 61 D 385, USSR and Satellites Documents 1953–56. Top Secret. A January 11 covering memorandum from Elmer B. Staats, Executive Officer of the Operations Coordinating Board, to the Operations Coordinating Board, noted that at its January 5 meeting the Board approved the recommendations in the paper. No further record of this meeting has been found.

[2] See Document 190 and footnote 1 thereto.

[3] See footnote 2, Document 190.

At their meeting of August 13, 1954,[4] the Board Assistants agreed that Albania should not be considered as an "important" satellite for the purposes of this study.

2. The Working Group first reviewed existing intelligence estimates of the political situation concerning all of the Eastern European satellites. Then a study was made of the methods that might be used to detach a satellite. U.S. capabilities for such action were reviewed and conclusions flowing from the analysis were drawn. Studies on the vulnerabilities of East Germany and Czechoslovakia were prepared especially for this review.

3. The analysis indicates that the instrumentalities of Soviet dominion in the political, economic and cultural fields, backed by military force, continue to be effective in maintaining control over the satellites. The progressive sovietization of the political, social and economic structure of the satellites, the orientation of the local economies towards the East and the concentrated effort at indoctrination of the rising generation have served further to support Moscow's control over the satellite areas. The Soviet orbit nevertheless has vulnerabilities which are susceptible to exploitation by the United States.

4. Without attempting to be categorical, it is the opinion of the Working Group that soft treatment cannot be expected to effect the basic changes in the nature of communist regimes which would conform to U.S. objectives; and that therefore, except when relaxations are calculated to obtain carefully defined limited objectives within a short time span or to protect the people against the regime under special circumstances of internal tension, pressures should be increased against any part of the Soviet orbit where suitable opportunities appear. The importance of this subject justifies study of appropriate implementing actions consistent with U.S. policy as it develops.

Recommendation

It is recommended that the Board concur in the following:

a. At present, given the strength of the Soviet position, no major Soviet satellite presents vulnerabilities of such extent that their exploitation can be expected to result in its detachment from the Soviet bloc.

b. U.S. capabilities under present conditions are not sufficient to accomplish the detachment of any major Soviet satellite by means short of war.

c. Unless the power balance between the United States and the Soviet Union changes drastically in our favor, there is little likelihood

---

[4] No record of this meeting has been found.

of detaching a major satellite at any time without grave risk of war except by negotiation. The only satellite which now lends itself to possible detachment by this means is East Germany. If an effort against this satellite were to be undertaken with any hope of success it would require a concentration of political, economic and psychological measures directed to this end. A study of the requirements of such a concentrated effort should now be undertaken with East Germany as a target in order that advantage may be taken of any future development making possible the unification of Germany by negotiation on terms acceptable to the U.S.

[Omitted here are 36 pages of analysis supporting the summary.]

---

204. Director of Central Intelligence Directive No. 5/1[1]

Washington, January 11, 1955.

COORDINATION OF THE FOREIGN CLANDESTINE
COLLECTION ACTIVITIES OF THE ARMED SERVICES WITH
THOSE OF THE CENTRAL INTELLIGENCE AGENCY

Pursuant to the provisions of the National Security Act of 1947, as amended,[2] and for the purpose of defining under NSCID No. 5,[3] those clandestine collection activities which the Armed Services conduct in

---

[1] Source: National Archives, RG 59, S/P–NSC Files: Lot 62 D 1, NSC Intelligence Directives. Secret. On January 11, NSC Executive Secretary Lay circulated this directive by memorandum to the National Security Council and noted that the Director of Central Intelligence would make reference to it and other directives in his quarterly oral report at the January 13 NSC meeting. (Ibid.) In a January 12 memorandum to the Secretary of State, Armstrong also transmitted this directive and described it as follows: "Specifically, DCID 5/1, attached, defines the respective areas of responsibility of CIA and the armed services in the field of clandestine intelligence. As such it represents a long sought agreement between Defense and CIA in this very sensitive, very complex, but very important field. Neither the NSC nor DCI Intelligence Directive provides for coordination with the Department on clandestine intelligence activities which bear upon foreign policy, although coordination of this kind is specifically provided in directives pertaining to covert [psychological] Operations. *I do not, however, recommend that any revision be made at this time.*" (Ibid., S/S–NSC Files: Lot 66 D 95, National Intelligence Objectives) Brackets and emphasis in the original.

[2] Pursuant to P.L. 216 of August 10, 1949, National Security Act amendments of 1949, the Department of Defense was established to coordinate and direct the U.S. Army, Navy, and Air Force. (63 Stat. 578)

[3] Document 255.

order to carry out their responsibilities and assigned missions, and to protect the security of their foreign based military commands or installations, and for the purpose of coordinating such activities with those of the Central Intelligence Agency (except in areas where United States armed forces are engaged in active combat operations, in which event the provisions of paragraph 10 of NSCID #5 shall be deemed applicable), the following is established:

1. Where United States military commands or installation are located outside of the United States and its possessions, the commanders thereof may conduct such foreign clandestine collection activities as they deem essential to the execution of their assigned missions, in accordance with the principles and procedures set forth hereinafter.

2. Review and coordination of plans for the clandestine collection activities of the Armed Services and plans of the Central Intelligence Agency for the clandestine collection of information of interest to the Armed Services will be accomplished with each service to the extent practicable at the national level.

3. In order to assure field coordination of clandestine collection activities, the designated representatives of the military commanders concerned and of the Director of Central Intelligence will review together all such activities of those military commanders, as well as the operational plans and procedures therefor. They will also review together those clandestine collection activities of the Central Intelligence Agency which are undertaken in direct support of the military commanders concerned. Coordination may involve the creation and utilization of common support facilities, the exchange of operational information, and the establishment of informal committees.[4]

4. In the event that the designated representative of the Director of Central Intelligence considers an activity, plan or agent to be potentially harmful to the over-all clandestine effort, the proposed action will not be carried out except as provided in paragraph 5 below, without prior approval resulting from agreement between the appropriate military service intelligence chief and the Director of Central Intelligence.

5. In those instances when the military commander considers the action proposed in paragraph 4 above to be essential to the immediate conduct of his mission or critical to the security of his forces, and time does not permit referral of the issue to Washington, the action may proceed on the responsibility of the military commander, pending resolution in Washington. The military commander will inform the designated representative of the Director of Central Intelligence as to his action.[5]

---

[4] Upon the issuance of this Directive, a systematic review and adjustment, where necessary, of ongoing operations will be made in the field in conformity with the provisions of this Directive. [Footnote in the original.]

[5] Printed from an unsigned copy.

205. Memorandum From the National Security Council
Representative on Internal Security (Coyne) to the President's
Special Assistant for National Security Affairs (Cutler) and the
Executive Secretary of the National Security Council (Lay)[1]

Washington, February 8, 1955.

RE

CIA–The Doolittle Report on CIA's Covert Activities

Last Friday night[2] at the invitation of Allen Dulles, General Doolittle, Bill Franke and I dined with Mr. Dulles and several of his key officials (Messrs. Cabell, Kirkpatrick, Wisner, White, Bissell, Helms, Balmer, Scott, Angleton and Roosevelt). Following the dinner Mr. Dulles and his associates gave us a detailed fill-in on the progress made thus far by CIA in its efforts to implement the recommendations of the Doolittle Report.[3] Highlights of their oral progress report follow.

1. *NSCID #5:*[4] Agreement has been reached between CIA and the military services with respect to the conduct of certain espionage and counterespionage operations overseas. (I think this will mark a very substantial step forward, if it serves to clarify those areas of "agreed activities" which have been the subject of considerable controversy for several years.)

2. *Operational Security Clearances:* An agreement has been drawn with respect to the security clearance of agent, service and proprietary personnel which is satisfactory to the DD/P and SO areas of the Agency.

3. *Counterespionage:* A highly experienced official has been newly installed as the Chief of this area of the DD/P complex and improved procedures are being put into effect.

4. *Polygraph Program:* The backlog of unpolygraphed personnel has been virtually eliminated.

5. *Cover Problems:* Renewed efforts are underway to cope with the very difficult, practical problem of developing varied covers suitable for CIA's needs on both long-term and short-term bases. Allen Dulles thinks more might be done on this score, including increased use of aliens.

6. *Buildings:* Varied and repeated efforts are being made with little success to improve the present office-housing situation which finds

---

[1] Source: Central Intelligence Agency, Executive Registry, Job 86–B00269R, Box 3, Folder 9. Top Secret. Drafted by Coyne. Coyne forwarded a copy to DCI Dulles under cover of a February 18 memorandum, commenting that the President had seen the memorandum and could be preparing to talk with Dulles about it.

[2] February 4.

[3] Document 192.

[4] For NSCID No. 5 Revised, see Document 256.

CIA, through no fault of its own, located in 34 buildings in the Washington area.

7. *DD/Support:* All normal functions of the Agency, exclusive of DD/I, DD/P, and IG have been combined under the newly created office of the Deputy Director for Support. By this action, personnel, administration, fiscal, communications and related matters are pulled together under one head. Allen Dulles believes—and I agree—that this should have the effect of rendering more coordinated and better support to the various operational segments of the Agency.

8. *Organization of the DD/P Offices:* Steps have been initiated to streamline the DD/P set-up. Allen Dulles and Wisner are pressing to get this done.

9. *Training:* Continuing efforts are being made to improve the training of personnel. Specific programs have been initiated for this purpose.

10. *Projects Review:* A new Review Committee is about to be set up which will continue the complicated task of examining projects with a view to eliminating those which are less essential so that available resources may be allocated to those of greater importance to the Agency's mission.

11. *Long-Range Planning:* Continued emphasis is being afforded this matter and expert scientific and other outside personnel (such as Land and Killian) are being tapped to assure maximum results.

As Mr. Dulles and his assistants briefed us our views were solicited and were quite freely given.

I was impressed, but not at all surprised, at the very constructive approach which Allen Dulles and all of his associates have taken to the Doolittle Report. I am convinced that assiduous efforts are being made by the Agency to profit by such of the recommendations contained therein as may be meritorious. The fact that Allen Dulles would take the time to consult members of an extinct committee is as unusual as it is desirable, and it speaks well of Allen Dulles' continuing efforts to improve the performance of the many important national security responsibilities which devolve upon CIA. (The use of the participants in the Doolittle survey in a continuing, consultative capacity strikes me as being highly desirable in view of the background which they have accumulated concerning the covert operations of CIA. Allen Dulles has in mind consulting with these same people on future occasions.)

I suggest that you give the President a brief oral fill-in on the foregoing when the opportunity presents itself. I suggest also that a word of appreciation from the President to Allen Dulles would be well deserved.

J. Patrick Coyne[5]

---

[5] Printed from a copy that bears this typed signature.

206. Memorandum of Agreement Between the Central Intelligence Agency and the Department of Justice[1]

Washington, February 10, 1955.

Memorandum of Agreement Between the Attorney General of the United States and the Central Intelligence Agency for the Entry of Aliens of Interest to the Central Intelligence Agency Under Special Circumstances

The Central Intelligence Agency has frequent need for the covert temporary entry of aliens into the United States for intelligence and operational purposes within its jurisdiction.

To effectuate entry in such cases, the Central Intelligence Agency will submit each such alien's case in writing to the Commissioner of Immigration and Naturalization with the request to defer inspection of the subject upon arrival and parole to the Central Intelligence Agency under the authority of Section 212(d)(5) of this Immigration and Nationality Act.

In order that the intelligence benefits to be derived from such entries not be outweighed by the dangers, if any, to the internal security of the United States by the presence of such aliens, the Central Intelligence Agency agrees that it will take all necessary steps to establish the bona fides of each prospective entrant prior to submittal to the Immigration and Naturalization Service. It further agrees: (a) That this method of entry will only be utilized where it is strictly in the national interest; (b) That each request will be accompanied by a summary of pertinent background and biographical data with particular emphasis on aspects bearing on internal security and admissibility under the immigration laws, as well as the result of a current check of the FBI files; and (c) That the place, time and manner of arrival will be coordinated with the Service in advance thereof.

Each alien whose entry is authorized by the Commissioner under the foregoing procedure will be paroled for such period of time as may be agreed on by the Central Intelligence Agency and the Service, in no instance to exceed one year. Further extensions of parole, similarly

---

[1] Source: Central Intelligence Agency, Executive Registry, Job 95–G00278R, Box 1. Secret. Dulles also sent a February 10 memorandum to Wisner stressing CIA's responsibility for determining the bona fides of aliens admitted under this agreement and directing him to ensure that all elements of the CIA under his control be informed of the contents of the memorandum. (Ibid.)

limited, may be authorized thereafter on a written statement of need, which will include the results of a current security check.

Upon arrival each alien will execute an agreement acknowledging parole status in a form satisfactory to the Central Intelligence Agency and the Service.

After parole of such aliens, the Central Intelligence Agency will assume responsibility for care, supervision and control of a kind and degree it believes consistent with the internal security needs of the United States during continuance of their parole status. Further, in the case of any alien whose physical custody is not to be maintained or is to be terminated, the Central Intelligence Agency will keep the Service informed as to his activities and whereabouts for the duration of his parole status. In addition, the Central Intelligence Agency will arrange for presentation of each alien for registration pursuant to law at a time and place satisfactory to the Service.

Upon completion of their intelligence or operational purposes in the United States, or if internal security reasons so require, these aliens will be removed therefrom through the arrangements and at the expense of the Central Intelligence Agency, except in these cases in which other disposition is made of a nature satisfactory to the Service. Also, the Central Intelligence Agency will inform the Service sufficiently in advance of each proposed departure as to permit verification thereof if the Service so elects.

In accordance with past practice, the Service will apprise the FBI of the entry and departure or other disposition of these aliens.

The Service will maintain separate and secure files under this agreement.

Herbert Brownell, Jr.
Attorney General

Allen W. Dulles[2]
Director of Central Intelligence

---

[2] Printed from a copy that indicates Brownell and Dulles signed the original.

207. National Security Council Directive[1]

NSC 5511   Washington, February 14, 1955.

DIRECTIVE ON A NET EVALUATION SUBCOMMITTEE

1. Pursuant to the recommendations of the National Security Council in NSC Action No. 1260–b (November 4, 1954) and my subsequent approval thereof,[2] I hereby establish a permanent procedure to provide integrated evaluations of the net capabilities of the USSR, in the event of general war, to inflict direct injury upon the continental U.S. and key U.S. installations overseas, and to provide a continual watch for changes which would significantly alter those net capabilities.

2. Each integrated evaluation should:

a. Cover all types of attack, overt or clandestine;
b. Include consideration of the several courses of action which the USSR is capable of executing; and
c. Take into account the estimated future status of approved military and non-military U.S. defense programs.

3. Each integrated evaluation report should estimate from the practical standpoint the extent and effect of direct injury, including radioactive fall-out, upon the continental U.S. and key U.S. installations overseas, resulting from the most probable types and weights of attacks which the USSR is capable of delivering during approximately

---

[1] Source: National Archives, RG 273, NSC 5511. Top Secret. This directive was circulated by Acting Executive Secretary Gleason to the National Security Council. Copies were sent to the Secretary of the Treasury, Attorney General, Director of the Bureau of the Budget, Chairman of the Atomic Energy Commission, Federal Civil Defense Administrator, Chairman of the Joint Chiefs of Staff, Director of Central Intelligence, Chairman of the Interdepartmental Intelligence Conference, and Chairman of the Interdepartmental Committee on Internal Security, with a note stating that the directive had been approved by the President on the same date. See also *Foreign Relations, 1955–1957*, vol. XIX, pp. 56–57; and for the subcommittee's presentations to the National Security Council in 1955, 1956, and 1957, see ibid., pp. 126–130 and 672–676.

[2] This NSC action reads: "Adopted the recommendation of the Net Capabilities Evaluation Subcommittee that there be established a permanent procedure to insure a continuous evaluation of the general nature of the one made by this Subcommittee, and a continual watch for significant changes; such procedure to provide for a report to the National Security Council at least once a year and, in any event, at whatever time changes become apparent that would significantly alter the net capabilities of the USSR to inflict direct injury upon the continental U.S. and key U.S. installations overseas." President Eisenhower subsequently approved this recommendation "with the understanding that the nature of the permanent procedures, including appropriate staffing, would be subject to future determination by the President." (National Archives, RG 59, S/S–NSC (Miscellaneous) Files: Lot 66 D 95, Records of Action by the National Security Council, Box 102)

the first thirty days of general war, taking into account the effect of U.S. counterattacks during this period. A separate evaluation will be made, assuming each of the following types of initial attack:

a. An initial surprise attack, based on a USSR decision to give first priority to damage to the continental U.S., with no strategic warning but with tactical warning intervals appropriate to target location and type of attack.

b. An initial attack, based on a USSR decision to balance all factors involved in initiating general war; preceded by the amount of strategic warning estimated to be most likely under those circumstances.

c. An initial attack preceded by sufficient strategic warning to place U.S. military and non-military defenses in a condition of full alert and to initiate U.S. retaliatory action.

4. Integrated evaluations should be submitted to the Council on or before October 1 of each year, and relate to the situation on a critical date normally about three years in the future. In addition to these annual integrated evaluations, an integrated evaluation should be submitted to the Council at such times as the Subcommittee feels that a change has become apparent that would significantly alter the net capabilities of the USSR to inflict direct injury upon the continental U.S. and key U.S. installations overseas. The first integrated evaluation should be submitted to the Council on or before October 1, 1955.

5. In order to prepare these integrated evaluations I hereby establish a Net Evaluation Subcommittee of the National Security Council, composed of the Chairman of the Joint Chiefs of Staff, who will serve as Chairman, the Director of the Office of Defense Mobilization, the Federal Civil Defense Administrator, the Director of Central Intelligence, the Chairman of the Interdepartmental Intelligence Conference, and the Chairman of the Interdepartmental Committee on Internal Security. Each Subcommittee member shall be consulted regarding and given ample opportunity to review the following prior to adoption by the Subcommittee: (a) subsidiary terms of reference, (b) the assumptions to be used as a basis for each evaluation report, (c) the complete evaluation report (less background material, which shall be made available only on a "need to know" basis), and (d) any recommendations which the Subcommittee may choose to submit. The Chairman of the Subcommittee, in consultation with the Director, will prepare regulations and establish procedures for the handling of highly sensitive information[3] required in the preparation of an evaluation report so as to safeguard its security on a strict "need to know" basis and to

---

[3] Information such as that relating to war plans, new weapons and equipment, techniques and tactics for their employment, the vulnerability of U.S. defenses, and domestic and foreign intelligence sources and methods. [Footnote in the original.]

preclude the assembly of an unwarranted amount of sensitive information in one document.

6. In all matters relating to AEC activities, it is expected that the Subcommittee shall consult with and obtain the advice and assistance of the Chairman of the Atomic Energy Commission.

7. Subcommittee members are designated to act as individuals, but each shall have the right to consult, at his discretion and under appropriate security safeguards, with his agency or committee prior to Subcommittee action on matters normally within the cognizance of his committee or agency. In subscribing to the reports and recommendations of the Subcommittee the individual members shall not be expected to assume responsibility for technical matters or conclusions not normally within the cognizance of his own parent committee or agency. Reports as submitted to the Council should show, so far as possible by textual footnotes, any dissents by Subcommittee members.

8. The Subcommittee will have a staff, composed of individuals assigned by member agencies, as required by the Director, and under the direction of a Director whom I shall designate. The Director may be compensated through the National Security Council from contributions by the member agencies.

9. The Net Evaluation Subcommittee hereby established is empowered under the terms of this Directive to call on any agency of the Government for relevant information, evaluations, and estimates, subject only to establishment of appropriate security regulations and procedures for the handling of highly sensitive information as provided under paragraph 5, above.

10. Distribution of each completed Subcommittee report will be determined at the time by me.

Dwight D. Eisenhower[4]

---

[4] Printed from a copy that bears this typed signature.

208.   Executive Order No. 10598[1]

Washington, February 28, 1955.

AMENDING EXECUTIVE ORDER NO. 10483, ESTABLISHING THE OPERATIONS COORDINATING BOARD

By virtue of the authority vested in me by the Constitution and statutes, and as President of the United States, it is ordered that subsections (b) and (d) of Section 1 of Executive Order No. 10483 of September 2, 1953 (18 F.R. 5379)[2] be, and they are hereby, amended to read, respectively, as follows:

"(b) The Board shall have as members the following: (1) the Under Secretary of State, who shall represent the Secretary of State and shall be the chairman of the Board, (2) the Deputy Secretary of Defense, who shall represent the Secretary of Defense, (3) the Director of the Foreign Operations Administration, (4) the Director of Central Intelligence, (5) the Director of the United States Information Agency, and (6) one or more representatives of the President to be designated by the President. Each head of agency referred to in items (1) to (5), inclusive, in this Section 1 (b) may provide for an alternate member who shall serve as a member of the Board in lieu of the regular member representing the agency concerned when such regular member is for reasons beyond his control unable to attend any meeting of the Board; and any alternate member shall while serving as such have in all respects the same status as a member of the Board as does the regular member in lieu of whom he serves."

"(d) The Special Assistant to the President for National Security Affairs may attend any meeting of the Board."

Dwight D. Eisenhower[3]

---

[1] Source: Central Intelligence Agency, Executive Registry, Job 86–T00268R, Box 9. Unclassified. Reprinted from *Federal Register* 55–1831, Vol. 20, Number 41, March 1, 1955.

[2] Document 157.

[3] Printed from a copy that bears this typed signature.

209. National Security Council Report[1]

NSC 5509   Washington, March 2, 1955.

STATUS OF UNITED STATES PROGRAMS FOR NATIONAL
SECURITY AS OF DECEMBER 31, 1954

[Omitted here are Parts 1–6.]

Part 7—The Foreign Intelligence Program
(Prepared by the Central Intelligence Agency
and Concurred in by the Intelligence
Advisory Committee)

[Omitted here is the Table of Contents.]

Note: Paragraph 10a of NSC 162/2[2] sets forth the primary missions
of the US intelligence system in support of basic national security requirements. This report presents a statement and evaluation of capabilities to carry out these objectives as of December 31, 1954. Section I
of the report is addressed primarily to the first of these three objectives
(warning of aggression) and Section II to the other two (capabilities
and intentions of foreign countries). Section III deals with problems of
collection related to all three objectives. Problems of covert collection
are considered in Section IV.

I. Warning of Aggression

*"Collecting and analyzing indications of hostile intentions that would
give maximum prior warning of possible aggression or subversion in any area
of the world."* NSC 162/2, para. 10a(1)

1. *National Intelligence Objectives.* Pursuant to NSCID #4[3] the IAC
on December 14, 1954, approved a new statement of "Priority National
Intelligence Objectives" (DCID 4/4)[4] which was prepared in the light
of NSC 162/2. This basic revision of priority national intelligence
objectives, which will be reviewed semi-annually, provides improved

---

[1] Source: National Archives, RG 59, S/S–NSC: Lot 63 D 351, NSC 5509 Memoranda,
Box 85. Top Secret. NSC 5509, prepared by various U.S. Government agencies for the
National Security Council, is described in *Foreign Relations*, 1955–1957, vol. XIX, pp. 58–59
Ellipsis in the original.
[2] Superseded by NSC 5501, approved January 7, 1955. The missions of the US in-
telligence system are reaffirmed in the same words (para. 56). [Footnote in the original.
For NSC 162/2, see ibid., 1952–1954, vol. II, Part 1, pp. 577–597. For NSC 5501, "Basic
National Security Policy," January 7, 1955, see ibid., 1955–1957, vol. XIX, pp. 24–39.]
[3] See ibid., 1945–1950, Emergence of the Intelligence Establishment, Document 422.
[4] Document 201.

guidance to research and collection throughout the intelligence community and focuses attention upon those intelligence area of greatest security concern.

2. *Watch Committee of the IAC.* For the purpose of supporting the mission of the IAC Watch Committee "to provide earliest possible warning to the United States Government of hostile action by the USSR, or its allies, which endangers the security of the United States" there has now been established, under the direction of the committee, an Indications Center. This center is staffed by representatives of the intelligence agencies who, in coordination with their parent agencies, analyze information from all sources and select and collate indications of Soviet/Communist hostile action or intentions affecting U.S. national security for the consideration of the Watch Committee. This function is in counterdistinction to the warning provided through radar, spotters, and filter centers. For further support of the mission of the Watch Committee, there was issued on November 30, 1954, NSC 5438, "Transmittal of Information to the IAC Watch Committee,"[5] which authorizes and directs appropriate departments and agencies of the Government to make fully available to the IAC Watch Committee all information and intelligence pertinent to its mission and functions.

3. *Evaluation of U.S. Warning Capabilites.* On September 14, 1954, the IAC approved SNIE 11–8–54, "Probable Warning of Soviet Attack on the U.S. Through Mid-1957,"[6] which estimates the amount of advance warning to be expected in the event of various types of attack which might be initiated by the USSR. It concludes that the U.S. could expect possibly as much as six months and not less than 30 days warning of Soviet preparations for a full-scale ground, sea, and air attack in the event of prior mobilization. It also concludes, however, that particularly by 1957 only a few hours or in some cases no specific warning, other than that provided by early warning radar, could be relied upon in event of various types and scales of surprise attack. A periodic review and revision of this estimate is contemplated.

Our advance warning largely depends on sifting a large quantity of material to discover those indications of enemy activity which suggest that measures are being taken to implement a decision to attack. The enemy's choice of the type of attack greatly affects our advance warning capability. We are largely dependent on radar and forward observation stations for early warning of air attack, in the event that our intelligence fails to discover indications of preparations therefor and if the USSR should risk launching such an attack without prior

---

[5] See Document 187 and footnote 4 thereto.

[6] Not printed. (National Archives, RG 263, Soviet NIE's, 1950–1955, #68, Box 1)

mobilization. We lack adequate penetrations of the Soviet Bloc that can be relied on to provide warning in the event that the enemy is willing to risk a surprise attack without extensive mobilization. Reports of troop movements and logistical activity are usually reported too late or are too inconclusive to give adequate early warning in such an event. We are exploiting all available sources of information and constantly striving to develop new and improved means of detection of attack.

As stated in SNIE 11–8–54, "The warning process is . . . affected by the whole context of events in which it operates, including psychological factors and even pure chance. It cannot be regarded as a mechanical process which it is possible for intelligence to set up once and for all and which thereafter operates automatically."

II. Estimating the Capabilities and Intentions of Foreign Countries

"Accurately evaluating the capabilities of foreign countries, friendly and neutral as well as enemy, to undertake military, political, economic, and subversive courses of action affecting U.S. security." NSC 162/2, para. 10a(2)

"Forecasting potential foreign developments having a bearing on U.S. national security." NSC 162/2, para. 10a(3)

1. *National Intelligence Objectives.* DCID 4/3[7] and 4/4 set up, respectively, comprehensive objectives for all countries and areas, and priority objectives for specific countries and subjects. DCID 4/4 particularly delineates more precisely than has been done heretofore the specific aspects of capabilities and intentions of certain countries that deserve priority attention.

2. *National Intelligence Estimates.* Since the last report (NSC 5430, Part 8),[8] several major estimates have been produced dealing with Soviet Bloc capabilities and probable courses of action. Included in this group were three basic annual reviews: "Soviet Capabilities and Probably Courses of Action Through Mid-1959,"[9] "Communist Courses of Action in Asia Through 1957,"[10] and "Probable Developments in the European Satellites Through Mid-1956."[11] In addition, three estimates were produced directly or indirectly in support of the NSC Study of "Net Capabilities of the USSR to Inflict Direct Injury Upon the Conti-

---

[7] Document 200.

[8] NSC 5430, Part 8, "The Foreign Intelligence Program and Related Activities," dated August 18, 1954, is in National Archives, RG 59, S/S–NSC Files: Lot 63 D 351, NSC 5430 Series.

[9] Reference is to NIE 11–4–54, September 14, 1954; extracts are in *Foreign Relations, 1952–1954,* vol. VIII, pp. 1235–1238.

[10] Reference is to NIE 10–7–54, November 23, 1954; ibid., vol. XIV, pp. 930–944.

[11] Reference is to NIE 12–54, August 24, 1954, not printed. (National Archives, RG 59, INR Files: Lot 78 D 394, Record Sets of NIE's SE's and SNIE's)

nental U.S. and Key U.S. Installations Overseas":[12] "Soviet Gross Capabilities for Attacks on the U.S. and Key Overseas Installations Through 1 July 1957,"[13] "Probable Warning of Soviet Attack on the U.S. as of Mid-1957," and "Soviet Capabilities and Probable Programs in the Guided Missile Field."[14] Seventeen estimates were produced on countries outside the Soviet Bloc. Much emphasis was given to the Far East, particularly to Indochina. Of the 24 NIE's published during the six-month period, 16 were related to specific NSC papers or policy decisions.

Continuing evaluation is taking place on means for improving the quality of National Intelligence Estimates. The entire production of 1953 and the first six months of 1954 have been reviewed in order to identify and correct intelligence deficiencies. In addition, there is now before the IAC a special detailed "post-mortem" of NIE 11–6–54, "Soviet Capabilities and Probable Programs in the Guided Missile Field."

3. *Basic Intelligence.* The initial world coverage of the National Intelligence Survey is essentially 45% completed, including 2400 individual sections, mainly on JCS high priority areas. Present production is slightly below the scheduled rate of approximately 8 equivalent NIS per year. The over-all quality is being improved by better collection in support of the program

4. *Military Intelligence*

a. *General.* At the present time, military intelligence is generally adequate to provide broad measurements of the military, logistic, industrial, and governmental control strengths of the USSR, Communist China, and the Satellites. However, significant detailed information available is fragmentary and it is essential to develop means to overcome present deficiencies in the collection field in order adequately to support U.S. military plans, programs, and operations.

Limited gains were made during the past six months in the following fields: analysis of performance characteristics of new types of Soviet aircraft; data on the development of Soviet nuclear weapons, information on modifications of Soviet tactical doctrine in nuclear warfare; technical methods and devices for intelligence collection; Chinese Communist ground force dispositions; and knowledge of Soviet warship construction.

---

[12] Not found. Soviet capabilities were discussed by the National Security Council on November 4, 1954; see *Foreign Relations, 1955–1957,* vol. XIX, p. 25, footnote 5.

[13] Reference is to SNIE 11–7A–54, September 14, 1954, not printed. (National Archives, RG 263, Soviet NIE's, Box 1, # 67)

[14] Reference is to NIE 11–6–54, October 5, 1954, not printed. (Ibid., RG 59, INR Historical Files: Lot 78 D 394, Record Sets of NIE's, SE's and SNIE's)

Nevertheless, military intelligence on the USSR and, to a lesser extent on Communist China and the Satellites, is inadequate in many critical fields. There is a serious lack of specific and detailed information on the following: the development, production, and deployment of guided missiles; other unconventional weapons; newly developed or modified conventional weapons; delivery systems, logistical capabilities and support; some components of the air defense system; and scientific and technical strengths as they affect military capabilities. Our knowledge continues to be inadequate on the movements and dispositions of Soviet Bloc forces, particularly in the USSR. The cessation of hostilities in Indochina has resulted in a reduction of military intelligence on the Viet Minh.

Our knowledge of Soviet atomic energy progress is referred to in paragraph 7b below. With respect to information on: (1) specific allocations by the USSR of available nuclear materials to types of weapons in the small, medium and large yield categories; (2) specific allocations of nuclear weapons and warheads to various delivery systems; and (3) actual disposition of nuclear weapons and warheads, our requirements continue to be unfulfilled.

b. *Target Materials Production.* Approximately 80% of the minimal requirements for air target materials, in the Air Objective Folder Program (OAFP), in support of joint war plans are complete. The remaining 20% of the minimal requirements are scheduled for completion by the end of CY 1955. Other air target materials, desired by the Services for development of the optimum opportunities for air action, are approximately 50% satisfied. Production to satisfy the remainder of these requirements continues to the maximum extent practicable and consonant with priority emphasis on highest and earliest readiness in support of joint war plans.[15]

---

[15] The Director of Naval Intelligence notes that the rate of production of air target materials for the highest priority (all-weather) Navy targets continues to be a matter of concern. The Target Area Analysis Radar (TAAR) is considered to be the most significant piece of target material developed and produced for-all weather, medium to high altitude operations. Between July 1952 and July 1954 the Navy nominated 632 all-weather targets for inclusion in the Air Objectives Folder Program for production of TAAR's. As of December 1, 1954, TAAR production had not been started for 52%. TAAR production was in process for 22%, and TAAR had been completed for 26%. The TAAR is seldom useful for low-level, all-weather mining but charts can serve adequately where there are steep gradients along the shore. In other cases the capability for conducting these operations is greatly reduced. No intelligence solution appears possible. Low-level, high-speed aircraft missions require special charts for navigation and approach which are not now available. However, such charts are under development. [Footnote in the original.]

5. *Political Intelligence*

a. *The Soviet Bloc and Communist China.* Political intelligence on the Soviet Orbit is built mainly upon the careful screening and evaluation of overt materials from the Soviet and Chinese Communist press, radio, and other information media. The flow of current material, plus the accumulated body of evaluated data and the development of a group of experienced analysts, make possible a reasonably accurate interpretation of political developments in the Soviet/Communist world.

Recent defections of fairly high level Soviet officials have served to confirm important aspects of existing intelligence analysis. Similarly, the observed course of events over the past year has borne out in most substantial particulars the intelligence estimates of probable post-Stalin developments in the USSR.

Our capability for assessing specific short-term intentions of the USSR and Communist China is inherently limited by the closed character of the Soviet and Communist Chinese decision-making systems. Although the Soviet/Communist regimes cannot mask their general international aims and attitudes, only a very high level penetration of these governments would make possible fully assured assessments of particular Soviet/Communist plans and intended actions.

b. *The Free World.* As a part of a long term look at the prospects in the cold war, special emphasis has been placed during the past six months on the situation in the underdeveloped areas of Asia, Africa, and Latin America; Communist capabilities in the Free World; and attitudes and reactions in the Free World and in the Soviet Bloc to nuclear weapons developments.

The revolution which overthrew a Communist regime in Guatemala and the disclosure of the Tudeh[16] ring in the Iranian army have made available to U.S. intelligence a new body of material on Communist tactics of infiltration and control. Analysis of these materials is expected to provide an improved understanding of Communist subversive capabilities in underdeveloped countries.

6. *Economic Intelligence*

a. *General.* Economic intelligence, like political intelligence, is essentially the product of collation and analysis of data from primarily overt sources. Economic intelligence on the Soviet Bloc has improved as a result of additional systematic analysis of the Soviet potential industries. Experimentation is under way on new economic research techniques for the evaluation of Soviet capabilities for supporting

---

[16] Iranian Communist Party.

specialized weapons programs. Among the major unsolved problems are Soviet defense expenditures and Soviet agricultural growth capabilities.

b. *Communist China*. Economic research effort and the flow of intelligence materials on Communist China have increased, resulting in a better appreciation of Chinese Communist productive capabilities and of Sino-Soviet economic relationships. The output of certain basic industries, such as electric power, and iron and steel, is reasonably well established. Further information and research are required to determine agricultural and handicraft output, chemical and munitions output, transportation capabilities, and over-all per capita consumption.

c. *Economic Defense*. In addition to a continuing review of major commodity problems for East-West trade controls, intelligence support for economic defense includes an assessment of possible long-run economic developments within the Soviet Bloc as they relate to economic defense policies. Intelligence support for enforcement of economic defense measures has been maintained in spite of diminishing information on trade transactions. Intelligence on shipping engaged in Soviet Bloc trade continues to be good, and there has been some improvement in cargo information. Continued joint conferences with the UK have produced substantial agreement on intelligence concerning Free World trade with Communist China, although significant differences still exist as to the type and quantity of cargoes reaching Communist China from or via Hong Kong and other trans-shipment points. Moreover, information on unrecorded shipments remains inadequate.

d. *Free World*. Economic intelligence production on the Free World has concentrated on analysis of (a) improved economic conditions in Western Europe; (b) the unfavorable outlook for Japanese foreign trade; and (c) the problem of economic development in underdeveloped areas. The results of this effort have been satisfactory.

e. *Coordination*. The Economic Intelligence Committee (EIC) has taken a more active part in guiding economic intelligence production and has continued its surveys to uncover economic research and collection deficiencies. In September, the EIC coordinated a draft DCID 15/1,[17] later approved by the IAC, which delineates IAC agency responsibilities for production and coordination of foreign economic intelligence related to national security.

7. *Scientific and Technical Intelligence*

a. *General*. Through intensified collection and research our understanding of Soviet basic scientific capabilities, including the quality and quantity of their scientific manpower, has improved. In specific

---

[17] Document 191.

fields of science and technology, however, vast gaps in our knowledge still exist. Substantial improvement will require successful application of new collection techniques and improved analytical processes now under development.

b. *Atomic Energy.* The most significant advances in atomic energy intelligence have resulted from the extensive Soviet nuclear weapons test program and the return of German technical personnel from the USSR. Data from the weapons test program and related information received during the past six months have made more clear the current status of Soviet nuclear development and indicate that several nuclear weapon types are probably being stockpiled. These same data and information furnish guidelines for estimating the future course of Soviet nuclear developments. Interrogation of German returnees has confirmed previous reports of the activities of German scientists in the Soviet atomic program and has provided information that raises somewhat the level of confidence in the estimates of Soviet U-235 production given in NIE 11–3–54.[18] The apportionment between weapons types of the Soviet fissionable material stockpile, although susceptible of estimate by indirect methods of varying reliability, cannot yet be confirmed by direct evidence.

c. *Guided Missiles.* Preparation of the first NIE on guided missiles revealed critical gaps in our knowledge. While certain new collection techniques and data reduction methods give promise of better information, their development has not yet progressed to the point of providing the information required. A U.S./UK intelligence conference on Soviet guided missiles capabilities, held in London in November, found the independently prepared U.S. and UK estimates to be relatively close.[19]

d. *Biological Warfare.* Following production of SEC 2–54, "Soviet Biological Warfare Capabilities Through 1960",[20] the first community-wide estimate in this field, a joint study of critical deficiencies in biological warfare intelligence and recommended means for their elimination has been undertaken. Coordinated all-source research by IAC member agencies on certain suspected Soviet biological warfare installations has been largely completed. Despite these efforts, positive knowledge of the existence and nature of a Soviet BW program has yet to be established.

---

[18] Not printed. (National Archives, RG 263, Soviet NIE's, 1950–1955, Box 1)

[19] IAC–D–81/6, "Reports of the US/UK Intelligence Conferences on Electronics and Guided Missiles," January 27, 1955, is not printed. (Central Intelligence Agency, Executive Registry, Job 85–S00362R, Box 5, Folder 8)

[20] Not printed. (Ibid., Transnational Issues Job 79–R00825A, Box 105)

8. *Intelligence Support for Foreign Information and Psychological Warfare Programs*

The survey of USIA's intelligence needs and assets reported in IAC–D–55/7[21] was approved by the DCI, USIA, and the Department of State. Pertinent recommendations were approved by the IAC. The survey report defined the types of intelligence and intelligence information required to meet USIA's essential needs, which are, in the main, also the needs of other agencies with related programs. Arrangements have now been made to insure that USIA, to the maximum extent possible, will receive the pertinent products of the existing intelligence organizations. To strengthen existing facilities, increased funds have been allocated for the expansion and acceleration of production of relevant parts of the NIS program. To meet the specialized needs of USIA, utilizing the intelligence produced by other agencies as required, an intelligence unit has been established with USIA accompanied by the abolition of certain USIA offices. It is expected in the near future that certain intelligence assets of USIA will be made available to the intelligence community.

III. Collection

1. *The Foreign Service.* Reporting from and collection by the Foreign Service, a primary overt source of intelligence information, continues for the most part to meet expectations.

a. *Reporting from behind the Iron Curtain.* Reporting remains inadequate in the political and sociological fields, principally because of restrictions on movement and the size of missions. Generally speaking, reporting from and on the USSR from the intelligence point of view has shown some slight gain; in the case of the Satellites, there has been a decline, at least in political reporting. Some improvement in reporting has been hoped for because of the greater cordiality of Soviet Bloc officials in their contacts with Western representatives, but little is yet evident. On the other hand, a decrease in the flow of overtly collected materials is expected as a result of probable retaliatory action by the governments of the USSR and Satellites to recent and pending U.S. travel and access restrictions on Soviet diplomatic personnel.

b. *Reporting outside the Bloc.* The principal handicap to improved Foreign Service reporting is reduced staff. However, strengthened inter-agency coordination of collection and requirements has contributed to improved reporting, especially in the economic field.

---

[21] Not printed. (Ibid., History Staff, Job 84–00161R, Box 3, Folder 6) It was the basis for Acting Director of Central Intelligence Cabell's recommendation that the NSC designate CIA to disseminate national intelligence to USIA. His memorandum is in National Archives, RG 59, S/P–NSC Files: Lot 62 D 1, NSCID's.

c. *Publications Procurement.* The continued absence of satisfactory publications procurement from London and the Middle East is having a cumulative effect and for some areas is beginning to impair analysis-in-depth.

d. *Map Procurement.* Collection of maps from the Soviet Bloc has been limited, by continued security restrictions, to atlases and small-scale maps. There has been a marked decrease in the procurement of maps and map intelligence from Latin America and from Northwest Europe, because of lack of specialized collectors in these areas.

2. *Agricultural Reporting.* Under recent legislation, agricultural attachés will report directly to the Department of Agriculture. However, by subsequent agreement between the Department of Agriculture and the Department of State, the latter will continue to be responsible for agricultural reporting from the Soviet Bloc.

3. *Military Attaché System.* The attaché system continues to be a major source of military intelligence. It provides good coverage outside the Soviet Bloc, but the capabilities of attachés in countries within the Bloc continue to be drastically restricted by counter-intelligence measures. In view of these basic restrictions, active consideration is being given to training of military attachés in special observation techniques, including photography and recording. Also, an improved program of collection guidance has been initiated to relate attaché activities more directly to urgent requirements. However, these measures will still leave overt collection capabilities far short of being able to meet military intelligence requirements in Soviet Bloc areas. Substantial improvement in military intelligence collection under present personnel, equipment and operating expense limitations will depend upon improved coordination, guidance, and the development of new collection techniques.

4. *Overseas Command.* Overseas commands continue to be important sources of information on Communist armed forces and war potential within the limitations noted in II–4 and IV.

5. *Aerial Reconnaissance.* The trend toward exploiting aerial reconnaissance opportunities continues together with improving capabilities. Reconnaissance operations continue to be performed within the framework of policy considerations of other than an intelligence nature. Research and development are producing promising results in equipment and techniques. Establishment of an Army Photo Interpretation Center has been approved.

6. *Exploitation of Defectors.* Soviet and Satellite defectors as well as East German scientists who, after working under contract in the USSR, were returned to East Germany and defected to the West, continue to provide valuable intelligence on the Soviet Orbit. The rate of defection remains constant. In the last six months, 10 Satellite and 7 Soviet bona

fide defectors were received at the Defector Reception Center, Germany, while 28 German scientists were received by the Returnee Exploitation Group. MVD[22] defectors Yuri Rastvorov, Nikolai Khokhlov and an unsurfaced lieutenant colonel, and the Polish Security Official, Josef Swiatlo, although defecting early in 1954, made outstanding contributions to U.S. intelligence and psychological warfare programs during this period. The U.S. also received the intelligence benefits from defectors received by various other friendly Western countries.

7. *Domestic Collection.* This continues to be productive. The possibility of increased travel by private U.S. individuals within the Soviet Union may expand the collection potential of such sources. Further progress has been made in the coordination of the activities of CIA and the military services in the collection of foreign scientific and technical information from U.S. sources within the framework of NSCID #7.[23]

8. *Foreign Radio Broadcasts.* World-wide radio monitoring coverage continues at approximately the same level as a year ago. However, installations have been improved and the processing of monitored material has been further perfected.

9. *Foreign Materials and Equipment.* Continuing Soviet efforts to increase the export of Bloc products and more extensive Soviet participation in international trade fairs have facilitated the collection of Soviet and Satellite non-military items. There has been a steady increase in the acquisition of factory markings data on Soviet Bloc equipment. With the exploitation of available military equipment nearly completed, emphasis is now directed toward the exploitation of civilian equipment available through commercial channels.

10. *Programs in Electronics*

a. *Monitoring of Radio Jamming.* Monitoring of the reception of U.S. broadcasts to the Soviet Bloc, increased under the authority of NSC 169[24] by the use of intercept facilities at U.S. embassies behind the Iron Curtain, contributed significantly to VOA and RFE operations, and was therefore accelerated. In addition, a project to locate and collect data on the Soviet radio jamming system has had significant results.

b. *Non-Communications Electronic Intercept (ELINT).* ELINT collection activities have assisted materially in gathering information on Soviet equipment and systems, including identification of AI radar in op-

---

[22] Soviet Ministry of Internal Affairs. The Soviet foreign intelligence apparatus had been renamed the KGB in 1954.

[23] See *Foreign Relations, 1945–1950, Emergence of the Intelligence Establishment,* Document 427.

[24] NSC 169, "Electro-Magnetic Communications," October 27, 1953, received final approval by the President on October 22, 1953. (National Archives, RG 59, S/S–NSC Files: Lot 63 D 351, Serial Master Files of NSC Documents)

erational use and the establishment of the general nature of Soviet navigational systems. Much remains to be done before a satisfactory integration of the U.S. ELINT effort can be achieved. Meanwhile, liaison with foreign activities in this field, primarily those of the UK, has improved.

11. *Travel Folder Program.* The 1955 schedule for revision of Travel Folders will reflect the priority selections of the entire U.S. intelligence community. It will involve 29 routes and 39 town briefs in the USSR and country questionnaires for 5 Satellites.

12. *Foreign Language Publications.* Further progress has been made in the coordination of foreign publications procurement, particularly from Communist China, and a greater and speedier flow of publications from that area is expected in 1955.

IV. Covert Collection of Intelligence Relating to the Soviet Bloc

1. During the last six months, clandestine operating conditions within the Soviet Orbit have been affected by two opposed trends—a tightening of internal security measures in both the Far East and Europe on the one hand, and a relaxation of travel restrictions to and from the Orbit on the other. One has made the maintenance of clandestine mechanisms and assets in Communist countries increasingly difficult; the other has opened up new opportunities to exploit legal travellers; i.e., Communist officials who travel in the West and Western officials, businessmen, and students who travel in the Orbit. This legal-traveller program in 1954 resulted in 335 positive intelligence reports.

2. A greater counterespionage effort and closer cooperation with friendly intelligence services have resulted in a heavier flow of both positive and operational data which will make possible a more concentrated effort directed towards Soviet and Satellite personalities and installations abroad. In this connection, the constantly expanding use of technical surveillance facilities to cover Soviet and Satellite installations abroad has been found increasingly valuable. In addition, some new approaches to denied area operations such as ELINT are being further developed.

3. In order to coordinate more effectively intelligence collection with outstanding requirements capabilities, a program designed to give better guidance to the field is being completed. Although an overall increase in the quantity of intelligence is noted, deficiencies in the quality of information and the specific coverage of priority targets still exist.

4. In certain categories, however, the quality of intelligence information obtained on the USSR has improved. Intelligence information of considerable significance has been obtained on Soviet Army tactical doctrine and on modifications thereof for nuclear warfare.

210.   Memorandum From the Director of the Bureau of the Budget (Hughes) to President Eisenhower[1]

Washington, March 3, 1955.

SUBJECT

Coordination of Economic, Psychological, Political Warfare, and Foreign Information Activities (NSC Actions Nos. 1183[2] and 1197)[3]

1. When you assigned this study to the Bureau of the Budget, you indicated that its primary purpose should be to answer two questions: (1) What is the present status of this work and how are responsibilities placed, and (2) What were my recommendations for improving planning methods and effectiveness?

2. On November 23, 1954,[4] I reported to you on the first question by supplying you with (1) a chart and narrative description indicating

---

[1] Source: National Archives, RG 59, S/S–NSC Files: Lot 66 D 148, Coordination of Psychological and other Warfare Activities. Secret. Sent on March 3 to members of the National Security Council for discussion at the March 10 NSC meeting. (Ibid.) In a February 7 memorandum, Comptroller of the Department of State, Isaac W. Carpenter, Jr., had informed Under Secretary of State Hoover that all Department of State Assistant Secretaries opposed the proposals and recommendations in this memorandum. (Ibid.) For example, Special Assistant for Intelligence and Research Armstrong opposed creation of the "Rockefeller Board" as duplicative in a February 3, memorandum to Carpenter. (National Archives, RG 59, INR Files: Lot 58 D 776, 1945–60, Box 2, Rockefeller Board) In a February 4 memorandum to Deputy Under Secretary of State for Administration Henderson, Max Bishop, Operations Coordinator, Office of the Under Secretary of State, also opposed the proposal as diluting the authority of the Operations Coordinating Board. (Ibid., Records of the Bureau of Administration: Lot 62 D 220, TS Records on Interagency Relations, 1948–61, OCB) Despite Department of State opposition, the President approved the proposal on March 10. See *Foreign Relations, 1955–1957*, vol. XIX, p. 62.

[2] At its 207th meeting on July 22, 1954, the National Security Council, in NSC Action No. 1183, "Coordination of Economic Warfare Activities," noted the President's request that the Bureau of the Budget study and prepare recommendations for NSC consideration on placing responsibility within the Executive Branch for coordinating all U.S. economic warfare activities. The NSC later transmitted NSC Action No. 1183 to the Director of the Bureau of the Budget for implementation. (National Archives, RG 59, S/S–NSC (Miscellaneous) Files: Lot 66 D 95, Records of Action by the National Security Council)

[3] See Document 187 and footnote 7 thereto.

[4] In the November 24, 1954, memorandum to the President, Hughes wrote that he would await the report on economic warfare then being prepared by Joseph M. Dodge, Special Assistant to the President for foreign economic affairs, before formally submitting the study requested by the President. Accompanying that memorandum were preliminary reports on the existing organization of the Executive Branch involved in the forward planning and coordination of economic, psychological, and political warfare, and information and a summary of the principal problems raised by that organization. (National Archives, RG 59, S/S–NSC Files: Lot 66 D 148, Coordination of Economic, Psychological and Political Warfare and Foreign Information Activities)

the functions of agencies involved, committee memberships, etc., which were found to be in existence at the time our study was launched, and (2) a summary of the principal problems raised by the organization as it then existed. Copies of those papers, together with a copy of my memorandum of transmittal to you, have been supplied to the members of the National Security Council and to the Secretary of the Treasury, the Director of Central Intelligence, and the Chairman, Joint Chiefs of Staff.[5]

3. The results of this study have been reviewed by a group consisting of Presidential Assistants Cutler and Rockefeller, Under Secretary of State Hoover,[6] Deputy Secretary of Defense Anderson, Director of Central Intelligence Dulles, and former Under Secretary of State Smith.[7] The recommendations contained in this memorandum are based upon their advice and have their concurrence.

4. Two closely related organizational studies were conducted concurrently with our review. One was the study of our information activities made for you by Mr. William H. Jackson.[8] The other was the study conducted by Mr. Joseph M. Dodge of executive branch organization for planning and coordinating foreign economic policy.[9] This latter study was conducted in close cooperation with the Bureau of the Budget and with your Advisory Committee on Government Organization.

---

[5] Enclosure to Memo for NSC from Executive Secretary, same subject, dated December 13, 1954. [Footnote in the original.]

[6] On January 29, Hughes prepared a draft memorandum to respond to the President's request for a study on the coordination of economic, psychological, and political warfare and foreign information activities. That draft was reviewed by officers in the Department of State. Commenting on the January 29 paper, Robert R. Bowie of S/P recommended to Acting Secretary of State Herbert Hoover, Jr., on February 4 that "every effort be made to head off the formation" of what he perceived as a potential cold war strategy board to be headed by Nelson Rockefeller. On February 14 Hughes sent a revised draft to Under Secretary of State Hoover, DCI Dulles, and Deputy Under Secretary of Defense Anderson. Presumably, the remarks appearing in this memorandum are in response to the revised draft of February 14. (National Archives, RG 59, S/S–NSC Files: Lot 66 D 148, Planning Coordination Group)

[7] Walter Bedell Smith.

[8] See Document 184.

[9] Apparently this refers to a staff study prepared by Dodge in response to a July 12, 1954, request by President Eisenhower. On November 22, 1954, Dodge presented the President with the final draft of his report, entitled "The Development and Coordination of Foreign Economic Policy." As a result of the Dodge study, the Council on Foreign Economic Policy was established, and on December 11, 1954, President Eisenhower appointed Dodge as the first chairman of that council. ("Organization, Procedures and Accomplishments of the Council on Foreign Economic Policy;" Eisenhower Library, Council on Foreign Economic Policy: Records, 1954–1961) The White House press release of December 11, 1954, announcing Dodge's appointment is in Department of State Bulletin, December 27, 1954, pp. 987–988.

5. At your request, the Budget Bureau and the Advisory Committee on Government Organization are currently working with Mr. Stassen and Mr. Dodge to develop for your consideration a pattern of organization for the conduct of foreign assistance programs. This matter is scheduled to be disposed of soon as it involves basic considerations which must affect your request in the near future to the Congress for authority to carry on foreign aid programs in fiscal year 1956 and subsequent years.

6. In addition, the following recent decisions have been made which affect the subject matter of this report:

a. The appointment of Mr. Dodge as Special Assistant to the President for foreign economic affairs and the establishment of the Council on Foreign Economic Policy.

b. The appointment of Mr. Nelson Rockefeller as Special Assistant to the President to provide leadership on your behalf in the development of increased understanding and cooperation among all peoples and in reviewing and developing methods and programs by which the various departments and agencies of the Government may effectively contribute to such cooperation and understanding.

c. The assignment to a Special Committee chaired by Mr. Rockefeller of responsibility for coordinating the implementation of the policies contained in NSC 5505/1[10] and NSC 5502/1.[11]

7. In addition to placing into effect the above-mentioned reorganizations, I should like to recommend further proposals for improving planning methods and effectiveness in the area which you requested us to study.

Organization in Connection with Planning Coordination

A. The Present Situation

1. In making recommendations for improving planning methods and coordination of economic, psychological, political warfare and foreign information activities, and their relation to the military program, certain existing responsibilities have been kept clearly in mind.

a. The NSC Planning Board, utilizing the resources and staffs of the component agencies (assisted by a small NSC staff), is responsible for developing recommendations for national security policy for consideration by the NSC and transmittal to the President. Neither the

---

[10] NSC 5505/1, "Exploitation of Soviet and European Satellite Vulnerabilities," January 31, is printed in *Foreign Relations, 1955–1957*, vol. XXIV, pp. 20–22.

[11] NSC 5502/1, "U.S. Policy Toward Russian Anti-Soviet Political Activities," January 31, is printed ibid., pp. 12–19.

NSC nor its Planning Board has any responsibility for developing operating programs under approved national security policy.

b. When the President has approved a national security policy, recommended by the NSC, the agencies of Government which have functions germane to its execution are responsible to him for devising plans and taking actions to carry such policy into effect.

c. The Operations Coordinating Board has two major responsibilities:

(1) Whenever the President directs, as to an approved national security policy, the OCB shall (a) advise with the operating agencies concerned as to the coordination of the interdepartmental aspects of the detailed operational plans developed by such agencies to carry out such policy and as to the timely and coordinated execution of such operational plans, and (b) initiate proposals for action within the framework of national security policies in response to opportunity and changes in the situation. The operating agencies concerned have the responsibility for developing and carrying out their respective programs under approved national security policies or other approved policies transmitted by the President to OCB.

(2) Under NSC 5412,[12] the Central Intelligence Agency's charter for covert operations, the members of OCB are advised in advance of major programs involving covert operations relating to policies and the OCB is the normal channel for securing coordination of support for covert work among the Departments of State and Defense and the CIA. Later in this paper it is recommended that NSC 5412 be amended to remove any conflict with the functions assigned to the Special Committee referred to in d. below and with the duties recommended below to be given to the Planning Coordination Group.

d. As indicated above, the President recently approved the establishment of a Special Committee under the Chairmanship of Special Assistant Nelson Rockefeller to coordinate the implementation of policies contained in NSC 5502/1 and NSC 5505/1. Besides the Special Assistant as Chairman, this Special Committee is composed of the Under Secretary of State, the Deputy Secretary of Defense, and the Director of Central Intelligence (each of whom may be represented in day-to-day operations by deputies appointed by them), with participation as appropriate of representatives of the Department of Justice, the Foreign Operations Administration, the U.S. Information Agency, and other interested departments and agencies. The duties of this Special Committee include reviewing current programs and developing new programs to carry out the above-mentioned national security policies, ensuring coordination of actions taken thereunder, and

---

[12] Document 171.

making evaluative progress reports to the President through the National Security Council. This Special Committee mechanism was established in this connection because of need for high-level, restricted attention to developing the sensitive programs, and the coordination of actions thereunder, called for by the above-mentioned national security policies.

e. At present, except for operations exclusively covert, the OCB, through working committees representative of the responsible agencies, coordinates the implementation of the plans and programs proposed by such agencies to carry out approved policies. In the case of covert operations, other than under NSC 5502/1 and NSC 5505/1, such coordination is effected through direct liaison between the CIA and the Departments of State and Defense and other departments and agencies as well as through the members of the OCB as prescribed in NSC 5412.

B. Proposals

1. As stated above, the working up of plans and programs to implement national security policies rests with the agencies primarily responsible therefor. But there is a continuing need in Government to infuse in such plans and programs dynamic, new and imaginative ideas, to diagnose precisely how best to meet the over-all problems of a given country or area, to bring into balance all aspects of a problem and all resources available to solve it, to find ways effectively to utilize U.S. private organizations and foreign individuals and groups and foreign public and private organizations. The promotion of such imaginative planning, based on the best intelligence obtainable, should materially aid in coordinating economic, psychological, political warfare, and foreign information activities so as to further international cooperation and understanding, to reduce the Communist threat, to strengthen friendly ties with the U.S., to promote the freedom, well being, and dignity of the individual man, and to improve the world climate of opinion.

2. It is believed that a small, high-level group should be given responsibility for meeting the need just referred to. This group would aid in developing planning in both overt and covert fields.

3. To accomplish this objective, it is recommended as follows:

a.[13] The above-mentioned Special Committee, consisting of the Special Assistant, Mr. Rockefeller, the Under Secretary of State, the Deputy Secretary of Defense, the Director of Central Intelligence (plus representation from other agencies when appropriate), established to coordinate the implementation of policies under NSC 5502/1 and 5505/1 should be reestablished, within the framework of OCB, where

---

[13] A note in the margin reads: "approved by the President March 4, 1955."

it might be designated as the Planning Coordination Group. This body would be a special grouping of OCB members chaired by Mr. Rockefeller and reporting directly to the Chairman of OCB. It would have such small staff as might be convenient to its special purpose, including the duties assigned to it under c. below. Such staff, while distinct from the OCB staff, could call upon OCB for housekeeping services and other administrative assistance. The Chairman of OCB will, from time to time, transmit progress reports of the Planning Coordination Group to the President through the National Security Council.

b. The Special Assistant, Mr. Rockefeller, should be designated a member of the OCB under Section 1 (b) (5) of Executive Order No. 10,483[14] and should also be designated vice chairman of the Board.

c. The Planning Coordination Group, with reference to overt and covert actions to implement those national security policies appropriate to its functions, including those assigned to OCB for coordination, should advise and assist the responsible operating agencies in the coordinated development of plans and programs to carry out such national security policies. The implementation of such plans and programs, with respect to overt actions, will be coordinated by the Operations Coordinating Board. In addition, the Planning Coordination Group should hereafter be advised in advance of major covert programs initiated by the Central Intelligence Agency under NSC 5412 or as otherwise directed, and should be the normal channel for giving policy approval for such programs as well as for securing coordination of support therefor among the Departments of State and Defense and the Central Intelligence Agency. With reference to NSC 5502/1 and NSC 5505/1: the necessary action should be taken to revise NSC Action No. 1314–d, January 27, 1955,[15] to substitute the Planning Coordination Group for the above mentioned Special Committee and to bring the resulting arrangement into conformity with the foregoing provisions of this paragraph.

d. The Planning Coordination Group should keep close and continuing contact with the work of the Operations Coordinating Board.

---

[14] Document 157.

[15] NSC Action No. 1314–d, "Exploitation of Soviet and European Satellite Vulnerabilities," was discussed at the 234th meeting of the National Security Council on January 27. The cited paragraph concerned the NSC recommendation that the President designate a special committee to be headed by Nelson A. Rockefeller to review programs to carry out policy stated in NSC 5505, "Exploitation of Soviet and European Satellite Vulnerabilities," dated January 18. On March 10 at the 240th meeting of the National Security Council, the special committee was replaced by the Planning Coordination Group through an amendment to NSC Action No. 1314–d by NSC Action No. 1349, "Coordination of Economic, Psychological and Political Warfare and Foreign Information Activities." (National Archives, RG 59, S/S–NSC (Miscellaneous) Files: Lot 66 D 95, Records of Action by the National Security Council, 1955)

The Planning Coordination Group would not itself engage in operations or enter into the stream of agency operations.

e. Because action respecting covert operations should be restricted so far as possible to those who have a need to know and should be kept at a high level, it is recommended that NSC 5412 be amended so as to substitute therein the members of the Planning Coordination Group specifically mentioned in 3 a. above for the members of the OCB, and to bring the resulting arrangement into conformity with the foregoing provisions of 3 c. above.

f. The location of the Planning Coordination Group within the framework of OCB is in line with the basic principle of integration in national security policy formulation and implementation. The work to be done by this group can contribute greatly to the imaginative dynamic quality and the effectiveness of coordinated agency planning to carry out approved national security policies.[16]

Rowland Hughes[17]

----

[16] On March 10 President Eisenhower designated Rockefeller a member of the Operations Coordinating Board and the OCB Vice Chairman. The President also asked Rockefeller to serve as chairman of the Planning Coordination Group. (Eisenhower Library, Whitman File, Administration Series, Rockefeller, Nelson, 1952–1955) At its 240th meeting that same day, the National Security Council noted that the President had signed the March 10 letter requesting Rockefeller to assume the responsibilities. The NSC then approved the recommended amendments to NSC 5412. (Eisenhower Library, Whitman File, NSC Meetings, 1955) See Document 212.

[17] Printed from a copy that indicates Hughes signed the original.

----

211. Editorial Note

In the course of a discussion on the Formosa crisis in the President's office at 2:30 p.m. on March 11, 1955, which was attended by Secretary of State Dulles, DCI Dulles, Chairman of the Joint Chiefs of Staff Radford, Chief of Staff of the Air Force Twining, Chief of Naval Operations Carney, the President's Staff Secretary Goodpaster, and Special Assistant for National Security Affairs Cutler, President Eisenhower also raised some more general questions regarding U.S. intelligence, as follows:

"i. The President complained about conflicting intelligence information coming to him. He said he wanted steps taken to centralize and centrally evaluate all intelligence. It was agreed that the NIC should be 'beefed up' and put on a 24 hour basis. Secretary Dulles said there are three aspects to intelligence:

"a. rapid communication of intelligence from the field
"b. coordination of intelligence in Washington
"c. obtaining accurate intelligence as to Chinat loyalty on Formosa

"The President said that—under emergent circumstances like the present—he wanted (1) intelligence transmitted from the field to Washington very fast; (2) a prompt evaluation of such intelligence at a central point where all interested agencies were represented, so as to obtain a commonly agreed assessment as quickly as possible; (3) in the case of something 'hot', a warning to himself and other key persons, pending such central evaluation." (Memorandum for the Record prepared by Cutler; Eisenhower Library, Whitman File, Miscellaneous Series, Formosa—Visit to CINCPAC) The full text of Cutler's memorandum is printed in *Foreign Relations, 1955–1957*, volume II, pp. 355–360.

---

212. National Security Council Directive[1]

NSC 5412/1   Washington, March 12, 1955.

COVERT OPERATIONS

1. The National Security Council, taking cognizance of the vicious covert activities of the USSR and Communist China and the governments, parties and groups dominated by them (hereinafter collectively referred to an "International Communism") to discredit and defeat the aims and activities of the United States and other powers of the free world, determined, as set forth in NSC directives 10/2[2] and 10/5[3] that, in the interests of world peace and U.S. national security, the overt foreign activities of the U.S. Government should be supplemented by covert operations.

---

[1] Source: Eisenhower Library, Special Assistant to the President for National Security Affairs Records. Top Secret. This Directive was circulated under cover of a March 12 note from Executive Secretary Lay to the National Security Council. The note indicates that the President approved the directive, which superseded NSC 5412, that same day. The NSC approved the amendments to NSC 5412 (Document 171) at its March 10 meeting. See Document 210 and footnote 16 thereto.

[2] *Foreign Relations, 1945–1950*, Emergence of the Intelligence Establishment, Document 292.

[3] Document 90.

2. The Central Intelligence Agency had already been charged by the National Security Council with conducting espionage and counter-espionage operations abroad. It therefore seemed desirable, for operational reasons, not to create a new agency for covert operations, but, subject to directives from the NSC, to place the responsibility for them on the Central Intelligence Agency and correlate them with espionage and counter-espionage operations under the overall control of the Director of Central Intelligence.

3. The NSC has determined that such covert operations shall to the greatest extent practicable, in the light of U.S. and Soviet capabilities and taking into account the risk of war, be designed to:

a. Create and exploit troublesome problems for International Communism, impair relations between the USSR and Communist China and between them and their satellites, complicate control within the USSR, Communist China and their satellites, and retard the growth of the military and economic potential of the Soviet bloc.

b. Discredit the prestige and ideology of International Communism, and reduce the strength of its parties and other elements.

c. Counter any threat of a party or individuals directly or indirectly responsive to Communist control to achieve dominant power in a free world country.

d. Reduce International Communist control over any areas of the world.

e. Strengthen the orientation toward the United States of the peoples and nations of the free world, accentuate, wherever possible, the identity of interest between such peoples and nations and the United States as well as favoring, where appropriate, those groups genuinely advocating or believing in the advancement of such mutual interests, and increase the capacity and will of such peoples and nations to resist International Communism.

f. In accordance with established policies and to the extent practicable in areas dominated or threatened by International Communism, develop underground resistance and facilitate covert and guerrilla operations and ensure availability of those forces in the event of war, including wherever practicable provision of a base upon which the military may expand these forces in time of war within active theaters of operations as well as provision for stay-behind assets and escape and evasion facilities.

4. Under the authority of Section 102(d)(5) of the National Security Act of 1947, the National Security Council hereby directs that the Director of Central Intelligence shall be responsible for:

a. Ensuring, through designated representatives of the Secretary of State and of the Secretary of Defense, that covert operations are planned and conducted in a manner consistent with United States foreign and military policies and with overt activities, and consulting with and obtaining advice from the Planning Coordination Group of the Operations Coordinating Board and other departments or agencies as appropriate.

b. Informing, through appropriate channels and on a need-to-know basis, agencies of the U.S. government, both at home and abroad (including diplomatic and military representatives), of such operations as will affect them.

5. In addition to the provisions of paragraph 4, the following provisions shall apply to wartime covert operations:

a. Plans for covert operations to be conducted in active theaters of war and any other areas in which U.S. forces are engaged in combat operations will be drawn up with the assistance of the Department of Defense and will be in consonance with and complementary to approved war plans of the Joint Chiefs of Staff.

b. Covert operations in active theaters of war and any other area in which U.S. forces are engaged in combat operations will be conducted under such command and control relationships as have been or may in the future be approved by the Department of Defense.

6. As used in this directive, "covert operations" shall be understood to be all activities conducted pursuant to this directive which are so planned and executed that any U.S. Government responsibility for them is not evident to unauthorized persons and that if uncovered the U.S. Government can plausibly disclaim any responsibility for them. Specifically, such operations shall include any covert activities related to: propaganda, political action; economic warfare; preventive direct action, including sabotage, anti-sabotage, demolition; escape and evasion and evacuation measures; subversion against hostile states or groups including assistance to underground resistance movements, guerrillas and refugee liberation groups; support of indigenous and anti-comunist elements in threatened countries of the free world; deception plans and operations; and all activities compatible with this directive necessary to accomplish the foregoing. Such operations shall not include: armed conflict by recognized military forces, espionage and counter-espionage, nor cover and deception for military operations.

7. This directive supersedes and rescinds NSC 10/2, NSC 10/5, and NSC 5412. Subparagraphs "a" and "b" under the heading "Additional Functions of the Operations Coordinating Board" on page 1 of the President's memorandum for the Executive Secretary, National Security Council, supplementing Executive Order 10483,[4] are superseded by the following provisions:

a. Except as the President otherwise directs, the regular members of the Planning Coordination Group shall hereafter be advised in advance of major covert programs initiated by the Central Intelligence Agency under this policy or as otherwise directed, and shall be the normal channel for giving policy approval for such programs as well as

---

[4] Document 157. The President's memorandum is Document 158.

for securing coordination of support therefor among the Departments of State and Defense and the Central Intelligence Agency.

b. The designated representatives of the Secretaries of State and Defense referred to in paragraph 4-a above shall keep the members of the Planning Coordination Group from their respective departments advised as to matters on which they are consulted by the Director of Central Intelligence, and which have been or are to be referred to the Planning Coordination Group.

---

213.   Memorandum From the Executive Secretary of the National Security Council (Lay) to the National Security Council[1]

Washington, March 15, 1955.

SUBJECT

The Foreign Information Program and Psychological Warfare Planning

REFERENCES

A. NSC 59/1[2]
B. NSC 127/1[3]
C. NSC Action. Nos. 1197[4] and 1198[5]
D. Memo for NSC from Executive Secretary, same subject, dated February 8, 1955[6]

1. The attached NSC Staff memorandum sets forth a brief review of measures which have been periodically considered or adopted within the Executive Branch to provide organizational arrangements and principles for coordination and planning in the field of psychological operations. It illustrates the difficulties and divergences of opinion hitherto encountered in attempting to provide adequate direction and coordination for psychological operations at a high governmental

---

[1] Source: National Archives, RG 59, S/P–NSC Files: Lot 62 D 1, NSC 127/1. Top Secret. Copies were sent to the Secretary of the Treasury, Director of the Bureau of the Budget, Chairman of the Joint Chiefs of Staff, and Director of Central Intelligence. All ellipses in the original.

[2] Document 2.

[3] Document 123.

[4] See footnote 3, Document 210.

[5] In NSC Action No. 1198, "The Foreign Information Program and Psychological Warfare Planning," the National Security Council, on August 5, 1954, noted that NSC 59/1 and NSC 127/1 had been deemed obsolete. The Council, however, deferred further action pending completion of the Bureau of the Budget study on coordination of economic, psychological and political warfare and foreign information activities. (National Archives, RG 59, S/S–NSC (Miscellaneous) Files: Lot 66 D 95, Records of Action by the National Security Council, 1954)

[6] Not found; see numbered paragraph 6 below.

level. It also affords a historical record to those presently concerned with the desirability of providing further policy and organizational arrangements in this area.

2. NSC 59/1 ("The Foreign Information Program and Psychological Warfare Planning", March 9, 1950) and NSC 127/1 ("Plan for Conducting Psychological Operations During General Hostilities", July 25, 1952) have clearly become obsolete in many of their provisions due to major change in Executive branch organization during the past few years. Therefore, they should be rescinded, revised, or otherwise dealt with.

3. The current status of action on these policies has developed in the following manner.

a. A special memorandum from the President to the NSC, dated September 3, 1953,[7] transferred the functions of the POCC (established pursuant to NSC 59/1) to the OCB. The OCB continued only the POCC Subcommittee, the "X-Day Working Group", charged with developing plans for psychological operations in support of hostilities.

b. The "X-Day Working Group" was authorized by OCB in the latter part of 1953 to propose revisions in NSC 127/1 deemed necessary in the light of the numerous Executive Branch organizational changes brought about since the adoption of the policy in question.

c. In carrying out their task, the X-Day Committee found itself unable to make agreed recommendations on several major issues due to departmental conflict of views.

d. As a result, the OCB in its report to the NSC dated July 23, 1954,[8] recommended recision of NSC 59/1` and NSC 127/1, "without prejudice to the principles of operation and the responsibilities of departments and agencies to engage in psychological warfare and psychological warfare planning enunciated therein or elsewhere".

4. On August 3, 1954, the Joint Chiefs of Staff submitted recommendations to the NSC opposing recision of NSC 59/1 and NSC 127/1, pointing out that these policies, although obsolete in some respects, contained "essential formal statements of national policy on psychological warfare matters".[9]

5. The NSC on August 5, 1954, deferred further action with respect to NSC 59/1 and NSC 127/1, pending receipt of a study from the Bureau of the Budget which was to include "the placing of responsibility within the Executive Branch for coordinating economic

---

[7] Document 158.

[8] Not found, but for a memorandum of discussion of this paper by the National Security Council on August 5, 1954, see Document 187.

[9] Not printed, but see Document 187.

warfare, psychological warfare and foreign information activities".[10] However, the study in question does not deal specifically with the problems posed by NSC 59/1 and NSC 127/1.

6. In a memorandum for the Secretary of Defense dated January 11, 1955, subsequently circulated to the NSC on February 8, 1955 with a supporting memorandum from the Secretary of Defense, the Joint Chiefs of Staff reaffirmed their views of August 3, 1954 and additionally set forth certain provisions which should be contained in any revised policy.[11]

7. As suggested by the attached historical summary, a number of major issues are identifiable, which must be dealt with in any attempt to provide for organizational arrangements in this area:

a. *Departmental Responsibility.* State's primary prerogative for giving in this area in peacetime policy guidance, with related responsibilities, has been generally recognized. Military prerogatives in wartime have been likewise generally recognized. However, the organizational expression of carrying out these responsibilities has varied considerably (ICS, IFIO, NPSB, PSB, OCB).

b. *The Necessity of Continuity.* This concept has been approached in various ways, including:

(1) The organization for coordination of planning in this area should be the same in peace and war;

(2) Peacetime arrangements should generally prevail on a temporary basis during the first stages of general war—to be modified or replaced later by a permanent organization whose nature and authority would subsequently by determined;

(3) A special *interim organization* should be provided for in peacetime to be activated during the initial stages of general hostilities (or limited war);

(4) A *permanent* organization should be provided for in peacetime for the period of general war, or some variant of this concept with (3);

(5) No binding decision should be made at this time on the nature of the permanent organization for coordination and planning during general hostilities.

c. *The Governmental Level of Responsibility.*

(1) Should the organization be at the Assistant Secretary level or higher?

(2) Should the organization have the authority to make psychological warfare policy and to issue directives, operational and other, or should it be more exclusively coordinating in nature?

---

[10] This was NSC Action No. 1198; see footnote 9, Document 187.

[11] Not found but see numbered paragraph 31 in the attachment printed below.

(3) To what extent should the organization have an independent staff?

(4) What provision should be made for access to the top policy-making levels in the Government and to the President?

(5) To what extent should the directing officer of such an organization be independent from the departments and have direct access to the President?

(6) To what extent does the changed nature of general war as presently envisaged bear on the necessity and importance of establishing in peacetime an organization for the conduct of psychological operations in the initial stages of general war?

(7) To what extent is it necessary in peacetime to provide, in the psychological warfare area, trained personnel and stockpiled resources for use in wartime?

8. In view of the past history in this field and the nature of the issues identified in the preceding paragraph, it is believed that a high level review of the existing arrangements in the light of NSC 59/1 and NSC 127/1 should be undertaken with a view to preparing appropriate recommendations for consideration by the National Security Council. Such a review should be undertaken with a full understanding of the existing arrangements and current plans and programs in this field, as well as the status of planning for the possibility of limited or general war.

9. Mr. Cutler therefore recommends that the responsibility for making such a review and recommendations be assigned to Mr. Nelson Rockefeller as Special Assistant to the President "to provide leadership in the development of increased understanding and cooperation among all peoples and in reviewing and developing methods and programs by which the various departments and agencies of the Government may effectively contribute to such cooperation and understanding". In this assignment Mr. Rockefeller should be provided with such advice and assistance as he requires from the Bureau of the Budget, the Office of Defense Mobilization and the Operations Coordinating Board as well as the responsible operating departments and agencies.

10. Mr. Rockefeller and the NSC Planning Board concur in the above recommendation.

James S. Lay, Jr.[12]

---

[12] Printed from a copy that bears this typed signature.

Attachment[13]

SUMMARY OF PSYCHOLOGICAL WARFARE ARRANGEMENTS
WITHIN THE U.S. GOVERNMENT SINCE WORLD WAR II
(with particular respect to the problems posed by
NSC 59/1 and 127/1)

World War II

1. Approximately six months after U.S. entry into World War II, the OWI (Office of War Information) was established by Executive Order in June 1942.[14] The OWI was responsible for domestic and overt foreign information programs and answered directly to the President. Policy guidance was provided by the Committee on War Information, chaired by the Director of OWI, with representation which included the departments of State, War, and Navy.

2. Subsequently, in 1943, the OSS (Office of Strategic Services) was established and made responsible, among other functions, for the conduct of covert information and propaganda activities abroad, answering to the Joint Chiefs of Staff.

3. There was no psychological warfare organization for the services as a whole, although there was created within SHAEF a special psychological warfare staff division on a level with G–2. In theaters of military operations, each commander set up his own psychological warfare organization and coordinated psychological warfare with his combat operations.

Post-World War II

4. Following the end of the war, the OSS was dissolved and certain overt activities of the OWI, including the VOA facilities, were transferred to the Department of State. At the same time the CIA took over the intelligence and covert psychological warfare activities of the OSS. The military services retained their psychological warfare units on a greatly reduced scale, though they conducted significant activities in this area through the reorientation program necessitated by the occupation of Germany and Japan. This was the status of organization within the Government in early 1947 when the exigencies of the current cold war posed increased challenges and demands on U.S. activities in this field.

---

[13] Top Secret. No drafting information appears on the paper.
[14] President Franklin D. Roosevelt signed Executive Order No. 9182 on June 13, 1942. (Department of State *Bulletin*, June 27, 1942, p. 566)

5. At the end of 1947, by interdepartmental agreement, the State Department was charged with the responsibility for current peacetime propaganda activities (NSC 4 Dec. 9, 1947).[15] To provide for closer policy coordination and integration of facilities and programs, an Interdepartmental Coordinating Staff (ICS) was established under the direction of the Assistant Secretary of State for Public Affairs. Representatives of State, Army, Navy, Air Force and CIA participated on this joint staff. The organization was to develop psychological objectives for cold war programs and to coordinate the activities of the operating agencies.

6. This agreement accordingly placed responsibility upon the Secretary of State for peacetime psychological operations during the cold war; the question of wartime conduct of psychological warfare was not covered by this early agreement but was left for further study. Early in 1949, interdepartmental agreement was reached on the establishment in the State Department of a planning organization to develop plans for interim arrangements for foreign and domestic information programs and overt psychological operations abroad during the initial stages of war (NSC 43, March 9, 1949).[16] The director of this planning staff was appointed by the Secretary of State in consultation with directly interested agencies. The staff was composed of State and military personnel, with liaison representatives from CIA and NSRB. Policy consultants to the director of the staff were designated by the Secretary of State and Defense, the Director of CIA and the Chairman of the NSRB. The functions and personnel of this staff overlapped to a considerable degree with the Interdepartmental Coordinating Staff (ICS). This condition and subsequent experience led to a review of existing arrangements (see NSC 43/1, Aug. 2, 1949).[17]

NSC 59/1

7. As a result, in March 1950 revised basic principles for handling psychological warfare planning and operations were adopted and put into effect. (NSC 59/1, March 9, 1950). The principle that propaganda in both peace and war is a continuing mechanism of national policy directed toward the achievement of national aims was reaffirmed. Under NSC 59/1, the Secretary of State was charged with responsibility for:

---

[15] See *Foreign Relations*, 1945–1950, Emergence of the Intelligence Establishment, Documents 252–265.

[16] NSC 43, "Planning for Wartime Conduct of Overt Psychological Warfare," is in National Archives, RG 59, S/S–NSC Files: Lot 63 D 351, NSC 43 Series.

[17] Ibid.

a. The formulation of policy and plans for the National Foreign Information program during peacetime.

b. The formulation of national psychological warfare policy in time of national emergency or threat of war and during the initial stages of war.

c. The coordination of policy and plans for these activities with other appropriate agencies. The policy and planning for periods of emergency and the initial stages of war were to be coordinated with the joint war plans of the Department of Defense, and where such plans had a direct impact on war plans, they were to be subject to JCS concurrence.

8. In accordance with NSC 59/1, a revised central planning and coordinating mechanism based on the consolidation of the former Staffs was established to deal with these responsibilities. The ICS became the Interdepartmental Foreign Information Staff (IFIS). The director was appointed by the Secretary of State and was in fact the Assistant Secretary of State for Public Affairs. The group of consultants was retained. This combined mechanism became the Interdepartmental Foreign Information Organization (IFIO).[18]

9. Again there was avoided coming fully to grips with the issue of jurisdictional responsibility for psychological warfare policy and direction during war, because of the fundamental differences between State and the military services on the question. Agreement had been reached only for planning through the initial stages of war, but even this concept was left without precise definition. This arrangement proved unsatisfactory and the cause of friction from many aspects.

10. The IFIS joint staff was charged with planning for emergency and wartime psychological operations and completed a study shortly after the outbreak of war in Korea on the assignment of psychological warfare responsibilities for the initial stages of war (defined as D plus 90) and for the subsequent stages of war. This study was transmitted to the departments for adoption in July 1950.[19] It provided that:

a. During the initial stages of war, the Secretary of State would:
(1) Formulate psychological warfare policy and issue policy guidance directives to operating agencies.

---

[18] The IFIO became the body charged with psychological warfare policy in time of national emergency or during the initial stages of war. Following the Presidential directive of April 4, 1951, establishing the PSB, the IFIO was redesignated the POCC, Psychological Operations Coordinating Committee. The POCC created a subcommittee, the X-Day working group, to prepare the required plans. [Footnote in the original. For the April 4 directive, see Document 60.]

[19] The study cited presumably is NSC 74 of July 10, 1950, "A Plan for National Psychological Warfare," which was sent to NSC members and the Secretary of the Treasury. The NSC did not formally approve NSC 74. A copy is in National Archives, RG 59, S/S–NSC Files: Lot 63 D 351, NSC 74. See also Document 17.

(2) Coordinate these functions with agencies executing psychological warfare functions.

(3) Prepare detailed plans and programs for implementation of policies.

(4) In areas other than theaters of military operations, execute overt psychological warfare programs, provide for coordination with covert psychological warfare and coordinate U.S. psychological warfare policies and operations with our allies.

b. To handle psychological warfare during the subsequent stages of war, there should be established an independent agency:

(1) Authorized to issue directives to operating agencies.

(2) Providing for representation of the operating agencies.

(3) Authorized to provide coordination with our allies.

(4) Having direct access to the President, but recognizing the authority of the State Department in areas other than theaters of military operations, the Department of Defense having authority in such theaters.

11. Furthermore, for the initial stages of war, an interdepartmental board was to be established within the State Department to act as the "executive agent" of the Secretary of State in formulating policy plans for, and coordination of, the world-wide conduct of psychological warfare.

12. The transition from the peacetime organization to the initial stages of war organization was to take place on D-Day, or earlier at the discretion of the President. The IFIO would be designated the Interim Psychological Warfare Board and strengthened; as executive agent for the Secretary of State, it would issue directives.

13. These recommendations led to further controversy. In the fall of 1950 Secretary of Defense Johnson advocated the immediate establishment of the Interim Psychological Warfare Board in the Executive Office of the President and immediate consideration of the question of composition and urgency of a National Psychological Warfare Board. He proposed that the latter Board would be independent of existing departments and have full-time public members in the majority. On the other hand, the Department of State was not willing to accept establishment of the Interim Board as an executive agent for the Secretary of State at that time. The issue was posed as to whether or not such an interim board would impair the Secretary of State's responsibility for the conduct of foreign affairs. Accordingly, an impasse developed.

14. Meanwhile, in August 1950, in the light of the Korean developments, State strengthened the IFIO organization. The interdepartmental consultants group was expanded and renamed the National Psychological Strategy Board. It was headed by the Assistant Secretary of State for Public Affairs and was composed of representatives of the Secretary of Defense, the JCS, the Director of CIA and the Army as Executive Agent of the JCS for the conduct of psychological warfare in Korea.

15. Attempting to break the organizational deadlock, State proposed in December 1950 a new concept, emphasizing continuing psychological effort (rather than phased operations) for both peace and war. The conclusion was that the same organization should be responsible for formulation of policy and programs in both peace and war. It was proposed to place responsibility for all phases in the Secretary of State with an interdepartmental coordinating agent to advise the Secretary on policy and to coordinate planning operations. This proposal was rejected by Defense.

16. A new memorandum of agreement and disagreement was then worked out interdepartmentally. It set forth the issue somewhat as follows. Agreement was reached on the following points:

a. The peace-to-war phasing was eliminated and the need for organizational and policy continuity recognized. The responsibility of the JCS in theaters of military operations and of State in other areas was reaffirmed.

b. A single official, designated by the President:

(1) Should be responsible for formulation of psychological policy within the framework of approved national policy and coordination and evaluation of the psychological effort; and

(2) Should be authorized to issue policy guidance to the operating agencies.

c. Representatives at the policy levels, also agencies executing major portions of the psychological effort, should advise this official and coordinate operations.

17. There was disagreement as to whether or not the single official designated by the President should be the Secretary of State or an independent official responsible to the President. Arguments were put forth for both propositions, and the matter was referred to the President for decision in January 1951.

Establishment of the Psychological Strategy Board.

18. The problem was worked on by the BOB, the NSC Staff, and a final agreement was negotiated by the agencies concerned. This resulted in the directive of the President on June 20, 1951, establishing the Psychological Strategy Board.[20] The principle of psychological operations was recognized. However the designation of a single official as the focus of responsibility was replaced by the concept of a Board composed of the Undersecretary of State, the Undersecretary of Defense, and the Director of CIA. A director appointed by the President served under the Board, and was placed in a position to take initiative

---

[20] See Document 60.

in, and give direction to, government-wide psychological operations. The Board was directed particularly to:

a. provide more effective plans of psychological operations within the framework of approved national policies;
b. coordinate psychological operations of all departments and agencies of government, and
c. evaluate the effectiveness of the national psychological effort.

19. In the meantime the IFIO have been continuing to struggle with the formulation of a "national psychological warfare plan" for general war, to include principles of operation, delineation of responsibilites and organizational principles, etc. Since the PSB now had been given authority for such planning, the IFIO plan along with alternate departmental versions was, accordingly, referred for further study and action to the PSB.

NSC 127/1

20. The PSB in due course resubmitted the plan for conducting psychological operations during general hostilities to the NSC for approval, (NSC 127/1). It provided, among other things:

a. A statement of national objectives which will maintain in a condition of general hostilities (based on NSC 20/4).[21]
b. Basic principles of operations.
c. Delineation of responsibilities, including:
(1) PSB responsibility for formulation and promulgation as guidance of over-all national psychological objectives, policies and programs, and for the coordination and evaluation of the national psychological effort (para. 7, NSC 127/1).
(2) The JCS to be responsible, in conformity with national policy and PSB guidance, for planning and execution of U.S. psychological operations in military theaters of operations (para. 8, NSC 127/1).
(3) State in conformity with national policy and PSB guidance responsible for the planning and execution of U.S. overt psychological operations in areas other than military theaters of operations (para. 9, NSC 127/1).
(4) "In situations in which a military theater of operations embraces territory of a government which exercises civil authority and to which a U.S. diplomatic mission is accredited . . . the Department of State shall be responsible for the U.S. information program directed toward the nations of the country concerned". (para. 10, NSC 127/1).
(5) "The Psychological Strategy Board shall insure through the government agency or agencies appropriate . . . any necessary coordination of national psychological operations, policies, or plans with the appropriate agencies of other governments" (para. 14, NSC 127/1).

---

[21] NSC 20/4, "U.S. Objectives With Respect to the USSR To Counter Soviet Threats to U.S. Security," November 23, 1948, is printed in *Foreign Relations, 1948*, vol. I, Part 2, pp. 662–669.

21. NSC 127/1 further provides that plans for the transfer of facilities and personnel from State and other overt agencies to military control in military theaters of operations should be coordinated through the organization established pursuant to NSC 59/1 (the POCC). Originally the PSB draft of 127/1 had provided for such coordination by the PSB, but this was changed subsequent to a recommendation by the Bureau of the Budget. In approving NSC 127/1 the President made clear that this policy was to serve as a basis for emergency planning relating to sudden general hostilities and "directed that the subsidiary plans and measures authorized provide maximum flexibility whenever the President deems it desirable to determine the ultimate organization appropriate to protracted full-scale general hostilities" (NSC 127/1, Note by the Executive Secretary, July 25, 1952).

Establishment of the Operations Coordinating Board

22. The effort of the Psychological Strategy Board to carry out its variegated mission was not a happy one. In reviewing its activities the Jackson Committee[22] found that:

"there is no 'strategic concept for psychological operations' separate and distinct from a strategic concept for gaining national aims without war. When PSB has developed, for example, a 'regional psychological plan', it has really formulated a plan for the achievement of national aims involving the use of propaganda, diplomacy, economic pressure and military strength in various combinations. It is this fact which has caused so much controversy between PSB and the established planning agencies within the State Department".

Accordingly, the Jackson Committee recommended abolishment of the PSB and the establishment of the OCB as a coordinating body which would:

a. Aid in coordinating the implementation of detailed operational plans prepared by responsible departments and agencies to carry out approved NSC policies.
b. Assure the timely and coordinated carrying out of such plans.
c. Initiate new proposals for action within the framework of national security policies in response to opportunity and other changes in the situation.
d. Assure that each project or action was so executed as to make its full contribution to the particular "climate of opinion" which the United States is seeking to achieve in the war.

---

[22] See Document 151.

Subsequent Arrangements for X-Day Planning

23. The Jackson Committee noted that the POCC, which had existed as a mechanism through which the State Department could coordinate the Foreign Information Program, was responsive to a necessary function, but recommended that the POCC be abolished and its function made a responsibility of the OCB and the OCB staff.

24. As a result, in a special memorandum to the NSC by the President, dated September 3, 1953 the functions of the POCC were transferred to the OCB. The OCB did not immediately abolish the POCC, but after the lapse of a little time discontinued it as a separate coordinating arrangement. However, the OCB continued an ad hoc committee on X-Day planning to carry on the work of developing plans for conducting psychological operations in support of hostilities, which had been the function of the "X-Day Committee" of the now defunct POCC.

25. In the fall of 1953 the ad hoc Committee on X-Day planning reported to the OCB that due to reorganization measures within the Government subsequent to NSC 127/1, revision of this policy was necessary in order that the X-Day Committee could go ahead with their tasks. Reorganization Plan No. 8 had established the USIA.[23] Executive Order No. 10483 had established the OCB, and the functions of the POCC had been transferred to the former. The X-Day working group felt that 127/1 could be revised easily in order to take into account these changes within the Government structure. Accordingly, it was authorized to present proposals for such revisions to the OCB for transmittal to the NSC. These proposals did not long remain "non-controversial" as was originally hoped. On March 22 the X-Day Working Committee presented proposals to the OCB for the revision of NSC 127/1, which in effect reopened many of the old arguments between the agencies concerning jurisdiction and the conduct of psychological operations during wartime. The matter was further complicated by trying to propose revisions to cover all types of hostilities, in order that "support planning should anticipate as far as possible every such situation from limited combat, as in Korea, to general war". There was no agreement within the Committee on the following major issues:

a. DOD, USIA and CIA representatives supported the position that in time of hostilities the Operations Coordinating Board should be responsible for "the formulation of national psychological objectives" and "the coordination of psychological operations and programs".

---

[23] On June 1, 1953, President Eisenhower submitted Reorganization Plan No. 8 to Congress. The text and supplementary information on that plan are printed in Department of State *Bulletin*, June 14, 1953, pp. 849–856.

b. The State representative supported the position that the OCB should be responsible for "assuring the formulation and coordination of guidance" and "the coordination of programs" for psychological operations in time of hostilities. (This would leave to the OCB to determine where the organization to provide guidance should be established, within the OCB or outside, etc.).

c. On the military enclave situation (NSC 127/1, para. 10), Defense, CIA and USIA supported the position that the military commander should have the responsibility of coordinating over-all psychological operations, with the USIA operations "insofar as practicable" being placed under his direction as an entity in charge of a designee of the USIA when the former deems it necessary for support of the military operations.

d. State supported the position that in this situation USIA should operate under the direction of the State Department Chief of Mission. The area of disagreement was possibly even broader, however, for the State Department representative with the X-Day Working Group reserved State's rights throughout to reconsider further at a higher level.

26. The OCB considered this problem (primarily at the Board Assistants' level) for some time and in its report to the NSC on the subject, dated July 21, 1954, generally came to the conclusion that the jurisdictional issues raised concerning final authority over psychological operations during general war were (a) difficult of resolution at the present time, and (b) did not perhaps need to be resolved at the present time.

27. The OCB recommended:

a. That the NSC rescind NSC 59/1 and NSC 127/1 "without prejudice to the principles of operation and the responsibilities of departments and agencies to engage in psychological warfare and psychological warfare planning enunciated therein or elsewhere."

b. "That the NSC note that the OCB serves as the body for dealing with requirements for interdepartmental coordination concerning overseas information and psychological warfare activities in carrying out NSC assignments or upon specific request by participating departments and agencies."

c. "That the NSC note that the OCB developed, on an urgent basis, a detailed contingency plan for information and psychological warfare activities in Indochina and that the OCB will not develop any further detailed subsidiary plans of this type for designated areas unless so directed by the NSC." (the implication being that if and when limited, rather than general, war should occur the OCB could develop plans and coordinating arrangements for Psywar operations which would be appropriate in the circumstances).

Current Status

28. The Joint Chiefs of Staff in their views dated 3 August 1954 objected to the recision of NSC 59/1 and 121/1 on the grounds that "although obsolete in certain organizational respects, (they) contain essential formal statements of national policy on psychological warfare

matters. Without a formal statement of responsibilities of governmental agencies concerned, there can be no valid basis for psychological warfare planning". The JCS further recommended that NSC 59/1 and NSC 127/1 should be revised or superseded.

29. On August 5, 1954, by NSC Action No. 1198, further action with respect to NSC 59/1 and NSC 127/1 was deferred pending receipt of an expanded study by the Bureau of the Budget (NSC Action No. 1197) which was "to include the placing of responsibility within the executive branch for coordinating economic warfare, psychological warfare, political warfare, and foreign information activities". However, the Bureau of the Budget was not specifically directed to propose a solution to the organizational and jurisdictional problems concerning psychological warfare operations during hostilities which are raised by NSC 127/1 and which have such a long history, and its projected report does not propose a solution to this matter.

30. In a letter to the Director, Office of Defense Mobilization dated February 7, 1955,[24] the Executive Officer of the Operations Coordinating Board noted that the OCB is currently responsible for the coordination of the transfer of overt information facilities, personnel, etc., to the theater commander in a period of general war "and that adequate authority and procedures exist utilizing the OCB structure to carry out this responsibility in a limited conflict." However, he further commented that in the absence of detailed plans for full mobilization in time of war, it did not appear to be feasible for the OCB to develop such plans for psychological warfare to be applicable in the event of general war.

31. In a memorandum dated January 11, 1955, subsequently circulated to the NSC on February 8, 1955, with a supporting memorandum from the Secretary of Defense, the Joint Chiefs of Staff reaffirmed their views of August 3, 1954, and specifically proposed that any document designed to supersede NSC 59/1 and NSC 127/1 should:

"a. Contain an approved definition of psychological warfare.
"b. Contain an approved definition of psychological operations.
"c. Adequately define responsibility and authority for the conduct of psychological warfare under conditions of declared war or hostilities involving the engagement of U.S. forces under conditions short of declared war.
"d. Delineate agency responsibility for use of facilities within a theater.
"e. Provide guidance for the orderly transfer of facilities at the beginning of hostilities.
"f. Provide for a coordinated psychological warfare effort by all agencies of government."

---

[24] Not found.

214. Memorandum of Discussion at the 247th Meeting of the National Security Council[1]

Washington, May 5, 1955.

SUBJECT

Discussion at the 247th Meeting of the National Security Council, Thursday, May 5, 1955

[Omitted here is a paragraph listing the participants at the meeting.]

1. Status of United States Programs for National Security As of December 31, 1954: The Internal Security Program (NSC 5509, Part 8)[2]

Mr. Coyne introduced his presentation with a brief analysis of the internal security arrangements under the National Security Council, with particular reference to the functions, responsibilities and membership of the Interdepartmental Intelligence Conference (IIC) and the Interdepartmental Committee on Internal Security (ICIS). He thereafter indicated that he would confine his presentation to five major problems relating to internal security. He added that he would pause at the end of his discussion of each of these five problems, to answer any questions.

Mr. Coyne then analyzed the Communist movement in the United States, using charts to illustrate his major points. At the conclusion of this discussion the President inquired, apropos of Mr. Coyne's statement that publishing activities helped to provide revenues for the Communist Party, USA, what publishing houses were maintained by the Communist Party and what kinds of material they published. Mr. Coyne and others described the publications, and the President then inquired whether such publications were clearly tabbed as Communist in character. Mr. Coyne replied that this was not normally the case, but that it was not difficult to discover their character after a brief reading.

The Vice President inquired as to the character of the firm which published the Matusow book.[3] Mr. J. Edgar Hoover explained the backgrounds of Angus Cameron and Albert Kahn, who had published this volume.

---

[1] Source: Eisenhower Library, Whitman File, NSC Records. Top Secret. Prepared by Gleason on May 6.

[2] A copy of NSC 5509, Part 8, is in the National Archives, RG 59, S/S–NSC Files: Lot 63 D 351, NSC 5509 Series.

[3] Reference is to Harvey Matusow, *False Witness* (New York: Cameron and Kahn, 1955).

At the conclusion of this discussion Mr. Coyne continued with his presentation, dealing successively with the following subjects: (1) Soviet bloc intelligence targets, overt and covert; (2) legal and illegal entry of foreign persons and materials into the United States; (3) the security of critical facilities; and (4) the security of vital information. (A copy of Mr. Coyne's report is filed with the minutes of the meeting.)[4]

At the conclusion of the presentation the President referred to the account given by Mr. Coyne of the manner in which a Czech courier had brought into Idlewild from Montreal six diplomatic pouches containing 1500 pounds of contents, while managing to avoid either customs or immigration inspection. The President said he could not imagine how an individual with so much material could have avoided some kind of customs inspection. Mr. Coyne replied that the courier in question had simply managed to fool both the customs and immigration officials, and had removed his pouches in an automobile which had been sent for that purpose.

The President said that despite the privileges of diplomatic immunity, would it not be right that if we catch an individual planning to evade our regulations, that individual should lose his diplomatic inviolability?

Mr. Coyne said that he would prefer that members of the State Department answer the President's question. Secretary Hoover stated that while it would be possible to go after a particular man, it would be extremely difficult to change the system which allowed for the inviolability of the diplomatic pouch. We could declare an individual persona non grata. Mr. Rose,[5] acting for the Secretary of the Treasury, recalled the circumstances of the case Mr. Coyne had cited, and indicated that the Embassy of Czechoslovakia had firmly denied that its courier had evaded regulations.

The President said he was sure of at least one thing. He would not feel that he was a very good and effective administrator if he could not think up some way to delay such an individual as this Czech courier long enough to discover what were the contents of his baggage and pouches without actually opening them.

Secretary Wilson said that was it not obvious that there was consistent abuse of the pouch privilege by Soviet bloc people. The President replied that of course they consistently abused the privilege, but the difficulty was that the United States in turn was dependent on being able to transmit diplomatic pouches to and from its missions in countries behind the Iron Curtain. Indeed, in one respect at least it

---

[4] Not found.

[5] H. Chapman Rose, Assistant Secretary of the Treasury.

needed these pouches more than the Soviet bloc diplomats, because it was necessary in many cases to send food in the pouches.

Mr. Allen Dulles said that he was convinced that there were certain additional steps which the United States could take to reduce Soviet bloc abuse of the pouch privilege, although, he said, many of his people in the Central Intelligence Agency did not agree with this point of view.

The President said that he hated to be a sucker when he knew that the other fellow was fooling and abusing him.

Mr. Coyne assured the President that certain members of the Council, including Admiral Radford, not to mention the members of the two internal security committees, were hard at work to see what additional actions we could take to cope with this problem

Admiral Radford said that he was indeed interested, and had tried to canvass the three Services as to possible reduction of their dependence on pouch material sent to Washington by the Military Attachés. He had not been very successful in persuading them that it was unnecessary to rely so heavily on this pouch material. Nevertheless, he still felt personally that the United States loses more than it gains by its strict adherence to the inviolability of the diplomatic pouch as a means of securing intelligence materials on the Soviet bloc.

The President said that he thought it would be a good idea to contact our Embassies in the Soviet bloc countries and to ascertain from them just how important our own pouches really are. If this importance proved not to be vital, we might contemplate new regulations. In any event, said the President, he admitted that the problem of controlling abuse of the pouch was not as easy as it looked on the surface.

Mr. Dillon Anderson then inquired of the President whether he wished further study and recommendations by the two internal security committees on this subject. The Attorney General, Mr. J. Edgar Hoover and Mr. Coyne pointed out that the two committees were already engaged in restudying the problem.

Governor Stassen, reverting to the problem of illegal entries into the United States from foreign countries, which Mr. Coyne had underlined, inquired whether the time may not be close at hand when everyone in the United States must be compelled to have an identification card. It might, for example, be possible to insist on such identification cards under cover of the requirements for civil defense. The President replied that of course the system of identification cards had been common in many European countries for a good many years, but he believed that an attempt to introduce this system in the United States would raise a great political storm, although it might be possible to get by with a civil defense cover.

The National Security Council:[6]

a. Noted and discussed an oral briefing on the subject by the NSC Representative on Internal Security, based upon Part 8 or NSC 5509.

b. Noted that the internal security committees are preparing a report for Council consideration on the internal security problems created by Soviet bloc use of the diplomatic pouch in relation to U.S. use of the diplomatic pouch in the Soviet bloc countries.

Note: The action in b above subsequently transmitted to the Chairmen, IIC and ICIS.

[Omitted here are the remaining agenda items.]

---

[6] Paragraphs a–b and the Note that follow constituted NSC Action No. 1390. (National Archives, RG 59, S/S–NSC (Miscellaneous) Files: Lot 66 D 95, Records of Action of the National Security Council)

---

215. Memorandum From Director of Central Intelligence Dulles to the Special Assistant to the Secretary of Defense (Erskine)

Washington, May 7, 1955.

[Source: Central Intelligence Agency, Executive Registry, Job 95–G00278B, Box 1, Folder 29. Top Secret. 1 page not declassified.]

---

216. Memorandum From the Chief of Foreign Intelligence, Central Intelligence Agency (Steward) to Director of Central Intelligence Dulles

Washington, May 10, 1955.

[Source: Central Intelligence Agency, Office of the Deputy Director of Operations, Job 79–01228A, Box 30. Secret. 3 pages not declassified.]

217. Memorandum From the Assistant Director of the Office of Research and Reports, Central Intelligence Agency (Guthe) to the Assistant to the Deputy Director for Intelligence (Planning), Central Intelligence Agency[1]

Washington, May 13, 1955.

SUBJECT

    Sovmat[2] Program

REFERENCE

    Memorandum from Assistant to DD/I (Planning) to AD/RR, dated 20 April 1955, same subject[3]

1. The collection and exploitation of Soviet Bloc materials has long been considered by this Office to be a potential source of valuable, positive, economic intelligence information. The potential of this source has also been recognized by the ORR [Office of Research and Reports][4] Panel of Economic Consultants in at least two of their annual reports. Economic intelligence information to be derived in this fashion could either be confirmatory or could provide economic information unobtainable from other sources.

2. The development of the Sovmat Program has not been, for the most part, as was initially anticipated. While collection of the majority of Sovmat type items is a matter of opportunity and consequently can be geared only to a long range research program, this Office has not been completely satisfied with respect to the length of time involved, the cost and the responsiveness of exploitation reports for these items. The answers to the specific questions raised in the referenced memorandum reflect the nature of our dissatisfaction.

3. The research programs of this Office require information such as that sought through the Sovmat Program. Because of the many disappointing results from the Sovmat Program, serious consideration is being given to other sources which while lacking the same potential, can provide somewhat similar information on the same items which would be more timely and responsive to our requirements. This would also effect a considerable savings of money for what appears to be unjustifiable expense for exploitation.

---

[1] Source: Central Intelligence Agency, History Staff, Job 84–B00389R, Box 4. Secret. Drafted by J.M. Ault in the Office of Research and Reports.

[2] Soviet Materials.

[3] Not found.

[4] Brackets in the original.

4. The following comments concerning the Sovmat Program are submitted in response to the specific questions raised in the referenced memorandum:

a) Do you consider the time between levying the requirements and receipt of report of exploitation excessive?

[Answer][5] It has been the experience of this Office that economic exploitation requirements are usually fulfilled by the following general categories of exploitation facilities:

[*Heading and 1 paragraph (10 lines) not declassified*]

2) *Exploitation Facilities of the Armed Services*

The Sovmat Staff has direct contact with the separate Services through their representation to the Joint Technical Intelligence Sub-committee (JTIS). After serving our exploitation requirements on the Services, the Sovmat Staff has indicated by memoranda to this Office that they have no further responsibility for the requirements and that the Office of Collection and Dissemination is the proper channel for obtaining exploitation reports. The exploitation reports prepared by the Services are not published in the Sovmat "OO-T" series, but follow their own format. A check of some of these reports which have been received by this Office indicates that the time between receipt of the item by the Services and receipt of the published exploitation report will vary between one and two years.

Recently, a JTIS publication identified all exploitation reports prepared by the various Services and CIA. According to this publication, the exploitation reports vary in their degree of availability and are not all disseminated. There is not sufficient description of the reports listed in this publication to indicate whether the exploitation requested by this Office has been accomplished.

An inquiry was made of Liaison Division/DCD [Domestic Contact Division, DDP][6] to ascertain the method by which exploitation reports were acquired from the Services in response to our requirements. It was discovered that DCD has no record of the requirements which are served on the Services by Sovmat Staff and has no follow-up instruction from the Sovmat Staff. Hence, no reports will be received in direct response to our requirements and we will receive only such reports as will be disseminated by the Services.

---

[5] Brackets in the original.
[6] Brackets in the original.

A specific document request was made through Liaison Division, OOD for an exploitation report on Soviet ammunition, which was described as a "Preliminary Report" by the Ordnance Corps and was never disseminated nor was it listed in the JTIS publication. We discovered that the report contained [2 lines not declassified]. Such information was of considerable value to this Office. A similar situation was discovered in requesting a non-disseminated report from another Service with respect to Soviet ball bearings.

Under these circumstances, the time interval between levying requirements and the receipt of exploitation reports is certainly excessive and there is no certainty that an exploitation report will be received, or if exploitation is accomplished, that it will include our requirements.

3) *Exploitation Facilities of Non-Military Government Agencies*

This Office does not consider the time interval between levying requirements and receipt of exploitation reports to be excessive where the exploitation is accomplished by non-military government agencies.

b. Do you consider that the best and most economical means are used for exploitation of Sovmat materials?

The Sovmat Staff notifies this Office of the cost of exploitation only in those instances where in their judgment there is an unusual charge or where they feel that additional justification, other than the requirement, is warranted. This Office has, therefore, no knowledge of the exploitation cost of a great majority of the exploitation accomplished in response to our requirements.

In most instances where this Office has been made aware of the exploitation cost, it does appear that there is excessive cost for the exploitation contemplated in a number of our requirements and the best and most economical means are not always used for exploitation. It is felt that greater reliance should be placed on this Office by the Sovmat Staff for substantive guidance, interpretation of our requirements, and suggestions for exploiting facilities and companies with a view toward minimizing the cost of exploitation.

[1 paragraph (16 lines) not declassified]

There are additional instances which have tended to create the impression in this Office that the cost of exploitation is excessive. As for example, where we had requested that an exploiting facility prepare a brief evaluation of a Sovmat item, the exploitation report forwarded by the Sovmat Staff for evaluation by this Office contained the results of elaborate testing and comprehensive technical description, far in excess of our request. On the exploitation reports, the Office checked to evaluate the reports in the requesting Office or an Office with a major interest. Since this Office was the only Office requested to evaluate, it was presumed that we were the only requester. On other exploitation reports where ORR and OSI [the Office of Scientific Intelligence,

DDI][7] were both indicated as requesting Offices, informal discussion between interested analysts of the two Offices has revealed that the report goes far beyond the interest of either Office.

c. [2 paragraphs (12 lines) not declassified]

d. Do you have any suggestions for improvement of the Sovmat Program?

This Office has frequently made suggestions to the Sovmat Staff for improvement in the Sovmat Program through regular channels. For example, in January 1954 this Office forwarded comments by Ambassador [Joseph][8] Flack of Embassy Warsaw and Mr. George Atkins, a former employee of Embassy Moscow, which described difficulties in the Sovmat Program. Comments received by this Office from returning attachés and State personnel regarding lack of adequate collection guidance have been informally discussed with the Sovmat Staff. A continuous flow of evaluations from this Office call to the attention of the Sovmat Staff specific instances where the exploitation reports might better be focused on requirements of this Office.

Some of the major suggestions of this Office which might be considered for improvement of the Sovmat Program are outlined below and stem in part from the comments in preceding paragraphs:

1. The Sovmat Staff should arrange for adequate follow-up on exploitation requirements served on the Services to insure, insofar as possible, that the requirements are accomplished by the Services and that exploitation reports are received in response to these requirements.

2. The Sovmat Staff should provide exploitation cost information and whenever possible, total procurement costs to enable the requesting Offices to consider this factor in the preparation of the periodic revisions of the Sovmat Collection Guide. This information will have a direct influence in the preparation of collection requests for the same or similar items. In this way, adequate prior consideration will be given to insure that the value of the information to be derived from the item is commensurate with the cost of procurement and exploitation.

3. The Sovmat Staff should utilize the special knowledge of the requesting Offices for substantive guidance, interpretation of requirements, and suggestions for exploiting facilities. It cannot be expected that the Offices can provide adequate support to the Sovmat Staff in a mere exchange of memoranda. [19 lines not declassified]

---

[7] Brackets in the original.
[8] Brackets in the original.

4. Greater emphasis should be made by the Sovmat Staff in coordinating the common interests of several Offices in certain types of items to establish periodic collection and standard exploitation of the items. This would eliminate any possibility of duplication of collection, incomplete exploitation, and excessive administrative and exploitation costs. As examples of programs which can be effected where there is this community of interest in similar items, [2 *lines not declassified*] there is mutual interest in the same type products. Standard collection procedures have been arranged. The result is a minimum of administrative detail and cost and complete and satisfactory exploitation for all interested Agencies.

5. The Sovmat Staff should take greater advantage of the suggested exploitation section of the [1 *line not declassified*] in order to anticipate exploitation for those items which are expected to be purchased or have been purchased and are awaiting shipment.

6. The Sovmat Staff should consider the practicality of having one or two industry experts evaluate an item at CIA facilities together with representatives of the respecting Offices prior to formulation of extensive exploitation requirements. An example of the value of this practice can be shown in the examination of a [2 *lines not declassified*]. This examination evaluation precluded costly and comprehensive exploitation.

7. The Sovmat Staff should provide more adequate collection support and cooperation in those instances where high priority collection and exploitation is required by this Office. As an example of the lack of cooperation and support we have received from the Sovmat Staff in this respect, our recent priority requirements for collection and exploitation of a [10 *lines not declassified*]. Furthermore, the Sovmat Staff advised this Office that they preferred to rely on existing procedures for such collection and exploitation. As we could not provide detailed information on the collection of the sample and because of the reluctance of the Sovmat Staff to interfere with regular channels, we were required to obtain the information on the basis of informal relationships and outside of liaison channels which were available to the Sovmat Staff.

Otto B. Guthe[9]

---

[9] Printed from a copy that bears this typed signature.

218.   Circular Airgram From the Department of State to All Diplomatic and Consular Posts[1]

CA–7918   Washington, May 14, 1955.

SUBJECT

The Watch Committee and the National Indications Center

The purpose of this instruction is to review the responsibility of the *Watch Committee* of the Intelligence Advisory Committee (IAC) of the National Security Council, and to provide notice of the establishment of the *National Indications Center* (NIC), which has been set up to increase the Watch Committee's capability to discharge its mission. The instruction is being circulated to Foreign Service posts to provide information on how posts should cooperate in carrying out the responsibility the Department bears to the Watch Committee and the NIC.

The Watch Committee is chaired by the Deputy Director of the Central Intelligence Agency, at present Lt. Gen. Cabell, and his senior representatives from each of the following: State, Army, Navy, Air Force, JIG, CIA, AEC, and the FBI. Its mission is: "To provide earliest possible warning to the United States Government of hostile action of the USSR, or its allies, which endangers the security of the United States." ("Hostile action" is defined as aggressive action by armed forces or organizations or individuals in support of military strategy.)

The Watch Committee has the following functions:

1. To analyze and evaluate information and intelligence, both current and cumulative furnished by IAC agencies relating to the imminence of hostilities, and to develop therefrom conclusions as to indications of:

a. Soviet/Communist intentions to initiate hostilities against the continental US, US possessions, or US forces abroad; US Allies or their forces; areas peripheral to the Soviet Orbit.

b. Any other development, actual or potential, susceptible of direct exploitation by Soviet/Communist hostile action which would jeopardize the security of the U.S.

2. To report promptly their conclusions to the principals of the IAC and to other appropriate recipients. If immediate action or decision on the part of the President or the National Security Council seems

---

[1] Source: National Archives, RG 59, Central Files 1955–60, 101. 2/5–1455. Secret. Drafted by McAfee on May 3, cleared in 10 bureaus, and approved by Furnas.

to be required a meeting of the IAC will be convened by the Director of Central Intelligence.

The Watch Committee is always on call for emergency sessions and meets regularly on Wednesday of each week.

The *National Indications Center* has been established to provide a central staff devoting full time to the problems faced by the Watch Committee. It is charged, among other responsibilities with:

1. Developing and operating the Watch Committee Intelligence plan for world wide collection of information pertinent to the Watch Committee mission;

2. Arranging for exploitation of all sources of information bearing on the mission;

3. Arranging with IAC agencies for systematic screening of all information and intelligence received by them for the purpose of forwarding to the Indications Center all items which contain indications of Soviet/Communist intentions.

In support of the Watch Committee and NIC, the President on 30 November 1954 approved NSC 5438,[2] directing all appropriate departments and agencies of the Government:

"1. To make fully available to the IAC Watch Committee all information and intelligence of reasonable credibility pertinent to its mission and functions without restriction because of source, policy or operational sensitivity.

"2. To keep the IAC Watch Committee informed concerning significant diplomatic, political, military, or other courses of action by the U.S., approved for immediate implementation or in process of execution, which might bring about military reaction or early hostile action by the USSR, or its allies, thus endangering the security of the U.S. This information is for the explicit and express use of the Watch Committee and those members of the National Indications Center who need to know of it in order to perform their functions."

The Department of State's responsibility to the *Watch Committee* and the *National Indications Center* covers evaluation of political and economic indications which might bear on Soviet/Communist intent to initiate hostilities. Within the Department, the Office of the Special Assistant, Intelligence (R) bears the responsibility for the discharge of the Department's commitments. However, the responsibility to be checking constantly for such indications is shared by the other areas of the Department and by Foreign Service posts. Information on any

---

[2] Regarding NSC 5438, see Document 187 and footnote 4 thereto.

such indications should be brought immediately to the attention of the Department by telegram when appropriate, and should be followed up when necessary by dispatch containing available further information, including information on the source and reliability of the report.[3]

At posts where Service Attachés or CAS are present, the information should also be passed to those officers.

Directly bearing on the question of Soviet/Communist intent to initiate hostilities, of course, would be information on attempts to smuggle fissionable material or other types of unconventional warfare weapons or sabotage devices into the country. Any information of this type should be reported immediately by telegram and followed by dispatch providing full details as to the source and reliability of the information, the origin and destination of the material and the alleged use to be made of it. At posts having CAS or Legal Attachés, all available information should also be passed to them.

This instruction neither supersedes nor modifies any other extant instruction concerning the requirements of other government agencies for specialized information having to do with threats to the security of the United States (e.g. Secret Circular Instruction, June 17, 1952 concerning the smuggling into the U.S. of radiological, biological, chemical, and other weapons, or sabotage devices.)[4]

Hoover

---

[3] McAfee elaborated on the watch functions of the Department of State in an August 19 memorandum to Robert G. Barnes, Director of the Executive Secretariat, for distribution throughout the Department. According to McAfee, the Department was charged with evaluating diplomatic indications of Soviet/Chinese intent to initiate hostilities and for reporting to the Watch Committee significant Soviet/Communist hostile reactions to certain U.S. diplomatic negotiations and economic measures. In particular, Department officials were asked to look for such indications when reviewing memoranda of conversation and observing Soviet reactions to U.S. negotiations for base rights, military assistance pacts, or transit rights with states adjacent to the Soviet orbit, and to such steps as preclusive purchasing, embargoes, blockade, and interference with Soviet/Communist marine or air transport. (National Archives, RG 59, Central Files 1955–60, 101.2/8–1955)

[4] Not found.

219. Editorial Note

NSC 5520, "U.S. Scientific Satellite Program," was discussed by the National Security Council at its May 26, 1955, meeting and approved by the President on May 27. The potential for intelligence collection was a major factor in the decision to proceed with satellite development. NSC 5520 is printed in *Foreign Relations*, 1955–1957, volume XI, pages 723–732.

---

220. Report by the Task Force on Intelligence Activities of the Commission on Organization of the Executive Branch of the Government[1]

Washington, May 1955.

PREFACE

Scope of the Study

"Intelligence"—A Definition

The fate of the nation well may rest on accurate and complete intelligence data which may serve as a trustworthy guide for top-level governmental decisions on policy and action in a troubled world where so many forces and ideologies work at cross purposes.

The Congress has recognized the importance of the role of intelligence in our national security. It has authorized the expenditure of vast

---

[1] Source: Central Intelligence Agency, Executive Registry, Job 86–B00269R, Box 1. Top Secret. Regarding the background to this report, see Document 185. This report, which includes two appendices, is attached to a transmittal letter from the task force members to Herbert Hoover, May 1955, not printed. The letter outlined the task force's awareness of "the grave responsibility implicit in its assigned mission," and it expressed the members' "personal appreciation for the wholehearted and enthusiastic cooperation given us by the departments and agencies involved." It also noted, however, that "the task force was severely hampered by the security restrictions imposed upon it in its survey of the clandestine operations of the Central Intelligence Agency. While the necessity for carefully safeguarding sensitive material is well recognized, the fact remains that the restrictions complicated the conduct of the survey of this vital segment of our national intelligence community." The letter also transmitted the unclassified report, which was subsequently published and sent to Congress (Document 221). Only the Preface and Introduction to the classified report are printed here.

sums of money by appropriate departments and agencies to carry on this work.

Immediately after World War II, at the suggestion of the Chief Executive of our Government, the Congress approved the creation of a new agency unique and in many ways strange to our democratic form of government. It is known as the Central Intelligence Agency (CIA).

The CIA operates without the customary legislative restraints and reins under which other departments must function. Its work is veiled in secrecy, and it is virtually a law unto itself.

In order to evaluate the extent and effectiveness of intelligence as carried out under these conditions, the Task Force on Intelligence Activities found that it was confronted at the outset with the problem of arriving at a common understanding and agreement on the meaning of the word "intelligence," as applied to its own areas of work and investigation.

The word has many definitions and is subject to varying shades of interpretation and meaning. In a certain context it might refer to "ability to learn"; in another context, "intellect," or perhaps "ability to meet a new situation"; and in yet another sense, "common sense."

In the search for an acceptable definition as applied to our own field of study, it was found that each department or agency surveyed had its own definition. Many of these definitions were lengthy, and involved use of words requiring additional interpretation or delimitation to get to their precise application.

The task force sought a definition as simple and clear as possible and arrived at the following:

"Intelligence deals with all the things which should be known in advance of initiating a course of action."

Useful for our purposes, also, as a supplemental and expanded definition is that given in the Dictionary of United States Military Terms for Joint Usage:

"INTELLIGENCE—The product resulting from the collection, evaluation, analysis, integration, and interpretation of all available information which concerns one or more aspects of foreign nations or of areas of operations, and which is immediately or potentially significant to planning."

Scope of Task Force Study Refined

Initially, this task force was instructed by the Commission on Organization of the Executive Branch of the Government, hereinafter referred to as the Commission or the Hoover Commission, to study and make recommendations as to the structure and administration of the Central Intelligence Agency and other kindred intelligence activities.

Later, those instructions were changed by the Commission to embrace studies of *all* intelligence activities of the Federal Government and to submit recommendations to effect changes considered necessary to promote economy, efficiency, and improved service in this field.

The task force gave thorough consideration to the decision of the Commission to broaden the scope of the task-force studies to include all intelligence activities of the Federal Government. It developed that there are at least twelve major departments and agencies which, in one manner or another, are engaged in intelligence. Among these are the Department of State, the Department of Defense (including the Army, Navy, Air Force, and Joint Chiefs of Staff), the Central Intelligence Agency, the Atomic Energy Commission, the Department of Commerce, and the Department of Agriculture. In addition, there are ten or more minor agencies or activities which expend public funds directly or indirectly on behalf of the intelligence effort of the Government.

Thus, under the broad definition of its terms of reference, the task force was confronted with the Herculean job of studying and reporting on more than twenty major and minor departments and agencies. It readily became apparent that any attempt to spread the efforts of the task force over such a large area would mean either that only minor results could be expected within the allotted time or the work period should be extended beyond the date contemplated for dissolution of the Commission on May 31, 1955. Therefore, it was apparent that the scope of the task-force work had to be refined if any useful results were to be derived from its efforts and expenditure of funds.

Positive Foreign Intelligence Vital

The most pressing need under present conditions is for those officials in responsible positions in Government, especially those responsible for foreign policy, to have readily available full and factual foreign intelligence. The word "foreign" as used here denotes the target of information as distinct from the geographical source.

Thus, it appeared to the task force that within the given time limit the best interests of the Government would be served if the task force directed its attention to the departments and agencies whose entire or primary responsibilities lie in the field of positive foreign intelligence as it pertains to national defense and security, and in whose care vast sums of money and unique authority have been entrusted. These are the Department of State, the Department of Defense, the Central Intelligence Agency, the National Security Council, the Federal Bureau of Investigation (to the extent that it deals in security intelligence), and the intelligence activities of the Atomic Energy Commission.

Directive to the Task Force

Accordingly, a proposal to delimit the scope of the task-force studies was made to and approved by the Commission, as follows:

1. *Survey the work of the Central Intelligence Agency.* Cover all activities of CIA, wherever located, including but not limited to collection, evaluation, and dissemination of intelligence, obligation and expenditure of funds, examination of auditing of funds, security, personnel, projects carried out through other agencies, relationship and coordination with other governmental intelligence agencies, communications, supply and storage; a determination of the responsibilities of the agency, as prescribed by legislative enactment or administrative action, and a study as to whether the responsibilities have been adequately defined and are being implemented.

2. *Survey the intelligence activities of the Department of Defense.* Cover all intelligence activities, wherever located, of the Department of Defense, Joint Chiefs of Staff, National Security Agency, Army, Navy, and Air Force, including, but not limited to, collection, evaluation, and dissemination of intelligence, obligation and expenditure of funds, security, personnel, projects carried out through other agencies, communications, relationship and coordination with other governmental intelligence agencies, supply and storage; a determination of the responsibilities of the Department and all its elements for intelligence, as prescribed by legislative enactment or administrative action, and a study as to whether the responsibilities have been adequately defined and are being implemented. No survey will be made of the organization or organizational structure of tactical units in the Army, Navy, and Air Force engaged primarily in producing tactical or combat intelligence.

3. *Survey the intelligence activities of the Department of State.* Cover all intelligence activities related to national defense, wherever located, of the Department of State, including but not limited to, collection, evaluation, and dissemination of intelligence, obligation and expenditure of funds, security, personnel, projects carried out through other agencies, communications, relationship and coordination with other governmental intelligence agencies, and supply; a determination of the responsibilities of the Department for intelligence, as prescribed by legislative enactment or administrative action, and a study as to whether the responsibilities have been adequately defined and are being implemented.

4. *Survey the intelligence activities of the National Security Council.* Include a study of the history, legislation, development, organization, and operations of the National Security Council as they affect intelligence activities. Include study of the Operations Coordinating Board, the Intelligence Advisory Committee, and related activities.

5. *Survey limited segments of the intelligence activities of other agencies.* The segments to be studied would be developed as the task force gathers information.

6. *General Considerations.* Determine which of the intelligence services, activities, and functions performed by any of the agencies surveyed are (a) essential; (b) not necessary; (c) of similar nature, and what consolidations are in the public interest; (d) non-essential, and which are competitive with private enterprise; and (e) duplicate or overlap those of other agencies.

This requires a determination in the basic surveys outlined in paragraphs 1 to 5 as to what services, activities, and functions are being performed by each agency studied. Upon completion of the basic surveys, a functional survey of the work done by the agencies would be undertaken from the data developed. With such a scope, the task force would cover, among other things:

(1) The intelligence function of the National Security Council.
(2) The value and effectiveness of the information supplied by the operating agencies.
(3) The effectiveness of the coordination of intelligence agencies.
(4) The organization, procedures, methods, and performance of the several Government agencies in the field of overt and covert intelligence.
(5) An examination of the operation and physical plant of the agencies as to economy, adequacy, effect on efficiency, and utilization.
(6) The various programs of the several agencies in such fields as training, research and development, stockpiling, reference material, and security.
(7) The personnel policies and manpower utilization.
(8) All programs and procedures for the collection, development, and dissemination of information to include collection apparatus and dissemination media.
(9) The interrelationship between the several areas thus assigned and actual areas of coverage, mutual support of one another.

In the execution of this extensive undertaking, the task force, in certain areas, had to employ the "sampling" method, particularly in the case of the study of those activities of the agencies overseas.

Sensitive Portions of Agencies Surveyed

In giving its approval of the foregoing proposal, the Commission directed that a first paragraph be added as follows:

"1. The study and survey of the sensitive portions of the agencies will be undertaken by General Clark with a minimum staff on a 'need-to-know' basis."

Pursuant to the foregoing directive, arrangements were made orally between Mr. Allen Dulles, Director of the Central Intelligence Agency, and General Mark W. Clark, chairman of the Task Force on Intelligence Activities, initially for General Clark and Colonel Herman O. Lane, a member of the task-force staff, to have access to CIA activities, both overt and covert. Shortly after this arrangement was implemented, it developed that a requirement existed for at least one additional member of the task force to have access to covert activities of the agency. Accordingly, Admiral Richard L. Connolly's name was added to the list.

This arrangement continued until a decision was made that certain members of the task force and staff should inspect intelligence activities in the European and Far East areas. Since General Clark was unable to take part in one of these inspection trips, the problem confronting the task forces, as a result of the existing restrictions on the clearance of the task force to sensitive material of the agency, was presented to the Director of Central Intelligence. The following quoted letter was received from the director:

CENTRAL INTELLIGENCE AGENCY
Washington 25, D.C.
Office of the Director
27 January 1955

General J.G. Christiansen
Staff Director
Task Force on Intelligence Activities
Commission on Organization of the Executive Branch of the Government
Washington D.C.

Dear General Christiansen:

With further reference to your letter of 20 January 1955,[2] and our telephone conversations of yesterday evening and today, I have arranged clearance for Mr. Henry Kearns and for you to have access to CIA activities, both overt and covert, in connection with your trip to the Pacific area. It is also understood that all members of the Task Force and you, yourself, will be cleared to consider the report with respect to both overt and covert activities of the CIA which may be submitted by those members of your staff who have been cleared for on-the-spot investigation of those activities. I quite appreciate that this is necessary in connection with the preparation of the Task Force report.

This procedure has been cleared with Governor Adams.

Faithfully yours,

Allen W. Dulles
Director

Cost of the Intelligence Effort

Precise figures on the cost in money and manpower engaged in intelligence activities in the interest of national defense and security are not a matter of record. Any attempt to compile such data accurately would require the expenditure of money out of all proportion to the value of the findings. The task force estimates, however, that the annual expenditure is in the order of $800 million.

---

[2] Not found.

Organization of the Task Force

Security Impact on Selection of Personnel

The Task Force on Intelligence Activities was the last to be authorized by the Hoover Commission. The director and deputy of the staff assumed their duties on October 1, 1954. The limited pool of available personnel in the United States with prior experience in the intelligence field influenced to some extent the structure of the staff and its methods of operation.

Personnel of the Intelligence Task Force and of the staff had to be screened carefully for background security and possible prejudicial interest arising from prior association with departments and agencies under investigation.

Before a member of the task force or staff could have access to any material, a security background investigation was conducted and the individual declared by proper authority to be eligible for access to "Top Secret" information. In each case where the inquiry involved access to atomic energy data, a special clearance was obtained.

It was found that each department and agency had evolved its criteria, practices, and standards for clearance. The task force adopted a policy in conformity with the policies and requirements of the department or agency involved in each specific investigation.

In the interest of security and economy, the task force also decided to keep its staff as compact as possible. Sensitive material was studied generally on the premises of the agencies.

Staff Organization

After careful consideration by the task force of the possible methods of organizing the staff and its work, it was decided that the most practical course would be to assign some teams composed of one or two staff members to study specific agencies, and to delegate to other teams specific across-the-board survey functions. Individual task force members were assigned across-the-board responsibilities paralleling the work of designated staff teams. Thus, all members would be in a position to interject their influence and guidance in the staff activities and at the same time obtain valuable first-hand knowledge of the overall problem.

Initially, five staff study groups were organized. Some were assigned responsibility for study of a single department; others, where feasible, covered two or more agencies.

The restrictions imposed on the staff in its survey of the Central Intelligence Agency necessitated that the work be broken down into two classifications, with one group studying the covert aspects of CIA, and the other surveying the overt operations of the Agency. These two teams carefully coordinated and correlated their studies, except where information on the more sensitive areas of the Agency's work was restricted to designated individuals. This arrangement proved very cumbersome, was time-consuming, and seriously interfered with the conduct of the survey.

As each task group completed the study of a particular department or agency, it was assigned to studies of specific functions common to two or more agencies.

Procedures for Gathering Data

The task force scrupulously avoided the use of questionnaires. The statistical matter which appears throughout this report was extracted from documentary files maintained by the departments and agencies.

The task force and staff had the benefit of detailed briefings by each agency studied. These briefings were characterized by informality. Oral questions and answers were the rule rather than the exception. No verbatim transcriptions of the conversations and comments of witnesses were deemed necessary. In some instances, however, copies of the prepared briefings were furnished to the staff for ready reference.

Discussions were had with all echelons of personnel in each department and agency, from the clerk at the working level to and including the Secretary of State, the Secretary and Deputy Secretary of Defense, and the Director of Central Intelligence.

The task force also had the benefit of expert advice from many individuals who are not in Government employ but who previously occupied positions of prime responsibility in the development of our present intelligence operations and organization. Their help and advice were of inestimable value.

Some of these witnesses appeared before the task force at no expense to the Government and at considerable personal sacrifice. The task force wishes to express its unqualified appreciation to these public-spirited individuals in private life who gave freely of their time, and who by their objective approach to the problem materially enlightened the task force.

Teams Make First-Hand Studies Abroad

In order to obtain a clearer picture of intelligence operations, two teams, each composed of a member or members of the task force and members of the staff, were sent abroad for on-the-spot investigations. One team visited the European sector and the other went to the Far East.

These staff groups had discussions with the senior United States representatives, senior military commanders, and representatives of the Central Intelligence Agency in the countries visited. The visits and discussions afforded the task force first-hand information which could be obtained in no other fashion.

The conclusions reached and the recommendations contained in this report reflect the benefits of those personal tours of inspection.

Results of the Recommendations Made in 1948 by the First Hoover Commission As They Related to Intelligence

The first Hoover Commission[3] directed its attention primarily to the functional responsibilities and relationships of the heads of the various departments and agencies established under the National Security Act. The principal recommendation relating directly to intelligence was incorporated in the following general recommendation:

"That more adequate and effective relations be developed at working level among the appropriate committees of the Joint Chiefs of Staff on one hand, and the National Security Council, Central Intelligence Agency, Research and Development Board, Munitions Board, and the National Security Resources Board on the other hand. That vigorous steps be taken to improve the Central Intelligence Agency and its work."

Results

The Reorganization Plan No. 3 of 1953[4] transferred the functions of the National Security Resources Board and Munitions Board to the Office of Defense Mobilization. The functions of the Research and Development Board were transferred to the Secretary of Defense by Reorganization Plan No. 6 of 1953,[5] where they are incorporated in the functions of the Assistant Secretary of Research and Development. There are apparently no relationships on working levels in the intelligence field between the Joint Chiefs of Staff and the Office of Defense Mobilization, except through the representation of the Secretary of Defense in the National Security Council. As far as the intelligence relations between the Joint Chiefs of Staff and the Central Intelligence Agency on working levels are concerned, they are implicit in the representation of the joint intelligence group of the Joint Staff, Joint Chiefs of Staff, on the Intelligence Advisory Committee. The degree of coordination effected through these relationships will be discussed more fully in this report in the section devoted to the Joint Chiefs of Staff. The steps taken subsequent to the publication of the report of the first Hoover Commission to improve the Central Intelligence Agency are

---

[3] Some documentation on the first Hoover Commission (1948) is in *Foreign Relations*, 1945–1950, Emergence of the Intelligence Establishment, Documents 351–352, 360, and 399.

[4] Effective June 12, 1953; 67 Stat. 634.

[5] Effective June 30, 1953; 67 Stat. 638.

discussed in the following paragraphs relating to the recommendations of the task force of the first Hoover Commission.

*Observations, Recommendations, and Results of the Task Force on
Intelligence Activities within the National Defense Organization*

The task force of the first Hoover Commission confined its observations and recommendations to the Central Intelligence Agency, its internal problems, and its relationships with the Joint Chiefs of Staff, the State Department, the National Security Council, and the intelligence agencies of the three military services.

The present task force has been unable to determine the degree to which these observations and recommendations were published and disseminated, except as they are reflected in the recommendation of the Commission discussed previously. However, as they influenced to some degree the direction of the efforts of this task force, a brief discussion of the observations of this task force in the same areas is believed to be pertinent.

*Observations of the Task Force of First Hoover Commission and Comments
of this Task Force Thereon*

1. "Judgment as to the effectiveness of the CIA must be tempered by considerations of its apparent youth, its lack of tradition and established, time-tried procedures, and of continuity of personnel." The soundness of that observation is self-evident and is supported by the observations of this task force as set forth in its report.

2. "There seems to be an excess of administrative personnel, and there is undue interference with operating agencies. Reduction of administrative overhead is possible and desirable, and interference with operating agencies should be eliminated." There still exists some excess of administrative personnel because of considerations relating to compartmentalization for security reasons, and because of the fact that the agency is now scattered among thirty-four buildings. This administrative overhead is a matter of constant concern and study to the agency. Plans for new construction have been initiated and funds will be requested.

3. "The CIA is scattered among twenty-two buildings, causing many administrative difficulties, although some scattering may be desirable for security reasons." The number of buildings now occupied by the agency has been increased to thirty-four, thus magnifying the administrative difficulties.

4. "The CIA has fallen short of its objectives as a source of national intelligence, especially in the fields of scientific intelligence, including medical. This information should be evaluated centrally." This observation will be commented upon in the discussion following recommendation 3 below.

5. "The CIA's main problem is one of securing and retaining qualified personnel. This is also true of other intelligence agencies." The securing and retaining of qualified personnel has been largely solved by the agency as it has had sufficient funds to attract the best qualified people, sometimes, unfortunately, at the expense of the intelligence agencies of the three services. This situation will be discussed more fully in the section covering the Central Intelligence Agency and the military services.

6. "The services must rid their intelligence estimates of service bias." Attempts on the part of service intelligence agencies to present honest intelligence estimates particular to that agency are sometimes "slanted" by the command echelons of the services in support of budgetary requests. This tendency should not be charged to intelligence agencies, which on the whole, are doing an honest job as far as this task force has been able to observe.

7. [1 paragraph (7 lines) not declassified]

8. "Thought should be given to desirability of splitting CIA in time of war, and transferring operational services, such as open and covert collection, to the Department of Defense. Changes should be made in peacetime organization to facilitate this split." Much thought has been given by the officials of the CIA and the military services concerning the proper relationships in time of war between the CIA and the military services. Present plans of the CIA do not contemplate the transfer of any of CIA's current functions and responsibilities to the Department of Defense in time of war. However, current plans (approved by the Secretary of Defense and the DCI) envisage the transfer of operational control over CIA's component forces in active theaters of war where American Forces are engaged to the military commander thereof, who will exercise such control in the same manner as control is exercised by him over components of the Army, Navy, and Air Force assigned to the same command (see Appendix II). The task force believes that the seriousness of this ever-present problem warrants continued study to arrive, if possible, at the most suitable solution prior to the outbreak of war.

9. "The military services, including Joint Chiefs of Staff, tend to withhold details of operational information and military plans on the grounds of security." This situation has not been solved to the complete satisfaction of all interested parties.

10. "The ties binding the JCS, among others, to the CIA are too tenuous." This observation resulted in recommendation 3 of the task force and will be commented on in the discussion following that recommendation.

11. "Any proposals for the revision of laws so as to permit conviction, regardless of intent, in cases of dangerous disclosures by indiscreet

and irresponsible persons, should be examined most carefully by Congress in the light of our concepts of freedom." As far as this task force has been able to determine, no statutory authority exists or is contemplated which covers the situation of former employees who may, negligently or otherwise, *without intent,* make unauthorized disclosures.

12. "The National Security Organization, as established by the National Security Act of 1947, is soundly conceived. In order to improve operations, the NSC should give more thought and attention to the relationships of CIA with other agencies, and by working through the Secretaries of State and Defense, should encourage the improvement of other intelligence agencies." This observation is incorporated in recommendation 1 of the task force below.

13. "Such of the reforms as suggested by this committee, as well as those of the Dulles Committee,[6] should be made promptly, but when action has been taken, the agencies affected should be permitted a period of internal development free from examination and its attendant publicity." Any comment on this sound observation would be redundant.

Recommendations of the Task Force of the First Hoover Commission

1. "That more adequate and effective relations be established at the working levels between appropriate committees of the JCS and the Joint Staff and their countermembers in (1) the National Security Council, (2) the Central Intelligence Agency, (3) the Research and Development Board, (4) the Munitions Board, and (5) the National Security Resources Board, to the end that in their strategic planning the JCS will weigh adequately and on a systematic, reciprocal basis, considerations of foreign policy, intelligence, scientific research and development, and economic capabilities." This recommendation is substantially the same as the recommendation of the commission, and the results will be discussed in the sections of this report devoted to the Joint Chiefs of Staff.

2. "That the Secretary of Defense be the sole representative of the national military establishment on the National Security Council. The Committee suggests, however, in order that the JCS may be fully and currently posted on our national policy, that they be invited, as a general rule, to attend meetings of the NSC, but without membership thereon. The civilian departmental secretaries, although not members, should also be invited to attend council meetings in appropriate circumstances." The National Security Act of 1947, as amended, now provides that the Secretary of Defense is the sole National Defense Establishment member. However, secretaries and under secretaries of the military departments may serve as members at the pleasure of the Pres-

---

[6] For a summary of the Dulles Committee Report, see *Foreign Relations, 1945–1950, Emergence of the Intelligence Establishment,* Document 358.

ident. The law also provides that the Joint Chiefs of Staff will be the principal military advisers to the President, the National Security Council, and the Secretary of Defense. It has been observed by this task force that the Chairman of the Joint Chiefs of Staff habitually attends the meetings of the National Security Council and the other members attend for those items in which the Joint Chiefs are concerned. When departmental matters are before the Council which are of concern to the Secretaries of the Army, Navy, or Air Force, the secretary concerned will be invited and may bring his military chief as an adviser, in which case that military chief will not be attending in his role as a member of the JCS.

3. "That vigorous efforts be made to improve the internal structure of the CIA and the quality of its product, especially in the fields of scientific and medical intelligence; that there be established within the agency at the top echelon an evaluation board or section composed of competent and experienced personnel who would have no administrative responsibility and whose duties would be confined solely to intelligence evaluation; and that positive efforts be made to foster relations of mutual confidence between the CIA and the several departments and agencies it serves." This task force has observed that positive efforts have been made to improve the quality of scientific and medical intelligence. The Office of Scientific Intelligence is adequately staffed to include medical personnel. In the quality of its products, this agency is definitely handicapped by the inability of the intelligence community as a whole to collect information from the Soviet bloc. The Office of National Estimates is a top-echelon evaluation board, composed of competent and experienced personnel with no administrative responsibilities and whose duties are confined solely to intelligence evaluation, the product of which appears in the form of national estimates. Specific recommendations with regard to deficiencies in the relations of the Central Intelligence Agency with the services will be found in those sections devoted to CIA and the Department of Defense.

4. "That the Research and Development Board and the CIA, as a joint undertaking, establish immediately within one or the other agency an efficient and capable unit to collect, collate, and evaluate scientific and medical intelligence, in order that our present glaring deficiencies in this field be promptly eliminated." The Research and Development Board has been dissolved and its functions transferred to the Secretary of Defense. Progress made by the Central Intelligence Agency in the field of scientific and medical intelligence is fully discussed in the section of this report devoted to that agency.

INTRODUCTION

The machinery for accomplishing our intelligence objectives, hereinafter called the intelligence community when referred to as a whole, includes the Central Intelligence Agency, the National Security Council, the National Security Agency, the Federal Bureau of Investigation, and the intelligence sections of the Department of State, of the Army, the Navy, and the Air Force, and of the Atomic Energy Commission. Some of these agencies approach or exceed the operations of the CIA in functions and in expenditures. However, since CIA is charged with the overall responsibility for coordinating the output of all intelligence forces, the task force gave special attention to the work of that Agency.

Our investigations showed that the sensitive and vital work of the intelligence community is being led by a group which is sincere, and dedicated to the service of the nation. We discovered no valid ground for the suspicion that the CIA or any other element of the intelligence family was being effectively contaminated by any organized subversive or Communistic clique. Charges were made by some individuals alleging a few members of the intelligence community to be poor security risks. All such cases, except those obviously without merit, were investigated by proper authority, or investigations are in the process of being made.

On the basis of its comprehensive studies, the task force feels that the American people can and should give their full confidence and support to the intelligence program, and contribute in every possible way to the vital work in which these agencies are engaged. We found the Director of Central Intelligence to be industrious, objective, selfless, enthusiastic, and imaginative. We are convinced, however, that in his enthusiasm he has taken upon himself too many burdensome duties and responsibilities on the operational side of CIA's activities. The task force feels that certain administrative flaws have developed in the CIA, which must be corrected to give proper emphasis and direction to its basic responsibilities

The major aim would be greater concentration on the collection of intelligence information from our primary target—Russia and her satellites, and Communist China.

The task force is deeply concerned over the lack of adequate intelligence data from behind the Iron Curtain. The information we need on the political plans, scientific progress, and military potential of the Communists is there to be had, and we must exert every conceivable and practicable effort to get it. Proper directional emphasis, aggressive leadership, boldness and persistence are essential to achieve the desired results.

The glamor and excitement of some angles of our intelligence effort must not be permitted to overshadow other vital phases of the work or cause neglect of primary functions. A majority of the task force is convinced that an internal reorganization of the CIA is necessary to give assurance that each of these functions receives adequate attention without diversionary interest.

The task force further is concerned over the absence of satisfactory machinery for surveillance of the stewardship of the Central Intelligence Agency. It is making recommendations which it believes will provide the proper type of "watch-dog" commission as a means of reestablishing that relationship between the CIA and the Congress so essential to and characteristic of our democratic form of government, but which was abrogated by the enactment of Public Law 110[7] and other statutes relating to the Agency. It would include representatives of both Houses of Congress and of the Chief Executive. Its duties would embrace a review of the operations and effectiveness not only of the CIA, but also of all other intelligence agencies.

One of the aims in the creation of a compact commission of this type would be to keep the public assured of the essential and trustworthy accomplishments of our intelligence forces, and to enlist public support and participation in the intelligence effort.

Action of this sort is needed to promote a general awareness and appreciation among the people of the significance and objectives of the intelligence program. There is a corollary demand for clarification of misunderstandings which have arisen in the public mind, largely as a result of the misapplication of secrecy. However, it must be recognized that intelligence operations require a large element of secrecy as an essential to success.

The task force further is greatly concerned about the inadequate guidance being given to NSA by the United States Communication Intelligence Board, and about certain aspects of communications. Recommendations to improve the current status are made in Appendix I, Parts 1 and 2.

The intelligence community should draw more widely on the available pool of retired citizens with wide previous business experience in the foreign field, and among retired military personnel who have specialized over a long period in the intelligence field. It should develop a more attractive program of career incentives for its officials, and of benefits for its overseas employees.

Recommendations to achieve these desirable results are being offered by the task force.

[Omitted here are the body of the report and the Appendices.]

---

[7] A reference to the Central Intelligence Agency Act of 1949, approved June 20, 1949, which exempted the Central Intelligence Agency from disclosure of certain information concerning its organization such as functions, official titles, and number of personnel. (63 Stat. 208)

221. Report by the Commission on Organization of the Executive Branch of the Government to the Congress[1]

Washington, June 1955.

[Omitted here are a list of the members of the Commission and of the Task Force on Intelligence Activities, a transmittal letter, table of contents, acknowledgments, and preface.]

PART I

The task force, in order to give assurance to the Nation that all segments of the Intelligence Activities are efficiently carried out and that the expenditures are properly administered, recommends that a permanent "watchdog" committee be created. They recommend that such a committee be created from Members of the Senate and House, together with eminent citizens serving part time as needed, to be appointed by the President.

The Commission believes, however, that while mixed congressional and citizens committees for temporary service are useful and helpful to undertake specific problems and to investigate and make recommendations, such committees, if permanent, present difficulties. We therefore make the following recommendation.

Recommendation

(a) That the President appoint a committee of experienced private citizens, who shall have the responsibility to examine and report to him periodically on the work of Government foreign intelligence activities. This committee should also give such information to the public as the President may direct. The committee should function on a part-time and per diem basis.

(b) That the Congress consider creating a Joint Congressional Committee on Foreign Intelligence, similar to the Joint Committee on Atomic Energy. In such case, the two committees, one presidential and the other congressional, could collaborate on matters of special importance to the national security.

Other measures requiring legislation or of an administrative character are recommended by the task force and we suggest these for the consideration of the Congress and the Departments concerned.

---

[1] Source: Central Intelligence Agency, Executive Registry, Job 86–B00269R, Box 14. Unclassified. The title page of Part II bears the date May 1955, but it was released with the rest of this publication on June 29, 1955. Regarding the preparation of this report, see Document 220 and footnote 1 thereto. For Eisenhower's Implementation of Recommendation (a) above, see *Public Papers: Eisenhower, 1956*, p. 72.

The unclassified report of the task force requires no detailed review, and we therefore include it in full as Part II of this report.

PART II

Report on Intelligence Activities in the Federal Government

[Omitted here are the title page of Part II, names of the commissioners and task force personnel, a table of contents, acknowledgments, transmittal letter, and preface.]

Introduction

The machinery for accomplishing our Intelligence objectives hereafter called the Intelligence community when referred to as a whole, includes the Central Intelligence Agency, the National Security Council, the National Security Agency, the Federal Bureau of Investigation, and the Intelligence sections of the Department of State, of the Army, the Navy, and the Air Force, and of the Atomic Energy Commission. Some of these agencies approach or exceed the operations of the CIA in functions and in expenditures. However, since CIA is charged with the overall responsibility for coordinating the output of all Intelligence forces, the task force gave special attention to the work of that agency.

Our investigations showed that the sensitive and vital work of the Intelligence community is being led by a group which is sincere and dedicated to the service of the Nation. We discovered no valid ground for the suspicion that the CIA or any other element of the Intelligence family was being effectively contaminated by any organized subversive or communistic clique. Charges were made by some individuals alleging a few members of the Intelligence community were poor security risks. All such cases, except those obviously without merit, were investigated by proper authority, or investigations are in the process of being made.

On the basis of its comprehensive studies, the task force feels that the American people can and should give their full confidence and support to the Intelligence program, and contribute in every possible way to the vital work in which these agencies are engaged. We found the Director of Central Intelligence to be industrious, objective, selfless, enthusiastic, and imaginative. We are convinced, however, that in his enthusiasm he has taken upon himself too many burdensome duties and responsibilities on the operational side of CIA's activities. The task force feels that certain administrative flaws have developed in the CIA, which must be corrected to give proper emphasis and direction to its basic responsibilities.

The major aim would be greater concentration on the collection of Intelligence information from our primary target—Russia and her satellites, and Communist China.

The task force is deeply concerned over the lack of adequate Intelligence data from behind the Iron Curtain. Proper directional emphasis, aggressive leadership, boldness, and persistence are essential to achieve the desired results.

The glamor and excitement of some angles of our Intelligence effort must not be permitted to overshadow other vital phases of the work or to cause neglect of primary functions. A majority of the task force is convinced that an internal reorganization of the CIA is necessary to give assurance that each of these functions gets adequate attention with diversionary interest.

The task force further is concerned over the absence of satisfactory machinery for surveillance of the stewardship of the Central Intelligence Agency. It is making recommendations which it believes will provide the proper type of "watch-dog" commission as a means of reestablishing that relationship between the CIA and the Congress so essential to and characteristic of our democratic form of government, but which was abrogated by the enactment of Public Law 110[2] and other statutes relating to the Agency. It would include representatives of both Houses of Congress and of the Chief Executive. Its duties would embrace a review of the operations and effectiveness not only of the CIA, but also of all other intelligence agencies.

One of the aims in the creation of a compact commission of this type would be to keep the public assured of the essential and trustworthy accomplishments of our Intelligence forces, and to enlist public support and participation in the Intelligence effort.

Action of this sort is needed to promote a general awareness and appreciation among the people of the significance and objectives of the Intelligence program. There is a corollary demand for clarification of misunderstandings which have arisen in the public mind, largely as a result of the misapplication of secrecy. However, it must be recognized that Intelligence operations require a large element of secrecy as an essential to success.

The Intelligence community should draw more widely on the available pool of retired citizens with wide previous business experience in the foreign field, and among retired military personnel who have specialized over a long period in the Intelligence field. It should develop a more attractive program of career incentives for its officials, and of benefits for its overseas employees.

Recommendations to achieve these desirable results are being offered by the task force.

---

[2] See footnote 7, Document 220.

Scope of the Studies

Early Instructions

Initially, this task force was instructed by the Commission on Organization of the Executive Branch of the Government (hereafter referred to as the Hoover Commission or the Commission) to study and make recommendations as to the structure and administration of the Central Intelligence Agency.

Later, those instructions were changed by the Commission to embrace studies of *all* Intelligence operations of the Federal Government and recommendations for changes necessary to promote economy, efficiency, and improved service in this field.

The task force gave thorough consideration to the decision of the Commission to broaden the scope of the studies. It found at least 12 major departments and agencies engaged in Intelligence in one form or another. In addition, 10 or more minor agencies or activities expend public funds directly or indirectly in behalf of the Intelligence effort of the Government.

Thus, under the broad definition of its terms of reference, the task force was confronted with the Herculean job of studying and reporting on more than a score of major and minor departments and agencies. It quickly became evident that any attempt to spread its investigations over such a large area would mean that only sketchy results could be achieved within the allotted time.

Task Force Procedure Revised

The most pressing need under present conditions is for officials in important positions in Government, particularly those responsible for foreign policy, to have readily available full and factual foreign Intelligence. (The word "foreign" as used here denotes the target of information as distinct from the geographical source.)

Accordingly, the task force suggested to the Commission that the best results could be obtained if the dimensions of the inquiry were limited to certain key departments and agencies.

This proposal was approved by the Commission with the understanding that the task force would determine which of the Intelligence services, activities, and functions of the agencies surveyed it considered essential; those not necessary, or of similar nature and requiring consolidation in the public interest; those nonessential and competitive with private enterprise; and those representing duplication or overlapping of work between agencies. Under this revised program, the task force would cover, among other matters:

(1) The Intelligence functions of the National Security Council.
(2) The value and effectiveness of the information supplied by the operating agencies.

(3) The effectiveness of the coordination of Intelligence activities.

(4) The organization, procedures, methods, and performance of the Government agencies in the field of Intelligence.

(5) An examination of the operation and physical plant of the agencies as to economy, adequacy, effect on efficiency, and utilization.

(6) The various programs of the agencies in such fields as training, research and development, stockpiling, reference material, and security.

(7) Personnel policies and manpower utilization.

(8) All programs and procedures for the collection, development, and dissemination of Intelligence information within the Government, including collection apparatus and dissemination media.

(9) Effectiveness of the coverage by the various agencies of their specific areas of assignment, and extent of teamwork between these agencies.

Two Reports Prepared

In the preparation of this report, the task force was motivated by a sincere desire to present as complete an account of its findings as considered judgment indicated would best serve the public interest. Certain other facts and recommendations prepared by the task force have been omitted from this report on the ground that their disclosure publicly might give aid and comfort to our potential enemies or might jeopardize our national defense and security. These findings have been incorporated in a separate, highly classified, comprehensive report which has been placed in the hands of the Chairman of the Commission.

Teams Make Firsthand Studies Abroad

In order to obtain a clearer picture of intelligence operations, two teams were sent abroad for on-the-spot investigations. Each team was composed of a member or members of the task force and members of the staff. One group visited the European sector and the other went to the Far East.

These staff groups held conferences with the senior United States representatives and senior military commanders in the countries visited. The visits and discussions provided the task force with firsthand information which could have been obtained in no other fashion.

The conclusions reached and the recommendations contained in this report, and in the more comprehensive report to the Chairman of the Commission, reflect the benefit of those personal tours of inspection.

Organization of the Task Force

Security Impact on the Selection of Personnel

The Task Force on Intelligence Activities was the last investigative group authorized by the Hoover Commission. The director and deputy of the staff assumed their duties on October 1, 1954. The limited pool of available personnel in this country with prior experience in the Intelligence field influenced to some extent the structure of the staff and its methods of operation.

The task force personnel and staff had to be screened carefully for background security and possible prejudicial interest arising from prior association with departments and agencies embraced in the survey.

Before a member of the task force or staff could have access to any material, a security background investigation was conducted and the individual declared by proper authority to be eligible for access to "Top Secret" information. In each case where the inquiry involved access to atomic energy data, a time-consuming special clearance was obtained.

It was found that each department and agency had developed its own criteria, practices, and standards for clearance. The task force adopted a policy in conformity with the policies and requirements of the department or agency involved in each specific inquiry.

In the interest of security and economy, the task force also decided to keep its staff as compact as possible. Sensitive material generally was studied on the premises of the agencies.

Staff Organization

After careful consideration by the task force of various possible methods of organizing the staff and its work, it was decided that the most practical course would be to assign teams composed of 1 or 2 staff members to study specific agencies, and to delegate to other teams specific across-the-board survey functions. Individual task force members were assigned across-the-board responsibilities paralleling the work of designated staff teams.

Thus, all task force members were in a position to interject their influence and guidance in the staff activities and at the same time obtain valuable firsthand knowledge of the overall problem.

Procedures for Gathering Data

The task force and staff had the benefit of detailed briefings by top officials and employees of each agency studied. These briefings were characterized by informality. Oral questions and answers usually were employed. In some instances, however, copies of prepared briefings were furnished to the staff for ready reference.

Discussions were had with many echelons of personnel in each department and agency, from the clerks up to and including the heads of the executive departments.

In the execution of its extensive undertaking, the task force in certain areas found it necessary to employ the "sampling" method, particularly in the case of the study of activities overseas.

The task force also received expert advice from many individuals no longer in Government employ, but who previously occupied positions of prime responsibility in the development of our present Intelligence operations and organization. Some of these witnesses appeared before the task force at no expense to the Government and at considerable personal sacrifice. Their help and suggestions were of inestimable value.

"Intelligence"—A Definition

[Omitted here is language similar to the Preface of Document 220.]

I. The Intelligence Community—National Level

The National Security Council

The function of the National Security Council is to advise the President with respect to the integration of domestic, foreign, and military policies relating to the national security so as to enable the military services and the other departments and agencies of the Government to cooperate more effectively in matters involving national security.

The Council is composed of the President, the Vice President, the Secretaries of State and Defense, the Director of the Foreign Operations Administration, the Director of the Office of Defense Mobilization, the Secretaries and Under Secretaries of other executive departments and military departments when appointed by the President, to serve at his pleasure.

The Council, in addition to performing such other functions as the President may direct, for the purpose of coordinating more effectively the policies and functions of the departments and agencies of the Government relating to national security, subject to the direction of the President, shall:

1. Assess and appraise the objectives, commitments, and risks of the United States in relation to our actual and potential military power, in the interest of national security, for the purpose of making recommendations to the President to meet these problems.

2. Consider policies on matters of common interest to the departments and agencies of the Government concerned with the national security, and make recommendations to the President on these matters.

In order to accomplish its mission, the National Security Council has at its disposal several groups which function in varying degrees within the field of national Intelligence.

Duties of Special Assistant to the President

The Council is linked closely to the President, not only because the Chief Executive is Chairman and a member of it, but also because of the designation by him of a Special Assistant to the President for National Security Affairs who, as a member of the White House Staff, has constant and direct access to the President and enjoys his complete confidence.

This Special Assistant to the President is, in fact if not in name, the Executive Officer of the NSC and is chairman of the highly important Planning Board of the NSC.

He personally briefs the President on national security affairs, and with the President's approval prepares the agenda for the NSC meetings. This Special Assistant to the President does not preside at any NSC meeting, but sits (just beneath the Council itself) at the apex of the NSC administrative machinery.

Progress in National Intelligence Policies

The National Security Council has issued several Intelligence directives.[3] They express the policy by which the Intelligence effort is guided and coordinated; establish, within the Intelligence community, committees for the fulfillment of specific Intelligence functions; and pinpoint the responsibility for specific duties in designated fields of Intelligence.

The national Intelligence policy, as expressed in these directives, calls for integration of all departmental Intelligence relating to national security through a process of coordination of effort by the Director of Central Intelligence and correlation of Intelligence by the Central Intelligence Agency.

Other groups have been established as appendages to the Council, through some of which Intelligence, advice, and recommendations have been received by the Council for its use in advising and making recommendations to the President.

The Central Intelligence Agency

The Central Intelligence Agency, created by the National Security Act of 1947,[4] is charged with the responsibility of coordinating, evaluating, and distributing Intelligence data affecting the national security. The Director of Central Intelligence gives advice and recommendations to the National Security Council on such matters.

The CIA well may attribute its existence to the surprise attack on Pearl Harbor and to the postwar investigation into the part Intelligence or lack of Intelligence played in the failure of our military forces to receive adequate and prompt warning of the impending Japanese attack.

That investigation of events leading up to the "day of infamy" impressed upon Congress the fact that information necessary to anticipate the attack actually was available to the Government; but that there was no system in existence to assure that the information, properly

---

[3] National Security Council Intelligence Directives (NSCIDs) issued from 1950–1955 are printed at the end of this volume. Earlier directives are in *Foreign Relations, 1945–1950, Emergence of the Intelligence Establishment*.

[4] 61 Stat. 343.

evaluated, would be brought to the attention of the President and his chief advisers so that appropriate decisions could be made and timely instructions transmitted to the interested military commanders.

It also demonstrated that in the prewar Government organization no single official was responsible for whatever failure of Intelligence was involved; and the blame for the military surprise fell, justly or unjustly, on the military commanders present and immediately involved in the debacle.

Therefore, in 1947, when legislation for a national Intelligence organization was being considered, there was a widespread feeling among members of the Congress that responsibility for the coordination of the production of national Intelligence, as distinguished from departmental Intelligence, and for its dissemination, must be centered at one point.

Creation of the Central Intelligence Agency, with its Director charged with the coordination of the Intelligence effort, was authorized to fill this need. The Director of Central Intelligence, in the performance of this responsibility, receives pertinent information from all branches of the Government engaging in collection of Intelligence, including the Atomic Energy Commission.

The Central Intelligence Agency Act of 1949 provides for the administration of the Agency and grants the Director wide autonomous authority.

II. The Intelligence Community—Departmental Level

Department of Defense

Office of Special Operations (OSO)

Authority, Responsibility, and Functions

The responsibility of the Secretary of Defense for Intelligence Activities in the military services is not specifically defined in legislation or Executive order, but is implicit in the following provision of the National Security Act of 1947:

The Secretary of Defense shall be the principal assistant to the President in all matters relating to the Department of Defense. Under direction of the President, and subject to the provisions of this Act, he shall have direction, authority, and control over the Department of Defense.

The Assistant to the Secretary of Defense (Special Operations) was designated to fulfill a requirement for staff participation and representation in matters affecting defense and national Intelligence efforts. His authority and responsibilities are set forth in various directives and memoranda of the Secretary of Defense.

The organization is small and is neither intended nor prepared to exercise administrative control over day-to-day Intelligence activities of the armed services.

Joint Chiefs of Staff

Joint Intelligence Unit

As an adjunct of the Joint Chiefs of Staff, there is a Joint Intelligence Committee composed of the Intelligence chiefs of the members of the Joint Chiefs of Staff. The committee members are: the Deputy Director for Intelligence of the Joint Staff, who acts as committee chairman; the G–2 of the Army; the Director of Naval Intelligence; and the Director of Intelligence, Air Force.

The Deputy Director for Intelligence of the Joint Staff heads the Joint Intelligence Group, performing the Intelligence functions and duties assigned to him by the Joint Chiefs of Staff through the Director of the Joint Staff.

Inasmuch as the Joint Chiefs of Staff and the Joint Staff are within the Department of Defense, the Joint Intelligence Group supports the Secretary of Defense in Intelligence matters.

Department of the Army

Responsibilites of the Assistant Chief of Staff, G–2, Intelligence (AC/S, G–2)

The AC/S, G–2, under supervision of the Deputy Chiefs of Staff—and of the Comptroller of the Army, within his scope of responsibility—plans, coordinates and supervises the collection, evaluation and dissemination of Intelligence information pertaining to the war potential, topography, military forces and military activities of foreign nations, and the strategic vulnerability of the United States and its possessions.

The AC/S, G–2, also gives staff guidance and coordination to the Counter-Intelligence Corps (CIC) and to the Army Intelligence Center (AIC).

Attaché System

Army efforts in the Intelligence collection field are carried out largely through its Attaché System which maintains stations in many foreign countries.

Officers are assigned in the Attaché System on a highly selective basis in conformity with rigid requirements and standards established for candidates for this type of duty.

After selection, officers are assigned to language and Intelligence schools to prepare them for their assignments.

G–2 Training Interest

G–2's training interest lies principally in the areas of policy guidance and planning. The training division establishes the policies under which Intelligence and language schools operate, and monitors their program.

Elements of the division also monitor training programs in the Intelligence field, which are conducted by the various field commands and agencies, to insure conformance with G–2's guidance.

Counter-Intelligence Corps

This Corps operates under the command of a major general, who is also, in effect, a deputy of AC/S, G–2, for CIC matters. However, while the Corps commander is responsible for certain administrative and security functions, he does not exercise a true command control over the personnel of the Corps. Based on the principle that security is a function of command, elements of the Corps generally are assigned to field units and operate directly under command of the unit to which they are assigned.

The mission of the CIC is to ferret out any treason, sedition, subversive activity or disaffection, and to detect and prevent enemy espionage or sabotage within the Army Establishment and its area of jurisdiction.

In the pursuit of their primary functions, members of the Army's Counter-Intelligence Corps acquire some intelligence data, and these are fed into the Intelligence system.

Relationship to Other Agencies

G–2 operates generally in a healthy atmosphere of cooperation and understanding in its relationship with other segments of the Intelligence community. Committee, subcommittee, and working groups provide for ready interchange of material, practices, methods, and other pertinent Intelligence information.

Much of the effectiveness of this system is achieved through personal contacts. Material of an urgent nature can be disseminated throughout the Intelligence community through these contacts without being delayed to await scheduled committee meetings. There is positive evidence of an aggressive willingness and desire among those engaged at the working level to promote the overall Intelligence effort.

Language Training Program

Language training for the Attaché System and for the Foreign Area Specialist Training (FAST) is conducted at the Army Language School in Monterey, Calif. Use also is made of the Naval Language School in Washington, D.C., and civilian colleges. The Army conducts language courses for CIC personnel at Fort Holabird, Md.

Department of the Navy

Office of Naval Intelligence (ONI)

The Office of Naval Intelligence is part of the organization of the Office of the Chief of Naval Operations. The Director of Naval

Intelligence is designated as an Assistant Chief of Naval Operations, and reports directly to the Vice Chief of Naval Operations. He also has a direct responsibility to the Secretary of the Navy.

Under the authority and direction of the Chief of Naval Operations, the Director of Naval Intelligence is required to administer, operate, and maintain an Intelligence service fulfilling the Intelligence and counterintelligence requirements of the Department of the Navy for the purpose of:

1. Informing the Naval Establishment of the war-making capabilities and intentions of foreign nations.

2. Providing the Naval Establishment with the Intelligence needed for plans and operations.

3. Warning naval authority of threats to security of the Naval Establishment.

4. Providing the naval contributions to joint, national, and international Intelligence.

5. Promoting the maximum Intelligence readiness of the operating forces and other components of the Naval Establishment.

6. Coordinating the Intelligence effort of the Naval Establishment.

7. Developing and promulgating, subject to approval of the Secretary of the Navy, policies for the protection of classified matter, including such policies applicable to industrial security.

8. Advising the Chief of Naval Operations concerning all matters relating to naval Intelligence and security policies for the protection of classified matter.

Organization in the Field

In the field, three organizations assist in carrying out the Intelligence mission of the Navy:

1. Naval District Intelligence Officers, who are under ONI's management control and operate in the continental United States and in certain outlying areas.

2. Intelligence organizations within the forces afloat, which, although directly under their respective commanders, are still under ONI's technical supervision.

3. The Naval Attaché System, which also is under jurisdiction of the ONI.

The primary functions of the District Intelligence Officers are the conduct of counterintelligence and the implementation of security policies. The District Intelligence Officer serves on the staff of his Naval District Commandant, and in certain designated districts has additional duty on the staff of the commander of the sea frontier in which his district is located. The Naval District Intelligence Offices are the major source of domestic counterintelligence of special concern to the Navy.

In the forces afloat, each area, fleet, type and task force commander, and all flag officers exercising command have a staff Intelligence section. This is headed by an Intelligence officer who is responsible for the collection, processing, and dissemination of Intelligence for the command. ONI supports their Intelligence requirements and assigns them collection missions within their capabilities to execute.

Naval Attaché System

Naval attachés and their staffs are officially a part of ONI, but they also have a responsibility to the Ambassador or Minister who is the chief of the diplomatic mission to which they are assigned. Normally, attachés are stationed only in those countries which are of primary naval interest to ONI.

Each of the ambassadors to countries having ports of call for our naval elements would like to have a naval attaché to take care of many problems arising from these visits and the attendant shore leaves.

Administration

Administrative work in the Office of Naval Intelligence is handled by the Assistant Director of Naval Intelligence, Administration. Manpower and management surveys are conducted continuously by this division to maintain efficiency and economy throughout ONI.

"Special Duty Only"

Most of the military personnel assigned to Intelligence duties are line officers, not specialists. The Military Personnel Act of 1947[5] made provision for Intelligence specialists in the Regular Navy. However, since by law none of these "Special Duty Only" officers may succeed to command, and since command is the usual stepping stone to flag rank, the "Special Duty Only" class of service is unpopular among line officers.

Department of the Air Force

Organization for Intelligence Work

The civilian staff of the Secretary of the Air Force includes a Special Assistant for Intelligence who is responsible for review and evaluation of all matters pertaining to plans, policies, and programs relative to the Air Force Intelligence program. He is also charged with supervision and ultimate review of the personnel security program, both military and civilian.

---

[5] 61 Stat. 512.

The Deputy Chief of Staff, Operations, is responsible for the Air Force Intelligence activities, communications activities, and atomic energy matters.

The Department's Inspector General is responsible to the Chief of Staff, USAF. Among his other duties, he conducts investigations of matters involving major crimes, violations of public trust, subversive activities, sabotage and espionage; and performs related counterintelligence functions for the Department.

The Director of Intelligence, Headquarters, USAF, is directly responsible to the Deputy Chief of Staff, Operations. This organizational relationship places him in a position subordinate to a Deputy Chief of Staff. The interposing of an echelon between the major Intelligence element of the Air Force and the Department's Chief of Staff and certain other functional Deputy Chiefs of Staff, such as the Comptroller, affects adversely the efficiency of staff operation. Elevation of the Director of Intelligence to the level of Deputy Chief of Staff would greatly enhance the prestige of Intelligence in the Air Force. This is a desirable and appropriate step in view of the tremendous importance of Intelligence in the overall mission of the Air Force.

Air Force Intelligence Training

Recognizing the need for continuing Intelligence training, the Air Force has established such a program for officers and airmen, embracing courses ranging from those of an introductory nature to those appropriate for staff officers in higher headquarters.

In addition to the service schools, college facilities are used for language training and special studies. Training courses are also available for Air Force reserve personnel.

The Air Force training program generally is adequate for current requirements, even in technical areas where the personnel turnover is heavy. Periodic studies should be made, however, to assure the adequacy of training facilities in relation to worldwide staff requirements. The staffing of foreign posts with inadequately trained personnel may be not only uneconomical, but might result also in the loss of opportunities to collect Intelligence.

Department of State

Responsibility for Foreign Policy

A primary function of the Secretary of State is to act as principal adviser to the President in the determination of American foreign policy and to implement and supervise its execution by diplomatic means. By virtue of the authority the Secretary exercises over all the activities of the Department and the Foreign Service, he derives principal support for the accomplishment of this task from the Under Secretaries, the Administrator of the Bureau of Security and Consular Affairs, the Special Assistant—Intelligence, and the Director of the Policy Planning Staff.

The Special Assistant—Intelligence, with rank equivalent to that of an Assistant Secretary, develops and implements a coordinated program for foreign Intelligence for the Department and for producing reports essential to determination and execution of foreign policy.

Effect of Diplomacy on the Overall Collection of Intelligence

The task force has recognized the incompatibility in method between the practice of diplomacy and the more direct and active operations incident to the collection of Intelligence and the conduct of cold war.

While all contribute to the end in view, conflicts between them must be resolved, usually on a high level, and always in the national interest. It must be realized that diplomacy is not an end in itself; that, while political ends must be served and unjustifiable risks avoided, the collection of Intelligence is a vital element in the fight to preserve our national welfare and existence. Instances have come to the attention of the task force where too conservative an attitude has prevailed, often to the detriment of vigorous and timely action in the field.

Creation of the Intelligence Area

Prior to World War II, Intelligence for the support of American foreign policy was produced by the inadequate research staffs of departmental policy offices which had many other duties to perform. Creation of the Intelligence Area of that Department, by Executive Order 9621 of September 20, 1945, recognized the need for improving the quality of Intelligence demanded by the tense international situation.

The Secretary of State is a member of the National Security Council. The Intelligence Area provides staff assistance to the Secretary and senior policy officers of the Department of State, and maintains liaison with the other members of the Intelligence community in the discharge of the Department's responsibility in the total Intelligence program of the Government.

Better Quarters Needed

The Intelligence Area maintains its offices and records in a converted apartment building, which does not constitute satisfactory quarters for this special type of work. The cost of adequate security measures consequently is high.

Existing plans for an addition to the New State Building, if approved under the provisions of Public Law 519, would improve working conditions and efficiency, produce savings through the vacating of leased spaces, and reduce costs of security, maintenance, and miscellaneous services for this branch of the Intelligence effort.

Federal Bureau of Investigation (FBI)

A Bureau of Investigation was created, under jurisdiction of the Attorney General of the United States, by Executive order of July 26, 1908. The policies now followed in the administration of the Federal Bureau of Investigation were established in 1924, and in July 1935, this agency became known as the Federal Bureau of Investigation.

In view of the limited activities of the FBI in the positive and foreign Intelligence fields, a detailed study of this agency was not made. However, its functions in the counterintelligence effort were studied with deep interest by the task force, in order to fill out the Intelligence picture.

We found the Director of the FBI, through his forcefulness, initiative, and managerial ability, to have developed his agency into a model organization of its kind. We are confident that in the FBI we have a most effective counterintelligence service.

FBI Responsibilities in Counterintelligence

Among other assigned responsibilities, the FBI has jurisdiction over investigations relating to espionage, sabotage, treason, and other matters pertaining to the internal security of the United States. This jurisdiction places the FBI directly in the field of counterintelligence.

Executive Order 10450 (May 27, 1953),[6] which established the security procedure covering "all persons seeking the privilege of employment or privileged to be employed in the departments and agencies of the Government," provides that:

All investigations conducted by any other agencies, which develop adverse information involving loyalty or information showing coercion of an employee to act contrary to the interests of the national security, shall be referred promptly to the Federal Bureau of Investigation for a full field investigation.

Relationship to Other Departments and Agencies

The Director of the FBI—along with the Assistant Chief of Staff, G–2, Department of the Army; the Director of Naval Intelligence, Department of the Navy; and the Director of Special Investigations, the Inspector General, Headquarters, U.S. Air Force—is a member of the Interdepartmental Intelligence Conference (IIC) which is responsible for the coordination of the investigation of all domestic espionage, counterespionage, sabotage, subversion, and other related Intelligence matters affecting internal security.

---

[6] 18 FR 2489 and 26 FR 6967.

The IIC Charter does not disturb the responsibilities of the member agencies, but makes mandatory such action of those agencies as is necessary to insure complete investigative coverage of this field without duplication of effort, through appropriate exchange and coordination of information and action among the various pertinent agencies and departments of the Government.

III. Foreign Intelligence

Evolution of Our Plans

Traditionally, Americans are a peace-loving people. But, a philosophy of peace is no guarantee of peace. In a tortured world where greed, intrigue, and lust for power exist, protection of liberty and assurance of survival lie in alertness and strength. Alertness involves adequate Intelligence data on which to base adequate preparedness.

From the beginning, the United States has tried consistently to maintain relationships with other countries openly and to refrain from participation in secret treaties. This principle likewise established the early pattern for the conduct of our Intelligence activities. The collection of information concerning political and military policies and plans of foreign governments was accomplished openly and with the full knowledge of the foreign powers. The work was performed through the offices of our diplomatic representatives abroad and accredited military attachés.

A substantial volume of material was collected, but there was no machinery at home to pull this information together into a cohesive mass and to draw from it logical conclusions upon which to base national policy and future plans.

On July 11, 1941, the Chief Executive, in his capacity as Commander-in-Chief of the Armed Forces, established an Office of the Coordinator of Information to

collect and analyze information data, military or otherwise, which may bear upon national defense strategy; to interpret and correlate such strategic information; to make it available to the President and such other officials as the President may determine, and to carry out, when requested by the President, such supplementary activities as may facilitate the securing of strategic information not available to the Government.

This office came into being only 5 months before Pearl Harbor.

Through a process of evolution, there finally emerged the Office of Strategic Services as an operating agency of the Joint Chiefs of Staff. This organization remained intact until the end of World War II.

Postwar Organization

In the fall of 1944, the Chief Executive wrote to the Director of Strategic Services requesting recommendations as to the organization of a postwar Intelligence organization. The Director submitted a plan for the creation of a central Intelligence service. The plan placed the proposed central Intelligence service in the Executive Office of the President and called for the appointment by the President of a Director of Intelligence who would discharge and perform his functions and duties under the direction and supervision of the President.

It also provided for the establishment of an Intelligence Advisory Board consisting of the Secretaries of State, War, and Navy, and such others as the President deemed necessary. The duties of the board would be to advise and assist the Director of Intelligence.

The plan placed in the hands of the Director the work of coordinating, collecting, evaluating, and disseminating Intelligence for national purposes. It also recognized that various departments of the Government should have their own Intelligence bureaus for the collection and processing of such information and material as might be needed in the performance of their daily functions and duties. Each of these bureaus would be under the sole control of its department head and would not be encroached upon or impaired by the functions granted to any other governmental Intelligence agency.

The plan further contemplated that in time of war or unlimited emergency, all programs of such an agency in areas of actual or projected military operations would be coordinated with military plans and be subject to the approval of the Joint Chiefs of Staff; or in case of the consolidation of the armed services, under the supreme commander.

Functions Divided

Under the pressure of prompt dissolution of wartime agencies, the Chief Executive, on September 20, 1945, divided the functions, personnel, and physical resources of the Office of Strategic Services between the State Department and the War Department. The research and presentation element was transferred to the State Department, to be absorbed or liquidated so that the element would cease to exist on December 31, 1945.[7]

On January 22, 1946, the Chief Executive created the National Intelligence Authority consisting of the Secretaries of State, War, and Navy, and the President's personal representative, to plan, develop, and coordinate Federal foreign Intelligence activities so as to assure the most effective accomplishment of the Intelligence mission for national security. This presidential directive also created a Central Intelligence Group (CIG) under the direction of a Director of Central Intelligence (DCI), designated by the President to assist the National

---

[7] See *Foreign Relations*, 1945–1950, Emergence of the Intelligence Establishment, for key documents dealing with the organization and administration of U.S. Government intelligence organizations during that period.

Intelligence Authority (NIA) and to be responsible to it. The directive specified that the head of the CIG would sit as a member of the NIA.

It charged the Central Intelligence Group with the task of correlating, evaluating, and disseminating Intelligence relating to the national security; with coordinating such activities of the Intelligence agencies of the State, War, and Navy Departments as related to the national security; and with performing other services of common concern.

By the National Security Act of 1947, as amended (Public Law 253, 80th Cong., July 26, 1947), the Congress established a National Security Council (NSC) which took the place of the old National Intelligence Authority; and created under the National Security Council a Central Intelligence Agency (CIA) with a Director of Central Intelligence (DCI) as its head. The National Intelligence Authority ceased to exist.

Under the provisions of this act, the National Security Council established an Intelligence Advisory Committee (IAC) made up of the various Intelligence chiefs, to advise the Director of Central Intelligence in his efforts to coordinate the Intelligence activities of the Nation.

[Omitted here is Section IV, Intelligence Personnel and Security.]

V. "Watchdog" Commission

The task force fully realizes that the Central Intelligence Agency, as a major fountain of Intelligence for the Nation, must of necessity operate in an atmosphere of secrecy and with an unusual amount of freedom and independence. Obviously, it cannot achieve its full purpose if subjected to open scrutiny and the extensive checks and balances which apply to the average governmental agency.

Because of its peculiar position, the CIA has been freed by the Congress from outside surveillance of its operations and its fiscal accounts. There is always a danger that such freedom from restraints could inspire laxity and abuses which might prove costly to the American people.

Although the task force has discovered no indication of abuse of powers by the CIA or other Intelligence agencies, it nevertheless is firmly convinced, as a matter of future insurance, that some reliable, systematic review of all the agencies and their operations should be provided by congressional action as a checkrein to assure both the Congress and the people that this hub of the Intelligence effort is functioning in an efficient, effective, and reasonably economical manner.

Within the Armed Services Committee, there is a liaison channel between the Congress and CIA which serves a worthy purpose, but which cannot include private citizens in its membership and has not attempted to encompass the wide scope of service and continuity which this task force considers essential for "watchdog" purposes.

The task force recognizes that secrecy is necessary for proper operation of our foreign Intelligence Activities but is concerned over the possibility of the growth of license and abuses of power where disclosure of costs, organization, personnel, and functions are precluded by law.

On the other hand, sporadic investigations in this field might inadvertently result in unauthorized disclosure of classified information to the detriment of the Intelligence effort. Periodic audits or studies by some qualified, impartial agency would remove both of these dangers and would also allay any suspicions and distrust which have developed in the public mind by the complete secrecy of these operations. Such a procedure also might serve to shield our Intelligence program from unjustifiable attacks upon the agencies concerned, and enhance public confidence and support of this vital work.

The Central Intelligence Agency Act of 1949 legalized the administrative procedures for the Agency. It was passed by the Congress on the unanimous recommendation of the Armed Services Committee.

Agency Gets Wide Exemptions

The Act exempts the Agency from compliance with any provision of law limiting transfers of appropriations; any requirements for publication or disclosure of the organization, functions, names, official titles, salaries or numbers of personnel employed by the Agency; and any regulations relating to the expenditure of Government funds.

The widespread conviction among Members of Congress that this situation should be corrected is indicated by the fact that more than a score of resolutions have been introduced in the current session calling for a review or watch over our Intelligence activities, usually by a large joint committee of the two Houses.

The task force, however, envisions as the proper agency for this watchdog job a small, permanent commission modeled after the Commission on Organization of the Executive Branch of the Government— a bipartisan group including members of both Houses of Congress and distinguished private citizens appointed by the President.

Members chosen from private life to serve on this proposed watchdog commission should come from a select group of loyal, qualified, and public-spirited citizens who command the respect and confidence of the American people.

Comprehensive periodic studies of the foreign Intelligence Activities of the United States would be made by the commission, with special attention to the questions of whether the assigned work of these Intelligence agencies is being carried on efficiently and effectively; whether there is any unnecessary overlapping or duplication of effort between civilian and military Intelligence agencies; whether the staffs are a size justified by their assigned functions and producing the Intelligence required for the security of the Nation; whether expenditures are within budget authorizations and in keeping with the expressed intent of the Congress; whether fiscal policies and procedures are in conformity with sound accounting principles and practices to the maximum extent possible; whether any of their activities or policies are in conflict with the foreign policy aims and program of the United States; and whether the effort of any of these Intelligence agencies is being dissipated or adversely affected by assignment of added functions alien to Intelligence. The commission would require a small permanent staff, with the usual provisions for employing attorneys, experts, consultants, and auditors, for expenses and for compensation of members and employees. It would be empowered to hold hearings and to subpoena witnesses, under adequate safeguards to prevent the public disclosure of classified defense information which it might receive; but would have the authority to demand and receive from any source any information it might need for its own use.

The overall aim would be the promotion of aggressive leadership which would unify the Intelligence effort, make it more productive, and inspire a higher spirit of teamwork through elimination of petty competitive jealousies.

Would Study Complaints

The proposed commission should hold itself available to receive and to study all complaints against any of our Intelligence agencies; to maintain a familiarity with the activities of these agencies as a safeguard against the abuse of their proper functions; to consider requests of the agencies for legislation, and, where advisable, to support the needs of the Intelligence community before the Congress, and advise the Congress on the effects of proposed legislation on our Intelligence effort. An integral part of its duties would be reports of its findings and its recommendations to the President and to the Congress annually and at such other times as might be appropriate or necessary.

One of the fundamental purposes of these reports would be to keep the public informed, within the bounds of security, of the value and the vital accomplishments of the Intelligence community and provide an answer to unfounded complaints and criticisms which have tended to arouse fears and distrust of the Intelligence effort in the minds of the people.

Public support thus engendered certainly would improve the effectiveness of the Intelligence operations, and foster public participation in the collection of overt Intelligence data. The people who support these operations are entitled to assurance that the investment is paying dividends. With such assurance, they would develop an enthusiasm and alertness which could bring in valuable information at times to supplement the work of the regular Intelligence forces.

VI. Functional Intelligence

Map Procurement

The task force found map requirements and production for Intelligence purposes well coordinated. Through the years, there has developed by mutual cooperation among the departments and agencies, a committee whose primary function is to prevent duplication in map procurement.

There is established within the Bureau of the Budget an Examiner of Surveys and Maps, who coordinates all map-making programs to avoid duplication and overlapping of functions. The system seems to be efficient and effective.

Trustworthy and up-to-date Intelligence cartography is one of the major elements utilized in Intelligence operations. The cost of this phase of the work is substantial, but we found this expense to be justified by the results achieved.

Intelligence Libraries

On the basis of visits made to the Intelligence libraries maintained by the military services, the CIA, and the State Department, the task force believes that these libraries in general are efficiently operated. There is a workable system in effect among the agencies for notification of availability and exchange of information.

There has been considerable discussion of the idea of putting all the material in the possession of all Intelligence agencies in one central library.

The value of a library depends on the ready accessibility of its material to the users. Its use and effectiveness declines when those who need it must become involved in complicated procedures and delays in obtaining material.

The task force feels that a central library would foster the development of private desk-side libraries and the retention by individuals of material for protracted periods, with the resultant denial or delay in access to others. Establishment of a central library, therefore, seems impracticable.

However, for the purpose of providing ready reference and more facile access to the various Intelligence data by any department or agency, the task force suggests that all departments within the Defense Establishment and the Department of State adopt the single-index system based on the Intelligence subject code now in use by the CIA and the Air Force libraries. The value of such a standardized procedure probably would be well worth the expense involved.

Various elements in the Intelligence family have come up with divergent definitions and interpretations of certain words and phrases in common use by the Intelligence community. The resultant confusion could be eliminated by standardization. To that end, the task force proposes that the National Security Council produce an agreed glossary of terms and definitions and provide for periodic review of this glossary.

VII. Conclusions and Recommendations

In summarizing its findings and its recommendations, the task force at the outset found, in general, that the Intelligence effort is being pursued in a diligent and dedicated manner. It noted throughout the Intelligence community an atmosphere of urgency and a desire to get on with the job of breaking through security barriers erected by our potential enemies.

However, instances of inefficient practices were disclosed, and recommendations to correct them have been made.

The domestic counterintelligence effort was found to be effectively coordinated among the departments and agencies concerned. Positive direction and mutual support are provided through the operations of the Interdepartmental Intelligence Conference and the Interdepartmental Committee on Internal Security. Specific responsibility in the domestic area of each counterintelligence agency is established partially by statute, and is further definitively specified by a "Delimitations Agreement" to prevent overlapping and duplication of effort.

Recommendations covering overseas counterintelligence operations, carried out by the military services and the Central Intelligence Agency, are contained in our classified report.

The domestic security and counterintelligence functions of the Federal Bureau of Investigation were found to be conducted efficiently and effectively. This Bureau renders competent and highly cooperative assistance to other Government Intelligence agencies and performs an essential and important function in the overall intelligence effort.

The National Intelligence Survey is an invaluable publication which provides the essential elements of basic Intelligence in all areas of the world. While its production involves an extensive and expensive effort, all members of the Intelligence community derive an immediate benefit from the contributions they make to it and profit from the final product. There always will be a continuing requirement for keeping this survey up to date.

Administrative Flaws Noted

The task force concluded that the legislation and organizational setup for Intelligence purposes are soundly conceived, but that administrative flaws are in evidence. Accordingly, it has pointed most of its suggestions in that direction.

Failure to produce certain elements of Intelligence has been due in part to the restrictive effects of some of our national attitudes and policies toward the collection of Intelligence so necessary for effective resistance to Soviet aggression. Also, among some of those responsible for implementation of our foreign policy by diplomacy and negotiation, there seems to exist an abhorrence to anything that might lead to diplomatic or even protocol complications.

This negative attitude, usually at the desk level, at times has stifled initiative and action in the collection of Intelligence. Some of these efforts, if permitted to proceed properly, might have brought direct and immediate results and made positive contributions to the national welfare that would have justified the attendant political risks and possible inconsequential diplomatic embarrassment.

Data on Soviet Bloc Inadequate

Security measures adopted by the Communists have been provokingly conceived and boldly employed. They have been quite effective in comparison with our security measures, which have permitted the collection of vital secrets in this country with relative ease. The information we need, particularly for our Armed Forces, is potentially available. Through concentration on the prime target we must exert every conceivable and practicable effort to get it. Success in this field depends on greater boldness at the policy level, a willingness to accept certain calculated political and diplomatic risks, and full use of technological capabilities.

The task force is of the opinion that the Director of Central Intelligence should employ an Executive Director, or "chief of staff," of the Agency so that the DCI might be relieved of the chore of many day-to-day administrative and operational problems, and thus be able to give more time to the broad, overall direction of the Agency and the coordination of the entire Intelligence effort.

Recommendations With Respect to Personnel

The effectiveness of our national Intelligence effort is measured to a large degree by the character and ability of the personnel, both military and civilian, engaged in this work. The diligent and dedicated effort of the Intelligence community was evident to the task force.

Some problems, however, exist in the personnel management field. These problems, taken collectively, seriously affect the morale, the availability, and the quality of the Intelligence personnel.

The task force presents detailed recommendations later in this report, with a view to improving the prestige of the civilian analyst;

developing real career incentives in Intelligence; relieving the critical shortage of qualified Intelligence personnel by tapping the valuable pool of retired civilian business men and experience abroad, and of especially trained and qualified retired military personnel; broadening the base of civilian employment to provide greater flexibility of recruitment of the best qualified individuals; improving the conditions of service of CIA personnel stationed abroad, and increasing the salaries of certain key officials in CIA.

Recommendation No. 1

That the Central Intelligence Agency be reorganized internally to produce greater emphasis on certain of its basic statutory functions;[8] and

That the Director of Central Intelligence employ an executive officer or "Chief of Staff" of that Agency.

Recommendation No. 2

That a small, permanent bipartisan commission, composed of members of both Houses of the Congress and other public-spirited citizens commanding the utmost national respect and confidence, be established by act of Congress to make periodic surveys of the organization, functions, policies, and results of the Government agencies handling foreign Intelligence operations; and to report, under adequate security safeguards, its findings and recommendations to the Congress, and to the President, annually and at such other times as may be necessary or advisable. The proposed "watchdog" commission should be empowered by law to demand and receive any information it needed for its own use. It would be patterned after the Commission on Organization of the Executive Branch of the Government (Hoover Commission). Appointments by the President of persons from private life to the proposed Commission should be made from a select list of distinguished individuals of unquestioned loyalty, integrity, and ability, with records of unselfish service to the Nation.

The tremendous importance to our country of the Intelligence function, and the unpublicized and selfless duties performed, demand that the prestige of this function, and of the personnel involved, be recognized through the use of adequate career incentives and benefits to encourage full development of talent within the Intelligence community.

---

[8] Details and supporting factual matter relating to this recommendation are contained in the separate classified report of the task force. They cannot be incorporated in this public report for security reasons. [Footnote in the original.]

Recommendation No. 3

That the Executive Pay Bill of 1949[9] be amended to increase the annual salary of the Director of Central Intelligence to the equivalent of the pay of the Deputy Secretary of Defense (now $20,000); to bring the compensation of the Deputy Director of Central Intelligence up to $17,500, the same as that of most Under Secretaries of the executive branch; and to provide operating directors of areas of responsibility in Intelligence with proportionate salaries; and

That the chiefs of the various Intelligence units of the military services be elevated in the organizational structure to the level of Deputy Chiefs of Staff in the Army and the Air Force, and Deputy Chief of Naval Operations in the Navy; and

That the Central Intelligence Agency Act of 1949 be amended to provide:

(a) Additional medical and hospital benefits and services for dependents of CIA employees when stationed overseas, similar to the benefits authorized for dependents of members of the Foreign Service.

(b) Statutory leave benefits (and accumulation of leave) for employees of CIA overseas, as now applied to members of the Foreign Service.

Retired civilians with long business experience in the foreign field constitute a possible source of important contributions to the Intelligence effort, and this resource should be exploited fully. There is also a valuable reservoir of retired military personnel with foreign experience which might well be utilized. One major advantage in the exploitation of these groups would be the speed with which they could be fitted into the Intelligence picture because they would come in with a large part of the necessary training already behind them.

Recommendation No. 4

That the Central Intelligence Agency Act of 1949 be amended to authorize employment by the CIA of retired military personnel of the armed services without any arbitrary limitation on the number of such employees (the limit now is 15) and without regard to the law limiting their compensation; except that such personnel should be authorized to accept either their military retirement pay plus any difference between their retired pay and the proper pay of the office they would hold in CIA or the proper pay of the office, but not both; and

That the Department of Defense make extensive use of Schedule A of the Civil Service Regulations (non-competitive appointments) in

---

[9] P.L. 359, approved October 15, 1949. (63 Stat. 880)

the employment by the military services of civilian Intelligence analysts and other specialists in order to provide the necessary flexibility in the recruitment of qualified civilian personnel (to include retired citizens with wide previous business experience in the foreign field) and to facilitate the interchange of such personnel between zone of interior competitive service and the overseas excepted service.

The task force is satisfied that the personnel security program and procedures within the Intelligence community are adequate to minimize the possibility of security risks and to make extremely unlikely their employment in sensitive positions in the Intelligence agencies, except in the procedure for systematic rechecking of all personnel to make sure that the passage of time has not altered the trustworthiness of any employee, and to make certain that none has succumbed to some weakness of intoxicants or sexual perversion, or developed some other shortcoming that would disqualify him from further sensitive work. The Federal Bureau of Investigation has adequate safeguards against such a danger.

Recommendation No. 5

That measures be instituted in all agencies for rechecking the security status of all personnel engaged in Intelligence activities at periodic intervals not to exceed 5 years in any individual case.

Our Government and its Intelligence forces are not fully exploiting the possibilities of valuable military and technological data potentially available in scientific reports and technical publications issued in foreign countries. The State Department now is charged with this duty. Under this arrangement, we lack adequate collection facilities and staff experts to evaluate the material.

Recommendation No. 6

That the responsibility for procurement of foreign publications and for collection of scientific Intelligence be removed from the State Department and placed in the hands of the CIA, with authority to appoint such scientific attachés as may be necessary to carry on this work abroad.

Efficient handling of Intelligence information demands modern quarters for the personnel and the records. The Central Intelligence Agency, after 8 years of operation, still lacks such facilities.

Recommendation No. 7

That the Congress appropriate as soon as practicable the funds necessary to construct adequate headquarters facilities for CIA in or near Washington, D.C.

The task force believes not only that great care must be taken in the selection of highly qualified persons, both technologically and

Intelligence-wise, for the group supervising atomic energy data, but that changes in the group should be made as infrequently as possible.

Recommendation No. 8

That steps be taken to introduce highly selective methods of choosing members of the coordinating committee on atomic energy Intelligence, not only to get the benefit of service by the most competent individuals, but also to assure long tenure in this important assignment.

Lack of adequate linguistic preparation often has proved to be a serious handicap to our representatives abroad. This became painfully apparent during the Korean war. The ability to write and speak the language fluently, and to interpret foreign words and idioms accurately always helps an American to get around in an alien land, to win the confidence of its people, and to understand them.

Recommendation No. 9

That a comprehensive, coordinated program be developed to expand linguistic training among American citizens serving the Intelligence effort; and

That the Department of Defense expand and promote language training by offering credit toward reserve commissions to ROTC students and drill credit to Reserve personnel for completion of selected language courses.

---

222. Editorial Note

[*text not declassified*]

223.   **Central Intelligence Agency Comments on the Report of the Technological Capabilities Panel**[1]

NSC 5522   Washington, June 8, 1955.

[Omitted here are a June 8 note from the NSC Executive Secretary to the NSC, a memorandum of July 1 to all holders of NSC 5522, a table of contents, an index to agency comments, a summary of agency comments, and Annexes A and B containing comments by the Department of State and Department of Defense, respectively.]

ANNEX C[2]

TAB A

Technological Capabilities Panel Recommendations on Which the Central Intelligence Agency Has Full Responsibility for Study and Report to the National Security Council

Specific Recommendation C. 4

1.   This recommendation reads as follows:

"We need to examine intelligence data more broadly, or to invent some new technique, for the discovery of hoaxes. As a first step, we recommend a National Intelligence Estimate, with adequate safe-

---

[1] Source: Eisenhower Library, Records of White House Staff Secretary, Comments on the Report to the President by the Technological Capabilities Panel. Top Secret. A typed notation at the bottom of the first page reads: "Revised 7/26/55." On February 14, the Technological Capabilities Panel (the Killian Panel) of the Science Advisory Committee reported to President Eisenhower on "Meeting the Threat of Surprise Attack." Background on that report and extracts from it are printed in *Foreign Relations, 1955–1957*, vol. XIX, pp. 41–56. See also the editorial note, ibid., p 83. The full report is in National Archives, RG 59, S/S–RD Files: Lot 71 D 171, Top Secret Restricted Data. On June 8, Executive Secretary of the National Security Council Lay circulated to NSC members a paper entitled "Comments on the Report to the President by the Technological Capabilities Panel of the Science Advisory Committee" under NSC Action No. 1355. (Ibid., S/S–NSC (Miscellaneous) Files: Lot 66 D 95, Records of Action of the National Security Council) Comments on the February 14 Panel Report were submitted by the Departments of State and Defense, Office of Defense Mobilization, Atomic Energy Commission, Bureau of the Budget, Interdepartmental Intelligence Conference–Interdepartmental Committee on Internal Security, the Special Committee established to coordinate the implementation of NSC 5513/1, the NSC Planning Board, and the Central Intelligence Agency. (Eisenhower Library, Records of White House Staff Secretary, Comments on the Report to the President by the Technological Capabilities Panel) Also see *Foreign Relations, 1955–1957*, vol. XIX, pp. 95–108. The judgment of the report at that time "that the United States had no reliable early warning and the Strategic Air Command was vulnerable, perhaps tempting, the Soviets to attempt a surprise attack" was to have a significant impact on the course of the nascent U–2 program.

[2] The CIA comments in Annex C were sent to the Executive Secretary of the National Security Council under cover of a June 6 memorandum from Director of Central Intelligence Dulles. (Ibid.)

guards, of our success in keeping secret our most useful techniques of intelligence. This estimate would suggest the extent to which an enemy might be manipulating the information obtained through these sources."

2. Discussion:

The problem of ascertaining the validity of information concerning the USSR, collected through various sources available to us, is a continuing one in the intelligence process. Thus, while no attempt has been made in the past to prepare a comprehensive estimate concerning Soviet attempts at deception, and the effect of such activity on the validity of National Intelligence Estimates, a considerable amount of research and analytical time has been expended. This effort could fruitfully be brought to bear in the preparation of a study of Soviet success in penetrating our most useful techniques of intelligence. A comprehensive study will be initiated through an appropriate mechanism. Our initial investigations do not reveal any requirements for additional personnel or funds for the accomplishment of this task.

[Omitted here are Specific Recommendation C. 9 and discussion of it.]

Specific Recommendation C. 10

1. This recommendation reads as follows:

"A heavy long-term investment should be made in the preparation of covert agents as eventual sources of high-level intelligence."

2. Discussion:

This recommendation, as amplified by the pertinent discussion in the report,[3] has implicit in it the expansion of clandestine networks in non-communist areas looking to the time, perhaps even twenty years from now, when some of these areas may be critically important. It suggests the slow and careful preparation of agents in the event of a political coup, a threatened coup, or some similar governmental crisis; and finally, the use of such agents in legal travel operations against the communist countries and in the penetration of communist and pro-communist groups outside of the communist-controlled areas.

---

[3] "It has become exceedingly difficult to obtain significant information from covert operations inside Russia. The security zones at the border, the general restrictions in the interior, the thousands of security police, and the innumerable informers among the population are brutally effective in limiting the infiltration, exfiltration, and usefulness of agents. Therefore, we must more and more depend upon science and technology to assist and complement the best efforts of classical intelligence." (National Archives, RG 59, S/S–RD Files: Lot 71 D 171, The Report to the President of the Technological Capabilities Panel)

It is noted that a recent recapitulation of high-level intelligence efforts with long-term potential shows that the CIA possesses several score agent assets of this type situated in almost every sensitive nonorbit area of the world and in many areas which, though not presently significant, could become so in the years to come. It is this type of agent facility which has contributed to the success of certain political operations which have been reported to the NSC.

The CIA accepts and endorses the emphasis placed in the report on the importance of using individuals of great intelligence, training and experience [1½ lines not declassified]. This type of activity has been a part of our operational program for some time but it clearly deserves an effort above that which we are now putting forth. It is most difficult to locate people who are not too selfish, too insecure, or too naive to produce material of value within such a program. The security precautions erected by the Russians, the Chinese and the Satellites have imposed very rigid requirements in the selection of such individuals. Therefore, an expansion of our present activities is certainly called for, including the availability of additional manpower to make possible slow and careful development of highly intelligent penetration agents.

Laying the groundwork for extensive covert operations in every country available to our agents, to the extent outlined above, would require additional effort through intensification and limited expansion of our U.S. case officer selection and training facilities, an increase in our case officer corps, and a limited broadening of our several support structures (administrative, communications, and technical). A general estimate of the proportion of the required increases in terms of case officer personnel would be approximately 10%.

TAB B

Recommendations On Which CIA Has Primary Responsibility for Reporting to the NSC, Subject to Coordination With Other Agencies

General Recommendation 6 and Specific Recommendation C 7:

1. These recommendations read as follows:

GR6: The National Security Council establish policies and take actions which will permit the full exploitation of the intelligence and other advantages which can be made available to us through the establishment [1 line not declassified].

[1 paragraph (4 lines) not declassified]

2. Discussion:

The Central Intelligence Agency, in coordination with the Department of Defense, concurs in these recommendations. [4 lines not declassified]

[4 paragraphs (48 lines) not declassified]

Specific Recommendation C 3

1. This recommendation reads as follows:

We *must* find ways to increase the number of hard facts upon which our intelligence estimates are based, to provide better strategic warning, to minimize surprise in the kind of attack, and to reduce the danger of gross overestimation or gross under-estimation of the threat. To this end, we recommend adoption of a vigorous program for the extensive use, in many intelligence procedures, of the most advanced knowledge in science and technology.

2. Discussion:

The CIA agrees with these statements and recommendations. The Director of Central Intelligence has developed plans for implementation in the near future which will make possible a further step toward the achievement of the objective underlying the TCP recommendation, namely: to "use the ultimate in science and technology to improve our intelligence take."

The Agency has created a permanent Scientific Advisory Board, composed largely of former members of the Technological Capabilities Panel, to advise the Director and to supplement existing activities.

The Agency's plans envisage:

a. The establishment of a suitable unit, with its supporting laboratory facility, to insure the continual creation, recognition and application of new scientific and technical methods for the acquisition, processing, and production of all forms of foreign intelligence,

b. The establishment of procedures for developing the concomitant equipment and instrumentation peculiar to the production of intelligence, and

c. The establishment of close working relationships between the unit mentioned in paragraph a. above, and all correlative developmental divisions within the intelligence community and in particular with the Office of the Assistant Secretary of Defense (R&D).

TAB C

Recommendations Under Which Primary Responsibility Was
Assigned to Other Agencies Subject to Coordination
With the Central Intelligence Agency

[Omitted here are the CIA comments on General Recommendation 11 and Specific Recommendations A. 9, B. 12c, C. 1, C. 5, and C. 6.]

Specific Recommendation C. 8

1. This recommendation reads as follows:

"Intelligence applications warrant an immediate program leading to very small artificial satellites in orbits around the earth. Construction of large surveillance satellites must wait upon adequate solutions to some extraordinary technical problems in the information gathering and reporting and its power of supply, and should wait upon development of the intercontinental ballistic missile rocket propulsion system. The ultimate objective of research and development on the large satellite should be continuous surveillance that is both extensive and selective and that can give fine scale details sufficient for the identification of objects (airplanes, trains, buildings) on the ground."

2. Discussion:

The psychological warfare value of launching the first earth satellite makes its prompt development of great interest to the intelligence community and may make it a crucial event in sustaining the international prestige of the United States.

There is an increasing amount of evidence that the Soviet Union is placing more and more emphasis on the successful launching of the satellite. Press and radio statements since September 1954 have indicated a growing scientific effort directed toward the successful launching of the first satellite. Evidently the Soviet Union has concluded that their satellite program can contribute enough prestige of cold war value or knowledge of military value to justify the diversion of the necessary skills, scare material and labor from immediate military production. If the Soviet effort should prove successful before a similar United States effort, there is no doubt but that their propaganda would capitalize on the theme of the scientific and industrial superiority of the communist system.

The successful launching of the first satellite will undoubtedly be an event comparable to the first successful release of nuclear energy to the world's scientific community, and will undoubtedly receive comparable publicity throughout the world. Public opinion in both neutral and allied states will be centered on the satellite's development. For centuries scientists and laymen have dreamed of exploring outer space. The first successful penetration of space will probably be the small satellite vehicle recommended by the Technological Capabilities Panel. The nation that first accomplishes this feat will gain incalculable prestige and recognition throughout the world.

The United States' reputation as the scientific and industrial leader of the world has been of immeasurable value in competing against Soviet aims in both neutral and allied states. Since the war the reputation of the United States' scientific community has been sharply challenged by Soviet progress and claims. There is little doubt but that the Soviet Union would like to surpass our scientific and industrial reputation in order to further her influence over neutralist states and to shake the confidence of states allied with the United States. If the Soviet Union's scientists, technicians and industrialists were apparently to surpass the United States and first explore outer space, her propaganda machine would have sensational and convincing evidence of Soviet superiority.

If the United States successfully launches the first satellite, it is most important that this be done with unquestionable peaceful intent. The Soviet Union will undoubtedly attempt to attach hostile motivation to this development in order to cover her own inability to win this race. To maximize our cold war gain in prestige and to minimize the effectiveness of Soviet accusations, the satellite should be launched in an atmosphere of international good will and common scientific interest. For this reason the CIA strongly concurs in the Department of Defense's suggestion that a civilian agency such as the U.S. National Committee of the IGY supervise its development and that an effort be made to release some of the knowledge to the international scientific community.

The small scientific vehicle is also a necessary step in the development of a larger satellite that could possibly provide early warning information through continuous electronic and photographic surveillance of the USSR. A future satellite that could directly collect intelligence data would be of great interest to the intelligence community.

The Department of Defense has consulted with the Agency, and we are aware of their recommendations, which have our full concurrence and strong support.

[Omitted here are annexes bearing comments by other U.S. departments and agencies on the Technological Capabilities Panel report of February 14, 1955.]

---

224. Editorial Note

A group of national security experts headed by Nelson A. Rockefeller met in Quantico, Virginia June 5–10, 1955, to explore vulnerabilities of the Communist bloc. See *Foreign Relations, 1955–1957*, volume XIX, page 84. A summary of the recommendations of the Quantico Panel is printed ibid., 1955–1957, volume V, page 216. Walt W. Rostow, then at the Massachusetts Institute of Technology and a member of the panel, published an account of the Quantico deliberations in *Open Skies: Eisenhower's Proposal of July 21, 1955* (Austin: University of Texas Press, 1982).

Another panel called together by Rockefeller in late August 1955 met in Washington, D.C. and Quantico to discuss and review the psychological aspects of U.S. national security policy. The Quantico II Panel, as it was often called, submitted its recommendations to President Eisenhower in early December 1955. See *Foreign Relations, 1955–1957*, volume XIX, pages 153–154.

225.   Minutes of a Meeting of the Intelligence Advisory Committee[1]

IAC–M–200   Washington, June 14, 1955, 10:45 a.m.

Director of Central Intelligence
Allen W. Dulles
Presiding[2]

Deputy Director of Central Intelligence
Lieutenant General Charles P. Cabell
Presiding[2]

MEMBERS PRESENT

Mr. W. Park Armstrong, Special Assistant for Intelligence, Department of State
Major General Robert A. Schow, acting for Assistant Chief of Staff, G–2,
    Department of the Army
Rear Admiral Carl F. Espe, Director of Naval Intelligence, Department of the Navy
Major General John A. Samford, Director of Intelligence, Headquarters,
    United States Air Force
Rear Admiral Edwin T. Layton, Deputy Director for Intelligence, The Joint Staff
Mr. Charles H. Reichardt, acting for Atomic Energy Commission Representative
    to the IAC
Mr. M.W. Kuhrtz, acting for Assistant to the Director, Federal Bureau of
    Investigation

ALSO PRESENT

Mr. Sherman Kent, Central Intelligence Agency
Mr. H. Marshall Chadwell, Central Intelligence Agency
Mr. Otto E. Guthe, Central Intelligence Agency
Mr. Abbot E. Smith, Central Intelligence Agency
[name not declassified], Central Intelligence Agency
[name not declassified], Central Intelligence Agency
[name not declassified], Central Intelligence Agency
[name not declassified], Central Intelligence Agency
Mr. Edward W. Proctor, Central Intelligence Agency
[name not declassified], Central Intelligence Agency
Mr. P.A. Trezise, Department of State
Mr. Howard Furnas, Department of State
Colonel J. H. Montgomery, Department of the Army

---

[1] Source: Central Intelligence Agency, Executive Registry Job 85–500362R, Box 2, Folder 6. Secret. The meeting was held in the Director's Conference Room in the Administration Building in the Central Intelligence Agency.

[2] Part of meeting. [Footnote in the original.]

Lieutenant Colonel W.J. Lage, Department of the Army
Lieutenant Colonel V.J. Fenili, Department of the Army
Captain Bruce E. Wiggin, Department of the Navy
Mr. Lawrence Healey, Department of the Navy
Colonel P.D. Wynne, United States Air Force
Lieutenant Colonel Van A. Woods, Jr., United States Air Force
Mr. John A. Power, United States Air Force
Colonel John E. Leary, USA, The Joint Staff
Colonel Robert Totten, USAF, The Joint Staff
Captain Ralph Metcalf, USN, The Joint Staff

[Omitted here is discussion of agenda items 1. Approval of the minutes of the June 7, 1955 meeting, and 2. Noting of Watch Committee Report No. 253.]

3. Proposed DCID 3/6: Establishment of a Guided Missile Intelligence Committee (IAC–D–81/9, 31 May 1955)[3]

a. The Chairman stressed the importance to the security of the US of doing everything possible to improve intelligence on guided missiles. He stated that he would not wish to take the responsibility for not going forward with some community approach which was responsive to the need. He further stated that he realized that the suggested draft was not the only way to get at the problem and that he was more anxious to press for the principle of interagency cooperation in this field than for the details of the present proposal.

b. The Service members generally took exception in principle to the proposed draft as an invasion of the weapons field now allocated to the services under DCID 3/4.[4] Moreover, they tended to view the key gap in the field of guided missiles intelligence as collection. This has been given a high priority by the services and it is not clear how the establishment of another committee would improve current efforts.

c. The Air Force member referred to the Air Force program to attack the problem more broadly and indicated that while collection was an important aspect of the problem, there also were possibilities in the field of research and analysis. He suggested that an alternative to setting up a new committee would be to broaden the charter of the Scientific Estimates Committee.

d. The State member stated that he would support the proposal but indicated that his department had a less direct interest in this subject than did the other members. The AEC member was in favor of the proposal. His agency has been pleased with the JAEIC approach to an

---

[3] Not found.
[4] Document 126.

important problem and he felt that the establishment of a GMIC might help AEC augment its contribution in this field. He believed that the biggest gain would be in the development of new techniques and methods for exploiting intelligence in this field. The FBI member had no objection to any proposal designed to improve the end-product but indicated his agency would not be competent to sit on the committee if formed.

e. The Chairman and General Cabell reiterated that the proposal was in no way designed to supersede individual efforts but to give them added impetus. Mr. Kent pointed out that under the present setup it is not clear who takes the action called for in agreed post-mortem findings in this field. The pulling together of all individual efforts is thus left largely undone.

f. *Action:* The IAC deferred action on the draft directive pending the receipt in two weeks of a report prepared by the SEC in coordination with EIC. The SEC report is to include a proposal of how the objectives of the draft DCID could be met by SEC, the changes in SEC's charter which an assumption of this responsibility would entail, and an evaluation of current Air Force efforts in the field of guided missile intelligence.

[Omitted here is discussion of agenda item 4. The North African and Arab-Israeli Situations.]

---

226.   Letter From the Chief of the Office and Research and Intelligence, U.S. Information Agency (Loomis) to the Country Public Affairs Officer at the Embassy in South Africa (Graves)[1]

Washington, June 22, 1955.

Dear Mr. Graves:

Several weeks ago an addition to your operating manual was sent to all posts for inclusion in Part 1, Section 223.[2] This addition included

---

[1] Source: National Archives, RG 306: USIA Files Lot 63 A 190, B. 172, IRI Memoranda (IAN), 1954–56. Confidential; Official–Informal. A cover letter from Clary Thompson, Deputy Assistant Director, Near East, South Asia and Africa, U.S. Information Agency, to Dear _____, June 22, 1955, suggests that the letter was intended to be sent to multiple U.S. posts abroad.

[2] Not further identified.

about four pages describing the organization and functions of the Office of Research and Intelligence (IRI). While this statement described what we are supposed to do, it was, of necessity, written in formal Government language.

I thought it might be helpful if I filled you in more completely and more informally, with particular emphasis on how we hope to be of service to you.

When IIA was part of the Department of State,[3] it depended on the Intelligence Area of the Department (OIR) to collect and produce the kind of intelligence needed for policy and programming. This arrangement was never completely satisfactory since OIR had insufficient resources to devote to our requirements, and of course became impossible after USIA was separated from the Department.[4]

About a year ago Mr. Streibert[5] went to Mr. Allen Dulles and asked him to take a look at the problem of how best to supply USIA with all the information it required to function. Mr. Dulles accepted the job, and appointed a task force which studied the issue for several months in great detail both in Washington and in selected posts overseas.

Both the National Security Council's Intelligence Advisory Committee (IAC) and the Agency accepted the recommendations of the task force[6] and they were put into effect in September 1954.

The survey team first identified six types of information which were needed by USIA. I am enclosing an excerpt from the Report which describes these in detail.

The survey team concluded on the basis of these requirements that the intelligence needs of USIA did not differ *in kind* from the intelligence required to support the political, economic, and military activities of the Government, but that USIA did require such intelligence "with an emphasis, a detail and a form not normally required in intelligence produced for other purposes". I should point out that "intelligence", as used in this letter and with respect to USIA in general, does not mean covert or "cloak and dagger" operations. Rather, it refers to the entire process of overt collection, collation, evaluation and dissemination of information and analyses on subjects relevant to USIA activities.

---

[3] For documentation on the establishment and responsibilities of the International Information Administration (IIA) on January 16, 1953, see *Foreign Relations, 1952–1954*, vol. II, Part 2, pp. 1591ff.

[4] For documentation on the creation of the U.S. Information Agency (USIA) later in 1953, see ibid., pp. 1709–1711.

[5] Theodore E. Streibert, Director of the U.S. Information Agency.

[6] The task force and its recommendations have not been further identified, but many features of the report are summarized below and quoted in the enclosure.

The survey concluded further that:

(a) The total available intelligence of the types required by USIA had been inadequate in character and quantity, and should be increased;

(b) The primary responsibility for the provision of the types of intelligence required by USIA should continue to be assigned to the Department of State and in a lesser degree to the other agencies of the Intelligence Community;

(c) USIA should establish its own intelligence organization to tailor the output of the other intelligence agencies to the particular and peculiar applied needs of the Information Agency.

This, in a nutshell, is our primary function.

The survey group also concluded that on occasion the U.S. Information Agency, particularly its field staff, was a unique source of intelligence information. This would include information that field officers pick up about the organization and operations of foreign and communist media in a particular country. The survey group concluded that USIS should, therefore, have the responsibility of reporting this special type of information in coordination with the reporting by the other sections of the Embassy. You can use the most convenient channel for this reporting; the psychological section of the WEEKA, State Department despatches, or USIA despatches. One point was stressed—USIS field personnel should not be expected to undertake activities for the sole purpose of gathering information. Rather, their responsibility is to report information which they had gathered as a by-product to their regular activities in support of the general USIA program.

Another point stressed by the Survey group was the function of evaluation. The group concluded, and we strongly concur, that the responsibility for evaluating the program cannot be separated from the executive responsibility for running and planning the program. We believe that IRI's job is to provide to the responsible USIA executives all the facts and figures which are available, and upon which they can base their judgment as to what actions they should take.

For example, if IRI were asked—"Is the radio program in the Union of South Africa[7] any good?"—we would say that it was not our function to answer that question since it involves judgment—program judgment. We would try to work out with you the questions to which we wanted answers, such as:

"How many people listen to USIS radio programs as compared to the competition?"

"What type of people listen?"

---

[7] The words "Southern Rhodesia" are crossed out and "the Union of South Africa" has been inserted by hand.

"Why do they listen to the programs?"
"What is their opinion of the programs?"

etc. We would then present those findings to all levels concerned; you, your radio officer, IBS, the Area Directors, etc. You all could argue as to whether or not the findings indicated that the program was good, bad or indifferent, and whether or not the program needed change. IRI will follow the same principles as the FBI, which, as you know, has always been scrupulously careful never to tell any operating unit what to do as a result of its findings. Our mission in IRI, therefore, is completely a service mission to provide both the USIS field missions, and the headquarters elements of USIA, with the information they want about foreign programs, issues and conditions. Specifically, IRI is not responsible for gathering or analyzing statistics about the output of USIS programs. That is the responsibility of each media concerned.

The survey team found that the following four separate units, dealing with various phases of research and intelligence, existed within USIA: the Evaluation Staff (IEV) (which, among other things, contracted for research studies with universities and private research firms); the Coordinator of Psychological Intelligence (CPI) (which was a group of some 35 people assigned to the State Department, but paid by USIA); the Research and Library Section of IBS; and the IPS Library. Upon approval of the Report, these units were abolished and a new central organization was established called the Office of Research and Intelligence (IRI).

After the usual delays caused by the merging of functions and organizations and the slow recruitment and appointment of qualified personnel, IRI is now getting to the point where it can begin to carry out its responsibilities.

As a manual outlines, IRI is composed of four divisions: Collection and Liaison, Library, Production, and External Research. The first of these, the *Collection and Liaison Division,* is primarily responsible for collecting the raw and finished intelligence from other intelligence agencies, both within this Government and from foreign governments; falling within the six categories spelled out in the IAC Survey. In addition, this division has the job of trying to convince other agencies to produce finished intelligence for us. To the extent that it succeeds, the work of the Production Division is simplified.

The Collection Division also disseminates the raw and finished intelligence which it collects to all elements of USIA. They distribute to USIS in the field, and to other Government agencies, the finished production turned out by IRI. They are the people responsible for getting scripts declassified which have utilized paraphrases of some classified material in their preparation.

Another major responsibility of the Collection and Liaison Division is to formulate intelligence requirements. Normally, people come to us with a vague desire for "all the facts" on a given subject. We then must get them to refine and sharpen their requirements until we know exactly what they want, and how they plan to use the information. We then list the minimum information which must be collected.

The Division lays requirements on the other intelligence agencies (State, Defense, CIA) to do production for us when they are better equipped. It will lay requirements on the field to collect information when you are the best source. As I mentioned above, this will primarily be where we are anxious to learn about the Communist and indigenous activities in the various media. In other words, this Division is the middleman between the user of intelligence and those who collect and produce it.

The Collection and Liaison Division is headed by Ed Carroll, who had a lot of wartime service with OSS in Europe, and was with the Intelligence Collection group in the Department of State for the past nine years.

The second Division is the *Library Division.* The nucleus of the collection and personnel of this Division is the old IBS and IPS libraries. The Division is headed by Roth Newpher, who headed the IBS Library and Research Staffs for 12 years. The Library has four rather distinct collections.

The first section is the *book and periodical collection.* We have some 25,000 volumes and 260 periodicals and newspapers. The collection is heavily weighted with Russian and Communist materials, but does cover the waterfront. Also, of course, we have excellent relationships with all other libraries, both Government and private, so that the Library can obtain almost any book on very short notice.

The second section is the *unclassified morgue,* which has more than 5 million items, classified under 80,000 headings. This is a unique facility in Government. Nowhere else is there such a large amount of unclassified intelligence material.

The third section is the *classified file.* This resembles the unclassified, except that all documents in it are classified. This is a new section for the Agency, and is rapidly expanding. We have excellent relationships with the CIA Library so that if we do not have a classified document ourselves, we can get it shortly from CIA.

The fourth section is the *propaganda collection,* which is unique among collections in or out of the intelligence community. It represents an extensive collection of the published propaganda of foreign countries, and contains some 30,000 items organized by country of distribution. It is extensively cross-indexed. We must rely heavily on you to send us examples from your area. Many have already contributed significantly.

This material is constantly used by the Director and other headquarters personnel because it is particularly effective in demonstrating the opposition.

The Library Division is prepared to give you very rapid service. The Library provides reference service for Agency personnel in Washington. It can do so by telegram or despatch for you.

The third IRI division is the *Production Division*, headed by Lou Olom, who for three years was Chief of the CPI unit located in the State Department, and who has been in intelligence for the last 15 years.

The Production Division has the responsibility of answering questions from any part of USIS or USIA. Sometimes these questions can be answered on the telephone very speedily. Sometimes they require considerable work and result in a memorandum of some length.

The Production Division does not always answer these questions itself. If a large and comprehensive study is required, we will lay the requirement on other appropriate intelligence organizations—State, CIA, Defense as well as non-IAC agencies such as Labor, Agriculture and Commerce Departments. The Production Division will make every effort to meet any deadline which you establish. We are a "quick and dirty" shop completely geared to the operational needs of the Agency. We will give you whatever information we are able to obtain within your time limit—an hour, a day, or a week. We believe you, the user, rather than we, should establish the deadline, since you know how and when you expect to use the information. Obviously, the shorter the deadline, the more superficial the answer.

Requests from the field for information can be sent either directly to IRI or to IPS, depending on the type of product desired. Both IPS and IRI often work on the same requests. We in IRI do the research, and try to obtain all the facts bearing on the subject and place them in some logical order, irrespective of whether they help or hinder our cause. IPS utilizes these facts, as appropriate in its output. There is, therefore, no reason for you to change whatever system you are now using. However, if you only wish a fact or an intelligence analysis rather than a story, it might be a little quicker if you made that request to IRI.

The Production Division has seven branches—the five regular areas, the USA Branch, and the Functional Branch.

The Functional Branch is responsible for following international Communism, front organizations as well as local and national party propaganda methods and activities. They also follow media activities worldwide, so that we can detect and analyze changes in emphasis or procedures in Communist radio, Communist movies, etc. Paul Phillips is Acting Chief.

The USA Branch is headed by Dick Fitzpatrick, and is responsible for providing background information on the United States, which you and other elements of this Agency request. Again, if you want an article about some facet of the United States, or American life, we often provide the material to IPS and they, of course, do the final writing.

The Soviet-Satellite Branch is responsible for obtaining the facts and figures about the Soviet and European Satellites, and for following their activities, particularly their current propaganda lines and operations. The Division is headed by Mike Fodor, who has lived in the area for many years, and most recently was the editor of the *Neue Zeitung*.

Your Branch, the Near East Branch, does not yet have a Branch Chief, although Joe Dees is acting in that capacity. Joe was at one time in the operational intelligence division of the Voice, but came to us from Radio Liberation.

The fourth Division is the External Research Division, which has the mission of supplementing classical intelligence, using the unique techniques of social science. The most obvious area not touched by traditional intelligence seems to be public opinion surveys. We believe that surveys of public opinion are a unique and important addition to other sources of information, such as newspaper comment, editorial comment, and estimates of the situation by qualified observers.

We are now using the survey technique to get two different types of information. The first is opinion on political matters, particularly as they concern our global themes—such matters as:

What is your opinion of the United States?—of Russia?
In your opinion, how are the relations between your country and the United States at the present time?
Do you think the local Communist party is an independent party or is it controlled by the Soviet Union?
If Western Europe were attacked with atomic or hydrogen bombs, would you approve or disapprove of the use of such bombs on enemy cities?

Survey techniques also provide unique information on specific USIS activities, such as exhibits, radio programs, etc. In these surveys we ask such questions as:

What radio programs did you listen to last night?
How often do you listen to _____ program?
What is your opinion of the program?
Which do you think gives you more reliable reports of the news—radio or newspaper?
What is your opinion of the exhibit you have just seen?
What part did yo like the best?
Which the least? Why?

etc.

Through the science of sampling and questionnaire research, the opinions of small, carefully selected groups can be used to estimate the attitudes of larger groups with a high degree of accuracy (3–5% with the sample-size generally employed). This tool can be used to study the opinions of the entire adult population, or just of certain groups—the youth, the educated, the city dweller, or whatever particular segment you are interested in.

We are now conducting political surveys every four months in four countries of Western Europe, which we are calling Barometer Reports. We began survey operations in Western Europe, in part because public opinion in the American sense of the word is more meaningful there, and in part because the local research concerns were further developed. We believe that one of the chief values of these surveys is that it allows both us and you to chart trends in opinion with more accuracy than any other method. We plan to extend these surveys to the other major countries of the world as rapidly as possible. We have just finished an exploratory survey in four countries of Latin America, and hope to put them also on a regular basis.

The External Research Division is very small—only five professionals—since the work is essentially a field function. The Agency has thus far established a TO of twelve research officers overseas, seven are already assigned as follows: England, France, Germany, Austria, Italy, Brazil and Mexico. We hope to establish research offices soon in India, Thailand, Japan, Egypt and Iran. These officers will be regular members of the PAO's staff, reporting to him, spending his GOE, in order to provide the PAO with the facts and figures he needs, through individual research, local contractors, or any other means available.

If some headquarters' element in Washington, or some other Agency, such as the National Security Council, desires local survey information, we will lay that requirement on the Public Affairs Officer. Under this system, the Research Officer becomes really familiar with his country and can produce rapid, efficient, and meaningful research studies. This is particularly true of research dealing with the impact of the USIS programs. During the initial stages, we are supplementing the post's GOE with additional funds, earmarked for research, but this is only an interim measure until the Public Affairs Officer can include research in his regular budget. However, whenever IRI places an additional requirement on any post, which is over and above its normal concern, we will provide the Public Affairs Officer with additional funds so that these special requirements will not be a financial burden.

The function of the External Research Division is to provide technical backstopping services to these research officers. Also, the Division prepares the detailed requirements, such as questions to be asked in order to satisfy headquarters' needs. In the case of those countries which do not have a research officer, the External Research Division will provide as much help as possible to the Public Affairs Officer. If the PAO has some particularly pressing problem, IRI is prepared to send one of its Washington staff on TDY for as long as necessary to obtain the information required by the PAO.

The Division is headed by Leo Crespi, who was Research Officer in Germany for six years. This Division will no longer emphasize long-range basic studies. It, like the Production Division, is now a service shop trying to provide information as quickly as possible, so that it can be of practical use to all elements of USIS and USIA.

I am afraid this letter has become a little long, but I wanted to describe in some detail our assets, and our mission, so that you could understand it better, and therefore use it. Our sole mission is to be of service, and we will change our methods and procedures as required to give you what you want.

I will be very glad to get your comments on our service, both good and bad, particularly any recommendations which you may have for improvement.

Sincerely,

Henry Loomis[8]

Enclosure[9]

IDENTIFICATION OF INTELLIGENCE NEEDS

USIA has essential needs for the following types of intelligence and intelligence information:

1. *Selected segments of societies:* selected classes, groups, organizations (public and private), and their leadership, present and potential

a) Size, composition, ideologies and attitudes, predispositions, and reactions to: (1) the United States, the USSR and other countries of greatest significance and their basic policies, (2) critical foreign and internal problems.
b) The patterns of influence among groups, organizations, and leaders (including the government); specifically, who is influential, on whom, how, and how much

2. *Media Research and Analysis:*

a) Communication habits and types of media in the country (press, publications, radio, motion pictures, TV).
b) Organizational aspects of each medium, including location, key personnel, finance, distribution and exhibition outlets, and a description of the facilities of the media.

---

[8] Printed from a copy that bears this typed signature.
[9] Confidential.

c) The political orientation of the media.
d) The content of the communications output by the media.
e) Location, size and type of audience receiving the output of the media.
f) The reactions of the audience to the media, and why.

3. *Foreign Propaganda,* both friendly and unfriendly, including exchange of persons or cultural exchange

a) Facilities and personnel.
b) Program content and plans.
c) Estimate of probable courses of foreign propaganda.
d) Analyses of foreign propaganda vulnerabilities.

4. Impact of factors affecting public opinion and attitudes and the net impact of such factors on people of a country. Such factors would include historical attitudes of people, and the influence of current domestic and foreign official and unofficial activities.

5. *Descriptive Detail,* that is, unclassified or declassified intelligence information to supplement the content of USIA media with items of local interest in order to make the output appear more interesting and more authoritative, particularly in denied areas.

6. *International Communism:*

a) International organizations, personalities, programs, fiscal support, methods and success or failure of operations.
b) Local applications, including counterespionage information, with emphasis on communications facilities.

---

227. Editorial Note

In an effort to improve coordination of intelligence collection in the field, Secretary of State Dulles on June 23, 1955, instructed 71 diplomatic posts on domestic and field procedures for acquiring intelligence and requested those posts to report on their current handling of intelligence collection coordination. The Secretary suggested that missions with USIA and FOA staffs could include representatives of those agencies in the collection activities. (CA–9152, June 23, 1955; National Archives, RG 59, Central Files 1955–60, 120.201/6–2355)

228.   Letter From Director of Central Intelligence Dulles to the Director of the Bureau of the Budget (Hughes)[1]

Washington, June 25, 1955.

Dear Mr. Hughes:

For some time I have been concerned with the adequacy of the resources of the Department of State's intelligence organization. I have consulted with Mr. W. Park Armstrong on this question and studied in detail the proposed strengthening of the State Department's intelligence program as reflected in the Department's FY 1957 budget estimates. On the basis of this study I am convinced that the increases in personnel and funds sought must be granted in order to avoid serious impairment of the national intelligence effort.

The intelligence framework of the Government has its particular problems in that, to a degree not often found in other governmental functions, each intelligence agency is heavily dependent upon others, and the President and the National Security Council are dependent upon the community as a whole, not simply upon one or several of its parts. I might add that this governmental area differs from others also in that the Director of Central Intelligence has certain statutory responsibilities with regard to the coordination of the activities of the several intelligence agencies; this indeed accounts for, and I believe justifies, my present comment.

A careful review of the intelligence produced by the Department of State for National Intelligence Estimates and for other purposes of direct concern to this Agency indicates the need for increased positions, particularly in the following fields of endeavor:

Special Intelligence—In this period of intensive diplomatic activity the Department's particular responsibilities in this field must be discharged promptly and thoroughly, and the present limited staff is badly overstretched.

Intelligence on the Soviet Orbit and Its Integration—We are entering a period of significant change in the organization of the Communist Bloc and relations between Communist parties and governments. Our ability to anticipate major Communist moves and to conduct appropriate cold war countermeasures requires a major stepping-up of our analysis of the techniques, strengths, and weaknesses of the Communist Bloc mechanism. This can only be accomplished by the most de-

---

[1] Source: National Archives, RG 59, INR Historical Files: Lot 59 D 27, Box 73. Secret. Drafted by Robert Amory, Deputy Director for Intelligence, on June 24.

tailed scrutiny of each item of evidence, whether overtly or covertly obtained, by highly competent political analysts.

Intelligence on Underdeveloped Areas—The ferment that exists in the large and highly populated areas of the world in which the U.S. and the USSR are engaged in an acute struggle for men's minds requires far more detailed knowledge, both economic and political, than we have as yet been able to produce. Here the problem does not lie in the paucity of information but in adequate resources for compiling and analyzing data.

Public Opinion Analysis—We are only just beginning to develop adequate barometers of public opinion in the Free World and are becoming more and more aware of the need to respond to and influence such if our leadership of the Free World coalition is to be effective. USIA's efforts to collect raw data in this field must be supported by highly competent evaluation by political intelligence experts.

Watch Function—With the approval of the NSC, the National Indications Center has been established on a 24-hour basis. Moreover, the Watch Committee's activities have materially stepped up as a result of a constantly increasing danger of devastating damage to the U.S. in the event major aggression caught us flat-footed. The Department of State's political intelligence is as vital a contribution to this work as is the military contributions; hence the additional positions requested for this work are indispensable to the over-all discharge of our early warning responsibility.

United Nations and International Conference Biographic Support—In an era of intensive diplomatic activity including special conferences and lengthy sessions of the United Nations, the Department's biographic resources have been found badly overstrained. This condition is enhanced by the large number of personalities included in Communist delegations and by the growing need to handle effectively the representatives of small but crucial countries.

Private Research—The need to maximize the contribution to intelligence by private and institutional research is obvious, not only because of its substantive merit, but because in the long run it involves a saving to the tax payer. Every effort is being made to insure that the intelligence agencies carefully coordinate their efforts in this field, and a considerable work load falls on the Department of State. Their work contributes not only to the Department but to the entire intelligence community.

Summing up the foregoing, I would like to emphasize that the increases sought by the Department are necessary to the *national* intelligence effort. They will not constitute a duplication of effort currently expended by the intelligence community nor could they be more logically performed by another intelligence agency. I would like also to stress the care with which the necessity for the proposed increases has been scrutinized. This is in part borne out by the fact that if all the proposed increases are granted, the intelligence organization of the Department of State will still be substantially smaller than in FY 1953.

I strongly recommend that the Bureau of the Budget give its support to the proposed intelligence program of the Department of State for FY 1957.

Sincerely,

Allen W. Dulles[2]

---

[2] Printed from a copy that indicates Dulles signed the original.

---

229. Editorial Note

The U.S. Air Force had been developing the concept of plastic balloon reconnaissance since 1946. After studying the use of plastic balloons as carriers of photographic and electronic reconnaissance equipment since 1948, the Air Force by 1953 was experimenting and testing the balloons directed at the Soviet bloc. By the middle of 1954 the Air Force had test-launched over 500 reconnaissance balloons in Project Moby Dick and had by fall 1954 drawn up a basic operational concept for all future important reconnaissance programs. On March 23, 1955, Air Force headquarters assigned the Strategic Air Command to undertake a pioneer reconnaissance of Soviet territory. (Memorandum of conversation by Robert F. Packard, July 22; National Archives, RG 59, INR Files: Lot 61 D 67, Genetrix; John T. Bohn, "History of the First Air Division," unpublished history done in SAC History Division, Office of Information, Headquarters, SAC, November, 1956, vol. 1, pp. 2–3)

Project Genetrix, the codename ultimately adopted for the first U.S. Air Force large-scale, unmanned, high altitude balloon intelligence operation, was conceived and designed by the RAND Corporation for the Air Force as a means of overcoming the lack of photographic and meteorological intelligence on the Soviet bloc land mass. SAC was charged with operational responsibility for Genetrix. The plans for Genetrix initially called for free flight of balloons from west to east across the Soviet land mass from launching sites in either England, northern Europe, or the eastern Mediterranean. On June 28, the Air Force requested concurrence of the Department of State for conducting negotiations with German, Norwegian, and Turkish authorities to obtain cooperation on Genetrix activities on their territories.

By August 19, the German and Turkish Governments had assented to the operation, and, according to the Ambassador to Norway, the Norwegian Government was expected soon to accept the U.S. plans for Genetrix operations within its boundaries. (Memorandum of conversation by W. Park Armstrong, Jr., November 29; National Archives, RG 59, Central Files 1955–60, 700.5411/11–2955; memoranda of conversation by Robert F. Packard, July 22 and August 22; both ibid., INR Files: Lot 61 D 167, Genetrix)

While British Prime Minister Sir Anthony Eden consented to cooperation on Genetrix, he told President Eisenhower on August 19 that if Genetrix followed soon after the Geneva Foreign Ministers' conference scheduled for October, the Soviet Government could conceivably contrast the balloon operation with the President's aerial inspection proposals made at the July summit conference. Consequently, President Eisenhower agreed on August 23 to postpone the initiation of Genetrix from November 1 until after the United States could assess the results of the Geneva Foreign Ministers' meeting. (Memorandum by W. Park Armstrong, Jr., August 23; letter from Secretary of State Dulles to Sir Robert Scott, British Embassy, August 23; copy of an undated letter to President Eisenhower from Sir Anthony Eden, noted as received by the President on August 19 in a memorandum by John W. Hanes, Jr., August 24; all ibid.)

President Eisenhower described his proposal on mutual aerial observation to the Soviet Government in Geneva on July 21 and in his July 27 White House press conference. (*Public Papers: Eisenhower, 1955*, pages 713–716, 731–733)

---

230. Department of Defense Directive[1]

S–3115.2   Washington, July 13, 1955.

SUBJECT

    Electronics Intelligence (ELINT)

---

[1] Source: National Security Agency, Accession 23034, H02–0106–1, Folder 2, Correspondence–Memos concerning ELINT. Secret.

I. Establishment

Pursuant to the authority vested in the Secretary of Defense and subject to his authority, direction and control, and in accordance with NSCID 17,[2] the Secretary of the Air Force is hereby assigned the responsibility and delegated the necessary authority to direct and supervise the consolidated processing, analysis, and dissemination of information on foreign non-communication electromagnetic radiations and to guide and coordinate Electronics Intelligence (ELINT) activities of all agencies of the Department of Defense. In the development and application of ELINT policies and procedures, the Secretary of the Air Force will give due consideration to recommendations of the U.S. Communications Intelligence Board and the advice of the Joint Chiefs of Staff.

II. Purpose

The objectives of this directive are to consolidate Department of Defense ELINT analysis activities under a single direction, to guide and coordinate Department of Defense collection of ELINT information and to provide for optimum interaction and mutual support between ELINT and COMINT in order to produce efficiently the best possible ELINT results for all users, and to provide for the establishment of a Technical Processing Center pursuant to NSCID 17. The Secretary of the Air Force will bring about the orderly consolidation of the separate ELINT analysis and processing centers heretofore operated by the several military Departments and agencies. In carrying out these objectives, the Secretary of the Air Force will not abridge the authority of operational commanders over integral ELINT resources in support of their operations nor the freedom of such commanders to exchange ELINT materials for their mutual support. Consistent with the over-all policies established by the Secretary of the Air Force, operational commanders will be authorized to establish such policies, procedures, and mechanisms as they deem necessary for the rapid lateral interchange of ELINT information.

III. Mission

The Secretary of the Air Force will provide common services for ELINT, specifically to include:

1. Organization and administration of the Technical Processing Center for central technical analysis based on all ELINT observations and other relevant information. The results of the central technical analysis will be made directly available to all consumers of this type of information.

---

[2] Document 259.

2. Effective and timely guidance to Department of Defense field collection agencies and advice to the Central Intelligence Agency. Such guidance shall be expeditiously transmitted through appropriate channels as prescribed by the several Departments and agencies concerned. Such guidance will reflect the interests of all users and will provide for the coordination of and technical assistance to field activities to maximize their total usefulness.

3. Guidance and advice, as in paragraph III. 2. above, concerning methods and procedures for the improvement and standardization of the operations and equipment related to ELINT collection, analysis, evaluation, and dissemination, and recommendations concerning research and development programs as appropriate.

4. Technical support to the Department of State in its negotiations for the acquisition of intercept sites in foreign countries; technical support to designated representatives of the U.S.; and technical representation on behalf of the Department of Defense in ELINT discussions.

IV. Administration

The Assistant Secretary of Defense (Comptroller) shall arrange with the Secretary of the Air Force, the Secretaries of the other two Military Departments, the Director of Central Intelligence, and heads of other appropriate Departments and Agencies for the financing of the consolidated activities provided for by this directive.

The Secretary of the Air Force may reassign his responsibilities for the ELINT activities as prescribed by this directive within the command structure of the Department of the Air Force. It is the intent of this directive that the Secretary of the Air Force will provide for the performance of the functions of the consolidated activities within the organizational structure of his Department and that he shall not establish a joint agency for that purpose, although individuals drawn from other Departments and the Central Intelligence Agency may be integrated therein. This provision, however, will not preclude the establishment of such advisory committees or groups as may be considered necessary for the effective administration of the consolidated activities.

The Secretaries of the Military Departments shall assure active participation by their Departments through the detail of qualified military and civilian personnel to staff the consolidated activities and through such other measures as may be mutually agreed.

The Secretary of the Air Force, in collaboration with the heads of the other Military Departments and Agencies, will issue the necessary implementing instructions to accomplish actions required by this directive. The Secretary of the Air Force will periodically report on the activities under this directive to the Secretary of Defense.

V. Participation

The Secretary of the Air Force will collaborate fully with the Central Intelligence Agency as an active collector and user in the field of ELINT, as well as with other interested agencies, and will provide for the participation of the Central Intelligence Agency in the operation of the Technical Processing Center, in accordance with NSCID 17.

RB Anderson
Acting Secretary of Defense

---

231.   Memorandum of Conversation

Washington, July 19, 1955.

[Source: National Archives, RG 59, Central Files 1950–55, 101.21/7–1955. Top Secret. 2 pages not declassified.]

---

232.   Memorandum of Conversation Between President Eisenhower and Secretary of State Dulles.[1]

Washington, August 5, 1955, 12:30 p.m.

SUBJECT

Nelson Rockefeller

I raised with the President the situation re Nelson Rockefeller, stating that I simply wanted the President to know at this stage that we were having a very difficult time working with him and that, although I was trying to work the situation out, I was not at all sure that I would be successful in doing so. I then described to the President briefly my own thinking as to the proper role that someone in Rockefeller's posi-

---

[1] Source: Eisenhower Library, Papers of John Foster Dulles. Confidential; Personal and Private; Eyes Only. Drafted by R.L. O'Connor of the Secretary's staff. The memorandum bears the handwritten notation "Copy to Mr. Hoover."

tion should play. I said that I felt that his primary function was to screen the many ideas, written and oral, that came into the White House in the field of foreign affairs and to see to it that the worthwhile ones were put into proper Government channels for further consideration and followed up. I said that I recognized that the regular departments were often so tied to daily routines that they did not have time or resourcefulness in dealing with new ideas. However, I said that if somebody like Nelson Rockefeller built up a staff of his own, as he appeared to have every intention of doing, he in turn became a bureaucrat and defeated the whole purpose of the exercise.

I then showed the President the copy of the memorandum Governor Adams had given me from Nelson Rockefeller to the President outlining his staff requirements.[2] The President expressed some surprise at the size and complexity of the proposed staff and said that he had been unaware of all these arrangements.

JFD

---

[2] Not found.

---

233. **Memorandum From the Deputy Under Secretary of State for Political Affairs (Murphy) to the Secretary of State's Special Assistant for Intelligence and Research (Armstrong)**

Washington, August 18, 1955.

[Source: National Archives, RG 59, Central Files 1950–55, 101.21/7–1955. Top Secret. 1 page not declassified.]

234.   National Security Council Report[1]

NSC 5525   Washington, August 31, 1955.

STATUS OF UNITED STATES NATIONAL SECURITY PROGRAMS
AS OF JUNE 30, 1955

[Omitted here are Parts 1–6.]

Part 7—THE FOREIGN INTELLIGENCE PROGRAM

(Prepared by the Central Intelligence Agency and concurred in by
the Intelligence Advisory Committee)[2]

[Omitted here is a Table of Contents.]

(*Note:* The intelligence community was recently investigated by
the Clark Task Force of the Hoover Commission.[3] The findings of the
Commission, which are presently under advisement, are not covered
or commented on in this report. The comments of the organizations reported on are being transmitted separately to the White House in accordance with customary procedure.)

I. Summary

   A. Evaluation of U.S. Capabilities to Provide Warning of Attack

We believe, as we did at the time of our previous report, that the
U.S. could expect possibly as much as six months and not less than 30
days warning of Soviet preparation for full-scale land, sea, and air attack, providing that the Soviets went to full, or nearly full mobilization prior to the attack.

The current estimate of the growing air capabilities of the USSR
has made us somewhat more pessimistic than we were last year regarding our ability to give advance intelligence warning of surprise air
attack. Should the USSR attempt a major surprise air attack against the
U.S. from forward bases in 1955, the preparations might be detected,

---

[1] Source: National Archives, RG 59, S/S–NSC Files: Lot 63 D 351, NSC 5525. Top
Secret. The full report was transmitted to the National Security Council under cover of
an August 31 memorandum from Acting Executive Secretary of the National Security
Council Gleason.

[2] On July 19, A. Sidney Buford III, Director of the Office of Libraries and Intelligence Acquisition, Department of State, sent to the IAC the State Department's contribution to the IAC's semi-annual report on the Foreign Intelligence Program to the National Security Council. The Department of State report is in National Archives, RG 59,
INR Files: Lot 58 D 776, IAC–D–55 Series on Foreign Intelligence Program.

[3] See Document 220. For the public report by the task force on intelligence, see Document 221.

and if they were, would provide a generalized degree of warning of several days, and specific warning of unusual and possibly threatening air activity on the order of 18–24 hours. A lesser scale of attack, involving about 250 aircraft, if accompanied by an extraordinary security effort could be launched as early as 1955 with no assurance of specific advance warning to U.S. intelligence (apart from that provided by early warning radar). Attacks against U.S. bases or forces overseas, or against U.S. allies, could be made with equal or greater likelihood of being accomplished without advance warning.

In the period between now and 1958, Soviet capabilities for surprise attacks will almost certainly increase. Furthermore, the USSR will have a progressively increasing capability for launching attacks on the U.S. from interior Soviet bases. Such a method of attack would probably provide no specific advance warning to U.S. intelligence.

The USAF now operates world-wide on a 24-hour basis an Indications System for detecting imminent Communist attacks, especially air attack with nuclear weapons. Major air commands have subsidiary centers tied in with Washington by preferential use channels of communication for flash transmission of early warning intelligence. This system is in turn tied in with the unified command indications centers and with the National Indications Center in Washington, which is maintained on a 24-hour basis by the Watch Committee of the IAC.[4]

B. Evaluation of Soviet Capabilities and Intentions

Intelligence to support over-all assessments of the strengths of the USSR, Communist China, and the Satellites is generally improving. The general limitations of intelligence on the USSR are evident in the process of attempting to measure the forces shaping Soviet policy. We can illuminate the broad outlines of the chief problems confronting Soviet leadership, but we are still unable to determine the degree to which these problems, such as allocation of Soviet economic resources and German rearmament, generate pressures on Soviet policy. The main questions of political intelligence often involve matters of judgment on which little or no factual evidence can be brought to bear—the degree of independence enjoyed by Communist China in matters of major policy, the degree of likelihood that the USSR will withdraw from East Germany, the likelihood of open intervention by the USSR in hostilities between the U.S. and Communist China which threatened the existence of the latter.

We have made progress in economic intelligence on the USSR, most notably in improving techniques for measuring economic growth.

---

[4] For a description of the National Indications Center and the Watch Committee of the IAC, see Document 218.

However, there remains the basic problem, that of determining the extent to which the Soviet economy is capable of meeting the competing claims for resources arising from the various internal and external commitments of Soviet policy. In an effort to find some solution to this problem, we have recently focused attention on a particularly difficult aspect of intelligence on Soviet resources allocation, the estimated economic cost of the over-all Soviet military effort.

New techniques for acquiring and analyzing data have advanced our knowledge of Soviet scientific and technological capabilities. Progress has been made in intelligence on Soviet development of guided missiles and electronic equipment, and on the Soviet nuclear program. Despite advances in these and other fields, important questions such as the characteristics of various guided missiles, the existence and nature of a Soviet biological warfare program, and the apportionment of nuclear material among various types of weapons and systems, remain to be answered.

Although we have succeeded in collecting much information on the separate branches of the Soviet armed forces, we have yet to construct the picture of probable Soviet strategy so essential to estimating general trends in the Soviet military establishment, probable Soviet choices in weapons systems, or the strength of particular military components. The requirement for such estimates is particularly urgent at the present time because of recent indications that Soviet military thinking is adjusting to the impact of modern military technology.

C. Collection

In most respects there has been little over-all change in our collection capabilities within the Bloc, largely because of the continued strict enforcement of Sino-Soviet security and counterintelligence measures. However, there has been a considerable improvement in the collection of intelligence data through technological means such as ELINT, together with increasing use of aerial reconnaissance. Evacuation of U.S. forces from Austria will deprive the military services of a significant intelligence base. Service collection units in Austria will be transferred to West Germany, where operational requirements are being carefully considered in U.S.-West German negotiations on a new Forces Arrangement.[5]

---

[5] Under the terms of the Austrian State Treaty signed in Vienna on May 15 all World War II allied occupying powers were scheduled to evacuate Austria within 90 days of the treaty coming into force. (See Foreign Relations, 1955–1957, vol. V) This provision is in Article 20 of the treaty, which is printed in full in Department of State Bulletin, Vol. XXXII, June 6, 1955, pp. 916ff. In preparation, the U.S. Government was negotiating a new status of forces agreement with the West German government. (Foreign Relations, 1955–1957, vol. XXVI, pp. 242 and 300)

235. Letter From the Chairman of the Planning Coordination Group (Rockefeller) to the Director of the Bureau of the Budget (Hughes)[1]

Washington, September 23, 1955.

Dear Rowland:

This is to confirm our conversation in which I recommended to you that the Planning Coordination Group be abolished, and that I resign as Vice Chairman of the Operations Coordinating Board. We are preparing an informal memorandum for you setting forth the problems that must be considered in regard to the functions of the Group.

I would suggest that December thirty-first be considered the termination date as this would give time to arrange for the orderly transfer of existing responsibilities and completion of the work in progress.

I am sorry to make this recommendation. However, it is clear after six months experience that this mechanism will not be able to accomplish the objectives set forth in the memorandum of March 3, 1955,[2] which was approved by the President.

A meeting of the Planning Coordination Group members will be held next week. At that time I will discuss this recommendation with them.[3]

Sincerely,

Nelson A. Rockefeller[4]
Special Assistant

---

[1] Source: National Archives, RG 59, S/S–NSC Files: Lot 66 D 148, PCG, Coordination of Psychological and other Warfare Activities. Confidential.

[2] Document 210.

[3] Rockefeller informed the PCG of his intention at the Group's September 26 meeting. Item 4 of the minutes of this meeting reads:

"The Chairman announced his conviction that after six months' experience the PCG cannot discharge its functions and made a recommendation that it be abolished on December 31, 1955. The CIA representative indicated no objection to this recommendation and discussed briefly methods by which the coordination of major covert programs could be handled after the abolishment of PCG. The State and Defense representatives reserved position on the recommendation by the Chairman. Copies of a letter from the Chairman, PCG, to the Director, Bureau of the Budget, dated September 23, 1955, recommending the abolishment of PCG, were furnished the PCG members." (Minutes of Third Meeting, September 26; National Archives, RG 59, S/S–NSC Files: Lot 66 D 148, PCG, Coordination of Psychological and other Warfare Activities.)

[4] Printed from a copy that indicates Rockefeller signed the original.

236. Letter From the Secretary of State's Special Assistant for Intelligence and Research (Armstrong) to Director of Central Intelligence Dulles[1]

Washington, October 5, 1955.

Dear Allen:

The Task Force on Intelligence Activities ("Clark Committee") of the Commission on Organization of the Executive Branch of the Government (Hoover Commission), in its *public* Report to the Congress on Intelligence dated May 1955, but released in June,[2] makes a number of disparaging statements concerning the attitude of the Department of State toward intelligence collection activities. In the Conclusions and Recommendations (Part VII, pages 37–38) it is stated:

". . . Also among some of those responsible for implementation of our foreign policy by diplomacy and negotiation, there seems to exist an abhorrence to anything that might lead to diplomatic or even protocol complications.

"This negative attitude, usually at the desk level, at times stifled initiative and action in the collection of intelligence. Some of these efforts, if permitted to proceed properly, might have brought direct and immediate results and made positive contributions to the national welfare that would have justified the attendant political risks and possible inconsequential diplomatic embarrassment."

Further on, referring to the inadequacy of data on the Soviet Bloc, the Report says that:

". . . Success in this field depends on greater boldness at the policy level, a willingness to accept certain calculated political and diplomatic risks, and full use of technological capabilities."

The Department is naturally concerned at such allegations and desires to learn what the basis for them might be. In the Top Secret Task Force Report dated May 1955,[3] I can find no substantiating data or argumentation for the implied charges against the Department made in the public report. However, according to the *Top Secret* Report, Appendix II, which has not been available to the Department, fully discusses [*less than 1 line not declassified*]. Would it be possible for you to make this Appendix available to me on a highly restricted basis? Alternatively, could you send to us a statement, generally summarizing

---

[1] Source: National Archives, RG 59, Central Files 1955–60, 711.5200/11–2555. Secret. Drafted by Fisher Howe on October 5, concurred in by W. Tapley Bennett, Jr. (G), Robert G. Barnes (S/S), and Loy Henderson (O). All ellipses in the original.

[2] Document 220.

[3] Document 221.

the Report's position on this matter, as was, I believe, suggested by the President's Military Secretary.

Directly related to the question of what was said by the public Task Force Report would be the views of your Agency on the question of the Department's attitude toward intelligence and intelligence operations. Naturally the Department would wish to know it if this analysis is correct in your view, and would wish promptly to take remedial action if legitimate intelligence activities are inhibited by the actions of Foreign Service or Departmental officers.

Sincerely,

W. Park Armstrong, Jr.[4]

---

[4] Printed from a copy that indicates Armstrong signed the original.

---

237. Memorandum From the Acting Assistant Secretary of State for European Affairs (Barbour) to the Under Secretary of State (Hoover)[1]

Washington, October 18, 1955.

SUBJECT

Abolition of the Planning Coordination Group

At a PCG Alternates meeting this morning we discussed the attached draft documents[2] to accomplish the abolition of the Planning Coordination Group.[3]

Substantive comment was made on the following two points in the proposed memorandum to the Chairman of the OCB.[4]

1. CIA proposed that Par. 4(a) be redrafted to amend NSC 5412/1[5] to specify the individuals originally designated in Sec. 4(a) of that NSC

---

[1] Source: National Archives, RG 59, S/S–NSC Files: Lot 66 D 148, PCG. No classification marking.

[2] Not printed.

[3] See Document 235 and footnote 3 thereto.

[4] The Under Secretary of State was chairman of the Operations Coordinating Board.

[5] Document 212.

paper, i.e. a representative of the Secretary of State and Secretary of Defense and to omit reference to members of the OCB. The reasoning advanced was that while the State Department representative is the same as the representative designated for this purpose in 5412,[6] it is not clear whether the Defense representatives will be the same. (The question was not (repeat not) raised but it may be noted that the effect of this CIA proposal would be, unless further altered, to exclude Nelson Rockefeller. The "representative of the President" is not mentioned in NSC 5412.

2. Defense (Charlie Sullivan) questioned whether in Par. 3 of the memorandum to the Chairman of OCB it is sufficient to state that the original objectives of the PCG continue valid and other means should be sought to achieve these objectives. Sullivan thought the PCG might consider suggesting some alternative means. I took the line and was supported by Nelson and CIA that that statement went far enough for the time being and we should not consider alternative mechanisms now.

One additional point was raised by Nelson Rockefeller, namely to explain the reason for his resignation as Vice Chairman of the OCB. His explanation was that the Budget Bureau have never liked the idea of establishing a Vice Chairman of the OCB. He did not expand further on the matter.

I took the general position on these points that in your absence I could not give Departmental approval but that we would consider them further when submitted.

---

[6] Document 171.

238. Director of Central Intelligence Directive No. 4/5[1]

Washington, October 18, 1955.

PRIORITY NATIONAL INTELLIGENCE OBJECTIVES

1. Pursuant to National Security Council Intelligence Directive No. 4,[2] paragraph 2, the following list of priority national intelligence objectives is established as a guide for the coordination of intelligence collection and production in response to requirements relating to the formulation and execution of national security policy.

2. By definition, all items in this listing are deemed to be critical national intelligence factors requiring priority attention and effort. Distinction is made, however, between three levels of priority within the general priority category. Order of listing within these three groups is a matter of convenience in presentation and has no significance with respect to the relative priority of specific items within the group.

3. In order to afford a stable basis for intelligence planning, this directive is designed to remain valid over an extended period. It will be reviewed annually, or on the request of any member of the IAC. It is recognized that urgent interim requirements may arise requiring ad hoc treatment, and that the criteria on which the following priorities are established shall remain under continuing review. These criteria were issued in IAC–D–50/7, 16 August 1955,[3] and define categories of priority as follows:

a. First Priority Intelligence Objectives are those which will permit the US: (1) to anticipate and counter those policies or actions of foreign states which would occasion gravest consequences to the US; and (2) to stimulate policies or actions of foreign states (or actions within them) which could occasion greatest benefit to the US.

b. Second Priority Intelligence Objectives are those which will permit the US: (1) to anticipate and counter those policies or actions of

---

[1] Source: National Archives, RG 59, S/P–NSC Files: Lot 62 D 1, NSC Intelligence Directives. Secret. On December 7, the Department of State sent this directive to all diplomatic posts and Hong Kong and Singapore in Circular Airgram 4388, to aid the Department in improving the organization and coordination of intelligence reporting from the field. (Ibid., Central Files 1955–60, 101.21/12–755)

[2] See *Foreign Relations,* 1945–1950, Emergence of the Intelligence Establishment, Document 422.

[3] Documentation on IAC–D–50/7, "Criteria for Determining Priority National Intelligence Objectives," August 16, is in National Archives, RG 59, INR Files: Lot 58 D 776, Box 27.

foreign states which would have serious consequences for the US; and (2) to stimulate policies or actions of foreign states (or actions within them) which could occasion great benefit to the US.

c. Third Priority Intelligence Objectives are those which will permit the US: (1) to anticipate and counter those policies or actions of foreign states which would have harmful consequences to the US; and (2) to stimulate policies or actions of foreign states (or actions within them) which could occasion substantial benefits to the US.

4. DCID 4/4 is hereby rescinded.[4]

I. First Priority Objectives[5]

a. Soviet over-all politico-military strategy, intentions, and plans, particularly with respect to initiating hostilities using Soviet or Satellite armed forces, and to disarmament and arms inspection.

b. Chinese Communist over-all politico-military strategy, intentions, and plans, particularly with respect to initiating hostilities using Chinese Communist armed forces.

c. Present and probable future Soviet capabilities for nuclear attack on the United States or key US overseas installations and for defense against air attack.

d. Soviet capabilities, plans, and intentions for the clandestine delivery of nuclear, biological, or chemical weapons against the US or key US overseas installations.

II. Second Priority Objectives[6]

The USSR and European Satellites

a. The Soviet estimate of US and allied capabilities and intentions; of US and allied economic and political stability, and of the strength, cohesion, and probable development of the NATO Bloc.

b. Major Soviet international political objectives and courses of action, including economic policies and actions, with particular reference to courses designed to weaken and disrupt the NATO alliance or to foment antagonism between Western and Asian powers.

c. Soviet political strengths and weaknesses: the actual locus of political power in the USSR; actual or potential personal or policy con-

---

[4] DCID 4/4, "Priority List of Critical National Intelligence Objectives," was issued 14 December 1954. [Footnote in the original. For DCID 4/4, see Document 201.]

[5] *Note:* Order of listing within Category I is a matter of convenience in presentation and has no significance with respect to the relative priority of specific items within that category. [Footnote in the original.]

[6] *Note:* Order of listing within Category II is a matter of convenience in presentation and has no significance with respect to the relative priority of specific items within that category. [Footnote in the original.]

flicts within the ruling group; Soviet-Satellite relations, with particular reference to the character and degree of Soviet control; the strengths and weaknesses of the Soviet and Satellite apparatus of police control; the extent of actual disaffection and of potential resistance in the Soviet and Satellite populations.

d. The strength and weaknesses of the Soviet (including Satellite) economy, with particular reference to its ability to support a major war; the motivation, character, and magnitude of current economic development programs, their implementation, and their effect upon the economic, political, and military strength of the Soviet Bloc; the capabilities and vulnerabilities of the Soviet and Satellite internal communications systems.

e. Soviet and Satellite scientific and technical strengths and weaknesses substantially affecting Soviet military, economic, and political capabilities.

f. The general capabilities of the Soviet and Satellite armed forces.

[9 *headings and 31 paragraphs (96 lines) not declassified*]

Allen W. Dulles[7]
Director of Central Intelligence

---

[7] Printed from a copy that bears this typed signature.

---

239. Paper Prepared in the Department of Defense[1]

Washington, undated.

COMMENTS OF THE DEPARTMENT OF DEFENSE ON THE
RECOMMENDATIONS OF THE HOOVER COMMISSION TASK
FORCE ON INTELLIGENCE ACTIVITIES OF THE GOVERNMENT

The following comments are addressed to the Recommendations of the Task Force which are applicable to the Department of Defense.

---

[1] Source: Defense Intelligence Agency Files. No classification marking. The paper was enclosed in a November 10 letter from Secretary of Defense Wilson to President Eisenhower, and both were under cover of a November 10 letter from Wilson to Rowland R. Hughes. Attached to the paper, but not printed, is Tab A, a draft of Department of Defense comments on all nine recommendations. Both of Wilson's letters indicate that the responses were to the unclassified Hoover Commission Report on Intelligence Activities. For extracts from this unclassified report, see Document 221.

Recommendations (a) and (b) of the Commission itself, and Recommendations Nos. 1, 2, and 7 of the Task Force, are considered not to be sufficiently applicable to the Department of Defense to justify comment by it.

Recommendation No. 3

"That the chiefs of the various intelligence units of the military services be elevated in the organizational structure to the level of Deputy Chiefs of Staff in the Army and the Air Force, and Deputy Chief of Naval Operations in the Navy."

Non-concur

Comment

The Department of Defense agrees that it is essential that intelligence be given adequate weight and representation in the staff organization of the military services if it is to function with optimum efficiency,—but it considers that this can be assured without the recommended organizational changes at this time.

Implementation: None at this time.

Recommendation No. 4

"That the Department of Defense make extensive use of Schedule A of the Civil Service Regulations (non-competitive appointments) in the employment by the military services of civilian intelligence analysts and other specialists in order to provide the necessary flexibility in the recruitment of qualified civilian personnel (to include retired citizens with wide previous business experience in the foreign field) and to facilitate the interchange of such personnel between zone of interior competitive service and the overseas excepted service."

Concur

Comment

Each of the three Services has taken or is developing measures to apply Schedule A to elements of its civilian intelligence staff. In addition, the Department of Defense is studying the matter with a view to finding an optimum balance between desirable flexibility in hiring and rotation of skilled career personnel on the one hand and providing the fullest practicable job security and incentive (as a vital morale factor) on the other.

Implementation: Take action in accordance with the results of such study.

Recommendation No. 5

"That measures be instituted in all agencies for rechecking the security status of all personnel engaged in intelligence activities at periodic intervals not to exceed 5 years in any individual case."

Concur in principle

Comment

It is considered that the current security practices and the procedures for acting on adverse information essentially fulfill the objectives of these recommendations. Within the objectives, however, it is desirable to leave to each individual service reasonable latitude in the method of implementation. For example, it may in some cases aid the investigation not to alert the individual involved by suspending him. Measures are taken, of course, in such cases to insure that classified information is adequately safeguarded. This general subject is being reviewed in order to insure that the underlying objectives of these recommendations are adequately served.

Implementation: Additional precautions indicated by such review.

Recommendation No. 6

"That the responsibility for procurement of foreign publications and for collection of scientific intelligence be removed from the State Department and placed in the hands of CIA, with authority to appoint such scientific attachés as may be necessary to carry on this work abroad."

Concur in part

Comment

The collection of scientific intelligence is one of the most important intelligence activities of the Government. It is of vital concern to the Department of Defense. The CIA should have coordinating responsibility but it would be unwise and inefficient to give it or any other agency a monopoly in this field, nor does any one agency now have such a monopoly. The Department of Defense considers it inappropriate for the Central Intelligence Agency to have overt attachés stationed abroad.

Implementation: None by Department of Defense.

Recommendation No. 8

"That steps be taken to introduce highly selective methods of choosing members of the coordinating committee on atomic energy intelligence, not only to get the benefit of service by the most competent individuals, but also to assure long tenure in this important assignment."

Concur

Comment

The salaries the Department of Defense can pay for top-flight talent in this field compare unfavorably with those offered outside the Government, and this makes it difficult to insure long-term continuity.

Implementation: The Department of Defense will use its best efforts to carry out this Recommendation.

Recommendation No. 9

"That a comprehensive, coordinated program be developed to expand linguistic training among American citizens serving the Intelligence effort; and

"That the Department of Defense expand and promote language training by offering credit toward reserve commissions to ROTC students and drill credit to Reserve personnel for completion of selected language courses."

Concur in principle

Comment

The Department of Defense endorses the importance of a comprehensive program of foreign language and area specialist training for persons serving the national intelligence effort and allied activities. It and its elements have taken various measures during the past years to further such a program. But in the case of ROTC and reserves, the Department of Defense is reluctant to provide for additional language training if such training must be at the expense of training in primary military subjects. Specifically, the Task Force's recommendation would make for wider participation but would, not by itself, produce well-trained linguists.

Implementation: The various existing programs are being studied in the light of this recommendation with a view to achieving an optimum balance between qualitative and quantitative standards.

---

240. Memorandum of Telephone Conversation Between Secretary of State Dulles and Director of Central Intelligence Dulles[1]

Washington, November 22, 1955, 3:39 p.m.

The Sec. referred to Grayback.[2] Radford has written Wilson,[3] who took it up with the Pres., requesting that he be authorized to proceed.

---

[1] Source: Eisenhower Library, Papers of John Foster Dulles, Telephone Conversations, General. No classification marking. Drafted by Phyllis D. Bernau. Secretary Dulles placed the call.

[2] Formerly known as Project Genetrix. See Document 229.

[3] Memorandum from the Chairman of the Joint Chiefs of Staff to the Secretary of Defense, November 16. (National Archives, RG 59, Central Files 1955–60, 711.5261/11–1655)

The Sec. has reservations about it—this is a dangerous and cumbersome way of going about it. AWD said there are two feelings in Defense. AWD talked with Quarles the other day. AWD thinks it will get them so alerted it will spoil other things he thinks have more potential.[4] The Sec. has to make a decision. AWD suggested they, Radford, Wilson and Quarles get together—AWD does not feel he knows enough about the potential to pass good judgment. The Sec. said they want authority here before December 1. The Sec. may call Wilson to see if it can wait until next week, or maybe Hoover can handle it. The Sec. said the Pres. is dubious about it on general principles. The Sec. said a lot of money was spent on it. The Sec. will find out how fast it has to move.

AWD said Strauss will use "megaton" instead of "large" in the release for Thursday's papers. The Sec. said o.k.

---

[4] Dulles is alluding to the U–2 which would fly over Eastern Europe in June 1956.

---

241. Letter From Director of Central Intelligence Dulles to the Secretary of State's Special Assistant for Intelligence and Research (Armstrong)[1]

Washington, November 25, 1955.

Dear Park:

This is with reference to your letter of 5 October 1955[2] concerning the statements made in the report of the Task Force on Intelligence Activities (Clark Committee)[3] regarding the attitude of the Department of State toward intelligence collection activities.

As you point out, there is no substantiating data or argumentation for the implied charges made against the Department of State in the Top Secret Task Force Report, dated May 1955—at least not in that

---

[1] Source: National Archives, RG 59, Central Files 1955–60, 711.5200/11–2555. Top Secret. The letter is attached to a November 29 memorandum from Armstrong indicating that Dulles' letter was being forwarded to Hoover, Murphy, and MacArthur.

[2] Document 236.

[3] Documents 220 and 221.

portion of the report, which excludes pages 76–204,[4] made available to this Agency.

We have once again carefully reviewed Appendix II which deals with certain aspects of CIA's work.[5] The pertinent portions of this report appear to be:

"The allocation of funds for all projects of psychological warfare to specific areas, more particularly for propaganda, has been consistently influenced and too frequently interfered with by low-level State Department representatives since the beginning of the cold-war program. This intervention in the program by such representatives, whose interests are narrow and restricted to their assigned country areas, has at times in the past resulted not only in misdirected efforts on the part of the Clandestine Services, but in serious financial losses to the Government also, without a fair measure of gainful return. These might have been avoided had the DCI been given long-range national policy guidance at higher State Department level and had been permitted then to act on his own judgment, or, better still, had NSC more clearly defined the prerogatives of the DCI in carrying out his cold-war mission. To the surveying officer it is significant that NSC gave to the DCI the sole responsibility for carrying out cold-war operations aimed at the Communist bloc. Nowhere in NSC directives pertaining to this mission is it indicated that the DCI's responsibility therefor may be delegated to, or shared with, any other Government agency. . . . While there is no evidence revealed in this survey concerning any serious disagreement between CIA officials and these same representatives with respect to psychological warfare, it is clearly indicated that, as far as the Office of the Secretary of State is concerned, such policy advice has come on a piece-meal basis and too often not from specifically designated representatives of that agency."

[1 paragraph (3½ lines) not declassified]

I consider that there is no real basis of fact for the above allegations regarding the State Department's attitude. As regards policy guidance, the Department has been wholly cooperative and I do not consider that there has been any improper "intervention" or "interference" in the carrying out by CIA of cold war programs. [3 lines not declassified]

Sincerely,

Allen W. Dulles

---

[4] Pages 76–88 concerned the Department of State and pages 89–205 examined the intelligence role of the Department of Defense. (Memorandum from Dillon Anderson to Goodpaster, February 14, 1956; Eisenhower Library, Hoover Commission Report on Intelligence Activities, May 1955–October 1956)

[5] Appendix II, which discussed the clandestine service of the Central Intelligence Agency, is not printed.

242.   Memorandum From Secretary of State Dulles to President Eisenhower[1]

Washington, December 1, 1955.

SUBJECT

"Operation Grayback"[2]

I have been fully briefed by the Air Force on "Operation Grayback".[3] It is my view that while I would not today start the operation in view of possible newer techniques, nevertheless the operation is already mounted at a cost of approximately $70,000,000, with personnel all over the world. The operation will probably produce intelligence data of considerable significance. Also, reasonable cover has been devised in that similar operations have, in fact, been conducted from a good many points in the United States and elsewhere, designed to obtain meteorological data. This cover will probably not fool the Soviets, but it will create a situation such that they cannot take any very great offense publicly.[4]

On balance, I would be inclined to go ahead with it if Sir Anthony Eden is also prepared to do so. While some operations will be started from Norway, Germany and Turkey, there is, I believe, primary dependence upon the British Isles.

I would suggest your authorizing me to advise Eden of the foregoing attitude on our part and see what his reaction is.[5]

JFD

---

[1] Source: National Archives, RG 59, Central Files 1955–60, 711.5261/12–1555. Top Secret.

[2] Formerly known as Project Genetrix. See Document 229.

[3] The Secretary of State received an Air Force briefing on Grayback on November 29. (Memorandum of conversation by Armstrong; National Archives, RG 59, INR Files: Lot 58 D 766, Genetrix)

[4] According to the memorandum of the November 29 briefing, the Air Force proposed to say that the balloons were part of a worldwide meteorological research survey that the U.S. Government had been conducting for years. (Ibid.)

[5] A handwritten note on the memorandum reads: "I concur C.E. Wilson O.K." Below this note President Eisenhower wrote: "Original query to be of a *non*-pressure type. D." Secretary Dulles wrote a December 1 letter to British Ambassador Sir Roger Makins in which he noted that he had discussed "Grayback" with the President who had asked him to notify Prime Minister Eden, through Makins, that he, the President, was disposed to let the operation proceed. He would, however, not take final action until he had Eden's response. (Ibid., Central Files 1955–60, 711.5261/12–155) On December 3, Secretary Dulles informed Secretary of Defense Wilson that he had solicited Eden's views and would let Wilson know of Eden's response. He added: "I showed the President my memorandum with your concurrence with respect to 'Grayback'. The President said that he was disposed to go along, provided Eden concurred. However, the President asked me, in putting it up to Eden, to make clear that the President was not trying to pressure him. I gathered that the President has not much enthusiasm for the project." (Ibid., INR Files: Lot 61 D 67, Genetrix)

243.   Memorandum From Director of Central Intelligence Dulles to the Secretary of State's Special Assistant for Intelligence and Research (Armstrong)

Washington, December 3, 1955.

[Source: National Archives, RG 59, Central Files 1955–60, 101.21/ 12–355. Top Secret. 5 pages not declassified.]

---

244.   Memorandum From Director of Central Intelligence Dulles to Secretary of Defense Wilson[1]

Washington, December 3, 1955.

SUBJECT

Research on Psychochemicals

1. For the past four years the Central Intelligence Agency has been actively engaged in research on a group of powerful chemicals affecting the human mind called psychochemicals. We have developed extensive professional contacts, experience and a considerable amount of information on many psychochemicals including in particular a material known as LSD. This Agency is continuing its interest in this field, and in the light of its accumulated experience offers its cooperation and assistance to research and development programs which the Department of Defense is considering at this time.

2. The Agency became interested in the potential importance of psychochemicals, primarily because of the enthusiasm and foresight of Dr. L. Wilson Greene, Technical Director of the Chemical and Radiological Laboratories at the Army Chemical Center. Dr. Greene's ideas were included in a report written by him in 1949 entitled "Psychochemical Warfare, a New Concept of War".

3. Since 1951 this Agency has carried out a program of research which has provided important information on the nature of the abnormal behavior produced by LSD and the way this effect varies with such factors as size of dose, differences in the individual and environment. The behavioral effects of repeated doses given over a long time

---

[1] Source: Central Intelligence Agency, Executive Registry, Job 80–B01731R, Box 15. Secret.

has been studied. We have established that individuals may develop a tolerance to LSD. A search for possible antidotes is being made. It has been found that LSD produces remarkable mental effects when taken in exceedingly small doses. The foregoing became increasingly interesting when it was recently discovered that LSD could be synthesized in quantity.

4. There are many characteristics of LSD and other psychochemicals which either have not been studied or require further study. We are continuing to search for a satisfactory antidote for LSD as well as other defensive measures. More data should be accumulated if it is desired to predict the precise effect upon a given individual under given circumstances. It would appear to be important that field trials be made to determine the effects on groups of people or on individuals engaged in group activities.

5. This Agency's scientists who have been responsible for this research in psychochemicals have maintained close and effective liaison with various research and development groups in the Department of Defense who are aware of our interest and, in varying degrees, of our progress in psychochemicals. Some of these individuals are:

Dr. L. Wilson Greene, Technical Director, Chemical Corps, Chemical and Radiological Laboratories, Army Chemical Center
Dr. Bruce Dill, Scientific Director, Chemical Corps, Medical Laboratory, Army Chemical Center
Dr. Amendeo Marrazzi, a scientist at the Medical Laboratory, Army Chemical Center
Capt. Clifford P. Phoebus, Chief, Biological Sciences Division, Office of Naval Research
Brig. Gen. Don D. Flickinger, ARDC, U.S.A.F.
Lt. Col. Alexander Batlin, Office of the Assistant Secretary of Defense (Research and Development)

6. In addition, this Agency has provided financial support for certain projects in the field of psychochemicals being conducted by the Chemical Corps and by the Office of Naval Research. We have noted with considerable interest the current Department of Defense study of the potential importance of certain psychochemical materials including LSD which is being carried out by the Ad Hoc Study Group on Psychochemicals under the Technical Advisory Panel on CW and BW of the Office of the Assistant Secretary of Defense for Research and Development. If our accumulated information, experience and professional contacts can be of any assistance, this Agency gladly offers its co-operation in this program.

Allen W. Dulles[2]

---

[2] Printed from a copy that bears this typed signature.

245.   Minutes of a Meeting of the Intelligence Advisory Committee[1]

IAC–M–222   Washington, December 13, 1955, 10:45 a.m.

Director of Central Intelligence
Allen W. Dulles
Presiding[2]

Deputy Director of Central Intelligence
Lieutenant General Charles P. Cabell
Presiding[2]

MEMBERS PRESENT

Mr. W. Park Armstrong, Special Assistant for Intelligence, Department of State
Major General Ridgely Gaither, Assistant Chief of Staff, G–2, Department of the Army
Rear Admiral Carl F. Espe, Director of Naval Intelligence, Department of the Navy
Major General John A. Samford, Director of Intelligence, Headquarters, United States Air Force
Rear Admiral Edwin T. Layton, Deputy Director for Intelligence, The Joint Staff
Mr. Harry S. Traynor, Atomic Energy Commission representative to the IAC
Mr. Alan H. Belmont, Assistant Director, Federal Bureau of Investigation

1. *Report of the IAC Ad Hoc Guided Missile Intelligence Survey Committee* (IAC–D–81/13, 25 November 1955)[3]

a. Colonel White, Chairman, Ad Hoc Guided Missile Intelligence Survey Committee led off the discussion by summarizing briefly the conclusions reached by the Committee.

b. Admiral Layton, supported by Admiral Espe and General Gaither, took the position that under existing NSC directives, guided missiles intelligence, being intelligence on weapons, fell clearly within the responsibility of the Department of Defense. In short, that guided missiles intelligence is departmental intelligence. He further expressed the view that the creation of an IAC subcommittee on guided missiles was not the answer to what is basically a collection problem.

c. General Samford stated that, based on the experience of the Air Force as the primary collector of guided missiles intelligence, he be-

---

[1] Source: Central Intelligence Agency, Executive Registry, Job 85–500362R, Box 2, Folder 6. Secret. The meeting was held in the IAC Conference Room, Administration Building, Central Intelligence Agency.

[2] Part of meeting. Lieutenant General Ralph Canine, Director, National Security Agency, attended part of the meeting. [Footnote in the original.]

[3] Not found.

lieved that there was merit in the idea of a coordinated community approach. This approach had demonstrated its value in the field of atomic energy intelligence.

d. Mr. Dulles expressed the view that guided missiles intelligence was national intelligence of the highest priority, probably of even greater ultimate importance to our national security than atomic energy intelligence. A concerted attack on the problem by the community, under the guidance of an IAC guided missiles committee, is therefore essential if he and the community are to discharge their responsibilities under existing NSC directives.

e. It was agreed that Mr. Dulles would draw up his views for presentation to the National Security Council under the procedure provided in NSCID No. 1, paragraph 3 a.[4]

---

[4] Document 255.

---

246. Memorandum From the Chairman of the Planning Coordinating Group (Rockefeller) to the Chairman of the Operations Coordinating Board (Hoover)[1]

Washington, December 14, 1955.

SUBJECT

Report of the Planning Coordination Group

I. Background

1. The Planning Coordination Group was established within the framework of the OCB by letter of the President of March 10, 1955.[2] The Group's functions and composition are described in the Budget

---

[1] Source: National Archives, RG 59, S/S–NSC Files: Lot 66 D 148, PCG, Part 2. Top Secret. Attached to Rockefeller's memorandum was a December 14 letter from the Director of the Bureau of the Budget expressing concurrence in the abolition of the Planning Coordination Group. When Hoover sent Rockefeller's memorandum to President Eisenhower under cover of a December 16 memorandum, he recommended that the proposal to abolish the PCG be approved. (Ibid.)

[2] See footnotes 1 and 16, Document 210.

Director's memorandum to the President of March 3, which the President approved March 4, subject: "Coordination of Economic, Psychological, Political Warfare, and Foreign Information Activities."[3]

2. Paragraph 3 a of the Budget Director's memorandum states that the Planning Coordination Group should report directly to the Chairman of OCB, who would from time to time transmit progress reports of the Group to the President through the National Security Council. Accordingly, this report is submitted with the request that it be so transmitted.[4]

II. Report

3. The Planning Coordination Group was established to aid in developing planning in both overt and covert fields and to advise and assist the responsible operating agencies in the coordinated development of plans and programs to carry out those national security policies appropriate to its functions. After seven months' experience, it is clear to the four members of the Group that the Planning Coordination Group mechanism will not be able to accomplish these objectives. The Group therefore *recommends* that the President abolish the Planning Coordination Group effective December 31, 1955.

4. The Planning Coordination Group was also given specific responsibilities for being advised of and channeling support to major covert programs (NSC 5412/1)[5] and for being the coordinating agency for the statements of policy in NSC 5505/1 and NSC 5502/1.[6]

a. Respecting covert operations, the Group *recommends* that the President approve that paragraph 7 a of NSC 5412/1 be amended so as to read substantially as follows:

"Except as the President otherwise directs, the designated representatives of the Secretary of State and of the Secretary of Defense referred to in paragraph 4 a, above, and a designated representative of the President whenever one has been designated for this purpose, shall hereafter be advised in advance of major covert programs initiated by CIA under this policy or as otherwise directed, and shall be the normal channel for giving policy approval for such programs as well as for securing coordination of support therefor among the Departments of State and Defense and the CIA."

---

[3] Document 210.

[4] Document 248.

[5] Document 212.

[6] For NSC 5505/1, see *Foreign Relations*, 1955–1957, vol. XXIV, pp. 20–22. For NSC 5502/1, see ibid., pp. 12–19.

and that paragraphs 4 a and 7 b of NSC 5412/1 be amended as necessary to take account of the termination of the PCG and to conform to the substance of the language quoted above.[7]

b. Respecting the coordination of NSC 5505/1, the OCB has forwarded to the Special Assistant for National Security Affairs the Group's recommendation that that policy statement (as well as the related policy statement in NSC 174[8]) should be reviewed by the NSC Planning Board in the light of and subsequent to the pending revision of NSC 5501.[9] By December 31, 1955, the Group will have transmitted to the NSC a progress report on NSC 5505/1. The Group *recommends* that the President designate the OCB as the coordinating agency for the statements of policy in NSC 5505/1 and NSC 174 effective December 31, 1955.

c. Respecting the coordination of NSC 5502/1, the Group *recommends* that the President designate OCB as the coordinating agency effective December 31, 1955.

(With reference to the recommendations in this paragraph, the necessary action should be taken to revise NSC Action 1349, March 10, 1955,[10] to reflect the President's actions.[11])

Nelson A. Rockefeller

---

[7] In NSC Action No. 1497, "Abolition of the Planning Coordination Group," December 28, the National Security Council amended NSC 5412/1 to take account of the abolition of the PCG. (National Archives, RG 59, S/S–NSC (Miscellaneous) Files: Lot 66 D 95, Records of Action by the National Security Council) For NSC 5412/2, see Document 250.

[8] For NSC 174, "U.S. Policy Toward the Soviet Satellites in Eastern Europe," December 11, 1953, see *Foreign Relations, 1952–1954*, vol. VIII, pp. 110–127.

[9] Ibid., 1955–1957, vol. XIX, pp. 24–38.

[10] In NSC Action No. 1349, "Coordination of Economic, Psychological and Political Warfare and Foreign Information Activities," the National Security Council approved amendments to NSC 5412 at its March 10 meeting. (National Archives, RG 59, S/S–NSC (Miscellaneous) Files: Lot 66 D 95, Records of Action by the National Security Council) See footnote 16, Document 210.

[11] On December 20, President Eisenhower approved the recommendations to abolish the Planning Coordination Group and to designate the Operations Coordinating Group as the coordinating agency for NSC 5505/1, NSC 5502/1, and NSC 174 effective December 31. The National Security Council was notified of the President's action by a December 27 memorandum from Executive Secretary of the National Security Council Lay. (National Archives, RG 59, S/S–NSC (Miscellaneous) Files: Lot 66 D 148, Box 127, Coordination of Economic, Psychological and Political Warfare and Foreign Information Activities)

247. Memorandum From the Secretary of State's Special Assistant for Intelligence and Research (Armstrong) to Secretary of State Dulles[1]

Washington, December 22, 1955.

SUBJECT

Board of Consultants for the Central Intelligence Agency

Mr. Allen Dulles informed me today that the White House will soon announce the appointment by the President of a Board of Consultants on Foreign Intelligence Activities, with broad authority to keep itself informed and to advise the President on matters falling within that field.[2] Subject to final acceptance in the case of some individuals, the following are expected to make up the Board:

Gen. John E. Hull, USA (Ret.)
Adm. Richard E. Connolly, USN (Ret.)
Gen. James Doolittle, USAF (Ret.)
Mr. James Killian, President of MIT
Mr. David Bruce
Mr. Benjamin Fairless, U.S. Steel Corp.
Mr. Morris Hadley

Mr. Allen Dulles pointed out that all of the above, except Mr. Fairless, have had extensive experience in the use of intelligence or on committees that have made detailed surveys in the intelligence field. This move, at least in part, is intended to blunt the drive manifesting itself on the Hill to set up a joint committee in Congress to supervise foreign intelligence activities.

W. Park Armstrong, Jr.

---

[1] Source: National Archives, RG 59, Central Files 1955–60, 101.21/12–2255. Official Use Only. Copies were sent to Murphy, Henderson, MacArthur, and Bowie. A handwritten notation on the memorandum by Dulles' secretary Phyllis D. Bernau reads, "Sec. saw."

[2] The President's Board of Consultants on Foreign Intelligence Activities was established by President Eisenhower's Executive Order 10656, February 6, 1956. It was succeeded by the President's Foreign Intelligence Advisory Board (PFIAB), established by Executive Order 10938, May 4, 1961, in the wake of the failed Bay of Pigs invasion of Cuba and increased attention to the role and activities of the intelligence community.

248. Editorial Note

Under a December 27, 1955, covering memorandum to the National Security Council, Executive Secretary Lay transmitted an undated report prepared by Nelson Rockefeller, "Coordination of Foreign Political, Military, Economic, Informational, and Cover Operations," which recommended farreaching changes in military theater and command organization and in the Operations Coordinating Board. (Eisenhower Library, Special Assistant for National Security Affairs, William H. Jackson, Records, President's Papers) Rockefeller was scheduled to defend his views before the NSC Planning Board on February 20, 1956. Documentation on the Department of State's opposition to Rockefeller's recommendations is in National Archives, RG 59, S/S–NSC Files: Lot 62 D 430.

Subsequently, Eisenhower's Assistant, Sherman Adams, asked the Special Assistant to the President for National Security Affairs, William H. Jackson, to examine Rockefeller's proposal. Jackson prepared a critical memorandum on April 2, 1956. (Eisenhower Library, Special Assistant to the President for National Security Affairs Records, OCB Organization) Finally, on March 26, 1957, following the issuance of Executive Order 10700 of February 25, 1957 (22 *Federal Register* 1111), which amended E.O. 10483 of September 2, 1953, by placing the Operations Coordinating Board within the National Security Council structure, Eisenhower agreed that Rockefeller's report could be removed from the NSC's agenda. At the same time, however, he referred the relevant recommendations for wartime responsibility for foreign information and psychological operations to the Director of the Office of Defense Mobilization to prepare plans. (National Archives, RG 59, S/P–NSC Files: Lot 62 D 1, 1935–62, Box 115)

---

249. Memorandum of Conference With President Eisenhower[1]

Washington, December 27, 1955.

OTHERS PRESENT

Secretary Dulles
Assistant Secretary Gardner (Air Force)
General Twining

---

[1] Source: Eisenhower Library, Records of White House Staff Secretary, Intelligence Matters. Top Secret. Drafted by Goodpaster on December 28.

General Cabell
Colonel Randall
Colonel Goodpaster

The President said that the background regarding project "Gray-back"[2] was very hazy in his mind. He did not know how it had gotten started, although he did recall that it had been mentioned by Dr. Land in his office at the time of the Killian Report.[3] He now understood that it represents about a $75 million investment, and that it is ready for initiation very soon. General Twining said that Admiral Radford had stated that he had presented the matter to the President for consideration, and he also said that Mr. Quarles had also stated that the matter had been presented to the President. He said that there is nothing in the records about this. Secretary Dulles recalled that just prior to the Geneva meeting he had raised with the President the question whether it should be held in abeyance.[4]

The President then said that regardless of how the matter progressed, it is timely to consider what should be done now. He understood that a plane that is being developed is coming along very well.[5] It also appeared that if the balloons were discovered, as they will be, certain questions become important—such as what will public reaction be in the UK and Japan, how many of them are likely to be shot down, whether their release will spur the development of higher altitude radar, etc. General Twining said it is practically impossible to pick these up by radar. It is also practically impossible to intercept them—our Air Force has made extensive attempts to do so and has never succeeded.

Replying to a question by the President, Mr. Gardner said there are approximately 2500 of these balloons. It is expected that 500 to 600 would pass through to the Western coast of the Pacific. One-half would travel at about 40,000 feet and the other half could be sent much higher. The project is manned with 4400 people in the United States and 1400 overseas. The President asked whether the project should not be presented as meteorological, with pictures taken to show ground speed, etc. Secretary Dulles said a further question is whether to do it at all. Mr. Gardner said that by late April or May four alternative items, with trained crews, should be available and capable of operating at

---

[2] Previously known as Project Genetrix. See Documents 229, 240, and 242.

[3] Headed by James R. Killian, President of Massachusetts Institute of Technology, the Technological Capabilities Panel of the Science Advisory Committee prepared a study, issued on February 14, requested by the President on U.S. technological capability to reduce the threat of surprise attack. See Document 223.

[4] See Document 229.

[5] The U–2, a joint CIA–U.S. Air Force reconnaissance aircraft.

approximately 80,000 feet.[6] General Cabell viewed the present project as a supplement, and thought if the balloons were kept below 50,000 feet they would not stimulate a "crash" radar program. There was discussion whether possible political reaction might tend to prevent use of the alternative when it is ready—in that case it might be well to consider delaying the whole project a year. The President said that there is a natural tendency toward reluctance for a bold program. If the results seem necessary, he would do it, but that is the question. He thought that an effort involving 2500 in a few months might cause alarm, where a dozen or so a week would not have a "crash" significance (Secretary Dulles asked what would be lost if the action were delayed for a year—Mr. Gardner said that the force will have to be largely disbanded and material would crack and disintegrate).

Mr. Gardner said that low altitude winds are satisfactory throughout the year except in July and August, and that if the lower altitudes were used—which seem desirable—the release could be phased out. The President thought they should be released at a number of points throughout the world. Mr. Dulles felt an agreed news release will be extremely important, and the President said it must tell a good story. General Cabell suggested that other countries be approached to ask them to return the equipment gondolas when they come down. Mr. Dulles agreed that it made a great difference if they were released a few at a time and in many places all over the world. The President thought that the announcement should be on the basis that when the winds are right, we will get off a number from all stations. He thought that if this is presented as a meteorological operation, it would be all right; he did not feel it could be done just in January and February, i.e., it should not be a "crash" program. Mr. Dulles suggested the following as points on which to agree: Launchings should be spread over time; medium altitudes should be used—50 to 55 thousand feet; some should be released from Japan, Honolulu and Alaska; notice should be given to other countries and to the world at large. The President indicated agreement and suggested that this notice bring out that we would like to have the items returned; that if any country wanted to develop the prints, they should take care not to destroy the negatives; that all languages should be used on the request for return, including Russian; that State Department should review the cover plan (Secretary Dulles to get a little group together to look at this); that the long-term aspect of the thing should be emphasized, bringing out that efforts in the past have been too intermittent and relating it to the "jet stream" shift responsible for the recent floods in California. To a question by Secretary Dulles as to how the photographing operation is to be

---

[6] Gardner apparently is alluding to the U–2.

explained, it was indicated that operations are well advanced to inform the authorities of the International Geophysical Year[7] of this activity as a means of mapping cloud formations (which is, in fact, all that most photographs will show.)[8]

AJG
Colonel, CE, US Army

---

[7] The International Geophysical Year was scheduled to begin July 1, 1957, with worldwide scientific observations of earth and astronomical phenomena. It would continue for one and a half years.

[8] President Eisenhower was given a technical briefing on December 27. On the next day Secretary Dulles told Fisher Howe that those attending the briefing included Secretary Dulles, General Twining, Trevor Gardner, and an aide to Secretary of Defense Wilson. The Secretary indicated at the briefing that the British had given their go ahead on December 25, and the President approved the operation subject to "certain modifications," which included slowing down the rate of launching, extending the time period of the operation, and resubmission of the program to Secretary Dulles to whom the President "delegated authority for the final decision and triggering of the operation." (Memorandum by Fisher Howe, December 28; National Archives, RG 59, INR Files: Lot 61 D 67, Genetrix) Another account of this December 27 briefing is in a telegram from Bergquist to General LeMay, December 28. (Ibid.)

---

250. National Security Council Directive[1]

NSC 5412/2   Washington, undated.

COVERT OPERATIONS

1. The National Security Council, taking cognizance of the vicious covert activities of the USSR and Communist China and the governments, parties and groups dominated by them (hereinafter collectively referred to as "International Communism") to discredit and defeat the aims and activities of the United States and other powers of the free world, determined, as set forth in NSC directives 10/2[2] and 10/5,[3] that, in the interests of world peace and U.S. national security, the overt

---

[1] Source: Eisenhower Library, Special Assistant to President for National Security Affairs Records, President's Papers. Top Secret. This directive was transmitted to the NSC under cover of a December 28 note from NSC Executive Secretary Lay. Lay stated that the President had approved the directive on the same date.

[2] See *Foreign Relations, 1945–1950, Emergence of the Intelligence Establishment,* Document 292.

[3] Document 90.

foreign activities of the U.S. Government should be supplemented by covert operations.

2. The Central Intelligence Agency had already been charged by the National Security Council with conducting espionage and counter-espionage operations abroad. It therefore seemed desirable, for operational reasons, not to create a new agency for covert operations, but, subject to directives from the NSC, to place the responsibility for them on the Central Intelligence Agency and correlate them with espionage and counter-espionage operations under the over-all control of the Director of Central Intelligence.

3. The NSC has determined that such covert operations shall to the greatest extent practicable, in the light of U.S. and Soviet capabilities and taking into account the risk of war, be designed to:

a. Create and exploit troublesome problems for International Communism, impair relations between the USSR and Communist China and between them and their satellites, complicate control within the USSR, Communist China and their satellites, and retard the growth of the military and economic potential of the Soviet bloc.

b. Discredit the prestige and ideology of International Communism, and reduce the strength of its parties and other elements.

c. Counter any threat of a party or individuals directly or indirectly responsive to Communist control to achieve dominant power in a free world country.

d. Reduce International Communist control over any areas of the world.

e. Strengthen the orientation toward the United States of the peoples and nations of the free world, accentuate, wherever possible, the identity of interest between such peoples and nations and the United States as well as favoring, where appropriate, those groups genuinely advocating or believing in the advancement of such mutual interests, and increase the capacity and will of such peoples and nations to resist International Communism.

f. In accordance with established policies and to the extent practicable in areas dominated or threatened by International Communism, develop underground resistance and facilitate covert and guerrilla operations and ensure availability of those forces in the event of war, including wherever practicable provision of a base upon which the military may expand these forces in time of war within active theaters of operations as well as provision for stay-behind assets and escape and evasion facilities.

4. Under the authority of Section 102(d)(5) of the National Security Act of 1947, the National Security Council hereby directs that the Director of Central Intelligence shall be responsible for:

a. Ensuring, through designated representatives of the Secretary of State and of the Secretary of Defense, that covert operations are planned and conducted in a manner consistent with United States foreign and military policies and with overt activities, and consulting with and obtaining advice from the Operations Coordinating Board and other departments or agencies as appropriate.

b. Informing, through appropriate channels and on a need-to-know basis, agencies of the U.S. Government, both at home and abroad (including diplomatic and military representatives), of such operations as will affect them.

5. In addition to the provisions of paragraph 4, the following provisions shall apply to wartime covert operations:

a. Plans for covert operations to be conducted in active theaters of war and any other areas in which U.S. forces are engaged in combat operations will be drawn up with the assistance of the Department of Defense and will be in consonance with and complementary to approved war plans of the Joint Chiefs of Staff.

b. Covert operations in active theaters of war and any other areas in which U.S. forces are engaged in combat operations will be conducted under such command and control relationships as have been or may in the future be approved by the Department of Defense.

6. As used in this directive, "covert operations" shall be understood to be all activities conducted pursuant to this directive which are so planned and executed that any U.S. Government responsibility for them is not evident to unauthorized persons and that if uncovered the U.S. Government can plausibly disclaim any responsibility for them. Specifically, such operations shall include any covert activities related to: propaganda; political action; economic warfare; preventive direct action, including sabotage, anti-sabotage, demolition; escape and evasion and evacuation measures; subversion against hostile states or groups including assistance to underground resistance movements, guerrillas and refugee liberation groups; support of indigenous and anti-communist elements in threatened countries of the free world; deception plans and operations; and all activities compatible with this directive necessary to accomplish the foregoing. Such operations shall not include: armed conflict by recognized military forces, espionage and counter-espionage, nor cover and deception for military operations.

7. Except as the President otherwise directs, designated representatives of the Secretary of State and of the Secretary of Defense of the rank of Assistant Secretary or above, and a representative of the President designated for this purpose, shall hereafter be advised in advance of major covert programs initiated by CIA under this policy or as otherwise directed, and shall be the normal channel for giving policy approval for such programs as well as for securing coordination of support therefor among the Departments of State and Defense and the CIA.

8. This directive supersedes and rescinds NSC 10/2, NSC 10/5, NSC 5412,[4] NSC 5412/1,[5] and subparagraphs "a" and "b" under the

---

[4] Document 171.
[5] Document 212.

heading "Additional Functions of the Operations Coordinating Board" on page 1 of the President's memorandum for the Executive Secretary, National Security Council, supplementing Executive Order 10483.[6]

---

[6] Document 157.

---

251. Paper Prepared by J. Patrick Coyne of the National Security Council Staff[1]

Washington, undated.

Report on Intelligence Activities in the Federal Government
Prepared for the Commission on Organization of the Executive
Branch of the Government
By the Task Force on Intelligence Activities

CHAPTER I—Brief History of U.S. Foreign Intelligence Activities
(Pages 1–12)

This Chapter contains no recommendations.

CHAPTER II—The Central Intelligence Agency (Pages 13–75)

Recommendation 1 (page 72): That "covert intelligence" and "cold war" functions of the current DD/P be assigned to separate Deputy Directors whose areas of responsibility shall be administratively and logistically self-supporting. (A minority of the Task Force members did not concur in this recommendation, believing that "covert intelligence" and "cold war" operations should be under the staff and operating control of a single operating Deputy Director—as at present.)

---

[1] Source: Eisenhower Library, Records of White House Staff Secretary, Subject Series, Alphabetical Subseries, Box 13, Hoover Commission Report on Intelligence Activities, May 1955–October 1956. Top Secret. President Eisenhower had referred the classified Clark Task Force Report (Document 221), along with departmental and agency comments on applicable sections of it, to Dillon Anderson, the President's Special Assistant, on December 15 for further action and recommendations as appropriate. This report is Coyne's compilation of the departmental and agency responses, including his added "Additional Action Required" and "Observations," which he completed in early 1956. (Memorandum from Anderson to Goodpaster, February 14, 1956; Eisenhower Library, Hoover Commission Report on Intelligence Activities, May 1955–October 1956, and memorandum from Coyne to NSC Executive Secretary Lay, January 20, 1956; ibid.) Some documentation on departmental and agency responses to the Clark Task Force Report are ibid. and in the National Archives, RG 59, Central Files 1955–60, 711.52 and 711.5200. All ellipses in the original.

Agency Comment: CIA opposes the recommendation on the grounds that: (1) "the experience of CIA during the period of separate operation prior to 1952 proved the operational disadvantages of attempting to conduct, on a secure and efficient basis, two world-wide clandestine organizations, each compartmented from the other"; and (2) organizations of separate supporting elements for each of the clandestine services would be duplicative, costly and ineffective.

Additional Action Required: Presidential decision as to whether the Task Force (majority) recommendation or the contrary views of CIA should be adopted.

Observation: CIA's view should be adopted since the majority proposal of the Task Force has been tried previously and found less satisfactory than present organizational arrangements which combine the covert and cold war functions of CIA. (The CIA view is consistent with that of the Doolittle Committee[2] whose survey of CIA's clandestine services was much more extensive than that made by the Task Force.)

Recommendation 2 (page 73): That CIA be reorganized with a Director, a Deputy Director, an Executive Director, a general Secretariat, necessary staff sections and offices of the administrative and logistic services and an operating Deputy Director of Intelligence with seven operating offices thereunder, including an Office of Basic Intelligence.

Agency Comment: CIA concurs in the creation of, and has established, an Office of Basic Intelligence. CIA notes that the balance of this recommendation consists of suggesting that the names of four of the offices under the Deputy Director of Intelligence be changed. CIA will change the name of one of these offices shortly, but believes that little will be accomplished in effecting the other name changes suggested.

Additional Action Required: None.

Recommendation 3 (page 73): That CIA re-establish the Office of Executive Director to relieve the DCI of the necessity of having to devote a large part of his time to the solution of many daily administrative and minor operational problems.

Agency Comment: CIA is opposed on the grounds that the interposition of another command echelon would not necessarily accomplish the intended objective. CIA is giving this recommendation further study, however.

Additional Action Required: None by the White House or the NSC.

Observation: This recommendation does not involve any major policy considerations. Internal reorganizations of the type recommended should be left to the sound discretion of the agency head.

---

[2] Document 192.

Recommendation 4 (page 73): That the status of the three major operating Deputy Directors be changed from Civil Service appointees (now Grade GS-18) to Public Law Presidential appointees, at an annual salary of $16,000.

Agency Comment: CIA concurs in the recommended pay increases but thinks it unwise that the Operating Deputy Directors require Senatorial approval, particularly where an individual's background and competence in clandestine operations would have to be reviewed. CIA has received no indication of any Senatorial desire to review CIA appointments, other than the appointments of the DCI and his Deputy.

Additional Action Required: None by the White House or NSC. CIA is taking action through appropriate channels in an effort to obtain the pay increases recommended.

Recommendation 5 (page 73): That the "cold war" operating deputy director be designated as CIA's representative on the Operations Coordinating Board to free the DCI to devote a greater share of his time to the Agency's intelligence functions.

Agency Comment: CIA is opposed. It notes that the DCI is required to personally attend OCB meetings by virtue of a Presidential Directive, and that his participation in OCB meetings is not unduly burdensome. CIA notes further that the Deputy Director/Plans is closely associated with OCB activity in that CIA members of OCB working groups are drawn from CIA's clandestine services.

Additional Action Required: Presidential decision as to whether the Task Force recommendation should be adopted.

Observation: Because the benefits derived from DCI's participation in OCB meetings outweighs the burdens occasioned by such participation, the Task Force recommendation should be rejected. If this observation is concurred in advice should be communicated to CIA as to the President's reaffirmation of the directive which provides for DCI's membership on the OCB.

Recommendation 6 (page 73): That a comprehensive internal management survey of the Agency be conducted by CIA within a year following the reorganization of CIA, as recommended by the Task Force.

Agency Comment: CIA presently has in progress three concurrent programs of an internal management nature.

Additional Action Required: None, at this time.

Recommendation 7 (page 74): That all NSC, IAC, and DCI Intelligence Directives be reviewed by the IAC and others concerned, with a view to establishing clearer areas of responsibility and to allocating intelligence tasks in accord with each agency's capability, interest, and paramount national responsibilities.

Agency Comment: The DCI will recommend the establishment of an IAC Subcommittee to review all such Intelligence Directives, as necessary, to clarify areas of responsibility or reallocate tasks.

Additional Action Required: Action at appropriate levels (IAC, DCI, NSC) to be taken on the basis of the review of Intelligence Directives being initiated by CIA.

Recommendation 8 (page 74): That responsibility for procurement of foreign publications and collection of scientific intelligence be shifted from State to CIA, and that CIA be authorized to appoint scientific attachés to U.S. diplomatic missions as necessary.

Agency Comment: CIA agrees that facilities for procurement of foreign publications and collection of scientific intelligence should be strengthened. The substance of this recommendation is under active study by State and CIA and it is hoped that an agreement thereon will be reached at an early date.

Additional Action Required: None by the White House or the NSC.

Recommendation 9 (page 74): That the Scientific Estimates Committee be abolished and in lieu thereof there be established under the IAC a Scientific Intelligence Committee with appropriate subcommittees to insure community-wide coordination.

Agency Comment: CIA is in general agreement with this recommendation. The substance thereof is under active consideration in the IAC.

Additional Action Required: None, other than the normal actions which will flow from IAC consideration of the recommendation.

Recommendation 10 (page 74): That the effectiveness of CIA's security program be re-evaluated to establish a system assuring personnel security rechecks on a minimum five year basis.

Agency Comment: CIA reports that the recommended program has been in effect as of March 26, 1955 and, in addition, that there is a continuing review made of the security of its employees, including automatic rechecks in the case of personnel actions, such as transfers, promotions, appointments to special activities, etc.

Additional Action Required: None.

Recommendation 11 (page 74): That Congress be requested to appropriate funds to construct adequate CIA housing facilities in or near Washington.

Agency Comment: CIA reports this has been done.

Additional Action Required: None.

Recommendation 12 (page 74): That the CIA Act of 1949 be amended to authorize employment of "any" (instead of 15 now authorized) retired officers or warrant officers of the Armed Services; and to authorize overseas personnel additional dependent medical benefits and employee leave accumulations equivalent to those authorized for Foreign Service personnel.

Agency Comment: CIA would welcome an increase in the number of retired officers of the Armed Services authorized to be employed by the Agency. It believes that the authorized number should be between twenty-five and fifty. CIA concurs in granting additional Foreign Service benefits for dependents as well as leave benefits and leave accumulations for CIA employees.

(Current inquiry of CIA reflects the Agency has prepared draft legislation—now being processed by the Budget Bureau—designed to authorize employment of as many as forty retired officers of the Armed Services, as well as draft legislation designed to carry into effect the Task Force recommendations concerning CIA personnel, their leave accumulations, and additional medical benefits for dependents of CIA employees stationed abroad.)

Additional Action Required: None.

Recommendation 13 (page 75): That legislation be sought to increase the annual salary of the DCI to $20,000; to increase the compensation of the Deputy DCI to $17,500; and to authorize the appointment of an Executive Director of CIA at an annual salary of $16,000.

Agency Comment: The recommended increases in the salaries of the DCI and the Deputy DCI have been included in proposed amendments to the Executive Pay Bill of 1949.[3] CIA, as indicated in Recommendation 3 above, opposes establishing the office of Executive Director, but is giving further study to the Task Force recommendation on this point.

Additional Action Required: None.

CHAPTER III—The Department of State (Pages 76–88)

Recommendation 1 (page 87): That the personnel strength of the Intelligence Area be maintained at a level consistent with functional responsibilities and work load.

Agency Comment: State concurs. An increase of ten persons for the present fiscal year has been authorized for the Intelligence Area. State is budgeting a substantial increase for its intelligence function in fiscal year 1957.

Additional Action Required: None.

Recommendation 2 (page 88): That NSCID No. 10[4] be revised to place responsibility for collection of information in the basic sciences in CIA.

---

[3] See footnote 10, Document 221.

[4] Dated January 19, 1949; text is in *Foreign Relations, 1945–1950*, Emergence of the Intelligence Establishment, Document 429.

Agency Comment: State reports that while it is not possible to comment favorably or unfavorably on this recommendation at this time, meetings on the subject are being held with CIA and every effort will be made to develop a satisfactory solution.

Additional Action Required: Action is dependent upon the outcome of the State–CIA meetings mentioned above and on the IAC review of all Intelligence Directives (to which reference is made in Chapter II, Recommendation 7).

Recommendation 3 (page 88): That State finalize its plans for the periodic review of all personnel coming within the provisions of Executive Order 10450.[5]

Agency Comment: State has given substantial thought to the matter and agrees that a program for periodic review should be carefully considered. Through its normal channels State will pursue the matter with interested agencies, such as Justice and the Civil Service Commission.

Additional Action Required: None, beyond that indicated in State's comment.

Recommendation 4 (page 88): That intelligence personnel occupying positions which have been designated as Foreign Service assignments be included in State's program for accelerated language and area training.

Agency Comment: State reports that such personnel are eligible for participation in these programs and that the Intelligence Area is represented in the planning and selection process for such training.

Additional Action Required: None.

Recommendation 5 (page 88): That in implementing the Foreign Service Integration Program due regard should be given the special qualifications of intelligence personnel transferred to foreign posts; and to the extent practicable special qualifications developed should be safeguarded upon reassignment.

Agency Comment: State concurs and is developing procedures to accomplish the intent of this recommendation.

Additional Action Required: None.

CHAPTER IV—The Department of Defense (Pages 89–205)

A. Office of Special Operations (Pages 89–94)

Recommendation 1 (page 94): That DOD Directive 5105.7[6] be examined with a view to clarifying and eliminating any ambiguities which would lead to a misinterpretation of the functions and misapplication

---

[5] Security Requirements for Government Employment, April 27, 1953. (18 F.R. 2489)
[6] Not found.

of the authority of OSO; and that the relationships of OSO with the intelligence organization of the JCS and the military departments be spelled out more specifically to reduce possibilities of friction and misunderstanding.

Agency Comment: DOD does not consider that the Directive is ambiguous. However, DOD will give continuing attention to the operations of OSO under the Directive.

Additional Action Required: None, beyond that referred to in DOD's comment.

B. *The Joint Chiefs of Staff (Pages 94–99)*

This Section contains no recommendations.

C. *Department of the Army (Pages 99–137)*

Recommendation 1 (page 137): That the Army Attaché System be manned to permit full exploitation of its collection potential and that present personnel ceilings imposed by DOD be lifted in order to achieve greater flexibility and permit more extensive prior training of assigned personnel.

Agency Comment: DOD agrees with the concept calling for maximum exploitation of the intelligence potential of the Attaché System. It does not agree that present personnel ceilings are seriously inhibitive. DOD reports that its ceilings on Attaché strength (in the three services) are flexible; that DOD now has underway a program for consolidating and simplifying the Attaché functions of the services; and that it is studying ways of improving selection and training of Attachés.

Additional Action Required: Final decision by DOD as to lifting personnel ceilings in the Attaché System.

Recommendation 2 (page 137): That the (Army) Assistant Chief of Staff, Intelligence, be elevated to the level of Deputy Chief of Staff.

Agency Comment: DOD does not concur. It notes that the top staff of the Army was recently reorganized following a balanced consideration of all its aspects and it concludes that it would be premature to reorganize now as recommended, particularly since legislation would be necessary to achieve the Task Force's recommendation.

Additional Action Required: None by the White House or the NSC.

Observation: This recommendation does not involve any major policy considerations. Internal reorganizations of the type recommended should be left to the sound discretion of the agency head.

Recommendation 3 (page 137): That the National Security Council revise NSCID No. 5[7] to provide for clandestine intelligence activity on

---

[7] Document 256.

the part of the Military Services consistent with their capabilities and statutory responsibilities under the National Security Act of 1947.

Agency Comment: DOD notes that this recommendation "reflects the strong and unanimous views of the Services" and that "it involves a fundamental issue within the intelligence community." Because of the importance of this particular recommendation the remainder of the Defense comment thereon is quoted in full:

"NSCID No. 5 has been interpreted as assigning to CIA the exclusive right to control and conduct covert foreign intelligence operations. Such activities as the services have been allowed to conduct during the past 7 or 8 years in this important field even in war theaters have been essentially on the sufferance of CIA. Meanwhile, however, CIA's record of performance in covert intelligence operations of direct interest to the mission of the Armed Services has been disappointing, particularly against primary Soviet orbit intelligence targets. The services, which consider that they have generally a longer record of experience in this work, are convinced that they can produce through covert operations more effectively than CIA various needed categories of intelligence related to their particular missions and requirements. They point out moreover that CIA's covert operations are conducted to a large extent under military cover.

The Agreed Activities paper (DCID No. 5/8)[8] represents a cautious compromise, which is not altogether satisfactory to the services. It provides for a measure of participation by them in covert operations on a best-qualified basis. The services believe their right to participate should be explicit in a NSCID and not dependent on a subsidiary agreement.

It is too early to judge whether this agreement will prove workable. First steps have been taken by CIA to function under the agreement, and the services are proceeding to strengthen their covert collection resources. Each side tends to be wary of the other; and more generosity and good will than has been shown in the past will be necessary if the present tentative arrangement is to work.

Monitorship over this problem has been assigned to the Assistant to the Secretary of Defense (Special Operations) who has been directed to keep the developments under continuing review. If events develop favorably under the Agreed Activities paper, revision of NSCID No. 5 may prove to be unnecessary."

Additional Action Required: Further action may be taken by IAC and NSC now or it may be delayed, depending upon: (1) developments

---

[8] A copy is in the Central Intelligence Agency, History Staff, Job 84–B00389R, Box 4.

under the "Agreed Activities Paper," as revised, or (2) the outcome of the proposed review of all NSC, DCI and IAC Intelligence Directives, as set forth in Chapter II, Recommendation 7 of the Task Force Report.

Observation: It is to be noted that: (1) the Task Force Report and the comments thereon present only the military side of this controversy; and (2) CIA, despite its primary responsibility in the field, is not cognizant of—and, therefore, has had no opportunity to comment on this and other military-related segments of the Task Force Report which are germane to the primary mission of CIA. The controversy over NSCID No. 5 has raged too long (several years); IAC and, if necessary, NSC should act upon it at an early date.

Recommendation 4 (page 137): That the implementation of NSCID No. 13[9] be extended to permit participation in the Soviet and Satellite defector inducement program by the Military Services and CIA in direct proportion to the capabilities of each.

Agency Comment: DOD reports that the three Services strongly support this and related recommendations, believing that at the working level CIA has often tended unnecessarily to restrict their participation in this area of intelligence operations which is of vital importance to them. The Military Services believe they have substantial present and potential capabilities in the inducement of defection of which full use should be made. DOD will undertake to negotiate with the Director of Central Intelligence to bring about optimum participation by the Services and fullest realization of their potential in the defector program.

Additional Action Required: NSCID No. 13 should be expeditiously reviewed by IAC and modified by NSC, if modification is determined to be necessary.

Observation: This recommendation of the Task Force appears to be somewhat at variance with its Recommendation 6, Appendix II, wherein it proposes "that the inducement phase of the Defector Program, as applicable to active participation by diplomatic and *military* representatives serving overtly abroad, be discontinued."

Recommendation 5 (page 137): That consideration be given to more extensive use of "Schedule A"[10] in the employment of civilian analysts and other intelligence specialists in the Department of the Army, in order to achieve necessary flexibility.

---

[9] Document 252.

[10] The U.S. Civil Service Commission defined "Schedule A" positions as those jobs that were other than confidential or policy determining in character, and for which it was impractical to require examinations. "Schedule A" positions also were excepted from the regular competitive U.S. Civil Service. (5 *CFR*, 1956 *SUPP.*, 6.100)

Agency Comment: DOD concurs in general and has initiated a thorough study of the problem.

Additional Action Required: Decision by DOD following its study of the problem.

Recommendation 6 (page 137): That the Army aggressively attack the linguist problem by developing and using outside sources for training in colleges and universities through the method of (for example) its comprehensive ROTC and Reserve programs.

Agency Comment: DOD reports that considerable use is now being made of civilian facilities for the purpose indicated, but that the problem involves quality rather than quantity and is most acute in the case of rare languages. The recommendation concerning ROTC language training requires further study.

Additional Action Required: Decision by DOD following its further study.

Recommendation 7 (page 137): That measures be instituted for the periodic security rechecking of personnel assigned in sensitive areas at intervals not to exceed 5 years.

Agency Comment: DOD believes that its current security practices essentially fulfill the objectives of this recommendation. The general subject will be reviewed by DOD however to insure that the underlying objective of the recommendation is adequately served.

Additional Action Required: Apart from the review referred to by DOD, no additional action is required.

D. *Department of the Navy (Pages 138–156)*

Recommendation 1 (page 156): That the Navy put its counterintelligence program on a wider base so as to bring its worldwide protection up to an adequate level.

Agency Comment: DOD concurs but believes that the actual method of expansion should be further investigated.

Additional Action Required: Further investigation as suggested by DOD, followed by action consistent with its investigative findings and with the objective of establishing an adequate counterintelligence program in the Navy.

Recommendation 2 (page 156): That the Navy provide for periodic review of the security status of intelligence personnel who come within the provisions of Executive Order 10450.

Agency Comment: DOD believes that its current security practices essentially fulfill the objectives of this recommendation. The general subject will be reviewed by DOD however to insure that the underlying objective of the recommendation is adequately served.

Additional Action Required: None.

Recommendation 3 (page 156): That the Navy expand its intelligence collection effort.

Agency Comment: See DOD's comment on Recommendation 1 of the Task Force Report on the Department of the Army, (page 7, above).

Additional Action Required: Final decision by DOD as to lifting personnel ceilings in the Attaché System.

Recommendation 4 (page 156): That the Navy continue and expand its efforts to improve intelligence consciousness at all ranks and levels of the Department.

Agency Comment: DOD concurs. Instruction on the mission and role of intelligence is included in the regional training schools, intelligence centers, and in the curricula of line schools at all levels.

Additional Action Required: None.

E. *Department of the Air Force (Pages 156–179)*

Recommendation 1 (page 178): That the position of Director of Intelligence, Air Force, be raised to that of a Deputy Chief of Staff.

Agency Comment: DOD does not concur. It notes that the Task Force made a similar recommendation (which DOD opposes) with respect to the Director of Intelligence, Army, but that it made no recommendation respecting the position of the Director of Naval Intelligence.

Additional Action Required: None by the White House or the NSC.

Observation: This recommendation does not involve any major policy considerations. Internal reorganizations of the type recommended should be left to the sound discretion of the agency head.

Recommendation 2 (page 178): That a limited number of civilian personnel spaces for Air Force Intelligence be exempt from certain Civil Service requirements.

Agency Comment: DOD concurs in general and has initiated a thorough study of the problem.

Additional Action Required: Decision by DOD following its study of the problem.

Recommendation 3 (page 178): That a board or commission be established to make an equitable and coordinated allocation among the member agencies of personnel spaces exempt from certain Civil Service requirements.

Agency Comment: DOD has initiated a thorough study of the problem.

Additional Action Required: None, pending the completion of DOD's study.

Recommendation 4 (page 178): That the Air Attaché System be maintained at a level which will insure an adequate collection capability and that Air Attaché qualifications be commensurate with the collection potential of the station.

Agency Comment: See DOD's comment on Recommendation 1 of the Task Force's Report on the Department of the Army (page 7, above).

Additional Action Required: Final decision by DOD as to the Attaché System, its adequacy, personnel strength, training, qualifications, etc.

Recommendation 5 (page 179): That an Intelligence Research Center be established under CIA to guide the total intelligence research program.

Agency Comment: DOD notes that each service intelligence agency and CIA conduct research programs and it agrees that a common research service would be desirable. However, it believes that the effort to establish such a center "should be under the DCI acting for the IAC and not under the CIA."

Additional Action Required: Joint consideration of this recommendation by the IAC agencies.

Observation: It would appear desirable that CIA be apprised of, and be afforded an opportunity to comment on, this recommendation. This is particularly so if the "additional action" indicated above is not taken (if such action is taken, CIA will automatically have such an opportunity by virtue of its identification with the IAC).

Recommendation 6 (page 179): That a board be established to supervise declassification of security information.

Agency Comment: DOD does not concur. It believes such a procedure would be cumbersome, and is of the view that its present practices in this area are adequate.

Additional Action Required: None, because ultimate responsibility for such matters is lodged in the head of the Department concerned.

Recommendation 7 (page 179): That a periodic examination be made of Air Force intelligence publications to assure justification for both the publication and distribution thereof.

Agency Comment: DOD concurs; the recommended action is now being implemented.

Additional Action Required: None.

Recommendation 8 (page 179): That mechanical and electronic devices to analyze, classify, file, and produce intelligence information be put into use at the earliest possible moment.

Agency Comment: DOD concurs. It believes that automation in intelligence production has undoubted value and it notes that considerable investigation has been conducted along the lines indicated in this recommendation.

Additional Action Required: Implementation of the recommendation by DOD.

Recommendation 9 (page 179): That all possible resources be used to exploit technological means for intelligence collection.

Agency Comment: DOD concurs, advising that the recommendation is currently receiving attention.

Additional Action Required: None (assuming the attention being afforded this matter by DOD results in the implementation of this recommendation).

Recommendation 10 (page 179): That the use of "overflights" to secure vital information receive constant consideration.

Agency Comment: DOD concurs, noting that the constant support of other U.S. Government agencies is required if full results are to be achieved. (DOD observes that upon resolution of some of the details involved in this recommendation, it may be advisable to seek NSC action thereon.)

Additional Action Required: Presidential and/or NSC consideration following receipt of DOD's recommendation on the subject.

Recommendation 11 (page 179): That the Air Force develop adequate procedures for the periodic security review of personnel occupying sensitive positions.

Agency Comment: DOD believes that its current security practices essentially fulfill the objective of this recommendation. The general subject will be reviewed by DOD however to insure that the underlying objective of the recommendation is adequately served.

Additional Action Required: Apart from the review referred to by DOD, no additional action is required.

F. Covert Operations—Department of Defense (Pages 179–205)

Recommendation 1 (page 204): That under the terms of the "Agreed Activities" paper, the services expand their clandestine collection efforts with primary emphasis focused on targets in the Soviet Union and Communist China. Personnel and funds to accomplish this objective should be made available to the military intelligence services.

Agency Comment: DOD concurs and suggests that the satellites, including areas of Southeast Asia, should be added to the primary target area.

Additional Action Required: This recommendation should be reviewed and acted upon by the IAC and, if necessary, the NSC. (See Chapter II, Recommendation 7, which calls for IAC review of all NSC, DCI, and IAC Intelligence Directives and Chapter IV, C, Recommendation 3, which calls for revision of NSCID No. 5 in particular.)

Observation: It is noted that CIA has not been advised of, nor otherwise afforded an opportunity to comment on, this recommendation, which involves one of the primary missions of that Agency. (This situation will be remedied if the additional action mentioned above is carried into effect.)

Recommendation 2 (page 204): That the intelligence community establish adequate and positive measures for the identification and listing of all clandestine operators as provided in IAC Directive No. 54, approved July 24, 1952.[11] Mutual trust regarding the divulgence of intelligence sources should be cultivated within the community.

Agency Comment: DOD concurs, noting that an effort has been made under the IAC Directive to create a national source control mechanism. DOD thinks it probable that the recommendation can be implemented effectively on some clearly mutual basis, such as rotating the chairmanship of the source control mechanism.

Additional Action Required: None for the reasons set forth in the following paragraph.

Observation: The Task Force seems in its recommendation to have missed the point of IAC–D–54. This directive is designed to identify for the entire intelligence community "papermills" and "fabricators" who have been exposed as such. It does not provide that each intelligence agency disclose to the others the identities of their "clandestine operators"—such a practice would be foolhardy. Current inquiry reflects that in the main the intelligence agencies are exchanging information concerning fabricators, frauds, etc., as provided in IAC–D–54.

Recommendation 3 (page 204): That the defector program, including inducement policies, early access to the defector and prompt determination of the use to which he is to be put, be improved, with the objective of making defection more attractive and of deriving greater benefit for the entire intelligence community.

Agency Comment: DOD's comments on this general subject are set forth under Recommendation 4, Chapter IV (page 9, above). CIA was not furnished with the section of the report which contains this recommendation.

Additional Action Required: IAC review of NSCID No. 13.

Recommendation 4 (page 205): That the military services be permitted greater latitude in offering inducements to potential defectors.

Agency Comment: DOD concurs. The gist of DOD's comments on this and related aspects of the defector program are summarized under Chapter IV, Recommendation 4 (page 9, above).

Additional Action Required: As set forth under Chapter IV, Recommendation 4.

Observation: This recommendation of the Task Force is, in part at least, contrary to its Recommendation 6, Part II, wherein it is proposed

---

[11] IAC–D–54, approved July 24, 1952. (Central Intelligence Agency, Community Management Staff, Job 82–00400R, Box 2, Folder 9)

that the inducement phase of the Defector Program, as applicable to active participation by diplomatic and military representatives serving overtly abroad, be discontinued.

Recommendation 5 (page 205): That the National Security Council review present assets and direct the necessary action to assure adequate preparation for evasion and escape and support of guerrilla warfare.

Agency Comment: DOD concurs. To facilitate the review recommended DOD suggests that CIA and DOD report the pertinent facts to the NSC with recommendation for necessary action. To that end DOD will initiate a proposal looking to the preparation of an appropriate report.

Additional Action Required: None, pending preparation of the referenced report.

Recommendation 6 (page 205): [*14 lines not declassified*]

Recommendation 7 (page 205): That when military cover is used steps be taken to insure that the person so covered lives in consonance with the cover position and duties.

Agency Comment: DOD concurs, noting that an interim effort is being made to insure that all persons wearing the uniform are qualified to play the role convincingly.

Additional Action Required: None, other than continuing effort along the lines mentioned above.

CHAPTER V—Atomic Energy Intelligence (Pages 206–220)

Recommendation 1 (page 220): That CIA pay special attention to the production of atomic energy intelligence.

Agency Comment: CIA reports that that agency and the entire intelligence community long ago agreed that the highest priority be accorded this subject. Continuous attention at the highest level is directed to seeing that this program is energetically implemented.

DOD concurs, noting that in CIA's appointed role as coordinator for the production of national intelligence it should pay special attention to the *coordination* of the production of atomic energy intelligence. DOD believes that the Joint Atomic Energy Intelligence Committee is an adequate instrument for this purpose and is now being so used.

Additional Action Required: None, since CIA reports that the highest priority and continuous attention is already being accorded this subject by the entire intelligence community.

Recommendation 2 (page 220): That the responsibility of AEC for intelligence be defined in an NSC Intelligence Directive and that an NSC Intelligence Directive set forth the responsibility, authority, functions, and composition of the Joint Atomic Energy Intelligence Committee.

Agency Comment: AEC agrees. It is of the belief that this two-fold recommendation may be accomplished by one NSC Intelligence Directive; that such a Directive should also establish the responsibilities of the other IAC agencies for atomic energy intelligence "in order that ambiguities of present directives . . . be clarified."

CIA advises that AEC's intelligence responsibilities are now under discussion between CIA and AEC, and that at the appropriate time an intelligence directive thereon will be proposed to the NSC.

DOD concurs in this two-fold recommendation. It favors an NSCID for the purpose of defining AEC's intelligence responsibility; but it believes that since the JAEIC is a subcommittee of the IAC, a DCID (rather than an NSCID) will suffice to carry out the latter part of the recommendation.

Additional Action Required: None, pending completion of IAC's processing of the directives envisaged by this recommendation.

Recommendation 3 (page 220): That the AEC define the responsibility and functions of its Division of Intelligence.

Agency Comment: AEC reports that its Division of Intelligence has received the informal concurrence of the other intelligence agencies as to its national intelligence responsibilities. Following Commission consideration thereof, the intelligence agencies will be formally notified of same.

Additional Action Required: None.

Recommendation 4 (page 220): That each of the member agencies of the Joint Atomic Energy Intelligence Committee insure that it is represented on that Committee by the best qualified individual available concerning the matter under discussion, and that changes in representation be made as infrequently as practicable.

Agency Comment: AEC concurs. AEC reports that every effort has been and will continue to be made to comply with this recommendation.

CIA reports that it has pressed for the assignment of the best qualified personnel to the Committee, and it notes that the record of the Committee in the matter of continuity and length of tenure is a very favorable one.

DOD concurs in this recommendation noting that it will continue to make every effort to insure the fulfillment thereof.

State reports that it has been following the practice recommended by the Task Force.

Additional Action Required: None.

Recommendation 5 (page 220): That there be a thorough review of the processes for development of the atomic energy portions of National Intelligence Estimates to insure, in the first place, that everything practicable is done to develop intelligence regarding intentions, plans, programs, policies, doctrines and capabilities of the Soviet Union with regard to war-time use of atomic energy and, secondly, that the National Intelligence Estimates reflect the full extent of available intelligence in those matters.

Agency Comment: AEC strongly endorses this recommendation, noting that the accuracy and completeness of estimates on foreign atomic energy capabilities are of deep concern to it.

CIA reports that its Board of Estimates is already carrying out this recommendation; that the Board is not only going into Soviet war-time use of atomic energy, but is working on peace-time applications as well; and that it goes without saying that every effort is being made to have the National Intelligence Estimates reflect the full extent of available knowledge on the subject.

DOD concurs in this recommendation.

State concurs. In order that the National Intelligence Estimates may reflect the full extent of available intelligence in this field, State recommends specific courses of action which appear appropriate for IAC consideration.

Additional Action Required: Consideration by the IAC.

CHAPTER VI—The Federal Bureau of Investigation (Pages 221–226)

This Chapter contains no recommendations.

CHAPTER VII—Intelligence Production (Pages 227–244)

Recommendation 1 (page 244): That an agreed glossary of intelligence terms be produced and reviewed periodically.

Agency Comment: DOD agrees and suggests that an IAC Subcommittee be appointed to produce it.

State has no particular difficulty in this area, but it will be pleased to assist IAC in implementing the recommendation.

CIA reports that it has compiled a glossary of intelligence terms and that action will be taken through the IAC to secure acceptance thereof as the authoritative dictionary of intelligence nomenclature.

Additional Action Required: Completion of the project by the IAC.

Recommendation 2 (page 244): That positive measures be taken to increase the quantity and improve the quality of information collected, with special emphasis on the primary target area, to include the revision of existing directives to assign more explicit responsibility to agencies which can fulfill the requirement.

Agency Comment: DOD concurs, adding that in its opinion and in the opinion of the military services the briefing and debriefing for intelligence purposes of U.S. travelers (now exclusively the prerogative of CIA) could profitably be decentralized to some extent. It believes that review of "official cover" requirements may indicate that certain intelligence operations now being performed by CIA may be more effectively conducted by other agencies. As to the Task Force recommendation that there be special emphasis on the primary target area, DOD notes that, in general, the service intelligence agencies have their sights set on the primary target.

CIA notes that NSC, IAC and CIA intelligence directives are being reviewed with a view to revision where appropriate (as indicated in Chapter II, above). As to the Task Force exhortation that, in the collection of intelligence, there be special emphasis on the primary target area, CIA notes that the entire intelligence community has invariably accorded the Soviet Union the highest priority as a target of intelligence.

Additional Action Required: None, other than that now being carried out, or that which may be indicated by current intelligence or by the review of Intelligence Directives referred to by CIA.

Observation: The oft-repeated exhortations of the Task Force that primary emphasis be placed upon the USSR as the primary intelligence target are in a sense misleading in that they could leave the casual reader with the erroneous impression that the USSR is not the primary intelligence target. Individually and collectively the intelligence forces of the United States Government concentrate on the USSR, its satellites, and International Communism in general, as the primary U.S. intelligence target. U.S. intelligence agencies are not satisfied with the quality or quantity of intelligence gained thus far with respect to this primary target, but they have felt it better to accept criticism such as that leveled in the Task Force Report and in the published report on the subject rather than risk disclosure of highly sensitive operations which do indicate that some inroads are being successfully made on the primary target.

CHAPTER VIII—Functional Intelligence (Pages 245–254)

Recommendation 1 (page 254): That the intelligence community actively give recognition to this primary intelligence target, i.e., the Soviet Union, and take such actions as are necessary to present a concerted effort for the single purpose of breaking this vital intelligence block.

Agency Comment: State notes that the intelligence community has been doing precisely this for some time and it adds that it is prepared to give continuing support to this intelligence priority.

Defense and CIA (as indicated previously) have commented (in the several instances wherein the point of this recommendation has been made) that the intelligence community is concentrating upon the USSR as a primary intelligence target.

Recommendation 2 (page 254): That the State Department's programs for integration and expansion of the Foreign Service and for acceleration of language and area training be pursued vigorously.

Agency Comment: State reports that this matter is the subject of vigorous action at all levels of the Department on a continuous and top priority basis.

CHAPTER IX—Personnel (Pages 255–274)

Recommendation 1 (page 273): That DOD give consideration to the exploitation of the ROTC and reserve intelligence programs for language training purposes by offering credit toward reserve commissions and drill credits respectively, for the completion of selected language courses.

Agency Comment: DOD notes that considerable use is now being made of civilian facilities for the purpose indicated in this recommendation; that the problem involves quality rather than quantity; that the recommendations concerning ROTC language training require thorough study; and that it would be unwise to give blanket accreditation for language work regardless of the type of service for which the trainee is destined.

Additional Action Required: Completion of DOD's study and consideration of the recommendation.

Recommendation 2 (page 273): That DOD conduct periodic surveys of service personnel procedures to insure that adequate consideration is being given to the requirements of the intelligence agencies for their share of the best qualified military personnel.

Agency Comment: DOD does not concur. DOD believes its current practices are adequate. It agrees that the highest practicable standards should be applied in the selection of attaché personnel.

Additional Action Required: None, assuming DOD's current practices are in fact adequate.

Recommendation 3 (page 273): That DOD require that the Military Services study the problem of improving the prestige of the civilian analyst vis-à-vis his military colleagues.

Agency Comment: DOD concurs, noting that in practical terms there is no easy solution to this problem. DOD reports much has been done on the problem and that it will keep same under review.

Recommendation 4 (page 273): That DOD facilitate the employment as intelligence specialists of qualified retired military personnel by initiating action toward amending the laws concerning Federal employment of retired military personnel, with a view to removing the present ceiling on the Federal pay of such individuals.

Agency Comment: DOD believes present laws on this subject are too restricted; on the other hand it is fearful lest statutory amendments be such as to permit retired officers with intelligence experience to automatically find employment as civilian intelligence analysts. DOD reports that the CSC has developed a proposal to relax existing legislative requirements along the general lines of this recommendation.

Additional Action Required: Executive Branch processing of CSC's legislative proposal and submission thereof for Congressional consideration.

Recommendation 5 (page 273): That DOD give consideration to more extensive use of "Schedule A" in the employment of civilian analysts and other intelligence specialists, in order to provide necessary flexibility in the recruitment of qualified civilian personnel by the military services, and to facilitate the interchange of such personnel between the Zone of Interior competitive service and the overseas excepted service.

Agency Comment: DOD agrees that greater flexibility in hiring and in the ability to shift civilian personnel between the Zone of the Interior and foreign stations is essential. It believes a degree of relaxation of Civil Service regulations is desirable to deal with these problems. DOD has initiated a thorough study of the matter.

Additional Action Required: Appropriate action by DOD following completion of its study of the problem.

Recommendation 6 (page 273): That DOD, in the consideration of future economies, give proper weight to the importance of intelligence in peace time, so as to avoid serious reductions-in-force in our centers of intelligence production.

Agency Comment: DOD concurs, noting that the purpose of this recommendation can be further served by applying such reductions-in-force as do occur to overhead positions rather than to basic productive elements.

Recommendation 7 (page 274): That DOD take prompt action to insure that proper consideration in personnel planning is given to the impact of the time lag involved in our present clearance requirements for filling sensitive positions.

Agency Comment: DOD believes this recommendation requires further study.

Additional Action Required: Further study and appropriate action by DOD.

CHAPTER X—Security (Pages 275–283)

Recommendation 1 (page 273): That any individual employed in an intelligence organization "about whom sufficient doubt concerning his security has been raised . . . should be removed from employment pending final determination of his case."

Agency Comment: DOD considers that its current security practices and procedures essentially fulfill the objectives of this recommendation. However, it reports that the general subject will be reviewed in order to insure that those objectives are adequately served.

CIA reports that it is carrying out the intent of this recommendation in that it adheres carefully to Executive Order 10450 which provides for the suspension of Federal employees when a reasonable doubt exists as to their security status. State reports that "this recommendation requires no implementation in the Department of State" . . . since State's regulations do not preclude employee suspensions in such circumstances.

Additional Action Required: Strict adherence to Executive Order 10450 by the agencies concerned—such adherence will accomplish the objective of this recommendation.

Observation: State has missed the point of this recommendation. All agencies now have the authority to suspend employees under the circumstances indicated in the recommendation. The point the Task Force appears to be making is that some of the agencies fail to suspend when there is sufficient cause and it is the Task Force's view that in the intelligence organizations of our government in particular, such suspension should occur pending final determination of the employee's case.

Recommendation 2 (page 283): That the "findings and proposed disposition of those cases which were reported as still in process at the time the survey by this Task Force was concluded should be reported to the President."

Agency Comment: DOD did not comment on this point.

CIA noted that under normal reporting procedures as established by Executive Order 10450, information is furnished to the Civil Service Commission or the FBI on such cases, and that thereafter the status of such cases is available to the President, through the executive agencies he has designated, to report on the implementation of Executive Order 10450.

State advises that detailed reports concerning the very small percentage of such employees in its Intelligence Area have been made available to the Civil Service Commission, and that CSC makes a composite report periodically on such cases in all government agencies.

Observation: CIA and State seem to have missed the point of this recommendation. (DOD did not comment upon it at all.) If the recommendation is deemed to have validity, the White House may wish to request that the heads of the intelligence agencies concerned report the findings and disposition of alleged security risk cases (in their intelligence areas) in process at the time the Task Force concluded its survey.

Recommendation 3 (page 283): That measures be instituted in all agencies to recheck the security status of all personnel engaged in intelligence activities at periodic intervals not to exceed 5 years in any individual case.

Agency Comment: CIA reports that this is now being done in that agency. State reports that the problem of periodic review of such cases is being given serious study, following which State will bring its views thereon to the attention of the agencies concerned, such as the CSC and the Department of Justice.

DOD considers that its current security practices essentially fulfill the objectives of this recommendation. However, the general subject will be reviewed to insure that the underlying objectives of the recommendation are adequately served.

Additional Action Required: This recommendation should be rejected.

Observation: This recommendation has been made in varying forms on a number of occasions in the Task Force report. In theory it has ostensible merit; in practice it is unsound. In lieu of subjecting employees to reinvestigations at least every 5 years a good counterintelligence program is what is needed. When employees are initially brought on board they should be exhaustively checked. Thereafter they should not be harassed by reinvestigations, but should be accepted as loyal, bona fide Americans unless counterintelligence discloses reasons for contrary views. Wholesale investigations of the type called for by the Task Force would constitute unjustifiable use of manpower and money, would not be productive of substantial results, and would be harmful to the morale of the employees concerned. Reinvestigations should be made on a selective, rather than wholesale, basis and only when there is reasonable cause therefor.

CHAPTER XI—Counterintelligence (Pages 284–292)

Recommendation 1 (page 292): That the Navy give due consideration to the requirement for additional competent and trained counterintelligence personnel in order to provide adequate security for its personnel and facilities.

Agency Comment: DOD concurs in principle, but believes that the actual method of expansion should be investigated.

Additional Action Required: Further investigation as suggested by DOD, followed by action consistent with its investigative findings and with the objective of providing adequate security for naval personnel and facilities. (See Recommendation 1, Chapter IV, D, page 10, above.)

CHAPTER XII—Maps and Libraries (Pages 293–305)

Recommendation 1 (page 305): That the IAC consider the adoption of a single index system based on the Intelligence Subject Code now in use by CIA.

Agency Comment: CIA and DOD concur. CIA reports that this recommendation is currently under study in a special subcommittee of the IAC. The subcommittee is expected to report to the IAC within the next few weeks.

CHAPTER XIII—Coordination in Overseas Areas (Pages 306–309)

Recommendation 1 (page 309): That senior military commanders in the field be given greater flexibility in their use of information on a need-to-know basis, giving due regard to the protection of its source.

Agency Comment: CIA comments that it is not aware of any complaints of restrictions on use of information supplied. CIA reports that it is fully cognizant of its obligation and responsibility to get information to the senior officer responsible for action and policy.

DOD considers that "current practices in the DOD are satisfactory within the regulations imposed by other agencies."

CHAPTER XIV—Development of New Equipment and Techniques
(Pages 310–311)

Recommendation 1 (page 311): That the IAC take positive action to insure that a definite and concerted effort is made to develop new techniques, methods and equipment for the collection and production of intelligence and insure that a free exchange of information concerning such projects is accomplished within the intelligence community.

Agency Comment: CIA reports that compliance with this recommendation will be accomplished in conjunction with IAC actions currently underway and that the means of producing intelligence on the Soviet/Sino Bloc are "always under continuous scrutiny."

DOD concurs, stating that continuing efforts are being devoted to fulfillment of this recommendation. DOD observes that in all cases full effectiveness can be achieved only with a frank and free interchange of information.

State concurs, noting that it has initiated a number of steps in social science, psychological and research areas, all of which are designed to further the objective of this recommendation.

CHAPTER XV—"Watch-Dog" Commission (Pages 312–317)

Recommendation 1 (page 317): That a small, permanent, bipartisan commission, composed of members of both Houses of the Congress and other public-spirited citizens commanding the utmost national respect and confidence, be established by Act of Congress to make periodic surveys of the organization, functions, policies, and results of the Government agencies handling foreign intelligence operations; and to report, under adequate security safeguards, its findings and recommendations to the Congress, and to the President, annually and at such other times as may be necessary or advisable. The proposed "watch-dog" commission should be empowered by law to demand and receive any information it needs for its own use. It would be patterned after the Commission on Organization of the Executive Branch of the Government (Hoover Commission). Appointments by the President of persons from private life to the proposed commission should be made from a select list of distinguished individuals of unquestioned loyalty, integrity, and ability, with records of unselfish service to the nation.

Agency Comment: CIA does not concur in this recommendation. CIA believes, with the Hoover Commission itself, that "while mixed Congressional and citizens committees for temporary service are useful and helpful to undertake specific problems and to investigate and make recommendations, such committees, if permanent, present difficulties." CIA points out that it now reports to the Armed Services Committees of the Senate and House, and to the Senate and House Appropriations Committees. As a consequence CIA does not consider that a Joint Congressional Committee would add any essential helpful element. CIA does concur, however, in the appointment (as recommended by the Hoover Commission, but not by its Task Force) by the President of a committee of experienced private citizens to examine and report periodically on the work of the Government's foreign intelligence activities.

DOD believes that the permanent, bipartisan commission recommended by the Task Force would afford improved protection for, as well as efficiency in, foreign intelligence operations.

Additional Action Required: None, in view of the establishment on January 13, 1956 by the President of a Board of Consultants[12] to review periodically the foreign intelligence activities of the Government.

CHAPTER XVI—Summary of Conclusions and Recommendations (Pages 318–348)

This Chapter is merely repetitive of information appearing earlier in the Report. Conclusions and recommendations are restated in verbatim fashion in some instances; in other instances they are paraphrased and combined with still other opinions and recommendations contained in the body of the report. This Chapter does not appear to contain any new information. It merely restates, repeats, and reemphasizes certain of the points previously made.

Appendix

The recommendations discussed below are from Appendix I of the Task Force Report. The Department of Defense comments are supplementary to those submitted by the Director of Central Intelligence for the United States Communications Intelligence Board (USCIB) and the

---

[12] Regarding the creation of this board, see *Public Papers: Eisenhower, 1956,* pp. 72–74.

United States Communications Security Board (USCSB), in which the Department of Defense and the three Services concur.

Recommendation No. 1

"That the National Security Council direct USCIB to establish COMINT realities and consideration of capabilities of other intelligence sources. This operational guidance to NSA should be so clear and succinct as to require minimum interpretation by the Director, NSA, of what is required and its degree of importance. USCIB should be primarily concerned with end products and the Director, NSA, should determine the best way of producing the end product. If USCIB fails after a reasonable length of time to provide more adequate guidance to the Director, NSA, then the latter should be made a member of the Intelligence Advisory Committee."

Department of Defense Position:

1. Concur, subject to comment.

2. *Comment:*

It is doubtful that IAC membership for the Director, NSA, would solve the problem; it would probably raise additional complications.

In this connection, the Department of Defense considers that the present status and membership of the IAC give rise to ambiguity which this particular recommendation would only sharpen. The IAC is unique in being neither a policy nor an operational body, but a mixture of the two. This is the result partly of unforeseen evolution within the IAC, and partly of significant changes which have occurred within the Department of Defense since the IAC was established.

To the extent that the NSC intended the IAC to serve as a policy body, its Defense membership (the three Services and JCS) is at once diffuse and incomplete in that the Service representation is largely at an operating rather than a policy level and the Secretary of Defense is not directly represented, although the JCS representative (Chairman, Joint Intelligence Committee) coordinates with the appropriate elements of OSD. On the other hand, to the extent that the IAC serves as a body concerned with the coordination and formulation of intelligence estimates and the coordination of operational intelligence matters, its present formalized structure may not be entirely necessary. The three Service intelligence chiefs are suitable representation in this context, and although the Chairman, JIC, does not conduct operations, he is the appropriate indirect representative of the Secretary of Defense for these matters. In its dual capacity the IAC works, but in an unnecessarily complicated and probably uneconomical context of differing levels of activity.

The Department of Defense considers that a more desirable ultimate organization of the top structure of U.S. intelligence would involve a single board with policy cognizance over all aspects of intelligence. The Secretary of Defense's representative would be an appropriate civilian official, competent to act for him. Under this board would be several specialist committees to deal with operational matters; one concerned with communications and electronics intelligence and communications security (as recommended by the Clark Task Force); another with intelligence operations; a third with intelligence production; and possibly others. Representation on these committees would be provided by the Service intelligence chiefs and other operators (such as the Director, NSA) when appropriate.

The following main points summarize the views that are crystallizing in the Department of Defense on the general subject of intelligence:

1. The Secretary of State and the Secretary of Defense must assume final responsibility for guidance and control over all aspects of intelligence.

2. The Director of Central Intelligence as the actual executive agent must have adequate and clearly defined coordinative powers under the Secretaries of State and Defense.

3. National intelligence policy is under the cognizance of the National Security Council. However, because of the sensitive nature of important elements of intelligence, intelligence matters might most appropriately be dealt with by a Special Committee of the NSC (which is now the case, to the satisfaction of all concerned, with respect to COMINT and COMSEC matters: the Secretaries of State and Defense, and the Attorney General for matters under his cognizance, with the advice of the Director of Central Intelligence, constitute the Special Committee of the NSC).

4. The concept behind USCIB has proved to be the most satisfactory solution so far in one important intelligence area. Appropriately modified, it could usefully be applied to the entire intelligence field.

The changes which this general concept would involve do not require legislation. Internal reorganization within the IAC and probably an executive order to establish the new organization would suffice.

The Department of Defense proposes to discuss this subject further with the Director of Central Intelligence and the Department of State, and hopes in due course together with them to arrive at an agreed proposal for submission.

Recommendation No. 2

"That the Director, NSA, be given clearcut directives which will enable him to make much greater and continuing effort to produce high-level communications intelligence. This is of such great importance that monetary considerations should be waived and an effort at least equal to the Manhattan Project should be exerted at once."

Department of Defense Position:

With respect to that portion of the Recommendation advocating "an effort at least equal to the Manhattan Project" [*1 line not declassified*] the Department of Defense considers some expansion on the USCIB comments is warranted.

[*24 lines not declassified*]

With this objective in mind the Department of Defense has authorized the Director, NSA, to bring the best possible analytical brains from outside NSA to bear on the problem (if they can be found); and USCIB has recommended that this country undertake a maximum effort to [*1½ lines not declassified*].

The Department of Defense considers that [*1½ lines not declassified*] as to warrant the full force of the government behind both projects.

Recommendation No. 6

"That the Department of Defense carefully study the organizational structure and proper positioning within its respective services of the three cryptologic agencies—AFSS, ASA, and NSG—with a view toward improving their prestige and effectiveness, thereby strengthening their personnel assignment policies and logistical support."

Department of Defense Position:

USCIB considered that this recommendation pertains to an internal problem within the Department of Defense, and has accordingly referred it to this Department for comment.

The Department of Defense has long recognized that high professional standards and opportunity for a rewarding career for military and civilian personnel engaged in the communications intelligence effort must be strengthened if we are to deal successfully with the increasingly difficult technical problems confronting that effort. One means of achieving this objective is to constitute the Service cryptologic agencies as major commands. These should be subordinate neither to the intelligence nor to the communications elements within the Services, but should in each case report directly to the chief of staff. Adequate recognition of cryptology as a major operational career field cannot be otherwise achieved.

The Air Force cryptologic agency, the Security Service (AFSS), has been so constituted for approximately seven years. The AFSS is responsible for COMINT production [*less than 1 line not declassified*] and COMSEC activities, and in addition operated the Air Force's ground-based ELINT stations and its SSO (Special Security Officer) system for the dissemination of COMINT. Largely because of its status as a major command, the AFSS has developed a dynamic and promising program for recruiting, developing and holding on to technically qualified military career personnel.

Until recently the Army cryptologic agency (the Army Security Agency (ASA)) was responsible for COMINT production [less than 1 line not declassified] and for COMSEC. It was subordinate to G–2. On 23 June 1955, the ASA was designated as a major command responsible to the Chief of Staff, with virtually complete cognizance over all Army aspects of COMINT, COMSEC, ELINT and communications electromagnetic countermeasures (ECM). It is anticipated that this action will facilitate development of an energetic Army cryptologic career program paralleling that of the Air Force.

The Navy cryptologic activity, the Navy Security Group (NSG), is not so constituted. It operates at a lower echelon and under divided intelligence and communications cognizance. The NSG does not nominally have a commanding officer; it functions under the Chief of Security Branch who in turn reports to the Director, Naval Communications. The responsibilities of the NSG include COMINT production [less than 1 line not declassified] COMSEC, and ELINT.

The Secretary of Defense proposes in the near future to ask the Secretary of the Navy to review the placement of the Navy cryptologic organization to determine whether a subordination and structure more closely paralleling that of the Army and the Air Force might not be advantageous.

Recommendation No. 7

"That the military Services give greater attention to selecting officers for COMINT duties, assign regular or 'career' reserve officers to the maximum extent possible, indoctrinate officers in COMINT prior to sending them to command field stations, and establish career opportunities for specialists equal to those of the line or general service officers. Rotation and replacement procedures should be improved. The feasibility of using [less than 1 line not declassified] should be thoroughly tested.

"It is also recommended that the Congress enact legislation to authorize the National Security Agency to employ specially qualified retired military personnel as presently authorized the Central Intelligence Agency and with no restriction on the number so employed. Such legislation should also permit the Secretary of Defense to recall retired officers to active duty with NSA and have those officers counted against the authorized strength of NSA but not of the respective military services."

Department of Defense Position:

The Department of Defense submits the following additional observations in expansion of the USCIB comment on this recommendation. As set forth in its comments on Recommendation No. 6, the Department of Defense believes that the establishment of major cryptologic commands in each of the military services will do much to promote the career possibilities advocated in Recommendation No. 7. Also, with the support of this Department, the Army and NSA are already embarked on a program to develop [*less than 1 line not declassified*]. Recently the Secretary of Defense endorsed a Navy proposal to augment the Naval Security Group with civilians.

With respect to the employment by NSA of specially qualified retired military personnel, the Department of Defense supports this proposal for NSA in principle as an element of the Department, but would emphasize that the highest objective standards of professional or technical skill should be applied in hiring such persons, in order to avoid possible abuses which could seriously prejudice career civilian morale.

Full consideration of the application of this proposal is currently in progress among personnel and legislative experts within the Department of Defense.

Recommendation No. 8

"That the Secretary of Defense give further consideration to the allocation of an appropriate number of 'super grades' and positions under Public Law 313[13] to NSA; to the possibility of further inducements or higher pay to selected consultants; and to privileges extended to civilians overseas."

Department of Defense Position:

The Department of Defense is supporting the efforts of the Director, NSA, to obtain additional super grades from the Civil Service Commission. Further, the Assistant Secretary of Defense (Manpower and Personnel) is seeking as a priority matter (within existing legislation) to meet the request of the Director, NSA, for further inducements to selected consultants and privileges for civilians employed overseas. The consultant problem is not confined to NSA alone, and the Department prefers to resolve it for NSA as part of an over-all Department of Defense solution. Such additional legislation as may be required to achieve these objectives is also under consideration.

---

[13] Reference presumably is to the law relating to the compensation of the professional and scientific services in the War and Navy Departments, approved August 1, 1947. (61 Stat. 715)

Appendix I[14]

Part 1—The National Security Agency (Pages 1–58)

Recommendation 1 (page 46): That NSC direct USCIB to establish COMINT requirements in the light of COMINT realities and consideration of capabilities of other intelligence sources. This operational guidance to NSA should be so clear and succinct as to require minimum interpretation of what is required and of its degree of importance. USCIB should be primarily concerned with end products and the Director, NSA, should determine the best way of producing same. If USCIB fails after a reasonable length of time to provide more adequate guidance to the Director, NSA, the latter should be made a member of the IAC.

Agency Comment: USCIB considers the first part of this recommendation to be in hand in that a revised COMINT requirements list, prepared with NSA participation, has been approved by a Working Committee within USCIB and will soon be presented for USCIB approval. With respect to the second part of the recommendation, USCIB does not believe that NSA membership on the IAC should be related to the development of or failure to develop USCIB directives or requirements.

DOD concurs, but is doubtful that the problem to which the latter part of the recommendation is addressed would be solved by making the Director, NSA, a member of the IAC. DOD is presently crystalizing its views on the general subject of intelligence and on the ultimate organization of the top structure of U.S. intelligence. DOD proposes to discuss the matter with State and CIA and hopes in due course, together with those agencies, to arrive at an agreed proposal for submission.

Additional Action Required: As to COMINT requirements—none. As to NSA's membership on the IAC—defer decision pending a determination as to whether USCIB's revised COMINT requirements constitute sufficient guidance for NSA. (In the interim consideration should be given to granting observership status on the IAC to the Director, NSA.)

Recommendation 2 (page 48): That the Director, NSA, be given clear cut directives which will enable him to make much greater and continuing effort to produce high level communications intelligence. This is of such great importance that monetary considerations should be waived and an effort at least equal to the Manhattan Project should be exerted at once. (It is noted that in forwarding Appendix I, Part 1, the

---

[14] This section of Coyne's report was classified Top Secret; U.S. Eyes Only; Handle Via COMINT Channels Only.

Task Force indicated that "the importance of the adoption of Recommendation 2 is especially emphasized—this is believed to be vital to the intelligence effort.")

Agency Comment: USCIB does not concur in the implication that guidance or lack thereof has adversely affected the production of high level communications intelligence. USCIB notes that "emphasis upon the guidance factor has tended to obscure the real, and critical, weakness which does exist, namely, [*4 lines not declassified*]. As to the proposed initiation of efforts in this field along the lines of the Manhattan Project, USCIB states that it is not now in a position to determine the nature and scope of the increased effort which might be applied to the solution of COMINT's chief problem [*less than 1 line not declassified*]. USCIB believes it will be in a better position to decide this matter as a result of NSA's plan for implementing the new COMINT objectives list, or as a result of a special study which is being undertaken by highly qualified, technical experts in an effort to [*less than 1 line not declassified*] problem referred to above. USCIB is convinced that maximum assistance would be provided to NSA in the solution of its major problem by the [*2 lines not declassified*]. Based thereon, the Special Committee of the NSC for COMINT (Sec/State and Sec/Def) has agreed that an optimum, if not indeed a prerequisite, step toward [*2 lines not declassified*] and should be accorded maximum priority. To that end the Special Committee has authorized marshalling of all relevant [*less than 1 line not declassified*] resources of the intelligence agencies.

Additional Action Required: Reconsideration by NSC's Special Committee for COMINT of the recommended expansion of NSA's efforts.

Observation: Such reconsideration should be deferred pending completion of the study and related steps referred to by USCIB and summarized above.

Recommendation 3 (page 49): That ELINT and COMINT be integrated to the extent of placing ELINT under NSA for analysis of the product and guidance and coordination in the collection and dissemination of ELINT. The authority of operational commanders over the integral ELINT resources, however, should not be abridged. USCIB or the combined board which is recommended in this report to replace it should exercise only policy control over ELINT matters.

Agency Comment: USCIB believes this recommendation has been overtaken by the issuance of NSCID No. 17[15] and by the DOD Direc-

---

[15] Document 259.

tive on ELINT dated July 13, 1955.[16] USCIB believes no further action should be taken on this recommendation until these recent directives have been implemented and tried.

Additional Action Required: Following a reasonable trial period the reference directives should be re-examined in the light of this recommendation.

Observation: The USCIB response is unclear. By inference it appears that ELINT has not been placed under NSA, as recommended by the Task Force.

Recommendation 4 (page 50): That the military services and NSA continue to strive for a higher degree of cryptographic security; that the problem of communications security be restudied by USCSB (or the combined board as recommended in this report) with a view to reducing to the lowest practicable level the quantity of information released through telecommunications; and that NSC 168[17] be re-examined to ascertain if the Director, NSA, has sufficient authority to carry out his COMSEC responsibilities.

Agency Comment: USCIB agrees with the need for a higher degree of communications security and feels that efforts to attain this end should continue; however, it does not consider that the recommendation falls within the purview of USCIB.

USCSB reports that, at all times, the military services and NSA keep the problem of cryptographic security under thorough review. USCSB concurs in the recommended review of NSC 168, but notes that in essence this review is already underway pursuant to the provisions of NSC 168 itself.

Recommendation 5 (page 51): That a single board with appropriate technical subcommittees have policy guidance over communications intelligence and communications security. If the recommendation to place the evaluation and analysis of ELINT under NSA is adopted, then policy guidance for ELINT as well as COMINT and COMSEC should be exercised by the proposed single board.

Agency Comment: USCIB is not now willing to recommend establishment of a single board "because the basic functions and organizational arrangements within a number of the interested agencies are sufficiently divergent to justify the continued separate existence of USCIB and USCSB." USCSB opposes the recommendation because of the difficulties of implementation which would result from the establishment of a single board, as proposed.

---

[16] Document 230.

[17] The title of NSC 168, November 1953 was "Communications Security." Documentation on this NSC paper is in the National Archives, RG 273, Policy Papers.

Recommendation 6 (page 51): That DOD study the organizational structure and proper positioning within its respective services of the three cryptologic agencies—AFSS, ASA, and NSG—with a view toward improving their prestige and effectiveness, thereby strengthening their personnel assignment policies and logistic support.

Agency Comment: USCIB endorses the aim of this recommendation but considers it a problem internal to DOD. DOD believes that one means of achieving the objective of this recommendation is to constitute the service cryptologic agencies as major commands. The Air Force Cryptologic Agency (AFSS) has been so constituted for about seven years. The Army Cryptologic Agency (ASA) was designated as a major command following the submission of the Task Force Report. The Navy Cryptologic activity (NSG) is not so constituted at present; DOD will in the near future ask the Secretary of the Navy to review his cryptologic organization to determine whether it might be re-established on a basis paralleling that of the Army and the Air Force.

Recommendation 7 (page 52): That the military services give greater attention to selecting officers for COMINT duties, assign regular or "career" reserve officers to the maximum extent possible, indoctrinate officers in COMINT prior to sending them to command field stations, and establish career opportunities for specialists equal to those of the line or general service officers. Rotation and replacement procedures should be improved. The feasibility of using civilian intercept operators should be tested. It is also recommended that Congress enact legislation to authorize NSA to employ especially qualified retired military personnel with no restriction on the number so employed. Such legislation should also permit Sec. Def. to recall active officers to duty with NSA and have those officers counted against the authorized strength of NSA, but not of the respective military services.

Agency Comment: USCIB concurs in this recommendation. DOD reports that full consideration of these proposals is currently in progress within DOD.

Recommendation 8 (page 54): That the Secretary of Defense give further consideration to the allocation of an appropriate number of "super grades" and positions under Public Law 313 to NSA; to the possibility of further inducements or higher pay to selected consultants; and to privileges extended to civilians overseas.

Agency Comment: USCIB concurs in this recommendation. DOD also concurs and is taking the steps it deems appropriate in an effort to accomplish the objectives of this recommendation.

Recommendation 9 (page 55): That USCIB or its successor board clarify the objectives and functions of intelligence liaison detachments with NSA, establish uniform procedures to be followed for such detachments in their relationship with NSA, and specify maximum numbers of personnel to be assigned for liaison duties after examining the extent of interest of each agency concerned. Intelligence personnel assigned to liaison duty with NSA should be required to attend an indoctrination course conducted by NSA.

Agency Comment: USCIB does not concur in this recommendation. It agrees that mutual familarization with the requirements, capabilities and operations of both NSA and consumer agencies is desirable; it feels, however, that because the necessary functions of intelligence liaison detachments vary continuously with the missions of the consumer agencies and the character of COMINT production activities, the arrangements called for by this recommendation cannot successfully be rendered uniform.

Additional Action Required: Decision as to whether the view of the Task Force or the view of USCIB should be adopted.

Observation: USCIB's view is most sound. The Task Force recommendation should be rejected.

Recommendation 10 (page 56): That NSA and the three cryptologic services give greater emphasis to, and continue to develop mutual cooperation in, improving the technical factors of intercept stations.

Agency Comment: USCIB concurs. Greater emphasis has been given this matter and USCIB considers the arrangements which have been undertaken in this regard to be satisfactory.

Recommendation 11 (page 56): That more thorough periodic reinvestigations of personnel be made. Particular effort should be concentrated on persons occupying the more sensitive positions.

Agency Comment: USCIB has established a special committee to investigate the matter, and USCIB is prepared to act on whatever recommendations are made by that committee.

Observation: See "Observation" Section of Chapter X, Recommendation 3.

Recommendation 12 (page 57): That the Director, NSA, be given authority to inspect the service cryptologic schools and make appropriate recommendations for improvement where COMINT is affected.

Agency Comment: USCIB concurs.

Part 2—Communications and Electronics in Support of Intelligence
Activities (Pages 1–44)

Recommendation 1 (page 37): That an Intelligence Communications and Electronics Subcommittee (ICES) to the Combined Intelligence Board (this assumes that USCIB and USCSB have been combined into a single board, as proposed elsewhere in the report) be established to review and produce recommendations to the Combined Intelligence Board with respect to all communications and electronics proposals from intelligence activities which call for facilities, equipments, or additional personnel which cannot be obtained from existing resources; and to supply technical advice to the Board on such matters as it might request.

Agency Comment: USCIB does not agree. It believes that the spirit of this recommendation is being accomplished by expert communications and electronics advice provided from within the agencies concerned with the subject.

Additional Action Required: None, assuming the USCIB comment on this recommendation is accurate.

Recommendation 2 (page 38): That more effective use be made within DOD of the high potential value and know-how available in the Joint Communications-Electronics Committee of the Joint Chiefs of Staff to deal with communications and electronics problems related to the broad intelligence field. Responsibility should be placed on that group for reviewing and commenting on communications and electronics requirements that the NSA considers necessary to meet the intelligence objectives, and the demands being placed by NSA on the special communications and electronics groups in the military services under NSA operational control; and for submitting recommendations to the Secretary of Defense on ways and means to insure maximum coordination and effectiveness in the over-all communications and electronics effort in support of intelligence.

Agency Comment: USCIB considers that existing procedures for reviewing and commenting on NSA requirements are satisfactory.

Recommendation 3 (page 38): That more effective technical advice be injected into USCIB deliberations to permit development of more appropriate statements of the intelligence objectives to be accomplished by communications or electronics means.

Agency Comment: USCIB agrees with the spirit of this recommendation and believes that it is now being carried into effect.

Recommendation 4 (page 38): That the present basic policy for the provision of point-to-point communications services to intelligence community activities from existing governmental or civil communications services be continued. That any attempt to set up separate, duplicate, or paralleling point-to-point communications facilities be authorized only when the necessity therefor has been fully reviewed and agreed to by the Intelligence Communications and Electronics Subcommittee recommended in Recommendation 1, above.

Agency Comment: USCIB concurs in the first sentence of the recommendation. It agrees with the second sentence to the extent of believing that no separate facilities should be established for intelligence use without full consideration by appropriate authority.

Recommendation 5 (page 39): That a basic policy of utilizing existing facilities, services, and equipment to the maximum degree be applied wherever it is determined to be technically feasible in the COMINT, ELINT, and COMSEC operations (this applies particularly to certain aspects of the technical training phases, operational procedures, and logistics); that exceptions to this policy be authorized only when the necessity therefor has been fully reviewed and agreed to by the Intelligence Communications and Electronics Subcommittee recommended in Recommendation 1, above.

Agency Comment: USCIB considers that the spirit of this recommendation is now being carried out. It does not agree that the additional review (called for in the last sentence) is either necessary or desirable.

Recommendation 6 (page 39): That any arrangements with respect to centralized control of ELINT give adequate consideration to the immediate and vital interest of the military in this field and the need to keep electronic countermeasures (ECM)—a tactical weapon—clearly under military operational control.

Agency Comment: USCIB believes that this recommendation has been overtaken by the issuance of NSCID 17 and the related Department of Defense Directive of July 13, 1955.

Recommendation 7 (page 39): That all planning and operation of communications and electronics efforts in support of intelligence activities include full consideration of the following to meet national emergency conditions:

a. Day-to-day operation and training be based on realism in light of the situation and facilities expected to be available in time of war or national emergency. This applies in a special manner to planning operations to be effective in case of heavy jamming operations.

b. Key intelligence installations, served by costly, hard-to-replace electronics equipment and associated records be located outside established target areas. That these installations have integrated plans for national emergency or disaster operations. That all agencies involved in planning new, alternate, or emergency locations for Federal agencies expedite action to assist NSA in its current efforts to obtain a suitable site.

c. Pending accomplishment of b, that effective interim disaster plans be developed promptly for each key intelligence installation to include as a minimum (1) alternate site, (2) installed and tested minimum equipment with necessary basic records at the alternate site, and (3) adequate knowledge of disaster plans by key personnel.

Agency Comment: USCIB concurs in Recommendation 7-a and considers that it is now being carried out. USCIB agrees in principle with Recommendation 7-b but notes that the great extension of target areas by fallout hazards would require relocation at such great distances that reduction in operational efficiency would be unacceptable and the agency concerned would be unable to retain or attract key personnel.

USCIB reports that plans for the location of alternate NSA sites are now being developed by DOD. USCIB concurs in Recommendation 7-c and reports that it is being carried into effect except for bulky, costly, and complex cryptoanalytic machinery.

Recommendation 8 (page 40): That the present basic communications (cryptographic) security plan, providing for centralized control with effective decentralization of operations, be continued; that each agency and service maintain effective inspection and vigorous training programs to reduce to the minimum cryptographic operational security violations.

Agency Comment: USCSB concurs, noting that the Communications Security Plan referred to represents, in reality, a number of communications security arrangements each of which is considered satisfactory.

Recommendation 9 (page 40): That NSC determine ways and means to control more effectively release of valuable intelligence to potential enemies via clear text messages being transmitted over government and civil communication networks.

Agency Comment: USCSB considers that the policy responsibility for control of governmental clear text messages falls within its charter. It reports that it has long recognized this problem and is working toward its solution. It does not believe that the problem is one for NSC consideration. USCSB considers that the policy responsibility for control of nongovernmental clear text messages over civil communications networks is outside its purview.

Additional Action Required: Referral of the nongovernmental aspects of the subject to Commerce for consideration in the light of its NSC-assigned responsibilities relating to the safeguarding of unclassified strategic information.

Recommendation 10 (page 40): That the general tendency within the communications intelligence and the communications security agencies to overemphasize the special security facets of their operations with respect to basic communications and electronics features be examined objectively and comprehensively by [a] competent, technically qualified authority to insure that such overemphasis is not producing unnecessary duplication of facilities and operations in peacetime which will grow to completely unrealistic figures in wartime, and producing a system which may fail in an emergency because it will require considerable readjustment of basic operational practices at a critical time.

Agency Comment: USCIB believes existing procedures for review of communications requirements are adequate. USCIB does not believe that the security aspects of COMINT are significantly overemphasized. Accordingly, USCIB opposes creation of the special committee called for by this recommendation. USCSB, in essence, concurs in USCIB's view; it believes that no separate examination of the problem is required.

Recommendation 11 (page 41): "SPECIAL RECOMMENDATION": That the President set up a special commission composed of technically qualified civil and military communications and electronics representatives, to survey and produce recommendations as to ways and means to insure the more effective utilization of all communications and electronics resources of the United States in the national interests in case of war or national emergency. (This recommendation was singled out by the Task Force as one worthy of special emphasis and as one believed to be of great importance.)

Agency Comment: ODM expressed the view (7/6/55)[18] that the Report which was shortly thereafter to be made to the NSC by the Science Advisory Committee would contain organizational recommendations somewhat more far reaching than those suggested in the Task Force Report and, if adopted, would probably satisfy the recommendations of the Task Force Report.

Additional Action Required: DOD, ODM and CIA views should be obtained on this recommendation, including recommendations as to its implementation. (The ODM comment of 7/6/55 is not specific enough to assess the validity of the Task Force recommendation.)

Appendix II[19]

The Clandestine Services of the Central Intelligence Agency

Recommendation 1 (page 42): That the "covert intelligence" and "cold war functions" of the Deputy Director/Plans be assigned to separate Deputy Directors whose areas of responsibility should be administratively and logistically self-supporting.

Agency Comment: CIA does not concur, noting that the recommended system had been tried prior to 1952 and abandoned; that CIA's experience during the period of separate operations proved the operational disadvantages of attempting to conduct on a secure and efficient basis two worldwide clandestine organizations, each compartmented from the other.

Additional Action Required: See Chapter II, Recommendation 1, Page 1, above.

Recommendation 2 (page 42): That the part of CIA's July 15, 1952 Directive appointing area division chiefs as executives of the DCI and providing for their direct dealing with him and senior overseas representatives[20] be rescinded.

---

[18] Not found.

[19] This section of Coyne's report was classified Top Secret.

[20] Printed in Warner, ed., *The CIA Under Harry Truman*, pp. 465–467.

Agency Comment: CIA reports this Directive has been reviewed and rescinded.

Recommendation 3 (page 42): That the DCI re-establish the office of Executive Director of that agency.

Agency Comment: CIA is opposed to this recommendation on the ground that the interposition of another command echelon would not necessarily accomplish the intent of the recommendation. Further study, however, is being given the subject.

Observation: Because this is purely of an intra-agency character, it would seem appropriate to defer to DCI's judgment thereon.

Recommendation 4 (page 42): That CIA's espionage and counterespionage programs against Soviet targets be intensified.

Agency Comment: CIA concurs fully, noting that it is assiduously pursuing the course recommended. Recent organizational changes have stimulated a more intensified effort on the part of the clandestine services in the espionage and counterespionage fields.

Recommendation 5 (page 42): That the proposed annual CIA psychological warfare budget and allocations be submitted for NSC approval and subsequent changes presented by DCI to the OCB.

Agency Comment: CIA does not agree. CIA notes that the recommendation is inconsistent with the charter and function of the NSC; that NSC is an organ for the formulation of basic policy; that NSC does not have the time and staff required to consider details of budgets and funds allocation. CIA notes that in developing its psychological warfare budget, it is careful to conform to policy established by the Council, and to request Council authorization for any proposed action which is not covered by existing policy. In addition it is the practice of DCI to keep the NSC closely informed concerning psychological warfare programs.

Additional Action Required: Decision as to whether the Task Force recommendation should be adopted.

Observation: In view of the reasons advanced by CIA, all of which are valid, the Task Force recommendation should not be adopted.

Recommendation 6 (page 42): That the inducement phase of the Defector Program, as applicable to active participation by diplomatic and military representatives serving overtly abroad, be discontinued.

Agency Comment: CIA does not concur. It notes that cover employed by CIA personnel overseas often precludes direct contact with potential defectors and the use of overt diplomatic and military personnel for this purpose is a natural and essential adjunct to the defector program, provided their activities are closely coordinated with CIA. CIA believes that the fact that such work may result in occasional embarrassment is a calculated risk which it considers worthwhile inasmuch as the intelligence and cold war gains for defection or recruitment of Soviet personnel are considerable.

Additional Action Required: Expeditious review of NSCID No. 13 by IAC and, if necessary, NSC.

Observation: This recommendation of the Task Force is not fully consistent with its recommendations on pages 137 and 205. (On page 137 the Task Force recommends greater participation by the military services in the Soviet and Satellite defector inducement program; on page 205 the Task Force recommends that the military services be permitted greater latitude in offering inducements to potential defectors.)

Recommendation 7 (page 43): That the program for training of specialists in covert intelligence collection and for the development of linguists be intensified.

Agency Comment: CIA concurs and has in effect a number of measures the objectives of which coincide with this recommendation. A mandatory quota of five per cent of all clandestine service personnel are in training at all times.

Recommendation 8 (page 43): That submission of individual budgets to the CIA Project Review Committee by the area division chiefs be discontinued and funds for each cold war component be prepared under the supervision of its chief and submitted for the component to the Project Review Committee.

Agency Comment: CIA observes that this recommendation is based on a separation of CIA "cold war" and "covert intelligence functions" with which CIA does not concur. It notes, however, that in relation to its existing organization the programming system of the clandestine services now being put into operation assures a review by the DDP and his staff of the budget recommendations of the area divisions of CIA clandestine services.

Recommendation 9 (page 43): That the number of auditors of the regular CIA audit staff be increased materially.

Agency Comment: CIA concurs. This action is being taken as rapidly as possible in line with an internal organization survey made by CIA several months ago.

Recommendation 10 (page 43): That greater efforts be exerted to establish long-range deep cover for CIA personnel serving covertly overseas.

Agency Comment: CIA concurs. It has been working toward the objective of this proposal for many years. As a result of a current review of all aspects of "cover," recommendations are now being studied which are designed to produce better results in this complex field.

Recommendation 11 (page 43): That the NSC render a specific interpretation of the provisions of paragraph 4-b, NSC 5412/1 as it affects the several members of the intelligence community.

Agency Comment: CIA notes that the reference paragraph directs that the DCI shall be responsible for "informing through appropriate channels and on a 'need-to-know' basis, agencies of the U.S. government, both at home and abroad, including diplomatic and military representatives, of such operations as will affect them." CIA reports that it has been scrupulously careful to keep other agencies appropriately informed pursuant to the "need-to-know" principle; and that it is trying constantly to remedy and prevent individual instances of failure on the part of its personnel in their efforts to strike the difficult balance between the proper range of interests of another agency and the restrictive principle of "need-to-know." CIA points out that as a standard procedure it provides individual briefings for Ambassadors and other State personnel, Defense Commanders, Chiefs of Military Missions, Attachés, etc.

Recommendation 12 (page 43): That the CIA Act of 1949 be amended to authorize the employment of "any" (instead of fifteen now authorized) retired officers or warrant officers of the armed services.

Agency Comment: See Chapter II, Recommendation 12, Page 4, above.

National Security Council Intelligence Directives, 1950–1955

252. National Security Council Intelligence Directive No. 13[1]

Washington, January 19, 1950.

EXPLOITATION OF SOVIET AND SATELLITE DEFECTORS OUTSIDE THE UNITED STATES

Pursuant to the provisions of Section 102(d)(4) of the National Security Act of 1947,[2] as amended, Section 4(a)(7) of NSC 50,[3] and NSCID No. 5,[4] the National Security Council hereby authorizes and directs that:

1. It is in accord with the best U.S. tradition to endeavor to protect and assist those fleeing from persecution. Under present conditions, and with due regard for the effects of such action on the diplomatic and political interests of the United States, it is also in the important interests of national security that defectors be welcomed and assisted in obtaining a degree of personal and economic security and made to feel that there is a place for them in a free society. The best sources of information and intelligence on the Soviet world, necessary in the interests of the national security, are defectors from Soviet control. The most effective agents to destroy the communist myth of the Soviet paradise are defectors who are able to tell the truth about conditions of life behind the Iron Curtain.

2. The term "defectors" is here employed to denote individuals who escape from the control of the USSR or countries in the Soviet orbit, or who, being outside such jurisdiction or control, are unwilling to return to it, *and* who are of special interest to the U.S. Government (a) because they are able to add valuable new or confirmatory information to existing U.S. knowledge of the Soviet world, (b) because they are of operational value to a U.S. agency, or (c) because their defection can be exploited in the psychological field.

a. A *potential defector* is a person who may reasonably be expected to become a defector if he is induced to do so.

---

[1] Source: National Archives, RG 59, S/S–NSC (Miscellaneous) Files: Lot 66 D 95, NSCIDs. Top Secret. NSCID No. 13 received NSC approval by memorandum action on January 19. (Ibid., Records of Action by the National Security Council)

[2] 61 Stat. 495–510.

[3] See *Foreign Relations*, 1945–1950, Emergence of the Intelligence Establishment, Document 384.

[4] Ibid., Document 423.

b. A *declared defector* is a person who has left the service of his country and therefore requires protection and assistance.

c. *Inducement* means the commission of an act by, or manifestly at the instigation of, an American official which is demonstrably intended to bring about a defection and for which the U.S. Government might, if the act were discovered, be called upon to account.

Potential Defectors

3. CIA shall be responsible for inducing the defection of potential defectors, except in the cases where it is manifestly in the interest of security or efficiency that representatives of other agencies undertake such action.

Declared Defectors

4. The ranking American official in the area concerned shall be responsible for determining the manner and degree to which the acceptance or rejection of a declared defector may affect the diplomatic and political interests of the United States. Any overt publicity and propaganda exploitation of a defector shall be coordinated with the Department of State.

5. The Central Intelligence Agency shall be responsible for the covert exploitation of defectors, and shall, within the framework of paragraph 4, coordinate all matters concerned with the handling and disposition of declared defectors from the Soviet Union and the satellite states in order to assure the effective exploitation of all defectors for operational, intelligence, or psychological purposes by the U.S. Government.

6. CIA shall seek the guidance of the appropriate Departments to insure that no action taken under this directive jeopardizes the military, security, political, or diplomatic interests of the United States and shall keep the other IAC agencies adequately informed of actions taken with respect to individual defector cases.

7. Subject to the over-all direction of the Chief of Mission, CIA representatives in the field shall have operating responsibility outside U.S. occupied areas for:

a. Providing secure facilities and preliminary assessment of a defector's bona fides and his intelligence or other potential value to the U.S. Government.

b. Assuring that the other IAC agencies have adequate opportunity to exploit a defector for intelligence or operational purposes, including immediate access to the defector in the field.

c. Arranging secure movement of defectors as required.

8. In U.S. occupied areas CIA shall establish, together with the Department of State and that military department having executive authority in the area, adequate procedures designed to carry out the obligations listed in paragraphs 7 a–c.

9. Field representatives of the IAC agencies shall be responsible for:

a. Informing promptly the ranking American official and the CIA representative of any potential or declared defector who comes to their attention.

b. Directly or through questionnaires, representing the intelligence interests of their respective agencies in the debriefing of such defectors.

10. To the extent that there are available funds, CIA shall be responsible for the final disposal and rehabilitation of defectors. The IAC agencies shall provide all possible assistance to CIA in establishing rapid and effective means of disposal.

11. If it appears to be in the national interest to bring a defector to the United States for intelligence purposes or operational use, CIA shall be responsible for coordinating with the interested departments and agencies for policy approval and for making necessary arrangements in advance for entry. CIA shall also be responsible for handling and disposal of the defector in agreement with the interested departments or agencies. In each case, notice and full available biographic and background information will be given to the Federal Bureau of Investigation in advance. No commitments for entry for intelligence purposes or operational use will be made by any United States official without coordination and notice as set forth in this paragraph.

---

253. National Security Council Intelligence Directive No. 14[1]

Washington, March 3, 1950.

EXPLOITATION OF DEFECTORS AND OTHER ALIENS WITHIN THE UNITED STATES

Pursuant to the provisions of the National Security Act of 1947,[2] as amended, and Section 4 of NSC 50,[3] the National Security Council,

---

[1] Source: National Archives, RG 59, S/S–NSC (Miscellaneous) Files: Lot 66 D 95, NSCIDs. Top Secret. NSCID No. 14 received NSC approval by memorandum action on March 3. (Ibid., Records of Action by the National Security Council)

[2] 61 Stat. 495–510.

[3] See *Foreign Relations*, 1945–1950, Emergence of the Intelligence Establishment, Document 384.

with the concurrence of the Attorney General of the United States, hereby authorizes and directs that:

1. Exploitation of aliens within the U.S. for internal security purposes shall be the responsibility of the Federal Bureau of Investigation. Exploitation of aliens as sources of foreign intelligence information or for other foreign intelligence purposes shall be the responsibility of the Central Intelligence Agency. This allocation to the Federal Bureau of Investigation and to the Central Intelligence Agency of separate areas of alien exploitation responsibility does not preclude joint exploitation, which must be encouraged whenever feasible. It further carries with it the obligation for each agency to give to the other, without delay and directly, all information pertinent to the activities and responsibilities of that other agency, such as the FBI notifying CIA promptly of aliens of potential foreign intelligence interest who may come to its attention and CIA notifying FBI of information it obtains relating to internal security problems.

2. Exploitation of aliens by the Central Intelligence Agency or by the other member agencies of the Intelligence Advisory Committee shall be conducted for the following purposes:

a. To obtain foreign intelligence information required in the interests of national security or by the member agencies of the Intelligence Advisory Committee.

b. To obtain internal security information or other data required by the Federal Bureau of Investigation in the discharge of its domestic responsibilities.

c. For such other purposes as the National Security Council shall deem to be in the interests of national security.

3. In the case of any official, employee, or other individual officially attached to a foreign government or one of its agencies, an official of a political party officially recognized by its government, or an official of an international organization, in an overt or covert capacity, who defects within the United States, the Federal Bureau of Investigation shall:

a. Immediately notify CIA, as well as the other IAC members and other interested agencies, of the actual or potential defection.

b. Determine insofar as is possible the legitimacy of such reported potential or actual defection within the United States, and whether the individual's determination to defect or his defection is or is not known to his government.

c. Immediately notify the Attorney General and the Department of State of the identity of the individual concerned and his official connection with a foreign government, as well as his status as a defector. Comments and observations will be solicited from the Attorney General and the State Department.

d. Be initially responsible for exploitation of all such actual or potential defectors, and maintain sole jurisdiction over them until completion of its internal security exploitation, unless it is jointly determined that the foreign intelligence interest shall be paramount in the particular case.

e. Determine whether such potential defector can be utilized in a clandestine capacity and when so utilized provide through CIA, or the other interested agency, for satisfaction of foreign intelligence requirements. Appropriate security restrictions will be agreed upon in individual cases. If, for operational reasons, it is not possible for the FBI to immediately fulfill foreign intelligence requirements of the other agency, such notice will be provided to CIA and the other agency.

f. Make immediately available to CIA with copies to interested IAC members all foreign intelligence information resulting from the initial exploitation of such a defector, and provide, through established channels, for his interview by other member agencies of the IAC upon their request, prior to the full exhaustion of internal security requirements if feasible.

g. On request by CIA, arrange for the transfer of such a defector to the jurisdiction of the CIA upon completion of its internal security exploitation, unless it is jointly determined that the foreign intelligence interest is paramount prior to that time. The CIA will assume responsibility for necessary maintenance and custody during the period of its exploitation and shall be responsible for the final disposal and rehabilitation of all such defectors. Internal security problems will remain the responsibility of the Federal Bureau of Investigation. The final disposition of the alien and reimbursement of maintenance expenses will be determined by mutual agreement in advance among the CIA and interested agencies in each case, based upon future operational considerations.

h. Pursuant to the provisions of Section 102(e) of the National Security Act of 1947, as amended, upon the written request of the Director of Central Intelligence, provide all available information and pertinent observations with respect to the internal security factors involved in the exploitation of each defector for foreign intelligence information.

4. In the case of aliens within the U.S., other than those covered in paragraph 3 above, CIA shall:

a. Be responsible for their exploitation for foreign intelligence under the provisions of NSCID No. 7.[4]

---

[4] Ibid., Document 427.

b. In order that the statutory responsibilities and domestic intelligence jurisdiction of the Federal Bureau of Investigation may be adequately handled and in order to prevent confusion in internal security matters, the CIA or any other authorized intelligence agency will, prior to exploiting an alien within the United States, advise the FBI in advance of the exploitation. The FBI will then provide information it has which may be of assistance in the exploitation by the other agency and will make such observations as are pertinent, including notice that exploitation by the other agency would interfere with matters involved in internal security or execution of the statutory obligations of the FBI.

c. After determining priorities, arrange for exploitation of the alien for foreign intelligence purposes by any other IAC agency or agencies which may request independent exploitation of the alien. The CIA will assume responsibility for necessary maintenance and custody during the period of exploitation. During the period of such maintenance, internal security problems will remain the responsibility of the Federal Bureau of Investigation, except as is provided below. Reimbursement of maintenance expenses will be determined by mutual agreement in advance among the CIA and interested agencies in each case.

d. Notify the FBI immediately of information obtained through its own facilities or from other IAC agencies that an alien within the U.S. has defected or may defect. To accomplish this end, the other IAC agencies will transmit without delay all such pertinent information to the CIA and the FBI.

5. If it appears to be in the national interest to bring a defector to the United States for intelligence purposes or operational use under the provisions of this Directive, CIA shall be responsible for coordinating with the other interested departments and agencies for policy approval and for making necessary arrangements in advance for entry. CIA shall also be responsible for handling and disposal of the defector in agreement with the interested departments or agencies, and until such disposal will make adequate provisions to insure that the defector does not endanger the internal security of the United States. In each case, notice and full available biographic and background information will be given to the Federal Bureau of Investigation in advance. No commitments for entry for intelligence purposes or operational use will be made by any United States official without coordination and notice as set forth in this paragraph.

6. Any overt publicity and propaganda exploitation of a defector shall be coordinated with the Department of State.

254. National Security Council Intelligence Directive No. 15[1]

Washington, June 13, 1951.

COORDINATION AND PRODUCTION OF FOREIGN ECONOMIC INTELLIGENCE

Pursuant to the provisions of Section 102 (d) of the National Security Act of 1947,[2] as amended, the National Security Council hereby authorizes and directs the Central Intelligence Agency to perform the following functions with respect to foreign economic intelligence relating to the national security:

1. Maintain a continuing review of the requirements of the United States Government for foreign economic intelligence relating to the national security, and of the facilities and arrangements available to meet those requirements, making from time to time such recommendations to the National Security Council concerning improvements as may require National Security Council action.

2. Insure through regular procedures that the full economic knowledge and technical talent available in the Government is brought to bear on important issues involving national security, including issues on which assistance is requested by the National Security Council or members thereof.

3. Evaluate, through regular procedures, the pertinence, extent, and quality of the foreign economic data available bearing on national security issues, and develop ways in which quality could be improved and gaps could be filled.

4. Conduct, as a service of common concern, such foreign economic research and produce such foreign economic intelligence as may be required (a) to supplement that produced by other agencies either in the appropriate discharge of their regular departmental missions or in fulfillment of assigned intelligence responsibilities; (b) to fulfill requests of the Intelligence Advisory Committee.

---

[1] Source: Truman Library, President's Secretary Files, Subject File. Confidential. NSCID No. 15 was approved by the NSC at its 94th meeting on June 13 (NSC Action No. 495). (National Archives, RG 59, S/S–NSC (Miscellaneous) Files: Lot 66 D 95, Records of Action by the National Security Council) A correction to NSCID No. 15 was issued on June 22. The text was unchanged, the only change being a minor adjustment to format.

[2] 61 Stat. 495–510.

255.   National Security Council Intelligence Directive No. 5 Revised[1]

Washington, August 28, 1951.

ESPIONAGE AND COUNTERESPIONAGE OPERATIONS

Pursuant to the provisions of Section 102 (d) of the National Security Act of 1947,[2] the National Security Council hereby authorizes and directs that:

1. The Director of Central Intelligence shall conduct all organized Federal espionage operations outside the United States and its possessions for the collection of foreign intelligence information required to meet the needs of all Departments and Agencies concerned, in connection with the national security, except for certain agreed activities by other Departments and Agencies.

2. The Director of Central Intelligence shall conduct all organized Federal counterespionage operations outside the United States and its possessions and in occupied areas, provided that this authority shall not be construed to preclude the counter-intelligence activities of any army, navy or air command or installation and certain agreed activities by Departments and Agencies necessary for the security of such organizations.

3. The Director of Central Intelligence shall be responsible for coordinating covert and overt intelligence collection activities.

4. When casual agents are employed or otherwise utilized by an IAC Department or Agency in other than an overt capacity, the Director of Central Intelligence shall coordinate their activities with the organized covert activities.

5. The Director of Central Intelligence shall disseminate such intelligence information to the various Departments and Agencies which have an authorized interest therein.

6. All other National Security Council Intelligence Directives or implementing supplements shall be construed to apply solely to overt intelligence activities unless otherwise specified.

---

[1] Source: National Archives, RG 273, NSCIDs. Top Secret. This revision of NSCID No. 5, December 12, 1947 (see *Foreign Relations, 1945–1950,* Emergence of the Intelligence Establishment, Document 423) added paragraphs 7–10. These paragraphs were proposed by the Department of Defense and circulated to the NSC under cover of July 30 and August 8 memoranda from NSC Executive Secretary Lay. (Truman Library, President's Secretary's Files, Subject File) The revised NSCID No. 5 was approved by the NSC by memorandum action on August 28 (NSC Action No. 534). It was circulated to Council members by Lay by a memorandum of the same date. (Ibid.)

[2] 61 Stat. 495–510.

7. In an occupied area, the representative of the Director of Central Intelligence will coordinate espionage and counterespionage operations in or from the area with the senior U.S. Representative and keep the Senior U.S. Military Commander informed in general of the clandestine collection activities conducted by DCI in or from such area.

8. In an area other than theaters of war or occupied areas, the representative of the Director of Central Intelligence will keep the senior U.S. Representative appropriately advised of the espionage and counterespionage operations in or from the area.

9. When CIA requires Service support for espionage and counterespionage projects, such support as may be authorized by the Department of Defense will be planned jointly with the Joint Chiefs of Staff.

10. In time of war or when the President directs, the Director of Central Intelligence will coordinate espionage and counterespionage operations in or from a theater of active military operations with the Joint Chiefs of Staff. In active theaters of war, where American forces are engaged, representatives of the Director of Central Intelligence conducting espionage and counterespionage operations in or from the theater shall be under the direct command of the United States theater commander.

---

256. National Security Council Intelligence Directive No. 1 Revised[1]

Washington, March 28, 1952.

DUTIES AND RESPONSIBILITIES

Pursuant to the provisions of Section 102 of the National Security Act of 1947,[2] and for the purposes enunciated in paragraphs (d) and

---

[1] Source: National Archives, RG 273, NSCIDs. Secret; Security Information. This revised version of NSCID No. 1 was approved by the National Security Council by memorandum action on March 28 (NSC Action No. 623). (National Archives, RG 59, S/S–NSC Files: Lot 66 D 95, Records of Action by the National Security Council). NSCID No. 1 as originally adopted by the NSC on December 12, 1947, is printed in *CIA Cold War Records, The CIA Under Harry Truman,* pp. 169–171. For the revision of July 7, 1949, see *Foreign Relations,* 1945–1950, Emergency of the Intelligence Establishment, Document 385 and Document 431, footnote 2. For the revision of January 19, 1950, see ibid., Document 432.

[2] 61 Stat. 495–510.

(e) thereof, the National Security Council hereby authorizes and directs that:

1. To maintain the relationship essential to coordination between the Central Intelligence Agency and the intelligence organizations, an Intelligence Advisory Committee consisting of the Director of Central Intelligence, who shall be chairman thereof, the Director, Federal Bureau of Investigation, and the respective intelligence chiefs from the Departments of State, Army, Navy, and Air Force, and from the Joint Staff (JCS), and the Atomic Energy Commission, or their representatives, shall be established to advise the Director of Central Intelligence. The Director of Central Intelligence will invite the chief, or his representative, of any other intelligence Agency having functions related to the national security to sit with the Intelligence Advisory Committee whenever matters within the purview of his Agency are to be discussed.

2. To the extent authorized by Section 102 (e) of the National Security Act of 1947, the Director of Central Intelligence, or representatives designated by him, by arrangement with the head of the department or agency concerned, shall make such surveys and inspections of departmental intelligence material of the various Federal Departments and Agencies relating to the national security as he may deem necessary in connection with his duty to advise the NSC and to make recommendations for the coordination of intelligence activities.

3. Coordination of intelligence activities should be designed primarily to strengthen the over-all governmental intelligence structure. Primary departmental requirements shall be recognized and shall receive the cooperation and support of the Central Intelligence Agency.

a. The Director of Central Intelligence shall, in making recommendations or giving advice to the National Security Council pertaining to the intelligence activities of the various Departments and Agencies, transmit therewith a statement indicating the concurrence or non-concurrence of the members of the Intelligence Advisory Committee; provided that, when unanimity is not obtained among the Department heads of the National Military Establishment, the Director of Central Intelligence shall refer the problem to the Secretary of Defense before presenting it to the National Security Council.

b. Recommendations of the Director of Central Intelligence shall, when approved by the National Security Council, issue as Council Directives to the Director of Central Intelligence. The respective intelligence chiefs shall be responsible for insuring that such orders or directives, when applicable, are implemented within their intelligence organizations.

c. The Director of Central Intelligence shall act for the National Security Council to insure full and proper implementation of Council directives by issuing such supplementary DCI directives as may be required. Such implementing directives in which the Intelligence Advisory Committee concurs unanimously shall be issued by the Director of Central Intelligence, and shall be implemented within the Departments and Agencies as provided in paragraph b. Where disagreement arises between the Director of Central Intelligence and one or more members of the Intelligence Advisory Committee over such directives, the proposed directive, together with statements of non-concurrence, shall be forwarded to the NSC for decision as provided in paragraph a.

4. The Director of Central Intelligence shall produce intelligence relating to the national security, hereafter referred to as national intelligence. In so far as practicable, he shall not duplicate the intelligence activities and research of the various Departments and Agencies but shall make use of existing intelligence facilities and shall utilize departmental intelligence for such production purposes. For definitions see NSCID No. 3.[3]

5. a. The Director of Central Intelligence shall disseminate National Intelligence to the President, to members of the National Security Council, to the Intelligence Chiefs of the IAC Agencies, and to such Governmental Departments and Agencies as the National Security Council from time to time may designate. Intelligence so disseminated shall be officially concurred in by the Intelligence Agencies or shall carry a statement of substantially differing opinions.

b. Unless otherwise provided by law or NSC Directive, the Director of Central Intelligence is authorized to disseminate National Intelligence on a strictly controlled basis to foreign governments and international bodies upon determination by the Director of Central Intelligence, concurred in by the Intelligence Advisory Committee, that such action would substantially promote the security of the United States; provided that any disclosure of classified military information included in such national intelligence is in accordance with the policies laid down in the U.S. National Disclosure Policy (MIC 206/29),[4] such determination to be made by the Army, Navy, and Air Force; and provided further that any disclosure of FBI intelligence information will be cleared with that Agency prior to dissemination.

6. Whenever any member of the Intelligence Advisory Committee obtains information that indicates an impending crisis situation, such as the outbreak of hostilities involving the United States, or a condition which affects the security of the United States to such an extent that immediate action or decision on the part of the President or the

---

[3] See *Foreign Relations, 1945–1950*, Emergence of the Intelligence Establishment, Document 426.

[4] For a partial text of the National Disclosure Policy, see ibid., 1948, vol. I, Part 2, p. 575.

National Security Council seems to be required, he shall immediately furnish the information to the other members of the Intelligence Advisory Committee as well as to other officials or agencies as may be indicated by the circumstances. The Director of Central Intelligence shall immediately convene the Intelligence Advisory Committee. After receiving the views of the Intelligence Advisory Committee members, the Director of Central Intelligence shall promptly prepare and disseminate the national intelligence estimate in accordance with paragraphs 4 and 5 above.

7. When Security Regulations of the originating Agency permit, the Director of Central Intelligence shall disseminate to the Federal Bureau of Investigation and other Departments or Agencies intelligence or intelligence information which he may possess when he deems such dissemination appropriate to their functions relating to the national security.

8. The Director of Central Intelligence shall perform for the benefit of the existing intelligence Agencies such services of common concern to these Agencies as the National Security Council determines can be more efficiently accomplished centrally.

9. The intelligence organizations in each of the Departments and Agencies shall maintain with the Central Intelligence Agency and with each other, as appropriate to their respective responsibilities, a continuing interchange of intelligence information and intelligence available to them.

10. The intelligence files in each intelligence organization, including the CIA, shall be made available under security regulations of the Department or Agency concerned to the others for consultation.

11. The intelligence organizations within the limits of their capabilities shall provide, or procure, such intelligence as may be requested by the Director of Central Intelligence or by one of the other Departments or Agencies.

12. The Director of Central Intelligence shall make arrangements with the respective Departments and Agencies to assign to the Central Intelligence Agency such experienced and qualified officers and members as may be of advantage for advisory, operational, or other purposes, in addition to such personnel as the Director of Central Intelligence may directly employ. In each case, such departmental personnel will be subject to the necessary personnel procedures of each Department.

257.   National Security Council Intelligence Directive No. 9 Revised[1]

Washington, December 29, 1952.

COMMUNICATIONS INTELLIGENCE

Pursuant to the provisions of Section 101 and Section 102 of the National Security Act of 1947,[2] as amended, and to the Presidential directive approved October 24, 1952,[3] which

a. Stated that the communications intelligence (COMINT) activities of the United States are a national responsibility, and that they must be so organized and managed as to exploit to the maximum the available resources in all participating departments and agencies and to satisfy the legitimate intelligence requirements of all such departments and agencies;

b. Designated the Secretaries of State and Defense as a Special Committee of the National Security Council for COMINT, which Committee shall, with the assistance of the Director of Central Intelligence, establish policies governing COMINT activities, and keep the President advised of such policies through the Executive Secretary of the National Security Council (The President in approving this directive also directed that the Attorney General shall be a member of the

---

[1] Source: Truman Library, President's Secretary's Files, Subject File. Top Secret. The March 10, 1950, version of NSCID No. 9, is *Foreign Relations, 1945–1950, Emergence of the Intelligence Establishment*, Document 435. For the original July 1, 1948, version, see ibid, Source note. This version was originally issued on October 24, 1952. (Truman Library, President's Secretary's Files, Subject File) After its issuance, on October 31 the Director of the Federal Bureau of Investigation J. Edgar Hoover wrote to Executive Secretary of the National Security Council Lay with three "observations." First, Hoover wrote, the Attorney General should be a member of the Special Committee whenever matters of interest to the FBI were before the Committee. Second, the right of the USCIB "to investigate and study the standards and practices of its member agencies" was too broad. Third, the authority of the NSA Director to "have direct access" and "technical control" of "any elements" of the member agencies also was too broad (Ibid.) In his December 17 reply, Lay informed Hoover the decision of the Special Committee to amend NSCID No. 9. There were three changes. First the sentence in parentheses at the end of preambular paragraph "b" was added. Second, in paragraph 1 d. (1) the Secretary of Defense and the Director of the Federal Bureau of Investigation were added to those who were given two votes. Finally, paragraph 4 was added. (Ibid.) Montague has an interesting account of the interagency sensitivities involved in this episode in *General Walter Bedell Smith As Director of Central Intelligence, October 1950-February 1953*, p. 253.

[2] 61 Stat. 495–510.

[3] By memorandum of October 28, Executive Secretary of the National Security Council Lay informed the Secretaries of State and Defense that President Truman had approved this revised version of NSCID No. 9 on October 24. (Truman Library, President's Secretary's Files, Subject File)

Special Committee whenever matters of interest to the Federal Bureau of Investigation are before that Committee.); and

c. Further designated the Department of Defense as executive agent of the Government, for the production of COMINT information;

the Special Committee of the National Security Council for COMINT hereby authorizes and directs that:

1. *Directive to the United States Communications Intelligence Board (USCIB).*

a. USCIB shall be reconstituted as a body acting for and under the Special Committee, and shall operate in accordance with the provisions of this directive. Only those departments or agencies represented in USCIB are authorized to engage in COMINT activities.

b. The Board shall be composed of the following members:

(1) The Director of Central Intelligence, who shall be Chairman of the Board.
(2) A representative of the Secretary of State.
(3) A representative of the Secretary of Defense.
(4) A representative of the Director of the Federal Bureau of Investigation.
(5) The Director of the National Security Agency (NSA).
(6) A representative of the Department of the Army.
(7) A representative of the Department of the Navy.
(8) A representative of the Department of the Air Force.
(9) A representative of the Central Intelligence Agency.

c. The Board shall have a staff headed by an executive secretary who shall be appointed by the Chairman with the approval of the majority of the Board.

d. It shall be the duty of the Board to advise and make recommendations to the Secretary of Defense, in accordance with the following procedure, with respect to any matter relating to communications intelligence which falls within the jurisdiction of the Director of NSA:

(1) The Board shall reach its decision by a majority vote. Each member of the Board shall have one vote except the representatives of the Secretary of State, the Secretary of Defense, the Director of the Federal Bureau of Investigation, and of the Central Intelligence Agency who shall each have two votes. The Director of Central Intelligence, as Chairman, will have no vote. In the event that the Board votes and reaches a decision, any dissenting member of the Board may appeal from such decision within 7 days to the Special Committee. In the event that the Board votes but fails to reach a decision, any member of the Board may appeal within 7 days to the Special Committee. In either event the Special Committee shall review the matter, and its determination thereon shall be final. Appeals by the Director of NSA and/or the representatives of the Military Departments shall only be filed with the approval of the Secretary of Defense.

(2) If any matter is voted on by the Board but

(a) no decision is reached and any member files an appeal;
(b) a decision is reached in which the representative of the Secretary of Defense does not concur and files an appeal;

no action shall be taken with respect to the subject matter until the appeal is decided, provided that, if the Secretary of Defense determines, after consultation with the Secretary of State, that the subject matter presents a problem of an emergency nature and requires immediate action, his decision shall govern, pending the result of the appeal. In such an emergency situation the appeal may be taken directly to the President.

(3) Recommendations of the Board adopted in accordance with the foregoing procedures shall be binding on the Secretary of Defense. Except on matters which have been voted on by the Board, the Director of NSA shall discharge his responsibilities in accordance with his own judgment, subject to the direction of the Secretary of Defense.

(4) The Director of NSA shall make such reports and furnish such information from time to time to the Board, either orally or in writing, as the Board may request, and shall bring to the attention of the Board either in such reports or otherwise any new major policies or programs in advance of their adoption by him.

e. It shall also be the duty of the Board as to matters not falling within the jurisdiction of NSA:

(1) To coordinate the communications intelligence activities among all departments and agencies authorized by the President to participate therein;

(2) To initiate, to formulate policies concerning, and subject to the provisions of NSCID No. 5,[4] to supervise all arrangements with foreign governments in the field of communications intelligence; and

(3) To consider and make recommendations concerning policies relating to communications intelligence of common interest to the departments and agencies, including security standards and practices, and, for this purpose, to investigate and study the standards and practices of such departments and agencies in utilizing and protecting COMINT information.

f. Any recommendation of the Board with respect to the matters described in paragraph e above shall be binding on all departments or agencies of the Government if it is adopted by the unanimous vote of the members of the Board. Recommendations approved by a majority, but not all, of the members of the Board shall be transmitted by it to the Special Committee for such action as the Special Committee may see fit to take.

g. The Board will meet monthly, or oftener at the call of the Chairman or any member, and shall determine its own procedures.

2. *Directive to the Secretary of Defense.*

a. Subject to the specific provisions of this directive, the Secretary of Defense may delegate in whole or in part authority over the Director of NSA within his department as he sees fit.

---

[4] Document 255.

b. The COMINT mission of the National Security Agency (NSA) shall be to provide an effective, unified organization and control of the communications intelligence activities of the United States conducted against foreign governments, and to provide for integrated operational policies and procedures pertaining thereto. As used in this directive, the terms "communications intelligence" or "COMINT" shall be construed to mean all procedures and methods used in the interception of communications other than foreign press and propaganda broadcasts and the obtaining of information from such communications by other than the intended recipients,[5] but shall exclude censorship and the production and dissemination of finished intelligence.

c. NSA shall be administered by a Director, designated by the Secretary of Defense after consultation with the Joint Chiefs of Staff, who shall serve for a minimum term of 4 years and who shall be eligible for reappointment. The Director shall be a career commissioned officer of the armed services on active or reactivated status, and shall enjoy at least 3-star rank during the period of his incumbency.

d. Under the Secretary of Defense, and in accordance with approved policies of USCIB, the Director of NSA shall be responsible for accomplishing the mission of NSA. For this purpose all COMINT collection and production resources of the United States are placed under his operational and technical control. When action by the Chiefs of the operating agencies of the Services or civilian departments or agencies is required, the Director shall normally issue instructions pertaining to COMINT operations through them. However, due to the unique technical character of COMINT operations, the Director is authorized to issue direct to any operating elements under his operational control task assignments and pertinent instructions which are within the capacity of such elements to accomplish. He shall also have direct access to, and direct communication with, any elements of the Service or civilian COMINT agencies on any other matters of operational and technical control as may be necessary, and he is authorized to obtain such information and intelligence material from them as he may require. All instructions issued by the Director under the authority provided in this paragraph shall be mandatory, subject only to appeal to the Secretary of Defense by the Chief of Service or head of civilian department or agency concerned.

e. Specific responsibilities of the Director of NSA include the following:

(1) Formulating necessary operational plans and policies for the conduct of the U.S. COMINT activities.

---

[5] See Public Law 513, 81st Congress, 1950. [Footnote in the original. P.L. 513, May 13, 1950 (64 Stat. 159) deals with the safeguarding of communications intelligence information.]

(2) Conducting COMINT activities, including research and development, as required to meet the needs of the departments and agencies which are authorized to receive the products of COMINT.

(3) Determining, and submitting to appropriate authorities, requirements for logistic support for the conduct of COMINT activities, together with specific recommendations as to what each of the responsible departments and agencies of the Government should supply.

(4) Within NSA's field of authorized operations prescribing requisite security regulations covering operating practices, including the transmission, handling and distribution of COMINT material within and among the COMINT elements under his operational or technical control; and exercising the necessary monitoring and supervisory control, including inspections if necessary, to ensure compliance with the regulations.

(5) Subject to the authorities granted the Director of Central Intelligence under NSCID No. 5, conducting all liaison on COMINT matters with foreign governmental communications intelligence agencies.

f. To the extent he deems feasible and in consonance with the aims of maximum over-all efficiency, economy, and effectiveness, the Director shall centralize or consolidate the performance of COMINT functions for which he is responsible. It is recognized that in certain circumstances elements of the Armed Forces and other agencies being served will require close COMINT support. Where necessary for this close support, direct operational control of specified COMINT facilities and resources will be delegated by the Director, during such periods and for such tasks as are determined by him, to military commanders or to the Chiefs of other agencies supported.

g. The Director shall exercise such administrative control over COMINT activities as he deems necessary to the effective performance of his mission. Otherwise, administrative control of personnel and facilities will remain with the departments and agencies providing them.

h. The Director shall make provision for participation by representatives of each of the departments and agencies eligible to receive COMINT products in those offices of NSA where priorities of intercept and processing are finally planned.

i. The Director shall have a civilian deputy whose primary responsibility shall be to ensure the mobilization and effective employment of the best available human and scientific resources in the field of cryptologic research and development.

j. Nothing in this directive shall contravene the responsibilities of the individual departments and agencies for the final evaluation of COMINT information, its synthesis with information from other sources, and the dissemination of finished intelligence to users.

3. The special nature of COMINT activities requires that they be treated in all respects as being outside the framework of other or general intelligence activities. Orders, directives, policies, or recommen-

dations of any authority of the Executive Branch relating to the collection, production, security, handling, dissemination, or utilization of intelligence, and/or classified material, shall not be applicable to COMINT activities, unless specifically so stated and issued by competent departmental or agency authority represented on the Board. Other National Security Council Intelligence Directives to the Director of Central Intelligence and related implementing directives issued by the Director of Central Intelligence shall be construed as non-applicable to COMINT activities, unless the National Security Council has made its directive specifically applicable to COMINT.

4. Nothing in this directive shall be construed to encroach upon or interfere with the unique responsibilities of the Federal Bureau of Investigation in the field of internal security.

---

258.   National Security Council Intelligence Directive No. 16[1]

Washington, March 7, 1953.

FOREIGN LANGUAGE PUBLICATIONS

Pursuant to the provisions of Section 102 of the National Security Act of 1947,[2] as amended, and for the purposes enunciated in paragraphs (d) and (c) thereof, the National Security Council hereby authorizes and directs that:

1. The Director of Central Intelligence shall insure the coordination of the procurement of foreign language publications for intelligence purposes, it being understood that captured documents are excepted from this provision.

2. The Director of Central Intelligence shall provide, as a primary responsibility, for the following services to the IAC agencies.

a. Preparing and disseminating English language excerpts, summaries, abstracts, and compilations from foreign language publications.

b. Developing and maintaining indexes, accession lists, and reference services regarding foreign language publications of intelligence interest.

---

[1] Source: National Archives, RG 273, NSCIDs. Confidential. NSCID No. 16 received NSC approval by memorandum action on March 7 (NSC Action No. 732). (National Archives, RG 59, S/S-NSC (Miscellaneous) Files: Lot 66 D 95, Records of Action by the National Security Council)

[2] 61 Stat. 495–510.

3. The Director of Central Intelligence shall insure the coordination of the above activities, as well as the coordination of translation services, with similar activities maintained by the intelligence agencies in accordance with their needs; such coordination shall not prejudice the maintenance of facilities necessary to meet departmental demands.

4. The intelligence agencies of the Government shall grant to the Director of Central Intelligence, upon request, access to foreign language publications in their possession.

5. An Advisory Committee on Foreign Language Publications shall be established to assist the Director of Central Intelligence in the implementation of this directive. It shall be composed of the IAC agencies and other agencies of the Government will be invited to sit with the Committee on matters which concern them.

---

259.   National Security Council Intelligence Directive No. 17[1]

Washington, May 16, 1955.

"ELECTRONIC INTELLIGENCE" (ELINT)

Pursuant to Sections 101 and 102, as amended, of the National Security Act of 1947,[2] The National Security Council authorizes and directs that:

The following organization and procedures are hereby established in order that Electronics Intelligence, hereinafter called ELINT, may be made most effective.

1. *Definition:* The term ELINT is defined as the collection (observation and recording), and the technical processing for later intelligence purposes, of information on foreign, non-communications, electromagnetic radiations emanating from other than atomic detonation sources.

2. The USCIB, in addition to its authority and responsibility as defined in NSCID #9,[3] and operating under the procedures established

---

[1] Source: National Archives, RG 59, S/P–NSC Files: Lot 62 D 1, NSC Intelligence Directives. Secret. NSCID No. 17 was approved by the NSC by memorandum action on May 16. All members of the Intelligence Advisory Committee concurred in NSCID No. 17, except the FBI which had "no comment" on the directive. (Ibid.)

[2] 61 Stat. 495–510.

[3] Document 257.

under paragraph 1-(f) of that Directive, shall be the national policy body for ELINT, including policy in relation to the Technical Processing Center provided by paragraph 4 below, arrangements with foreign governments in the field of ELINT, and recommendations concerning research and development requirements.

3. Subject to the provisions of paragraph 2 above, the Department of Defense and the Central Intelligence Agency shall be responsible for their respective ELINT collection activities.

4. The technical processing of all ELINT shall be accomplished in a center to be organized and administered by the Department of Defense. However, parallel processing in the field may be accomplished for essential immediate operational or tactical purposes. This center shall be jointly staffed by individuals detailed from the Department of Defense and the CIA in a proportion to be determined by the Secretary of Defense and the DCI.

5. All data collected by the collection agencies shall be made available forthwith to the Technical Processing Center, subject only to minimum delays necessitated by prior exploitation in the field for urgent tactical or operational purposes.

6. The Technical Processing Center shall effect fullest and most expeditious processing possible and furnish the results thereof to the interested Departments and agencies, and to the extent practicable, in the form desired by them.

Index

References are to document numbers

Acheson, Dean:
  CIA budget issues, 30
  CIA changes made at request of NSC,
    110
  Economic intelligence relating to
    national security, 144
  Europe (Eastern), 144
  National Intelligence Surveys, 41
  Psychological warfare planning, 49
  Soviet Union, 144
Ackerman, Gen. John B., 136
Adams, Sherman, 248
Advisory Committee on Government
  Organization, 210
Aerial/photo reconnaissance:
  Air Force, recommendations made by
    U.S., 102
  Balloons used in, 164, 229, 240, 242,
    249
  Dulles's (John F.) assessments, 240,
    242
  Eisenhower authorizes production of
    thirty high performance aircraft,
    199
  Eisenhower-Dulles (Allen W.)
    communications, 197, 198
  Foreign Information Program, 146,
    155
  Lockheed-Air Force (U.S.) meetings,
    196
  NSC Papers:
    NSC 142, 146
    NSC 161, 155
    NSC 5509, 209
  Project Genetrix, 229
  Project Grayback, 240, 249
  Smith's (Walter B.) assessments, 164
  Technological Capabilities Panel, 194
Africa, 61, 125, 127, 155
Agricultural reporting, 209
Agriculture Department, U.S. (USDA),
  220
Ainsworth, Donald H., 175
Air America, 15
Air Force, U.S.:
  Aerial/photo reconnaissance, 102,
    164, 194, 196, 198, 199, 229, 242

Air Force, U.S.—Continued
  Collection (intelligence) requirements,
    coordination of, 202
  Commission on the Organization of
    the Executive Branch of the
    Government, 220, 221, 234, 251
  Cryptographic systems, 251
  Disclosure of classified military
    information, 255
  Electronic intelligence, 230
  Europe (Eastern), 142
  Missiles, guided, 225
  NSC-Air Force relations, 256
  NSCID 1, 256
  Project Genetrix, 229
  Project Grayback, 240, 241, 242, 249
  Psychological warfare planning, 124,
    213
  Search projects, special electronic
    airborne, 6
  Soviet Union's capability to injure the
    U.S., evaluating the, 173
  Warning facilities of the intelligence
    community, information/
    recommendations concerning,
    234
  Watch Committee, IAC, 91, 218
Air Objective Folder Program (AOFP),
  209
Air Resupply and Communications
  (ARC) Wing program, 147
Air Technical Intelligence Center
  (ATIC), 202
Albania, 59, 190
Aliens into U.S. for intelligence/
  operational purposes, 206
Allen, Raymond B., 104
American Committee for Freedom,
  15
Amory, Robert, Jr., 115, 137, 175, 176,
  177, 193, 228
Anderson, Dillon, 214, 241
Anderson, Robert B., 230
Appleton, John B., 41
Armas, Carlos C., 154
Armed Forces Security Agency (AFSA),
  21, 40, 99, 121

Armstrong, W. Park, Jr., 9, 19, 35, 39,
    115, 175, 197, 233, 243
  Aerial/photo reconnaissance, 229
  Bureau of the Budget's study for
      coordinating economic/
      psychological/political warfare
      and foreign information
      activities, 210
  Central Intelligence Agency:
    Board of Consultants on Foreign
        Intelligence Activities, 247
    Budget issues, 30
    Changes made at CIA in response
        to requests from NSC, 110
    Defense Department-CIA relations,
        204
    State Department-CIA relations, 24,
        46
  Commission on the Organization of
      the Executive Branch of the
      Government, 236, 241
  Covert operations, 70, 71
  Foreign Service, 159
  Intelligence Advisory Committee,
      policies and procedures of the,
      29
  Missiles, guided, 225
  National Intelligence Estimates, 37
  NSC Paper 50, 110
  Office of Special Operations, 24
  Psychological warfare planning, 59
  Scientific/technical intelligence,
      112
  Soviet Union's capability to injure the
      U.S., evaluating the, 172
  State Department-Defense
      Department Staff Study on
      intelligence, 22
  Troy Report, 59
Army, U.S.:
  CIA–Army relations, 95
  Collection (intelligence) requirements,
      coordination of, 202
  Commission on the Organization of
      the Executive Branch of the
      Government, 220, 221, 251
  Communications intelligence, 99
  Coordination of economic/
      psychological/political warfare
      and foreign information
      activities, 213
  Cryptographic systems, 251
  Disclosure of classified military
      information, 256

Army, U.S.—Continued
  NSC-Army relations, 256
  NSC Intelligence Directives:
    NSCID 1, 256
    NSCID 5, 95
  Psychological warfare planning, 124,
      213
  Watch Committee, IAC, 91, 218
Ashcraft, 50
Asia, Southeast:
  Aid/personnel to, American, 59
  Air Resupply and Communications
      Wing program, 147
  Committee for a Free Asia, 15, 94
  Covert activities, 68
  Foreign Information Program, 155
  Psychological warfare planning:
    NSC Paper 135, 127
    Progress report (PSB) as of August
        1, 1952, 125
    Progress report (PSB) as of October
        30, 1952, 133
    Progress report (PSB) as of January
        5, 1953, 143
    Progress report (PSB) as of July 29,
        1953, 153
  Radio Free Asia, 94
  Troy Report, 59
  War plans, CIA/OPC strategic, 61
Assessing the Soviet Threat: The Early
    Cold War Years (Kuhns), 12
Atkins, George, 217
Atomic Energy Commission (AEC),
    207, 218, 221, 225
Atomic energy/war/weapons, 59, 126,
    155, 209, 251
Attaché system, military, 202, 209, 214,
    221
Ault, J.M., 217
Austria, 127, 234
Ayers, Fred, 164, 196

Babbitt, Theodore, 27
Bacteriological warfare, 124
Bahrein Petroleum Company, 105
Baker, James G., 194, 198
Balloons used for aerial/photo
    reconnaissance, 164, 229, 240, 242,
    249
Balloons used for propaganda, 26, 59, 92
Balmer, Gen. Jesmond D., 108, 111, 142,
    167, 205
Barbour, Walworth, 94, 118, 142, 237
Barnard, John L., 37, 41

Barnes, C. Tracy, 104, 129
Barnes, Robert G., 48, 218, 236
Barrett, Edward W., 7, 26, 52, 78
  Crusade for Freedom, 100
  Psychological warfare planning:
    Cabinet Committee, 47
    Interdepartmental Foreign
        Information Organization, 57
    Psychological Strategy Board, 67,
        74
    Supervise, debate on who should,
        49
    Troy Report, 59
  Radio Free Europe, 94
  Voice of America, 94
Barry, James P., 175
Batlin, Alexander, 244
Belmont, Alan H., 245
Benjamin, Donald F., 175
Bennett, W. Tapley, Jr., 236
Beria, Lavrenty, 161
Berle, Adolph, 94
Berry, J. Lampton, 130, 145
Bieri, B.M., 189
Biographic information on foreign
    personalities, 146, 155, 206
Biological warfare, 209
Bishop, Max, 210
Bissell, Richard, 31, 193, 205
Boggs, Marion W., 187
Bohlen, Charles, 85, 96, 106
Bohn, John T., 229
Bohnaker, W.J., 57
Bolling, Gen. A.R., 35, 65
Borel, Paul, 115
Bowie, Robert R., 187, 210
Braden, Thomas, 94, 100
Bradley, Gen. Omar N.:
  CIA–Defense Department relations,
      54, 56
  Covert operations, 83
  Search operations, special electronic
      airborne, 6
  Security of the United States, project
      to provide a more adequate basis
      for planning the, 80
  Soviet Union's capability to injure the
      U.S., evaluating the, 138, 148, 149
  Support bases, overseas CIA
      logistical, 140
  Taiwan and China, conflict between,
      106
British Broadcasting Company, 146
Broadcast monitoring, foreign, 24

Brownell, George A., 99
Brownell, Herbert, Jr., 206
Brownell Committee Report, 99, 121
Bruce, David, 247
  Oil issues, 105
  Psychological warfare planning:
    Cold War, 139
    NSC Paper 10/5, 139
    Progress Report (State Department)
        as of May 7, 1952, 109
    Psychological Operations
        Coordinating Committee,
        124
    Smith's (Walter B.)
        recommendations to
        consolidate/strengthen the
        PSB, 135
  Soviet Union's capability to injure the
      U.S., evaluating the, 138
Buford, Sidney, III., 234
Bulgaria, 190
Bull, Gen. Harold R., 150, 172, 173, 175,
    176, 177
Bundy, William P., 115, 149, 172
Bureau of European Affairs, 37
Bureau of the Budget, 52, 92, 210, 212,
    213
Burgin, Miron, 172
Buying, organized/coordinated
    program of covert preclusive,
    116

Cabell, Gen. Charles P., 29, 106, 159,
    168, 172, 174, 196, 199, 205
  Aerial/photo reconnaissance, 249
  Missiles, guided, 225, 245
  Project Grayback, 249
  U.S. Information Agency, 209
Cameron, Angus, 214
Campaign of Truth, 69
Canine, Maj. Ralph J., 29, 121, 136
Carpenter, Issac W., 210
Central Intelligence Agency (CIA) (see
    also Dulles, Allen W.; Foreign
    Information Program; Intelligence
    Advisory Committee; Operations
    Coordinating Board; Psychological
    warfare planning; Smith, Walter B.):
  Aerial/photo reconnaissance, 102,
      194, 196
  Army (U.S.)-CIA relations, 95
  Board of Consultants on Foreign
      Intelligence Activities, 247
  Budget issues, 24, 30, 111

Central Intelligence Agency (CIA)—
  Continued
  Buildings/offices, improving, 205
  Central Intelligence Act of *1949*, 220,
    221, 251
  Central Intelligence Group, 221
  Collection (intelligence) requirements,
    coordination of, 202
  Commission on the Organization of
    the Executive Branch of the
    Government, 186, 220, 221, 234,
    236, 239, 251
  Communications intelligence, 107
  Coordination of economic/
    psychological/political warfare
    and foreign information
    activities, 210, 213
  Cover problems, 205
  Covert operations (*see also* Office of
    Policy Coordination *and* Office of
    Special Operations *below*):
    Aliens into U.S. for
      intelligence/operational
      purposes, 206
    Commission on the Organization
      of the Executive Branch of the
      Government, 251
    Doolittle Report, 184, 185, 188, 192,
      193, 205
    JCS's assessments, 83
    Johnson's (Louis) support of, 1
    Joint Subsidiary Plans Division,
      93
    Joyce's assessments, 145
    NSCID *5*, 255
    NSC *5412*, 171
    NSC *5412/1*, 212
    NSC *5412/2*, 250
    Planning Coordination Group to be
      advised before operations
      initiated by CIA, 212
    Policy Planning Staff's
      assessments, 145
    Private organizations/businesses
      used by, 15
    Scope and pace of, 68, 70, 83
    Support bases, overseas logistical,
      140
    Watch Committee, IAC, 3
  Crusade for Freedom, 100
  Current Intelligence Bulletin, 51, 53
  Daily Summary, 48, 53
  Defectors, using/exploiting, 107,
    253

Central Intelligence Agency (CIA)—
  Continued
  Defense Department-CIA relations:
    Budget/finance/personnel issues,
      34
    Director of Central Intelligence
      Directive *5/1*, 204
    Doolittle Report, 205
    Dulles (Allen W.)-Kyes
      communications, 165
    Marshall's (George C.) analysis of
      U.S. intelligence, 32
    Smith (Walter B.)-Bradley
      communications, 54, 56
  Director of Central Intelligence
    Directives:
    DCID *1/2*, 179, 187, 202
    DCID *3/3*, 126
    DCID *3/4*, 126, 155, 172, 225
    DCID *4/1*, 200
    DCID *4/2*, 25, 202
    DCID *4/3*, 200, 209
    DCID *4/4*, 200, 201
    DCID *4/5*, 238
    DCID *5/1*, 204
    DCID *14/1*, 18
    DCID *15/1*, 169, 191
  Duties and responsibilities, 256
  ECA–CIA relations, 31
  Economic intelligence relating to
    national security, 72, 144
  Electronic intelligence, 230, 259
  Europe (Eastern), 144
  Foreign Service, 159
  Guerrilla warfare, 75
  Interdepartmental Economic
    Intelligence Committee, 107
  International Information Activities
    Committee, 151, 153, 173, 189
  Japan, 101
  JCS–CIA relations, 77, 176, 220, 255
  Joyce's assessments, 145
  Korean War, 12
  Kyes's assessments, 165
  Maritime sources for intelligence
    purposes, exploitation of, 113
  Middle East, 105
  National Intelligence Estimates, 37
  Net intelligence estimates of the
    capabilities/intentions of other
    nations, 177, 189
  NSC–CIA relations, 8, 107, 110, 256
  NSC Intelligence Directives:
    NSCID *1*, 256

Central Intelligence Agency (CIA)—
    Continued
NSC Intelligence Directives—
    Continued
    NSCID 5, 255
    NSCID 13, 252
    NSCID 14, 253
    NSCID 16, 258
    NSCID 17, 259
NSC Papers:
    NSC 26/2, 84
    NSC 50, 110
    NSC 174, 190
    NSC 5525, 234
Office of National Estimates, 27, 107
Office of Policy Coordination:
    Acheson-Barrett communications,
        49
    Budget estimates/studies, 8
    CIA–OPC relations, 96, 130, 145
    Covert operations, 108
    Economic intelligence relating to
        national security, 92
    Europe (Eastern), 71
    Expansion of, 145
    Guerrilla warfare, 42
    Intelligence Advisory Committee,
        policies and procedures of the,
        29
    Joint Subsidiary Plans Division, 93
    Korean War, 12
    NSC Paper 10/2, 111
    NSC Paper 10/5, 108
    NSC Paper 68, 8
    Office of Special Operations,
        merging with, 50, 130
    Personnel problems, 71
    Poland, U.S. spies captured in, 142
    Policy guidance, 7, 26
    Political background, 145
    Private organizations/businesses,
        using, 15
    PSB–OPC relations, 96
    Radio Free Asia, 94
    Scope of operations, increased, 70
    State Department-CIA relations, 24
    State Department-OPC relations,
        129
    Taiwan and China, conflict
        between, 71
    United States, policy governing
        conduct within the, 33
    War plans, OPC/CIA strategic, 61,
        111

Central Intelligence Agency (CIA)—
    Continued
Office of Reports and Estimates, 46
Office of Research and Reports, 107
Office of Special Operations:
    Armstrong's assessments, 24
    Commission on the Organization
        of the Executive Branch of the
        Government, 221
    Doolittle Report, 192
    History of the organization, 87
    Joint Subsidiary Plans Division, 93
    Office of Policy Coordination,
        merging with, 50, 130
    Reorganization, 152
Office of Special Projects, 4
Operational planning,
        interrelationship between
        intelligence and, 107
Pearl Harbor, surprise attack on, 221
Planning, long-range, 205
Planning Coordination Group-CIA
        relations, 212, 237, 246
Polygraph program, 205
Priority National Intelligence
        Objectives, 25, 238
Problems facing, 23, 29
Publication procurement, foreign,
        258
Radio Free Europe, 94
Satellites, developing/using, 122
Scientific/technical intelligence, 107,
        112, 120, 126, 155
Security, NSC's status reports on
        national:
    June 30, 1952, 127
    December 31, 1953, 170
    June 30, 1955, 234
Security clearances, operational, 205
Security of the United States, project
        to provide a more adequate basis
        for planning the, 80, 107, 121,
        131
Soviet Union:
    Aerial/photo reconnaissance, 102
    Capability to injure the U.S.,
        evaluating the, 80, 131, 173,
        207
    Director of Central Intelligence
        Directive 15/1, 169
    REDCAP program, 87
    REDSKIN program, 87
    REDSOX program, 87
    Satellites, developing/using, 122

Central Intelligence Agency (CIA)—
  Continued
  Soviet Union—*Continued*
    Sovmat Program (Soviet materials),
      217
  State Department-CIA relations:
    Armstrong's assessments, 24
    Daily Summary, 48
    Jackson (William H.)-Armstrong
      communications, 46
    Joyce's assessments, 129
    Memorandum of agreement, 34, 51
  State Department-Defense
    Department Staff Study on
    intelligence, 20
  Taiwan and China, conflict between,
    106
  Technological Capabilities Panel,
    223
  Training issues, 205
  Voice of America, 94, 107
  Warning facilities of the intelligence
    community, information/
    recommendations concerning, 186
  War plans, OPC/CIA strategic, 61,
    111
  Watch Committee, IAC, 91, 107,
    189
Chadwell, H. Marshall, 172, 175, 225
Chennault, Claire, 15
China, Communist (*see also* China,
    conflict with *under* Taiwan), 234
  Civil Air Transport's application for
    commercial rights in Okinawa,
    101
  Collection (intelligence) requirements,
    coordination of, 202
  Commission on the Organization of
    the Executive Branch of the
    Government, 220, 221, 234
  Covert operations to wartime needs,
    conversion of peacetime, 61
  Director of Central Intelligence
    Directives:
    DCID 4/4, 201
    DCID 4/5, 238
  Foreign Information Program, 146,
    155
  Intelligence objectives, Smith's
    (Walter B.) priority list of critical
    national, 117
  NSC Papers:
    NSC 5412/1, 212
    NSC 5509, 209

China, Communist—*Continued*
  Operations Coordinating Board, 158
  Psychological warfare planning, 26,
    59, 92, 125, 153
  Security Council, admission to the, 26
  Troy Report, 59
Christiansen, Gen. J.G., 220
CIA. *See* Central Intelligence Agency.
CIA Under Harry Truman, The (Warner),
    29, 42, 90, 251, 255
Civil Air Transport (CAT), 101
Civil War, U.S., 59
Clark, Mark W., 184, 185, 220
Clark, Ralph, 115
Clark Task Force of the Hoover
    Commission. *See* Commission on
    the Organization of the Executive
    Branch of the Government.
Clausewitz, Carl von, 59
Coast Guard, U.S., 79
Colby, Walter F., 29, 35
Cold War:
  Air Resupply and Communications
    Wing program, 147
  Commission on the Organization of
    the Executive Branch of the
    Government, 251
  Joyce's assessments, 142
  NSC Paper *162/2*, 163
  Psychological warfare planning, 127,
    129, 133, 139
  Real war, Cold War operations *vs.*
    preparation for, 70
  Smith's (Walter B.) recommendations
    to consolidate/strengthen the
    PSB, 129
  Support bases, overseas CIA
    logistical, 140
  Collection and Liaison Division of the
    Office of Research and Intelligence,
    226
Collins, J. Lawton, 21
Commerce Department, U.S., 79, 144, 220
Commission on the Organization of the
    Executive Branch of the
    Government:
  Air Force, U.S., 220, 221, 234, 251
  Army, U.S., 220, 221, 251
  Atomic energy, 251
  Central Intelligence Agency, 186, 220,
    221, 234, 236, 239, 251
  China, Communist, 200, 221, 234
  Communications intelligence, 220,
    251

Commission on the Organization of the
    Executive Branch of the
    Government—*Continued*
Cost of the intelligence effort, 220
Covert operations, 251
Defense Department, U.S., 220, 239,
    251
Dulles (Allen W.)-Armstrong
    communications, 236, 241
Eisenhower-Doolittle
    communications, 185
Europe (Eastern), 220, 251
Evolution of foreign intelligence, 221,
    251
Federal Bureau of Investigation, 220,
    221, 251
Functional intelligence, 251
Hoover Commission, First (1948), 220
Intelligence, defining, 220, 221
Introduction, 221
Joint Chiefs of Staff, 221, 251
Library facilities, 221, 251
Map procurement, 221, 251
National Security Council, 200, 221,
    234
Navy, U.S., 220, 221, 251
NSC Paper 5525, 234
Office of Special Operations, 221
Office of the Coordinator of
    Information, 221
Organization of the task force, 220,
    221
Origins of, 184
Personnel, 251
Positive foreign intelligence, 220
Scientific/technical intelligence, 251
Scope of the task force, 221
Security clearances, operational, 251
Sensitive data and a need-to-know
    basis, 220
Soviet Union, 220, 221, 234, 251
State Department, U.S., 221, 251
Summary/conclusions, 221, 251
Committee for a Free Asia, 15, 94
Communications intelligence
    (COMINT) (*see also* Electronic
    intelligence):
Brownell Committee Report, 99, 121
Central Intelligence Agency, 107
Commission on the Organization of
    the Executive Branch of the
    Government, 220, 251
Doolittle Report, 192
Expansion of, 19

Communications intelligence
    (COMINT)—*Continued*
Lay-Hoover (J. Edgar)
    communications, 141
NSCID 9, 136, 257
Smith's (Walter B.) assessments, 97
Truman's assessments, 132
Communications Intelligence Board,
    U.S. (USCIB), 19, 121, 132, 141, 220,
    257, 259
Communism outside the Soviet orbit,
    146, 155, 214
Compton, Wilson S., 96
Congress for Cultural Freedom, 15
Connolly, Adm. Richard E., 220, 247
Connors, W. Bradley, 57
Conway, Rose A., 63
Cooper, Chester, 115
Covert operations (*see also*
    Psychological warfare planning;
    under Central Intelligence Agency
    and National Security Council;
    individual subject headings), 251
Coyne, J. Patrick, 79, 205, 214, 251
Crespi, Leo, 226
Crusade for Freedom, 94, 100
Cryptographic systems, 121, 251
Current Intelligence Bulletin, 53, 55
Cutler, Robert, 160, 161, 173, 174, 187,
    205, 210, 211, 213
Czechoslovakia, 92, 100, 153, 190

Daniel, Adm. H.C., 172, 175
Davison, Phillips, 67
Dees, Joe, 226
Defectors, using/exploiting:
    Intelligence Advisory Committee,
        202, 252, 253
    Interagency Defector Committee, 18
    NSC Intelligence Directives:
        NSCID 13, 252
        NSCID 14, 253
    NSC Papers:
        NSC 86/1, 107
        NSC 5509, 209
    Psychological warfare planning, 92
    REDCAP program, 87
    State Department-CIA relations, 24
    Troy Report, 59
Defense Department, U.S. (*see also*
    Defense *and* Office of Special
    Operations *under* Central
    Intelligence Agency):
    Aerial/photo reconnaissance, 199

Defense Department, U.S.—*Continued*
Commission on the Organization of
the Executive Branch of the
Government, 220, 239, 251
Communications intelligence, 132,
257
Coordination of economic/
psychological/political warfare
and foreign information
activities, 210, 213
Covert operations:
JCS's assessments, 83
NSC *10/2*, 171
NSC *10/5*, 171
NSC *5412*, 171
NSC *5412/1*, 212
NSC *5412/2*, 250
Electronic intelligence, 230
European migrants, 127
NSC Intelligence Directive *9*, 257
Psychological warfare planning, 28,
124, 125, 129, 135
Soviet Union's capability to injure the
U.S., evaluating the, 173
State Department-Defense
Department study on
intelligence, 20, 22
Taiwan and China, conflict between,
106
Technological Capabilities Panel, 223
Watch Committee, IAC, 107
DeFlorez, Adm. Luis, 122
DeLoach, C.D., 35
Devine, John E., 94, 100
Dill, Bruce, 244
Director of Central Intelligence
Directives (DCID). *See under*
Central Intelligence Agency.
Disclosure of classified military
information, 256
Dodge, Joseph M., 174, 210
Doolittle, Gen. James H., 184, 185, 192,
193, 205, 247
Doolittle Report, 184, 185, 188, 192, 193,
205
Drain, Richard D., 115, 172, 175
DuBridge, L.A., 122
Duff, Gen. Robinson E., 136
Dulles, Allen W., 100, 160, 166, 196, 215,
216, 243
Aerial/photo reconnaissance, 164,
197, 198
Air Resupply and Communications
Wing program, 147

Dulles, Allen W.—*Continued*
Aliens into U.S. for intelligence/
operational purposes, 206
Appointment as director of Central
Intelligence Agency, 145
Board of Consultants on Foreign
Intelligence Activities, 247
Bull, communications with, 177
Bureau of the Budget's study for
coordinating economic/
psychological/political warfare
and foreign information
activities, 210
CIA changes made at request of NSC,
110
Commission on the Organization of
the Executive Branch of the
Government, 220, 221, 236, 241
Comprehensive National Intelligence
Objectives, 200
Covert operations, 43, 205
Crusade for Freedom, 94
Defense Department-CIA relations,
165
Director of Central Intelligence
Directive *4/5*, 238
Economic intelligence requirements
relating to national security, 191
Eisenhower-Doolittle meetings, 193
Europe (Eastern), 167, 174
Foreign persons/materials into the
U.S., 214
JCS–CIA relations, 176
Missiles, guided, 225, 245
Net intelligence estimates of the
capabilities/intentions of other
nations, 150
NSC Intelligence Directive *5*, 168
NSC Papers:
NSC *10/2*, 162
NSC *10/5*, 162
Office of Policy Coordination and
Office of Special Operations,
merging the, 50
Priority National Intelligence
Objectives, 201, 238
Project Grayback, 241
Psychochemicals, 244
Psychological warfare planning, 67,
78
Radio Free Europe, 94
Soviet Union, 149, 161, 172
State Department intelligence,
assessments of, 228

Dulles, Allen W.—*Continued*
Superpower competition, 195
Taiwan and China, conflict between,
106
Technological Capabilities Panel, 223
Voice of America, 94
Warning facilities of the intelligence
community,
information/recommendations
concerning, 187
Watch Committee, IAC, 175
Dulles, John F.:
Aerial/photo reconnaissance, 199,
240, 242, 249
Coordination of economic/
psychological/political warfare
and foreign information
activities, 227
Covert operations, 212
Project Grayback, 240, 242, 249
Rockefeller and, relations between, 232

East, Near/Far (*see also* Asia, Southeast;
Middle East), 68, 92
Easton, John, 172
ECA. *See* Economic Cooperation
Administration.
Economic Cooperation Administration
(ECA), 28, 31
Economic Defense Advisory
Committee, 116
Economic Intelligence Committee:
Collection (intelligence) requirements,
coordination of, 202
Director of Central Intelligence
Directive 15/1, 169, 191
Foreign Information Program, 155
NSC 5509, 209
Smith's (Walter B.) assessments, 107
Terms of reference for, 72
Economic intelligence relating to
national security:
Collection (intelligence) requirements,
coordination of, 202
Commission on the Organization of
the Executive Branch of the
Government, 220
Coordination of economic/
psychological/political warfare
and foreign information
activities, 210, 213, 248, 254
Director of Central Intelligence
Directive 15/1, 169, 191
Europe (Eastern), 144

Economic intelligence relating to
national security—*Continued*
Foreign Information Program, 146,
155
Jackson's (William H.) assessments,
73
NSC Action 1183, 187
NSC Intelligence Directive 15, 254
NSC Papers:
NSC 142, 146
NSC 161, 155
NSC 5509, 209
Psychological Operations
Coordinating Committee, 92
Soviet Union, 144, 169, 191
Ecuador, 153
Eden, Anthony, 229, 242
Edwards, Gen. Idwal H., 149, 173,
189
Edwards Report, 149
Efteland, Robert G., 82
Eisenhower, Dwight D.:
Aerial/photo reconnaissance, 197,
198, 199, 229, 240, 242, 249
Board of Consultants on Foreign
Intelligence Activities, 247
Cold War, 163
Commission on the Organization of
the Executive Branch of the
Government, 184, 185, 220, 221,
239, 251
Communist movement in the U.S.,
214
Coordination of economic/
psychological/political warfare
and foreign information
activities, 210, 213, 248
Covert operations, 171
Doolittle, meetings with, 193
Doolittle Report, 184, 185, 193, 205
Dulles (John F.)-Rockefeller relations,
232
Economic intelligence relating to
national security, 187
Europe (Eastern), 174
Executive Orders:
10450, 251
10483, 157, 158, 171, 208, 248, 250
10598, 208
10700, 248
Foreign persons/materials into the
U.S., 214
International Information Activities
Committee, 151, 153, 173, 189

Eisenhower, Dwight D.—*Continued*
  Net Evaluation Subcommittee, 207
  NSC Papers:
    NSC 59/1, 2, 187
    NSC 127/1, 2, 187
  Operations Coordinating Board, 157,
    158, 183, 208, 210
  Planning Coordination Group, 246
  Project Grayback, 242, 249
  Psychological warfare planning, 2,
    187
  Quantico Panel I/II, 224
  Soviet Union's capability to injure the
    U.S., evaluating the, 207
  Taiwan and China, conflict between,
    211
  Technological Capabilities Panel, 223
  Warning facilities of the intelligence
    community, information/
    recommendations concerning,
    187
  Watch Committee, IAC, 218
Electronic intelligence (ELINT):
  Commission on the Organization of
    the Executive Branch of the
    Government, 251
  Communications Intelligence Board,
    U.S., 259
  Defense Department's assessments,
    230
  NSCID 17, 259
  NSC 5509, 209
  Search operations, special electronic
    airborne, 6
Erskine, Gen. Graves, 152, 164, 165,
  215
Espe, Adm. Carl F., 197, 225, 245
Europe (Eastern):
  Collection (intelligence) requirements,
    coordination of, 202
  Commission on the Organization of
    the Executive Branch of the
    Government, 220, 221, 251
  Covert operations, 68
  Defectors, using/exploiting, 252, 253
  Director of Central Intelligence
    Directives:
    DCID 4/4, 201
    DCID 4/5, 238
  Doolittle Report, 192
  Economic intelligence relating to
    national security, 144, 191
  Explosives/demolition materials,
    OCB and the stockpiling of, 167

Europe (Eastern)—*Continued*
  Foreign Information Program, 146,
    155
  Foreign persons/materials into the
    U.S., 214
  Free Europe Committee, 188
  Joyce's assessments, 142
  National Committee for Free Europe,
    15, 26, 94, 100
  NSC Intelligence Directives:
    NSCID 13, 252
    NSCID 14, 253
  NSC Papers:
    NSC 174, 190
    NSC 5509, 209
  Office of Research and Intelligence,
    226
  Provisional Committee for the
    Movement of Migrants from
    Europe, 127
  Psychological warfare planning, 127,
    142, 143, 153
  Quantico Panel I/II, 224
  Radio Free Europe, 15, 68, 94, 100,
    125, 188
  Satellites, developing/using, 203
  Search operations, special electronic
    airborne, 6
  Security, NSC's status report on
    national, 127
  Smith's (Walter B.) assessments, 71
  State Department personnel/funding,
    Dulles's (Allen W.) request for
    increase in, 228
  Surveillance of Soviet Bloc diplomatic
    representatives, 174
  Troy Report, 59
  Uprisings in, policy guidelines for
    CIA Planning to capitalize on,
    167
  Volunteer Freedom Corps, 148
  Warning facilities of the intelligence
    community, information/
    recommendations concerning,
    186
  War plans, CIA/OPC strategic, 61
Europe (Western):
  Covert operations, 68
  Foreign Information Program, 146,
    155
  National Committee for Free Europe,
    15, 26, 94, 100
  Psychological warfare planning, 125,
    133, 153

Europe (Western)—*Continued*
Security, NSC's status report on
national, 127
Troy Report, 59
War plans, CIA/OPC strategic, 61
European Defense Community (EDC),
178
Evans, Allan, 35, 175
Executive Orders:
10450, 251
10483, 157, 158, 208, 248, 250
10598, 208
10700, 248
Export of strategic materials, authority
to control the, 79
External Research Division of the Office
of Research and Intelligence, 226

Facilities Protection Board, 79
Fairless, Benjamin, 247
False Witness (Matusow), 214
FBI. *See* Federal Bureau of
Investigation.
Fechteler, Adm. William M., 106
Federal Bureau of Investigation (FBI)
(*see also* Hoover, J. Edgar):
Commission on the Organization of
the Executive Branch of the
Government, 220, 221, 251
Defectors, using/exploiting, 253
Europe (Eastern), 174
NSC–FBI relations, 256
NSC Intelligence Directives:
NSCID *1*, 256
NSCID *14*, 253
Watch Committee, IAC, 91, 218
Federal Civil Defense Administration
(FCDA), 131, 172, 173, 207
Federal Communication Commission
(FCC), 79
Fenili, Vasco J., 172, 175, 225
Ferguson, John H., 96, 106
Finan, William F., 78
Fitzpatrick, Dick, 226
Fleming, Arthur S., 173
Flickinger, Don D., 244
Ford, Harold, 115
Foreign Broadcast Information Division
(FBID), 202
Foreign Information Program
(*see also* Psychological warfare
planning):
Aerial reconnaissance, 146, 155
Africa, 155

Foreign Information Program—
Continued
Armed forces intelligence, 146
Asia, Southeast, 155
Biographic information, 146, 155
China, Communist, 146, 155
Collection, 146, 155
Communism, world, 155
Coordination of economic/
psychological/political warfare
and foreign information
activities, 146, 155, 210, 213
Domestic collection, 146, 155
Economic intelligence, 146, 155
Europe (Eastern), 146, 155
Europe (Western), 146, 155
Foreign language publications, 155
Foreign Service, 155
Geographic intelligence, 146, 155
Industrialization information, 155
Japan, 155
Joint Chiefs of Staff, 146
Korean War, 155
Latin America, 155
Library facilities, 146, 155
Map procurement and reference
service, 155
Materials/equipment, foreign, 146
National Intelligence Estimates, 146,
155
National Intelligence Surveys, 146, 155
National Security Council's
assessments, 2, 128
North Atlantic Treaty Organization,
146, 155
NSC Papers:
NSC *161*, 155
NSC *5509*, 209
Operations Coordinating Board
taking over functions of, 183
Order of battle intelligence and
equipment, 155
Overseas commands, 146, 155
Photographs and motion picture
films, 146, 155
Political/social/cultural intelligence,
146, 155
Radio, 146, 155
Scientific/technical intelligence, 146,
155
Service Attaché System, 146, 155
Soviet Union, 146, 155
Support and collation facilities, 146,
155

Foreign Information Program—
Continued
Targeting, 146, 155
Travel folder program, 155
Watch Committee, IAC, 155
Foreign Operations Administration,
210
Foreign persons/materials into the U.S.,
206, 214
Foreign Service, 155, 159, 209
Formosa. See Taiwan.
Fosdick, Dorothy, 96
Foster, William C., 31, 137
France, 100, 125, 127, 153
Franke, William B., 185, 192, 205
Free Europe Committee (FEC), 188
Furnas, Howard, 225

Gaither, Gen. Ridgely, 245
Gardner, Trevor, 196, 249
General Services Administration (GSA),
79
General Walter Bedell Smith as Director of
Central Intelligence (Montague), 23,
29, 63, 257
Geographic intelligence, 146, 155
Germany (East), 92, 127, 153, 190
Germany (West), 92, 127, 153, 190, 229,
234, 242
Gibbons, Willis A., 122
Gillis, Charles F., 115, 172
Gleason, S. Everett, 76, 131, 207, 234
Godel, William H., 160
Goodpaster, Andrew, 199, 241, 249
Gray, Gordon, 78, 82, 85
Great Britain, 84, 100, 124, 145, 153, 229,
242, 249
Greece, 127, 139, 153, 190
Greene, L. Wilson, 244
Greenstein, J.L., 122
Guatemala, 154, 209
Guthe, Otto, 217, 225
Guzman, Jacobo A., 154

Hadley, Morris, 185, 192, 247
Hanes, John W., Jr., 229
Harriman, W. Averell, 31, 144
Harvey, Mose L., 115
Healey, Lawrence, 175, 225
Helms, Richard, 50, 103, 167, 205
Henderson, Loy, 210, 236
Henderson, Malcolm C., 29, 115
Hillenkoetter, Adm. Roscoe, 10, 11
Communications intelligence, 19

Hillenkoetter, Adm. Roscoe—Continued
Defector Committee, Interagency, 18
Intelligence objectives, priority list of
critical national, 25
Office of Special Projects, 4
State Department-Defense
Department Staff Study on
intelligence, 20, 22
Hong Kong Press Monitoring Service,
202
Hooker, Robert J., 110
Hoover, E.M., 189
Hoover, Herbert, 184, 185, 220, 221
Hoover, Herbert, Jr.:
Bureau of the Budget's study for
coordinating economic/
psychological/political warfare
and foreign information
activities, 210
Doolittle Report, 188
Foreign persons/materials into the
U.S., 214
Planning Coordination Group, 237,
246
Watch Committee, IAC, 218
Hoover, J. Edgar, 115
Communications intelligence, 141, 257
Communist movement in the U.S., 214
Emergency situation, action plan for,
16
Interdepartmental Intelligence
Committee, 65, 66
NSCID 9, 257
Hoover Commission. See Commission on
the Organization of the Executive
Branch of the Government.
Hopkins, Armand, 82
Horsey, Outerbridge, 145
Houston, Lawrence, 23, 168
Howe, Fisher, 13, 29, 39, 118, 145, 184,
236, 249
Howze, Hamilton, 29
Hughes, John, 94
Hughes, Rowland R., 210, 235, 239
Hulick, Charles E., Jr., 26, 188
Hull, Gen. John E., 106, 247
Humelsine, Carlisle, H., 7, 13, 24, 30,
34, 45, 47
Hungary, 190

IAC. See Intelligence Advisory
Committee.
Immigration and Naturalization
Service, 79, 206

Indochina, 92
Industrial information/security, 79, 155
Industry Evaluation Board, 79
Intelligence Advisory Committee (IAC)
    (see also Commission on the
    Organization of the Executive
    Branch of the Government):
  CIA, problems facing the, 23
  Collection (intelligence) requirements,
    coordination of, 202
  Communications intelligence, 19
  Defectors, using/exploiting, 202, 218,
    252, 253
  Director of Central Intelligence
    Directive 4/5, 238
  Duties and responsibilities, 256
  Economic Intelligence Committee, 72,
    155, 169, 191, 202
  Economic intelligence relating to
    national security, 144
  Europe (Eastern), 144
  Foreign Service, 159
  Interagency Defector Committee, 18
  Interdepartmental Committee on
    Internal Security, 79
  Meetings:
    October 20, 1950, 29
    December 7, 1950, 35
    June 5, 1952, 115
    March 16, 1954, 172
    May 4, 1954, 175
    December 20, 1954, 202
    June 14, 1955, 225
  Missiles, guided, 225, 245
  National Indications Committee/
    Center, 186, 211, 234
  National Intelligence Estimates, 29, 155
  National Security Act of 1947, 29
  NSC Intelligence Directives:
    NSCID 1, 256
    NSCID 13, 252
    NSCID 14, 253
  NSC Paper 5525, 234
  Policies and procedures, 29
  Political/social/cultural intelligence,
    155
  Priority National Intelligence
    Objectives, 209
  Scientific/technical intelligence, 126
  Security, NSC's status report on
    national, 234
  Security of the United States, project
    to provide a more adequate basis
    for planning the, 80

Intelligence Advisory Committee
    (IAC)—Continued
  SNIE 11–8–54, 209
  Soviet Union (see also Watch
    Committee, IAC under Soviet
    Union), 80, 115, 131, 172
  State Department-CIA relations, 24
  Warning facilities of the intelligence
    community, information/
    recommendations concerning,
    186, 187, 209
Intelligence Communications and
    Electronics Subcommittee (ICES),
    251
Intelligence Estimates. See National
    Intelligence Estimates; Special
    National Intelligence Estimates.
Intelligence Working Group (IWG),
    144
Interagency Defector Committee, 18
Interdepartmental Committee on
    Internal Security (ICIS):
  NSC Meeting, May 5, 1955, 214
  NSC Paper 5511, 207
  Psychological Operations
    Coordinating Committee, 74
  Psychological Strategy Board, 74
  Security of the United States, project
    to provide a more adequate basis
    for planning the, 79, 80, 86
  Soviet Union's capability to injure the
    U.S., evaluating the, 80, 131, 137,
    138, 173, 207
Interdepartmental Coordinating Staff
    (ICS), 213
Interdepartmental Economic
    Intelligence Committee, 107
Interdepartmental Foreign Information
    Organization (IFIO), 57, 92, 213
Interdepartmental Foreign Information
    Staff (IFIS), 28, 213
Interdepartmental Intelligence
    Committee (IIC):
  Hoover's (J. Edgar) assessments, 65,
    66
  NSC Action 543, 86
  NSC Meeting, May 5, 1955, 214
  Smith's (Walter B.) assessments, 65,
    66
  Soviet Union's capability to injure the
    U.S., evaluating the, 131, 137,
    138, 173, 207
International Broadcasting Division
    (IBD), 94

International Information Activities
  Committee, 151, 153, 173, 189
International Information
  Administration (IIA), 226
International Information and
  Educational Exchange, 69
Iran, 143, 153, 209
Italy, 125, 127, 139, 153

Jackson, C.D., 158, 160, 161, 248
Jackson, William H., 35, 85, 88, 99,
  142
  Bureau of the Budget's study for
    coordinating economic/
    psychological/political warfare
    and foreign information
    activities, 210
  CIA changes made at request of NSC,
    110
  Covert operations, 68
  Crusade for Freedom, 100
  Defense Department-CIA relations, 34
  ECA–CIA relations, 31
  Economic intelligence relating to
    national security, 73
  Guerrilla warfare, 42
  Intelligence Advisory Committee,
    policies and procedures of the,
    29
  National Intelligence Estimates, 29
  Office of Special Operations, 87
  State Department-CIA relations, 46
  Voice of America, 44
Japan, 249
  Civil Air Transport's application for
    commercial rights in Okinawa,
    101
  Emergency assistance, 153
  Foreign Information Program, 155
  Kaji case, 145
  Psychological warfare planning:
    NSC Paper 135, 127
    Progress report (PSB) as of August
      1, 1952, 125
    Progress report (PSB) as of January
      5, 1953, 143
    Progress report (PSB) as of July 29,
      1953, 153
  Psychological Operations
    Coordinating Committee, 124
JCS. See Joint Chiefs of Staff.
Jessup, Phillip, 30
Johnson, Alexis, 101
Johnson, Charles E., 24, 82, 153

Johnson, Clarence K., 196
Johnson, Adm. Felix L., 29, 35, 113, 115
Johnson, Louis, 1, 6, 213
Johnston, Kilbourne, 93
Johnston, S. Paul, 185
Joint Atomic Energy Intelligence
  Committee (JAEIC), 126, 149, 225,
  251
Joint Chiefs of Staff (JCS) (see also
  Bradley, Gen. Omar N.):
  Aerial/photo reconnaissance, 202,
    240
  Air Resupply and Communications
    Wing program, 147
  Armed Forces Security Agency, 21, 40
  Central Intelligence Agency:
    Defense Department-CIA relations,
      64
    JCS–CIA relations, 77, 176, 220, 256
    Problems facing the, 23
  Collection (intelligence) requirements,
    coordination of, 202
  Commission on the Organization of
    the Executive Branch of the
    Government, 220, 221, 251
  Communications intelligence, 99, 132
  Coordination of economic/
    psychological/political warfare
    and foreign information
    activities, 213
  Covert operations:
    Joint Subsidiary Plans Division, 93
    Joyce's assessments, 43
    NSC Intelligence Directive 5, 255
    NSC 10/3, 43
    NSC 5412, 171
    NSC 5412/2, 250
    Scope and pace of, 83, 85, 111
    Support bases, overseas CIA
      logistical, 140
    Wartime needs, conversion of
      peacetime to, 61
  Foreign Information Program, 146
  Guerrilla warfare, 75
  Joint Intelligence Committee-JCS
    relations, 95
  Middle East, 105
  Net intelligence estimates of the
    capabilities/intentions of other
    nations, 189
  NSC Intelligence Directives:
    NSCID 1, 256
    NSCID 5, 255
    NSC–JCS relations, 255

Joint Chiefs of Staff (JCS)—*Continued*
    NSC 10/2, 111
    Office of Policy Coordination's war
        plan, approval of, 111
    Office of Special Projects, 4
    Project Grayback, 240
    Psychological warfare planning:
        Psychological Operations
            Coordinating Committee, 124
        Psychological Strategy Board, 28,
            78, 129, 135
        Smith's (Walter B.)
            recommendations to
            consolidate/strengthen the
            PSB, 129, 135
    Search operations, special electronic
        airborne, 6
    Security of the United States, project
        to provide a more adequate basis
        for planning the, 80, 131, 138
    Soviet Union:
        Capability to injure the U.S., 80,
            131, 137, 138, 149, 173, 189, 207
        CIA's assessments, 173
        Kennan's assessments, 118
        Weakening the power/will to wage
            cold/hot war, 83
    Taiwan and China, conflict between,
        106
    Warning facilities of the intelligence
        community, information/
        recommendations concerning,
        186, 189
    Watch Committee, IAC, 91, 186
Joint Intelligence Committee (JIC), 95,
    115, 172
Joint Intelligence Indications
    Committee (JIIC), 91
Joint Press Reading Service (JPRS), 202
Joint Subsidiary Plans Division (JSPD),
    93
Joint Technical Intelligence
    Subcommittee (JTIS), 202, 217
Joyce, Robert P., 7, 38, 52, 70, 75, 85,
    100, 104, 108
    Central Intelligence Agency:
        Changes made at request of NSC,
            110
        Matthews, communications with,
            145
        OPC–CIA relations, 130
    Cold War, 142
    Covert operations:
        Europe (Eastern), 142

Joyce, Robert P.—*Continued*
    Covert operations—*Continued*
        NSC 10/3, 43
        Scope and pace of, 43, 111, 145
        Poland, U.S. spies captured in, 142
    Psychological warfare planning:
        Assessments of, 142
        Europe (Eastern), 142
        Psychological Strategy Board, 129,
            135
        Smith's (Walter B.)
            recommendations to
            consolidate/strengthen the
            PSB, 129, 135
    Radio Free Europe, 94
    Voice of America, 94
Justice Department, U.S., 210

Kahn, Albert, 214
Kaji, Waturu, 145
Kearns, Henry, 220
Keay, Victor P., 35, 172
Kennan, George F., 4, 15, 118, 129
Kennedy, John R., 41
Kennedy, Joseph W., 194, 198
Kent, Sherman, 115, 120, 172, 225
Khokhlov, Nikolai, 209
Killian, James, 198, 247, 249
Kirk, Alan G., 129, 133
Kirkpatrick, Lyman, 35, 50, 87, 88, 95,
    205
Koch, Henry, 96
Kohler, Foy D., 94, 100
Kolb, Roland L., 172
Korean War:
    Air America, 15
    Armistice negotiations, 127
    CIA devoting massive efforts to, 12
    Coordination of economic/
        psychological/political warfare
        and foreign information
        activities, 213
    Covert operations to wartime needs,
        conversion of peacetime, 61
    Foreign Information Program, 155
    NSC Intelligence Directive 5, 168
    Psychological warfare planning:
        Interdepartmental Foreign
            Information Organization, 57
        Office of Policy Coordination, 26
        Prisoners, forcible repatriation of,
            143
        Progress report (PSB) as of August
            1, 1952, 125

Korean War—*Continued*
  Psychological warfare planning—
    Continued
    Progress report (PSB) as of October
      30, *1952*, 133
    Progress report (PSB) as of January
      5, *1953*, 143
    Progress report (PSB) as of July *29,*
      1953, 153
    Progress report (State Department)
      as of October *17, 1950*, 28
    Progress report (State Department)
      as of November *8, 1951*, 92
    Progress report (State Department)
      as of July *31, 1952*, 124
    Psychological Operations
      Coordinating Committee, 124
    Psychological Strategy Board, 127
    Security, NSC's status report on
      national, 127
Krentz, Kenneth C., 129, 130
Kretzman, Roger, 94
Kuhrtz, Meffert, 29, 175, 225
Kuwait, 105
Kyes, Roger M., 152, 164, 165, 166

Labor Department, U.S., 79
Ladue, L.K., 40
Lage, W.J., 225
Lalor, Capt. W.G., 6, 40
Land, Edwin H., 194, 198, 249
Lane, Herman O., 220
Langer, William L., 35
Lansing, Samuel M., 115, 172, 175
Latin America:
  Covert operations, 68
  Psychological warfare planning:
    NSC 10/2, 127
    Progress report (PSB) as of August
      1, *1952*, 125
    Progress report (PSB) as of January
      5, *1953*, 143
    Progress report (PSB) as of July *29,*
      1953, 153
    Security, NSC's status report on
      national, 127
Lauritsen, C.C., 122
Lawton, Fred, 47, 119
Lay, James S., Jr., 2, 16, 19
  Buying, organized/coordinated
    program of covert preclusive, 116
  Commission on the Organization of
    the Executive Branch of the
    Government, 251

Lay, James S., Jr.—*Continued*
  Communications intelligence, 97, 141,
    257
  Coordination of economic/
    psychological/political warfare
    and foreign information
    activities, 213, 248
  Covert operations:
    Buying, preclusive, 116
    NSC Action No. 400, 38
    NSCID 5, 255
    NSC 10/2, 38
    NSC 10/3, 43
    NSC 5412, 171
    Scope and pace of, 68, 85, 89, 90
  Defense Department-CIA relations,
    204
  Economic intelligence relating to
    national security, 73
  Guerrilla warfare, 42
  Middle East, 105
  NSC Intelligence Directives:
    NSCID 5, 255
    NSCID 9, 257
  NSC Papers:
    NSC 10/3, 63
    NSC 10/4, 63
    NSC 10/5, 90, 162
    NSC 59/1, 183
    NSC 127/1, 183
    NSC 135, 127
  Operations Coordinating Board, 158
  Planning Coordination Group, 246
  Psychological warfare planning:
    Key Data Book, 134
    Progress report (PSB) as of October
      30, *1952*, 133
    Progress report (PSB) as of July *29,*
      1953, 153
    Progress report (State Department)
      as of October *17, 1950*, 28
    Progress report (State Department)
      as of March *19, 1951*, 57
    Progress report (State Department)
      as of November *8, 1951*, 92
    Smith's (Walter B.)
      recommendations to
      consolidate/strengthen the
      PSB, 135
  Security, NSC's status report on
    national, 127
  Security of the United States, project
    to provide a more adequate basis
    for planning the, 131

Lay, James S., Jr.—*Continued*
  Soviet Union's capability to injure the
    U.S., evaluating the, 131, 138
  Warning facilities of the intelligence
    community, information/
    recommendations concerning,
    186, 187
Layton, Adm. Edwin T., 175, 176, 197,
  225, 245
Leary, John E., 225
Legislation (*see also* National Security
  Act of 1947):
  Central Intelligence Act of 1949, 220,
    221, 251
  Executive Pay Bill of 1949, 221, 251
  Immigration and Nationality Act,
    206
Library facilities, 69, 146, 155, 221, 226,
  251
Lloyd, Gates, 50, 94, 100
Lockheed Aircraft Corporation, 194,
  196
Loomis, Henry, 226
Lovett, Robert:
  Communications intelligence, 136
  Covert operations, 4
  NSC Papers:
    NSC 10/3, 63
    NSC 10/4, 63
  Office of Policy Coordination, 129
  Psychological warfare planning, 47,
    78, 82
  Taiwan and China, conflict between,
    98
LSD (lysergic acid diethylamide), 244
Lydman, J.W., 172
Lysergic acid diethylamide (LSD), 244

MacArthur, Gen. Douglas, 28
MacArthur, Douglas, II, 241
Magruder, Gen. John, 1, 22, 26, 38, 43,
  82, 85, 99, 104, 108
  Covert operations, 70
  Guerrilla warfare, 75
  Poland, U.S. spies captured in, 142
  Psychological warfare planning, 78,
    129, 142
Mails used as an access point to Soviet
  Union, 59
Makins, Roger, 242
Malpass, Ray E., 172, 175
Manchuria, 155
Manfull, Melvin L., 48
Maples, H.N., 115, 175

Maps, procurement of foreign-
  published, 155, 202, 209, 221, 251
Marchant, J.C., 35
Maritime sources for intelligence
  purposes, exploitation of, 113
Marrazzi, Amendeo, 244
Marshall, Gen. George C., 4
  CIA-Defense Department relations,
    36, 64
  CIA–JCS relations, 77
  Covert operations, 83, 129
  Intelligence, analysis of U.S., 32
  Security of the United States, project
    to provide a more adequate basis
    for planning the, 80
Martin, James G., 172
Massachusetts Institute of Technology,
  57, 92
Matthews, H. Freeman, 30, 52, 104, 118,
  142, 145
Matusow, Harvey, 214
McCool, Capt. R.G., 29, 35
McFadden, William, 111, 130, 145
McKee, Samuel, Jr., 35
Media research/analysis and Office of
  Research and Intelligence, 226
Megee, Gen. Vernon E., 29
Metcalf, Ralph, 225
Middle East, 61
  CIA's assessments, 127
  NSC Paper 135, 127
  Oil issues, 61, 105
  Psychological warfare planning:
    Progress report (PSB) as of August
      1, 1952, 125
    Progress report (PSB) as of October
      30, 1952, 133
    Progress report (PSB) as of January
      5, 1953, 143
    Progress report (State Department)
      as of November 8, 1951, 92
  Security, NSC's status report on
    national, 127
Military attaché system, 202, 209, 214,
  221
Missiles, guided, 209, 225, 245
Montague, Ludwell, 23, 27, 29, 35, 115,
  175
Montgomery, J.H., 225
Moore, Gen. Ernest B., 29, 35
Morgan, George A., 160, 161, 183
Morrow, John J., 172, 175
Motion picture films, 69, 155
Muccio, John J., 28

Murphy, Robert, 241
Mutual Security Agency, 125
Mutual Trade Security Advisory
    Committee, 116

Nash, Frank C., 68, 70, 85, 106
National Committee for a Free Europe
    (NCFE), 15, 26, 94, 100
National Cryptographic Security Board,
    121
National Indications Committee/Center
    (NIC), 186, 211, 234
National Intelligence Authority (NIA),
    221
National Intelligence Estimates (NIE):
    Barnard's assessments, 37
    Commission on the Organization of
        the Executive Branch of the
        Government, 251
    Foreign Information Program, 155
    Intelligence Advisory Committee,
        29
    NIE:
        10–7–54, 209
        11–3–54, 209
        11–4–54, 209
        11–6–54, 209
        11–7A–54, 209
        12–5–54, 209
        27, 189
        59, 144
        64, 155
        65, 115, 155
    NSC 5509, 209
    Operational assumptions and facts,
        distinguishing between, 189
    Soviet Union's capability to injure the
        U.S., evaluating the, 209
    Technological Capabilities Panel, 223
National Intelligence Surveys (NIS), 41,
    146, 155
National Psychological Strategy, 26, 96
National Security Act of 1947:
    Collective responsibility, doctrine of,
        20
    Commission on the Organization of
        the Executive Branch of the
        Government, 220, 221
    Communications intelligence, 97, 257
    Coordination of economic/
        psychological/political warfare
        and foreign information
        activities, 254
    Covert operations, 38, 43, 171

National Security Act of 1947—Continued
    Defectors, using/exploiting, 252, 253
    Duties and responsibilities of
        National Security Council, 256
    Electronic intelligence, 259
    Espionage and counterespionage
        operations, 255
    Intelligence Advisory Committee, 29,
        155
    JCS–CIA relations, 77
    National Security Organization, 220
    NSCID 15, 254
    NSC Papers:
        NSC 5412/1, 212
        NSC 5412/2, 250
    Publication procurement, foreign, 258
National Security Agency (NSA):
    Collection (intelligence) requirements,
        coordination of, 202
    Commission on the Organization of
        the Executive Branch of the
        Government, 220, 221, 251
    Communications intelligence, 132,
        136, 141, 257
    NSCID 9, 257
National Security Council (NSC) (see
        also Intelligence Advisory
        Committee; Operations
        Coordinating Board):
    Actions:
        No. 282, 73
        No. 283, 2
        No. 367, 84
        No. 400, 38
        No. 519, 86
        No. 534, 256
        No. 543, 86, 131, 137, 138
        No. 623, 256
        No. 687, 138
        No. 873, 189
        No. 873-d, 173
        No. 1183, 187, 210
        No. 1195, 187
        No. 1195-b, 187
        No. 1197, 187, 210, 213
        No. 1198, 213
        No. 1260, 207
        No. 1314-d, 210, 246
        No. 1349, 210, 246
    Aerial/photo reconnaissance, 209
    Agricultural reporting, 209
    Air Force (U.S.)-NSC relations, 256
    Air target materials in the Air
        Objective Folder Program, 209

National Security Council (NSC)—
Continued
Army (U.S.)-NSC relations, 256
Atomic energy/war/weapons, 209
Biological warfare, 209
Buying, organized/coordinated
program of covert preclusive, 116
Central Intelligence Agency:
Budget issues, 30
CIA changes made at request of
NSC, 107, 110
NSC–CIA relations, 8, 107, 110,
255
Classified government information,
clearance for access to, 79
Collection (intelligence) requirements,
coordination of, 234
Commission on the Organization of
the Executive Branch of the
Government, 220, 221, 234, 251
Communications intelligence, 19, 132,
136, 257
Communist movement in the U.S., 214
Coordination of economic/
psychological/political warfare
and foreign information
activities, 210, 213, 254
Covert operations (*see also*
Psychological warfare planning
below):
Doolittle Report, 192
NSCID 5, 255
NSC 10/2, 38, 162, 171
NSC 10/3, 24, 43, 171
NSC 10/5, 162, 171
NSC 5412, 171
NSC 5412/1, 212
NSC 5412/2, 171, 250
Office of Policy Coordination, 8
Office of Special Projects, 4
Planning Coordination Group,
212
Scope and pace of, 68, 70, 71, 75,
76, 83, 85, 89, 90, 108
Soviet Union and its satellites, 5
Defectors, using/exploiting, 209, 252,
253
Domestic collection, 209
Duties and responsibilities, 256
Economic intelligence relating to
national security, 73, 144, 187,
209
Edwards Report, 149
Electronic intelligence, 259

National Security Council (NSC)—
Continued
Europe (Eastern), 144, 174
FBI–NSC relations, 256
Foreign Information Program, 2,
128
Foreign persons/materials into the
U.S., 214
Foreign Service, 209
Guerrilla warfare, 42
Intelligence Directives:
NSCID 1, 155, 169, 179, 191, 245, 256
NSCID 2, 202
NSCID 3, 169, 191, 256
NSCID 4, 201, 209, 238
NSCID 4/2, 201
NSCID 5, 38, 43, 64, 77, 95, 132,
145, 168, 185, 192, 202, 204,
205, 251, 255, 257
NSCID 5/8, 251
NSCID 6, 202
NSCID 7, 202, 253
NSCID 9, 44, 132, 136, 141, 152, 257
NSCID 10, 112, 251
NSCID 10/2, 212, 250
NSCID 10/5, 212, 250
NSCID 11/1, 202
NSCID 13, 18, 192, 251, 252
NSCID 14, 18, 253
NSCID 15, 73, 169, 191, 254
NSCID 16, 155, 258
NSCID 17, 230, 251, 259
Interdepartmental Committee on
Internal Security, 79
JCS–NSC relations, 256
Maps, procurement of foreign-
published, 209
Materials/equipment, collecting
foreign, 209
Meetings:
June *18, 1948*, 4
June *13, 1951*, 254
May *20, 1953*, 148
May *27, 1953*, 149
March *4, 1954*, 170
March *11, 1954*, 170
March *25, 1954*, 170
July *22, 1954*, 210
August *5, 1954*, 187, 210
January *27, 1955*, 210
March *10, 1955*, 210
May *5, 1955*, 214
Middle East, 105
Military attaché system, 209

National Security Council (NSC)—
  Continued
  Missiles, guided, 209
  National Security Act of 1947, 38, 43
  Net Capabilities Evaluation
    Subcommittee, 182, 207
  OCB–NSC relations, 160
  Office of Research and Intelligence, 226
  Papers:
    NSC 4, 52
    NSC 10/2, 8, 29, 33, 38, 42, 43, 52,
      64, 68, 76, 77, 81, 83, 96, 104,
      108, 111, 140, 145, 152, 158,
      162, 171
    NSC 10/3, 24, 42, 43, 63, 81, 171
    NSC 10/4, 63
    NSC 10/5, 90, 104, 107, 108, 129,
      135, 139, 152, 158, 162, 171
    NSC 17, 158
    NSC 20/4, 125, 139, 213
    NSC 26/2, 84, 105
    NSC 26/4, 105
    NSC 26/5, 105
    NSC 43, 52, 213
    NSC 48/5, 76, 90, 106
    NSC 50, 8, 20, 29, 37, 107, 110, 145,
      253
    NSC 59, 49, 52
    NSC 59/1, 2, 28, 57, 81, 92, 96, 109,
      124, 139, 152, 158, 183, 187,
      213
    NSC 66/1, 44, 107, 146, 155
    NSC 68, 5, 8, 68, 101, 108
    NSC 74, 17, 49, 52, 213
    NSC 86/1, 107
    NSC 104/2, 116
    NSC 114/3, 114
    NSC 127/1, 123, 183, 187, 213
    NSC 135, 127, 128
    NSC 140, 189
    NSC 140/1, 149, 189
    NSC 142, 146, 155
    NSC 159, 173, 189
    NSC 161, 155, 170
    NSC 162/2, 163, 179, 190, 209
    NSC 165/1, 181
    NSC 169, 209
    NSC 174, 167, 190, 203, 246
    NSC 5401/1, 190
    NSC 5407, 170
    NSC 5408, 174
    NSC 5412, 171, 185, 188, 192, 210,
      250
    NSC 5412/1, 212, 237, 246, 250

National Security Council (NSC)—
  Continued
  Papers—*Continued*
    NSC 5412/2, 171, 250
    NSC 5430, 209
    NSC 5432, 182
    NSC 5438, 187, 218
    NSC 5501, 209
    NSC 5502/1, 210, 246
    NSC 5505, 210
    NSC 5505/1, 210, 246
    NSC 5509, 209, 214
    NSC 5511, 207
    NSC 5520, 219
    NSC 5525, 234
  Political intelligence, 209
  Priority National Intelligence
    Objectives, 209
  Psychological warfare planning:
    CIA's assessments, 127
    Cold War, 139
    National Psychological Warfare
      Plan for General War, 92
    NSC 10/5, 139
    NSC 135, 127
    PSB–NSC relations, 28, 78, 104
    Smith's (Walter B.)
      recommendations to
      consolidate/strengthen the
      PSB, 135
    Summary of psychological warfare
      arrangements within U.S.
      government since World War
      II, 213
    Truman's approval of, 2
  Publication procurement, foreign,
    209, 258
  Radio broadcasts, foreign, 209
  Satellites, developing/using, 219
  Scientific/technical intelligence,
    209
  Security, status reports on national:
    June 30, 1952, 127
    February 10, 1953, 146
    December 31, 1953, 170
    March 2, 1955, 209
    May 5, 1955, 214
    June 30, 1955, 234
  Security of the United States, project
    to provide a more adequate basis
    for planning the, 86, 131, 138
  Soviet Union's capability to injure the
    U.S., evaluating the, 131, 137,
    138, 173, 207, 234

National Security Council (NSC)—
Continued
State Department-Defense
Department Staff Study on
intelligence, 20, 22
Taiwan and China, conflict between,
106
Technological Capabilities Panel,
223
Travel Folder Program, 209
Voice of America, 44
Volunteer Freedom Corps, 148
Warning facilities of the intelligence
community, information/
recommendations concerning,
187, 209, 234
National Security Organization, 220
National Security Resources Board
(NSRB), 28, 213, 220
National Student Association, 15
Navy, U.S.:
Air target materials in the Air
Objective Folder Program,
209
Collection (intelligence) requirements,
coordination of, 202
Commission on the Organization of
the Executive Branch of the
Government, 220, 221, 251
Communications intelligence, 99
Cryptographic systems, 251
Disclosure of classified military
information, 255
Maritime sources for intelligence
purposes, exploitation of, 113
NSCID 1, 256
NSC-Navy relations, 256
Psychological warfare planning, 124,
213
Search operations, special electronic
airborne, 6
Target Area Analysis Radar, 209
Watch Committee, IAC, 91, 218
Netherlands, 153
Newpher, Roth, 226
NIE. See National Intelligence
Estimates.
Nitze, Paul H.:
Covert operations, 68, 70
Psychological warfare planning:
Cold War, 139
National strategic concept for
psychological action,
formulating a, 96

Nitze, Paul H.—Continued
Psychological warfare planning—
Continued
NSC Paper 10/5, 139
Psychological Strategy Board, 62,
81
Troy Report, 59
Taiwan and China, conflict between,
106
Nixon, Richard M., 214
Nobel Project, 109
Nordbeck, Theodore M., 41
North Atlantic Treaty Organization
(NATO), 109, 146, 155, 238
Norway, 229, 242
NSC. See National Security Council.

OCB. See Operations Coordinating
Board.
Ocker, Capt. John, 29, 35
Office of Defense Mobilization (ODM),
173, 189, 194, 207, 213, 248, 251
Office of National Estimates, 107
Office of Naval Intelligence (ONI), 221
Office of Policy Coordination (OPC).
See under Central Intelligence
Agency.
Office of Research and Intelligence
(IRI), 226
Office of Special Operations (OSO). See
under Central Intelligence Agency.
Office of Special Projects, 4
Office of Strategic Services (OSS), 12,
87, 213, 221
Office of the Coordinator of
Information, 221
Oil issues, 61, 105
Olom, Lou, 226
OPC. See Office of Policy Coordination
under Central Intelligence Agency.
Operations Coordinating Board (OCB):
China, Communist, 158
Collection (intelligence) requirements,
coordination of, 202
Commission on the Organization of
the Executive Branch of the
Government, 251
Coordination of economic/
psychological/political warfare
and foreign information
activities, 210, 213, 248
Doolittle Report, 192
Europe (Eastern), 167, 203
European Defense Community, 178

Operations Coordinating Board
    (OCB)—*Continued*
  Executive Order *10483*, 157, 158, 208
  Executive Order *10598*, 208
  Explosives/demolition materials, 167
  Foreign Information Program, 183
  Gray activities, principles to assure
      coordination of, 181
  Guatemala, 154
  International Information Activities
      Committee, 151
  Meetings:
    September *17, 1953*, 160
    May *5, 1954*, 178
  NSC–OCB relations, 160
  NSC Papers:
    NSC *59/1*, 183, 187
    NSC *127/1*, 183, 187
    NSC *174*, 190
    NSC *5412*, 171
    NSC *5412/2*, 250
  Planning Coordination Group:
    Abolition of, talks about the, 237
    Bureau of the Budget's study for
        coordinating economic/
        psychological/political warfare
        and foreign information
        activities, 210
    Taking over responsibilities of,
        246
  Psychological warfare planning:
    PSB's staff/resources to be used by,
        160
    Psychological Operations
        Coordinating Committee, 158,
        213
    Summary of psychological warfare
        arrangements within U.S.
        government since World War
        II, 213
  Rockefeller as chairman of,
      Eisenhower designates, 210
  Rockefeller's resignation, 235, 237
  Satellites, developing/using, 203
OSO. *See* Office of Special Operations
    under Central Intelligence Agency.

Packard, Robert F., 229
Pakistan, 153
Parrott, Thomas A., 26
Partridge, Gen. Richard C., 115
Pawley, William D., 185, 192
Pearl Harbor, surprise attack on, 221
Penn, Perry H., 172

People's Republic of China. *See* China,
    Communist.
Philbin, T.R., 96
Phillips, Joseph B., 26, 96
Phoebus, Clifford, 244
Photographs (*see also* Aerial/photo
    reconnaissance), 146, 155
Pinay, Antoine, 127
"Plan for National Psychological
    Warfare," 17
Planning Coordination Group:
  Abolition of Group, consideration of,
      235, 237, 246
  Bureau of the Budget's study for
      coordinating economic/
      psychological/political warfare
      and foreign information
      activities, 210
  CIA-Planning Coordination Group
      relations, 212, 237, 246
  NSC Paper *5412/1*, 212
  OCB taking over responsibilities of, 246
  Status Report as of December *14,
      1955*, 246
"Planning for Wartime Conduct of
    Overt Psychological Warfare," 2
Plutonium production, 155
Poland, 142, 145, 190
Political warfare (*see also* Psychological
    warfare planning), 59
Polygraph program, 205
Population growth, 59
Porter, Gen. Edward H., 115, 136, 175, 176
Port security, 79
Power, John A., 172, 225
Press monitoring, 202
Press program and Campaign of Truth,
    69
Prisoners, 92, 143, 202
Private organizations/businesses used
    by the CIA, 15
Proctor, Edward W., 225
Production Division of the Office of
    Research and Intelligence, 226
"Production of National Intelligence,"
    20, 22
Project Brain Wave, 57
Project Genetrix, 229
Project Grayback, 240, 241, 242, 249
Project Nobel, 57, 109
Project Vagabond, 57
Provisional Committee for the
    Movement of Migrants from
    Europe (PICMME), 127

PSB. *See* Psychological Strategy Board
    under Psychological warfare
    planning.
Psychochemicals, 244
Psychological Operations Coordinating
    Committee (POCC). *See under*
    Psychological warfare planning.
"Psychological Operations Newsletter,"
    109
Psychological Strategy Board (PSB). *See*
    under Psychological warfare
    planning.
Psychological warfare planning (*see also*
    Foreign Information Program;
    under Korean War *and* Operations
    Coordinating Board):
    Balloons used for propaganda, 26, 59,
        92
    Cabinet Committee, 47
    Campaign of Truth, 69
    China, Communist, 26, 59, 92, 125,
        153
    CIA's assessments, 127
    Cold War, 127, 129, 133, 139
    Coordination of economic/
        psychological/political warfare
        and foreign information
        activities, 210, 213, 248
    Covert operations, 83
    Defectors, using/exploiting, 92
    Europe (Eastern), 142
    Kennan's assessments, 4
    Key Data Book, 134
    NSC Papers:
        NSC 10/5, 139
        NSC 59/1, 2, 28, 57, 81, 92, 96, 109,
            124, 139, 152, 158, 183, 187, 213
        NSC 74, 52
        NSC 127/1, 123
        NSC 135, 127
        NSC 5509, 209
    Office of Policy Coordination, 26
    Office of Special Operations, 152
    Office space, 78
    Operations Coordinating Board
        taking over functions of, 158, 183
    Origins of, 2
    Program planning, 69
    Progress report (State Department) as
        of October 17, 1950, 28
    Progress report (State Department) as
        of March 19, 1951, 57
    Progress report (State Department) as
        of November 8, 1951, 92

Psychological warfare planning—
    Continued
    Progress report (State Department) as
        of May 7, 1952, 109
    Progress report (State Department) as
        of July 31, 1952, 124
    Psychological Operations
        Coordinating Committee:
        Bacteriological warfare, 124
        Defectors, 92
        Economic intelligence relating to
            national security, 92
        Interdepartmental Committee on
            Internal Security, 74
        Japan, 124
        North Atlantic Treaty Organization,
            109
        Operations Coordinating Board
            taking over functions of, 158,
            213
        Prisoners-of-war, 92
        Project Nobel, 109
        "Psychological Operations
            Newsletter," 109
        Security, State Department's status
            report on national, 124
        Soviet Union, 92, 109
        Television in propaganda, 109
        Training program, 109
        Troop acceptability program, 109
        United Nations, 109, 124
        X–Day planning, 124, 127, 213
        Yugoslavia, 124
    Psychological Strategy Board:
        Acheson-Souers meetings, 49
        Africa, 125
        Anti-American attitudes, 133
        Asia, Southeast, 125, 127, 133
        China, Communist, 125, 153
        Cold War, 127, 133, 139
        Conduct of board meetings, new
            procedures for expediting the,
            57
        Covert operations, scope and pace
            of, 85, 89
        Draft directive on, 45, 47
        Emergency assistance provided to
            other countries, 153
        Europe (Eastern), 127, 143
        Europe (Western), 133, 153
        Executive Order 10483, 157, 158
        Expanded charter, 71
        France, 125, 127, 153
        Functions of, 78, 82

Psychological warfare planning—
  Continued
Psychological Strategy Board—
  Continued
  Funding issues, 78, 82
  Germany, 127
  Great Britain, 153
  Guerrilla warfare, 76
  Interdepartmental Committee,
    74
  Italy, 125, 127, 153
  Japan, 125, 127, 153
  JCS–PSB relations, 78
  Joyce's assessments, 142
  Latin America, 125, 153
  Meetings: July 2, 1951, 78
  Meetings: August 13, 1951, 82
  Meetings: December 5, 1951, 96
  Middle East, 125, 133
  National Psychological Strategy, 96
  National Psychological Warfare
    Plan for General War, 92
  National strategic concept for
    psychological action,
    formulating a, 96
  New PSB, plans for a, 67
  Nitze's assessments, 62, 81
  NSCID 135, 127
  NSC 10/2, 127
  NSC 10/5, 108, 127
  NSC 74, 52
  NSC–PSB relations, 28, 78, 104
  OPC–PSB relations, 96
  Operations Coordinating Board
    taking over functions of,
    160
  Origins of, 17, 28, 60, 74, 213
  Procedures for the conduct of
    business, 82, 104
  Progress report (PSB) as of August
    1, 1952, 125
  Progress report (PSB) as of October
    30, 1952, 133
  Progress report (PSB) as of January
    5, 1953, 143
  Progress report (PSB) as of July 29,
    1953, 153
  Project Brain Wave, 57
  Project Nobel, 57
  Project Vagabond, 57
  Radio, 69, 133
  Radio Free Europe, 125
  Satellites, developing/using, 122
  Scope of, 28

Psychological warfare planning—
  Continued
Psychological Strategy Board—
  Continued
  Smith's (Walter B.) recom-
    mendations to consolidate/
    strengthen the, 129, 135
  Soviet Union, 122, 125, 153
  Stalin, Joseph, 127
  Summary of psychological warfare
    arrangements within U.S.
    government since World War
    II, 213
  Taiwan, 125
  Trade policies, 153
  Troy Report, 57, 59
  Truman's assessments, 119
  Voice of America, 125
  War, plan for the conduct of
    psychological operations in the
    event of a general, 125, 127
  Weapons, public statements with
    respect to certain, 127
  Security, NSC's status report on
    national, 127
  Summary of psychological warfare
    arrangements within U.S.
    government since World War II,
    213
  Supervise, debate on who should,
    49
  Troy Report, 59, 62, 92
  Truman signs NSC Paper 59/1, 2
Publication procurement, foreign, 155,
  202, 209, 258
Purcell, Edward M., 194, 198
Putnam, Palmer, 122
Putt, Gen. Donald, 196, 199

Qatar, 105
Quantico Panel I/II, 224
Quarles, Donald A., 249

Radar reconnaissance, 146
Radford, Adm. Arthur W., 176, 177, 189,
  211, 214, 240, 249
Radio and political warfare (*see also*
  Voice of America):
  Collection (intelligence) requirements,
    coordination of, 202
  Foreign Information Program, 146, 155
  NSC Paper 5509, 209
  Office of Research and Intelligence,
    226

Radio and political warfare—*Continued*
Psychological warfare planning, 69,
133
Radio Free Asia, 94
Radio Free Europe, 15, 68, 94, 100,
125, 188
Soviet Union, 153
Rand, William, 160
RAND Corporation, 122, 229
Rastvorov, Yuri, 209
Reber, James Q., 48, 51, 72, 78, 115, 172,
202
REDCAP program, 87
REDSKIN program, 87
REDSOX program, 87
Reed, Allan, L., 172
Reichardt, Charles H., 172, 175
Republic of China. *See* Taiwan.
Research and Development Board
(RDB), 115, 220
Roach, Ralph R., 197
Rockefeller, Nelson:
Coordination of economic/
psychological/political warfare
and foreign information
activities, 210, 213, 248
Dulles (John F.) and, relations
between, 232
Operations Coordinating Board:
Resigning as vice chairman, 235, 237,
246
Vice chairman, appointment as, 210
Planning Coordination Group:
Abolished, Rockefeller's
recommendation that group
be, 235, 237, 246
Status report from group as of
December 14, 1955, 246
Quantico Panel I/II, 224
Rockwell, Samuel S., 175
Romania, 61, 153, 169, 190
Roosevelt, Franklin D., 213
Rostow, Walt W., 224
ROTC, 251

Samford, Gen. John A., 164, 172, 175,
197, 225, 245
Sargeant, Howland H., 7, 69, 78, 100
Satellites, developing/using, 122, 219,
223
Saudi Arabia, 105
Savage, Carlton, 96
Scammon, R.M., 115
Schow, Gen. Robert A., 225

Schwinn, Walter K., 96
Scientific/technical intelligence:
Areas, field subdivided into three
basic, 126
Armstrong's assessments, 112
Central Intelligence Agency, 107, 112,
120, 126, 155
Collection (intelligence) requirements,
coordination of, 202
Commission on the Organization of
the Executive Branch of the
Government, 251
Coordinating mechanisms, 126
Director of Central Intelligence
Directive 3/4, 126
Economic intelligence relating to
national security, 209
Electronic intelligence, 230
Foreign Information Program, 146,
155
Intelligence Advisory Committee, 126
Interdepartmental Committee on
Internal Security, 79
Kent's assessments, 120
Missiles, guided, 209, 225, 245
NSC Paper 5520, 219
Policies and procedures, 126
Psychochemicals, 244
Satellites, developing/using, 122, 219,
223
Scientific Estimates Committee, 126,
146, 155, 225, 251
Search operations, special electronic
airborne, 6
Soviet Union's capabilities, IAC's
assessment of, 115
Sovmat Program (Soviet materials),
217
State Department-CIA relations, 24
Technological Capabilities Panel, 194,
223
Troy Report, 57, 59, 62, 92
Scott, Robert, 229
Scott, W.K., 52
Search projects, special electronic
airborne, 6
Security clearances, operational, 205,
251
Service Attaché System, 146, 155
Sheldon, Huntington D., 175
Smith, Abbot E., 225
Smith, Brad J., 164
Smith, N.E., 175
Smith, R. Jack, 175

Smith, Walter B., 12, 24, 47, 58
  Bureau of the Budget's study for
      coordinating economic/
      psychological/political warfare
      and foreign information
      activities, 210
  Changes made at CIA in response to
      requests from NSC, 107, 110
  Communications intelligence, 97
  Covert operations:
      Guerrilla warfare, 75
      Joyce's assessments, 111
      NSC 10/2, 38
      NSC 10/3, 43
      Scope and pace of, 68, 70, 71, 75,
          111
  Current Intelligence Bulletin, 53, 55
  Defense Department-CIA relations,
      36, 54, 56
  ECA–CIA relations, 31
  Europe (Eastern), 71
  Intelligence Advisory Committee,
      29
  Interdepartmental Intelligence
      Committee, 65, 66
  JCS–CIA relations, 77
  Joyce's assessments, 145
  Marshall's (George C.) analysis of
      U.S. intelligence, 32
  National Intelligence Estimates, 29
  Net intelligence estimates of the
      capabilities/intentions of other
      nations, 189
  NSC Papers:
      NSC 10/3, 63
      NSC 10/4, 63
      NSC 26/2, 84
  Objectives, priority list of critical
      national intelligence, 117
  Operations Coordinating Board,
      160
  Psychological warfare planning:
      Progress Report by the Director, 82
      Psychological Strategy Board, 67,
          74, 78, 82, 129, 135
      Truman's assessments, 119
  Resignation of, 145
  Scientific/technical intelligence, 126
  Security of the United States, project
      to provide a more adequate basis
      for planning the, 80, 131
  Soviet Union's capability to injure the
      U.S., evaluating the, 115, 131,
      137, 138, 148, 189

Smith, Walter B.—Continued
  Support bases, overseas CIA
      logistical, 140
  Taiwan and China, conflict between,
      98
  Volunteer Freedom Corps, 148
  Watch Committee, IAC, 35
SNIE. See Special National Intelligence
      Estimates.
Snyder, John, 17
Somoza, Anastasio, 154
Sontag, R.J., 115
Souers, Adm. Sidney W., 4, 16, 47, 49,
      52
Soviet Union (see also Europe (Eastern)):
  Aerial/photo reconnaissance over,
      102, 194, 197, 198
  Aircraft (U.S.) shot down in Baltic, 6
  Biological warfare, 209
  Collection (intelligence) requirements,
      coordination of, 202
  Commission on the Organization of
      the Executive Branch of the
      Government, 220, 221, 234, 251
  Covert operations, 5, 61
  Defectors, using/exploiting, 252,
      253
  Director of Central Intelligence
      Directives:
      DCID 4/4, 201
      DCID 4/5, 238
  Doolittle Report, 192
  Economic intelligence requirements
      relating to national security, 144,
      169, 191
  Edwards Report, 149
  Ethnic groups, non-Russian, 161
  Foreign Information Program, 146,
      155
  Intelligence Advisory Committee, 80,
      115, 131, 172
  Kennan's assessment of military
      intelligence-gathering services in,
      118
  Mails used as an access point into,
      59
  NIE 65, 115
  Non-Russian ethnic groups, 161
  NSC Action 543, 131
  NSC Intelligence Directives:
      NSCID 13, 252
      NSCID 14, 253
  NSC Papers:
      NSC 162/2, 163

Soviet Union—*Continued*
  NSC Papers—*Continued*
    NSC *174*, 190
    NSC *5412/1*, 212
    NSC *5509*, 209
  Office of Research and Intelligence, 226
  Political warfare aimed at, 59
  Press monitoring, 202
  Psychological warfare planning:
    NSC Paper *10/5*, 139
    Progress report (PSB) as of August
      1, *1952*, 125
    Progress report (PSB) as of July *29,
      1953*, 153
    Progress report (State Department)
      as of November *8, 1951*, 92
    Progress report (State Department)
      as of May *1, 1952*, 109
    Psychological Operations
      Coordinating Committee, 92
  Satellites, developing/using, 122
  Radio, 153
  REDCAP program, 87
  REDSKIN program, 87
  REDSOX program, 87
  Satellites, developing/using, 122, 203
  Scientific/technical intelligence, 112,
    115, 120
  Security, NSC's status report on
    national, 127
  Security of the United States, project
    to provide a more adequate basis
    for planning the, 80, 86, 115, 127,
    131, 138
  Smith's (Walter B.) assessments, 117
  Sovmat Program (Soviet materials),
    217
  State Department personnel and
    funding, Dulles's (Allen W.)
    request for increase in, 228
  Superpower competition, 195
  Technological Capabilities Panel, 223
  Troy Report, 57, 59, 62, 92
  U.S. evaluation of the possibility of
    being injured by:
    CIA's assessments, 173, 189
    Intelligence Advisory Committee,
      115, 172
    Interdepartmental Committee on
      Internal Security, 80, 131, 137,
      138, 173, 207
    Interdepartmental Intelligence
      Committee, 131, 137, 138, 173,
      207

Soviet Union—*Continued*
  U.S. evaluation of the possibility of
    being injured by—*Continued*
    Joint Chiefs of Staff, 80, 131, 137,
      138, 149, 173, 189, 207
    Lay's assessments, 138
    NSC No. *543*, 86, 131, 138
    NSC No. *1260*, 207
    NSC *5509*, 209
    NSC *5511*, 207
    NSC *5525*, 234
    NSC's senior staff's assessments,
      137
    SNIE *11–8–54*, 209
  Voice of America, 44, 57, 59
  Warning facilities of the intelligence
    community, information/
    recommendations concerning,
    186, 209
  Watch Committee, IAC:
    CIA's assessments, 81, 107, 189
    DCID *1/2*, 179, 187
    Fact sheet, 91
    Foreign service posts, State
      Department airgram to all,
      218
    JCS's assessments, 186
    Meetings: December *7, 1950*, 35
    Meetings: May *4, 1954*, 175
    Meetings: June *14, 1955*, 225
    NSC *142*, 146
    NSC *161*, 155
    NSC *5509*, 209
    NSC *5525*, 234
    Trueheart's assessments, 3
    Weakening the power/will to wage
      cold/hot war, 83
Spalding, Hobart A., 41
Special Cryptologic Advisory Group,
  121
Special electronic airborne search
  operations (SESP), 6
Special National Intelligence Estimates
  (SNIE):
  SNIE *11–8–54*, 209
Staats, Elmer B., 178, 203
Stalin, Joseph, 59, 127
Stassen, Harold, 210, 214
State Department, U.S. (*see also*
  Acheson, Dean; Armstrong, W.
  Park, Jr.; Dulles, John F.; Hoover,
  Herbert, Jr.; National Intelligence
  Estimates; Operations Coordinating
  Board):

State Department, U.S.—*Continued*
CIA-State Department relations:
Armstrong's assessments, 24
Daily Summary, 48
Jackson (William H.)-Armstrong
communications, 46
Joyce's assessments, 129
Memorandum of agreement, 34, 51
Commission on the Organization of
the Executive Branch of the
Government, 221, 241, 251
Defense Department-State
Department study on
intelligence, 20, 22
Dulles's (Allen W.), assessment of
intelligence produced by, 228
Personnel and funds, Dulles's (Allen
W.) request for increases in, 228
Propaganda policy guidance, 7
Psychological warfare planning:
Progress report as of October 17,
1950, 28
Progress report as of March 19,
1951, 57
Progress report as of November 8,
1951, 92
Progress report as of May 7, 1952,
109
Progress report as of July 31, 1952,
124
Stelle, Charles C., 96
Stevens, Adm. Leslie, 38, 67, 70, 75, 96,
104, 139
Steward, Gordon, 216
Stone, Adm. Earl E., 40
Stout, R.F., 113
Strauss, Lewis L., 240
Streibert, Theodore E., 226
Strong, Robert C., 145
Sullivan, Charlie, 237
Support bases, overseas CIA logistical,
140
Swiatlo, Josef, 209
Sykes, O.B., 115

Taiwan:
China, conflict with:
Chinese Nationalist Forces on
Taiwan, 98
Eisenhower's complaints about
conflicting intelligence
information, 211
Guerrilla warfare, 71, 75, 76, 98
NSC 10/2, 108

Taiwan—*Continued*
China, conflict with—*Continued*
NSC 10/5, 108
NSC 135, 127
Security, NSC's status report on
national, 127
Smith's (Walter B.) assessments, 98
State/JCS/Defense/NSC/CIA,
joint meeting between, 106
Psychological warfare planning, 125
Talbott, Harold E., 196, 198
Target Area Analysis Radar (TAAR), 209
Taylor, Robert, 31
Technological Capabilities Panel, 194,
223
Television in propaganda, 109
Thompson, Clary, 226
Thorburn, James G., Jr., 172
Tod, Roy, 35, 95
Tolman, John D., 115
Totten, Robert, 175, 225
Travel Folder Program, 155, 209
Traynor, Harry S., 197
Treasury Department, U.S., 79
Trezise, Philip H., 96, 225
Troy Report, 57, 59, 62, 92
Trudeau, Gen. Arthur G., 168, 172, 197
Trueheart, William C., 3, 35, 115, 172
Truman, Harry S., 58
Buying, organized/coordinated
program of covert preclusive, 116
CIA–JCS relations, 77
Classified government information,
clearance for access to, 79
Communications intelligence, 97, 99,
132, 257
Covert operations, 5, 76, 89
Current Intelligence Bulletin, 53, 55
Foreign Information Program, 2, 128
NSC Intelligence Directive 9, 257
NSC Paper 26/2, 84
Psychological warfare planning:
Cold War, 139
Key Data Book, 134
NSC Paper 10/5, 139
NSC Paper 127/1, 123
Origins of, 2
Psychological Strategy Board, 49,
60, 74, 119, 213
Security of the United States, project
to provide a more adequate basis
for planning the, 138
Soviet Union's capability to injure the
U.S., evaluating the, 138

Tufts, Robert W., 96
Tukey, John W., 194, 198
Turkey, 127, 153, 229, 242
Tuttle, Elbert P., 187
Twining, Gen. Nathan, 106, 186, 196, 198, 199, 211, 249

United Fruit Company, 154
United Nations, 26, 109, 124, 143
United States Communications Intelligence Board (USCIB), 19, 44
United States Communications Security Board (USCSB), 251
U.S. Information Agency (USIA), 181, 183, 209, 210, 213, 226
U.S. Information and Education (USIE) Program, 69, 94

Vandenberg, Gen. Hoyt S., 101
Van Slyck, Forrest, 27
Venona: Soviet Espionage and the American Response, 1939–1957 (Benson & Warner), 87
Villard, Henry S., 96
Visa and Passport Divisions, 79
Voice of America (VOA):
   CIA's assessments, 127
   Crusade for Freedom, 100
   Foreign Information Program, 146
   NSC Paper 66/1, 44, 107
   NSC Paper 135, 127
   Psychological warfare planning, 125, 213
   Radio Free Europe's displaced personnel taken care of by, 94
   Troy Report, 57, 59, 62, 92
Volunteer Freedom Corps, 148

Wage issues, 221, 251
Warner, Michael, 29
Washburn, Abbott, 94, 100
Watch Committee, IAC. See under Soviet Union.
Watson, E.C., 122
Watts, Phillip H., 96
Webb, James E., 9, 11
   CIA-State Department relations, 24
   Office of Special Projects, 4
   Psychological warfare planning:
      Cabinet Committee, 47
      Interdepartmental Committee, 74
      Nitze's assessments, 62
      NSC 10/5, 104
      NSC 74, 52

Webb, James E.—Continued
   Psychological warfare planning— Continued
      Office of Policy Coordination, 26
      Program planning, 69
      Progress report (State Department) as of November 8, 1951, 92
      Psychological Operations Coordinating Committee, 92
      Psychological Strategy Board, 60, 67, 74, 82, 92
      State Department-Defense Department Staff Study on intelligence, 22
Weckerling, Gen. John, 64, 91
Whearty, Raymond P., 79
Willems, Gen. John M., 175
Wilson, Charles E., 186, 239, 240, 242
Wisner, Frank G., 7, 50, 67, 82, 100, 180, 205
   Aliens into U.S. for intelligence/operational purposes, 206
   CIA–OPC relations, 130, 145
   Civil Air Transport's application for commercial rights in Okinawa, 101
   Covert operations, 71, 85, 111, 188
   ECA–CIA relations, 31
   Eisenhower-Doolittle meetings, 193
   Europe (Eastern), 167
   Intelligence Advisory Committee, 29
   NSC–CIA coordination, 8
   NSC 10/2, 162
   NSC 10/5, 162
   Office of Policy Coordination, 33
   Office of Special Projects, 4
   Psychological warfare planning, 129
   Radio Free Europe, 94
   Soviet Union, 161
   Taiwan and China, conflict between, 106
   Voice of America, 94
Woods, Van A., Jr., 225
Wright, Edwin M., 41, 142
Writ of habeas corpus, 16
Wyman, W., 50, 93
Wynne, P.D., 225

Yalu River, 155
Yeager, Joseph, 115
Young, Frederick R., 57, 142
Yugoslavia, 59, 124, 139, 190

References are to document numbers

ISBN 0-16-076468-8

9 780160 764684

90000